Contracting Law

Contracting Law

FIFTH EDITION

Amy Kastely
Deborah Waire Post
Nancy Ota
Deborah Zalesne

CAROLINA ACADEMIC PRESS
Durham, North Carolina

ISBN 978-1-59460-989-3
LCCN 2015943125

CAROLINA ACADEMIC PRESS
700 Kent Street
Durham, North Carolina 27701
Telephone (919) 489-7486
Fax (919) 493-5668
www.cap-press.com

Printed in the United States of America
2020 Printing

Contents

Table of Cases

Table of Additional Sources

Personal Acknowledgments

I thank many classes of first year law students at St. Mary's University School of Law and the University of Hawai'i William S. Richardson School of Law for the joy of studying contract law with them, with special thanks to Francell Mokihana Marquardt, Joyce McCarty, Jill Nunakawa, Mike Simpson, Shawna Soderstein, Isabel de la Riva, Judy Saenz, and Denise Mejia. Thanks also to the secretarial staffs of St. Mary's University School of Law and of the University of Hawai'i School of Law, particularly Jane Tanaka and Frieda Honda, for excellent work and kind encouragement. I am indebted to the able and engaged research assistance of Christine Dahilig, Bonnie Oppermann, Suzanna Meredith, Karen Corby, Judy Saenz, Conry Davidson, Stephanie Hebert, and Laura Winfield. Among many generous colleagues I owe a special thanks to Yvonne Cherena Pacheco, Elise Garcia, Maivan Clech Lam, Ana Novoa, Judy Scales-Trent, Rey Valencia, and Judy Weightman. I am grateful to the buena gente of the Esperanza Peace & Justice Center, to Graciela Sanchez, Gloria Ramirez, Antonia Castaneda, Maria Berriozabal, and many others, with whom I have learned a practice of community cultural activism that gives shape to a life-long yearning for justice. I thank J. Kastely, Joe Kastely, and Christina Rose Kastely for loving conversation and engaging play. Finally I thank Graciela Sanchez for her mighty and courageous love, and Isabel, Enrique, Xavier, Fernando, Bernard, Gustavo, and Leticia Sanchez for enormous generosity of spirit and family.

—Amy Kastely

This new edition of Contracting Law is a first step in reorganizing the presentation of contracts doctrine in a first year casebook. It is our intention to retain a critical, outsider perspective while focusing attention on significant changes that have occurred in the past twenty years, including the redefinition or elimination of the requirement of consent or assent in consumer contracts. In that respect, the contracts workshop hosted by Nancy Ota and Albany Law School in 2012 was critical and I would like to thank our participants: Aditi Bagchi, Danni Hart, Hosea Harvey, Emily Houh, Eboni Nelson, Patricia Williams, and Erick Zacks. There is a wider community that I would like to acknowledge as well: the inclusive, supportive and informative annual contracts section conferences that have expanded, informed and shaped my understanding of contracts. Finally, it goes without saying that there would be no book without the collaboration, friendship and support of wonderful co-authors: Amy Kastely, Nancy Ota, and Deborah Zalesne.

—Deborah Post

Thanks to all who paved the way and created the opportunity for me to enter the profession of legal education. I am in awe and indebted to you for your encouragement, especially Francisco Valdes, Julia M.C. Friedlander, Margaret Jane Radin, Emma Coleman Jordan, Mari Matsuda, Bill Ong Hing, Laura Gomez, and Gerald Lopez. I have had tons of support from many colleagues at Albany Law School and I am especially grateful for the fabulous assistance provided by Sherri Ann Meyer and Kimberly Waldin. Thanks also to Albany Law School for supporting a Contracts Workshop and all of the participants who provided food for thought for Amy, Deborah, Deborah, and me to chew on including: Aditi Bagchi, Danni Hart, Hosea Harvey, Emily Houh, Eboni Nelson, Patricia Williams, and Eric Zacks. I have learned immensely from my amazing colleagues, Amy, Deborah, and Debbie, and I am grateful for the opportunity to work with them. Thanks to all of my students who make this endeavor meaningful and fun. And finally, I would not be doing any of this without the love and support of my family, but especially Victor and Laura, whose love and companionship sustain me.

—Nancy K. Ota

I would like to extend my thanks to the faculty of CUNY School of Law, whose encouragement and open-mindedness about the teaching of law made this project possible. In particular, I thank my dear friends and co-conspirators, Jeff Kirchmeier, Andrea McArdle, and David Nadvorney, whose influence is immeasurable. I also thank my wonderful students, whose energy and curiosity make the teaching of law fun and interesting and who challenge me in new ways each year. I am grateful to my co-authors, Amy, Deborah, and Nancy, for the inspiration of their work, as well as their endless patience and brilliance. I owe a special debt to Sharon Hom, who paved the way for me as one of the original co-authors of this book. Finally, I thank my parents, Saul and Shelly, and all the Zalesnes (and Retiks and Levins), for always being there for me with their love and support, and my wonderful partner Michael and amazing daughter Ella, for the inspiration and happiness they bring to me each day.

—Deborah Zalesne

Acknowledgments

Robert Braucher, *Interpretation and Legal Effect in the Second Restatement of Contracts*, © 1981 by Columbia Law Review. Excerpt reprinted with the permission of Columbia Law Review.

Raymond Carver, *A Small Good Thing*, from Cathedral, Copyright © 1983 by Raymond Carver. Reprinted by permission of Alfred A. Knopf Inc.

Denise Chávez, *The Wedding*, first published in Daughters of the Fifth Sun: A Collection of Latina Fiction and Poetry, published by Riverhead Books, a division of G.P. Putnam's Sons, New York, Copyright © by Denise Chávez. Reprinted with the permission of the publisher and the author.

John Cheever, *Artemis, the Honest Well Digger* from The World of Apples by John Cheever, Copyright © 1973 by John Cheever. Reprinted by permission of Alfred A. Knopf Inc.

Marcus Cicero, De Officiis, Book III, translated by Walter Miller, Copyright © Harvard University 1913. Excerpt reprinted by permission of the publishers and the Loeb Classical Library.

Richard Danzig and Geoffrey R. Watson, The Capability Problem in Contract Law: Further Readings on Well-known Cases, Copyright © 2004 by West Academic Publishing. Excerpt reproduced and reprinted with the permission of the publisher.

Sue Doro, Blue Collar Goodbye, Copyright © 1993 by Sue Doro. Reprinted with the permission of the author.

Laurie Kindel Fett, *The Reasonable Expectations Doctrine: An Alternative to Bending and Stretching Traditional Tools of Contract Interpretation*, 18 William Mitchell Law Review 1113 (1992). Copyright © 1992 by Laurie Kindel Fett. Excerpt reproduced with permission of the author and William Mitchell Law Review.

Jonathan Franzen, *The Corrections*, Excerpts from "Corecktail: It's the Future" from The Corrections by Jonathan Franzen. Copyright © 2001 by Jonathan Franzen. Reprinted by permission of Farrar, Straus and Giroux, LLC.

Dominic Gates and Alicia Mundy, *Boeing Lawyer Warns of Company's Legal Peril*, Jan. 31, 2006 Seattle Times. Copyright © 2006 by the Seattle Times. Reprinted with permission of the Seattle Times.

Mary Gordon, Final Payments, Copyright © 1978 by Mary Gordon. Excerpt reprinted by permission of Random House Inc.

bell hooks, Homeplace: A Site of Resistance, reprinted from bell hooks, Yearning: Race, Gender and Cultural Politics. Copyright © 1990 by Gloria Watkins. South End Press, Boston, Massachusetts.

Nancy Kim, Wrap Contracts: Foundations and Ramifications, Copyright © 2013 by Nancy Kim. Reprinted by permission of Oxford University Press.

Jane Smiley, A Thousand Acres, Copyright © 1991 by Jane Smiley. Excerpt reproduced with permission of Ballantine Publishing Group a division of Random House Inc., New York.

John Steinbeck, The Grapes of Wrath, Copyright © 1939, renewed 1967 by John Steinbeck. Excerpt reproduced with permission of publisher.

Amy Tan, *Mother Tongue*, Copyright © 1980 by Amy Tan. First appeared in The Threepenny Review. Reprinted by permission of the author and the Sandra Dijkstra Literary Agency.

Lea S. VanderVelde, *The Gendered Origins of the Lumley Doctrine: Binding Men's Consciences and Women's Fidelity*, 101 Yale L.J. 775 (1991-1992). Copyright © 1992 The Yale Law Journal Co. Excerpt reprinted with permission of The Yale Law Journal Co. and Fred B. Rothman & Co. from The Yale Law Journal.

Hiroshi Wagatsuma & Arthur Rosett, *Cultural Attitudes towards Contract Law: Japan and the United States Compared*, 2 UCLA Pac. Basin L.J. 76 (1983). Copyright © by Hiroshi Wagatsuma and Arthur Rosett. Excerpt reproduced with permission by authors.

Paulette Childress White, *Getting the Facts of Life*, from Memory of Kin, Stories About Family by Black Writers, edited by Mary Helen Washington, Copyright © 1989 by Paulette Childress White. Excerpt reproduced with permission by the author.

Patricia J. Williams, *Alchemical Notes: Reconstructing Ideals from Deconstructed Rights*, 22 Harv. C.R.-C.L. L. Rev. 401 (1987) Copyright © 1987 by the President and Fellows of Harvard College. Excerpt reproduced with permission by Harvard Civil Rights Civil Liberties Law Review.

Restatement Third, Restitution and Unjust Enrichment, copyright © 2011 by The American Law Institute. All rights reserved. Reproduced with permission.

Editors' Note

We have edited the cases, articles, and book excerpts for readability and relevance to the subject matter. In most cases, deletions are noted with ellipses. In some instances, citations and footnotes are omitted without notation. Cases and articles retain the original footnote numbers where included. We also attempted to achieve some uniformity with formatting styles and so the cases may look different from the official published version. And finally, we have included the first names of the judges who authored the opinions.

Contracting Law

Chapter One

Introduction to Contract Law

A. Lawyering and Legal Education

Lawyers do different tasks in a variety of settings. The work includes counseling, negotiating, investigating facts, drafting documents, organizing corporations, lobbying legislatures, drafting statutes and regulations, testifying before legislative committees and government agencies, developing and executing public relations strategies, organizing community groups, and litigating. These tasks occur in local, state, federal, or international forums, and require a variety of different skills. This Textbook and the accompanying Contracting Law Student Workbook have two goals of equal importance: (1) to help students develop skills of working with words, ideas, legal principles, doctrines, and authoritative texts; and (2) to help students learn current contract law, by which we mean contract principles and doctrine as articulated or recognized by contemporary judges, lawyers, and legislators.

Contracting Law examines current contract law and its impact on groups and individuals. We explore the historical, narrative, moral, and economic aspects of contract law and the influence of these on decisions made by courts, legislatures, agencies, arbitrators, counselors, and private negotiators. In addition, we focus on the skills of legal analysis, argument, and judgment. Lawyers work in situations in which something has to be decided, and people disagree, or are unsure, about what the decision should be. Should the not-for-profit community center enter a partnership with a privately owned employment service? Should the city council prohibit political leafleting in the museum lobby? Should the Department of Commerce require contractors to provide group medical insurance to their employees? Should Ace Construction Company be required to pay Melinda Leong compensation for its failure to use the kind of tile specified in the contract between them? These are not questions that can be decided by deductive or inductive logic alone, and the questions cannot be answered with absolute certainty. Instead, they require practical decisions, made for the purpose of action. Decisions of this sort require fact finding and the ability to assemble a coherent picture and a narrative that organizes those facts into a coherent account of the situation; plus they require some assessment of arguments made in favor of and against alternative decisions. Thus the skills of critical reading, narrative, and normative analysis are fundamental lawyering skills.

B. The Study of Contract Law

Contract law addresses the legal recognition and consequences of promises, agreements, and exchanges. If one person claims that another agreed or promised to do something, lawyers will classify that, at least initially, as a contract law claim. Because a basic tenet of contract law is that only voluntarily made promises and agreements ought to be binding, a central focus of contract law is the nature of voluntary choice. Another important focus of contract law is market exchange: money for products, services for money, food for products, services for housing, and the like. Contract law can be seen as setting out some of the "rules of the game" for a market economy.

The emphasis on choice in contract law reflects an emphasis on choice in political, moral, and economic thinking in the United States today. As a consequence, contract has become an important lens through which we see the world. Americans comfortably describe a broad range of relationships as "contractual," including such diverse arrangements as a car loan, a marriage, and membership in human society (as in "the social contract"). Through this lens, human relationships appear voluntary and negotiable. We also use the concept of contract to describe a methodology, a process of organizing and maintaining relationships. In family counseling, for example, spouses, lovers, parents, and children are sometimes asked to "negotiate" and to "make contracts" regarding responsibilities and privileges in their home lives. Many colleges have instituted "contract requirements" systems in which individual students and their professors negotiate a course of study for which the student will be responsible. In these instances and others, contract negotiation is used as a methodology for the creation of good, healthy, or productive relationships.

"Market," too, is a central concept in the United States and throughout the world. People speak of a "free market" of ideas or a "market" of political organizations. People say they are "in the market" for a dating partner or spouse. Like contract, market is used as a methodology: "market" bidding is viewed as a just system for hiring government employees, allocating public services, and selecting sites for international conferences. Throughout, "market" is linked with freedom, with structural impartiality, and with deference to individual preference, however formed. Together, contract and market are the dominant metaphors of the twentieth century. Much of current contract law corresponds with and reinforces these cultural metaphors and the visions of human relationships that are constructed by them. Yet the metaphors of contract and market are not the only images of human relationship in dominant culture; other images, including some that conflict with the metaphors of contract and market, play an important role in the dominant culture and in current law.

What are some of the conflicting images of human relationships in dominant culture? Think about the obligations you feel to other people. Are they "voluntarily created and assumed," as the contract and market metaphors would describe them? What about the obligations of parenthood? Or of friendship? Those are "voluntarily assumed," aren't they? Or are the obligations of parenthood imposed by the state, through statutes that define the minimal care, support, and education that a parent must give to his or her child, or by religions, through the good parenting prescribed by religious teachings? Are the obligations of friendship imposed by custom, through the many stories of generosity and loyalty that people tell and retell in stories, books, movies, and television shows? What about a transaction as simple as the purchase of an automobile? If it is a new car, why does a buyer usually assume that the seller is obligated to ensure that the car functions reasonably well? Is that obligation of the seller, if it exists, voluntarily created and assumed, imposed by the state, dictated by religions, or followed as customary practice?

The idea of voluntariness in human relations is in turn connected to the idea of self-determination—the "right to be oneself" or the idea that people can and should make their own choices about their lives. Many believe that a person decides whether to complete high school and college, whether and whom to date or to marry, what job to take, where to live, whether to hold religious beliefs or to practice a particular faith, whether to have children and if so, how many to have.

Yet sociologists and other social scientists tell a very different story: they say that the "choices" we make about these life-determining matters are readily predictable according to our class, race, ethnicity, gender, religion, and geographic location. Our choices are constrained by our sense of duty or obligation to others and the presence or absence of meaningful opportunities in our lives. Some individuals do follow unusual paths and overcome what are insurmountable obstacles for others. Indeed, for a variety of reasons, many current law students have defied predictions. But for every working-class heterosexual white woman in law school, for example, there are thousands of others whose choices closely conform to those the sociologists would predict. And for every middle class Mexican-American man in law school, for another example, there are thousands more who have made choices more in line with those that are statistically predictable.

This predictability of individual choice is acknowledged in casual ways: people say that he became a doctor because his father was a doctor, or that she had to drop out of high school because her family needed her to work or because she was pregnant, or that he got a job as an electrician because his uncle was in the union, or that she took a low-paying job as a waitress because she knew she wouldn't be hired in a higher-paying construction job. People in the United States acknowledge social determination of individual choice in these and many other ways. Yet this acknowledgment does not cause people to abandon the idea of individual freedom of choice—the two ideas, individual freedom of choice and the constraints of social positioning that determine or guide individual choices, merely co-exist, harmoniously or not, in our thoughts and actions. Because contract law concerns the obligations that arise from human relationships, it reflects both of these sometimes conflicting ideas.

As one studies legal arguments and legal rules, it is important to ask why some might be persuasive to a judge and why others might not. Frequently, the persuasiveness of an argument or the strength of a rule depends upon its correspondence with contemporary images of human relationships. Judges are people; they inherit and participate in culture and their perceptions and thoughts are informed by their cultures just as with other people. In addition, judges are rightly concerned about the impact their decisions will have on future thought and behavior and rightly consider the ways in which a decision will contribute to dominant views of human obligation. The interaction between law and culture is multidimensional and multidirectional: law is influenced by current political, ethical, and economic thought, and law in turn influences political, ethical, and economic thought; law is formed both in gradual evolution with social institutions and ideologies and, at times, in fundamental schism with traditional norms and practices.

On the History of Contract Law

Since modern contract law emphasizes choice, some tell the history of contract law as a progressive, evolutionary growth of the idea of choice as a foundation for modern society. For example, Sir Henry Maine, an English lawyer, wrote in 1864:

> The movement of the progressive societies has been uniform in one respect. Through all its course it has been distinguished by the gradual dissolution of family dependency, and the growth of individual obligation in its place.... Nor is it difficult to see what is the tie between man and man which replaces by degrees those forms of reciprocity in rights and duties which have their origin in the Family. It is Contract.... [W]e may say that the movement of the progressive societies has hitherto been a movement from Status to Contract.

Sir Henry Maine, Ancient Law 163–65 (1864).

This statement, accurate or not, reflects the enthusiasm of the era and the hold the idea of progress had on some groups in Europe and the United States at the end of the nineteenth century. It also reflects the racist view that human development has evolved in a unilinear manner, with European cultures representing the apex of human civilization. This view has been challenged and discredited, but the truth in Maine's statement is its focus on social change as characteristic of nineteenth-century life and imagination. The ties created by kinship and family—ties of affection, economics, and politics—were breaking down. People were on the move—from the countryside to the city, from the "old world" to the "new."

In the United States of the eighteenth century, the idea of choice as fundamental to human life was promoted and expanded as a political slogan of the American Revolution. In the nineteenth century the idea offered hope and inspiration in the struggle for the freedom of those who were bought and sold as chattel. During the end of the nineteenth century, the idea of choice was transmuted to fit the needs and aspirations of those in the United States who sought economic growth and expansion, and by the early twentieth century, the idea of economic freedom had become a prominent feature in the ideal of human choice. The idea of individual choice thus originated not as the product of evolutionary development, but as a slogan of social and political revolution in a variety of forms. *See* John Dewey, The Public and its Problems 85–103 (1927, reprint 1985). Choice has been a liberatory notion. Yet as John Dewey, the influential philosopher and educator, observed, the ideas of individual autonomy we inherit have left untouched numerous forms of association, "overlooked" as "matters of course." "Indeed," Dewey wrote, "any attempt to touch them, notably the established form of family and the legal institution of property, were looked upon as subversive, as license, not liberty, in the sanctified phrase." *Id.* at 100–101. "Freedom of choice," as we inherit it, has specific meanings and established boundaries that reflect its social and political past. The tension between these historically determined boundaries of human choice and broader aspirations of freedom is an important element in contract law.

Contract law, as a separate legal field, is also relatively new and somewhat revolutionary. The first treatises in English to treat contract law as an autonomous area were published during the mid-nineteenth century. Harvard University Professor Christopher Columbus Langdell edited the first "casebook" on contract law in 1871. Langdell taught that contract law is separate from other areas of the law because it is uniquely based on individual consent and that the whole of contract law can be derived from fundamental elements of consensual obligation. This theory of contract law, developed and promoted by Langdell, Samuel Williston, Oliver Wendell Holmes, and others during the end of the nineteenth and the beginning of the twentieth centuries, is now labeled "classical contract theory" or "classical contract law." Classical contract law treats agreement as the product of discrete, voluntary, communicative acts (as in the rules of offer and acceptance) and it emphasizes bargained-for exchange as the basis for contractual obligation (as in the doctrine of consideration). It also features the idea of "objectivity"—as measured by "the reasonable man" or, more recently, "the reasonable person"—as the appropriate legal standard for evaluating words and behavior.

At the same time that the philosophy of law or contract theory that is labeled "Classical" was emerging, there were contractual relationships in which the idea of choice in the formation of contracts was accompanied by a regime of enforcement that included criminal sanctions. Criminal punishment for laborers who abandoned their work was not unknown. In 1790, the nascent United States Congress enacted An Act for the government and regulation of Seamen in the merchants service, Act of July 20, 1790, ch.

29, 1 Stat. 131 (1790), which criminalized the breach of contract by sailors. After the Civil War, legislation criminalizing breach of contract was enacted in several southern states and subsequently challenged in a series of cases denominated the "peonage cases" that came before the United States Supreme Court in the early 20th century. In one of these cases, *Bailey v. Alabama*, 219 U.S. 219 (1911), Supreme Court Justice Oliver Wendell Holmes, who had been a soldier in the civil war, dissented from the majority decision invaliding the Alabama statute. Holmes believed that a state has the right to pass laws which incentivize "right conduct" and which punish "wrong conduct." According to Holmes, "[b]reach of legal contract without excuse is wrong conduct, even if the contract is for labor, and if a state adds to civil liability a criminal liability to fine, it simply intensifies the legal motive for doing right; it simply does not make the laborer a slave." That is not the opinion that prevails today and we recoil at the idea, but it is certainly as clear a statement as there can be of the power of the state to develop rules, and to exert social control over and to regulate private actors in the realm of economic exchange.

The focus on choice has been so pervasive in American society and in contract law that it distracts attention from the fact that anything that is labeled "law" signals the exercise of power by the state. There are many statutes and regulatory regimes created by the federal government and state legislatures that govern the creation and performance of contemporary contracts. The case law of contract that we study, however, is primarily concerned with the claims brought before a court by someone who claims that the promises or agreements made by him with another party are legally enforceable. The state ensures that the injured party receives some sort of recompense for the injury sustained when the agreement is not fulfilled, the promises not kept. Contracts may be negotiated privately, but when there is a failure to perform, the injured party has the right to seek a remedy in a court of law. Courts may refuse to enforce contracts and this action too can be a form of social control. There are contract doctrines that disallow the claims of those who engage in conduct that violates shared norms with respect to integrity or fairness and contract doctrines that allocate risk of loss when there is no fault. Courts, as arms of the state, are concerned with more than right conduct and wrong conduct of the participants in the market. They are also motivated by a desire to create rules that foster economic growth as well as rules that protect the integrity of the market. For some judges, this means enforcing the "reasonable expectations" of the parties. For others this might mean adopting rules that are "liability limiting." In the latter case, judges sometimes refer to rules that reduce "transaction costs" or "efficient" legal rules. In the introductory case included in this section, the opinion of Chief Justice Harris in *H. J. Coolidge v. Pua'aiki and Kea* is informed by the political and economic conditions in Hawai'i at the time the case was decided and by a singular pragmatism with respect to the industry that was developing in Hawai'i at that time.

And while change is a singular feature of the law, so is continuity and recurrence of themes and ideas. It is not surprising then that we find in this 19th century decision rules and law that have been abandoned and principles and rules that continue to be applied in contemporary cases. Many of the ideas and doctrines associated with classical contract law have persisted in the twentieth century, while many others have been challenged and either rejected or reformulated. Lawyers, judges, and other critics have argued that classical contract law leads to unjust results and thus conflicts with the ultimate purpose of law — justice. Responding to these criticisms, judges and lawyers have developed alternative theories and doctrine, drawing from pre-classical law as well as from a variety of cultural images and values.

Current contract law is not a coherent product of unilinear evolution. It has a complex ancestry that includes not only the Anglo-American common law tradition, but also European and colonial civil and canon law traditions, Asian legal traditions, international natural law traditions, and many indigenous legal traditions, including Native American, Eskimo, Hawaiian, Mexican, and Puerto Rican traditions. Current contract law also is comprised of many different and sometimes conflicting values, ideas, images, and aspirations, articulated and pursued in many local, national, and international forums. In this course we will examine some of the many histories and contemporary threads of contract law.

On Reading Cases in Context

We begin our study with a case decided in 1877, by the Supreme Court of the Kingdom of Hawai'i. The history of Hawai'i excerpted in this section places the contract dispute in a wider context. The case is distant enough in time and place to allow us to see more clearly the political, economic, and social conditions that influenced the judge in this decision. At the same time, the rules with respect to agency, certainty, and mutuality of obligation are remarkably modern. Political ideology and social and economic conditions matter in contemporary case law as well but it is not always as easy to understand or see these connections. Nonetheless, it is important to read cases with an appreciation for the importance of context.

The 1870s were significant in Hawaiian history, just as they were in the formation of classical contract law. At the same time that Christopher Columbus Langdell was teaching contract law to students at Harvard using the case-method, the society, politics, and economics of the Kingdom of Hawai'i were undergoing rapid change. During the one hundred years following first contact with Europeans, the Hawaiian people suffered great losses at the hands of and by the diseases of the foreigners. The Hawaiian population dropped from a pre-contact number estimated to have been at least 800,000 to less than 50,000. In addition, during the 1830s and 1840s, Americans assumed important roles in the Hawaiian government and pressured King Kamehameha III and other traditional leaders to adopt a system of private ownership of land—and a system of contract law modeled on Anglo-American law that allowed foreigners (non-Hawaiians) to buy land. These changes had the desired effect of transferring ownership and control of the land to European-Americans. By 1890, European-Americans owned or controlled seventy-five percent of the land designated for private ownership.

A significant portion of this land was made into sugar plantations. In 1876, American sugar planters and their allies, including Chief Justice Charles Harris, the author of *Coolidge v. Pua'aiki and Kea*, negotiated a Treaty of Reciprocity with the United States under which Hawaiian-grown sugar could be imported and sold in the United States without tariffs. In fact in 1865, Justice Harris introduced sugarcane to the Ko'olaupoko area where this case takes place. He originally partnered with Queen Kalama, wife of King Kamehameha III, to introduce agriculture, and when she died in 1870 he purchased the land from her estate. Planters such as Justice Harris responded to the Treaty with an almost immediate expansion of sugar production, doubling output between 1874 and 1879, and increasing the number of sugar plantations from twenty in 1875 to sixty-three by 1880. This expansion increased the need for low-paid labor, the essential ingredient for the huge profits reaped by American plantation owners.

To meet this need, sugar planters increased the recruitment of Hawaiian workers like Pua'aiki and Kea, and with their governmental ally, the Bureau of Immigration, arranged for recruitment and immigration of thousands of workers from China, Japan, the Pacific Islands, Portugal, and later the Philippines and Korea. As part of their efforts to keep workers on the plantations, sugar planters consciously encouraged interethnic hostility among different groups of plantation workers. Workers were paid very low wages, graduated by race and gender, and were required to rent over-crowded housing that lacked adequate water and sanitation facilities and to buy food at plantation-owned stores. Plantation owners restricted private farming by Hawaiian and immigrant families, thereby increasing their dependence on plantation work and stores. In addition, for some years, plantation owners withheld a portion of each immigrant worker's wages; the stated reason for this was that the worker could not otherwise afford to pay for passage back to his or her home country. One effect of this practice was to create an incentive for the worker to stay on the plantation, because the money was forfeited if the worker fled.

Although the record in this case does not detail the circumstances of Pua'aiki's and Kea's contracts, there are historical accounts of plantation owners' general contracting practices during the 1870s. The system was managed by the Royal Hawaiian Agricultural Society, an organization of sugar and pineapple planters and various Hawaiian government officials. Professor Ronald Takaki describes plantation labor contracts with Chinese workers during this period:

> After their arrival in the city, Chinese workers were herded into a labor market for assignment to the plantations. They were marched to a yard near the customhouse and guarded by soldiers. The planters and their agents inspected the laborers and made their selections. The Chinese laborers were then made to sign labor contracts that specified the period of service required, wages, board, housing, medical care, and other terms. A labor contract in 1870, for example stated:

> Honolulu, Hawaiian Islands

> _____ 1870

> I _____ Party of the first part, a native of China, a free and voluntary Passenger to the Sandwich Islands, do bind myself to labor on any of the said Islands, at any work that may be assigned me, by the Party of the Second part, or their agents, upon the terms and in the manner within specified, for the term of Five Years from this date.

> _____ Party of the second part, do agree and bind themselves, or agents, to conform fully to the within Agreement,

> Witness _____ Signed _____

> _____ Signed _____

> Memorandum of Agreement by the Agent of the Hawaiian Government.

> No Contract can be made in Hongkong.

> All Emigrants must go as Free Passengers.

> Each Emigrant shall be given him, 1 heavy Jacket, 1 light Jacket; 1 Waterproof Jacket, 2 pairs Pants, 1 pair shoes, 1 pair Stockings, 1 Hat, 1 Mat, 1 Pillow, 1 Blanket.

> A Present of Ten dollars to be paid the day before the ship sails. In no instance will any deduction from wages be made for Clothes or Money advanced in Hongkong.

> A free passage to Sandwich Islands, with food, water, and Medical care, given each Emigrant.

The Master to pay all Government personal Taxes.

All Children to be taught in the Public Schools, free of any expense to the Parents.

Each Man to receive $6 for each month labor performed of 26 days.

Each Woman to receive $5 for each month labor performed of 26 days.

The wages to be paid in Silver, upon the first Saturday after the end of the month.

No labor shall be exacted upon the Sabbath, only in case of emergency, when it shall be paid for extra.

All emigrants who are employed as House Servants, when their duties compel them to labor Sundays and evenings, shall receive for men 7 dollars per month, for women 6 dollars per month.

Three days Holiday shall be given each Emigrant at Chinese New Year and a present of $2.

These three days time to be counted the same as if employed.

In all cases, the Master to provide good and sufficient food and comfortable House Room.

In case of sickness, Medical attendance and care free.

No wages during illness.

Each Emigrant to find his own Bed clothing.

Each Emigrant, upon arrival in the Sandwich Islands, to sign a contract (to work for such Master as may be chosen for him by the Government Agent) for the term of Five Years from the time of entering upon his duties, to work faithfully and cheerfully according to the laws of the Country, which compel both Master and Servant to fulfill their Contracts.

Families shall not be separated, the Government particularly desire that men will take their wives.

Every Emigrant shall have all the rights and protection under the law that are given to any Citizen of the Country.

At the expiration of the Five Years each Emigrant has a right to remain in the Country, or to leave it.

> Saml. G. Wilder
> H. H. M. Commissioner of
> Immigration.

Ronald Takaki, Pau Hana: Plantation Life and Labor in Hawai'i 1835–1920, 32–33 (1983).

This was what we would now call a "standard-form contract." Its terms were specified by statute, the Masters and Servants Law of 1850, enacted by the legislature of the Kingdom of Hawai'i with the support of European and American planters who, in the weeks prior to the enactment of the law, had organized the Royal Hawai'i an Agricultural Society. Labor contracts in this form were routinely enforced against workers caught fleeing the plantations. Under the Masters and Servants Law, an employee who left a plantation or refused to work was subject to fines, corporal punishment, and forced labor on the plaintiff-employer's plantation (the statute allowed two days labor as punishment for every one day of unexcused absence from work). Under this law, refusing to perform plantation work was treated as a criminal violation. From twenty-first century perspectives, this seems harsh: current law treats employment as a private relationship and breach of employment contract as a matter of civil liability. Criminal punishment is the most coercive form of government regulation; its use against employees was repudiated in most of the United States by the late nineteenth century, along with slavery and indentured servitude. It is true that the statute endorsed symmetry in the criminal treatment of contract breaches in the Kingdom of Hawai'i: the statute defined the employer's obligations (as are incorporated in the Memorandum of Agreement quoted above) and provided punishment by fines for violation of these obligations. Yet in practice the symmetry did not exist—the law was used almost exclusively to enforce workers' obligations.

Court records reveal very few cases brought against plantation owners even though some plantation owners were notoriously abusive. On some plantations, workers were not fully paid or debt was wrongly charged against them. On some plantations the living conditions were extremely crowded and unsanitary, and disease ran rampant. Medical providers were sometimes incompetent and always served in the conflicted role of disciplinarian: workers who became ill and could not work faced either no pay, if the plantation doctor granted permission not to work, or fines of two days' pay for each day of absence, if the doctor refused to grant permission. Many plantation owners refused to listen to workers' complaints and brutally punished any organized effort by workers to seek better working conditions. On many plantations, field workers were prohibited from speaking to one another as they worked. There was no systematic effort by government agents or plantation owners to inform workers of their rights and of avenues of legal recourse. The Public Prosecutor rarely sought enforcement of a plantation owner's obligations and workers did not have the means to contact and hire lawyers. When workers were prosecuted, courts rarely acknowledged their counterclaims against plantation owners.

By the end of the nineteenth century, reformers had managed to repeal the criminal penalties for breach of labor contracts, but plantation owners established private police forces to exercise coercive control over workers on the plantations. The government police force was enlarged in order to recover and control the many workers who sought to flee the plantations. With some changes and much violent repression, this system lasted until the 1940s, when plantation workers finally were able to organize under the protection of the National Labor Relations Act and force plantation owners to deal with the workers' unions.

All of the Hawai'i Supreme Court Justices on the panel that decided H.J. Coolidge v. Pua'aiki and Kea and all of the lawyers involved in the case were European-Americans who were educated in the United States. The court based its decision on ideas drawn from Anglo-American contract law, as well as enactments of the legislature of the Kingdom of Hawai'i. Coolidge vs. Pua'aiki and Kea was initiated by the Public Prosecutor as a criminal case entitled King vs. Pua'aiki and Kea, as were all such cases prior to this one. The Hawai'i Supreme Court decided to rename the case by inserting H.J. Coolidge, the name of the owner of the plantation from which Pua'aiki and Kea had fled, in place of the King. In this way, the Court signaled its decision to treat the dispute as "contractual," involving the relationship between a plantation owner and a plantation worker, and not the relationship between the government and a citizen, despite the fact that the employer's rights were enforced by criminal punishment.

The decision to treat the relationship as contractual was crucial to defining the kinds of arguments that could be made by the litigants. As you read the case, notice that one consequence of this categorization is the assumption, expressed by the court, that the workers had the power to negotiate particular details of their work, including the particular kind of work to be done and the specific plantation to which the worker would be assigned — contrary to the provision in the contract above allocating the power to assign workers to certain masters to the government agent. Once this power is assumed, then defenses to enforcement of the contractual obligation are significantly limited: if a person had the power to create the obligation (the power to choose which promises to make), then that person ought not be allowed to evade the obligation unless something significant has changed in the relevant circumstances. The only logical alternative, given the assumption of power, is to argue that the person who had the power to create the obligation (the power of choice) was somehow defective or improperly constrained so that his or her decisions should not have the binding effect that they otherwise would.

This set of assumptions about the structural relationships between employers and employees continues today. By assuming equality of choice, contract law renders inequality of power between these groups irrelevant to the determination of rights and obligations in employment contracts. In this way contract law serves to protect employers' power to determine wages and working conditions and to maintain low wages for many workers.

Professor Karl Llewellyn, an influential legal realist and principal drafter of the Uniform Commercial Code, observed, in 1931, that the study of contract law has not sufficiently examined the consequences of contract law for groups of people and the significance of social groups (including groups defined by class and other social, political, and economic positioning) in the distribution of power within society. Describing his own study of the tension between contract interpretation and inequality of power between individuals, Llewellyn wrote:

> Too late for remedy I note that this whole paper is thrown off center by failure to carry throughout the discussion an awareness of the groupwise (as contrasted with an individualistic) structure of society.... An effective and sustained integration of such a view of group-wise structure with the subject of the paper, and of both together with the property-system, is difficult ... [because of] the vicious heritage of regularly viewing "parties" to a deal as single individuals.

Karl N. Llewellyn, What Price Contract? An Essay in Perspective, 40 Yale L.J. 704, 733 n.63 (1931). This book, Contracting Law, pursues Llewellyn's insight regarding the importance of understanding the effects of contract law on the allocation of power among groups. Throughout, we focus on the significance of legal rules and analysis to groups such as employers, employees, farmers, bankers, manufacturers, franchisors, franchisees, men, women, racial and ethnic minorities, speakers of languages other than English, lesbian women, gay men, and physically- and mentally-challenged people. Throughout, we invite attention to the effects of contract law on the structures of our social, political, and economic lives.

H.J. Coolidge v. Pua'aiki and Kea

Supreme Court of the Kingdom of Hawai'i
3 Haw. Rep. 810 (1877)

CHARLES COFFIN HARRIS, CHIEF JUSTICE

These are two actions originally brought in the Police Court of Honolulu on contracts for labor; the first contract being for a term of five months, dated the 3d of November 1876, at $12 per month, upon which an advance of $39 is acknowledged to have been received; and the second is dated the 13th of November 1875, for twelve months, at $10

Plantation workers' homes at Wainaku, Hawai'i, circa 1890. Photo by Charles Furneaux reproduced courtesy of the Bishop Museum Archives.

per month, upon which an advance of $35 has been received. The first one is signed by H.J. Coolidge, per M.A. Coolidge; and the second signed by H.J. Coolidge.

It is made to appear that, at the time of signing the contract with Pua'aiki, Mr. Coolidge was out of the country, temporarily, and had left his plantation in charge of his wife, who conducted all the business, and carried on the plantation generally.

Now it is said that this contract is not binding upon Pua'aiki, because [that] Mrs. Coolidge had no authority, in writing, from her husband, and could not bind him so as to make him liable to the penal terms of the 1423 section of the Civil Code, which enacts: That if, on complaint of the servant, the master should be found "guilty of any cruelty, misusage or violation of any of the terms of the contract, the laborer shall be discharged from all obligations of service, and the master shall be fined in a sum not less than five nor more than one hundred dollars, and in default of the payment thereof be imprisoned at hard labor until the same is paid."

It is not alleged that there has been any violation of any terms of the contract on the part of the employer; and it is admitted that Mr. Coolidge returned to the country after the contract had been made in his name, and resumed the carrying on of the plantation himself.

The point in the case seems to be that there is no denial of Mrs. Coolidge's authority, but on the contrary an admission of it, and indeed an express recognition of it by her husband in this and similar cases after his return. She was acting as manager of the plantation during her husband's absence and did all the duties of a manager.

Now if we were to hold that it was necessary for her to have an authority in writing to do this especial act of hiring labor, it would be necessary for any other manager to have it. The employment of labor seems to fall within her authority as manager, and if she were lawfully authorized to act as manager, it was not necessary that she should be authorized in writing. Her act certainly bound her husband to the performance of every condition of the contract contained, not only in the contract itself, but those required by the statute; and therefore there is no failure of "mutuality" of contract, and, indeed, Mr. Coolidge's subsequent adoption of her acts was equivalent to his previous authority. There seems to have been a mistake made at the argument in the idea that this act did not fall within her authority as wife. Neither did it, but it did fall within her authority as manager of the plantation, and in our opinion, even bound her husband to the penalties of the 1423 section, so far as they could be enforced at any time against the owner of any plantation. It will be observed that the imprisonment clause in said section is a mere means of enforcing the payment of the fine. The question raised under the 1423 section seems to be not of much weight, for it would be impossible to imprison an absentee owner or a company of shareholders, and yet when the agent keeps all the terms of the contract the other party to the contract would be bound by it ...

[Further], it is urged against these contracts that they do not indicate in what labor the defendants are to be employed, and that they are not sufficiently particular with regard to the place of performing the labor; and the 1417 section is quoted to support that proposition. The section reads as follows: "Any person who has attained the age of twenty years, may bind himself or herself, by written contract, to serve another in any art, trade, profession or other employment, for any term not exceeding five years."

Pua'aiki's contract reads "that the said party of the second part promises to perform such labor for H.J. Coolidge or his agent in the district of Koolaupoko, Island of Oahu, as the said party of the first part shall direct." This is a clear contract to perform services as a general laborer or servant; and the Hawaiian version, which is not a literal rendering (as it ought to be perhaps) has it "ma ka mahiai, etc." that is to say "farming, etc." and the place designated in Pua'aiki's contract is in the district of Koolaupoko. This is a clear contract to perform reasonable, ordinary acts of labor as he may be directed in the employer's usual and ordinary business.

Now there is no allegation that the men have been required to perform any unusual and extraordinary labor. The most that can be said of the contracts is that they are loose as far as regards the style of labor to be performed and were probably meant to be so by both parties—so likewise with regard to the place where it was to be performed. The laborers signed the contract intelligently and there is no allegation made that either of the parties here have been sent to any place or subjected to any exposure which was not reasonably contemplated by themselves when they signed the contract. If they wished to confine themselves to any particular kind of labor, they should have themselves caused it to have been designated in their contract; so likewise, if they had wished the space, over which they were to be sent, to have been specially limited, they should have caused it to be inserted in their contract. The contracts themselves are not unusual or unreasonable in their forms and requirements.

These cases were entitled *King vs. Pua'aiki*, and *King vs. Kea*. The King is not a proper complainant in such cases. In no respect do they fall within the duties of the public prosecutor. The employer in this case is seeking to enforce his private contract and makes use of the provisions of the law for that purpose. The intitulation should be in this case *H.J. Coolidge vs. Pua'aiki*, as we have made it, by consent, and if a different habit has prevailed, the entering of cases of this nature hereafter should be in accordance with this ruling. The judgment of the Police Magistrate is affirmed.

Anatomy of a Judicial Decision

Lawyers frequently distinguish between law and fact when analyzing a case. In this context, law refers to "[t]he aggregate of legislation, judicial precedents, and accepted legal principles; ... the body of rules, standards, and principles that the courts of a particular jurisdiction apply ..." and fact refers to "actual occurrences, and relationships ... also states of mind such as intentions and the holding of opinion." Bryan A. Garner, Black's Law Dictionary 709, 1015 (10th ed. 2014). The law is "articulated" or "recognized" by the judge and "applied" by either the judge or the jury to decide the rights and obligations of the parties, while facts are "found" or "determined" by the trier-of-fact (in some cases the judge, in others the jury) based on the evidence presented by both parties. Although this distinction cannot be maintained for all purposes and we will reconsider it at various points during this course, it is helpful right now to look more closely at these two as separate parts of a case and to introduce some important aspects of each.

Law

What is "the law"? When lawyers focus on the legal part of a case, what do they see? Although it is not possible to give a simple answer to that question, there are three important aspects of the law side of any case that first year law students should notice: first, there are legal categories into which cases are fitted. Looking at a particular dispute, a judge or lawyer will think "this is a contract dispute," "this is a tort claim," or "this is a Fair Housing Act case." Frequently, a single dispute will involve several legal categories. For instance, a consumer may allege both breach of contract and the tort of negligence in a suit against a manufacturer whose product has caused injury.

Second, the law always involves some idea (or ideas) seen as having special significance to the determination of parties' rights and obligations. The idea is sometimes embodied in a legislative enactment (such as Civil Code section 1423 in Coolidge), but in contract law, the significant ideas are much more frequently statements of principles or doctrine—legal rules, tests, or standards. The term doctrine has both a broad and a more narrow meaning, and the two meanings are in conflict: the broad meaning of doctrine applies to a wide range of rules, terms, principles, values, theories, tenets, beliefs, or philosophies that are treated as authoritative by lawyers and courts; Garner, *id.* at 585; William P. Statsky, Legal Thesaurus/Dictionary 254 (1985); the more narrow meaning is an acknowledged set of rules and terms that are widely recognized as fundamental to a particular category of law. These two meanings conflict because in the more narrow usage, doctrine is treated as distinct from "theory," "principles," "values," and the like, while in the broad definition, these are a part of doctrine. Although this inconsistent usage is confusing for law students and lawyers both, it is so far firmly entrenched. In this course, we will generally use the term doctrine in the more narrow usage, referring to the rules, definitions, and tests (or terms of art) that comprise contract doctrine and we will make it clear when we are using its broader meaning. We will use the term principle to refer to a general value or idea, or more accurately, a cluster of general values and ideas. For now, it is more useful to focus on the concept of a rule in legal doctrine, as we do below.

The third aspect of law that lawyers look for and use are authoritative texts that enact, recognize, or explain a legal rule or term. In contract law the most frequently used authoritative texts are judicial decisions. In addition, legislative and other official enactments, including the Uniform Commercial Code (UCC), address particular kinds of contracts.

Finally, some commentary is very influential in contract law, particularly the Restatements of Contracts drafted by the prestigious American Law Institute.

Let us consider each of these three aspects of the law in more detail.

Legal Categories

In the last paragraph of *Coolidge v. Pua'aiki and Kea*, Chief Justice Harris wrote:

> These cases were entitled *King vs. Pua'aiki*, and *King vs. Kea*. The King is not a proper complainant in such cases. In no respect do they fall within the duties of the public prosecutor. The employer in this case is seeking to enforce his private contract and makes use of the provisions of the law for that purpose. The intitulation should be in this case *H.J. Coolidge vs. Pua'aiki*, as we have made it, by consent, and if a different habit has prevailed, the entering of cases of this nature hereafter should be in accordance with this ruling.

The name of the case was important to the Hawai'i Supreme Court because it signified the legal category into which the dispute fell. By categorizing the cases as contract disputes, instead of criminal cases, for example, or property disputes, the court evoked the set of legal doctrines that it considered appropriate to resolution of the dispute. Three important consequences flowed from this categorization.

First, the choice of legal category makes available and limits the kinds of arguments that appropriately or effectively can be made by each party. Once the relationship was categorized as contractual, any defenses asserted by Pua'aiki and Kea had to be made in the language of contract: they could and did argue that there was no contract, or they could have argued that they should be excused from the contract because of some breach of the contract by Coolidge.

Could the workers have argued that their earlier decisions to enter the contracts should not bind them later? Upon what basis could they have made such an argument? It is difficult, isn't it, to argue that one's present self should not be held responsible for the actions of one's past self? Could Pua'aiki and Kea have said that their past selves, who formed the contract, lacked information necessary to make well-reasoned decisions? Or that the Hawaiian translation of the contract document they were given was not accurate and therefore that they did not understand the terms of the contract? Or that they acted against reason, because of need, stress, anxiety, or fear?

Could Pua'aiki and Kea have said that Coolidge misbehaved in some way and therefore should not be allowed to enforce the contract? Was the employer's misbehavior relevant to the enforcement of the worker's obligation? What about the behavior of other people who were not "parties" to the "contract," such as the government officials who negotiated and facilitated the transformation of land usage; the Hawaiian Sugar Planters' Association representatives who drafted the contract form and convinced government officials to allow enforcement by plantation owners; the Board of Immigration officers who negotiated with foreign governments for the "purchase" of workers for plantation work; or the private police forces that maintained owners' control on the plantations? Would misbehavior by these other people ever be relevant to Pua'aiki's and Kea's "contractual" obligations? These are the lines of argument that are either made available or eliminated by the characterization of these disputes as contractual.

A second consequence of categorizing the dispute as a contract case is that the court then treats it as a situation involving only private individuals, with the state merely giving effect to the choices of the parties. If the court had categorized the case as criminal, in contrast, the involvement of the state would have been a featured element. Although the state clearly played an important role in the enforcement of the contract labor system on the plantations in Hawai'i, this role is not "seen" by the law and thus is not given any weight in evaluating the legal rights and obligations of the individuals. The state had a direct interest in the sugar industry's and later the pineapple industry's ability to retain plantation workers and the court may well have been influenced by this interest in deciding against the workers, yet the state's interest is not examined or explained in the decision. In this way and others, the decision reflects the ideological framework of classical contract law: the ideal of contract as a system of private social ordering that results from the exercise of individual freedom. It is striking to see this framework applied to a case involving criminal penalties, to see the power of this image of freedom control the court's analysis even as the state's coercive force is directly applied. The myth of private ordering (that is, the portrayal of commercial exchanges as unaffected by government action) has had a powerful influence on contract law in the United States.

A third consequence of the court's choice of contract law as the category in which to evaluate the dispute is to incorporate the set of factual assumptions that inform much of contract doctrine as a part of the court's "factual" evaluation. This is one way in which the fact-law distinction blurs—embedded in any area of law are a set of assumptions about the world; antitrust law, for example, rests on assumptions about the functioning of market exchange; labor law embodies assumptions about wage labor; and so on. Contract doctrine too, rests on a set of assumptions about the world. In Coolidge, the court's decision to categorize the cases as contract disputes and the relationships between Pua'aiki and Kea and H.J. Coolidge as employment contracts (rather than, say, to characterize the cases as criminal prosecutions and the relationships as indentured servitude) made it possible for the court to conclude that the workers had power to affect the terms of their relationships with Coolidge, and this factual assumption justified the holding that the two men were legally obligated to work under the terms of the contract.

Legal Rules

Lawyers and judges use the word "rule" often, and the notion of a legal "rule" is crucial to the working of the legal system. A "rule" in law functions very differently from the rules you may encounter elsewhere. Judges and lawyers often talk of a court "defining a new rule of law," or "making new law," as if it were appropriate for the court to use these new rules in evaluating the parties' past behavior. In Coolidge, the court discussed the rule suggested by the defendants: that an agent does not have the authority to hire workers without the principal's written authorization. If the court had decided to adopt such a rule, Mrs. Coolidge's actions taken on behalf of her husband would have been ineffective. The court also discussed the meaning in this case of the existing rule that a contract should not be enforced if its terms are indefinite.

What does it mean to say that there is a "rule," if the rule can be created by the court after the events in the case have already occurred? Imagine playing a game of Rummy: you pick up and discard cards with great skill until you are one card short of being able to "go out," which would make you the winner of the game. But suddenly one of the other players says that he thinks players should have to meld sequences of cards that are not in the same suit—a king of diamonds, queen of spades, jack of hearts, ten of clubs. The rule in Rummy is that you have to have a sequence of four cards in the same suit, hearts for instance, or of the same rank, like four queens. His proposed new rule would mean that all the cards you have melded or laid down are worthless while he would win the game. He admits that his rule is not the traditional rule, but argues that the game would be improved by this change. He insists that the traditional rule is boring and that the new rule would make the game more lively. Whatever the merits of his arguments, and whatever the outcome of the discussion he has initiated, this innovator is not playing Rummy. It may be that he will invent a new and better game, but it will be a new game.

The so-called "rules of law" are not at all like rules of a card game, because in Anglo-American legal practice, in the resolution of a specific dispute, lawyers and judges argue and deliberate not only about whether a particular rule applies to the dispute or whether the rule has been violated; they actually argue, after the fact, about what the rule is or what it should be. In law, it is appropriate for a litigant to challenge the content of a doctrinal rule, to argue that it should be abandoned or changed in some way, even after the events subject to the rule have taken place. The durability of a rule in law depends on a variety of factors, including the institutional setting in which it was articulated (e.g., in legislation, in regulations of administrative agencies, or by courts of high authority) and the degree to which it corresponds or conflicts with deeply held or widely accepted political or ethical values. This is one important reason why law professors emphasize legal reasoning or arguments in law as having significance equal to or even greater than particular doctrinal rules.

Many rules of law are simple and uncontroversial (e.g., a person may not lawfully park in a no-parking zone), and lawyers are not often needed or sought in situations where those uncontroverted rules are applied. When controversy exists—when people disagree about what the law ought to be or to mean in a particular situation—lawyers are needed. And lawyers in these situations need to know not only the current statements of law, but also which of these statements are likely to be disputed, reformulated, limited, or expanded, and how this may occur. So in a case like *Coolidge v. Pua'aiki and Kea*, where the practice involved had already been the subject of social and political debate, the most basic legal issues—like the legal category in which the case belongs and the laws to be applied—become the subject of active debate.

Authoritative Texts in Contract Law

In *Coolidge v. Pua'aiki and Kea*, the court referred to sections 1417 and 1423 of the Civil Code of the Kingdom of Hawai'i. It is unusual that the court did not also cite court decisions, particularly cases discussing agency contracts, the contract doctrine of "mutuality of obligation," and the rule regarding indefiniteness of contract terms.

In contemporary contract law, three types of authoritative texts are most important: (a) judicial decisions; (b) legislation and other official enactments, including the Uniform Commercial Code and the United Nations Convention on Contracts for the International Sale of Goods (hereinafter "CISG"); and (c) commentary, including the Restatements (First and Second) of Contracts. The following is a brief description of these types of authoritative texts.

Judicial Decisions

The most frequently cited authoritative texts in contract law are judicial decisions. These are the precedents that comprise the body of common law. Many of the states in the United States, with the exception of Louisiana, have, by statute, adopted the common law of England, as interpreted by courts in the United States and England, and as adapted or appropriate to the particular state, its people, history, and customs.[1] The general system

---

1. *See, e.g.,* Fla. Stat. § 2.01 ("Common law and certain statutes declared in force. The common law and statute laws of England which are of a general and not a local nature, with the exception

of judicial authority, embodied in the formal structures of state and federal courts and in the doctrine of *stare decisis*, makes decisions of courts authority for future decisions. Generally, a court must accept prior decisions of higher courts within its jurisdiction as authoritative, while it is free to follow decisions by courts in other jurisdictions if the court finds those decisions persuasive.

Legislation and Other Official Enactments

The Uniform Commercial Code was written and promulgated by the National Conference of Commissioners on Uniform State Laws and the American Law Institute. Professor Karl Llewellyn was the reporter and principal drafter of Article 2, dealing with the sale of goods. Goods are defined in the Code as "all things moveable"—virtually all the things that students would buy as consumers—but other things you might not expect such as crops that can be harvested, the unborn young of animals, and minerals that can be removed from under the earth. The Code was written during the late 1940s, subjected to discussion and legislative effort throughout the 1950s, and first adopted by most states in the 1960s. Now every state has adopted all or some part of the Code. We will look closely at several Code provisions, particularly as they incorporate a version of contract law that is different from classical contract law. The Code is more organic or holistic in its approach to contract formation, for example, and it incorporates community norms much more directly than does classical contract law. Specific provisions of Article 2 (governing contracts for the sale of goods) reformulate or reject rules of classical contract law. These provisions have not only changed the rules applicable to contracts governed by Article 2, they have encouraged courts to change the doctrine applicable to other contracts as well.

The United Nations Convention on Contracts for the International Sale of Goods was written by the United Nations Committee on International Trade, with active participation by governmental and nongovernmental representatives from throughout the world. Once the Convention is ratified by a nation, it applies to contracts between its citizens and citizens of another ratifying nation or to contracts where the applicable law is the law of a ratifying nation. The CISG was completed in 1980, after years of negotiation and drafting. It went into force in 1988, after ratification by the necessary number of eleven nations. As of 2014, the Convention had been ratified by the United States and eighty-three other nations, including many of the United States' major trading partners, such as Mexico, Canada, France, Germany, and China. The CISG addresses many specific issues of contract law and in many instances departs from both the Anglo-American common law and the Uniform Commercial Code.

Numerous other federal, state, and local statutes and regulations apply to particular types or aspects of contract. Agencies such as the federal Equal Employment Opportunity Commission, and federal and state consumer protection agencies have adopted rules and guidelines applying to various kinds of contracts. It is important for a lawyer to research

---

herein mentioned, down to the fourth day of July 1776, are declared to be of force in this state; provided, the said statutes and common law be not inconsistent with the constitution and laws of the United States and the acts of the legislature of this state."); Utah Code Ann. §68-3-1 ("Common Law Adopted. The common law of England so far as it is not repugnant to, or in conflict with, the constitution or laws of the United States, or the constitution or laws of this state, and so far only as it is consistent with and adapted to the natural and physical conditions of this state and the necessities of the people hereof, is hereby adopted, and shall be the rule of decision in all courts of this state.").

any statutes or regulations applicable to a contract on which she or he is working. In this course we will direct our attention to the basic issues of contract formation, interpretation, and enforcement and look at statutes of this sort only occasionally.

Commentary

In the United States, courts often cite legal commentary as authoritative text. Commentary includes law review articles, treatises, encyclopedias such as Corpus Juris Secundum and American Jurisprudence, and, most importantly, the Restatement (Second) of Contracts. The Restatement was prepared by the American Law Institute, a prestigious organization of lawyers, judges, and law professors. The Restatement resembles a statute or a compilation of numerous rules of law. In addition, commentary and illustrations are provided for many sections. Although the Restatements purport to be restatements of the common law—the reduction of court decisions to rule-like form—many provisions are attempts to reform particular aspects of the law. In this course, we pay close attention to the Restatement (Second) of Contracts in part because it has wide influence among lawyers, judges, and bar examiners, and in part because it sets out to explain and justify all of current contract doctrine.

Facts

Many people assume that the main reason for a trial is to resolve disagreements about what happened. Indeed, most lawyers would agree that a significant part of any trial is the presentation of evidence leading to findings of fact by the "trier of facts" (either a jury or the judge). But look again at *Coolidge v. Pua'aiki and Kea*: the Hawai'i Supreme Court's opinion mentions a number of facts about the case, most of which apparently were not contested. The parties did not disagree that M.A. Coolidge signed a document that purported to record a contract between her husband, H.J. Coolidge, and Pua'aiki at a time when H.J. Coolidge was away from Hawai'i that H.J. Coolidge signed a paper that purported to record a contract between H.J. Coolidge and Kea; that both Pua'aiki and Kea received some money from Coolidge; and that both Pua'aiki and Kea refused to work on Coolidge's plantation. The parties basically agreed about what happened, when the events happened, and who participated in the events. The "factual" dispute in the case was not so much over what happened as over the meaning and legal significance of those events. And this case is not unusual in that regard. The contest over meaning is often at the heart of legal disputes.

Story-Telling

We ascribe meaning to acts and events. A part of the meaning involves their connection to other acts and events. We construct these connections in the telling of stories (or "histories" or "statements of fact" or "narratives"). These stories then help to identify which doctrine or rule applies. What is a story of the dispute in *Coolidge*? A man named Pua'aiki and a woman named M.A. Coolidge signed a paper; M.A.'s husband, H.J. Coolidge, was away from Hawai'i at the time. A man named Kea and H.J. Coolidge signed another paper. Because M.A. Coolidge hired the two employees while her husband was away, the lawyers for Pua'aiki raised the issue of agency. The Public Prosecutor for the Kingdom of Hawai'i initiated criminal prosecution of Pua'aiki and Kea in the Police Court of Honolulu. Because breach of contract involved criminal sanctions, the lawyers for Pua'aiki and Kea argued that the wife had to be authorized in writing. If you were Pua'aiki's or Kea's attorney, what additional information would you collect and offer in evidence? What facts would you highlight, what story would you tell?

Judicial opinions frequently begin with a story—a telling of the acts and events involved in the dispute. One important purpose of this judicial story-telling is to convey the court's interpretation of the acts and events, so that readers can understand the decision and be persuaded by it. The audience for a judicial opinion includes other judges on a panel, the litigants and the attorneys, appellate courts reviewing the decision, judges deciding other cases, attorneys forming advice or arguments in other cases, legislators considering reform legislation, and business or community groups working on similar issues.

Before writing a final version of an opinion, judges usually read written arguments submitted by the lawyers and litigants, listen to oral arguments, ask questions, and write drafts of an opinion. Often, judges change their minds about cases during this process of reading, listening, questioning, and drafting. The crafting and re-crafting of the story of the case can be an important part of this process, allowing a judge to examine a variety of issues and arguments, from several different perspectives. The process of story-telling is entwined with activities of discovery, analysis, and persuasion.

The way the story of the dispute is told by lawyers involved in the case can be critically important, because a story (or history or statement of facts) invites the listener or reader to think about and evaluate the dispute in certain ways. In pleadings, motions, and hearings the judge is told competing narratives and, at various stages, in small rulings and in a final decision, the judge must choose or compose her own persuasive version of the events. The judge must determine an account of the acts and events in dispute that he or she finds persuasive, believable, satisfying as an explanation of the evidence, taken as a whole. The judge is guided in part by doctrine or statute: sometimes explicitly, as when doctrine includes factual presumptions, and sometimes implicitly, as in Coolidge, when the doctrines of the law of agency directed the court to pay attention to whether the husband later acknowledged the actions taken on his behalf. The judge is also guided by her or his legal education (which trains her or him or her to anticipate certain connections among events), by arguments of counsel (including explicit or implicit claims about the political and ethical significance of different stories), and by the complex understandings about people and the world that judges bring to their work as historically and socially rooted individuals. This last element is worth considering directly.

Background Assumptions

Chief Justice Harris fit the events of Pua'aiki and Kea's relationship with Coolidge into a framework of "background assumptions" or "stories" about human communication and expectations. He apparently assumed that a person can "sell" his or her labor, that people create obligations by particular acts, and that the exercise of "choice" is morally significant. All of these are culturally specific notions: they are not shared by all people. Moreover, they are "deep" or "buried" assumptions: people who have them do not perceive them as assumptions about reality, but as reality itself. This is a phenomenon of culture: the "perspectives" or "culture" of others appear to us as "a different perspective" or "a different culture," while our own perspective or culture seems "real" and functions as the standard with which we measure "difference." So in ascribing meaning to events or in choosing among alternative stories, unexamined assumptions play a large part in what "makes sense" or "seems likely."

In jury trials, the jury is given the responsibility to decide the facts. Professor Scheppele observes:

What are we to make of this practice? We might say, first, that the delegation of fact finding to the jury shows that the selection of the best version of a story is to be made against the backdrop of the community's implicit rules for the construction of reality. If this community does not view orders by spirits to be a reasonable motive for a killing, for example, then a version of reality that incorporates such an account is unlikely to be persuasive to a jury in a murder trial. If the version of reality that the defendant urges is removed far enough from ordinary narrative conventions that the account is unintelligible to typical community members, then the defendant may be found to be insane. Even when a judge composes statements of facts as part of her opinion, the statements generally follow more broadly accepted conventions of storytelling.

Most of the time, the implicit standards for the description of reality work tolerably well. There are large areas of social life where the commonly understood backdrop is so clear that the relevant description of events is obvious. The question "How was your day?" asked by a husband of his wife produces answers that make sense against the backdrop of what they have come to expect from each other. The wife may reasonably answer that the department meeting went well or that she'd finished an article she was working on, but she will probably not say to her husband that she passed three red cars in a row in the university parking lot. The latter statement would generally be seen as irrelevant in that particular context. Similarly, the instruction to a guard to shoot any of his captives who moved does not mean that the guard should then shoot all the prisoners because they are moving around the earth's axis and around the sun. Some things, while part of a description of the "whole truth," generally "go without saying." The array of things that could be said as part of a description is so large that we must have some way of sorting through the huge morass of detail. And those standards are part of the things that one learns growing up as a conventionally socialized member of a culture.

In fact, an account, a story, a version of "what happened" only makes sense against a background that limits the range of things that might be said. To describe the whole truth is impossible; to describe a coherent partial truth means having some background standards for deciding what is relevant and what is not. And judgments of relevance are necessarily local. They depend on things like the social context and the purposes for which the description will be used. What is surprising is how much of social life proceeds with standards for description being implicit, but well-understood, highly complex, but used in practice by a great many social actors.

Agreement over what is true and what has happened does not extend to all areas of social life, however. Perceptual fault lines run through social life in locations where the competing visions of differently socialized groups come into contact, and, when the pressure is great enough, eventually force the perceptions of one group or the other to buckle. Although they may coexist for a long time without serious conflicts, radically different perceptions create the potential for devastating social earthquakes. The pressures of lawsuits, out of which one version or another emerges victorious, make such disasters more likely.

Kim Lane Scheppele, The Re-Vision of Rape Law, 54 U. Chi. L. Rev. 1095, 1107–08 (1987).

Traditional descriptions of litigation focus on disputes about particular facts, the meaning of events, legal categories, and rules of law, but not explicit disputes over background assumptions of reality. Nevertheless, skillful lawyers know that background assumptions about the world profoundly influence a judge's or a juror's perception and interpretation of disputed issues of fact and law. Skillful lawyers attempt, sometimes consciously and sometimes unconsciously, to replace or, at least, to complicate assumptions that may inform a particular decision. Methods for challenging background assumptions include explicitly identifying the assumption, providing more detailed information on the case or on more general matters, and using surprising or otherwise shocking names or labels in order to illuminate unseen aspects or consequences of the assumption.

In Hawai'i, for example, some people challenged the contract labor system by naming it "slavery." Some explicitly questioned the assumption that the relationships between American plantation owners and Portuguese, Hawaiian, Japanese, Chinese, Filipino, Korean, and other workers were the result of workers' "free choice" and "agreement" to the terms written down and they questioned the assumption that the workers had the power to change the terms of the documents they were required to sign. Those who sought to reform or abolish the contract labor system were able to publicly question the set of assumptions underlying surface justifications for the system. As you read cases throughout this course, watch for situations in which lawyers and judges might have used techniques of this sort.

Law, Fact, and Legal Reduction

As you read the materials in this and other courses, it will be important to notice one further element of law and fact. That element is the oversimplification that inheres in the legal practices you study and the legal skills you acquire.

> That life is complicated is a fact of great analytic importance. Law too often seeks to avoid this truth by making up its own breed of narrower, simpler, but hypnotically powerful rhetorical truths. Acknowledging, challenging, playing with these as rhetorical gestures is, it seems to me, necessary for any conception of justice.

Patricia J. Williams, The Alchemy of Race and Rights 10 (1991).

The term "rhetorical truths" used by Professor Williams refers to the classical art of rhetoric, which can be understood generally as "the art of rendering an indeterminate situation determinate for the purposes of action." As Aristotle described it, rhetoric is the art one uses when "things can be other than they appear to be," meaning when people hold different opinions about something (e.g., a plan for the future, an evaluation of past actions, an assessment of a painting, or the meaning of justice) and yet someone has to resolve or select among the different opinions in order to act. The art of rhetoric is the mode of analysis appropriate where scientific or logical proof is not possible.

Rhetoric is the mode through which one characterizes a situation as accurately or usefully or justly as one can and then acts as if that characterization were true. When making a hard decision, it is necessary to pick out aspects of the situation that seem important to the decision. In doing so, one reduces the complexity of the situation by ignoring some aspects and distilling others, but that reduction cannot be avoided. Most work that lawyers do is within the art of rhetoric. Indeed, until the middle of the nineteenth century, lawyers were called rhetors and trained by rhetoricians (including John Adams, Professor of Rhetoric, the first law teacher at Harvard University). This naming ended when, for other reasons, rhetoric came to be viewed in a negative light, as an art of deception or manipulation (this is the origin of the negative connotations of the word "rhetoric" or "mere rhetoric" now in popular use).

One great risk in the art of rhetoric is that people will mistake temporary reductions of complexity, done merely to facilitate action when action was required, for universal truth. In legal disputes, lawyers and judges must characterize and reduce the enormous complexity of motives, emotions, history, and responsibility for the purpose of deciding who will be held legally liable for what. Whether the lawyers and judges do this well or badly in a particular case is itself subject to dispute. But significantly, any such rendition is made for the purposes of that particular case. The rendition and decision made by one court may guide others faced with similar cases in the future (as the doctrine of *stare decisis* provides in most cases), but a prior rhetorical determination is not necessarily the only or the best guide to future determinations. The mistake too often made in the law is to think that past renditions and decisions are statements of universal truth that must be accepted in the future. As Professor Williams suggests, this mistake may block the possibility of justice in particular cases.

Compare the court's discussion of M.A. Coolidge's authority to act on her husband's behalf and its discussion of whether the contract should be enforced. In discussing the agency issue, the court analyzed many factual details and a wide range of factors: that Mrs. Coolidge had managed the plantation in the past; that Mr. Coolidge returned after the contract had been made, resumed management of the plantation, and both explicitly and implicitly acknowledged Mrs. Coolidge's actions on his behalf; that a ruling that a writing was required would apply to plantation managers generally (and, the court implies, this would be unduly burdensome or inefficient). In discussing enforcement of the contracts with Pua'aiki and Kea, in contrast, the court did not give any details about the contract signing that would aid in an analysis of the fairness of forcing them to perform the agreement, although in an aside, the court did say that the contract papers had not been accurately ("literally") translated into Hawaiian ("as it ought to be perhaps"). Instead, the court recited an idealized version of contract methodology:

> The laborers signed the contract intelligently and there is no allegation made that either of the parties here have been sent to any place or subjected to any exposure which was not reasonably contemplated by themselves when they signed the contract. If they wished to confine themselves to any particular kind of labor, they should have themselves caused it to have been designated in their contract; so likewise, if they had wished the space, over which they were to be sent, to have been specially limited, they should have caused it to be inserted in their contract.

The question of whether the contract should be enforced cannot be solved through scientific or logical analysis. It involves a choice among competing values, a choice among competing rhetorical truths. It is important that contractual commitments be taken seriously, that people be required to make promises carefully and to carry out those promises seriously made. It is also important that the government respect private arrangements and individual choice. On the other hand, the court's recitation is unsatisfying because it ignores the difficult political, ethical, and economic questions raised by enforcement of this contract. Commitment to individual freedom suggests that the court should look closely to see if the contractual commitments actually were made with full understanding. The rhetorical truth offered by this court is unsatisfying because many of the details that seem most important are not available. The historical record suggests that the inclusion of more facts in the decision would have undermined the court's decision to enforce the contract, but we cannot know that for sure because the opinion oversimplifies and thus conceals the details of this dispute.

This move to oversimplification in legal analysis is one of the reasons that this book includes works of fiction, history, poetry, economics, philosophy, and political theory.

These materials offer contextual details and experiential insights that are not available in judicial opinions or legislation read in isolation. The interdisciplinary materials also offer theoretical perspectives and narrative techniques that assist lawyers in working with contract principles and doctrine.

———————

Chapter Two

Principles of Contract Law

Good lawyers are skilled at the art of argument. They are able to analyze alternative categories and rules, use authoritative texts, engage in story-telling, and illuminate or challenge background assumptions. Good lawyers are able to identify the legal and factual choices that provide the structure and logic of an argument and to anticipate and formulate alternatives. These skills of persuasion are needed in counseling, drafting, negotiating, litigating, and in a variety of other routine lawyering activities. Thus, a part of legal education is developing the skills of argument.

This chapter discusses the three most influential principles in contract law and the clusters of values and ideas associated with them. The chapter is designed to give you an initial guide to the analysis of arguments in contract law. Spotting these familiar ideas will provide a first step in your analysis of different arguments, rules, and theories in contract law.

The first of these influential principles is called "bargain," the second "reliance," and the third "restitution." Each provides an independent set of reasons for legal intervention to prevent or remedy a particular injury or injustice. The claims of injury and entitlement are familiar. For instance, someone might say "She promised to pay me if I would ___"; or "Because he promised to give me ___, I gave up ___"; or "She owes me because I gave her ___." The blanks may be filled with anything of value: property, money, services, or even something intangible, such as an idea, an opportunity, or a legal right. These statements reference a set of values, including the importance of exchange, trust, or reciprocity. They also trigger different questions that are evaluative of the claims. Did you do what she asked? What made you think you could depend on his promise? Why would you expect her to give you something in return?

It is worthwhile to study each principle separately. It is also true, however, that the values and beliefs associated with each principle overlap in important ways, so that values of one will reappear in association with another. The areas of overlap can be as interesting and instructive as the areas of difference. The imperative of reciprocity, for example, which is central to the restitution principle, is also associated with the bargain principle.

The materials in this chapter focus on the array of values, terms, and arguments associated with each of these three principles.

A. The Bargain Principle

The bargain principle includes the central belief that an agreement to exchange one thing for another gives rise to mutual obligations. "A deal is a deal." This idea is a commonplace in the United States. It is also highly controversial. People disagree, for example, whether "a deal is a deal" if it was made under conditions of coercion, duress, or inequality of power and resources, and people disagree whether coercion, duress, and inequality of power and resources are rare or prevalent in exchange transactions. In our time, deep controversy exists regarding the nature and significance of individual action and interpersonal obligation. The bargain principle is influential throughout contract law, and consequently, the controversies associated with it are pervasive as well.

What values underlie the bargain principle? Why do people think that the act of agreeing to an exchange should result in obligation? Some say it is because of the meaning we assign to the convention of promising. If a person says "I promise" or "I assure you" or makes some equivalent statement, we usually think the person ought to do whatever it is that he or she promised—that is what it means to make a promise. Yet we don't hear all promises in the same way. The statement "I promise not to interrupt" is qualitatively different from the statement "I promise to sell you my car for $3,000." If a promise is part of a "deal," many people think of it as more obligatory than it would be if it were isolated from any exchange.

Having identified this commonplace, a next step is to locate its rationale. This is a process in the traditional art of rhetoric. A "commonplace" is an idea, story, or other belief that is widely held. It is a metaphoric "place"—a place in thought—where people can meet and from which shared ideas and arguments can be drawn. Having met in the common place, we can investigate together: What beliefs make up this place, what reasons might people give for why deals are obligatory? Here are some possibilities:

1. Both sides are committed. When you get something, you give something in return.

2. The other person will count on the deal and spend money or make commitments because he or she believes the deal will be fulfilled.

3. Deal making is the way people make a living—and so the promises made in this context are particularly serious and therefore obligatory.

4. Commercial exchange is crucial to our economy, and if people do not live up to their deals, business people will be unable to plan for the future, people won't be willing to make deals, businesses will shut down, people will be unemployed, etc.

5. Deals and the fulfillment of deals are crucial to a free market system and a free market is essential to individual freedom.

What other reasons might people give to explain and justify this commonplace?

The rationale for a commonplace can be, and often is, controversial. Ideas that seem obvious often seem that way just because they are frequently repeated and seldom examined. But consider: if an idea seems obvious to you, it probably seems obvious to some other people. Some of those people may be judges, and the idea may well influence their decisions. In the same way, though, if an idea seems obvious to you, it might not seem obvious, or it might have a very different meaning, to some other people, including some judges. "Common sense" can refer to a familiarity with the rules and practices of a particular institution, school, family, or job, but rules and practices vary among different institutions and therefore "common sense" varies according to individual experience. The cultural institution of medical care, for example, includes a set of expectations regarding the behavior of doctors towards patients and patients towards doctors; doctors are regarded as having unquestionable authority: the doctor tells the patient what to do, and the patient does it. But these are contested: some doctors and patients think that a different set of norms ought to apply—that doctor and patient should be thought of as "partners" sharing authority in pursuit of the mutual goal of the patient's physical well-being—and they are working to change them; others are not troubled by the existing norms and may perceive them as "intuitively" correct, as "seeming" or "feeling" right or appropriate. Common sense can also reference the respect given to behavior that a particular community views as productive or honorable. So if future-planning or risk-taking is admired, many people will feel these as "intuitively" valuable qualities. Common sense is informed by individual political sensibilities as well. Faith in or skepticism about other human beings or a perception of the world as economically and politically uncertain, for instance, can influence a person's sense of the meaning and rationale for commonplace ideas.

A next step after identifying possible rationales for a commonplace is to interrogate them. One might ask, for example, why is it thought that a person who gets something should give something in return? Who is benefited and who burdened by that belief? Are there some situations where a person is not expected to give something in return? And one might ask of the second belief identified above, is it true that a person will rely on a deal? If so, why is that? Are people more likely to rely on deals than on gifts? If so, why is that? Who benefits and who is burdened by that practice? Are there situations in which we want to discourage reliance on a deal?

To be effective as a lawyer, one must be able to anticipate and address the different ways that decision-makers think about a particular issue or dispute and to challenge what seems "intuitively correct," "obvious," or "natural." That is why law professors frequently ask students to identify familiar ideas associated with a legal doctrine, to investigate their various rationales, and then to interrogate them. This is a way to discover and map the relevant intellectual or ideological terrain. Intuition or "common sense" is only the starting point for legal analysis—reflection and careful interrogation must follow. As you read the materials in this section, formulate your own answers to the question, "Why is a deal, a deal?" and consider critically the answers that are suggested by contract doctrines. The following case suggests a different form of the same question: what is the difference between a promise to make a gift and a promise to make an exchange and why isn't the first just as obligatory as the second?

Kirksey v. Kirksey
Supreme Court of Alabama
8 Ala. 131 (1845)

Assumpsit by the defendant, against the plaintiff in error.[*] The question is presented in this court, upon a case agreed, which shows the following facts:

The plaintiff was the wife of defendant's brother, but had for some time been a widow, and had several children. In 1840, the plaintiff resided on public land, under a contract of lease, she had held over, and was comfortably settled, and would have attempted to secure the land she lived on. The defendant resided in Talladega County, some sixty, or seventy miles off. On the 10th October, 1840, he wrote to her the following letter:

> Dear sister Antillico—Much to my mortification, I heard, that brother Henry was dead, and one of his children. I know that your situation is one of grief, and difficulty. You had a bad chance before, but a great deal worse now. I should like to come and see you, but cannot with convenience at present. . . . I do not know

---

* Editors: Assumpsit was the early writ, or cause of action, for breach of contract. More information on the history of the action for breach of contract and the consideration doctrine is in Chapter Four, infra.

whether you have a preference on the place you live on, or not. If you had, I would advise you to obtain your preference, and sell the land and quit the country, as I understand it is very unhealthy, and I know society is very bad. If you will come down and see me, I will let you have a place to raise your family, and I have more open land than I can tend; and on the account of your situation, and that of your family, I feel like I want you and the children to do well.

Within a month or two after the receipt of this letter, the plaintiff abandoned her possession, without disposing of it, and removed with her family, to the residence of the defendant, who put her in comfortable houses, and gave her land to cultivate for two years, at the end of which time he notified her to remove, and put her in a house, not comfortable, in the woods, which he afterwards required her to leave.

A verdict being found for the plaintiff, for two hundred dollars, the above facts were agreed, and if they will sustain the action, the judgment is to be affirmed, otherwise it is to be reversed.

JOHN J. ORMOND, JUDGE

The inclination of my mind, is, that the loss and inconvenience, which the plaintiff sustained in breaking up, and moving to the defendant's, a distance of sixty miles, is a sufficient consideration to support the promise, to furnish her with a house, and land to cultivate, until she could raise her family. My brothers, however, think that the promise on the part of the defendant, was a mere gratuity, and that an action will not lie for its breach. The judgment of the court below must therefore be reversed, pursuant to the agreement of the parties.

———————

O. Henry (William Sydney Porter), The Gift of the Magi

(1905)

One dollar and eighty-seven cents. That was all. And sixty cents of it was in pennies. Pennies saved one and two at a time by bulldozing the grocer and the vegetable man and the butcher until one's cheeks burned with the silent imputation of parsimony that such close dealing implied. Three times Della counted it. One dollar and eighty-seven cents. And the next day would be Christmas.

There was clearly nothing to do but flop down on the shabby little couch and howl. So Della did it. Which instigates the moral reflection that life is made up of sobs, sniffles, and smiles, and sniffles predominating.

While the mistress of the home is gradually subsiding from the first stage to the second, take a look at the home. A furnished flat at $8 per week. It did not exactly beggar description, but it certainly had that word on the lookout for the mendicancy squad.

In the vestibule below was a letter-box into which no letter would go, and an electric button from which no mortal finger could coax a ring. Also appertaining thereunto was a card bearing the name "Mr. James Dillingham Young."

The "Dillingham" had been flung to the breeze during a former period of prosperity when its possessor was being paid $30 per week. Now, when the income was shrunk to $20, the letters of "Dillingham" looked blurred, as though they were thinking seriously of contracting to a modest and unassuming D. But whenever Mr. James Dillingham Young came home and reached his flat above he was called "Jim" and greatly hugged by Mrs. James Dillingham Young, already introduced to you as Della. Which is all very good.

Della finished her cry and attended to her cheeks with the powder rag. She stood by the window and looked out dully at a gray cat walking a gray fence in a gray backyard. Tomorrow would be Christmas Day, and she had only $1.87 with which to buy Jim a present. She had been saving every penny she could for months, with this result. Twenty dollars a week doesn't go far. Expenses had been greater than she had calculated. They always are. Only $1.87 to buy a present for Jim. Her Jim. Many a happy hour she had spent planning for something nice for him. Something fine and rare and sterling—something just a little bit near to being worthy of the honor of being owned by Jim.

There was a pier-glass between the windows of the room. Perhaps you have seen a pier-glass in an $8 flat. A very thin and very agile person may, by observing his reflection in a rapid sequence of longitudinal strips, obtain a fairly accurate conception of his looks. Della, being slender, had mastered the art.

Suddenly she whirled from the window and stood before the glass. Her eyes were shining brilliantly, but her face had lost its color within twenty seconds. Rapidly she pulled down her hair and let it fall to its full length.

Now, there were two possessions of the James Dillingham Youngs in which they both took a mighty pride. One was Jim's gold watch that had been his father's and his grandfather's. The other was Della's hair. Had the Queen of Sheba lived in the flat across the air shaft, Della would have let her hair hang out the window some day to dry just to depreciate Her Majesty's jewels and gifts. Had King Solomon been the janitor, with all his treasures piled up in the basement, Jim would have pulled out his watch every time he passed just to see him pluck at his beard from envy.

So now Della's beautiful hair fell about her rippling and shining like a cascade of brown waters. It reached below her knee and made itself almost a garment for her. And then she did it up again nervously and quickly. Once she faltered for a minute and stood still while a tear or two splashed on the worn red carpet.

On went her old brown jacket; on went her old brown hat. With a whirl of skirts and with the brilliant sparkle still in her eyes, she fluttered out the door and down the stairs to the street.

Where she stopped a sign read: "Mme. Sofronie. Hair Goods of All Kinds." One flight up Della ran, and collected herself, panting. Madame, large, too white, chilly, hardly looked the "Sofronie."

"Will you buy my hair?" asked Della.

"I buy hair," said Madame. "Take yer hat off and let's have a sight at the looks of it."

Down rippled the brown cascade.

"Twenty dollars," said Madame, lifting the mass with a practiced hand.

"Give it to me quick," said Della.

Oh, and the next two hours tripped by on rosy wings. Forget the hashed metaphor. She was ransacking the stores for Jim's present.

She found it at last. It surely had been made for Jim and no one else. There was no other like it in any of the stores, and she had turned all of them inside out. It was a platinum fob chain simple and chaste in design, properly proclaiming its value by substance alone and not by meretricious ornamentation—as all good things should do. It was even worthy of The Watch. As soon as she saw it she knew that it must be Jim's. It was like him. Quietness and value—the description applied to both. Twenty-one dollars they took from her for it, and she hurried home with the 87 cents. With that chain on his watch Jim might be properly anxious about the time in any company. Grand as the watch was, he sometimes looked at it on the sly on account of the old leather strap that he used in place of a chain.

When Della reached home her intoxication gave way a little to prudence and reason. She got out her curling irons and lighted the gas and went to work repairing the ravages made by generosity added to love. Which is always a tremendous task, dear friends — a mammoth task.

Within forty minutes her head was covered with tiny, close-lying curls that made her look wonderfully like a truant schoolboy. She looked at her reflection in the mirror long, carefully, and critically.

"If Jim doesn't kill me," she said to herself, "before he takes a second look at me, he'll say I look like a Coney Island chorus girl. But what could I do — oh! What could I do with a dollar and eighty-seven cents?"

At 7 o'clock the coffee was made and the frying-pan was on the back of the stove hot and ready to cook the chops.

Jim was never late. Della doubled the fob chain in her hand and sat on the corner of the table near the door that he always entered. Then she heard his step on the stair way down on the first flight, and she turned white for just a moment. She had a habit of saying little silent prayers about the simplest everyday things, and now she whispered: "Please God, make him think I am still pretty."

The door opened and Jim stepped in and closed it. He looked thin and very serious. Poor fellow, he was only twenty-two — and to be burdened with a family! He needed a new overcoat and he was without gloves.

Jim stopped inside the door, as immovable as a setter at the scent of quail. His eyes were fixed upon Della, and there was an expression in them that she could not read, and it terrified her. It was not anger, nor surprise, nor disapproval, nor horror, nor any of the sentiments that she had been prepared for. He simply stared at her fixedly with that peculiar expression on his face.

Della wriggled off the table and went for him.

"Jim, darling," she cried, "don't look at me that way. I had my hair cut off and sold it because I couldn't have lived through Christmas without giving you a present. It'll grow out again — you won't mind, will you? I just had to do it. My hair grows awfully fast. Say 'Merry Christmas!' Jim, and let's be happy. You don't know what a nice — what a beautiful, nice gift I've got for you."

"You've cut off your hair?" asked Jim, laboriously, as if he had not arrived at that patent fact yet even after the hardest mental labor.

"Cut it off and sold it," said Della. "Don't you like me just as well, anyhow? I'm me without my hair, ain't I?"

Jim looked about the room curiously.

"You say your hair is gone?" he said, with an air almost of idiocy.

"You needn't look for it," said Della. "It's sold, I tell you — sold and gone, too. It's Christmas Eve, boy. Be good to me, for it went for you. Maybe the hairs of my head were numbered," she went on with a sudden serious sweetness, "but nobody could ever count my love for you. Shall I put the chops on, Jim?"

Out of his trance Jim seemed quickly to wake. He enfolded his Della. For ten seconds let us regard with discreet scrutiny some inconsequential object in the other direction. Eight dollars a week or a million a year—what is the difference? A mathematician or a wit would give you the wrong answer. The magi brought valuable gifts, but that was not among them. This dark assertion will be illuminated later on.

Jim drew a package from his overcoat pocket and threw it upon the table.

"Don't make any mistake, Dell," he said, "about me. I don't think there's anything in the way of a haircut or a shave or a shampoo that could make me like my girl any less. But if you'll unwrap that package you may see why you had me going a while at first."

White fingers and nimble tore at the string and paper. And then an ecstatic scream of joy; and then, alas! A quick feminine change to hysterical tears and wails, necessitating the immediate employment of all the comforting powers of the lord of the flat.

For there lay The Combs—the set of combs, side and back, that Della had worshiped for long in a Broadway window. Beautiful combs, pure tortoise shell, with jeweled rims— just the shade to wear in the beautiful vanished hair. They were expensive combs, she knew, and her heart had simply craved and yearned over them without the least hope of possession. And now, they were hers, but the tresses that should have adorned the coveted adornments were gone.

But she hugged them to her bosom, and at length she was able to look up with dim eyes and a smile and say: "My hair grows so fast, Jim!"

And then Della leaped up like a little singed cat and cried, "Oh, oh!"

Jim had not yet seen his beautiful present. She held it out to him eagerly upon her open palm. The dull precious metal seemed to flash with a reflection of her bright and ardent spirit.

"Isn't it a dandy, Jim? I hunted all over town to find it. You'll have to look at the time a hundred times a day now. Give me your watch. I want to see how it looks on it."

Instead of obeying, Jim tumbled down on the couch and put his hands under the back of his head and smiled.

"Dell," said he, "let's put our Christmas presents away and keep 'em a while. They're too nice to use just at present. I sold the watch to get the money to buy your combs. And now suppose you put the chops on."

The magi, as you know, were wise men—wonderfully wise men—who brought gifts to the Babe in the manger. They invented the art of giving Christmas presents. Being wise, their gifts were no doubt wise ones, possibly bearing the privilege of exchange in case of duplication. And here I have lamely related to you the uneventful chronicle of two foolish children in a flat who most unwisely sacrificed for each other the greatest treasures of their house. But in a last word to the wise of these days let it be said that of all who give gifts these two were the wisest. Of all who give and receive gifts, such as they are wisest. Everywhere they are wisest. They are the magi.

Note

William Sydney Porter, otherwise known as O. Henry, was born in 1862 in North Carolina. He began his career as a writer of short stories in earnest after he was convicted of embezzlement in 1898 and sent to prison in Ohio for three years. Porter moved to New

York after his release and during the next nine years before his death in 1910, he published more than 300 stories and became one of the most popular writers of the time. "The Gift of the Magi" is one of O. Henry's most famous stories. "The Gift of the Magi" seems at first to confirm the opposition between market exchange and exchange between family members. Do the generalizations we make about market exchange apply in all of Della's transactions? Do Della and Jim have expectations of one another that do not involve individual benefit or profit? Is there any exchange between the two? What is the distinction, if there is one, between exchanges involving family members and exchanges in the market?

What makes one promise a "mere gratuity" and another part of a market exchange? Does the fact that a promise is made in a family setting lead you to think, as the majority of the Alabama Supreme Court thought, that the promise had to be an act of charity or a gift rather than a bargain? Was Judge Ormond inclined to enforce the promise because he thought the parties had bargained?

The distinction between gift and enforceable bargain that is suggested in *Kirksey* implies that the distributions of resources that take place in one kind of human interaction are qualitatively different from those that take place in another. Why might someone assume that one mode of economic distribution, a promise of a gift, should be excluded from the realm of legal liability while another, bargain, is included? One rationale for this commonplace is that it is possible and worthwhile to distinguish between market transactions and non-market transactions. And why? The answer to this question is difficult to locate. To many Americans, it just seems intuitively correct that market transactions define a realm separate from non-market transactions between family members, lovers, neighbors, and the like.

Intuitions are difficult to interrogate. It is helpful to consider alternative commonplaces, alternative intuitions, as a way to get outside of one's own. For example, interest in cross-cultural comparison of economic beliefs and practices ("market ideology") was stimulated by the great economic success of Japan during the period from the 1960s to the 1980s and by the recognition and promotion of the concept of a "global economy." Businesspeople and others in the United States have examined the differences between the United States and Japan in the way market transactions are considered and practiced. Market ideology is radically different in the two nations.

In the United States, market transactions are thought to involve exchanges between people who are not otherwise obligated to each other, that is, "arm's length" transactions. The relationship between buyer and seller or between employer and employee is viewed as economic, not "social" or "personal." In Japan, in contrast, market transactions are thought to include important social and personal elements. As you read John Elemans' essay describing employment relations in large Japanese corporations, consider the differing ideas about market transactions in Japan and the United States.

John Elemans, The Gift Economy

(1990)

One area in which American companies are always at a disadvantage when operating in Japan is that of personnel. American managers frequently complain that they are unable to attract the best Japanese people to work for them. Americans are often at a loss to explain this problem: compared to Japanese employers these companies offer exceptional wages, longer holidays, shorter work hours, challenges and other benefits that would make these jobs seem like great opportunities to anyone. Why then do Japanese people refuse to work for these companies?

The answer? The factors that Americans find important in selecting a job are not important to Japanese. The traditional business analysis does not work. In fact, the rules of a market economy are not the rules that apply in the Japanese employment world; rather the rules of a gift economy apply.

...

When an American takes a job, he or she is entering into an exchange that takes place almost totally in the market economy: the company is buying that person's labor. Although some degree of company loyalty may develop, compared to the Japanese, Americans find it easy to change jobs and do so more often. When another job that is more interesting pays more or is more convenient comes along, people switch jobs. This is accepted as a societal norm.

When a Japanese person takes a job, he or she is entering into a series of exchanges that take place almost totally in a gift economy....

Japanese companies give gifts to their employees on all of the occasions in which gifts are exchanged between ordinary individuals; weddings and deaths are the two most common. In these cases the company is personified by the department manager, who must also attend the ceremonies associated with these events. Both require the exchange of gifts between both parties; the company also receives gifts from the employee. At a Japanese wedding, guests bring gifts of money, and guests receive a physical gift of about the same value as the monetary gift (the amount is generally approximated in advance by the level of one's income and social station). At funerals, guests also bring money and receive food at the wake, as well as salt and tea or sweets to take home. In these cases the company provides the money to be given by the manager. It is important to note that the manager is not paid extra for his time on these jobs. This reinforces his symbolic representation of the company (he is not a hireling doing the job for money).

...

The largest gift-giving occasion in the West is obviously Christmas. The Japanese have adapted this custom, blending it with o-sei-bo (literally "year end gift"). Japanese also have adopted a similar Chinese custom called Chu-gen. Chu-gen takes place in July (not on any fixed day). On each of these occasions Japanese people give gifts to people with whom they have certain relationships (friends and debt or obligation relationships). On these occasions companies also give an important gift to employees in the form of cash payments. The word used to describe the money is borrowed from English, "bonus," but it has completely different connotations and meaning from the English word. Notably the total value of the bonus in Japan is from four to twelve times (occasionally higher) the value of one's monthly salary. The level varies roughly with the economic well-being of the company. Furthermore, no Japanese treats this money as a bonus in the Western sense. It is necessary for survival....

Any company in Japan must give a constant stream of small gifts to any company that buys its product or service. These gifts, which take the form of cookies, cakes, cooking oil, soap, soy sauce, fruit, canned goods, tea, coffee, and so on, are exchanged by visiting personnel. As they are received by the company, they are passed on to the employees who share them. Especially large amounts of these gifts are passed out a Christmas and at Chu-gen, but continue year 'round.

Another important event in Japan is the New Year celebration. This is so large and complex that it commonly begins in early December. Like the Chu-gen, gift-giving is not fixed on a single day (like Christmas Day); the actual event is more hazy. New Year celebrations are more like big communal birthday parties. In the Chinese tradition a person's age is counted from New Year, not the physical birthday. Two of several important celebrations at this time are the bo-nen-kai ("to forget the year gathering") and shin-nen-kai ("new year gathering"). Again, almost all companies arrange these parties for their employees (as well as separate ones for customers).

. . .

Another Western custom adopted (and adapted) by the Japanese relates to Valentine's Day. It is common in Japan for females to give chocolates to two groups of men on February 14. One group consists of men (usually one man) they are romantically interested in. In the second case, gifts of chocolate are given to anyone to whom the woman feels indebted or under obligation. These gifts are called giri-choco ("duty-chocolate"). Virtually all women in Japan give such gifts to their managers.

The main gift given by the employees to their company for all the gifts just described is their labor. Work is done with great concern for accuracy, for quality and for promptness. This does not take place only in limited areas of production but pervades the society. As one visitor to Japan remarked after he had some papers photocopied: the job was flawless. Each page was perfectly centered, and each page matched the others. It was the extraordinary care shown to what would normally (by Westerners) be considered an insignificant job that impressed him.

. . .

Rather than looking at how American companies can compete inside Japan, perhaps Japan's economic success brings into question the usefulness or validity of the current employee/employer relationship in America.

In the environment I have tried to describe, each employee develops a rich sense of belonging and security. No amount of money, number of holidays (without the rest of the group), or opportunity for advancement can equal these things. In the Japanese norm, a "job" has a deep context and meaning which an American "job" does not....

Note — On Markets and Market Ideologies

A common definition of a market economy is a system in which goods and services are allocated through a regime of individual property ownership and voluntary exchange. By this definition, the Japanese economy, including the particular system of labor in large Japanese corporations that Elemans describes, surely is a "market economy." The description of the Japanese economy as a "gift economy" adopted by John Elemans, a North American, is misleading in as much as it suggests that the Japanese system is not a "market economy." The Japanese market economy is instead *different* from the U.S. market economy, because the two systems are informed by different beliefs and values. The common understanding of market transactions in Japan, as described by Elemans, does not rest upon the same distinction between market and non-market transactions that is so important to market ideology in the United States.

Market ideology in the United States features competition as a fundamental element of the market system, and this idea reinforces the perceived distinction between market and non-market transactions. U.S. market theory assumes that it is robust competition that will lead to lower prices and higher quality and views gift-giving as an inappropriate interference with competition over price and quality. Yet gifts are given by companies in the United States in a variety of different contexts and some U.S. companies have traditions of family picnics, Christmas parties, retirement dinners, or gifts (the symbolic gold watch) that are expressions of community and interdependence. There also has been a proliferation of "loyalty" programs in a variety of industries that sell to consumers. Reward points earned on credit card expenditures, discount cards, airline loyalty programs, and points from retailers for every purchase of more than a certain amount. These programs are meant to promote return business and additional purchases.

But still, many people in the United States are suspicious of gifts and personal loyalty in business relationships. Business gifts and personal loyalty are thought to "distort" market competition: many think that a gift to a purchasing agent by a seller's representative, for example, may encourage the agent to buy from the gift-giver even though her or his price is higher than that of others or that personal loyalty may lead to "sweetheart deals" in which lower quality goods or services are purchased merely because of personal loyalty. Price and quality are viewed as the only "legitimate" grounds for purchasing decisions and considerations of friendship or personal loyalty are seen as improper—gift-giving and personal loyalty in business become bribery or extortion. Conversely, economic interactions are thought to corrupt friendships. "Never lend money to a friend," Americans say. The perception of these risks lends support to the idea that a clear line can and should be drawn between private friendship and business exchange.

Although loyalty by an employee to a company is seen as motivation for high productivity, loyalty by management towards individual employees is viewed as potentially disruptive of a company's profit-maximizing goals. Professional managers often view acts of benevolence by management towards individual employees as fiscally wasteful and disruptive of healthy competition. Business managers in the United States generally consider competition important in the labor market and treat loyalty and benevolence as distorting extras, to be omitted especially in times of recession, where wage reductions, plant closings, layoffs, worker replacement, and forced retirement are common management strategies.

Closely linked to U.S. market ideology, the bargain principle features the idea that it is possible and desirable to distinguish between "gift promises" and "promises made in exchange." The comparison with Japanese gift-giving practices reveals the cultural specificity of the distinction between "market" and "non-market" transactions.

Neo-Classical Economics and Contract Law

Elemans suggests that the "obvious" distinction between market and non-market transactions—between exchanges and gifts—reflects one among many different ways to understand and organize resource allocations and transfers. By featuring voluntary, arm's length exchange as a central basis for human obligation, contract law in the United States adopts one among many theories for understanding and organizing the allocation of goods and services in our society and one among several models of market exchange

The economic theory most closely associated with the bargain principle is neo-classical economics. Professor Robin Malloy, an economist and legal scholar, describes some of the basic assumptions on which neo-classical economics relies and the values that inform and are informed by these assumptions. The assumptions of neo-classical economics are:

- People act in their own self interest;
- In the pursuit of self interest, people act rationally;
- People have access to perfect information (this assumption means that people have the knowledge necessary to act rationally);

- People and resources are freely moveable;
- There are no artificial restrictions on entry to the marketplace (relying on this assumption we must conclude that the marketplace remains competitive because buyers and sellers are free to move in and out of the market and thereby effectuate the free mobility of people and resources);
- The current distribution of wealth and resources is taken as a given (acceptance of the current distribution is an important assumption in the neo-classical model because the allocation of resources and rights derived from the model is determined by people casting wealth-based economic votes. In other words, to the extent people cast their votes in the marketplace by spending dollars, the initial allocation of dollars will affect the outcome of the voting).

The values associated with neo-classical economics are:

First, because people are able to act rationally to make decisions in their own self interest, it becomes a value to say that they do. This value ... presumes that these self interested choices in the aggregate are an expression of the best choices for society.

Second, the notion that people have perfect information implies that there is no economic or educational bias in the ability to process this information. The value expressed here accepts the current distribution of educational and economic resources, leading to disparate results in the processing by otherwise equally possessed human beings.

Third, the ability to freely move implies a value judgment against the hardship claims of those that fail to uproot their families and relocate. It is a value judgment that dehumanizes the experience of relocating and, therefore, treats the mobility of people as inanimate objects.

Fourth, free exit and entry into the market is essential to competition and the results of competition are presumed to be desirable.

Fifth, and finally, acceptance of the current allocation is fair and equitable or at least that there is no fair or equitable means of substantially improving or changing the current situation.

Robin Paul Malloy, Law and Economics: A Comparative Approach to Theory and Practice 54–55 (1990).

Unlike earlier beliefs of *laissez faire* free market economics, neo-classical economic theory sees an important role for law in facilitating and regulating market transactions. Should judges pursue economic goals in deciding contract cases? It is possible and desirable, some lawyers argue, to have law be entirely separate and independent of economic concerns. This view is often coupled with the argument that law is also separate and independent of morality and politics. Others reject this view of law, arguing that it is neither possible nor desirable to maintain rigid boundaries between law, economics, politics, and morality, because each of these four areas is concerned with justice, and they overlap in important ways. Judges and lawyers draw upon economic, moral, and political arguments in legal decision-making largely because they see these as relevant to matters of justice. The relevant question may not be whether judges and lawyers should pursue economic goals but rather whether judges, lawyers, and others should be aware and willing to admit that they are doing this. The idea that law has its own special reasoning and that it is "neutral," devoid of moral, political or economic content or consequence, is appealing. But again, so long as the law is understood to be an instrument of justice, then legal issues, arguments,

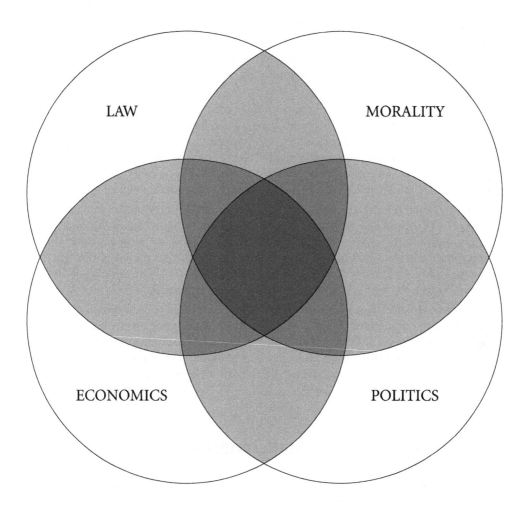

and value choices will be influenced by and will influence the discourse and practices of economics, morality, and politics.

Earlier we offered a definition of law as "[t]he aggregate of legislation, judicial precedents, and accepted legal principles; ... the body of rules, standards and principles that the courts of a particular jurisdiction apply...." *Economics* can be defined as "of, relating to, or based on the production, distribution, and consumption of goods and services"; *politics* (from *polis*, meaning a group of people living as a community) can be defined as "an activity or art associated with the relations among people in society"; and *morality* or *ethics* (from *ethos*, meaning habit or character) can be defined as "related to matters of right and wrong behavior or good and bad character" (although there are important differences in the connotations of the different words morality and ethics, we will treat them as roughly equivalent).

Specialists working in one or another of these areas have claimed that their area predominates over the others: some political scientists, for example, have argued that law, morality, and economics are merely manifestations of politics; some economists have claimed that morality, law, and politics are merely expressions of economic concerns; some moral philosophers have contended that issues of morality underline all economic, political, and legal matters; and some legal theorists have argued that law is the framework within which all moral, economic, and political concerns must be expressed. Others have argued that each of the four areas are autonomous, unconnected to any other. In our study of contract law, we treat these four areas as overlapping spheres, each of which offers important ideas and concerns about justice, which can be defined as "right or good ordering of human life."

As you read judicial opinions in this and other courses, watch for arguments and assumptions drawn from political, economic, moral, and legal discourse. Sometimes judges draw distinctions between moral and legal responsibility or between a "legal" question and a "political" or "policy" question, saying the latter should be addressed by the legislature and not the courts. In other cases, judges, without apology, make explicitly moral, economic, or political arguments as an integral part of their legal analysis.

Professor Malloy comments on the need for lawyers to become familiar with economic arguments: "[J]udicial decisions and legal argument are oftentimes built on underlying assumption[s] which are ideologically based. Thus, the good lawyer needs to be able to decipher hidden ideological bias in legal argumentation so that the most effective case can be made for one's own cause." Robin Paul Malloy, *id.* at 49. The same could be said for the value of learning to discern moral and political arguments.

As Professor Malloy suggests, one advantage in studying economic, moral, and political assumptions and arguments in law is that it enables one to understand, use, or contest them in particular cases. In your study of contract law, it is important to see the connection between the bargain principle and neo-classical economic assumptions and arguments and also to see the ways that current law varies from those assumptions and arguments.

B. Reliance: Trust, Responsibility, Injury

The reliance principle begins with the idea that people do rely upon each other in many situations and that such reliance often is morally and politically valuable. In its best form, reliance flows from and is an indication of trust. Trust is important to human life, both at a level of social trust, where people believe that even strangers will not harm them, and at a personal level, where one has some confidence that another person will do as she or he says. Trust is so pervasive in our lives that we tend not to notice it. Yet we trust others, including many strangers, on a daily basis in many ways. We rely on grocery stores to sell food that is not poisoned; we rely on doctors we have never met before to give us appropriate medical care; we trust bus drivers, train engineers, and airplane pilots to carry our bodies safely at high speeds; we trust child care providers, schools, and camps with our children; we trust carpenters and mechanics with our homes and belongings. Most human activities and achievements require trust, reliance, and cooperation.

In the United States, however, many people are concerned that social and personal trust has waned. "People increasingly [have] become resigned to a society in which taking advantage of others when one can is standard and accepted behavior. All seem to feel they must take part in the struggle to advance their own interests, or others will do so at their expense." Virginia Held, Rights and Goods 62–63 (1984). People are less trusting: businesspeople are less willing to extend credit; some consumers do not trust "mainstream" grocery stores and agricultural producers to sell healthy foods; many do not trust public hospitals and other medical care providers; many do not trust lawyers; and many do not trust their children to educational institutions, resorting instead to home schooling. Weakening of social and personal trust shifts the meaning of reliance and interdependence. In the absence of trust, reliance occurs only when people have no alternatives; in the absence of trust, relying on others is a burden that must be assumed only by those who have little power or resources.

Some maintain that decreasing levels of trust in the United States is a consequence of our political and economic beliefs: "The teachings that students and citizens absorb frequently extol rather than question egoism: the liberal tradition asserts that government is justified only if it serves individual self-interest; the myth of Adam Smith, on which capitalism and market economies rest, asserts that if all pursue their own selfish interests, this will add up to what is best for everyone; the novels of Ayn Rand and the theories of libertarians carry the excesses of egoism to new heights of popularity.... But trust and co-operation cannot be built on egoism." Malloy, *supra*, at 63. Recognition of the significance and value of trust and interdependence is at the core of the reliance principle in contract law and so questions regarding the weakening of trust and the political, moral, and economic meaning of reliance have become a significant part of contemporary contract law.

Laurie Kuribayashi, Freeway Poem

(1986)

He's right.
Freeway driving, like everything else
she's afraid of trying,
isn't as impossible as she'd thought.
He taught her, out of necessity
more than love, to synchronize
their travel with the other cars.
She learned not to think,
while winding around the curve
between Moanalua and Halawa,
about the parallel impact between
crashing at 50 mph on asphalt
and falling fifteen stories
to land spread-eagled on cement.
Images of Lee being gutted
by his stick shift on the H-1
and Clara's windshield guillotine
no longer come to mind
as she accelerates on the onramp
above Church of the Crossroads.
But he knows it's not enough
to face fear with rationality
and necessary action: he knows
freeway driving, like everything else
that frightens her, is filled
with uncertainty and so requires
a certain amount of faith,
in herself and others,

that she so rarely finds: as always
there are just too many variables
juxtaposing at too high a speed.
And she still can't tell, no matter
how she peers into that little mirror
screwed onto the car door,
how fast a car is coming at them;
she still feels that mystical anxiety
whenever the shadow of an overpass
passes through the car so fast
that it's almost non-existent;
and she still wishes she had that faith
to merge with the minimum of panic,
to believe that together
they could move safely forward,
parallel with the others.

Note

The reliance principle values trust and seeks to protect those who rely on others; the principle is concerned with the existence and strength of trust among us. However, the reliance principle also includes the belief that there should be limits on trust and reliance. Self-sufficiency is valued along with interdependence. Imposing oneself and one's needs on others is not thought admirable. This potential conflict is sometimes reconciled in the statement, "reasonable reliance ought to be valued and protected." Yet it is the notion of "reasonableness" in this context that is hotly contested. Some people maintain that it is "reasonable" to rely on another person in a variety of different circumstances. Others maintain that it is reasonable to rely on another person only if that person has promised to do something or otherwise voluntarily invited the reliance. This second position echoes the modern emphasis on choice: one ought not to rely on someone unless he or she has chosen to assume the burden of your reliance. If the person has not chosen to be reliable, then it is wrong or at least unreasonable for you to rely on that person. This idea, that reliance is reasonable only when the other person has voluntarily assumed the burden of your reliance, is both pervasive and persistently challenged in current law.

As a result of this limitation, the reliance principle in current law emphasizes promises — the belief that promises should be kept, and, in a more controversial way, the question whether obligation should ever be imposed in the absence of a promise. At the same time, however, the reliance principle features a different set of ideas regarding harm and responsibility. The reliance principle draws from the idea that a central purpose of legal action is to correct wrongs. It focuses on harm, in the concrete form of out-of-pocket losses, and on the belief that one who causes harm should be accountable for it. The difference between the bargain principle and the reliance principle is the difference between distributive and corrective (or restorative) justice. The bargain principle provides that the existence of a bargain entitles each person to the benefit he or she expected from ᵗ exchange (a distributive claim). The reliance principle, in contrast, holds that a person ᵗ has been injured ought to be compensated for that injury (a corrective or restorative). Just as restorative justice sometimes has been seen as more compelling than the claim for distributive justice, the reliance principle in contract law has been seen by many as more compelling than the bargain principle. *See, e.g.,* Lon Fuller & William Purdue, The Reliance Interest in Contract Law, 46 Yale L.J. 52 (1936); Patrick S. Atiyah, The Rise and Fall of Freedom of Contract (1979).

Historically, protection for reasonable reliance predated classical contract law and its emphasis on the bargain principle. Following the development of classical contract law, reliance rather quickly resurfaced as a major challenge to the classical model of bargained-for exchange. The following case, *Ricketts v. Scothorn,* is a leading case for the doctrine of "promissory estoppel," which is the most direct manifestation of the reliance principle in current contract law.

Andrew Ricketts v. Katie Scothorn

Supreme Court of Nebraska
77 N.W. 365 (1898)

JOHN JOSEPH SULLIVAN, JUDGE

In the District Court of Lancaster County the plaintiff, Katie Scothorn, recovered judgment against the defendant, Andrew D. Ricketts, as executor of the last will and testament of John C. Ricketts, deceased. The action was based upon a promissory note, of which the following is a copy: "May the first, 1891. I promise to pay to Katie Scothorn on demand, $2,000, to be at 6 per cent. per annum. J.C. Ricketts." In the petition the plaintiff alleges that the consideration for the execution of the note was that she should surrender her employment as bookkeeper for Mayer Bros., and cease to work for a living. She also alleges that the note was given to induce her to abandon her occupation, and that, relying on it, and on the annual interest, as a means of support, she gave up the employment in which she was then engaged. These allegations of the petition are denied by the administrator. The material facts are undisputed. They are as follows: John C. Ricketts, the maker of the note, was the grandfather of the plaintiff. Early in May—presumably on the day the note bears date—he called on her at the store where she was working. What transpired between them is thus described by Mr. Flodene, one of the plaintiff's witnesses: "A. Well, the old gentleman came in there one morning about nine o'clock, probably a little before or a little after, but early in the morning, and he unbuttoned his vest, and took out a piece of paper in the shape of a note; that is the way it looked to me; and he says to Miss Scothorn, 'I have fixed out something that you have not got to work any more.' He says, none of my grandchildren work, and you don't have to. Q. Where was she? A. She took the piece of paper and kissed him, and kissed the old gentleman, and commenced to cry." It seems Miss Scothorn immediately notified her employer of her intention to quit work, and that she did soon after abandon her occupation. The mother of the plaintiff was a witness, and testified that she had a conversation with her father, Mr. Ricketts, shortly after the note was executed, in which he informed her that he had given the note to the plaintiff to enable her to quit work; that none of his grandchildren worked, and he did not think she ought to. For something more than a year the plaintiff was without an occupation, but in September 1892, with the consent of her grandfather, and by his assistance, she secured a position as bookkeeper with Messrs. Funks & Ogden. On June 8, 1894, Mr. Ricketts died. He had paid one year's interest on the note, and a short time before his death expressed regret that he had not been able to pay the balance. In the summer or fall of 1892 he stated to his daughter, Mrs. Scothorn, that if he could sell his farm in Ohio he would pay the note out of the proceeds. He at no time repudiated the obligation. We quite agree with counsel for the defendant that upon this evidence there was nothing to submit to the jury, and that a verdict should have been directed peremptorily for one of the parties. The testimony of Flodene and Mrs. Scothorn, taken together, conclusively establishes the fact that the note was not given in consideration of the plaintiff pursuing, or agreeing to pursue, any particular line of conduct. There was no promise on the part of the plaintiff to do, or refrain from doing, anything. Her right to the money promised in the note was not made to depend upon an abandonment of her employment with Mayer Bros., and future abstention from like service. Mr. Ricketts made no condition, requirement, or request. He exacted no quid pro quo. He gave the note as a gratuity, and looked for nothing in return. So far as the evidence discloses, it was his purpose to place the plaintiff in a position of independence, where she could work or remain idle, as she might choose. The abandonment of Miss Scothorn of her position as bookkeeper was altogether voluntary. It was not an act done in fulfillment of any contract obligation assumed when she accepted the note. The instrument in suit, being given without any valuable consideration, was nothing more than a promise to make a gift in the future of the sum of money therein named. Ordinarily, such promises are not enforceable, even when put in the form of a promissory note. *Kirkpatrick v. Taylor*, 43 Ill. 207; *Phelps v. Phelps*, 28 Barb. 121; *Johnston v. Griest*, 85 Ind. 503; Fink v. Cox, 18 Johns. 145. But it has often been held that an action on a note given to a church, college, or other like institution, upon the faith of which money has been expended or obligations incurred, could not be successfully defended on the ground of a want of consideration. *Barnes v. Perinea*, 12 N.Y. 18; *Philomath College v. Hartless*, 6 Or. 158; *Thompson v. Board*, 40 Ill. 379; *Irwin v. Lombard University*, 46 N.E. 63 (Ohio). In this class of cases the note in suit is nearly always spoken of as a gift or donation, but the decision is generally put on the ground that the expenditure of money or assumption of liability by the donee on the faith of the promise constitutes a valuable and sufficient consideration. It seems to us that the true reason is the preclusion of the defendant, under the doctrine of estoppel, to deny the consideration. Such seems to be the view of the matter taken by the supreme court of Iowa in the case of *Simpson Centenary College v. Tuttle*, 33 N.W. 74 (Iowa), where Rothrock, J., speaking for the court, said: "Where a note, however, is based on a promise to give for the support of the objects referred to, it may still be open to this defense [want of consideration], unless it shall appear that the donee has, prior to any revocation, entered into engagements, or made expenditures based on such promise, so that he must suffer loss or injury if the note is not paid. This is based on the equitable principle that, after allowing the donee to incur obligations on the faith that the note would be paid, the donor would be estopped from pleading want of consideration." And in the case of *Reimensnyder v. Gans*, 2 Atl. 425 (Pa.), which was an action on a note given as a donation to a charitable object, the court said: "The fact is that, as we may see from the case of *Ryerss v. Trustees*, 33 Pa. St. 114, a contract of the kind here involved is enforceable rather by way of estoppel than on the ground of consideration in the original undertaking." It has been held that a note given in expectation of the payee performing certain services, but without any contract binding him to serve, will not support an action. *Hulse v. Hulse*, 84 E.C.L. 709. But when the payee changes his position to his disadvantage in reliance on the promise, a right of action does arise. *McClure v. Wilson*, 43 Ill. 356; *Trustees v. Garvey*, 53 Ill. 401.

Under the circumstances of this case, is there an equitable estoppel which ought to ~clude the defendant from alleging that the note in controversy is lacking in one of the ntial elements of a valid contract? We think there is. An estoppel in pais is defined to right arising from acts, admissions, or conduct which have induced a change of position in accordance with the real or apparent intention of the party against whom they are alleged." Mr. Pomeroy has formulated the following definition: "Equitable estoppel is the effect of the voluntary conduct of a party whereby he is absolutely precluded, both at law and in equity, from asserting rights which might, perhaps, have otherwise existed, either of property, of contract, or of remedy, as against another person who in good faith relied upon such conduct, and has been led thereby to change his position for the worse, and who on his part acquires some corresponding right, either of property, of contract, or of remedy." 2 Pom. Eq. Jur. 804. According to the undisputed proof, as shown by the record before us, the plaintiff was a working girl, holding a position in which she earned a salary of $10 per week. Her grandfather, desiring to put her in a position of independence, gave her the note, accompanying it with the remark that his other grandchildren did not work, and that she would not be obliged to work any longer. In effect, he suggested that she might abandon her employment, and rely in the future upon the bounty which he promised. He doubtless desired that she should give up her occupation, but, whether he did or not, it is entirely certain that he contemplated such action on her part as a reasonable and probable consequence of his gift. Having intentionally influenced the plaintiff to alter her position for the worse on the faith of the note being paid when due, it would be grossly inequitable to permit the maker, or his executor, to resist payment on the ground that the promise was given without consideration. The petition charges the elements of an equitable estoppel, and the evidence conclusively establishes them. If errors intervened at the trial, they could not have been prejudicial. A verdict for the defendant would be unwarranted. The judgment is right and is affirmed.

Note

Judge Sullivan weaves a new doctrine out of several existing threads. First he cites a number of cases involving gifts to churches and other charities. Next he cites the doctrine of equitable estoppel, which can be explained in the following way: if a person makes a representation about a fact, in a situation in which another person is likely to rely on the truth of that fact (sometimes in the context of litigation and sometimes in other contexts), then the first person is barred ("estopped") from denying the truth of the fact as he or she stated it. So in litigation, for example, if at a crucial stage the defendant alleges that the traffic light was green, the court may estop her from later claiming that it was red. In *Ricketts v. Scothorn*, Judge Sullivan applied that idea to a promise, instead of a statement of fact. So under *Ricketts*, if a person says, in effect, "I will do this," in a situation in which reliance is reasonable and foreseeable, he or she may later be estopped from saying "I will not do this" or "My promise is not enforceable." Judge Sullivan's evocation of the estoppel doctrine in this context has been the most influential part of the case.

By evoking the estoppel doctrine, Judge Sullivan also evokes the residual judicial power to "do equity" within the body of law called "equity," which is characterized by relatively open claims to justice. Evocation of this power and this body of law allows courts to move beyond more limited existing doctrines to broader evaluations of fairness and culpability.

Another significant aspect of *Ricketts* is the remedy that the court allowed. If the reason that Ricketts' estate is liable to Scothorn is because Scothorn relied on her grandfather and lost income as a result, then shouldn't the measure of damages be the amount of income she lost? Instead, the court enforced Ricketts' promise in full, requiring the estate to pay $2,000. Reliance, in this case, was a reason to enforce the promise, but it was not the measure of injury. Today, most courts treat reliance or promissory estoppel as a reason to enforce a promise—as an alternative to bargained-for exchange. *See* Restatement (Second) of Contracts § 90 (Contract Enforceable Without Consideration: Promise Reasonably Inducing Action or Forbearance).

Some lawyers have argued that the doctrine of promissory estoppel blurs the line between the realms of "private ordering" (classical contract) and "public obligation" (tort law). But as we have seen, the values associated with the bargain principle are not merely private—both the bargain and the reliance principles include social values. These two principles suggest different visions of contract law, with one featuring exchange and the other featuring trust, and the two are sometimes in conflict. It is the nature of law to reflect and to reconcile (sometimes only temporarily) conflicting values and interests.

C. Restitution: Unjust Enrichment and the Duty to Right Other Wrongs

The restitution principle holds that one who violates a duty or commits some wrong ought to be required to repair any injury she or he has caused. In current law, the principle is most closely associated with (or reduced to) the idea that one ought to pay for a benefit unjustly retained. The ideas and values associated with this principle are evident throughout contract law. In addition, however, there is a body of law called Restitution that is different from Contract law because it imposes liability apart from any promise, agreement, or market exchange. The prestigious American Law Institute has published Restatements of the Law of Restitution which are distinct from its Restatements of Contracts, Torts, Property, and the like. Yet most U.S. law schools do not offer courses in Restitution. Most lawyers think of restitution as a remedy, an alternative basis for recovery, and a principle that is more likely to appear in contract disputes than in other sorts of litigation. As a consequence, the study of restitution is included in most contract law courses.

Restitution features the idea of duty—"what a man should do, he should be made to do," as some courts put it. To some, this idea sounds antiquated, an echo of bygone eras in which individual freedom was encumbered by status-based obligations. And it sounds anachronistic, an echo of moral directives that now sound inappropriately self-righteous or authoritarian. There is much to this insight; the language of duty, the values and lines of analysis suggested by that language, seem strangely inappropriate in our time. Yet "duty" still has significance for many Americans in a variety of different settings, including those of family, friendship, faith, and civic responsibility. People speak of duties that arise in connection with a variety of roles, some of which involve exchange transactions and some of which do not: we speak, for example, of the duties of an employer, an employee, a creditor, a debtor, a merchant, a consumer, a landlord, a tenant, an artist, a politician, a reporter, a doctor, or a mechanic. People speak also of duties that arise from certain circumstances, including gift-giving, need, dependence, and privilege. But when does "duty" give rise to a legally enforceable obligation?

Contemporary Restitution Law emphasizes the duty to return or pay for a benefit unjustly retained. This privileging of unjust enrichment is evident in the title of the current restatement of restitution: the *Restatement (Third) of Restitution and Unjust Enrichment*. As the *Restatement (Third)* explains:

The law of restitution is predominantly the law of unjust enrichment, but "unjust enrichment" is a term of art. The substantive part of the law of restitution is concerned with identifying those forms of enrichment that the law treats as "unjust" for purposes of imposing liability.

...

Restitution is the law of nonconsensual and nonbargained benefits in the same way that torts is the law of nonconsensual and nonlicensed harms. Both subjects deal with the consequences of transactions in which the parties have not specified for themselves what the consequences of their interaction should be. The law of torts identifies those circumstances in which a person is liable for injury inflicted, measuring liability by the extent of the harm; the law of restitution identifies those circumstances in which a person is liable for benefits received, measuring liability by the extent of the benefit.

Restatement (Third) of Restitution and Unjust Enrichment § 1, Comments (b), (d) (2011).

Accordingly, in contemporary law, the word "restitution," which at one time was understood to mean "restoring a just order" after some breach of duty had occurred, is now understood by many lawyers to refer to "restoring a benefit" that has been unjustly retained.

Why do many contemporary courts and commentators limit restitution to unjust enrichment? Perhaps it is out of discomfort with the explicit moral content of the restitution principle or with its suggestion of social structuring beyond individual choice. There clearly is tension between the classical liberal claim of legal neutrality and the explicitly moral claims of traditional restitution law. Unlike other restitutionary ideas, unjust enrichment can be reconciled somewhat with the bargain principle (by supposing that unjust enrichment occurs where the benefactor and the beneficiary would have made a contract if they could have) and thus made to appear "morally neutral."

At the same time that restitution is narrowed to unjust enrichment, many courts and commentators view unjust enrichment as a particularly compelling basis for liability because it frequently involves both a breach of duty and an out-of-pocket loss. Thus, despite courts' discomfort with its explicitly moral arguments, restitution-as-unjust-enrichment continues to be an influential principle in contemporary law.

Bargain, reliance, and restitution all include moral claims. Yet these are often concealed in arguments drawn from the bargain principle and understated in those drawn from the reliance principle. Arguments based upon the restitution principle, in contrast, are sometimes explicitly moral, and they are often framed in terms of duty. For this reason, restitutionary arguments may sound less "rational," more "naive," "thinner" or "shallower," or more conclusory to contemporary ears than other legal arguments. To understand the complicated influence of the restitution principle in contemporary law, consider the complicated state of moral discourse in our time.

Alasdair MacIntyre, A Disquieting Suggestion

(1984)

Imagine that the natural sciences were to suffer the effects of a catastrophe. A series of environmental disasters are blamed by the general public on the scientists. Widespread riots occur, laboratories are burnt down, physicists are lynched, books and instruments are destroyed. Finally a Know-Nothing political movement takes power and successfully abolishes science teaching in schools and universities, imprisoning and executing the remaining scientists. Later still there is a reaction against this destructive movement and enlightened people seek to revive science, although they have largely forgotten what it was. But all that they possess are fragments: a knowledge of experiments detached from any knowledge of the theoretical context which gave them significance; parts of theories unrelated either to the other bits and pieces of theory which they possess or to experiment; instruments whose use has been forgotten; half chapters from books, single pages from articles, not always fully legible because torn and charred. Nonetheless all these fragments are re-embodied in a set of practices which go under the revived names of physics, chemistry, and biology. Adults argue with each other about the respective merits of relativity theory, evolutionary theory and phlogiston theory, although they possess only a very partial knowledge of each. Children learn by heart the surviving portions of the periodic tables and recite as incantations some of the theorems of Euclid. Nobody, or almost nobody, realizes that what they are doing is not natural science in any proper sense at all. For everything that they do and say conforms to certain canons of consistency and coherence and those contexts which would be needed to make sense of what they are doing have been lost perhaps irretrievably.

In such a culture men would use expressions such as "neutrino," "mass," "specific gravity," "atomic weight" in systematic and often interrelated ways which would resemble in lesser or greater degrees the ways in which such expressions had been used in earlier times before scientific knowledge had been so largely lost. But many of the beliefs presupposed by the use of these expressions would have been lost and there would appear to be an element of arbitrariness and even of choice in their application which would appear very surprising to us. What would appear to be rival and competing premises for which no further argument could be given would abound.... This imaginary possible world is very like one that some science fiction writers have constructed. We may describe it as a world in which the language of natural science, or parts of it at least, continues to be used but is in a grave state of disorder....

...

What is the point of constructing this imaginary world inhabited by fictitious pseudo scientists ... ? The hypothesis which I wish to advance is that in the actual world which we inhabit the language of morality is in the same state of grave disorder as the language of natural science in the imaginary world which I described. What we possess, if this view is true, are the fragments of a conceptual scheme, parts which now lack those contexts from which their significance derived. We possess indeed simulacra of morality, we continue to use many of the key expressions. But we have — very largely, if not entirely — lost our comprehension, both theoretical and practical, of morality.

But how could this be so? The impulse to reject the whole suggestion out of hand will certainly be very strong. Our capacity to use moral language, to be guided by moral reasoning, to define our transactions with others in moral terms is so central to our view of ourselves that even to envisage the possibility of our radical incapacity in these respects is to ask for a shift in our view of what we are and do which is going to be difficult to achieve.... [A] prerequisite for understanding the present disordered state of the imaginary world was to understand its history, a history that had to be written in three distinct stages. The first stage was that in which the natural sciences flourished, the second that in which they suffered the catastrophe and the third that in which they were restored but in damaged and disordered form. Notice that this history, being one of decline and fall, is informed by standards. It is not an evaluatively neutral chronicle. The form of the narrative, the division into stages, presuppose standards of achievement and failure, of order and disorder.

Note

Professor MacIntyre's parable offers an account of the current state of moral discourse. Although some forms of moral discourse, some religious discourses for example, do not suffer the kind of disarray MacIntyre describes, other forms clearly do. Duty-based morality, the traditional basis of restitution, surely is fragmented in many of the ways MacIntyre described. The words of duty-based morality are used and many of the ideas still carry weight, yet

> many of the beliefs presupposed by the use of these expressions ... have been lost and there ... appear[s] to be an element of arbitrariness and even of choice in their application which would appear very surprising to [someone more accustomed to this discourse]. What ... appear to be rival and competing premises for which no further argument ... [can] be given ... abound.

In legal, political, economic and moral discourse, the bargain principle, together with the related principles of individualism, have tended to crowd out competing ideas, silencing or trivializing the language of duty and obligation. Recently some courts, lawyers, and commentators have worked to recover and reconstruct a duty-based theory of obligation as a vibrant part of contemporary contract law. Some of this effort entails increased use of restitution as a basis for liability and some focus on the enforcement of "promises made in recognition of a past benefit," which we will examine at greater length in Chapter Five.

In the following case, the court takes care to be conceptually precise in its analysis of doctrine, to recognize the political interests at stake in the decision, and to identify the moral imperatives that warrant recovery in restitution. After you have read the opinion, think carefully about the significance of duty in this case.

————————

T.T. Cotnam v. F.L. Wisdom et al.

Supreme Court of Arkansas
104 S.W. 164 (Ark. 1907)

Action by F. L. Wisdom and another against T. T. Cotnam, administrator of A. M. Harrison, deceased, for services rendered by plaintiffs as surgeons to defendant's intestate. Judgment for plaintiffs. Defendant appeals. Reversed and remanded.

Instructions 1 and 2, given at the instance of plaintiffs, are as follows: "(1) If you find from the evidence that plaintiffs rendered professional services as physicians and surgeons to the deceased, A. M. Harrison, in a sudden emergency following the deceased's injury in a street car wreck, in an endeavor to save his life, then you are instructed that plaintiffs are entitled to recover from the estate of the said A. M. Harrison such sum as you may find from the evidence is a reasonable compensation for the services rendered. (2) The character and importance of the operation, the responsibility resting upon the surgeon performing the operation, his experience and professional training, and the ability to pay of the person operated upon, are elements to be considered by you in determining what is a reasonable charge for the services performed by plaintiffs in the particular case."

JOSEPH M. HILL, C. J. (AFTER STATING THE FACTS).

The reporter will state the issues and substance of the testimony and set out instructions 1 and 2 given at instance of appellee, and it will be seen therefrom that instruction 1 amounted to a peremptory instruction to find for the plaintiff in some amount.

The first question is as to the correctness of this instruction. As indicated therein the facts are that Mr. Harrison, appellant's intestate, was thrown from a street car, receiving serious injuries which rendered him unconscious, and while in that condition the appellees were notified of the accident and summoned to his assistance by some spectator, and performed a difficult operation in an effort to save his life, but they were unsuccessful, and he died without regaining consciousness. The appellant says: "Harrison was never conscious after his head struck the pavement. He did not and could not, expressly or impliedly, assent to the action of the appellees. He was without knowledge or will power. However merciful or benevolent may have been the intention of the appellees, a new rule of law, of contract by implication of law, will have to be established by this court in order to sustain the recovery." Appellant is right in saying that the recovery must be sustained by a contract by implication of law, but is not right in saying that it is a new rule of law, for such contracts are almost as old as the English system of jurisprudence. They are usually called "implied contracts." More properly they should be called "quasi contracts" or "constructive contracts." *See* 1 Page on Contracts, § 14; also 2 Page on Contracts, § 771.

The following excerpts from *Sceva v. True*, 53 N. H. 627, are peculiarly applicable here: "We regard it as well settled by the cases referred to in the briefs of counsel, many of which have been commented on at length by Mr. Shirley for the defendant, that an insane person, an idiot, or a person utterly bereft of all sense and reason by the sudden stroke of an accident or disease may be held liable, in assumpsit, for necessaries furnished to him in good faith while in that unfortunate and helpless condition. And the reasons upon which this rest are too broad, as well as too sensible and humane, to be overborne by any deductions which a refined logic may make from the circumstances that in such cases there can be no contract or promise, in fact, no meeting of the minds of the parties. The cases put it on the ground of an implied contract; and by this is not meant, as the defendant's counsel seems to suppose, an actual contract—that is, an actual meeting of the minds of the parties, an actual, mutual understanding, to be inferred from language, acts, and circumstances by the jury—but a contract and promise, said to be implied by the law, where, in point of fact, there was no contract, no mutual understanding, and so no promise. The defendant's counsel says it is usurpation for the court to hold, as a matter of law, that there is a contract and a promise, when all the evidence in the case shows that there was not a contract, nor the semblance of one. It is doubtless a legal fiction, invented and used for the sake of the remedy. If it was originally usurpation, certainly it has now become very inveterate, and firmly fixed in the body of the law. Illustrations might be multiplied, but enough has been said to show that when a contract or promise implied by law is spoken of, a very different thing is meant from a contract in fact, whether express or tacit. The evidence of an actual contract is generally to be found either in some writing made by the parties, or in verbal communications which passed between them, or in their acts and conduct considered in the light of the circumstances of each particular case. A contract implied by law, on the contrary, rests upon no evidence. It has no actual existence. It is simply a mythical creation of the law. The law says it shall be taken that there was a promise, when in point of fact, there was none. Of course this is not good logic, for the obvious and sufficient reason that it is not true. It is a legal fiction, resting wholly for its support on a plain legal obligation, and a plain legal right. If it were true, it would not be a fiction. There is a class of legal rights, with their correlative legal duties, analogous to the obligationes quasi ex contractu of the civil law, which seem to lie in the region between contracts on the one hand, and torts on the other, and to call for the application of a remedy not strictly furnished either by actions ex contractu or actions ex delicto. The common law supplies no action of duty, as it does of assumpsit and trespass;

and hence the somewhat awkward contrivance of this fiction to apply the remedy of assumpsit where there is no true contract and no promise to support it."

This subject is fully discussed in Beach on the Modern Law of Contracts, 639 et seq., and 2 Page on Contracts, 771 et seq. One phase in the law of implied contracts was considered in the case of *Lewis v. Lewis*, 75 Ark. 191, 87 S. W. 134. In its practical application it sustains recovery for physicians and nurses who render services for infants, insane persons, and drunkards. 2 Page on Contracts, §§ 867, 897, 906. And services rendered by physicians to persons unconscious or helpless by reason of injury or sickness are in the same situation as those rendered to persons incapable of contracting, such as the classes above described. *Raoul v. Newman*, 59 Ga. 408; Meyer v. K. of P., 70 N. E. 111, 178 N. Y. 63, 64 L. R. A. 839. The court was therefore right in giving the instruction in question.

The defendant sought to require the plaintiff to prove, in addition to the value of the services, the benefit, if any, derived by the deceased from the operation, and alleges error in the court refusing to so instruct the jury. The court was right in refusing to place this burden upon the physicians. The same question was considered in *Ladd v. Witte*, 116 Wis. 35, 92 N. W. 365, where the court said: "That is not at all the test. So that a surgical operation be conceived and performed with due skill and care, the price to be paid therefor does not depend upon the result. The event so generally lies with the forces of nature that all intelligent men know and understand that the surgeon is not responsible therefor. In absence of express agreement, the surgeon, who brings to such a service due skill and care, earns the reasonable and customary price therefor, whether the outcome be beneficial to the patient or the reverse."

The court permitted to go to the jury the fact that Mr. Harrison was a bachelor, and that his estate would go to his collateral relatives, and also permitted proof to be made of the value of the estate, which amounted to about $18,500, including $10,000 from accident and life insurance policies. There is a conflict in the authorities as to whether it is proper to prove the value of the estate of a person for whom medical services were rendered, or the financial condition of the person receiving such services. In *Robinson v. Campbell*, 47 Iowa, 625, it was said: "There is no more reason why this charge should be enhanced on account of the ability of the defendants to pay than that the merchant should charge them more for a yard of cloth, or the druggist for filling a prescription, or a laborer for a day's work." On the other hand, *see Haley's Succession*, 24 South. 285 (La.), and *Lange v. Kearney*, 4 N. Y. Supp. 14, 51 Hun, 640, which was affirmed by the Court of Appeals, 28 N. E. 255 (N.Y.), holding that the financial condition of the patient may be considered. Whatever may be the true principle governing this matter in contracts, the court is of the opinion that the financial condition of a patient cannot be considered where there is no contract and recovery is sustained on a legal fiction which raises a contract in order to afford a remedy which the justice of the case requires. In *Morrissett v. Wood*, 26 South. 307 (Ala.), the court said: "The trial court erred in admitting testimony as to the value of the patient's estate, against the objection of the defendant. The inquiry was as to the value of the professional services rendered by the plaintiff to the defendant's testator, and, as the case was presented below, the amount or value of the latter's estate could shed no legitimate light upon this issue nor aid in its elucidation. The cure or amelioration of disease is as important to a poor man as it is to a rich one, and, prima facie at least, the services rendered the one are of the same value as the same services rendered to the other. If there was a recognized usage obtaining in the premises here involved to graduate professional charges with reference to the financial condition of the person for whom such services are rendered, which had been so long established and so universally acted upon as to have ripened into a custom of such character that it might be considered that these services were rendered and accepted in contemplation of it, there is no hint of it in the evidence."

There was evidence in this case proving that it was customary for physicians to graduate their charges by the ability of the patient to pay, and hence, in regard to that element, this case differs from the Alabama case. But the value of the Alabama decision is the reason given which may admit such evidence, viz., because the custom would render the financial condition of the patient a factor to be contemplated by both parties when the services were rendered and accepted. The same thought differently expressed is found in *Lange v. Kearney*, 4 N. Y. Supp. 14, 51 Hun, 640. This could not apply to a physician called in an emergency by some bystander to attend a stricken man whom he never saw or heard of before; and certainly the unconscious patient could not, in fact or in law, be held to have contemplated what charges the physician might properly bring against him. In order to admit such testimony, it must be assumed that the surgeon and patient each had in contemplation that the means of the patient would be one factor in determining the amount of the charge for the services rendered. While the law may admit such evidence as throwing light upon the contract and indicating what was really in contemplation when it was made, yet a different question is presented when there is no contract to be ascertained or construed, but a mere fiction of law creating a contract where none existed in order that there might be a remedy for a right. This fiction merely requires a reasonable compensation for the services rendered. The services are the same be the patient prince or pauper, and for them the surgeon is entitled to fair compensation for his time, service, and skill. It was therefore error to admit this evidence, and to instruct the jury in the second instruction that in determining what was a reasonable charge they could consider the "ability to pay of the person operated upon."

It was improper to let it go to the jury that Mr. Harrison was a bachelor and that his estate was left to nieces and nephews. This was relevant to no issue in the case, and its effect might well have been prejudicial. While this verdict is no higher than some of the evidence would justify, yet it is much higher than some of the other evidence would justify, and hence it is impossible to say that this was a harmless error.

Judgment is reversed, and cause remanded.

Note

A claim for unjust enrichment is generally said to require proof of three elements:

1. The plaintiff conferred a benefit on the defendant;

2. The plaintiff did not confer the benefit as a gift (it is not unjust to keep a birthday present); and

3. The plaintiff was not acting "voluntarily" in conferring the benefit. This element is sometimes described as proof that the plaintiff did not "pass up" an opportunity to enter into a contract with the defendant before conferring the benefit. To avoid the charge of voluntariness, the plaintiff must show some good reason (like emergency, lack of information, or mistake) for why she did not negotiate a contract with the defendant before conferring the benefit.

In *Cotnam v. Wisdom*, the Arkansas Supreme Court discussed the conceptual framework in which Dr. Wisdom's claim against Harrison's estate should be analyzed. The claim was based upon a legal duty that Harrison allegedly owed to Dr. Wisdom to repay him for professional medical care given to Harrison when he was unconscious. The basis for the alleged legal duty was not a contract — Dr. Wisdom did not claim that Harrison had promised to pay for the medical services. Rather, the alleged duty to pay was based upon Harrison's having received the medical services in circumstances in which it would be unjust not to pay for them. Accordingly, it was irrelevant that Harrison was unconscious and therefore unable to enter a contract. Citing *Sceva v. True*, the Court recognized that the idea of a "contract implied in law" or a "quasi-contract" is a fiction — there was no contract, but the law of restitution draws an analogy to contract law in order to fashion a remedy for unjust enrichment.

This recognition of these fictions is instructive. Current law includes numerous legal fictions, and courts often resort to a legal fiction where important political and moral concerns conflict. In the area of restitution, a deep conflict exists between the sense that one person may be obliged to another for a wide variety of culturally-specific reasons, only some of which are consensual, and the belief that freedom of contract, and freedom generally, requires that a person be obligated to do only that which he or she intentionally and explicitly promised to do.

D. The Principles in Action

Contract law governs the legal consequences of promises, agreements, and exchanges, and one of its core tenets is that not every promise generates legally enforceable obligations. As we have seen, contract law recognizes three general situations that result in legal obligations: (1) when a promise is made as part of an agreed exchange ("bargain contract" or just "contract"); (2) when a promise is made in circumstances in which the promisor should have expected that someone else would rely on the promise ("promissory estoppel"); and (3) when a material benefit conferred gives rise to an enforceable obligation ("restitution"). These are the three bases for liability, or causes of action, in contract law. The remainder of this book will focus on the details of these promissory and non-promissory claims.

Although we deal with these claims individually in the chapters that follow, they do not occur so distinctly when people are involved in legal disputes. When a party brings a complaint for redress, that party must assert a set of facts that establishes the basis for a legal obligation. A corresponding "claim," "theory of recovery," or "cause of action" is a translation of the facts into a form that is recognized by courts as a claim that an obligation has been breached, an injury has occurred, and a judicial remedy is warranted. A cause of action may be stated as a simple rule or it may have multiple parts or "elements," which are the component facts necessary to establish a particular cause of action.

The following case, Allison v. J.P. Morgan Chase Bank, shows how multiple claims arise out of a single set of facts. In this case, the Allisons are in the early stages of their legal dispute with J.P. Morgan Chase Bank. The plaintiffs are asserting numerous claims that fall into various legal categories, and we can see the three principles — bargain, reliance, and restitution — at work. As you read the case, pay attention to the different causes of action addressed by the court, the necessary elements of each one, and the court's ruling regarding each claim. How many allege an obligation based on a promise? What areas of law govern the other claims?

Allison v. J.P. Morgan Chase Bank

United States District Court

2012 WL 4633177, 2012 U.S. Dist. Lexis 142522, (E.D. Tex. 2012)

KEITH F. GOBLIN, UNITED STATES MAGISTRATE JUDGE

In accordance with 28 U.S.C. § 636(c), the Local Rules for the United States District Court for the Eastern District of Texas, the parties' consent, and order of the District Court, the above-captioned civil action is before the undersigned United States Magistrate Judge for consideration of all matters, trial, and entry of judgment. The Court previously issued a brief order granting in part and denying in part the defendants' Motion to Dismiss Pursuant to Rule 12(b)(6).... The Court now issues this opinion and order specifically setting forth the findings and legal conclusions in support of that ruling....

Procedural Background and Plaintiffs' Claims

On June 11, 2011, the plaintiffs, Michael and Tracy Allison ("the Allisons" or "plaintiffs"), filed suit ... against defendants J.P. Morgan Chase Bank, N.A. and Chase Home Finance LLC ("Chase" or "defendants"). Plaintiffs allege that on August 7, 2007, they obtained a mortgage loan with Chase Home Finance for the property and residence located at 186 Tiger Lily Street, Bridge City, Texas. The Allisons live in this residence with their three children, one of whom is disabled. They further state that in September 2008, their residence was flooded as a result of Hurricane Ike. The Allisons allege that they lost their home and business but continued to make their mortgage payments at this time, exhausting their life savings.

The Allisons further aver that in the spring and summer of 2009, they "got behind on their mortgage loan payments." They state that Chase "suggested and offered to modify the terms of the mortgage loan, a program for persons affected by Hurricane Ike." The plaintiffs further state that Chase "represented to the Allisons that [they] are required to be behind on their mortgage payments for two months to qualify for the modification program." The plaintiffs "did as they were instructed and did not pay the mortgage for two months." The plaintiffs state that over the course the next sixteen months, Chase, "either by negligence or intentional mismanagement, clumsily performed the administering of the modification to the loan." The Allisons allege that despite their "diligence and co-operation," "the employees and departments at Chase, through Chase's own internal bureaucracy, were incapable of sending and communicating between its own departments." Chase would lose documents and/or property received from the Allisons and the modification process had to "start all over again." The Allisons received a notice of foreclosure but Chase advised that the foreclosure notice was a mistake and the modification process was ongoing. The Allisons contend that this process occurred several times.

On May 1, 2011, Chase notified the plaintiffs that their mortgage loan had been transferred from Chase Finance, LLC ("Chase Finance") to JP Morgan Chase Bank, N.A. ("JP Morgan"). On May 5, 2011, Chase served the Allisons with a forcible detainer and eviction suit filed in the Justice of the Peace Court, Precinct 3, in Orange County, Texas. The Allisons contend that Chase improperly filed the eviction suit and that Chase did not have standing to file the suit because the loan had been transferred to JP Morgan before Chase Finance filed the suit.

Based on these factual allegations, the Allisons assert the following causes of action. First, they contend that the defendants are vicariously liable for the [negligent and otherwise tortious] acts of their employees. The plaintiffs also specifically claim causes of action against both defendants for breach of contract, promissory estoppel, quantum meruit..., and wrongful foreclosure in violation of the Texas DTPA. The plaintiffs are seeking actual damages, exemplary damages, injunctive relief precluding the taking of their property, attorneys' fees, costs, interest, and judgment for title to and possession of the property at issue. . . .

The Defendant's Motion to Dismiss

In this motion, Chase contends that each of the plaintiffs' purported causes of action fail as a matter of law. Chase also argues that the plaintiffs have failed to plead sufficient facts to support each cause of action. . . .

Discussion

A. Relevant Legal Standards ... Rule 12(b)(6) Motion to Dismiss

"To survive a motion to dismiss, a complaint must contain sufficient factual matter, accepted as true, 'to state a claim to relief that is plausible on its face.'" *Ashcroft v. Iqbal*, 556 U.S. 662 (2009) (quoting *Bell Atlantic Corp. v. Twombly*, 550 U.S. 544, 570, (2007)). To be plausible, the complaint's "[f]actual allegations must be enough to raise a right to relief above the speculative level." *In re Great Lakes*, 624 F.3d at 210 (quoting *Twombly*, 550 U.S. at 555). . . .

B. Application to Plaintiffs' Claims ...

Breach of Contract

The petition asserts that Chase breached a contract to modify the terms of the original mortgage contract for the Allisons' residence. Under Texas law, the elements of a breach of contract claim include: (1) existence of a valid contract; (2) plaintiff's performance or tender of performance; (3) defendant's breach of the contract; and (4) the plaintiff must incur damages as a result of the breach. *Prime Prod. Inc. v. SSI Plastics*, 97 S.W.3d 631, 636 (Tex. Ct. App. 2002) ...

Assertion of the existence of a verbal contract to modify an existing mortgage and promise to refrain from foreclosure may support a valid claim. *See Brandon*, 2011 U.S. Dist. Lexis 145812, 2011 WL 6338832 (E.D. Tex. 2011). In *Brandon*, Judge Mazzant addressed issues similar to those presented here. After the plaintiff lost this job and became arrear in mortgage payments, the defendants allegedly promised to modify mortgage and refrain from foreclosing on the property. Wells Fargo told the plaintiff he qualified for a special program for homeowners who had lost their jobs. Despite compliance with all requirements to participate in the modification program by the plaintiff and promises that the modification process was ongoing, Wells Fargo sold the mortgage at auction to Freddie Mac and began foreclosure and eviction processes. In *Brandon*, the court found that the pled facts supported the existence of an oral agreement between the parties, fulfillment of the plaintiff's end of the bargain, a letter from Wells Fargo memorializing the oral agreement, and breach by foreclosure and sale of the property constituted a valid claim for breach of contract.

Here, the plaintiffs assert that a contract(s) existed between the Allisons and Chase regarding the modification of the original mortgage loan. As in *Brandon*, plaintiffs have pled that Chase informed the Allisons that they qualified for a special modification program offered to those affected by Hurricane Ike. According to the petition, the Allisons were required to submit certain financial documentation and to default on two months of payments prior to the modification. In response, the Allisons submitted all required documentation and ceased making payments in return for a modification and delayed foreclosure. As in *Brandon*, the Allisons assert that they have fully performed and fulfilled

precedence

their end of the bargain by submitting the necessary financial documentation and halting monthly payments at the request of Chase employees.

Reading the petition in the most favorable light, the plaintiffs assert that Chase breached the contract by rejecting payment, failing to execute the modification, foreclosing prior to the execution of the modification, and selling the property to JP Morgan. They claim damages which include the loss of their home as well as financial loss incurred as a result of the alleged breach. Similar to *Brandon*, the factual allegations asserted here constitute a valid claim for breach of contract. While this case can be distinguished from *Brandon* in that the Allisons have not asserted the existence of a written letter memorializing the agreement, the Allisons have pled facts from which it can be reasonably inferred that an oral agreement for modification existed and defendants breached this agreement by foreclosing prematurely. Additionally, evidence from the discovery process may prove the existence of a valid claim. Therefore, the motion to dismiss the breach of contract claim should be denied....

Promissory Estoppel

Plaintiffs allege that their reliance on Chase's promise to modify the contract was to their detriment, and Chase's breach of the promise caused them damage, namely the loss of their home. Promissory estoppel makes a promise enforceable even without consideration if (1) the promisor should have reasonably expected the promisee to rely on the promise and (2) the promisee actually relied on the promise to its detriment. *See* Michol O'Connor, O'Connor's Texas Causes of Action (2012) at 114. As an independent claim alternative to breach of contract, the elements of a promissory estoppel action include: (1) the defendant made a promise to the plaintiff; (2) the plaintiff reasonably and substantially relied on the promise to its detriment; and (3) the plaintiff's reliance was foreseeable by the defendant. *See Henry Schein, Inc. v. Stromboe*, 102 S.W.3d 675, 686 n. 25 (Tex. 2002); *English v. Fisher*, 660 S.W.2d 521, 524 (Tex. 1983).

Plaintiffs assert Chase employees promised to enter into a modification agreement regarding the terms of the original loan. Further, the plaintiffs contend that they stopped making payments at the request of Chase to accomplish the modification process. In response, Chase foreclosed on the Allisons' home. Plaintiffs assert that they relied to their detriment (the loss of their home) on promises to modify made by employees of Chase and further state that a reasonable person in their position would not forego mortgage payments absent the promise made by the mortgage company or extenuating circumstances. Although the defendants contest this fact in their motion, according to the facts pled in the petition, the Allisons stopped making payments after instructed to do so by Chase. Taking the pled facts as true, the Allisons' allegations are sufficient to sustain promissory estoppel claim and should survive a motion to dismiss.

Quantum Meruit

The theory of recovery of quantum meruit is founded on the principle of unjust enrichment. *Bashara v. Baptist Mem'l Hosp. Sys.*, 685 S.W.2d 307, 310 (Tex. 1985). The elements of quantum meruit include: (1) valuable services rendered or materials furnished; (2) for the defendant; (3) services/materials were accepted by defendant; and (4) reasonable notification that the plaintiff expected to be compensated by the defendant. *See also Johnson v. Kruse*, 261 S.W.3d 895, 901 (Tex. Ct. App. 2008).

Defendants argue that the claim should be dismissed because there is no authority supporting the contention that an action in quantum meruit can be based on payment of money. After a review of the applicable case law, the Court agrees. The Court also notes that the undersigned has already determined that the breach of contract survives dismissal. Quantum meruit is an equitable remedy which does not arise out of a contract, but it is independent of it. Based on the facts pled, the Court finds that the motion to dismiss should be granted as to the quantum meruit claim....

Trespass to Real Property

Trespass to real property is defined as an unauthorized entry upon the land of another. O'Connor's Texas Causes of Action 971 (2012) (collecting cases). The elements include: (1) plaintiff owns or has a lawful right to possess the real property; (2) defendant entered the plaintiff's land; (3) the entry was physical, intentional, and voluntary; and (4) caused injury to the plaintiff. *Wilen v. Falkenstein*, 191 S.W.3d 791, 797–98 (Tex. Ct. App. 2006). The Allisons' petition does not include any facts alleging that any of the named defendants physically entered the property in question. In their response, the Allisons concede that the factual allegations in the pleading are insufficient. This claim must be dismissed.

Private Nuisance

Plaintiffs assert that the defendants interfered with their interest in the home, and the defendants' actions constitute a private nuisance under state law. Private nuisance is non-trespassory invasion of another's interest in the private use and enjoyment of land, and it may include "emotional harm to a person from the deprivation of the enjoyment of his property through fear, apprehension, or loss of peace of mind." *Kane v. Cameron Int'l Corp.*, 331 S.W.3d 145, 147–48 (Tex. Ct. App. 2011). A person with a right to occupy land can maintain an action for private nuisance. *See Schneider v. Nat'l Carriers, Inc. v. Bates*, 147 S.W.3d 264, 268 n. 2 (Tex. 2004).

Here, the facts pled indicate that the Allisons had an interest in their home and the defendants interfered with that interest by prematurely foreclosing on the property. The Allisons contend that the premature foreclosure caused emotional harm by depriving the Allisons enjoyment of their home, the fear of foreclosure, and loss of peace of mind. For these reasons, the motion to dismiss the private nuisance claim should be denied....

DTPA

Plaintiffs assert that the defendants' actions violated the Texas Deceptive Trade Practices—Consumer Protection Act (DTPA). The DTPA was enacted to protect consumers and allow recovery when certain deceptive acts cause economic damages. Tex. Bus. & Com. Code Ann. § 17.50 (2011). To recover under the DTPA, a plaintiff must prove: (1) plaintiff is a consumer; (2) defendant is a proper defendant under the DTPA; (3) defendant committed a violation of the statute; and (4) the violation caused plaintiff damages. Brandon, at 8 (applying Texas state law in a diversity action). Consumer" is limited to individuals or entities who purchase or lease goods or services. Tex. Bus. & Com. Code Ann. § 17.45 (West 2011).

The determination of whether the plaintiff is a consumer is a question of law, and courts look at the object of the transaction to make the determination. Brandon, at 9. For DTPA purposes, Texas courts have held that a purchaser of a loan could sue the bank under the DTPA for an unconscionable course of conduct in foreclosing on a home. *See Flenniken v. Longview Bank & Trust Co.*, 661 S.W.2d 705 (Tex. 1983). The courts focus on the transaction from the perspective of the purchaser and have concluded that when the objective of the transaction is to actually acquire a car or house, for example, rather than just borrow money, the plaintiff may qualify as a consumer. *See La Sara Grain Co. v. First Nat'l Bank*, 673 S.W.2d 558, 566–67 (Tex. 1984). The plaintiffs have alleged facts which, read in the most favorable light, support their status as consumers under the

DTPA. They have also pled facts throughout the petition in the context of this and other causes of action which could sustain a claim for DTPA violations. The Court concludes that the motion to dismiss should be denied as to the DTPA claim.

[Editors: in omitted sections, the Court denied the defendants' motion to dismiss plaintiffs' tort claim for negligent misrepresentation and granted the motion to dismiss all other claims.]

Chapter Three

Contract Formation

Agreement, or *mutual assent*, is fundamental to contract liability, as it is fundamental to the bargain principle and the commonplace that a "deal is a deal." This chapter examines the doctrines that guide courts in evaluating whether the parties reached an agreement and thus whether a contract was formed. While Chapter Two focused on the broad *principles* (or clusters of ideas and values) that weave through contract law, this chapter begins our detailed examination of the *doctrines* (*rules*, *definitions*, *tests*, and *terms of art*) of contract law.

In most of the cases in this chapter, one person alleges that another has breached a contract and the other person defends himself or herself by arguing that there is no contract because there was no agreement or mutual assent. Most often, the parties did communicate or interact in some way, but they contest the significance of their interaction. Were they negotiating? Did they agree to something? Did they complete their negotiations or was there an understanding that more negotiation was necessary? Does it matter whether they left some aspects of the transaction open for future agreements? These are the questions raised by the cases in this chapter.

The chapter focuses on the doctrines of offer and acceptance, which facilitate analysis of communication and the formation of agreements by dividing complex interactions into discrete units. Before beginning our examination of the doctrines of offer and acceptance, however, it is necessary to examine the doctrine of "objective interpretation." This doctrine concerns the interpretation of words and behavior.

A. Difference and Meaning in Communication

Disputes over the meanings of words, conduct, and events arise frequently. The different meanings people ascribe to the same situations and their conflicting interpretations of events often reflect differences in language, culture, and experience. The first set of materials in this section focuses on the "objective theory" of interpretation, which provides that words and conduct should be interpreted as a "reasonable person" (or, until recently, a "reasonable man") would interpret them. This approach is applied throughout contract law, to disputes over formation, interpretation, and performance. In this chapter, we will study the objective theory as it applies to contract formation. The "objective theory" assumes that a standard of shared meaning already exists or that one ought to exist, and this assumption is controversial. Chapter Seven examines another traditional approach to conflicts in meaning: the doctrine of misunderstanding. Contemporary courts generally apply it only when they cannot find an "objective" meaning and so the parties' misunderstanding of each other precludes agreement. In Chapter Nine, we will see the objective theory applied to interpretation of the content of a contract.

As you read the cases in this section, look closely at the different meanings that each party and the court ascribe to words and conduct. How does each court resolve the dispute? Should courts attempt to measure reasonableness from the perspective of an outside observer, or should they attempt to take on the perspective of participants in the situation? Also consider the time and effort required for accurate communication: who should bear the burden of this time and effort? Whose responsibility should it be to assure understanding—a speaker or a listener, a writer or a reader? Finally, consider alternatives to the reasonable person standard—should the objective test be abandoned in favor of some other standard? If so, what should that new standard be?

The Objective Theory of Interpretation

Charles R. Embry v. Hargadine, McKittrick Dry Goods Company

Missouri Court of Appeals

105 S.W. 777 (1907)

RICHARD LIVINGSTON GOODE, JUDGE

We dealt with this case on a former appeal, 115 Mo. App. 130, 91 S.W. 170. It has been retried, and is again before us for the determination of questions not then reviewed. The appellant was an employee of the respondent company under a written contract to expire December 15, 1903, at a salary of $2,000 per annum. His duties were to attend to the sample department of respondent, of which he was given complete charge. It was his business to select samples for the traveling salesmen of the company, which is a wholesale dry goods concern, to use in selling goods to retail merchants. Appellant contends that on December 28, 1903, he was re-engaged by respondent, through its president, Thomas H. McKittrick, for another year at the same compensation and for the same duties stipulated in his previous written contract. On March 1, 1904, he was discharged, having been notified in February that, on account of the necessity of retrenching expenses, his services and that of some other employees would no longer be required. The respondent company contends that its president never re-employed appellant after the termination of his written contract, and hence that it had a right to discharge him when it chose. The point with which we are concerned required an epitome of the testimony of appellant and the counter testimony of McKittrick, the president of the company, in reference to the alleged re-employment. Appellant testified: That several times prior to the termination of his written contract on December 15, 1903, he had endeavored to get an understanding with McKittrick for another year, but had been put off from time to time. That on December 23d, eight days after the expiration of said contract, he called on McKittrick, in the latter's office, and said to him that as appellant's written employment had lapsed eight days before, and as there were only a few days between then and the 1st of January in which to seek employment with other firms, if respondent wished to retain his services longer he must have a contract for another year, or he would quit respondent's service then and there. That he had been put off twice before and wanted an understanding or contract at once so that he could go ahead without worry. That McKittrick asked him how he was getting along in his department, and appellant said he was very busy, as they were in the height of the season getting men out—had about 110 salesmen on the line and others in preparation. That McKittrick then said: "Go ahead, you're all right. Get your men out, and don't let that worry you." That appellant took McKittrick at his word and worked until February 15th without any question in his mind. It was on February 15th that he

AN UNIDENTIFIED TRAVELING SALESMAN photographed behind the J.H. Hill Store, Russell, Kansas. Photo courtesy of the Kansas State Historical Society.

was notified his services would be discontinued on March 1st. McKittrick denied this conversation as related by appellant, and said that, when accosted by the latter on December 23d, he (McKittrick) was working on his books in order to get out a report for a stockholders' meeting, and, when appellant said if he did not get a contract he would leave, that he (McKittrick) said: "Mr. Embry, I am just getting ready for the stockholders' meeting tomorrow. I have no time to take it up now. I have told you before I would not take it up until I had these matters out of the way. You will have to see me at a later time. I said: 'Go back upstairs and get your men out on the road.' I may have asked him one or two other questions relative to the department, I don't remember. The whole conversation did not take more than a minute."

Embry also swore that, when he was notified he would be discharged, he complained to McKittrick about it, as being a violation of their contract, and McKittrick said it was due to the action of the board of directors, and not to any personal action of his, and that others would suffer by what the board had done as well as Embry. Appellant requested an instruction to the jury setting out, in substance, the conversation between him and McKittrick according to his version, and declaring that those facts, if found to be true, constituted a contract between the parties that defendant would pay plaintiff the sum of $2,000 for another year, provided the jury believed from the evidence that plaintiff commenced said work believing he was to have $2,000 for the year's work. This instruction was refused, but the court gave another embodying in substance appellant's version of the conversation, and declaring it made a contract "if you (the jury) find both parties thereby intended and did contract with each other for plaintiff's employment for one year from and including December 23, 1903, at a salary of $2,000 per annum."

... Therefore it remains to determine whether or not this part of the instruction was a correct statement of the law in regard to what was necessary to constitute a contract between the parties; that is to say, whether the formation of a contract by what, according to Embry, was said, depended on the intention of both Embry and McKittrick. Or, to put the question more precisely: Did what was said constitute a contract of reemployment on the previous terms irrespective of the intention or purpose of McKittrick?

Judicial opinion and elementary treatises abound in statements of the rule that to constitute a contract there must be a meeting of the minds of the parties, and both must agree to the same thing in the same sense. Generally speaking, this may be true; but it is not literally or universally true. That is to say, the inner intention of parties to a conversation subsequently alleged to create a contract cannot either make a contract of what transpired, or prevent one from arising, if the words used were sufficient to constitute a contract. In so far as their intention is an influential element, it is only such intention as the words or acts of the parties indicate; not one secretly cherished which is inconsistent with those words or acts. The rule is thus stated by a text-writer, and many decisions are cited in support of his text: "The primary object of construction in contract law is to discover the intention of the parties. This intention in express contracts is, in the first instance, embodied in the words which the parties have used and is to be deduced therefrom. This rule applies to oral contracts, as well as to contracts in writing, and is the rule recognized by courts of equity." 2 Paige, Contracts § 1104 ... In *Smith v. Hughes*, L.R. 6 Q.B. 597, 607, it was said:

> If, whatever a man's real intention may be, he so conducts himself that a reasonable man would believe that he was assenting to the terms proposed by the other party, and that other party upon that belief enters into the contract with him, the man thus conducting himself would be equally bound as if he had intended to agree to the other party's terms.

And that doctrine was adopted in *Phillip v. Gallant*, 62 N.Y. 256. In 9 Cyc. 245, we find the following text:

> The law imputes to a person an intention corresponding to the reasonable meaning of his words and acts. It judges his intention by his outward expression and excludes all questions in regard to his unexpressed intention. If his words or acts,

judged by a reasonable standard, manifest an intention to agree in regard to the matter in question, that agreement is established, and it is immaterial what may be the real, but unexpressed, state of his mind on the subject....

In view of those authorities, we hold that, though McKittrick may not have intended to employ Embry by what transpired between them according to the latter's testimony, yet if what McKittrick said would have been taken by a reasonable man to be an employment, and Embry so understood it, it constituted a valid contract of employment for the ensuing year.

The next question is whether or not the language used was of that character, namely, was such that Embry, as a reasonable man, might consider he was re-employed for the ensuing year on the previous terms, and act accordingly. We do not say that in every instance it would be for the court to pronounce on this question, because, peradventure, instances might arise in which there would be such an ambiguity in the language relied on to show an assent by the obligor to the proposal of the obligee that it would be for the jury to say whether a reasonable mind would take it to signify acceptance of the proposal.... With these rules of law in mind, let us recur to the conversation of December 23d between Embry and McKittrick as related by the former. Embry was demanding a renewal of his contract, saying he had been put off from time to time, and that he had only a few days before the end of the year in which to seek employment from other houses, and that he would quit then and there unless he was re-employed. McKittrick inquired how he was getting along with the department, and Embry said they, i.e., the employees of the department, were very busy getting out salesmen. Whereupon McKittrick said: "Go ahead, you are all right. Get your men out, and do not let that worry you." We think no reasonable man would construe that answer to Embry's demand that he be employed for another year otherwise than as an assent to the demand, and that Embry had the right to rely on it as an assent. The natural inference is, though we do not find it testified to, that Embry was at work getting samples ready for the salesmen to use during the ensuing season. Now, when he was complaining of the worry and mental distress he was under because of his uncertainty about the future, and his urgent need, either of an immediate contract with respondent, or a refusal by it to make one, leaving him free to seek employment elsewhere, McKittrick must have answered as he did for the purpose of assuring appellant that any apprehension was needless, as appellant's services would be retained by the respondent. The answer was unambiguous, and we rule that if the conversation was according to appellant's version, and he understood he was employed, it constituted in law a valid contract of re-employment, and the court erred in making the formation of a contract depend on a finding that both parties intended to make one. It was only necessary that Embry, as a reasonable man, had a right to and did so understand.

Some other rulings are assigned for error by the appellant, but we will not discuss them because we think they are devoid of merit.

The judgment is reversed, and the cause remanded. All concur.

Note

What are the unspoken expectations between employee and employer? Do you think McKittrick should have been more clear in communicating with Embry if he did not intend to renew Embry's contract? In evaluating the meaning of McKittrick's words and behavior, the court evaluated what a reasonable man in Embry's position would understand

McKittrick's words and behavior to mean. This is the "objective" approach to interpretation. What aspects of Embry's situation should be relevant to this evaluation? Should it matter that he had worked for the company for many years? Or that his past agreements with the company had been made orally, without written documentation? Should it matter that other dry goods companies also have relatively informal contracts with their sales employees? Should it matter that Embry had told McKittrick that he needed to know about his employment renewal right away, and that both Embry and McKittrick were particularly busy at that time of the year? What other information may be relevant to interpretation of McKittrick's words and behavior under the objective theory?

Arthur Miller, The Death of a Salesman

(1949)

HOWARD: Say, aren't you supposed to be in Boston?

WILLY: That's what I want to talk to you about, Howard. You got a minute? *He draws a chair in from the wing.*

HOWARD: What happened? What're you doing here?

WILLY: Well …

HOWARD: You didn't crack up again, did you?

WILLY: Oh, no. NO …

HOWARD: Geez, you had me worried there for a minute. What's the trouble?

WILLY: Well, tell you the truth, Howard. I've come to the decision that I'd rather not travel any more.

HOWARD: Not travel! Well, what'll you do?

WILLY: Remember, Christmas time, when you had the party here? You said you'd try to think of some spot for me here in town.

HOWARD: With us?

WILLY: Well, sure.

HOWARD: Oh, yeah, yeah. I remember. Well, I couldn't think of anything for you, Willy.

WILLY: I tell ya, Howard. The kids are all grown up, y'know. I don't need much any more. If I could take home—well, sixty-five dollars a week, I could swing it.

HOWARD: Yeah, but Willy, see I—

WILLY: I tell ya why, Howard. Speaking frankly and between the two of us, y'know— I'm just a little tired.

HOWARD: Oh, I could understand that, Willy. But you're a road man, Willy, and we do a road business. We've only got a half-dozen salesmen on the floor here.

WILLY: God knows, Howard, I never asked a favor of any man. But I was with the firm when your father used to carry you in here in his arms.

HOWARD: I know that, Willy, but—

WILLY: Your father came to me the day you were born and asked me what I thought of the name of Howard, may he rest in peace.

HOWARD: I appreciate that, Willy, but there just is no spot here for you. If I had a spot I'd slam you right in, but I just don't have a single solitary spot.

He looked for his lighter. Willy has picked it up and gives it to him. Pause.

WILLY, *with increasing anger*: Howard, all I need to set my table is fifty dollars a week.

HOWARD: But where am I going to put you, kid?

WILLY: Look, it isn't a question of whether I can sell merchandise, is it?

HOWARD: No, but it's a business, kid, and everybody's gotta pull his own weight.

WILLY, *desperately*: Just let me tell you a story, Howard—

HOWARD: 'Cause you gotta admit, business is business.

WILLY, *angrily*: Business is definitely business, but just listen for a minute. You don't understand this.

When I was a boy—eighteen, nineteen—I was already on the road. And there was a question in my mind as to whether selling had a future for me. Because in those days I had a yearning to go to Alaska. See, there were three gold strikes in one month in Alaska, and I felt like going out. Just for the ride, you might say.

HOWARD, *barely interested*: Don't say.

WILLY: Oh, yeah, my father lived many years in Alaska. He was an adventurous man. We've got quite a little streak of self-reliance in our family. I thought I'd go out with my older brother and try to locate him, and maybe settle in the North with the old man. And I was almost decided to go, when I met a salesman in the Parker House. He name was Dave Singleman. And he was eighty-four years old, and he'd drummed merchandise in thirty-one states. And old Dave, he'd go up to his room, y'understand, put on his green velvet slippers—I'll never forget—and pick up his phone and call the buyers, and without leaving his room, at the age of eighty-four, he made his living. And when I saw that, I realized that selling was the greatest career a man could want. 'Cause what could be more satisfying than to be able to go, at the age of eighty-four, into twenty or thirty different cities, and pick up a phone, and be remembered and loved and helped by so many different people? Do you know? When he died—and by the way he died the death of a salesman, in his green velvet slippers in the smoker of the New York, New Haven and Hartford, going into Boston—when he died, hundreds of salesmen and buyers were at his funeral. Things were sad on a lotta trains for months after that. *He stands up. Howard has not looked at him.* In those days there was personality in it, Howard. There was respect, and comradeship, and gratitude in it. Today, it's all cut and dried, and there's no chance for bringing friendship to bear—or personality. You see what I mean? They don't know me any more.

HOWARD, *moving away, to the right*: That's just the thing, Willy.

WILLY: If I had forty dollars a week—that's all I'd need. Forty dollars, Howard.

HOWARD: Kid, I can't take blood from a stone, I—

WILLY, *desperation is on him now*: Howard, the year Al Smith was nominated, your father came to me and—

HOWARD, *starting to go off*: I've got to see some people, kid.

WILLY, *stopping him*: I'm talking about your father! There were promises made across this desk! You mustn't tell me you've got people to see—I put thirty-four years into this firm, Howard, and now I can't pay insurance! You can't eat the orange and throw the peel away—a man is not a piece of fruit!

Arthur Miller was one of the most accomplished writers in the United States and Death of a Salesman may be his most famous play. The preceding excerpt from the Pulitzer Prize winning tragedy has both irony and pathos. These two men have known each other for many years. Do they understand one another? Which parts of their conversation support your conclusion?

R.L.M. Dist. Co. v. W.A. Taylor, Inc.

723 F. Supp. 421 (D. Ariz. 1988)

ROGER G. STRAND, DISTRICT JUDGE.

. . .

The parties both acknowledge that there was no express agreement, either written or oral, relating to the transferability of their commercial relationship. RLM contends that there was an implied agreement between the parties concerning transferability which arose by virtue of the custom and practice relating to transferability that exists within the liquor industry.

Basic contract law does not require that agreements be made exclusively through verbal or written communications. Contracts may be implied in whole or in part through conduct alone or through usage of trade. *See Cook v. Cook*, 691 P.2d 664 (Ariz. 1984); Restatement (Second) Contracts § 4, comment a; *Id.* § 5 comment a; 1 Corbin on Contracts § 18 (1963). Therefore, even though RLM and Taylor never discussed the issue of transferability, an implied agreement concerning this subject may arise in the absence of a specific agreement to the contrary if custom or practice in the industry provides for such an understanding.

In the present case, the evidence at trial established that while spirituous liquor suppliers and distributors often do not discuss, orally or in writing, the terms of their transfer rights, the custom in the industry is that distribution rights may be transferred, with the consent of the supplier, upon sale of the distributor's business or transfer of the business.

The court finds and concludes that custom and practice in the industry and the course of conduct between RLM and Taylor was sufficient to imply an agreement between the parties relating to transferability. . . .

United Steelworkers of America, Local 1330 v. United States Steel

United States District Court for the Northern District of Ohio
492 F. Supp. 1 (1980)

THOMAS DEMETRIOS LAMBROS, JUDGE

. . .

In this action, the workers at the Mahoning Valley, Ohio, plants of United States Steel Corporation seek to enforce the alleged promise of the company to keep those plants open so long as they remain profitable. This suit was precipitated by the announced plan of the company to shut down the steel mills. On February 28, 1980, this Court temporarily enjoined the company from closing the plants; trial on the merits was advanced to March 17, 1980, so that the important issues embodied in this action might be given full and prompt consideration.

I.

This nation is in the throes of growing pains of similar intensity to the traumatic changes brought by the advent of the steam engine and the Industrial Revolution. From the turn of the century until the decade prior to this, the United States has been in an expansionary period brought on by plentiful energy and raw materials, technological leadership, and the insatiable maw of four major wars. Steel was the backbone of this expansion, and the dominance of the automobile in this period was a major source of support to the burgeoning steel industry. In the 1960s it appeared that this expansion and economic dominance had no limiting factor and that a rising gross national product and standard of living could be expected to become a permanent part of American Life.

The 1970s, however, were a time of serious reappraisal. The country's energy supplies were limited and controlled by a foreign cartel. The technological success of our allies, especially the Federal Republic of Germany and Japan, although welcome from the standpoint of the strengthening of the free world, made it clear that economic cooperation and not coercion would be the order of the new decade. This shift in economic power had a particularly strong effect in the automotive industry, and the influx of foreign cars meant the influx of foreign steel. Perhaps most importantly, the advent of peace after the conflict in Vietnam and the continuation from that period of a foreign policy of détente and non-interference have required a massive reallocation of capital, labor and technological research. The beating of swords into ploughshares is and will be a painful process of relocation and restructuring, though the prospect of a more permanent peace suggests that the changes must be made.

This lawsuit is a symptom of the changes discussed above. . . . United States Steel decided to close its plants in the Mahoning Valley, and approximately 3,500 workers became victims of the economic shifts forced on this nation by recent events.

The workers asked this Court for injunctive relief to keep the plants operating and their jobs intact. United States Steel answered that lack of profitability forced it to close and that it had a right to make this management decision, and the issues were thereby joined.

. . .

The Second Amended Complaint suggests four theories in support of injunctive relief— breach of contract, promissory estoppel, violation of anti-trust statutes and property right.

The breach of contract and detrimental reliance claims are based on a series of communications by employees of defendant to the workers at the Mahoning Valley plants. Plaintiffs allege these communications constitute a promise by the company to keep the mills operating if and so long as the workers made the mills profitable. These statements are set forth in paragraph ten of the Complaint.

. . .

The statements by employees of the company to the workers are crucial to the contract and estoppel claims because they are at the heart of the two basic issues the Court must decide: were the statements offers to enter into a unilateral contract that were binding on the corporation? and, should the company reasonably have expected the workers to rely on those statements?

. . .

Many of the statements were messages communicated to the employees by an internal telephone network called the "hot-line." William Kirwin, Manager of the Youngstown facilities, explained in testimony that various members of the management and public relations sectors of the company would record a short tape message. That message would then be connected to a system of in-plant telephones so that a worker could pick up a special hot-line telephone receiver and hear the recorded message. The message could not be heard on conventional telephones outside the plant.

The hot-line messages never make clear a promise to remain open if the workers made the plant profitable. A September 1, 1977, message said there were "no immediate plans to permanently shut down" and that "the continued operation of these plants is absolutely dependent upon their being profit-makers." However, the statement that lack of profitability would close the plants does not imply the converse that the plants will not close if they are profitable. William Kirwin's numerous hot-line remarks (on January 4, 1978, January 11, 1978, April 7, 1978, November 8, 1978 and December 21, 1978) come close to embodying the promise alleged by plaintiffs, especially such comments as these: "With your help, this effort will continue and if and when there will be a phase-out depends on the plants' profitability, but no timetable has been set." "Our future is what we make it." "I am asking each of you to consider how you may help in keeping Youngstown the going plant it is today."

Mr. Kirwin's remarks, however, must be considered in the context of their delivery. The hot-line was begun, according to Kirwin, as a mechanism for communicating safety tips to the workers, and was later expanded into a tool for correcting false rumors that might be spread through the plant and appear in the media. This Court has carefully read and reread Mr. Kirwin's messages, attempting to put itself in the place of a steelworker hearing those messages during 1977, 1978 and 1979. The Court concludes that the reasonable understanding to be drawn from those messages is this: The United States Steel plants in the Mahoning Valley are in trouble and a shutdown is imminent; the board of directors of the corporation will base the shutdown decision largely on profitability; if the plants become profitable it may affect management's shutdown decision; therefore, the most effective thing the workers can do to save their jobs is to work efficiently to help the profitability picture.

It is clear to this Court that Mr. Kirwin was dedicated to his job and to the employees of the steel plants. He believed that steel could be effectively produced in the Mahoning Valley. He wanted desperately to save the mills. Toward that goal he embarked on a "morale" program to attempt to get the workers in Youngstown to make steel profitable. Although this speaks highly of Mr. Kirwin's ability and dedication, it also suggests that his statements were not necessarily those of the national company management. For example, on January 3, 1978, Edgar Speer, then Chairman of the Board of Directors of United States Steel, affirmed that at some point the Ohio and McDonald Works would have to be closed. Mr. Kirwin's hot-line remarks of January 4, 1978 and January 11, 1978, were directed toward explaining Mr. Speer's remark. It was at this point that Mr. Kirwin stated "if and when there will be a phase-out depends on the plant's profitability."

The other remarks alleged in paragraph ten of the Complaint are less troubling. Remarks made to the media by various employees of the company cannot reasonably be construed as embodying a promise made to the workers, especially when the statements were made by public relations people and not company officers (see the statements of Frederick Foote and Randall Walthius).

It is this Court's considered opinion that a reasonable understanding of all of the statements alleged in paragraph ten of the Complaint would suggest that national company management wanted to close the plant for lack of profitability and that the call for increased worker productivity was a plan William Kirwin was presenting as a final effort for the workers to sway national management opinion. Mr. Kirwin's plan was courageous and well conceived, but it did not represent a promise made by the corporation on which the workers should reasonably have relied.

...

Note

Approximately 4,000 workers lost their jobs in the U.S. Steel Youngstown, Mahoning Valley, plant closings. In an effort to regain their jobs and to renew the economic vitality of their communities, a group of laid-off workers and community groups organized the Community Steel Corporation and sought to buy the facilities from U.S. Steel. As Bob Vasquez, president of Local 1330 explained: "If U.S. Steel doesn't want to make steel in Youngstown, the people of Youngstown will make steel in Youngstown." Staughton Lynd, *The Genesis of the Idea of a Community Right to Industrial Property in Youngstown and Pittsburgh, 1977–1987*, J. Amer. Hist. 926, 938 (1987).

U.S. Steel, however, refused to consider an offer from the Community Steel Corporation, explaining that it was unwilling to sell to a worker-owned company because a worker-owned company might qualify for loans from the government and thus might have a competitive advantage. Because of this concern, U. S. Steel explained, it would not negotiate for sale of the plant to any association of employees. The plaintiffs in *United Steelworkers, Local 1330 v. United States Steel* included one count alleging that U.S. Steel's refusal to consider an offer by workers to purchase violated federal anti-trust laws. In an omitted part of the opinion above, Judge Lambros held that the antitrust claim was premature because U.S. Steel had not yet disposed of the plant facilities.

Under pressure from the court, U.S. Steel delayed its decision on the Community Steel Corporation's offer to buy, but in 1981, Community Steel Corporation withdrew from its efforts to buy the Youngstown plants because the Economic Development Administration (the EDA) of the Commerce Department denied its application for a loan. Staughton Lynd, attorney for the Community Steel Corporation, later explained: "The EDA was very close to the steel industry, and they may well have been less than enthusiastic about another competitor in a poor market—we really don't know." Craig R. Waters, *Born-Again Steel, Inc.*, November 1984, page 52. The Community Steel Corporation then agreed to settle its anti-trust claim against U.S. Steel on the condition that U.S. Steel sell some of its Youngstown facilities to another company, McDonald Steel Corporation. McDonald Steel Corporation, with David S. Houck, a former U.S. Steel manager, as its President, reopened two mills and recorded a profit of $7.5 million in its first year of operation, 1982. *See* Rosemary Armao, *A Steel Mill is Reopening*, United Press International, Regional News, June 9, 1983. In 1993, the corporation reported net sales of $23 million and announced a new Employee Stock Ownership Plan. *McDonald Steel Launches ESOP*, 10 Youngstown Business Journal, March 15, 1994, page 20.

In the aftermath of the steel plant closings involved in this and other cases, Congress enacted the *Worker Adjustment and Retraining Notification Act*, 29 U.S.C. §§ 2101–2109 (1988), which requires companies with 100 or more employees to give workers sixty days' notice of plant closings and mass layoffs. However, there are numerous exceptions to the notification requirement, and enforcement of the Act is left solely to individual litigation.

Many critics have argued that the Act has had no impact on the hardships of plant closings and that it is routinely ignored by employers. *See, e.g.,* Stephen D. Ake, *Evolving Concepts in Management Prerogatives: Plant Closures, Relocations, and Mass Layoffs,* 24 Stetson L. Rev. 241 (1994) ("[C]ommentators generally acknowledge that the WARN Act has had no significant impact on the length of advance notice given to employees. This is largely a result of exemptions, lack of enforcement mechanisms, and uncertainty or ignorance of WARN's requirements. Results from a General Accounting Office (GAO) Report to Congressional Committees indicate that more than one-half of the employers expecting a plant closure failed to provide sixty days' advance notice even when the event appeared to meet the WARN Act's criteria."). *See generally,* Jessica L. Stein, *The Worker Adjustment Retraining and Notification Act (Warn),* 19 Seton Hall Legis. J. 648 (1995).

One reason for such high levels of noncompliance with the WARN Act might be that employers have much to gain from keeping employees ignorant of plant closing plans. In some cases, like the U.S. Steel plant closings, employers want employees to know that plant closings are possible, but not certain, in order to convince employees to agree to wage and benefit reductions. In other cases, employers want employees to know nothing about possible plant closings so employees will continue their employment, productivity, and company loyalty. This apparently was the Maytag Company's motivation in misleading its employees regarding plans to close its Narco-Dixie plant in Ranson, West Virginia. In 1989, Maytag announced the construction of a new manufacturing plant in Williston, South Carolina. Immediately, employees at Maytag's Ranson plant became concerned that construction of the new facility indicated a company plan to close the Ranson facility and asked the company for information. Maytag officials responded with a series of promises and representations, including the assurance that Ranson employees' "jobs [were] safe," and that they could "buy [their] cars and houses" without fear of losing their jobs. Despite these assurances, Maytag closed the Ranson plant in 1991. As one of the plaintiffs explained, "They told us buy our homes and cars because your job's secure; we're not going anywhere.... [And then] [t]hey moved. They left. They sent termination notices to everybody." *Transcript,* Sunday Morning, September 3, 1995. Laid off workers filed suit for breach of contract and promissory estoppel, alleging that at the time its officials made these promises and representations plans to close the plant were already formulated. Amended Complaint, *Henry v. Maytag Corporation* (Civil Action No. 92-C-417, Circuit Court of Jefferson County, West Virginia). In 1995, Maytag agreed to pay $16.5 million to former employees of its Ranson plant in settlement of this suit.

Sue Doro, Blue Collar Goodbyes

(1993)

blue collar goodbyes are a jumpstart
on a frozen battery midnight parking lot
peering out of second shift propped open coffee eyes
from a toolbox back at the radial drill machine
in Allis Chalmers Tractor Shop
where the only African American on the housing line
teams up with the only female in the maintenance repair
to move those tractors out the door
now Bill Dunlop's powerful hands fasten jumper cables
to plus and minus inside car hoods exposed to winter in Wisconsin

my '71 Ford and Bill's bran' new step up van's competent motor
vibrating powdered snow like sifted cake flour
off a gleaming waxed finish revealing
Bill's stencil painted signature design
DADDY HIGH POCKETS
and his wife Bernice's
LADY LOW POCKETS
in the cold moon glow blue brightness
as my engine finally turns over
warming up goodbyes satisfying
as Bill and Bernice's faces across their kitchen table
heavy with the platters of deep Southern fried catfish
and hot cornbread put out for company
my home partner Larry and I over for Saturday night
and Bill waits inside his van to be sure
I'm not stuck in ice ruts
then fifteen years and a plant closure later
Bill's gone
I'm gone
Allis Chalmers is gone
blue collar goodbyes become letters and phone calls
from back home Bill and Bernice
and Milwaukee road buddies Earl, Don, and Verona
veterans of yet another plant closing down, another buy out
by a hungrier corporation
another selling out up the hill
with nothing but our lunch buckets
more forced layoffs, a few paid severances
don't know how many transfers to Chicago or Minneapolis
where the Soo Line promised jobs then
four years later about to go belly up too,
it offers those same people a chance to buy
their own failing railroad
in a town they never wanted to live in
blue collar goodbyes report Wisconsin to California
on lined school notebook paper start and strong
THERE'S BACK PAY COMING ... YOU BETTER CALL
and phoning find the Soo Line
would've kept my blood-earned money
if I had not known
the hearts of survivors
that corporate minds will never know
survivors of shutdowns and forty-below-zero wind chills
work friends like family separated
by job change and cross country miles
people who hold ear and remember lunch buckets
Saturday catfish and goin' home car rides that never say never
'cause we'll see you sometime
goodbyes like sparks of electricity through jumper cables
in a midnight parking lot

In the Matter of the Estate of Virgil A. Steffes, Deceased Mary Lou Brooks v. Terry V. Steffes, Personal Representative

Supreme Court of Wisconsin
290 N.W.2d 697 (1980)

SHIRLEY S. ABRAHAMSON, JUSTICE

The question on appeal is whether the plaintiff, who engaged in an adulterous relationship with the deceased, may recover from the estate for unpaid salary, wages, or other compensation for personal services rendered to the deceased within the two-year period preceding his death.

Virgil Steffes died without a will on July 17, 1976. His gross estate was valued at $733,644.65. Steffes was survived by a son, who is an heir and the personal representative of the estate, and children of a deceased son, who are heirs. The plaintiff, Mary Lou Brooks, filed a claim against the estate in the amount of $29,200.00 for personal services rendered to the deceased during the last two years of his life (July 17, 1974–July 17, 1976). The estate refused to pay the claim and this litigation ensued. The trial court rendered judgment allowing the claim against the estate in the amount of $14,600.00.

There is no dispute that plaintiff rendered services for Steffes on the farm and in his home and that she gave him excellent nursing care during his lengthy last illness. Steffes' son had been a guest in his father's home before his father's death, and he testified that he had eaten meals cooked by the plaintiff, that his father's home was kept in good condition, and that the plaintiff took good care of his ill father.

The son, as personal representative, appeals the judgment on three grounds: (1) that the facts do not sustain the trial court's findings that the plaintiff rendered services at the request of and with the knowledge of the deceased and with the expectation of compensation; (2) that any services rendered are presumed to be gratuitous because plaintiff lived for more than six years as a member of Steffes' household and that the requirement that there be an express promise to pay for such services was not met; and (3) that the plaintiff cannot recover compensation for the work she performed in the house and on the farm, because Steffes and the plaintiff had engaged in sexual intercourse.

We affirm the judgment of the trial court.

I.

The facts are not in dispute. Mary Lou Brooks, the plaintiff, met Virgil Steffes, the deceased, in 1969, while the plaintiff was working in a tavern, and soon thereafter she moved to Steffes' farm home where she resided until his death. Plaintiff and Steffes were each married to other persons. Plaintiff knew Steffes was a married man, and he continued to be married until his wife died in 1974. The plaintiff had been married in 1963 and had two children. She continued to be married while she lived in the deceased's house, initiating divorce proceedings after Steffes' death. Plaintiff admitted having sexual relations with Virgil Steffes until about a year before Steffes' death. Plaintiff and numerous witnesses testified that neither plaintiff nor Steffes had represented her as Mrs. Virgil Steffes.

According to the plaintiff's undisputed testimony she performed the following chores in the house and on the farm: she cleaned the house, did the cooking, washing, and ironing; she helped fix farm fences; she picked the corn crop; she ran the combine and loaded the corn into a "semi" during late 1974; she chased animals which escaped from the pasture; from the end of October until May (1974–1975) she loaded silage; she aided the deceased in pouring concrete walls around the feedlot; she aided the deceased in re-modeling his home by "tearing out partitions" and by setting forms, pouring concrete, and pulling the forms; she wrote all the deceased's checks (with one or two exceptions) under the deceased's direction over the two-year period in question, signing his name along with her initials; and she cleaned and prepared machinery for the April 1975 farm sale. The amount of work performed by the plaintiff may be gauged by the size of the farming operation. In July, 1974, there were 80 head of Charolais cattle and approximately 20 registered Morgan horses on the farm. There were also 325 acres of corn on the farm in the spring of 1975.

The plaintiff also described the nursing care she gave Steffes. In the fall of 1974, his health began to deteriorate. He suffered from headaches and dizzy spells. In March, 1975 he was hospitalized and tests revealed a brain tumor; surgery was performed. Plaintiff stayed in a chair beside Steffes' bed for four days and nights while he was in the hospital. For twenty-eight consecutive days after Steffes' surgery, plaintiff drove him to the hospital for cobalt treatments. Steffes' condition continued to worsen during 1976 and plaintiff's care continued. Plaintiff's testimony relating to the care she gave Steffes during his illness was summarized by the estate's counsel as follows:

> ... In the summer of 1975 after surgery, Virgil still had headaches and had so much pressure from the tumor. He went blind in his left eye. I took him for eye tests and he got a little weak in his right side in 1976. In the fall of 1975 there was only horses left.... The remodeling of the house was completed in April, 1976. The slight stroke or weakening of Virgil Steffes was when we were working in the house about three weeks before we moved in. We moved in around April 1st. He called me. He couldn't use his leg it was so weak and his arm. We were still working there. Laudel Culver and Don Urbanek and Bill and Daisy Crubaugh, we were all in the house working that evening and Virgil and I went up to the other place. He said he did not know what was wrong, his legs seemed weak and that. Then I exercised his leg and his arm by working his leg up and down, back and forth, trying to keep the strength in it and his arm. I took him back to La Crosse for a checkup and they took x-rays and the doctor showed me the x-rays where the tumor was coming back and I told him about Virgil's leg and that and he says to exercise it, and so I did and that's when they put him on some pills and he had to have them every four hours. They were to keep the pressure off where the tumor was coming back. Virgil got kidney infection and I took him back, and they gave him pills. They wanted to use a catheter and he said no. I bought a urinal and sat beside him. If he could, for awhile he could help himself when he had to use it and then he got that he couldn't use it. If he wet himself I changed his clothes and if he had an accident in bed, I would change the bed in the middle of the night. This went on during June, 1976. After March, 1976 he had a stroke that affected the whole one side of him and so then in order for him to walk I would slide my foot under his and pick his foot up and walk him that way. He was going to the doctor and the hospital during this time. I took him for his checkups. I would lift him out of the chair and then I would slide my foot under his and put my arm around him, put my arm around him and he would lean on me and we would get to the car that way. Be the same thing at the hospital. If I had to park some place out in the parking lot too far away, then I would go and get or Greg Gebhard might go with me. Sometimes Mike Urbanek rode along and they would run in and get a wheel chair and bring it out and then I would wheel him into the hospital and wheel him out to the car. Then

towards the last when his whole side went I couldn't even walk him no more. I went into Bohlman's Drug Store and rented a wheel chair for at the house too.... Mr. Steffes died July the 17th '76.

Plaintiff testified that she received the following items from the deceased during this two-year period: food and lodging; approximately $7,200.00 from the sale of horses and cows which deceased had given to plaintiff to take care of; $3,200.00 towards a $4,544.00 Pontiac which was purchased June 22, 1976 and titled in the plaintiff's name.

The trial court summarized the plaintiff's efforts as follows: "Now this lady although she was not a mason (she) did cement work, and although she was not a carpenter she did carpentry work, and although she wasn't an accountant she did bookkeeping work, although she was not a nurse she rendered nursing services."

Plaintiff testified that she expected to receive something for the services she performed for Virgil Steffes during the last two years of his life. The deceased's brother-in-law and friends of both the plaintiff and the deceased testified that Steffes had indicated that he wanted to provide for the plaintiff and that he wanted her to have the house and farm on his death. However, Steffes did not execute a will and sold part of the farm on land contract and gave the purchasers an option to purchase farm property.

II.

The trial court found that the plaintiff went into the deceased's home as a housekeeper, that the housekeeping, farming and nursing services "rendered by her were performed at the instance and with his knowledge of the decedent"; and that the plaintiff expected compensation for these services over and above room and board and the gratuities she received from Mr. Steffes. These findings are significant because this court, in a long line of cases, has held that where services are performed at the special instance of the deceased and with his knowledge and are performed by the claimant with expectation of reasonable compensation, recovery may be allowed on the basis of a contract to pay, implied in fact or law. The trial court concluded that a contract for services can be implied from the facts and can also be implied in law (quasi-contract) on the ground of unjust enrichment and that plaintiff can recover the reasonable value of services rendered to the deceased.

The personal representative asserts that the evidence does not support the trial court's findings of fact that the services were rendered at the instance of and the knowledge of the decedent and with the expectation of compensation.

The personal representative's brief acknowledges that the plaintiff's services were performed with the knowledge of the decedent and that while he was ill in the hospital, he asked her to stay and asked her to help him so that he did not have to have a catheter. Nevertheless the personal representative argues that the trial court's finding that the services were performed at the deceased's instance and request cannot be sustained because the plaintiff moved to the home of the decedent and became a part of his household and family. The personal representative argues that because all services were performed as a member of the household the performance was not "at the decedent's instance and request" but was expected under the circumstances. The personal representative further argues that plaintiff's expectations were fulfilled when she was compensated by room, board, companionship, and gifts.

In effect the personal representative is asking this court to hold that, because the plaintiff was treated as a member of the household and performed services and because there was no direct evidence that the plaintiff was hired as a housekeeper, the trial court erred, as a matter of law, in concluding that the services were rendered at the decedent's instance and request. The personal representative cites no authority for this proposition of law, and we can find none.

In *Kramer v. Bins*, 205 Wis. 562, 238 N.W. 307 (1931), the claimant moved into the defendant's home and cared for him and his ailing father. The defendant alleged that the claimant performed services under an agreement that the parties would be married later and that the services were rendered without cost to the defendant. The claimant asserted that she performed services at his special instance and request and that she expected payment. The trial court submitted two questions, inter alia, to the jury: (1) Did the claimant render services to the defendant at the defendant's request, and (2) were the services rendered pursuant to a marriage agreement that each was to work for the other without pay? The jury concluded that the defendant had requested that services be rendered but that the parties had agreed that no compensation should be paid. This court upheld the verdict of the jury. There is nothing in the *Kramer v. Bins* opinion to indicate that services performed by a person who is treated as a member of the household but who was not hired as a housekeeper are, as a matter of law, expected and cannot, as a matter of law, be performed "at the instance and request" of the defendant. Indeed the opinion indicates that it is for the trier of facts to determine whether services of a person treated as a member of the household are performed at the request and special instance of the defendant and with the expectation of compensation.

. . .

We conclude there is no legal or factual basis to support the personal representative's argument that because plaintiff was treated as a member of the household the evidence does not support the trial court's findings that she went into Steffes' home as a housekeeper with the expectation of payment for services and that her services were rendered at the instance of the deceased and with his knowledge.

III.

The personal representative next argues that the trial court erred in holding that the plaintiff could prevail on proof of an implied contract. The trial court held in the instant case that there was a contract implied in fact and law to pay; it concluded that there was no express contract to pay the full value of the services rendered.

We start with the principle well-grounded in human experience that where one renders valuable services for another payment is expected. This court has frequently stated that "if one merely accepts services from another which are valuable to him, in general, the presumption of fact arises that a compensation equivalent is to pass between the parties, and the burden of proof is upon the recipient of the service to rebut such presumption if he would escape from rendering such equivalent." *Wojahn v. National Union Bank*, 144 Wis. 646, 667, 129 N.W. 1068, 1077 (1911).

The personal representative's theory is that a presumption that the services were performed gratuitously applies in the instant case. Where there is a close family or marriage relationship, the law presumes the services are performed gratuitously, and the law will not imply from the mere rendition of services by one family member to another a promise to pay. This presumption of gratuitous service is, as is the presumption that services are rendered for compensation, well-grounded in human experience and rebuttable. It is clear that the plaintiff is not related to the deceased by blood or marriage. The personal representative argues that the presumption of gratuitous service should apply anyway because the plaintiff was part of Steffes' family, the term "family" being used to include anyone who is a member of the household. The basis for applying the presumption of gratuitous service to persons cohabiting but not related by marriage is that in the ordinary course of life persons living together in a close relationship perform services for each other without expectation of payment in the usual sense because the parties mutually care for each other's needs and perform services for each other out of a feeling of affection or a sense of obligation.

The personal representative asserts that the law in Wisconsin is that if a presumption of gratuitous service applies, the party seeking compensation must prove the existence of an express contract for compensation. The personal representative relies on *Estate of Goltz*, 205 Wis. 590, 594, 238 N.W. 374, 376 (1931), in which this court said:

> The law is well established that "where near relatives by blood or marriage reside together as one common family, and one of them renders services to another, and such other furnishes him board and lodging or other necessaries or comforts, a presumption arises that neither party intended to receive or to pay compensation for the services rendered on the one hand, or for the board and lodging or other necessaries or comforts on the other; that they were intended as mutual acts of kindness done or furnished gratuitously"....

> Since the facts of this case bring it within the rule stated and give rise to the presumption of gratuitous services, it was incumbent upon the claimant to prove an express contract by direct and positive evidence or to prove by unequivocal facts and circumstances that which is the equivalent of direct and positive proof of an express contract.

Cases decided by this court since *Goltz* have departed from the principle that a presumption that services were rendered gratuitously may be rebutted only by proof of an express contract. This court has upheld judgments awarding compensation on the basis of a contract implied in fact even though the claimant was related to the decedent by blood or marriage.

We do not think it is necessary in the instant case to determine whether a presumption of gratuitous service arises where persons live in the same household in a meretricious relationship, because whether the initial presumption is that services were to be compensated or that they were rendered gratuitously, the final determination of whether the services were to be compensated depends on the circumstances relating to the plaintiff's entry into and her stay in the Steffes household. If an express promise to pay is proved or a promise to pay can be implied from the facts, then the plaintiff is entitled to compensation regardless of the fact that she rendered services with a sense of affection, devotion and duty.

As we explained in *Estate of Detjen*, 34 Wis. 2d 46, 52–53, 148 N.W.2d 745, 748 (1967):

> ... And, whatever the initial presumptions may be, the final determination, we have said in the *Estate of Kuepper* (1961), 12 Wis. 2d 577, 107 N.W.2d 621, depends not on a rule of law which awards or denies compensation for services rendered depending on the family relationship of the parties or the house they live in, but upon the existence or nonexistence of an express promise, or one implied in fact, that the services were to be paid for.

> In respect to the payment of decedent's debts in her lifetime, when there is no express promise of repayment, one may be implied or negated in fact from the conduct of the parties, the nature of the bill, the amount of payments, the relationship and affection or lack of it between the parties, and whether such payments are usually made under such circumstances as to indicate or negate a promise of repayment. Thus the circumstances may support a presumption or an inference of an implied promise or negate its existence, but whatever the

direct evidence is and whatever inferences may be drawn from other evidence, the burden of proving an implied agreement existed between the claimant and the decedent falls upon the claimant. *Estate of Kuepper, supra*; *Wojahn v. National Union Bank* (1911), 144 Wis. 646, 129 N.W. 1068; *Estate of St. Germain* (1945), 246 Wis. 409, 17 N.W.2d 582.

In the case at bar the plaintiff had been employed in a tavern when she met the deceased. The trial court concluded that she left a paying job to take care of deceased's home; that she went to the deceased's farm and performed labor usually performed by a housekeeper, farm-hand, mason, carpenter, bookkeeper and nurse; and that she worked long and hard doing heavy work and performing unpleasant tasks. She testified she expected compensation. Witnesses testified that the decedent said he wanted to leave real estate to her and wanted to provide for her. Several of the services plaintiff performed were of a commercial variety, and the deceased hired employees to perform services similar to those rendered by the plaintiff.

The trial court in the instant case carefully reviewed the relation and situation of the parties, the nature and character of the services rendered, and all the facts and circumstances and concluded that the plaintiff entered this home and remained there as a housekeeper for the deceased; that although there was a warm and affectionate relation between the plaintiff and the deceased and the deceased made gifts to the plaintiff, the plaintiff expected payment for the services and the deceased expressed his intent to provide for the plaintiff; and that an agreement between the plaintiff and the deceased that he would pay for such services can be implied from the circumstances.

The trial court's conclusion in the case at bar is consistent with prior decisions of this court holding that under the facts of the particular case an implied promise to pay for services was proved....

...

In *Estate of Grossman*, 250 Wis. 457, 461, 27 N.W.2d 365, 367 (1947), a father requested an adult daughter who lived 100 miles from the parent's home to come to her parents' home and help care for her ailing mother. After the mother died, the father became ill, and the daughter again left her job and home to return to the parents' home to care for the father. The daughter sought reasonable compensation for these services from the father's estate. She did not prove an express contract for payment. Noting that the intention of the parties may be gathered from the acts, deeds and words of the parties and the surrounding circumstances, this court concluded that the daughter's evidence, although "not too strong," was "sufficient to overcome the presumption (that the services were gratuitously performed) and sustain the trial court in granting judgment for the services rendered...."

...

We hold that there is sufficient evidence in the case at bar to support the trial court's finding that there was an implied promise to pay for the services plaintiff rendered.

For the foregoing reasons, we affirm the judgment of the trial court.

Judgment affirmed.

JOHN L. COFFEY, JUSTICE, DISSENTING

The plaintiff, Mrs. Brooks, left her husband and two children to live in an adulterous relationship with the deceased, a much older man who was also married. They maintained an intimate sexual relationship until his health no longer permitted it. The "services" she performed for the deceased were owed to her husband under her solemn marriage vows.

After the deceased became ill, she took care of him and performed some of the farm work. But this was not a separate undertaking. It was a continuation of the meretricious relationship she had established earlier.

The majority claims that Mrs. Brooks provided the decedent with "excellent nursing care during his lengthy last illness." Moreover, they claim that the decedent's son testified that when he visited his father's home he found it was kept in good condition and that Mrs. Brooks was taking good care of his ill father. I find, after a thorough examination of the record, no evidence to substantiate the majority's opinion that Mrs. Brooks provided "excellent nursing care," but rather she provided "intermediate care" as he was not totally independent in taking care of his own needs. Secondly, the record also fails to substantiate that the decedent's son testified that Mrs. Brooks "took good care of his ill father," but rather he testified as follows:

Q. And what's the condition of the house when you were here?

A. It was in good shape.

Q. And did she cook meals for you at that time?

A. Yes.

Q. And your father?

A. Yes.

Q. When was the last time that you saw your father?

A. I saw him about the first week in May of 1976.

Q. And that was at his home?

A. Right, that was at the south house.

Q. And did you observe Mary Lou Brooks do anything for him at that time?

A. Yes, I did.

Q. And what did she do?

A. She cooked dinner and she cooked meals for us.

Q. Did she assist him in any way in getting around?

A. She prepared his food for him and gave him a fork and he ate with his left hand.

Q. Did she have to help him walk?

A. No, not on that date.

Q. He was able to walk all by himself?

A. Yes.

Out of a misguided sense of fairness, the author of the majority opinion implies a promise to pay from the "circumstances relating to the plaintiff's entry into and her stay in the Steffes household." I have examined the circumstances cited and can only reach the conclusion that sexual intimacy, in violation of their marriage vows, was the underlying motivation for Mrs. Brooks' entry into and stay in the home of the deceased. In *Estate of Fox*, 178 Wis. 369, 190 N.W. 90 (1922) this court said that: "Courts are practically unanimous in holding that when a woman voluntarily and knowingly lives in illicit relations with a man she cannot recover on an implied contract for services rendered him during the period of such relationship. 29 L.R.A., N.S. 787." *Id.* at 371, 190 N.W. at 91.

The majority opinion says Mrs. Brooks testified she expected compensation. I disagree. Her actual testimony was as follows:

Q. Did you receive any wages from Mr. Steffes?

A. No sir.

Q. From July of '74 until his death?

A. No sir.

Q. Did you expect to receive any money for the work that you did?

A. No.

Q. Pardon?

A. No, but he always told me that.

By Mr. Antoine: I would object to what he said. That's hearsay and she's not competent to testify to it.

By the Court: I'll sustain the objection.

By Mr. Urban: Q. Did you understand that question?

A. No.

Q. Let me ask you differently. Did you expect to receive anything for the services you performed for Virgil Steffes from July 17, 1974, until the time of his death?

By Mr. Antoine: Object to that. It's already been answered.

By the Court: No, the previous question was a little different. The other question was, do you expect to receive any money, and this question is, do you expect to receive anything, and that's a different question. Answer the question.

A. Yes.

In *Estate of Detjen*, 34 Wis. 2d 46, 148 N.W.2d 745 (1967) this court held that:

Whether the claim involves services rendered to the decedent or payments made for her benefit, the foundation for recovery generally is the same—a contract express or implied. And, whatever the initial presumptions may be, the final determination, we have said in the *Estate of Kuepper* (1961), 12 Wis. 2d 577, 107 N.W.2d 621, depends not on a rule of law which awards or denies compensation for services rendered depending on the family relationship of the parties or the house they live in, but upon the existence or nonexistence of an express promise, or one implied in fact, that the services were to be paid for.

Id. at 52, 53, 148 N.W.2d at 748.

Furthermore, in *In the Matter of Guardianship of Kordecki*, 95 Wis. 2d 275, 290 N.W.2d 693 (1980) this court, quoting from *Estate of Detjen, supra*, held, with regard to the general rule of implied-in-fact contracts, that: " … a promise to pay will not be implied if a benefit is conferred with no expectation of payment but is conferred from motives of friendliness, neighborliness, kindliness or charity." *Id.* at 280, 290 N.W.2d at 695.

In this case, Mrs. Brooks did not expect to be paid, although it should be pointed out that Mrs. Brooks did not go uncompensated, she received clothing, board, food, lodging, plus $7,200 from the sale of horses and cattle and $3,200 towards the purchase of a car while living with the deceased. She expected the deceased to leave her the farm, but he sold it before his death and did not leave her the proceeds. Of this fact she was well aware, but still did not leave and return to her husband and children she had abandoned. Now the majority gives her money compensation she never expected as a consolation prize.

The amount of money compensation that the majority awards to the plaintiff is minor in comparison to the total value of the decedent's gross estate. However, the fact that the plaintiff's recovery is small when compared to the gross value of the estate does not support the court's holding because the total value of the estate is immaterial. Likewise, the amount of money taken in an armed robbery or the amount of money obtained in a check forgery scheme are immaterial, but the underlying principle of law is this court's granting of a consolation prize to a woman who has abandoned her family and entered an adulterous relationship with a married man in violation of the laws of this state. In affirming the trial court's award of $14,600 from the estate to Mrs. Brooks, are we not depriving the decedent's lawful heirs, his children, of their just and complete inheritance? Is she also allowed to inherit from her own lawful husband should he predecease her and before a lawful divorce? Is she entitled to her dower-elective share rights? Within the past six months, the Illinois Supreme Court, when confronted with a similar problem, commented in *Hewitt v. Hewitt*, 77 Ill. 2d 49, 31 Ill. Dec. 827, 394 N.E.2d 1204 (1979) as follows:

> The issue of unmarried cohabitants' mutual property rights, however, as we earlier noted, cannot appropriately be characterized solely in terms of contract law, nor is it limited to considerations of equity or fairness as between the parties to such relationships. There are major public policy questions involved in determining whether, under what circumstances, and to what extent it is desirable to accord some type of legal status to claims arising from such relationships. Of substantially greater importance than the rights of the immediate parties is the impact of such recognition upon our society and the institution of marriage. Will the fact that legal rights closely resembling those arising from conventional marriages can be acquired by those who deliberately choose to enter into what have heretofore been commonly referred to as 'illicit' or 'meretricious' relationships encourage formation of such relationships and weaken marriage as the foundation of our family-based society? In the event of death shall the survivor have the status of a surviving spouse for purposes of inheritance, wrongful death actions, workmen's compensation, etc.? And still more importantly: what of the children born of such relationships? What are their support and inheritance rights and by what standards are custody questions resolved? What of the sociological and psychological effects upon them of that type of environment? Does not the recognition of legally enforceable property and custody rights emanating from nonmarital cohabitation in practical effect equate with the legalization of common law marriage at least in the circumstances of this case? And, in summary, have the increasing numbers of unmarried cohabitants and changing mores of our society ... reached the point at which the general welfare of the citizens of this State is best served by a return to something resembling the judicially created common law marriage our legislature outlawed in 1905?

Id. 31 Ill. Dec. at 830–831, 394 N.E.2d at 1207–08.

In the case at bar, there could not be a common-law marriage without a lawful divorce. Mrs. Brooks and the deceased were content to maintain their prior marital status while living together in open defiance of their vows and the laws of the state of Wisconsin. This court ought not to allow Mrs. Brooks to assert a right to compensation growing out of a relationship which offends the standards of decency of any age. Their lifestyle has not been condoned, but has been rejected by our legislature. Moreover, the majority's decision contravenes the intent and policy of "The Family Code" of this state as recited in sec. 245.001(2), Stats., which reads in part as follows:

(2) Intent. It is the intent of chs. 245 to 248 to promote the stability and best interests of marriage and the family. Marriage is the institution that is the foundation of the family and of society. Its stability is basic to morality and civilization, and of vital interest to society and the state. The consequences of the marriage contract are more significant to society than those of other contracts, and the public interest must be taken into account always....

The majority, in its opinion, cites a California Supreme Court case, *Marvin v. Marvin*, 18 Cal. 3d 660, 134 Cal. Rptr. 815, 557 P.2d 106 (1976) as establishing the existence of certain mutual property rights between parties living together outside of marriage. California, unlike Wisconsin, has repealed its statute imposing criminal sanctions for sexual activity between unmarried, consenting adults. Thus, in California there is no barrier to adults living together out of wedlock. However, where a state has established a statutory barrier to cohabitation between unmarried adults that law should be given full force and effect and not be undermined. Attempts have been made in Wisconsin, in fact as recently as the current legislative session to abolish or eliminate the statutory barrier preventing consenting adults who are married to another person from living together and engaging in adulterous behavior but these attempts have been unsuccessful. In a recent tax case, *Ensminger v. Commissioner of Internal Revenue*, 610 F.2d 189 (1979) the 4th Circuit Court of Appeals held that a taxpayer could not claim as a dependent a 21 year old woman, not his wife, with whom he lived and supported because their relationship "(was) in violation of local law." In that case North Carolina had a statute holding that lewd and lascivious cohabitation between a man and woman not married to each other was a misdemeanor. The court also stated that: "The regulation of marriage, family life and domestic affairs 'has long been regarded as a virtually exclusive province of the states.'" *Id.* at 191.

I believe the majority has resorted to an unfortunate form of judicial surgery that can only serve to accelerate the growth of the self-destructive cancer of the '70s "immorality" and the decline of the family. If there is to be a direct, frontal assault on the traditional values, principles, ideals and pattern of family life, the very lifeline and backbone of our American society, it should be accomplished within the confines of the legislative halls not in the courts. The judicial system is ill equipped to deal with a social change of this magnitude because we are without the benefit of up-to-date economic, social and psychological data in the field of domestic relations and the far reaching implications of court approved abandonment and the problems accompanying fatherless and motherless children in the decades ahead. With this decision are we not condoning abandonment? Broken homes? Are not 95% of all juvenile law violators from broken homes? Are not by far the vast majority of welfare problems directly attributable to abandonment? If there is a need for a change in this far reaching public policy question, and I fail to see the necessity, let it be done after a legislative fact-finding hearing where a more thorough discussion can only lead to greater knowledge and expertise in the solving of this most delicate question. The Illinois Supreme Court in *Hewitt v. Hewitt, supra*, held that the decision of whether the present law should be changed so as to grant legal rights or status to a non-marital relationship, such as existed in this case, is best left to the legislature:

> ... The question whether change is needed in the law governing the rights of parties in this delicate area of marriage-like relationships involves evaluations of sociological data and alternatives we believe best suited to the superior investigative and fact-finding facilities of the legislative branch in the exercise of its traditional authority to declare public policy in the domestic relations field.

Id. 31 Ill. Dec. at 832, 394 N.E.2d at 1209.

Therefore, I would reverse.

Note — On Informal Contracts and the Objective Theory

Informal Contracts

The court in *Embry* held that a contract could have been formed between Embry and McKittrick even though they did not sign any document, shake hands, or use the words "promise," "commitment," or "contract." In *Steffes* the court found that an agreement between Brooks and Steffes, including a promise by Steffes to pay Brooks for her household and nursing services, was implied in their words, conduct, and circumstances. Informal contracts are enforceable. The only significant limitation on this rule is the statute of frauds (or, more accurately, statutes of frauds, because there are many, applicable to different kinds of contracts). We will examine some aspects of the statute of frauds in Chapter Six. As a general rule, oral contracts are enforceable; there is no general common law rule requiring written evidence of a contract.

Objective Theory: Rationale and Criticisms

The recognition of informal contracts means that problems of interpretation are multiplied many-fold. Informal agreements are manifested in words, conduct, and circumstances sometimes occurring over many years. Where one person says that a complex combination of words, conduct, and circumstances constitutes agreement and another person says it does not, how should the court decide? The court in *Embry* applied one version of the objective theory of contract interpretation: " ... if what McKittrick said would have been taken by a reasonable man to be an employment, and Embry so understood it, it constituted a valid contract of employment for the ensuing year." Under this approach, the meaning of words, conduct, and circumstances is determined from the perspective of a reasonable person. This approach is distinguished from the "subjective theory," under which the court would evaluate what both people actually thought (by indirect evidence, of course) and the court would find a contract only if their thoughts were the same, i.e., if there had been a "meeting of the minds." This was the approach taken by the trial court in *Embry* and rejected by the court of appeals.

The current justification for the "objective theory" in contract law is that it is practical: for courts, it focuses attention on readily available evidence of words and behavior and does not require courts to determine the "unknowable" subjective intent; and for contracting parties, it allows reliance by "average people" on their "normal perceptions" and does not require them to make detailed inquiries regarding the other party's actual understandings and expectations. Current law also justifies the objective theory with the moral argument that one ought to be responsible for the effect one has on other people and ought not be permitted to escape responsibility with the claim "I did not mean to do it."

The nineteenth century rationale for the doctrine was different: its promoters argued that an "objective" approach to interpretation of words and conduct would require groups and individuals to conform their language and behavior to that of members of the majority. Justice Oliver Wendell Holmes and Professor Samuel Williston, both influential proponents of the "objective theory," emphasized the importance of encouraging such conformity in the interests of business efficiency and social order.

During the 1930s and 1940s, in the generation after Williston, several prominent contracts scholars and practitioners argued that the objective theory unfairly burdened those who do not conform to "average" language usage and behavior. Many urged reform or rejection of the doctrine. Professor Malcolm Sharp, for example, argued that application of the "objective theory" to bind a speaker to an obligation that he or she did not intend should be limited to situations where the contracting party has actually relied upon a "reasonable" but incorrect interpretation of a speaker's words and conduct. In other cases, where the contracting party has not yet relied on a communication, the speaker should not be obligated and courts should find merely that the parties have failed to reach agreement on the topic. More recently, critics argue that the reasonableness standard unjustly reflects class biases of judges who have tended to think that employers and merchants ought not to be burdened with responsibilities towards their workers or consumers.

Three Variations on the Objective Test

Although the objective theory is widely embraced, courts differ in their application of its *reasonable person* test. Three variations can be discerned: one treats the "reasonable person" as a "universal" observer who is positioned outside of the history and circumstances of the parties and who hears or sees the words and conduct apart from the context in which they were uttered or performed. This version of the objective theory is associated with a formalist approach to law and legal interpretation that is not generally followed today, although it continues to have some impact in contract interpretation, as discussed in Chapter Nine.

The second variation of the *reasonable person* test interprets the meaning of words and conduct according to the understanding of a "universal" observer who is *placed in the position of the recipient of the communication.* This was the test employed by the court in *Embry v. McKittrick.* Although the court does not describe the personal characteristics or history of the reasonable person used in its analysis, the opinion suggests that the reasonable person does have Embry's job, employment history, and contextual knowledge and concerns. This "positioned" reasonableness analysis is the most commonly used variation of the objective test.

The third variation of the *reasonable person* test interprets the meaning of words and conduct according to the understanding of an observer who is placed in the position of the recipient of the communication but who also has the *social identity* of the recipient. In *Local 1330*, Judge Lambros explained his use of the objective theory by saying: "This Court has carefully read and reread Mr. Kirwin's messages, attempting to put itself in the place of a steelworker hearing those messages during 1977, 1978 and 1979." By attempting to place himself not merely in the position of a "reasonable person" examining the communications from U.S. Steel officials, but in the *identity* of a steelworker, Judge Lambros appeared to endorse this third variation of the objective theory. We could call this a "socially situated" reasonableness analysis, if we take the phrase, "socially situated" to mean not merely in the position of the recipient of the communication, Embry, but also having the social identity of the recipient (or, in the words of the United Nations Sales Convention, being "of the same kind" as the recipient).

The "socially situated" reasonableness test draws support from Article 8 of the *United Nations Convention on Contracts for the International Sale of Goods,* which provides that statements and conduct of contracting parties should be interpreted according to the parties' own shared meanings; but if these cannot be ascertained, then the statements and conduct should be interpreted according to the understanding that "a reasonable person *of the same kind* as the other party would have had in the same circumstances." This Article reflects the concerns voiced by representatives of Third World Nations, who strenuously objected to provisions that would hold Third World traders to "reasonable" meanings or practices that had been developed among traders from Western industrialized nations without participation of Third World traders and with the distinct purpose of furthering the interests of Western traders. It is not that Third World traders would not want to engage in developing such shared understandings and practices, but rather that they should not be required to submit to those already formed. As one government representative maintained:

> [T]he subordination of ... [interpretive rules] to normative and interpretive usages and practices could result in the imposition of unfair usages and inequitable practices ... which in standard contracts were usually laid down by the economically stronger party to the detriment of the weaker party.

Analysis of Replies and Comments by Governments on Hague Conventions of 1964: Report of the Secretary-General, U.N. Doc. A/CN.9/31, *reprinted in* [1970] Y.B. Int'l L. Comm'n 159, 169, U.N. Doc. A/CN.9/SER.A/1970 (statement of Mexican government). If Third World traders were bound by existing understandings and practices, representatives argued, their local understandings would be denied validity, and they would, in effect, be required to submit to interpretations that worked to their disadvantage. By requiring interpretation according to the understanding of a person "of the same kind" (which should include nationality, culture, religion, and the like), and "in the same circumstances," Article 8 offers the possibility of an objective interpretation that would avoid the issues raised by Third World representatives.

Perhaps the most important consequence flowing from the choice among these three different variations of the objective test is the kinds of evidence each allows. Under the first variation, the only relevant evidence is the specific words and conduct being interpreted. Under the positioned reasonable person test, in contrast, evidence of the history of the parties' relationship and of the circumstances surrounding the communications should be admitted as relevant to the interpretation. And under the socially situated test, relevant evidence would include not only the history and circumstances of the communications but also the practices of the parties' trades or communities and their own experiences in negotiations of this sort. In a plant closing case, for example, a steelworker's reasonable understanding of company communications may be influenced by a long history of interdependence between the company and a community. Although this history may be irrelevant from a universal observer's perspective, it may be very significant to a worker's understanding.

Critics of the socially situated reasonableness test argue that it is not realistic to think that judges can perceive standards of reasonableness other than their own, and that this variation of the objective test does more harm than good by leading courts to think they actually are able to switch perspectives and by allowing them to foreclose challenges. *Cf.* Naomi Cahn, *The Looseness of Legal Language: The Reasonable Woman Standard in Theory and in Practice*, 77 Cornell L. Rev. 1398 (1992). Look closely at Judge Lambros' analysis—are you persuaded that he has been able to take on the perspective of a steelworker? The weakness in the socially situated reasonableness test is similar to the weakness in the traditional subjective theory: both require the court to determine the understanding of some other person, and success at this effort is unlikely. It is better, critics argue, to directly challenge class and other bias in the objective theory than to invite judges to indulge stereotypical versions of others' perspectives. The aspiration to impartiality in the objective theory is valuable; rather than abandon the approach, judges ought to interrogate their own perceptions of reasonableness, take seriously the claims of class and other bias raised by lawyers and others, and give wide leeway to the range of evidence that will be admitted on issues of interpretation. In response to this criticism, defenders of the socially situated approach argue that this test can be effective in reminding the judge that he or she must attend carefully to the possibility of different perspectives. Under the guidance of this doctrine, advocates argue, judges are led to look more carefully at the evidence of differences (between the parties and between the judge and a party) than they would otherwise.

All approaches to interpretation require the interpreter to create an account of what happened — to tell a coherent story that connects events and gives meaning to words and conduct. And responsible choice among competing stories requires not only an assessment of which "seems more likely" but also an examination of the assumptions and expectations about "normal" human interaction that underlie one's sense of what is "likely." One way to illuminate these assumptions and expectations is to learn what others assume and expect. Moreover, a judge's choice among competing stories will have significance for others in a variety of ways, so it is incumbent on a judge to reflect carefully on his or her choice. It is a shortcoming of the objective theory that it has invited judges to reaffirm, rather than question, their own perceptions. The mere existence of "three variations" in the objective approach today reflects some courts' dissatisfaction with the theory's narrowing effects.

Patricia J. Williams, Alchemical Notes: Reconstructing Ideals from Deconstructed Rights

22 Harv. C.R.-C.L. L. Rev. 401 (1987)

Some time ago, Peter Gabel and I taught a contracts class together. Both recent transplants from California to New York, each of us hunted for apartments in between preparing for class and ultimately found places within one week of each other. Inevitably, I suppose, we got into a discussion of trust and distrust as factors in bargain relations. It turned out that Peter had handed over a $900 deposit, in cash, with no lease, no exchange of keys and no receipt, to strangers with whom he had no ties other than a few moments of pleasant conversation. Peter said that he didn't need to sign a lease because it imposed too much formality. The handshake and the good vibes were for him indicators of trust more binding than a distancing form contract. At the time, I told Peter I thought he was stark raving mad, but his faith paid off. His sublessors showed up at the appointed time, keys in hand, to welcome him in. Needless to say, there was absolutely nothing in my experience to prepare me for such a happy ending.[13]

I, meanwhile, had friends who found me an apartment in a building they owned. In my rush to show good faith and trustworthiness, I signed a detailed, lengthily-negotiated, finely-printed lease firmly establishing me as the ideal arm's length transactor.

As Peter and I discussed our experiences, I was struck by the similarity of what each of us was seeking, yet in such different terms, and with such polar approaches. We both wanted to establish enduring relationships with the people in whose houses we would be living; we both wanted to enhance trust of ourselves and to allow whatever closeness, whatever friendship, was possible. This similarity of desire, however, could not reconcile our very different relations to the word of law. Peter, for example, appeared to be extremely

---

13. In fact, I remain convinced that, even if I were of a mind to trust a lessor with this degree of informality, things would not have worked out so successfully for me; many Manhattan lessors would not have trusted me, a black person, enough to let me in the door in the first place — paperwork, references and credit check notwithstanding.

self-conscious of his power potential (either real or imagistic) as a white or male or lawyer authority figure. He therefore seemed to go to some lengths to overcome the wall which that image might impose. The logical ways of establishing some measure of trust between strangers were for him an avoidance of conventional expressions of power and a preference for informal processes generally.[14]

I, on the other hand, was raised to be acutely conscious of the likelihood that, no matter what degree of professional or professor I became, people would greet and dismiss my black femaleness as unreliable, untrustworthy, hostile, angry, powerless, irrational and probably destitute.[15] Futility and despair are very real parts of my response. Therefore it is helpful for me, even essential for me, to clarify boundary; to show that I can speak the language of lease is my way of enhancing trust of me in my business affairs. As a black, I have been given by this society a strong sense of myself as already too familiar, too personal, too subordinate to white people. I have only recently evolved from being treated as three-fifths of a human,[16] a subpart of the white estate.[17] I grew up in a neighborhood where landlords would not sign leases with their poor, black tenants, and demanded that rent be paid in cash; although superficially resembling Peter's transaction, such "informality" in most white-on-black situations signals distrust, not trust. Unlike Peter, I am still engaged in a struggle to set up transactions at arm's length, as legitimately commercial, and to portray myself as a bargainer of separate worth, distinct power, sufficient rights to manipulate commerce, rather than to be manipulated as the object of commerce.

Peter, I speculate, would say that a lease or any other formal mechanism would introduce distrust into his relationships and that he would suffer alienation, leading to the commodification of his being and the degradation of his person to property. In contrast, the lack of a formal relation to the other would leave me estranged. It would risk a figurative isolation from that creative commerce by which I may be recognized as whole, with which I may feed and clothe and shelter myself, by which I may be seen as equal — even if I am stranger. For me, stranger-stranger relations are better than stranger-chattel.

. . .

One summer when I was about six, my family drove to Maine. The highway was very straight and hot and shimmered darkly in the sun. My sister and I sat in the back seat of the Studebaker and argued about what color the road was. I said black. My sister said purple. After I had successfully harangued her into admitting that it was indeed black, my father gently pointed out that my sister still saw it as purple. I was unimpressed with the relevance of that at the time, but with the passage of years, and much more observation, I have come to see endless overheated highways as slightly more purpley than black. My sister and I will probably argue about the hue of life's roads forever. But, the lesson I learned from listening to her wild perceptions is that it really is possible to see things—

---

14. See generally Delgado, Dunn, Brown, Lee & Hubbert, Fairness and Formality: Minimizing the Risk of Prejudice in Alternative Dispute Resolution, Wis. L. Rev. 1359 (1985).

15. "Whatever else they learned in school, black children came to understand, as their parents had, that their color marked them as inferior in the eyes of whites, no matter how they conducted themselves. 'We came to understand,' a black woman would recall of her youth, 'that no matter how neat and clean, how law-abiding, submissive and polite, how studious in school, how church-going and moral, how scrupulous in paying our bills and taxes we were, it made no essential difference in our place.'" Litwack,"Blues Falling Down Like Hail": The Ordeal of Black Freedom, in New Perspectives on Race and Slavery in America 109, 118 (R. Abzug & S. Maizlish, eds. 1986).

16. See U.S. Const. art. I, §2.

17. As opposed to being a real part of the white estate. The lease of which I speak was for an apartment in Brooklyn; my search had started in Long Island, where two realtors had refused even to show me apartments in Port Washington and Roslyn.

even the most concrete things—simultaneously yet differently; and that seeing simultaneously yet differently is more easily done by two people than one; but that one person can get the hang of it with lots of time and effort.

In addition to our differing word usage, Peter and I had qualitatively different *experiences* of rights. For example, for me to understand fully the color my sister saw when she looked at a road involved more than my simply knowing that her "purple" meant my "black." It required as well a certain "slippage of perception" that came from my finally experiencing how much her purple *felt* like my black:

> Wittgenstein's experiments in some of the passages of his *Zettel* teach us about multiple perception, ellipsis and hinging, as well as about seeing and saying. He speaks of "entering the picture," and indeed his tricks try out our picture as our thought.... Ambivalence is assumed. It is as if the imagination were suddenly to be stretched: "Suppose someone were to say: 'Imagine this butterfly exactly as it is, but ugly instead of beautiful'?!" The transfer we are called upon to make includes ... stretching not just of the imagination, but of the transfer point: ... "It is as if I were told: 'Here is a chair. Can you see it clearly?—Good—now translate it into French.'"[23]

In Peter's and my case, such a complete transliteration of each other's experiences is considerably harder to achieve. If it took years for me to understand fully my own sister, probably the best that Peter and I can do—as friends and colleagues, but very different people—is to listen intently to each other so that maybe our respective children can bridge the experiential distance. Bridging such gaps requires listening at a very deep level to the uncensored voices of others.

B. Offer and Acceptance: The Mechanics of Contract Formation

The doctrines of offer and acceptance are analytic tools. Without such tools, a dispute over the existence of an agreement is difficult to evaluate: one side argues that the parties did agree, and the other maintains they did not. The rules of offer and acceptance direct the attention of the lawyer or judge to discrete parts of the process of agreement. Rather than merely asserting that "there was an agreement," for example, one can say "this communication was an offer and that one an acceptance," or, in a more complex case, "here was an offer, here it was rejected and a counter-offer was made, here the counter-offer lapsed and what would have been an acceptance of that counter-offer became an offer and it became irrevocable and was accepted." As tools, these doctrines are often very useful.

At the same time, the doctrines of offer and acceptance oversimplify the complexities of communication, eliminating many factors that influence understanding. Criticism of the reductive rules of offer and acceptance by legal realists, including that of Karl Llewellyn, led to changes in the doctrine that allow courts to focus more closely on contextual detail, including trade practices, the history and functions of the relationship between the parties, and other circumstances that give rise to unstated expectations and understandings.

---

23. Caws, Literal or Liberal: Translating Perception, 13 Crit. Inq. 49, 55 (1986) (citations omitted).

This section is divided into four subparts. The first focuses on the tests for an *offer* and the second on the common law tests for an *acceptance*. The third subpart examines the content of the acceptance and the developments resulting from the adoption of the *Uniform Commercial Code*. The fourth part concerns termination and revocation of offers and irrevocable offers.

Note — On the Polarity of the Offer-Acceptance Model

One consequence of the contract formation model of offer and acceptance is that the moment of acceptance is viewed as the moment of contract formation in a polar sense: before the acceptance was effective there was no contract; after the acceptance there was a contract. Off-On. This model does not allow for the possibility of a series of communications, which become increasingly obligatory, or a relationship growing in commitment over time. People do not experience most relationships, even most contractual relationships, in an off-on way: relationships, even commercial relationships, develop over time. In addition, the polar model of contract formation does not allow for equivocation or uncertainty. In the polar model, one either agrees or does not agree; there is no other possibility. The model simply renders irrelevant the complex ways that people actually establish working relationships.

In drafting Article Two of the *Uniform Commercial Code*, Professor Karl Llewellyn sought to reform this polar quality of contract formation doctrine in §2-204(b):

> (b) An agreement sufficient to constitute a contract for sale may be found even though the moment of its making is undetermined.

This provision allows courts to develop a flexible open-ended model of contract formation in contracts for the sale of goods. We will study contract formation under the *Uniform Commercial Code* in Part Three of this section.

---

1. Was There an Offer?

Application of the mechanical tool of offer and acceptance begins with a question: Which communication, if any, was the first to convey a "willingness to enter a bargain, so made as to justify [a reasonable person in the position of the other party] in understanding that his assent to that bargain is invited and will conclude it"? *See* Restatement (Second) §24. In other words, at what point in the communications did one party commit to the transaction, subject only to the other party's commitment. That communication is the first "offer."

J.W. Southworth v. Joseph C. Oliver and Arlene G. Oliver

Supreme Court of Oregon
587 P.2d 994 (1978)

Thomas H. Tongue, Justice

This is a suit in equity for a declaratory judgment that defendants "are obligated to sell" to plaintiff 2,933 acres of ranch lands in Grant County. Defendants appeal from a decree of specific performance in favor of plaintiff. We affirm.

Defendants contend on this appeal that a certain "writing" mailed by them to plaintiff was not an offer to sell such lands; that if it was an offer there was no proper acceptance of that offer and that any such offer and acceptance did not constitute a binding contract, at least so as to be specifically enforceable. Defendants also filed a demurrer in this court upon the ground that it appears from the face of plaintiff's complaint that the alleged agreement to sell such lands was void as in violation of the statute of frauds.

The Parties and the Property

Defendants are ranchers in Grant County and owned ranches in both the Bear Valley area and also in the John Day valley. In 1976 defendants came to the conclusion that they should "cut the operation down" and sell some of the Bear Valley property, as well as some of their Forest Service grazing permits. Defendant Joseph Oliver discussed this matter with his wife, defendant Arlene Oliver, and also with his son, and the three of them "jointly arrived" at a decision to sell a portion of the Bear Valley property. Joseph Oliver also conferred with his accountant and attorney and, as a result, it was decided that the sale "had to be on terms" rather than cash, for income tax reasons. Defendant Joseph Oliver then had "a discussion with Mr. Southworth (the plaintiff) about the possibility of ... selling this Bear Valley property." Plaintiff Southworth was also a cattle rancher in Bear Valley. The land which defendants had decided to sell was adjacent to land owned by him and was property that he had always wanted.

The Initial Meeting Between the Parties on May 20, 1976

According to plaintiff, defendant Joseph Oliver stopped by his ranch on May 20, 1976, and said that he (Oliver) was interested in "selling the ranch" and asked "would I be interested in buying it, and I said 'yes.'" Mr. Southworth also testified that "he thought I would be interested in the land and that Clyde (Holliday, also a neighbor) would be interested in the permits" and that "I told him that I was very interested in the land...." Plaintiff Southworth also testified that at that time defendant Oliver showed him a map, showing land that he "understood them to offer for sale"; that there was no discussion at that time of price or terms of sale, or whether the sale of the land was contingent on sale of any of the permits, but that the conversation terminated with the understanding: "That he would develop and determine value and price and I would make an investigation to determine whether or not I could find the money and get everything arranged for a purchase. In other words, he was going to do A and then I would B."

According to plaintiff Southworth, defendant Oliver said that when he determined the value of the property he would send that information to Southworth so as to give him "notice" of "what he wanted for the land," but did not say that he was also going to give that same information to Mr. Holliday, although he did say that "he planned to talk to Clyde (Holliday) about permits," with the result that plaintiff knew that Oliver "might very well be ... talking to Clyde about the same thing he talked to you (plaintiff) about" and "give that information to Clyde Holliday as well as yourself."

According to defendant Joseph Oliver, the substance of that initial conversation with plaintiff was as follows:

> ... I told him we were going to condense our ranch down and sell some property and that we were in the process of trying to get some figures from the Assessor on it to determine what we wanted to sell and what we might want to do. Whenever we got this information together we were going to send it to him and some of my neighbors and give them first chance at it....

Mr. Oliver also testified that plaintiff said that "he was interested"; that he had a map with him; that he mentioned to plaintiff that he "was going to sell some permits," but that there was no discussion "about the permits going with the land at that time" and that he (Oliver) "talked along the lines that Clyde (Holliday) would probably be interested in those permits." On cross-examination Mr. Oliver also answered in the affirmative a question to the effect that the property which he and Mr. Southworth "delineated on the map" during that conversation "was the property" that he "finally decided to sell and made the general offering to the four neighbors."

Plaintiff also testified that on May 26, 1976, he called Clyde Holliday to ask if he was interested in buying the land and Mr. Holliday said "no," that he was interested only in the permits, but would be interested in trading some other land for some of the land plaintiff was buying from defendants.

The Telephone Call of June 13, 1976

Plaintiff testified that on June 13, 1976, he called defendant Oliver by telephone to "ask him if his plans for selling ... continued to be in force, and he said 'yes,'" that "he was progressing and there had been some delay in acquiring information from the Assessor, but they expected soon to have the information needed to establish the value on the land." Defendant Oliver's testimony was to the same effect, but he also recalled that at that time Mr. Southworth "said everything was in order and that I didn't have to worry, he had the money available and that everything was ready to go."

The Letters of June 17, June 21, and June 24, 1976

Several days later plaintiff received from defendants a letter dated June 17, 1976, as follows:

> "Enclosed please find the information about the ranch sales that I had discussed with you previously.
>
> "These prices are the market value according to the records of the Grant County Assessor.
>
> "Please contact me if there are any questions."

There were two enclosures with that letter. The first was as follows:

> "Joseph C. and Arlene G. Oliver
> 200 Ford Road
> John Day, OR 97845
>
> "Selling approximately 2933 Acres in Grant County in
>   T. 16 S., R. 31 E., W. M.
> near Seneca, Oregon at the assessed market value of:

LAND	$306,409
IMPROVEMENTS	<u>18,010</u>
Total	$324,419

> "Terms available—29% down—balance over 5 years at 8% interest. Negotiate sale date for December 1, 1976 or January 1, 1977.
>
> "Available after hay is harvested and arrangements made for removal of hay, equipment and supplies.
>
> "ALSO: Selling
>
> "Little Bear Creek allotment permit—100 head @ $225
>
> "Big Bear Creek allotment permit—200 head @ $250"

The second enclosure related to "selling approximately 6365 acres" in Grant County near John Day—another ranch owned by the Oliver family. Defendant Joseph Oliver testified that this letter and enclosures were "drafted" by his wife, defendant Arlene Oliver; that he then read and signed it; that he sent it not only to plaintiff, but also to Clyde Holliday and two other neighbors; that it was sent because "I told them I would send them all this information and we would go from there," that it was not made as an offer, and that it was his intention that the "property" and "permits" be transferred "together."

Upon receiving that letter and enclosures, plaintiff immediately responded by letter addressed to both defendants, dated June 21, 1976, as follows:

"Re the land in Bear Valley near Seneca, Oregon that you have offered to sell; I accept your offer."

Plaintiff testified that on June 23, 1976, Clyde Holliday called and said he needed to acquire a portion of the land "that I had agreed to buy from Joe (Oliver), and I said I have bought the land," and that we would "work out an exchange in accord with what we have previously mentioned," but that "(h)e said he needed more land."

Defendant Joseph Oliver testified that after receiving plaintiff's letter dated June 21, 1976, Clyde Holliday told him that "they (Holliday and plaintiff) were having a little difficulty getting this thing worked out," apparently referring to the "exchange" previously discussed between plaintiff and Holliday, and that he (Oliver) then told plaintiff that:

... (T)here seemed to be some discrepancies between what I was getting from the two parties and that I didn't exactly want to be an arbitrator or say you are right or you are wrong with my neighbors. I wished they would straighten the thing out, and if they didn't, I really didn't have to sell it, that I would pull it off the market, because I didn't want to get in trouble. I would have to live with my neighbors.

Finally, on June 24, 1976, defendants mailed the following letter to plaintiff:

"We received your letter of June 21, 1976. You have misconstrued our prior negotiations and written summaries of the lands which we and J. C. wish to sell. That was not made as or intended to be a firm offer of sale, and especially was not an offer of sale of any portion of the lands and permits described to any one person separately from the rest of the lands and permits described.

"The memorandum of ours was for informational purposes only and as a starting point for further negotiation between us and you and the others also interested in the properties.

"It is also impossible to tell from the attachment to our letter of June 17, 1976, as to the legal description of the lands to be sold, and would not in any event constitute an enforceable contract.

"We are open to further negotiation with you and other interested parties, but do not consider that we at this point have any binding enforceable contract with you.

This lawsuit then followed.

Defendants' Letter of June 17, 1976, Was an "Offer to Sell" the Ranch Lands

Defendants first contend that defendants' letter of June 17, 1976, to plaintiff was "not an offer, both as a matter of law and under the facts of this case." In support of that contention defendants say that their testimony that the letter was not intended as an offer was uncontradicted and that similar writings have been held not to constitute offers. Defendants also say that there is "authority for the proposition that all the evidence of surrounding circumstances may be taken into consideration in making that determination" and that the circumstances in this case were such as to require the conclusion that defendants did not intend the letter as an offer and that plaintiff knew or reasonably should have known that it was not intended as an offer because:

1. Defendants obviously did not intend it as an offer.

2. The wording of the "offer" made it clear that this was "information" that plaintiff had previously expressed an interest in receiving.

3. It did not use the term offer, but only formally advised plaintiff that defendants are selling certain lands and permits and set forth generally the terms upon which they would consider selling.

4. The plaintiff knew of the custom of transferring permits with land and had no knowledge from the writing or previous talk that defendants were selling any cattle.

5. Plaintiff knew and expected this same information to go to others.

Defendants conclude that

> "Considering the factors determined important by the authorities cited, these factors preponderate heavily that this was not an offer to sell the land only, or to sell at all, and should not reasonably have been so construed by the plaintiff."

In *Kitzke v. Turnidge*, 209 Or. 563, 573, 307 P.2d 522, 527 (1957), this court quoted with approval the following rule as stated in 1 WILLISTON ON CONTRACTS 49–50, § 22A (1957):

> ... In the early law of assumpsit stress was laid on the necessity of a promise in terms, but the modern law rightly construes both acts and words as having the meaning which a reasonable person present would put upon them in view of the surrounding circumstances. Even where words are used, "a contract includes not only what the parties said, but also what is necessarily to be implied from what they said." And it may be said broadly that "any conduct of one party, from which the other may reasonably draw the inference of a promise, is effective in law as such."

...

As also stated in 1 *Restatement of Contracts* § 25, Comment (A) (1932):

> It is often difficult to draw an exact line between offers and negotiations preliminary thereto. It is common for one who wishes to make a bargain to try to induce the other party to the intended transaction to make the definite offer, he himself suggesting with more or less definiteness the nature of the contract he is willing to enter into. Besides any direct language indicating an intent to defer the formation of a contract, the definiteness or indefiniteness of the words used in opening the negotiation must be considered, as well as the usages of business, and indeed all accompanying circumstances.

The difficulty in determining whether an offer has been made is particularly acute in cases involving price quotations, as in this case. It is recognized that although a price quotation, standing alone, is not an offer, there may be circumstances under which a price quotation, when considered together with facts and circumstances, may constitute an offer which, if accepted, will result in a binding contract. It is also recognized that such an offer may be made to more than one person. Thus, the fact that a price quotation is sent to more than one person does not, of itself, require a holding that such a price quotation is not an offer.

We agree with the analysis of this problem as stated in Murray on Contracts 37–40, §24 (1977), as follows:

"If A says to B, "I am going to sell my car for $500," and B replies, "All right, here is $500, I will take it," no contract results, assuming that A's statement is taken at its face value. A's statement does not involve any promise, commitment or undertaking; it is at most a statement of A's present intention....

However, a price quotation or advertisement may contain sufficient indication of willingness to enter a bargain so that the party to whom it is addressed would be justified in believing that his assent would conclude the bargain....

The basic problem is found in the expressions of the parties. People very seldom express themselves either accurately or in complete detail. Thus, difficulty is encountered in determining the correct interpretation of the expression in question. Over the years, some more or less trustworthy guides to interpretation have been developed....

The first and strongest guide is that the particular expression is to be judged on the basis of what a reasonable man in the position of the offeree has been led to believe. This requires an analysis of what the offeree should have understood under all of the surrounding circumstances, with all of his opportunities for comprehending the intention of the offeror, rather than what the offeror, in fact, intended. This guide may be regarded as simply another manifestation of the objective test. Beyond this universally accepted guide to interpretation, there are other guides which are found in the case law involving factors that tend to recur. The most important of the remaining guides is the language used. If there are no words of promise, undertaking or commitment, the tendency is to construe the expression to be an invitation for an offer or mere preliminary negotiations in the absence of strong, countervailing circumstances. Another guide which has been widely accepted is the determination of the party or parties to whom the purported offer has been addressed. If the expression definitely names a party or parties, it is more likely to be construed as an offer. If the addressee is an indefinite group, it is less likely to be an offer. The fact that this is simply a guide rather than a definite rule is illustrated by the exceptional cases which must be noted. The guide operates effectively in relation to such expressions as advertisements or circular letters. The addressee is indefinite and, therefore, the expression is probably not an offer. However, in reward cases, the addressee is equally indefinite and, yet, the expression is an offer. Finally, the definiteness of the proposal itself may have a bearing on whether it constitutes an offer. In general, the more definite the proposal, the more reasonable it is to treat the proposal as involving a commitment...." (Footnotes omitted)

Upon application of these tests to the facts of this case we are of the opinion that defendants' letter to plaintiff dated June 17, 1976, was an offer to sell the ranch lands. We believe that the "surrounding circumstances" under which this letter was prepared by defendants and sent by them to plaintiff were such as to have led a reasonable person to believe that defendants were making an offer to sell to plaintiff the lands described in the letter's enclosure and upon the terms as there stated.

That letter did not come to plaintiff "out of the blue," as in some of the cases involving advertisements or price quotations. Neither was this a price quotation resulting from an inquiry by plaintiff. According to what we believe to be the most credible testimony, defendants decided to sell the lands in question and defendant Joseph Oliver then sought out the plaintiff who owned adjacent lands. Defendant Oliver told plaintiff that defendants were interested in selling that land, inquired whether plaintiff was interested, and was told by plaintiff that he was "very interested in the land," after which they discussed the particular lands to be sold. That conversation was terminated with the understanding that Mr. Oliver would "determine" the value and price of that land, i.e., "what he wanted for the land," and that plaintiff would undertake to arrange financing for the purchase of that land. In addition to that initial conversation, there was a further telephone conversation in which plaintiff called Mr. Oliver "to ask him if his plans for selling ... continued to be in force" and was told "yes"; that there had been some delay in getting information from the assessor, as needed to establish the value of the land; and that plaintiff then told Mr. Oliver that "everything was in order" and that "he had the money available and everything was ready to go."

Under these facts and circumstances, we agree with the finding and conclusion by the trial court, in its written opinion, that when plaintiff received the letter of June 17th, with enclosures, which stated a price of $324,419 for the 2,933 acres in T.16 S.R.31 E.W.M. as previously identified by the parties with reference to a map, and stating "terms" of 29 percent down balance over five years at eight percent interest with a "sale date" of either December 1, 1976, or January 1, 1977, a reasonable person in the position of the plaintiff would have believed that defendants were making an offer to sell those lands to him.

This conclusion is further strengthened by "the definiteness of the proposal," not only with respect to price, but terms, and by the fact that "the addressee was not an indefinite group." *See* Murray, *supra* at 40.

As previously noted, defendants contend that they "obviously did not intend (the letter) as an offer." While it may be proper to consider evidence of defendants' subjective intent under the "objective test" to which this court is committed, it is the manifestation of a previous intention that is controlling, rather than a "person's actual intent." We do not agree with defendants' contention that it was "obvious" to a reasonable person, under the facts and circumstances of this case that the letter of June 17th was not intended to be an offer to sell the ranch lands to plaintiff.

We recognize, as contended by defendants, that the failure to use the word "offer," the fact that the letter included the "information" previously discussed between the parties, and the fact that plaintiff knew that the same information was to be sent to others, were important facts to be considered in deciding whether plaintiff, as a reasonable person, would have been led to believe that this letter was an "offer." *See also* Murray,*supra*, at 40. We disagree, however, with defendants' contention that these and other factors relied upon by defendants "preponderate" so as to require a holding that the letter of June 17th was not an offer.

The failure to add the word "offer" and the use of the word "information" are also not controlling, and, as previously noted, an offer may be made to more than one person. The question is whether, under all of the facts and circumstances existing at the time that this letter was received, a reasonable person in the position of the plaintiff would have understood the letter to be an offer by defendants to sell the land to him.

Defendants also contend that "plaintiff knew of the custom of transferring (Forest Service grazing) permits with the land and had no knowledge from the writing or previous talk that defendants were selling any cattle" (so as to provide such a basis for a transfer of the permits). Plaintiff testified, however, that at the time of the initial conversation, Mr. Oliver told plaintiff that he thought plaintiff "would be interested in the land and that Clyde would be interested in the permits." In addition, defendant Joseph Oliver, in response to questions by the trial judge, although denying that at that time he told plaintiff that he was "going to offer the permits to Mr. Holliday," admitted that he "knew Mr. Holliday was interested in the permits" and "could have" told plaintiff that he was "going to talk to Mr. Holliday about him purchasing the permits."

On this record we believe that plaintiff's knowledge of the facts noted by defendants relating to the transfer of such permits did not require a holding that, as a reasonable man, he did not understand or should not have understood that defendants' letter of June 17th was an offer to sell the ranch lands to him.

. . .

[Editors: In omitted sections, the court found that the letter of June 21 was an acceptance of the Olivers' offer and that the contract was not barred by indefiniteness or by the statute of frauds.]

For all of these reasons, the decree of the trial court is affirmed.

Note — Offer: A Manifestation of Willingness to Commit Was There an Offer?

Application of offer and acceptance doctrine begins with a question: Did there come a time, in the communications between the parties, when either person communicated a "willingness to enter a bargain, so made as to justify [a reasonable person in the position of the other party] in understanding that his assent to that bargain is invited and will conclude it"? *See* Restatement (Second) § 24. If so, then that communication will be characterized as an offer, and the next questions will be: Was this offer accepted?

Four Factors

As we saw in *Southworth v. Oliver*, the primary difficulty — and the primary area of potential dispute — in applying offer and acceptance doctrine is in deciding how to characterize specific communications. In deciding whether to characterize a particular communication as an offer, the court will consider a variety of factors, including:

1. Did the words of the communication indicate a willingness, at that moment, to make a commitment? If so, the communication appears more like an offer.

2. To how many people was the communication directed? If the communication was addressed to only one person, that generally makes it appear more like an offer.

3. Did the communication include detailed terms? If so, the communication appears more like an offer.

4. Are there any relevant community practices ("trade practices"), past conversations between the parties regarding transaction (as in *Southworth*), past contracts between parties ("course of dealings"), or other circumstances that would inform a reasonable person's interpretation of the communication? If so, these may make the communication appear more, or less, like an offer.

None of these factors is determinative: they are simply factors relevant to the underlying question whether the communication has expressed a present willingness to commit and therefore should be characterized as an "offer."

Generalizations

In addition to these four factors, there are some "general rules" or, more precisely some "generalizations" that may guide the court in this characterization.

1. Generally, advertisements addressed to the general public, other than those that offer rewards, should not be characterized as offers because they are addressed to a huge number of people;

2. Generally price quotes, catalogues, and price lists should not be characterized as offers because usually they are phrased in general terms, not focused on a specific order or job, and are distributed to many people;

3. Generally, putting a price tag on an item and placing it on a shelf in a retail store or market should not be characterized as an offer because the common practice allows sellers to change a price tag or remove an item from the shelf without notifying buyers.

When applying these generalizations, remember that they are not absolute or unrebuttable. Moreover, they are limited by their justifications: for example, courts often will characterize an advertisement as an offer if it limits the number of possible acceptances (e.g., "only available to the first caller") or if the advertisement requests readers to undertake a substantial action in response to the proposal (e.g., "use the Carbolic Smoke Ball for six weeks"; or "bring your car to us").

John D.R. Leonard v. Pepsico, Inc.

United States District Court, S.D. New York
88 F. Supp. 2d 116 (1999)

KIMBA WOOD, JUDGE

Plaintiff brought this action seeking, among other things, specific performance of an alleged offer of a Harrier Jet, featured in a television advertisement for defendant's "Pepsi Stuff" promotion. Defendant has moved for summary judgment pursuant to Federal Rule of Civil Procedure 56. For the reasons stated below, defendant's motion is granted.

I. Background

This case arises out of a promotional campaign conducted by defendant, the producer and distributor of the soft drinks Pepsi and Diet Pepsi.[1] The promotion, entitled "Pepsi Stuff," encouraged consumers to collect "Pepsi Points" from specially marked packages of Pepsi or Diet Pepsi and redeem these points for merchandise featuring the Pepsi logo. Before introducing the promotion nationally, defendant conducted a test of the promotion in the Pacific Northwest from October 1995 to March 1996. A Pepsi Stuff catalog was distributed to consumers in the test market, including Washington State. Plaintiff is a resident of Seattle, Washington. While living in Seattle, plaintiff saw the Pepsi Stuff commercial that he contends constituted an offer of a Harrier Jet.

A. The Alleged Offer

Because whether the television commercial constituted an offer is the central question in this case, the Court will describe the commercial in detail. The commercial opens upon

---

1. The Court's recitation of the facts of this case is drawn from the statements of uncontested facts submitted by the parties pursuant to Local Civil Rule 56.1. The majority of citations are to defendant's statement of facts because plaintiff does not contest many of defendant's factual assertions. Plaintiff's disagreement with certain of defendant's statements is noted in the text....

an idyllic, suburban morning, where the chirping of birds in sun-dappled trees welcomes a paperboy on his morning route. As the newspaper hits the stoop of a conventional two-story house, the tattoo of a military drum introduces the subtitle, "MONDAY 7:58 AM." The stirring strains of a martial air mark the appearance of a well-coiffed teenager preparing to leave for school, dressed in a shirt emblazoned with the Pepsi logo, a red-white-and-blue ball. While the teenager confidently preens, the military drumroll again sounds as the subtitle "T-SHIRT 75 PEPSI POINTS" scrolls across the screen. Bursting from his room, the teenager strides down the hallway wearing a leather jacket. The drumroll sounds again, as the subtitle "LEATHER JACKET 1450 PEPSI POINTS" appears. The teenager opens the door of his house and, unfazed by the glare of the early morning sunshine, puts on a pair of sunglasses. The drumroll then accompanies the subtitle "SHADES 175 PEPSI POINTS." A voiceover then intones, "Introducing the new Pepsi Stuff catalog," as the camera focuses on the cover of the catalog.[2]

The scene then shifts to three young boys sitting in front of a high school building. The boy in the middle is intent on his Pepsi Stuff Catalog, while the boys on either side are each drinking Pepsi. The three boys gaze in awe at an object rushing overhead, as the military march builds to a crescendo. The Harrier Jet is not yet visible, but the observer senses the presence of a mighty plane as the extreme winds generated by its flight create a paper maelstrom in a classroom devoted to an otherwise dull physics lesson. Finally, the Harrier Jet swings into view and lands by the side of the school building, next to a bicycle rack. Several students run for cover, and the velocity of the wind strips one hapless faculty member down to his underwear. While the faculty member is being deprived of his dignity, the voiceover announces: "Now the more Pepsi you drink, the more great stuff you're gonna get."

The teenager opens the cockpit of the fighter and can be seen, helmetless, holding a Pepsi. "[L]ooking very pleased with himself," the teenager exclaims, "Sure beats the bus," and chortles. The military drumroll sounds a final time, as the following words appear: "HARRIER FIGHTER 7,000,000 PEPSI POINTS." A few seconds later, the following appears in more stylized script: "Drink Pepsi — Get Stuff." With that message, the music and the commercial end with a triumphant flourish.

Inspired by this commercial, plaintiff set out to obtain a Harrier Jet. Plaintiff explains that he is "typical of the 'Pepsi Generation'... he is young, has an adventurous spirit, and the notion of obtaining a Harrier Jet appealed to him enormously." Plaintiff consulted the Pepsi Stuff Catalog. The Catalog features youths dressed in Pepsi Stuff regalia or enjoying Pepsi Stuff accessories, such as "Blue Shades" ("As if you need another reason to look forward to sunny days."), "Pepsi Tees" ("Live in 'em. Laugh in 'em. Get in 'em."), "Bag of Balls" ("Three balls. One bag. No rules."), and "Pepsi Phone Card" ("Call your mom!"). The Catalog specifies the number of Pepsi Points required to obtain promotional merchandise. The Catalog includes an Order Form which lists, on one side, fifty-three items of Pepsi Stuff merchandise redeemable for Pepsi Points. Conspicuously absent from the Order Form is any entry or description of a Harrier Jet. The amount of Pepsi Points required to obtain the listed merchandise ranges from 15 (for a "Jacket Tattoo" ("Sew 'em on your jacket, not your arm.")) to 3300 (for a "Fila Mountain Bike" ("Rugged. All-terrain. Exclusively for Pepsi.")). It should be noted that plaintiff objects to the implication that because an item was not shown in the Catalog, it was unavailable.

---

2. At this point, the following message appears at the bottom of the screen: "Offer not available in all areas. See details on specially marked packages."

The rear foldout pages of the Catalog contain directions for redeeming Pepsi Points for merchandise. These directions note that merchandise may be ordered "only" with the original Order Form. The Catalog notes that in the event that a consumer lacks enough Pepsi Points to obtain a desired item, additional Pepsi Points may be purchased for ten cents each; however, at least fifteen original Pepsi Points must accompany each order.

Although plaintiff initially set out to collect 7,000,000 Pepsi Points by consuming Pepsi products, it soon became clear to him that he "would not be able to buy (let alone drink) enough Pepsi to collect the necessary Pepsi Points fast enough." Reevaluating his strategy, plaintiff "focused for the first time on the packaging materials in the Pepsi Stuff promotion," and realized that buying Pepsi Points would be a more promising option. Through acquaintances, plaintiff ultimately raised about $700,000.

B. Plaintiff's Efforts to Redeem the Alleged Offer

On or about March 27, 1996, plaintiff submitted an Order Form, fifteen original Pepsi Points, and a check for $700,008.50. Plaintiff appears to have been represented by counsel at the time he mailed his check; the check is drawn on an account of plaintiff's first set of attorneys. At the bottom of the Order Form, plaintiff wrote in "1 Harrier Jet" in the "Item" column and "7,000,000" in the "Total Points" column. In a letter accompanying his submission, plaintiff stated that the check was to purchase additional Pepsi Points "expressly for obtaining a new Harrier jet as advertised in your Pepsi Stuff commercial."

On or about May 7, 1996, defendant's fulfillment house rejected plaintiff's submission and returned the check, explaining that:

> The item that you have requested is not part of the Pepsi Stuff collection. It is not included in the catalogue or on the order form, and only catalogue merchandise can be redeemed under this program.
>
> The Harrier jet in the Pepsi commercial is fanciful and is simply included to create a humorous and entertaining ad. We apologize for any misunderstanding or confusion that you may have experienced and are enclosing some free product coupons for your use.

Plaintiff's previous counsel responded on or about May 14, 1996, as follows:

> Your letter of May 7, 1996 is totally unacceptable. We have reviewed the video tape of the Pepsi Stuff commercial ... and it clearly offers the new Harrier jet for 7,000,000 Pepsi Points. Our client followed your rules explicitly....
>
> This is a formal demand that you honor your commitment and make immediate arrangements to transfer the new Harrier jet to our client. If we do not receive transfer instructions within ten (10) business days of the date of this letter you will leave us no choice but to file an appropriate action against Pepsi....

This letter was apparently sent onward to the advertising company responsible for the actual commercial, BBDO New York. In a letter dated May 30, 1996, BBDO Vice President Raymond E. McGovern, Jr., explained to plaintiff that:

> I find it hard to believe that you are of the opinion that the Pepsi Stuff commercial ("Commercial") really offers a new Harrier Jet. The use of the Jet was clearly a joke that was meant to make the Commercial more humorous and entertaining. In my opinion, no reasonable person would agree with your analysis of the Commercial.

On or about June 17, 1996, plaintiff mailed a similar demand letter to defendant.

...

II. Discussion

...

B. Defendant's Advertisement Was Not An Offer

1. Advertisements as Offers

The general rule is that an advertisement does not constitute an offer. The Restatement (Second) of Contracts explains that:

> Advertisements of goods by display, sign, handbill, newspaper, radio or television are not ordinarily intended or understood as offers to sell. The same is true of catalogues, price lists and circulars, even though the terms of suggested bargains may be stated in some detail. It is of course possible to make an offer by an advertisement directed to the general public (*see* § 29), but there must ordinarily be some language of commitment or some invitation to take action without further communication.

Restatement (Second) of Contracts § 26 cmt. b (1979). Similarly, a leading treatise notes that:

> It is quite possible to make a definite and operative offer to buy or sell goods by advertisement, in a newspaper, by a handbill, a catalog or circular or on a placard in a store window. It is not customary to do this, however; and the presumption is the other way.... Such advertisements are understood to be mere requests to consider and examine and negotiate; and no one can reasonably regard them as otherwise unless the circumstances are exceptional and the words used are very plain and clear.

1 Arthur Linton Corbin & Joseph M. Perillo, Corbin on Contracts § 2.4, at 116–17 (rev. ed. 1993); *see also* 1 E. Allan Farnsworth, Farnsworth on Contracts § 3.10, at 239 (2d ed. 1998); 1 Samuel Williston & Richard A. Lord, A Treatise on the Law of Contracts § 4:7, at 286–87 (4th ed. 1990). New York courts adhere to this general principle. *See Lovett v. Frederick Loeser & Co.*, 124 Misc. 81, 207 N.Y.S. 753, 755 (Mun. Ct. N.Y. City 1924) (noting that an "advertisement is nothing but an invitation to enter into negotiations, and is not an offer which may be turned into a contract by a person who signifies his intention to purchase some of the articles mentioned in the advertisement"); *see also Geismar v. Abraham & Strauss*, 109 Misc.2d 495, 439 N.Y.S.2d 1005, 1006 (Dist. Ct. Suffolk Cty. 1981) (reiterating *Lovett* rule); *People v. Gimbel Bros. Inc.*, 202 Misc. 229, 115 N.Y.S.2d 857, 858 (Ct.Spec.Sess. 1952) (because an "[a]dvertisement does not constitute an offer of sale but is solely an invitation to customers to make an offer to purchase," defendant not guilty of selling property on Sunday).

An advertisement is not transformed into an enforceable offer merely by a potential offeree's expression of willingness to accept the offer through, among other means, completion of an order form. In *Mesaros v. United States*, 845 F.2d 1576 (Fed.Cir. 1988), for example, the plaintiffs sued the United States Mint for failure to deliver a number of Statue of Liberty commemorative coins that they had ordered. When demand for the coins proved unexpectedly robust, a number of individuals who had sent in their orders in a timely fashion were left empty-handed. *See id.* at 1578–80. The court began by noting the "well-established" rule that advertisements and order forms are "mere notices and solicitations for offers which create no power of acceptance in the recipient." *Id.* at 1580; *see also Foremost Pro Color, Inc. v. Eastman Kodak Co.*, 703 F.2d 534, 538–39 (9th Cir. 1983) ("The weight of authority is that purchase orders such as those at issue here are not enforceable contracts until they are accepted by the seller.");[5] Restatement (Second) of Contracts §26 ("A manifestation of willingness to enter a bargain is not an offer if the person to whom it is addressed knows or has reason to know that the person making it does not intend to conclude a bargain until he has made a further manifestation of assent."). The spurned coin collectors could not maintain a breach of contract action because no contract would be formed until the advertiser accepted the order form and processed payment. *See id.* at 1581; *see also Alligood v. Procter & Gamble*, 594 N.E.2d 668 (Ohio Ct.App. 1991) (finding that no offer was made in promotional campaign for baby diapers, in which consumers were to redeem teddy bear proof-of-purchase symbols for catalog merchandise); *Chang v. First Colonial Savings Bank*, 410 S.E.2d 928 (Va. 1991) (newspaper advertisement for bank settled the terms of the offer once bank accepted plaintiffs' deposit, notwithstanding bank's subsequent effort to amend the terms of the offer). Under these principles, plaintiff's letter of March 27, 1996, with the Order Form and the appropriate number of Pepsi Points, constituted the offer. There would be no enforceable contract until defendant accepted the Order Form and cashed the check.

The exception to the rule that advertisements do not create any power of acceptance in potential offerees is where the advertisement is "clear, definite, and explicit, and leaves nothing open for negotiation," in that circumstance, "it constitutes an offer, acceptance of which will complete the contract." *Lefkowitz v. Great Minneapolis Surplus Store*, 86 N.W.2d 689, 691 (Minn. 1957). In *Lefkowitz*, defendant had published a newspaper announcement stating: "Saturday 9 AM Sharp, 3 Brand New Fur Coats, Worth to $100.00, First Come First Served $1 Each." *Id.* at 690. Mr. Morris Lefkowitz arrived at the store, dollar in hand, but was informed that under defendant's "house rules," the offer was open to ladies, but not gentlemen. *See id.* The court ruled that because plaintiff had fulfilled all of the terms of the advertisement and the advertisement was specific and left nothing open for negotiation, a contract had been formed. *See id.; see also Johnson v. Capital City Ford Co.*, 85 So.2d 75, 79 (La.Ct.App. 1955) (finding that newspaper advertisement was sufficiently certain and definite to constitute an offer).

The present case is distinguishable from *Lefkowitz*. First, the commercial cannot be regarded in itself as sufficiently definite, because it specifically reserved the details of the offer to a separate writing, the Catalog.[6]

The commercial itself made no mention of the steps a potential offeree would be required to take to accept the alleged offer of a Harrier Jet. The advertisement in *Lefkowitz*, in contrast, "identified the person who could accept." Corbin, *supra*, §2.4, at 119. *See generally United States v. Braunstein*, 75 F.Supp. 137, 139 (S.D.N.Y. 1947) ("Greater precision of expression may be required, and less help from the court given, when the parties are merely at the threshold of a contract."); Farnsworth, *supra*, at 239 ("The fact that a proposal is very detailed suggests that it is an offer, while omission of many terms suggests that it is not.").[7] Second, even if the Catalog had included a Harrier Jet among

---

5. Foremost Pro was overruled on other grounds by Hasbrouck v. Texaco, Inc., 842 F.2d 1034, 1041 (9th Cir.1987), aff'd, 496 U.S. 543 (1990). *See* Chroma Lighting v. GTE Products Corp., 111 F.3d 653, 657 (9th Cir.1997), cert. denied sub nom., Osram Sylvania Products, Inc. v. Von Der Ahe, 118 S.Ct. 357 (1997).

6. It also communicated additional words of reservation: "Offer not available in all areas. See details on specially marked packages."

7. The reservation of the details of the offer in this case distinguishes it from Payne v. Lautz Bros. & Co., 166 N.Y.S. 844 (City Ct. Buffalo 1916). In Payne, a stamp and coupon broker purchased massive quantities of coupons produced by defendant, a soap company, and tried to redeem them for 4,000 round-trip tickets to a local beach. The court ruled for plaintiff, noting that the advertisements

the items that could be obtained by redemption of Pepsi Points, the advertisement of a Harrier Jet by both television commercial and catalog would still not constitute an offer. As the *Mesaros* court explained, the absence of any words of limitation such as "first come, first served," renders the alleged offer sufficiently indefinite that no contract could be formed. *See Mesaros*, 845 F.2d at 1581. "A customer would not usually have reason to believe that the shopkeeper intended exposure to the risk of a multitude of acceptances resulting in a number of contracts exceeding the shopkeeper's inventory." Farnsworth, *supra*, at 242. There was no such danger in *Lefkowitz*, owing to the limitation "first come, first served."

The Court finds, in sum, that the Harrier Jet commercial was merely an advertisement. The Court now turns to the line of cases upon which plaintiff rests much of his argument.

2. Rewards as Offers

In opposing the present motion, plaintiff largely relies on a different species of unilateral offer, involving public offers of a reward for performance of a specified act. Because these cases generally involve public declarations regarding the efficacy or trustworthiness of specific products, one court has aptly characterized these authorities as "prove me wrong" cases. *See Rosenthal v. Al Packer Ford*, 374 A.2d 377, 380 (Md.Ct.Spec.App. 1977). The most venerable of these precedents is the case of *Carlill v. Carbolic Smoke Ball Co.*, 1 Q.B. 256 (Court of Appeal, 1892), a quote from which heads plaintiff's memorandum of law: "[I]f a person chooses to make extravagant promises ... he probably does so because it pays him to make them, and, if he has made them, the extravagance of the promises is no reason in law why he should not be bound by them." *Carbolic Smoke Ball*, 1 Q.B. at 268 (Bowen, L.J.).

Long a staple of law school curricula, Carbolic Smoke Ball owes its fame not merely to "the comic and slightly mysterious object involved," A.W. Brian Simpson. *Quackery and Contract Law: Carlill v. Carbolic Smoke Ball Company* (1893), in Leading Cases in the Common Law 259, 281 (1995), but also to its role in developing the law of unilateral offers. The case arose during the London influenza epidemic of the 1890s. Among other advertisements of the time, for Clarke's World Famous Blood Mixture, Towle's Pennyroyal and Steel Pills for Females, Sequah's Prairie Flower, and Epp's Glycerine Jube-Jubes, *see* Simpson, *supra*, at 267, appeared solicitations for the Carbolic Smoke Ball. The specific advertisement that Mrs. Carlill saw, and relied upon, read as follows:

> 100 £ reward will be paid by the Carbolic Smoke Ball Company to any person who contracts the increasing epidemic influenza, colds, or any diseases caused by taking cold, after having used the ball three times daily for two weeks according to the printed directions supplied with each ball. 1000 £ is deposited with the Alliance Bank, Regent Street, showing our sincerity in the matter.

> During the last epidemic of influenza many thousand carbolic smoke balls were sold as preventives against this disease, and in no ascertained case was the disease contracted by those using the carbolic smoke ball.

Carbolic Smoke Ball, 1 Q.B. at 256–57. "On the faith of this advertisement," *id.* at 257, Mrs. Carlill purchased the smoke ball and used it as directed, but contracted influenza nevertheless.[8] The lower court held that she was entitled to recover the promised reward.

---

were "absolutely unrestricted. It contained no reference whatever to any of its previous advertising of any form." *Id.* at 848. In the present case, by contrast, the commercial explicitly reserved the details of the offer to the Catalog.

8. Although the Court of Appeals' opinion is silent as to exactly what a carbolic smoke ball was, the historical record reveals it to have been a compressible hollow ball, about the size of an apple or

Affirming the lower court's decision, Lord Justice Lindley began by noting that the advertisement was an express promise to pay £100 in the event that a consumer of the Carbolic Smoke Ball was stricken with influenza. *See id.* at 261. The advertisement was construed as offering a reward because it sought to induce performance, unlike an invitation to negotiate, which seeks a reciprocal promise. As Lord Justice Lindley explained, "advertisements offering rewards ... are offers to anybody who performs the conditions named in the advertisement, and anybody who does perform the condition accepts the offer." *Id.* at 262; *see also id.* at 268 (Bowen, L.J.).[9] Because Mrs. Carlill had complied with the terms of the offer, yet contracted influenza, she was entitled to £100.

Like *Carbolic Smoke Ball*, the decisions relied upon by plaintiff involve offers of reward. In *Barnes v. Treece*, 549 P.2d 1152 (Wash.Ct.App. 1976), for example, the vice-president of a punchboard distributor, in the course of hearings before the Washington State Gambling Commission, asserted that, "I'll put a hundred thousand dollars to anyone to find a crooked board. If they find it, I'll pay it." *Id.* at 1154. Plaintiff, a former bartender, heard of the offer and located two crooked punchboards. Defendant, after reiterating that the offer was serious, providing plaintiff with a receipt for the punchboards on company stationery, and assuring plaintiff that the reward was being held in escrow, nevertheless repudiated the offer. *See id.* at 1154. The court ruled that the offer was valid and that plaintiff was entitled to his reward. *See id.* at 1155. The plaintiff in this case also cites cases involving prizes for skill (or luck) in the game of golf. *See Las Vegas Hacienda v. Gibson*, 359 P.2d 85 (Nev. 1961) (awarding $5,000 to plaintiff, who successfully shot a hole-in-one); *see also Grove v. Charbonneau Buick-Pontiac, Inc.*, 240 N.W.2d 853 (N.D. 1976) (awarding automobile to plaintiff, who successfully shot a hole-in-one).

Other "reward" cases underscore the distinction between typical advertisements, in which the alleged offer is merely an invitation to negotiate for purchase of commercial goods, and promises of reward, in which the alleged offer is intended to induce a potential offeree to perform a specific action, often for noncommercial reasons. In *Newman v. Schiff*, 778 F.2d 460 (5th Cir. 1985), for example, the Fifth Circuit held that a tax protestor's assertion that, "If anybody calls this show ... and cites any section of the code that says an individual is required to file a tax return, I'll pay them $100,000," would have been an enforceable offer had the plaintiff called the television show to claim the reward while the tax protestor was appearing. *See id.* at 466–67. The court noted that, like Carbolic Smoke Ball, the case "concerns a special type of offer: an offer for a reward." *Id.* at 465. *James v. Turilli*, 473 S.W.2d 757 (Mo.Ct.App. 1971), arose from a boast by defendant that the "notorious Missouri desperado" Jesse James had not been killed in 1882, as portrayed in song and legend, but had lived under the alias "J. Frank Dalton" at the "Jesse James Museum" operated by none other than defendant. Defendant offered $10,000 "to anyone who could prove me wrong." *See id.* at 758–59. The widow of the outlaw's son demonstrated, at trial, that the outlaw had in fact been killed in 1882. On appeal, the court held that defendant should be liable to pay the amount offered. *See id.* at 762; *see also Mears v. Na-*

---

orange, with a small opening covered by some porous material such as silk or gauze. The ball was partially filled with carbolic acid in powder form. When the ball was squeezed, the powder would be forced through the opening as a small cloud of smoke. *See* Simpson, supra, at 262–63. At the time, carbolic acid was considered fatal if consumed in more than small amounts. *See id.* at 264.

9. Carbolic Smoke Ball includes a classic formulation of this principle: "If I advertise to the world that my dog is lost, and that anybody who brings the dog to a particular place will be paid some money, are all the police or other persons whose business it is to find lost dogs to be expected to sit down and write a note saying that they have accepted my proposal?" Carbolic Smoke Ball, 1 Q.B. at 270 (Bowen, L.J.).

tionwide Mutual Ins. Co., 91 F.3d 1118, 1122–23 (8th Cir. 1996) (plaintiff entitled to cost of two Mercedes as reward for coining slogan for insurance company).

In the present case, the Harrier Jet commercial did not direct that anyone who appeared at Pepsi headquarters with 7,000,000 Pepsi Points on the Fourth of July would receive a Harrier Jet. Instead, the commercial urged consumers to accumulate Pepsi Points and to refer to the Catalog to determine how they could redeem their Pepsi Points. The commercial sought a reciprocal promise, expressed through acceptance of, and compliance with, the terms of the Order Form. As noted previously, the Catalog contains no mention of the Harrier Jet. Plaintiff states that he "noted that the Harrier Jet was not among the items described in the catalog, but this did not affect [his] understanding of the offer." It should have.[10]

Carbolic Smoke Ball itself draws a distinction between the offer of reward in that case, and typical advertisements, which are merely offers to negotiate. As Lord Justice Bowen explains:

> It is an offer to become liable to any one who, before it is retracted, performs the condition.... It is not like cases in which you offer to negotiate, or you issue advertisements that you have got a stock of books to sell, or houses to let, in which case there is no offer to be bound by any contract. Such advertisements are offers to negotiate—offers to receive offers—offers to chaffer, as, I think, some learned judge in one of the cases has said.

Carbolic Smoke Ball, 1 Q.B. at 268; *see also Lovett*, 207 N.Y.S. at 756 (distinguishing advertisements, as invitation to offer, from offers of reward made in advertisements, such as *Carbolic Smoke Ball*). Because the alleged offer in this case was, at most, an advertisement to receive offers rather than an offer of reward, plaintiff cannot show that there was an offer made in the circumstances of this case.

C. An Objective, Reasonable Person Would Not Have Considered the Commercial an Offer

Plaintiff's understanding of the commercial as an offer must also be rejected because the Court finds that no objective person could reasonably have concluded that the commercial actually offered consumers a Harrier Jet.

1. Objective Reasonable Person Standard

In evaluating the commercial, the Court must not consider defendant's subjective intent in making the commercial, or plaintiff's subjective view of what the commercial offered, but what an objective, reasonable person would have understood the commercial to convey. *See Kay-R Elec. Corp. v. Stone & Weber Constr. Co.*, 23 F.3d 55, 57 (2d Cir. 1994) ("[W]e are not concerned with what was going through the heads of the parties at the time [of the alleged contract]. Rather, we are talking about the objective principles of contract law."); *Mesaros*, 845 F.2d at 1581 ("A basic rule of contracts holds that whether an offer has been made depends on the objective reasonableness of the alleged offeree's belief that the advertisement or solicitation was intended as an offer."); Farnsworth, *supra*, § 3.10, at 237; Williston, *supra*, § 4:7 at 296–97.

If it is clear that an offer was not serious, then no offer has been made:

---

10. In his affidavit, plaintiff places great emphasis on a press release written by defendant, which characterizes the Harrier Jet as "the ultimate Pepsi Stuff award." Plaintiff simply ignores the remainder of the release, which makes no mention of the Harrier Jet even as it sets forth in detail the number of points needed to redeem other merchandise.

> What kind of act creates a power of acceptance and is therefore an offer? It
> must be an expression of will or intention. It must be an act that leads the offeree
> reasonably to conclude that a power to create a contract is conferred. This applies
> to the content of the power as well as to the fact of its existence. It is on this ground
> that we must exclude invitations to deal or acts of mere preliminary negotiation,
> and acts evidently done in jest or without intent to create legal relations.

Corbin on Contracts, § 1.11 at 30. An obvious joke, of course, would not give rise to a
contract. *See, e.g.,* Graves v. Northern N.Y. Pub. Co., 260 A.D. 900, 22 N.Y.S.2d 537 (App.Div.
4th Dept. 1940) (dismissing claim to offer of $1000, which appeared in the "joke column"
of the newspaper, to any person who could provide a commonly available phone number).
On the other hand, if there is no indication that the offer is "evidently in jest," and that an
objective, reasonable person would find that the offer was serious, then there may be a valid
offer. *See Barnes,* 549 P.2d at 1155 ("[I]f the jest is not apparent and a reasonable hearer
would believe that an offer was being made, then the speaker risks the formation of a contract
which was not intended."); *see also Lucy v. Zehmer,* 84 S.E.2d 516, 518, 520 (Va. 1954)
(ordering specific performance of a contract to purchase a farm despite defendant's protestation
that the transaction was done in jest as " 'just a bunch of two doggoned drunks bluffing' ").

2. Necessity of a Jury Determination

Plaintiff also contends that summary judgment is improper because the question of
whether the commercial conveyed a sincere offer can be answered only by a jury. Relying
on dictum from *Gallagher v. Delaney,* 139 F.3d 338 (2d Cir. 1998), plaintiff argues that a
federal judge comes from a "narrow segment of the enormously broad American socio-
economic spectrum," *id.* at 342, and, thus, that the question whether the commercial
constituted a serious offer must be decided by a jury composed of, inter alia, members
of the "Pepsi Generation," who are, as plaintiff puts it, "young, open to adventure, willing
to do the unconventional." Plaintiff essentially argues that a federal judge would view his
claim differently than fellow members of the "Pepsi Generation."

Plaintiff's argument that his claim must be put to a jury is without merit. *Gallagher*
involved a claim of sexual harassment in which the defendant allegedly invited plaintiff
to sit on his lap, gave her inappropriate Valentine's Day gifts, told her that "she brought
out feelings that he had not had since he was sixteen," and "invited her to help him feed
the ducks in the pond, since he was 'a bachelor for the evening.' " *Gallagher,* 139 F.3d at
344. The court concluded that a jury determination was particularly appropriate because
a federal judge lacked "the current real-life experience required in interpreting subtle
sexual dynamics of the workplace based on nuances, subtle perceptions, and implicit
communications." *Id.* at 342. This case, in contrast, presents a question of whether there
was an offer to enter into a contract, requiring the Court to determine how a reasonable,
objective person would have understood defendant's commercial. Such an inquiry is commonly performed by courts on a motion for summary judgment. *See Krumme,* 143 F.3d
at 83; *Bourque,* 42 F.3d at 708; *Wards Co.,* 761 F.2d at 120.

3. Whether the Commercial Was "Evidently Done In Jest"

Plaintiff's insistence that the commercial appears to be a serious offer requires the
Court to explain why the commercial is funny. Explaining why a joke is funny is a daunting
task; as the essayist E.B. White has remarked, "Humor can be dissected, as a frog can,
but the thing dies in the process...." The commercial is the embodiment of what defendant
appropriately characterizes as "zany humor."[11]

---

11. Quoted in Gerald R. Ford, Humor and the Presidency 23 (1987).

First, the commercial suggests, as commercials often do, that use of the advertised product will transform what, for most youth, can be a fairly routine and ordinary experience. The military tattoo and stirring martial music, as well as the use of subtitles in a Courier font that scroll terse messages across the screen, such as "MONDAY 7:58 AM," evoke military and espionage thrillers. The implication of the commercial is that Pepsi Stuff merchandise will inject drama and moment into hitherto unexceptional lives. The commercial in this case thus makes the exaggerated claims similar to those of many television advertisements: that by consuming the featured clothing, car, beer, or potato chips, one will become attractive, stylish, desirable, and admired by all. A reasonable viewer would understand such advertisements as mere puffery, not as statements of fact, *see, e.g., Hubbard v. General Motors Corp.*, 95 Civ. 4362 (AGS), 1996 WL 274018, at *6 (S.D.N.Y. May 22, 1996) (advertisement describing automobile as "Like a Rock," was mere puffery, not a warranty of quality); *Lovett*, 207 N.Y.S. at 756; and refrain from interpreting the promises of the commercial as being literally true.

Second, the callow youth featured in the commercial is a highly improbable pilot, one who could barely be trusted with the keys to his parents' car, much less the prize aircraft of the United States Marine Corps. Rather than checking the fuel gauges on his aircraft, the teenager spends his precious preflight minutes preening. The youth's concern for his coiffure appears to extend to his flying without a helmet. Finally, the teenager's comment that flying a Harrier Jet to school "sure beats the bus" evinces an improbably insouciant attitude toward the relative difficulty and danger of piloting a fighter plane in a residential area, as opposed to taking public transportation.[12]

Third, the notion of traveling to school in a Harrier Jet is an exaggerated adolescent fantasy. In this commercial, the fantasy is underscored by how the teenager's schoolmates gape in admiration, ignoring their physics lesson. The force of the wind generated by the Harrier Jet blows off one teacher's clothes, literally defrocking an authority figure. As if to emphasize the fantastic quality of having a Harrier Jet arrive at school, the Jet lands next to a plebeian bike rack. This fantasy is, of course, extremely unrealistic. No school would provide landing space for a student's fighter jet, or condone the disruption the jet's use would cause.

Fourth, the primary mission of a Harrier Jet, according to the United States Marine Corps, is to "attack and destroy surface targets under day and night visual conditions." United States Marine Corps, Factfile: AV-8B Harrier II (last modified Dec. 5, 1995) (www.hqmc.usmc.mil/factfile.nsf). Manufactured by McDonnell Douglas, the Harrier Jet played a significant role in the air offensive of Operation Desert Storm in 1991. *See id.* The jet is designed to carry a considerable armament load, including Sidewinder and Maverick missiles. *See id.* As one news report has noted, "Fully loaded, the Harrier can float like a butterfly and sting like a bee—albeit a roaring 14-ton butterfly and a bee with 9,200 pounds of bombs and missiles." Jerry Allegood, *Marines Rely on Harrier Jet, Despite Critics*, News & Observer (Raleigh), Nov. 4, 1990, at C1. In light of the Harrier Jet's well-documented function in attacking and destroying surface and air targets, armed reconnaissance and air interdiction, and offensive and defensive anti-aircraft warfare, depiction of such a jet as a way to get to school in the morning is clearly not serious even if, as

---

12. In this respect, the teenager of the advertisement contrasts with the distinguished figures who testified to the effectiveness of the Carbolic Smoke Ball, including the Duchess of Sutherland; the Earls of Wharncliffe, Westmoreland, Cadogan, and Leitrim; the Countesses Dudley, Pembroke, and Aberdeen; the Marchionesses of Bath and Conyngham; Sir Henry Acland, the physician to the Prince of Wales; and Sir James Paget, sergeant surgeon to Queen Victoria. *See* Simpson, supra, at 265.

plaintiff contends, the jet is capable of being acquired "in a form that eliminates [its] potential for military use."

Fifth, the number of Pepsi Points the commercial mentions as required to "purchase" the jet is 7,000,000. To amass that number of points, one would have to drink 7,000,000 Pepsis (or roughly 190 Pepsis a day for the next hundred years—an unlikely possibility), or one would have to purchase approximately $700,000 worth of Pepsi Points. The cost of a Harrier Jet is roughly $23 million dollars, a fact of which plaintiff was aware when he set out to gather the amount he believed necessary to accept the alleged offer. Even if an objective, reasonable person were not aware of this fact, he would conclude that purchasing a fighter plane for $700,000 is a deal too good to be true.[13]

Plaintiff argues that a reasonable, objective person would have understood the commercial to make a serious offer of a Harrier Jet because there was "absolutely no distinction in the manner" in which the items in the commercial were presented. Plaintiff also relies upon a press release highlighting the promotional campaign, issued by defendant, in which "[n]o mention is made by [defendant] of humor, or anything of the sort." These arguments suggest merely that the humor of the promotional campaign was tongue in cheek. Humor is not limited to what Justice Cardozo called "[t]he rough and boisterous joke ... [that] evokes its own guffaws." *Murphy v. Steeplechase Amusement Co.*, 250 N.Y. 479, 483, 166 N.E. 173, 174 (1929). In light of the obvious absurdity of the commercial, the Court rejects plaintiff's argument that the commercial was not clearly in jest.

...

[In omitted sections, the court concluded that the statute of frauds would preclude enforcement of the alleged contract, that plaintiff could not prevail on his claim of misrepresentation, because the commercial did not make a false representation of fact, and that further discovery should not be permitted. —Eds.]

III. Conclusion

In sum, there are three reasons why plaintiff's demand cannot prevail as a matter of law. First, the commercial was merely an advertisement, not a unilateral offer. Second, the tongue-in-cheek attitude of the commercial would not cause a reasonable person to conclude that a soft drink company would be giving away fighter planes as part of a promotion. Third, there is no writing between the parties sufficient to satisfy the Statute of Frauds.

For the reasons stated above, the Court grants defendant's motion for summary judgment. The Clerk of Court is instructed to close these cases. Any pending motions are moot.

Note—On Interpretation and Context

Southworth and *Pepsico* illustrate a variety of analyses appropriate under the common law doctrines of offer and acceptance. In *Southworth*, the court evaluated each

---

13. In contrast, the advertisers of the Carbolic Smoke Ball emphasized their earnestness, stating in the advertisement that £1,000 is deposited with the Alliance Bank, shewing our sincerity in the matter." Carbolic Smoke Ball, 1 Q.B. at 257. Similarly, in Barnes, the defendant's "subsequent statements, conduct, and the circumstances show an intent to lead any hearer to believe the statements were made seriously." Barnes, 549 P.2d at 1155. The offer in Barnes, moreover, was made in the serious forum of hearings before a state commission; not, as defendant states, at a "gambling convention."

communication to determine at what point one party manifested a willingness to enter the exchange, and the court decided that the Olivers had indicated such an intent to Southworth in the June 17 mailing. The court's principal concern in making this evaluation was what a person in Southworth's position would think about the Olivers' intention. In deciding the June 17th letter was an offer to Southworth, the court does not have to decide whether it was also an offer to the other recipients; indeed, the court's analysis suggests that it would not be, because they did not have the same series of conversations that Southworth had with Joseph Oliver. The court's decision that the letter was an offer to Southworth was contextually specific. In *Pepsico*, the court interpreted the meaning of the complex communication in a television ad that was textured with the pictures and sounds of put-on and posturing. Throughout, the courts' interpretations of words and conduct were influenced by what legal significance the interpretations would have and by the political and moral context in which the courts' interpretations were made.

2. The Assent Invited: Acceptance

As we have seen, an *offer* is a manifestation of willingness to enter into the exchange, conditional only on acceptance by the offeree. An *acceptance* is a manifestation of willingness to enter into the exchange as offered. An offer creates a *power of acceptance* in the offeree. As this power of acceptance is said to be "created by the offeror," its scope is "defined by the offeror"; or, as courts often recite, "the offeror is master of the offer." In other words, the appropriate manner and content of acceptance is defined by the offer, and an attempted acceptance is not effective unless it conforms to the manner and content indicated by the offer. There are, however, recognized exceptions and limitations to this rule.

The first case in this subsection, *Panhandle Eastern Pipe Line v. Nowlin Smith*, raises issues regarding both the *manner* and the *content* of an acceptance. The two cases immediately following *Panhandle Eastern Pipe Line* focus on the *manner* (or mode) of acceptance; in the first, *CIM Insurance Corporation v. Cascade Auto Glass, Inc.*, the court found that the offer required acceptance by performance. The acceptance, which simultaneously completed performance, created a *unilateral* contract. In the second case, *Russell v. Texas Co.*, the court found that silence could be acceptance of an offer.

Panhandle Eastern Pipe Line Co. v. Nowlin Smith, Jr.

Wyoming Supreme Court
637 P.2d 1020 (1981)

CHARLES S. BROWN, JUSTICE

Panhandle Eastern Pipe Line Company (Panhandle) appeals a district court judgment granting damages to its former employee Nowlin Smith, Jr., for breach of contract. Panhandle asserts that no contract ever existed.... It also maintains that if this court decides a contract did exist, we should nevertheless reverse the damage award because it was not supported by sufficient evidence.

We affirm.

Panhandle fired Mr. Smith in October, 1979. Mr. Smith followed the grievance procedure provided by a collective bargaining agreement to the third and final level of intracompany proceedings, which was a meeting with company officials at the division office. After that meeting, Panhandle initially decided to uphold the decision to fire Mr. Smith, but changed its mind after Mr. Smith's union representative requested that it reconsider. By letter dated December 13, 1979, the company offered to withdraw the discharge if Mr. Smith would agree to comply with certain terms and conditions. Mr. Smith signed the letter under the typewritten words, "Understood, Agreed To and Accepted," added some handwritten notations, and again signed his name. The union representative also signed the letter and returned it to the company.

Because Mr. Smith wrote on the letter, Panhandle argues that no contract existed, claiming that Mr. Smith failed to use the mode of acceptance which it prescribed. As Panhandle conceded at oral argument, it would have contested any words being added to the letter, even ones as innocuous as, "Have a nice day." Panhandle also argues that Mr. Smith made a counteroffer by adding terms and conditions which showed he was trying to modify the offer.... Appellant [Panhandle] cautioned this court not to confuse the two theories of "mode of acceptance" and "counteroffer," although appellant tried to interweave them in its brief. Because we want to avoid any confusion, we have decided to address both the "mode of acceptance" argument and the "counteroffer" argument.

I.

An offeror has the right to demand an exclusive mode of acceptance from an offeree. The mode of acceptance can be unreasonable or difficult if the offeror clearly expresses his intention to exclude all other modes of acceptance. This intention must be expressed in the communicated offer itself. *Crockett v. Lowther*, Wyo., 549 P.2d 303, 309 (1976), citing 1 CORBIN, CONTRACTS § 88, at 373 (1963). The letter of December 13, 1979, contained the offer to withdraw Mr. Smith's discharge. The letter directed that both Mr. Smith and the union had to agree in writing to the terms of the offer, and that the signatures were a condition precedent to the withdrawal of the discharge.[1] It went on to reiterate that the withdrawal of the discharge was contingent upon receipt of written acceptance by Mr. Smith and the union.

Panhandle insists that it modified this offer by demanding of Mr. Smith during a telephone conversation that he just sign the letter and not add anything. Mr. Smith, however, does not remember the conversation that way, and we must view the evidence on appeal most favorably to him. *Madrid v. Norton*, Wyo., 596 P.2d 1108 (1979). Here, Mr. Smith testified he did not understand that any addition to the letter would be considered a rejection of the offer. Panhandle, therefore, did not orally modify the written offer of December 13, 1979; it failed to "clearly express, in the terms of the communicated offer itself," its intention to exclude all other modes of acceptance. *Crockett v. Lowther, supra*. Panhandle was explicit only in stating that the terms and conditions had to be agreed to in writing.

The offeror is master of the offer, but we think fairness demands that when there is a dispute concerning mode of acceptance, the offer itself must clearly and definitely express

---

1. [The letter said:]

    ... The Company has, therefore, determined that Mr. Smith will be given one more opportunity to rehabilitate himself and his discharge shall hereby be withdrawn under the terms and conditions listed below, which terms and conditions must be agreed to in writing by both Mr. Smith and the Union as a condition precedent to the withdrawal of the discharge.

    The letter then said, "The terms and conditions are: ..." and set out eight additional terms and conditions, some of which will be discussed later.

an exclusive mode of acceptance. There must be no question that the offeror would accept the prescribed mode and only the prescribed mode. Corbin comments, "The more unreasonable the method appears, the less likely it will be that a court will interpret his offer as requiring it (a specific mode of performance) and the more clear and definite must be the expression of his intention in words." 1 CORBIN ON CONTRACTS § 88, at 373 (1963). The only motivation we could surmise for the requirement that no handwriting be added to the paper, regardless of content, would be that the offeror had an inordinate fondness for tidy sheets of paper. The requirement strikes us as unreasonable, and strikes out as a prescribed mode of acceptance unless the offeror's intention is explicitly set out. We agree that the mode of acceptance rule " … has been enforced with a rigor worthy of a better cause." We are not eager to enforce it if there is any question about the mode of acceptance or about the clarity with which the demand was made. Had Panhandle seriously been proposing an exclusive mode of acceptance calling for the absence of any writing on the paper other than signatures, the letter should have explicitly demanded that exact and exclusive mode of performance.

II.

The requirement that no terms or conditions be added to change the contract is a different matter. The law of contract formation dictates that one who modifies an offer has usually rejected the offer and made a counteroffer, and that no contract exists unless the original offeror accepts the counteroffer. *Trautwein v. Leavey*, Wyo., 472 P.2d 776 (1970).

Panhandle contends that Mr. Smith made a counteroffer by adding a request on the letter to see his personnel file and to contest any mistakes he found there. An offer must be accepted unconditionally; but there is, as always, an exception to the rule. An acceptance is still effective if the addition only asks for something that would be implied from the offer and is therefore immaterial. 1 Corbin on Contracts § 86, p. 368 (1963). A Panhandle supervisor, Mr. Smith, and a company machinist, who was also a union representative, all testified that all Panhandle employees had the right to see their personnel files. Panhandle's offer to withdraw its discharge and eventually reinstate Mr. Smith carried with it the implication that he would be able to see his personnel record when he was once again an active employee.

Besides reserving the right to see his personnel file, Mr. Smith wrote that his personnel file contained mistakes, and that he was having financial problems, apparently as a result of the company's actions. Williston has described the kind of acceptance Mr. Smith made as one showing "an abundance of caution," and Corbin has called it a "grumbling acceptance," which in this case it certainly appeared to be. The acceptance was unenthusiastic to be sure, but it was an acceptance nevertheless. Mr. Smith signed his name under the words "Understood, Agreed To and Accepted." He wrote that he agreed to the terms and conditions. He began performance by seeking medical help and by sending in a check to keep his insurance current. Mr. Smith wanted to be sure that he would be able to see his personnel file when he returned to work. His effort to insure that right should not block him from benefits that Panhandle had already offered to him. His "grumbling acceptance" should stand.

We therefore affirm.

The Manner of Acceptance

As a general rule, an offer may specify any manner of acceptance that the offeror desires. Thus, an offeror can say "the exclusive manner of acceptance of this offer is to stand on your head and recite the names of all of the Presidents of the United States." Assuming this is not unconscionable or vulnerable to other objections based on fairness or public policy, the offeree must do the specified feat in order to accept the offer. Most frequently, however, offerors do not specify a manner of acceptance or if they do (e.g., by having a signature line on a form) they do not say this is the "exclusive" manner of acceptance. Usually, if the offeror does not specify that a particular manner of acceptance is the only appropriate manner, courts will interpret the offer to allow acceptance in any reasonable manner. In *Panhandle*, the company argued that the offer had specified a particular manner of acceptance: "just sign and don't add anything," and that Smith's response did not conform to this because he added something. However, the court found the offer did not specify an *exclusive* manner of acceptance and Smith's response of signing and adding a note was a reasonable manner of acceptance. This decision is typical of many contemporary decisions. Although courts continue to recite the rule that the offeror is the "master of the offer," and they will enforce a clear restriction on the manner of acceptance, as a general rule most courts assume that offers do not specify exclusive manners of acceptance. They reason that in most cases, in drafting the offer, the offeror is interested merely in getting an acceptance and does not care in what form it comes. This approach is encouraged by U.C.C. section 2-206 that provides, *"Unless otherwise un-ambiguously indicated* by the language or circumstances, ... an offer to make a contract shall be construed as inviting acceptance in any manner and by any medium reasonable in the circumstances"* (emphasis added).

Acceptance by Promise (Express or Implied): Bilateral Contracts

Usually, an acceptance will take the form of an express or implied promise. For example, in Southworth v. Oliver, the court found that Southworth accepted the Olivers' offer in a letter that said "Re the land in Bear Valley near Seneca, Oregon that you have offered to sell; I accept your offer." Did Southworth promise anything?

Yes. Surely a reasonable person in the Olivers' position would perceive that Southworth was promising to pay $324,419, the amount listed in the Olivers' earlier letter.

Southworth accepted the offer by making a promise, and this concluded the agreement. This agreement forms the basis of what contract doctrine calls a "bilateral contract," because the contract includes one or more promises by both parties.

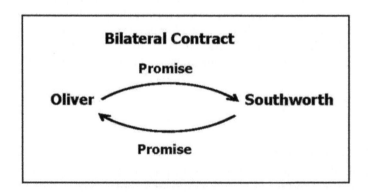

Bilateral Contract

Promise

Oliver — Southworth

Promise

Of course, the offeree may express the return promise in words (e.g., "Sure, I'll sell you my motorcycle for $5,000"); may imply the return promise in words and actions (e.g., "let's shake on it" while extending the hand); or may imply the return promise in actions alone (e.g., handing the motorcycle keys to the offeror).

In one common form of acceptance by implied promise, the offeree begins doing the work requested in the offer. For example, an offeree could accept the offer "I'll pay you $300 if you remove the old paint from the exterior of my house" by picking up a scrapper and beginning to remove the paint. This would be an acceptance by return promise because the offeree's actions would convey his or her promise to do the whole job.

When an offeree accepts by making a return promise, the resulting contract is a "bilateral contract" because it consists of one promise (or a set of promises) from the offeror to the offeree and a return promise (or set of promises) from the offeree to the offeror.

Acceptance by Full Performance: Unilateral Contracts

An acceptance completes the formation of a contract, thereby binding both offeror and offeree. If the offer permits an acceptance by promise, then both parties are bound by the contract as soon as the return promise is made and both are obligated to perform as promised. Because the contract includes promises by both parties ("cross-promises"), it is called a *bilateral contract.* If the offer specifies that it can be accepted only by full performance, then the contract is not formed until the offeree fully performs everything that is sought by the offer. After the contract is formed, then only the offeror is obligated to perform, because the offeree has already fully performed. Because only one party is obligated after the contract is formed, this is called a *unilateral contract.* For example, suppose a seller has 10 used snowmobiles with a sign that says, "TAKE ALL 10 FOR $8,000." A buyer approaches the seller with $8,000 cash and hands it to the seller. In this situation, the offeree's performance (handing over the cash) is both the acceptance, which creates the contract, and the completion of the offeree's part of the exchange. A contract formed in this way is a "unilateral contract" because the contract that is created by the acceptance leaves only the offeror's obligation to perform (in this example, the duty to transfer ownership of the 10 snowmobiles).

In the past, some judges and scholars viewed the unilateral contract as a rarity in the real world, limited to rewards ("$500 if you find my lost dog") and contests ("a new set of clubs if you sink a hole-in-one"). Yet today, it is undeniable that a wide variety of contracts do fit the unilateral model. Consider a standard insurance contract: the insurance company promises to reimburse the insured for various possible losses if the insured pays

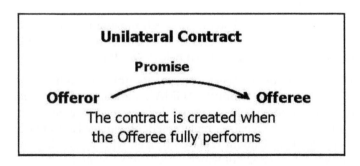

a premium; the insured accepts this offer by paying the premium. Does the insured promise to pay the premium? No, generally not: if the insured fails to pay, the insurance company can't sue the insured for breach of contract, the company simply is not obligated to reimburse losses.

Similarly, consider an "at-will" employment contract. The employee is told that she will be paid a certain amount of money for a period of work (for example, a coffee shop cashier is told he will be paid $10 an hour for a 40 hour per week schedule) and that she is an "at will" employee, meaning that she can be fired at any time and the employer is free to make whatever personnel changes he wants. Frequently, courts have characterized this as a unilateral contract: the employer makes a new offer each day (unless and until he decides to replace the employee or eliminate the job) and the employee accepts these offers by going to work each day. If the employee does not show up for work, she has not breached a contract, but the employer doesn't have to pay her for that time.

With these examples in mind, one can see that many contemporary contracting relationships fit the unilateral contract pattern. Courts have articulated rules relevant to this pattern:

1. When the offer indicates that it can be accepted by any reasonable means, then the offeree *may* accept by making a promise or by fully performing the actions sought by the offer, *see* Restatement (Second) of Contracts § 32 ("In case of doubt an offer is interpreted as inviting the offeree to accept either by promising to perform what the offer requests or by rendering the performance, as the offeree chooses.").

2. Sometimes, an offer will expressly require an acceptance by promise or an acceptance by full performance as an exclusive mode of acceptance.

3. Although, as a general rule, an offer must clearly and unambiguously state that an acceptance must be in a particular form, an offer will implicitly require full performance if it requests the offeree to do something dangerous, risky, or unlikely to occur. For example, a reasonable offeree would understand that she could not accept the offer "I'll give you $250 if you find my lost dog" by a promise ("ok, I promise to find your lost dog."), but only by full performance (finding the dog).

CIM Insurance Corporation, et al. v. Cascade Auto Glass, Inc.

Court of Appeals of North Carolina
660 S.E.2d 907 (2008)

Barbara A. Jackson, Judge

Cascade Auto Glass, Inc. ("Defendant") appeals the granting of summary judgment in favor of CIM Insurance Corporation and seventeen other named Plaintiffs in the instant case on 5 April 2007. For the reasons stated below, we affirm.

Defendant is an automobile glass replacement company doing business in North Carolina. The eighteen named Plaintiffs ("GMAC") are all GMAC-affiliated insurance companies providing comprehensive automobile insurance coverage to insureds within North Carolina, including the repair or replacement of damaged automobile windshields. Between 1999 and 2004, Defendant replaced broken windshield glass in at least 2,284 GMAC-insured vehicles, over 525 of which were North Carolina vehicles.

Prior to 1999, GMAC administered its own glass coverage program, and generally paid the full amounts billed by Defendant for work performed for its insureds. In 1999, GMAC entered into an agreement with Safelite Solutions—an affiliate of Safelite Auto Glass ("Safelite")—to serve as third-party administrator of its auto glass program. Thereafter, Safelite communicated the prices that GMAC would agree to pay Defendant for its services, which generally were lower than what GMAC previously had paid.

Defendant disputed the Safelite prices. Notwithstanding Defendant's protests, once an insured filed a claim, Safelite would send Defendant a confirmation fax, including the previously stated price GMAC would pay, and a statement that "[p]erformance of services constitutes acceptance of the above price...." Defendant then would perform repair or replacement services and bill GMAC the rates it deemed "fair and reasonable." Defendant also disputed the prices Safelite provided in the confirmation faxes.

GMAC, through Safelite, submitted payments to Defendant according to the prices it quoted in its various communications with Defendant. Defendant accepted the payments from GMAC and deposited the money into its corporate accounts ...

Defendant has had similar pricing disputes in Idaho and Washington, and brought suit in those states seeking to recover "'unpaid' balances" from insurance carriers in those states. Defendant also threatened to file a complaint against GMAC. Consequently, on 15 February 2005, GMAC brought the instant action for declaratory judgment, seeking a declaration of the rights of the parties. In response, on 21 March 2005, Defendant counterclaimed for breach of contract as to the alleged unpaid balances.

On 29 September 2006, GMAC filed a motion for summary judgment, which was heard on 19 February 2007. By that time, both the Idaho and Washington appellate courts had issued opinions affirming their respective lower courts' granting of summary judgment against Defendant. *See* Cascade Auto Glass, Inc. v. Idaho Farm Bureau Ins. Co., 115 P.3d 751 (Idaho 2005); Cascade Auto Glass v. Progressive Casualty Ins., 145 P.3d 1253 (Wa. 2006). The trial court in the instant case also granted summary judgment against Defendant by order filed 5 April 2007. Defendant appeals.

. . .

In its 5 April 2007 order, the trial court based its judgment on three grounds: (1) GMAC complied with the terms of its insurance contract; (2) GMAC paid Defendant in accordance with unilateral contracts GMAC entered into with Defendant; and (3) Defendant's actions in cashing checks sent to it by GMAC, knowing that GMAC considered those payments "final," constituted an accord and satisfaction of any potential claim Defendant might assert. "If the granting of summary judgment can be sustained on any grounds, it should be affirmed on appeal." Shore v. Brown, 428, 378 S.E.2d 778, 779 (N.C. 1989).

A unilateral contract is formed when one party makes a promise and expressly or impliedly invites the other party to perform some act as a condition for making the promise binding on the promisor. *See* Gurvin v. Cromartie, 33 N.C. 174, 179 (1850)

. . .

In the instant case, GMAC, through Safelite, communicated the prices it was willing to pay Defendant for services rendered to its insureds. These prices were communicated in several ways: (1) via letter to Defendant's shops, (2) via telephone when initial claims were made, (3) via confirmation fax after claims were made but before work was performed, and (4) via eventual payment of invoices at the GMAC rate rather than Defendant's rate. The confirmation faxes stated, "[p]erformance of services constitutes acceptance of the above price...." Although Defendant protested the stated prices, these protests admitted that the confirmation faxes constituted offers — "The purpose of this letter is to address [the confirmation faxes] and to dispel any notion that we are in agreement with the offered pricing."

"It is a fundamental concept of contract law that the offeror is the master of his offer. He is entitled to require acceptance in precise conformity with his offer before a contract is formed." MacEachern v. Rockwell International Corp., 254 S.E.2d 263, 265 (N.C. 1979). Here, the offer stated that acceptance was by performance. Because Defendant performed the requested repairs or replacements, it accepted the terms of GMAC's offers, forming valid unilateral contracts at GMAC's stated prices. See Id. at 266 ("[W]hen the offer so provides, it may be accepted by performing a specific act rather than by making a return promise.").

GMAC paid Defendant pursuant to the terms of the unilateral contracts entered into between the parties. Defendant has not been "underpaid" and is due no further payments. Therefore, summary judgment was properly granted against Defendant.

Affirmed.

Acceptance by Silence

Is it possible to accept an offer by doing and saying nothing? What if the offer specifies "your silence will indicate your acceptance of this offer." If the offeree does nothing, is he or she then bound to a contract? Seems unfair to the offeree, doesn't it? What if the offer says: "If you eat dinner tonight, that will indicate your acceptance of this offer."?

Concerned with the possibility of such unfairness, courts have articulated the general rule that "silence cannot be acceptance." Like most legal rules, however, rigid application of the rule would lead to unjust results. Courts have recognized several situations, therefore, in which silence can operate as an acceptance:

1. when the parties explicitly agree that silence will constitute acceptance (e.g., "If you don't hear from me by Friday, you can assume that the offer is accepted by us.");

2. when the parties' past dealings have established a practice in which silence is understood to convey acceptance (i.e., when the parties have implicitly agreed that silence will be acceptance); and

3. when the offeree has already received the benefits of the offered contract.

Theodore B. Russell v. Texas Co.
United States Court of Appeals for the Ninth Circuit
238 F.2d 636 (1956)

Sherrill Halbert, District Judge

Plaintiff-appellant, Russell, claims title to certain real property, which will be referred to in this opinion as section 23. Russell's predecessors in interest acquired their interest in this property from the Northern Pacific Railway Company, defendant-appellee herein, through a contract followed by a warranty deed executed in 1918. In both the contract and the deed was a reservation of mineral rights by the grantor. The Texas Company, defendant-appellee and cross-appellant herein, has been conducting extensive operations on section 23 since 1952 under an oil and gas lease granted by Northern Pacific Railway Company. The Texas Company has also made use of the surface of section 23 in connection with operations carried on by it on lands other than section 23.

Russell, as plaintiff, instituted this action seeking relief under three causes of action. By the second and third causes of action, Russell seeks to recover damages from The Texas Company for its use of the surface of section 23 in connection with its operations on section 23 and on adjacent lands.

. . .

The evidence shows that The Texas Company received on October 30, 1952, an offer from Russell for a revocable license to cover the use of section 23 in connection with operations on adjacent lands for the sum of $150.00 a day, which offer contained the express proviso that, "your continued use of the roadway, water and/or materials will constitute your acceptance of this revocable permit." The evidence further shows that The Texas Company did so continue to use section 23 until November 22, 1952, and it was not until sometime in December of that year that Russell finally received a communication from the Company to the effect that the offer was rejected. Neither party depends in any material respect on this purported rejection.

. . .

Judgment was entered in favor of Russell and against The Texas Company in the amount of $3,837.60, which consisted of $3,600.00 due under the revocable license and $237.60 due for the use of the land under the terms of the mineral reservation.

The Texas Company appeals from that portion of the judgment which awarded Russell $3,600.00 as the amount due under the terms of the revocable license, contending that the court erred as a matter of law in finding that the offer for the said license was accepted.

Russell appeals from that portion of the judgment against the Texas Company which awarded him $237.60, claiming that the court, in arriving at the measure of compensation, applied the wrong rule of damages. . . .

The Texas Company argues that the revocable license, which Russell offered to it in connection with its wrongful use of section 23, was never accepted, because the Company had no intention of accepting it. Appellant presents for our consideration numerous passages from the *Restatement of Contracts* and *Williston on Contracts* dealing with the necessity of the offeree's intent to accept where an ambiguous act is selected by the offeror to signify acceptance, or where silence and inaction can be considered an acceptance. None of these citations deal with the precise question that we are confronted with in this case. The question here is whether an offeree may vitiate a contract by a claim of lack of intention to accept an offer when he accepts and retains the benefits offered to him by the offeror, with a positive and affirmative proviso by the offeror that such acceptance of the benefits will, in and of itself, be deemed by the offeror to be an acceptance. To put the problem in homely terms, may an offeree accept all of the benefits of a contract and then declare that he cannot be held liable for the burdens because he secretly had said, "King's Ex"? We think not. A rule with such effect would be unconscionable and is not in line with either fairness or justice. The correct rule, we believe, is found in 72(2) of the *Restatement of Contracts,* wherein it is stated:

> Where the offeree exercises dominion over things which are offered to him, such exercise of dominion in the absence of other circumstances showing a contrary intention is an acceptance. *If circumstances indicate that the exercise of dominion is tortious the offeror may at his option treat it as an acceptance, though the offeree manifests an intention not to accept.* (Emphasis added.)

Russell's offer of the license in clear and unambiguous terms stated that the continued use of section 23 in connection with activities and operations on other lands would constitute an acceptance of the offer of the license. The trial court found on the evidence that The Texas Company did so continue to use section 23, and hence unequivocally came within the terms specified for acceptance. It is a well established principle of property law that the right to use the surface of land as an incident of the ownership of mineral rights in the land, does not carry with it the right to use the surface in aid of mining or drilling operations on other lands (*See* 36 Am. Jur., *Mines and Minerals*, 177, 180 and 181; Anno.: 48 A.L.R. 1406, 1407). That such use by The Texas Company was tortious admits of no doubt. But even in the absence of a tortious use, the true test would be whether or not the offeror was reasonably led to believe that the act of the offeree was an acceptance, and upon the facts of this case it seems evident that even this test is met.

. . .

The conclusion reached by the trial court on this phase of the case was correct.

. . .

The judgment is affirmed as to both appellants.

―――――――

Judicial Interpretation of Unread Boilerplate

"Sometimes I click as many as six I AGREEs before breakfast," said the 21st-Century Queen of the rabbit-hole.

What is the legal significance of clicking "I agree"? Have you ever actually read the "terms and conditions" to which you are agreeing? Have you ever clicked without reading the terms and conditions? Does it trouble you that U.S. Supreme Court Chief Justice Roberts does not read the "terms and conditions" before clicking "I Agree"?* Wouldn't you be more troubled if you read a news report saying that the Chief Justice of the United States Supreme Court spent twelve hours reading the iTunes Terms and Conditions? Is it a rational use of your time to read the terms and conditions? Would a reasonable person in the position of the website owner understand your click to mean that you agree to all of the terms and conditions that are linked to the website?

U.S. buyers spent an estimated $304.9 billion in internet purchases in 2014. Estimates for global e-commerce sales project about $1.5 trillion in business to consumer transactions. A lot of people are clicking the box marked I AGREE or browsing websites that treat any visit as agreement to all linked terms.

―――――――

Kevin Khoa Nguyen, an individual, on behalf of himself and all others similarly situated v. Barnes & Noble, Inc.

United States Court of Appeals for the Ninth Circuit
763 F.3d 1171 (2014)

JOHN T. NOONAN, CIRCUIT JUDGE

Barnes & Noble, Inc. ("Barnes & Noble") appeals the district court's denial of its motion to compel arbitration against Kevin Khoa Nguyen ("Nguyen") pursuant to the arbitration agreement contained in its website's Terms of Use. In order to resolve the issue of arbitrability, we must address whether Nguyen, by merely using Barnes & Noble's

―――――――

* *See* Debra Cassens Weiss, Chief Justice Roberts Admits He Doesn't Read the Computer Fine Print—ABA Journal (Oct 20, 2010).

website, agreed to be bound by the Terms of Use, even though Nguyen was never prompted to assent to the Terms of Use and never in fact read them. We agree with the district court that Barnes & Noble did not provide reasonable notice of its Terms of Use, and that Nguyen therefore did not unambiguously manifest assent to the arbitration provision contained therein.

We also agree with the district court that Nguyen is not equitably estopped from avoiding arbitration because he relied on the Terms of Use's choice of law provision.

We therefore affirm the district court's denial of Barnes & Noble's motion to compel arbitration and to stay court proceedings.

I. Background

A.

The underlying facts are not in dispute. Barnes & Noble is a national bookseller that owns and operates hundreds of bookstores as well as the website <www.barnesandnoble.com>. In August 2011, Barnes & Noble, along with other retailers across the country, liquidated its inventory of discontinued Hewlett–Packard Touchpads ("Touchpads"), an unsuccessful competitor to Apple's iPad, by advertising a "fire sale" of Touchpads at a heavily discounted price. Acting quickly on the nationwide liquidation of Touchpads, Nguyen purchased two units on Barnes & Noble's website on August 21, 2011, and received an email confirming the transaction. The following day, Nguyen received another email informing him that his order had been cancelled due to unexpectedly high demand. Nguyen alleges that, as a result of "Barnes & Noble's representations, as well as the delay in informing him it would not honor the sale," he was "unable to obtain an HP Tablet during the liquidation period for the discounted price," and was "forced to rely on substitute tablet technology, which he subsequently purchased ... [at] considerable expense."

B.

In April 2012, Nguyen filed this lawsuit in California Superior Court on behalf of himself and a putative class of consumers whose Touchpad orders had been cancelled, alleging that Barnes & Noble had engaged in deceptive business practices and false advertising in violation of both California and New York law. Barnes & Noble removed the action to federal court and moved to compel arbitration under the Federal Arbitration Act ("FAA"), arguing that Nguyen was bound by the arbitration agreement in the website's Terms of Use.

The website's Terms of Use are available via a "Terms of Use" hyperlink located in the bottom left-hand corner of every page on the Barnes & Noble website, which appears alongside other hyperlinks labeled "NOOK Store Terms," "Copyright," and "Privacy Policy." These hyperlinks also appear underlined and set in green typeface in the lower lefthand corner of every page in the online checkout process.

Nguyen neither clicked on the "Terms of Use" hyperlink nor actually read the Terms of Use. Had he clicked on the hyperlink, he would have been taken to a page containing the full text of Barnes & Noble's Terms of Use, which state, in relevant part: "By visiting any area in the Barnes & Noble.com Site, creating an account, [or] making a purchase via the Barnes & Noble.com Site ... a User is deemed to have accepted the Terms of Use." Nguyen also would have come across an arbitration provision, which states:

XVIII. DISPUTE RESOLUTION

Any claim or controversy at law or equity that arises out of the Terms of Use, the Barnes & Noble.com Site or any Barnes & Noble.com Service (each a "Claim"), shall be resolved through binding arbitration conducted by telephone, online or based solely upon written submissions where no in-person appearance is required.

> In such cases, arbitration shall be administered by the American Arbitration Association under its Commercial Arbitration Rules (including without limitation the Supplementary Procedures for Consumer–Related Disputes, if applicable), and judgment on the award rendered by the arbitrator(s) may be entered in any court having jurisdiction thereof.

...

> Any claim shall be arbitrated or litigated, as the case may be, on an individual basis and shall not be consolidated with any Claim of any other party whether through class action proceedings, class arbitration proceedings or otherwise.

...

> Each of the parties hereby knowingly, voluntarily and intentionally waives any right it may have to a trial by jury in respect of any litigation (including but not limited to any claims, counterclaims, cross-claims, or third party claims) arising out of, under or in connection with these Terms of Use. Further, each party hereto certifies that no representative or agent of either party has represented, expressly or otherwise, that such a party would not in the event of such litigation, seek to enforce this waiver of right to jury trial provision. Each of the parties acknowledges that this section is a material inducement for the other party entering into these Terms of Use.

Nguyen contends that he cannot be bound to the arbitration provision because he neither had notice of nor assented to the website's Terms of Use. Barnes & Noble, for its part, asserts that the placement of the "Terms of Use" hyperlink on its website put Nguyen on constructive notice of the arbitration agreement. Barnes & Noble contends that this notice, combined with Nguyen's subsequent use of the website, was enough to bind him to the Terms of Use. The district court disagreed, and Barnes & Noble now appeals.

II. Standard of Review

"We review the denial of a motion to compel arbitration de novo." *Cox v. Ocean View Hotel Corp.*, 533 F.3d 1114, 1119 (9th Cir.2008). Underlying factual findings are reviewed for clear error, *Balen v. Holland Am. Line Inc.*, 583 F.3d 647, 652 (9th Cir.2009), while "[t]he interpretation and meaning of contract provisions" are reviewed de novo, *Milenbach v. Comm'r*, 318 F.3d 924, 930 (9th Cir.2003).

III. Discussion

A.

The FAA, 9 U.S.C. § 1 *et seq.*, requires federal district courts to stay judicial proceedings and compel arbitration of claims covered by a written and enforceable arbitration agreement. *Id.* § 3. The FAA limits the district court's role to determining whether a valid arbitration agreement exists, and whether the agreement encompasses the disputes at issue. *See Chiron Corp. v. Ortho Diagnostic Sys., Inc.*, 207 F.3d 1126, 1130 (9th Cir.2000). The parties do not quarrel that Barnes & Noble's arbitration agreement, should it be found enforceable, encompasses Nguyen's claims. The only issue is whether a valid arbitration agreement exists.

In determining whether a valid arbitration agreement exists, federal courts "apply ordinary state—law principles that govern the formation of contracts." *First Options of Chicago, Inc. v. Kaplan*, 514 U.S. 938, 944, 115 S.Ct. 1920, 131 L.Ed.2d 985 (1995). Federal courts sitting in diversity look to the law of the forum state—here, California—when making choice of law determinations. *Hoffman v. Citibank (S.D.), N.A.*, 546 F.3d 1078, 1082 (9th Cir.2008) (per curiam). Under California law, the parties' choice of law will govern unless section 187(2) of the Restatement (Second) of Conflict of Laws dictates a different result. *Id.*

Here, the parties agree that the validity of the arbitration agreement is governed by New York law, as specified by the Terms of Use's choice of law provision. But whether the choice of law provision applies depends on whether the parties agreed to be bound by Barnes & Noble's Terms of Use in the first place. As the district court acknowledged in its order, we need not engage in this circular inquiry because both California and New York law dictate the same outcome. Thus, in evaluating the validity of Barnes & Noble's arbitration agreement, we apply New York law, to the extent possible.

For the reasons that follow, we hold that Nguyen did not enter into Barnes & Noble's agreement to arbitrate.

B.

"While new commerce on the Internet has exposed courts to many new situations, it has not fundamentally changed the principles of contract." *Register.com, Inc. v. Verio, Inc.,* 356 F.3d 393, 403 (2d Cir.2004). One such principle is the requirement that "[m]utual manifestation of assent, whether by written or spoken word or by conduct, is the touchstone of contract." *Specht v. Netscape Commc'ns Corp.,* 306 F.3d 17, 29 (2d Cir.2002) (applying California law).

Contracts formed on the Internet come primarily in two flavors: "clickwrap" (or "click-through") agreements, in which website users are required to click on an "I agree" box after being presented with a list of terms and conditions of use; and "browsewrap" agreements, where a website's terms and conditions of use are generally posted on the website via a hyperlink at the bottom of the screen. *See Register.com,* 356 F.3d at 428–30. Barnes & Noble's Terms of Use fall in the latter category.

"Unlike a clickwrap agreement, a browsewrap agreement does not require the user to manifest assent to the terms and conditions expressly ... [a] party instead gives his assent simply by using the website." *Hines v. Overstock.com, Inc.,* 668 F.Supp.2d 362, 366–67 (E.D.N.Y.2009) (citation and quotation marks omitted) (alteration in original). Indeed, "in a pure—form browsewrap agreement, 'the website will contain a notice that—by merely using the services of, obtaining information from, or initiating applications within the website—the user is agreeing to and is bound by the site's terms of service.'" *Fteja v. Facebook, Inc.,* 841 F.Supp.2d 829, 837 (S.D.N.Y.2012) (quoting *United States v. Drew,* 259 F.R.D. 449, 462 n. 22 (C.D.Cal.2009)). Thus, "by visiting the website—something that the user has already done—the user agrees to the Terms of Use not listed on the site itself but available only by clicking a hyperlink." *Id.* "The defining feature of browsewrap agreements is that the user can continue to use the website or its services without visiting the page hosting the browsewrap agreement or even knowing that such a webpage exists." *Be In, Inc. v. Google Inc.,* No. 12-CV-03373-LHK, 2013 WL 5568706, at *6 (N.D.Cal. Oct. 9, 2013). "Because no affirmative action is required by the website user to agree to the terms of a contract other than his or her use of the website, the determination of the validity of the browsewrap contract depends on whether the user has actual or constructive knowledge of a website's terms and conditions." *Van Tassell v. United Mktg. Grp., LLC,* 795 F.Supp.2d 770, 790 (N.D.Ill.2011) (citing *Sw. Airlines Co. v. BoardFirst, LLC,* No. 06-CV-0891-B, 2007 WL 4823761, at *4 (N.D.Tex. Sept. 12, 2007)); *see also* Mark A. Lemley, *Terms of Use,* 91 Minn. L. Rev. 459, 477 (2006) ("Courts may be willing to overlook the utter absence of assent only when there are reasons to believe that the [website user] is aware of the [website owner's] terms.").

Were there any evidence in the record that Nguyen had actual notice of the Terms of Use or was required to affirmatively acknowledge the Terms of Use before completing his online purchase, the outcome of this case might be different. Indeed, courts have consistently enforced browsewrap agreements where the user had actual notice of the agreement. *See, e.g., Register.com*, 356 F.3d at 401–04 (finding likelihood of success on the merits in a breach of browsewrap claim where the defendant "admitted that ... it was fully aware of the terms" of the offer); *Sw. Airlines Co.*, 2007 WL 4823761, at *4–6 (finding proper contract formation where defendant continued its breach after being notified of the terms in a cease and desist letter); *Ticketmaster Corp. v. Tickets.Com, Inc.*, No. CV-997654, 2003 WL 21406289, at *2C (C.D.Cal. Mar. 7, 2003) (denying defendants' summary judgment motion on browsewrap contract claim where defendants continued breaching contract after receiving letter quoting the browsewrap contract terms). Courts have also been more willing to find the requisite notice for constructive assent where the browsewrap agreement resembles a clickwrap agreement — that is, where the user is required to affirmatively acknowledge the agreement before proceeding with use of the website. *See, e.g., Zaltz v. JDATE*, 952 F.Supp.2d 439, 451–52 (E.D.N.Y.2013) (enforcing forum selection clause where prospective members had to check box confirming that they both read and agreed to the website's Terms and Conditions of Service to obtain account); *Fteja*, 841 F.Supp.2d at 838–40 (enforcing forum selection clause in website's terms of service where a notice below the "Sign Up" button stated, "By clicking Sign Up, you are indicating that you have read and agree to the Terms of Service," and user had clicked "Sign Up").

But where, as here, there is no evidence that the website user had actual knowledge of the agreement, the validity of the browsewrap agreement turns on whether the website puts a reasonably prudent user on inquiry notice of the terms of the contract. *Specht*, 306 F.3d at 30–31; *see also In re Zappos.com, Inc. Customer Data Sec. Breach Litig.*, 893 F.Supp.2d 1058, 1064 (D.Nev.2012). Whether a user has inquiry notice of a browsewrap agreement, in turn, depends on the design and content of the website and the agreement's webpage. *Google*, 2013 WL 5568706, at *6. Where the link to a website's terms of use is buried at the bottom of the page or tucked away in obscure corners of the website where users are unlikely to see it, courts have refused to enforce the browsewrap agreement. *See, e.g., Specht*, 306 F.3d at 23 (refusing to enforce terms of use that "would have become visible to plaintiffs only if they had scrolled down to the next screen"); *In re Zappos.com*, 893 F.Supp.2d at 1064 ("The Terms of Use is inconspicuous, buried in the middle to bottom of every Zappos.com webpage among many other links, and the website never directs a user to the Terms of Use."); *Van Tassell*, 795 F.Supp.2d at 792–93 (refusing to enforce arbitration clause in browsewrap agreement that was only noticeable after a "multi-step process" of clicking through non-obvious links); *Hines*, 668 F.Supp.2d at 367 (plaintiff "could not even see the link to [the terms and conditions] without scrolling down to the bottom of the screen — an action that was not required to effectuate her purchase"). On the other hand, where the website contains an explicit textual notice that continued use will act as a manifestation of the user's intent to be bound, courts have been more amenable to enforcing browsewrap agreements. *See, e.g., Cairo, Inc. v. Crossmedia Servs., Inc.*, No. 04-04825, 2005 WL 756610, at *2, *4–5 (N.D.Cal. Apr. 1, 2005) (enforcing forum selection clause in website's terms of use where every page on the website had a textual notice that read: "By continuing past this page and/or using this site, you agree to abide by the Terms of Use for this site, which prohibit commercial use of any information on this site"). *But see Pollstar v. Gigmania, Ltd.*, 170 F.Supp.2d 974, 981 (E.D.Cal.2000) (refusing to enforce browsewrap agreement where textual notice appeared in small gray print against a gray background). In short, the conspicuousness and placement of the "Terms of Use" hyperlink, other notices given to users of the terms of use, and the website's general design all contribute to whether a reasonably prudent user would have inquiry notice of a browsewrap agreement.

Barnes & Noble argues that the placement of the "Terms of Use" hyperlink in the bottom left-hand corner of every page on the Barnes & Noble website, and its close proximity to the buttons a user must click on to complete an online purchase, is enough to place a reasonably prudent user on constructive notice. It is true that the location of the hyperlink on Barnes & Noble's website distinguishes this case from *Specht*, the leading authority on the enforceability of browsewrap terms under New York law. There, the Second Circuit refused to enforce an arbitration provision in a website's licensing terms where the hyperlink to the terms was located at the bottom of the page, hidden below the "Download" button that users had to click to initiate the software download. *See Specht*, 306 F.3d at 30. Then-Second Circuit Judge Sotomayor, writing for the panel, held that "a reference to the existence of license terms on a submerged screen is not sufficient to place consumers on inquiry or constructive notice of those terms." *Id.* at 32. By contrast, here the "Terms of Use" link appears either directly below the relevant button a user must click on to proceed in the checkout process or just a few inches away. On some pages, the content of the webpage is compact enough that a user can view the link without scrolling. On the remaining pages, the hyperlink is close enough to the "Proceed with Checkout" button that a user would have to bring the link within his field of vision in order to complete his order.

But the proximity or conspicuousness of the hyperlink alone is not enough to give rise to constructive notice, and Barnes & Noble directs us to no case law that supports this proposition.[1] The most analogous case the court was able to locate is *PDC Labs., Inc. v. Hach Co.*, an unpublished district court order cited by neither party. No. 09-1110, 2009 WL 2605270 (C.D.Ill. Aug. 25, 2009). There, the "Terms [and Conditions of Sale] were hyperlinked on three separate pages of the online ... order process in underlined, blue, contrasting text." *Id.* at *3. The court held that "[t]his contrasting text is sufficient to be considered conspicuous," thereby placing a reasonable user on notice that the terms applied. *Id.* It also observed, however, that the terms' conspicuousness was reinforced by the language of the final checkout screen, which read, " 'STEP 4 of 4: *Review terms*, add any comments, and submit order,' " and was followed by a hyperlink to the Terms. *Id.* (emphasis added).

As in *PDC*, the checkout screens here contained "Terms of Use" hyperlinks in underlined, color-contrasting text. But *PDC* is dissimilar in that the final screen on that website contained the phrase "Review terms." *PDC Labs.*, 2009 WL 2605270, at *3. This admonition makes *PDC* distinguishable, despite the court's explanation that the blue contrasting hyperlinks were sufficiently conspicuous on their own. That the *PDC* decision couched its holding in terms of procedural unconscionability rather than contract formation further distinguishes it from our case. *See id.*

In light of the lack of controlling authority on point, and in keeping with courts' traditional reluctance to enforce browsewrap agreements against individual consumers,[2]

---

1. Indeed, in cases where courts have relied on the proximity of the hyperlink to enforce a browsewrap agreement, the websites at issue have also included something more to capture the user's attention and secure her assent. *See, e.g.*, 5381 Partners LLC v. Sharesale.com, Inc., No. 12-CV-4263 JFB AKT, 2013 WL 5328324, at *7 (E.D.N.Y. Sept. 23, 2013) (in addition to hyperlink that appeared adjacent to the activation button users had to click on, website also contained a text warning near the button that stated "By clicking and making a request to Activate, you agree to the terms and conditions in the [agreement]"); Zaltz, 952 F.Supp.2d at 451–52 (users required to check box confirming that they had reviewed and agreed to website's Terms and Conditions, even though hyperlink to Terms and Conditions was located on the same screen as the button users had to click on to complete registration).

2. *See* Woodrow Hartzog, *Website Design as Contract*, 60 Am. U. L. Rev. 1635, 1644 (2011) (observing that courts "tend to shy away from enforcing browsewrap agreements that require no

we therefore hold that where a website makes its terms of use available via a conspicuous hyperlink on every page of the website but otherwise provides no notice to users nor prompts them to take any affirmative action to demonstrate assent, even close proximity of the hyperlink to relevant buttons users must click on — without more — is insufficient to give rise to constructive notice. While failure to read a contract before agreeing to its terms does not relieve a party of its obligations under the contract, *Gillman v. Chase Manhattan Bank, N.A.*, 73 N.Y.2d 1, 11, 537 N.Y.S.2d 787, 534 N.E.2d 824 (1988), the onus must be on website owners to put users on notice of the terms to which they wish to bind consumers. Given the breadth of the range of technological savvy of online purchasers, consumers cannot be expected to ferret out hyperlinks to terms and conditions to which they have no reason to suspect they will be bound.

Barnes & Noble's argument that Nguyen's familiarity with other websites governed by similar browsewrap terms, including his personal website <www. kevinkhoa.com>, gives rise to an inference of constructive notice is also of no moment. Whether Nguyen has experience with the browsewrap agreements found on other websites such as Facebook, LinkedIn, MySpace, or Twitter, has no bearing on whether he had constructive notice of Barnes & Noble's Terms of Use. There is nothing in the record to suggest that those browsewrap terms are enforceable by or against Nguyen, much less why they should give rise to constructive notice of Barnes & Noble's browsewrap terms.

C.

Barnes & Noble argues in the alternative that the district court erroneously rejected its argument that Nguyen should be equitably estopped from avoiding arbitration because he ratified the Terms of Use by relying on its choice of law provision in his complaint and asserting class claims under New York law. Reviewing the district court's decision for abuse of discretion, *Kingman Reef Atoll Invs., LLC v. United States*, 541 F.3d 1189, 1195 (9th Cir.2008), we reject Barnes & Noble's argument for two reasons.

First, the doctrine of direct benefits estoppel does not apply to the facts at hand. Federal courts have recognized that the obligation to arbitrate under the FAA does not attach only to one who has personally signed the arbitration provision. *Thomson-CSF, S.A. v. Am. Arbitration Ass'n*, 64 F.3d 773, 776 (2d Cir.1995). Instead, a non-signatory to an arbitration agreement may be compelled to arbitrate where the nonsignatory "knowingly exploits" the benefits of the agreement and receives benefits flowing directly from the agreement. *See MAG Portfolio Consultant, GMBH v. Merlin Biomed Grp. LLC*, 268 F.3d 58, 61 (2d Cir.2001); *see also Belzberg v. Verus Invs. Holdings Inc.*, 21 N.Y.3d 626, 977 N.Y.S.2d 685, 999 N.E.2d 1130, 1134 (.2013). But Nguyen is not the type of non-signatory contemplated by the rule. Equitable estoppel typically applies to third parties who benefit from an agreement made between two primary parties. *See, e.g., Wash. Mut. Fin. Grp., LLC v. Bailey*, 364 F.3d 260, 267–68 (5th Cir.2004) (estopping nonsignatory wife of borrower from avoiding arbitration clause of loan agreement made between her husband and lender); *Parillo v. Nataro*, 34 Misc.2d 800, 229 N.Y.S.2d 492, 493–94 (Sup.Ct.1962) (applying equitable estoppel to third-party beneficiary of insurance contract). Here, Nguyen is not a third-party beneficiary to Barnes & Noble's Terms of Use, and whether he is a primary party to the Terms of Use lies at the heart of this dispute.

Second, we are unable to find any case law holding that reliance on a contract's choice of law provision in itself constitutes a "direct benefit." The closest case is *HD Brous & Co.*,

---

outward manifestation of assent"); Lemley, 91 Minn. L. Rev. at 472–77 ("An examination of the cases that have considered browsewraps in the last five years demonstrates that the courts have been willing to enforce terms of use against corporations, but have not been willing to do so against individuals.").

Inc. v. Mrzyglocki, an unpublished district court decision, in which the court compelled arbitration against a nonsignatory petitioner in part because the non-signatory had sought to limit the respondent's choice of substantive law by relying on the agreement's choice of law provision. No. 03 Civ.8385(CSH), 2004 WL 376555, at *8 (S.D.N.Y. Feb. 26, 2004). But *HD Brous* is distinguishable because the agreement there served as the foundational document for the business relationship between the parties and explicitly named the petitioner as the intended beneficiary. *Id.* It can hardly be said here that the choice of New York law — chosen unilaterally by Barnes & Noble — was intended to benefit Nguyen. Any benefit derived by Nguyen under New York law — whether it be the possibility of statutory or treble damages on Nguyen's nationwide class claims — is merely incidental.

In light of these distinguishing facts, the district court did not abuse its considerable discretion in rejecting Barnes & Noble's estoppel argument.

We hold that Nguyen had insufficient notice of Barnes & Noble's Terms of Use, and thus did not enter into an agreement with Barnes & Noble to arbitrate his claims.

Karl Llewellyn, The Form or Boiler-Plate "Agreement"

(1960)

I know of few "private" law problems which remotely rival the importance, economic, governmental, or "law" — legal, of the form-pad agreement; and I know of none which has been either more disturbing to life or more baffling to lawyers.

The impetus to the form-pad is clear, for any business unit; by standardizing terms, and by standardizing even the spot on the form where any individually dickered term appears, one saves all the time and skill otherwise needed to dig out and record the meaning of variant language; one makes check-up, totaling, follow-through, etc., into routine operations; one has duplicates (in many colors) available for administration of multidepartment business; and so on more. The content of the standardized terms accumulates experience, it avoids or reduces legal risks and also confers all kinds of operating leeways and advantages, all without need of either consulting counsel from instance to instance or of bargaining with the other parties. Not to be overlooked, either, is the tailoring of the crude misfitting hand-me-down pattern of the "general law" "in the absence of agreement" to the particular detailed working needs of your own line of business — whether apartment rentals, stock brokerage, international grain trade, installment selling of appliances, flour milling, sugar beet raising, or insurance. It would be a heart-warming scene, a triumph of private attention to what is essentially private self-government in the lesser transactions of life or in those areas too specialized for the blunt, slow tools of the legislature — if only all businessmen and all their lawyers would be reasonable.

But power, like greed, if it does not always corrupt, goes easily to the head. So that the form-agreements tend either at once or over the years, and often by whole lines of trade, into a massive and almost terrifying jug-handled character; the one party lays his head into the mouth of a lion — either, and mostly, without reading the fine print, or occasionally in hope and expectation (not infrequently solid) that it will be a sweet and gentle lion. The more familiar instances, perhaps, are the United Realtors' Standard Lease, almost any bank's collateral note or agreement, almost any installment sale form, an accident insurance policy, a steamship ticket, a beet sugar refinery contract with a farmer or a flour miller's with its customer; or, on a lesser scale, the standard nonwarranty given by seed companies or auto manufacturers. In regard to such, one notes four things: (1)

sometimes language which seems at first sight horrifying may have good human and economic stimulus; thus, suits for loss of crop before a farmer jury are pretty terrible things to face for the price of a few bags of seed; and (2) there are crooked claims and there are irrationally unreasonable ones — each with its jury risk — as well as solid ones; and only a clause which in law bars the claim absolutely can free an outfit like an insurance company to deal fairly though "in its discretion" with the latter class. On the other hand, (3) boiler-plate clauses can and often do run far beyond any such need or excuse, sometimes (thus, as early as our *Lake v. Columbus Ins. Co.*, 13 Ohio 48 (1844), and distressingly today in, e.g., the cheap furniture business) involving flagrant trickery; and (4) not all "dominant" parties are nice lions, and even nice lions can make mistakes.

There is a fifth and no less vital thing to note: Where the form is drawn with a touch of Mr. Dooley's "gentlemanly restraint," or where, as with the overseas grain contracts or the Pacific Coast dried fruit contracts or the Worth Street Rules on textiles, two-fisted bargainers on either side have worked out in the form a balanced code to govern the particular line or trade or industry, there is every reason for a court to assume both fairness and wisdom in the terms, and to seek in first instance to learn, understand, and fit both its own thinking and its action into the whole design. Contracts of this kind (so long as reasonable in the net) are a road to better than official-legal regulation of our economic life; indeed, they tend to lead into the setting up of their own quick, cheap, expert tribunals.

. . .

Such is the background of a phenomenon which has been gaining in importance for more than a century, its well-done pieces tending, as stated, to slide off out of court or "legal" notice because of dispute avoidance, ready adjustment, or arbitration. For the work of official law that has been unfortunate. It has tended to keep out of the familiar law books, where they might stir imitation and imagination of other lawyers, the balanced type of boiler-plate. It has tended also to keep away from the appellate courts enough contact with the balanced type of form to let that type grow into a recognized pattern and a welcomed standard against which hog-drafting can be spotted, measured, and damned, so that the two different approaches and technique-lines of construction which are needed could be made articulate and reserved each to its appropriate sphere. Instead, the material which has come into court and into the American books has been in the main the jug-handled, mess-making stuff. What, then, of that?

For the courts, the story is quick to tell, though the cases must run into the thousands, and with no reckonability anywhere in sight. Unpredictably, they read the document for what it says, drop a word about freedom of contract, or about opportunity to read or improvident use of the pen, or about powerlessness of the court to do more than regret, or the like, and proceed to spit the victim for the barbecue. With equal unpredictability, they see the lopsided document as indecent, and evade it[.] ... Above all, the sound impulse for fairness — better, against outrage — fails to cumulate into any effective or standard techniques, except in a very few areas such as life and fire insurance....

. . .

The answer, I suggest, is this: Instead of thinking about "assent" to boiler-plate clauses, we can recognize that so far as concerns the specific, there is no assent at all. What has in fact been assented to, specifically, are the few dickered terms and the broad type of the transaction, and but one thing more. That one thing more is a blanket assent (not a specific assent) to any not unreasonable or indecent terms the seller may have on his form, which do not alter or eviscerate the reasonable meaning of the dickered terms. The fine print which has not been read has no business to cut under the reasonable meaning of those dickered terms which constitute the dominant and only real expression of agreement, but much of it commonly belongs in.

The queer thing is that where the transaction occurs without the fine print present, courts do not find this general line of approach too hard to understand: thus in the cases Prausnitz gathers, in regard to what kind of policy an oral contract for insurance contemplates; nor can I see a court having trouble, where a short memo agrees in due course to sign "our standard contract," in rejecting an outrageous form as not being fairly within the reasonable meaning of the term. The clearest case to see is the handing over of a blank check: no court, judging as between the parties, would fail to reach for the circumstances, in determining whether the amount filled in had gone beyond the reasonable.

Why, then, can we not face the fact where boiler-plate is present? There has been an arm's length deal, with dickered terms. There has been accompanying that basic deal another which, if not on any fiduciary basis, at least involves a plain expression of confidence, asked and accepted, with a corresponding limit on the powers granted: the boiler-plate is assented to en bloc, "unsight, unseen," on the implicit assumption and to the full extent that (1) it does not alter or impair the fair meaning of the dickered terms when read alone, and (2) that its terms are neither in the particular nor in the net manifestly unreasonable and unfair. Such is the reality, and I see nothing in the way of a court's operating on that basis, to truly effectuate the only intention which can in reason be worked out as common to the two parties, granted good faith. And if the boiler-plate party is not playing in good faith, there is law enough to bar that fact from benefiting it. We had a hundred years of sales law in which any sales transaction with explicit words resulted in two several contracts for the one consideration: that of sale, and the collateral one of warranty. The idea is applicable here, for better reason; any contract with boiler-plate results in *two* several contracts: the *dickered* deal, and the collateral one of *supplementary* boiler-plate.

Rooted in sense, history, and simplicity, it is an answer which could occur to anyone.

Nancy Kim, Wrap Contracts: Foundations and Ramifications (2013) Problems of Form

The form of a contract affects the way it is perceived by the consumer. It also affects the volume and nature of the legal terms capable of being compressed into the form.

. . .

The length of the contract signals the importance of a transaction to the customer. Even if consumers generally don't read their contracts, they may view with suspicion a thick contract handed to them to complete a simple transaction. Even if the customer is unable to negotiate, she will likely flip through the pages and skim the terms. An unusually hefty document for a minor transaction is likely to arouse the customer's suspicion....

With digital contracts, consumers typically are not able to assess at a glance whether the contract contains multiple pages or just a couple. Although they are unlikely to read contracts, consumers handed a multipage document may be more likely to scan the pages and catch an unsavory term. The terms of online contracts are not immediately visible. Because they typically require a click on a hyperlink or scrolling in order to read their terms, the likelihood of a chance encounter with an unusual or objectionable term is reduced.... the problems associated with wrap contracts—indeed, with any standard form contract—can be traced to the bastardized version of blanket assent. The notion of blanket assent is not outrageous in its original physical world context. Someone signing a form agreement has indicated by his or her signature that he or she has read and agreed to the terms. When Karl Llewellyn referred to assent in the context of standard form contracts, he understood that there was no specific assent to any particular provision. Rather, there was actual assent to the negotiated terms and the type of transaction and blanket assent to those terms that were not unreasonable or indecent. Llewellyn hadn't foreseen wrap contracts.

---

3. The Content of an Acceptance

The "Mirror-Image" Rule

To create a contract, the offeree has to agree to the terms proposed in the offer; that is what it means to "agree" or to "accept" an offer. This is the rationale for the "mirror image rule," which provides that an effective acceptance must express agreement to all of the terms in the offer and may not add any additional terms (i.e., the acceptance must be a "mirror image" of the offer). If the offeree does include any new or altered terms in her or his response, then courts will characterize the response as a "rejection" of the original offer (which normally terminates the offer) and a new offer (a "counter-offer") inviting acceptance by the original offeror. The mirror-image rule is meant to prevent formation of a contract that the offeror never offered to make.

Despite the clarity and apparent force of its logic, the mirror image rule has proved to be an awkward tool. The fact is that people rarely communicate in the "mirroring" fashion envisioned by the rule. Offerees often include language in their responses that does not appear in the offers to which they are responding or that corresponds to usual practices or terms. Strict application of the mirror image rule, then, would frustrate the purposes of offer and acceptance doctrine.

To avoid this result, courts have developed three "exceptions" in which a response does operate as an acceptance even though it appears to supplement or alter the words in the offer:

1. When the court concludes that the apparently "new" terms in the acceptance were implied terms of the offer and therefore do not alter the offer;

2. When the additional or altered terms were "immaterial" or "minor" when compared to the overall purpose of the contract; and

3. When the additional or altered terms could be characterized as mere "requests" for a modification or mere "grumbling" accompanying an acceptance.

The defendant in *Panhandle* argued that Smith's response on the contract document added a term to the offer and therefore was not an acceptance but a counteroffer. The court rejected this argument, reasoning that all employees at Panhandle had a right to examine their personnel files and that access to the file was an implied term of the offer; therefore Smith's response did not add a term but merely made explicit an implied term of the offer. Any remaining addition, the court then said, was mere "grumbling" on Smith's part and not a new term of the contract. Even with sophisticated analysis, however, the mirror image rule can have the effect of denying the existence of a contract even where the parties themselves believe and act as if there was a contract.

In the next section, we will see how the mirror image rule has been altered by Article 2 of the Uniform Commercial Code, applicable to contracts for the sale of goods and

Article 19 of the United Nations Convention for the International Sale of Goods. For all other contracts, however, the mirror image rule, with these three "exceptions," continues to be an important part of contract formation doctrine.

Article 2 of the Uniform Commercial Code: Contract Formation

Article 2 of the Uniform Commercial Code supplements or modifies some, but certainly not all, doctrines of the common law with respect to contracts for the sale of goods. As a practical matter, a contract for the sale of goods is subject to the general contract doctrine, except when Article 2 changes a particular rule of formulation. For example, Article 2 does not deal with when a communication should be characterized as an offer, so if one of the parties to an alleged sales contract claims that the parties did not create a contract, the court will begin its analysis by applying the same doctrines employed by the court in *Southworth v. Oliver, supra* to determine whether one of the communications could be characterized as an offer. For the next step, however, to determine whether the offer was accepted, the court must first decide whether the Article 2 applies and if so, the court must apply UCC §§ 2-204, 2-206, and 2-207 because these do alter the common law rules governing an acceptance.

Many people mistakenly believe that the UCC applies to only transactions involving merchants or commercial players, and they are surprised to learn that the UCC applies to transactions such as garage sales, Girl Scout cookie sales, and fast-food dining. So before we examine contract formation governed by UCC §§ 2-204, 2-206, and 2-207 in earnest, we need to look at how the courts decide which contracts are subject to Article 2. This issue is most difficult regarding contracts that involve both goods and services. The next case involves an issue of this sort.

―――――――――

Brenda Golden v. Den-Mat Corporation and Dr. Carissa M. Gill

Court of Appeals of Kansas
276 P.3d 773 (Kan. 2012)

G. Gordon Atcheson, J.

...

In late 2004, Brenda Golden wanted to replace the veneers on her teeth with new ones that would give her smile what she described as a "super white" appearance. Veneers are synthetic panels cemented to the front of a person's teeth, thereby covering discoloration or other imperfections in the natural dentition. Golden saw a magazine advertisement for Cerinate veneers, a proprietary product Den-Mat manufactures. In response to her telephone call to the number in the advertisement, Den-Mat sent Golden a brochure describing the Cerinate veneers as "thin porcelain shields ... bonded to the front of" the teeth "to create dramatic changes in your smile." The brochure touted "long-term clinical research" showing the Cerinate veneers would last up to 16 years "with no discoloration" and "100% retention." The brochure also explained that the porcelain veneers "are stronger and more durable" than comparable products made from plastic. According to the brochure, "[s]ometimes plastic composites stain and discolor with age, whereas, Cerinate Veneers maintain their beautiful luster and vitality." The brochure referred several times to the durability of the veneers and promoted the "strong, patented adhesive" used to attach them.

...

Golden decided to get the Cerinate veneers and contacted Den-Mat for a dentist in the Wichita area. Den-Mat supplied Golden with Dr. Gill's name and contact information as the nearest professional authorized to apply Cerinate veneers. Dr. Gill worked in Wellington, some 35 miles south of Golden's home.

Golden first met with Dr. Gill on November 8, 2004, and they discussed Golden's desire for "really white" teeth. Golden wanted the whitest veneers Den-Mat produced. Golden showed Dr. Gill the Den-Mat brochure and specifically asked about the durability of the veneers and the potential for discoloration.... Dr. Gill assured Golden that porcelain would not discolor. Dr. Gill recalled telling Golden that the whitest veneers might not be the best choice cosmetically because they could look artificial rather than natural. But Golden was adamant she wanted the whitest shade.

Dr. Gill removed the old veneers, took impressions of Golden's teeth, and ordered the new veneers from Den-Mat. On January 10, 2005, Dr. Gill attached the Cerinate veneers to Golden's upper teeth....

Golden later testified in her deposition that she felt the veneers seemed darker or less white as soon as they had been affixed to her teeth. Nonetheless, Golden returned to Dr. Gill 3 weeks later and had the remaining veneers applied to her lower teeth. By then, one of the upper veneers had come loose and another appeared to have a crack in it. Dr. Gill ordered replacement veneers and later applied them; she did not charge Golden for that work.

Golden paid $9,875.25 for the Cerinate veneers. The payment was made to Dr. Gill. The record on appeal is unclear as to whether Golden made a single payment or paid a portion of the cost as a deposit. The record does not indicate when Golden tendered any payments. Neither a bill nor an invoice has been included among the evidentiary materials.

Another veneer came off about 6 months later. Dr. Gill reapplied the veneer, again at no cost to Golden. In late March 2007, another veneer came off. Dr. Gill ordered a replacement veneer from Den-Mat. The replacement veneer was considerably whiter than the veneers Golden already had. On April 23, 2007, Dr. Gill spoke with a Den-Mat representative who said it was possible that Golden's veneers had become stained or had darkened over time. Dr. Gill recounted the conversation to Golden the same day.

Later on April 23, 2007, Golden wrote a letter to Dr. Gill expressing her dissatisfaction with the veneers and her belief they had developed "a gray cast" in the 15 months since they were placed on her teeth. Golden asked for Dr. Gill's help in obtaining a new set of veneers from Den-Mat at no cost. Dr. Gill's staff noted the letter in her office chart a week later. Den-Mat declined to replace Golden's veneers.

In the first part of 2008, Golden went to her regular dentist to have the Cerinate veneers removed from her upper teeth and replaced with a similar product from another manufacturer. The replacements cost about $4,500. In the summary judgment materials, Golden submitted a close-up photograph of her teeth after the upper veneers had been replaced. In the photograph, the lower teeth, with the Cerinate veneers, are noticeably duller than the replacement veneers and seem to have what could be stains.

On January 9, 2008, Golden filed a petition against the Den-Mat entities and Dr. Gill alleging breach of express warranties regarding the veneers and breach of implied warranties of merchantability and fitness for a particular purpose....

The district court granted summary judgment to the defendants on all of Golden's claims. In a short letter ruling issued on August 17, 2009, without citing supporting statutes or caselaw, the district court found that warranty claims [against] Dr. Gill, ...

[were claims for] professional negligence and, thus, governed by a 2-year statute of limitations that expired before Golden filed suit.

UCC Coverage

Dr. Gill contends there was "no transaction in goods" between her and Golden and, therefore, the UCC does not apply. Beneath that overstatement of the circumstances lurks an actual controversy that should be left for the jury. As we have said, Article 2 of the UCC regulates the sale of goods. The UCC defines goods expansively as meaning "all things (including specially manufactured goods) which are movable at the time of identification to the contract for sale," except for the money to be paid under the contract for the goods, investment securities, and legal rights to things or property. K.S.A. 84-2-105(1).

Goods — the Cerinate veneers — were plainly involved in and integral to the transaction involving Golden and Dr. Gill, as we have already indicated. Golden met with Dr. Gill, as Den-Mat's recommended dentist, and ordered the veneers through her. Dr. Gill received the veneers and then applied them to Golden's teeth. Golden paid Dr. Gill. But a sale does not come within the scope of the UCC merely because the contract *includes* the transfer of goods. Many contracts also entail services associated with the goods. The arrangement here was of that sort, and Dr. Gill provided services essential for Golden's use of the veneers. In UCC parlance, those transactions involving goods and services are commonly known as mixed or hybrid contracts.

The UCC does not address mixed contracts as such. So courts have created common-law rules to determine if those transactions should be treated as sales of goods covered under the UCC or service contracts outside the Code's regulation. Some 30 years ago, the Kansas Supreme Court adopted the "predominant purpose" test for classifying mixed contracts. *Care Display, Inc. v. Didde-Glaser, Inc.,* 589 P.2d 599 (Kan. 1979). The predominant purpose test has become the commonly accepted, if not the near universal, standard. *See* 1 *White & Summers, Uniform Commercial Code,* ch. 9, §9-2, p. 606 (5th ed. 2006). As the name suggests, the test attempts to discern the principal nature of the transaction: Is the buyer seeking services to which the goods are incidental, or is the buyer acquiring goods to which the services are auxiliary? *Care Display,* 589 P.2d at 605 ("'The test for inclusion or exclusion [of mixed contracts under the UCC] is ... whether their predominant factor, their thrust, their purpose, reasonably stated, is the rendition of service, with goods incidentally involved ... or is a transaction of sale, with labor incidentally involved.'" (*quoting Bonebrake v. Cox,* 499 F.2d 951, 960 (8th Cir. 1974).) ...

The predominant purpose test, however, is not especially predictive in the abstract. It looks at and depends upon the factual circumstances of the transaction being litigated. *Care Display,* 589 P.2d at 605 ("[E]ach case must be determined on an individual basis, and ... broad statements of principles are of little assistance in deciding a particular case."). Kansas ... courts have developed some general considerations in looking at mixed contracts [involving sales of computer software and related services].

In that context, the Kansas Supreme Court recognized that the UCC should be applied if the services would have been unnecessary without the purchase of the software. *Wachter Management,* 144 P.3d at 750–751. Reiterating the need to look at each contract individually under the predominant purpose test, this court held that the sale of a commercial off-the-shelf software program was covered under the UCC, even though the seller also provided installation and training services as part of the contract. *Systems Design,* 788 P.2d at 882–883....

Courts have split over whether the predominant purpose of a mixed contract presents an issue of law for the court or a question of fact for the jury. *See Higgins v. Lauritzen,*

530 N.W.2d 171 (Mich. Ct. App. 1995) (question of fact); *Valley Farmers' Elevator v. Lindsay Bros.*, 398 N.W.2d 553, 556 (Minn. 1987) (generally question of law), *overruled on other grounds Hapka v. Paquin Farms*, 458 N.W.2d 683, (Minn. 1990); *MBH, Inc. v. John Otte Oil & Propane*, 727 N.W.2d 238 (Neb. 2007) ("whether goods or nongoods predominate a contract is generally a question of law"); *Quality Roofing v. Hoffmann-La Roche*, A.2d 1077 (N.J. 1997) (question of fact). The Kansas appellate courts apparently have not directly addressed the point.

… Given the case-specific inquiry and the factually driven nature of the determination, essentially considering all of the circumstances bearing on the transaction, we conclude the issue of predominance of goods or services in a mixed contract is fundamentally one of fact. As such, it typically should be left for the trier of fact rather than resolved on summary judgment.

But, of course, a court may decide an issue of fact if the material circumstances are undisputed in a given case. Absent a factual dispute, the question presented effectively becomes one of law. *See, e.g., St. Clair v. Denny*, 781 P.2d 1043 (Kan. 1989); *Lay v. Kansas Dept. of Transportation*, 928 P.2d 920 (Kan. Ct. App. 1996), *rev. denied* 261 Kan. 1085 (1997). By the same token, even if the predominate purpose of a mixed contract were a question of law, any conflicts in the material historical facts would have to be resolved at trial with the jury providing answers to special interrogatories to inform the court's legal determination.…

Having concluded the predominant purpose of a mixed contract to be a question of fact, we turn to whether the transaction here, nonetheless, must be considered one principally for services rather than goods based on the summary judgment record. If so, the UCC would be inapplicable, as Dr. Gill argues.

Unlike most medical or dental procedures, Golden's acquisition of the veneers was purely for cosmetic purposes. She was not seeking treatment for some illness or injury. The transaction was materially different from, for example, a dentist filling a cavity. In that instance, the patient or buyer has a malady, perhaps a painful one, and seeks a cure from the dentist. The dentist may drill and fill the cavity, though there might be other treatment options, such as installing a crown or pulling the offending tooth. The patient has received services in the form of a diagnosis, a recommended course of care, and actual treatment. The patient has also received whatever material the dentist used to fill the cavity. The filling itself would likely be a form of goods under the UCC, and the contract between the patient and dentist would be a mixed one. But the services would plainly seem to predominate. The patient wanted treatment for the cavity and principally sought diagnostic and therapeutic services from the dentist to accomplish that purpose. The patient had no particular interest in what the dentist used to fill the cavity and likely left the decision to the dentist's professional judgment. We think that would be true of the vast majority of transactions between a patient and a healthcare provider for treatment of illness or injury in which there were a single contract.

Golden, however, suffered from no malady and sought no professional diagnosis or treatment. She simply wanted whiter teeth and sought replacements for the veneers she had been wearing. Golden had received information from Den-Mat containing representations about the characteristics of its Cerinate veneers making them appear to be a satisfactory choice. Although disputed in the record, there is evidence Golden shared that information with Dr. Gill and received some assurance from her as to the accuracy of a critical characteristic—the veneers, being made of porcelain, would not stain or dull over time. Golden then purchased Den-Mat's Cerinate veneers through Dr. Gill, who applied them to Golden's teeth.

Viewing the record favorably to Golden, as we must in considering her opposition to summary judgment, she did not go to Dr. Gill with a problem — dull or aesthetically un-appealing teeth — for which she wanted a professional consultation about various corrective options. Golden wanted Cerinate veneers and understood from Den-Mat that Dr. Gill could provide and apply that product. To be sure, Dr. Gill also provided services in that she removed the existing veneers, sized and ordered the Cerinate veneers, and applied the new veneers to Golden's teeth. But a jury could fairly conclude Golden wanted the veneers, while the services were simply part of the means of accomplishing that purpose. That would be consistent with the notion that but for the buyer's acquisition of the goods, the services would have been unnecessary, making the contract predominately one for the goods, as the Kansas Supreme Court has suggested. *Wachter Management*, 144 P.3d at 750–751.

The predominance of the veneers as goods also seems plausible and, thus, within a jury's reasonable consideration when the transaction is compared with orthodontics, another form of dentistry often used for largely cosmetic purposes. To straighten the patient's teeth, the orthodontist applies braces and other devices, often over an extended time period. The goods, those devices, are an integral part of the process. But the orthodontist makes a professional judgment about the types of braces to achieve the ultimate purpose of realigning the patient's teeth. Again, the contract is a mixed one for goods and services. But the patient's purpose is not the acquisition of braces but of straight teeth. The braces are temporary appliances, used by the orthodontist, for achieving that end. In those circumstances, the orthodontist's services would seem to predominate over the goods.

The same degree of professional skill and judgment is lacking here in that Golden essentially selected the goods independently, though she sought affirmation of that selection from both Dr. Gill and representatives of Den-Mat regarding particular characteristics of the goods. And, unlike braces, the veneers themselves, once applied, provided the desired cosmetic result. The result continued only so long as the veneers remained in place and performed as Golden understood they would.

Finally, nothing in the record evidence shows Dr. Gill contracted separately with Golden for professional services apart from the purchase of the veneers. The parties do not argue there were separate or distinct contracts for the veneers, on the one hand, and Dr. Gill's services, on the other. The transaction was unitary, combining goods and services. Likewise, there is no evidence Golden was charged separately for the veneers and for Dr. Gill's services or that the services were even broken out as a distinct component or cost in the contract or in any billing. *See* 1 *White & Summers, Uniform Commercial Code*, ch. 9, §9-2, p. 606 (relative costs of goods and services and undifferentiated or itemized billing of them frequently considered in assessing predominant purpose of mixed contract); *Van Sistine v. Tollard*, 291 N.W.2d 636 (Wis. 1980) (contract primarily for services where property owner supplied some of the siding to be installed on home and installer's labor costs exceeded cost of siding and other materials installer provided).

. . .

In short, the record evidence fails to support a finding as a matter of law for Dr. Gill that the transaction with Golden was one in which acquisition and use of services pre-dominated over the purchase of goods so that the UCC would not apply. Summary judgment could not be granted to Dr. Gill on the UCC claims on that basis....

Uniform Commercial Code § 2-207

Section 2-207 ("Additional Terms in Acceptance or Confirmation") of the Uniform Commercial Code modifies (or refines) the mirror image rule for contracts for the sale of goods. Professor John Murray explains the "simple purpose" of this section:

> Without a doubt, 2-207 is based on the assumption that merchants do not read or understand the printed terms of their exchanged forms. 39 Vand. L. Rev. 1307, 1385 (1986).... The common law "mirror-image" rule requires the acceptance to match the terms of the offer. Where a response to an offer contains different or additional terms in boilerplate clauses, the mirror-image rule insists that the response must be a "conditional acceptance," i.e., a counteroffer, even though it reasonably appears to be a definite expression of acceptance. In the paradigm transaction, a buyer sends a purchase order (offer) and the seller's response is an acknowledgment form that appears to be an acceptance but contains variant terms in the boilerplate clauses such as a disclaimer of warranty, an arbitration clause, or an exclusion of consequential damages. Since the seller's response is a counteroffer, there is no contract [under the mirror-image rule] via the exchange of forms. The seller, however, ships the goods, which the buyer accepts, thereby unwittingly accepting the seller's terms in the counteroffer that had been fired as the "last shot" in the battle. Though the buyer is unfairly surprised to learn that the contract contains the seller's terms, this is the result ordained under the "last shot" principle. Section 2-207 was designed to remedy this injustice.

John E. Murray, Jr., *The Definitive "Battle of the Forms": Chaos Revisited*, 20 J.L. Com 1, 2–3 (2000).

Subsection 2-207(1) achieves this result:

> A definite and seasonable expression of acceptance or a written confirmation which is sent within a reasonable time operates as an acceptance even though it states terms additional to or different from those offered or agreed upon, unless acceptance is expressly made conditional on assent to any different or additional terms.

The next two cases, *Defontes & Long v. Dell* and *Step-Saver Data Systems v. Wyse Technologies*, deal with the difficult problem of "box-top," "shrink-wrap," and other terms that are sent to a buyer on the box or packed with the goods themselves. Should these terms be binding on the buyer? Does U.C.C. section 2-207 apply to this situation? If so, how should it apply? If not, what other line of analysis is appropriate? These are pressing questions, especially affecting all purchasers of expensive computer hardware or software.

Mary E. DeFontes and Nicholas T. Long, individually and on behalf of a class of persons similarly situated v. Dell, Inc., et al.

Supreme Court of Rhode Island

984 A.2d 1061 (2009)

Frank J. Williams, Chief Judge (Ret.)

. . .

I

Facts and Travel

This litigation began on May 16, 2003, when Mary E. DeFontes, individually and on behalf of a class of similarly situated persons, brought suit against Dell, alleging that its collection of taxes from them on the purchase of Dell optional service contracts violated the Deceptive Trade Practices Act, G.L. 1956 chapter 13.1 of title 6. Ms. DeFontes asserted that service contracts, such as the option service contract offered by Dell, were not taxable within the State of Rhode Island. Nicholas Long joined the suit as a plaintiff, and an amended complaint was filed on July 16, 2003, that also added Dell subsidiaries Dell Catalog and Dell Marketing, and two service providers, QualxServ and BancTec as defendants.[1]

Dell is an international computer hardware and software corporation. Within the Dell corporate umbrella, Dell Catalog and Dell Marketing primarily are responsible for selling computers via the internet, mail-order catalogs, and other means to individual and business consumers. Dell ships these orders throughout all fifty states from warehouses located in Texas and Tennessee. As part of these purchases, Dell offers consumers an optional service contract for on-site repair of its products, with Dell often acting as an agent for third-party service providers, including BancTec and QualxServ. Parties opting to purchase a service contract are charged a "tax," which is either paid to the State of Rhode Island directly or collected by the third-party service provider and then remitted to the state.

The two initial plaintiffs, Ms. DeFontes and Mr. Long, engaged in slightly different transactions. Ms. DeFontes purchased her computer through Dell Catalog and selected a service contract with BancTec. She paid a total of $950.51, of which $13.51 was characterized as tax on the service contract. Mr. Long purchased his computer through Dell Marketing and opted for a service contract managed by Dell. In total, he paid $3,037.73, out of which $198.73 was designated as tax paid on the service contract. There is no allegation that Dell improperly retained any of the collected tax. Several months after plaintiffs filed their amended complaint, defendants filed a motion to stay proceedings and compel arbitration, citing an arbitration provision within the parties' purported agreements.[2] The defendants argued that the arbitration provision was part of a "Terms and Conditions Agreement," which they contended plaintiffs had accepted by accepting delivery of the goods. Specifically, they averred that plaintiffs had three separate opportunities to review the terms and conditions agreement, to wit, by selecting a hyperlink on the Dell website, by reading the terms that were included in the acknowledgment/ invoice that was sent to plaintiffs sometime after they placed their orders, or by reviewing the copy of the terms Dell included in the packaging of its computer products.

---

1. The plaintiffs also added a common-law negligence claim to their amended complaint.

2. The arbitration clause in Ms. DeFontes' "Terms and Conditions Agreement," quoted by the hearing justice in his decision, provided,

"ANY CLAIM, DISPUTE, OR CONTROVERSY (WHETHER IN CONTRACT, TORT, OR OTHERWISE, WHETHER PREEXISTING, PRESENT OR FUTURE, AND INCLUDING STATUTORY, COMMON LAW, INTENTIONAL TORT AND EQUITABLE CLAIMS) AGAINST DELL, its agents, employees, successors, assigns or affiliates ... arising from or relating to this Agreement, its interpretation, or the breach, termination or validity thereof, the relationships which result from this Agreement (including, to the full extent permitted by applicable law, relationships with third parties who are not signatories to this Agreement), Dell's advertising, or any related purchase SHALL BE RESOLVED EXCLUSIVELY AND FINALLY BY BINDING ARBITRATION ADMINISTERED BY THE NATIONAL ARBITRATION FORUM (NAF) under its Code of Procedure then in effect .... The arbitration ... will be limited solely to the dispute or controversy between Customer and Dell .... Any award of the arbitrator(s) shall be final and binding on each of the parties, and may be entered as a judgment in any court of competent jurisdiction."

The arbitration provision in the terms and conditions agreement sent to Mr. Long contained substantially similar language.

The hearing justice issued a written decision on January 29, 2004. He first addressed which state law to apply to the parties' dispute. After determining that the choice-of-law provision included in the terms and conditions agreement, which identified Texas as the controlling jurisdiction, was enforceable, he then analyzed whether the parties had, in fact, agreed to be bound by the terms and conditions agreement. The hearing justice found that although plaintiffs had three opportunities to review the terms, none was sufficient to give rise to a contractual obligation. First, he noted that plaintiffs could have reviewed the terms and conditions agreement had they clicked a hyperlink that appeared on Dell's website. The hearing justice found, however, that this link was "inconspicuously located at the bottom of the webpage" and insufficient to place customers on notice of the terms and conditions.[3] Nevertheless, the hearing justice noted that the terms and conditions agreement also appeared both in the acknowledgment that Dell sent to plaintiffs when they placed their orders and later within the packaging when the computers were delivered.[4]

The hearing justice noted that "courts generally recognize that shrinkwrap agreements,[5] paper agreements enclosed within the packaging of an item, are sufficient to put consumers on inquiry notice of the terms and conditions of a transaction." He also observed, however, that shrinkwrap agreements generally contain an express disclaimer that explains to consumers that they can reject the proposed terms and conditions by returning the product. The crucial test, according to the hearing justice, was "whether a reasonable person would have known that return of the product would serve as rejection of those terms." He looked to the introductory language of the terms and conditions agreement, which he quoted as follows,[6]

> "PLEASE READ THIS DOCUMENT CAREFULLY! IT CONTAINS VERY IMPORTANT INFORMATION ABOUT YOUR RIGHTS AND OBLIGATIONS, AS WELL AS LIMITATIONS AND EXCLUSIONS THAT MAY APPLY TO YOU. THIS DOCUMENT CONTAINS A DISPUTE RESOLUTION CLAUSE.
>
> "This Agreement contains the terms and conditions that apply to purchases by Home, Home Office, and Small Business customers from the Dell entity

---

3. We also note that Mr. Long appears to have purchased his computer over the telephone and it is unclear from the record whether he viewed the Dell website in relation to his purchase.

4. In his analysis of whether plaintiffs had accepted the terms and conditions agreement, the hearing justice did not distinguish the acknowledgment/invoice that plaintiffs received from the nearly identical documents contained in the computer packaging. We note that although defendants provided the hearing justice with evidence of the date plaintiffs received their respective acknowledgments, they did not provide the date of Dell's shipment of the computer systems. On appeal, defendants assert simply that "many customers receive the invoice or acknowledgment before the computer system is shipped ...." As we may review on appeal only the evidence presented to the hearing justice, we express no opinion regarding the significance, if any, of evidence showing that plaintiffs had received the terms and conditions agreement before shipment of the computer systems. *See* Carroll v. Yeaw, 850 A.2d 90, 92 (R.I. 2004) (record for review in this Court must be made in the trial court). *See generally* 1 White & Summers, Uniform Commercial Code §§ 1-4 (5th ed. 2006) (discussing whether terms contained in an invoice can be differentiated from terms found on or inside the packaging).

5. A "shrinkwrap agreement" refers to the common commercial practice of including additional terms and conditions either on the outside of a package or within it when it is shipped to the consumer. Often these packages are covered in plastic or cellophane which must be breached to open.

6. The hearing justice appears to have conflated the slightly different language of the terms and conditions agreements sent to Mr. Long and Ms. DeFontes. Although similar, some differences do exist. Significantly, the documents sent to Ms. DeFontes contained an express disclaimer advising her that "[i]f for any reason Customer is not satisfied with a Dell-branded hardware system, Customer may return the system under the terms and conditions of Dell's Total Satisfaction Return Policy ...."

named on the invoice ('Dell'). By accepting delivery of the computer systems, related products, and/or services and support, and/or other products described on that invoice. [sic] You ('Customer') agrees [sic] to be bound by and accepts [sic] these terms and conditions ... These terms and conditions are subject to change without prior written notice at any time, in Dell's sole discretion."

The hearing justice found that this language was insufficient to give a reasonable consumer notice of the method of rejection. He found that defendants' failure to include an express disclaimer meant that they could not prove that plaintiffs "knowingly consent[ed]" to the terms and conditions of the agreement. Accordingly, the hearing justice found that Plaintiffs could not be compelled to enter arbitration.

Although the hearing justice noted that it was unnecessary to address plaintiffs' alternative arguments that the contract was both illusory and unconscionable, he discussed them in his decision "for the sake of completeness." First, he rejected plaintiffs' argument that the agreement was unconscionable because it prevented them from asserting rights as a class. He found that there was no right under Texas law to proceed as a class action litigant. *See Autonation U.S.A. Corp. v. Leroy*, 105 S.W.3d 190, 199–200 (Tex. App. 2003).

Second, the hearing justice addressed whether the agreement was illusory. He found that the arbitration agreement was not illusory merely because it required plaintiffs to submit to arbitration while allowing defendants to litigate any of its claims in court....

II

Discussion

We review the trial court's denial of a motion to compel arbitration *de novo. See Kristian v. Comcast Corp.*, 446 F.3d 25, 31 (1st Cir. 2006). The parties acknowledge that because their transactions involved interstate commerce, the Federal Arbitration Act (FAA) is applicable. *See* 9 U.S.C. §§ 1 through 16. Congress enacted the FAA to "overrule the judiciary's longstanding refusal to enforce agreements to arbitrate." *Dean Witter Reynolds Inc. v. Byrd*, 470 U.S. 213, 219–20, 105 S. Ct. 1238, 84 L. Ed. 2d 158 (1985). It requires enforcement of privately negotiated arbitration agreements "save upon such grounds as exist at law or in equity for the revocation of any contract." 9 U.S.C. § 2. Thus, once a court is "satisfied that the making of the agreement for arbitration or the failure to comply therewith is not an issue" it "shall make an order directing the parties to proceed to arbitration in accordance with the terms of the agreement." 9 U.S.C. § 4.

Yet, the United States Supreme Court has been equally insistent that "arbitration is a matter of contract and a party cannot be required to submit to arbitration any dispute which he has not agreed so to submit." *Howsam v. Dean Witter Reynolds, Inc.*, 537 U.S. 79, 83, 123 S. Ct. 588, 154 L. Ed. 2d 491 (2002) (quoting *United Steelworkers of America v. Warrior & Gulf Navigation Co.*, 363 U.S. 574, 582, 80 S. Ct. 1347, 4 L. Ed. 2d 1409 (1960)); *see also Mirra Co. v. School Administrative District No. 35*, 251 F.3d 301, 304 (1st Cir. 2001) ("Arbitration is a contractual matter, and no party may be forced to arbitrate a dispute unless she has expressly agreed to do so by contract."). The determination of whether the parties have formed an agreement to arbitrate is a matter of state contract law. *See* 9 U.S.C. § 2; *First Options of Chicago, Inc. v. Kaplan*, 514 U.S. 938, 944, 115 S. Ct. 1920, 131 L. Ed. 2d 985 (1995). Moreover, a hearing justice's determination of "[w]hether a party has agreed to be bound by arbitration is a question of law subject to this Court's de novo review." *Stanley-Bostitch, Inc. v. Regenerative Environmental Equipment Co.*, 697 A.2d 323, 325 (R.I. 1997) (citing *Providence Teachers' Union v. Providence School Committee*, 433 A.2d 202, 205 (R.I. 1981)).

...

We therefore evaluate whether plaintiffs are bound by the terms and conditions agreement by resorting to a careful review of the provisions of the U.C.C. Under U.C.C. § 2-204, contracts for the sale of goods may be formed "in any manner sufficient to show agreement, including conduct by both parties which recognizes the existence of such a contract." Tex. Bus. & Com. Code Ann. § 2.204 (Vernon 1994). The U.C.C. creates the assumption that, unless circumstances unambiguously demonstrate otherwise, the buyer is the offeror and the seller is the offeree. *See Klocek v. Gateway, Inc.*, 104 F. Supp. 2d 1332, 1340 (D. Kan. 2000). Moreover, U.C.C. § 2-206 provides in relevant part,

> "(a) Unless otherwise unambiguously indicated by the language or circumstances,

> "(1) an offer to make a contract shall be construed as inviting acceptance in any manner and by any medium reasonable in the circumstances;

> "(2) an order or other offer to buy goods for prompt or current shipment shall be construed as inviting acceptance either by a prompt promise to ship or by the prompt or current shipment of conforming or nonconforming goods ...." Tex. Bus. & Com. Code Ann. § 2.206 (Vernon 1994)."

If contract formation occurred at the moment Dell's sales agents processed the customer's credit card payment and agreed to ship the goods, as plaintiffs argue, then any additional terms would necessarily be treated as "[a]dditional [t]erms in [a]cceptance or [c]onfirmation" under U.C.C. § 2-207[10] or offers to modify the existing contract under U.C.C. § 2-209. Yet, the modern trend seems to favor placing the power of acceptance in the hands of the buyer after he or she receives goods containing a standard form statement of additional terms and conditions, provided the buyer retains the power to "accept or return" the product.

The eminent Judge Frank Easterbrook has authored what are widely considered to be the two leading cases on so-called "shrinkwrap" agreements. In *ProCD, Inc. v. Zeidenberg*, 86 F.3d 1447, 1452–53 (7th Cir. 1996), the court challenged the traditional understanding of offer and acceptance in consumer transactions by holding that a buyer of software was bound by an agreement that was included within the packaging and later appeared when the buyer first used the software. 11 *Id.* The court first held that U.C.C. § 2-207 was inapplicable because in cases involving only one form, the "battle-of-the-forms" provision was irrelevant. *ProCD, Inc.*, 86 F.3d at 1452. It then proceeded to evaluate the agreement under U.C.C. § 2-204 and reasoned that "[a] vendor, as master of the offer, may invite acceptance by conduct, and may propose limitations on the kind of conduct that constitutes acceptance. A buyer may accept by performing the acts the vendor proposes to treat as

---

10. Tex. Bus. & Com. Code Ann. § 2.207 (Vernon 1994) provides:
   "(a) A definite and seasonable expression of acceptance or a written confirmation which is sent within a reasonable time operates as an acceptance even though it states terms additional to or different from those offered or agreed upon, unless acceptance is expressly made conditional on assent to the additional or different terms.
   "(b) The additional terms are to be construed as proposals for addition to the contract. Between merchants such terms become part of the contract unless:
   "(1) the offer expressly limits acceptance to the terms of the offer;
   "(2) they materially alter it; or
   "(3) notification of objection to them has already been given or is given within a reasonable time after notice of them is received.
   "(c) Conduct by both parties which recognizes the existence of a contract is sufficient to establish a contract for sale although the writings of the parties do not otherwise establish a contract. In such case the terms of the particular contract consist of those terms on which the writings of the parties agree, together with any supplementary terms incorporated under any other provisions of this title."

acceptance." ProCD, Inc., 86 F.3d at 1452. In *Hill v. Gateway 2000, Inc.*, 105 F.3d 1147, 1148–49 (7th Cir. 1997), the court expanded its earlier holding in *ProCD* beyond transactions involving software where the consumer is prompted to accept or decline the terms when he first uses the program. It determined that when a merchant delivers a product that includes additional terms and conditions, but expressly provides the consumer the right to either accept those terms or return the product for a refund within a reasonable time, a consumer who retains the goods beyond that period may be bound by the contract. *Id.* Judge Easterbrook explained,

> "Practical considerations support allowing vendors to enclose the full legal terms with their products. Cashiers cannot be expected to read legal documents to customers before ringing up sales. If the staff at the other end of the phone for direct-sales operations such as Gateway's had to read the four-page statement of terms before taking the buyer's credit card number, the droning voice would anesthetize rather than enlighten many potential buyers. Others would hang up in a rage over the waste of their time. And oral recitation would not avoid customers' assertions (whether true or feigned) that the clerk did not read term X to them, or that they did not remember or understand it." *Id. at 1149.*

The defendants argue that *ProCD* represents the majority view and we have found considerable support for their contention. *See, e.g., O'Quin v. Verizon Wireless,* 256 F. Supp. 2d 512, 515–16 (M.D. La. 2003) ("Terms and Conditions Pamphlet" binding where acceptance expressed by activation and use of wireless services as long as "opportunity to return"); *Bischoff v. DirecTV, Inc.,* 180 F. Supp. 2d 1097, 1101 (C.D. Cal. 2002) ("Customer Agreement" mailed to each customer along with the first billing statement valid when clearly advised "[i]f you do not accept these terms, please notify us immediately and we will cancel your service"); *Brower v. Gateway 2000, Inc.,* 246 A.D.2d 246, 676 N.Y.S.2d 569, 572 (N.Y. App. Div. 1998) (arbitration clause of standard terms and conditions agreement valid where consumer informed that by keeping product beyond thirty days after delivery he was accepting terms); *M.A. Mortenson Co., v. Timberline Software Corp.,* 140 Wn.2d 568, 998 P.2d 305, 308 (Wash. 2000) (adopting *ProCD* analysis but noting shrinkwrap agreement explicitly instructed consumers "IF YOU DO NOT AGREE TO THESE TERMS AND CONDITIONS, PROMPTLY RETURN ... TO THE PLACE OF PURCHASE AND YOUR PURCHASE PRICE WILL BE REFUNDED"). Moreover, as plaintiffs' counsel has initiated nationwide litigation, a number of sister jurisdictions have decided more or less the precise issue put before us in defendants' favor. For instance, in *Stenzel v. Dell, Inc.,* 2005 ME 37, 870 A.2d 133 (Me. 2005), the Maine Supreme Judicial Court reviewed a similar terms and conditions agreement sent to Dell customers that included the language,

> "By accepting delivery of the computer systems, related products, and/or services and support, and/or other products described on that invoice [, the customer] agrees to be bound by and accepts these terms and conditions. If for any reason Customer is not satisfied with a Dell-branded hardware system, Customer may return the system under the terms and conditions of Dell's Total Satisfaction Return Policy ...." *Id. at 140.*

The court held that by "accepting delivery of the computers, and then failing to exercise their right to return the computers as provided by the agreement, [the plaintiffs] expressly manifested their assent to be bound by the agreement ...." *Id.; see also Carideo v. Dell, Inc.,* 520 F. Supp. 2d 1241, 1244 (W.D. Wash. 2007); *Omstead v. Dell, Inc.,* 473 F. Supp. 2d 1018, 1025–26 (N.D. Cal. 2007); *Adams v. Dell Computer Corp.,* No. CIV AC-06-089, 2006 U.S. Dist. LEXIS 66774, 2006 WL 2670969 (S.D. Tex. Sept. 18, 2006); *Sherr v. Dell,*

Inc., No. 05 CV 10097(GBD) 2006 U.S. Dist. LEXIS 51864, 2006 WL 2109436, *3 (S.D.N.Y. July 27, 2006) ("customer need only return the product according to the return policy in order to reject the Agreement"); *Falbe v. Dell, Inc.*, No. 04-C-1425, 2004 U.S. Dist. LEXIS 13188, 2004 WL 1588243, *3 (N.D. Ill. 2004) ("Our analysis begins, and could end, with … *Hill v. Gateway 2000, Inc.*").

Courts have not been universal in embracing the reasoning of *ProCD* and its progeny, however. In *Step-Saver Data Systems, Inc. v. Wyse Technology,* 939 F.2d 91, 98 (3d Cir. 1991), the court determined that when parties exchange the shipment of goods for re-muneration the existence of a contract is not in doubt; rather, any dispute relates solely to the nature of its terms. After deciding that U.C.C. § 2-207 applies to situations in which a party sends a confirmatory document that claims to establish additional terms of the contract, the court held that U.C.C. § 2-207 "establishes a legal rule that proceeding with a contract after receiving a writing that purports to define the terms of the parties's contract is not sufficient to establish the party's consent to the terms of the writing to the extent that the terms of the writing either add to, or differ from, the terms detailed in the parties's earlier writings or discussions." *Id.* at 99.[12] The court therefore held that a licensing agreement affixed to the packaging constituted a proposal for additional terms that was not binding unless expressly agreed to by the purchaser. *Id.* at 100; *see also Klocek,* 104 F. Supp. 2d at 1339, 1341 (finding buyer's "act of keeping the computer past five days was not sufficient to demonstrate that plaintiff expressly agreed to the Standard Terms" and criticizing the *Hill* court's summary dismissal of U.C.C. § 2-207 by stating "nothing in its language precludes application in a case which involves only one form"); *Licitra v. Gateway, Inc.,* 189 Misc. 2d 721, 734 N.Y.S.2d 389, 396 (N.Y. Civ. Ct. 2001) (construing arbitration clause of a shrinkwrap agreement as a proposal for additional terms under U.C.C. § 2-207 because it materially altered the existing agreement).

The Supreme Court of Oklahoma, which has also been drawn into this nationwide class-action suit against defendants, has rejected *Hill*'s reasoning as well. *See Rogers,* 138 P.3d at 833. Although remanding the case to determine whether the arbitration provision was included in the parties' agreement, it noted,

> "The plaintiffs' accepting the computers and not returning them is consistent with a contract being formed at the time that the orders were placed and cannot be construed as acquiescing in the 'Terms and Conditions of Sale' document whether included with the invoice or acknowledgment or with the computer packaging. If the contracts were formed at the time the orders were placed, *see* U.C.C. § 2-206(1), the 'Terms and Conditions of Sale' document, including the arbitration provision, would be an additional term of the contracts under section 2-207. The arbitration provision would not be part of the contracts but proposals to add it as a term to the contracts." *Rogers,* 138 P.3d at 833 (citing U.C.C. § 2-207).[13]

---

12. The official comment to U.C.C. § 2-207 indicates that the provision applies "where an agreement has been reached orally or by informal correspondence between the parties and is followed by one or both of the parties sending formal memoranda embodying the terms so far agreed upon and adding terms not discussed." U.C.C. § 2-207 Official Comment 1 (2001).

13. It appears that the drafters of the Uniform Commercial Code were themselves flummoxed by this issue. Amended U.C.C. § 2-207, which, although not adopted, could provide some insight into any evolving consensus among commercial law scholars and practitioners, states in Official Comment 5,

> "The section omits any specific treatment of terms attached to the goods, or in or on the container in which the goods are delivered. This article takes no position on whether a court should follow the reasoning in Step-Saver Data Systems, Inc. v. Wyse Technology, 939 F.2d 91 (3d Cir. 1991) and Klocek v. Gateway, Inc., 104 F. Supp. 2d 1332 (D. Kan. 2000) (original

After reviewing the case law pertaining to so-called "shrinkwrap" agreements, we are satisfied that the *ProCD* line of cases is better reasoned and more consistent with contemporary consumer transactions. It is simply unreasonable to expect a seller to apprise a consumer of every term and condition at the moment he or she makes a purchase. A modern consumer neither expects nor desires to wade through such minutia, particularly when making a purchase over the phone, where full disclosure of the terms would border on the sadistic. Nor do we believe that, after placing a telephone order for a computer, a reasonable consumer would believe that he or she has entered into a fully consummated agreement. *See Axelson, Inc. v. McEvoy-Willis, a Division of Smith International (North Sea), Ltd.,* 7 F.3d 1230, 1232–33 (5th Cir. 1993) ("An offer is an act that leads the offeree reasonably to believe that assent (i.e., acceptance) will conclude the deal."). Rather, he or she is aware that with delivery comes a multitude of standard terms attendant to nearly every consumer transaction.

We therefore decline to adopt the minority view, as urged by plaintiffs, that a contract is fully formed when a buyer orders a product and the seller accepts payment and either ships or promises to ship. Instead, formation occurs when the consumer accepts the full terms after receiving a reasonable opportunity to refuse them. Yet in adopting the so-called "layered contracting"[14] theory of formation, we reiterate that the burden falls squarely on the seller to show that the buyer has accepted the seller's terms after delivery. Thus, the crucial question in this case is whether defendants reasonably invited acceptance by making clear in the terms and conditions agreement that (1) by accepting defendants' product the consumer was accepting the terms and conditions contained within and (2) the consumer could reject the terms and conditions by returning the product.

On the first question, defendants notified plaintiffs that "[b]y accepting delivery of the computer systems, related products, and/or services and support, and/or other products described on that invoice[,] You ('Customer') agrees to be bound by and accepts those terms and conditions." This language certainly informed plaintiffs that defendants intended to bind them to heretofore undisclosed terms and conditions, but it did not advise them of the period beyond which they will have indicated their assent to those terms. The defendants argue that the meaning of the term "accepting delivery" is apparent to a reasonable consumer. We are not so sure. *See Licitra,* 734 N.Y.S.2d at 392 ("All terms of the 'Agreement' should not be enforced merely because the consumer retains the equipment for 30 days after receipt, especially because it is unclear when the 30-day period to protest begins. Does it commence upon delivery of the goods to the carrier since the 'Agreement' states that title passes upon 'delivery to the carrier' ... or does it commence upon receipt by the consumer? Is the time period stayed in the all too common situation where a parent buys the computer as a present for a student and does not give the gift for several weeks or is the clock ticking while the equipment sits in the box?"). "Acceptance of goods" has a technical meaning not easily discernable to the average consumer.[15] A consumer may

---

2-207 governs) or the contrary reasoning of Hill v. Gateway 2000, 105 F.3d 1147 (7th Cir. 1997) (original 2-207 inapplicable)." Amended § 2-207, Comment 5 (2003).

14. This phrase is taken from the Supreme Court of Washington and is meant to denote that "while some contracts are formed and their terms fully defined at a single point in time, many transactions involve a rolling or layered process." M.A. Mortenson Co. v. Timberline Software Corp., 140 Wn.2d 568, 998 P.2d 305, 313 n.10 (Wash. 2000) (quoting the Uniform Computer Information Transactions Act § 208 cmt. 3 (Approved Official Draft)).

15. Tex. Bus. & Com. Code Ann. § 2.606 (Vernon 1994) provides in relevant part:
   "(a) Acceptance of goods occurs when the buyer
      "(1) after a reasonable opportunity to inspect the goods signifies to the seller that the goods are conforming or that he will take or retain them in spite of their non-conformity; or

believe that simply by opening the package he or she has agreed to be bound by the terms and conditions contained therein. Indeed, many of the courts that have enforced so-called "approve-or-return" agreements cite language informing the consumer of a specific period after which he or she will have accepted the terms. *See, e.g., Hill,* 105 F.3d at 1148 (terms govern if consumer retains beyond thirty days); *Brower,* 676 N.Y.S.2d at 570 ("By keeping your Gateway 2000 computer system beyond thirty (30) days after the date of delivery, you accept the Terms and Conditions."). The more problematic issue, however, is whether plaintiffs were aware of their power to reject by returning the goods.

Significantly, the agreement sent to Ms. DeFontes, who is no longer a plaintiff in this case, contained additional language advising her of the method of rejection. The introductory provision of the terms and conditions agreement that defendants sent to her stated, "[i]f for any reason Customer is not satisfied with a Dell-branded hardware system, Customer may return the system under the terms and conditions of Dell's Total Satisfaction Return Policy ...." In doing so, defendants explicitly contrasted acceptance of the terms with rejection of the goods, albeit while retaining some ambiguity whether rejection of defendants' proposed terms could reasonably be construed as dissatisfaction with "Dell-branded hardware." Many of the cases upholding shrinkwrap agreements cite explicit disclaimers advising consumers of their right to reject the terms. *See, e.g., ProCD, Inc. v. Zeidenberg,* 908 F. Supp. 640, 644 (W.D. Wis. 1996) ("If you do not agree to the terms of this License, promptly return all copies of the software, listings that may have been exported, the discs and the User Guide to the place where you obtained it."); *Bischoff,* 180 F. Supp. 2d at 1101 ("[i]f you do not accept these terms, please notify us immediately and we will cancel your service"); *M.A. Mortenson Co.,* 998 P.2d at 308 ("IF YOU DO NOT AGREE TO THESE TERMS AND CONDITIONS, PROMPTLY RETURN ... TO THE PLACE OF PURCHASE AND YOUR PURCHASE PRICE WILL BE REFUNDED"). Such explicit language is also present in some of the foreign cases in which defendants have prevailed. *See, e.g., Sherr,* 2006 U.S. Dist. LEXIS 51864, 2006 WL 2109436, at *1 ("[a]greement informs the consumer that by returning the product or refusing delivery in accordance with Dell's return policy, he can reject the terms and conditions"). Although the above language is significantly clearer, the terms and conditions agreement sent to Ms. DeFontes nevertheless made the important connection between acceptance of the terms by accepting delivery and rejection by returning the goods.

That this language is absent in the documents sent to current plaintiffs Mr. Long and Ms. Ricci is troubling and raises the specter that they were unaware of both their power to reject and the method with which to do so. The introductory provision that purportedly bound plaintiffs does not mention either the "Total Satisfaction Return Policy" or the thirty-day period in which a consumer may exercise his or her right to return the product. Rather, this policy is explained, if at all, in a distinct section of the terms and conditions agreement, which confusingly informed plaintiffs that "Dell Branded Hardware systems and parts that are purchased directly from Dell by an end-user Customer may be returned by Customer in accordance with Dell's 'Total Satisfaction Return Policy' in effect on the date of the invoice." Thus, the consumer is left to construe these provisions together and infer that his or her right to reject the terms extends beyond what would commonly be understood as the moment of delivery. This separate provision not only fails to establish

---

"(2) fails to make an effective rejection (Subsection (a) of Section 2.602), but such acceptance does not occur until the buyer has had a reasonable opportunity to inspect them; or

"(3) does any act inconsistent with the seller's ownership; but if such act is wrongful as against the seller it is an acceptance only if ratified by him."

a clear relationship between the consumer's acceptance of the terms by retaining the goods and his or her right to reject the terms by returning the product, but it further obscures the matter by forcing the consumer to refer to a separate document if he or she wants to discover the full terms and conditions of the "Total Satisfaction Return Policy." Even if the consumer reviews the total satisfaction return policy, we are not convinced that the policy clearly explains to a reasonable consumer that his or her right to return the product includes rejection of the terms and conditions agreement. We believe the hearing justice rightly concluded that although "Dell does provide a 'total satisfaction policy' whereby a customer may return the computer, this return policy does not mention the customer's ability to return based on their unwillingness to comply with the terms."

In reviewing the language of the terms and conditions agreement it cannot be said that it was reasonably apparent to the plaintiffs that they could reject the terms simply by returning the goods. We believe that too many inferential steps were required of the plaintiffs and too many of the relevant provisions were left ambiguous. We are not persuaded that a reasonably prudent offeree would understand that by keeping the Dell computer he or she was agreeing to be bound by the terms and conditions agreement and retained, for a specified time, the power to reject the terms by returning the product....

III

Conclusion

For the reasons set out above, the judgment of the Superior Court is affirmed. The papers of the case are returned to the Superior Court.

Step-Saver Data Systems, Inc. v. Wyse Technology and The Software Link, Inc.

United States Court of Appeals for the Third Circuit
939 F.2d 91 (1991)

JOHN M. WISDOM, CIRCUIT JUDGE

The "Limited Use License Agreement" printed on a package containing a copy of a computer program raises the central issue in this appeal. The trial judge held that the terms of the Limited Use License Agreement governed the purchase of the package, and, therefore, granted the software producer, The Software Link, Inc. ("TSL"), a directed verdict on claims of breach of warranty brought by a disgruntled purchaser, Step-Saver Data Systems, Inc. We disagree with the district court's determination of the legal effect of the license, and reverse and remand the warranty claims for further consideration.

Step-Saver raises several other issues, but we do not find these issues warrant reversal. We, therefore, affirm in all other respects.

I. Factual and Procedural Background

The growth in the variety of computer hardware and software has created a strong market for these products. It has also created a difficult choice for consumers, as they must somehow decide which of the many available products will best suit their needs. To assist consumers in this decision process, some companies will evaluate the needs of particular groups of potential computer users, compare those needs with the available technology, and develop a package of hardware and software to satisfy those needs. Beginning in 1981, Step-Saver performed this function as a value added retailer for International Business Machine (IBM) products. It would combine hardware and software to satisfy the word processing, data management, and communications needs for offices of physicians and lawyers. It originally marketed single computer systems, based primarily on the IBM personal computer.

As a result of advances in micro-computer technology, Step-Saver developed and marketed a multi-user system. With a multi-user system, only one computer is required. Terminals are attached, by cable, to the main computer. From these terminals, a user can access the programs available on the main computer.

After evaluating the available technology, Step-Saver selected a program by TSL, entitled Multilink Advanced, as the operating system for the multi-user system. Step-Saver selected WY-60 terminals manufactured by Wyse, and used an IBM AT as the main computer. For applications software, Step-Saver included in the package several off-the-shelf programs, designed to run under Microsoft's Disk Operating System ("MS-DOS"), as well as several programs written by Step-Saver. Step-Saver began marketing the system in November of 1986, and sold one hundred forty-two systems mostly to law and medical offices before terminating sales of the system in March of 1987. Almost immediately upon installation of the system, Step-Saver began to receive complaints from some of its customers.

Step-Saver, in addition to conducting its own investigation of the problems, referred these complaints to Wyse and TSL, and requested technical assistance in resolving the problems. After several preliminary attempts to address the problems, the three companies were unable to reach a satisfactory solution, and disputes developed among the three concerning responsibility for the problems. As a result, the problems were never solved. At least twelve of Step-Saver's customers filed suit against Step-Saver because of the problems with the multi-user system.

Once it became apparent that the three companies would not be able to resolve their dispute amicably, Step-Saver filed suit for declaratory judgment, seeking indemnity from either Wyse or TSL, or both, for any costs incurred by Step-Saver in defending and resolving the customers' law suits. The district court dismissed this complaint, finding that the issue was not ripe for judicial resolution. We affirmed the dismissal on appeal. Step-Saver then filed a second complaint alleging breach of warranties by both TSL and Wyse and intentional misrepresentations by TSL. The district court's actions during the resolution of this second complaint provide the foundation for this appeal....

. . .

II. The Effect of the Box-Top License

The relationship between Step-Saver and TSL began in the fall of 1984 when Step-Saver asked TSL for information on an early version of the Multilink program. TSL provided Step-Saver with a copy of the early program, known simply as Multilink, without charge to permit Step-Saver to test the program to see what it could accomplish. Step-Saver performed some tests with the early program, but did not market a system based on it.

In the summer of 1985, Step-Saver noticed some advertisements in Byte magazine for a more powerful version of the Multilink program, known as Multilink Advanced. Step-Saver requested information from TSL concerning this new version of the program, and allegedly was assured by sales representatives that the new version was compatible with ninety percent of the programs available "off-the-shelf" for computers using MS-DOS. The sales representatives allegedly made a number of additional specific representations of fact concerning the capabilities of the Multilink Advanced program.

Based on these representations, Step-Saver obtained several copies of the Multilink Advanced program in the spring of 1986, and conducted tests with the program. After these tests, Step-Saver decided to market a multi-user system which used the Multilink Advanced program. From August of 1986 through March of 1987, Step-Saver purchased and resold 142 copies of the Multilink Advanced program. Step-Saver would typically purchase copies of the program in the following manner. First, Step-Saver would telephone TSL and place an order. (Step-Saver would typically order twenty copies of the program at a time.) TSL would accept the order and promise, while on the telephone, to ship the goods promptly. After the telephone order, Step-Saver would send a purchase order, detailing the items to be purchased, their price, and shipping and payment terms. TSL would ship the order promptly, along with an invoice. The invoice would contain terms essentially identical with those on Step-Saver's purchase order: price, quantity, and shipping and payment terms. No reference was made during the telephone calls, or on either the purchase orders or the invoices with regard to a disclaimer of any warranties.

Printed on the package of each copy of the program, however, would be a copy of the box-top license. The box-top license contains five terms relevant to this action:

(1) The box-top license provides that the customer has not purchased the software itself, but has merely obtained a personal, non-transferable license to use the program.[7]

(2) The box-top license, in detail and at some length, disclaims all express and implied warranties except for a warranty that the disks contained in the box are free from defects.

(3) The box-top license provides that the sole remedy available to a purchaser of the program is to return a defective disk for replacement; the license excludes any liability for damages, direct or consequential, caused by the use of the program.

(4) The box-top license contains an integration clause, which provides that the box-top license is the final and complete expression of the terms of the parties' agreement.

(5) The box-top license states: "Opening this package indicates your acceptance of these terms and conditions. If you do not agree with them, you should promptly return the package unopened to the person from whom you purchased it within fifteen days from date of purchase and your money will be refunded to you by that person."

The district court, without much discussion, held, as a matter of law, that the box-top license was the final and complete expression of the terms of the parties' agreement. Because the district court decided the questions of contract formation and interpretation as issues of law, we review the district court's resolution of these questions de novo.

Step-Saver contends that the contract for each copy of the program was formed when TSL agreed, on the telephone, to ship the copy at the agreed price.[9] The box-top license,

---

7. When these form licenses were first developed for software, it was, in large part, to avoid the federal copyright law first sale doctrine. Under the first sale doctrine, once the copyright holder has sold a copy of the copyrighted work, the owner of the copy could "sell or otherwise dispose of the possession of that copy" without the copyright holder's consent. *See* Bobbs-Merrill Co. v. Straus, 210 U.S. 339, 350, 28 S. Ct. 722, 726, 52 L. Ed. 1086 (1908); 17 U.S.C.A. § 109(a) (West 1977)....

9. *See* UCC § 2-206(1)(b) and comment 2. Note that under UCC § 2-201, the oral contract would not be enforceable in the absence of a writing or part performance because each order typically involved more than $500 in goods. However, courts have typically treated the questions of formation and interpretation as separate from the question of when the contract becomes enforceable. *See, e.g.,* C. Itoh & Co. v. Jordan Int'l Co., 552 F.2d 1228, 1232–33 (7th Cir. 1977); Southeastern Adhesives Co. v. Funder America, 89 N.C. App. 438, 366 S.E.2d 505, 507–08 (N.C. Ct. App. 1988); United Coal & Commodities Co. v. Hawley Fuel Coal, Inc., 363 Pa. Super. 106, 525 A.2d 741, 743 (Pa. Super. Ct.), *app. denied,* 517 Pa. 609, 536 A.2d 1333 (1987).

argues Step-Saver, was a material alteration to the parties' contract which did not become a part of the contract under UCC § 2-207.

TSL argues that the contract between TSL and Step-Saver did not come into existence until Step-Saver received the program, saw the terms of the license, and opened the program packaging. TSL contends that too many material terms were omitted from the telephone discussion for that discussion to establish a contract for the software. Second, TSL contends that its acceptance of Step-Saver's telephone offer was conditioned on Step-Saver's acceptance of the terms of the box-top license. Therefore, TSL argues, it did not accept Step-Saver's telephone offer, but made a counteroffer represented by the terms of the box-top license, which was accepted when Step-Saver opened each package. Third, TSL argues that, however the contract was formed, Step-Saver was aware of the warranty disclaimer, and that Step-Saver, by continuing to order and accept the product with knowledge of the disclaimer, assented to the disclaimer....

A. Does UCC § 2-207 Govern the Analysis?

As a basic principle, we agree with Step-Saver that UCC § 2-207 governs our analysis. We see no need to parse the parties' various actions to decide exactly when the parties formed a contract. TSL has shipped the product, and Step-Saver has accepted and paid for each copy of the program. The parties' performance demonstrates the existence of a contract. The dispute is, therefore, not over the existence of a contract, but the nature of its terms. When the parties' conduct establishes a contract, but the parties have failed to adopt expressly a particular writing as the terms of their agreement, and the writings exchanged by the parties do not agree, UCC § 2-207 determines the terms of the contract.

As stated by the official comment to § 2-207:

1. This section is intended to deal with two typical situations. The one is the written confirmation, where an agreement has been reached either orally or by informal correspondence between the parties and is followed by one or more of the parties sending formal memoranda embodying the terms so far as agreed upon and adding terms not discussed....

2. Under this Article a proposed deal which in commercial understanding has in fact been closed is recognized as a contract. Therefore, any additional matter contained in the confirmation or in the acceptance falls within subsection (2) and must be regarded as a proposal for an added term unless the acceptance is made conditional on the acceptance of the additional or different terms.

...

To understand why the terms of the license should be considered under § 2-207 in this case, we review briefly the reasons behind § 2-207. Under the common law of sales, and to some extent still for contracts outside the UCC, an acceptance that varied any term of the offer operated as a rejection of the offer, and simultaneously made a counteroffer. This common law formality was known as the mirror image rule, because the terms of the acceptance had to mirror the terms of the offer to be effective. If the offeror proceeded with the contract despite the differing terms of the supposed acceptance, he would, by his performance, constructively accept the terms of the "counteroffer," and be bound by its terms. As a result of these rules, the terms of the party who sent the last form, typically the seller, would become the terms of the parties' contract. This result was known as the "last shot rule."

The UCC, in § 2-207, rejected this approach. Instead, it recognized that, while a party may desire the terms detailed in its form if a dispute, in fact, arises, most parties do not expect a dispute to arise when they first enter into a contract. As a result, most parties will proceed with the transaction even if they know that the terms of their form would not be enforced.[18] The insight behind the rejection of the last shot rule is that it would be unfair to bind the buyer of goods to the standard terms of the seller, when neither party cared sufficiently to establish expressly the terms of their agreement, simply because the seller sent the last form. Thus, U.C.C. section 2-207 establishes a legal rule that proceeding with a contract after receiving a writing that purports to define the terms of the parties' contract is not sufficient to establish the party's consent to the terms of the writing to the extent that the terms of the writing either add to, or differ from, the terms detailed in the parties' earlier writings or discussions.[19] In the absence of a party's express assent to the additional or different terms of the writing, section 2-207 provides a default rule that the parties intended, as the terms of their agreement, those terms to which both parties have agreed, along with any terms implied by the provisions of the UCC.

The reasons that led to the rejection of the last shot rule, and the adoption of section 2-207, apply fully in this case. TSL never mentioned during the parties' negotiations leading to the purchase of the programs, nor did it, at any time, obtain Step-Saver's express assent to, the terms of the box-top license. Instead, TSL contented itself with attaching the terms to the packaging of the software, even though those terms differed substantially from those previously discussed by the parties. Thus, the box-top license, in this case, is best seen as one more form in a battle of forms, and the question of whether Step-Saver has agreed to be bound by the terms of the box-top license is best resolved by applying the legal principles detailed in section 2-207.

B. Application of Section 2-207

TSL advances several reasons why the terms of the box-top license should be incorporated into the parties' agreement under a §2-207 analysis. First, TSL argues that the parties' contract was not formed until Step-Saver received the package, saw the terms of the box-top license, and opened the package, thereby consenting to the terms of the license.... TSL argues that the box-top license was a conditional acceptance and counter-offer under §2-207(1). Third, TSL argues that Step-Saver, by continuing to order and use the product with notice of the terms of the box-top license, consented to the terms of the box-top license.

...

The box-top license as a counter-offer?

TSL advances two reasons why its box-top license should be considered a conditional acceptance under UCC §2-207(1). First, TSL argues that the express language of the box-top license, including the integration clause and the phrase "opening this product indicates your acceptance of these terms," made TSL's acceptance "expressly conditional on assent

---

18. As Judge Engel has written: Usually, these standard terms mean little, for a contract looks to its fulfillment and rarely anticipates its breach. Hope springs eternal in the commercial world and expectations are usually, but not always, realized. McJunkin Corp. v. Mechanicals, Inc., 888 F.2d at 482.

19. As the Mead Court explained:

Absent the [UCC], questions of contract formation and intent remain factual issues to be resolved by the trier of fact after careful review of the evidence. However, the [UCC] provides rules of law, and section 2-207 establishes important legal principles to be employed to resolve complex contract disputes arising from the exchange of business forms. Section 2-207 was intended to provide some degree of certainty in this otherwise ambiguous area of contract law. In our view, it is unreasonable and contrary to the policy behind the [UCC] merely to turn the issue over to the uninformed speculation of the jury left to apply its own particular sense of equity.

Mead Corp., 654 F.2d at 1206 (citations omitted).

to the additional or different terms." Second, TSL argues that the box-top license, by permitting return of the product within fifteen days if the purchaser does not agree to the terms stated in the license (the "refund offer"), establishes that TSL's acceptance was conditioned on Step-Saver's assent to the terms of the box-top license, citing *Monsanto Agricultural Products Co. v. Edenfield*.[28] While we are not certain that a conditional acceptance analysis applies when a contract is established by performance,[29] we assume that it does and consider TSL's arguments.

To determine whether a writing constitutes a conditional acceptance, courts have established three tests. Because neither Georgia nor Pennsylvania has expressly adopted a test to determine when a written confirmation constitutes a conditional acceptance, we consider these three tests to determine which test the state courts would most likely apply.

Under the first test, an offeree's response is a conditional acceptance to the extent it states a term "materially altering the contractual obligations solely to the disadvantage of the offeror." Pennsylvania, at least, has implicitly rejected this test. In *Herzog Oil Field Service, Inc.*,[32] a Pennsylvania Superior Court analyzed a term in a written confirmation under UCC § 2-207(2), rather than as a conditional acceptance even though the term materially altered the terms of the agreement to the sole disadvantage of the offeror.[33]

Furthermore, we note that adopting this test would conflict with the express provision of UCC § 2-207(2)(b). Under § 2-207(2)(b), additional terms in a written confirmation that "materially alter [the contract]" are construed "as proposals for addition to the contract," not as conditional acceptances.

A second approach considers an acceptance conditional when certain key words or phrases are used, such as a written confirmation stating that the terms of the confirmation are "the only ones upon which we will accept orders."[34] The third approach requires the offeree to demonstrate an unwillingness to proceed with the transaction unless the additional or different terms are included in the contract.[35]

Although we are not certain that these last two approaches would generate differing answers,[36] we adopt the third approach for our analysis because it best reflects the understanding of commercial transactions developed in the UCC. Section 2-207 attempts to distinguish between: (1) those standard terms in a form confirmation, which the party would like a court to incorporate into the contract in the event of a dispute; and (2) the actual terms the parties understand to govern their agreement. The third test properly

---

28. 426 So. 2d 574 (Fla. Dist. Ct. App.1982).

29. Even though a writing is sent after performance establishes the existence of a contract, courts have analyzed the effect of such a writing under UCC § 2-207....

32. 391 Pa. Super. 133, 570 A.2d 549 (Pa. Super. Ct.1990).

33. The seller/offeree sent a written confirmation that contained a term that provided for attorney's fees of 25 percent of the balance due if the account was turned over for collection. 570 A.2d at 550.

34. Ralph Shrader, Inc. v. Diamond Int'l Corp., 833 F.2d 1210, 1214 (6th Cir.1987)....

35. *See, e.g.*, Daitom, Inc., 741 F.2d at 1576; Idaho Power Co. v. Westinghouse Elec. Corp., 596 F.2d 924, 926 (9th Cir. 1979).

36. Under the second approach, the box-top license might be considered a conditional acceptance, but Step-Saver, by accepting the product, would not be automatically bound to the terms of the box-top license. *See* Diamond Fruit Growers, Inc., 794 F.2d at 1444. Instead, courts have applied UCC § 2-207(3) to determine the terms of the parties's agreement. The terms of the agreement would be those "on which the writings of the parties agree, together with any supplementary terms incorporated under any other provisions of this Act." UCC § 2-207(3). Because the writings of the parties did not agree on the warranty disclaimer and limitation of remedies terms, the box-top license version of those terms would not be included in the parties' contract; rather, the default provisions of the UCC would govern.

places the burden on the party asking a court to enforce its form to demonstrate that a particular term is a part of the parties' commercial bargain.

Using this test, it is apparent that the integration clause and the "consent by opening" language is not sufficient to render TSL's acceptance conditional. As other courts have recognized,[38] this type of language provides no real indication that the party is willing to forego the transaction if the additional language is not included in the contract.

The second provision provides a more substantial indication that TSL was willing to forego the contract if the terms of the box-top license were not accepted by Step-Saver. On its face, the box-top license states that TSL will refund the purchase price if the purchaser does not agree to the terms of the license.[39] Even with such a refund term, however, the offeree/counterofferor may be relying on the purchaser's investment in time and energy in reaching this point in the transaction to prevent the purchaser from returning the item. Because a purchaser has made a decision to buy a particular product and has actually obtained the product, the purchaser may use it despite the refund offer, regardless of the additional terms specified after the contract formed. But we need not decide whether such a refund offer could ever amount to a conditional acceptance; the undisputed evidence in this case demonstrates that the terms of the license were not sufficiently important that TSL would forego its sales to Step-Saver if TSL could not obtain Step-Saver's consent to those terms.

As discussed, Mr. Greebel testified that TSL assured him that the box-top license did not apply to Step-Saver, as Step-Saver was not the end user of the Multilink Advanced program. Supporting this testimony, TSL on two occasions asked Step-Saver to sign agreements that would put in formal terms the relationship between Step-Saver and TSL. Both proposed agreements contained warranty disclaimer and limitation of remedy terms similar to those contained in the box-top license. Step-Saver refused to sign the agreements; nevertheless, TSL continued to sell copies of Multilink Advanced to Step-Saver.

Additionally, TSL asks us to infer, based on the refund offer, that it was willing to forego its sales to Step-Saver unless Step-Saver agreed to the terms of the box-top license. Such an inference is inconsistent with the fact that both parties agree that the terms of the box-top license did not represent the parties' agreement with respect to Step-Saver's right to transfer the copies of the Multilink Advanced program. Although the box-top license prohibits the transfer, by Step-Saver, of its copies of the program, both parties agree that Step-Saver was entitled to transfer its copies to the purchasers of the Step-Saver multi-user system. Thus, TSL was willing to proceed with the transaction despite the fact that one of the terms of the box-top license was not included in the contract between TSL and Step-Saver. We see no basis in the terms of the box-top license for inferring that a reasonable offeror would understand from the refund offer that certain terms of the box-top license, such as the warranty disclaimers, were essential to TSL, while others such as the non-transferability provision were not.

Based on these facts, we conclude that TSL did not clearly express its unwillingness to proceed with the transactions unless its additional terms were incorporated into the

---

38. *See, e.g.,* Idaho Power Co., 596 F.2d at 926–27.

39. One Florida Court of Appeals has accepted such an offer as a strong indication of a conditional acceptance. Monsanto Agricultural Prods. Co., 426 So. 2d at 575–76. Note that the Monsanto warranty label was conspicuous and available to the purchaser before the contract for the sale of the herbicide was formed. When an offeree proceeds with a contract with constructive knowledge of the terms of the offer, the offeree is typically bound by those terms, making the conditional acceptance finding unnecessary to the result reached in Monsanto.

parties' agreement. The box-top license did not, therefore, constitute a conditional acceptance under UCC § 2-207(1).

Did the parties' course of dealing establish that the parties had excluded any express or implied warranties associated with the software program?

TSL argues that because Step-Saver placed its orders for copies of the Multilink Advanced program with notice of the terms of the box-top license, Step-Saver is bound by the terms of the box-top license. Essentially, TSL is arguing that, even if the terms of the box-top license would not become part of the contract if the case involved only a single transaction, the repeated expression of those terms by TSL eventually incorporates them within the contract.

Ordinarily, a "course of dealing" or "course of performance" analysis focuses on the actions of the parties with respect to a particular issue.[40] If, for example, a supplier of asphaltic paving material on two occasions gives a paving contractor price protection, a jury may infer that the parties have incorporated such a term in their agreement by their course of performance.[41] Because this is the parties' first serious dispute, the parties have not previously taken any action with respect to the matters addressed by the warranty disclaimer and limitation of liability terms of the box-top license. Nevertheless, TSL seeks to extend the course of dealing analysis to this case where the only action has been the repeated sending of a particular form by TSL. While one court has concluded that terms repeated in a number of written confirmations eventually become part of the contract even though neither party ever takes any action with respect to the issue addressed by those terms,[42] most courts have rejected such reasoning.[43]

For two reasons, we hold that the repeated sending of a writing which contains certain standard terms, without any action with respect to the issues addressed by those terms, cannot constitute a course of dealing which would incorporate a term of the writing otherwise excluded under § 2-207. First, the repeated exchange of forms by the parties only tells Step-Saver that TSL desires certain terms. Given TSL's failure to obtain Step-Saver's express assent to these terms before it will ship the program, Step-Saver can reasonably believe that, while TSL desires certain terms, it has agreed to do business on other terms — those terms expressly agreed upon by the parties. Thus, even though Step-Saver would not be surprised[44] to learn that TSL desires the terms of the box-top license, Step-Saver might well be surprised to learn that the terms of the box-top license have been incorporated into the parties' agreement.

Second, the seller in these multiple transaction cases will typically have the opportunity to negotiate the precise terms of the parties' agreement, as TSL sought to do in this case. The seller's unwillingness or inability to obtain a negotiated agreement reflecting its terms

---

40. A "course of performance" refers to actions with respect to the contract taken after the contract has formed. *UCC* § 2-208(1). "A course of dealing is a sequence of previous conduct between the parties to a particular transaction which is fairly to be regarded as establishing a common basis of understanding for interpreting their expressions and other conduct." UCC § 1-205.

41. *See* Nanakuli Paving & Rock Co. v. Shell Oil Co., 664 F.2d 772 (9th Cir. 1981).

42. *See* Schulze & Burch Biscuit Co. v. Tree Top, Inc., 831 F.2d 709, 714–15 (7th Cir.1987)....

43. *See, e.g.*, Trans-Aire Int'l v. Northern Adhesive Co., 882 F.2d at 1262–63 & n.9; Diamond Fruit Growers, Inc., 794 F.2d at 1445; Tuck Industries v. Reichhold Chemicals, Inc., 542 N.Y.S.2d 676, 678, 151 A.D.2d 566 (N.Y. App. Div.1989); Southeastern Adhesives Co., 366 S.E.2d at 507–08.

44. *Cf.* UCC § 2-207, comment 4 (suggesting that terms that "materially alter" a contract are those that would result in "surprise or hardship if incorporated without express awareness by the other party").

strongly suggests that, while the seller would like a court to incorporate its terms if a dispute were to arise, those terms are not a part of the parties' commercial bargain. For these reasons, we are not convinced that TSL's unilateral act of repeatedly sending copies of the box-top license with its product can establish a course of dealing between TSL and Step-Saver that resulted in the adoption of the terms of the box-top license.

With regard to more specific evidence as to the parties' course of dealing or performance, it appears that the parties have not incorporated the warranty disclaimer into their agreement. First, there is the evidence that TSL tried to obtain Step-Saver's express consent to the disclaimer and limitation of damages provision of the box-top license. Step-Saver refused to sign the proposed agreements. Second, when first notified of the problems with the program, TSL spent considerable time and energy attempting to solve the problems identified by Step-Saver.

Course of conduct is ordinarily a factual issue. But we hold that the actions of TSL in repeatedly sending a writing, whose terms would otherwise be excluded under UCC § 2-207, cannot establish a course of conduct between TSL and Step-Saver that adopted the terms of the writing.

. . .

C. The Terms of the Contract

Under section 2-207, an additional term detailed in the box-top license will not be incorporated into the parties' contract if the term's addition to the contract would materially alter the parties' agreement. Step-Saver alleges that several representations made by TSL constitute express warranties, and that valid implied warranties were also a part of the parties' agreement. Because the district court considered the box-top license to exclude all of these warranties, the district court did not consider whether other factors may act to exclude these warranties. The existence and nature of the warranties is primarily a factual question that we leave for the district court, but assuming that these warranties were included within the parties' original agreement, we must conclude that adding the disclaimer of warranty and limitation of remedies provisions from the box-top license would, as a matter of law, substantially alter the distribution of risk between Step-Saver and TSL. Therefore, under UCC § 2-207(2)(b), the disclaimer of warranty and limitation of remedies terms of the box-top license did not become a part of the parties' agreement.

Based on these considerations, we reverse the trial court's holding that the parties intended the box-top license to be a final and complete expression of the terms of their agreement. Despite the presence of an integration clause in the box-top license, the box-top license should have been treated as a written confirmation containing additional terms. Because the warranty disclaimer and limitation of remedies terms would materially alter the parties' agreement, these terms did not become a part of the parties' agreement. We remand for further consideration the express and implied warranty claims against TSL.

. . .

VI.

We will reverse the holding of the district court that the parties intended to adopt the box-top license as the complete and final expression of the terms of their agreement. We will remand for further consideration of Step-Saver's express and implied warranty claims against TSL. Finding a sufficient basis for the other decisions of the district court, we will affirm in all other respects.

William S. Klocek v. Gateway, Inc., et al.

United States District Court for the District of Kansas

104 F. Supp. 2d 1332 (2000)

KATHRYN HOEFER VRATIL, DISTRICT JUDGE

William S. Klocek brings suit against Gateway, Inc.... on claims arising from purchases of a Gateway computer.... This matter comes before the Court on the *Motion to Dismiss* which Gateway filed November 22, 1999....

Gateway's Motion to Dismiss

Plaintiff brings individual and class action claims against Gateway, alleging that it induced him and other consumers to purchase computers and special support packages by making false promises of technical support. Individually, plaintiff also claims breach of contract and breach of warranty, in that Gateway breached certain warranties that its computer would be compatible with standard peripherals and standard internet services.

Gateway asserts that plaintiff must arbitrate his claims under Gateway's Standard Terms and Conditions Agreement ("Standard Terms"). Whenever it sells a computer, Gateway includes a copy of the Standard Terms in the box which contains the computer battery power cables and instruction manuals. At the top of the first page, the Standard Terms include the following notice:

NOTE TO THE CUSTOMER:

This document contains Gateway 2000's Standard Terms and Conditions. By keeping your Gateway 2000 computer system beyond five (5) days after the date of delivery, you accept these Terms and Conditions.

The notice is in emphasized type and is located inside a printed box which sets it apart from other provisions of the document. The Standard Terms are four pages long and contain 16 numbered paragraphs. Paragraph 10 provides the following arbitration clause:

DISPUTE RESOLUTION. Any dispute or controversy arising out of or relating to this Agreement or its interpretation shall be settled exclusively and finally by arbitration. The arbitration shall be conducted in accordance with the Rules of Conciliation and Arbitration of the International Chamber of Commerce. The arbitration shall be conducted in Chicago, Illinois, U.S.A. before a sole arbitrator. Any award rendered in any such arbitration proceeding shall be final and binding on each of the parties, and judgment may be entered thereon in a court of competent jurisdiction.[2]

Before granting a stay or dismissing a case pending arbitration, the Court must determine that the parties have a written agreement to arbitrate. *See* 9 U.S.C. §§ 3 and 4; *Avedon Engineering, Inc. v. Seatex,* 126 F.3d 1279, 1283 (10th Cir. 1997). When deciding whether

---

2. Gateway states that after it sold plaintiff's computer, it mailed all existing customers in the United States a copy of its quarterly magazine, which contained notice of a change in the arbitration policy set forth in the Standard Terms. The new arbitration policy afforded customers the option of arbitrating before the International Chamber of Commerce ("ICC"), the American Arbitration Association ("AAA"), or the National Arbitration Forum ("NAF") in Chicago, Illinois, or any other location agreed upon by the parties. Plaintiff denies receiving notice of the amended arbitration policy. Neither party explains why—if the arbitration agreement was an enforceable contract—Gateway was entitled to unilaterally amend it by sending a magazine to computer customers.

the parties have agreed to arbitrate, the Court applies ordinary state law principles that govern the formation of contracts. *First Options of Chicago, Inc. v. Kaplan,* 514 U.S. 938, 944 (1995). The existence of an arbitration agreement "is simply a matter of contract between the parties; [arbitration] is a way to resolve those disputes—but only those disputes—that the parties have agreed to submit to arbitration." *Avedon,* 126 F.3d at 1283 (quoting *Kaplan,* 514 U.S. at 943–945, 115 S.Ct. 1920). If the parties dispute making an arbitration agreement, a jury trial on the existence of an agreement is warranted if the record reveals genuine issues of material fact regarding the parties' agreement. *See Avedon,* 126 F.3d at 1283.

...

The Uniform Commercial Code ("U.C.C.") governs the parties' transaction under both Kansas and Missouri law. *See* K.S.A. §84-2-102; V.A.M.S. §400.2-102 (U.C.C. applies to "transactions in goods."); Kansas Comment 1 (main thrust of Article 2 is limited to sales); K.S.A. §84-2-105(1); V.A.M.S. §400.2-105(1) ("'Goods' means all things ... which are movable at the time of identification to the contract for sale...."). Regardless whether plaintiff purchased the computer in person or placed an order and received shipment of the computer, the parties agree that plaintiff paid for and received a computer from Gateway. This conduct clearly demonstrates a contract for the sale of a computer. *See, e.g., Step-Saver Data Sys., Inc. v. Wyse Techn.,* 939 F.2d 91, 98 (3d Cir. 1991). Thus the issue is whether the contract of sale includes the Standard Terms as part of the agreement.

State courts in Kansas and Missouri apparently have not decided whether terms received with a product become part of the parties' agreement. Authority from other courts is split. *Compare Step-Saver,* 939 F.2d 91 (printed terms on computer software package not part of agreement); *Arizona Retail Sys., Inc. v. Software Link, Inc.,* 831 F.Supp. 759 (D.Ariz. 1993) (license agreement shipped with computer software not part of agreement); *and U.S. Surgical Corp. v. Orris, Inc.,* 5 F.Supp.2d 1201 (D.Kan. 1998) (single use restriction on product package not binding agreement); *with Hill v. Gateway 2000, Inc.,* 105 F.3d 1147 (7th Cir.), *cert. denied,* 522 U.S. 808, 118 S.Ct. 47, 139 L.Ed.2d 13 (1997) (arbitration provision shipped with computer binding on buyer); *ProCD, Inc. v. Zeidenberg,* 86 F.3d 1447 (7th Cir. 1996) (shrinkwrap license binding on buyer);[6] *and M.A. Mortenson Co., Inc. v. Timberline Software Corp.,* 140 Wash.2d 568, 998 P.2d 305 (2000) (following *Hill* and *ProCD* on license agreement supplied with software). It appears that at least in part, the cases turn on whether the court finds that the parties formed their contract *before* or *after* the vendor communicated its terms to the purchaser. *Compare Step-Saver,* 939 F.2d at 98 (parties' conduct in shipping, receiving and paying for product demonstrates existence of contract; box top license constitutes proposal for additional terms under §2-207 which requires express agreement by purchaser); *Arizona Retail,* 831 F.Supp. at 765 (vendor entered into contract by agreeing to ship goods, or at latest by shipping goods to buyer; license agreement constitutes proposal to modify agreement under §2-209 which requires express assent by buyer); *and Orris,* 5 F.Supp.2d at 1206 (sales contract concluded when vendor received consumer orders; single-use language on product's label was proposed modification under §2-209 which requires express assent by purchaser); *with ProCD,* 86 F.3d at 1452 (under §2-204 vendor, as master of offer, may propose limitations on kind of conduct that constitutes acceptance; §2-207 does not apply in case with only one form);

---

6. The term "shrinkwrap license" gets its name from retail software packages that are covered in plastic or cellophane "shrinkwrap" and contain licenses that purport to become effective as soon as the customer tears the wrapping from the package. *See ProCD,* 86 F.3d at 1449.

Hill, 105 F.3d at 1148–49 (same); *and Mortenson,* 998 P.2d at 311–314 (where vendor and purchaser utilized license agreement in prior course of dealing, shrinkwrap license agreement constituted issue of contract formation under § 2-204, not contract alteration under § 2-207).

Gateway urges the Court to follow the Seventh Circuit decision in *Hill.* That case involved the shipment of a Gateway computer with terms similar to the Standard Terms in this case, except that Gateway gave the customer 30 days — instead of 5 days — to return the computer. In enforcing the arbitration clause, the Seventh Circuit relied on its decision in *ProCD,* where it enforced a software license which was contained inside a product box. *See Hill,* 105 F.3d at 1148–50. In *ProCD,* the Seventh Circuit noted that the exchange of money frequently precedes the communication of detailed terms in a commercial transaction. *See ProCD,* 86 F.3d at 1451. Citing UCC § 2-204, the court reasoned that by including the license with the software, the vendor proposed a contract that the buyer could accept by using the software after having an opportunity to read the license. *ProCD,* 86 F.3d at 1452. Specifically, the court stated:

> A vendor, as master of the offer, may invite acceptance by conduct, and may propose limitations on the kind of conduct that constitutes acceptance. A buyer may accept by performing the acts the vendor proposes to treat as acceptance.

ProCD, 86 F.3d at 1452.

The *Hill* court followed the *ProCD* analysis, noting that "[p]ractical considerations support allowing vendors to enclose the full legal terms with their products." *Hill,* 105 F.3d at 1149.[9]

The Court is not persuaded that Kansas or Missouri courts would follow the Seventh Circuit reasoning in *Hill* and *ProCD.* In each case the Seventh Circuit concluded without support that UCC § 2-207 was irrelevant because the cases involved only one written form. *See ProCD,* 86 F.3d at 1452 (citing no authority); *Hill,* 105 F.3d at 1150 (citing *ProCD*). This conclusion is not supported by the statute or by Kansas or Missouri law. Disputes under § 2-207 often arise in the context of a "battle of forms," *see, e.g., Diatom,*

---

9. Legal commentators have criticized the reasoning of the Seventh Circuit in this regard. *See, e.g.,* Jean R. Sternlight, Gateway Widens Doorway to Imposing Unfair Binding Arbitration on Consumers, Fla. Bar J., Nov. 1997, at 8, 10–12 (outcome in Gateway is questionable on federal statutory, common law and constitutional grounds and as a matter of contract law and is unwise as a matter of policy because it unreasonably shifts to consumers search cost of ascertaining existence of arbitration clause and return cost to avoid such clause); Thomas J. McCarthy et al., Survey: Uniform Commercial Code, 53 Bus. Law. 1461, 1465–66 (Seventh Circuit finding that UCC § 2-207 did not apply is inconsistent with official comment); Batya Goodman, Honey, I Shrink-Wrapped the Consumer: the Shrinkwrap Agreement as an Adhesion Contract, 21 Cardozo L. Rev. 319, 344–352 (Seventh Circuit failed to consider principles of adhesion contracts); Jeremy Senderowicz, Consumer Arbitration and Freedom of Contract: A Proposal to Facilitate Consumers' Informed Consent to Arbitration Clauses in Form Contracts, 32 Colum. J.L. & Soc. Probs. 275, 296–299 (judiciary (in multiple decisions, including Hill) has ignored issue of consumer consent to an arbitration clause). Nonetheless, several courts have followed the Seventh Circuit decisions in Hill and ProCD. *See, e.g.,* M.A. Mortenson Co., Inc. v. Timberline Software Corp., 140 Wash.2d 568, 998 P.2d 305 (license agreement supplied with software); Rinaldi v. Iomega Corp., 1999 WL 1442014, Case No. 98C-09-064-RRC (Del.Super. Sept. 3, 1999) (warranty disclaimer included inside computer Zip drive packaging); Westendorf v. Gateway 2000, Inc., 2000 WL 307369, Case No. 16913 (Del. Ch. March 16, 2000) (arbitration provision shipped with computer); Brower v. Gateway 2000, Inc., 246 A.D.2d 246, 676 N.Y.S.2d 569 (N.Y.App.Div.1998) (same); Levy v. Gateway 2000, Inc., 33 UCC Rep. Serv.2d 1060 (N.Y.Sup. Oct. 31, 1997) (same).

Inc. v. Pennwalt Corp., 741 F.2d 1569, 1574 (10th Cir. 1984), but nothing in its language precludes application in a case which involves only one form. The statute provides:

Additional terms in acceptance or confirmation.

(1) A definite and seasonable expression of acceptance or a written confirmation which is sent within a reasonable time operates as an acceptance even though it states terms additional to or different from those offered or agreed upon, unless acceptance is expressly made conditional on assent to the additional or different terms.

(2) The additional terms are to be construed as proposals for addition to the contract [if the contract is not between merchants]....

K.S.A. §84-2-207; V.A.M.S. §400.2-207.

By its terms, §2-207 applies to an acceptance or written confirmation. It states nothing which requires another form before the provision becomes effective. In fact, the official comment to the section specifically provides that §§2-207(1) and (2) apply "where an agreement has been reached orally ... and is followed by one or both of the parties sending formal memoranda embodying the terms so far agreed and adding terms not discussed." Official Comment 1 of UCC §2-207. Kansas and Missouri courts have followed this analysis. *See Southwest Engineering Co. v. Martin Tractor Co.*, 205 Kan. 684, 695, 473 P.2d 18, 26 (1970) (stating in dicta that §2-207 applies where open offer is accepted by expression of acceptance in writing or where oral agreement is later confirmed in writing); *Central Bag Co. v. W. Scott and Co.*, 647 S.W.2d 828, 830 (Mo.App. 1983) (§§2-207(1) and (2) govern cases where one or both parties send written confirmation after oral contract). Thus, the Court concludes that Kansas and Missouri courts would apply §2-207 to the facts in this case. *Accord Avedon,* 126 F.3d at 1283 (parties agree that §2-207 controls whether arbitration clause in sales confirmation is part of contract).

In addition, the Seventh Circuit provided no explanation for its conclusion that "the vendor is the master of the offer." *See ProCD*, 86 F.3d at 1452 (citing nothing in support of proposition); *Hill*, 105 F.3d at 1149 (citing *ProCD*). In typical consumer transactions, the purchaser is the offeror, and the vendor is the offeree. *See Brown Mach., Div. of John Brown, Inc. v. Hercules, Inc.*, 770 S.W.2d 416, 419 (Mo.App. 1989) (as general rule orders are considered offers to purchase); *Rich Prods. Corp. v. Kemutec Inc.*, 66 F.Supp. 2d 937, 956 (E.D.Wis. 1999) (generally price quotation is invitation to make offer and purchase order is offer). While it is possible for the vendor to be the offeror, *see Brown Machine*, 770 S.W.2d at 419 (price quote can amount to offer if it reasonably appears from quote that assent to quote is all that is needed to ripen offer into contract), Gateway provides no factual evidence which would support such a finding in this case. The Court therefore assumes for purposes of the motion to dismiss that plaintiff offered to purchase the computer (either in person or through catalog order) and that Gateway accepted plaintiff's offer (either by completing the sales transaction in person or by agreeing to ship and/or shipping the computer to plaintiff).[11] *Accord Arizona Retail*, 831 F.Supp. at 765 (vendor entered into contract by agreeing to ship goods, or at latest, by shipping goods).

---

11. UCC §2-206(b) provides that "an order or other offer to buy goods for prompt or current shipment shall be construed as inviting acceptance either by a prompt promise to ship or by the prompt or current shipment ..." The official comment states that "[e]ither shipment or a prompt promise to ship is made a proper means of acceptance of an offer looking to current shipment." UCC §2-206, Official Comment 2.

Under § 2-207, the Standard Terms constitute either an expression of acceptance or written confirmation. As an expression of acceptance, the Standard Terms would constitute a counter-offer only if Gateway expressly made its acceptance conditional on plaintiff's assent to the additional or different terms. K.S.A. § 84-2-207(1); V.A.M.S. § 400.2-207(1). "[T]he conditional nature of the acceptance must be clearly expressed in a manner sufficient to notify the offeror that the offeree is unwilling to proceed with the transaction unless the additional or different terms are included in the contract." *Brown Machine*, 770 S.W.2d at 420.[12]

Gateway provides no evidence that at the time of the sales transaction, it informed plaintiff that the transaction was conditioned on plaintiff's acceptance of the Standard Terms. Moreover, the mere fact that Gateway shipped the goods with the terms attached did not communicate to plaintiff any unwillingness to proceed without plaintiff's agreement to the Standard Terms. *See, e.g., Arizona Retail*, 831 F.Supp. at 765 (conditional acceptance analysis rarely appropriate where contract formed by performance but goods arrive with conditions attached); *Leighton Indus., Inc. v. Callier Steel Pipe & Tube, Inc.*, 1991 WL 18413, *6, Case No. 89-C-8235 (N.D.Ill. Feb. 6, 1991) (applying Missouri law) (preprinted forms insufficient to notify offeror of conditional nature of acceptance, particularly where form arrives after delivery of goods).

Because plaintiff is not a merchant, additional or different terms contained in the Standard Terms did not become part of the parties' agreement unless plaintiff expressly agreed to them. *See* K.S.A. § 84-2-207, Kansas Comment 2 (if either party is not a merchant, additional terms are proposals for addition to the contract that do not become part of the contract unless the original offeror expressly agrees).[13] Gateway argues that plaintiff demonstrated acceptance of the arbitration provision by keeping the computer more than five days after the date of delivery. Although the Standard Terms purport to work that result, Gateway has not presented evidence that plaintiff expressly agreed to those Standard

---

12. Courts are split on the standard for a conditional acceptance under § 2-207. *See* Daitom, 741 F.2d at 1576 (finding that Pennsylvania would most likely adopt "better" view that offeree must explicitly communicate unwillingness to proceed with transaction unless additional terms in response are accepted by offeror). On one extreme of the spectrum, courts hold that the offeree's response stating a materially different term solely to the disadvantage of the offeror constitutes a conditional acceptance. *See* Daitom, 741 F.2d at 1569 (citing Roto-Lith, Ltd. v. F.P. Bartlett & Co.,   297 F.2d 497 (1st Cir.1962)). At the other end of the spectrum, courts hold that the conditional nature of the acceptance should be so clearly expressed in a manner sufficient to notify the offeror that the offeree is unwilling to proceed without the additional or different terms. *See* Daitom, 741 F.2d at 1569 (citing Dorton v. Collins & Aikman Corp., 453 F.2d 1161 (6th Cir.1972)). The middle approach requires that the response predicate acceptance on clarification, addition or modification. *See* Daitom, 741 F.2d at 1569 (citing Construction Aggregates Corp. v. Hewitt-Robins, Inc., 404 F.2d 505 (7th Cir.1968)). The First Circuit has since overruled its decision in Roto-Lith, *see* Ionics, Inc. v. Elmwood Sensors, Inc., 110 F.3d 184, and the Court finds that neither Kansas nor Missouri would apply the standard set forth therein. *See* Boese-Hilburn Co. v. Dean Machinery Co., 616 S.W.2d 520(Mo.App.1981) (rejecting Roto-Lith standard); Owens-Corning Fiberglas Corp. v. Sonic Dev. Corp., 546 F.Supp. 533, 538 (D.Kan.1982) (acceptance is not counteroffer under Kansas law unless it is made conditional on assent to additional or different terms (citing Roto-Lith as comparison)); Daitom, 741 F.2d at 1569 (finding that Dorton is "better" view). Because Gateway does not satisfy the standard for conditional acceptance under either of the remaining standards (Dorton or Construction Aggregates), the Court does not decide which of the remaining two standards would apply in Kansas and/or Missouri.

13. The Court's decision would be the same if it considered the Standard Terms as a proposed modification under UCC § 2-209. *See, e.g.*, Orris, 5 F.Supp.2d at 1206 (express assent analysis is same under §§ 2-207 and 2-209).

Terms. Gateway states only that it enclosed the Standard Terms inside the computer box for plaintiff to read afterwards. It provides no evidence that it informed plaintiff of the five-day review-and-return period as a condition of the sales transaction, or that the parties contemplated additional terms to the agreement.[14] *See Step-Saver*, 939 F.2d at 99 (during negotiations leading to purchase, vendor never mentioned box-top license or obtained buyer's express assent thereto). The Court finds that the act of keeping the computer past five days was not sufficient to demonstrate that plaintiff expressly agreed to the Standard Terms. *Accord Brown Machine*, 770 S.W.2d at 421 (express assent cannot be presumed by silence or mere failure to object). Thus, because Gateway has not provided evidence sufficient to support a finding under Kansas or Missouri law that plaintiff agreed to the arbitration provision contained in Gateway's Standard Terms, the Court overrules Gateway's motion to dismiss.

. . .

4. Termination and Revocation of the Offer Prior to Acceptance

Note — On Termination of an Offer and the Power to Accept

As we have seen, the doctrine of offer and acceptance provide that a contract is formed if an offer is accepted before the offer terminates. The doctrine also provides that an offer is terminated by:

(1) rejection or counteroffer (*e.g.*, a response that violates the mirror-image rule);

(2) revocation of the offer — this is examined in depth in the next section;

(3) lapse, in which the offer is said to simply expire after passage of a specified or reasonable period of time (a general rule is that oral offers lapse at the end of the conversation or after a time specified by the offeror and that written offers lapse after a "reasonable" time or a time specified by the offeror), *see Restatement (Second) of Contracts* § 41; and

(4) death of the offeror or the offeree, *see Restatement (Second) of Contracts* § 48.

Under classical contract theory, no contract exists until there is an offer and acceptance, and therefore no obligation exists until there is an offer and acceptance. Thus, as a matter of logical deduction, an offeror is free to revoke her or his offer at any time prior to acceptance, because she or he has no obligation to the offeree, not even the obligation to leave the offer open. The rule of nineteenth- and early twentieth-century Anglo-American law was that an offer could be revoked at any time prior to acceptance, even if the offeror had promised not to revoke. This rule is in conflict with rules of negotiation in other

---

14. The Court is mindful of the practical considerations which are involved in commercial transactions, but it is not unreasonable for a vendor to clearly communicate to a buyer — at the time of sale — either the complete terms of the sale or the fact that the vendor will propose additional terms as a condition of sale, if that be the case.

legal systems, which provide that an offer must be left open for a reasonable period of time. In the United States, the rule has been seen as unjust, and courts have developed several exceptions to the general rule.

————————

George Dickinson v. John Dodds

Court of Appeal, Chancery Division2 Ch. D. 463 (1876)

On Wednesday, the 10th of June, 1874, the Defendant John Dodds signed and delivered to the Plaintiff, George Dickinson, a memorandum, of which the material part was as follows:—

> "I hereby agree to sell to Mr. George Dickinson the whole of the dwelling-houses, garden ground, stabling, and outbuildings thereto belonging, situate at Croft, belonging to me, for the sum of £800. As witness my hand this tenth day of June, 1874.

> "£800.   (Signed) *John Dodds.*"

> "P.S.—This offer to be left over until Friday, 9 o'clock, A.M. J.D. (the twelfth), 12th June, 1874.

> (Signed) *J. Dodds.*"

The bill alleged that Dodds understood and intended that the Plaintiff should have until Friday 9 A.M. within which to determine whether he would or would not purchase, and that he should absolutely have until that time the refusal of the property at the price of £800, and that the Plaintiff in fact determined to accept the offer on the morning of Thursday, the 11th of June, but did not at once signify his acceptance to Dodds, believing that he had the power to accept it until 9 A.M. on the Friday.

In the afternoon of the Thursday the Plaintiff was informed by a Mr. Berry that Dodds had been offering or agreeing to sell the property to Thomas Allan, the other Defendant. Thereupon the Plaintiff, at about half-past seven in the evening, went to the house of Mrs. Burgess, the mother-in-law of Dodds, where he was than staying, and left with her a formal acceptance in writing of the offer to sell the property. According to the evidence of Mrs. Burgess this document never in fact reached Dodds, she having forgotten to give it to him.

On the following (Friday) morning, at about seven o'clock, Berry, who was acting as agent for Dickinson, found Dodds at the Darlington railway station, and handed to him a duplicate of the acceptance by Dickinson, and explained to Dodds its purport. He replied that it was too late, as he had sold the property. A few minutes later Dickinson himself found Dodds entering a railway carriage, and handed him another duplicate of the notice of acceptance, but Dodds declined to receive it, saying, "You are too late. I have sold the property."

It appeared that on the day before, Thursday, the 11th of June, Dodds had signed a formal contract for the sale of the property to the Defendant Allan for £800, and had received from him a deposit of £40.

The bill in this suit prayed that the Defendant Dodds might be decreed specifically to perform the contract of the 10th of June, 1874; that he might be restrained from conveying the property to Allan; that Allan might be restrained from taking any such conveyance; that, if any such conveyance had been or should be made, Allan might be declared a trustee of the property for, and might be directed to convey the property to, the Plaintiff; and for damages.

The cause came on for hearing before Vice-Chancellor Bacon on the 25th of January, 1876.

. . .

[A decree for specific performance was entered, and the Defendants appealed.]

Court of Appeal, Chancery Division2 Ch. D. 463 (1876)

WILLIAM MILBOUME JAMES, LORD JUSTICE, AFTER REFERRING TO THE DOCUMENT OF THE 10TH OF JUNE, 1874, CONTINUED:

The document, though beginning "I hereby agree to sell," was nothing but an offer, and was only intended to be an offer, for the Plaintiff himself tells us that he required time to consider whether he would enter into an agreement or not. Unless both parties had then agreed there was no concluded agreement then made; it was in effect and substance only an offer to sell. The Plaintiff, being minded not to complete the bargain at that time, added this memorandum—"This offer to be left over until Friday, 9 o'clock A.M., 12th June, 1874." That shows it was only an offer. There was no consideration given for the undertaking or promise, to whatever extent it may be considered binding, to keep the property unsold until 9 o'clock on Friday morning; but apparently Dickinson was of opinion, and probably Dodds was of the same opinion, that he (Dodds) was bound by that promise, and could not in any way withdraw from it, or retract it, until 9 o'clock on Friday morning, and this probably explains a good deal of what afterwards took place. But it is clear settled law, on one of the clearest principles of law, that this promise, being a mere nudum pactum, was not binding, and that at any moment before a complete acceptance by Dickinson of the offer, Dodds was as free as Dickinson himself. Well, that being the state of things, it is said that the only mode in which Dodds could assert that freedom was by actually and distinctly saying to Dickinson, "Now I withdraw my offer." It appears to me that there is neither principle nor authority for the proposition that there must be an express and actual withdrawal of the offer, or what is called a retraction. It must, to constitute a contract, appear that the two minds were as one, at the same moment of time, that is, that there was an offer continuing up to the time of the acceptance. If there was not such a continuing offer, then the acceptance comes to nothing. Of course it may well be that the one man is bound in some way or other to let the other man know that his mind with regard to the offer has been changed; but in this case, beyond all question, the Plaintiff knew that Dodds was no longer minded to sell the property to him as plainly and clearly as if Dodds had told him in so many words, "I withdraw the offer." This is evident from the Plaintiff's own statements in the bill.

The Plaintiff says in effect that, having heard and knowing that Dodds was no longer minded to sell to him, and that he was selling or had sold to someone else, thinking that he could not in point of law withdraw his offer, meaning to fix him to it, and endeavoring to bind him, "I went to the house where he was lodging, and saw his mother-in-law, and left with her an acceptance of the offer, knowing all the while that he had entirely changed his mind. I got an agent to watch for him at 7 o'clock the next morning, and I went to the train just before 9 o'clock, in order that I might catch him and give him my notice of acceptance just before 9 o'clock, and when that occurred he told my agent, and he told me, you are too late, and he then threw back the paper." It is to my mind quite clear that before there was any attempt at acceptance by the Plaintiff, he was perfectly well aware that Dodds had changed his mind, and that he had in fact agreed to sell the property to Allan. It is impossible, therefore, to say there was ever that existence of the same mind between the two parties which is essential in point of law to the making of an agreement.

I am of opinion, therefore, that the Plaintiff has failed to prove that there was any binding contract between Dodds and himself.

GEORGE MELLISH, LORD JUSTICE

I am of the same opinion. The first question is, whether this document of the 10th of June, 1874, which was signed by Dodds, was an agreement to sell, or only an offer to sell, the property therein mentioned to Dickinson; and I am clearly of the opinion that it was only an offer, although it is in the first part of it, independently of the postscript, worded as an agreement. I apprehend that, until acceptance, so that both parties are bound, even though an instrument is so worded as to express that both parties agree, it is in point of law only an offer, and, until both parties are bound, neither party is bound. It is not necessary that both parties should be bound within the Statute of Frauds, for, if one party makes an offer in writing, and the other accepts it verbally, that will be sufficient to bind the person who has signed the written document. But, if there be no agreement, either verbally or in writing, then, until acceptance, it is in point of law an offer only, although worded as if it were an agreement. But it is hardly necessary to resort to that doctrine in the present case, because the postscript calls it an offer, and says, "This offer to be left over until Friday, 9 o'clock a.m." Well, then, this being only an offer, the law says—and it is a perfectly clear rule of law—that, although it is said that the offer is to be left open until Friday morning at 9 o'clock, that did not bind Dodds. He was not in point of law bound to hold the offer over until 9 o'clock on Friday morning. He was not so bound either in law or in equity. Well, that being so, when only the next day he made an agreement with Allan to sell the property to him, I am not aware of any ground on which it can be said that that contract with Allan was not as good and binding a contract as ever was made. Assuming Allan to have known (there is some dispute about it, and Allan does not admit that he knew of it, but I will assume that he did) that Dodds had made the offer to Dickinson, and had given him till Friday morning at 9 o'clock to accept it, still in point of law that could not prevent Allan from making a more favorable offer than Dickinson, and entering at once into a binding agreement with Dodds.

Then Dickinson is informed by Berry that the property has been sold by Dodds to Allan. Berry does not tell us from whom he heard it, but he says that he did hear it, that he knew it, and that he informed Dickinson of it. Now, stopping there, the question which arises is this—If an offer has been made for the sale of property, and before that offer is accepted, the person who has made the offer enters into a binding agreement to sell the property to somebody else, and the person to whom the offer was first made receives notice in some way that the property has been sold to another person, can he after that make a binding contract by the acceptance of the offer? I am of opinion that he cannot. The law may be right or wrong in saying that a person who has given to another a certain time within to accept an offer is not bound by his promise to give that time; but, if he is not bound by that promise, and may still sell the property to someone else, and if it be the law that, in order to make a contract, the two minds must be in agreement at some one time, that is, at the time of the acceptance, how is it possible that when the person to whom the offer has been made knows that the person who has made the offer has sold the property to someone else, and that, in fact, he has not remained in the same mind to sell it to him, he can be at liberty to accept the offer and thereby make a binding contract? It seems to me that would be simply absurd. If a man makes an offer to sell a particular horse in his stable, and says, "I will give you until the day after tomorrow to accept the offer," and the next day goes and sells the horse to somebody else, and receives the purchase-money from him, can the person to whom the offer was originally made then come and say, "I accept," so as to make a binding contract, and so as to be entitled to recover damages for the non-delivery of the horse? If the rule of law is that a mere offer to sell property, which can be withdrawn at any time, and which is made dependent on the acceptance of the person to whom it is made, is a mere nudum pactum, how is it possible that the person to whom the offer has been made can by acceptance make a binding contract after he knows that the person who has made the offer has sold the property to someone else? It is admitted law that, if a man who makes an offer dies, the offer cannot be accepted after he is dead, and parting with the property has very much the same effect as the death of the owner, for it makes the performance of the offer impossible. I am clearly of opinion that, just as when a man who has made an offer dies before it is accepted it is impossible that it can then be accepted, so when once the person to whom the offer was made knows that the property has been sold to someone else, it is too late for him to accept the offer, and on that ground I am clearly of opinion that there was no binding contract for the sale of this property by Dodds to Dickinson, and even if there had been, it seems to me that the sale of the property to Allan was first in point of time. However, it is not necessary to consider if there had been two binding contracts, which of them would be entitled to priority in equity, because there is no binding contract between Dodds and Dickinson.

State of Washington v. Richard Lee Wheeler

Washington Supreme Court
95 Wash. 2d 799, 631 P.2d 376 (1981)

ROBERT UTTER, JUSTICE

Richard Wheeler, by direct appeal from a verdict and judgment of second degree assault with a firearm, raises four issues. These involve the enforceability of a plea bargain, the admission of both altered testimony and hearsay, and a jury instruction defining "knowledge." We find no reversible error and accordingly affirm.

Early on the morning of December 26, 1978, Richard Wheeler, a white, middle-aged shipyard worker, returned to his houseboat from a Christmas party to find that the boat had been burglarized for the second time that month. Kelly, a younger white male whom Wheeler had met the previous day, was with Wheeler, and the two had been drinking heavily.

Wheeler had reported the first burglary to the police, but was dissatisfied with their investigation. Neighbors had given Wheeler descriptions of two black males who allegedly had been in the marina on several occasions. Wheeler and Kelly returned to Wheeler's pickup and left. Wheeler had a .410 gauge shotgun in the truck.

At about 2 a.m. Wheeler and Kelly drove alongside three young black males, two of whom ostensibly fit the description given by Wheeler's neighbors, and engaged the three in conversation. Two of the three soon fled, either because they recognized Wheeler or because they saw the shotgun. Wheeler and Kelly caught the third, a 15-year-old, and Wheeler knocked him down, allegedly to examine the tread on his shoes to determine if they matched prints left on the boat. Wheeler then struck the youth on the side of the head, tearing one ear in a manner that required several stitches to mend. The victim's mother and sister came running out of a nearby house to protest, and Wheeler shouted something at them, apparently to the effect that they would never see their boy again.

Wheeler and Kelly then forced the victim into the pickup and drove him to a secluded area about 6 miles away. During the trip, Wheeler threatened the youth, struck him with his elbow, and knocked his head into the back cab window, giving him a black eye, several facial cuts, and a bruised and bloodied scalp. Once they arrived, Wheeler physically kicked the youth out of the vehicle and, as the boy was running away, fired a shot either at him or into the air.

Wheeler and Kelly were apprehended before the youth was located, and in an inadvertent confrontation at the police station, Wheeler told the boy's mother that he had killed her son. Wheeler testified, however, that he never intended to seriously injure the youth, but only wanted to teach him a lesson and to scare him into telling where the stolen property was located.

Prior to trial the defendant's attorney and the trial prosecutor entered into a plea bargain negotiation whereby the defendant offered to plead guilty to second degree assault with a deadly weapon and the prosecution apparently agreed to drop the firearm allegation, to drop the kidnapping charge, and to recommend a 3-year deferred sentence conditioned on 120 days in jail (with work release), restitution, and payment of costs.

There is substantial evidence that the bargain was first accepted by the prosecutor who then revoked the acceptance shortly before the guilty plea was to be entered. The trial prosecutor maintains, however, that no formal acceptance occurred. A motion for specific performance was heard before Judge Barbara Rothstein on March 23, 1979. Judge Rothstein, assuming but not finding that an agreement had been reached, held that the plea bargain was not enforceable.

The trial prosecutor evidently changed her mind regarding the merits of entering into the plea bargain as a result of her interviews with witnesses and because of the reaction of the victim's family to the agreement. The plea bargain was officially retracted, however, by Prosecuting Attorney Norm Maleng, who announced a new departmental policy of personally reviewing all of the evidence in difficult cases and deciding whether "manifest injustice" would occur if an agreement were allowed to stand.

On May 1, 1979, after several continuances, Wheeler and Kelly were tried together by jury in a consolidated action. Defendant Wheeler was convicted of second degree assault with a firearm and was sentenced to prison.

. . .

I.

The defendant seeks specific performance of the prosecutor's initial offer. He contends that the prosecutor could not legally rescind the offer until he had an opportunity to accept it. The issue, as framed by his argument, is one of first impression in this state.

The weight of authority is that, absent some detrimental reliance by the defendant, the State may withdraw from any plea agreement prior to the actual entry of a guilty plea. *Government v. Scotland*, 614 F.2d 360 (3d Cir. 1980). That result has been reached by strictly applying contract principles and characterizing the plea bargain as a unilateral contract. That is, only the defendant's plea, or some other detrimental reliance upon the arrangement, constitutes an acceptance of the agreement; and consequently the bargain can be revoked if neither has occurred. Those courts have further reasoned that enforcing bargains made before the plea would inhibit the prosecutor's use of plea bargaining; and that the defendant, because she or he can still get a jury trial, has an adequate remedy for the State's revocation.

Only one case has deviated from that conclusion. *Cooper v. United States*, 594 F.2d 12 (4th Cir. 1979). *Cooper* held that a defendant was entitled to specific performance of a plea bargain, even though it was rescinded by the government prior to defendant's acceptance.…

Like the other jurisdictions, we reject the *Cooper* analysis. A defendant does not have a constitutional right to plea bargain, *see Weatherford v. Bursey*, 429 U.S. 545, 51 L. Ed. 2d 30, 97 S. Ct. 837 (1977), and thus the failure to enforce a plea proposal, as opposed to an "accepted" offer, cannot violate substantive due process. Substantive due process protects those rights which are "so rooted in the traditions and conscience of our people as to be ranked as fundamental," … or are "implicit in the concept of ordered liberty." *Rochin v. California*, 342 U.S. 165, 169, 96 L. Ed. 183, 72 S. Ct. 205, 25 A.L.R.2d 1396 (1952), quoting *Snyder v. Massachusetts*, 291 U.S. 97, 105, 78 L. Ed. 674, 54 S. Ct. 330, 90 A.L.R. 575 (1934), and *Palko v. Connecticut*, 302 U.S. 319, 325, 82 L. Ed. 288, 58 S. Ct. 149 (1937). The right to specific performance of a plea proposal, if it can be called a right, is not rooted in the "traditions and conscience of our people." … While the defendant is to be treated with fairness, *State v. Tourtellotte*, 88 Wn.2d 579, 564 P.2d 799 (1977), which in most cases would dictate that the prosecutor comply with any extended offer, we cannot conclude that the right to any specific offer is so fundamental and so instrumental to our system of justice that it rises to constitutional magnitude.

…

We conclude that absent a guilty plea or some other detrimental reliance by the defendant, the prosecutor may revoke any plea proposal. Since the defendant has alleged only "psychological" reliance on the prosecutor's offer, and without a showing that the prosecutor has abused its discretion by routinely rescinding its offers, the trial court correctly declined to enforce it.

Note — On Revocation of Offers

The General Rule that Offers are Revocable until Acceptance

What is the rationale for the Anglo-American rule that an offeror may revoke the offer any time prior to acceptance? What rationale was given by the court in *Dickinson v. Dodds*? Do you find it persuasive? What counter-arguments can be made? If "a deal is a deal" in part because both parties are obligated and because there is a mutuality to the commitments, is it a corollary that one party should not be obligated if the other is not? Is it unjust if one party is obligated while the other is not? Perhaps this idea is based on concern with speculation, or with oppression.

The Anglo-American rule allowing revocation of an offer applies even if the offeror promised not to revoke, as the court held in *Dickinson v. Dodds*. Does this conflict with freedom of contract?

Irrevocable Offers

Four exceptions to the general rule allowing revocation of an offer are now recognized in most states in the U.S. An offeror loses the power to revoke an offer in the following scenarios:

1. True Option Contract

An offer cannot be revoked if the parties create a true option contract, in which the offeree gives separate consideration for the offeror's promise not to revoke as described in *Restatement (Second) of Contracts* § 87(1):

§ 87. Option Contract

(1) An offer is binding as an option contract if it

(a) is in writing and signed by the offeror, recites a purported consideration for the making of the offer, and proposes an exchange on fair terms within a reasonable time; or

(b) is made irrevocable by statute;

2. Uniform Commercial Code § 2-205

§ 2-205 Firm Offers.

An offer by a merchant to buy or sell goods in a signed writing which by its terms gives assurance that it will be held open is not revocable, for lack of consideration, during the time stated or if no time is stated for a reasonable time, but in no event may such period of irrevocability exceed three months; but any such term of assurance on a form supplied by the offeree must be separately signed by the offeror;

3. Restatement (Second) of Contracts § 45: Beginning Performance in Response to an Offer that can be Accepted only by Full Performance

§ 45. Option Contract Created by Part Performance or Tender

(1) Where an offer invites an offeree to accept by rendering a performance and does not invite a promissory acceptance, an option contract is created when the offeree tenders or begins the invited performance or tenders a beginning of it.

(2) The offeror's duty of performance under any option contract so created is conditional on completion or tender of the invited performance in accordance with the terms of the offer.;

4. Restatement (Second) § 87(2) An Offer that Has Been Foreseeably and Substantially Relied Upon by the Offeree (see Drennan v. Star Paving)

§ 87. Option Contract

(2) An offer which the offeror should reasonably expect to induce action or forbearance of a substantial character on the part of the offeree before acceptance and which does induce such action or forbearance is binding as an option contract to the extent necessary to avoid injustice.

Additionally, under Article 16 of the *United Nations Convention on Contracts for the International Sale of Goods*, offers can be revoked except in specified circumstances:

Article 16

(1) Until a contract is concluded an offer may be revoked if the revocation reaches the offeree before he has dispatched an acceptance.

(2) However, an offer cannot be revoked:

(a) if it indicates, whether by stating a fixed time for acceptance or otherwise, that it is irrevocable; or

(b) if it was reasonable for the offeree to rely on the offer as being irrevocable and the offeree has acted in reliance on the offer.

———————

Note—On Offers "Becoming Irrevocable," "Irrevocable Offers," and "Contracts," Including "Option Contracts"

The *Restatement (Second) of Contracts* § 45 does not say an offer that can be accepted only by full performance becomes irrevocable after the offeree begins performance. Instead, it says that where such an offer is made, "an option contract is created when the offeree tenders or begins the invited performance...." Why is the idea of an option contract introduced here? The answer lies in the formalist approach of Samuel Williston, principle drafter of the *Restatement (First) of Contracts*. A debate recorded in the proceedings of the American Law Institute reveals Williston's approach to § 45:

JUDGE CARDOZO: Are there any suggestions as to ... Section 45?

...

MR. WILLIS: I wonder if there is not an inaccuracy in Section 45.... Under such circumstances as we find in Section 45, we do not have a contract of course ... yet it says the offeror is bound by a contract. I wonder if that is not misleading. The actual fact is that in our most recent cases and the modern development of the law the power of revocation on the part of the offeror is destroyed, and therefore the offeree has the power to go on if he wants to and complete his acceptance. If he does we finally get a contract, but if he does not go on and perform the rest of the work of course there is no contract....

MR. WILLISTON: I call an irrevocable offer a contract. The offeror has promised to do something and he is liable if he does not do it.

MR. WILLIS: I beg your pardon, you do not want to call this an irrevocable offer, do you?

MR. WILLISTON: That is what you called it, did you not?

MR. WILLIS: Oh, no.

MR. WILLISTON: You stated the power to revoke is destroyed.

MR. WILLIS: It becomes irrevocable—

MR. WILLISTON: All right. When it becomes irrevocable it is an irrevocable offer.

MR. WILLIS: But it does not seem to me that that is so; it seems to me that a contract is one thing and an irrevocable offer is another.

MR. WILLISTON: We are apart on that. An irrevocable [offer] is not *the* contract which the offer proposes, but being a binding promise, it is a contract.

Drennan v. Star Paving Company

California Supreme Court
51 Cal. 2d 409, 333 P.2d 757 (1958)

ROGER J. TRAYNOR, JUSTICE

Defendant appeals from a judgment for plaintiff in an action to recover damages caused by defendant's refusal to perform certain paving work according to a bid it submitted to plaintiff.

On July 28, 1955, plaintiff, a licensed general contractor, was preparing a bid on the "Monte Vista School Job" in the Lancaster school district. Bids had to be submitted before 8:00 p.m. Plaintiff testified that it was customary in that area for general contractors to receive the bids of subcontractors by telephone on the day set for bidding and to rely on them in computing their own bids. Thus on that day plaintiff's secretary, Mrs. Johnson, received by telephone between fifty and seventy-five subcontractors' bids for various parts of the school job. As each bid came in, she wrote it on a special form, which she brought into plaintiff's office. He then posted it on a master cost sheet setting forth the names and bids of all subcontractors. His own bid had to include the names of subcontractors who were to perform one-half of one per cent or more of the construction work, and he had also to provide a bidder's bond of ten per cent of his total bid of $317,385 as a guarantee that he would enter the contract if awarded the work.

Late in the afternoon, Mrs. Johnson had a telephone conversation with Kenneth R. Hoon, an estimator for defendant. He gave his name and telephone number and stated that he was bidding for defendant for the paving work at the Monte Vista School according to plans and specifications and that his bid was $7,131.60. At Mrs. Johnson's request he repeated his bid. Plaintiff listened to the bid over an extension telephone in his office and posted it on the master sheet after receiving the bid form from Mrs. Johnson. Defendant's was the lowest bid for the paving. Plaintiff computed his own bid accordingly and submitted it with the name of defendant as the subcontractor for the paving. When the bids were opened on July 28th, plaintiff's proved to be the lowest, and he was awarded the contract.

On his way to Los Angeles the next morning plaintiff stopped at defendant's office. The first person he met was defendant's construction engineer, Mr. Oppenheimer. Plaintiff testified:

> I introduced myself and he immediately told me that they had made a mistake in their bid to me the night before, they couldn't do it for the price they had bid, and I told him I would expect him to carry through with their original bid because I had used it in compiling my bid and the job was being awarded them. And I would have to go and do the job according to my bid and I would expect them to do the same.

Defendant refused to do the paving work for less than $15,000. Plaintiff testified that he "got figures from other people" and after trying for several months to get as low a bid as possible engaged L & H Paving Company, a firm in Lancaster, to do the work for $10,948.60.

The trial court found on substantial evidence that defendant made a definite offer to do the paving on the Monte Vista job according to the plans and specifications for $7,131.60, and that plaintiff relied on defendant's bid in computing his own bid for the school job and naming defendant therein as the subcontractor for the paving work. Accordingly, it entered judgment for plaintiff in the amount of $3,817.00 (the difference between defendant's bid and the cost of the paving to plaintiff) plus costs.

Defendant contends that there was no enforceable contract between the parties on the ground that it made a revocable offer and revoked it before plaintiff communicated his acceptance to defendant.

There is no evidence that defendant offered to make its bid irrevocable in exchange for plaintiff's use of its figures in computing his bid. Nor is there evidence that would warrant interpreting plaintiff's use of defendant's bid as the acceptance thereof, binding plaintiff, on condition he received the main contract, to award the subcontract to defendant. In sum, there was neither an option supported by consideration nor a bilateral contract binding on both parties.

p claims

Plaintiff contends, however, that he relied to his detriment on defendant's offer and that defendant must therefore answer in damages for its refusal to perform. Thus the question is squarely presented: Did plaintiff's reliance make defendant's offer irrevocable?

Section 90 of the *Restatement of Contracts* states: "A promise which the promisor should reasonably expect to induce action or forbearance of a definite and substantial character on the part of the promisee and which does induce such action or forbearance is binding if injustice can be avoided only by enforcement of the promise." This rule applies in this state. *Edmonds v. County of Los Angeles*, 40 Cal. 2d 642, 255 P.2d 772.

Defendant's offer constituted a promise to perform on such conditions as were stated expressly or by implication therein or annexed thereto by operation of law. (*See* 1 WILLISTON, CONTRACTS (3rd. ed.), § 24A, p. 56, § 61, p. 196.) Defendant had reason to expect that if its bid proved the lowest it would be used by plaintiff. It induced "action of a definite and substantial character on the part of the promisee."

Had defendant's bid expressly stated or clearly implied that it was revocable at any time before acceptance we would treat it accordingly. It was silent on revocation, however, and we must therefore determine whether there are conditions to the right of revocation imposed by law or reasonably inferable in fact. In the analogous problem of an offer for a unilateral contract, the theory is now obsolete that the offer is revocable at any time before complete performance. Thus section 45 of the *Restatement of Contracts* provides:

> If an offer for a unilateral contract is made, and part of the consideration requested in the offer is given or tendered by the offeree in response thereto, the offeror is bound by a contract, the duty of immediate performance of which is conditional on the full consideration being given or tendered within the time stated in the offer, or, if no time is stated therein, within a reasonable time.

In explanation, comment b states that the

> main offer includes as a subsidiary promise, necessarily implied, that if part of the requested performance is given, the offeror will not revoke his offer, and that if tender is made it will be accepted. Part performance or tender may thus furnish consideration for the subsidiary promise. Moreover, merely acting in justifiable reliance on an offer may in some cases serve as sufficient reason for making a promise binding (*see* § 90).

Whether implied in fact or law, the subsidiary promise serves to preclude the injustice that would result if the offer could be revoked after the offeree had acted in detrimental reliance thereon. Reasonable reliance resulting in a foreseeable prejudicial change in position affords a compelling basis also for implying a subsidiary promise not to revoke an offer for a bilateral contract.

. . .

When plaintiff used defendant's offer in computing his own bid, he bound himself to perform in reliance on defendant's terms. Though defendant did not bargain for this use of its bid neither did defendant make it idly, indifferent to whether it would be used or not. On the contrary it is reasonable to suppose that defendant submitted its bid to obtain the subcontract. It was bound to realize the substantial possibility that its bid would be the lowest, and that it would be included by plaintiff in his bid. It was to its own interest that the contractor be awarded the general contract; the lower the subcontract bid, the lower the general contractor's bid was likely to be and the greater its chance of acceptance and hence the greater defendant's chance of getting the paving subcontract. Defendant had reason not only to expect plaintiff to rely on its bid but to want him to. Clearly defendant had a stake in plaintiff's reliance on its bid. Given this interest and the fact that plaintiff is bound by his own bid, it is only fair that plaintiff should have at least an opportunity to accept defendant's bid after the general contract has been awarded to him.

It bears noting that a general contractor is not free to delay acceptance after he has been awarded the general contract in the hope of getting a better price. Nor can he reopen bargaining with the subcontractor and at the same time claim a continuing right to accept the original offer. In the present case plaintiff promptly informed defendant that plaintiff was being awarded the job and that the subcontract was being awarded to defendant.

Defendant contends, however, that its bid was the result of mistake and that it was therefore entitled to revoke it. It relies on the rescission cases of *M. F. Kemper Const. Co. v. City of Los Angeles*, 37 Cal. 2d 696, 235 P.2d 7, and *Brunzell Const. Co. v. G. J. Weisbrod, Inc.*, 134 Cal. App. 2d 278, 285 P.2d 989. *See also, Lemoge Electric v. San Mateo County*, 46 Cal. 2d 659, 662, 297 P.2d 638. In those cases, however, the bidder's mistake was known or should have been known to the offeree, and the offeree could be placed in status quo. Of course, if plaintiff had reason to believe that defendant's bid was in error, he could not justifiably rely on it, and section 90 would afford no basis for enforcing it. *Robert Gordon, Inc. v. Ingersoll-Rand, Inc.*, 7 Cir., 117 F.2d 654, 660. Plaintiff, however, had no reason to know that defendant had made a mistake in submitting its bid, since there was usually a variance of 160 per cent between the highest and lowest bids for paving in the desert around Lancaster. He committed himself to performing the main contract in reliance on defendant's figures. Under these circumstances defendant's mistake, far from relieving it of its obligation, constitutes an additional reason for enforcing it, for it misled plaintiff as to the cost of doing the paving. Even had it been clearly understood that defendant's offer was revocable until accepted, it would not necessarily follow that defendant had no duty to exercise reasonable care in preparing its bid. It presented its bid with knowledge of the substantial possibility that it would be used by plaintiff; it could foresee the harm that would ensue from an erroneous underestimate of the cost. Moreover, it was motivated by its own business interest. Whether or not these considerations alone would justify recovery for negligence had the case been tried on that theory (*see Biakanja v. Irving*, 49 Cal. 2d 647, 650, 320 P.2d 16), they are persuasive that defendant's mistake should not defeat recovery under the rule of section 90 of the *Restatement of Contracts*. As between the subcontractor who made the bid and the general contractor who reasonably relied on it, the loss resulting from the mistake should fall on the party who caused it.

…

There is no merit in defendant's contention that plaintiff failed to state a cause of action, on the ground that the complaint failed to allege that plaintiff attempted to mitigate the damages or that they could not have been mitigated. Plaintiff alleged that after defendant's default, "plaintiff had to procure the services of the L & H Co. to perform said asphaltic paving for the sum of $10,948.60." Plaintiff's uncontradicted evidence showed that he spent several months trying to get bids from other subcontractors and that he took the lowest bid. Clearly he acted reasonably to mitigate damages. In any event any uncertainty in plaintiff's allegation as to damages could have been raised by special demurrer. Code Civ. Proc. § 430, subd. 9. It was not so raised and was therefore waived. Code Civ. Proc. § 434.

The judgment is affirmed.

———————

Karl Llewellyn, Our Case-Law of Contract: Offer and Acceptance

48 Yale L.J. 1 (1938)

The Magic of Offer and Acceptance

Even case-law judges persist in an urge to shape results to the life-situation as they see it. Through open confusion and conflict runs their desire to find a doctrinal definition of any situation which is just to that situation in life. Through the covert confusion of result typically attendant on accepted doctrine which either is at odds with life or is non-significant, runs the same urge and sap, unevenly and unpredictably choked back by some doctrinal block, or else bursting through. *No large-scale doctrinal dichotomy, then, which too much misfits life can hope to fit the cases;* the more outlandish the one misfit, the more probable and pervasive the other.

The great dichotomy in the orthodox doctrine of Offer and Acceptance is that between bilateral and unilateral contract.[61] But there have been signs over thirty years or more of difficulty with it and its implications. Perhaps it is time to recanvass the *life-situation* with which it has to deal. And so to recanvass the cases which its office is to reflect and to guide.

This will not be easy doing. The rules of Offer and Acceptance have been worked over; they have been written over; they have been shaped and rubbed smooth with pumice, they wear the rich deep polish of a thousand class rooms; they have a grip on the vision and indeed on the affections held by no other rules "of law," real or pseudo. For it was Offer and Acceptance which first led each of us out of laydom into The Law. Puzzled, be-fogged, adrift in the strange words and technique of cases, with only our sane feeling of what was decent for a compass, we felt the warm sun suddenly, we knew that we were arriving, we knew we too could "think like a lawyer": That was when we learned to down seasickness as A revoked when B was almost up the flag-pole. Within the first October, we had achieved a technical glee in justifying judgment then for A; and succulent memory lingers, of the way our dumber brethren were pilloried as Laymen still. This is therefore no area of "rules" to be disturbed. It is an area where we *want* no disturbance, and will brook none. It is the Rabbit-Hole down which we fell into the Law, and to him who has gone down it, no queer phenomenon is strange; he has been magicked; the logic of Wonderland we then entered makes mere discrepant decision negligible. And it is not only hard, it is obnoxious, for any of us who have gone through that experience to even conceive of Offer and Acceptance as perhaps in need of re-examination.

I, too, am of the generation to whom Offer and Acceptance in traditional garb were as the rising of the sun. It had always been; it would always be; and it somehow was good. And the Law said, "Let there be Promise for a Promise *or* Promise for an Act." And that binds eyes as ancient China did a little lady's feet. Our generation will not easily regain a normal vision. But it does help a little to realize that it was not really so in the beginning. Story's remarks on Offer and Acceptance were largely not law when written in 1844, and still are not. Parsons, in 1853, attempted to open the subject on the cases; but Langdell could not stomach Parsons' views. Nor are they what we have learned. The analysis which to all of us has been as if eternal, with its neatly boxed "Did A want a promise *or* an act?,"

---

61. The argument is that the classical bilateral-unilateral distinction dies as it approaches fact either of life or of case decision. I put forward as a major piece of evidence the prominence which that distinction has in the table of contents of 1 Williston and Thompson, *op. Cit. supra* note 58, and the lack of correspondence of the text, and much more of the notes, to the suggestions in the table of contents. The Restatement shows the distinction only in the background, coloring much, but not explicitly, as a fundamental cleavage.

its straight-line rigid consequences, its integration into an equally neat theory of consideration, that analysis appears in print first less than seventy years ago. A good part of the cases we still study antedate it—and their decisions are far from squaring with it, especially with its class-room implications.

––––––––––

C. Complicating Assent: "Indefinite" Agreements

Concern with indefiniteness surfaces twice in formation doctrine. First, as we have seen, the definiteness, or degree of detail, in a communication is a factor in deciding whether it was an offer. As *Southworth* suggests, if a communication (or a series of communications) does not include the terms of the proposed contract with some degree of detail, courts are less likely to find that the communication was a "manifestation of intent to enter the exchange." Second, a separate doctrine provides that *indefinite contracts* are not enforceable. The cases in this section examine this doctrine of indefiniteness.

The rationale for this doctrine is that indefiniteness indicates lack of genuine agreement, requiring courts to "write a contract for the parties" (by filling in the gaps), and this is an inappropriate exercise of the court's power. Many judges, lawyers, and scholars have argued that this rationale is unpersuasive, and indefinite contracts should be binding since people actually do make contracts that they think are binding even though the contracts are indefinite. And like the mirror image rule, the doctrine allows people to escape liability on a "technicality."

As a result of criticism of this sort, the doctrine of indefiniteness has been substantially curtailed. Rather than refuse to enforce an indefinite contract, most contemporary courts will consider first whether the parties intended to be bound. If they did, then the court will attempt to find a way to fill the gaps in the contract in order to enforce it. The first three cases in this section illustrate changes in the indefiniteness doctrine during the twentieth century. The last case, *Oglebay Norton v. Armco*, involves the particular problem of *agreements to agree*.

––––––––––

George A. Varney v. Isaac E. Ditmars

Court of Appeals of New York
217 N.Y. 223, 111 N.E. 822 (1916)

EMORY ALBERT CHASE, JUDGE

This is an action brought for an alleged wrongful discharge of an employee. The defendant is an architect employing engineers, draftsmen and other assistants. The plaintiff is an architect and draftsman. In October, 1910, he applied to the defendant for employment and when asked what wages he wanted, replied that he would start for $40 per week. He was employed at $35 per week. A short time thereafter he informed the defendant that he had another position offered to him and the defendant said that if he would remain with him and help him through the work in his office he thought he could offer him a better future than anybody else. He continued in the employ of the defendant and became acquainted with a designer in the office and said designer and the plaintiff from time to time prior to the 1st of February, 1911, talked with the defendant about the work in his office. On that day by arrangement the two remained with the defendant after the regular office hours and the defendant said:

> I am going to give you $5 more a week; if you boys will go on and continue the way you have been and get me out of this trouble and get these jobs started that were in the office three years, on the first of next January I will close my books and give you a fair share of my profits....

The plaintiff was given charge of the drafting. Thereafter suggestions were made by the plaintiff and said designer about discharging many of the defendant's employees and employing new men and such suggestions were carried out and the two worked in the defendant's office overtime and many Sundays and holidays. At least one piece of work that the defendant said had been in his office for three years was completed. The plaintiff on his cross-examination told the story of the employment of himself and said designer as follows:

> And he says at that time "I am going to give you $5 more a week starting this week." This was about Thursday. He says "You boys go on and continue the work you are doing and the first of January next year I will close my books and give you a fair share of my profits." Those were his exact words.

Thereafter the plaintiff was paid $40 a week. On November 6, 1911, the night before the general election in this state, the defendant requested that all of his employees that could do so, should work on election day. The plaintiff told the defendant that he wanted to remain at home to attend an election in the village where he lived. About four o'clock in the afternoon of election day he was taken ill and remained at his house ill until a time that as nearly as can be stated from the evidence was subsequent to December 1, 1911. On Saturday, November 11, the defendant caused to be delivered to the plaintiff a letter in which he said:

> I am sending you herewith your pay for one day's work of seven hours, performed on Monday, the 6th inst. On Monday night, I made it my special duty to inform you that the office would be open all day Election Day and that I expected you and all the men to report for work. Much to my surprise and indignation, on Tuesday you made no appearance and all the men remained away, in obedience of your instructions to them of the previous evening. An act of this kind I consider one of extreme disloyalty and insubordination and I therefore am obliged to dispense with your services.

After the plaintiff had recovered from his illness and was able to do so he went to the defendant's office (the date does not appear) and told him that he was ready, willing and able to continue his services under the agreement. The defendant denied that he had any agreement with him and refused to permit him to continue in his service. Thereafter and prior to January 1, 1912, the plaintiff received for special work about $50.

The plaintiff seeks to recover in this action for services from November 7, 1911, to December 31, 1911, inclusive, at $40 per week and for a fair and reasonable percentage of the net profits of the defendant's business from February 1, 1911, to January 1, 1912, and demands judgment for $1,680.

At the trial he was the only witness sworn as to the alleged contract and at the close of his case the complaint was dismissed.

The statement alleged to have been made by the defendant about giving the plaintiff and said designer a fair share of his profits is vague, indefinite and uncertain and the amount cannot be computed from anything that was said by the parties or by reference to any document, paper or other transaction. The minds of the parties never met upon any particular share of the defendant's profits to be given the employees or upon any plan by which such share could be computed or determined. The contract so far as it related to the special promise or inducement was never consummated. It was left subject to the will of the defendant or for further negotiation.

It is urged that the defendant by the use of the word "fair" in referring to a share of his profits, was as certain and definite as people are in the purchase and sale of a chattel when the price is not expressly agreed upon, and that if the agreement in question is declared to be too indefinite and uncertain to be enforced a similar conclusion must be reached in every case where a chattel is sold without expressly fixing the price therefor.

The question whether the words "fair" and "reasonable" have a definite and enforceable meaning when used in business transactions is dependent upon the intention of the parties in the use of such words and upon the subject-matter to which they refer. In cases of merchandising and in the purchase and sale of chattels the parties may use the words "fair and reasonable value" as synonymous with "market value." A promise to pay the fair market value of goods may be inferred from what is expressly agreed by the parties. The fair, reasonable or market value of goods can be shown by direct testimony of those competent to give such testimony. The competency to speak grows out of experience and knowledge. The testimony of such witnesses does not rest upon conjecture. The opinion of this court in *United Press v. N.Y. Press Co.* (164 N.Y. 406) was not intended to assert that a contract of sale is unenforceable unless the price is expressly mentioned and determined.

In the case of a contract for the sale of goods or for hire without a fixed price or consideration being named it will be presumed that a reasonable price or consideration is intended and the person who enters into such a contract for goods or service is liable therefor as on an implied contract. Such contracts are common, and when there is nothing therein to limit or prevent an implication as to the price, they are, so far as the terms of the contract are concerned, binding obligations.

The contract in question, so far as it relates to a share of the defendant's profits, is not only uncertain but it is necessarily affected by so many other facts that are in themselves indefinite and uncertain that the intention of the parties is pure conjecture. A fair share of the defendant's profits may be any amount from a nominal sum to a material part according to the particular views of the person whose guess is considered. Such an executory contract must rest for performance upon the honor and good faith of the parties making it. The courts cannot aid parties in such a case when they are unable or unwilling to agree upon the terms of their own proposed contract.

It is elementary in the law that, for the validity of a contract, the promise, or the agreement, of the parties to it must be certain and explicit and that their full intention may be ascertained to a reasonable degree of certainty. Their agreement must be neither vague nor indefinite, and, if thus defective, parol proof cannot be resorted to. *United Press v. N.Y. Press Co., supra.*

…

The rule stated from the *United Press* case does not prevent a recovery upon quantum meruit in case one party to an alleged contract has performed in reliance upon the terms thereof, vague, indefinite and uncertain though they are. In such case the law will presume a promise to pay the reasonable value of the services. Judge Gray, who wrote the opinion in the *United Press* case, said therein:

> I entertain no doubt that, where work has been done, or articles have been furnished, a recovery may be based upon quantum meruit, or quantum valebat; but, where a contract is of an executory character and requires performance over

a future period of time, as here, and it is silent as to the price which is to be paid to the plaintiff during its term, I do not think that it possesses binding force. As the parties had omitted to make the price a subject of covenant, in the nature of things, it would have to be the subject of future agreement, or stipulation. (p. 412.)

. . .

So, in this case, while I do not think that the plaintiff can recover anything as extra work, yet if the work actually performed as stated was worth more than $40 per week, he having performed until November 7, 1910, could, on a proper complaint, recover its value less the amount received.

. . .

The judgment should be affirmed, with costs.

BENJAMIN CARDOZO, JUDGE, READS DISSENTING OPINION, AND WILLARD BARTLETT, CHIEF JUDGE, AND JOHN HOGAN, JUDGE, CONCUR:

I do not think it is true that a promise to pay an employee a fair share of the profits in addition to his salary is always and of necessity too vague to be enforced. The promise must, of course, appear to have been made with contractual intent. But if that intent is present, it cannot be said from the mere form of the promise that the estimate of the reward is inherently impossible. The data essential to measurement may be lacking in the particular instance, and yet they may conceivably be supplied. It is possible, for example, that in some occupations an employee would be able to prove a percentage regulated by custom. The difficulty in this case is not so much in the contract as in the evidence. Even if the data required for computation might conceivably have been supplied, the plaintiff did not supply them. He would not have supplied them if all the evidence which he offered, and which the court excluded, had been received. He has not failed because the nature of the contract is such that damages are of necessity incapable of proof. He has failed because he did not prove them.

. . .

On the ground that the plaintiff failed to supply the data essential to computation, I concur in the conclusion that profits were not to be included as an element of damage. I do not concur, however, in the conclusion that he failed to make out a case of damage to the extent of his loss of salary. The amount may be small, but none the less it belongs to him. The hiring was not at will. The plain implication was that it should continue until the end of the year when the books were to be closed. The evidence would permit the jury to find that the plaintiff was discharged without cause, and he is entitled to damages measured by his salary for the unexpired term.

The judgment should be reversed and a new trial granted, with costs to abide the event.

Cobble Hill Nursing Home, Inc. v. Henry and Warren Corp.

Court of Appeals of New York
548 N.E.2d 203 (1989)

JUDITH S. KAYE, JUDGE

Contrary to the trial court and the Appellate Division, we conclude that the price term is sufficiently definite, and therefore grant judgment to plaintiff requiring specific performance of the contract.

The agreement at issue arose in connection with the nursing home scandals of the 1970s. Eugene Hollander, then a prominent figure in the industry, had for years been the operator of several nursing homes, until his felony convictions in 1976. He was and remains president of defendant Henry and Warren Corporation, owner of the Brooklyn property plaintiff seeks to purchase; his wife was and remains the corporation's sole shareholder. Prior to his convictions Hollander and his wife leased this property from defendant corporation, and operated the Congress Nursing Home there.

In July 1975 Hollander was indicted by State and Federal Grand Juries for crimes involving unwarranted health and medical care reimbursements. Faced with possible loss of operating certificates and preclusion from the nursing home business, Hollander during plea negotiations asked that the Department of Health appoint receivers who would continue to operate his nursing homes and pay rent to Henry and Warren Corporation.* Negotiations ensued for the appointment of plaintiff—a not-for-profit hospital corporation organized by community residents—as receiver for the Congress Nursing Home. Hollander's efforts at similar arrangements for his other nursing homes proved fruitless, as did his litigation to compel appointment of receivers for those facilities.

Talks regarding plaintiff's receivership continued through year-end. At a meeting in December, the Department informed Hollander that the maximum rent payable by a receiver would be calculated pursuant to the Medicaid reimbursement regulations (10 NYCRR part 86), which provided for reimbursement based upon a facility's historical cost. Thus calculated, projected rent for Congress was approximately half the amount defendant was then receiving. The Department refused to reconsider the matter, and indeed advised Hollander that it would take steps to revoke his operating certificates if a receiver was not soon installed.

In May 1976 Hollander entered a plea to the Federal charges and was sentenced to a five-year term of imprisonment (which was suspended), fined $10,000 and placed on probation for five years; a condition of his probation was that he "divest himself of all connections, direct or indirect, with any occupation that requires the custody or care of other people." Hollander had earlier pleaded guilty in State Supreme Court to the felonies of grand larceny in the second degree and offering a false instrument for filing in the first degree, but sentencing on the State charges was postponed because of the ongoing negotiations involving the transfer to plaintiff.

On May 17, 1976, a receivership agreement was signed by plaintiff, defendant, the Hollanders and the Department. On that same date, plaintiff and defendant additionally entered into a lease for the premises, assuring defendant continuing income from the operation of the nursing home, with rent to be "determined ... by [the Department of Health] pursuant to all applicable statutes, rules and regulations." Both the receivership agreement and the lease—each incorporating the other—contain the following purchase option:

> During the Term of the Lease, [plaintiff] shall have an option to purchase the premises (including without limitation the improvements thereon and the items

---

* Hollander's request was made pursuant to Public Health Law § 2810(1), which provides: "The owner or owners of any residential health care facility may at any time request the department to take over the operation of such facility by the appointment of a receiver. Upon receiving such a request, the department may, if it deems such action desirable, enter into an agreement with any such owners on the appointment of a receiver to take charge of the facility under whatever conditions as shall be found acceptable by both parties. Receivership commenced in accordance with the provisions of this subdivision shall terminate at such time as is agreed upon by the parties, or at such time as either party notifies the other in writing that he wishes to terminate such receivership."

set forth on the Inventory) at any time during said Term at a price determined by the Department in accordance with the Public Health Law and all applicable rules and regulations of the Department without prejudice to the remedies, if any, of the parties herein.

The very day after these agreements were signed—May 18, 1976—Hollander was sentenced to five years' probation conditioned on payment of a fine of $250,000 and $1,000,000 restitution to the State, as well as permanent divestiture of all his nursing home interests. The receivership agreement and lease enabled Hollander to represent to the sentencing court that he was completely out of the nursing home business.

More than three years later, in fall 1979, plaintiff notified the Department that it elected to exercise its option, and asked the Department to set the price. The Department in turn supplied "a computation of the Medicaid allowable transfer price which is the Price as called for by the Receiver Agreement." As the Department explained: "The Medicaid allowable transfer price (as well as Medicaid reimbursement for capital cost) is based upon the original historical cost of a facility as reported to the Department, subject to Departmental review. The original historical cost of a facility is also called the initial allowed facility cost and is defined in 10 NYCRR 86-2.21(a)(6)." This cost serves as the basis for a capital cost component in the Medicaid reimbursement rate determined pursuant to 10 NYCRR 86-2.21(e). The Department determined that as of January 1, 1980, the initial price defined in the purchase option provisions of the agreements was $3,046,352.

Plaintiff exercised the option, and delivered its down payment. Defendant, however, refused stating that it had "no intention of selling the facility in question to Cobble Hill at a price to be established by the Department in accordance with the Public Health Law as it is presently constituted." Defendant objected that the transfer price established by those provisions was "confiscatory," in that it bore "no relation to market value or any other reasonable criteria of true value for this facility." Defendant filed suit in the United States District Court for the Eastern District of New York, alleging due process violations and unjust taking. Those charges were dismissed for failure to state a claim, and the pendent State law claims were dismissed for want of jurisdiction.

Plaintiff meanwhile commenced an action in the State Supreme Court for specific performance of the option; defendant counterclaimed for rescission or adjustment of rent payments to fair market value. Defendant also separately sued the Department and the Commissioner of Health (intervenor on this appeal) challenging the determinations of rent and price as less than fair value. Both State court actions were consolidated into the present suit.

In response to plaintiff's motion for summary judgment, the parties entered into a stipulation. By agreement, Supreme Court awarded plaintiff partial summary judgment and struck defendant's affirmative defenses and the counterclaims except for "financial matters," which were reserved for the court. If the parties could not themselves reach an amicable resolution by June 16, 1986, they were to return to court for a hearing on those matters. In December 1986, at a hearing on the open financial matters, Supreme Court *sua sponte* vacated the stipulation and proceeded to hear argument on the validity of the option. Defendant at that point contended that the option was void for indefiniteness of the price term, in that no provision of the Public Health Law or the Department's rules and regulations provide a method for fixing the sales price of real property.

Supreme Court dismissed the complaint, finding that the option agreement was unenforceable for failure to specify a method by which price could be determined, and a divided Appellate Division affirmed. The court concluded that the specified law and regulations did not provide an explicit mechanism for determining purchase price, and that the parties had therefore failed to state an essential term, rendering the option unenforceable. The dissenting Justice, by contrast, found an enforceable contract, because the option expressed the parties' intent that the price be fixed by a third party, or because the agreement set forth a practicable method by which price was to be determined, or because the question was foreclosed by the parties' stipulation for partial summary judgment (144 A.D.2d 518, 524–527, 534 N.Y.S.2d 399).

After dismissal for nonfinality of a motion for leave to appeal to this court, Supreme Court granted defendant's application to direct plaintiff to surrender possession of the nursing home—at the time housing more than 500 elderly residents—and denied a cross motion for a stay. We then granted leave to appeal as well as a stay, and now reverse.

Few principles are better settled in the law of contracts than the requirement of definiteness. If an agreement is not reasonably certain in its material terms, there can be no legally enforceable contract (*Martin Delicatessen v. Schumacher*, 52 N.Y.2d 105, 109, 436 N.Y.S.2d 247, 417 N.E.2d 541; Restatement (Second) of Contracts § 33 (1981)). The doctrine of definiteness serves two related purposes.

First, unless a court can determine what the agreement is, it cannot know whether the contract has been breached, and it cannot fashion a proper remedy (*see, Metro-Goldwyn-Mayer v. Scheider*, 40 N.Y.2d 1069, 1070–1071, 392 N.Y.S.2d 252, 360 N.E.2d 930; Restatement (Second) of Contracts § 33(2) (1981)). This is particularly significant where specific performance is sought. *Second*, the requirement of definiteness assures that courts will not impose contractual obligations when the parties did not intend to conclude a binding agreement (*see*, Restatement (Second) of Contracts § 33(3) (1981)).

While the settled principles are easily articulated, their proper application has sometimes proved elusive. The difficulty is that the concept of definiteness cannot be reduced to a precise, universal measurement (Calamari & Perillo, Contracts § 2-9, at 53 (3d ed.)). The standard is necessarily flexible, varying for example with the subject of the agreement, its complexity, the purpose for which the contract was made, the circumstances under which it was made, and the relation of the parties (*id.*, at 54; Farnsworth, Contracts §§ 3.27, 3.29 (1982)).

Moreover, at some point virtually every agreement can be said to have a degree of indefiniteness, and if the doctrine is applied with a heavy hand it may defeat the reasonable expectations of the parties in entering into the contract (*see, Cohen & Sons v. Lurie Woolen Co.*, 232 N.Y. 112, 114, 133 N.E. 370 [Cardozo, J.]; Murray, Contracts § 27, at 47 (2d ed. 1974)). While there must be a manifestation of mutual assent to essential terms, parties also should be held to their promises and courts should not be "pedantic or meticulous" in interpreting contract expressions (1 Corbin, Contracts § 95, at 396 (1963); *see also*, UCC 2-204(3)). Before rejecting an agreement as indefinite, a court must be satisfied that the agreement cannot be rendered reasonably certain by reference to an extrinsic standard that makes its meaning clear (1 Williston, Contracts § 47, at 153–156 (3d ed. 1957)). The conclusion that a party's promise should be ignored as meaningless "is at best a last resort." (*Cohen & Sons v Lurie Woolen Co.*, 232 N.Y., at 114, 133 N.E. 370, *supra*.)

Passing from the general to the particular, a price term is not necessarily indefinite because the agreement fails to specify a dollar figure, or leaves fixing the amount for the future, or contains no computational formula. Where at the time of agreement the parties have manifested their intent to be bound, a price term may be sufficiently definite if the amount can be determined objectively without the need for new expressions by the parties; a method for reducing uncertainty to certainty might, for example, be found within the agreement or ascertained by reference to an extrinsic event, commercial practice or trade usage (*Metro-Goldwyn-Mayer v. Scheider*, 40 N.Y.2d 1069, 1070–1071, 392 N.Y.S.2d 252, 360 N.E.2d 930, *supra*; Annotation, *Requisite Definiteness of Price to Be Paid in Event of Exercise of Option for Purchase of Property*, 2 A.L.R.3d 701). A price "so arrived at would have been the end product of agreement between the parties themselves." (*Martin Delicatessen, supra*, at 110, 436 N.Y.S.2d 247, 417 N.E.2d 541.)

That standard is met here. Applying the foregoing principles to the facts, we conclude that the price term was sufficiently definite for an enforceable contract.

Addressing first the language of the agreement, the option manifests the parties' unmistakable intent that price was to be fixed by a third person—the Department of Health—itself providing an objective standard without the need for further expressions by the parties (*compare, Martin Delicatessen, supra; see also,* UCC 2-305(1)(c); 1 Corbin, §98, at 435–436; Farnsworth, §3.28, at 198; Knapp, *Enforcing the Contract to Bargain*, 44 N.Y.U. L. Rev. 673, 696 (1969)). That the agreement additionally directed the Department to fix the price "in accordance with the Public Health Law and all applicable rules and regulations" does not render the term indefinite.

Defendant urges that there is in fact no "applicable" rule or regulation for fixing the sales price of real property and therefore the essential term is illusory. But it is apparent from the agreement that these parties reposed discretion in the Department to make the price determination, limited only by the requirement that it apply provisions that were suitable, pertinent and appropriate for the task at hand. As the dissenting Justice below correctly observed, while the regulations did not authorize the Department to set a purchase price they did provide a means of fixing one—which is all these parties required. "The Public Health Law contemplates 'Medicaid' reimbursement to nursing home operators for 'real property costs' (*see,* Public Health Law §2808), including reasonable rent (*see,* 10 NYCRR 86-2.21(c)) and, where the operator is the owner, the reasonable costs of acquisition, e.g., amortization, interest and 'return of equity' (*see,* 10 NYCRR 86-2.21(e))." (144 AD2d, at 525, 534 N.Y.S.2d 399 [*dissenting opn.*].)

That the Department could indeed calculate a price by reference to its rules and regulations is evidenced by the fact that it did exactly that. As reflected in its letter fixing the price, the Department followed its regulations by referring to historical cost, then reducing that figure by the amount paid by the Medicaid program as capital cost reimbursement as of January 1980, and announcing the option price.

Beyond the contract language, the undisputed circumstances in which this agreement was made further confirm that the Department was to have the authority it exercised in fixing the price.

This was hardly an ordinary contract concluded between two private parties. Hollander's overriding objective was to avoid incarceration for his crimes; only the binding agreement he had reached with plaintiff literally on the eve of sentencing permitted him to make the representations to the court necessary to attain that objective. The Department's interest was to ensure the continuing operation of the nursing home, on a financial basis that would attract a responsible operator yet meet the cost-containment standards set by law for this largely publicly funded program.

The agreements repeatedly refer to plaintiff's limited resources and inability to pay more than reimbursable amounts. The receivership agreement states that plaintiff is a not-for-profit corporation having minimum capital, that plaintiff may not receive any fee as a receiver, and that "[n]otwithstanding anything to the contrary contained herein or in the Lease, the liability of [plaintiff] for rent, additional rent or other liability due to the Landlord or the Operator hereunder shall be limited to amounts finally determined by the Department or other applicable authority to be reimbursable under the Medicaid program." Likewise, the lease reflects the parties' recognition that plaintiff expects that "the primary source of its revenues" from the operation of the nursing home would be Medicaid payments and that this expectation was "a substantial and material inducement" to enter into the lease.

In these circumstances, when the parties designated the Department to fix the option price, that designation was obviously not for the purpose of calculating the nursing home's market value (*see*, Farnsworth, §3.28, at 198, n.20 [noting the risks of third-party valuation]). Defendant's contention that, under this agreement, it is somehow entitled to the equivalent of fair market value is simply without substance.

Bearing in mind the two objectives served by the definiteness requirement in contract law, there is no legal justification for voiding this agreement. The terms of agreement and the appropriate remedy can be readily determined, and it is plain that the parties intended this to be a complete and binding contract. Far from being a necessary "last resort," to declare this defendant's promise legally meaningless — thus allowing it to walk away with its property after enjoying the benefits of the bargain — defeats the reasonable expectations of the parties in entering into the contract and is a misuse of the definiteness doctrine.

Given an enforceable agreement that permitted the Department of Health to fix the option price as it did, and given defendant's refusal to comply, there can be no question that defendant has breached the contract. Where, as here, the agreement is for the conveyance of real property, specific performance rather than damages is the appropriate remedy (*see, Van Wagner Adv. Corp. v. S & M Enters.*, 67 N.Y.2d 186, 192, 501 N.Y.S.2d 628, 492 N.E.2d 756).

Accordingly, the order of the Appellate Division should be reversed, with costs, and judgment granted in plaintiff's favor.

Mary Gordon, Final Payments

(1978)

And now they were burying my father, because something had to be done with the bodies of the dead. It was the end of my life as well. After they lowered his body, I would have to invent an existence for myself. Care of an invalid has this great virtue: one never has to wonder what there is to do. Life is simple and inevitable and straightforward. Even the tedium has its seduction; empty time has always been earned. One can, if one chooses, leave it simply empty. My life had the balletic attraction of routine. Eleven years of it: bringing him breakfast, shaving him, hating to look at his face, twisted from the stroke in a way that made me forget the possibility of beauty.... And then I would put him in the chair and wheel him into the kitchen because, after all that, the morning was gone and it was time to make lunch.

And with his mouth twisted and his eye half shut he would try to talk to me. If I did not understand him, he would throw or break something, so that I would pretend (my ironic father to whom irony was no longer possible) always to understand.

In the afternoon he would try to read or sleep, and I would go to the store and try to clean the house. But it always seemed impossible. Life had accumulated around me in the house before I was old enough to fight it; life had grown into the walls so that I began to confuse it with the dust that was everywhere and the magazines that collected, that my father did not want thrown away, and the old letters and the grime that I could never get out of the furniture.

At supper I would cut my father's food up for him and wheel him into the living room where I would read to him for an hour. And then it would be time to get him ready for bed. The slow, long business of dying tired him daily. It was impossible to explain to anyone how long it takes to do the most ordinary things for an invalid. The whole day goes into the needs of a dying animal. And as with each new stroke he was able to do less for himself, the days were filled, and I grew dull. I slept when he slept. Sometimes he slept most of the day.

Note

When Mary Gordon's book, *Final Payments*, was published in 1978, it sold over 1,000,000 copies in paperback. This excerpt illustrates, as does *Cobble Hill Nursing Home* that care for elderly parents is a significant problem for adult children. Since Medicaid was enacted in the 1960s, nursing home or long term care has been an option for elderly people who suffer from serious illness. Although eligibility for Medicaid is need-based, the practice of "voluntary impoverishment" — middle-class elderly people transferring assets to other family members in order to qualify as medically indigent — is widespread. According to various estimates, Medicaid funds more than two-thirds of nursing home residents. Even so, only 1.4 million or so of the 40 million people over the age of 65 actually live in nursing homes. But, the proportion of people in nursing homes increases for the segment of senior citizens over the age of 75. L. Harris-Kojetin, M. Sengupta, E. Park-Lee, R. Valverde R., *Long-term Care Services in the United States: 2013 Overview*. National health care statistics reports; no 1., National Center for Health Statistics. 2013.

In the wake of Congressional cuts to Medicaid funding, governors and state legislators observed that "Medicaid can no longer be the financing mechanism for the nation's long term care costs ..." Robert Pear, *States Proposing Sweeping Change to Trim Medicaid*, N.Y. Times, Sec. A, Col. 6 May 9, 2005. What will be the effect of such a change? Note that U.S. Census Bureau projects the population of people over the age of 65 to increase by roughly 18 million and within that group, the number of people over the age of 85 will increase by 1.4 million. 2014 National Population Projections; Table 3 *available at* http://www.census.gov/population/projections/data/national/2014/summarytables.html. Is home care preferable to treatment in facilities with skilled nursing and medical staff? Who bears the cost of home care for the elderly? Would it be easier to place an elderly parent in either an assisted living facility (where they have some autonomy) or a nursing home if you could be sure they would be cared for adequately and their dignity preserved? Does your view of this issue affect your reading of *Cobble Hill Nursing Home, Inc.*?

Oglebay Norton Co. v. Armco, Inc.

Ohio Supreme Court
52 Ohio St. 3d 232, 556 N.E.2d 515 (1990)

PER CURIAM

...

On January 9, 1957, Armco Steel Corporation, n.k.a. Armco, Inc., appellant, entered into a long-term contract with Columbia Transportation Company, which later became a division of Oglebay Norton Company, appellee. The principal term of this contract required Oglebay to have adequate shipping capacity available and Armco to utilize such shipping capacity if Armco wished to transport iron ore on the Great Lakes from mines in the Lake Superior district to Armco's plants in the lower Great Lakes region.

In the 1957 contract, Armco and Oglebay established a primary and a secondary price rate mechanism which stated:

> Armco agrees to pay ... for all iron ore transported hereunder *the regular net contract rates for the season* in which the ore is transported, *as recognized by the leading iron ore shippers* in such season for the transportation of iron ore.... *If*, in any season of navigation hereunder, *there is no regular net contract rate recognized by the leading iron ore shippers* for such transportation, *the parties shall mutually agree upon a rate* for such transportation, *taking into consideration the contract rate being charged for similar transportation* by the leading independent vessel operators engaged in transportation of iron ore from The Lake Superior District. (Emphasis added.)

During the next twenty-three years, Armco and Oglebay modified the 1957 contract four times. With each modification Armco agreed to extend the time span of the contracts beyond the original date. Both parties acknowledged that the ever-increasing requirements capacity Armco sought from Oglebay would require a substantial capital investment from Oglebay to maintain, upgrade, and purchase iron ore carrier vessels.

The fourth amendment, signed in 1980, required Oglebay to modify and upgrade its fleet to give each Oglebay vessel that Armco utilized a self-unloading capability. It is undisputed that Oglebay began a $95 million capital improvement program at least in part to accommodate Armco's new shipping needs. For its part, Armco agreed to pay an additional twenty-five cents per ton for ore shipped in Oglebay's self-unloading vessels and agreed to extend the running of the contract until December 31, 2010.

During trial, the court recognized Armco's and Oglebay's close and long-standing business relationship, which included a seat for Armco on Oglebay's Board of Directors, Armco's owning Oglebay Norton stock, and a partnership in another venture. In fact, one of Oglebay's vessels was named "The Armco." This relationship is perhaps best characterized by the language contained in the 1962 amendment, wherein the parties provided:

> ... Armco has a vital and unique interest in the continued dedication of ... [Oglebay's] bulk vessel fleet ... since such service is a necessary prerequisite to Armco's operation as a major steel producer.... Armco's right to require the dedication of ... [Oglebay's] bulk vessels to Armco's service ... is the essence of this Agreement[.] ...

The amendment also granted to Armco the right to seek a court order for specific performance of the terms of the contract.

From 1957 through 1983 the parties established the contract shipping rate that Oglebay charged Armco by referring to a specified rate published in "Skillings Mining Review," in accordance with the 1957 contract's primary price mechanism. The published rate usually represented the price that Innerlake Steamship Company, a leading independent iron ore shipper, charged its customers for a similar service. Oglebay would quote this rate to Armco, which would then pay it to Oglebay.

Unfortunately, in 1983 the iron and steel industry suffered a serious downturn in business. Thus, in late 1983, when Oglebay quoted Armco the shipping rate for the 1984 season, Armco challenged that rate. Due to its weakened economic position, Armco requested that Oglebay reduce the rate Oglebay was going to charge Armco. The parties then negotiated a mutually satisfactory rate for the 1984 season.

In late 1984 the parties were unable to establish a mutually satisfactory shipping rate for the 1985 season. Oglebay billed Armco $7.66 ($.25 self-unloading vessel surcharge included) per gross ton, and Armco reduced the invoice amount to $5 per gross ton. Armco then paid the $5 per ton figure, indicating payment in full language on the check to Oglebay, and explaining its position in an accompanying letter. In late 1985, the parties again attempted to negotiate a rate, this time for the 1986 season. Again they failed to reach a mutually satisfactory rate.

On April 11, 1986, Oglebay filed a declaratory judgment action requesting the court to declare the rate set forth in the contract to be the correct rate, or in the absence of such a rate, to declare a reasonable rate for Oglebay's services. Armco's answer denied that the $7.41 rate sought by Oglebay was the "contract rate," and denied that the trial court had jurisdiction to declare this rate of its own accord, as a "reasonable rate" or otherwise. During the 1986 season, Oglebay continued to ship iron ore for Armco. Armco paid Oglebay $4.22 per gross ton for ore shipped prior to August 1, 1986 and $3.85 per gross ton for ore shipped after August 1, 1986. On August 12, 1987, Armco filed a supplemental counterclaim seeking a declaration that the contract was no longer enforceable, because the contract had failed of its purpose due to the complete breakdown of the rate pricing mechanisms.

After a lengthy bench trial, the trial court on November 20, 1987 issued its declaratory judgment, which made four basic findings of fact and law. First, the court held that it was apparent from the evidence presented that Oglebay and Armco intended to be bound by the 1957 contract, even though the rate or price provisions in the contract were not settled.

Second, the court held that where the parties intended to be bound, but where a service contract pricing mechanism based upon the mutual agreement of the parties fails, "then the price shall be the price that is 'reasonable' under all the circumstances at the time the service is rendered."

Third, the trial court held that the parties must continue to comply with the alternative pricing provision contained within paragraph two of the 1957 contract. That alternative pricing provision mandates that the parties consider rates charged for similar services by leading independent iron ore vessel operators.

Fourth, the trial court held that if the parties were unable to agree upon a rate for the upcoming seasons, then the parties must notify the court immediately. Upon such notification, the court, through its equitable jurisdiction, would appoint a mediator and require the parties' chief executive officers " ... to meet for the purpose of mediating and determining the rate for such season, i.e., that they 'mutually agree upon a rate.'" The court of appeals affirmed the judgment of the trial court.

The cause is now before the court upon the allowance of a motion to certify the record.

Per Curiam

This case presents three mixed questions of fact and law. First, did the parties intend to be bound by the terms of this contract despite the failure of its primary and secondary pricing mechanisms? Second, if the parties did intend to be bound, may the trial court establish $6.25 per gross ton as a reasonable rate for Armco to pay Oglebay for shipping Armco ore during the 1986 shipping season? Third, may the trial court continue to exercise its equitable jurisdiction over the parties, and may it order the parties to utilize a mediator if they are unable to mutually agree on a shipping rate for each annual shipping season? We answer each of these questions in the affirmative and for the reasons set forth below affirm the decision of the court of appeals.

I.

Appellant Armco argues that the complete breakdown of the primary and secondary contract pricing mechanisms renders the 1957 contract unenforceable, because the parties never manifested an intent to be bound in the event of the breakdown of the primary and secondary pricing mechanisms. Armco asserts that it became impossible after 1985 to utilize the first pricing mechanism in the 1957 contract, i.e., examining the published rate for a leading shipper in the "Skillings Mining Review," because after 1985 a new rate was no longer published. Armco asserts as well that it also became impossible to obtain the information necessary to determine and take into consideration the rates charged by leading independent vessel operators in accordance with the secondary pricing mechanism. This is because that information was no longer publicly available after 1985 and because the trial court granted the motions to quash of non-parties, who were subpoenaed to obtain this specific information. Armco argues that since the parties never consented to be bound by a contract whose specific pricing mechanisms had failed, the trial court should have declared the contract to be void and unenforceable.

The trial court recognized the failure of the 1957 contract pricing mechanisms. Yet the trial court had competent, credible evidence before it to conclude that the parties intended to be bound despite the failure of the pricing mechanisms. The evidence demonstrated the long-standing and close business relationship of the parties, including joint ventures, interlocking directorates and Armco's ownership of Oglebay stock. As the trial court pointed out, the parties themselves contractually recognized Armco's vital and unique interest in the combined dedication of Oglebay's bulk vessel fleet, and the parties recognized that Oglebay could be required to ship up to 7.1 million gross tons of Armco iron ore per year.

Whether the parties intended to be bound, even upon the failure of the pricing mechanisms, is a question of fact properly resolved by the trier of fact. *Normandy Place Assoc. v. Beyer* (1982), 2 Ohio St. 3d 102, 106, 2 OBR 653, 656, 443 N.E.2d 161, 164. Since the trial court had ample evidence before it to conclude that the parties did so intend, the court of appeals correctly affirmed the trial court regarding the parties' intent. We thus affirm the court of appeals on this question.

II.

Armco also argues that the trial court lacked jurisdiction to impose a shipping rate of $6.25 per gross ton when that rate did not conform to the 1957 contract pricing mechanisms. The trial court held that it had the authority to determine a reasonable rate for Oglebay's services, even though the price mechanism of the contract had failed, since the parties intended to be bound by the contract. The court cited 1 *Restatement of the Law 2d, Contracts* (1981) 92, section 33, and its relevant comments to support this proposition. Comment e to section 33 explains in part:

> ... Where [the parties] intend to conclude a contract for the sale of goods ... and the price is not settled, the price is a reasonable price at the time of delivery if ... (c) the price is to be fixed in terms of some agreed market or other standard as set or recorded by a third person or agency and it is not so set or recorded. Uniform Commercial Code § 2-305(1).

As the trial court noted, section 33 was cited with approval by the Court of Appeals for Cuyahoga County in *Mr. Mark Corp. v. Rush, Inc.* (1983), 11 Ohio App. 3d 167, 11 OBR 259, 464 N.E.2d 586. *Restatement* Section 33, Comment e follows virtually identical language contained in Section 2-305(1) of the *Uniform Commercial Code*, which was adopted in Ohio as R.C. 1302.18(A)....

The court therefore determined that a reasonable rate for Armco to pay to Oglebay for transporting Armco's iron ore during the 1986 shipping season was $6.00 per gross ton with an additional rate of twenty-five cents per gross ton when self-unloading vessels were used. The court based this determination upon the parties' extensive course of dealing, " ... the detriment to the parties respectively, and valid comparisons of market price which reflect [the] economic reality of current depressed conditions in the American steel industry."

The court of appeals concluded that the trial court was justified in setting $6.25 per gross ton as a "reasonable rate" for Armco to pay Oglebay for the 1986 season, given the evidence presented to the trial court concerning various rates charged in the industry and given the intent of the parties to be bound by the agreement.

The court of appeals also held that an open price term could be filled by a trial court, which has the authority to review evidence and establish a "reasonable price," when the parties clearly intended to be bound by the contract. To support this holding, the court cited *Restatement of the Law 2d, Contracts, supra,* at 92, Section 33, and its comments, and 179, Section 362, and its comments.

Section 33, Comment A provides in part:

> ... [T]he actions of the parties may show conclusively that they have intended to conclude a binding agreement, even though one or more terms are missing or are left to be agreed upon. In such cases courts endeavor, if possible, to attach a sufficiently definite meaning to the bargain. An offer which appears to be indefinite may be given precision by usage of trade or by course of dealing between the parties. Terms may be supplied by factual implication, and in recurring situations the law often supplies a term in the absence of agreement to the contrary....

Id. at 92.

As the court of appeals noted, we have held that "agreements to agree," such as the pricing mechanisms in the 1957 contract, are enforceable when the parties have manifested an intention to be bound by their terms and when these intentions are sufficiently definite to be specifically enforced. *Normandy Place Assoc., supra,* 2 Ohio St. 3d at 105–106, 2 OBR at 656, 443 N.E.2d at 164. We have also held that "[i]f it is found that the parties intended to be bound, the court should not frustrate this intention, if it is reasonably possible to fill in some gaps that the parties have left, and reach a fair and just result." *Litsinger Sign Co. v. American Sign Co.* (1967), 11 Ohio St. 2d 1, 14, 40 O.O.2d 30, 37, 227 N.E.2d 609, 619.

The court of appeals conducted an extensive review of the evidence presented to the trial court and concluded that the $6.25 per gross ton figure was a "reasonable rate" in this situation. The court of appeals noted that Oglebay presented evidence from Jesse J. Friedman, an economic and financial expert, who testified that $7.44 per gross ton was a reasonable rate for such services. Further evidence showed that Armco paid $5.00 per gross ton to Oglebay for the 1985 season, even though the published rate for that season was $7.41 per gross ton.

There was also testimony that Oglebay quoted Armco $5.66 per gross ton as the rate for the 1987 season. The evidence also showed that LTV Steel, prior to its bankruptcy renegotiations with Oglebay, had paid Oglebay the published rate of $7.41 per gross ton. Evidence also indicated that American Steamship Co. had quoted Armco a $5.90 per gross ton rate for the 1986 season.

The court of appeals concluded that the $6.25 per gross ton figure fell acceptably between the rate range extremes proven at trial. The court found this to be a reasonable figure. We find there was competent, credible evidence in the record to support this holding and affirm the court of appeals on this question.

III.

Armco also argues that the trial court lacks equitable jurisdiction to order the parties to negotiate or in the failure of negotiations, to mediate, during each annual shipping season through the year 2010. The court of appeals ruled that the trial court did not exceed its jurisdiction in issuing such an order. 3 *Restatement of the Law 2d, Contracts* (1981) 179, Section 362, entitled "Effect of Uncertainty of Terms," is similar in effect to Section 33 and states: "Specific performance or an injunction will not be granted unless the terms of the contract are sufficiently certain to provide a basis for an appropriate order."

Comment B to Section 362 explains:

> ... Before concluding that the required certainty is lacking, however, a court will avail itself of all of the usual aids in determining the scope of the agreement.... Expressions that at first appear incomplete may not appear so after resort to usage ... or the addition of a term supplied by law ...

Id. at 179.

Ordering specific performance of this contract was necessary, since, as the court of appeals pointed out, " ... the undisputed dramatic changes in the market prices of great lakes shipping rates and the length of the contract would make it impossible for a court to award Oglebay accurate damages due to Armco's breach of the contract." We agree with the court of appeals that the appointment of a mediator upon the breakdown of court-ordered contract negotiations neither added to nor detracted from the parties' significant obligations under the contract.

It is well-settled that a trial court may exercise its equitable jurisdiction and order specific performance if the parties intend to be bound by a contract, where determination of long-term damages would be too speculative. *See* 3 Restatement of the Law 2d, Contracts, *supra*, at 171–172, Section 360(a), Comment b; *Columbus Packing Co. v. State, ex rel. Schlesinger* (1919), 100 Ohio St. 285, 294, 126 N.E. 291, 293–294. Indeed, the court of appeals pointed out that under the 1962 amendment, Armco itself had the contractual right to seek a court order compelling Oglebay to specifically perform its contractual duties.

The court of appeals was correct in concluding that ordering the parties to negotiate and mediate during each shipping season for the duration of the contract was proper, given the unique and long-lasting business relationship between the parties, and given their intent to be bound and the difficulty of properly ascertaining damages in this case. The court of appeals was also correct in concluding that ordering the parties to negotiate and mediate with each shipping season would neither add to nor detract from the parties' significant contractual obligations. This is because the order would merely facilitate in the most practical manner the parties' own ability to interact under the contract. Thus we affirm the court of appeals on this question.

The court of appeals had before it competent, credible evidence from which to conclude that the parties intended to be bound by the terms of the contract, to conclude that the

$6.25 per gross ton figure was a "reasonable rate" under the circumstances, and to conclude that the trial court's exercise of continuing equitable jurisdiction was proper in this situation. Accordingly, we affirm the decision of the court of appeals. Judgment affirmed.

CHRISTOPHER COLUMBUS LANGDELL

OLIVER WENDELL HOLMES, JR.

ARTHUR L. CORBIN

SAMUEL WILLISTON

KARL N. LLEWELLYN

LON FULLER

Chapter Four

The Consideration Doctrine

Not all promises are enforceable. "Formation of a contract requires a bargain in which there is a manifestation of mutual assent to the exchange and a consideration." (Restatement (Second) of Contracts, § 17(1)). So, even where there is assent, a promise might not be enforced for lack of consideration. "To constitute consideration, a performance or a return promise must be bargained for." Restatement (Second) of Contracts, § 71(1). Comment b to § 71 explains:

> "In the typical bargain, the consideration and the promise bear a reciprocal relation of motive or inducement: the consideration induces the making of the promise and the promise induces the furnishing of the consideration...."

Because a promisor may be legally bound for other reasons, however, a more accurate statement of the current consideration doctrine would include a qualification: lack of consideration makes a promise unenforceable, unless enforcement of the promise is warranted on some alternative ground such as reliance or receipt of a past benefit.

This chapter begins with a brief history of the consideration doctrine. Contract scholars writing in the late nineteenth and early twentieth centuries shaped this doctrine as the political and jurisprudential center of classical contract law. The consideration doctrine embodies the "laissez-faire" and "free market" attitude of the U.S. business and legal elite following the Civil War. Fueled by the burst of industrialization and the promise of huge profits and fearful of the increasing size and desperate poverty of the urban underclass, laissez-faire economic and legal theory promoted noninterference or indifference as a high virtue of government. The consideration doctrine was the site of many spoken and unspoken political struggles throughout the twentieth century and into the twenty-first. This history is crucial to understanding the peculiar incoherence of the current consideration doctrine.

Judges, lawyers, and commentators have searched in vain for either persuasive justifications for the consideration doctrine or definitive arguments against it. Courts have created explicit exceptions to it and have implicitly narrowed or circumvented it in a variety of different settings. Yet regardless of the on-going struggle and the unending criticism, courts continue to recite and apply the doctrine. Perhaps this is because judges view the core ideas of consideration as harmonious with popular beliefs about market exchange or perhaps it is because the doctrine provides a tool with which judges can refuse enforcement of transactions they view as unfair or otherwise socially harmful.

Following the historical introduction, Part B examines the first element in the definition of consideration, "a return promise or performance" and the related rule that "courts will not inquire into the adequacy of consideration." Part C explores the second element of this definition: "that is bargained for" and related rules.

A. Origins of the Consideration Doctrine

The legal phrase "consideration for a promise" is approximately four hundred years old, but its meaning has changed significantly over that period. In this section, we will highlight four phases in the long history of this doctrine: (1) the early view of consideration, as it developed in the sixteenth and seventeenth centuries; (2) the "classical" reformulation of consideration during the second half of the nineteenth century; (3) the reinterpretation of consideration as one of several bases for contractual liability during the 1940s and 50s; and (4) a contemporary, emerging view of consideration as a device for regulating the process and content of transactions.

1. The Early View of Consideration

The phrase "consideration for a promise" began with an idea drawn from the Roman notion of "causa," meaning the reason or motive for a promise—what the promisor was thinking about or "considering" when she or he made the promise. The purpose for identifying a "consideration" was to make the allegation of a promise credible, to give the court some idea of the context in which the promise was made. The fact that the promisor was already under some obligation to the promisee, as when the promisee had already loaned the promisor money or had done something for the promisor, clearly would satisfy the consideration requirement in this early meaning of the phrase. "Because you gave my son food and medical care when he needed it, I promise to pay you $1,000" would be a promise with consideration. Courts could understand why such a promise would be made and were thus prepared to believe that it was a serious commitment. In an almost complete turn-about, however, the late nineteenth century version of the consideration requirement, as it was developed by classical contract theorists, did not recognize this "past consideration" as sufficient because it was not "bargained-for."

2. The Classical Reformulation

During the second half of the nineteenth century, leading contract theorists repositioned the consideration doctrine to the center of classical contract theory and reformulated it to require a "bargained for" exchange. Perhaps the most influential advocate for the "new" doctrine of consideration was Oliver Wendell Holmes. In *The Common Law* (1881), Holmes observed "The doctrine of contract has been so thoroughly remodeled to meet the needs of modern times, that there is less necessity here than elsewhere for historical research." *Id.* at 247. Having thus asserted the birth of a new contract law, Holmes does offer historical analysis, but it is explicitly offered to show the centrality of bargaining to the consideration doctrine and contract liability. As Holmes explains:

> Debt throws most light upon the doctrine of consideration.
>
> Our law does not enforce every promise that a man may make. Promises made, as ninety-nine promises out of a hundred are, by word of mouth or simple writing, are not binding unless there is a consideration for them. That is, as it is commonly explained, unless the promisee has either conferred a benefit on the promisor, or incurred a detriment, as the inducement to the promise.

Id. at 253.

Holmes elaborated on the element of inducement featured in the new consideration doctrine:

> It is said that any benefit conferred by the promisee on the promisor, or any detriment incurred by the promisee, may be a consideration....
>
> ... [A]lthough the courts may have sometimes gone a little far in their anxiety to sustain agreements, there can be no doubt of the principle which I have laid down, that the same thing may be a consideration or not, as it is dealt with by the parties. This raises the question how a thing must be dealt with, in order to make it a consideration.
>
> It is said that consideration must not be confounded with motive. It is true that it must not be confounded with what may be the prevailing or chief motive in actual fact. A man may promise to paint a picture for five hundred dollars, while his chief motive may be a desire for fame. A consideration may be given and accepted, in fact, solely for the purpose of making a promise binding. But nevertheless, it is the essence of a consideration, that, by the terms of the agreement, it is given and accepted as the motive or inducement of the promise. Conversely, the promise must be made and accepted as the conventional motive or inducement for furnishing the consideration. The root of the whole matter is the relation of reciprocal conventional inducement, each for the other, between consideration and promise.

Id. at 289–94.

Holmes continued with an explanation of why a promise made in recognition of a benefit already received should not be enforceable:

> If the foregoing principles be accepted, they will be seen to explain a doctrine which has given the courts some trouble to establish. I mean the doctrine that an executed consideration will not sustain a subsequent promise. It has been said, to be sure, that such a consideration was sufficient if preceded by a request. But the objections to the view are plain. If the request was of such a nature, and so put, as reasonably to imply that the other person was to have a reward, there was an express promise, although not put in words, and that promise was made at the same time the consideration was given and not afterwards. If, on the other hand, the words did not warrant the understanding that the service was to be paid for, the service was a gift, and a past gift can no more be a consideration than any other act of a promisee not induced by the promise.

Id. at 295–96.

With this rejection of "past benefit" as a basis for enforcing a promise, the transformation of consideration doctrine was complete. The doctrine of consideration became the theoretical heart of classical contract law — the sole basis for contractual liability. Implementing this vision required discounting many actual decisions, but it had the advantage of simplicity and the endorsement of many influential lawyers.

Christopher Columbus Langdell was among the most influential proponents of this new theory. His *Selection of Cases on the Law of Contracts*, first published in 1871 and reissued periodically, was the foundation for generations of lawyers' understandings of contract law. Like Holmes, Langdell saw the newly formulated theory of contract as the articulation of sound principles that should be implemented despite their break with prior judicial decisions. In the preface to his casebook, Langdell wrote:

Law, considered as a science, consists of certain principles or doctrines. To have such a mastery of these as to apply them with constant facility and certainty to the over-tangled skein of human affairs, is what constitutes a true lawyer; and hence to acquire that mastery should be the business of every earnest student of law.... [A]nd much the shortest and the best, if not the only way of mastering the doctrine effectually is by studying the cases in which it is embodied. But the cases which are useful and necessary for this purpose at the present day bear an exceedingly small proportion to all that have been reported. The vast majority are useless and worse than useless for any purpose of systematic study. Moreover, the number of fundamental legal doctrines is much less than is commonly supposed.

Christopher Columbus Langdell, Selection of Cases on the Law of Contracts vi (1871).

3. The Reinterpretation of Consideration as One among Many

During the 1920s, Arthur Corbin and others argued strenuously for recognition of the idea that some promises are enforced even though they lack bargained for consideration. Most persuasively, these advocates argued that courts frequently enforce gratuitous promises that have been relied upon, particularly in the context of charitable contributions and gratuitous bailments. Much of the debate over this idea focused on the drafting of the American Law Institute's *Restatement of the Law of Contracts*. The principal drafter of the *Restatement* was Samuel Williston, an influential classical contract theorist. Although Williston was reluctant to include any suggestion that consideration was not the sole basis for contractual liability, and Oliver Wendell Holmes condemned the idea, still the *Restatement*'s explicit purpose was to "restate" the law as it actually existed. Corbin was able to present so many decisions enforcing gratuitous promises because of reliance that Williston was compelled to agree to the inclusion of section 90. With the publication of the *Restatement* in 1932, then, the primacy of consideration was called into serious question and the path to a second reformulation of the consideration doctrine was laid out.

In 1941, the Columbia Law Review published a series of articles on consideration, with a forward and concluding article penned by Karl Llewellyn. The other contributors to this volume were Lon Fuller, Malcolm Sharp, Paul Hays, and Malcolm Mason. This Symposium came after several years of direct scholarly challenges to the consideration doctrine, including an article that advocated outright rejection of the consideration doctrine, written by a well-known English jurist and published in the Harvard Law Review. Lord Wright, *Ought the Doctrine of Consideration to be Abolished from the Common Law*, 49 Harv. L. Rev. 1225 (1936). Llewellyn's *Foreword* describes the disarray of consideration theory:

..."Consideration" is not in any meaningful sense a topic....

There is instead an historically collected agglomeration of states of fact—like pebbles in pudding-stone—held together by the sole tie of being allegedly covered by "the same" legal doctrine. But the legal doctrines concerned are not "the same"; they are not a single body. The *Restatement of Contracts* achieves a semi-unity of concept and doctrine on "consideration" in the formation of promissory obligation; but it does so only at the expense of express recognition that its consideration doctrine does *not* cover the field of fact with which the same *Restatement* is concerned....

Karl Llewellyn, *On the Complexity of Consideration: A Foreword*, 41 Colum. L. Rev. 777, 778 (1941).

Llewellyn then argues that three devices have been used to maintain the illusion of a unified consideration doctrine. The first device is a narrow definition of contract, which excludes such "problem" types as waivers and non-promissory agreements. He continues:

> The second device has been to throw out any discrepant bodies of case-material as wrong, and so not to be worried over; at worst, they can be treated … as intrusive cysts upon a body which "is," nonetheless, a unity. What I shall treat as the third device is the natural result of the first two and goes to the practical work with law, which must be done despite the absence of appropriate theory. That third device is to retain the body of general (though inadequate) doctrine, always capable of use and pressing for use, but to build beside it a body of escape-doctrine applicable to precisely the same situations (if they are at all problematical); the two bodies remaining in actual, but latent conflict. This is what my brother Patterson has well called "back-door building." Along with it goes a type of overt, but unnoticed, semi-conflict: the building of two explicit general rules, each of overbroad reach, which overlap the problematical area from different directions....
>
> What all this comes to, is that "the field" is bound, for a while, to mean different things to [different people] … It is no wonder that philosophers exploring it have been unable to find any single policy-theory on which "the" doctrine rested. There is more wonder that there has not come a more adequately emphatic recognition that this is not for one reason, but for two. It is not only because "consideration" expresses a considerable number of policies, often at odds and not worked out in full harmony. It is, even more, because there is no single doctrine or body of doctrine to be found either under or near the label. The conglomerate nature of relevant doctrine on what "consideration" is, and when it is or is not necessary, is an expression of the successive differential pressures of the different policies at different times or in different circumstances, pressures felt quite as much situation by situation, or even case by case, as they have been felt in terms either of broad policy or of need for doctrinal unity.

Id. at 779–80.

In addition, the reformulation of this period includes the important emphasis on the ends served by the consideration doctrine, with a recognition that it may serve multiple and conflicting ends. Another entry in the Columbia symposium is an article entitled *Consideration and Form* written by Lon Fuller, an influential legal theorist who had already co-authored, with law student William Purdue, an important article on the reliance principle in contract law. In *Consideration and Form*, Fuller argues that consideration serves both formal and substantive purposes in contract law.

As a formality, Fuller argues, consideration provides evidence, serves as a caution against undeliberated promises, and provides a channel for the expression of an intent to be bound. To evaluate the substantive functions of consideration, Fuller first defines three substantive bases of contractual liability: the promotion of private autonomy (including exchange), the protection of reliance, and the prevention of unjust enrichment. Fuller then analyzes the effectiveness of the consideration doctrine in implementing these three principles and finds that in many instances the doctrine promotes these principles, while in some circumstances it does not. In conclusion, Fuller argues that the consideration doctrine should not be abolished but that some rules associated with it should be reformed and other doctrines developed:

> It has sometimes been proposed that the doctrine of consideration be "abolished." Such a step would, I believe, be unwise, and in a broad sense even

impossible. The *problems* which the doctrine of consideration attempts to solve cannot be abolished. There can be little question that some of these problems do not receive a proper solution in the complex of legal doctrine now grouped under the rubric "consideration." It is equally clear that an original attack on these problems would arrive at some conclusions substantially equivalent to those that result from the doctrine of consideration as now formulated. What needs abolition is not the doctrine of consideration but a conception of legal method which assumes that the doctrine can be understood and applied without reference to the ends it serves. When we have come again to define consideration in terms of its underlying policies the problem of adapting it to new conditions will largely solve itself.

Lon Fuller, *Consideration and Form*, 41 Colum. L. Rev. 799, 824 (1941).

In these articles and elsewhere, Llewellyn, Fuller, and others reformulated the consideration doctrine as one among other tests for the enforceability of promises and agreements. Professor Edwin Patterson noted this reformulation in a 1958 article entitled *An Apology for Consideration*. Patterson set out the following propositions, drawn from the reformulation by Llewellyn, Fuller, and others. These propositions well describe the consideration doctrine as it has been understood by lawyers since the 1950s and 1960s:

1) Consideration implies a thing and a process;

2) Consideration may be a sufficient basis of promissory liability without being the exclusive one; and

3) Some supposed corollaries of consideration need not be defended.

Edwin Patterson, *An Apology for Consideration*, 58 Colum. L. Rev. 929, 932–941 (1958).

4. An Emerging Use of Consideration as a Tool for Implementing Fairness and a Variety of Other Public Policies

During the last decades of the twentieth century, the view that consideration is but one among many bases for contractual liability gained support from the work of "reliance theorists," including Patrick Atiyah and others, and from a variety of jurisprudential contracts theories offered during that period, including "relational contract theory," "economic analysis of contract," "responsive contract theory," "contract as promise," "consensual contract law," and "post-modern contract law." While it is difficult and risky to name "emerging" ideas, there appears to have been not only a development of the idea of consideration as one of many, but also a shift in courts' use of the consideration doctrine in recent years. Part of this shift is a more practical, or perhaps skeptical, attitude towards the consideration doctrine. Grant Gilmore's provocative book, *The Death of Contract* may have been influential in development of this attitude.

In 1970, Grant Gilmore delivered a series of lectures at the Ohio State University Law School that he then compiled and published in 1973 under the engaging title *The Death of Contract*. A mere 103 pages long, this book has inspired reviews, responsive articles, and long discursive footnotes. In this book, Gilmore, a widely respected professor of law, debunked, with wit and passion, classical contract theory, Christopher Columbus Langdell, Oliver Wendell Holmes, and the doctrine of consideration. With the publication of *The Death of Contract*, the sting of laughter significantly weakened many lawyers' belief in the consideration doctrine as a principle of abstract truth. Gilmore portrays the consideration doctrine as an artificially constructed, deeply political, yet nevertheless potentially useful tool.

Gilmore described the classical theory of contract as "dedicated to the proposition that no one should be liable to anyone for anything. Since the ideal was not attainable, the compromise was to restrict liability within the narrowest possible limits." *Id.* at 14. As to the ascendency of this theory, Gilmore cites Lawrence Friedman's analysis of the correspondence between classical contract theory and laissez-faire economic theory:

> I suppose that laissez-faire economic theory comes down to something like this: If we all do exactly as we please, no doubt everything will work out for the best. Which seems to mean about the same thing that the contract theory comes down to, with liability reduced to a minimum.

Id. at 95. Gilmore further surmised:

> It seems apparent to the twentieth century mind, as perhaps it did not to the nineteenth century mind, that a system in which everybody is invited to do his own thing, at whatever cost to his neighbor, must work ultimately to the benefit of the rich and powerful, who are in a position to look after themselves and to act, so to say, as their own self-insurers. As we look back on the nineteenth century theories, we are struck most of all, I think, by the narrow scope of social duty which they implicitly assumed. No man is his brother's keeper; the race is to the swift; let the devil take the hindmost.

Id.

About Langdell, Gilmore writes:

> To judge by the casebook and the Summary, Langdell was an industrious researcher of no distinction whatever either of mind or ... of style. But it is with Langdell that we first see Contract as ... an "abstraction"—a remote, impersonal, bloodless abstraction.... The casebook was to contain—and presumably did contain—all the important contract cases that had ever been decided. "All the cases" turned out to be mostly English cases, arranged in historical sequence from the seventeenth century down to the date of publication; the English cases were occasionally supplemented by comparable sequences of cases from New York and Massachusetts—no other American jurisdictions being represented. The Summary, which runs to a hundred and fifty pages or so, is devoted almost entirely to explaining which of the cases in the main part of the casebook are "right" and which are "wrong." The explanation, typically, is dogmatic rather than reasoned; Langdell knew right from wrong, no doubt by divine revelation, and that should suffice for the student. This aspect of the Summary of the Law of Contracts throws an entertaining light on the origins of case-method teaching. At least in Langdell's version, it had nothing whatever to do with getting students to think for themselves; it was, on the contrary, a method of indoctrination through brainwashing.

Id. at 13.

Gilmore describes Holmes as the brilliant yet deceptive advocate who turned Langdell's vision into a "monstrous machine," looking with "stone-eyed indifference" at the claims of those who would trust without a bargain. Gilmore wrote: "In the elaboration of consideration theory much wit and learning was devoted to the game, popularized by Holmes, of pretending that bargain theory was not only philosophically, economically, and socially sound but that it also had the sanction of history."

Grant Gilmore's *The Death of Contract* set the stage for a genuine embracing of Fuller's insight that consideration must be understood in terms of the ends it serves (or can be made to serve) rather than as an abstract rule or principle. In a 1995 article, Mark Wessman reported the results of his survey of some 300 cases decided since the mid-1970s in which courts refused enforcement to a promise or agreement because of lack of consideration. Wessman concludes that in a significant number of those cases, courts were influenced by their desire to prevent enforcement of exchanges that were unfair or to implement some other policy goal. See Mark B. Wessman, *Should We Fire the Gatekeeper? An Examination of the Doctrine of Consideration*, 48 U. Miami L. Rev. 45 (1993). Wessman finds this use of the consideration doctrine troubling because it "obscure[s] the true factual or policy issues and lead[s] to dubious case dispositions." Other lawyers and courts see this emerging use of the consideration as a positive development, empowering the courts to resist unfairness and other injustice in contractual relationships. Yet, as Wessman suggests, there is a serious risk that courts will use this power deceptively. And there is a serious risk that some courts will use it to implement policies unjustly benefiting some groups while burdening others.

B. "A Return Promise or Performance" and "Courts Will Not Inquire into the Adequacy of Consideration"

There are several definitions of consideration. Most courts use a relatively broad definition such as *any performance (including forbearance) or return promise done or given as inducement for the promise.* Another definition used by some courts is *some benefit or detriment given or suffered as an inducement for the promise.* This second definition is less favored by contemporary courts because it suggests that some actual benefit or detriment must be proved, and that is not accurate. Still a third alternative defines consideration as *something of legal value* transferred, undertaken, or foregone *as an inducement for the promise.* This definition is also disfavored by many courts because it wrongly suggests that there is a clear category of things that have "legal value."

The *Restatement (Second) of Contracts*, in section 71, defines consideration as a "bargained-for" "performance or ... return promise," in accordance with the first definition above. Section 71 specifies further that a performance "may consist of ... an act other than a promise, or ... a forbearance, or ... the creation, modification, or destruction of a legal relation" and that "the performance or return promise may be given to the promisor or to some other person. It may be given by the promisee or by some other person." Restatement (Second) of Contracts § 71. The *Restatement (Second)* explicitly disapproves a definition of consideration that focuses on "benefit" or "detriment"; section 79 (a) says: "If the requirement of consideration is met, there is no additional requirement of ... a gain, advantage, or benefit to the promisor or a loss, disadvantage, or detriment to the promisee."

Contemporary consideration doctrine provides that there must be a "reciprocal relation of motive or inducement" between the promise and return promise or performance. A promise is defined in Restatement (Second) of Contracts § 2: "A promise is a manifestation of intention to act or refrain from acting in a specified way, so made as to justify a promisee in understanding that a commitment has been made." Section 71(2) and (3) of the Restatement (Second) of Contracts provide further guidance:

(2) A performance or return promise is bargained for if it is sought by the promisor in exchange for his promise and is given by the promisee in exchange for that promise.

(3) The performance may consist of

    (a) an act other than a promise, or

    (b) a forbearance, or

    (c) the creation, modification, or destruction of a legal relation.

In this section, we look at the "performance or promise" requirement. In *Hamer v. Sidway*, the court applies the general rule that *any* promise or performance is sufficient, without regard to whether it is valuable or "beneficial" to the promisor or costly to the promisee. This rule is usually stated in words of judicial restraint: the court will not inquire into the adequacy of the consideration. The rationale for this rule draws on the ideology of "freedom of contract." In this view, individuals should be free to set their own values and to engage in the free exchange of goods and services without interference from the government, including the judiciary. The rule reflects the belief that courts ought not to impose upon the parties their own views regarding the value of the goods or services being exchanged. Despite its historical significance, the continued viability of the rule precluding inquiry into the adequacy of consideration is uncertain, because contemporary contract law includes doctrines that require courts to evaluate the fairness of an exchange, particularly if one party is unusually vulnerable, if inequality in parties' bargaining power is unusually great, if a term of the contract conflicts with some public policy, or if the contract is unusually one-sided. We will explore this idea in our discussion of "unconscionability" in Chapter Seven.

Hamer v. Sidway

Court of Appeals of New York
27 N.E. 256 (N.Y. 1891)

... The plaintiff presented a claim to the executor of William E. Story, Sr., for $5,000 and interest from the 6th day of February, 1875. She acquired it through several mesne assignments from William E. Story, 2d. The claim being rejected by the executor, this action was brought. It appears that William E. Story, Sr., was the uncle of William E. Story, 2d., that at the celebration of the golden wedding of Samuel Story and wife, father and mother of William E. Story, Sr., on the 20th day of March, 1869, in the presence of the family and invited guests, he promised his nephew that if he would refrain from drinking, using tobacco, swearing, and playing cards or billiards for money until he became 21 years of age, he would pay him the sum of $5,000. The nephew assented thereto, and fully performed the conditions inducing the promise. When the nephew arrived at the age of 21 years, and on the 31st day of January, 1875, he wrote to his uncle, informing him that he had performed his part of the agreement, and had thereby become entitled to the sum of $5,000. The uncle received the letter, and a few days later, and on the 6th day of February, he wrote and mailed to his nephew the following letter:

    Buffalo, Feb. 6, 1875.

    W. E. Story, Jr.—Dear Nephew: Your letter of the 31st ult. came to hand all right, saying that you had lived up to the promise made to me several years ago.

I have no doubt but you have, for which you shall have five thousand dollars, as I promised you. I had the money in the bank the day you was twenty-one years old that I intend for you, and you shall have the money certain. Now, Willie, I do not intend to interfere with this money in any way till I think you are capable of taking care of it, and the sooner that time comes the better it will please me. I would hate very much to have you start out in some adventure that you thought all right and lose this money in one year. The first five thousand dollars that I got together cost me a heap of hard work. You would hardly believe me when I tell you that to obtain this I shoved a jack-plane many a day, butchered three or four years, then came to this city, and, after three months' perseverance, I obtained a situation in a grocery store. I opened this store early, closed late, slept in the fourth story of the building in a room 30 by 40 feet, and not a human being in the building but myself. All this I done to live as cheap as I could to save something. I don't want you to take up with this kind of fare. I was here in the cholera season of '49 and '52, and the deaths averaged 80 to 125 daily, and plenty of smallpox. I wanted to go home, but Mr. Fisk, the gentleman I was working for, told me, if I left them, after it got healthy he probably would not want me. I stayed. All the money I have saved I know just how I got it. It did not come to me in any mysterious way, and the reason I speak of this is that money got in this way stops longer with a fellow that gets it with hard knocks than it does when he finds it. Willie, you are twenty-one, and you have many a thing to learn yet. This money you have earned much easier than I did, besides acquiring good habits at the same time, and you are quite welcome to the money. Hope you will make good use of it. I was ten long years getting this together after I was your age. Now, hoping this will be satisfactory, I stop....

Truly yours, W. E. Story.

P. S. You can consider this money on interest.

The nephew received the letter, and thereafter consented that the money should remain with his uncle in accordance with the terms and conditions of the letter. The uncle died on the 29th day of January, 1887, without having paid over to his nephew any portion of the said $5,000 and interest.

ALTON BROOKS PARKER, JUSTICE, AFTER STATING THE FACTS AS ABOVE

The question which provoked the most discussion by counsel on this appeal, and which lies at the foundation of plaintiff's asserted right of recovery, is whether by virtue of a contract defendant's testator, William E. Story, became indebted to his nephew, William E. Story, 2d, on his twenty-first birthday in the sum of $5,000. The trial court found as a fact that "on the 20th day of March, 1869, ... William E. Story agreed to and with William E. Story, 2d, that if he would refrain from drinking liquor, using tobacco, swearing, and playing cards or billiards for money until he should become twenty-one years of age, then he, the said William E. Story, would at that time pay him, the said William E. Story, 2d, the sum of $5,000 for such refraining, to which the said William E. Story, 2d, agreed," and that he "in all things fully performed his part of said agreement." The defendant contends that the contract was without consideration to support it, and therefore invalid. He asserts that the promisee, by refraining from the use of liquor and tobacco, was not harmed, but benefited; that which he did was best for him to do, independently of his uncle's promise, — and insists that it follows that, unless the promisor was benefited, the contract was without consideration, — a contention which, if well founded, would seem to leave open for controversy in many cases whether that which the promisee did or omitted to do was in fact of such benefit to him as to leave no consideration to support the enforcement of the promisor's agreement. Such a rule could not be tolerated, and is without foundation in the law. The exchequer chamber in 1875 defined "consideration" as follows: "a valuable consideration, in the sense of the law, may consist either in some right, interest, profit, or benefit accruing to the one party, or some forbearance, detriment, loss, or responsibility given, suffered, or undertaken by the other." Courts "will not ask whether the thing which forms the consideration does in fact benefit the promisee or a third party, or is of any substantial value to any one. It is enough that something is promised, done, forborne, or suffered by the party to whom the promise is made as consideration for the promise made to him." Anson, Cont. 63. "In general a waiver of any legal right at the request of another party is a sufficient consideration for a promise." Pars. Cont. "Any damage, or suspension, or forbearance of a right will be sufficient to sustain a promise." 2 Kent, Comm. (12th ed.). Pollock in his work on Contracts (page 166), after citing the definition given by the exchequer chamber, already quoted, says:

> The second branch of this judicial description is really the most important one. 'Consideration' means not so much that one party is profiting as that the other abandons some legal right in the present, or limits his legal freedom of action in the future, as an inducement for the promise of the first.

Now, applying this rule to the facts before us, the promisee used tobacco, occasionally drank liquor, and he had a legal right to do so. That right he abandoned for a period of years upon the strength of the promise of the testator that for such forbearance he would give him $5,000. We need not speculate on the effort which may have been required to give up the use of those stimulants. It is sufficient that he restricted his lawful freedom of action within certain prescribed limits upon the faith of his uncle's agreement, and now, having fully performed the conditions imposed, it is of no moment whether such performance actually proved a benefit to the promisor, and the court will not inquire into it; but, were it a proper subject of inquiry, we see nothing in this record that would permit a determination that the uncle was not benefited in a legal sense.

. . .

Note — Consideration and the Market

Does the rule that courts will not inquire into the adequacy of consideration have an impact on the distribution of goods in our society? Two important assumptions of neo-classical market economics are "people and resources can move freely" and "there are no artificial restrictions on entry into the marketplace." This suggests that market pricing will reflect the value each person places on the item being exchanged. Assume, for example, I have a refrigerator that I value at approximately $400. In other words, if someone offered me $380 for the refrigerator, I would not sell it, but if someone offered me $420, I would. The value I place on my refrigerator in part reflects the cost and inconvenience of replacing or doing without it and in part reflects my appreciation of the refrigerator's color or the small scratch on the side that reminds me of my cousin's visit five years ago. Now assume that my neighbor, Sarah, likes or wants my refrigerator more than I do. Perhaps she has a large family and could save a significant amount of money by having an extra refrigerator and my refrigerator is precisely the size that will fit into an available space in her apartment. Sarah offers to pay me $450 for my refrigerator — I am inclined to promise to sell it to her. But before I do, you ask me to sell the refrigerator to you. As it happens, you value my refrigerator even more than Sarah or I do: you like its unusual color and its unusually large freezer compartment (you have a taste for ice cream, perhaps), and your old refrigerator just stopped cooling. You offer to pay me $550 for the refrigerator and I accept.

This situation fits the assumptions of market economics. The refrigerator is moveable and so is your money. There are no barriers to entry: I am open to anyone's offer. Should the court declare that $550 is an "exorbitant" price for the refrigerator? Neo-classical economics suggests that the answer is no. The difference between the price Sarah is willing to pay and the price you are willing to pay is due solely to how much you each value my refrigerator and it would be inappropriate for anyone, most especially the government, to say your priorities are wrong. This tenet of neo-classical economics echoes a commonplace of liberal and libertarian thought: that the government should be impartial regarding disputes of value among the citizenry.

Is every market transaction like this one? This story of the refrigerator sale follows a standard story about market transactions and pricing that we learn from teachers, newspapers, and television. Yet just as sociologists report that an individual's important life choices are predictable according to the person's class, gender, race, ethnicity, and sexuality, economic analysts tell us that pricing in the United States tends to vary according to economic class, race, and gender. Poor people pay more for many comparable goods, housing, and services than do middle-class and wealthy people; women pay more than men, and people of color pay more than white people.

Does poverty operate as an "artificial" barrier or obstacle to entry in the marketplace? In other words, are poor people limited in how they can spend their money or sell their labor or products because they are excluded from or restrained in some exchanges? Does race operate as a basis of exclusion from or restriction in some transactions? Does gender?

Numerous studies show that prices charged for merchandise, housing, and services in poor neighborhoods are significantly higher than in more wealthy neighborhoods. Various reasons for these disparities have been suggested. Increased insurance payments, security costs, and theft loss account for only a portion of the increased prices, and these are often offset by lower commercial rents and labor costs in poor neighborhoods. Some analysts have concluded that price disparities exist mainly because poor communities are isolated from wider markets—poor transportation systems, racial and class hostility, discrimination in the credit industry, inadequate police protection, and lack of information combine to prevent low-income consumers from shopping in areas other than their immediate neighborhoods. Because the markets are isolated, competition is limited, and so traders, landlords, and service providers can charge more.

What about systems of disparate pricing in which women are routinely charged higher prices than men for comparable goods and services? The clothing, dry cleaning, and hair cutting industries are well-known examples. And in some industries, there is both gender and racial price disparity. In a study of 180 independent negotiations for new car purchases conducted at ninety different automobile dealerships in the Chicago area, Professor Ian Ayres found that both starting prices and final prices varied according to the race and gender of the purchaser. In this study, all of the testers were middle-class:

> Testers of different races and genders entered new car dealerships separately and bargained to buy a new car, using a uniform negotiation strategy. The study tests whether automobile retailers react differently to this uniform strategy when potential buyers differ only by gender or race.

The tests reveal that white males receive significantly better prices than blacks and women.... [W]hite women had to pay forty percent higher markups than white men; black men had to pay more than twice the markup, and black women had to pay more than three times the markup of white male testers.

Ian Ayres, *Fair Driving: Gender and Race Discrimination in Retail Car Negotiations*, 104 Harv. L. Rev. 817, 818–19 (1991). In a follow-up study, Ayres found:

The results of the expanded audit confirm the previous finding that dealers systematically offer lower prices to white males than to other tester types. But the more comprehensive data reveal a different ordering of discrimination than in the prior study: as in the original study, dealers offered all black testers significantly higher prices than white males, but unlike the original study, the black male testers were charged higher prices than the black female testers.

Ian Ayres, *Further Evidence of Discrimination in New Car Negotiations and Estimates of its Cause*, 94 Mich. L. Rev. 109 (1995) (Professor Ayres speculates that sellers' behavior in the second study may have been influenced by extensive publicity on the first study, id. at 142–43.).

There are several possible explanations for gender and racial price disparities. In some industries, such as the clothing and dry cleaning industries, gender price differences are traditional practice. At one time they may have reflected actual differences in the goods or services being provided, but the practice of different pricing continued after any significant differences in goods and services ended. Perhaps consumers do not notice the different pricing and merchants do not clearly disclose it. Moreover, individual merchants apparently have not wanted to lower prices for women, even though that would give them a competitive advantage.

In other industries (it appears that the new car industry is one) the dynamics of race and gender operate to put some consumers at an advantage and others at a disadvantage in negotiations over price. After evaluating different explanations for the "strong dealer tendency to offer lower prices to white males" revealed in his study of new car negotiations, Professor Ayres concludes that discrimination is caused by both "hatred" and "profits," by both "animus-based" and "profit-based" actions. Ayres, *Further Evidence of Discrimination*, 94 Mich. L. Rev. at 112.

Examining "animus-based" discrimination, Ayres distinguishes between "associational animus," where a seller dislikes interacting with some groups, and "consequential animus," where a seller desires to disadvantage some groups. Ayres concludes that the desire to disadvantage some groups, particularly black men, is widespread among new car dealers and has a substantial effect on pricing, while "associational animus," the desire to avoid interaction, is not. Examining "profit-based" discrimination, Ayres distinguishes between "cost-based" discrimination, where a seller acts as if transactions with some groups of buyers will take more of the seller's time and resources than another because of credit issues or service needs, for example, and "revenue-based" discrimination, where the seller acts as if some groups of buyers will be willing to pay a higher price than another. Ayres found evidence of both forms of "profit-based" discrimination.

One factor in "revenue-based" discrimination may be a dynamic of social and cultural control that influences negotiations and other personal interactions. Studies in other settings have concluded that race and gender hierarchies affect individual relations, including negotiations, in multiple ways. *See, e.g.,* Trina Grillo, *The Mediation Alternative: Process Dangers for Women*, 100 Yale L. J. 1545 (1991). A part of race and gender privilege is a sense of confidence and entitlement in relation to others, while a part of race and gender subordination is a dual sense of being on the one hand unseen or disbelieved by others and on the other hand closely scrutinized and judged by others. *See generally* Peggy MacIntosh, *White Privilege and Male Privilege, in* Race, Class, and Gender 76 (Margaret Andersen & Patricia Hill Collins, eds., 1995). This contrast of privilege and subordination is one of many ways in which race and gender influence daily interactions. And this difference in positioning may significantly influence the outcome of negotiations, reinforcing sellers' expectations that some groups of buyers will be "willing" to pay more.

Given all this, is it wrong for merchants to charge more in poor neighborhoods? Is it wrong for merchants to charge women and men of color more than they do white women and men? Is it wrong to charge black men more than black women? The rule that courts should not look at the adequacy of exchange prevents or shields courts from having to answer these questions. Yet courts are influenced by the substantive fairness of the contract in a particular case, aren't they? One doctrine that explicitly directs the court to examine the fairness of an exchange is the doctrine of unconscionability, which provides that "unconscionable" contracts or contract terms will not be enforced. We will examine this doctrine in Chapter Seven.

———————

C. The Consideration Must Be "Bargained-For"

"Bargained-for" means that the return promise or performance was sought by the promisor in exchange for the promise; that the promise or performance was the reason or "inducement" for the promise. The doctrine adds that getting the promise or performance does not have to be the *actual* or predominant motive of the promisor. What is required, instead, is the objective *appearance* of a bargained-for exchange, structured so that the return promise or performance is the "price" of the promise. Recall Holmes' example: "A man may promise to paint a picture for five hundred dollars, while his chief motive may be a desire for fame." Five hundred dollars is the bargained-for consideration for the painting, despite the painter's actual motive.

As we saw in *Hamer v. Sidway*, courts refrain from inquiring into the "adequacy" of consideration. Nonetheless, courts might examine the "sufficiency" of consideration. A court looking for sufficient consideration determines whether there is reciprocal exchange. Thus, the rule barring judicial inquiry into the adequacy of consideration does not preclude a court from looking into the sufficiency of the return promise or performance. One such categorical exclusion is a promise or performance of "love and affection," which courts routinely dismiss as "insufficient" to serve as consideration. And, the notion of "insufficiency" underlies the unenforceability of promises made in exchange for illegal promises, illusory promises, and for nominal consideration.

In the first part of this section, we will review *Kirksey v. Kirksey* and the rationale for the consideration doctrine. In the next part, we will look at the distinction between a bargained-for exchange and a "gift promise with a condition" that the court discusses in *Langer v. Superior Steel Corp.* In the third part, we will introduce the "nominal consideration" doctrine, in which courts say, in effect, "I will not be made a fool by accepting that a valuable promise was induced by a worthless one!"

1. Bargained-For Means that the Promise Was "Induced By" the Return Promise or Performance and Vice-Versa

Please review *Kirksey v. Kirksey* in Chapter Two. Judge Ormond said that he thought the brother-in-law's promise to provide a house for his brother's widow and children was given in exchange for bargained-for consideration, but he was out-voted. Kirksey gave up her preference and moved her family, so the requirement of a promise or performance was met, but a majority of the judges concluded that her actions were not the inducement for the brother-in-law's promise.

Kirksey v. Kirksey *Redux*

Even though Judge Ormond discusses the transaction as outside of the realm of bargain and markets, he is sympathetic to Angelico Kirksey's claim (Angelico is misspelled as "Antillico" in the quoted letter), but he has no legal doctrine to help her. What is curious, however, is that there were facts that could have resulted in a better outcome for Angelico. In their article, *Dear Sister Antillico … The Story of Kirksey v. Kirksey*, 94 Geo. L.J. 321 (2006), detailing the facts, gaps, and history of the case, Professors William R. Casto and Val D. Ricks reveal that Isaac Kirksey invited his sister-in-law to Talladega in part so that she could hold a preference for him on public land. With Angelico living the land, he thought he would be able buy the land later from the United States government at a discount. Their extensive research discovered that, "He was bargaining for her to act as a placeholder, and she knew it …" 94 Geo. L.J. at 325. Isaac later evicted Angelico because the law had changed. Since Angelico was living on the property, she, not Isaac, would be eligible to purchase it. Moreover, she wanted to buy the land. In order to preserve his opportunity to keep the land, Isaac had to evict her and occupy the land himself.

When the court inserted Isaac's invitation to "Sister Antillico" they omitted a portion of the letter. The letter in its entirety reads (omitted portion is highlighted):

> Dear Sister Antillico [sic] — Much to my mortification, I heard that brother Henry was dead, and one of his children. I know that your situation is one of grief and difficulty. You had a bad chance before, but a great deal worse now. I should like to come and see you, but cannot with convenience at present. *I am not well at present, my family has been generally well, all but myself and my youngest son. We have not been very sick. The health of the County is tolerably good at present. I should like to know your situation.* I do not know whether you have a preference on the place you live on or not. If you had, I would advise you to obtain your preference, and sell the land and quit the country, as I understand it is very unhealthy, and I know society is very bad. If you will come down and see me, I will let you have a place to raise your family, and I have more open land than I can tend; and on account of your situation, and that of your family, I feel like I want you and the children to do well.

Isaac needed Angelico to come hold his preference because he and his son were unable to hold it and he suggests to her that she sell the land she was occupying (for a profit) and help him with the open land that he is unable to tend. In the context during the 1830s and 1840s, "open land" meant land open to the public for settlement. 94 Geo. L.J. at 344.

Professors Casto and Ricks surmise that Angelico's lawyer did not make the argument that she and Isaac had a deal because it did not serve her goal, which was to obtain the land. 94 Geo. L.J. 352–353. Making the claim was difficult given legal circumstances that complicated the very claim. So in the end, absent any proffer of evidence of their bargain, she is unable to recover.

United States of America [Small Business Administration] v. Betty Jo Meadors

United States Court of Appeals for the Seventh Circuit
753 F.2d 590 (7th Cir. 1985)

RICHARD DICKSON CUDAHY, CIRCUIT JUDGE.

Appellant Meadors appeals an order of the district court granting the Small Business Administration (the "SBA") summary judgment in its action to collect from appellant as guarantor on a loan. The district court found ... that no independent consideration was necessary for her signature as a guarantor.... We reverse and remand.

I.

In January, 1977, M.J.D., Inc. ("MJD") applied to the Bargersville State Bank (the "Bank") for a loan to pay off debts and to provide for additional working capital for a lumber company MJD owned in Bargersville, Indiana. The Bank's board of directors approved the loan subject to a guaranty by the SBA. In April, 1977, the SBA approved the request for a 56% guaranty of the $281,000 loan, but required the principals Melton Meadors, Jay Judd and Harold Ducote and Ducote's wife Marie to sign a guaranty on SBA Form 148. In the January application, listed on page four as possible guarantors had been: "Melton E. Meadors—a single person, Jay A. Judd & Wife, Harold A. Ducote, Jr., & Wife." After considering the loan application and attached balance sheets, the SBA chose to have Meadors, Judd, Ducote and Ducote's wife sign the required guaranty.

On April 2, 1977, Melton Meadors and Betty, appellant here, were married. At the April 19 closing the three principals and their wives were all present. Although the SBA had provided places on its Form 148 for the signatures only of Meadors, Judd, Ducote, & Ducote's wife, and although no one from the SBA was present to request additional signatures, all six—the three principals and their wives—signed the guaranty form. Neither the SBA nor the Bank required Betty to sign any document as a prerequisite for disbursing loan proceeds. These facts are not disputed by either side.

MJD defaulted on its loan, and the Bank asked the SBA to take over the guaranteed portion of the loan. MJD turned over the collateral securing the loan to the SBA in July, 1980 and it was later sold. An action was subsequently instituted in district court to collect the deficiency from the guarantors, including Betty Meadors. Appellant raised several defenses, including lack of consideration ... In November, 1983 appellee SBA filed a motion for summary judgment which was granted by the district court on February 2, 1984. It is from that grant of summary judgment that Betty Meadors appeals....

III.

Betty Meadors argues ... that she received no consideration for her signature on the guaranty form. She reasons that the signature of a volunteer, who happens upon an agreement after the negotiations have been concluded and the terms set, and who signs as a guarantor although neither side has required her to sign, has not received consideration and therefore is not bound by the agreement.

Consideration has long and consistently been treated as an essential element of every contract. Yet there is little agreement about just what consideration is, and that fact makes it difficult to assess a defense of want of consideration in a novel setting. We venture that the setting in which it is raised here is very nearly unique, and the validity of the defense would seem to depend on which interpretation of the doctrine we adopt.

Every interpretation has serious faults. It used to be said that consideration was either a benefit to the promisor, or a detriment to the promisee. In other words, the one who made the promise receives consideration if he gets something, or if the one to whom he makes the promise gives something up. Either alternative will do. If I promise you a thousand dollars if you quit smoking, and you do quit, then even though there may be no benefit to me, I have received consideration: you have given something up. Similarly, I can promise you a thousand dollars if you teach my daughter to sing. If you do teach her—or if you promise to—then I have received consideration even if all the practice sessions and even the final result are of no real benefit to me.

But reflection shows that benefit-detriment is neither necessary nor sufficient for consideration. I may promise to give you a thousand dollars if you quit smoking—I may even do it in writing—and you may give up smoking, and yet my promise may be unenforceable and may be the sort of thing that everyone would agree was without consideration. For you may have given up smoking without ever having learned of my promise. So the detriment in isolation is not sufficient for consideration. On the other hand, I might agree to pay you for something that was neither a benefit to me nor a detriment to you. I might promise to pay you for bringing a benefit on yourself. The reasoning in the classic case of *Hamer v. Sidway*, 124 N.Y. 538, 27 N.E. 256 (N.Y.App.1891), suggests that the courts will find consideration in such a case. An uncle had promised his nephew $5000 on his twenty-first birthday if the nephew would refrain from drinking, smoking, swearing and playing cards until that time. The nephew evidently fulfilled his part of the deal, but the uncle's executor resisted his claim against the estate. The court found the promise enforceable:

> The defendant contends that the contract was without consideration to support it, and therefore invalid. He asserts that the promisee, by refraining from the use of liquor and tobacco was not harmed, but benefitted; that that which he did was best for him to do, independently of his uncle's promise,—and insists that it follows that, unless the promisor was benefitted, the contract was without consideration.... Such a rule would not be tolerated and is without foundation in the law.... Courts will not ask whether the thing which forms the consideration does in fact benefit the promisee or a third party, or is of any substantial benefit to anyone. It is enough that something is *promised*, done, forborne or suffered by the party to whom the promise is made as consideration for the promise made to him.

Id. at 257 (emphasis added).

Perhaps because of such difficulties, the benefit-detriment account of consideration was replaced by a "bargain" theory: there is consideration when each promise or performance has been bargained for, when each has been offered as inducement for the other:

> [I]t is the essence of a consideration, that, by the terms of the agreement, it is given and accepted as the motive or inducement of the promise. Conversely, the promise must be made and accepted as the conventional ... inducement for furnishing the consideration. The root of the whole matter is the relation of reciprocal conventional inducement, each for the other, between consideration and promise.

O.W. Holmes, The Common Law 293–94 (1881).[2] The bargain-exchange account fits rather neatly into an economic analysis of common law, which sees in this version of the doctrine of consideration an attempt to select out for enforcement those contracts — namely bargained-for exchanges — that promote the increase of value in society.

> The state has an independent interest in the enforcement of [bargain] promises. Exchange creates surplus, because each party presumably values what he gets more highly than what he gives. A modern free-enterprise system depends heavily on private planning and on credit transactions that involve exchanges over time. The extent to which private actors will be ready to engage in exchange, and are able to make reliable plans, rests partly on the probability that bargain promises will be kept. Legal enforcement of such promises increases that probability.

Eisenberg, *Principles of Consideration*, 67 Cornell L. Rev. 640, 643 (1982)[3] ...

Of course, if any theory could persuade us that the cases that stand as counterexamples to it were wrongly decided, we might accept the theory in spite of the cases. But the tendency in the courts has been to favor the accumulated wisdom of the common law over the simplicity of any generalized theory. Thus Eisenberg argues that consideration is a guise under which judges have tried to deal fairly with contract difficulties, and argues that it is time now to relegate the doctrine and its epicycles to the history books, and bring fairness out into the open in decision-making.

> In the past courts decided issues of fairness covertly, and expressed their decisions through the manipulation of rules and exceptions purportedly designed for other ends.... The agenda for the legal community is ... to encourage the courts to perform such review openly.

67 Cornell L. Rev., at 640–41.[4]

Although it is a beguiling thought to drop the mask and do justice openly, the present case seems to us to make manifest the emptiness of such an approach. Having dropped the guise of consideration, what is the fair outcome in a case in which a wife (apparently)

---

2. "Going back into the past, there was an indefinite number of cases which had imposed liability, in the name of consideration, where nothing like Holmes's 'reciprocal conventional inducement' was anywhere in sight." G. Gilmore, Death of Contract 63 (1974). Gilmore saw Holmes as trying to change the law, and succeeding. "There is never any point in arguing with a successful revolution. What Holmes told the young lawyers who flocked to his lectures in the spring of 1881 promptly became the truth — the indisputable truth — of the matter for his own and succeeding generations." *Id.* at 21.

This position is subject to two different sorts of criticism: (1) unilateral promises also increase surplus, Posner, Gratuitous Promises in Economics and Law, 6 J. Legal Stud. 411, 412 (1977); and (2) if it is the promotion of exchanges in the market place that is sought, why extend enforcement to, for example, intrafamilial contracts or the contract between me and the fellow who sells me his car? C. Fried, Contract as Promise 36–37 (1981).

3. This position is subject to two different sorts of criticism: (1) unilateral promises also increase surplus, Posner, Gratuitous Promises in Economics and Law, 6 J. of Legal Stud. 411, 412 (1977); and (2) if it is the promotion of exchanges in the market place that is sought, why extend enforcement to, for example, intrafamilial contracts or the contract between me and the fellow who sells me his car? C. Fried, Contract as Promise 36–37 (1981).

4. "The movement in the law rather suggests that we may have in the not too distant future a more candid set of principles to determine which promises should be enforceable in terms of the fairness of each type. We are moving in that direction as a result of decisions and statutes lending validity to types of promises whose legitimacy had been in doubt under the doctrine of consideration.... Secondly, we are moving in that direction as a result of a more open willingness to stigmatize certain promises as unfair or unconscionable and to deny enforcement on that ground rather than on the ground of insufficient consideration." C. Fried, *supra*, at 39.

gratuitously affixes her name to a guaranty intended for her husband? Where the rules of contract law clearly dictate one result or the other (and there is no fraud or unconscionability) then the fair outcome might be to enforce that result. But to find such rules we are driven back to the doctrine of consideration and its exceptions.[5]

Since the just solution does not leap out at us, therefore, let us begin by pressing the doctrine of consideration as far as it will go. Where there is no consideration, it has been the general rule that the contract is not enforceable. In this case, under the versions of the doctrine we are acquainted with, there has been no consideration. The government suffered no detriment: its undertaking would have been precisely the same (on the account we have before us) whether or not Mrs. Meadors had signed the guaranty. She gained no benefit, either; whatever benefit passed to her and her husband because of the loan would have passed without her signature. And no bargain was involved. The SBA gave up nothing to induce Mrs. Meadors to sign; her signature induced no act or promise on the part of the SBA. Since there has been no consideration, the general rule would deny the government enforcement of the contract.

The general rule applies to guaranties. If there has been no consideration for a guaranty, the guaranty is not enforceable. But the mindless application of that rule tends to produce unacceptable results; for example, a guarantor ought not to be able to raise the defense that he received no *separate* consideration for his agreement to act as guarantor — no guaranty would ever be enforceable in such a case unless it could be shown that the guarantor had been paid for his undertaking. And so an apparent exception to the rule arose: no *independent* consideration is necessary for a guaranty signed at the same time as the principal agreement. The exception is only apparent since it does not deny that consideration is necessary; it only denies that *separate* consideration is necessary. In other words, the loan made by the promisee may be made in consideration for the signatures both of the principal and the guarantor: he may have been unwilling to make the loan in the absence of either.

> If the promises of the principal and the surety are made simultaneously, they may be made for a single consideration; the loan of money by the creditor to the principal is a sufficient consideration for the promises of both principal and surety.

Corbin on Contracts § 213.[6] That rule, on its face, suggests that because the signing was simultaneous the appellant here cannot raise the defense of lack of consideration. On a benefit-detriment theory, there is nothing more to be said about it.

We believe, however, that that outcome is wrong, and — although cases on this point are naturally rare — we are supported in our belief by the commentators and by the bargain-exchange interpretation of the doctrine of consideration.[7] This is not the ordinary

---

5. It may seem that, in our effort to find a rule that gives the just result, we have given considerations of simplicity short shrift. Although we think that the best argument for a result different from the one we reach here would be based on the simplicity of a rule that automatically bound signers, the same argument could be made for any per se rule and does not seem to us to weigh heavily in the balance.

6. Corbin distinguishes guaranties made subsequent to the principal agreement as requiring separate consideration. There are cases holding that even in such circumstances no separate consideration is necessary, but in each such case it is clear that the guaranty had been bargained for with the main agreement, or there is some other explanation for the apparent discrepancy.

7. Whether or not the contract-as-promise theory yields the same result would seem to depend on what we mean by "promise," if one condition of something being a promise from X to Y is that Y be aware of it, then there would seem to be no contract in this case. In Fried's version of the theory communication of the promise to Y is an essential element of promising; Fried sees communication as one of the elements that the doctrine of consideration, in its own befuddled way, has tried to provide. C. Fried, *supra*, at 41–42.

case of the guarantor signing simultaneously with the principal; this is more like the case mentioned earlier in which X promises to pay Y a thousand dollars if Y gives up smoking, and Y gives up smoking without ever learning of X's promise. Whether or not there has been benefit to one party or detriment to the other, there has been no bargain here, and the SBA made the loan apparently in ignorance of Mrs. Meadors' signature. If those are the facts, then we believe that not only has there been no independent consideration, there has been no consideration at all.

In *Banco Credito y Ahorro Ponceno v. Scott*, 250 A.2d 387 (Del.Super.1969), the problem was the inverse of the one we have here: the guarantor's signature had been bargained for but, without the creditor's knowledge, the guarantor failed to sign. The court relied on Corbin § 213 ("[b]ut for the promise of any surety that is made subsequently to the advancement of the money to the principal, there must be a new consideration") to conclude that his later signing could not bind him without new consideration. In the most recent Corbin (1984 Supplement), the editor discusses that opinion:

> [I]t is questionable whether [the rule relied on by the court] was properly applied to the facts alleged. If the guarantee by Scott was at all times contemplated to be given by the parties, then the debt was not "pre-existing" but actually substantially contemporaneous, though considerable time passed before Scott actually got around to signing it.... *On the other hand, if Scott's signature was not originally contemplated as part of the deal, then the debt was "pre-existing" though Scott signed within the hour.*

C. Kaufman, Corbin on Contracts § 213 (1984 Supplement) (emphasis added). And this last alternative Corbin contemplates is just the case before us.

For Corbin, the lack of consideration is clear from the fact that the signature was not originally contemplated as part of the deal. Where the creditor does not even know of the signature — as we are assured by both parties is the case here — the lack of a bargain and consequent lack of consideration is even clearer:

> Even if the promisee takes some action subsequent to the promise (so that there is no problem of past consideration), and even if the promisor sought that action in exchange for his promise, ... that action is not bargained for unless it is given by the promisee in exchange for the promise. In other words, just as the promisor's purpose must be to induce an exchange, so the promisee's purpose must be to take advantage of the proposed exchange. *In practice, the principal effect of this requirement is to deny enforcement of the promise if the promisee takes the action sought by the promisor without knowledge of the promise. As might be supposed, examples are infrequent.*

E. Farnsworth, Contracts 64 (1982).[8] On the undisputed facts, this case is one of Farnsworth's infrequent examples.

...

---

8. Eisenberg also suggests the rarity of such cases:
    The proposition that bargains involving the performance of a pre-existing contractual duty are often gratuitous is empirically far-fetched. Perhaps a few such cases could be found, but I have never run across one. In any event, if such cases really do arise, they neither need nor justify a special rule. As Comment a [to § 573 of the Restatement Second of Contracts] points out, "[i]f the performance was not in fact bargained for and given in exchange for the promise, the case is not within this section: in such cases there is no consideration...."
67 Cornell L. Rev., at 644–45.

We hold, therefore, that summary judgment for plaintiff was not appropriate on this point. Although the parties have apparently agreed on the relevant facts, we feel that it would also be inappropriate for us to decide as a matter of law that the guaranty is unenforceable. The district court, relying on a different construction of the law, did not take evidence on the question. Construing the law as we have construed it, it must be resolved whether in fact Betty Meadors' signature was in any respect whatsoever required, anticipated, requested or relied upon (or, in fact, known of); because if it was not, it was wholly irrelevant to the transaction and does not create an enforceable obligation.

Reversed and Remanded.

----

a. A Distinction: Bargained versus Gift with a Condition

The consideration doctrine does not offer much guidance in determining when a promise or performance is bargained for, but the distinction discussed by the court in *Langer*, between a promise given for a bargained-for consideration and gift promise with a condition, does give us two categories and a name for each.

Langer v. Superior Steel Corporation

Superior Court of Pennsylvania
161 A. 571 (1932)

THOMAS J. BALDRIGE, JUDGE

This is an action of assumpsit to recover damages for breach of a contract. The court below sustained questions of law raised by defendant, and entered judgment in its favor.

The plaintiff alleges that he is entitled to recover certain monthly payments provided for in the following letter:

August 31, 1927.

Mr. Wm. F. Langer,

Dear Sir: As you are retiring from active duty with this company, as Superintendent of the Annealing Department, on August 31, we hope that it will give you some pleasure to receive this official letter of commendation for your long and faithful service with the Superior Steel Corporation.

The Directors have decided that you will receive a pension of $100.00 per month as long as you live and preserve your present attitude of loyalty to the Company and its Officers and are not employed in any competitive occupation. We sincerely hope that you will live long to enjoy it and that this and the other evidences of the esteem in which you are held by your fellow employees and which you will today receive with this letter, will please you as much as it does us to bestow them.

Cordially yours,

[Signed] Frank R. Frost, President

The defendant paid the sum of $100 a month for approximately four years when the plaintiff was notified that the company no longer intended to continue the payments.

The issue raised by the affidavit of defense is whether the letter created a gratuitous promise or an enforceable contract. It is frequently a matter of great difficulty to differentiate between promises creating legal obligations and mere gratuitous agreements. Each case depends to a degree upon its peculiar facts and circumstances. Was this promise supported by a sufficient consideration, or was it but a condition attached to a gift? If a contract was created, it was based on a consideration, and must have been the result of an agreement bargained for in exchange for a promise. *Kirkpatrick v. Muirhead*, 16 Pa. 117. It was held in *Presbyterian Board of Foreign Missions v. Smith*, 209 Pa. 361, 363, 58 A. 689, that

> a test of good consideration is whether the promisee, at the instance of the promisor, has done, forborne, or undertaken to do anything real, or whether he has suffered any detriment, or whether, in return for the promise, he has done something that he was not bound to do, or has promised to do some act, or has abstained from doing something.

Mr. Justice Sadler pointed out in *York Metal & Alloys Co. v. Cyclops S. Co.*, 124 A. 752, 754 (Pa.) that a good consideration exists if one refrains from doing anything that he has a right to do, "whether there is any actual loss or detriment to him or actual benefit to the promisor or not."

The learned court below held that there was not a sufficient consideration, as the plaintiff was not bound to refrain from taking other employment, or continuing his loyalty to the defendant. That he had the alternative of receiving the monthly payment or endeavoring to seek other employment does not determine the existence or nonexistence of a consideration. But an agreement is not invalid for want of consideration because one party has an option while the other has not; it may be obligatory on one and optional with the other. 13 C.J. 336; *York Metal & Alloys Co. v. Cyclops S. Co.*, *supra*.

The plaintiff, in his statement, which must be admitted as true in considering the statutory demurrer filed by defendant, alleges that he refrained from seeking employment with any competitive company, and that he complied with the terms of the agreement. By so doing, has he sustained any detriment? Was his forbearance sufficient to support a good consideration? Professor Williston, in his treatise on Contracts § 112, states:

> It is often difficult to determine whether words of condition in a promise indicate a request for consideration or state a mere condition in a gratuitous promise. An aid, though not a conclusive test in determining which construction of the promise is more reasonable is an inquiry whether the happening of the condition will be a benefit to the promisor. If so, it is a fair inference that the happening was requested as a consideration.... In case of doubt where the promisee has incurred a detriment on the faith of the promise, courts will naturally be loath to regard the promise as a mere gratuity, and the detriment incurred as merely a condition.

It is reasonable to conclude that it is to the advantage of the defendant if the plaintiff, who had been employed for a long period of time as its superintendent in the annealing department, and who, undoubtedly, had knowledge of the methods used by the employer, is not employed by a competitive company; otherwise, such a stipulation would have been unnecessary. That must have been the inducing reason for inserting that provision. There is nothing appearing of record, except the condition imposed by the defendant, that would have prevented this man of skill and experience from seeking employment elsewhere. By receiving the monthly payments, he impliedly accepted the conditions imposed, and was thus restrained from doing that which he had a right to do. This was a sufficient consideration to support a contract.

The appellee refers to *Kirksey v. Kirksey*, 8 Ala. 131, which is also cited by Professor Williston in his work on Contracts § 112, note 51, as a leading case on this subject under discussion. The defendant wrote his sister-in-law, the plaintiff: "If you will come down and see me, I will let you have a place to raise your family and I have more open land than I can tend: and on the account of your situation and that of your family, I feel like I want you and the children to do well." The plaintiff left her home and moved her family a distance of 67 miles to the residence of the defendant, who gave her the house and land, and, after a period of two years, requested her to leave. The court held that the promise was a mere gratuity. In that case, as well as in *Richards' Ex'r v. Richards*, 46 Pa. 78, there was no benefit to be derived by the promisor, as in the case at bar, and therefore a good consideration was lacking.

. . .

Judgment is reversed, and the defendant is hereby given permission to file an affidavit of defense to the merits of the plaintiff's claim.

Note

In *Langer v. Superior Steel*, the defendant, Superior Steel, asserted that its promise to Langer was not enforceable because it was gratuitous, without consideration. In response, the plaintiff argued that consideration existed in Langer's *performance* of "remaining loyal" to Superior Steel and refraining from taking a job with another company. Further, Langer's attorney argued, the company' promise apparently was "induced" by the performance and the performance was "induced by" the promise: they were "bargained-for." As evidence of this mutual inducement, Langer pointed to the statement in Superior Steel's letter to him: "you will receive a pension of $100.00 per month as long as you live and preserve your present attitude of loyalty to the Company and its Officers and are not employed in any competitive occupation."

Superior Steel apparently made two arguments in response. First, Superior Steel argued that Langer's refraining from employment elsewhere could not be consideration for its promise because Langer was not *obligated* (i.e., he had not promised) to refrain from working for another company and he remained free to take such employment whenever he chose to do so. In support of this argument, the company likely evoked the so-called "rule of mutuality of obligation," which suggests that one party's promise is not enforceable unless the other party is similarly obligated. Judge Baldrige rejected this argument, holding that Langer's forbearance was a performance that constituted consideration even though he had not promised to continue that performance. The court's rejection of the company's "mutuality of obligation" argument is consistent with the current majority view. The Restatement (Second) of Contracts, for example, explicitly rejects the "rule of mutuality of obligation" in Section 79: "If the requirement of consideration is met, there is no additional requirement of ... mutuality of obligation."

Superior Steel's second argument was that Langer's performance in refraining from other employment was not "bargained for" in exchange for Superior Steel's promise to pay him $100 a month for the rest of his life. In support of this argument, Superior Steel cited *Kirksey v. Kirksey*. Judge Baldrige rejected this argument and distinguished this case from *Kirksey* by observing that in Kirksey, the promisor, the brother-in-law, "was not benefited" by his sister-in-law's moving and therefore her moving was more likely a "condition of a gift" than a "consideration of a promise," under the analysis suggested by Williston. This line of analysis, offering a way to distinguish gifts-with-a-condition from promises-with-consideration, remains viable under the reformulated view of the consideration doctrine.

b. Nominal Consideration Is Not Credibly Bargained-For

"Nominal" means "in name or form only." One rule associated with the consideration doctrine is that "nominal consideration is not sufficient to satisfy the consideration requirement." This rule seems to contradict the rule of *Hamer v. Sidway*, that courts will not inquire into the adequacy of consideration. Nevertheless, the rule precluding nominal consideration is generally accepted in current contract law.

Consider this example: Alice promises to sell an antique rocking chair (with an appraised value of approximately $5,000) to her friend Bret for $1. Alice then changes her mind and refuses to let Bret take the rocking chair and refuses to take the $1 bill that Bret tries to hand her. Bret then sues Alice for breach of contract. Alice responds to Bret's claim by asserting that there is no contract between her and Bret and her promise is not enforceable, because it was not given in exchange for a bargained-for consideration. Bret would respond, of course, that his promise to pay Alice $1 is a return promise that certainly appears to be the bargained-for consideration for Alice's promise.

How would you rule if you were the judge in this case? Would you apply the rule that "courts will not inquire into the adequacy of consideration" and decide in Bret's favor? Does that result seem correct? If you were inclined to say that Alice's promise is not enforceable, what would be the reasoning behind that result?

The history of the nominal consideration rule is interesting. During the early twentieth century, a second or third generation of classical contract theorists asserted that "nominal" consideration should satisfy the consideration requirement because, in their view, a market economy requires that each party be free to assign his or her own value to whatever is the subject of the exchange (in our example, the rocking chair). If Alice believes that the chair is worth $1, the courts should honor her assessment. In addition, classical theorists of that time argued that individuals should have the ability to deliberately designate some gift promises as enforceable (a routine practice during the nineteenth century, through use of the personal seal).

Accordingly, the drafters of the first Restatement of Contracts (published in 1932) maintained that nominal consideration should be sufficient to satisfy the consideration requirement. Section 84 states that "Consideration is not insufficient because of the fact that (a) the obtaining of it was not the motive or a material cause inducing the promisor to make the promise, ..." Illustration 1 to section 84 of the Restatement of Contracts read:

> A wishes to make a binding promise to his son B to convey to B Blackacre, which is worth $5000. Being advised that a gratuitous promise is not binding, A writes to B an offer to sell Blackacre for $1. B accepts. B's promise to pay $1 is sufficient consideration. (emphasis added)

Yet, despite this endorsement by the First Restatement, courts rejected this idea. With few exceptions, courts held, with little explanation, that nominal consideration does not satisfy the "bargained-for consideration" requirement, By 1981, when the Restatement (Second) of Contracts was published, its drafters had little choice but to admit defeat. Illustration 5 to section 71 of the Restatement (Second) of Contracts specifies::

> A desires to make a binding promise to give $1000 to his son B. Being advised that a gratuitous promise is not binding, A offers to buy from B for $1000 a book worth less than $1. B accepts the offer knowing that the purchase of the book is a mere pretense. There is no consideration for A's promise to pay $1000. (emphasis added)

So why were courts unwilling to adopt the nominal consideration device urged in the First Restatement? Essentially, the device was just too artificial, too much of a fiction, for courts to swallow. Consideration is an awkward doctrine constructed in order to feature market exchange as the center of contract law. So the consideration doctrine requires courts to employ the illusive concepts and distinctions we have been discussing: adequacy of consideration as opposed to sufficiency of consideration, inducement for promise as distinguished from motive for a promise, and the like. Then, in a case involving nominal consideration, such as the one in Illustration 5, one lawyer stands before the court and insists that her client's promise to give his father a used and battered book worth less than $1 was bargained for consideration for the father's promise to pay $1,000. Surely this would try the judge's patience. Indeed, a judge may well be insulted by the lawyer's argument!

The Drafters' Comment b to Section 71 supports this explanation for courts' refusal to enforce promises that purport to be made in exchange for nominal consideration:

> [A] mere pretense of bargain does not suffice, as where there is a false recital of consideration or where the purported consideration is merely nominal. In such cases there is no consideration.

This, then, is the "rationale" for the rule that a court may "inquire into the adequacy of consideration" at least for the purpose of finding that nominal consideration does not satisfy the bargained-for consideration requirement: such scrutiny is sometimes necessary to protect the court from the insult of an obviously sham transaction.

---

2. The "Pre-Existing Duty Rule" — A First Look

The "pre-existing duty rule" provides that a promise to do something that one is already obligated to do is not bargained-for consideration for a promise by the other party. In *White v. Village of Homewood*, below, for example, the court held that the fire department's agreement to let Angela White take the firefighter/paramedic qualifying physical agility test was not the bargained-for consideration for her agreement releasing the department from all claims arising from the test, and therefore that she was not bound by the release. This rule makes sense if you think about it from the fire department's perspective: did the fire department let her take the test because she gave them a release? No, the fire department let her take the test because a statute required it to do so. Her release was unconnected to anything the fire department did and therefore it was gratuitous and not enforceable.

In Chapter Eight we will study the pre-existing duty rule as it has been applied to contract modifications, where several exceptions have been recognized.

Angela White v. Village of Homewood and Village of Homewood Fire and Police Commission

Appellate Court of Illinois
628 N.E.2d 616 (1993)

JUSTICE ALLEN HARTMAN DELIVERED THE OPINION OF THE COURT

Plaintiff, Angela White, appeals the dismissal of her negligence action as barred by an exculpatory agreement that she signed. The sole issue presented for review is whether the exculpatory agreement relieved defendants of liability.

Plaintiff's amended complaint against defendants arose from personal injuries she sustained in June 1990 while taking a physical agility test to become a firefighter/paramedic for the Homewood Fire Department. While traversing horizontal bars as part of the test, plaintiff fell and was injured. Count II of the amended complaint, the only count relevant to this appeal, alleged that defendants were negligent in administering the test.

Defendants moved to dismiss the negligence count pursuant to section 2-619 of the Civil Practice Law, asserting that the exculpatory agreement signed by plaintiff before taking the test released them from liability. The exculpatory agreement, attached as an exhibit, stated:

Agility Test

Release of All Liabilities

The undersigned, for good and valuable considerations, hereby releases, remises and discharges the Village of Homewood, a Municipal Corporation, its officers, servants, agents and employees of and from any and all claims, demands, and liabilities to me and on account of any and all injuries, losses and damages, to my person that shall have been caused, or may, at any time, arise as a result of a certain Fire Examination Agility Test conducted by the Board of Fire and Police Commissioners of said Village of Homewood, the intention hereof being to completely, absolutely, and finally release said Village of Homewood, and its officers, servants, agents and employees of and from any and all liability arising wholly or partially from the cause aforesaid.

Plaintiff filed a response in which she admitted signing the exculpatory agreement before taking the test, but stated she only did so to obtain employment. She maintained that the exculpatory agreement is unenforceable.

The circuit court granted defendants' motion and dismissed with prejudice the ordinary negligence count. Plaintiff appeals.

Plaintiff contends that the exculpatory agreement is unenforceable because it lacks consideration and violates public policy. She seeks reinstatement of her ordinary negligence count.

Under certain circumstances exculpatory contracts may act as a total bar to a plaintiff's negligence claim. *Harris v. Walker*, 519 N.E.2d 917, 919 (Ill. 1988). This is because public policy strongly favors the freedom to contract. *Harris*, 519 N.E.2d 917, 919 (Ill. 1988), quoting *McClure Engineering Associates, Inc. v. Reuben H. Donnelley Corp.*, 447 N.E.2d 400, 402 (Ill. 1983).

To be efficacious in a court of law, however, a release must be based upon consideration. *Toffenetti v. Mellor*, 153 N.E. 744, 746 (Ill. 1926). The same rules apply to an exculpatory agreement. (*See Sexton v. Southwestern Auto Racing Association, Inc.*, 394 N.E.2d 49, 50 (Ill. App. 1979). *But see* Restatement (Second) of Torts § 496B cmt. a, at 565 (1965).) Valuable consideration for a contract consists either of some right, interest, profit or benefit accruing to one party, or some forbearance, detriment, loss of responsibility given, suffered or undertaken by the other. *De Fontaine v. Passalino*, 584 N.E.2d 933, 939 (Ill. App. 1991). The pre-existing duty rule provides that where a party does what it is already legally obligated to do, there is no consideration as there is no detriment. For example, where a guest was by statute entitled to use a hotel safe to store valuables, a promise by the guest to limit the liability of the hotel in exchange for using the safe is not supported by consideration because of the pre-existing duty rule. *Goncalves v. Regent International Hotels, Ltd.*, 447 N.E.2d 693, 700 (N.Y. 1983).

Defendants maintain that, in consideration of the exculpatory agreement, they administered the physical agility test and allowed plaintiff to participate. Analysis reveals, however, that defendants gave no consideration for the exculpatory agreement. According to the Illinois Municipal Code, defendants were required by law to administer the physical agility test, and plaintiff had a legal right to participate. 65 IL.C.S. 5/10-2.1-6 (West 1992). Consideration cannot flow from an act performed pursuant to a pre-existing legal duty. As a result, the exculpatory agreement is unenforceable as a matter of law.

We reject defendants' claim that *Radloff v. Village of West Dundee*, 489 N.E.2d 356 (Ill. App. 1986), controls this issue. There, plaintiff signed an exculpatory agreement before taking a physical aptitude test to become a village police officer. The release specifically stated that it was in "consideration of said Village arranging for the administration of said test." While scaling a seven-foot barricade during the test, plaintiff injured herself. The circuit court dismissed plaintiff's cause of action, finding that the exculpatory agreement she signed relieved the village of liability. The appellate court affirmed, saying it was unpersuaded by the public policy arguments set forth by plaintiff. Defendants aver that the consideration contemplated by the release in *Radloff* is the same as the consideration contemplated in the instant case: administration of the physical agility test, and the benefit to plaintiff of participating therein. Defendants fail to note that the issue of lack of consideration never was raised in *Radloff*. Consequently, *Radloff* provides no precedent for the case *sub judice*.

Defendants correctly point out that, generally, courts will not inquire into the sufficiency of consideration to support a contract between two parties. *Ahern v. Knecht*, 563 N.E.2d 787, 792 (Ill. App. 1990). As long as the agreement is bargained for, and the amount of consideration is not so grossly inadequate as to shock the conscience of the court, the adequacy of the consideration will not be challenged. Here, however, adequacy is not the issue for absolutely no consideration flowed between the parties. Defendants' cited authority is irrelevant to the disposition of this case.

In the alternative, plaintiff argues that the exculpatory agreement is unenforceable because it involves a matter of public concern and defendants were in a dominant position, relying on two cases. In the first, *Campbell v. Chicago, Rock Island & Pacific Ry. Co.*, 90 N.E. 1106 (Ill. 1910), the court held unenforceable an exculpatory clause between an employer and employee: "Public policy will not permit the master by contract with his servant to relieve himself from liability for injuries occasioned by his own negligence." *Campbell*, 90 N.E. at 1108. In the second, *Parkhill Truck Co. v. State of Illinois* (1965), 25 Ill. Ct. Cl. 172, the court of claims held unenforceable an exculpatory clause between the State and a truck driver; the clause was contained in a permit issued by the State granting the truck driver the right to travel across State highways, and it relieved the State from its own negligence. The court held the exculpatory clause violative of public policy as it involved a matter of public concern and the State was in a dominant position. *Parkhill Truck Co.*, 25 Ill. Ct. Cl. at 175.

The general rule is to enforce exculpatory agreements unless (1) it would be against settled public policy of the State to do so, or (2) there is something in the social relationship of the parties militating against upholding the agreement. *Harris*, 519 N.E.2d at 919, quoting *Jackson v. First National Bank*, 114 N.E.2d 721, 725 (Ill. 1953). Exculpatory agreements that are contrary to public policy include those (1) between an employer and employee; (2) between the public and those charged with a duty of public service, such as involving a common carrier, an innkeeper, a public warehouseman or a public utility; and (3) between parties where there is such a disparity of bargaining power that the agreement does not represent a free choice on the part of the plaintiff, such as a monopoly or involving a plaintiff without a reasonable alternative. Restatement (Second) of Torts §496B comments e–j, at 567–69 (1965).

The exculpatory agreement signed in this case is against public policy; the social relationship of the parties militates against upholding the agreement. *See Harris*, 519 N.E.2d at 919. The disparity of bargaining power here was such that the exculpatory agreement was not plaintiff's free choice. She was required to sign the exculpatory agreement in order to complete her job application for the position of village firefighter/paramedic. This requirement put her, as a job applicant, at the mercy of her potential employer's negligence, no matter how great. Defendants contend that plaintiff freely chose to apply for the position; that they did not have a monopoly on the job market, as plaintiff could apply elsewhere; and, therefore, that plaintiff had reasonable alternatives than to sign the exculpatory agreement. These arguments ignore the economic compulsion facing those in search of employment. To suppose that plaintiff here had any bargaining power whatsoever defies reality. Had plaintiff refused to sign the exculpatory agreement, she would not have been allowed to participate in the physical agility test and, consequently, could not have qualified for the position. Defendants do not contend otherwise. Indeed, they admit in their brief that "[h]ad [plaintiff] not signed the release, [she] would not have received the benefit of participating in the test." We find this result unconscionable and will not enforce this exculpatory agreement.

Additionally, we note that the relationship between defendants and plaintiff, as potential employer and job applicant, is akin to the relationship between an employer and employee. As earlier noted, exculpatory agreements between an employer and employee that relieve an employer from liability for the employer's own negligence have long been found contrary to public policy. *Campbell*, 90 N.E. at 1108; Restatement (Second) of Torts §496B, comment f, at 567 (1965). Our decision is merely an extension of this policy.

Defendants' attempt to distinguish this case from *Parkhill Truck Co.*, 25 Ill. Ct. Cl. 172, fails. Defendants claim that *Parkhill Truck Co.* involved a disparity of bargaining power between the parties as the "necessity of the truck driver to operate on State highways in order to conduct his business causes the truck driver to be under an economic compulsion to execute the exculpatory agreement. The economic compulsion in the present case is at least as great as that in *Parkhill Truck Co.* Additionally, this case involves a matter of public concern, as did *Parkhill Truck Co.*

. . .

For the reasons set forth above, we reverse the dismissal and remand to the circuit court with instructions to reinstate the ordinary negligence count of plaintiff's complaint.

Reversed and remanded with instructions.

Profile: Engine Company Number Three All-Women Firefighting Crew in San Diego

(1995)

Bryant Gumbel, host: The state of California recently registered yet another first, this time in the field of firefighting. As other fire departments across this country have struggled with change, a unique group of firefighters has emerged in San Diego; and remarkably, they've come together more by chance than by design. NBC's Kelly O'Donnell explains.

Kelly O'Donnell reporting: It's just an average day in the San Diego Fire Department.

Ms. Linda Morse: Was it a traffic accident?

O'Donnell: Engine Company Number Three answering an emergency call.

Ms. Morse: Engine three on the scene. We're here to help you.

O'Donnell: But nothing's average about this fire crew. They are all women, the first female engine company in the country. Captain Linda Morse, engineer Lisa Blake, and fire-fighters Carol Ringe and Leilani Cerruto.

Unidentified Woman #1: One, two, three.

O'Donnell: They've had to fight to come this far. Women haven't always been welcome in this traditionally male world. But in San Diego, they're making their own traditions.

Ms. Carol Ringe: I think we've proved that women can do the job, and they are trainable, and they can do the job just as well as men.

O'Donnell: In San Diego, 8 percent of firefighters are women. That's the highest among major cities. This, when other places like New York have fewer than 1 percent and are still struggling to integrate women into fire departments.

Ms. Lisa Blake: Engine three.

O'Donnell: The debate has centered on the issue of strength.

[Firefighter]: I might use technique over strength, but with the combination of the two I still get the job done.

O'Donnell: Captain Linda Morse says the public they serve has no reservations.

Ms. Morse: If they're going to call 911, they're not going to judge you as you come in the door. They're going to be so happy to see you, they're not going to say, you know, 'This is a woman.'

O'Donnell: Even though their job is considered dangerous, the hardest part of their day is often leaving home. Because three of these firefighters are mothers, the conversation at the fire station is a little different than what you'd normally hear.

[Ringe Child]: My mommy's a firefighter. I'm going to grow up to be a firefighter, too.

O'Donnell: But when they're working, Battalion Chief John Hale says there's no difference between men and women.

Chief John Hale: You have to remember that this job is a very strenuous, physical job, regardless of your gender. You have to be able to do that, and the people that pass the system are the ones that can do that, men or women. There are lots of men that can't do this job, and that have been turned down.

O'Donnell: Training and fitness are a big part of the job. Drills prepare them for whatever the 24-hour shift demands.

Ms. Morse: Truck One from Engine Three, we are pumping 100 pounds.

Unidentified Woman #2: One, two, three.

Ms. Morse: On the fire ground you don't have a lot of time to talk. So you need to anticipate how the other person works, how they think, and then with very little verbal commands, be able to accomplish a task.

O'Donnell: Do you feel any different knowing there's a woman protecting your back than if it were a male firefighter protecting your back?

Ms. Lisa Blake: Not at all. The only thing that's important to me is that the person next to me is competent, and that's not a problem with this crew.

Ms. Leilani Cerruto: We're going to help you. We're going to help you.

Ms. Morse: Relax, we're here to help you ...

O'Donnell: As pioneers in their field, these women are under a great deal of pressure. Add to that a job that's already incredibly tough. But they understand the risks involved and are proud of the work they do.

[Firefighter]: We feel that, you know, we're making a step into history as the all-women crew, and we're happy to be a part of that.

O'Donnell: Lots of little boys want to be firefighters. When you were five or six years old, did you ever dream you'd be wearing the badge?

Ms. Morse: Absolutely not.

Ms. Ringe: Absolutely not.

Ms. Cerruti: Unh-unh.

Ms. Morse: I think about when my son is in elementary school, and he studies history, and maybe they'll be shocked that gender was such a big issue. I think about the time when it's not an issue, and I think that will be the time when we've finally made it.

O'Donnell: For *Today*, Kelly O'Donnell, NBC News, San Diego.

---

3. "Illusory Promises"

Sometimes a statement may sound like a promise, but really isn't one. Here's an example: "I promise to sell you my antique oak desk, unless I decide not to."

The essential element of "promise" is commitment. To make a "promise," one must pledge or commit oneself to some future action or inaction. The rule of "illusory promises" recognizes that the mere use of promissory language (e.g., "I promise") without an actual commitment cannot be characterized as a "promise" and therefore cannot be consideration for another party's promise. The example involving my Oak desk is a paradigm illusory promise. The paradigm presents an easy example. In many cases the determination whether a "promise" is illusory is more difficult. See the comments to Section 77 of the Restatement (Second) of Contracts for numerous examples of illusory promises.

The two cases that follow, *Flemma v. Halliburton Energy Services, Inc.* and *Wood v. Lucy, Lady Duff-Gordon*, deal with the notion of legally enforceable return promises in distinct situations. In *Flemma*, the court considers whether an employee's promise to arbitrate disputes is supported by consideration when the employer can unilaterally revoke the dispute resolution process after an employee's claim has accrued. In *Wood v. Lucy, Lady Duff-Gordon*, Judge Benjamin Cardozo analyzes the commercial circumstances in which the parties' relationship exists and concludes that there must be an implied return obligation. Are the promises illusory? In contrast, the court in *Lawrence v. Ingham County Health Dept. Family Planning/Pre-Natal Clinic* is unable to see the relationship between the Lawrences and their health care provider as more than charity and relying on the outdated notion of "mutuality of obligation" finds no consideration. Yet the problem of unenforceability does not mean that the return promise in *Lawrence* is illusory. Instead, the decision suggests that Ms. Lawrence's promise is somehow categorically insufficient.

Edward R. Flemma v. Halliburton Energy Services, Inc., Rick Risinger, Richard Montman, and Karl E. Madden

Supreme Court of New Mexico
303 P.3d 814 (2013)

BARBARA J. VIGIL, JUSTICE

...

I. Background

Defendant Halliburton Energy Services (Halliburton) hired Plaintiff Edward Flemma (Flemma) to work as a cement equipment operator in Houma, Louisiana, in January of 1982. During his twenty-six years of employment with Halliburton, Flemma was promoted several times and worked for the company in Louisiana, Texas, Angola, and New Mexico. The last position he held was as district manager in Farmington, New Mexico, where he worked from 2006 until the time of his termination in 2008.

As district manager, Flemma was involved in a company initiative to consolidate three Farmington facilities into one suitable facility. Halliburton considered two locations for the consolidated facility: Troy King, located within the Farmington city limits, and Crouch Mesa, located outside the city limits. The company preferred the Troy King location partly due to tax incentives offered by the city. Flemma opposed the Troy King facility for various reasons, including concerns about the safety of the general public.

Flemma alleged that in August 2006, he and Defendant Karl Madden, a district sales manager for Halliburton, received a warning from Defendant Richard Montman, Flemma's supervisor, that "if you value your career, you will keep your mouth shut about the Troy King property." The day after this warning, Rick Grisinger, a Vice President of Halliburton, told Flemma to stop making "negative comments" regarding the Troy King location. Flemma did not heed Grisinger's warning, and in July 2007, Flemma continued to express his concerns when he prepared an executive summary comparing the two locations and reiterating the public safety issues at the Troy King location.

In April 2008, Montman informed Flemma, "Today is your last day with the company, you are not meeting my expectations." Montman gave Flemma the option of signing a resignation, general release, and settlement agreement, as well as accepting twelve weeks of base salary, or being terminated. Flemma refused to sign the documents and was terminated. He stated in an affidavit that he was terminated in retaliation for "not keeping [his] mouth shut" about his concerns related to the Troy King facility. As a result, Flemma filed a complaint in district court on December 22, 2008, against Halliburton and others for wrongful and retaliatory discharge.

After answering Flemma's complaint, Halliburton filed a motion to compel arbitration, alleging that Flemma agreed to a binding arbitration provision in the company's Dispute Resolution Program (DRP), which was adopted in 1997. In support of its motion, Halliburton attached documentary evidence that on four separate occasions, Halliburton mailed Flemma materials notifying him that continued employment with the company constituted his acceptance of the terms of the DRP. According to Halliburton, the four mailings were essentially identical and expressly stated that continuing employment with Halliburton would constitute an agreement with Flemma to abide by the DRP.

The first two alleged notifications occurred in December 1997 and spring 1998 while Flemma was working in Texas. The third alleged notification occurred in the summer of 1999 while Flemma was working in Louisiana. The fourth alleged notification occurred in October 2001 while Flemma was again working in Texas. Halliburton stated that it maintained a record of all the DRP-related mailings that were returned to Halliburton as undeliverable and none of the mailings sent to Flemma were returned as such. Thus, Halliburton alleged that Flemma must have received the mailings, which it asserted means that he was on notice that he agreed to arbitrate any employment-related disputes by continuing his employment.

Flemma responded to Halliburton's motion to compel, arguing ... that the DRP is invalid because Halliburton's promise to arbitrate is illusory, as it allows Halliburton to amend or terminate the DRP after a claim accrues.

After briefing by the parties and a hearing, the district court denied Halliburton's motion to compel arbitration.

... Halliburton appealed the denial of its motion to the Court of Appeals. In a split decision, the Court of Appeals reversed the district court.

... Flemma appealed the Court of Appeals' opinion and argues ... that Halliburton's ability to modify the terms of the arbitration agreement after a claim has accrued, but before an arbitration proceeding has been initiated, renders the arbitration agreement illusory and thereby unenforceable.... [W]e conclude that there is no valid agreement to arbitrate due to a lack of consideration since Halliburton's ability to revoke its promise to arbitrate after a claim has accrued makes the promise illusory.

II. Discussion.

...

A Valid Agreement to Arbitrate Was Not Formed Under New Mexico Law.

Applying New Mexico law to the alleged agreement, we conclude that Flemma and Halliburton never formed a valid agreement to arbitrate because the agreement fails for lack of consideration. It fails because Halliburton's promise to arbitrate is illusory since Halliburton retains the right to unilaterally amend the agreement's terms after an employee's claim has accrued.

There is no dispute that Halliburton made an offer to arbitrate. However, the facts of the case do not support the conclusion that it gave valid consideration for Flemma's promise to arbitrate. Halliburton argues that in exchange for Flemma's promise to arbitrate his claims, it promised to arbitrate its claims, and that these mutual promises are consideration to support enforcement of the arbitration agreement. We disagree. Because the terms of the agreement allow Halliburton to amend the agreement after a claim has accrued, but before arbitration proceedings are initiated, Halliburton can decide that it does not want to use alternative dispute resolution, or it may alter the terms on which alternative dispute resolution is based.

The existence of a valid agreement to arbitrate is required to compel arbitration. *See Mitsubishi Motors Corp. v. Soler Chrysler-Plymouth, Inc.*, 473 U.S. 614, 626, (1985) (holding that the existence of a valid agreement to arbitrate is also a prerequisite to compelling arbitration under the FAA); *see also McMillan v. Allstate Indem. Co.*, 84 P.3d 65 (N.M. 2004) (explaining that New Mexico's Uniform Arbitration Act does not permit a court to grant a motion to compel arbitration where no agreement to arbitrate exists). "Whether a valid contract to arbitrate exists is a question of state contract law." *DeArmond*, 81 P.3d 573 (N.M. 2003) (citing *First Options of Chicago, Inc. v. Kaplan*, 514 U.S. 938, 944–45 (1995)). For a contract to be legally valid and enforceable, it "must be factually supported by an offer, an acceptance, consideration, and mutual assent." *Garcia v. Middle Rio Grande Con-*

servancy Dist., 918 P.2d 7 (N.M. 1996) (internal quotation marks and citation omitted). The burden of proof is on the party asserting that a valid contract exists. *See Camino Real Mobile Home Park P'ship v. Wolfe*, 891 P.2d 1190, 1196 (1995)....

A promise is illusory if it consists of "words in promissory form that promise nothing." 2 Joseph M. Perillo & Helen Hadjiyannakis Bender, Corbin on Contracts § 5.28 at 142 (rev. ed. 1995). According to the Restatement (Second) of Contracts § 77 (1981), "A promise or apparent promise is not consideration if by its terms the promisor or purported promisor reserves a choice of alternative performances ..." A party's promise to arbitrate is also illusory where it retains the ability to unilaterally change the arbitration agreement. *See id.* cmt. a ("Words of promise which by their terms make performance entirely optional with the 'promisor' do not constitute a promise."); *Dumais v. Am. Golf Corp.*, 299 F.3d 1216, 1219 (10th Cir. 2002) ("[A]n arbitration agreement allowing one party the unfettered right to alter the arbitration agreement's existence or its scope is illusory."); *Salazar v. Citadel Commc'ns Corp.*, 90 P.3d 466 (N.M. 2004) ("Under general New Mexico contract law, an agreement that is subject to unilateral modification or revocation is illusory and unenforceable.")....

The district court stated that Flemma's case "[fell] nicely" between the cases of *Salazar* and *Sisneros v. Citadel Broad. Co.*, 142 P.3d 34 (N.M. 2006). In *Salazar*, this Court ruled that an arbitration agreement annexed to an employment agreement was unenforceable. 90 P.3d at 469–470. The Court found that the policy gave the employer the unrestricted right to amend or terminate its agreement to arbitrate disputes at any time, thereby making it unenforceable. 90 P.3d at 468. The Court of Appeals distinguished *Salazar* in *Sisneros*. The arbitration agreement at issue in Sisneros restricted the employer's right to terminate or amend the agreement to arbitrate. 142 P.3d at 42–43. "[A]ny termination or amendment [would] not apply to claims which accrued before the amendment or termination." 142 P.3d at 43. (added emphasis omitted) (internal quotation marks and citation omitted). Therefore, once a claim accrued, the employer and employee were bound to arbitrate the dispute under the rules that applied when the claim accrued. 142 P.3d at 43.

The reason that this case falls between *Salazar* and *Sisneros* is that, as the district court found, the arbitration agreement leaves a period of time between when a claim accrues and when a proceeding is initiated, during which Halliburton retains the authority to unilaterally amend the agreement. A claim for common law tort arising from employment termination accrues when an employee's job is terminated. 142 P.3d at 43. According to the October 2001 agreement sent to Flemma, "[N]o amendment shall apply to a Dispute for which a proceeding has been initiated pursuant to the Rules." (Emphasis added.) In *Salazar*, the employer retained authority to amend the agreement throughout. P.3d at 468. In *Sisneros*, the employer could not amend the agreement after a claim accrued, i.e., after a termination. 142 P.3d at 43. Halliburton's agreement only partially fixes the deficiencies highlighted by *Salazar* by providing that no amendment can be made after arbitration proceedings are initiated, but it fails to meet the requirement set by *Sisneros*.

Halliburton's DRP is contrary to *Sisneros* because it can amend the DRP after a claim accrues. In addition, Halliburton retains sole discretion to revoke the DRP at any time. Although Halliburton cannot modify the DRP unless it gives advance notice to current employees, terminated employees such as Flemma would not receive advance notice of changes to the agreement. Therefore, Halliburton's DRP is illusory because it retains the authority to unilaterally amend the agreement even after a claim accrues.

III. Conclusion

We conclude that the district court did not err in refusing to compel arbitration in this case.... [W]e conclude that no valid agreement to arbitrate exists, as the agreement lacks consideration because Halliburton can unilaterally amend or revoke its promise to arbitrate after a claim has accrued. In the context of this case, we must ensure that the employee, who has apparently agreed to arbitrate employment-related disputes, has received consideration for this promise. This is particularly crucial where the employer's authority to terminate employment is the cause for the need for dispute resolution. Here, Halliburton made what appears to be a return promise to arbitrate, but a closer evaluation of its promise reveals that it only created the illusion of such a promise because it could amend the DRP or do away with it all together after Flemma's claim accrued. This type of illusory promise is insufficient consideration for Flemma's promise to arbitrate employment-related disputes, and it is patently unfair in the context of the imbalanced at-will employee-employer relationship.

Accordingly, we reverse the Court of Appeals and affirm the district court's denial of the motion to compel arbitration. We remand this matter to the district court for further proceedings on Flemma's employment claims.

IT IS SO ORDERED.

Otis Wood v. Lucy, Lady Duff-Gordon

Court of Appeals of New York
118 N.E. 214 (N.Y. 1917)

JUDGE BENJAMIN NATHAN CARDOZO

The defendant styles herself 'a creator of fashions.' Her favor helps a sale. Manufacturers of dresses, millinery, and like articles are glad to pay for a certificate of her approval. The things which she designs, fabrics, parasols, and what not, have a new value in the public mind when issued in her name. She employed the plaintiff to help her to turn this vogue into money. He was to have the exclusive right, subject always to her approval, to place her indorsements on the designs of others. He was also to have the exclusive right to place her own designs on sale, or to license others to market them. In return she was to have one-half of 'all profits and revenues' derived from any contracts he might make. The exclusive right was to last at least one year from April 1, 1915, and thereafter from year to year unless terminated by notice of 90 days. The plaintiff says that he kept the contract on his part, and that the defendant broke it. She placed her indorsement on fabrics, dresses, and millinery without his knowledge, and withheld the profits. He sues her for the damages, and the case comes here on demurrer.

The agreement of employment is signed by both parties. It has a wealth of recitals. The defendant insists, however, that it lacks the elements of a contract. She says that the plaintiff does not bind himself to anything. It is true that he does not promise in so many words that he will use reasonable efforts to place the defendant's indorsements and market her designs. We think, however, that such a promise is fairly to be implied. The law has outgrown its primitive stage of formalism when the precise word was the sovereign talisman, and every slip was fatal. It takes a broader view today. A promise may be lacking, and yet the whole writing may be 'instinct with an obligation,' imperfectly expressed (Scott, J., in *McCall Co. v. Wright*, 117 N. Y. Supp. 775; *Moran v. Standard Oil Co.*, 105 N. E. 217, 228 (N.Y.)). If that is so, there is a contract.

The implication of a promise here finds support in many circumstances. The defendant gave an exclusive privilege. She was to have no right for at least a year to place her own indorsements or market her own designs except through the agency of the plaintiff. The acceptance of the exclusive agency was an assumption of its duties. We are not to suppose that one party was to be placed at the mercy of the other. Many other terms of the agreement point the same way. We are told at the outset by way of recital that:

> 'The said Otis F. Wood possesses a business organization adapted to the placing of such indorsements as the said Lucy, Lady Duff-Gordon, has approved.'

The implication is that the plaintiff's business organization will be used for the purpose for which it is adapted. But the terms of the defendant's compensation are even more significant. Her sole compensation for the grant of an exclusive agency is to be one-half of all the profits resulting from the plaintiff's efforts. Unless he gave his efforts, she could never get anything. Without an implied promise, the transaction cannot have such business 'efficacy, as both parties must have intended that at all events it should have.' Bowen, L. J., in the *Moorcock*, 14 P. D. 64, 68. But the contract does not stop there. The plaintiff goes on to promise that he will account monthly for all moneys received by him, and that he will take out all such patents and copyrights and trade-marks as may in his judgment be necessary to protect the rights and articles affected by the agreement. It is true, of course, as the Appellate Division has said, that if he was under no duty to try to market designs or to place certificates of indorsement, his promise to account for profits or take out copyrights would be valueless. But in determining the intention of the parties the promise has a value. It helps to enforce the conclusion that the plaintiff had some duties. His promise to pay the defendant one-half of the profits and revenues resulting from the exclusive agency and to render accounts monthly was a promise to use reasonable efforts to bring profits and revenues into existence. For this conclusion the authorities are ample. [citations omitted].

The judgment of the Appellate Division should be reversed, and the order of the Special Term affirmed, with costs in the Appellate Division and in this court.

Note

Benjamin Nathan Cardozo was appointed to the New York Court of Appeals (the state's highest court) in 1914 and was the first Jew to serve on the court. While on the court he earned wide acclaim, and, in 1927, Cardozo was elected Chief Judge, having been the nominee of both the Democratic and Republican parties. In 1932, Cardozo was appointed to the U.S Supreme Court by Herbert Hoover. The nomination was met with anti-Semitic protests and threats, but this opposition was overcome by Cardozo's strong bipartisan support. Justice Cardozo served on the U.S. Supreme Court until his death in 1938.

Justice Cardozo's influence on the common law of contracts and torts in the United States is without rival. His judicial opinions and other writing, including The Nature of the Judicial Process (1921), Growth of the Law (1924), The Paradoxes of Legal Science (1928), and a collections of essays entitled Law and Literature and Other Essays and Addresses (1931), continue to shape contemporary law and legal practice.

Ethel Lawrence, Individually and As Next Friend of Jessica Lawrence, a Minor, and Douglas J. Lawrence v. Ingham County Health Department Family Planning/Pre-Natal Clinic, and A. Breck, M.D., William C. Carley, M.D., L. Sanborn, M.D., D. Holden, M.D., A. Crow, M.D., Edward W. Sparrow Hospital, St. Lawrence Hospital, Robert Posey, M.D., and J. C. Leshock, M.D.

Court of Appeals of Michigan
408 N.W. 2d 461 (Mich. 1987)

MICHAEL J. KELLY, PRESIDING JUDGE

Plaintiffs appeal as of right from an order of summary disposition granted under MCR 2.116(C)(8) in favor of defendant Ingham County Health Department Family Planning/ Pre-Natal Clinic. We affirm.

Plaintiffs filed this three-count complaint following the birth of their daughter, Jessica Lawrence. According to the allegations in the complaint, which are taken as true for purposes of deciding and reviewing a motion under MCR 2.116(C)(8), plaintiff Ethel Lawrence first visited defendant clinic on December 13, 1979, for a pregnancy test. She reported her last menstrual period as October 19, 1979, and tested positive for pregnancy. Plaintiff then continued routine prenatal treatment with the clinic. On August 19, 1980, she appeared at defendant St. Lawrence Hospital in labor, where she underwent an emergency Caesarean section. Jessica Lawrence suffered fetal distress and prenatal asphyxia, which plaintiffs theorized could have been prevented by applying standard procedures for postmature fetuses. Following the delivery, Jessica was resuscitated and transferred to defendant Edward W. Sparrow Hospital. She sustained permanent, serious brain damage.

Plaintiffs' original complaint alleged various acts of negligence on the part of the individual physicians, the clinic and the two hospitals. Defendant clinic was granted summary disposition as to the negligence claims on the ground of governmental immunity. See *Ross v. Consumers Power Co.* (on rehearing), 363 N.W. 2d 641 (Mich. 1984). Plaintiffs do not appeal from that ruling.

Plaintiffs' third amended complaint included two counts of breach of contract.[1] In paragraphs 4 and 5 of Count II of their third amended complaint, plaintiffs allege breach of an enforceable agreement between plaintiffs Ethel and Douglas Lawrence and the clinic and clinic physicians:

4. That thereafter, Defendant Ingham County Health Department Family Planning/Prenatal Clinic agreed to accept Plaintiff Ethel Lutman Lawrence as a patient and plaintiff Ethel Lutman Lawrence agreed to follow the directions of the physicians and other medical personnel at the Defendant Clinic for the benefit of her unborn child.

---

1. Although plaintiffs plead contract implied in law, we interpret their claims as a breach of a contract implied in fact. In determining whether there is a contract implied in fact, the courts look to the acts and conduct of the parties to determine whether the essential elements of an express contract have been established. 6A Michigan Law & Practice, Contracts § 3, at 69–70.

5. That an implied contract in law was created as a result of the Defendant Clinic's offer to provide medical services to Plaintiff Ethel Lutman Lawrence within the then-existing and applicable standard of care and Plaintiff Ethel Lutman Lawrence's acceptance of said offer by agreeing to follow the directions of the Defendant Clinic's physicians and other medical personnel for the benefit of her unborn child.

Plaintiffs allege that Jessica Lawrence is a third-party beneficiary of this contract between her parents and the clinic.

In Count III of the third amended complaint, plaintiffs allege breach of an implied contract between the clinic and the hospital. However, plaintiffs admitted at oral argument on the motion for summary disposition that Count III did not state a claim against defendant clinic and we will therefore not address Count III on appeal.

The lower court found that plaintiffs failed to state a cause of action for breach of contract and granted summary disposition in favor of defendant clinic. Summary disposition on this ground tests the legal basis of the complaint, not whether it can be factually supported, and is proper only when the claim is so clearly unenforceable as a matter of law that no factual development can possibly justify a right to recover. *Bradford v. Michigan*, 153 Mich. App. 756, 761, 396 N.W. 2d 522 (1986). The trial court concluded that plaintiffs failed to plead facts that would support a finding of adequate consideration and that plaintiffs' contract claim must therefore fail.

Plaintiffs argue that the consideration provided by plaintiff Ethel Lawrence was her agreement not to have an abortion and her agreement to follow the directions of the clinic medical staff. Plaintiffs contend that, by entering into these agreements, Ethel Lawrence refrained from doing that which she was legally privileged to do and thereby rendered valuable consideration in return for defendant clinic's promise to provide adequate prenatal care. Since plaintiffs have not alleged in their complaint that Ethel Lawrence agreed not to have an abortion in return for the promise of medical care, we will not consider this argument further.[2]

The contract described by plaintiffs involves an exchange of promises: Ethel Lawrence's promise to follow directions in exchange for the clinic's promise to provide appropriate prenatal care. In order for Ethel Lawrence's promise to rise to the level of consideration sufficient to support a contract implied in fact, however, that promise must be of some value to defendant clinic. We think this means the promise must be enforceable. Although we recognize that mutuality of obligation is not always a necessary element to every contract, we are persuaded that, in the context of this case, lack of mutuality of obligation translates into lack of consideration:

Inasmuch as a promise by one person is merely one of the kinds of consideration that will support a promise by another, mutuality of obligation is not an essential element in every contract. Therefore, to say the least, language which is susceptible of the interpretation that consideration and mutuality of obligation are two distinct elements lacks precision in that, while consideration is essential, mutuality of obligation is not, *unless the want of mutuality would leave one party without a valid or available consideration for his promise.* [17 Am. Jur. 2d Contracts § 11, at 347–48. *Emphasis added.*]

Plaintiff Ethel Lawrence's agreement to follow the advice of the clinic's medical staff regarding prenatal health care is not a legally enforceable promise. Contrary to the position

---

2. We note, however, that our analysis would be the same on sufficient consideration even if we did address this argument. We are saved from examining the public policy implications of such an anomalous agreement by plaintiffs' complaint.

of plaintiffs below, we are not persuaded that defendant clinic has or had a cause of action for breach of contract against plaintiff for failure on her part to follow its medical advice. Plaintiff Ethel Lawrence was given advice on health care conducive to the well-being of her unborn baby. We hold that her acceptance of that advice cannot be deemed consideration for a contract.

We are well aware that facts giving rise to a cause of action for negligence may also give rise to a cause of action for breach of contract. Where this occurs, the doctrine of governmental immunity bars only the negligence claim and does not prevent the party from pursuing the breach of contract claim based on the same facts. *See Rocco v. Dep't of Mental Health*, 363 N.W. 2d 641 (Mich. 1984). As in the instant case, the plaintiff's claim for breach of contract in Rocco was dismissed on the basis of inadequate pleadings. That order was reversed. In *Rocco*, however, the plaintiffs expressly alleged that they paid for the care and treatment rendered their decedent. The plaintiffs in *Rocco* did not plead consideration by way of their agreement to follow the defendant's medical advice.

We do not evaluate the adequacy of the consideration allegedly rendered in this case since that would be a question for the factfinder rather than for us in determining the adequacy of plaintiff's pleadings. We simply conclude that plaintiffs' claim of consideration is so clearly unenforceable as a matter of law that no factual development can possibly justify their right to recover on the theory of defendant's breach of an implied contract in fact.

Affirmed.

SAWYER, JUDGE, DISSENTING

I dissent.

Defendant health clinic made a promise to Ethel Lawrence that if she would come to the clinic and promise thereafter to follow its staff's directions, it would provide her and her unborn child with appropriate prenatal care. Despite these promises, which defendants must admit as true for purposes of the summary disposition motion, the majority concludes that Ethel's promise to follow the clinic's directions had no value to the clinic and, therefore, "is not a legally enforceable promise."

It is not the office of the courts to scrutinize the adequacy of consideration. *Harwood v. Randolph Harwood, Inc.*, 124 Mich. App. 137, 142, 333 N.W. 2d 609 (1983). In fact, even the majority concedes in its final paragraph that "the adequacy of the consideration ... [is] a question for the factfinder ..." How, then, can the majority now say that Ethel's promise is lacking in value? As I will explain more fully below, I am unable to sign my name to an opinion which on the one hand states that it will let the factfinder worry about the adequacy of consideration and, then, on the other hand holds that plaintiff Ethel Lawrence's consideration "is so clearly unenforceable as a matter of law."

I am unable to join the majority's opinion for one simple reason: it effectively ignores the fact that this matter comes before this Court by way of an appeal from a grant of summary disposition for failure to state a claim, MCR 2.116(C)(8), rather than from a jury verdict in favor of defendants or even from the grant of summary disposition under MCR 2.116(C)(10) (no genuine issue of material fact). While I am skeptical that plaintiffs will be able to prevail at trial, I am unwilling to deny them their day in court.

Summary disposition under MCR 2.116(C)(8) tests the legal basis of the complaint, not whether it can be factually supported, and is proper only when the claim is so clearly unenforceable as a matter of law that no factual development can possibly justify a right to recover. *Bradford v. Michigan*, 153 Mich. App. 756, 761, 396 N.W. 2d 522 (1986).

Regarding Count II of the complaint, plaintiffs allege that there was an implied contract which defendant health clinic breached.[1] The trial court concluded that there could be no contract as there was no consideration on plaintiffs' behalf:

Looking at the complaint in the light most favorable to the Plaintiff even if Plaintiff were able to sustain her proofs that she had not gotten an abortion and she had followed the directives [of the Health Department's physicians] when she was not obligated by law to do so, the Court does not believe that under any stretch of the imagination could that be considered as adequate or any form of consideration. I think to take that as consideration would expand the definition of the contract beyond all recognition.

The majority seems to follow this view, with which I disagree.

The concept of consideration was discussed in Calamari & Perillo, Contracts§ 4-1, at 133–134 (2d ed.):

Since the doctrine of consideration is an historical phenomenon and therefore in some of its aspects affected by fortuitous circumstances, an encompassing definition is perhaps impossible. Nonetheless, an attempt should be made. A learned judge [Cardozo, C.J., in *Allegheny College v. Nat'l Chautauqua Co. Bank*, 246 N.Y. 369, 159 N.E. 173 (1927)] has identified the three elements which must concur before a promise is supported by consideration.

(a) The promisee must suffer legal detriment; that is, do or promise to do what he is not legally obligated to do; or refrain from doing or promise to refrain from doing what he is legally privileged to do.

(b) The detriment must induce the promise. In other words the promisor must have made the promise because he wished to exchange it at least in part for the detriment to be suffered by the promisee.

(c) The promise must induce the detriment. This means in effect, as we have already seen, that the promisee must know of the offer and intend to accept.

---

1. While plaintiffs allege that there was an implied in law contract, my review of plaintiffs' allegations leads me to believe that any contract was an express contract, with part or all of the terms implied in fact. Plaintiffs' third amended complaint alleges that defendant health clinic offered to provide medical services and plaintiff Ethel Lawrence accepted the "offer by agreeing to follow the directions of the Defendant Clinic's physicians." A contract implied in law

is not a contract at all but an obligation imposed by law to do justice even though it is clear that no promise was ever made or intended. To illustrate, if a physician gives a child necessary medical care in the face of parental neglect, the physician may recover from the parents, in quasi contract, the value of his services.... The principal function of quasi contract is generally said to be that of prevention of unjust enrichment.

Calamari & Perillo, Contracts §§ 1–12, at 19–20 (2d ed.) (Footnotes omitted.)

The concept of an implied in fact contract differs:

When the parties manifest their agreement by words the contract is said to be express. When it is manifested by conduct it is said to be implied in fact. If A telephones a plumber to come to A's house to fix a broken pipe, it may be inferred that A has agreed to pay the plumber a reasonable fee for his services although nothing is said of this. The contract is partly express and partly implied in fact. There are cases of contracts wholly implied in fact. The distinction between this kind of contract and a contract expressed in words is unimportant: both are true contracts formed by a mutual manifestation of assent.

[*Id.* at 19.] Inasmuch as a plaintiffs allege that there was mutual agreement, I would view this as an express, rather than implied, contract. However, whether this is viewed as an express or implied contract is unnecessary to the resolution of this case. Rather, the question is whether plaintiffs allege the existence of consideration, which is a requirement for both express and implied contracts. Lowery v. Dep't of Corrections, 380 N.W.2d 99 (Mich. App. 1985).

In this case, plaintiffs argue that the consideration given by Ethel Lawrence was her agreement not to have an abortion and her agreement to follow the directions of the attending physicians.[2] Either of these agreements, if in fact they were made, would constitute a form of consideration. Her agreement not to have an abortion constitutes an agreement to refrain from doing that which she was legally privileged to do.[3] Her agreement to follow the advice of the physicians constitutes an agreement to do that which she was not legally obligated to do. Assuming that a factual development is made to show that Ms. Lawrence's agreements were made to induce defendant health clinic's agreement to provide services and, conversely, that defendant health clinic required Ms. Lawrence to make those agreements in order to receive the health services, then a contract would exist between the parties.

The flaw in the majority's reasoning is evident from the following statement: "Plaintiff Ethel Lawrence's agreement to follow the advice of the clinic's medical staff regarding prenatal health care is not a legally enforceable promise."

The majority, however, offers no authority for this conclusion. I am aware of no rule of law, be it statutory, regulatory or common law, which would operate to prevent a person from contractually obligating himself to following the advice of a physician. Since a person is free to do so, upon contractually binding oneself to following a physician's advice, that person exposes himself to a breach of contract action for a subsequent failure to follow the advice. The majority apparently confuses the unusualness of plaintiffs' theory in application with its viability in the abstract. That is, while I would be surprised to learn that it is common practice for patients to contractually agree to be bound by their physicians' advice, I do not believe such contracts are unenforceable as a matter of law.[4]

The same principle applies to plaintiffs' argument concerning the agreement not to have an abortion. While I am aware of no institution which demands such a promise, I can easily imagine that a private health clinic, run by a charitable or religious organization, might well offer free prenatal care as an inducement to prevent women from having an abortion.[5] While such an arrangement would undoubtedly prove difficult for a court to attempt to enforce or to provide a remedy for a breach of such an arrangement, I am unwilling to conclude at this time that such agreements are legally unenforceable.

Once the conclusion is reached that a person may legally bind himself to follow a physician's advice, or to forego an action he is legally privileged to take, it becomes a factual question whether he has made such an agreement. It is improper to resolve that factual question in the context of a motion brought pursuant to MCR 2.116(C)(8) or in an appeal from an order granted under that subrule.

---

2. I recognize that, as pointed out by the majority, plaintiffs did not allege in their complaint that Ethel Lawrence agreed to refrain from undergoing an abortion as a part of her agreement. However, plaintiffs did so argue in the trial court. Since plaintiffs could easily have added such an allegation to their complaint by way of amendment, and since amendments to complaints should be freely given, MCR 2.118(a)(2), Ben P. Fyke & Sons v. Gunter Co., 390 Mich. 649, 213 N.W.2d 134 (1973), I believe we can properly consider that argument as a part of plaintiffs' claim of consideration. However, I would reach the same result if I considered only plaintiffs' claim of consideration arising from the agreement to follow the physicians' advice.

3. *See* Roe v. Wade, 410 U.S. 113 (1973).

4. In fact, I can imagine situations in which a physician would wish to contractually bind his patient to take certain actions. For example, a physician may offer services for free or at a reduced fee in order to develop a new technique wherein the patient's obedience is essential to the physician's perfection and evaluation of the technique. While admittedly an uncommon occurrence, it does point to the flaw in the majority's broad-sweeping principle.

5. The question of a governmental agency demanding such a promise from a woman in exchange for services opens a Pandora's box which, fortunately, we have not yet been called upon to open.

The majority's and the trial court's alternative conclusion, that the consideration, if any, was inadequate is more easily disposed of. It is not ordinarily the role of the courts to question the adequacy of the consideration supporting the contract. Any consideration, no matter how economically insignificant, is sufficient to support a contract. *See Harwood*, *supra* at 142.[6]

To summarize, I would hold that a person may contractually obligate himself to follow the directions of a physician, or to forego an action he is legally privileged to perform. Where such an obligation is given in exchange for the promise of another to perform services, that obligation serves as consideration and a contract is established.

I would stress, however, the fact that this case comes to us by way of a motion for summary disposition for failure to state a claim. I express no opinion as to whether plaintiffs will be able to prove at trial, or even be able to survive a motion for summary disposition for no genuine issue of material fact, that Ms. Lawrence made her agreements in exchange for defendant health department's agreement to provide the health services. If the agreement of one did not induce the agreement of the other, then there is no contract. Similarly, we have not been called upon to consider whether defendant health department has provided consideration. Its only agreement appears to have been to provide health services. If, for example, it was under a preexisting legal duty to provide Ms. Lawrence with the health services, then its agreement to do so cannot constitute consideration. *Lowery v. Dep't of Corrections*, 146 Mich. App. 342, 359, 380 N.W. 2d 99 (1985).

While I recognize that plaintiffs' claim is, at best, novel and, at worst, tenuous, I do not believe that should provide the basis for summarily dismissing the complaint. Plaintiffs' theory is novel and, I suspect, it will prove difficult for them to establish the existence of the alleged promises and that the promise of each party induced the promise of the other. That is, I am not at all convinced that defendant health department required Ethel Lawrence to make the promises she allegedly did in order to receive medical attention. However, the point which seems to elude the majority and the trial court is that plaintiffs have not yet been called upon to convince anyone, be it this Court, the trial court, or a jury, that their claim can be borne out by the facts. To date, plaintiffs have only been called upon to state a claim. In my opinion, they have done so.

Judge Kelly once opined that "[as] in most *trials*, somebody wins and somebody loses."[9] However, the majority today would have plaintiffs lose before they have even had their day in court. To me, that is unconscionable.

I would reverse.[10]

Note — On Sovereign Immunity and Public Health Care

At the time of her pregnancy and this litigation, Ms. Lawrence was a woman of low income, seeking free medical care at a government clinic. The Ingham County Family Planning/Pre-Natal Clinic is a part of the Ingham County Health Department, a government

---

6. However, the adequacy of consideration may be relevant in certain instances, such as to determine the existence of fraud. Harwood, *supra* at 142.

9. Kovacs v. Chesapeake & O. R. Co., 351 N.W.2d 581 (Mich. App. 1984) (emphasis added).

10. However, I do agree with the majority that summary disposition on Count III of the complaint was appropriate in light of plaintiffs' admission in the trial court that Count III did not state a claim against defendant health department.

agency. The doctrine of sovereign immunity provides that the government (the "sovereign") cannot be sued unless, and then only to the extent that, it allows people to sue. The federal government and most state (and through them most local) governments have waived sovereign immunity with respect to contract claims. The rationale for waiving immunity regarding contract claims distinguishes between traditional activities of sovereignty, including criminal arrest and prosecution, military actions, taxation, and the like, and activities that are more like those of ordinary citizens and businesses, like making contracts to buy supplies. The federal government and most state governments have waived sovereign immunity regarding some, but not all, torts. Apparently Ingham County has not waived sovereign immunity regarding the torts alleged by Ethel and Douglas Lawrence. This is why the trial court dismissed the tort claims in this case and the Lawrences did not appeal that ruling.

What should be the scope of government liability when the government engages in the provision of medical care? Should the government and the doctors it employs be immune from liability for negligence in the provision of medical care?

Paulette Childress White, Getting the Facts of Life

(1989)

The August morning was ripening into a day that promised to be a burner. By the time we'd walked three blocks, dark patches were showing beneath Momma's arms, and inside tennis shoes thick with white polish, my feet were wet against the cushions. I was beginning to regret how quickly I'd volunteered to go.

"Dog. My feet are getting mushy," I complained.

"You should've wore socks," Momma said, without looking my way or slowing down.

I frowned. In 1961, nobody wore socks with tennis shoes. It was bare legs, Bermuda shorts and a sleeveless blouse. Period.

Momma was chubby but she could really walk. She walked the same way she washed clothes up-and-down, up-and-down until she was done. She didn't believe in taking breaks.

This was my first time going to the welfare office with Momma. After breakfast, before we'd had time to scatter, she corralled everyone old enough to consider and announced in her serious-business voice that someone was going to the welfare office with her this morning. Cries went up.

Junior had his papers to do. Stella was going swimming at the high school. Dennis was already pulling the *Free Press* wagon across town every first Wednesday to get the surplus food—like that.

"You want clothes for school, don't you?" That landed. School opened in two weeks.

"I'll go," I said.

"Who's going to baby-sit if Minerva goes?" Momma asked.

Stella smiled and lifted her small golden nose. "I will," she said. "I'd rather baby-sit than do *that*."

That should have warned me. Anything that would make Stella offer to baby-sit had to be bad.

A small cheer probably went up among my younger brothers in the back rooms where I was not too secretly known as "The Witch" because of the criminal licks I'd learned to give on my rise to power. I was twelve, third oldest under Junior and Stella, but I had long established myself as first in command among the kids. I was chief baby-sitter, biscuit-maker and broom wielder. Unlike Stella, who'd begun her development at ten, I still had my girl's body and wasn't anxious to have that changed. What would it mean but a loss of power? I liked things just the way they were. My interest in bras was even less than my interest in boys, and that was limited to keeping my brothers — who seemed destined for wildness — from taking over completely.

Even before we left, Stella had Little Stevie Wonder turned up on the radio in the living room, and suspicious jumping-bumping sounds were beginning in the back. They'll tear the house down, I thought, following mamma out the door.

We turned at Salliotte, the street that would take us straight up to Jefferson Avenue where the welfare office was. Momma's face was pinking in the heat, and I was huffing to keep up. From here, it was seven more blocks on the colored side, the railroad tracks, five blocks on the white side and there you were. We'd be cooked.

"Is the welfare office near the Harbor Show?" I asked. I knew the answer, I just wanted some talk.

"Across the street."

"Umm. Glad it's not way down Jefferson somewhere."

Nothing. Momma didn't talk much when she was outside. I knew that the reason she wanted one of us along when she had far to go was not for company but so she wouldn't have to walk by herself. I could understand that. To me, walking alone was like being naked or deformed — everyone seemed to look at you harder and longer. With Momma, the feeling was probably worse because you knew people were wondering if she were white, Indian maybe or really colored. Having one of us along, brown and clearly hers, probably helped define that. Still, it was like being a little parade, with Momma's pale skin and straight brown hair turning heads like the clang of cymbals. Especially on the colored side.

"Well," I said, "here we come to the bad part."

Momma gave a tiny laugh.

Most of Salliotte was a business street, with Old West-looking storefronts and some office places that never seemed to open. Ecorse, hinged onto southwest Detroit like a clothes closet, didn't seem to take itself seriously. There were lots of empty fields, some of which folks down the residential streets turned into vegetable gardens every summer. And there was this block where the Moonflower Hotel raised itself to three stories over the poolroom and Beaman's drugstore. Here, bad boys and drunks made their noise and did an occasional stabbing. Except for the cars that lined both sides of the block, only one side was busy — the other bordered a field of weeds. We walked on the safe side.

If you were a woman or a girl over twelve, walking this block — even on the safe side — could be painful. They usually hollered at you and never mind what they said. Today, because it was hot and early we made it by with only one weak *Hey baby* from a drunk sitting in the poolroom door.

"Hey baby yourself," I said but not too loudly, pushing my flat chest out and stabbing my eyes in his direction.

"Minerva girl, you better watch your mouth with grown men like that," Momma said, her eyes catching me up in real warning though I could see that she was holding down a smile.

"Well, he can't do nothing to me when I'm with you, can he?" I asked striving to match the rise and fall of her black pumps.

She said nothing, she just walked on, churning away under a sun that clearly meant to melt us. From here to the tracks it was mostly gardens. It felt like the Dixie Peach I'd used to help water-wave my hair was sliding down with the sweat on my face, and my throat was tight with thirst. Boy, did I want a pop. I looked at the last little store before we crossed the tracks without bothering to ask.

Across the tracks, there were no stores and no gardens. It was shady, and the grass was June green. Perfect-looking houses sat in unfenced spaces far back from the street. We walked these five blocks without a word. We just looked and hurried to get through it. I was beginning to worry about the welfare office in earnest. A fool could see that in this part of Ecorse, things got serious.

We had been on welfare for almost a year. I didn't have any strong feelings about it — my life went on pretty much the same. It just meant watching the mail for a check instead of Daddy getting paid, and occasional visits from a social worker that I'd always managed to miss. For Momma and whoever went with her, it meant this walk to the office and whatever went on there that made everyone hate to go. For Daddy, it seemed to bring the most change. For him, it meant staying away from home more than when he was working and a reason not to answer the phone.

At Jefferson, we turned left and there it was, halfway down the block. The Department of Social Services. I discovered some strong feelings. That fine name meant nothing. This was the welfare. The place for poor people. People who couldn't or wouldn't take care of themselves. Now I was going to face it, and suddenly I thought what I knew the others had thought, *What if I see someone I know?* I wanted to run back all those blocks to home.

I looked at Momma for comfort, but her face was closed and her mouth looked locked.

Inside, the place was gray. There were rows of long benches like church pews facing each other across a middle aisle that led to a central desk. Beyond the benches and the desk, four hallways led off to a maze of partitioned offices. In opposite corners, huge fans hung from the ceiling, humming from side to side, blowing the heavy air for a breeze.

Momma walked to the desk, answered some questions, was given a number and told to take a seat. I followed her through, trying not to see the waiting people — as though that would keep them from seeing me.

Gradually, as we waited, I took them all in. There was no one there that I knew, but somehow they all looked familiar. Or maybe I only thought they did, because when your eyes connected with someone's, they didn't quickly look away and they usually smiled. They were mostly women and children, and a few low-looking men. Some of them were white, which surprised me. I hadn't expected to see them in there.

Directly in front of the bench where we sat, a little girl with blond curls was trying to handle a bottle of Coke. Now and then, she'd manage to turn herself and the bottle around and watch me with big gray eyes that seemed to know quite well how badly I wanted a pop. I thought of asking Momma for fifteen cents so I could get one from the machine in the back but I was afraid she'd still say no so I just kept planning more and more convincing ways to ask. Besides, there was a water fountain near the door if I could make myself rise and walk to it.

We waited three hours. White ladies dressed like secretaries kept coming out to call numbers, and people on the benches would get up and follow down a hall. Then more people came in to replace them. I drank water from the fountain three times and was ready to put my feet up on the bench before us—the little girl with the Coke and her momma got called—by the time we heard Momma's number.

"You wait here," Momma said as I rose with her.

I sat down with a plop.

The lady with the number looked at me. Her face reminded me of the librarian's at Bunch school. Looked like she never cracked a smile. "Let her come," she said.

"She can wait here," Momma repeated, weakly.

"It's OK. She can come in. Come on," the lady insisted at me.

I hesitated, knowing that Momma's face was telling me to sit.

"Come on," the woman said.

Momma said nothing.

I got up and followed them into the maze. We came to a small room where there was a desk and three chairs. The woman sat behind the desk and we before it.

For a while, no one spoke. The woman studied a folder open before her, brows drawn together. On the wall behind her there was a calendar with one heavy black line drawn slantwise through each day of August, up to the twenty-first. That was today.

"Mrs. Blue, I have a notation here that Mr. Blue has not reported to the department on his efforts to obtain employment since the sixteenth of June. Before that, it was the tenth of April. You understand that department regulations require that he report monthly to this office, do you not?" Eyes brown as a wren's belly came up at Momma.

"Yes," Momma answered, sounding as small as I felt.

"Can you explain his failure to do so?"

Pause. "He's been looking. He says he's been looking."

"That may be. However, his failure to report those efforts here is my only concern."

Silence.

"We cannot continue with your case as it now stands if Mr. Blue refuses to comply with departmental regulations. He is still residing with the family, is he not?"

"Yes, he is. I've been reminding him to come in ... he said he would."

"Well, he hasn't. Regulations are that any able-bodied man, head-of-household and receiving assistance who neglects to report to this office any effort to obtain work for a period of sixty days or more is to be cut off for a minimum of three months, at which time he may reapply. As of this date, Mr. Blue is over sixty days delinquent, and officially, I am obliged to close the case and direct you to other sources of aid."

"Aid to Dependent Children would be the only source available to you. Then, of course, you would not be eligible unless it was verified that Mr. Blue was no longer residing with the family."

Another silence. I stared into the gray steel front of the desk, everything stopped but my heart.

"Well, can you keep the case open until Monday? If he comes in by Monday?"

"According to my records, Mr. Blue failed to come in May and such an agreement was made then. In all, we allowed him a period of seventy days. You must understand that what happens in such cases as this is not wholly my decision." She sighed and watched Momma with hopeless eyes, tapping the soft end of her pencil on the papers before her. "Mrs. Blue, I will speak to my superiors on your behalf. I can allow you until Monday next ... that's the"—she swung around to the calendar—"twenty-sixth of August, to get him in here."

"Thank you. He'll be in," Momma breathed. "Will I be able to get the clothing order today?"

Hands and eyes searched in the folder for an answer before she cleared her throat and tilted her face at Momma. "We'll see what we can do," she said, finally.

My back touched the chair. Without turning my head, I moved my eyes down to Momma's dusty feet and wondered if she could still feel them; my own were numb. I felt bodiless—there was only my face, which wouldn't disappear, and behind it, one word pinging against another in a buzz that made no sense. At home, we'd have the house cleaned by now, and I'd be waiting for the daily appearance of my best friend, Bernadine, so we could comb each other's hair or talk about stuck-up Evelyn and Brenda. Maybe Bernadine was already there, and Stella was teaching her to dance the bop.

Then I heard our names and ages—all eight of them—being called off like items in a grocery list.

"Clifford, Junior, age fourteen." She waited.

"Yes."

"Born? Give me the month and year."

"October, 1946," Momma answered, and I could hear in her voice that she'd been through these questions before.

"Stella, age thirteen."

"Yes."

"Born?"

"November 1947."

"Minerva, age twelve." She looked at me. "This is Minerva?"

"Yes."

No. I thought, no, this is not Minerva. You can write it down if you want to, but Minerva is not here.

"Born?"

"December 1948."

The woman went on down the list, sounding more and more like Momma should be sorry or ashamed, and Momma's answers grew fainter and fainter. So this was welfare. I wondered how many times Momma had to do this. Once before? Three times? Every time?

More questions. How many in school? Six. Who needs shoes? Everybody.

"Everybody needs shoes? The youngest two?"

"Well, they don't go to school ... but they walk."

My head came up to look at Momma and the woman. The woman's mouth was left open. Momma didn't blink.

The brown eyes went down. "Our allowances are based on the median costs for moderately priced clothing at Sears, Roebuck." She figured on paper as she spoke. "That will mean thirty-four dollars for children over ten ... thirty dollars for children under ten. It comes to one hundred and ninety-eight dollars. I can allow eight dollars for two additional pairs of shoes."

"Thank you."

"You will present your clothing order to a salesperson at the store, who will be happy to assist you in your selections. Please be practical as further clothing requests will not be considered for a period of six months. In cases of necessity, however, requests for winter outerwear will be considered beginning November first."

Momma said nothing.

The woman rose and left the room.

For the first time, I shifted in the chair. Momma was looking into the calendar as though she could see through the pages to November first. Everybody needed a coat.

I'm never coming here again, I thought. If I do, I'll stay out front. Not coming back in here. Ever again.

She came back and sat behind her desk. "Mrs. Blue, I must make it clear that, regardless of my feelings, I will be forced to close your case if your husband does not report to this office by Monday, the twenty-sixth. Do you understand?"

"Yes. Thank you. He'll come. I'll see to it."

"Very well." She held a paper out to Momma.

We stood. Momma reached over and took the slip of paper. I moved toward the door.

"Excuse me, Mrs. Blue, but are you pregnant?"

"What?"

"I asked if you were expecting another child."

"Oh. No, I'm not," Momma answered, biting down on her lips.

"Well, I'm sure you'll want to be careful about a thing like that in your present situation."

"Yes."

I looked quickly to Momma's loose white blouse. We'd never known when another baby was coming until it was almost there.

"I suppose that eight children are enough for anyone," the woman said, and for the first time her face broke into a smile.

Momma didn't answer that. Somehow, we left the room and found our way out onto the street. We stood for a moment as though lost. My eyes followed Momma's up to where the sun was burning high. It was still there, blazing white against a cloudless blue. Slowly, Momma put the clothing order into her purse and snapped it shut. She looked around as if uncertain which way to go. I led the way to the corner. We turned. We walked the first five blocks.

I was thinking about how stupid I'd been a year ago, when Daddy lost his job. I'd been happy.

"You-all better be thinking about moving to Indianapolis," he announced one day after work, looking like he didn't think much of it himself. He was a welder with the railroad company. He'd worked there for eleven years. But now, "Company's moving to Indianapolis," he said. "Gonna be gone by November. If I want to keep my job, we've got to move with it."

We didn't. Nobody wanted to move to Indianapolis—not even Daddy. Here, we had uncles, aunts and cousins on both sides. Friends. Everybody and everything we knew. Daddy could get another job. First came unemployment compensation. Then came welfare. Thank goodness for welfare, we said, while we waited and waited for the job that hadn't come yet.

The problem was that Daddy couldn't take it. If something got repossessed or somebody took sick or something was broken or another kid was coming, he'd carry on terribly until things got better—by which time things were always worse. He'd always been that way. So when the railroad left, he began to do everything wrong. Stayed out all hours. Drank and drank some more. When he was home, he was so grouchy we were afraid to squeak. Now when we saw him coming, we got lost. Even our friends ran for cover.

At the railroad tracks, we sped up. The tracks were as far across as a block was long. Silently, I counted the rails by the heat of the steel bars through my thin soles. On the other side, I felt something heavy rise up in my chest and I knew that I wanted to cry. I wanted to cry or run or kiss the dusty ground. The little houses with their sun-scorched lawns and backyard gardens were mansions in my eyes. "Ohh, Ma ... look at those collards!"

"Umm-humm," she agreed, and I knew that she saw it too.

"Wonder how they grew so big?"

"Cow dung, probably. Big Poppa used to put cow dung out to fertilize the vegetable plots, and everything just grew like crazy. We used to get tomatoes this big"—she circled with her hands—"and don't talk about squash or melons."

"I bet y'all ate like rich people. Bet y'all had everything you could want."

"We sure did," she said. "We never wanted for anything when it came to food. And when the cash crops were sold, we could get whatever else that was needed. We never wanted for a thing."

"What about the time you and cousin Emma threw out the supper peas?"

"Oh! Did I tell you about that?" she asked. Then she told it all over again. I didn't listen. I watched her face and guarded her smile with a smile of my own.

We walked together, step for step. The sun was still burning, but we forgot to mind it. We talked about an Alabama girlhood in a time and place I'd never know. We talked about the wringer washer and how it could be fixed, because washing every day on a scrub-board was something Alabama could keep. We talked about how to get Daddy to the Department of Social Services.

Then we talked about having babies. She began to tell me things I'd never known, and the idea of womanhood blossomed in my mind like some kind of suffocating rose.

"Momma," I said, "I don't think I can be a woman."

"You can," she laughed, "and if you live, you will be. You gotta be some kind of woman."

"But it's hard," I said, "sometimes it must be hard."

"Umm-humm," she said, "sometimes it is hard."

When we got to the bad block, we crossed to Beaman's drugstore for two orange crushes. Then we walked right through the groups of men standing in the shadows of the poolroom and the Moonflower Hotel. Not one of them said a word to us. I supposed they could see in the way we walked that we weren't afraid. We'd been to the welfare office and back again. And the facts of life, fixed in our minds like the sun in the sky, were no burning mysteries.

———

Paulette Childress White is a poet and short story writer. The Facts of Life was first published in an anthology: Memory of Kin: Stories about Family by Black Women Writers, edited by Mary Helen Washington. Why do you suppose this short story is called The Facts of Life? Which part of the Lawrence decision is most like what the welfare worker said to Minerva's mother?

---

4. Consideration and "Disfavored" Contract Terms: The Example of Job Security Terms

In most industrialized nations other than the United States, including Japan, Mexico, China, and the members of the European Community, most employees have job security. In contrast, most employees in the United States are subject to the "at-will employment doctrine," and can be terminated at any time, for any reason, or for no reason at all.

The at-will employment doctrine begins with a presumption about the meaning of contract terms: if an employment contract is for an indefinite period of time (which includes employment described as "permanent"), then it is presumed to be "at-will." The second part of the at-will doctrine is the rule that if a contract for an indefinite time does contain a term providing some measure of job security (such as "the employee will be fired only for cause"), that clause is unenforceable unless it was given in exchange for some "additional" consideration, beyond the normal employee's promise to work.

Jerry M. Worley v. Wyoming Bottling Company, Inc., d/b/a Coca-Cola of Casper
Supreme Court of Wyoming
1 P.3d 615 (2000)

LARRY LEHMAN, CHIEF JUSTICE

Jerry Worley contends that, after fifteen and a half years of faithful service, he was fired by appellee Wyoming Bottling. In turn, he filed suit claiming breach of employment contract ... The trial court granted Wyoming Bottling summary judgment on all claims. Because we conclude that disputed issues of material fact remain on Worley's claim for breach of contract..., we reverse and remand.

...

Facts

In accord with our standard of review, we present the facts in the light most favorable to Worley. When hired by Wyoming Bottling in May of 1980, Worley completed an employment application which contained an at-will employment disclaimer. Worley assumed the position of sales manager for the soft drink distributorship shortly after being hired, where he remained until his claimed firing in January of 1996. During his tenure, Worley established an exemplary work record, using three sick days in fifteen and a half years while earning numerous commendations, awards, and raises.

Also during Worley's tenure, Wyoming Bottling issued other at-will disclaimers. In 1991, Worley signed a non-compete agreement which included at-will employment language. Additionally, Wyoming Bottling issued an employee handbook in 1993 which contained several at-will employment disclaimers. The legal effect of these disclaimers, as well as the one contained in the 1980 application, is at issue in this appeal.

In 1995, due to increased sales goals and termination threats, Worley's work environment became stressful. After Worley's supervisor, area manager Herb McDonald, resigned, Worley began to question his own job security and spoke with Joe DeCora, the company president, about job security. Worley explained to DeCora that he was planning to make some major financial commitments, but first wanted to ensure that his job was secure. In his deposition, Worley testified that DeCora told him to make the financial commitments; that his job was secure; and the job would remain available to Worley as long as he wanted it. Following this discussion, Worley met for lunch with DeCora and the recently resigned McDonald. During lunch, and in McDonald's presence, DeCora's promise of job security was restated, as confirmed by McDonald's affidavit. In the same affidavit, McDonald asserts that Worley was the only employee left in the Casper office with the ability and experience to run the office until McDonald's successor could be found. It thus, McDonald explained, would have been difficult for Wyoming Bottling, without Worley, to continue normal operations for some time.

In December of 1995, Worley borrowed $18,000 by refinancing his home loan, using the proceeds to purchase a new car and new appliances for his home. Before finalizing the loan, Worley checked with his direct supervisor, Butch Gibson, to verify that his job performance was satisfactory. According to Worley, Gibson stated that everything was fine and "to go on about my affairs." In January of 1996, Wyoming Bottling demoted Worley one position level to route manager. The demotion included the loss of use of a company car, loss of use of a company credit card, and an $11,000 reduction in annual salary. Since Gibson had told him in December his work was fine, Worley was confused about the demotion and contacted DeCora. The parties contest what occurred during that conversation. Worley claims that DeCora fired him, repeating it three times in the midst of profanity, whereas Wyoming Bottling asserts that Worley quit.

. . .

Discussion

Wyoming recognizes the at-will employment doctrine, which allows either an employee or an employer to end the employment relationship at any time for any reason or for no reason. Although employment for an indefinite period of time is presumed to be at will, that presumption can be overcome by ... an express contract. *Davis v. Wyoming Medical Center*, Inc., 934 P.2d 1246, 1250 (Wyo.1997).Worley claims that he entered into an express oral contract with DeCora.

. . .

Worley asserts that during a conversation with DeCora, he entered into an express oral contract. In his deposition, Worley testified that he grew tired of job uncertainty and confronted DeCora with his intent to quit. DeCora responded: "Your job is secure. You can have that job for as long as you want it." Wyoming Bottling accepted Worley's version of events for summary judgment purposes and, therefore, does not contest that DeCora told Worley he had a job as long as he wanted it. . . .

Nevertheless, Worley must establish that he provided Wyoming Bottling with additional consideration to sustain an express oral employment contract altering the at-will presumption. *Wilder*, 868 P.2d at 218 (holding that employer promise of "permanent" employment does not alter the at-will presumption without additional consideration supplied by the employee or explicit language in the contract of employment stating that termination may only be for cause); *Bear v. Volunteers of America, Wyoming, Inc.*, 964 P.2d at 1250.... Worley claims, and his deposition testimony supports, that he intended to quit if he did not receive a promise of job security.[2]

Although Wyoming Bottling does not dispute the facts, it argues that Worley gave nothing up as consideration to support the contract because, even after his talk with DeCora, Worley was still free to leave at any time. Essentially, their argument is that there was no mutuality of obligation or that Worley's consideration was illusory. However, the demand for mutuality of obligation, although appealing in its symmetry, is simply a species of the forbidden inquiry into the adequacy of consideration, an inquiry in which this court has, by and large, refused to engage. *Pine River State Bank v. Mettille*, 333 N.W.2d 622, 629 (Minn. 1983). Worley testified that he agreed to stay on when he was free to leave. There being a question whether this consideration was bargained for, we conclude that Worley provided sufficient evidence on the issue of consideration to survive summary judgment.

Assuming Worley and Wyoming Bottling entered into an employment contract (either express or implied) allowing termination only for cause, a question also remains whether Worley was discharged for cause. Wyoming Bottling claims Worley was terminated for violating three personnel policies. Worley counters that termination for these violations was pretextual since the alleged violations were common, ordinary practices, and two fellow employees corroborated his claim. Whether an employee has been terminated for cause is generally a question of fact and, thus, summary judgment is premature under these disputed facts. *See Jewell*, 953 P.2d at 139; *Abell v. Dewey*, 847 P.2d 36, 41 (Wyo. 1993)....

Conclusion

Genuine issues of material fact exist on Worley's claim for breach of contract.... The district court's Order Granting Defendants' Motion for Summary Judgment is reversed and remanded....

―――――――

Note — On the At-Will Employment Doctrine

The at-will employment doctrine is among the most controversial in all of contract law. It has serious consequences for many people, and it conflicts with common expectations about "permanent" employment. Under the at-will rule, an employer can fire an employee for any reason or for no reason at all—even if an employee has passed a "probationary period," even if an employee has been hired on a "permanent" basis, and even if an employer promises an employee that he or she has "job security." Most people are surprised to learn of this rule, because it conflicts with our common-place understanding of the employment relationship. The following excerpt offers a political and ideological history of the at-will employment presumption.

The at-will rule was virtually unchallenged by courts until 1959, when the California Supreme Court held that an employer's discretion to fire an at-will employee could be limited by concerns of public policy. *Petermann v. Int'l. Brotherhood of Teamsters*, 344 P.2d 25 (Calif. 1959) (employee allegedly fired for refusing to lie to a legislative committee). During the 1960s through the early 1980s, several courts and legislatures endorsed

―――――――

2. A similar situation was discussed in Wilder, 868 P.2d at 219:The Restatement illustrates the operation of this rule with a hypothetical in which an employee is given a pay raise following a job offer from a competitor and a new contract of employment is written. The consideration for the new contract is provided by the employee refusing the job offer from the competitor. (citation omitted).

limitations on or exceptions to the at-will rule. After this initial period of reform, however, other courts and legislatures reaffirmed and reinforced the rule.

Courts in most states have held that the presumption created by the at-will doctrine is rebuttable, that employees may offer evidence to prove that the employer actually did promise to retain the worker unless the employee gives cause for termination, such as misconduct, failure to produce, or the like. *See, e.g., Taylor v. Canteen Corporation*, 69 F.3d 773 (7th Cir. 1995). Courts in most states also have concluded that such promises could be found expressed or implied in employee handbooks, personnel policies and procedures, and other such employer publications, *see, e.g., Pine River State Bank v. Mettille*, 333 N.W. 2d 622 (Minn. 1983), unless the publication includes a disclaimer of liability. *But cf. Farnum v. Brattleboro Retreat, Inc.*, 671 A.2d 1249 (Vt. 1995) (allowing the jury to decide whether employer's promises in a handbook are rendered ineffective by a boilerplate disclaimer). In several states, such a promise of job security is not binding unless the employee has given consideration in addition to the work for which he or she was hired, as in *Worley*. *See, e.g., Woo v. Centocor Inc.*, 1995 WL 672389 (E.D. Pa. 1995); *Merritt v. Edson Express, Inc.*, 437 N.W.2d 528 (S.D. 1989). In other states, an employer's promise that termination will occur only for cause is binding even if no additional consideration was given. *See, e.g., Toussaint v. Blue Cross & Blue Shield*, 292 N.W.2d 880, 886 (Mich. 1980). In some states an employer's promise may be enforceable under the doctrine of promissory estoppel (*see, e.g., Scholtes v. Signal Delivery Serv., Inc.*, 548 F. Supp. 487, 491 (W.D. Ark. 1982); *but see Hill v. Westchester Aeronautical Corp.*, 492 N.Y.S.2d 789, 791 (App. Div. 1985) (finding oral agreement insufficient when employment manual did not promise discharge for just and sufficient cause, and plaintiff did not show consideration greater than the ordinary services rendered incident to employment)), or some extension of reliance-based liability.

Following California, most states have recognized a limitation on an employer's discretion to terminate an at-will employee where the termination is in violation of public policy, which includes a fairly narrow range of circumstances such as termination in retaliation for cooperation with government officials. *See, e.g., Brockmeyer v. Dun & Bradstreet*, 335 N.W.2d 834 (Wis. 1983). Finally, while some courts have held that a general obligation of good faith may also limit employers' discretion to fire (some of which have held that good faith requires merely that the employer not fire an at-will employee in violation of public policy), *see, e.g., Metcalf v. Intermountain Gas Co.*, 778 P.2d 744 (Idaho 1989), several courts have refused to imply an obligation of good faith in at-will employment. *See, e.g., English v. Fischer*, 660 S.W.2d 521 (Tex. 1983).

Employers' power to terminate without cause is also limited by federal and state civil rights statutes, under which an employer may be held liable if he or she terminates an employee on the basis of race, sex, color, religion, national origin, disability, or age (or, in four states and several municipalities, sexual orientation), and the employee files a complaint within the short statute of limitations (usually 180 days) provided in such statutes. Similarly, an employer may be held liable under the National Labor Relations Act if he or she terminates an employee because of the employee's labor union activity and the employee files an appropriate grievance under the Act.

In 1987, Montana enacted a comprehensive job security act. The Montana Wrongful Discharge from Employment Act requires that employers terminate covered employees only for cause. Mont. Code Ann. § 39-2-901 et seq. Puerto Rican law also grants job security. *See* P.R. Laws Ann. tit. 29, § 185a (1990) (requiring good cause for terminating an employee). In 1991, the National Conference of Commissioners on Uniform State Laws adopted the Model Employment Termination Act, which requires good cause for termination of most employees. Model Employment Termination Act, National Conference of Commissioners on Uniform State Laws (1991). *See* Nina G. Stillman, Wrongful Discharge: Contract, Public Policy, and Tort Claims, Practicing Law Institute (1995). As of 2006, the model act had not been adopted in any state.

The at-will rule conflicts with many people's understanding of job security. Many workers are initially hired subject to a probationary period and, following successful completion of that period, are offered a full or "permanent" job. Many, if not most, employees in the United States believe that they will not be fired from "permanent employment" unless they fail to perform their job responsibilities or financial difficulties force the employer to reduce its workforce. Others maintain that our understanding should be quite different. Since the employer owns the business, they argue the employer can hire or fire employees as he or she sees fit, an understanding that is entirely harmonious with the at-will rule. The controversial character of this doctrine profoundly influences contemporary employment litigation. Writing for other practicing attorneys, Robert Fitzpatrick observed:

> Anyone who has labored in the vineyards of employment law ... is acutely aware that the doctrine of employment at-will is not consistent with the strongly held belief that an individual employee in this country is entitled to fair treatment. Anyone who has ever tried an employment case to a jury knows full well that the bottom line inquiry for the jurors is whether or not the employee was treated fairly. As a result of a spate of substantial jury verdicts in employment cases during the past decade defense attorneys and human resources professionals routinely advise employers that the best defense to wrongful discharge and employment discrimination litigation is to be consistent in one's treatment of employees and to base a termination on good cause.

Robert B. Fitzpatrick, Employment At-Will: Time for an Unjust Dismissal Statute, C953 ALI-ABA 681, Dec. 1, 1994.

Peter F. Drucker, a widely respected and influential management expert, discussed the complex issue of job security in a *Wall Street Journal* article entitled *The Job as Property*:

> [J]obs are rapidly turning into a kind of property. The mechanism differs from culture to culture; the results are very much the same.

> In Japan there is "lifetime employment" for the "permanent" (that is, primarily, male) employee in government and large businesses. This means, in effect, that short of bankruptcy the business is run primarily for the employee, whose right to the job has precedence over outside creditors and legal "owners" alike.

> In Europe, increasingly, employees cannot be laid off; they have to be bought out with "redundancy payments." In a few countries, such as Belgium and Spain, these payments are equivalent to a full salary or wage over the reminder of an employee's lifetime, for a worker with a few years of seniority. And the High Court of the European Community, in a decision which is considered binding for all member countries, has ruled that the claim to redundancy payments survives even an employer's bankruptcy and extends to the other assets of the owners of the employing firm.

> In the United States, recent legislation has given the employee's pension claim a great deal of the protection traditionally reserved for property. Indeed, in the event of bankruptcy or liquidation of the employing firm, employee pension claims take precedence over all other claims (except government taxes) for up to 30% of the employing firm's net worth.

The various fair-employment regulations in the U.S., whether on behalf of racial minorities, women, the handicapped, or the aged, treat promotion, training, job security and access to jobs as a matter of rights. It's getting harder to dismiss any employee except "for cause." . . .

Jobs, in effect, are being treated as a species of property rather than as contractual claims. Historically there have been three kinds of property: "real" property such as land; "personal" property such as money, tools, furnishings and personal possessions; and "intangible" property such as copyrights and patents. It is not too far-fetched to speak of the emergence of a fourth—"property in the job"—closely analogous to property in the land in pre-modern times. . . .

For the great majority of people in most developed countries, land was the true "means of production" until well in this century, often until World War II. It was property in land which gave access to economic effectiveness and with it to social standing and political power. It was therefore rightly called by the law "real" property.

In modern developed societies, by contrast, the overwhelming majority of the people in the labor force are employees of "organizations"—in the U.S. the figure is 93%—and the "means of production" is therefore the job. The job is not "wealth." It is not "personal property" in the legal sense. But it is a "right" in the means of production. . . . Today the job is the employee's means of access to social status, to personal opportunity, to achievement and to power.

For the great majority in the developed countries today, the job is also the one avenue of access to personal property. Pension claims are by far the most valuable assets of employees over 50, more valuable, indeed, than all his other assets taken together—his share in his house, his savings, his automobile and so on. And the pension claim is, of course, a direct outgrowth of the job, indeed part of the job.

The evolution of the job into a species of property can be seen as a genuine opportunity. It might be the right, if not the only, answer to the problem of "alienation" which Marx identified a century and a quarter ago as resulting from the divorce of the "worker" from the "means of production."

But as the long history of land tenure abundantly proves, such a development also carries a real danger of rigidity and immobility. In Belgium, for instance, the system of redundancy payments may prevent employers from laying off people. But it also keeps them from hiring workers they need, and thus creates more unemployment than it prevents or assuages. Similarly, lifetime employment may be the greatest barrier to the needed shift in Japan from labor intensive to knowledge intensive industries.

How can modern economies cope with the emergence of job property rights and still maintain the flexibility and social mobility necessary for adapting quickly to changes? At the very least, employing organizations will have to recognize that jobs have some of the characteristics of property rights and cannot therefore be diminished or taken away without due process. Hiring, firing, promotion and demotion must be subject to pre-established, objective, public criteria. And there has to be a review, a pre-established right to appeal to a higher judge in all actions affecting rights in and to the job.

Standards of review will, paradoxically, be forced on employers in the United States by the abandonment of fixed-age retirement. For companies to be able to dismiss even the most senile and decrepit oldster, they will have to develop impersonal standards of performance and systematic personnel procedures for employees of all ages.

The evolution of jobs into a kind of property also demands that there be no "expropriation without compensation," and that employers take responsibility to anticipate redundancies, retraining employees about to be laid off and finding and placing them in new jobs. It requires redundancy planning rather than unemployment compensation.

In the emerging "employee society," employees, through their pension funds, are beginning to own — and inevitably will also control — the large businesses in the economy. Jobs are becoming a nexus of rights and a species of property. This development is surely not what people mean when they argue about "capitalism," pro or con. But it is compatible with limited government, personal freedom and the rational allocation of resources through the free market. It may thus be the effective alternative to the "state capitalism" of the totalitarians which, under the name of "communism," makes government into absolute tyranny, and suppresses both freedom and rationality.

Chapter Five

Alternatives to the Bargain Model: Promises Reasonably Relied Upon, Promises Made in Recognition of a Past Benefit, and Unjust Enrichment

As the materials in Chapter Four reveal, modern contract law retains the doctrinal structure engineered by a relatively small group of scholars and jurists working in the second half of the nineteenth century. We now call this structure "classical contract law," but at the time of its creation, it was a radical innovation, the very opposite of "classical." Two inventions were at the core of this effort: first, the concept of "consideration" was redefined as "bargained-for exchange" and second, the consideration doctrine was positioned as the sole basis for promissory liability.

Without doubt, the promoters of classical contract law were hugely successful. Within a few decades, a disparate body of law, developed over centuries by wandering merchants, within feudal farming communities, and among burgeoning industrial centers, was re-formulated to promote the preeminence of market exchange in social ordering. This effort, together with those of market advocates throughout the business and professional classes, shaped the course of political and economic activity in the U.S. for most of the twentieth century.

Yet the market theorists of the late nineteenth century did not succeed in ending the practice of common law decision-making in the U.S. legal system, even though this was advocated strenuously by some of them. It is the nature of common law decision-making that conflicting ideas and values are never entirely silenced and this fact provides an important key to understanding the complexity of contract law today. Despite the enormous success of classical contract law and despite its bold claim that no promise should be legally enforced unless it was made as part of an exchange, competing ideas were not wholly rejected. Indeed, by the middle of the twentieth century, as we have seen, the claim of omnipotence for the consideration doctrine had to be abandoned by its most ardent proponents. By that time, courts and commentators had identified and elaborated two significant alternatives for promissory liability: reliance and recognition of past benefits. This chapter will examine those alternatives, as well as the area of non-promissory liability based on unjust enrichment.

A. Promises Reasonably Relied Upon: Restatement (Second), Section 90

It is clear that courts did enforce promises that were not made as part of an exchange (i.e., "gratuitous promises") both before and after the creation of classical contract law. Today, the idea that a promise upon which someone has foreseeably and reasonably relied may be enforced even though it was not given in exchange for consideration is firmly established. This doctrine, which is alternatively called "promissory estoppel," "detrimental reliance," or just "Section 90" has been recognized in almost every state. The few states that have not recognized promissory estoppel include the Supreme Court of Virginia, which has flatly rejected the doctrine, *W. J. Schafer Associates Inc. v. Cordant Inc.*, 493 S.E.2d 512, 521 (Va. 1997) ("Today, ... we hold that promissory estoppel is not a cognizable cause of action in the Commonwealth, and we decline to create such a cause of action."), *see also Mongold v. Woods*, 677 S.E.2d 288, 292 (Va. 2009) (citing *W. J. Schafer Associates Inc. v. Cordant Inc.* with approval and noting "We have not altered that position.") and the North Carolina Court of Appeals (*see Home Electric Co. of Lenoir, Inc. v. Hall & Underdown Heating and Air Conditioning Co.*, 358 S.E.2d 539, 541 (N.C. App. 1987) ("our Courts have never recognized [promissory estoppel] as a substitute for consideration, either in construction bidding, or in any other context."), *see also Penguin Restoration, Inc. v. Nationwide Mut. Ins. Co.*, 2013 WL 4419355, at *2 (E.D.N.C. Aug. 15, 2013) (refusing to apply the doctrine of promissory estoppel in a case governed by North Carolina law, based on the authority of *Home Electric Co. of Lenoir, Inc. v. Hall & Underdown Heating and Air Conditioning Co.*).

Pronouncing the end of consideration's hegemony, the Restatement (Second) of Contracts states only a qualified version of the classical consideration requirement in section 17 ("Requirement of a Bargain"):

(1) Except as stated in Subsection (2), the formation of a contract requires a bargain in which there is a manifestation of mutual assent to the exchange and a consideration.

(2) Whether or not there is a bargain a contract may be formed under special rules applicable to formal contracts or under the rules stated in §§ 82–94.

And in sections 82–94, the Restatement names a category of "Contracts Without Consideration" in which section 90 plays the most prominent role.

§ 90. Promise Reasonably Inducing Action or Forbearance

(1) A promise which the promisor should reasonably expect to induce action or forbearance on the part of the promisee or a third person and which does induce such action or forbearance is binding if injustice can be avoided only by enforcement of the promise. The remedy granted for breach may be limited as justice requires.

This is the doctrine of promissory estoppel recognized by *Ricketts v. Scothorn*, 77 N.W. 365 (Kan. 1898). Please reread *Ricketts v. Scothorn* in Chapter Two.

The doctrine articulated in Restatement (Second) § 90 rests on the idea that trust is important and worthy of protection in appropriate cases. So the question that shapes every case involving this doctrine is the large one of when, if ever, should a promisor expect that another person will rely on the promise and when, if ever, is it reasonable for a promisee or some third person to rely on a promise.

This subchapter explores these questions by looking at the two elements of promissory estoppel: (1) a promise and (2) expected and reasonable reliance.

1. The Promise

To allege a claim based on "Section 90" or "promissory estoppel," the plaintiff must assert that the defendant made a promise. As a general matter, contract law defines a promise as an expression of commitment:

> A promise is a manifestation of intention to act or refrain from acting in a specified way, so made as to justify a promisee in understanding that a commitment has been made.

Restatement (Second) of Contract § 2 (1). Notice that this definition incorporates both the objective approach to interpretation and the idea that commitment is the essence of promise.

In Chapters Three and Four, we saw some of the complexity involved in discerning and interpreting human communications. In legal decisions, these matters are shaped by the doctrinal context and purposes as to which the interpretations are made. In the context of promissory estoppel, as we have said, the focus is on the circumstances of trust, so the requirement of a promise is influenced by a court's views about the social dimension of trust. Some courts, for example, insist that reliance cannot be expected nor reasonable unless the promise is very formal: "clear and unambiguous." Other courts, focusing on informal practices of reliance that exist throughout our social interactions, find that mere "representations" can be sufficient expressions of commitment to induce expected and reasonable reliance. How do the following cases analyze the promise requirement?

State Bank of Standish v. Robert N. and Kathleen Curry

Supreme Court of Michigan
500 N.W.2d 104 (1993)

JUSTICE PATRICIA BOYLE

We granted leave in this case to determine whether there was sufficient evidence of a clear and definite promise to support a claim for relief on the theory of promissory estoppel. After careful review of the record, we find that there was. Accordingly, we affirm in part and reverse in part the decision of the Court of Appeals. We reinstate the jury's verdict in favor of the Currys and remand the case to the trial court for further proceedings consistent with this opinion.

I.

Robert and Kathleen Curry are dairy farmers. Beginning in 1975, the Currys annually obtained funds from the State Bank of Standish to purchase seed, fertilizer, and chemicals for spring planting. The sum of the operating loan varied little from year to year and was used solely for the planting of crops. Early each year, Mr. and Mrs. Curry would visit the bank to discuss the upcoming spring loan and crop plan with the bank's officers. The bank would complete the required paperwork and, after the initial visit with the Currys to discuss the loan, simply call the Currys back to the bank in March or April to sign the promissory note. Any outstanding balance on the previous year's loan was rolled over and added into a new loan bearing an interest rate of two points over the bank's prime rate, which was then amortized over a five-year period. Monthly payments were made directly from the Michigan Milk Producers Association (MMPA) by assignment of the proceeds from the Currys' milk contract. As collateral, the bank had a security agreement on all the Currys' personal property, which was, at a minimum, twice the value of the loan.

The federal government, in an attempt to stabilize prices in the dairy market in March 1986, implemented a dairy herd buy-out program.[1] Although never in default on any of his loans, Mr. Curry, discouraged by the increasing economic difficulties with dairy farming in the 1980s, seriously considered the program. The buy-out would have afforded him a debt-free termination of his dairy business. In addition to the money received from the government buy-out, the Currys' registered dairy herd could be sold in Canada for a greater amount than those unregistered herds in the program that would be slaughtered.

Mr. and Mrs. Curry went to the bank in January and February of that year with the sole purpose of discussing the government buy-out program to decide whether they should continue in or get out of the dairy farming business. At that time, Mr. Curry brought to the bank a written breakdown of the $20,000 needed for the upcoming spring loan. As usual, the Currys spoke with Mr. Garry, the assistant vice president and loan officer, and were later joined by Mr. Pelts, the executive vice president of the bank. The discussion centered on the current trying economic times and whether the Currys should enter the buy-out program. Mr. Curry testified that in the context of discussing whether he should continue dairy farming or get out of the dairy business, he asked the bank officers whether the bank would continue to support their farm. Mr. Garry and Mr. Pelts responded that the Currys were doing a good job and had made all their payments and that there was no reason to worry about their future in the dairy business because the bank would support them. Believing they had a promise for the upcoming spring loan on the basis of this conversation with bank officers, the Currys continued with their dairy farming operation and did not submit a serious bid in the government's March 1986 buy-out program.[2]

In mid-April, Mr. Curry stopped at the bank to request an additional $5,000 to tile a field and to inquire about the delay in signing the papers for the spring operating loan. Although it was now well into the spring planting season, Mr. Garry stated that "it would probably be a couple weeks before he got it all done." Mr. Curry contacted the bank in May and was informed by Mr. Garry that the bank would not renew their operating loan for 1986. Mr. Curry sought alternative financing from an arm of Farm Credit Services, but was told that he would first have to pay off his existing loan at the State Bank of Standish because it held all his personal property as collateral. He was unable to do so. To acquire the necessary cash to sustain the dairy operation, the Currys obtained credit from suppliers and subsequently defaulted on the outstanding promissory note with the bank. Because of late planting and necessary cutbacks, the production and health of the dairy herd declined.

The bank filed an action for claim and delivery. The Currys counterclaimed, alleging economic and emotional damages arising from breach of the bank's duty of good faith

---

1. Farmers participated in the program by submitting bids based on a price per hundred weight of milk. That figure was then multiplied by the volume of milk shipped off the farm. If the bid was accepted by the government, the farmer would receive a lump-sum payment, sell the dairy herd, and not reenter the dairy market for at least five years.

2. Mr. Curry, with the assistance of the farm's nutritionist, Dr. Scott LaBlond, determined that a competitive bid would be $20 per hundred weight of milk. Using that figure, the Currys' dairy operation would have been bought out for a sum between $400,000 and $500,000, affording them a profit of approximately $200,000. However, relying on the assurances of continued support by the bank, Mr. Curry submitted a bid of $50 per hundred. The low bid ultimately accepted by the government was $22.50 per hundred.

and fair dealing, fraud, duress, and promissory estoppel. The trial court granted the bank's motion for summary disposition pursuant to MCR 2.116(C)(8) on all counterclaims except promissory estoppel. The court also found no defense to the bank's claim and delivery action, but stayed judgment until after trial for the purpose of setoff, if any.

At trial, the jury found by special verdict that the bank made a clear and definite promise to loan money to the Currys for their 1986 farm operating needs and that the Currys had justifiably relied on that promise to their detriment. The jury award was set off against the amount due the bank on the promissory note, resulting in a judgment for the Currys of $56,243.44.

On appeal, conceding the facts alleged by the Currys as true, the bank contended that there was no evidence of a clear and definite promise by it to make the loan. The Court of Appeals agreed, reversed the trial court's judgment in favor of the Currys on the promissory estoppel claim, and affirmed the summary disposition on the fraud, duress, and good-faith and fair-dealing claims. We granted leave to appeal.

Because we agree with the Court of Appeals regarding summary disposition of the fraud, duress, and good-faith and fair-dealing claims, we address only the promissory estoppel issue. In its brief and at oral argument, the bank conceded reliance and did not raise the issues of consideration or damages. The only issue before us is whether the Court of Appeals correctly found insufficient evidence to permit the jury to sustain the Currys' claim of promissory estoppel.

II.

The Currys do not allege a promise to loan money on the basis of assurances by the bank that they were in compliance with the farm plan discussed the previous year, nor do they allege a promise solely on the basis of their ten-year financial relationship with the bank. What the Currys do claim is that the bank made a clear manifestation that it would continue to extend credit to finance their farming operation for the upcoming spring planting season, and that the material terms for that loan can be determined from the nature of that transaction and through the course of dealings between the parties. The bank, as counter-defendant, does not dispute the element of reliance. Rather, as appellant below, the bank argued only that there was no record support for a finding of a clear and definite promise as a matter of law.

The doctrine of promissory estoppel is set forth in 1 *Restatement Contracts*, 2d, § 90, p. 242:

> A promise which the promisor should reasonably expect to induce action or forbearance on the part of the promisee or a third person and which does induce such action or forbearance is binding if injustice can be avoided only by enforcement of the promise. The remedy granted for breach may be limited as justice requires.

Promissory estoppel developed to protect the ability of individuals to trust promises in circumstances where trust is essential. It is the value of trust that forms the basis of the entitlement to rely. However, the reliance interest protected by § 90 is *reasonable reliance,* and "reliance is reasonable only if it is induced by an actual promise." *School Dist. No. 69 of Maricopa Co. v. Altherr*, 458 P.2d 537 (Ariz. 1969).

In *Williston on Contracts*, Professor Lord observes that although the elements required to invoke the doctrine are straightforward, they necessarily involve a threshold inquiry into the circumstances surrounding both the making of the promise and the promisee's reliance as a question of law. The existence and scope of the promise are questions of fact and "a determination that the promise exists will not be overturned ... unless it is clearly erroneous." 4 *Williston, Contracts* (4th ed.), § 8:5, pp. 84–85, 102–103.[6] Thus, while we agree with the Court of Appeals in the instant case that the sine qua non of the theory of promissory estoppel is that the promise be clear and definite, we cannot agree with its narrow review of the record as evidence that such a promise did not exist.

The term promise is defined in the *Restatement (Second)*, Section 2, p. 8:

A promise is a manifestation of intention to act or refrain from acting in a specified way, so made as to justify a promisee in understanding that a commitment has been made.[7]

Courts are variably strict and flexible in determining whether a manifestation of intent may furnish a basis for promissory estoppel. The strict view, distinguishing promises that are future oriented from statements of belief, holds that a statement that is indefinite, equivocal, or not specifically demonstrative of an intention respecting future conduct, cannot serve as the foundation for an actionable reliance. This is usually determined by finding that the promisor's expression concerning his future conduct is insufficiently certain or defined. "Similarly, if the expression is made in the course of preliminary negotiations when material terms of the agreement are lacking, the degree of certainty necessary in a promise is absent." Feinman, [*Promissory Estoppel and Judicial Method*, 97 Harv. L. Rev. 678 (1984)] at 691–92.

Drawing heavily from the Restatement's definition of promise, it has been suggested that "[a] promise may be stated in words, either orally or in writing, or may be inferred wholly or partly from conduct.... Both language and conduct are to be understood in the light of the circumstances, including course of performance, course of dealing, or usage of trade." Farber & Matheson, [*Beyond Promissory Estoppel: Contract Law and the "Invisible Handshake,"* 52 U. Chi. L. Rev. 903 (1985)] at 932 n.104. In addition, "[a] promise must [also] be distinguished from a statement of opinion or a mere prediction of future events." Id. at 933. Variables such as the nature of the relationship between the parties, the clarity of the representation, as well as the circumstances surrounding the making of the representation, are important to the determination of whether the manifestation rises to the level of a promise. Both traditional contract and promissory estoppel theories of obligation use an objective standard to ascertain whether a voluntary commitment has been made. To determine the existence and scope of a promise, we look

---

6. In R. S. Bennett & Co. v. Economy Mechanical Industries, Inc., 606 F.2d 182, 186 (7th Cir. 1979), the court held:

Although the matter of avoidance of injustice might seem to be a question of law, the satisfaction of the other elements is a question of fact, and summary judgment therefore should not be granted if the record shows a genuine issue as to the existence of these elements. [Citations omitted.] ...

7. Comment a to § 90 cross references 1 Restatement Contracts, 2d, § 2. Comment a to § 2, p. 9, provides further explanation:

"Promise" as used in the Restatement of this Subject denotes the act of the promisor. If by virtue of other operative facts there is a legal duty to perform, the promise is a contract; but the word "promise" is not limited to acts having legal effect. Like "contract," however, the word "promise" is commonly and quite properly also used to refer to the complex of human relations which results from the promisor's words or acts of assurance, including the justified expectations of the promisee and any moral or legal duty which arises to make good the assurance by performance. The performance may be specified either in terms describing the action of the promisor or in terms of the result which that action or inaction is to bring about. See also 1 Williston, Contracts (4th Ed.) § 1:2, pp. 8–13; 1 Corbin, Contracts § 13, pp. 29–30.

to the words and actions of the transaction as well as the nature of the relationship between the parties and the circumstances surrounding their actions.

Lenders and borrowers frequently enter into preliminary discussions of whether a loan will be refinanced or further credit will be extended. And a lender should expect and "anticipate that a promise to lend needed money would induce a borrower to rely on the promise by making preparations for the loan ... or to cease searching to borrow the money elsewhere." *First Nat'l Bank of Logansport v. Logan Mfg. Co., Inc.*, 577 N.E.2d 949, 955 (Ind. 1991); *Malaker Corp. Stockholders Protective Committee v. First Jersey Nat'l Bank*, 395 A.2d 222, 227 (N.J. Super. Ct. 1978). However, general discussions of extending credit or "past renewals of credit should not lead a borrower to reasonably believe that credit will be extended or renewed again and again." Bahls, [*Termination of Credit for the Farm or Ranch: Theories of Lender Liability*, 48 Mont. L. Rev. 213 (1987)], at 224. Expressions of contingency, *Cincinnati Fluid Power, Inc. v. Rexnord, Inc.*, 797 F.2d 1386 (6th Cir. 1986), or of desire, *School Dist. No. 69 of Maricopa Co.*, *supra*, or reassurances regarding past performance, *Ho v. General Motors Corp.*, 661 F. Supp. 618 (E.D. Mich. 1987), *aff'd*, 852 F.2d 1287 (6th Cir. 1988), do not meet the promissory ideal. Nor does a course of past dealing where there has been a pattern of renewal in itself amount to sufficient assent to continue dealing or that renewal will be indefinite. Bahls, *supra*, at 220.

Although promissory estoppel has been used to enforce promises too indefinite or incomplete to constitute valid offers, *Hoffman v. Red Owl Stores, Inc.*, 133 N.W.2d 267 (Wis. 1965), it has been noted that considerable authority supports the proposition that maximizing the policy of contractual freedom "requires that the tests for the validity of the coincident promissory estoppel promise and contract offer be the same." Metzger & Phillips, *The Emergence of Promissory Estoppel as an Independent Theory of Recovery*, 35 Rutgers L.R. 472, 495 (1983). Thus, we observe that a promise "to continue to refinance or roll over [an existing] debt appears similar to an oral contract to [loan] money in the future," *Jamestown on Signal, Inc. v. First Federal Savings & Loan Ass'n*, 807 S.W.2d 559, 565 (Tenn. App. 1990); *Champaign Nat'l Bank v. Landers Seed Co., Inc.*, 519 N.E.2d 957 (Ill. App. 1988), *cert. denied*, 489 U.S. 1019 (1989),[11] and that other jurisdictions have held that an oral promise to loan money in the future is not void for indefiniteness where the essential terms are determinable.[12] For a promise to loan money in the future to be sufficiently clear and definite, some evidence must exist of the material terms of the loan, including the amount of the loan, the interest rate, and the method of repayment.[13]

---

11. Some jurisdictions have held promissory estoppel inapplicable in situations where mutual agreement has been reached upon all essential terms and that, regardless of either parties reliance, the true action lies in breach of an oral contract. See, for example, Gilmore v. Ute City Mortgage Co., 660 F. Supp. 437 (D. Colo. 1986).

12. First Nat'l Bank of Logansport, supra at 952–953. See also Union State Bank v. Woell, 434 N.W.2d 712 (N.D. 1989); Dennis Chapman Toyota, Inc. v. Belle State Bank, 759 S.W.2d 330 (Mo. App. 1988); Lohse v. Atlantic Richfield Co., 389 N.W.2d 352 (N.D. 1986); McErlean v. Union Nat'l Bank of Chicago, 414 N.E.2d 128 (Ill. Ct. App. 1980); Malaker Corp., supra; Hansen v. Snell, 354 P.2d 1070 (Utah 1960); Richards v. Oliver, 328 P.2d 544 (Ca. Ct. App. 1958).

13. Other courts have found that the terms of the promised loan need only be proven with a reasonable degree of certainty. See, for example, Wait v. First Midwest Bank/Danville, 491 N.E.2d 795 (Ill. Ct. App. 1986), where the Illinois Court of Appeals found that a promise to loan money was sufficiently definite where the duration of the loan could be established on the basis of custom or the terms of prior loans between the parties, and when the parties agreed that the interest rate would be the current variable rate charged.

Conversely, a minority of jurisdictions have determined that ambiguous or missing terms of a promise that are not essential to the reliance damage calculation will not preclude recovery under a promissory estoppel claim because the promise was too indefinite. *See Wheeler v. White*, 398 S.W.2d 93 (Tex. 1965); *First Nat'l Bank of Logansport, supra*; *Rosnick v. Dinsmore*, 457 N.W.2d 793 (Neb. 1990); *Hoffman v. Red Owl Stores, Inc., supra*. In *Hoffman*, the Wisconsin Supreme Court noted that § 90 does not require that the promise triggering reliance be so comprehensive in scope as to meet the requirements of an offer that would ripen into a contract if accepted by the promisee. The Court further observed that it would be a mistake to equate promissory estoppel to a breach of contract action. *Id.* at 699.

This approach is consistent with the general rule of contract that, where the parties have left open some matters to be determined in the future, enforcement is not precluded if there exists a method of determining the terms of the contract either by examining the agreement itself or by other usage or custom[14] that is independent of a party's mere "wish, will and desire." An enforceable agreement may be found "even though the determination is left to one of the contracting parties [as long as] he is required to make it 'in good faith' in accordance with [an] existing standard or with facts capable of objective proof." 1 Corbin, *Contracts* § 95, p. 402. The scope of an oral promise may also be identified by referring to the facts surrounding the loan where there exists a previous course of dealing between the parties, thereby supplying some objective method by which the missing terms could be supplied. Farber & Matheson, *supra* at 915 and n.45. *See also Nat'l Farmers Organization, Inc. v. Kinsley Bank*, 731 F.2d 1464, 1470 (10th Cir. 1984).

The evidence, viewed in a light most favorable to the Currys, showed that the Currys were not in default on their outstanding loan when they visited the bank in January and February 1986 to discuss the dairy buy-out program and the $20,000 loan for the upcoming spring planting season. As noted above, during the conversation, Mr. Curry inquired whether his dairy operation would continue to be supported by the bank as it had been in the past. While the bank asserts that its "assurances" were not made in the context of a specific discussion regarding whether a loan in a particular amount would be made, there was no real denial of Mr. Curry's testimony that he went to the bank for the express purpose of learning whether he would receive financing should he decide to continue in the dairy business. The bank's officers stated that the bank would continue to support the Currys, although they did not guarantee such support for the following year. Objectively viewed, the jury was entitled to find that these were not merely words of assurance or statements of belief, but of a promise of future action, *Esquire Radio & Electronics, Inc. v. Montgomery Ward & Co., Inc.*, 804 F.2d 787 (2d Cir. 1986).[15] *Compare Cincinnati Fluid*

---

14. Because a "promise" of job security arises in the context of a presumption of employment at will, we have held that orally grounded obligations must be clear and unequivocal. Rowe v. Montgomery Ward, 473 N.W.2d 268 (Mich. 1991).

15. Although the dissent correctly recognizes the standard of review in this case, that evidence must be viewed in a light most favorable to the Currys, it fails to do so. Instead, the dissent's conclusion that a promise did not exist here is premised on a review of the bank officer's testimony regarding the deteriorating financial status of the Currys to support his ultimate decision to refuse to make the loan. The question presented is not whether the bank would have been justified in denying the loan or the wisdom of the bank's decision in making it, but, rather, whether there was sufficient evidence to support a jury finding that the bank promised the Currys it would make the loan. We note, however, that the poor financial status of the Currys' dairy operation simply underscores their claim that they needed to know whether the bank would continue to support the farm if the Currys gave up the opportunity to submit a competitive bid in the buy-out program and get out of the dairy business.

Contrary to the dissent's assertions, we do not adopt a rule finding that "once a commercial lending relationship exists, debtors are entitled to rely upon vague affirmations of support to paralyze lenders' abilities to adjust to ever-changing market conditions." The bank conceded reliance and does not raise

Power, supra. Believing they had a promise for the spring loan, the Currys did not submit a serious bid in the government's dairy buy-out program.[16] Instead, they waited for the bank's call to come in and sign the paperwork for the spring loan, which would include the upcoming spring operating funds and a rollover of the outstanding balance on the previous year's loan at the usual terms of two points over the bank's prime, amortized over five years, and paid directly out of the monthly proceeds from their milk contract with the MMPA.[17]

Thus, the trial court did not err in leaving the question of the existence of a clear and definite promise to the jury where it could have found from the evidence that the bank had promised to make the loan, the terms of which could be objectively determined from the nature of the transaction, and the ten-year history of the customary loan practices between the parties.[18] Accordingly, we reverse in part and affirm in part the decision of the Court of Appeals. We reinstate the jury's verdict in favor of the Currys and remand the case to the trial court for further proceedings consistent with this opinion.

Judge Dorothy Comstock Riley, dissenting

I.

Because the statements at issue were not clear and definite promises necessary for the application of promissory estoppel, I respectfully dissent.

II.

The majority omits significant facts underlying this litigation, therefore I recite the pertinent facts. Robert and Kathleen Curry were dairy and cash crop farmers who financed their operations through a series of one-year loans with the State Bank of Standish. Beginning in 1975, the bank usually approved loans at 2 percent over the prime lending rate, and the balance of the previous years' loans were rolled over. *Ante.* This method of financing, however, slowly began to accumulate debt, and, by 1983, the Currys' outstanding balance totaled at least $110,000. The next year the debt reached $151,000, and in 1985, it rose to $167,000. Noting the mounting debt, in 1985 the parties agreed to abandon the rollover basis of payment, and agreed that operating loans were to be paid on a yearly basis. The Currys secured the loans with nearly all of their realty and personal property. *Ante.*

---

the issues of consideration or damages. We find only that there was sufficient evidence in the record that the bank promised the Currys a 1986 spring planting loan during their meeting to discuss the loan and the buy-out program.

16. The Court of Appeals statement that the Currys did not attempt to obtain the necessary funds elsewhere is erroneous. Mr. Curry and a representative of Farm Credit Services testified that, after the bank refused to make the loan for the spring of 1986, Mr. Curry sought funds from Production Credit Association, a lending arm of Farm Credit. However, because the State Bank of Standish and the Federal Land Bank held security agreements on all of the Currys' personal and real property, there was no collateral to secure a loan with a new lender.

17. The bank asserted that the course of dealings between the parties had changed because the previous year's loan, for the first time, had been guaranteed by the Farmers Home Guarantee Program. However, there was ample evidence to support a finding by the jury that there had been no change in the customary loan procedure between the parties. In 1985, the bank was still the actual lender of funds, the terms of the loan were unchanged, and, finally, it was the bank's loan officer who completed all the necessary paperwork for both the loan and the guarantee program. Mr. Curry testified that there was "[n]othing out of the ordinary" regarding the 1985 loan as compared to previous years, nor did he recall any discussion with bank officers informing him that future annual operating loans would have to be paid back on a yearly basis. Similarly, the bank's claim that there were errors in the farm report used for the 1986 loan was rebutted by the fact that these were chronic entry errors that the bank historically had been aware of and, as in prior years, had clarified and corrected them orally.

18. Nat'l Farmers Organization, supra at 1471.

In 1986, the Currys seriously considered submitting a bid to a federal program designed to reduce dairy surpluses by purchasing dairy farms.[1] The Currys discussed the program with Mr. Robert Garry, a vice president of the bank as well as the loan officer in charge of the Currys' file, and Mr. Matthew Pelts, an executive vice president. Mr. Curry testified that he "went down [to the bank] with the sole purpose and was very blunt about it, are you with me or against me. I wanted to know, should I continue farming, or should I get out, and, basically the bottom line was, you've done a good job, you've made your payments, we're with you." Mr. Curry repeatedly testified that the bank officers had pledged their "support" to the Currys.

In early 1986, Mr. Curry requested an annual loan of $20,000, which was later supplemented with an additional request for $5,000 to tile a field. As part of the loan application process, the Currys submitted a "Tel Farm" statement, a recordkeeping system which generates income and expense records for businesses such as dairy farms. The bank discerned errors in the statement, including obvious omissions detailing the outstanding debt owed to the bank, and informed the Currys that they should correct the form. The bank's request went unheeded. However, at the bank's request, the Currys did provide their prior year's tax return, which recorded losses of $72,000.

The Currys, assuming their loan request would be approved, purchased seed and supplies, but delayed planting corn while awaiting funds from the bank. The bank's financial projections regarding the farm and its mounting debt, combined with the Currys' previous year's losses of $72,000, however, ultimately led the bank to deny the loan request.

In October 1986, the bank filed suit when the Currys failed to pay their obligations on the outstanding debt. The Currys counterclaimed, alleging, inter alia, that the bank's refusal to approve the 1986 operating loan was a breach of the duties of good-faith performance and fair dealing that resulted in substantial damages. The trial court ruled that although the Currys did not have a defense regarding their outstanding debt, they had alleged detrimental reliance warranting a trial.

On May 4, 1988, a six-day trial concluded with a jury verdict in favor of the Currys for $127,575. The trial court found that with interest and costs the Currys were entitled to $157,000 along with a setoff of $101,000 of outstanding debt to the bank, and awarded the Currys $56,000. The court denied the bank's motion for judgment notwithstanding the verdict or, in the alternative, remitter. In May 1991, the Court of Appeals reversed the denial of judgment notwithstanding the verdict. The Court held "there was no clear and definite promise of a loan sufficient to warrant [the Currys] subsequent purchases and actions and, consequently, insufficient evidence to establish their theory of promissory estoppel." 476 N.W.2d 635, 638 (Mich. App. 1991).

This Court granted leave to appeal.

III.

The Court of Appeals reversed the trial court's denial of judgment notwithstanding the verdict because it found that there was insufficient evidence provided by the Currys

---

1. Farmers submitted selling bids to the government. If accepted, the government purchased the dairy herd and the farmer agreed not to reenter the dairy business for five years. If the Currys had submitted such a bid and it had been accepted, the Currys most likely would have received sufficient compensation to pay their debts and produce a profit.

to establish that the bank had made the clear and definite promise necessary for a successful assertion of promissory estoppel. In reviewing the decision of the Court of Appeals, this Court is to view the evidence in the light most favorable to the nonmoving party. Hence, the Currys' testimony must be assumed true, and all reasonable inferences must be drawn.

IV.

A.

Justice Cooley long ago explained the premise of promissory estoppel:

The doctrine of estoppel rests upon a party having directly or indirectly made assertions, promises or assurances upon which another has acted under such circumstances that he would be seriously prejudiced if the assertions were suffered to be disproved or the promises or assurances to be withdrawn. *Maxwell v. Bay City Bridge Co.*, 2 N.W. 639 (Mich. 1879). *See also Holt v. Stofflet*, 61 N.W.2d 28 (Mich. 1953).[2]

Because promissory estoppel is an exception to general contract principles in that it permits enforcement of a promise that may have no consideration, the general rule is:

In order that a statement or representation may be relied upon as creating an estoppel, its language must be clear and plain, or it must be clear and reasonably certain in its intendment, since estoppels must be certain and are not to be taken or sustained on mere argument or doubtful inference. 28 Am. Jur. 2d *Estoppel and Waiver* § 45, p. 654.

Hence, "a promise must be definite and clear." *McMath v. Ford Motor Co*, 259 N.W.2d 140 (Mich. Ct. App. 1977).

The requirement that promises be clear and definite is especially appropriate in the context of complex commercial financing. Hence, the majority recognizes that the finding of "general discussions of extending credit or 'past renewals of credit should not lead a borrower to reasonably believe that credit will be extended or renewed again and again.'" *Ante*, p. 87 (citation omitted). In fact, "a pattern of renewal in itself [does not] amount to sufficient assent to continue dealing or that renewal will be indefinite." *Ante* (citation omitted). Accordingly, the majority finds that "[f]or a promise to loan money in the future to be sufficiently clear and definite, some evidence must exist of the material terms of the loan, including the amount of the loan, the interest rate, and the method of repayment." *Ante*. This must be so because to enforce ambiguous promises of future financing is both inequitable and permits the speculative awarding of damages.[4]

---

2. More recently the doctrine has been articulated by four elements:
    (1) a promise, (2) that the promisor should reasonably have expected to induce action of a definite and substantial character on the part of the promisee, (3) which in fact produced reliance or forbearance of that nature, (4) in circumstances such that the promise must be enforced if injustice is to be avoided.
McMath v. Ford Motor Co., 259 N.W.2d 140 (Mich. 1977).
    4. The essential justification for the doctrine of promissory estoppel is the avoidance of substantial hardship or injustice were the promise not to be enforced. Too liberal an application of the concept will result in an unwitting and unintended undermining of the traditional rule requiring consideration for a contract. This is particularly true where the promise is the loan of money. Such promises, even when unsupported by consideration, do induce borrowers to neglect to secure the needed money elsewhere, and lenders must be held to anticipate such conduct. To hold as enforceable, however, a voluntary promise of a loan made to one who, in reliance thereon, fails to exercise a valueless right to seek the money elsewhere, would be tantamount to rendering all such voluntary promises of a loan enforceable without consideration. A determination declaring such a deviation from presently accepted

B.

In the instant case, the testimony reveals that the alleged promise was so ambiguous as to bar the application of promissory estoppel. In *Malaker Corp. Stockholders Protective Committee v. First Jersey Nat'l Bank*, 163 N.J. Super. 463, 480, 395 A.2d 222 (1978), the court ruled that a promise to loan an unspecified amount of money was not sufficient to constitute a clear and definite promise for the purposes of promissory estoppel:

At best, one could imply a promise of a loan of some indefinite amount guaranteed by additional collateral. We do not regard this kind of implied undertaking to lend an unspecified amount of money as the "clear and definite promise" that is required as an adequate foundation for estopping the bank to deny absence of consideration as a defense.

Similarly, the circumstances in the instant case do not constitute promissory estoppel. The vaporous and amorphous pledges of "support" were certainly not clear and definite promises. No terms of the loans were specified—the amount of the loan, the interest rates, the payment schedule, the method of payment were all undetermined. Nor were these statements of support formal agreements with merely some terms to be decided. The recent alteration of the terms of payment from a rollover to an annual payment basis, for instance, disproves any notion of "customary loan practices between the parties."[5] Moreover, the quickly souring financial circumstances of the Currys significantly altered any established customary norms between the parties.[6] Clearly the terms and approval of the annual loans were not fixed, but subject to annual renegotiation.[7] Furthermore, the majority relies heavily on the fact that Curry "went to the bank for the express purpose of learning whether he would receive financing should he decide to continue in the dairy business," and yet his intent is irrelevant to whether the bank made such a binding promise. Even after drawing all due inferences in favor of the Currys, the bank's statements were not a clear and definite promise sufficient to apply promissory estoppel because the bank clearly did not state the "material terms of the loan, including the amount of the loan, the interest rate, and the method of repayment." In the arena of highly complex financial

---

contract principles should only come from a confrontation with that issue, and not as an unintended consequence of the loose application of promissory estoppel to promises to lend money.

5. In fact, following the analysis of the majority to its logical conclusion, if a vague pledge of support occurred before 1985 and the Currys had relied upon the ability to roll over their debt, the bank would have been estopped from altering the payment schedule. Similarly, if instead of denying the loan request the bank had approved a loan with an increased interest rate, the majority would also declare such an offer estopped. In essence, the majority finds that once a commercial lending relationship exists, debtors are entitled to rely upon vague affirmations of support to paralyze lenders' abilities to adjust to ever-changing market conditions. Such a holding does extreme violence to the doctrine of promissory estoppel, as well as freedom of contract.

6. Contrary to the assertion of the majority, this opinion does not rest upon "a review of the bank officer's testimony regarding the deteriorating financial status of the Currys to support his ultimate decision to refuse to make the loan." In fact, I agree with the majority that the issue is "whether there was sufficient evidence to support a jury finding that the bank promised the Currys it would make the loan." Unlike the majority, I have examined those statements which plaintiffs suggest constitute a clear and definite promise and find them wanting. I simply note the Currys' deteriorating financial conditions to belie the notion that an established pattern of lending existed or could be expected to continue under the circumstances. Hence, the vague affirmation of support should not be understood to be so sufficiently clear and definite that it incorporated "the material terms of the loan, including the amount of the loan, the interest rate, and the method of repayment."

7. After all, the Currys did submit loan requests each year, and the bank did evaluate each request independently.

lending, the bank's statements are too vague and ambiguous to possess the necessary definiteness to justify a legitimate use of promissory estoppel.

V.

Because the statements at issue were not clear and definite promises necessary for the application of promissory estoppel, I respectfully dissent.

Note—On Farming, Reliance, and Trust

Agriculture, and "the family farm," are at the center of one important thread in dominant U.S. culture. This thread celebrates an ideal community of farmers, living egalitarian democracy, in which the virtues of perseverance, love of family, and respect for the land overcome the harshness of weather, rock, and human corruption. Many stories, songs, and images offer to generations of children an image of agricultural America as the "heartland," the place from which we come. Steinbeck's tenant men cry out: "but it's our land. We measured and broke it up. We were born on it, and we got killed on it, died on it. Even if it's not good, it's still ours. That's what makes it ours—being born on it, working it, dying on it. That makes ownership, not a paper with numbers on it." Cultural narratives associated with farming have influenced courts, as they evaluate the rights and obligations of farmer and bankers, and legislators, as they have enacted legislation dealing with farm subsidies and other agricultural support programs.

The character of agriculture in the United States has shifted from many smaller farms (6.5 million in 1935) to fewer farms (2.1 million in 2012), some of which are very large. The 2012 agricultural census tallied nearly $395 billion in sales of agricultural products, a 34 percent increase over the previous census in 2007. Three-quarters of the farms earned less than $50,000 in 2012, while only 11.9 percent of U.S. farms had annual sales exceeding $250,000. Less than 5 percent of all farms accounted for two-thirds of all agricultural products sold. Between 1935 and 2002, approximately 4.4 million families lost their farms. This trend is continuing: the number of farms decreased in all size categories except the largest between 2007 and 2012, while the total acreage decreased by a relatively small amount. U.S. Department of Commerce, Bureau of the Census, 1997 Census of Agriculture; 2012 Census of Agriculture.

Throughout this period, ownership of farms has remained largely family-based. Today, approximately 96.5% of U.S. farms are owned by individuals, families, or partnerships with only 3.5% owned by non-family corporations. Despite repeated alarms over the "demise of the family farm," the shift in agriculture is not from family to non-family, but rather from many, smaller, family-owned farms to fewer, larger, family-owned farms. Many, many families have lost their farms, but most have lost the farms to other families, not to corporations. Agribusiness is family-owned. The trend is not away from the family-owned farm, but rather away from the small farm.

The loss of small farms has been felt by some groups more than others. Many poor and working class families lost their farms in the years during and after the Depression. Many Japanese-American families lost their farms as a result of their illegal internment by the U.S. government during World War II. Many African-American families lost their farms in the rural South as a consequence of forced partition sales and numerous barriers to agricultural development erected by government licensing and the financial industry. The total number of minority-owned farms declined by 91 percent, from 481,601 in 1954 to 44,640 in 1987, while the number of white-owned farms declined by 51 percent, from 4,301,420 to 2,087,759 during the same time period. In 1954, minority-owned farms made up 10 percent of the total farms in the United States compared to 2 percent by 1987. Adell Brown, Jr., Ralph D. Christy, & Tesfa G. Gebremedhin, *Structural Changes in U.S. Agriculture: Implications for African-American Farmers*, 22 Rev. Black Pol. Econ. 51 (1994).

For those families who own large farms, an array of government programs provide protection against competition and uncertainties in the market. Many federal programs provide direct assistance payments and indirect farm subsidies. Although the total amount of assistance and subsidies is not available, census figures report approximately $8.1 billion a year in direct payments from the federal government to farmers. Indirect subsidies include purchases of wheat, feed grains, rice, and other crops by the Commodity Credit Corporation in order to decrease supply and increase retail prices on these farm products; low-interest and nonrecourse loans (a nonrecourse loan is one in which, in the event of default, the debtor is not liable for repayment beyond the value of the crop collateral); and dairy buy-outs such as that contemplated by the Currys in Bank of Standish. Estimates of the annual cost to the federal government of all direct and indirect farm subsidy programs are in the range of $30 billion.

Various reports have concluded that most of the federal assistance payments and subsidies go to the largest and wealthiest farmers. *See, e.g.*, Jones, Hezekiah, *Federal Agricultural Policies: Do Black Farm Operators Benefit?*, 22 Rev. Black Pol. Econ. 25 (1994); Greg Gordon, James Walsh, *After Farm Subsidy Cuts; Who'll Reap What's Left?*, Star Tribune, September 17, 1995, page 18A. Under section 1001 of the Food Security Act of 1985, Pub. L. No. 99-198, 99 Stat. 1354 (1985), the total annual payment that a person may receive under the programs for wheat, feed grains, upland cotton, extra long staple cotton, and rice is $50,000. The law also places a cap of $250,000 per person for total payments under all farm programs, see Food, Agriculture, Conservation, and Trade Act of 1990, 7 U.S.C. §§ 1308(1), 1308(2) (1988). Opposition to the farm subsidy programs has come from a wide variety of groups, including California vegetable farmers who have not received subsidies, environmental groups who argue that farm subsidies result in over-cultivation of land, "fiscal conservatives" who view farm subsidies as an unwarranted drain on the federal budget, and traders from Mexico and Canada who argue that farm subsidies result in artificially high prices for U.S. agricultural products. Although the agricultural subsidies have been justified as a means to ensure food supplies for the non-farming population, critics argue that they are not needed and do not serve this purpose but rather function merely as "welfare" for wealthy farmers. And despite much fanfare about the possibility of ending farm subsidies, payments from the federal government have continued to soar under both Democratic and Republican administrations.

Every claim of reliance requires the court to decide whether it is appropriate to grant a remedy in that particular case, and frequently courts are influenced by the nature of the relationship involved. *Ricketts v. Scothorn* involved a grandfather's promise to his granddaughter. Some would view this as a private matter, not appropriate for public concern. During the twentieth century, some argued that the doctrine of promissory estoppel ought to be limited to family settings, but as *Bank of Standish* illustrates, promissory estoppel now plays a significant role in commercial relationships.

In *Bank of Standish*, the Currys were dependent on the bank and the relationship was much more important to them than it was to the bank. Cultural narratives regarding the disparity in power between bankers and farmers lead observers to see and to emphasize this disparity. Do questions of trust, reasonable reliance, and responsibility turn on dynamics of power?

The philosopher Annette Baier argues that contract models are inadequate to evaluate trust in situations of power inequity: "[T]he more we ignore dependency relations between those grossly unequal in power and ignore what cannot be spelled out in an explicit acknowledgment, the more readily we will assume that everything that needs to be understood about trust and trustworthiness can be grasped by looking at the morality of contract." Annette Baier, *Trust and Antitrust*, 96 Ethics 231, 241 (1986). Although many courts have not yet developed sophisticated tools for description and analysis of power relations, the reliance principle and the doctrine of promissory estoppel encourage work in this direction.

It is helpful to note that the issue of formality often arises in disputes between people who are interdependent. The excerpt from John Steinbeck's classic Grapes of Wrath well portrays the complex relationship between farmers and banks. In good times, both farmers and banks profit from their transactions and establish trusting relationships; in bad times, the relative economic, social, and political power of the banks is revealed.

John Steinbeck, The Grapes of Wrath

(1939)

The owners of the land came onto the land, or more often a spokesman for the owners came. They came in closed cars, and they felt the dry earth with their fingers, and sometimes they drove big earth augers into the ground for soil tests. The tenants, from their sun-beaten dooryards, watched uneasily when the closed cars drove along the fields. And at last the owner men drove into the dooryards and sat in their cars to talk out of the windows. The tenant men stood beside the cars for a while, and then squatted on their hams and found sticks with which to mark the dust.

In the open doors the women stood looking out, and behind them the children—corn-headed children, with wide eyes, one bare foot on top of the other bare foot, and the toes working. The women and the children watched their men talking to the owner men. They were silent.

Some of the owner men were kind because they hated what they had to do, and some of them were angry because they hated to be cruel, and some of them were cold because they had long ago found that one could not be an owner unless one were cold. And all of them were caught in something larger than themselves. Some of them hated the mathematics that drove them, and some were afraid, and some worshiped the mathematics because it provided a refuge from thought and from feeling. If a bank or a finance company owned the land, the owner man said, the Bank—or the Company—needs—wants—insists—must have—as though the Bank or the Company were a monster, with thought and feeling, which had ensnared them. These last would take no responsibility for the banks or the companies because they were men and slaves, while the banks were machines and masters all at the same time. Some of the owner men were a little proud to be slaves to such cold and powerful masters. The owner men sat in the cars and explained. You know the land is poor. You've scrabbled at it long enough, God knows.

The squatting tenant men nodded and wondered and drew figures in the dust, and yes, they knew. God knows. If the dust only wouldn't fly. If the top would only stay on the soil, it might not be so bad.

The owner men went on leading to their point: You know the land's getting poorer. You know what cotton does to the land; robs it, sucks all the blood out of it.

The squatters nodded—they knew, God knew. If they could only rotate the crops they might pump blood back into the land.

Well, it's too late. And the owner men explained the workings and the thinkings of the monster that was stronger than they were. A man can hold land if he can just eat and pay taxes; he can do that.

Yes, he can do that until his crops fail one day and he has to borrow money from the bank.

But—you see, a bank or a company can't do that, because those creatures don't breathe air, don't eat side-meat. They breathe profits; they eat the interest on money. If they don't get it, they die the way you die without air, without side-meat. It is a sad thing, but it is so. It is just so.

The squatting men raised their eyes to understand. Can't we just hang on? Maybe the next year will be a good year. God knows how much cotton next year. And with all the wars—God knows what price cotton will bring. Don't they make explosives out of cotton? And uniforms? Get enough wars and cotton'll hit the ceiling. Next year, maybe. They looked up questioningly.

We can't depend on it. The bank—the monster has to have profits all the time. It can't wait. It'll die. No, taxes go on. When the monster stops growing, it dies. It can't stay one size.

Soft fingers began to tap the sill of the car window, and the hard fingers tightened on the restless drawing sticks. In the doorways of the sun-beaten tenant houses, women sighed and then shifted feet so that the one that had been down was now on top, and the toes working. Dogs came sniffing near the owner cars and wetted on all four tires one after another. And chickens lay in the sunny dust and fluffed their feathers to get the cleansing dust down to the skin. In the little sties the pigs grunted inquiringly over the muddy remnants of the slops.

The squatting men looked down again. What do you want us to do? We can't take less share of the crop—we're half starved now. The kids are hungry all the time. We got no clothes, torn an' ragged. If all the neighbors weren't the same, we'd be ashamed to go to meeting.

And at last the owner men came to the point. The tenant system won't work any more. One man on a tractor can take the place of twelve or fourteen families. Pay him a wage and take all the crop. We have to do it. We don't like to do it. But the monster's sick. Something's happened to the monster.

But you'll kill the land with cotton.

We know. We've got to take cotton quick before the land dies. Then we'll sell the land. Lots of families in the East would like to own a piece of land.

The tenant men looked up alarmed. But what'll happen to us? How'll we eat?

You'll have to get off the land. The plows'll go through the dooryard.

And now the squatting men stood up angrily. Grampa took up the land, and he had to kill the Indians and drive them away. And Pa was born here, and he killed weeds and snakes. Then a bad year came and he had to borrow a little money. An' we was born here. There in the door—our children born here. And Pa had to borrow money. The bank owned the land then, but we stayed and we got a little bit of what we raised.

We know that—all that. It's not us, it's the bank. A bank isn't like a man. Or an owner with fifty thousand acres, he isn't like a man either. That's the monster.

Sure, cried the tenant men, but it's our land. We measured and broke it up. We were born on it, and we got killed on it, died on it. Even if it's not good, it's still ours. That's what makes it ours—being born on it, working it, dying on it. That makes ownership, not a paper with numbers on it.

We're sorry. It's not us. It's the monster. The bank isn't like a man.

Yes, but the bank is only made of men.

No, you're wrong there—quite wrong there. The bank is something else than men. It happens that every man in a bank hates what the bank does, and yet the bank does it. The bank is something more than men, I can tell you. It's the monster. Men made it, but they can't control it.

The tenants cried, Grampa killed Indians, Pa killed snakes for the land. Maybe we can kill banks—they're worse than Indians and snakes. Maybe we got to fight to keep our land, like Pa and Grampa did.

And now the owner men grew angry. You'll have to go.

But it's ours, the tenant men cried. We—

No. The bank monster owns it. You'll have to go.

We'll get our guns, like Grampa when the Indians came. What then?

Well—first the sheriff, and then the troops. You'll be stealing if you try to stay, you'll be murderers if you kill to stay. The monster isn't men, but it can make men do what it wants.

But if we go, where'll we go? How'll we go? We got no money.

We're sorry, said the owner men. The bank, the fifty-thousand-acre owner can't be responsible. You're on land that isn't yours. Once over the line maybe you can pick cotton in the fall. Maybe you can go on relief. Why don't you go on west to California? There's work there, and it never gets cold. Why, you can reach out anywhere and pick an orange. Why, there's always some kind of crop to work in. Why don't you go there? And the owner men started their cars and rolled away.

The tenant men squatted down to their hams again to mark the dust with a stick, to figure, to wonder. Their sunburned faces were dark, and their sun whipped eyes were light. The women moved cautiously out of the doorways toward their men, and the children crept behind the women, cautiously, ready to run. The bigger boys squatted beside their fathers, because that made them men. After a time the women asked, What did he want?

And the men looked up for a second, and the smolder of pain was in their eyes. We got to get off. A tractor and a superintendent. Like factories.

Where'll we go? the women asked.

We don't know. We don't know.

And the women went quickly, quietly back into the houses and herded the children ahead of them. They knew that a man so hurt and so perplexed may turn in anger, even on people he loves. They left the men alone to figure and to wonder in the dust.

After a time perhaps the tenant man looked about—at the pump put in ten years go, with a goose-neck handle and iron flowers on the spout, at the chopping block where a thousand chickens had been killed, at the hand plow lying in the shed, and the patent crib hanging in the rafters over it.

The children crowded about the women in the houses. What we going to do, Ma? Where we going to go?

The women said, We don't know yet. Go out and play. But don't go near your father. He might whale you if you go near him. And the women went on with the work, but all the time they watched the men squatting in the dust—perplexed and figuring.

The tractors came over the roads and into the fields, great crawlers moving like insects, having the incredible strength of insects. They crawled over the ground, laying the track and rolling on it and picking it up. Diesel tractors, puttering while they stood idle; they thundered when they moved, and then settled down to a droning roar. Snub-nosed monsters, raising the dust and sticking their snouts into it, straight down the country, across the country, through fences, through dooryards, in and out of gullies in straight lines. They did not run on the ground, but on their own roadbeds. They ignored hills and gulches, water courses, fences, houses.

The man sitting in the iron seat did not look like a man; gloved, goggled, rubber dust mask over nose and mouth, he was part of the monster, a robot in the seat. The thunder of the cylinders sounded through the country, became one with the air and the earth, so that earth and air muttered in sympathetic vibration. The driver could not control it— straight across country it went, cutting through a dozen farms and straight back. A twitch at the controls could swerve the cat', but the driver's hands could not twitch because the monster that built the tractor, the monster that sent the tractor out, had somehow got into the driver's hands, into his brain and muscle, had goggled him and muzzled him— goggled his mind, muzzled his speech, goggled his perception, muzzled his protest. He could not see the land as it was, he could not smell the land as it smelled; his feet did not stamp the clods or feel the warmth and power of the earth. He sat in an iron seat and stepped on iron pedals. He could not cheer or beat or curse or encourage the extension of his power, and because of this he could not cheer or whip or curse or encourage himself. He did not know or own or trust or beseech the land. If a seed dropped did not germinate, it was nothing. If the young thrusting plant withered in drought or drowned in a flood of rain, it was no more to the driver than to the tractor.

He loved the land no more than the bank loved the land. He could admire the tractor—its machined surfaces, its surge of power, the roar of its detonating cylinders; but it was not his tractor. Behind the tractor rolled the shining disks, cutting the earth with blades—not plowing but surgery, pushing the cut earth to the right where the second row of disks cut it and pushed it to the left; slicing blades shining, polished by the cut earth. And pulled behind the disks, the harrows combining with iron teeth so that the little clods broke up and the earth lay smooth. Behind the harrows, the long seeders— twelve curved iron penes erected in the foundry, orgasms set by gears, raping methodically, raping without passion. The driver sat in his iron seat and he was proud of the straight lines he did not will, proud of the tractor he did not own or love, proud of the power he could not control. And when that crop grew, and was harvested, no man had crumbled a hot clod in his fingers and let the earth sift past his fingertips. No man had touched the seed, or lusted for the growth. Men ate what they had not raised, had no connection with the bread. The land bore under iron, and under iron gradually died; for it was not loved or hated, it had no prayers or curses.

At noon the tractor driver stopped sometimes near a tenant house and opened his lunch: sandwiches wrapped in waxed paper, white bread, pickle, cheese, Spam, a piece of pie branded like an engine part. He ate without relish. And tenants not yet moved away came out to see him, looked curiously while the goggles were taken off, and the rubber dust mask, leaving white circles around the eyes and a large white circle around nose and mouth. The exhaust of the tractor puttered on, for fuel is so cheap it is more efficient to leave the engine running than to heat the Diesel nose for a new start. Curious children crowded close, ragged children who ate their fried dough as they watched. They watched hungrily the unwrapping of the sandwiches, and their hunger-sharpened noses smelled the pickle, cheese and Spam. They didn't speak to the driver. They watched his hand as it carried food to his mouth. They did not watch him chewing; their eyes followed the hand that held the sandwich. After a while the tenant who could not leave the place came out and squatted in the shade beside the tractor.

"Why, you're Joe Davis's boy!"

"Sure," the driver said.

"Well, what you doing this kind of work for—against your own people?"

"Three dollars a day. I got sick of creeping for my dinner—and not getting it. I got a wife and kids. We got to eat. Three dollars a day, and it comes every day."

"That's right," the tenant said. "But for your three dollars a day fifteen or twenty families can't eat at all. Nearly a hundred people have to go out and wander on the roads for your three dollars a day. Is that right?"

And the driver said, "Can't think of that. Got to think of my own kids. Three dollars a day, and it comes every day. Times are changing, mister, don't you know? Can't make a living on the land unless you've got two, five, ten thousand acres and a tractor. Crop land isn't for little guys like us any more. You don't kick up a howl because you can't make Fords, or because you're not the telephone company. Well, crops are like that now. Nothing to do about it. You try to get three dollars a day someplace. That's the only way."

The tenant pondered. "Funny thing how it is. If a man owns a little property, that property is him, it's part of him, and it's like him. If he owns property only so he can walk on it and handle it and be sad when it isn't doing well, and feel fine when the rain falls on it, that property is him, and some say he's bigger because he owns it. Even if he isn't successful he's big with his property. That is so."

And the tenant pondered more. "But let a man get property he doesn't see, or can't take time to get his fingers in, or can't be there to walk on it—why, then the property is the man. He can't do what he wants he can't think what he wants. The property is the man, stronger than he is. And he is small, not big. Only his possessions are big—and he's the servant of his property. That is so, too."

The driver munched the branded pie and threw the crust away. "Times are changed, don't you know? Thinking about stuff like that don't feed the kids. Get your three dollars a day, feed your kids. You got no call to worry about anybody's kids but your own. You get a reputation for talking like that, and you'll never get three dollars a day. Big shots won't give you three dollars a day if you worry about anything but your three dollars a day."

"Nearly a hundred people on the road for your three dollars. Where will we go?"

"And that reminds me," the driver said, "you better get out soon. I'm going through the dooryard after dinner."

"You filled in the well this morning."

"I know. Had to keep the line straight. But I'm going through the dooryard after dinner. Got to keep the lines straight. And—well, you know Joe Davis, my old man, so I'll tell you this. I got orders wherever there's a family not moved out—if I have an accident—

you know, get too close and cave the house in a little—well, I might get a couple of dollars. And my youngest kid never had no shoes yet."

"I built it with my hands. Straightened out old nails to put the sheathing on. Rafters are wired to the stringers with baling wire. It's mine. I built it. You bump it down—I'll be in the window with a rifle. You even come too close and I'll pot you like a rabbit."

"It's not me. There's nothing I can do. I'll lose my job if I don't do it. And look—suppose you kill me? They'll just hang you, but long before you're hung there'll be another guy on the tractor, and he'll bump the house down. You're not killing the right guy."

"That's so," the tenant said. "Who gave you orders? I'll go after him. He's the one to kill."

"You're wrong. He got his orders from the bank. The bank told him, 'Clear those people out or it's your job.'"

"Well, there's a president of the bank. There's a board of directors. I'll fill up the magazine of the rifle and go into the bank."

The driver said, "Fellow was telling me the bank gets orders from the East. The orders were, 'Make the land show profit or we'll close you up.'"

"But where does it stop? Who can we shoot? I don't aim to starve to death before I kill the man that's starving me."

"I don't know. Maybe there's nobody to shoot. Maybe the thing isn't men at all. Maybe, like you said, the property's doing it. Anyway I told you my orders."

"I got to figure," the tenant said. "We all got to figure. There's some way to stop this. It's not like lightning or earthquakes. We've got a bad thing made by men, and by God that's something we can change." The tenant sat in his doorway, and the driver thundered his engine and started off, tracks falling and curving, harrows combing, and the phalli of the seeder slipping into the ground. Across the dooryard the tractor cut, and the hard, foot-beaten ground was seeded field, and the tractor cut through again; the uncut space was ten feet wide. And back he came. The iron guard bit into the house-corner, crumbled the wall, and wrenched the little house from it's foundation so that it fell sideways, crushed like a bug. And the driver was goggled and a rubber mask covered his nose and mouth. The tractor cut a straight line on, and the air and the ground vibrated with its thunder. The tenant man stared after it, his rifle in his hand. His wife was beside him, and the quiet children behind. And all of them stared after the tractor.

John Steinbeck was awarded the Nobel Prize for Literature in 1962. This excerpt is a chapter from Grapes of Wrath, which won the Pulitzer Prize in 1940. Do you think the relationship between the farmer and the land described in the book has changed over the years? Is there still a strong sentiment in favor of preserving the family farm? Why are creditors, the bankers, seen as the villains in this piece?

Dayton Malleable Clears $5 Million Capital Outlay

(Wall Street Journal, August 29, 1979)

Dayton, Ohio—Dayton Malleable Inc. said directors approved an initial capital expenditure of $5 million as part of a two-phase, $10 million modernization project at the Ohio division in Columbus.

The project is expected to take three years to complete but production will be maintained during that period, the company said. Orders for production equipment with extensive lead times have been placed, and construction is due to begin during the latter part of 1980.

"This first phase will provide the capability to produce Nodular iron castings, primarily for use in the truck and off-highway equipment markets," Leo W. Ladehoff, president and chief executive officer, said.

The maker of castings said that hourly employees agreed in June to help improve the division's financial condition, thereby maintaining operations at the Columbus facility. The employees agreed to extend the current labor contract one year, to Dec. 26, 1981, and to maintain the present wage level for the duration of the contract, Dayton Malleable said. The union also will assist the company in developing new productivity standards to improve efficiency.

Abbington v. Dayton Malleable, Inc.

United States District Court for the Southern District of Ohio
561 F. Supp. 1290 (1983)

ROBERT M. DUNCAN, DISTRICT JUDGE

This matter is before the Court on the motions of defendant Dayton Malleable and defendant United Steelworkers of America for summary judgment pursuant to Fed. R. Civ. P. 56. Plaintiffs filed a five-count complaint in this lawsuit asserting three claims against Dayton Malleable, Inc. (DMI) and asserting the remaining claims against United Steelworkers of America (union). Plaintiffs have brought this lawsuit pursuant to section 301 of the Labor Management Relations Act (LMRA), 29 U.S.C. § 185, alleging that defendant DMI violated the collective bargaining agreement between the union and DMI when it closed its Columbus foundry.

I. Statement of Facts

Both defendant DMI and defendant Steelworkers have filed motions for summary judgment claiming that based on the undisputed facts of this case, they are entitled to judgment as a matter of law. Based on the memoranda and supporting documents of the parties, as well as various statements of counsel during oral argument, a statement of the undisputed facts of this case follows. DMI is in the business of manufacturing rough commercial castings for major equipment manufacturing companies in the United States. The Columbus Division of DMI (the foundry) produced malleable iron primarily for manufacturers of trucks and farm equipment. DMI and the union were parties to a collective bargaining agreement effective from December 26, 1977 until December 26, 1980, which covered the Foundry and DMI's Ironton Division.

During the three-year period ending June 1979, the Foundry lost approximately $13 million. As a result of these financial losses, DMI informed a union representative,[2] as

---

2. The organizational structure of the United Steelworkers union deserves some elaboration at this point. In order to assist the international in performing its representational function, the international creates local affiliates. A representative of the international is assigned to each local. John T. Green was the international representative assigned to the local in this case. In addition, the international union is divided into geographic regions known as "districts," which are managed by district directors. The district director assigned to cover District 27, which encompasses the City of Columbus, was Harry E. Mayfield. It was Mayfield who was notified of DMI's intention to close the foundry sometime in December of 1978.

was required by the 1977 collective bargaining agreement, that DMI was planning on closing the Columbus plant. Thereafter, the company postponed the plant closing until March or April of 1979. At that time, a new president of DMI, Mr. Ladehoff, was selected, and another meeting between representatives of the company and union was held. Once again the financial difficulties of the company were discussed, as well as the declining market for the malleable iron products produced at the Columbus plant. The union's research department confirmed these losses, and it is undisputed that DMI was suffering severe financial trouble during the period of time in question.

A third meeting was held between management and union representatives at which time management made clear that the closing of the Columbus plant was inevitable unless certain changes were made. Among the changes proposed by the company were the following modifications of the collective bargaining agreement:

1.   A twelve-month extension, until December 26, 1981, of the existing collective bargaining agreement as it applied to the Columbus plant;

2.   A separation of the employees at the Columbus plant from employees at the Ironton plant into two bargaining units under separate agreements;

3.   A suspension of cost-of-living adjustments after June 1979 and a wage freeze for the duration of the contract; and

4.   Union and management cooperation in devising new production methods and in setting equitable incentive rates.

The management of DMI informed the union that if these concessions were made, DMI would make every effort to keep the Columbus plant open including making efforts to modernize the Foundry. The union believed that prior to making any decision on these matters, the employees were entitled to be consulted.

Therefore, management and union representatives agreed to hold two meetings in a tent to be erected on a lot next to the plant. At the June 8, 1979 tent meeting, employees were informed by DMI officials of the company's financial plight. At that time, Mr. Ladehoff, DMI's president, informed employees that DMI had only two options—closing the plant or attempting to convert and modernize the plant. Ladehoff went on to explain that the latter option would have to be approved by the board of directors. Thereafter, Ladehoff outlined the proposed modifications to the collective bargaining agreement which he considered "critical to convince our Board of Directors to allow us to invest 8 to 10 million new dollars in this plant."

At this tent meeting, a union representative also spoke to the employees. The proposed modifications to the collective bargaining agreement were reviewed and the union representative recommended that the concessions be approved. Thereafter, a question and answer session was held, and management gave employees an opportunity to consult with their union representatives privately.

The following day, Saturday, June 9, 1979, a secret ballot vote was conducted. Approximately 90% of the local union's membership turned out to vote. DMI's proposed modifications of the collective bargaining agreement were approved by a vote of 426 to 19. Thereafter, company and union officials met in an attempt to reduce these approved modifications to writing. After a series of meetings, the parties' differences were resolved and the modifications were formalized in a written memorandum of agreement. That memorandum of agreement expressly embodied the modifications to the collective bargaining agreement which had been approved the day following the tent meeting.[9]

Despite the poor performance of the Foundry in July 1979, in August 1979 DMI's Board of Directors voted an initial investment of $5 million to buy new equipment needed for the conversion to nodular iron production. Various press releases and letters from management confirmed the Board's approval of this initial expenditure for plant modernization.

In the fall of 1979, the financial condition of DMI continued to deteriorate. Nonetheless, it appears from the evidence that attempts to save the Columbus Foundry were still being made. In October of 1979 new equipment necessary for the conversion was purchased and installed. During this time discussion between company and union representatives concerning the effects of modernization were ongoing.

By December of 1979 financial losses to DMI were so great that the company was forced to shut down for a period of time and lay off many employees. In January 1980 and February 1980 the company continued to experience severe financial problems. In addition, the company could foresee little relief in the future since marketing forecasts suggested a continued decrease in demand for both malleable and nodular iron.

Finally, the Board of Directors of DMI concluded that the Columbus Foundry should be closed. On March 13, 1980, DMI representatives notified union officials that the Board of Directors had recommended that the Columbus Foundry be closed permanently. On March 20, 1980, the Board of DMI voted to shut down the Columbus plant as of May 31, 1980. The following day, the Foundry's general manager sent a letter to each employee notifying him or her of the decision to close the Foundry.

Thereafter in April 1980, the union and DMI met to negotiate a plant closing agreement. The plant closing agreement provided for severance pay in amounts equal to vacation entitlements and guaranteed payment of pension benefit levels provided for in the pension agreement. Thereafter, the union met with employees on several occasions to explain the terms of the plant closing agreement.

Thereafter in June 1980, plaintiffs commenced this action against DMI and the union. Both DMI and the union have filed motions for summary judgment. The Court will address the motions of each defendant separately.

II. Motion of Defendant DMI for Summary Judgment

A. Breach of the Collective Bargaining Agreement

Plaintiffs' first claim under section 301 of the Labor Management Relations Act is that DMI "breached the amended collective bargaining agreement by shutting down the Columbus Plant before December 26, 1981."

It is clear, however, that neither the collective bargaining agreement dated December 26, 1977 nor the Memorandum of Agreement required DMI to keep the Columbus Foundry open....

...

---

9. The Court also notes at this point that plaintiffs attempt to make much of the fact that no advance warning of the tent meetings was given to employees. Once again, the Court does not believe this fact is of great import. The employees were notified of the tent meetings a week before their occurrence. Furthermore, specific information concerning the purpose of the meeting and the proposed modification of the collective bargaining agreement was withheld in order to avoid the spread of rumors.

B. Promissory Estoppel

In addition to alleging breach of the alleged memorandum of agreement, plaintiffs allege a cause of action for breach of contract based on the doctrine of promissory estoppel. Relying largely on the Sixth Circuit's decision in Local 1330, United Steelworkers of America v. United States Steel Corporation, 631 F.2d 1264 (6th Cir. 1980), plaintiffs claim that contractual promises to modernize the Columbus Foundry and not to close the Foundry may be found based upon the equitable doctrine of promissory estoppel.

The Sixth Circuit in United Steelworkers specifically recognized the possibility of a cause of action based on the equitable doctrine of promissory estoppel. In that case, the Court stated that

The doctrine of promissory estoppel recognizes the possibility of the formation of a contract by action or forbearance on the part of a second party, based upon a promise made by the first party under circumstances where the actions or forbearance of the second party should reasonably have been expected to produce the detrimental results to the second party which they did produce....

In this case, plaintiffs' contractual claim of promissory estoppel is based upon oral statements made during the tent meeting concerning efforts to modernize and keep the Foundry open and the employee responses to these representations.

At the outset, there are a number of difficulties with plaintiffs' promissory estoppel argument. It is by no means clear that a claim of promissory estoppel based on oral representations is cognizable when the parties have executed a formal contract which addresses the precise matters which are the subject of those oral representations. This matter is raised only in passing, however, since even if this Court assumes that a claim of promissory estoppel based on oral representations is cognizable, it is clear that no such claim has been established on the undisputed facts of this case.

The doctrine of promissory estoppel requires that plaintiffs prove that defendant DMI made a promise which could reasonably be expected to induce action or forbearance. This Court's review of the undisputed facts in this case leads it to the inevitable conclusion that no statements by any officers of DMI at either the tent meetings or in various press releases constituted a definite promise to continue operation of or to modernize the Foundry.

The statements of DMI officials at the June 8 "tent meeting" cannot be read as promises. At that meeting the company president first reviewed the financial difficulties experienced by DMI. Mr. Ladehoff then stated:

Now that brings us to the first of several decisions that we must make as a company.

One choice we have is to simply stop losing money here and close it down. The second choice for Dayton Malleable is to invest somewhere between $8–10 million to convert this plant to produce primarily nodular iron.

Mr. Ladehoff then proceeded to address himself to each of the options available to DMI. He stated:

As for the first of those two choices, closing the foundry—it's an option that I, and I know that you, would like to avoid. I do not want to close this plant, but by the same token I cannot continue with an operation that loses millions of dollars each year....

That brings us to the second choice—to convert this plant to nodular iron production.

Thereafter, Mr. Ladehoff stated that prior to converting and modernizing the plant, the company would have to obtain the approval of the board of directors. It was further explained that in order to obtain approval of the conversion plan, the employees would have to convince the Board of Directors that they were willing to make certain concessions. The employees were then presented with the four contract modifications, which eventually became the subject of the memorandum of agreement. Mr. Ladehoff concluded his speech noting that

> It's not going to be easy for us either, but I'm confident that with the 4 points that I've outlined we have at least a chance to make this plant successful once again.

> Now the choice is yours—if you vote to support us, we're going to do our best to turn this plant into a winner so everybody here can win.

The Court is simply not convinced that any of these statements constitute promises which would reasonably be expected to induce action or forbearance.

Furthermore, none of the press releases issued by the company during the summer and fall of 1979 constitute a promise to continue operation of the plant. Having reviewed these press releases the Court concludes that the statements contained therein can be divided into two categories. First, certain press releases simply recite factual information concerning the Foundry—i.e., the board's approval of the $5 million investment to convert the plant to nodular iron production; the decision to purchase new equipment; and production goals. The remaining statements in press releases may basically be characterized as "congratulatory" insofar as they comment favorably on employee enthusiasm for and dedication to efforts to keep the plant operational. None of the statements in these press releases may be deemed a promise under the standard enunciated in Restatement (Second) of Contracts § 90.

In conclusion, therefore, the Court believes that plaintiffs' allegations of a right to recovery based upon the doctrine of promissory estoppel are without merit.

...

———————

Note

Judge Duncan held that the employees could not maintain their action for promissory estoppel because Mr. Ladehoff's statements did not constitute a "definite" promise and therefore could not reasonably have been expected to induce reliance by the employees. Here the court links the definiteness of the promise to section 90's specification that the promise be one that the promisor "should reasonably expect to induce ... [reliance] by the promisee or a third person." The court suggests that reliance should be expected only where the promise is definite, as other courts have held that reliance should be expected only where the promise is "clear and unambiguous" or "clear and definite" *see, e.g., Bank of Standish v. Curry.*

On Whether Ladehoff's Statements Were "Promises" and Whether He Reasonably Expected Them to Induce Reliance

Abbington and other employees presumably argued that a reasonable person in their position would understand Ladehoff's statements to be promises in the Restatement sense of a manifestation of willingness to commit to the arrangement. Which version of the objective test does this reference to the "reasonable person" suggest?

Abbington and the other employees also argued that their decisions to vote for wage and benefit reductions and productivity increases were induced by Ladehoff's statements and that he clearly expected that his statements would induce that reliance, for that was his explicit purpose in making the tent meeting speech. Knowing that the tent meeting was called for the purpose of discussing the company's request for wage, benefit, and productivity level concessions (which were to be voted upon the following day), Ladehoff began his speech as follows:

> Ladies and gentlemen I have come here today to talk with you about some decisions that we have to make, and decisions we have to make quickly. Decisions that will affect all of us. They will affect Dayton Malleable, our plant here in Columbus, and most importantly, you.

As Judge Duncan indicated, Ladehoff defined two options available to the company: to shut down or to convert; Ladehoff told the workers he wanted them to agree to wage cuts (suspension of the contractual increases and cuts in productivity incentive payments) and productivity increases; and he told the workers that although the Board would have to decide between these two options, the workers' concessions would be an important factor in the Board's decision. In describing the second option, Ladehoff emphasized that wages at the Columbus Foundry, which were then at an average of $9.03, were higher than wages paid at other foundries, including ones in Georgia (average: $4.25) and at Lynchburg(average: $6.30). Ladehoff continued:

> Now the Board of Directors of our company who represent the people who own it, the stockholders, would first have to give us permission to spend that kind of money (projected cost of $8–10 million for conversion) ... If they did approve the conversion, it would take between 2 and 3 years to complete the changeover, and that would include the purchase and installation of new electric furnaces and other allied equipment.... I would like to emphasize that during this 2 to 3 year period if we are to convert this plant we would not shut down — we would continue to operate with little interruption. (Emphasis added.)

Abbington v. Dayton Malleable, 561 F. Supp. at 1307.

Following Ladehoff's speech, each employee had to decide whether to vote for the concessions. Presumably each evaluated whether it would be better to receive full pay under the existing contract until the plant was shut down or to make the concessions in the hope that the Board would decide to convert, in which case, Ladehoff said, the plant would stay open for at least 2 to 3 years. The plaintiffs argued that a reasonable steelworker would have heard Ladehoff's words as an assurance that, if the Board chose to convert, then the plant would remain open for at least 2 to 3 years.

What do you think that a reasonable steelworker would have understood in these circumstances? What additional information do you want before answering this question? If you were a worker at the tent meeting, would you have relied on Ladehoff's assurance? Would you have trusted Ladehoff's explanation of the choices facing the Board and of the consequences of each one?

On the Issue of Injustice

If Ladehoff's statements would have been interpreted as commitments under the objective analysis and Ladehoff reasonably expected that these statements would induce the employees to agree to the Company's request, then the court's rationale for the requirement of a more "definite" promise appears weak. Could one argue that enforcement of Ladehoff's assurance that the Company would not shut down during the period of conversion is not necessary to avoid injustice? In other words, could one argue that there is no risk of injustice in these circumstances?

The Board voted to approve the conversion in August 1979. The company issued a press release announcing the Board's decision to convert the plant to production of nodular iron (Wall Street Journal, August 29, 1979, at 4) and began the process of conversion. In March 1980, however, the Board voted to shut down the foundry. Judge Duncan's opinion does not say what Ladehoff did or recommended to the Board during this period. Judge Duncan suggests that the Board's decision in March 1980 was made in response to "financial losses" and "deterioration" in "Dayton Malleable's financial condition" during the fall of 1979.

Was there injustice in the Company's benefiting from the employees' concessions and then closing the plant? What additional information do you want before answering this question? Because Judge Duncan decided that a "definite" promise was required and that the plaintiffs could not satisfy this requirement, he granted the company's motion for summary judgment and received no further evidence on the issue of injustice. However, following the decision, in 1984, company president Leo Ladehoff provided more information in an interview to the Foundry Management & Technology magazine.

During the interview, Ladehoff described the carefully planned "transformation" of the company from 1979 to 1983. Ladehoff joined the company as President in December 1978. "[In 1979], the industry was running at capacity. Our company had peak sales of $184 million that year …" (elsewhere, Dayton Malleable reported net profits of $3.13 million from the $184 million in sales for 1979, P.R. Newswire, March 18, 1980). Nevertheless, Ladehoff explained, Dayton Malleable decided to restructure its operations because of changes in the market for steel:

> The fuel crunch of the early '70s had forced automotive manufacturers to reduce the weight of new vehicles; and deregulation in the railroad and trucking industries, foreign competition, and material substitution were reducing demand for iron and steel casting.... [W]e carefully analyzed the changes that were occurring and concluded that the market changes were permanent.

The company devised a "growth plan" with an initial goal of completion by 1986–87. "Our objective was reached, however, in 1984, an accomplishment that we attribute to three factors: formulating the game plan early, using financial resources, and maintaining a steady determination." The "game plan" involved several steps: "The first phase (1979–81) involved closing the Columbus, Ohio, Foundry [and a plant in Buffalo, New York] and downsizing the Dayton and Ironton, Ohio, plants." The Dayton plant was subsequently closed. During the same period, the company acquired a new plant in Meridian, Mississippi. During the next phase, the company dropped its Ohio-associated name and adopted the name Amcast Industrial Corporation. In 1982, the company acquired several new subsidiaries, including Stanley G. Flagg and Co., which produced cast-metal products such as iron and bronze pipe fittings, Newman Foundry in 1982, and Elkhart Products Corp., a major producer of copper and bronze pipe fittings and valves. Jack C. Miske, Amcast — A New Company with a 117-year History, Foundry Management & Technology, April, 1984, at 52.

The financial picture painted by Ladehoff is quite different from that presented to the union and to Judge Duncan. While the "peak sales of $184 million" in 1979 dropped to $132–133 million following the plant closings in 1980 and 1981, the company quickly recovered. After acquiring the Meridian, Mississippi plant in 1981 and the new subsidiaries in 1982, the company experienced "record profits on record sales" in the September–November, 1983 quarter. Id.

The restructuring of Dayton Malleable was similar to that undertaken by many steel and other manufacturing companies during the 1980s. See Alan Downs, Corporate Executions: The Ugly Truth about Layoffs (1995); Fran Ansley, Standing Rusty and Rolling

Empty: Law, Poverty, and America's Eroding Industrial Base, 81 Geo. L.J. 1757 (1993). During the years from 1980 to 1995, more than 8 million workers were laid off, the largest number ever recorded. During the same period, corporate profits soared, and senior executives' salaries increased by 1,000 percent. In 2005, the average chief executive officer's salary was 431 times the average employee's pay, up from 301 times in 2003. Institute for Policy Studies/United for a Fair Economy, Executive Excess 2005.

In 1979, Dayton Malleable, like many other manufacturing companies, faced a problem and an opportunity. The problem was that its plants in Ohio and New York were obsolete. The directors and managers at Dayton Malleable, as at other companies, felt tremendous pressure to modernize in order to remain competitive, but this required investment in capital improvements, including the purchase of new equipment, and the implementation of new technology. In earlier times, improvements of this sort were financed by reinvesting profits into the business or by long-term borrowing. Owners bore the cost of capital improvements as a regular cost of doing business.

During the late 1970s and the 1980s, however, managers were unwilling to make shareholders bear these costs. Because of shifts in the stock market and the financial markets generally, there was an increasing emphasis on short-term investment and a "frenzy" of mergers and acquisitions. As a result, business managers felt great pressure to improve their net profits (the "bottom line") and distribute these to shareholders, in order to convince shareholders not to sell their stock to "corporate raiders" who seek to obtain voting control of the corporation. Managers generally oppose corporate acquisitions and other shifts in control, fearing that they will be replaced by new management personnel, that the new owners will resell the company or its assets for short term gains, or both. As Professor Ansley explains:

> Along with the ability to move capital fast and far has come the will to do so. A powerful tendency has emerged for managers and investors to seek the highest possible short-term returns on investment, and to display less and less commitment to any underlying product, place, or group of employees. Many plants are closed not because they fail to make a profit, but because they fail to make enough profit to hold the decision maker's interest when compared to some other marginally more profitable opportunity. When management fails to reinvest and modernize, productivity and profit margins most often do decline, thereby reinforcing the initial, casual decisions whose rhetoric often either places blame at the feet of labor, or speaks of these developments as if they constituted some natural and inevitable evolutionary path beyond anyone's control.

> Fueling and being fueled by this trend is the related explosion of mergers and acquisitions, many of which are quickly followed by downsizings, mass layoffs, and plant closings. More profit can often be made in less time by orchestrating a leveraged buyout than by managing the concrete manufacture of an actual product. The managerial culture of this merger "frenzy," with its emphasis on deal-driven profits over productivity or equity, has been noted with dismay and alarm by observers as diverse as the presidents of the United Auto Workers and of Harvard University.

Ansley, Standing Rusty, *supra* at 1765.

A manager cannot both reinvest most of the company's profits and pay large dividends, so managers of companies like Dayton Malleable needed to "find" money elsewhere with which to finance capital improvements. Many found it by reducing labor costs and abandoning obsolete buildings and equipment. This was the "opportunity" presented to

Dayton Malleable in 1979: by convincing the Dayton employees to agree to reduce wages and benefits and increase productivity, the company could save money to use in acquiring new plants. Then, by closing its plants in Ohio and New York and relocating to newer plants in areas with lower wage scales, Dayton Malleable could further reduce its labor costs. Finally, by abandoning its old facilities, the company could avoid the costs created by years of neglect and pass the expense of clean-up to the city of Dayton. Improvements in transportation services (due in large measure to subsidies by state and federal governments) meant that the company could move away from the traditional industrial centers of the northern states to areas with a lower wage scale. In his "tent meeting" speech, Leo Ladehoff emphasized that the company stood to gain much from closing its operations in Ohio and New York and acquiring new plants in Mississippi (where wages are lower than in any other state) and other low wage places.

In addition, in most states, under current law, it is possible for a company to abandon a plant without having to clear the land or otherwise rehabilitate deteriorated structures and equipment. *But see In re Indenture of Trust dated as of March 1, 1982, re City of Duluth $10,000,000 Indus. Dev. Revenue Bonds, Series 1982-1 (The Triangle Corporation Project)*, 437 N.W.2d 430 (Minn. Ct. App. 1989) (company had promised to keep equipment in Duluth in connection with issuance of $10 million municipal bonds; in suit by city, the court required the company to remain in operation for the life of the bonds); Ansley, Standing Rusty, *supra* at 1822–24, discussing *City of Norwood v. General Motors Corp., No. A8705920* (Ct. Common Pleas Hamilton County, Ohio filed Aug. 7, 1987, decision entered Sept. 2, 1988)(the complaint alleged that General Motors' abandoned plant constituted a nuisance; after the court held that the city may sue G.M. for nuisance, G.M. agreed to tear down the plant). Most often, abandoned plants are sold to a "demolition" or junk company for a minimal amount. The new owner takes whatever it can resell and then goes out of business, leaving useless land for local governments to clean up if they can. In most instances, the government cannot afford to clear the land and so abandoned plants are left as deteriorating waste.

This is what happened to the Dayton Malleable plant. In 1992, Dayton city officials declared the abandoned Dayton Malleable plant a nuisance. In response to this declaration, New Start Demolition, the plant's owner since 1988, began but did not finish cleaning up the large site. In July 1995, a murdered child was found in a pool of water in the ruins of Dayton Malleable's plant and media attention focused on dangerous conditions at the abandoned foundry. New Start's owner, John Peloquin, promised to do his best to resume the clean-up. During the fall of 1995, Peloquin and a small crew worked to fill in some of the most dangerous pits and raze some hazardous structures. City officials said they were satisfied with Peloquin's efforts, considering that Peloquin had but a small crew and the city itself could not afford to do the enormous clean-up. Tom Beyerlein, GHR Foundry Cleanup Lags but City Is Satisfied, Dayton Daily News, October 26, 1995.

The question raised by Abbington and other plant closing cases is whether it is just for companies to shift substantial portions of the costs of restructuring onto employees by forcing concessions and lower wages and onto communities by abandoning plants. In his opinion, Judge Duncan put great weight on the company's claim that it would suffer "continuing financial deterioration" if required to keep the Columbus foundry open. The financial information presented by Leo Ladehoff in his 1984 interview casts doubt on this characterization of Dayton Malleable's financial condition in 1979, but in any event, the court's treatment of this claim suggests one troubling answer to the question posed. A commonplace in the United States is that a business should never be required to lose money. This commonplace leads one to answer: that it is not unjust for a company to shift its costs for restructuring if necessary to avoid financial loss. This idea seems to underlie Judge Duncan's decision.

Judge Duncan did not reach the question of injustice under promissory estoppel and did not draw a connection between Ladehoff's assurances and the losses admittedly suffered by the employees as a consequence of their wage and benefit concessions. Perhaps Judge Duncan saw these as unconnected because he thought the workers would have agreed to concessions even if Ladehoff had not made any promise. Perhaps Judge Duncan thought that Abbington and the others agreed to concessions simply because that was the only chance they had to keep their jobs, and that they did not rely on the company in any way. What commonplaces inform that idea? That jobs are very important to employees and that employees know not to expect anything from their employers beyond a definite promise of pay for work done? That employees would or should know wage reductions that cause significant hardships for them and their families may be of little significance when compared to the large profit the company and its owners expect to earn from their investment?

If the court did see the situation in this way, then the "normal" course of events would be for the employees to make concessions and the company to retain its discretion to close down the plant. This course of events, the common narrative of employer-employee relations, could be altered only by a "definite" (clear, unambiguous …) promise by the company. Would it have been possible for the employees' lawyers to have challenged this story? What information would have been helpful in this effort? See Jack M. Beerman & Joseph W. Singer, Baseline Questions in Legal Reasoning: The Example of Property in Jobs, 23 Ga. L. Rev. 911, 946–56 (1989) (noting that the portrayal of employers as owners and employees as non-owners informs judicial decisions in employment cases and arguing for an alternative conception of jobs as a property right).

Postscript: The Company's Success and Return to Ohio

In 1994 Amcast Industrial recorded sales of $271.9 million and profits of $14.5. million. CEO Interview: Amcast Industrial Corp., The Wall Street Transcript, Dec. 19, 1994. In June 1995, Amcast announced plans to build a new plant in Wapakoneta, Ohio, which was the company's first significant investment in Ohio since the closing of the Columbus Foundry. Chairman Ladehoff explained the decision to return to Ohio by citing the reduction in the state's workers' compensation rates. "Specifically, Amcast executives are gushing about Gov. George Voinovich's promise to slash the state's workers' compensation rates. 'The costs were too high,' said Amcast Chairman Leo W. Ladehoff, 'until Governor Voinovich came along and tried to change it.'" Associated Press, Amcast to Build Plant in Wapakoneta, The Columbus Dispatch (Ohio), June 26, 1995. Amcast announced that the Wapakoneta plant would employ approximately 150 employees, at an average wage of $9.25 ($19,240 per year). Id.

Barbara Kingsolver, Why I Am a Danger to the Public

(1993)

Bueno, if I get backed into a corner I can just about raise up the dead. I'll fight, sure. But I am no lady wrestler. If you could see me you would know this thing is a joke — Tony, my oldest, is already taller than me, and he's only eleven. So why are they so scared of me I have to be in jail? I'll tell you.

Number one, this strike. There has never been one that turned so many old friends chingándose, not here in Bolton. And you can't get away from it because Ellington don't just run the mill, they own our houses, the water we drink and the dirt on our shoes and pretty much the state of New Mexico as I understand it. So if something is breathing, it's on one side or the other. And in a town like this that matters because everybody you know some way, you go to the same church or they used to babysit your kids, something. Nobody is a stranger.

My sister went down to Las Cruces New Mexico and got a job down there, but me, no. I stayed here and got married to Junior Morales. Junior was my one big mistake. But I like Bolton. From far away Bolton looks like some kind of all-colored junk that got swept up off the street after a big old party and stuffed down in the canyon. Our houses are all exactly alike, company houses, but people paint them yellow, purple, colors you wouldn't think a house could be. If you go down to the Big Dipper and come walking home loca you still know which one is yours. The copper mine is at the top of the canyon and the streets run straight uphill; some of them you can't drive up, you got to walk. There's steps. Oliver P. Snapp, that used to be the mailman for the west side, died of a heart attack right out there in his blue shorts. So the new mailman refuses to deliver to those houses; they have to pick up their mail at the P.O.

... [T]his was around the fourth or fifth week so everybody knew by then who was striking and who was crossing. It don't take long to tell rats from cheese, and every night there was a big fight in the Big Dipper. Somebody punching out his brother or his best friend. All that and no paycheck, can you imagine?

So it was Saturday and there was just me and Corvallis Smith up at the picket line, setting in front of the picket shack passing the time of day. Corvallis is un tipo, he is real tall and lifts weights and wears his hair in those corn rows that hang down in the back with little pieces of aluminum foil on the ends. But good-looking in a certain way. I went out with Corvallis one time just so people would have something to talk about, and sure enough, they had me getting ready to have brown and black polka dotted babies. All you got to do to get pregnant around here is have two beers with somebody in the Dipper, so watch out.

"What do you hear from Junior," he says. That's a joke; everybody says it including my friends. See, when Manuela wasn't hardly even born one minute and Tony still in diapers, Junior says, "Vicki, I can't find a corner to piss in around this town." He said there was jobs in Tucson and he would send a whole lot of money. Ha ha. That's how I got started up at Ellington. I was not going to support my kids in no little short skirt down at the Frosty King. That was eight years ago. I got started on the track gang, laying down rails for the cars that go into the pit, and now I am a crane operator. See, when Junior left I went up the hill and made such a ruckus they had to hire me up there, hire me or shoot me, one.

"Oh, I hear from him about the same as I hear from Oliver P. Snapp," I say to Corvallis. That's the rest of the joke.

It was a real slow morning. Cecil Smott was supposed to be on the picket shift with us but he wasn't there yet. Cecil will show up late when the Angel Gabriel calls the judgment, saying he had to give his Datsun a lube job.

"Well, looka here," says Corvallis. "Here comes the ladies." There is this club called Wives of Working Men, just started since the strike. Meaning Wives of Scabs. About six of them was coming up the hill all cram-packed into Vonda Fagham's daddy's air-conditioned Lincoln. She pulls the car right up next to where mine is at. My car is a Buick older than both my kids put together. It gets me where I have to go.

They set and look at us for one or two minutes. Out in that hot sun, sticking to our t-shirts, and me in my work boots—I can't see no point in treating it like a damn tea party—and Corvallis, he's an eyeful anyway. All of a sudden the windows on the Lincoln all slide down. It has those electric windows.

"Isn't this a ni-i-ice day," Says one of them, Doreen Carter. Doreen visited her sister in Laurel, Mississippi, for three weeks one time and now she has an accent. "Bein' payday an' all," she says. Her husband is the minister of Saint's Grace, which is scab headquarters....

"Well, yes, it is a real nice day," another one of them says. They're all fanning themselves with something paper. I look, and Corvallis looks. They're fanning theirselves with their husbands' paychecks.

I haven't had a paycheck since July. My son couldn't go to Morse with his basketball team Friday night because they had to have three dollars for supper at McDonald's. Three damn dollars.

The windows start to go back up and they're getting ready to drive off, and I say, "Vonda Fagham, vete al inferno."

The windows whoosh back down.

"What did you say?" Vonda wants to know.

"I said, I'm surprised to see you in there with the scab ladies. I didn't know you had went and got married to a yellow-spine scab just so somebody would let you in their club."

Well, Corvallis laughs at that. But Vonda just gives me this look. She has a little sharp nose and yellow hair and teeth too big to fit behind her lips. For some reason she was a big deal in high school, and it's not her personality either. She was the queen of everything. Cheerleaders, drama club, every school play they ever had, I think.

I stare at her right back, ready to make a day of it if I have to. The heat is rising up off that big blue hood like it's a lake all set to boil over.

"What I said was Vonda Fagham, you can go to hell."

"I can't hear a word you're saying," she says. "Trash can't talk."

"This trash can go to bed at night and know I haven't cheated nobody out of a living. You want to see trash, chica, you ought to come up here at the shift change and see what kind of shit rolls over that picket line."

Well, that shit I was talking about was their husbands, so up go the windows and off they fly. Vonda just about goes in the ditch trying to get that big car turned around.

. . .

That same day I came home and found Manuela and Tony in the closet. Like poor little kitties setting in there on the shoes. Tony was okay pretty much but Manuela was crying, screaming. I thought she would dig her eyes out.

Tony kept going, "they were up here looking for you!"

"Who was?" I asked him.

"Scab men," he said. "Clifford Owens and Mr. Alphonso and them police from out of town. The ones with the guns."

"The State Police?" I said. I couldn't believe it. "The State Police was up here? What did they want?"

"They wanted to know where you was at." Tony almost started to cry. "Mama, I didn't tell them."

"He didn't," Manuela said.

"Well, I was just up at the damn picket shack. Anybody could have found me if they wanted to." I could have swore I saw Owens's car go right by the picket shack, anyway.

"They kept on saying where was you at, and we didn't tell them. We said you hadn't done nothing."

"I haven't done nothing. Why didn't you go over to Uncle Manny's? He's supposed to be watching you guys."

"We was scared to go outside!" Manuela screamed. She was jumping from one foot to the other and hugging herself. "They said they'd get us!"

"Tony, did they say that? Did they threaten you?"

"They said stay away from the picket rallies," Tony said. "The one with the gun said he seen us and took all our pitchers. He said your mama's got too big a mouth for her own good."

At the last picket rally I was up on Lalo Ruiz's shoulders with a bull horn. I've had almost every office in my local, and sergeant-at-arms twice because the guys say I have no toleration for BS. They got one of those big old trophies down at the union hall that says on it "men of copper," and one time Lalo says, "Vicki ain't no Man of Copper, she's a damn stick of mesquite. She might break but she sure as hell won't bend."

Well, I want my kids to know what this is about. When school starts, if some kid makes fun of their last-year's blue jeans and calls them trash I want them to hold their heads up. I take them to picket rallies so they'll know that. No law says you can't set up on nobody with a bull horn. They might have took my picture, though. I wouldn't be surprised.

"All I ever done was defend my union," I told the kids. "Even cops have to follow the laws, and it isn't no crime to defend your union. Your grandpapa done it and his papa and now me."

Well, my grandpapa one time got put on a railroad car like a cow, for being a Wobbly and a Mexican. My kids have heard that story a million times. He got dumped out in the desert someplace with no water or even a cloth for his head, and it took him two months to get back. All that time my granny and Tía Sonia thought he was dead.

I hugged Tony and Manuela and then we went and locked the door. I had to pull up on it while they jimmied the latch because that damn door had not been locked one time in seven years.

————————

Barbara Kingsolver received the National Humanities Medal, the nation's highest honor for service through the arts, in 2000. She began her career as a science writer and free lance journalist. Her nonfiction work, Holding the Line: Women and the Great Arizona Mine Strike of 1983, is about the 18-month strike at the Phelps Dodge Copper Mine in Arizona. The experiences of Vicki Morales, the narrator in Why I am a Danger to the Public, is similar to that of many of the women of Phelps Dodge Copper Mine in Holding the Line.

What does Vicki feel about the copper mine and the mining company? What is her relationship with other workers? Are workers better off negotiating with their employers one on one or is there a place for collective action? What can you see in this story about the relationship between workers and also about the intensity of the struggle between management and owners and workers over the terms and conditions of employment?

2. Expected and Reasonable Reliance: Action or Forbearance by the Promisee or a Third Person

Section 90 says that a promise may be enforced if it is one that "the promisor should reasonably expect to induce action or forbearance on the part the promisee or a third person and which does induce such action or forbearance …" Some courts reformulate this element to require that the reliance be "reasonable" or "justified." The next two cases explore this requirement.

Carlisle v. T & R Excavating, Inc.

Court of Appeals of Ohio
704 N.E.2d 39 (Ohio App. 1997)

CLAIR DICKINSON, PRESIDING JUDGE.

Defendant T & R Excavating Inc. has appealed from a judgment of the Medina County Common Pleas Court that awarded $35,790.75 in damages for breach of contract to plaintiffs Janis Carlisle, Wishing Well Preschool Inc., and Janis Carlisle, trustee, The Enrichment Center of Wishing Well, Inc. Defendant has argued that the trial court incorrectly found that there was a contract between the parties because their agreement lacked sufficient consideration and definiteness. This court reverses the judgment of the trial court because there was no consideration for the agreement between the parties and, therefore, no contract existed.

I

Defendant T & R Excavating, Inc. is solely owned and operated by Thomas Carlisle. Plaintiff Janis Carlisle is the owner and director of Wishing Well, Inc. and trustee of The Enrichment Center of Wishing Well, Inc., both of which were also plaintiffs in this action.

Ms. Carlisle and Mr. Carlisle married in 1988.

During 1992, Ms. Carlisle decided to build a preschool and kindergarten facility. Mr. Carlisle helped her find a location for the preschool, and she purchased the land they selected. Following this, he helped her choose a general contractor for the construction of the preschool.

On September 25, 1992, T & R presented a "Proposal" to Ms. Carlisle in which it proposed the following:

> We hereby propose to do all of the excavation and site work at the above new Location. The total amount budgeted for this portion of the new building is $69,800.00. All labor, equipment costs, overhead and profit, necessary for the completion of this project, totaling $40,000.00 will be provided at no cost to Wishing Well Preschool, Inc. The $29,800.00 allotted for materials will be billed to Wishing Well Preschool, Inc. at T & R Excavating's cost.

On that same date, Ms. Carlisle signed an "Acceptance of Proposal," which was printed at the bottom of the "Proposal":

> The above prices, specifications and conditions are satisfactory and are hereby accepted. You are authorized to do the work as specified. Payment will be made as outlined above.

. . .

On February 1, 1993, the general contractor prepared and presented to Mr. Carlisle a standardized American Institute of Architects document, signed by Ms. Carlisle, entitled "Abbreviated Form of Agreement Between Owner and Contractor." Some information specific to the preschool project was typed into the appropriate blank areas of the document, and the last several pages of the agreement consisted of printed contract language. The typed-in information included a description of the site work to be done, an estimate of $29,325.00 for materials, a plan for how payment was to be made, a start date of February 1, 1993, and a completion date of June 25, 1993. Also typed in were the following statements:

> This contract is for material only. There is no charge for labor and equipment.

> The contract sum will be adjusted at the completion of this work to reflect the actual cost of materials installed.

Mr. Carlisle never signed the document.

Sometime during early 1993, T & R began performing excavation and site work for the preschool. [Mr. and Ms. Carlisle] separated during March 1993, and T & R continued working on the project until it abandoned it in late May or early June 1993. By that time, Wishing Well Inc. had paid approximately $35,000 for materials used by T & R for excavation and site work. Ms. Carlisle hired other workers to finish the excavation and site work. The preschool opened for business on August 28, 1993.... Ms. Carlisle, individually and as trustee of The Enrichment Center, and Wishing Well Preschool sued T & R for breach of contract. They requested damages equal to the amount it cost to have others finish the excavation and site work ... The trial court found that there was a contract for the excavation and site work and awarded plaintiffs $35,790.75 in damages for the cost of hiring others to finish that work after T & R left the project.... T & R timely appealed to this court.

II

T & R's sole assignment of error is that the trial court incorrectly found that there was a contract between the parties, because their agreement lacked sufficient consideration and definiteness. It has asserted that its offer to do the excavation and site work for the preschool was in the nature of a gift or a favor, and was not supported by any legally sufficient consideration....

Whether there is consideration at all ... is a proper question for a court. *Irving Leasing Corp. v. M & H Tire Co.* 475 N.E.2d 127, 129–130 (Ohio 1984). Gratuitous promises are not enforceable as contracts, because there is no consideration. Restatement of Contracts, supra, 172–174, Section 71, Comments a and b. *See, also, Murphey, Young & Smith Co., L.P.A. v. Billman* (Nov. 20, 1984). A written gratuitous promise, even if it evidences an intent by the promisor to be bound, is not a contract. 2 Corbin, Contracts (Rev.1995) 20, Section 5.3. Likewise, conditional gratuitous promises, which require the promisee to do something before the promised act or omission will take place, are not enforceable as contracts. Restatement of Contracts, supra, 174, Section 71, Comment c. While it is true, therefore, that courts generally do not inquire into the adequacy of consideration once it is found to exist, it must be determined in a contract case whether any "consideration" was really bargained for. If it was not bargained for, it could not support a contract.

There is no evidence in the record of any benefit accruing to T & R or any detriment suffered by Ms. Carlisle due to their agreement that could constitute consideration for a contract. Statements made during trial regarding the parties' agreement failed to show that there was consideration for T & R's promise. Mr. Carlisle testified that he wanted to help Ms. Carlisle with the preschool and that they both agreed the preschool would be a good retirement benefit for them. The trial judge, at one point, stated his opinion that Mr. Carlisle made his promise because he was "a nice guy and wanted to help [Ms. Carlisle] out," that the consideration for his promise was the "relationship," and that they both hoped to benefit from the preschool.

A desire to help cannot be consideration for a contract; rather, it is merely a motive. See Williston, Contracts, *supra*, 336–338, Section 7:17. Further, the possibility of sharing in the income from a spouse's business, which would be marital income, cannot be consideration for a contract because one is already entitled to share in marital income. *See, e.g., Schneider v. Schneider* 674 N.E.2d 769, 772–773 (Ohio 1996). No bargaining is necessary to obtain that which one already has. The decision to build the preschool to provide income later was more in the nature of a joint effort by Mr. Carlisle and Ms. Carlisle to obtain a single benefit together, than a bargained-for exchange. Finally, the relationship between Mr. Carlisle and Ms. Carlisle could not have been consideration for a contract. *See* Restatement of Contracts, *supra*, 173, Section 71, Comment a. *See also*, Corbin, Contracts, *supra*, 90, Section 5.18.

Nor did Ms. Carlisle's testimony about her understanding of the parties' agreement demonstrate that there was consideration for a contract. Ms. Carlisle testified at trial that she understood the agreement to consist of T & R's promise to do excavation and site work for no charge, and her promise to "pay [T & R] back for the supplies." The promise of reimbursement for out-of-pocket costs, standing alone, was not a benefit or detriment supporting a contract. Money changed hands, but the reimbursement was not a bargained-for benefit to the promisor or detriment to the promisee. No reasonable interpretation of Ms. Carlisle's testimony could support a conclusion that T & R promised to provide the free services in order to induce her to promise to reimburse it for materials only. Rather, the testimony suggested that there was a gratuitous promise by T & R to provide free services on the condition that Ms. Carlisle agree to reimburse it for the cost of materials that would be used in providing those services.

. . .

The only way Ms. Carlisle could have properly recovered the value of the services, therefore, is if she had ... proved, under a theory of promissory estoppel, that she had reasonably relied to her detriment on T & R's promise. *See Thatcher v. Goodwill Indus. of Akron*, 690 N.E.2d 1320, 1329–1330 (Ohio App. 1997). *See also*, Restatement of Contracts, supra, 242, Section 90, Comment a.... [Yet] the only evidence presented at trial suggesting reliance on the part of Ms. Carlisle was the following exchange during direct testimony:

Q   Did you, in securing financing, in part rely upon the proposal marked, the agreement marked Plaintiff's Exhibit 6?

A   This was requested by Huntington Bank. The banker I worked with, Doug Whitken, in trying to get the loans, saw this was collateral, and asked this be written into a contract to be used as collateral.

Q   Did you proceed in this project relying in part on this agreement with T & R Excavating?

A   Absolutely.

Q   Did T & R pull off the job before it had completed all the site work it was to do?

A   Yes.

Q.   Did your construction engineer have to go out and see other people to finish up the job?

A   Yes, he did.

Q   And were they paid?

A   Yes, they were paid.

Q   As a result of T & R pulling off the job, did this cause you any kind of a delay?

A   Yes, it did.

Following this, Ms. Carlisle testified about the various costs incurred as a result of delays she attributed to the failure of T & R to complete the work as originally planned.

The trial court found that Ms. Carlisle failed to prove that the delay in opening the preschool was attributable to T & R, and no other possible detriment other than delay-related expenses was suggested by Ms. Carlisle at trial. The fact that she may have relied on T & R's promise, as she testified, therefore, was not sufficient to recover under promissory estoppel, since she did not prove that the reliance was detrimental. *See Thatcher v. Goodwill Indus. of Akron, supra.* Simply paying other workers to finish the job does not establish detrimental reliance, even if she was forced to pay much more than she would have had to pay if T & R had finished it. Such payment merely left her in the position she would have been in had T & R never made its promise, assuming she would have built the preschool even without that promise. See Restatement of Contracts, *supra,* 246–247, Section 90, Comment f. *See also, e.g., Condon v. Body, Vickers & Daniels* 649 N.E.2d 1259, 1264–1265 (Ohio 1994). Nowhere in the record is there a suggestion that she would not have built the preschool, or built it as she did, without relying on the promise of free services by T & R. Moreover, the preschool cost approximately $800,000 to build, and T & R's fulfilled promise would have saved Ms. Carlisle only about $35,000, according to the trial court's decision and award. This amount is less than five percent of the building cost. There is, therefore, no argument, no evidence, and no basis for inferring that Ms. Carlisle relied to her detriment on T & R's promise.

Ms. Carlisle failed to establish that there was consideration for T & R's promise to do free excavation and site work for the preschool, or that she relied to her detriment on the promise. The promise, therefore, was not legally enforceable. *See Brads v. First Baptist Church of Germantown, Ohio and Thatcher v. Goodwill Indus. of Akron, supra.* T & R's assignment of error is sustained.

The judgment of the trial court is reversed.

Jo Laverne Alden v. Elvis Presley

Supreme Court of Tennessee
637 S.W.2d 862 (1982)

WILLIAM H.D. FONES, JUSTICE

This is an action against the estate of Elvis Presley to enforce a gratuitous promise to pay off the mortgage on plaintiff's home made by decedent but not consummated prior to his death.

The trial court denied recovery but the Court of Appeals found that plaintiff had relied upon the promise to her detriment and awarded plaintiff judgment on the theory of promissory estoppel.

Elvis Presley, 1956 Upi/Bettman.

I.

Plaintiff alleged that she relied to her detriment on a promise made by the decedent to pay off the mortgage indebtedness on plaintiff's home. Defendant did not deny a promise was made by decedent but contended that plaintiff's continued reliance upon that promise following decedent's death constituted an unreasonable and unjustified action on her part, and furthermore, that any damage done to plaintiff occurred as a result of affirmative action taken by her despite her knowledge of decedent's death and with full knowledge that decedent's executor had denied legal liability to fulfill the promise.

Plaintiff, Jo Laverne Alden, is the mother of Ginger Alden, the former girlfriend of the late Elvis Presley. Presley was a singer of great renown throughout the world and a man of substantial wealth. In January of 1977, Presley became engaged to Ginger Alden. He was quite generous to several members of the Alden family including Ginger and her mother, the plaintiff. Gifts to plaintiff included the funds for landscaping the lawn and installing a swimming pool for the Alden home. Due to his close relationship with plaintiff's daughter, Presley also became aware of plaintiff's desire to obtain a divorce from her husband. Presley offered to pay all expenses incurred in the divorce proceeding, including furnishing plaintiff an attorney; to advance plaintiff money to purchase her husband's equity in the Alden home; and to pay off the remaining mortgage indebtedness on the Alden home.

As a result of these promises, plaintiff filed for divorce on the grounds of irreconcilable differences. On August 1, 1977, a property settlement agreement was executed in which plaintiff paid her husband $5,325.00 for his equity in return for a deed conveying all of his interest in the home to plaintiff plus a release of the husband from all further liability upon the mortgage indebtedness on the Alden home. The mortgage indebtedness at the time of the execution of the settlement agreement was in the sum of $39,587.66, and it is this amount which is the subject of the present suit, all the other gifts and promises to plaintiff having been fulfilled. On August 16, 1977, Presley died suddenly leaving unpaid the mortgage indebtedness on the Alden home. On August 25, 1977, Drayton Beecher Smith, II, an attorney for the Presley estate, informed plaintiff that the estate would not assume liability for the mortgage indebtedness.

Plaintiff filed the present suit on February 14, 1978, to enforce the promise made by decedent to pay the home mortgage. On March 3, 1978, Smith informed plaintiff he could no longer represent her in the divorce action since he was serving as an attorney for decedent's estate. Plaintiff failed to employ new counsel and the divorce action was dismissed for failure to prosecute.

Plaintiff re-filed her divorce action in April, 1978, upon the same grounds and sought approval of the property settlement agreement executed in August, 1977, in conjunction with the original divorce suit. The divorce was granted in April, 1980, on the grounds of irreconcilable differences, and the property settlement was approved by the court. Plaintiff did not disclose to the court in the divorce case that decedent's estate had informed her it was not their intention to pay the mortgage on the Alden home

In the instant case, the trial court held that decedent did make a promise unsupported by consideration to plaintiff, that no gift was consummated for failure of delivery, that plaintiff and her husband suffered no detriment as she "wound up much better off after their association with Elvis A. Presley than either would have been if he had never made any promise to Jo Laverne Alden," and that plaintiff did not rely upon the promise since her divorce petition was filed subsequent to the present suit and subsequent to being told that decedent's estate would not accept legal responsibility for decedent's promise.

The Court of Appeals concurred in the trial court finding that there was no gift for failure of delivery, holding that delivery is not complete unless "complete dominion and control of the gift is surrendered by the donor and acquired by the donee," citing Pamplin v. Satterfield, 196 Tenn. 297, 265 S.W.2d 886 (1954); Brown v. Vinson, 188 Tenn. 120, 216 S.W.2d 748 (1949).

However, the Court of Appeals reversed the remainder of the trial court's decision by adopting and applying the doctrine of promissory estoppel holding that plaintiff had foregone remedies available to her in the divorce petition in reliance upon the promise made to her by decedent. The Court of Appeals reasoned the estate should be estopped from dishonoring that promise.

We concur in the reasoning of the trial court and Court of Appeals' findings that decedent did not make a gift of the money necessary to pay off the mortgage as there was no actual or constructive delivery. We find it unnecessary to address the question of whether or not Tennessee recognizes the doctrine of promissory estoppel because plaintiff has failed, as a matter of law, to prove essential elements of promissory estoppel, to-wit: detrimental reliance, and a loss suffered as a result of detrimental reliance.

II.

The Court of Appeals relied upon definitions of promissory estoppel found in the Restatement of Contracts and L. Simpson's, Law of Contracts. Since these works present representative definitions of promissory estoppel we quote with approval from the Court of Appeals' opinion as follows:

A concise statement concerning promissory estoppel is found in Restatement of Contracts, section 90, as follows:

A promise which the promisor should reasonably expect to induce action or forbearance of a definite and substantial character on the part of the promisee and which does induce such action or forbearance is binding if injustice can be avoided only by enforcement of the promise.

A more thorough examination of the doctrine, its elements and limitations is set forth in L. Simpson, Law of Contracts §61 (2d ed. 1965); to-wit:

Detrimental action or forbearance by the promisee in reliance on a gratuitous promise, within limits, constitutes a substitute for consideration, or a sufficient reason for enforcement of the promise without consideration. This doctrine is known as promissory estoppel. A promisor who induces substantial change of position by the promisee in reliance on the promise is estopped to deny its enforceability as lacking consideration. The reason for the doctrine is to avoid an unjust result, and its reason defines its limits. No injustice results in refusal to enforce a gratuitous promise where the loss suffered in reliance is negligible, nor where the promisee's action in reliance was unreasonable or unjustified by the promise. The limits of promissory estoppel are: (1) the detriment suffered in reliance must be substantial in an economic sense; (2) the substantial loss to the promisee in acting in reliance must have been foreseeable by the promisor; (3) the promisee must have acted reasonably in justifiable reliance on the promise as made.

III.

It is well established in this State that settlement agreements between husband and wife that purport to settle the legal obligations of alimony and child support, over which the Court has initial and continuing statutory authority to determine, are not binding until approved by the Court. See, e.g., Blackburn v. Blackburn, 526 S.W.2d 463 (Tenn. 1975); Penland v. Penland, 521 S.W.2d 222 (Tenn. 1975); Doty v. Doty, 260 S.W.2d 411 (Tenn. App. 1952); and Osborne v. Osborne, 197 S.W.2d 234 (Tenn. App. 1946). The terms of such agreements, "are merely evidential in value and may be followed by the court in its award of alimony—they should be given great consideration but are subject to close scrutiny by the court." 197 S.W.2d at 236.

The property settlement agreement that the Aldens entered into expressly provided that it was "subject to Court approval."

IV.

The residence of the Aldens and the mortgage indebtedness thereon was obviously subject to such disposition as alimony, as the circumstances of the parties justified at the time that the divorce was granted, April 1980.

Mrs. Alden did not inform the court that the estate had denied legal responsibility for the mortgage indebtedness, after she had entered into the property settlement agreement, but instead, affirmatively sought approval of the property settlement agreement. Beyond question, she was entitled to relief from that portion of the property settlement agreement wherein she assumed the mortgage indebtedness, upon revealing to the divorce court that she agreed to assume the mortgage only because decedent promised to pay it off gratuitously, but that the estate denied liability subsequent to the execution of the property settlement agreement. She was represented by counsel and must be charged with the knowledge that those facts constituted a change of circumstances that, as a matter of law, entitled her to relief from that portion of the agreement.

In this action plaintiff has shown that decedent's promise induced her to assume a $39,587 mortgage as part of a property settlement agreement dated August 1, 1977. However, the property settlement agreement was not binding upon plaintiff or her husband until approved by the court and the estate's denial of liability for decedent's gratuitous promise before submission of the agreement to the Court removed the element of detrimental reliance from the factual scenario of this case. It follows, plaintiff's reliance on the promise after August 25, 1977, was not reasonably justified and she suffered no loss as a result of justifiable reliance.

The judgment of the Court of Appeals is reversed and this case is dismissed.

Elvis Presley and Vera Matson, Love Me Tender

(1956)

Love me tender, love me sweet, never let me go.
You have made my life complete and I love you so.
Love me tender, love me true, all my dreams fulfill.
For, my darlin', I love you and I always will.
Love me tender, love me long, take me to your heart.
For its there that I belong and we'll never part.
Love me tender, love me true, all my dreams fulfill.
For, my darlin', I love you and I always will.
Love me tender, love me dear, tell me you are mine.
I'll be yours through all the years till the end of time
Love me tender, love me true, all my dreams fulfill.
For, my darlin', I love you and I always will.

B. Promises Made in Recognition of a Past Benefit

Under the consideration doctrine, something that happened (i.e., a promise or performance) before a promise is made cannot be consideration for that promise because, by definition, it is not "bargained for"—the promise was not made in order to induce the promisee to do something. The decision in *Mills v. Wyman*, below, applies this rule and refuses to enforce Wyman's promise to repay Mills for the expenses Mills had incurred in caring for Wyman's son, even though the promise was clearly proved, cautiously and seriously made, and surely one that most people would consider binding. Is this a good result?

Some courts and commentators, believing that promises like Mr. Wyman's should be enforced, have reasserted a second major alternative to consideration: a gratuitous promise may be enforced if it was given in recognition of a benefit that the promisee conferred on the promisor at some time in the past. *Webb v. McGowin*, below, is a leading modern case articulating this alternative. The doctrine was embraced in Restatement (Second) of Contracts section 86, published in 1981. This basis for enforcing a promise is not as frequently used in contemporary law as promissory estoppel, but its rationale is so compelling that many predict it will become an important part of contract law in the future: "By the time we get to Restatement (Third) it may well be that § [86] will have flowered like Jack's beanstalk in the same way that § 90 did between Restatement (First) and Restatement (Second)." Grant Gilmore, The Death of Contract 76 (1973).

In the next section, we look at the so-called "moral consideration" doctrine, an older, firmly established, version of this general idea that continues to be an important part of contemporary contract law.

---

1. The "Moral Obligation Doctrine"

Mills v. Wyman

Supreme Judicial Court of Massachusetts
3 Pick. [20 Mass.] 207 (1825)

This was an action of assumpsit brought to recover a compensation for the board, nursing, & c., of Levi Wyman, son of the defendant, from the 5th to the 20th of February 1821. The plaintiff then lived at Hartford, in Connecticut; the defendant, at Shrewsbury, in this county. Levi Wyman, at the time when the services were rendered, was about 25 years of age, and had long ceased to be a member of his father's family. He was on his return from a voyage at sea, and being suddenly taken sick at Hartford, and being poor and in distress, was relieved by the plaintiff in the manner and to the extent above stated. On the 24th of February, after all the expenses had been incurred, the defendant wrote a letter to the plaintiff, promising to pay him such expenses. There was no consideration for this promise, except what grew out of the relation which subsisted between Levi Wyman and the defendant, and Howe, J., before whom the cause was tried in the court of common pleas, thinking this not sufficient to support the action, directed a nonsuit. To this direction the plaintiff filed exceptions.

...

Isaac Parker, Chief Justice

General rules of law established for the protection and security of honest and fair-minded men, who may inconsiderately make promises without any equivalent, will sometimes screen men of a different character from engagements which they are bound in foro conscientiae to perform. This is a defect inherent in all human systems of legislation.

The rule that a mere verbal promise, without any consideration, cannot be enforced by action, is universal in its application, and cannot be departed from to suit particular cases in which a refusal to perform such a promise may be disgraceful.

The promise declared on in this case appears to have been made without any legal consideration. The kindness and services towards the sick son of the defendant were not bestowed at his request. The son was in no respect under the care of the defendant. He was twenty-five years old, and had long left his father's family. On his return from a foreign country, he fell sick among strangers, and the plaintiff acted the part of the good Samaritan, giving him shelter and comfort until he died. The defendant, his father, on being informed of this event, influenced by a transient feeling of gratitude, promises in writing to pay the plaintiff for the expenses he had incurred. But he has determined to break this promise, and is willing to have his case appear on record as a strong example of particular injustice sometimes necessarily resulting from the operation of general rules.

It is said a moral obligation is a sufficient consideration to support an express promise; and some authorities lay down the rule thus broadly; but upon examination of the cases we are satisfied that the universality of the rule cannot be supported, and that there must have been some preexisting obligation, which has become inoperative by positive law, to form a basis for an effective promise. The cases of debts barred by the statute of limitations, of debts incurred by infants, of debts of bankrupts, are generally put for illustration of the rule. Express promises founded on such preexisting equitable obligations may be enforced; there is a good consideration for them; they merely remove an impediment created by law to the recovery of debts honestly due, but which public policy protects the debtors from being compelled to pay. In all these cases there was originally a quid pro quo; and according to the principles of natural justice the party receiving ought to pay; but the legislature has said he shall not be coerced; then comes the promise to pay the debt that is barred, the promise of the man to pay the debt of the infant, of the discharged bankrupt to restore his creditor what by law he had lost. In all these cases there is a moral obligation founded upon an antecedent valuable consideration. These promises therefore have a sound legal basis. They are not promises to pay something for nothing; not naked pacts; but the voluntary revival or creation of obligation which before existed in natural law, but which had been dispensed with, not for the benefit of the party obliged solely, but principally for the public convenience. If moral obligation, in its fullest sense, is a good substratum for an express promise, it is not easy to perceive why it is not equally good to support an implied promise. What a man ought to do, generally he ought to be made to do, whether he promise or refuse. But the law of society has left most of such obligations to the interior forum, as the tribunal of conscience has been aptly called. Is there not a moral obligation upon every son who has become affluent by means of the education and advantages bestowed upon him by his father, to relieve the father from pecuniary embarrassment, to promote his comfort and happiness, and even to share with him his riches, if thereby he will be made happy? And yet such a son may, with impunity, leave such a father in any degree of penury above that which will expose the community in which he dwells, to the danger of being obliged to preserve him from absolute want. Is not a wealthy father under strong moral obligation to advance the interest of an obedient, well disposed son, to furnish him with the means of acquiring and maintaining a becoming rank in life, to rescue him from the horrors of debt incurred by misfortune? Yet the law will uphold him in any degree of parsimony, short of that which would reduce his son to the necessity of seeking public charity.

Without doubt there are great interests of society which justify withholding the coercive arm of the law from these duties of imperfect obligation, as they are called; imperfect, not because they are less binding upon the conscience than those which are called perfect, but because the wisdom of the social law does not impose sanctions upon them.

A deliberate promise, in writing, made freely and without any mistake, one which may lead the party to whom it is made into contracts and expenses, cannot be broken without a violation of moral duty. But if there was nothing paid or promised for it, the law, perhaps wisely, leaves the execution of it to the conscience of him who make it. It is only when the party making the promise gains something, or he to whom it is made loses something, that the law gives the promise validity. And in the case of the promise of the adult to pay the debt of the infant, of the debtor discharged by the statute of limitations or bankruptcy, the principle is preserved by looking back to the origin of the transaction, where an equivalent is to be found. An exact equivalent is not required by the law; for there being a consideration, the parties are left to estimate its value: though here the courts of equity will step in to relieve from gross inadequacy between the consideration and the promise.

These principles are deduced from the general current of decided cases upon the subject as well as from the known maxims of the common law. The general position, the moral obligation is a sufficient consideration for an express promise, is to be limited in its application, to cases where at some time or other a good or valuable consideration has existed.

A legal obligation is always a sufficient consideration to support either an express or an implied promise; such as an infant's debt for necessaries, or a father's promise to pay for the support and education of his minor children. But when the child shall have attained to manhood, and shall have become his own agent in the world's business, the debts he incurs, whatever may be their nature, create no obligation upon the father; and it seems to follow, that his promise founded upon such a debt has no legally binding force.

The cases of instruments under seal and certain mercantile contracts, in which considerations need not be proved, do not contradict the principles above suggested. The first import a consideration in themselves, and the second belong to a branch of the mercantile law, which has found it necessary to disregard the point of consideration in respect to instruments negotiable in their nature and essential to the interests of commerce.

Instead of citing a multiplicity of cases to support the positions I have taken, I will only refer to a very able review of all the cases in the note in 3 Bos. & P. 249. The opinions of the judges had been variant for a long course of years upon this subject, but there seems to be no case in which it was nakedly decided, that a promise to pay the debt of a son of full age, not living with his father, though the debt were incurred by sickness which ended in the death of the son, without a previous request by the father proved or presumed, could be enforced by action.

It has been attempted to show a legal obligation on the part of the defendant by virtue of our statute, which compels lineal kindred in the ascending or descending line to support such of their poor relations as are likely to become chargeable to the town where they have their settlement. But it is a sufficient answer to this position, that such legal obligation does not exist except in the very cases provided for in the statute, and never until the party charged has been adjudged to be of sufficient ability thereto. We do not know from the report any of the facts which are necessary to create such an obligation. Whether the deceased had a legal settlement in this commonwealth at the time of his death, whether he was likely to become chargeable had he lived, whether the defendant was of sufficient ability, are essential facts to be adjudicated by the court to which is given jurisdiction on this subject. The legal liability does not arise until these facts have all been ascertained by judgment, after hearing the party intended to be charged.

For the foregoing reasons we are all of opinion that the nonsuit directed by the court of common pleas was right, and that judgment be entered thereon for costs for the defendant.

On the "Moral Consideration" Doctrine

Reread Chief Judge Parker's discussion of the traditional doctrine of "moral consideration" in *Mills v. Wyman*. The Chief Judge emphasizes that the notion of a "moral obligation" in this doctrine is very limited, encompassing only the obligation that arises when an enforceable debt becomes unenforceable because of a statute of limitations or other "technicality." Because of this "moral obligation," a new promise to pay a debt that the promisor owes because of a prior contract is deemed to be enforceable because of the fiction of "moral consideration."

A slightly expanded variation of the moral consideration doctrine applies when a person promises to pay a debt that the promisor owes because of a prior *restitutionary* obligation. Recall, for example, the case of *Cotnam v. Wisdom*, in Chapter Two, in which Dr. Wisdom gave emergency medical care to A. M. Harrison, who, having been thrown from a street car by the force of a crash, lay unconscious on a public street. In the actual case, Harrison died without regaining consciousness and the Arkansas Supreme Court held that Harrison's estate may be obligated to pay the doctor for the professional medical services under the law of restitution (also called "contracts implied-in-law" or "quasi-contracts"). What if, in that case, Harrison survived his injuries, and in gratitude, promised to pay Dr. Wisdom for his life-saving professional services?

In our imagined case, Harrison's promise to pay Dr. Wisdom would be enforceable under the "expanded" version of the moral consideration doctrine.

Would this version of "moral consideration" justify enforcement of Lee Walter Taylor's promise in the following case? Did Taylor have an obligation to pay Harrington under the law of Restitution or Unjust Enrichment?

Lena Harrington v. Lee Walter Taylor

Supreme Court of North Carolina
225 N.C. 690, 36 S.E.2d 227 (1945)

PER CURIAM

The plaintiff in this case sought to recover of the defendant upon a promise made by him under the following peculiar circumstances:

The defendant had assaulted his wife, who took refuge in plaintiff's house. The next day the defendant gained access to the house and began another assault upon his wife. The defendant's wife knocked him down with an axe, and was on the point of cutting his head open or decapitating him while he was lying on the floor, and the plaintiff intervened, caught the axe as it was descending, and the blow intended for defendant fell upon her hand, mutilating it badly, but saving defendant's life.

Subsequently, defendant orally promised to pay the plaintiff her damages; but, after paying a small sum, failed to pay anything more. So, substantially, states the complaint.

The defendant demurred to the complaint as not stating a cause of action, and the demurrer was sustained. Plaintiff appealed.

The question presented is whether there was a consideration recognized by our law as sufficient to support the promise. The Court is of the opinion that, however much the defendant should be impelled by common gratitude to alleviate the plaintiff's misfortune, a humanitarian act of this kind, voluntarily performed, is not such consideration as would entitle her to recover at law.

The judgment sustaining the demurrer is affirmed.

Note on Harrington v. Taylor in Tort

After losing this action for breach of promise, Ms. Harrington sued Taylor in tort. The North Carolina Supreme Court affirmed dismissal of this action as well, in a brief opinion:

Harrington v. Taylor
Supreme Court of North Carolina
40 S.E.2d 367 (1946)

PER CURIAM

The action is against the defendant and not his wife who inflicted the injury. The plaintiff first sued on contract—defendant's promise to pay damages—reported in 225 N.C. 690, 36 S.E.2d 227. She now sues in tort.

The evidence is wanting in sufficiency to carry the case to the jury. The injury is not one which the defendant could have reasonably foreseen or anticipated. *Butner v. Spease*, 217 N.C. 82, 6 S.E.2d 808. The judgment of nonsuit will be upheld.

Affirmed.

The rule that a only professionals may recover for services rendered in an emergency is controversial, yet it continues to influence contemporary courts and it has been endorsed by the drafters of the Restatement (Third) of Restitution § 20 (Protection of Another's Life or Health):

> (1) A person who performs, supplies, or obtains professional services required for the protection of another's life or health is entitled to restitution from the other as necessary to prevent unjust enrichment, if the circumstances justify the decision to intervene without request.

...

The drafters explain:

> The present section authorizes a claim in respect of "professional services," whether the claim is asserted by the provider directly, by an institution or municipality that causes the services to be provided, or by a third party who pays for the services.... The word "professional" is used in a broad sense, to designate services that the provider is in the business of furnishing for money. An ambulance service that carries an unconscious patient to the hospital, acting in an emergency without an agreement for payment, has a claim by the rule of this section to its reasonable and customary charge. By contrast, the benefit conferred in an emergency by a nonprofessional rescuer does not create a liability in restitution on the part of the person rescued.

Restatement (Third) of Restitution § 20 Comment (a).

2. Promise Made in Recognition of a Past Benefit

Joe Webb v. Floyd McGowin

Court of Appeals of Alabama
168 So. 196 (Ala. 1935)

CHARLES RUSSELL BRICKEN, PRESIDING JUDGE

This action is in assumpsit. The complaint as originally filed was amended. The demurrers to the complaint as amended were sustained, and because of this adverse ruling by the court the plaintiff took a nonsuit, and the assignment of errors on this appeal are predicated upon said action or ruling of the court.

A fair statement of the case presenting the questions for decision is set out in appellant's brief, which we adopt.

On the 3d day of August 1925, appellant while in the employ of the W.T. Smith Lumber Company, a corporation, and acting within the scope of his employment, was engaged in clearing the upper floor of mill No. 2 of the company. While so engaged he was in the act of dropping a pine block from the upper floor of the mill to the ground below; this being the usual and ordinary way of clearing the floor, and it being the duty of the plaintiff in the course of his employment to so drop it. The block weighed about 75 pounds.

As appellant was in the act of dropping the block to the ground below, he was on the edge of the upper floor of the mill. As he started to turn the block loose so that it would drop to the ground, he saw J. Greeley McGowin, testator of the defendants, on the ground below and directly under where the block would have fallen had appellant turned it loose. Had he turned it loose it would have struck McGowin with such force as to have caused him serious bodily harm or death. Appellant could have remained safely on the upper floor of the mill by turning the block loose and allowing it to drop, but had he done this the block would have fallen on McGowin and caused him serious injuries or death. The only safe and reasonable way to prevent this was for appellant to hold to the block and divert its direction in falling from the place where McGowin was standing and the only safe way to divert it so as to prevent its coming into contact with McGowin was for appellant to fall with it to the ground below. Appellant did this, and by holding to the block and falling with it to the ground below, he diverted the course of its fall in such way that McGowin was not injured. In thus preventing the injuries to McGowin appellant himself received serious bodily injuries, resulting in his right leg being broken, the heel of his right foot torn off and his right arm broken. He was badly crippled for life and rendered unable to do physical or mental labor.

On September 1, 1925, in consideration of appellant having prevented him from sustaining death or serious bodily harm and in consideration of the injuries appellant had received, McGowin agreed with him to care for and maintain him for the remainder of appellant's life at the rate of $15 every two weeks from the time he sustained his injuries to and during the remainder of appellant's life; it being agreed that McGowin would pay this sum to appellant for his maintenance. Under the agreement McGowin paid or caused to be paid to appellant the sum so agreed on up until McGowin's death on January 1, 1934. After his death the payments were continued to and including January 27, 1934, at which time they were discontinued. Thereupon plaintiff brought suit to recover the unpaid installments accruing up to the time of the bringing of the suit.

1. The averments of the complaint show that appellant saved McGowin from death or grievous bodily harm. This was a material benefit to him of infinitely more value than any financial aid he could have received. Receiving this benefit, McGowin became morally bound to compensate appellant for the services rendered. Recognizing his moral obligation, he expressly agreed to pay appellant as alleged in the complaint and complied with this agreement up to the time of his death; a period of more than eight years.

Had McGowin been accidentally poisoned and a physician, without his knowledge or request, had administered an antidote, thus saving his life, a subsequent promise by McGowin to pay the physician would have been valid. Likewise, McGowin's agreement as disclosed by the complaint to compensate appellant for saving him from death or grievous bodily injury is valid and enforceable.

Where the promisee cares for, improves, and preserves the property of the promisor, though done without his request, it is sufficient consideration for the promisor's subsequent agreement to pay for the service, because of the material benefit received. *Pittsburg Vitrified Paving & Building Brick Co. v. Cerebus Oil Co.*, 100 P. 631 (Kan. 1909).

In *Boothe v. Fitzpatrick*, 36 Vt. 681 (1899), the court held that a promise by defendant to pay for the past keeping of a bull which had escaped from defendant's premises and been cared for by plaintiff was valid, although there was no previous request, because the subsequent promise obviated that objection; it being equivalent to a previous request. On the same principle, had the promise saved the promisor's life or his body from grievous harm, his subsequent promise to pay for the services rendered would have been valid. Such service would have been far more material than caring for his bull. Any holding that saving a man from death or grievous bodily harm is not a material benefit sufficient to uphold a subsequent promise to pay for the service, necessarily rests on the assumption that saving life and preservation of the body from harm have only a sentimental value. The converse of this is true. Life and preservation of the body have material, pecuniary values, measurable in dollars and cents. Because of this, physicians practice their profession charging for services rendered in saving life and curing the body of its ills, and surgeons perform operations. The same is true as to the law of negligence, authorizing the assessment of damages in personal injury cases based upon the extent of the injuries, earnings, and life expectancies of those injured.

In the business of life insurance, the value of a man's life is measured in dollars and cents according to his expectance, the soundness of his body, and his ability to pay premiums. The same is true as to health and accident insurance.

It follows that if, as alleged in the complaint, appellant saved J. Greeley McGowin from death or grievous bodily harm, and McGowin subsequently agreed to pay him for the service rendered, it became a valid and enforceable contract.

2. It is well settled that a moral obligation is a sufficient consideration to support a subsequent promise to pay where the promisor has received a material benefit, although there was no original duty or liability resting on the promisor. *Lycoming County v. Union County*, 53 Am. Dec. 575, 579, 580 (Pa. 1850). *Ferguson v. Harris*, 17 S.E. 782 (S.C. 1893); *Muir v. Kane*, 104 P. 153 (Wash. 1909); *State ex rel. Bayer v. Funk*; *Hawkes v. Saunders*, 1 Cowp. 290 (1902). In the case of *State ex rel. Bayer v. Funk*, 199 P. 592, 209 P. 113 (Ore. 1921), the court held that a moral obligation is a sufficient consideration to support an executory promise where the promisor has received an actual pecuniary or material benefit for which he subsequently expressly promised to pay.

The case at bar is clearly distinguishable from that class of cases where the consideration is a mere moral obligation or conscientious duty unconnected with receipt by promisor of benefits of a material or pecuniary nature. Here the promisor received a material benefit constituting a valid consideration for his promise.

3. Some authorities hold that, for a moral obligation to support a subsequent promise to pay, there must have existed a prior legal or equitable obligation, which for some reason had become unenforceable, but for which the promisor was still morally bound. This rule, however, is subject to qualification in those cases where the promisor, having received a material benefit from the promisee, is morally bound to compensate him for the services rendered and in consideration of this obligation promises to pay. In such cases the subsequent promise to pay is an affirmance or ratification of the services rendered carrying with it the presumption that a previous request for the service was made. *Chadwick v. Knox*, 31 N.H. 226; *Kenan v. Holloway*, 16 Ala. 53.

Under the decisions above cited, McGowin's express promise to pay appellant for the services rendered was an affirmance or ratification of what appellant had done raising the presumption that the services had been rendered at McGowin's request.

4. The averments of the complaint show that in saving McGowin from death or grievous bodily harm, appellant was crippled for life. This was part of the consideration of the contract declared on. McGowin was benefited. Appellant was injured. Benefit to the promisor or injury to the promisee is a sufficient legal consideration for the promisor's agreement to pay. *Fisher v. Bartlett*, 8 Greenl. (Me.) 122, 22 Am. Dec. 225; *State ex rel. Bayer v. Funk, supra.*

5. Under the averments of the complaint the services rendered by the appellant were not gratuitous. The agreement of McGowin to pay and the acceptance of payment by the appellant conclusively shows the contrary.

Note

The doctrine articulated in *Webb v. McGowin* is sometimes called the "material benefit" rule, because of the distinction between those moral or ethical obligations that arise because of family connection, our sense of justice, or the like, and the obligation that arises when one has received an actual material or pecuniary benefit from someone else.

The doctrine has also been called "promissory restitution" because of its focus on past benefit and because, in many cases, the promise can be seen as resolving any uncertainty about the appropriateness of recovery. We know, for example, that if McGowin had not made the promise to pay Webb for the remainder of his life, Webb, as a lay-rescuer, could not have recovered if he had filed an unjust enrichment claim against McGowin.

So why should McGowin's promise, made in gratitude for Webb's life-saving actions, but not given as part of an exchange, result in a different outcome for Webb's claim against McGowin? The Restatement (Second) of Contracts answers as follows:

> The law of restitution in the absence of promise severely limits recovery for necessaries furnished to a person under disability and for emergency services.... A subsequent promise in such a case may remove doubt as to the reality of the benefit and as to its value, and may negate any danger of imposition or false claim. A positive showing that payment was expected is not then required; an intention to make a gift must be shown to defeat restitution.

Restatement (Second) of Contracts, Section 86, Comment d.

We have concluded that if Webb had brought a claim against McGowin in restitution, for unjust enrichment, that claim would have been denied because Webb was a layperson and courts are uncertain as to the value of a layperson's care or intervention. But doesn't McGowin's promise to pay Webb supply convincing evidence that McGowin *himself* thought that Webb's intervention was valuable?

This is the notion of promissory restitution—that the promise resolves uncertainties that would arise in an unjust enrichment claim.

Do you agree with Grant Gilmore that the doctrine allowing enforcement of a promise made in recognition of a past benefit, will flower "like Jack's beanstalk?" *See* Grant Gilmore, The Death of Contract 76 (1973). Do you find the analysis and result in *Webb* more convincing than the analysis and result in *Mills v. Wyman*? The following case presents an alternative analysis of similar facts.

Robert M. Reece, Adm'r, C.T.A. of Estate of Ida M. Rhoads v. S. Earl Reece

Court of Appeals of Maryland
212 A2d 468 (Md. 1965)

WILSON K. BARNES, JUDGE

This is an appeal from a judgment entered by the Circuit Court for Garrett County in favor of S. Earl Reece, appellee (plaintiff below), in the amount of $34,200, for alleged personal services performed during the period 1930–1949 for appellant's decedent, Ida M. Rhoads. We are asked to reverse the judgment on the ground that there was no legally sufficient evidence upon which the appellee could recover....

The parties to this appeal are brothers, and both live in Westernport, in Allegany County. Ida M. Rhoads, was their aunt and also a resident of Westernport until her death on December 30, 1959. Upon her death the appellant, Robert M. Reece, probated a Last Will and Testament dated March 22, 1956 in the Orphans' Court for Allegany County and qualified as administrator *cum testamento annexo* of her estate. On August 5, 1960, four days before the administrator's notice to creditors was to expire, the appellee, S. Earl Reece, filed a claim against the estate in the amount of $53,500, a claim which the administrator rejected in writing on October 10, 1960. Earl then filed suit on April 7, 1961 in the Circuit Court for Allegany County; the case was later removed to Washington County, and then removed again to Garrett, where it was heard by the court without a jury on January 17, 1964.

Plaintiff claimed in his declaration that he had rendered personal services of substantial value to the Woodland Lumber Company, a corporation of which both he and Miss Rhoads were officers, directors, and stockholders, from 1930 until its dissolution in 1952, and that he had given advice to Miss Rhoads individually in connection with her business and personal affairs from 1930 until the date of her death in 1959. His cause of action is based upon two written documents, not under seal, both of which are dated December 2, 1949. Both are ... rough in appearance, and the typing on each, very poor.

...

The plaintiff's testimony does not reveal the nature of the services which he claims to have performed either for the lumber company or for Ida Mr. Rhoads individually. He did testify that he received 'not one cent' from the corporation during its entire existence, and that he had 'no salary arrangement whatever' with it. In reply to a question 'Why didn't you receive any money?', he stated 'Well, the Woodland Lumber Company, as it states right in those minutes, salaries were to be continued to Mr. Robinhold and Ida M. Rhoads ...'

...

A question presented by the defendant's motion to dismiss ... is whether the facts recited in the documents constitute sufficient legal consideration to support the promise of Miss Rhoads to pay for the past services of the plaintiff Reece. As we have indicated, the documents are not under seal. They were both dated December 2, 1949 and those documents indicate that the services for the Woodland Lumber Company and for Miss Rhoads ... had all been rendered prior to the signing by Miss Rhoads of the two documents. This is recited in both documents. The second document recites that he had not been paid for these services by either the company or Miss Rhoads. In the second document, Miss Rhoads promises to pay the plaintiff Reece for those services at the rate of $150.00 a month, without interest....

The general rule is that past consideration is insufficient to support a present promise. *Weil v. Free State Oil Company of Maryland*, 87 A.2d 826, 830 (Md. 1952). *See* 17 Am.Jur.2d Contracts, Section 125. *See also* 1 Williston, Contracts (3rd ed.), Section 142, where it is stated:

> Accordingly, something which has been given before the promise was made and, therefore, without reference to it, cannot, properly speaking, be legal consideration....

The doctrine that past consideration is no consideration represents the overwhelming weight of authority and is almost universally followed. This has been the law since early times.

There have been several exceptions, however, to this general principle of law. One of them is that a present promise to pay in consideration of an act previously done at the request of the promisor will be enforceable as supported by sufficient consideration even though that consideration consists of an act previously done. The request of the promisor may be either express or implied. Our predecessors, in *Pool v. Horner*, 20 A. 1036, 1038 (Md. 1885), quoted with approval from the notes to *Osbourne v. Rogers*, 1 Wm.Saund. 264b that it was a settled rule 'that a past consideration is not sufficient to support a subsequent promise, unless there was a request of the party express or implied, at the time of performing the consideration; ...' (emphasis supplied). As no express promise by Miss Rhoads at the beginning of the services in April 1930 is recited in either document, the question arises as to whether a request by Miss Rhoads to the plaintiff Reece to perform the services may be implied. We are of the opinion that such a request may be implied. The services rendered were of a business nature. In the second document Miss Rhoads states that the services were rendered 'for me at the office of the company I own' (emphasis supplied). She owned 685 shares of the entire 750 shares or in excess of 90% of the shares. She states that these services were "*rendered to me and the company for my financial and personal benefit.*" (emphasis supplied).

For these reasons, the judgment of the lower court will be affirmed.

Judgment affirmed, the appellant to pay the costs from the estate of Ida M. Rhoads

---

Note on Section 86 of the Restatement (Second) of Contracts

The drafters of the *Restatement (Second) of Contracts* incorporated the moral consideration doctrine and *Webb v. McGowin's* promissory restitution approach into a general rule in Section 86 (Promise for Benefit Received):

(1) A promise made in recognition of a benefit previously received by the promisor from the promisee is binding to the extent necessary to prevent injustice.

(2) A promise is not binding under Subsection (1)

(a) If the promisee conferred the benefit as a gift or for other reasons the promisor has not been unjustly enriched; or

(b) To the extent that its value is disproportionate to the benefit.

In Comment b), the drafters explained this Section:

> Rationale. Although in general a person who has been unjustly enriched at the expense of another is required to make restitution, restitution is denied in many cases in order to protect persons who have had benefits thrust upon them. [*For example, the rule against recovery for "volunteers."*] ... In other cases, restitution is denied by virtue of rules designed to guard against false claims, stale claims, claims already litigated, and the like. [*For example, the rule against recovery for lay-rescuers.*] In many such cases, a subsequent promise to make restitution removes the reason for the denial of relief, and the policy against unjust enrichment then prevails.... Enforcement of the subsequent promise sometimes makes it unnecessary to decide a difficult question as to the limits on quasi-contractual relief.

Restatement (Second) of Contracts, Section 86, Comment b (examples added).

C. Restitution — Non-Promissory Obligation Arising from Unjust Enrichment

As you will recall from Chapter Two, Restitution is a separate area of law, and, unlike Contract Law, it does not involve the enforcement of promises. Instead, liability in Restitution is based upon receipt of a benefit in circumstances in which it would be unjust not to return or pay for it.

Notice: the distinction between promissory liability and restitutionary liability is not difficult to understand. Too many lawyers, however, have found the distinction confusing, largely because, in fashioning a remedy for unjust enrichment, courts have analogized to contract law, explaining liability for unjust enrichment as "quasi-contract" or "contract implied in law." Consequently, contemporary courts continue to use the terms "quasi contract" and "contract implied in law" as synonymous with liability for unjust enrichment or restitution. You can avoid being confused by these terms if you remember that the term "quasi" can be roughly but usefully understood as "not really" and "implied in law" as "a fiction." Another term used by courts to describe liability based on unjust enrichment when the benefit conferred is work or service (as opposed to money or a thing), is "quantum meruit" (roughly, "the amount earned").

The next case provides an opportunity for you to examine the distinction between liability in contract ("an implied-in-fact contract") and liability in restitution (an "implied-in-law contract"). Plaintiff Howard Bailey sued Defendant Richard West for the reasonable value of the feeding and care of a horse, Bascom's Folly. Bailey alleged that West was obligated to pay under the law of restitution or unjust enrichment. However, the trial court, acting as the trier of fact, determined that there was an implied-in-fact contract between the parties, and entered judgment for a portion of the amount sought by the plaintiff. Both parties appealed this decision, and the Supreme Court of Rhode Island found it necessary to evaluate each of these alternative theories of recovery.

Howard E. Bailey v. Richard E. West

Supreme Court of Rhode Island
249 A.2d 414 (R.I. 1969)

Justice Thomas J. Paolino

This is a civil action wherein the plaintiff alleges that the defendant is indebted to him for the reasonable value of his services rendered in connection with the feeding, care and maintenance of a certain race horse named "Bascom's Folly" from May 3, 1962 through July 3, 1966. The case was tried before a justice of the superior court sitting without a jury, and resulted in a decision for the plaintiff for his cost of boarding the horse for the five months immediately subsequent to May 3, 1962 and for certain expenses incurred by him in trimming its hoofs. The cause is now before us on the plaintiff's appeal and defendant's cross appeal from the judgment entered pursuant to such decision.

The facts material to a resolution of the precise issues raised herein are as follows. In late April 1962, defendant, accompanied by his horse trainer, went to Belmont Park in New York to buy race horses. On April 27, 1962, defendant purchased "Bascom's Folly" from a Dr. Strauss and arranged to have the horse shipped to Suffolk Downs in East Boston, Massachusetts. Upon its arrival defendant's trainer discovered that the horse was lame, and so notified defendant, who ordered him to reship the horse by van to the seller at Belmont Park. The seller refused to accept delivery at Belmont on May 3, 1962, and thereupon, the van driver, one Kelly, called defendant's trainer and asked for further instructions. Although the trial testimony is in conflict as to what the trainer told him, it is not disputed that on the same day Kelly brought "Bascom's Folly" to plaintiff's farm where the horse remained until July 3, 1966, when it was sold by plaintiff to a third party.

While "Bascom's Folly" was residing at his horse farm, plaintiff sent bills for its feed and board to defendant at regular intervals. According to testimony elicited from defendant at the trial, the first such bill was received by him some two or three months after "Bascom's Folly" was placed on plaintiff's farm. He also stated that he immediately returned the bill to plaintiff with the notation that he was not the owner of the horse nor was it sent to plaintiff's farm at his request. The plaintiff testified that he sent bills monthly to defendant and that the first notice he received from him disclaiming ownership was " ... maybe after a month or two or so" subsequent to the time when the horse was left in plaintiff's care.

In his decision the trial judge found that defendant's trainer had informed Kelly during their telephone conversation of May 3, 1962, that " ... he would have to do whatever he wanted to do with the horse, that he wouldn't be on any farm at the defendant's expense...." He also found, however, that when "Bascom's Folly" was brought to his farm, plaintiff was not aware of the telephone conversation between Kelly and defendant's trainer, and hence, even though he knew there was a controversy surrounding the ownership of the horse, he was entitled to assume that " ... there is an implication here that, 'I am to take care of this horse.'" Continuing his decision, the trial justice stated that in view of the result reached by this court in a recent opinion[1] wherein we held that the instant defendant was liable to the original seller, Dr. Strauss, for the purchase price of this horse, there

---

1. See Strauss v. West, 100 R.I. 388, 216 A.2d 366.

was a contract "implied in fact" between the plaintiff and defendant to board "Bascom's Folly" and that this contract continued until plaintiff received notification from defendant that he would not be responsible for the horse's board. The trial justice further stated that " ... I think there was notice given at least at the end of the four months, and I think we must add another month on there for a reasonable disposition of his property."

In view of the conclusion we reach with respect of defendant's first two contentions, we shall confine ourselves solely to a discussion and resolution of the issues necessarily implicit therein, and shall not examine other subsidiary arguments advanced by plaintiff and defendant.

I.   The defendant alleges in brief and oral argument that the trial judge erred in finding a contract "implied in fact" between the parties. We agree.

The following quotation from 17 *C.J.S. Contracts* § 4 at pp. 557–560, illustrates the elements necessary to the establishment of a contract "implied in fact":

> ... A 'contract implied in fact,'... or an implied contract in the proper sense, arises where the intention of the parties is not expressed, but an agreement in fact, creating an obligation, is implied or presumed from their acts, or, as it has been otherwise stated, where there are circumstances which, according to the ordinary course of dealing and the common understanding of men, show a mutual interest to contract.

It has been said that a contract implied in fact must contain all the elements of an express contract. So, such a contract is dependent on mutual agreement or consent, and on the intention of the parties; and a meeting of the minds is required. A contract implied in fact is to every intent and purpose an agreement between the parties, and it cannot be found to exist unless a contract status is shown. Such a contract does not arise out of an implied legal duty or obligation, but out of facts from which consent may be inferred; there must be a manifestation of assent arising wholly or in part from acts other than words, and a contract cannot be implied in fact where the facts are inconsistent with its existence.

Therefore, essential elements of contracts "implied in fact" are mutual agreement, and intent to promise, but the agreement and the promise have not been made in words and are implied from the facts.

In the instant case, plaintiff sued on the theory of a contract "implied in law." There was no evidence introduced by him to support the establishment of a contract "implied in fact," and he cannot now argue solely on the basis of the trial justice's decision of such a result.

The source of the obligation in a contract "implied in fact," as in express contracts, is in the intention of the parties. We hold that there was no mutual agreement and "intent to promise" between the plaintiff and defendant so as to establish a contract "implied in fact" for defendant to pay plaintiff for the maintenance of this horse. From the time Kelly delivered the horse to him plaintiff knew there was a dispute as to its ownership, and his subsequent actions indicated he did not know with whom, if anyone, he had a contract. After he had accepted the horse, he made inquiries as to its ownership and, initially, and for some time thereafter, sent his bills to both defendant and Dr. Strauss, the original seller.

There is also uncontroverted testimony in the record that prior to the assertion of the claim which is the subject of this suit neither defendant nor his trainer had ever had any business transactions with plaintiff, and had never used his farm to board horses. Additionally, there is uncontradicted evidence that this horse, when found to be lame, was shipped by defendant's trainer not to plaintiff's farm, but back to the seller at Belmont Park. What is most important, the trial justice expressly stated that he believed the testimony of the defendant's trainer that he had instructed Kelly that defendant would not be responsible for boarding the horse on any farm.

From our examination of the record we are constrained to conclude that the trial justice overlooked and misconceived material evidence which establishes beyond question that there never existed between the parties an element essential to the formulation of any true contract, namely, an "intent to contract."

II. The defendant's second contention is that, even assuming the trial justice was in essence predicating defendant's liability upon a quasi-contractual theory, his decision is still unsupported by competent evidence and is clearly erroneous.

The following discussion of quasi-contracts appears in 12 *Am. Jur. Contracts* §4 (1988) at pp. 503 to 504:

> ... A quasi contract has no reference to the intentions or expressions of the parties. The obligation is imposed despite, and frequently in frustration of, their intention. For a quasi contract neither promise nor privity, real or imagined, is necessary. In quasi contracts the obligation arises, not from consent of the parties, as in the case of contracts, express or implied in fact, but from the law of natural immutable justice and equity. The act, or acts, from which the law implies the contract must, however, be voluntary. Where a case shows that it is the duty of the defendant to pay, the law imputes to him a promise to fulfill that obligation. The duty, which thus forms the foundation of a quasi contractual obligation, is frequently based on the doctrine of unjust enrichment....
>
> ... The law will not imply a promise against the express declaration of the party to be charged, made at the time of the supposed undertaking, unless such party is under legal obligation paramount to his will to perform some duty, and he is not under such legal obligation unless there is a demand in equity and good conscience that he should perform the duty.

Therefore, the essential elements of a quasi-contract are a benefit conferred upon defendant by plaintiff, appreciation by defendant of such benefit, and acceptance and retention by defendant of such benefit under such circumstances that it would be inequitable to retain the benefit without payment of the value thereof.

The key question raised by this appeal with respect to the establishment of a quasi-contract is whether or not plaintiff was acting as a "volunteer" at the time he accepted the horse for boarding at his farm. There is a long line of authority which has clearly enunciated the general rule that " ... if a performance is rendered by one person without any request by another, it is very unlikely that this person will be under a legal duty to pay compensation." 1 A Corbin, *Contracts* §234.

The *Restatement of Restitution* §2 (1937) provides: "A person who officiously confers a benefit upon another is not entitled to restitution therefor."* Comment a in the above-mentioned section states in part as follows:

> ... Policy ordinarily requires that a person who has conferred a benefit ... by way of giving another services ... should not be permitted to require the other to pay therefor, unless the one conferring the benefit had a valid reason for so

---

* The core idea in this provision is retained in the Restatement (Third) of Restitution §2(3) and (4). See Introduction to Subsection 1, below.

doing. A person is not required to deal with another unless he so desires and, ordinarily, a person should not be required to become an obligator unless he so desires.

Applying those principles to the facts in the case at bar it is clear that plaintiff cannot recover. The plaintiff's testimony on cross-examination is the only evidence in the record relating to what transpired between Kelly and him at the time the horse was accepted for boarding. The defendant's attorney asked plaintiff if he had any conversation with Kelly at that time, and plaintiff answered in substance that he had noticed that the horse was very lame and that Kelly had told him: "That's why they wouldn't accept him at Belmont Track." The plaintiff also testified that he had inquired of Kelly as to the ownership of "Bascom's Folly," and had been told that "Dr. Strauss made a deal and that's all I know." It further appears from the record that plaintiff acknowledged receipt of the horse by signing a uniform livestock bill of lading, which clearly indicated on its face that the horse in question had been consigned by defendant's trainer not to plaintiff, but to Dr. Strauss's trainer at Belmont Park. Knowing at the time he accepted the horse for boarding that a controversy surrounded its ownership, plaintiff could not reasonably expect remuneration from defendant, nor can it be said that defendant acquiesced in the conferment of a benefit upon him. The undisputed testimony was that defendant, upon receipt of plaintiff's first bill, immediately notified him that he was not the owner of "Bascom's Folly," and would not be responsible for its keep.

It is our judgement that the plaintiff was a mere volunteer who boarded and maintained "Bascom's Folly" at his own risk and with full knowledge that he might not be reimbursed for expenses he incurred incident thereto.

The plaintiff's appeal is denied and dismissed, the defendant's cross appeal is sustained, and the cause is remanded to the superior court for entry of judgement for the defendant.

———————

Enid Bagnold, National Velvet

(1949)

The piebald cropped in just such a field, on just such a Hullock as Velvet had dreamed. There was the haze and the ship. Mi, Edwina, Malvolia, Meredith and Velvet stood in a row leaning against the cobbled wall. There was a long and watchful silence. The wild thyme smelt warm and looked pink. The sea lay below, not blue but dove-grey. The coping of the wall was hot and rough.

"Stands marvelous," said Mi at length.

Another long appreciative silence.

"See his bone ..." said Mi.

...

The piebald looked up and saw them. Stared. Then cropped again.

"Seems quiet," said Edwina.

"Huh. No knowing. Think he's under fifteen hands?"

"Think he's more," said Velvet.

"See his white eye?"

They saw it. They saw everything. Their eyes, like birds' eyes, flickered over his startling patches of black and white. He was white in bold seas, and black in continents, marked in such a way that when he moved his white shoulders and his white quarters flashed, and his black body seemed to glide.

"Showy," said Mi.

Velvet climbed the wall into the field.

"He'll be off!" said Mally warningly.

Velvet went among the hot grasses towards him. She knew him. She had already ridden him in her dream. He cropped, head towards her, but watched her coming. She walked steadily and straight and began to talk in low tones. He raised his head and looked at her as firmly as she looked at him. She paused. He walked several paces towards her with confidence. No quirk or tremor or snort of doubt.

"See that!" said Mi, hanging against the wall.

They saw Velvet pat him and run her hand slowly down his neck on to his shoulder.

"She'll be that upset now," said Mi, "if she don't get him."

Velvet moved away. The animal followed her, flashing and jaunty. He had a white mane, a long white tail, pink hooves, a sloping pastern, and he struck his feet out clean and hard as he walked.

"Isn't his neck thick?" said Edwina.

"Bit," said Mi. "Bin gelded late."

The piebald, whose desires were gone, had kept his pride. He walked after Velvet like a stocky prince. Thick-necked, muscular, short and proud. He left her a few paces from the wall, and stood looking, then turned and cropped quietly.

"Gotter be back," said Mi.

Velvet hung a moment longer by the wall, then all five in silence turned downhill. There was a wild snort behind them and the thunder of feet.

"He's off!" said Mi, turning sharp. "It's set him off!"

The piebald had his white tail raised and his head arched like a Persian drawing. He was galloping down the field towards the corner.

"Stop! Stand! He's never going over that!"

The ground had dropped away so sharply at the far corner that the original builder of the cobbled wall, to keep his coping straight, had heightened the wall itself. It was five feet two at the end of the field, with a fine downhill take-off. The horse sailed over like a dappled flying boat. It was a double spring. As he was high in the air he saw also to his hind feet and drew them up sharply.

" … And to spare," said Mi quietly, nodding his head. "A horse like that'd win the National."

"You don't mean it, Mi!"

"Gets his hocks under. Got heart. Grand take-off. Then when he's up in the air he gives a kind of second hitch an' his feet tuck up so he's on'y a body without legs. See him look before he took off? See his ears flitch forward and back again? You on'y got to sit on him."

"Oh, Mi, why don't you ride?"

" … Got a nasty sort of look of Man-of-War too," pursued Mi, unheeding.

"Who was Man-of-War?"

"Man-eatin' stallion," said Mi.

"But a black and white horse like that doesn't look like anything to do with a race."

"Ever hear of the Tetrarch?"

"No."

"Looked like a rocking horse. Sorta dappled. Mr. Persse his trainer was. One mornin' he was sittin' eatin' his egg an' a stable lad rushed in an' screamed out, 'That coloured horse can beat anything!' an' rushed out again."

"And what did he win?"

"Didn't win anything so marvelous because they ran him as a two-year-old. But he sired twenty-seven thousand pounds!"

"How'd you know so much, Mi?"

"Used to read when I was up there," Mi jerked his finger north, away from the sea.

"Why did the stable boy rush in?"

"'Cause he won, didn't he, in the gallops in the morning."

"The piebald Tetrarch?"

"He wasn't piebald. Not even grey. He was coloured. Grey and roan and white. Mottled. They got him for a mascot. Just for a stable companion. And he brought them a fortune."

They walked down the slopes, wrapped in the eternal drama of the last being first.

---

1. Liability for Unjust Enrichment

The persistent question in the law of restitution is when is it unjust to retain a benefit that one has received. It is easier to describe circumstances in which it is NOT unjust to retain a benefit. One is if someone gives you a present on your birthday, it is not unjust for you to keep the gift without paying for it. Indeed, in that situation, the justice of the matter is so clear that the gift-giver would rightly be offended if you offered to pay! *See* Restatement (Third) of Restitution §2(1).

The second situation in which restitution law generally holds that one may justly retain a benefit without paying for it is the case of a layperson rendering medical or other professional services. This is the situation we discussed in the Note to *Webb v. McGowin*, above. As a general rule, justice does not require a person to pay for emergency services performed by a layperson. *See* Restatement (Third) of Restitution §20.

A third circumstance in which restitution law generally would not require payment is when the giver passes up an opportunity to ask the recipient if he or she wants the benefit. This is what restitution law labels a "voluntarily" or "officiously" conferred benefit for which the recipient is not obligated to pay. In *Bailey v. West*, Justice Paolino cited a "long line of authority" supporting the "general rule that if a performance is rendered by one person without any request by another, it is very unlikely that this person will be under a legal duty to pay compensation." Indeed, this was the basis for the court's decision rejecting Bailey's restitution claim. The court observed that the "key question" regarding Bailey's restitution claim was "whether or not plaintiff was acting as a 'volunteer' at the time he

Man O'War and Will Harbut at Faraway Farm in 1937. Photo by J.C. Skeets Meadors, courtesy of Keeneland Library.

accepted the horse for boarding at his farm," and then concluded that Bailey was "a volunteer" because he took the horse knowing that there was a dispute as to its ownership.

The basic idea underlying the "volunteer rule" is not difficult to understand. Imagine that you own a house with a cement walkway leading from the street to the front door. The walkway is rather old and weeds are growing up through the cracks, but it is not dangerous. One day, you return home to find that the cracked walkway removed and an entirely new cement walk installed in its place. As you stand in pleased surprise, a man approaches and hands you an invoice for $600 which he claims is the market value of the new walkway. Surely you should not have to pay the invoice! There is no reason why the man could not have asked if you wanted to hire him to replace the walkway and surely you have the right to decide if and when you should use your money in that way. If the man sued you for unjust enrichment, the court would rule in your favor, because the man acted as a "volunteer" or because his actions were "officious." Recall, however, that if the homeowner decides that she does want to pay the man something for his costs and materials, and she promises to pay him, then that promise may be enforceable under contract law, as a promise made in recognition of a past benefit.

The *Restatement (Third) of Restitution* restates the rule that recovery should be denied to one who confers an unrequested benefit without first making a contract with the recipient:

> (3) There is no liability in restitution for an unrequested benefit voluntarily conferred, unless the circumstances of the transaction justify the claimant's intervention in the absence of a contract.

> (4) Liability in restitution may not subject an innocent recipient to a forced exchange: in other words, an obligation to pay for a benefit that the recipient should have been free to refuse.

Restatement (Third) of Restitution § 2(3), (4). The drafters explain these subsection in Comments d) and e):

> d) *Benefits voluntarily conferred.* Instead of proposing a bargain, the restitution claimant first confers a benefit, then seeks payment for its value. When this manner of proceeding is unacceptable—as it usually is, if the claimant neglects an opportunity to contract—a claim based on unjust enrichment will be denied.

> The limitation of § 2(3) is traditionally expressed by denying restitution to a claimant characterized as "officious," an "intermeddler," or a "volunteer." This section states the same rule, substituting a functional explanation for the familiar epithets. Because contract is strongly preferred over restitution as a basis for private obligations (see Comment c), restitution is not usually available to a claimant who has neglected a suitable opportunity to make a contract beforehand.

> There are cases in which a claimant may indeed recover compensation for unrequested benefits intentionally conferred—because the claimant's intervention was justified under the circumstances, and because a liability in restitution will not prejudice the recipient. Chapter 3 of this Restatement constitutes a catalogue of the instances in which such recovery may be permitted....

> e) *Forced exchange.* Like the limits to restitution for unrequested benefits, the objection to restitution in circumstances that this Restatement sometimes characterizes as "forced exchange" would be expressed in traditional language by calling the claimant a "volunteer"...

The *Restatement's* "catalogue" of instances in which liability for unrequested benefits may be imposed include (1) benefits received in an emergency, in which the giver lacked time or opportunity to give the beneficiary a choice; (2) benefits conferred by mistake, in which the transferor was mistaken about the circumstances; (3) benefits wrongfully gained, as when a benefit is taken by fraud or theft; and (4) benefits conferred in situations involving a contract that turned out to be unenforceable or invalid.

Notice that the categories of benefits conferred in an emergency and benefits conferred by mistake are both defined by circumstances in which there was no opportunity for the parties to enter a contract before the benefit was given. People who conferred benefits in those circumstances did not have an opportunity to ask the recipients if they wanted the benefit. Accordingly, the benefits conferred in these circumstances were not given "voluntarily" or "officiously."

Cotnam v. Wisdom, in Chapter Two, involved benefits rendered in an emergency (item 1 in the list above). The case immediately following this discussion, *Toalson v. Madison*, involves a mistake (item 2). You probably have seen cases involving benefits wrongly obtained (item 3) in your Torts class. We will discuss benefits conferred under an unenforceable contract (item 4) in Chapters Six and Seven.

W. Rucker Toalson and F. E. Toalson v. Arch Madison

Kansas City Court of Appeals, Missouri
307 S.W.2d 32 (Mo. App. 1957)

Floyd L. Sperry, Commissioner

Plaintiffs Toalson, husband and wife, sued defendant Madison in equity for the reasonable value of betterments to a house owned by defendant, made by plaintiffs through mistake of ownership. Judgment was for defendant and plaintiffs appeal.

Mr. Toalson's testimony was to the effect that one Houston was the owner of Lots 17 and 18 in Woodland Addition to Columbia, Missouri; that Houston conveyed Lot 18 to defendant and, thereafter, conveyed Lot 17 to plaintiffs; that when Houston sold Lot 17 to plaintiffs he showed them the house and lot located at 221 Worley Street which, in fact, is Lot 18, and that he represented to them that it was Lot 17; that Houston walked around the house on Lot 18 and showed it; that, in fact, said Lot 18 had previously been sold to defendant; that plaintiffs notified the tenants of Lot 18 to vacate; that they moved out; that, beginning in January, 1955, plaintiffs made extensive improvements to the house thereon, including the construction of a room, bath and plumbing, installing gas, papering, painting, lights, and preparing the roof and flooring; that the total cost of said improvements was some $900; that, while improving the property, he saw defendant on the property but did not know who he was; that, after the improvements were completed, plaintiffs rented the property, from May 1, until August, for $30 per month; that, late in August, defendant's son or grandson came to the store and told plaintiffs that defendant owned the property; that thereafter plaintiffs made no further improvements and collected no further rents, and voluntarily surrendered possession to defendant. After learning of his mistake Mr. Toalson visited defendant to seek a settlement and defendant told him he did not care how much had been spent on the house, that "there is nothing I can do for you."

Mr. Menges testified to having worked for plaintiffs in improving the property; that he was paid $206 for his services.

Mr. Palmer, for plaintiffs, stated that he worked on the property and was paid $107 for services.

Mr. Logan stated that he dug up and moved an outside toilet from the front to the back yard; that defendant came onto the property and witness told him that Mr. Toalson was moving the stool into the house; that defendant merely grunted and walked away; that, while he was digging footings for the foundation, defendant again came over and asked what he was doing; that he was told that Mr. Toalson was going to build a new room on the house and that defendant 'turned and walked off.'

Mr. Coose testified to the effect that he saw defendant and Mr. Toalson talking, on the property, the day tile was unloaded for construction of the new room; that defendant told witness that Toalson 'was making a nice place out of it'; that he saw Toalson and defendant sitting together on the property a number of times while the work was going forward.

Mr. Limerick stated that defendant told him that he had seen the improvements being built but didn't tell plaintiffs to stop, that he didn't care how much money was spent on his property.

Defendant did not testify, but he offered the testimony of the city building inspector, to the effect that plaintiffs were issued a building permit for improvements on the property, estimated to cost $300.

. . .

The question here is whether plaintiffs, under the conditions shown in this record, may maintain this action in equity, independent of [any] statute, for improvements.

. . .

In 104 A.L.R. 588, note (b), it is said that certain cases, including *Valle v. Fleming*, 29 Mo. 152, *McLean v. Martin*, 45 Mo. 393, and *Calloway Bank v. Ellis*, 238 S.W. 844 (Mo. App.), support the general doctrine that even in the absence of fraud, acquiescence with knowledge, or other inequitable conduct on the part of the owner of land one who, mistakenly believing himself to be the owner, in good faith makes improvements on premises, may as plaintiff, recover therefor, by way of lien or otherwise, when the circumstances render such relief just and equitable; that that rule is "so asserted" in the case of *Calloway Bank v. Ellis*, *supra*.

. . . In *McLean v. Martin*, *supra*, plaintiff purchased land at sheriff's sale on a judgment, believing it to be defendant's land. Defendant also believed the land sold to be his and surrendered possession of his land to plaintiff. The purchase price was $850, and plaintiff made improvements to the value of $1,000. Later, it was learned that the land actually sold and conveyed was not the land of defendant, but that plaintiff had taken possession of and had improved the land actually owned by defendant. It was alleged that defendant had, in some manner, repossessed his land. Plaintiff sought judgment for $1,850. The trial court sustained a demurrer and the Supreme Court reversed and remanded for a new trial.

In *Calloway Bank v. Ellis*, *supra*, plaintiff purchased bonds from a school district. With the proceeds of the bonds a building was erected on land conveyed to the district by defendants. Thereafter, it was judicially determined that the district was illegally organized, that defendants' deed to the district was void, and that defendants never parted with title to the land upon which the improvements were made. The Springfield Court of Appeals decided the case on the principle that 'equity seeks to prevent the unearned enrichment of one at the expense of another,' and decreed a lien on the building erected on the land, in the amount due plaintiff; ordered that the building be sold and, after payment to defendants of such damages as had been sustained to the land, ordered the balance paid to plaintiff.

. . . We think the principle is established in Missouri that relief may be had in this type of case by a suit in equity, where equitable rights are involved, especially where the improvements were made with the knowledge and acquiescence of the landowner and if plaintiffs acted innocently, in good faith, and without notice . . .

There are many cases from other jurisdictions in harmony with our opinion herein, among which are *Voss v. Forgue*, 84 So.2d 563 (Fla.); *Ollig v. Eagles*, 78 N.W.2d 553, 557

(Mich.); *Bryant v. Carville*, 182 A. 162, 164 (Me.); *Murphy v. Benson*, 245 S.W. 249, 254 (Tex. App.). We have also found Missouri decisions, other than the three mentioned herein which, generally support our ruling. We think it unnecessary to refer more specifically to such cases, for it would extend the opinion and add but little of value.

The case below was apparently tried and decided on a wrong theory. There is no sufficient evidence in the record to determine the value by which the property was enhanced by the improvements made by plaintiffs, nor the amount of rents and profit collected by plaintiffs while in possession.

The judgment should be reversed and the cause remanded for a new trial.

---

2. Benefit Received

A claim for restitution, as we have seen, seeks compensation for a benefit that the defendant has received from the plaintiff, and if the claim is proved, then the defendant must pay plaintiff the fair market value of the benefit that he or she received.

Among the benefits that may give rise to restitutionary liability is the benefit of having an obligation fulfilled. In other words, one person may be obligated to compensate another who performs the first person's job or pays the first person's debt. Of course the other rules of restitution apply, so recovery would depend on there being some special circumstance justifying the intervention. Consider Restatement (Third) of Restitution §22 and the following case.

Emergency Physicians Integrated Care v. Salt Lake County
Supreme Court of Utah
167 P.3d 1080 (Utah 2007)

JUSTICE JILL N. PARRISH

Introduction

Emergency Physicians Integrated Care ("EPIC") is a Utah limited liability corporation formed for the purpose of providing billing and collection services to various emergency physicians around Utah. EPIC sued Salt Lake County (the "County") under a theory of quantum meruit, seeking compensation for medical services its physicians provided to county inmates. The district court entered summary judgment in favor of the County, holding that EPIC's services failed to "benefit" the County as required by the first prong of a quantum meruit* analysis. We reverse and remand for further proceedings consistent with this opinion.

Background

EPIC's suit against the County sought compensation for the value of the medical services provided by its physicians to county inmates from February 2000 to November 2004. The County denied any legal responsibility to pay for the services.

...

---

* Recall that some courts use the term "quantum meruit" to mean recovery for unjust enrichment (a/k/a restitution, quasi contract, implied in law contrat) when the benefit was work or service.

In May 2005, EPIC moved for partial summary judgment, arguing that the undisputed facts entitled it to judgment against the County under the equitable theory of quantum meruit. The County filed a cross-motion for summary judgment, arguing that ... EPIC's quantum meruit claim fails as a matter of law ...

The district court denied EPIC's motion for partial summary judgment and granted the County's motion "to the extent that [EPIC] has not shown that it is entitled to recover under a claim of quantum meruit." Reasoning that the inmates, rather than the County, were the primary beneficiaries of the services provided by EPIC physicians, the district court held that EPIC's quantum meruit claim failed as a matter of law because EPIC conferred only an incidental benefit on the County. In support of this conclusion, the district court observed that the EPIC physicians were required to bear the cost of inmate care because they had a statutory duty to provide emergency care regardless of a patient's ability to pay under the Emergency Medical Treatment and Active Labor Act ("EMTALA"), 42 U.S.C. §1395dd (2000). The district court also concluded that the County had no statutory obligation to pay physicians for the medical care they provided to inmates.... [T]he implication of the district court's ruling is that the County has no legal obligation to reimburse EPIC physicians at all for medical services provided to county inmates.

EPIC appealed to this court, arguing that (1) the County has an obligation to pay EPIC physicians for emergency medical services provided to inmates and (2) EPIC physicians are entitled to be reimbursed by the County for the reasonable value of these services. We have jurisdiction pursuant to Utah Code section 78-2-2(3)(j).

Analysis

We hold that the district court erred in entering summary judgment in favor of the County. The basis for the summary judgment was the district court's holding that EPIC could not establish the elements of its quantum meruit claim because the services provided to county inmates by EPIC physicians did not confer a benefit on the County. Because we disagree with this holding, we vacate the summary judgment and remand the case to the district court for further proceedings consistent with this opinion.

I. Quantum Meruit

Quantum meruit is an equitable tool that allows a plaintiff to receive restitution for the reasonable value of services provided to the defendant. See J & M Constr., Inc. v. Southam, 722 P.2d 779, 780 (Utah 1986) (per curiam); Christensen v. Abbott, 671 P.2d 121, 123 (Utah 1983); Foulger v. McGrath, 34 Utah 86, 95 P. 1004, 1007 (Utah 1908); Davies v. Olson, 746 P.2d 264, 269 (Utah Ct. App. 1987); Black's Law Dictionary 1255 (7th ed. 1999) ("A claim or right of action for the reasonable value of services rendered.")....

To prove the existence of a contract implied in law, a plaintiff must establish the following: "(1)[T]he defendant received a benefit; (2)an appreciation or knowledge by the defendant of the benefit; (3)under circumstances that would make it unjust for the defendant to retain the benefit without paying for it." Id. The district court entered summary judgment against EPIC after it concluded that EPIC could not establish the first element of a quantum meruit claim because the emergency services its physicians provided to county inmates did not confer a benefit on the County. We accordingly focus our discussion on this element.

Although EPIC's claim of quantum meruit is an equitable one, the nature of the benefit conferred on the County by EPIC is informed by the County's constitutional duty and is governed by statutory law. We consequently begin with an analysis of these issues.

A. Constitutional Duty to Provide Care

As acknowledged by both parties, the County has a constitutional obligation to provide medical care to those in its custody. The Eighth Amendment imposes on governments a duty to provide for the "'serious medical needs of prisoners.'" *City of Revere v. Ma. Gen. Hosp.*, 463 U.S. 239, 243–44, 103 S. Ct. 2979, 77 L. Ed. 2d 605 (1983) (quoting *Estelle v. Gamble*, 429 U.S. 97, 104, 97 S. Ct. 285, 50 L. Ed. 2d 251 (1976)). To an equal degree, the Fourteenth Amendment requires government entities to obtain medical care for injured pretrial detainees. Id. at 244–46 ("The Due Process Clause ... does require the responsible government or governmental agency to provide medical care to persons ... who have been injured while being apprehended by the police."); *see Bell v. Wolfish*, 441 U.S. 520, 535, 99 S. Ct. 1861, 60 L. Ed. 2d 447 (1979).

...

B. Statutory Duty to Pay for Medical Care

Because the County's duty to pay for the medical care of its inmates is a matter of state law, we consider whether Utah law allocates the costs of convicted and pretrial inmates' medical care to the County. EPIC contends that Utah Code section 17-50-319 renders the [county] liable for the cost of medical care provided to inmates, while the County contends that it does not.

Section 17-50-319 enumerates the charges for which counties are liable. Subsection (1)(c) of section 17-50-319 charges counties with the broad obligation to pay "expenses necessarily incurred in the support of persons charged with or convicted of a criminal offense and committed to the county jail." Utah Code Ann. 17-50-319(1)(c) (2005).

...

The district court agreed with the County and found the general provisions of subsection (1)(c) inapplicable, stating that nothing in that section "specifically allocated the costs of emergency physician services to counties." We disagree. The Constitution requires that the government provide medical care to persons convicted or detained by a government entity. *Revere*, 463 U.S. at 243–44. Consequently, medical care is logically included in subsection (1)(c)'s broad requirement that the County pay the expenses "necessarily incurred in the support" of pretrial or convicted inmates.[1]

Our conclusion in this regard is not changed by the fact that subsection (1)(k) explicitly charges the County with "expenses incurred by a *health care facility* in providing medical services at the request of a county sheriff for existing conditions of" convicted and pretrial inmates. Utah Code Ann. § 17-50-319(1)(k) (emphasis added). We acknowledge the well-settled principle of statutory construction that "when two provisions address the same subject matter and one provision is general while the other is specific, the specific provision controls." *Dairyland Ins. Co. v. State Farm Mut. Auto. Ins. Co.*, 882 P.2d 1143, 1146 (Utah 1994); *accord Lyon v. Burton*, 5 P.3d 616 (Utah). By their express terms, however, subsections (1)(k) and (2) govern only services provided by medical facilities, services that are distinct from medical care provided by physicians.

---

1. We recognize that under an earlier incarnation of Utah Code section 17-50-319(1)(c), we found no statutory duty to pay an attorney for legal services rendered to a man accused of murder. Pardee v. Salt Lake County, 118 P. 122, 124 (Utah 1911). We held in that case that the term "support" did not encompass an inmate's criminal defense. *Id. Pardee* is distinguishable, however, because unlike legal services, medical care does fall within the commonly understood definition of "support" as "[s]ustenance or maintenance." *See Black's Law Dictionary* 1453 (7th ed. 1999).

A facility is defined as "something (as a hospital, machinery, plumbing) that is built, constructed, installed, or established to perform some particular function or to serve or facilitate some particular end." Webster's Third New International Dictionary 812–13 (1986). Thus, under the plain language of the statute, the terms of subsections (1)(k) and (2) apply exclusively to those costs incurred by the entity associated with the physical structures in which the health care needs of the inmates are provided, rather than the costs incurred by individual health care providers. Because subsections (1)(k) and (2) do not address the County's obligation to compensate medical doctors who provide care to inmates, the County's obligation in this regard is controlled by the more general language of subsection (1)(c).

. . .

In sum, because subsections (1)(k) and (2) have no application to individual health care providers, the general provisions of subsection (1)(c) apply. Under this subsection, the County has a statutorily mandated duty to pay the physicians for the services provided.[2] We now consider how the County's constitutional and statutory obligations fit into EPIC's quantum meruit claim.

C. The Benefit the County Received from EPIC

We hold that EPIC physicians conferred a benefit on the County by providing the means by which it fulfilled its legal obligation to provide inmate care. While the inmates also benefitted from the services provided by EPIC physicians, it is not an element of quantum meruit that the benefit run exclusively to the party from which compensation is sought.

The district court acknowledged the County's constitutional duty, but held that the inmates were the true beneficiaries of EPIC's service and that any benefit to the County was merely incidental. In support of this conclusion, the district court relied on *Myrtle Beach Hospital, Inc. v. City of Myrtle Beach*, 532 S.E.2d 868, 869 (S.C. 2000), in which the South Carolina Supreme Court considered the city's obligation to pay for the medical treatment of pretrial detainees. The South Carolina Supreme Court rejected the hospital's quantum meruit claim, finding that the "detainee rather than the City" received the benefit conferred by the hospital. 532 S.E.2d at 873. It held that the city's constitutional obligation under *Revere* was fulfilled by " 'seeing that the detainees are taken promptly to a hospital' " for treatment. 532 S.E.2d at 873 (brackets omitted) (quoting *Revere*, 463 U.S. at 245). And it found that the services the hospital provided to the inmates only incidentally benefitted the city by helping it fulfill its constitutional obligation. 532 S.E.2d at 873 n.12.

We respectfully disagree with the South Carolina Supreme Court's conclusion that a government entity "receives [only] an incidental benefit" from a medical service provider treating inmates in its custody. *Id.*[3]

The first element of quantum meruit requires the court to measure the benefit conferred on the defendant by the plaintiff. *Berrett v. Stevens*, 690 P.2d 553, 557 (Utah 1984). The benefit conferred satisfies this requirement if the defendant's retention of the benefit would be unjust without providing compensation. 66 Am. Jur. 2d *Restitution and Implied Contracts* 13 (2001) ("It is not enough that a benefit was conferred on the defendant, and

---

2. Because we find a statutory duty to remunerate EPIC, we have no need to consider the possibility of a similar common law duty.

3. Further, we find that the facts of *Myrtle Beach* are distinguishable from those in this case. The City of Myrtle Beach had no statutory obligation to pay for the medical care of pretrial detainees because the statutes obligating payment covered only *convicted* inmates. Myrtle Beach, 532 S.E.2d at 871. As discussed above, however, Utah's statute obligates the County to pay for the medical care of pretrial and convicted inmates. *See supra* 15–22.

rather, the enrichment to the defendant must be unjust in that the defendant received a true windfall or 'something for nothing.'"); *Berrett*, 690 P.2d at 557 ("[T]he mere fact that a person benefits another is not by itself sufficient to require the other to make restitution."). While unjust enrichment does not result if the defendant has received only an incidental benefit from the plaintiff's service, id., this court has found that a large variety of items fall under the definition of "benefit," including an "interest in money, land, chattels, or choses in action; beneficial services conferred; satisfaction of a debt or duty owed by [the defendant]; or anything which adds to [the defendant's] security or advantage." *Baugh v. Darley*, 184 P.2d 335, 337 (Utah 1947).

We acknowledge that EPIC provided a physical benefit to the treated inmates, but the County also benefitted from EPIC's service.[4] In providing medical care to inmates, the County is not acting as a passive third party to a primary relationship between the physicians and inmates. Instead, the County has complete control over when and where medical services are provided and therefore dictates the means by which its constitutional obligation is fulfilled. For practical purposes, the County outsourced its constitutional duty to EPIC. Had it not done so, it would have been required to employ more on-site medical staff or bear increased liability for providing inadequate care. These are real benefits that are sufficient to establish the first prong of a quantum meruit claim.

In concluding that the County did not benefit from emergency services provided to its inmates, the district court reasoned that because EPIC has a duty to provide treatment to county inmates under EMTALA, 42 U.S.C. 1395dd, it is the physicians who must bear the cost of treatment, after the patients themselves.[5] The language of the statute does not support this conclusion. EMTALA requires hospital emergency departments to treat individuals who have emergency medical conditions without regard for their ability to pay. *See* 42 U.S.C. § 1395dd (2000). But it does not prohibit medical providers from recovering payment from emergency patients or their guardians after service has been provided.

II. Reasonable Value of Care

If EPIC proves its quantum meruit claim, it is entitled to the "reasonable value" of the services it provided. *Davies v. Olson*, 746 P.2d 264, 269 (Utah Ct. App. 1987); *accord Baugh v. Darley*, 112 Utah 1, 184 P.2d 335, 339 (Utah 1947) ("[I]n an action for unjust enrichment, in those cases where there is a proper equitable basis for the same, the measure of damages, by the great weight of authority, is the reasonable value of the services rendered.").... Because the determination of what constitutes a "reasonable value" for the physicians' services is dependent on the specific evidence presented and because the district court did not consider whether the evidence on this issue raised a factual dispute, we refrain from deciding this issue. Rather, we remand the matter to the district court for consideration of this argument and further proceedings consistent with this opinion.

---

4. Under Utah Code section 17-50-319(2)(a), medical services that a health care facility provides to inmates are the responsibility of the state only to the extent that they are not covered by private insurance. With this opinion, we do not absolve inmates for potential liability for care, but merely hold that EPIC provides a benefit to the County sufficient to fulfill the first element of a claim for quantum meruit.

5. The Supreme Court's *Revere* opinion contains dicta about *how* the costs of inmate care might be allocated, which may have formed some of the basis for the district court's reasoning here. *Revere* refers to federal grant money allocated to hospitals to cover indigent care and state laws requiring treatment without regard for a patient's ability to pay. 463 U.S. at 245. It then states that government entities might create their own hospitals or impose "on the willingness of hospitals and physicians" to treat inmates without consideration for payment. *Id.* The existence of these options, however, does not necessarily excuse government entities from paying for medical services provided to inmates or dictate that the cost of treatment be born by emergency physicians.

Conclusion

We reverse the district court's grant of summary judgment to Salt Lake County. EPIC physicians provided a benefit to the County when they provided medical services to pretrial and convicted county inmates by allowing the County to discharge its constitutional obligation to provide medical care to detainees and inmates and its statutory obligation to pay for the expenses necessarily incurred in support of county inmates. We therefore remand this case for consideration of the other arguments and defenses raised by the parties.

---

3. The Priority of Contract over Restitution

The *Restatement (Third) of Restitution*, includes the following "limiting principle":

> A valid contract defines the obligations of the parties as to matters within its scope, displacing to that extent any inquiry into unjust enrichment.

Restatement (Third) of Restitution § 2(2). As a general rule, if the parties have entered a valid, enforceable contract, and one party breaches that contract, the aggrieved party may recovery for breach of contract and may not elect to bring a restitution claim as an alternative. For example, imagine that A and B have entered a valid, enforceable contract specifying that A will pay B $100 to trim two pecan trees located in A's front yard. B does the work and A does not pay. Meanwhile, B learns that the fair market value of the work that he did is $150. If he could recover under restitution, for the fair market value of the work that A received, then B would get $150. This is the reason for the "limited principle quoted above, having agreed to work for $100, B ought not to gain a windfall from A's breach.

While the priority of contract is clear in a dispute between the parties to a valid, enforceable contract, the law is much less certain in cases involving a third party. Assume that A and B entered a valid, enforceable contract specifying that A, a general contractor, will pay B, a subcontractor, $10,000 to install wooden cabinets in a home owned by C. B completed the work. A then left town or went bankrupt, failing to pay B. Is C obligated to pay B for the wooden cabinets now installed in C's home? The uncertainty over the answer to this question can be seen by comparing the First Restatement of Restitution, adopted in 1939, with the Third Restatement, adopted in 2011 (Tentative Drafts of a Second Restatement of Restitution were circulated in 1983 and 1984, but work on the project was then suspended).

The *First Restatement* provided as follows:

> A person who has conferred a benefit upon another as the performance of a contract with a third person is not entitled to restitution from the other merely because of the failure of performance by the third person.

Restatement (First) of Restitution § 110. The only exception to this rule recognized in the *First Restatement* was if the agreement (between A and B) or performance (B's installation of the cabinets) was caused by fraud or mistake. See Restatement (First) of Restitution § 17.

In the Third Restatement, treatment of this topic is significantly changed. Consider Section 25 (Uncompensated Performance Under Contract with Third Person):

> (1) If the claimant renders to a third person a contractual performance for which the claimant does not receive the promised compensation, and the effect of the claimant's uncompensated performance is to confer a benefit on the de-

fendant, the claimant is entitled to restitution from the defendant as necessary to prevent unjust enrichment.

(2) There is unjust enrichment for purposes of subsection (1) only if the following three conditions are met:

    (a) Liability in restitution may not subject the defendant to a forced exchange (§ 2(4)). This condition is likely to be satisfied if the benefit realized by the defendant

        (i) is one for which the defendant has expressed a willingness to pay,

        (ii) saves the defendant an otherwise necessary expense, or

        (iii) is realized by the defendant in money.

    (b) Absent liability in restitution, the claimant will not be compensated for the performance in question, and the defendant will retain the benefit of the claimant's performance free of any liability to pay for it.

    c) Liability in restitution will not subject the defendant to an obligation from which it was understood by the parties that the defendant would be free.

. . .

The general denial of recovery in the First Restatement did not accurately reflect the range of results reached by courts both before and after its publication. Yet the decisions seemed torn between the priority of contract and the injustice of windfall benefits. The Third Restatement attempts to articulate these competing values. The drafters explain:

> b. Threshold limits to the claim. Under a traditional analysis, the restitution claim described in this section would often be barred by invoking a test of "privity." The rule here stated affords an equivalent protection to the interests of the defendant, without allowing the defendant to employ a formal test of privity to escape liability in cases of unmistakable unjust enrichment. The method adopted is to authorize restitution as necessary to prevent unjust enrichment, and to establish a rigorous test of unjust enrichment as a threshold requirement of the claim.

> Section 25 takes as a starting point the proposition, inherited from Restatement of Restitution § 110 (1937), that when A confers a benefit on B as the performance of A's contract with C, C's failure to render the performance promised to A does not necessarily mean that B has been enriched at A's expense; nor does it mean that any enrichment of B is necessarily unjust. The limited circumstances in which B might be unjustly enriched by A's performance are identified by two principal tests. The first is that restitution to A not subject B to what this Restatement calls a forced exchange (§ 2(4)). Circumstances in which this requirement are likely to be met are indicated by § 25(2)(a)(i)–(iii). The second fundamental requirement of unjust enrichment in these circumstances is that B must stand to obtain a valuable benefit at A's expense without paying anyone for it (§ 25(2) (b)). There is accordingly no unjust enrichment if B has paid the contract price to C; nor if B has paid in full (to C and to others, following C's default) the price originally fixed by contract for the work to which A has made an uncompensated contribution.

As you read the next two cases, consider how these provisions may apply to the facts in each case.

———————

Callano v. Oakwood Park Homes Corp.

Superior Court of New Jersey
219 A.2d 332 (N.J. 1966)

Donald G. Collester, Judge of the Appellate Division

Defendant Oakwood Park Homes Corp. (Oakwood) appeals from a judgment of $475 entered in favor of plaintiffs Julia Callano and Frank Callano in the Monmouth County District Court.

The case was tried below on an agreed stipulation of facts. Oakwood, engaged in the construction of a housing development, in December 1961 contracted to sell a lot with a house to be erected thereon to Bruce Pendergast, who resided in Waltham, Massachusetts. In May 1962, prior to completion of the house, the Callanos, who operated a plant nursery, delivered and planted shrubbery pursuant to a contract with Pendergast. A representative of Oakwood had knowledge of the planting.

Pendergast never paid the Callanos the invoice price of $497.95. A short time after the shrubbery was planted Pendergast died. Thereafter, on July 10, 1962 Oakwood and Pendergast's estate cancelled the contract of sale. Oakwood had no knowledge of Pendergast's failure to pay the Callanos. On July 16, 1962 Oakwood sold the Pendergast property, including the shrubbery located thereon, to Richard and Joan Grantges for an undisclosed amount.

The single issue is whether Oakwood is obligated to pay plaintiffs for the reasonable value of the shrubbery on the theory of quasi-contractual liability. Plaintiffs contend that defendant was unjustly enriched when the Pendergast contract to purchase the property was cancelled and that an agreement to pay for the shrubbery is implied in law. Defendant argues that the facts of the case do not support a recovery by plaintiffs on the theory of quasi-contract.

Contracts implied by law, more properly described as Quasi or constructive contracts, are a class of obligations which are imposed or created by law without regard to the assent of the party bound, on the ground that they are dictated by reason and justice. They rest solely on a legal fiction and are not contract obligations at all in the true sense, for there is no agreement; but they are clothed with the semblance of contract for the purpose of the remedy, and the obligation arises not from consent, as in the case of true contracts, but from the law or natural equity. Courts employ the fiction of Quasi or constructive contract with caution. 17 C.J.S. Contracts s 6, pp. 566–570 (1963).

In cases based on quasi-contract liability, the intention of the parties is entirely disregarded, while in cases of express contracts and contracts implied in fact the intention is of the essence of the transaction. In the case of actual contracts the agreement defines the duty, while in the case of quasi-contracts the duty defines the contract. Where a case shows that it is the duty of the defendant to pay, the law imparts to him a promise to fulfill that obligation. The duty which thus forms the foundation of a quasi-contractual obligation is frequently based on the doctrine of unjust enrichment. It rests on the equitable principle that a person shall not be allowed to enrich himself unjustly at the expense of another, and on the principle of whatsoever it is certain a man ought to do, that the law supposes him to have promised to do. *St. Paul Fire, etc., Co. v. Indemnity Ins. Co. of No. America*, 158 A.2d 825, 830 (N.J. 1960).

The key words are Enrich and Unjustly. To recover on the theory of quasi-contract the plaintiffs must prove that defendant was enriched, received a benefit, and that retention of the benefit without payment therefor would be unjust.

It is conceded by the parties that the value of the property, following the termination of the Pendegast contract, was enhanced by the reasonable value of the shrubbery at the stipulated sum of $475. However, we are not persuaded that the retention of such benefit by defendant before it sold the property to the Grantges was inequitable or unjust.

Quasi-contractual liability has found application in a myriad of situations. *See* Woodruff, Cases on Quasi-Contracts (3d ed. 1933). However, a common thread runs throughout its application where liability has been successfully asserted, namely, that the plaintiff expected remuneration from the defendant, or if the true facts were known to plaintiff, he would have expected remuneration from defendant, at the time the benefit was conferred. *See Rabinowitz v. Mass. Bonding & Insurance Co.*, 197 A. 44 (N.J. 1937). It is further noted that quasi-contract cases involve either some direct relationship between the parties or a mistake on the part of the person conferring the benefit.

In the instant case the plaintiffs entered into an express contract with Pendergast and looked to him for payment. They had no dealings with defendant, and did not expect remuneration from it when they provided the shrubbery. No issue of mistake on the part of plaintiffs is involved. Under the existing circumstances we believe it would be inequitable to hold defendant liable. Plaintiffs' remedy is against Pendergast's estate, since they contracted with and expected payment to be made by Pendergast when the benefit was conferred. *Cf. Service Fuel Oil Co. v. Hoboken Bank for Savings*, 191 A. 551 (N.J. 1937). A plaintiff is not entitled to employ the legal fiction of quasi-contract to 'substitute one promisor or debtor for another.' *Cascaden v. Magryta*, 225 N.W. 511, 512 (Mich. 1929).

Plaintiffs place reliance on *De Gasperi v. Valicenti*, 181 A.2d 862 (Pa. 1962), where recovery was allowed on the theory on unjust enrichment. We find the case inapposite. It is clear that recovery on quasi-contract was permitted there because of a fraud perpetrated by defendants. There is no contention of fraud on the part of Oakwood in the instant case.

Recovery on the theory of quasi-contract was developed under the law to provide a remedy where none existed. Here, a remedy exists. Plaintiffs may bring their action against Pendergast's estate. We hold that under the facts of this case defendant was not unjustly enriched and is not liable for the value of the shrubbery.

Reversed.

Lyle Dews v. Halliburton Industries, Inc.

Supreme Court of Arkansas
708 S.W.2d 67 (Ark. 1986)

JACK WILSON HOLT, CHIEF JUSTICE

At issue in this case is who is to pay eleven different companies approximately half of a million dollars for work performed while drilling an oil well. The chancellor held the appellant, Lyle Dews, and Bruce Massey are responsible for the debt. We agree. It is from that judgment that this appeal is brought. Our jurisdiction is pursuant to Sup. Ct. R. 29(1)(c) and (d).

Crystal Oil Co. owned certain leases covering lands in the southeast quarter and the north half of the southwest quarter, section 10, township 20S, range 25W, in Lafayette County, Arkansas. Crystal executed a farmout agreement of these leases with Dews on May 4, 1982. The terms of the farmout required Dews, at his expense, to drill a test well by May 15, 1982 and continue drilling to a depth sufficient to test the Cotton Valley

Formation. If production was obtained, Crystal was required to assign Dews an interest in the leasehold estate. Crystal reserved an overriding royalty interest. If the first well was drilled, the agreement gave Dews the option to drill additional wells on the remaining acreage. The agreement was extended until July 15, 1982. Dews paid no consideration for this farmout.

Dews then entered into an agreement with Bruce Massey whereby Massey would pay Dews $50,000 in exchange for Dews assigning to Massey his right to the leasehold estate under the Crystal-Dews agreement and subject to the terms of the Crystal-Dews agreement. Dews reserved 5% of the leasehold estate as an overriding royalty interest. Massey agreed in return to cause the well to be drilled as required by the Crystal-Dews farmout agreement.

Drilling operations began prior to July 15, 1982 and the well was completed as a producing well on November 14, 1982. All of the claimants in this case were hired by Massey to supply labor or material for drilling the well.

As a result of the drilling and completion of the well, Dews received his assignment of leases from Crystal. Dews never assigned his right to Massey pursuant to their agreement, because Massey never paid Dews the $50,000 in a manner satisfactory to Dews.

Some of the various companies responsible for drilling the well filed suit against Massey in an attempt to collect the money owed to them. Dews was brought in as a party defendant and Dews then cross-claimed against all of the companies.

The chancellor found that Massey did not appear and defend and was therefore in default, and that Massey and Dews were jointly and severally liable for the companies' claims. Each company was awarded a money judgment, for a total of $519,397.60 plus interest. In addition, all but one of the companies were allowed statutory liens against the leasehold estate, and all claimants were granted constructive, equitable liens upon all funds held by any purchaser of the oil or gas produced from the well.

Numerous issues are raised on appeal and on a cross-appeal filed by one of the companies. The chancellor based Dews' liability for the money owed on four alternative grounds. We agreed with one of the reasons, therefore, the chancellor is affirmed as to the money judgment.

I. Quasi-contract

In holding Dews liable under a quasi-contract theory, the chancellor found that the claimants provided valuable services and materials to the well, which services and materials were anticipated by the parties and were necessary to the completion of the well. Since Dews claims ownership of the well by virtue of the assignment from Crystal, and has accepted the well and the work performed by the claimants, the court held Dews would be unjustly enriched if he were not required to pay for the work.

Quasi-contracts, or contracts implied in law, are legal fictions, created by the law to do justice. They do not rest upon the express or implied assent of the parties. Rather, the underlying principle is that one person should not unjustly enrich himself at the expense of another. *Dunn v. Phoenix Village, Inc.*, 213 F. Supp. 936 (W.D. Ark 1963); Brill, Arkansas Law of Damages §15-3 (1984). To find unjust enrichment, a party must have received something of value, to which he was not entitled and which he must restore. There must also be some operative act, intent, or situation to make the enrichment unjust and compensable. Brill, *supra*; *Frigillana v. Frigillana*, 584 S.W.2d 30 (Ark. 1979). The basis for recovery under this theory is the benefit that the party has received and it is restitutionary in nature. Brill, *supra*. Recovery may be had under quasi-contract where services have been performed, whether requested or not, which have benefited a party. Dobbs, Handbook on the Law of Remedies§ 4.2 (1973). Courts, however, will only imply a promise to pay for services where they were rendered in such circumstances as authorized the party performing them to entertain a reasonable expectation of their payment by the party beneficiary. *Dunn, supra.* Quasi-contracts rest on the equitable principle that "whatsoever it is certain that a man ought to do, that the law supposes him to have promised to do ... Where a party has in good faith rendered a service, not illegal or contrary to public policy, and the other party has accepted and used the service, the former may recover." *Dunn, supra.*

That is the situation we are confronted with here. The appellees provided valuable services and materials for the well, without which the well never would have been drilled. Because the well was drilled and is producing, Dews received his assignment. Dews was undoubtedly enriched by appellees' actions.

As to the unjust aspect, the testimony at the trial demonstrated that Dews was aware that the companies were rendering valuable services to the well. Because Massey never paid Dews the $50,000 pursuant to their agreement, Dews at all times knew that Massey was in breach. Since Massey's authority to drill the well stemmed from the same agreement he had breached, Dews could not stand by and watch the companies perform services based on their agreements with Massey. Dews testified he decided to let Massey continue drilling in the hopes that he would finish the well. By making a conscious decision not to inform the companies that Massey was in breach of their agreement, and would therefore never receive the assignment, Dews allowed the debts to be incurred. He cannot permit such an injustice and still receive the benefit of the services rendered. Dews admitted as much during the course of the trial when he testified as follows:

> Q: If the situation occurs what I just said and you don't have to pay any lien claimants any money because you didn't contract with them according to your statement and you don't have to pay Mr. Massey because he is in breach of your contract and you have got an assignment from Crystal and the well is in [your] name, then you just get a free fall in this whole thing, is that just? Is that fair? For you to get something when you have got nothing in it except an assignment?
>
> Dews: I would say if I am paid I feel like ...
>
> Q: That is not my question.
>
> Dews: No sir, that is not fair.

The appellee companies, in good faith, performed services on the well. As the owner of the majority of the working interest in the producing well, Dews has accepted and used their services. The companies, therefore, may recover from him.

D. Review of Bases of Liability in Contract and Restitution

We have seen three bases of liability (or "causes of action") that feature promises: bargained-for exchange, promissory estoppel, and promise made in recognition of a past benefit. Contract law includes one further promissory basis of liability: promise under seal. The seal is a physical marking of formality and seriousness, usually made with wax or imprintation. The doctrine of contract under seal provides that a promise is enforceable if it is sealed. Before the nineteenth century, this was an important part of commercial law. Today, however, the doctrine has been rejected or repealed in over half of the states in the United States while in numerous others, bargained-for consideration or reliance on the sealed promise still is necessary for enforcement, and a seal is treated as merely rebuttable evidence that there was bargained-for consideration. Although some businesspeople continue to use seals to mark formal contract documents, the practice is much less common than in the past, and it is unlikely to be revived. Yet the need for some pure formality that would validate contracts continues to be felt and is reflected in some provisions of the Uniform Commercial Code. See, e.g., U.C.C. §§ 1-107, 2-205.

In contrast to these four promissory bases of liability, restitution imposes liability without any requirement of a promise. Restitution depends instead on a duty to right a wrong. The most common form of restitution today is unjust enrichment. In addition, cases involving restitution may feature a variety of other claims and asserted duties, including breach of a fiduciary duty, violation of a statutory duty, constructive trust, and replevin.

The following case provides an opportunity to review the bases of liability in contract. William Van Brundt sued Robert Rauschenberg, claiming breach of contract, promissory estoppel, unjust enrichment, constructive trust, conversion, and replevin. Could he also have argued that the promise was made in recognition of a past benefit? As you read the case, review your understanding of the bases of liability in contract and restitution.

One note of caution: In *Rauschenberg*, District Judge Martin, wrote that "New York does not recognize promissory estoppel as a valid cause [of] action when raised in the employment context." While this statement may be an accurate, although perhaps overly certain, statement of current New York law, it is not true of other jurisdictions, *see, e.g., Kinoshita v. Canadian Pacific Airlines*, 724 P.2d 110 (Haw. 1986) (finding employer, by distributing rules and policies, intended to create an atmosphere of job security and fair treatment constituting promises on which employees could rely).

William Edwin Van Brunt III v. Robert Rauschenberg

United States District Court for the Southern District of New York
799 F. Supp. 1467 (1992)

JOHN S. MARTIN, JR., DISTRICT JUDGE

. . .

Factual Background

Van Brunt met Rauschenberg in New York City in 1968 and the two maintained a continuous personal and business relationship until July 1990. The two spent substantial amounts of time together for purposes of business and pleasure. Van Brunt alleges that throughout their twenty-two year relationship, he assisted Rauschenberg in creating sculptures, photographs, drawings, paintings, print editions, mock-ups for posters, advertisements, magazine covers, catalogues, and books.

In his amended complaint, Van Brunt alleges that Rauschenberg repeatedly promised to provide him with various examples of each of the production phases of work created. Additionally, Rauschenberg allegedly promised Van Brunt that he would (1) pay his living expenses; (2) reimburse his business expenses; (3) pay Van Brunt's income taxes.

Before the Court is Van Brunt's amended complaint, alleging actions in contract, unjust enrichment, [and] promissory estoppel ... Rauschenberg moves to dismiss the complaint for failure to state a claim.

Robert Rauschenberg. Photo by Bruce Gilbert © 1990 NEWSDAY.

Discussion

A dismissal under 12(b)(6) for failure to state a claim should be granted only in certain limited circumstances. As the Second Circuit has stated:

> To dismiss a complaint for failure to state a claim upon which relief can be granted, a court must accept plaintiff's allegations at face value, ... must construe

the allegations in the complaint in plaintiff's favor, … and must dismiss the complaint only if "it appears beyond doubt that the plaintiff can prove no set of facts in support of his claim which would entitle him to relief."

Rapf v. Suffolk County of New York, 755 F.2d 282, 290 (2d Cir. 1985).

1. The Breach of Contract Claim

The essential elements to pleading a breach of contract under New York law are the making of an agreement, due performance by the plaintiff, breach by the defendant, and damage suffered by the plaintiff. *See Stratton Group, Ltd. v. Sprayregen*, 458 F. Supp. 1216, 1217 (S.D.N.Y. 1978).

…

Despite Van Brunt's ostensible compliance with pleading requirements, Rauschenberg argues that dismissal is nevertheless proper. First, Rauschenberg argues that dismissal is proper in that implied contracts arising out of personal relationships are not recognized in New York. Second, Rauschenberg contends that the alleged express promises are not sufficiently certain or specific to be enforceable. Third, Rauschenberg argues that parts of the contract claim must be dismissed as lacking in consideration or being barred by the statute of limitations and the statute of frauds.

Rauschenberg's argument that implied contracts arising out of personal relationships are not recognized in New York is quite simply irrelevant. While it is true that New York does not recognize such implied contracts, *see, e.g., Morone v. Morone*, 413 N.E.2d 1154 (N.Y. 1980), the plaintiff here does not seek to recover under an implied contract theory. Rather, Van Brunt alleges that various express agreements existed between him and Rauschenberg. In *Morone*, the New York Court of Appeals expressly reaffirmed the "long accepted … concept that an express agreement between unmarried persons living together is as enforceable as though they were not living together … provided only that illicit sexual relations were not 'part of the consideration of the contract'" (citations omitted). *Morone*, 429 N.Y.S.2d at 594. This is not a case involving an illicit sexual relationship. Nor is it a case where the services provided were of the type usually rendered gratuitously. *See, e.g., Trimmer v. Van Bomel*, 434 N.Y.S.2d at 85 (plaintiff provided companionship only). As such, an express agreement between Van Brunt and Rauschenberg is enforceable under New York law.

Rauschenberg next argues that the amended complaint fails to identify any agreement sufficiently definite to be enforceable. The argument is without merit. In his amended complaint, Van Brunt alleges that Rauschenberg agreed to (1) pay Van Brunt's living expenses; (2) reimburse business expenses incurred by Van Brunt on behalf of Rauschenberg; (3) annually supply Van Brunt with two drawings and two paintings destined for exhibition from each of the series of works that Rauschenberg and Van Brunt worked on; (4) provide Van Brunt with one of each edition and two of each multiple or poster that Rauschenberg and Van Brunt worked on together; (5) pay Van Brunt's income taxes; and (6) transfer to Van Brunt the property on Captiva Island known as the "Fish House." In consideration for these promises, Van Brunt alleges that he promised not only to devote his life, both personally and professionally, to Rauschenberg, but also to perform various duties, including coordinating exhibitions and providing administrative services. As such, the amended complaint sufficiently sets forth a cause of action for breach of contract and the motion to dismiss must fail. *Accord Kelley v. Galina-Bouquet, Inc.*, 155 A.D.2d 96, 552 N.Y.S.2d 305, 306 (1st Dep't 1990) (finding wife's breach of contract claim against husband sufficient where complaint alleged substantial business dealings prior to and during marriage).

This is not to say that the contract claims are to be sustained in their entirety. Specifically, Rauschenberg notes that some of the claims are for past consideration[2] and others are barred by the statute of limitations and the statute of frauds. It is elementary that "past consideration is no consideration." *Raymond Babtkis Assocs., Inc. v. Tarazi Realty Corp.*, 36 A.D.2d 694, 318 N.Y.S.2d 798 (1st Dep't 1971); 21 N.Y. Jur. 2d, Contracts 108 at 519 (1982). While past services may constitute valid consideration where there is a written agreement signed by the promisor, N.Y. Gen. Oblig. Law § 5-1105; *Sarama v. John Mee, Inc.*, 102 Misc. 2d 132, 422 N.Y.S.2d 582 (1979), the existence of a written agreement is not pleaded. Accordingly, the claims based on past consideration must be dismissed.

Similarly, other promises are barred by the statute of frauds and the applicable statute of limitations. Most notably, the allegations that Rauschenberg promised to transfer real property located in Captiva, Florida to Plaintiff must be dismissed since a promise to convey real property must be in writing to be enforceable.[3] N.Y. Gen. Oblig. Law § 5-703 (McKinney 1989); *Jonestown Place Corp. v. 153 W. 33rd St. Corp.*, 422 N.E.2d 820 (N.Y. 1981). However, the allegations that Rauschenberg promised to pay Van Brunt's tax obligations should not be dismissed. While a promise to "answer for the debt ... of another person" must be in writing to be enforceable by a creditor, see N.Y. Gen. Oblig. Law § 5-701(a)(2) (McKinney 1989); *Posner v. Minnesota Mining & Mfg. Co.*, 713 F. Supp. 562, 564 (E.D.N.Y. 1989), such a promise need not be in writing to be enforceable by the debtor.[4] *G. Carver Rice, Inc. v. Crawford*, 84 A.D.2d 866, (N.Y. 1981); Farnsworth, Contracts (2d) § 6.3, at 102 (1990); Calamari & Perillo, Contracts § 19-5, at 683 (2d ed. 1977).

Other claims are barred by the statute of limitations. In New York, breach of contract claims must be brought within six years from the time of the breach. N.Y. Civ. Prac. L. & R. § 213 (McKinney 1988); *Barr v. McGraw-Hill, Inc.*, 710 F. Supp. 95, 98 (S.D.N.Y. 1989). As such, the promises Van Brunt alleges as dating from 1969, 1979, 1982, and 1983 must be dismissed as time-barred.

It is noted that many of the contract allegations are too ambiguous to determine whether consideration was past or present. Other allegations fail to provide dates, making it difficult to ascertain whether or not they are barred by the applicable statute of limitations. While we are mindful that an order for a more definite statement should not serve as a substitute for discovery, we are also mindful that this is the second time the Plaintiff has appeared before the Court with vague allegations. Accordingly, pursuant to Fed. R. Civ. P. 12(e), we order the Plaintiff to file a new complaint containing concise paragraphs describing each promise, the date of the promise, the relevant consideration, and the specific damage resulting from the breach. In drafting the new complaint, Plaintiff is instructed to take cognizance of this Court's determinations. Claims which are for past consideration or are time-barred should not be re-alleged.

---

2. For example, Van Brunt alleges that in 1980 he was instrumental in helping Defendant settle a dispute. Afterwards, Plaintiff alleges "Rauschenberg, in consideration for the results achieved through Van Brunt's efforts, agreed to provide" Plaintiff with artwork. Similarly, Plaintiff alleges that in early 1969 he worked with Defendant on six drawings called the "Body Series" and that, after the series was exhibited, Defendant promised to provide Plaintiff with a drawing.

3. Recognizing this defect, Van Brunt does not press this claim in his amended complaint or in his opposition to the motion to dismiss.

4. Specifically, a surety agreement need not be in writing if "the promisee had no reason to know that the promisor was acting as a surety, or when the duties of the principal and surety are joint, or where the promise is made to the principal." Martin Roofing, Inc. v. Goldstein, 457 N.E.2d 700, 701 (N.Y. 1983). Here, the promise was made directly to Van Brunt, the principal.

Plaintiff's new complaint should be filed within fifteen (15) days of the date of this opinion and order. Failure to comply with the terms of this opinion may result in the imposition of sanctions.

2. The Unjust Enrichment Claim

Rauschenberg next argues that Van Brunt fails to state a claim for unjust enrichment.

To maintain a cause of action for unjust enrichment, a plaintiff must demonstrate that a) the defendant has been enriched; b) the enrichment was at the plaintiff's expense; and c) defendant's retention of the benefit would be unjust. *Hutton v. Klabal*, 726 F. Supp. 67, 72 (S.D.N.Y. 1989).

Here, Van Brunt alleges that Rauschenberg used Van Brunt's photographs, audiotapes and videotapes and thus contributed to the creation of art that has provided Rauschenberg with vast sums of money. Van Brunt alleges that he was solely responsible for the production of videotapes used by Rauschenberg in the ROCI exhibitions. Van Brunt further alleges that he was never properly compensated for the use of this property. Given the liberal pleading requirements under the Federal Rules, it is clear that Van Brunt's allegations are sufficient to state a claim for unjust enrichment. *Cf. Corto v. Fujisankei Communications Int'l, Inc.*, 177 A.D.2d 397, 576 N.Y.S.2d 139, 140 (1st Dep't 1991) (plaintiff's allegations that she created and helped produce a unique Japanese television show without credit or recompense sufficient to state a claim for unjust enrichment).

3. The Promissory Estoppel Claim

The elements of a promissory estoppel claim are a) a clear and unambiguous promise; b) reasonable and foreseeable reliance by the party to whom the promise is made; and c) an injury sustained by the party asserting the estoppel by reason of his reliance. *Ripple's of Clearview, Inc. v. Le Havre Assocs.*, 88 A.D.2d 120, 452 N.Y.S.2d 447, 449 (2d Dep't), appeal denied, 456 N.Y.S.2d 1026 (1982). While Van Brunt has alleged each element of promissory estoppel, the claim is nevertheless dismissed. This is because New York does not recognize promissory estoppel as a valid cause [of] action when raised in the employment context. *Dalton v. Union Bank of Switzerland*, 134 A.D.2d 174, 520 N.Y.S.2d 764, 766 (1st Dep't 1987); *Pancza v. Remco Baby, Inc.*, 761 F. Supp. 1164, 1172 (D.N.J. 1991) (applying New York law, "promises surrounding an employment relationship are insufficient to state a cause of action for promissory estoppel"); *Kelly v. Chase Manhattan Bank*, 717 F. Supp. 227, 235–36 (S.D.N.Y. 1989); *Tribune Printing Co. v. 263 Ninth Ave. Realty*, 88 A.D.2d 877, 452 N.Y.S.2d 590, 593 (1st Dep't 1982) ("In New York [promissory estoppel] is reserved for a limited class of cases based on unusual circumstances"). Accordingly, the motion to dismiss as to the promissory estoppel claim is granted.

. . .

Chapter Six

Restrictions on the Power to Contract

The doctrines of offer and acceptance, consideration, promissory estoppel, and promise made in recognition of a past benefit define circumstances in which promises and agreements will be enforced. These doctrines are stated in the language of private ordering, as if the question of enforceability depends solely or primarily on the parties' intentions. Although political, economic, and moral concerns profoundly influence the development and implementation of these doctrines, they nevertheless claim deference to private agreement. The doctrines we examine in this chapter, in contrast, deprive some private agreements of legal force. The various "statutes of frauds" preclude enforcement of certain kinds of contracts unless they are evidenced by some writing. The doctrines of illegality and violation of public policy refuse enforcement because the purpose or effect of the contract violates a law or conflicts with basic community values ("public policy"). And the doctrines of age and mental incapacity make contracts entered by young people and people who are mentally challenged voidable.

These doctrines are among those that are often called *contract defenses*. This term is accurate, but it can be misleading. It is true that each of these doctrines defines situations in which courts will not enforce private agreements so each of them can be asserted as a "defense" to a breach of contract action. But they also can be used as a basis for "rescinding" (canceling, undoing) or reforming (changing) a contract that no one has breached.

Under classical contract theory's commitment to freedom of contract, external restrictions are awkward. Why should people's promises, agreements, and market transactions be restricted? Contract defenses express a tension between the ideals of individual freedom and social regulation that is critical to our times. That tension cannot be neatly resolved. Most often, courts attempt to "balance" the competing interests or values, generating doctrine that is oddly complex or even incoherent. In addition, several of these doctrines are historically rooted in a political and intellectual context quite different from contemporary circumstances. The doctrines of capacity, for example, originated in a caste system: slaves, married women, men and women of non-European descent, and children were not permitted to enforce contracts, or were significantly limited in the contracts they were permitted to enforce. The rationale for the doctrine of capacity has changed, yet many of the rules and terms of the doctrine echo its caste-based history. This contrast between the historical roots and the newly developed rationale for these doctrines is another source of complexity in contemporary doctrine.

A. Statute of Frauds

Movie baron Samuel Goldwyn reportedly said, "A verbal contract ain't worth the paper it's written on." This may be good business advice, but it is not good legal advice. As a general rule, oral contracts are fully enforceable. The only exceptions to that rule are contracts covered by one or another statute that requires some written evidence before a contract will be legally enforced.

Most states have adopted a statute of frauds modeled on the English Act for the Prevention of Frauds and Perjuries, enacted in 1677. The original statute provided that a person may not sue for enforcement for six categories of promises "unless the agreement upon which such action shall be brought, or some memorandum or note thereof, shall be in writing, and signed by the party to be charged therewith." The categories of promises, agreements, and contracts covered by the 1677 act were:

(1) A promise of an executor or administrator to answer for the debt of his decedent;

(2) A promise to answer for the debt of another;

(3) An agreement made in consideration of marriage;

(4) A contract for the sale of an interest in land;

(5) Any agreement that is not to be performed within one year from the making thereof; and

(6) An agreement for the sale of goods for a price of more than ten pounds sterling.

Most state statutes include some version of these categories, including section 2-201 of the Uniform Commercial Code, which requires a writing for contracts involving the sale of goods for more than $500.

If a promise or agreement fits into one of these categories, then lawyers say it is "within" the statute of frauds. If an agreement is within the statute, then it is not enforceable unless there is some writing that "satisfies" the statute or the agreement fits within one of several exceptions to the statute of frauds.

To satisfy the statute of frauds, it is not necessary to prove that the parties created a "written contract." Instead, a writing will satisfy the statute if it describes or *refers* to the agreement and it is signed *or adopted* by the person against whom the contract is being enforced. Courts applying a statute of frauds have not required that the writing be formal or even that it have been seen or signed by both parties: a scrap of paper thrown to the bottom of a desk drawer can be sufficient.

One consequence of the statute of frauds is that a contract can be enforceable against one party (who signed or adopted the writing) while it is not enforceable against the other party (who may not have signed or adopted a writing). Courts do not require that the statute have the some consequences for both parties. If one party wrote down the agreement for his or her own files on company stationary (a printed letterhead can be a sufficient "signature"), and the other did not, then the contract might be enforceable against the first party, but not the second.

Similarly, it is not necessary that the writing be made at the time of the contract. An oral agreement is enforceable even if it is within the statute of frauds, so long as there is some writing that refers to the agreement and its terms, even if the writing repudiates the agreement, still it will serve to make the agreement enforceable!

Questions about the effect of recent advances in technology, especially the existence of computerized communications, have been answered by federal and state statutes that make electronic "signatures" legally effective for many purposes, including the statute of frauds. Some courts have held that a tape or video recording may satisfy the writing requirement, and some have held that these do not. *Compare Londono v. City of Gainesville*, 768 F.2d 1223 (11th Cir. 1985) *with Swink & Co. v. Carroll McEntee & McGinley*, 584 S.W.2d 393 (Ark. 1979).

Since enactment of the first statute of frauds, many judges and lawyers have resisted application of the statute of frauds, particularly in cases where the existence of the agreement or bargain is not really in dispute. In such cases, the statute of frauds is a "technical" escape that generates unjust results. The statute was repealed in England in 1954 and has been rejected by most legal systems and by the United Nations Convention on Contracts for the International Sale of Goods. *See* Article 11 ("A contract of sale need not be concluded in or evidenced by writing ..."). During drafting of the Convention, representatives from the United States and the former Union of Soviet Socialist Republics joined to insist that nations be permitted to retain local writing requirements. To accommodate these entities, a provision was added to allow a nation to opt out of Article 11. Article 12 ("Any provision of Article 11 ... that allows a contract of sale ... to be made in any form other than in writing does not apply where any party has his place of business in a Contracting State which has made a declaration under article 96 of the Convention ..."), and Article 96 ("A Contracting State whose legislation requires contracts of sale to be concluded in or evidenced by writing may at any time make a declaration in accordance with article 12 ...").

Despite its rejection in other parts of the world, the statute of frauds has been retained in the United States. Karl Llewellyn, principal drafter of the Uniform Commercial Code, was an influential advocate for retention of the statute, a position that put him in rare public disagreement with his mentor, Arthur Corbin. Llewellyn argued that even though the original purposes of the statute (which involved litigation procedures, long since repealed, where juries engaged in independent investigation and the parties themselves could not give testimony) are no longer meaningful, the statute of frauds should be retained because it encourages people to make written records of their contracts. Llewellyn waxed eloquent on this subject:

> That statute is an amazing product. In it, de Leon might have found his secret of perpetual youth. After two centuries and a half the statute stands, in essence better adapted to our need than when it first was passed.... The idea, which must in good part derive from the statute, that contracts at large will do well to be in writing, is fairly well abroad in the land.

Karl Llewellyn, What Price Contract? — An Essay in Perspective, 40 Yale L.J. 704, 747 (1931). *See generally* Zipporah Wiseman, Karl Llewellyn and the Merchant Rules, 100 Harv. L. Rev. 465, 515–539 (1987). Llewellyn and others argued that the benefits of the statute should be seen not in the complexity of judicial decisions but rather in the thousands of disputes that never are litigated. As one proponent wrote:

> [T]he cases that justify the statute are not primarily the litigated cases themselves, where it often looks as if a tricky defendant slides out of an honest bargain on the mere technicality of the lack of the statutory writing. The cases that justify the statute are the thousands of uncontested current transactions where misunderstanding and controversy are avoided by the presence of a writing, which the statute at least indirectly aided to procure.

Lawrence Vold, *The Application of the Statute of Frauds under the Uniform Sales Act*, 15 Minn. L. Rev. 391, 393–94 (1931).

Arthur Corbin, among others, was not persuaded by this argument. After analyzing thousands of cases on the statute of frauds in preparation of his treatise, The Working Rules of Contract Law § 275 (1950), he concluded:

> Such good as the statute renders in preventing the making of perjured claims and in causing important agreements to be reduced to writing is attained at a very great cost [of refusing contract] enforcement to many honest plaintiffs [and of adding] an immense complexity into the law, [but] repeal of the statute would involve such a wrench to the mental habits of the bench and bar that it is very unlikely to occur.

When Llewellyn and others discuss the "sensible" practice of writing things down, they call upon a cultural image of writing as orderly and well-disciplined. Writing is also associated with power and sacredness. "The power of the written word" evokes both the order and the authority associated with writing. Many religions honor sacred texts that are understood to have special power and meaning. *See generally* Henri-Jean Martin, The History and Power of Writing 102–15 (Linda G. Cochrane, trans. 1994). During the eighteen and nineteenth centuries, written declarations, including written constitutions, were treated as having special and transformative powers. As Professor Robert Clinton observed:

> The ultimate faith of the framers of the Constitution in the power of the written word is not surprising. Eighteenth-century American society emerged from western European traditions in which written documents played powerful roles in controlling human behavior and shaping the structure of, and limits on, governmental power.... The English legal tradition, while lacking a formal written constitution, had long relied on written documents to limit the prerogatives of the Crown and therefore the operation of government itself. These documents included the Magna Carta and the Bill of Rights.... The earliest colonists generally followed suit and chose the written word to structure their secular and religious relations with one another, producing such great early documents of governance as the Mayflower Compact.
>
> As the Revolution approached, protests against the Crown were presented in the form of written petitions and remonstrances or more informal written broadsides, sometimes published anonymously. When the American colonists finally broke with England, they again chose the written form to symbolize, commemorate, and legitimate the event with Thomas Jefferson's drafting of the Declaration of Independence for the Continental Congress. Continuing their love affair with the written word and its power to control human destiny and limit governmental abuses, most of the newly independent states soon adopted their own state constitutions and bills of rights. The new central government rapidly followed suit with the drafting in 1777 and the adoption in 1781 of the nation's first written constitution — the Articles of Confederation....
>
> It is difficult to read the debates of the Constitutional Convention without coming to the conclusion that the framers had a finite sense of the meaning of language and that they strove to use language precisely to control the governance of not only the contemporary generation, but also generations to come.

Robert Clinton, *Original Understanding, Legal Realism, and the Interpretation of "This Constitution,"* 72 Iowa L. Rev. 1177, 1187 (1987).

Schooled to honor this history as our own, many contemporary Americans view the written word as a powerful tool in the construction of human relations, including exchange relations. If it is written down, it is certain: it will happen.

So why doesn't the law say that all contracts must be evidenced by a writing? Would that be a better line of demarcation between enforceable and unenforceable promises than the consideration doctrine? The simplest answer is that such a rule would render many important commercial transactions unenforceable. Even as many people in the United States believe that writing is a powerful tool, they often do not feel any need to use it.

The law does not require written evidence for most contracts, and courts have engrafted numerous exceptions and fine distinctions on the statute of frauds. As a result, the question of whether a contract is covered by the statute or what it is that is needed to satisfy the statute is often contested. The complexity created by more than three hundred years of judicial interpretation resisting the statutes of frauds gives wide discretion to courts in applying statutes of frauds.

Given this discretion and the cultural context of the writing requirement, it is not surprising that courts tend not to apply the statute of frauds to transactions involving relatively sophisticated traders, apparently assuming that there is no need to "teach" or "encourage" those litigants to use written records. Instead, when sophisticated parties are involved, courts tend to defer and support the parties' agreement regardless of how it is expressed or proved. In contrast, if one or both of the litigants is perceived by the judge as "unsophisticated" or otherwise an "outsider," then the court frequently will apply the statute of frauds more rigidly, as if to teach a lesson to the newcomer.

Metz Beverage Company v. Wyoming Beverages, Inc.

Supreme Court of Wyoming
39 P.3d 1051 (2002)

JOHN C. BROOKS, DISTRICT JUDGE.

This case is brought by the appellant, Metz Beverage Company (Metz), against the appellee, Wyoming Beverages, Inc. (Wyoming Beverage), alleging the wrongful termination of a distributorship contract.

Metz had distributed Pepsi products for approximately 30 years in northeast Wyoming for Wyoming Beverage. In June 1997, Wyoming Beverage notified Metz that their long-term business arrangement would be terminated effective in October of 1997. Thereafter, Wyoming Beverage filed a declaratory action seeking a resolution of the relationship. Metz filed a counterclaim asserting, among other things, breach of contract, fraud, unjust enrichment, promissory estoppel, and a claim seeking an accounting.

After extensive discovery and the filing of voluminous motions, the district court granted summary judgment against Metz on Metz's breach of contract, fraud, and unjust enrichment claims. The matter is now before this court upon Metz's appeal of the district court's order and certification pursuant to W.R.C.P. 54(b).

Issue

The issue on appeal is straightforward:

> Did the District Court have a proper legal and factual basis to grant summary judgment against Metz as to Metz's claims of breach of contract ...

Factual Background

In 1967, Metz began to distribute Pepsi products in northeast Wyoming for Wyoming Beverage. That relationship, which continued for 30 years, started as an oral agreement between Forrest Clay of Wyoming Beverage and Buster Metz for Metz. The relationship and agreement appears to have been profitable and amicable for much of the 30 years.

In May of 1996, Buster Metz died. On June 12, 1997, Mr. Clay wrote a letter to Dorothy Metz, Buster's widow, stating:

> We believe that our oral agreement is terminable at will and that competitive circumstances and business necessities dictate termination of the distribution arrangement....
>
> It is our intention to accomplish the transfer to direct distribution on October 1, 1997[.]

It is undisputed that the original agreement made by Mr. Clay and Mr. Metz, in addition to being oral, was indefinite in terms of its duration. In 1990, the parties began discussing a written agreement. The initial attempts to reach a written agreement failed apparently as a result of the parties' inability to agree as to the proper length of the agreement. Metz sought an agreement that was significantly longer in duration than that proposed by Wyoming Beverage.

Between 1992 and 1994, Metz and Wyoming Beverage again tried to negotiate a written contract. Wyoming Beverage insisted on a limited three-year contract with no right of renewal. Metz continued to seek a longer agreement with a provision that any agreement could only be terminated for cause. During the negotiations, there was extensive communication and correspondence among Mr. Clay and Dorothy and Diana Metz. Diana Metz, Buster's daughter, had become deeply involved in the family business by that time.

Mr. Clay, in his correspondence with Metz, often expressed dissatisfaction with the performance of Metz's obligations under the contract and indicated that the failure to correct Metz's performance problems would result in termination of the oral agreement. Ultimately, the parties did not reach a written agreement. Buster Metz died in 1996. Wyoming Beverage terminated the relationship with Metz in October of 1997, and Wyoming Beverage itself took over direct distribution of the Pepsi products in northeast Wyoming.

...

Breach of Contract Claim

It is the position of Wyoming Beverage that any contract which existed with Metz was terminable at will by either party. Wyoming Beverage asserts that any such contract was unenforceable or limited because of the statute of frauds and the fact that the agreement had no specific duration. Metz, however, contends there was a valid enforceable contract that was only terminable for cause and that Wyoming Beverage breached its agreement with Metz by simply terminating the contract without cause.

A. The Contract

Wyoming Beverage has, at times in the record, contested the existence of a contract with Metz. Wyoming Beverage has instead referred to an arrangement or relationship with Metz. However, there is no doubt that an agreement of some nature existed between the parties from 1967 to 1997. The agreement was acknowledged in various pieces of correspondence sent by Mr. Clay to Metz. For example, in a letter to Diana Metz dated December 6, 1993, Mr. Clay stated:

If you fail to meet these obligations by the dates indicated, *the oral agreement between Wyoming Beverages and Metz Beverages* will be terminated, effective April 15, 1994. (Emphasis added.)

Similarly, on April 25, 1994, Mr. Clay wrote to Dorothy Metz:

As I mentioned to you then, we have no desire to cancel *our oral agreement.* (emphasis added).

We, therefore, conclude what the parties have essentially conceded that there was a contract between Metz and Wyoming Beverage.

B. The Statute of Frauds

Wyoming Beverage next contends that the agreement between the parties was void because it violated the statute of frauds. The parties acknowledge that the agreement in question was one for the sale of goods and, therefore, the Wyoming statutes incorporating the Uniform Commercial Code at §§ 34.1-2-101 et seq. apply.

The statute of frauds relating to the Uniform Commercial Code is found at Wyo. Stat. Ann. § 34.1-2-201 (2001), which provides as follows:

(a) Except as otherwise provided in this section a contract for the sale of goods for the price of five hundred dollars ($500.00) or more is not enforceable by way of action or defense unless there is some writing sufficient to indicate that a contract for sale has been made between the parties and signed by the party against whom enforcement is sought or by his authorized agent or broker. Writing is not insufficient because it omits or incorrectly states a term agreed upon but the contract is not enforceable under this paragraph beyond the quantity of goods shown in such writing....

(c) A contract which does not satisfy the requirements of subsection (a) but which is valid in other respects is enforceable:....

(ii) If the party against whom enforcement is sought admits in his pleading, testimony or otherwise in court that a contract for sale was made, but the contract is not enforceable under this provision beyond the quantity of goods admitted [.]

During discovery, Mr. Clay testified in a deposition as follows:

Q: You sold him [Metz] all the product he could order. It was that simple?

A: I sold him what he ordered that I could sell him, yes.

Pat Reed, one of Wyoming Beverage's managers, also testified as follows:

Q: Metz Beverages was encouraged to order however much product it could sell, wasn't it?

A: Yes.

Q: And Wyoming Beverages would supply to Metz Beverage, again, however much product Metz would require?

A: Yes.

From the foregoing letters, there is documentary evidence wherein Wyoming Beverage admitted that there was an agreement. Furthermore, there is evidence in the form of letters, testimony, and a 30-year ongoing business relationship that Wyoming Beverage would sell to Metz all of the Pepsi products that Metz needed to satisfy its customers. Thus, there is evidence of the agreement and that the agreement was a requirements contract.

This court has previously held that the Uniform Commercial Code parol evidence rule is intended to liberalize the rigidity of the common law. In addition, we noted the Uniform Commercial Code is intended to expand commercial practices through custom and usage as well as by agreement between the parties. *Century Ready-Mix Co. v. Lower & Co.*, 770 P.2d 692, 697 (Wyo. 1989). Thus, rigid adherence to the statute of frauds is contrary to the philosophy of the Uniform Commercial Code, and it is this court's policy to sustain a contact [*sic*] whenever possible. This court will not seek technical grounds for defeating a contract. *Century Ready-Mix*, at 697. The record reveals, through deposition testimony and other writings, that there was ample evidence to create an issue of fact as to any Uniform Commercial Code statute of frauds defenses raised by Wyoming Beverage.

Wyoming Beverage also relies on the general statute of frauds, Wyo. Stat. Ann. § 1-23-105 (2001), which states:

> (a) In the following cases every agreement shall be void unless such agreement, or some note or memorandum thereof be in writing, and subscribed by the party to be charged therewith:
>
> (i) Every agreement that by its terms is not to be performed within one (1) year from the making thereof[.]

This argument also fails for a number of reasons. As previously noted, there are in fact various writings acknowledging the existence of the agreement. The writings need not be made contemporaneously with the initial agreement, especially where, as here, the agreement was of long duration and the writings occurred during the performance of the contract. *Mead v. Leo Sheep Co.*, 232 P. 511, 513 (Wyo. 1925); *Laramie Printing Trustees v. Krueger*, 437 P.2d 856, 859 (Wyo. 1968).

Furthermore, this court has held that the general statute of frauds is inapplicable where there has been substantial part performance by one party. *Fowler v Fowler*, 933 P.2d 502, 504 (Wyo. 1997). Clearly, 30 years of performance by both parties would appear to satisfy the substantial part performance exception to the statute of frauds.

Finally, assuming this was a contract with no duration that was either terminable for cause or terminable at will, conceptually it could have been performed within one year. Therefore, it would not fall within the statute of frauds.

The purpose of the statute of frauds is to prevent the enforcement of alleged promises that never were made. The statute is not to be utilized to repudiate promises that in fact were made. *B&W Glass, Inc. v. Weather Shield Mfg., Inc.*, 829 P.2d 809, 816 (Wyo. 1992). The general Wyoming statute of frauds is inapplicable to this case.

. . .

Finally, as to the breach of contract claim, there is no dispute that Metz and Wyoming Beverage had done business for 30 years. During those years Wyoming Beverage imposed various requirements on Metz. Those included the requirement that Metz not sell competing products. Certainly, the imposition of such a restraint on Metz's operation, taken together with the Clay letters or the statements from Buster Metz, might give rise to the inference that Metz could only be terminated for cause. This court believes that there was sufficient evidence in the record to raise the inference that the parties had agreed that their oral contract was only terminable for cause. In light of that evidence, a jury could conclude that Wyoming Beverage breached its agreement with Metz by simply terminating the relationship. We must, therefore, hold that the district court was in error when it granted summary judgment as to the Metz breach of contract claim. . . .

We hold that the district court did not err when it granted summary judgment in favor of Wyoming Beverage on the fraud and unjust enrichment claims. However, the district court's entry of summary judgment as to Metz's breach of contract claim must be reversed in that material factual issues exist.

Reversed in part, and affirmed in part.

B. Illegality and Violation of Public Policy

1. Illegality

If Emma agrees to set fire to a school building in exchange for Bert's promise to pay her $10,000 in advance and Bert fails to pay her the $10,000, can Emma successfully sue Bert for breach of contract? Setting fire to the school building is illegal, so the answer is no. The explanation is two fold. First, in order to protect the integrity of the judicial system, the court will not allow itself to be used to facilitate criminal activity. Second, the court will attempt to discourage criminal activity by denying enforcement to any illegal agreements. Even if Emma does not intend to set the fire now (because of Bert's breach of contract), still she may not use the court to recover her expected profits. Because this doctrine is designed to protect the courts and the public generally, the defense or claim of illegality can be raised by the court on its own initiative, even if neither party mentions it.

Of course, actual disputes arise in circumstances that vary from this paradigm. What if the illegality is a technical violation of a licensing provision? Should the court determine the relative importance of various statutes and distinguish between contracts that violate "serious" prohibitions and those that violate merely "technical" ones? What if the illegality is just a small part of the contract? What if Bert has already paid Emma the money and Bert alleges that the whole plan was Emma's idea in the first place? Should the court act to "balance the equities" between two people, one of whom is more culpable than the other, or would even this amount of involvement compromise the integrity of the court and lend comfort to those who would go along with criminal or other prohibited behavior?

Segundo Jara and Carlos Huerta v. Strong Steel Doors, Inc., David Wei a/k/a Feng Qing Wei and Colonial Surety Company, et al.

Supreme Court, Appellate Division, Second Department, New York
871 N.Y.S.2d 363 (2009)

A. Gail Prudenti, P.J., Edward D. Carni, and Ariel E. Belen, J.J.

The defendants Strong Steel Door, Inc., and David Wei (hereinafter together Strong Steel Door) entered into several contracts with different municipalities for the performance of construction work. For that purpose, Strong Steel Door hired the plaintiff Carlos Huerta. Prior to doing so, Strong Steel Door requested that he provide documentation of his eligibility to work in the United States. Huerta complied by producing an alien registration card and Social Security card. Subsequently, Huerta's employment was terminated and, as a result, he, and others similarly situated, commenced this action seeking payment of a prevailing wage in accordance with Strong Steel Door's public works contracts. Meanwhile, Strong Steel Door learned that Huerta had provided false documentation, a fact which he does not dispute. Strong Steel Door moved, inter alia, for summary judgment dismissing the complaint insofar as asserted by Huerta against it and the Supreme Court denied that branch of its motion.... Strong Steel Door contends that Huerta entered into an illegal contract which renders it unenforceable as a matter of New York law. Additionally, it contends that Huerta's unclean hands preclude him from recovering in equity. We disagree.

As a general rule, illegal contracts are unenforceable (*see e.g. Lloyd Capital Corp. v. Pat Henchar, Inc.*, 603 N.E.2d 246 (N.Y.)). However, contrary to Strong Steel Door's contention, neither the contract at issue nor the work Huerta performed was illegal (*see Majlinger v. Cassino Contr. Corp.*, 802 N.Y.S.2d 56 ["As between the undocumented worker and the employer, however, there is a contract of employment, under which the worker is entitled to be paid for his or her work"], *affd. sub nom. Balbuena v. IDR Realty, LLC*, 845 N.E.2d 1246 (N.Y.) ["Although recoveries have been denied to parties who have engaged in illegal activities, in those cases it was the work being performed that was outlawed, whereas here, the construction work itself was entirely lawful"] [internal citations omitted]; *see also Matter of Sackolwitz v. Hamburg & Co.*, 67 N.E.2d 152, 156; *Noreen v. Vogel & Bros.*, 132 N.E. 102.

Nor is Strong Steel Door entitled to summary judgment dismissing Huerta's alternative claims for equitable relief under theories of unjust enrichment and quantum meruit. "The doctrine of unclean hands applies when the complaining party shows that the offending party is guilty of immoral, unconscionable conduct and even then only when the conduct relied on is directly related to the subject matter in litigation and the party seeking to invoke the doctrine was injured by such conduct" (*Columbo v. Columbo*, 856 N.Y.S.2d 159). Here, Strong Steel Door was not injured by Huerta's production of false documentation, as it received bargained-for labor (*see Fade v. Pugliani/Fade*, 779 N.Y.S.2d 568).

Finally, Strong Steel Door failed to satisfy its prima facie burden of establishing that it did pay Huerta a prevailing wage, which requires the denial of its motion regardless of the sufficiency of the opposing papers (*see Alvarez v. Prospect Hosp.*, 501 N.E.2d 572 (N.Y.)).

Accordingly, the Supreme Court properly denied that branch of Strong Steel Door's motion which was for summary judgment dismissing the complaint insofar as asserted by Huerta against it.

Pedro Montoya, Yodna Vivanco-Small, Village Taxi Corp., and Port Chester Taxi Corp v. Ramon Beltre, Janeth Campos, et al.

Supreme Court, Appellate Division, Second Department, New York
933 N.Y.S.2d 694 (2011)

JOHN M. LEVENTHAL, J.

A contract that violates municipal regulations which exist for the protection of public health or morals may be illegal and unenforceable (*see Benjamin v. Koeppel*, 650 N.E.2d 829 (N.Y.)). On this appeal, which arises from the sale of the outstanding capital stock and assets of certain taxi companies located within the Village of Port Chester, we consider, among other things, whether the Supreme Court correctly determined that so much of the subject contract as pertains to the sale of certain taxicab licenses is unenforceable and against public policy, mandating the summary dismissal of the fraud and breach of contract causes of action relating to those licenses. We answer this question in the affirmative.

Pursuant to a written agreement dated March 11, 2005 (hereinafter the agreement), the plaintiff Pedro Montoya and his wife, the plaintiff Yodna Vivanco-Small (hereinafter together the Buyers), purchased from the defendants Ramon Beltre and Janeth Campos (hereinafter together the Sellers) all of the outstanding capital stock and assets of two taxi companies, the plaintiffs Village Taxi Corp. (hereinafter Village Taxi) and Port Chester Taxi Corp. (hereinafter PC Taxi) for the sum of $300,000.... In September 2006, an addendum to the agreement was executed which states:

> The nine motor vehicles and the nine taxi licenses issue[d] by the Village of Port Chester is including [sic] in the transaction as part of the equipment sold by [the Sellers] to [the Buyers] during the sell [sic] and purchases of [Village Taxi and PC Taxi]. The purpose of this Agreement is to ratify the transfer of the nine cars and the nine licenses

The addendum lists the nine motor vehicles, as well as the licenses issued by the Village of Port Chester that were associated with each vehicle. Only Beltre signed the addendum.

In July 2007, the Buyers, Village Taxi, and PC Taxi (hereinafter collectively the plaintiffs), commenced this action against the Sellers, Carlos Pereyra, Leonardo Coronado, the Estate of Anthony Silvano (hereinafter the Estate), and Luso Taxi. Carlos Pereyra and Leonardo Coronado (hereinafter together the Drivers), as well as Anthony Silvano (now deceased), were taxicab drivers who previously worked for Village Taxi and PC Taxi when those companies were owned by the Sellers. The Drivers had continued to work for Village Taxi and PC Taxi for some time after they were sold to the Buyers. The defendant Luso Taxi is a Port Chester taxicab company and is the Drivers' current employer.

In their first cause of action seeking to recover damages for, in effect, fraudulent inducement against the Sellers, the plaintiffs alleged that the Sellers represented that the assets of Village Taxi and PC Taxi consisted of nine individual taxicab licenses which were issued by the Village "to operate vehicles for hire to carry persons pursuant to the Village of Port Chester Code." The plaintiffs alleged that the Sellers represented that those assets were "free and clear of any and all claims, liens, or encumbrances." The plaintiffs asserted that "[p]ursuant to the custom and practice within the Village of Port Chester, taxicab licenses were issued to individual drivers, and [Village Taxi and PC Taxi] were the beneficial owners of the licenses," and the Sellers represented as much. Specifically, the plaintiffs alleged that "during the entire course of ... negotiations," the Sellers "willfully and intentionally made [knowingly false] misrepresentations" to the Buyers regarding the status of the taxicab licenses to induce the Buyers to enter into the agreement, which the Buyers relied upon. The Buyers later learned that the "licenses were not properly held by [Village Taxi and PC Taxi]" and alleged that they have been forced to expend considerable sums "in order to establish and defend their rights to the licenses." According to the plaintiffs, the Buyers "would not have entered into the agreement to purchase the stock ... had they known that licenses were not in fact owned by [Village Taxi and PC Taxi]."

The second cause of action sought to recover damages for an unspecified breach of contract against the Sellers. The fourth cause of action sought to recover damages for breach of contract against the Drivers. The plaintiffs alleged that they were the "beneficial owners of the licenses and automobiles, currently in the name of [the Drivers], license numbers 12 and 38." The plaintiffs further claimed that "as a condition of their being granted permission to drive," the Drivers "agreed to work under the auspices and for the benefit of [Village Taxi and PC Taxi]." The Drivers allegedly breached that agreement in that they no longer drive for Village Taxi and PC Taxi.

In the sixth cause of action, the plaintiffs alleged, inter alia, that the Drivers exercised dominion and control over License Nos. 12 and 38, and the automobiles used in connection with those licenses. Accordingly, the plaintiffs sought to recover those licenses and vehicles.

Lastly, in the seventh cause of action, the plaintiffs stated, inter alia, that the action of the Drivers constituted "an unjust enrichment."

At her examination before trial, Vivanco-Small testified that she was familiar with the way the taxi companies did business in the Village of Port Chester. She testified that the industry standard or custom was not to put all the cars in the name of the corporation. Rather, Vivanco-Small acknowledged, it was her understanding that the taxicabs would be registered "in the name of individuals." Vivanco-Small added,

> I was informed [prior to purchasing Village Taxi and PC Taxi] that the Village of Port Chester requests the [taxicab] license to be under the person or the corporation which the insurance was. Meaning, insurance was issued to the individuals and those license [sic] should be issued to those individuals, not the corporation. At that time, they were not insured for the corporation.

According to Vivanco-Small, it was "quite difficult" to obtain insurance for a taxi corporation. Vivanco-Small initially testified at her deposition that the Buyers did not receive three of nine taxicab licenses, License Nos., 12, 38, or 57, for which they bargained in the addendum to the agreement. However, she later clarified that the Buyers did receive all nine taxicab licenses at closing, and kept those licenses for one year.

When the Buyers received License No. 12 in 2005, the license was initially in the name of a driver named Amabella Valdiviezo; Coronado and Montoya subsequently agreed to put that license in Coronado's name, despite knowing that the license was not transferrable. Vivanco-Small admitted that License No. 12 included the phrase "this license is not transferable" on the bottom. Nevertheless, Vivanco-Small testified that people generally "chang[ed] those license[s] among drivers." Vivanco-Small testified "that it was only for the purpose to run the business, keep for us [the Buyers] to keep run the business [sic]." Vivanco-Small agreed that Coronado's name was placed on License No. 12, with the consent of the Buyers, in order "to be able to operate a taxi [sic]." Montoya testified that the Buyers put License No. 12 in Coronado's name, rather than in the name of Village Taxi, "[b]ecause the corporation['s] insurance had not been approved."

As to License No. 38, which was in Pereyra's name prior to the closing, the Buyers testified at their deposition that they and Pereyra had agreed that Pereyra would keep License No. 38 in Pereyra's name, but the plaintiffs would be the true owners of that license. Vivanco-Small testified that License No. 57 was in the name of a nonparty prior to the closing, but was subsequently transferred to Silvano's name. Vivanco-Small admitted that the Buyers agreed that License No. 57 would be placed in Silvano's name. According to Vivanco-Small, after Silvano died, his son "claimed he owned that license."

In April 2009, following discovery, the Drivers moved, inter alia, for summary judgment dismissing the complaint insofar as asserted against them. The Drivers contradicted the plaintiffs' contentions regarding License Nos. 12 and 38, and argued that they fully complied with the provisions of Chapter 295 of the Port Chester Village Code, which addresses the Village's taxicab regulatory scheme.

Thereafter, the Sellers also moved for summary judgment dismissing the complaint insofar as asserted against them. The Sellers argued that the deposition testimony demonstrated that the Buyers knew at the time of the contract signing and closing that the taxi licenses were being held in the names of the respective license holders. The Sellers further asserted that the evidence demonstrated that the Buyers knew, at the time of the sale, that taxi licenses were held by those individuals.

In an order and judgment (one paper) dated August 3, 2009, the Supreme Court held that the Sellers and the Drivers established their prima facie entitlement to judgment as a matter of law dismissing the complaint insofar as asserted against them. The Supreme Court determined that while the Port Chester Village Code required the Buyers to apply for permission to transfer the subject taxi licenses, the Buyers conceded that they did not seek approval of any license transfer. The Supreme Court found that the defendants were "just as guilty [as the plaintiffs] in participating in this scheme," and that because the regulations at issue were established to protect public health and safety, the portion of the parties' addendum pertaining to the licenses was against public policy and therefore unenforceable. Moreover, the Supreme Court determined, it was "not disproportionate to decline to enforce the parties' agreement, especially since Plaintiffs have already reaped benefits from their fraudulent action."

On appeal, the plaintiffs contend that the agreement clearly and unambiguously provides that the Sellers would furnish the Buyers with good and marketable title to the nine taxicabs licenses. Thus, the plaintiffs assert that, as to the Sellers' and the Drivers' respective motions, the Supreme Court should not have considered any extrinsic evidence with respect to whether the agreement required the Sellers to convey the nine taxicabs and the nine taxicab licenses. Further, the plaintiffs contend that triable issues of fact exist as to the causes of action, in effect, to recover damages for fraudulent inducement and breach of contract asserted against the Sellers.

Discussion

The statutory scheme at issue is the Port Chester Village Code (hereinafter the Code) chapter 295. This Chapter, entitled "Taxicabs," regulates the taxi industry (*see* Town Law § 136[1] ["(t)he town board may provide by ordinance for the licensing and otherwise regulating of ... cabs"]; *see also* General Obligations Law § 7–201 [explaining that the purchaser of a licensed taxicab must be approved by the licensing agency]). Specifically, § 295–11(A) of the Code provides:

> It shall be unlawful for any person to own a motor vehicle to be operated as a taxicab upon the streets of the Village without first having obtained therefor a taxicab license under the provisions of this chapter from the office of the Village Clerk. Such license shall be issued as of July 1 and shall be valid to and including June 30 next succeeding, unless previously suspended or revoked. No license shall be issued unless said person and vehicle are affiliated with a dispatching company duly licensed under the provisions of this chapter. No license shall be issued to a person convicted of a felony.

A "taxicab operator" is defined as "[a]ny person who operates a taxicab, whether such person is the owner of such taxicab or registrant of such taxicab or employed to operate such taxicab" (Port Chester Village Code § 295–1). A "taxicab license" is defined as "[p]ermission granted to any person to own or register a vehicle for hire as a taxicab in [the] Village" (*id.*).

Section 295–12(A) of the Code provides that an "[a]pplication for a taxicab license shall be made by the owner," and specifies the information required on the application, including insurance information, any criminal history of the applicant, and a copy of the taxi operator's license. Section 295–13 of the Code discusses renewal of taxicab licenses, and notes that "transfers of the taxicab license shall be permitted and authorized upon the consent of the transferor/licensed vehicle owner provided that the transferee meets the license requirements of § 295–12" (Port Chester Village Code § 295–13 [D]). If a licensed vehicle is to be re-registered to another person or entity then such owner must provide a complete application containing the information required by the code (*see* Port Chester Village Code § 295–13[E]).

Code § 295–5(B) explains that the Village's taxi commission "may request any Village licensee to appear before it for a hearing based upon any complaint against such licensee relative to the provisions of this chapter." The taxi commission has authority to suspend or revoke a license "or take such other action as it may deem proper" (Port Chester Village Code § 295–5[B]). Moreover, under § 295–30(A) of the Code, the owner of a taxicab not properly licensed in accordance with the Code who engages in the taxicab business "shall be punished by a fine of not more than $250 or by imprisonment not exceeding 30 days, or by both such fine and imprisonment." Code § 295–30(C) similarly provides that "[u]pon conviction of any person for any violation of a provision of this chapter for which no punishment is specifically provided, the violation shall be punishable by a fine not exceeding $250 or by imprisonment not exceeding 30 days, or by both such fine and imprisonment."

"[P]arties should be free to chart their own contractual course" unless public policy is offended (*Welsbach Elec. Corp. v. MasTec N. Am., Inc.*, 859 N.E.2d 498, 502 (N.Y.)). However, illegal contracts are, as a general rule, unenforceable (*see e.g. Benjamin v. Koeppel*, 650 N.E.2d 829 (N.Y.); *Lloyd Capital Corp. v. Pat Henchar, Inc.*, 603 N.E.2d 246 (N.Y.); *Richards Conditioning Corp. v. Oleet*, 236 N.E.2d 639 (N.Y.); *Jara v. Strong Steel Door, Inc.*, 871 N.Y.S.2d 363). Although illegal contracts are generally unenforceable, in *Galbreath–Ruffin Corp. v. 40th & 3rd Corp.*, 227 N.E.2d 30, 40 (N.Y.), the Court of Appeals explained that where the statute or regulation requiring that a license be procured

> is merely for the purpose of raising revenue it would seem that acts performed without securing a license would be valid. But where the statute looks beyond the question of revenue and has for its purpose the protection of public health or morals or the prevention of fraud, a non-compliance with its terms would affect the legality of the business.

(*quoting Silinsky v. Lustig*, 192 N.Y.S. 837).

The Code, together with related regulations which are targeted at the taxicab industry, exist for the public's protection rather than for revenue-raising purposes (*see e.g. Bell v. Perrino*, 490 N.Y.S.2d 821, *affd.* 490 N.E.2d 1227 (N.Y.) ["(o)rdinances ... requiring the licensing of the taxicab industry ... are enacted for the benefit of the general public"]; *see generally Burbach v. City of New York*, 598 N.Y.S.2d 516 ["Ordinances requiring the licensing of the taxicab industry are enacted for the benefit of the general public, not for the benefit of a limited class of persons"]). The crux of the matter is that the agreement allowed for the conveyance of the taxicab licenses without the Village's involvement. The plaintiffs, for their part, maintain that the Sellers did not keep their end of the bargain. "[T]he courts are especially skeptical of efforts by clients or customers to use public policy 'as a sword for personal gain rather than a shield for the public good'" (*Benjamin v. Koeppel*, 650 N.E.2d 829 (N.Y.), *quoting Charlebois v. Weller Assoc.*, 531 N.E.2d 1288, 1284 (N.Y.)). Nevertheless, the Code makes clear that the parties were not authorized to bypass the Code by making private arrangements that were contrary to the regulatory scheme. The evidence submitted on the respective motions demonstrates that the Buyers were undoubtedly aware of this fact. That portion of the agreement relating to the licenses contravenes the primary purpose of the Code provisions: that is, the safety of the public. In this regard, in addition to provisions relating to insurance coverage and the safety of the vehicles, the Code mandates that taxicab license holders submit to criminal background checks and have, among other things, proper taxi operator's licenses and liability insurance.

We find that the denial of relief to the plaintiffs is not disproportionate to the requirements of public policy. Although the Buyers paid the sum of $300,000 for Village Taxi and PC Taxi's assets, only $75,000 of that sum went for equipment, which, according to the 2006 addendum, consisted of both cars and licenses. Here, the plaintiffs received all nine taxicabs and at least six of the licenses and, consequently, the loss of License Nos. 12, 38, and 57 would result in a minimal forfeiture. Indeed, we note that Vivanco-Small testified that the plaintiffs held all nine licenses for a year following the sale.

Construing the Code and the applicable public policy concerns, we conclude that the Supreme Court properly determined that the portion of the subject agreement which relates to the transfer of the licenses is unenforceable (*see e.g. Richards Conditioning Corp. v. Oleet*, 236 N.E.2d at 640 [where purpose of a regulatory scheme was to protect the public's health and safety, the plaintiff was barred from recovering on an agreement to install the air conditioning system since the plaintiff lacked an installer's license]). The conduct at issue has a direct connection to the fraudulent inducement and breach of contract causes of action since it concerned the transfer of the licenses. Consequently, the causes of action alleging, in effect, fraudulent inducement and breach of contract were properly dismissed.

. . .

The plaintiffs' remaining contentions are without merit.

Accordingly, the order and judgment is affirmed insofar as appealed from.

---

2. Violation of Public Policy

A second doctrine, closely tied to the doctrine of illegality, provides that a contract, or a contract term, should not be enforced if it violates public policy. This doctrine enables a court to refuse enforcement of a contract, or a specific contract term, even though it does not violate an official statute or regulation. While Constitutional provisions, statutes, legislative findings, executive directives, and judicial decisions may provide evidence of a "public policy," the doctrine allows courts to articulate public needs and interests beyond those authoritative materials. Thus, decisions involving this doctrine can be deeply controversial, as the following case demonstrates.

In the Matter of Baby "M" (A Pseudonym for an Actual Person)

Superior Court of New Jersey
525 A.2d 1128 (N.J. 1987)

HARVEY R. SORKOW, JUDGE

. . . .

Procedural History

This litigation began on May 5, 1986, when Mr. and Mrs. William Stern filed an ex-parte application for an order to show cause why this court should not issue an order for a summary judgment to enforce a surrogate-parenting contract.... [On July 31, the child, then four months old, was taken from the home of Ms. Whitehead's parents, in Holiday, Florida.]

The trial commenced on January 5, 1987.

Findings of Fact, Conclusions of Law and Opinion

An estimated 10% to 15% of all married couples are involuntarily childless. This calculation represents a three-fold increase of childless married couples over the last 20 years. It is estimated that between five-hundred thousand and one million married women are unable to have a child related to them genetically or gestationally without some kind of assisted fertilization or uterine implant.

The demand for this aid is more than the physical act of gestating and birthing a child. It follows from the social and psychological importance people attach to the ideal of having children who are genetically theirs. The desire to reproduce blood lines to connect future generations through one's genes continues to exert a powerful and pervasive influence. Being unable to bear a child excludes women and men from a range of human activity associated with child bearing and rearing.

. . . .

Use of a surrogate calls for the gestator to be artificially inseminated or implanted with a fertilized egg, carry the child to term and after delivery relinquish all parental rights and give the child to its natural father who was, of course, the sperm donor. (In some variations of alternative reproduction even this basic assumption need not be so.) The wife of the biological father then adopts the child.

. . . .

This court makes the following findings of fact:

William Stern was born in Berlin, Germany, on January 27, 1946. His parents were the sole surviving members of his family to escape the Holocaust. Shortly after his birth, the family settled in Pittsburgh, Pennsylvania, where he grew up in the midst of loving parents and financial insecurity. He became a United States citizen when his parents became citizens in 1954. His father, a banker in Germany, worked as a factory hand and short-order cook. His mother worked in a storm window factory. William Stern contributed to the support of his family by working at various after-school jobs. His father died when the boy was 12 years-of-age leaving his mother as his only surviving relative. Ultimately, Mr. Stern and his mother moved to New York where Mr. Stern began college. He graduated New York University and then attended graduate school at the University of Michigan. He has worked in the public sector and in private industry as a research scientist.

Mr. and Mrs. Stern met when they were both graduate students at the University of Michigan and began dating in 1969. The couple was married in East Lansing, Michigan, on July 27, 1974, by a minister friend of the family. By now, each had earned a Ph.D.— Mr. Stern in bio-chemistry and Mrs. Stern in human genetics.

With the death of his mother in 1983, Mr. Stern became the only surviving member of all branches in his family.

Elizabeth Stern is presently 41 years-of-age. She was born and grew up in East Lansing, Michigan, where her father was a professor of bio-chemistry at Michigan State University. Her father died in 1986. Her mother, who is in ill health, and her brother, who is unmarried, continue to live in East Lansing. After receiving her Ph.D., Mrs. Stern decided to go to medical school in order to work in a more people-oriented profession. She testified to being tired of "talking to test tubes." Her pediatric residency was completed in 1978. Mrs. Stern comes from a family background where religion and education have played important roles. As noted, her father was on the faculty at Michigan State University and was for a time, a lay reader at the family church.

The Sterns had discussed having children prior to and after their marriage but mutually concluded that until Mrs. Stern's pediatric residency was completed, her time to devote to family would be inadequate and thus unfair to the child. It was also concluded that post-residency earnings would make the family more economically secure.

In 1972 and 1978, Mrs. Stern had experienced several episodes of numbness in her fingers and toes and some leg weakness. In December 1979, while she was in her residency, a sharp turn in the progression of Mrs. Stern's malady occurred when she suffered what was ultimately diagnosed as optic neuritis. This is a symptom of multiple sclerosis. Being medically trained and aware of her symptoms, she concluded that she had multiple sclerosis. ...

The four experts called by the parties, both hypothetical and clinical, all concluded that Mrs. Stern has multiple sclerosis—albeit, in a mild form and the possibility of progression is limited to unknown. All experts agreed that current knowledge of the disease instructs that possibility of exacerbation during pregnancy is remote but in the late 1970s, the opposite was the prevailing view. However, in the post-partum period, the doctors now say the risk of exacerbation is from 5% to 40%. Exacerbation was defined as a chance of the disease symptoms worsening, that is, development of a new set of clinical symptoms. Dr. James Donaldson of the University of Connecticut Medical School testified that the type of exacerbation and whether the new symptoms would be temporary or permanent could not be determined. As well, the older a person gets, the higher the risk of a disability.

With regard to Mrs. Stern's disease, all the experts called on this issue, concluded that her decision not to become pregnant in light of her knowledge of her disease, her experienced symptomology, the accepted medical understanding of the medical profession at the time that risk of exacerbation was attendant to pregnancy was a medically reasonable and understandable decision. Once again, there is no apparent preventative only treatment after onset. While she testified to being willing to accept all risks of pregnancy for a 36-year-old woman, she was not willing to accept the added risks to her health that potential exacerbation of the multiple sclerosis would bring. For Mrs. Stern, onset of the disease would be too late. And while it appears that her disease is presently of the non-progressive type, there is no predictability of the course the disease will take. In Mrs. Stern's mind, there was fixed an understanding that she could not carry a child without great risk to her physical well-being. This understanding is well supported by the credible evidence in this case.

The Sterns explored the possibility of adoption but were discouraged in their inquiries. They learned that because they were of different religions and they were an "older couple," adoption of a newborn infant would be extremely difficult. Indeed, the multi-year wait would have them in their very late 30s to early 40s if a child were to become available. Moreover, following the death of William Stern's mother in 1983, the desirability of having his own biological offspring became compelling to William Stern, thus making adoption a less desirable alternative.

This court finds that the Sterns have a close network of friends and neighbors who function as an extended family and provide the Sterns with love and support which is returned in kind by the Sterns. Their friends live in reasonable proximity to plaintiffs, share family joys and sorrows and celebrate family milestones and holidays together.

In 1984, Mr. Stern read an ad from the Infertility Center of New York (hereinafter ICNY) and with the consent of Mrs. Stern, they decided to pursue surrogate parenting. ICNY is an agency that provides surrogate mother candidates to applicants seeking a child through an alternative means of reproduction.

Mary Beth Whitehead is presently 29 years old and is the sixth of eight children born to Joseph and Catherine Messer. Mrs. Whitehead decided to leave high school in mid-tenth grade at the age of 15 1/2 against the advice of her parents. While in school, she held a part-time job primarily as a hand in a pizza-deli shop. She began working at her brother's delicatessen where she met Richard Whitehead. The Whiteheads were married on December 3, 1973. Mrs. Whitehead was 16 years old. Mr. Whitehead was 24 years old. Richard Whitehead is 37 years old. He is employed as a driver for a waste carting company. He is one of four children born to Edward and June Whitehead. His parents separated about eight years ago. His father, a retired police officer, lives in Florida. His mother continues to live in New Jersey. Shortly after high school graduation, Mr. Whitehead was drafted into the United States Army, served 13 months in Vietnam and was honorably discharged as a specialist 4th class in 1971. As a result of a non-alcohol related accident, Mr. Whitehead lost the sight in his left eye.

Their first child, Ryan, was born on July 7, 1974. The Whiteheads had their second child, whom they named Tuesday, on January 27, 1976. Within several months after their daughter's birth, Richard and Mary Beth Whitehead decided that they did not want to have any more children, that they were "content" with the two children and thought they had the "perfect family." There was mutual agreement that Mr. Whitehead should have a vasectomy to prevent further impregnation of Mrs. Whitehead. The Whiteheads had created their family and wanted no further children.

From the date of the marriage in 1973, until moving in 1981 to the home in which they now live in Brick Township, the Whiteheads resided in many places. Indeed, from the date of their marriage through 1981 the Whiteheads moved at least 12 times, frequently living in the homes of other family members.

In or about 1978, the Whiteheads separated during which time Mrs. Whitehead received public assistance. The Monmouth County Welfare Board sued Mr. Whitehead to recover payments made to Mrs. Whitehead. An order for payment was entered against Mr. Whitehead. Eventually, after a warrant was issued for his arrest for non-payment, Mr. Whitehead repaid the monies owed to the Monmouth County Welfare Board.

The Whiteheads filed bankruptcy in or about 1983. The bankruptcy petition, made under oath, failed to disclose an interest the Whiteheads had in real estate and to list ownership of an automobile. To this day, Mrs. Whitehead drives a 1985 Honda registered in her maiden name in the State of Florida. It must be noted that this court document, made under oath and filed in the United States District Court, was, on cross-examination of Mrs. Whitehead, admitted not to be totally truthful and accurate, at least as to those two entries.

There are two mortgages on the Whiteheads' residence. The first mortgage is held by a financial institution. The second is a privately held second purchase money mortgage held by Mrs. Whitehead's sister and brother-in-law. When this suit started, both mortgages were in default and indeed foreclosure actions had begun on both of them. Mrs. Whitehead testified to obtaining a loan to bring the first mortgage current and out of foreclosure. The second mortgage continues in default and suit.

Mr. Whitehead has had various employments during the course of the marriage. Until obtaining his present employment in 1981, Mr. Whitehead has had seven different jobs in the last 13 years. There has also been at least one period of unemployment during which time Mr. Whitehead collected unemployment compensation.

Throughout the marriage and continuing to the present time, Mr. Whitehead has been an alcohol abuser. On two occasions, his driver's license has been suspended for alcohol-related accidents resulting in convictions for violating the motor vehicle laws of New Jersey. On two other occasions, his driving privileges were revoked for failing to comply with an alcoholic rehabilitation program. The revocation of Mr. Whitehead's driving privileges has affected his employment status. Uncontradicted is the fact that Mr. Whitehead has not actively pursued assistance to control his alcohol abuse for some time. Also uncontroverted is the fact that he admitted to a mental health expert that he had gone on two week binges at approximately six-month intervals. His last attendance at a meeting of AA appears to have been in 1980.

Equally of concern to this court is the finding that Mrs. Whitehead has characterized Mr. Whitehead's alcohol abuse as being "his problem." If she has concern that it may affect the family unit and its security, it was not apparent throughout her testimony. She minimized the effect by saying Mr. Whitehead is not a violent or abusive drunk.

Despite recommendations by the professionals who comprise her son's school district child study team, Mrs. Whitehead requested that their recommendations be disregarded and that her wishes be adopted. Dr. Metnick, the school psychologist, testified that in seven years only ten parents, out of hundreds of students tested, have rejected the child study team recommendations.

"Baby M" was born on March 27, 1986. On September 15, 1986 she was examined medically by a pediatrician, Dr. Donald I. Schiffman, and found to be in good health despite allegations by Mrs. Whitehead to the contrary. Dr. Donald Brodzinsky, Dr. Marshall Schechter and Dr. Harold Koplewicz evaluated the infant in December 1986, and January 1987. She has been found to be in the 97th percentile of development for height and weight; her gross and fine motor development are age appropriate and she is, in fact, advanced in several areas. She is a mellow, alert, easy-to-care-for child who is blessed with a "sunniness of disposition that is a delight to see." "Baby M" is a curious and social baby and adjusts to strangers and her social situations easily.

Mr. and Mrs. Whitehead have a son, age 12 and a daughter, age 11. Whether it is through the parents or counsel for the parents, from the early days of this litigation, there have been efforts to infuse these children into the dispute. Indeed, a motion was made for the court to grant leave to have the children intervene as parties and have one other than their father be appointed guardian ad litem. This application was denied. Mrs. Whitehead has on at least two occasions brought her daughter to the courthouse where she was caught up in a media crush—the child's anguish and fear forever captured in a graphic photo published in many newspapers. She sought to have her daughter testify about her feelings about the baby. This court finds that the issues raised by Mr. and Mrs. Whitehead that is, the effect on the Whiteheads' children of the removal of "Baby M" and her possible placement with Mr. and Mrs. Stern are non-issues. They relate neither to the issue of contract nor to the issue of "Baby M's" best interest. It is for this reason that there will be no fact finding about the two older Whitehead children. The treatment, attention and reaction of the Whiteheads to the care, education and welfare of their children will be of concern to this court and will be developed infra.

In or about August or September 1984, Mr. and Mrs. Stern made inquiries into several surrogate parenting programs throughout the United States. Initially, they had hoped to find a woman who would function as a gestational surrogate only; that is, a woman who would be implanted with an egg of Mrs. Stern fertilized by the sperm of Mr. Stern. At that time, however, in vitro fertilization was largely experimental and not a generally available option.

Mr. and Mrs. Stern contacted the Infertility Center of New York and were sent a brochure. The brochure explained in general terms the surrogate parenting procedure and the services which ICNY offered, including the screening of potential surrogate candidates. On December 3, 1984 Mr. Stern entered into an agreement with ICNY.

Over the next several months Mr. and Mrs. Stern were provided with various biographical data concerning potential surrogate candidates. Mr. and Mrs. Stern reviewed the material and attempted to set up interviews with several candidates. They were eventually told of a potential surrogate enrolled in the program who had been unsuccessful working with another couple for approximately eight months. The woman was described as being very dedicated and anxious to work with another couple. The candidate was Mary Beth Whitehead.

Mrs. Whitehead was enrolled in the ICNY surrogate program since the spring 1984. Mrs. Whitehead testified she was motivated to join the program in the hopes of "giving the most loving gift of happiness to an unfortunate couple." Mrs. Whitehead also felt that the surrogate's fee would assist her in providing for her children's long range educational goals. Her signed application also reveals these reasons.

Mrs. Whitehead had learned of surrogate parenting through an advertisement in The Asbury Park Press. Mrs. Whitehead spoke of her interest in the surrogacy program to no one other than Mr. Whitehead over the next week. Although Mr. Whitehead was initially opposed to Mrs. Whitehead's involvement in the surrogate program, he ultimately deferred to his wife's wishes. Mrs. Whitehead contacted ICNY and was provided with an application form, which she filled out and submitted to the center.

In or about April 1984 Mrs. Whitehead submitted to a psychological evaluation to determine her suitability as a potential surrogate. She was evaluated by interview and testing. The examiner reported that although Mrs. Whitehead expected to have strong feelings about giving up the baby at birth, she was sincere in her plan to become a surrogate mother and has thought extensively about the plan. Although the examiner noted that it would be important to explore with Mrs. Whitehead in more depth whether she would be able to relinquish the child in final analysis, Mrs. Whitehead was recommended as an appropriate candidate for a surrogate volunteer. This report was made for ICNY prior to Mrs. Whitehead working for her first childless couple. It was this fact of prior evaluation that the Sterns relied on. Mrs. Whitehead testified to receiving two counseling sessions at ICNY.

In or about May 1984 ICNY matched Mrs. Whitehead with a married couple (not Mr. and Mrs. Stern) who sought to engage Mrs. Whitehead as a surrogate. The prospective surrogate was presented with a proposed form of surrogate parenting agreement. The proposed agreement was almost identical to the agreement Mrs. Whitehead would later sign with Mr. Stern. As required by the center, she consulted independent counsel on May 24, 1984, who, after spending several hours discussing the possible legal ramifications of the agreement with both Mr. and Mrs. Whitehead, negotiated at Mrs. Whitehead's request several minor changes in the contract. The contract was signed by the Whiteheads and shortly thereafter, she began her efforts to conceive by artificial insemination. Her effort for this couple was unsuccessful. She was then introduced to Mr. and Mrs. Stern.

Mr. and Mrs. Stern met with Mr. and Mrs. Whitehead in January 1985 in New Brunswick, New Jersey. The site was chosen because it is approximately mid-way between the respective residences. The parties discussed the proposed surrogacy arrangement and other elements of their contemplated relationship, including Mrs. Whitehead's duty to relinquish custody of the child to Mr. and Mrs. Stern. Mrs. Whitehead made it clear she would not appear on the Sterns' doorstep. All she wanted was an annual picture and letter report of progress. At the conclusion of the meeting, it was agreed that Mrs. Whitehead would be the surrogate mother of a child to be born for Mr. and Mrs. Stern.

On February 6, 1986 Mr. Stern and Mr. and Mrs. Whitehead signed the surrogate parenting agreement. It was in all material respects the same contract that Mrs. Whitehead signed the spring of 1984. At that time, Mr. and Mrs. Whitehead had consulted with an attorney. As already noted, he read and explained the contract to them. Several minor changes were negotiated. Mrs. Whitehead believed the second contract to be as the first and thus, although able to do so, chose not to seek legal advice prior to signing the subject agreement. It is noted with more than passing importance that Mrs. Stern was not a signatory to the agreement. Mrs. Whitehead testified that her obligation was to attempt conception by artificial insemination, upon conception to carry the child to term, deliver and surrender the child to Mr. Stern renouncing at that time all of her parental rights and acknowledging that doing so would be in the child's best interest. It was also agreed that Mr. Stern's name would appear on the child's birth certificate.

In addition, the contract provided the following: Mrs. Whitehead would assume the risks of the pregnancy and child birth. She would submit to a psychiatric evaluation for which Mr. Stern would pay. Mr. Stern had the right to name the child. That in the event of the death of Mr. Stern, the child would be placed in the custody of Mr. Stern's wife. Mrs. Whitehead would not abort the child. In addition, she would undergo amniocentesis; and if the child were found to have a genetic or congenital abnormality, it would be aborted if Mr. Stern requested it.

That in the event the child possessed genetic or congenital abnormalities William Stern would assume legal responsibility for the child once it was born. The agreement also contained a severability clause.

The Whiteheads and the Sterns clearly understood the terms of the agreement and their obligations.

Mr. Whitehead acknowledged, pursuant to N.J.S.A. 9:17-44, that he refused to consent to the artificial insemination of his wife, and thus, pursuant to statute, he is not to be considered the father of the child born to his wife. Reference is made to the results of the HLA blood test (supra) which further confirms the issue of paternity.

Mrs. Whitehead was to be paid $10,000 and all medical expenses including dental expenses for performing her contractual obligations.

Under the present medical definition, Mrs. Whitehead had informed consent as to the procedure, if indeed, such consent was required. She was competent at the time of entering into the contract and was aware of its terms.

Subsequent to entering into the surrogate parenting agreement of February 6, 1985, Mrs. Whitehead was inseminated with the semenal fluid of Mr. Stern nine times. Finally, in July 1985 she conceived.

Mr. and Mrs. Stern were overjoyed with Mrs. Whitehead's pregnancy. They met with Mr. and Mrs. Whitehead and took them to dinner to celebrate.

Shortly after the pregnancy, in or about August 1985, Mr. Stern and Mrs. Stern, in anticipation of the birth of the child, executed new last wills and testaments naming the yet unborn child as a contingent beneficiary of their respective estates.

Over the next several months of Mrs. Whitehead's pregnancy, Mr. and Mrs. Stern papered and painted a room in their home that was to be the nursery.

Throughout the pregnancy Mr. and Mrs. Stern kept in close contact with Mrs. Whitehead telephonically and even visited on several occasions.

While the relationship between Mrs. Whitehead and Mr. Stern grew distant, her relationship with Mrs. Stern grew closer. The relationship subsequently deteriorated as Mrs. Stern insisted that Mrs. Whitehead undergo amniocentesis, take a prescription pharmaceutical in order to control the effects of the difference in blood type between Mr. Stern and Mrs. Whitehead and take certain precautions when Mrs. Whitehead reported an elevation in blood pressure in the last months of pregnancy.

Approximately one month prior to the birth of the child, in February 1986, Mr. and Mrs. Stern learned that Mrs. Whitehead had delayed signing the papers acknowledging Mr. Stern's paternity of the child. Mrs. Whitehead, nevertheless, indicated that she had no intention of repudiating her contract with Mr. Stern. Eventually, Mr. and Mrs. Whitehead signed the acknowledgment of paternity.

"Baby M" was born on March 27, 1986 at Monmouth Medical Center, Long Branch, New Jersey. Mr. and Mrs. Whitehead never told anyone at the hospital that Mrs. Whitehead was a surrogate mother. They prevailed on Mr. and Mrs. Stern not to reveal their relationship to the child. On March 27, 1986 Mr. and Mrs. Stern went to the hospital to see the infant and Mr. and Mrs. Whitehead. Because he was not identified as the child's father, Mr. Stern could not hold his newborn daughter. He could only view the infant through the nursery window. Mr. Whitehead's name appeared on the birth certificate as the child's father as did the name Sara Elizabeth Whitehead. This information was given to the hospital by either or both of the Whiteheads. Their unilateral action without consulting Mr. Stern was a violation of their understanding with Mr. and Mrs. Stern.

Mrs. Whitehead testified that throughout her pregnancy, she recognized the child being carried was not to be hers but was Mr. Stern's. This view was maintained throughout the pregnancy. Perhaps the delay in signing the adoption consents should have been a clue to a growing ambivalence on the part of Mrs. Whitehead. She testified that at the moment of birth she realized that she could not and would not give up the child. Until then, she understood what she promised to do, understood what she had to do, but when the time came to perform Mrs. Whitehead refused to perform her promise to give Mr. Stern his daughter.

When Mr. and Mrs. Stern visited Mrs. Whitehead and the baby in the hospital on March 28, 1986, Mrs. Whitehead informed them that she was not sure whether she could relinquish the child. Mr. and Mrs. Stern also testified that Mrs. Whitehead expressed sentiments to them to the effect that if she could not keep the child she could not go on living. Because of a failure to execute certain documents needed to adopt the child in Florida, Mr. and Mrs. Whitehead took the baby home to their house in Bricktown, New Jersey, on Sunday, March 30, 1986. Mr. and Mrs. Stern came to take the child in what has been described as an extremely emotional scene in which Mr. and Mrs. Stern expressed gratitude to Mr. and Mrs. Whitehead for what they had done for them and Mrs. Whitehead expressed her difficulties in relinquishing the child to Mr. and Mrs. Stern. There were indications that Mrs. Whitehead was extremely depressed and they questioned her ability to continue living without the child.

Mrs. Whitehead tells of passing a very restless emotional and depressed night. Mr. Whitehead, who said he never experienced such a night, finally told his wife to go to Tenafly and "get our baby."

On March 31, 1986, Mrs. Whitehead telephoned Mr. and Mrs. Stern and requested permission to visit the child. Mr. and Mrs. Stern agreed. At approximately 11:00 a.m. Mrs. Whitehead arrived at the Sterns' home with her sister, Joanne Cahill, a social worker. Mrs. Whitehead alternated between crying and speaking with a flat affectation. She told Mr. and Mrs. Stern that she did not want to live and that she had considered taking the entire bottle of valium pills the night before. Mrs. Whitehead said she wanted to take "Baby M" home with her for a one-week visit. Residence for the one week was offered by the Sterns but was rejected. Out of concern for Mrs. Whitehead's mental health, Mr. and Mrs. Stern acquiesced.

After listening to and observing Mr. Stern who testified about this wrenching moment, this court had no doubt that he fully expected to have his daughter returned to him after the week. His immense concern for Mrs. Whitehead and an almost naive belief in her good will was soon to be destroyed.

On April 1, 1986 Mrs. Whitehead telephoned Mr. and Mrs. Stern and indicated that she was going to be visiting with an aunt. She indicated that she would be unreachable. In fact, Mrs. Whitehead left the State of New Jersey on April 3, 1986 with the five-day old child and traveled to Florida to visit her parents.

The ostensible purpose of the visit was to show the infant to her parents and her son who was living with them. Mr. and Mrs. Stern did not know the five-day old was taken out of the State. They called the Whitehead house and Mr. Whitehead put off their inquiries and asked for their patience.

On April 4, 1986 Mrs. Whitehead telephoned Mrs. Stern. She indicated that she needed time to think about whether she wanted to keep the child. She told Mr. and Mrs. Stern that Mr. Whitehead had threatened to leave her if she kept the baby.

Mrs. Whitehead remained in Florida, unbeknownst to Mr. and Mrs. Stern, until April 8 or 9, 1986. During this period of time Mrs. Whitehead never indicated to her parents that she was considering keeping the child. Mrs. Whitehead returned to the State of New Jersey on or about April 9, 1986.

On April 9, 1986 Mrs. Stern telephoned the home of Mrs. Whitehead who advised Mrs. Stern that she would surrender custody of the child on Saturday, April 12, 1986. On April 11, 1986, however, Mrs. Whitehead telephoned the Sterns' household and advised Mr. Stern that she needed more time to consider her decision.

On April 12, 1986, Mr. and Mrs. Stern telephoned Mrs. Whitehead at approximately 6:00 a.m. They requested that they be permitted to visit the baby and Mrs. Whitehead agreed. Later that morning, Mr. and Mrs. Stern did, in fact, visit with the child.

During the visit of April 12, 1986 Mrs. Whitehead announced that she had decided to keep the child. Mrs. Whitehead indicated that if threatened with court intervention she would leave the country. Before leaving, Mrs. Stern requested that Mrs. Whitehead permit Mr. Stern to hold the baby one more time. Mrs. Whitehead refused and threatened to telephone the police. Mr. and Mrs. Stern left the Whitehead home without Mr. Stern's daughter.

On or about April 20, 1986 Mr. and Mrs. Whitehead listed their home for sale, indicating in the listing that they might be relocating to Florida.

On May 5, 1986, this court signed an order to show cause directing Mrs. Whitehead to deliver the infant to Mr. Stern.

On that same day, Mr. and Mrs. Stern accompanied the Bricktown police to the Whitehead residence. They brought with them the court order giving temporary custody of the child to Mr. and Mrs. Stern. The contents of this order were made known to Mr. and Mrs. Whitehead. Mr. Whitehead admitted his knowledge of the order. Mrs. Whitehead spoke to an attorney during the time when the police were attempting to enforce this court's order. Although Mr. and Mrs. Whitehead understood that they were being ordered by a court to return the child to Mr. and Mrs. Stern, during ensuing confusion Mrs. Whitehead took the child into a bedroom at the rear of the house and passed the child out the window to her waiting husband. That evening Mr. Whitehead took the child, first to his mother's house, and then to his sister's house in Neptune, New Jersey. After the police left, Mrs. Whitehead packed the belongings of the family, and was driven to the home of Mr. Whitehead's sister where the family remained overnight. The following morning, the Whitehead family: Mary Beth Whitehead, Richard Whitehead, their ten-year old daughter and the baby disappeared. Their whereabouts remained unknown to Mr. and Mrs. Stern for 87 days.

On May 6, 1986 Mr. and Mrs. Whitehead, their daughter and the infant child flew to the State of Florida where they were met by Mrs. Whitehead's parents (Catherine and Joseph Messer). Mr. and Mrs. Whitehead remained with the Messers until on or about May 20, 1986, at which time Mr. and Mrs. Whitehead and the infant child left the Messer household. Mr. and Mrs. Whitehead left the Messer household because they were afraid the local authorities would attempt to enforce the court order.

Mr. and Mrs. Stern hired a private detective in an effort to locate Mr. and Mrs. Whitehead and "Baby M." During their almost three months in Florida, Mr. and Mrs. Whitehead lived with Mr. and Mrs. Messer for approximately two to three weeks. They left their son and daughter in the care of the Messers and began a fugitive existence, staying in no less than 15 hotels, motels, and as well as with an assortment of relatives and friends. No pediatric care for the child was sought nor was she immunized against any of the childhood diseases during this period.

On May 20, 1986 Mr. Messer enrolled the Whiteheads' daughter in the Holiday, Florida, school system for the final two weeks of the school year. It was not yet decided whether the child would be attending school in Florida in September 1986, as such attendance was dependent upon whether Mr. and Mrs. Whitehead would be residing in the State of Florida or the State of New Jersey.

On or about July 15, 1986 Mr. Stern received a telephone call at his place of employment from Mrs. Whitehead. In addition to making demands for relief on Mr. Stern, Mrs. Whitehead threatened to kill herself and to take the life of the child, stating, "I'd rather see me and her (the infant child) dead before you get her," and "I gave her life. I can take her life," in addition to numerous other threats to the child's well-being. . . .

Mrs. Whitehead was hospitalized on or about July 28, 1986 in Stuart, Florida. On or about that date, Mr. Whitehead returned to the Messer home in Holiday, Florida, with the infant child.

On July 31, 1986 the child was taken into the care of Florida authorities and out of the Messer household by local law enforcement officials pursuant to a court order obtained in Florida under the Uniform Child Custody Jurisdiction Act. Physical custody of the child was subsequently transferred to Mr. and Mrs. Stern.

[Editors: In omitted sections, the Court reviewed the testimony of 38 witnesses, including 15 expert witnesses.]

This court is confronted with circumstances in which on February 6, 1985, the parties to this litigation, with great joy and expectation, entered into a surrogate arrangement. It was an arrangement where both the prospective family and the surrogate mother wanted the child; albeit, for different purposes. Even though the insemination is artificial, the parental attitude is real. Rosenblatt, "The Baby in the Factory," Time (February 14, 1983). The couple sought to bring into existence a child by conscious pre-arrangement which, as far as biologically possible, would be genetically their own. The surrogate consciously chose to bear a child for another couple with the understanding that she would not contest but would consent to their adoption of it.

[Editors: In the next section, the Court rejects Whitehead's argument that the surrogacy contract violates New Jersey's adoption statute, which prohibits the exchange of money in an adoption proceeding, and is therefore unenforceable under the doctrine of illegality. The Court finds that the surrogacy arrangement is not an adoption, and therefore is not covered by the adoption statute, because William Stern is the child's biological father. In the next section, the Court addresses whether the surrogacy contract violates a public policy. He considers and rejects various reasons why surrogacy contracts might be found inconsistent with public policy:]

It is argued that the child will not be protected. So long as there is no legislation and some court action in surrogacy arrangements is required, the child born of surrogacy will be protected in New Jersey. If there is compliance with the contract terms, adoption will be necessary; hence, court inquiry about best interests must take place. If there is non-compliance with the contract, as in this case, best interests is still litigated with protection to the child, with its own guardian and experts retained to aid the court in its best interests determination.

The second argument against surrogacy is that the surrogate mother will be exploited. To the contrary. It is the private adoption that has that great potential for, if not actual, exploitation of the mother. In the private adoption, the woman is already pregnant. The biological father may be unknown or at best uninterested in his obligations. The woman may want to keep the child but cannot do so for financial reasons. There is the risk of illegal consideration being paid to the mother. In surrogacy, none of these "downside" elements appear. The arrangement is made when the desire and intention to have a family exist on the couple's part. The surrogate has an opportunity to consult, take advice and consider her act and is not forced into the relationship. She is not yet pregnant.

The third argument is that to produce or deal with a child for money denigrates human dignity. With that premise, this court urgently agrees. The 13th Amendment to the United States Constitution is still valid law. The law of adoption in New Jersey does prohibit the exchange of any consideration for obtaining a child. The fact is, however, that the money to be paid to the surrogate is not being paid for the surrender of the child to the father. And that is just the point—at birth, mother and father have equal rights to the child absent any other agreement. The biological father pays the surrogate for her willingness to be impregnated and carry his child to term. At birth, the father does not purchase the child. It is his own biological genetically related child. He cannot purchase what is already his.

. . . .

The [next] argument against surrogacy is that it will undermine traditional notions of family. How can that be when the childless husband and wife so very much want a child? They seek to make a family. They intend to have a family. The surrogate mother could not make a valid contract without her husband's consent to her act. This statement should not be construed as antifeminist. It means that if the surrogate is married, her husband will, in all probability, have to sign the contract to establish his non-paternity pursuant to the New Jersey Parentage Law. Both sides of the equation must agree.

The … final argument suggests that an elite upper economic group of people will use the lower economic group of woman to "make their babies." This argument is insensitive and offensive to the intense drive to procreate naturally and when that is impossible, to use what lawful means are possible to gain a child. This intense desire to propagate the species is fundamental. It is within the soul of all men and women regardless of economic status.

. . . .

Fundamentally, when there were no time constraints, when Mrs. Whitehead was not pregnant, when each party had the opportunity to obtain advice (legal, medical and/or psychological), the parties expressed their respective offers and acceptances to each other and reduced their understanding to a writing. If the mutual promises were not sufficient to establish a valid consideration, then certainly there was consideration when there was conception. The male gave his sperm; the female gave her egg in their pre-planned effort to create a child—thus, a contract.

For the past year, there has been a child in being. She is alive and well. She is tangible proof of that which the Whiteheads and Mr. Stern in concert agreed to do. The child was conceived with a mutual understanding by the parties of her future life. Except now, Mrs. Whitehead has failed to perform one of her last promises, which was to surrender the child and renounce parental rights. She has otherwise performed the personal service that she had undertaken conception and carrying the child to term. The terms of the contract have been executed but for the surrender.

It is argued that Mrs. Whitehead should have a time period after delivery to determine if she wants to surrender the child. Such a rule has been developed in Kentucky by the use of Kentucky's private placement adoption statute. Use of laws not intended for their intended purpose creates forced and confusing results. There should be no use of the New Jersey adoption statutes to accommodate or deny surrogacy contracts. Indeed, again it is held that there is no law governing surrogacy contracts in New Jersey and the laws of adoption do not apply to surrogacy contracts. The sole legal concepts that control are parens patriae and best interests of the child. To wait for birth, to plan, pray and dream of the joy it will bring and then be told that the child will not come home, that a new set of rules applies and to ask a court to approve such a result deeply offends the conscience of this court. A person who has promised is entitled to rely on the concomitant promise of the other promisor. This court holds therefore that in New Jersey, although the surrogacy contract is signed, the surrogate may nevertheless renounce and terminate the contract until the time of conception. She may be subject then for such monetary damages as may be proven. Specific performance to compel the promised conception, gestation, and birth shall not be available to the male promisor. However, once conception has occurred the parties' rights are fixed, the terms of the contract are firm and performance will be anticipated with the joy that only a newborn can bring.

Having defined a new rule of law, this court hastens to add an exception. After conception, only the surrogate shall have the right, to the exclusion of the sperm donor, to decide whether to abort the fetus. Her decision to abort must comply with the guidelines set forth in *Roe v. Wade*, 410 U.S. 113, 93 S. Ct. 705, 35 L. Ed. 2d 147 (1973).

Roe, supra, establishes and recognizes the unique and singular quality of woman. That only woman has the constitutionally protected right to determine the manner in which her body and person shall be used. The surrogate parenting agreement fails to recognize this fact; hence, the clause it contains prohibiting abortion except as allowed by the male promisor is void and unenforceable.

. . . .

[Editors: in an omitted section, the court considers and rejects various additional arguments against enforcement of the surrogacy contract.]

It is further argued that the contract is illusory; that is to say, that only one of the parties has an obligation, the other only benefits, that there is no mutuality of obligation. This does not mean equality of obligation. *See Friedmann v. Tappan Development Corp.*, 22 N.J. 523 (1956); Williston, Contracts § 105A at 421. Such is not the case. Mr. Stern gave his sperm; Mrs. Whitehead gave her egg. Together the miracle of a new life was obtained. Mrs. Whitehead argues Mr. Stern does not have to take the child under certain circumstances which have not happened and are not before this court. She is arguing, hypothetically, "if." It is suggested again that this court is dealing with the facts before it. Even assuming arguendo, that the court were to address the issue of the illusory contract as stated by defendants, the conclusion would be the same. The Whiteheads argue that Mr. Stern does not have to take the baby if it is imperfect; but the fact is the contract does provide that there is an obligation and responsibility, that there is a life long responsibility by Mr. Stern for the child's support and welfare. The contract is not illusory.

....

For the foregoing reasons, this court concludes and holds that the surrogate-parenting agreement is a valid and enforceable contract pursuant to the laws of New Jersey.... This court further finds that Mrs. Whitehead has breached her contract in two ways: 1) by failing to surrender to Mr. Stern the child born to her and Mr. Stern and 2) by failing to renounce her parental rights to that child.

[Editors: In a final section, the Court holds that the discretionary remedy of specific performance — terminating the mother's parental rights and approving adoption of the child by Mrs. Stern — should be ordered only if it is in the best interests of the child. The Court then decides that the best interests of the child in this case does favor entry of an order of specific performance.]

Now having found that the best interests of the child will be enhanced and served in paternal custody, and ... having evaluated the equities, finds them weighted in favor of Mr. Stern. Enforcing the contract will leave Mr. and Mrs. Whitehead in the same position that they were in when the contract was made. To not enforce the contract will give them the child and deprive Mr. Stern of his promised benefits. This Court therefore will specifically enforce the surrogate-parenting agreement to compel delivery of the child to the father and to terminate the mother's parental rights....

In the Matter of Baby "M" (A Pseudonym for an Actual Person)

Supreme Court of New Jersey
109 N.J. 396, 537 A.2d 1227 (1988)

ROBERT WILENTZ, CHIEF JUSTICE

In this matter the Court is asked to determine the validity of a contract that purports to provide a new way of bringing children into a family. For a fee of $10,000, a woman agrees to be artificially inseminated with the semen of another woman's husband; she is to conceive a child, carry it to term, and after its birth surrender it to the natural father and his wife. The intent of the contract is that the child's natural mother will thereafter be forever separated from her child. The wife is to adopt the child, and she and the natural father are to be regarded as its parents for all purposes. The contract providing for this is called a "surrogacy contract," the natural mother inappropriately called the "surrogate mother."

We invalidate the surrogacy contract because it conflicts with the law and public policy of this State. While we recognize the depth of the yearning of infertile couples to have their own children, we find the payment of money to a "surrogate" mother illegal, perhaps criminal, and potentially degrading to women. Although in this case we grant custody to the natural father, the evidence having clearly proved such custody to be in the best interests of the infant, we void both the termination of the surrogate mother's parental rights and the adoption of the child by the wife/stepparent. We thus restore the "surrogate" as the mother of the child. We remand the issue of the natural mother's visitation rights to the trial court, since that issue was not reached below and the record before us is not sufficient to permit us to decide it *de novo*.

II. Invalidity and Unenforceability of Surrogacy Contract

We have concluded that this surrogacy contract is invalid. Our conclusion has two bases: direct conflict with existing statutes and conflict with the public policies of this State, as expressed in its statutory and decisional law.

One of the surrogacy contract's basic purposes, to achieve the adoption of a child through private placement, though permitted in New Jersey "is very much disfavored." *Sees v. Baber*, 74 N.J. 201, 217 (1977). Its use of money for this purpose—and we have no doubt whatsoever that the money is being paid to obtain an adoption and not, as the Sterns argue, for the personal services of Mary Beth Whitehead—is illegal and perhaps criminal. N.J. Stat. Ann. 9:3-54. In addition to the inducement of money, there is the coercion of contract: the natural mother's irrevocable agreement, prior to birth, even prior to conception, to surrender the child to the adoptive couple. Such an agreement is totally unenforceable in private placement adoption. *Sees*, 74 N.J. at 212–14. Even where the adoption is through an approved agency, the formal agreement to surrender occurs only *after* birth (as we read N.J. Stat. Ann. 9:2-16 and -17, and similar statutes), and then, by regulation, only after the birth mother has been offered counseling. N.J. Admin. Code 10:121A-5.4(c). Integral to these invalid provisions of the surrogacy contract is the related agreement, equally invalid, on the part of the natural mother to cooperate with, and not to contest, proceedings to terminate her parental rights, as well as her contractual concession, in aid of the adoption, that the child's best interests would be served by awarding custody to the natural father and his wife—all of this before she has even conceived, and, in some cases, before she has the slightest idea of what the natural father and adoptive mother are like.

. . . .

The surrogacy contract's invalidity, resulting from its direct conflict with the above statutory provisions, is further underlined when its goals and means are measured against New Jersey's public policy. The contract's basic premise, that the natural parents can decide in advance of birth which one is to have custody of the child, bears no relationship to the settled law that the child's best interests shall determine custody. . . .

The surrogacy contract guarantees permanent separation of the child from one of its natural parents. Our policy, however, has long been that to the extent possible, children should remain with and be brought up by both of their natural parents. . . .

The surrogacy contract violates the policy of this State that the rights of natural parents are equal concerning their child, the father's right no greater than the mother's. . . . The whole purpose and effect of the surrogacy contract was to give the father the exclusive right to the child by destroying the rights of the mother.

The policies expressed in our comprehensive laws governing consent to the surrender of a child . . . stand in stark contrast to the surrogacy contract and what it implies. Here there is no counseling, independent or otherwise, of the natural mother, no evaluation, no warning. . . .

Under the contract, the natural mother is irrevocably committed before she knows the strength of her bond with her child. She never makes a totally voluntary, informed decision, for quite clearly any decision prior to the baby's birth is, in the most important sense, un-informed, and any decision after that, compelled by a pre-existing contractual commitment, the threat of a lawsuit, and the inducement of a $10,000 payment, is less than totally voluntary. Her interests are of little concern to those who controlled this transaction.

Although the interest of the natural father and adoptive mother is certainly the predominant interest, realistically the *only* interest served, even they are left with less than what public policy requires. They know little about the natural mother, her genetic makeup, and her psychological and medical history. Moreover, not even a superficial attempt is made to determine their awareness of their responsibilities as parents.

Worst of all, however, is the contract's total disregard of the best interests of the child. There is not the slightest suggestion that any inquiry will be made at any time to determine the fitness of the Sterns as custodial parents, of Mrs. Stern as an adoptive parent, their superiority to Mrs. Whitehead, or the effect on the child of not living with her natural mother.

This is the sale of a child, or, at the very least, the sale of a mother's right to her child, the only mitigating factor being that one of the purchasers is the father. Almost every evil that prompted the prohibition on the payment of money in connection with adoptions exists here.

The differences between an adoption and a surrogacy contract should be noted, since it is asserted that the use of money in connection with surrogacy does not pose the risks found where money buys an adoption.

First, and perhaps most important, all parties concede that it is unlikely that surrogacy will survive without money. Despite the alleged selfless motivation of surrogate mothers, if there is no payment, there will be no surrogates, or very few....

Second, the use of money in adoptions does not *produce* the problem — conception occurs, and usually the birth itself, before illicit funds are offered. With surrogacy, the "problem," if one views it as such, consisting of the purchase of a woman's procreative capacity, at the risk of her life, is caused by and originates with the offer of money.

Third, with the law prohibiting the use of money in connection with adoptions, the built-in financial pressure of the unwanted pregnancy and the consequent support obligation do not lead the mother to the highest paying, ill-suited, adoptive parents. She is just as well-off surrendering the child to an approved agency. In surrogacy, the highest bidders will presumably become the adoptive parents regardless of suitability, so long as payment of money is permitted.

Fourth, the mother's consent to surrender her child in adoptions is revocable, even after surrender of the child, unless it be to an approved agency, where by regulation there are protections against an ill-advised surrender. In surrogacy, consent occurs so early that no amount of advice would satisfy the potential mother's need, yet the consent is irrevocable.

The main difference, that the unwanted pregnancy is unintended while the situation of the surrogate mother is voluntary and intended, is really not significant. Initially, it produces stronger reactions of sympathy for the mother whose pregnancy was unwanted than for the surrogate mother, who "went into this with her eyes wide open." On reflection, however, it appears that the essential evil is the same, taking advantage of a woman's circumstances (the unwanted pregnancy or the need for money) in order to take away her child, the difference being one of degree.

In the scheme contemplated by the surrogacy contract in this case, a middleman, propelled by profit, promotes the sale. Whatever idealism may have motivated any of the participants, the profit motive predominates, permeates, and ultimately governs the transaction. The demand for children is great and the supply small. The availability of contraception, abortion, and the greater willingness of single mothers to bring up their children has led to a shortage of babies offered for adoption.... The situation is ripe for the entry of the middleman who will bring some equilibrium into the market by increasing the supply through the use of money.

Intimated, but disputed, is the assertion that surrogacy will be used for the benefit of the rich at the expense of the poor.... In response it is noted that the Sterns are not rich and the Whiteheads not poor. Nevertheless, it is clear to us that it is unlikely that surrogate mothers will be as proportionately numerous among those women in the top twenty percent income bracket as among those in the bottom twenty percent. Put differently, we doubt that infertile couples in the low-income bracket will find upper income surrogates.

In any event, even in this case one should not pretend that disparate wealth does not play a part simply because the contrast is not the dramatic "rich versus poor." At the time of trial, the Whiteheads' net assets were probably negative—Mrs. Whitehead's own sister was foreclosing on a second mortgage. Their income derived from Mr. Whitehead's labors. Mrs. Whitehead is a homemaker, having previously held part-time jobs. The Sterns are both professionals, she a medical doctor, he a biochemist. Their combined income when both were working was about $89,500 a year and their assets sufficient to pay for the surrogacy contract arrangements.

The point is made that Mrs. Whitehead *agreed* to the surrogacy arrangement, supposedly fully understanding the consequences. Putting aside the issue of how compelling her need for money may have been, and how significant her understanding of the consequences, we suggest that her consent is irrelevant. There are, in a civilized society, some things that money cannot buy. In America, we decided long ago that merely because conduct purchased by money was "voluntary" did not mean that it was good or beyond regulation and prohibition.... Employers can no longer buy labor at the lowest price they can bargain for, even though that labor is "voluntary," 29 U.S.C. § 206 (1982), or buy women's labor for less money than paid to men for the same job, 29 U.S.C. § 206(d), or purchase the agreement of children to perform oppressive labor, 29 U.S.C. § 212, or purchase the agreement of workers to subject themselves to unsafe or unhealthful working conditions, 29 U.S.C. §§ 651–78. (Occupational Safety and Health Act of 1970). There are, in short, values that society deems more important than granting to wealth whatever it can buy, be it labor, love, or life. Whether this principle recommends prohibition of surrogacy, which presumably sometimes results in great satisfaction to all of the parties, is not for us to say. We note here only that, under existing law, the fact that Mrs. Whitehead "agreed" to the arrangement is not dispositive.

...

[Editors: In omitted sections, the Court decides that there was no basis for termination of Ms. Whitehead's parental rights and that the Constitution does not require enforcement of the surrogacy contract. Finally, the Court awards primary physical custody to the Sterns and visitation rights to Ms. Whitehead.]

Note on Narrative

Notice how Chief Judge Wilentz, the author of the New Jersey Supreme Court's majority opinion, tells the story of the case, with sympathy for all parties and appreciation for the Sterns' sincere desire to have a child and for Ms. Whitehead sympathetic wish to help infertile women and their husbands to conceive. The trial court's interpretation of the parties' motivation, particularly of Ms. Whitehead's motivation, was far different. Looking at the same evidence, the trial court concluded that "Mrs. Whitehead dominates the family. Mr. Whitehead is clearly in a subordinate role.... Mrs. Whitehead is ... unable to separate her own needs from those of the child.... She does not have the ability to subordinate herself to the needs of the child.... Mrs. Whitehead is manipulative, impulsive, and exploitative."

Indeed, much of the debate over surrogate mothering has focused on narrative. Is this baby-selling or generosity between women? Is it an exercise of class privilege, in which wealthy couples exploit working class and poor women, or an example of free market principles in operation? Is the transaction driven by gender privilege, in which a man is treated as the natural parent while the woman giving birth is a container, a womb for rent, or service provider? Is the "natural father's" wife the "legitimate" mother by virtue of marriage? Is surrogacy a technologically advanced solution to the tragic circumstance of infertility or genetic risk? Or are surrogate mothers strong women freely choosing to use their bodies as an economic resource?

How the story is told depends to a large extent on the speaker's beliefs and background assumptions about procreation, class, gender, and market exchange, and the beliefs of contemporary Americans vary widely on these matters. Lawyers arguing on Whitehead's behalf tried in numerous ways to challenge the assumption that William Stern's desire to have a child genetically related to him was "natural" and could not be altered or frustrated without significant loss to him. Whitehead's attorneys presented evidence showing details of the surrogacy arrangement in an effort to distinguish this arrangement from a tender story of child birth and parental love. They emphasized that the Sterns paid or would pay a total of $25,000 in the arrangement (including $10,000 to Mary Beth Whitehead, approximately $7,500 to the Infertility Center, and approximately $5,000 in medical expenses), that Elizabeth Stern was able to bear children but chose not to, and that the practice of surrogacy was part of a larger "commercialization" of childbearing driven by the profit-making motives of "brokers" like the Infertility Center. Evidence like this made it more difficult for courts to view surrogate parenting as a "natural" and therefore unalterable consequence of human desire and modern technology.

Further, Whitehead's attorneys tried to uncover and cast doubt on the assumptions that Ms. Whitehead must be a bad person (and thus a bad mother). The lawyers tried to do this by emphasizing the long-standing practice of women having babies for other women (including the Old Testament account of Hagar having a child to be cared for by Sara, the infertile wife of Abraham, the child's father), while at the same time emphasizing Ms. Whitehead's natural and honorable desire to care for her child.

On the Sterns' behalf, lawyers presented a competing narrative. They cast William Stern as a victim of fate and human cruelty — the only child of holocaust survivors — who desired merely to have a child to love and nurture, and they portrayed Whitehead as unstable and manipulative, an unworthy mother even to her other children. The foundation for this narrative was laid in the contract document, which named William Stern the "natural father" and Whitehead the "surrogate."

Stern's attorneys were effective in the trial court, persuading the trial court to order specific performance of the surrogacy agreement, including the termination of Whitehead's parental rights. In the New Jersey Supreme Court, however, Whitehead's attorneys were able to convince the Court that Whitehead and the surrogacy agreement were misjudged by the trial court and that Whitehead's parental rights should not be terminated. In an unusual passage, the N.J. Supreme Court explicitly criticized the lower court for its "harsh judgment" of Whitehead in the portrayal of her behavior and motivations:

It seems to us that given her predicament, Mrs. Whitehead was rather harshly judged—both by the trial court and by some of the experts. She was guilty of a breach of contract, and indeed, she did break a very important promise, but we think it is expecting something well beyond normal human capabilities to suggest that this mother should have parted with her newly born infant without a struggle.

In this way, the Supreme Court articulated and explicitly rejected some of the assumptions about gender and human motivation that otherwise might have influenced its decision in this case.

Another focus of the attorneys' arguments was that surrogate parenting contracts violate New Jersey's adoption and parental rights statutes and the state's public policy. Are you convinced that the surrogate parenting contract does violate the adoption and parental rights statutes? If not, are you persuaded by the Supreme Court's alternative holding that surrogate parenting contracts violate New Jersey's public policy? What, precisely, is the public policy that the contract violates?

The trial court held that the contract did not violate the adoption and parental rights statutes because Richard Stern is the child's biological father. In support of that conclusion Judge Sorkow said the adoption statute should be narrowly construed because surrogacy was not practiced at the time the statute was enacted. The Supreme Court, in contrast, held that the adoption and parental rights statutes reflect broad and important protections, particularly in the right of a parent to revoke consent to adoption given prior to the birth of a child and shortly thereafter, and therefore should be interpreted to apply to surrogate contracts. The interpretation of these statutes and the state's public policy require a determination of the social importance of protecting parental choice, particularly maternal choice. The trial court viewed these as relatively narrow concerns, while the N.J. Supreme Court viewed them quite broadly. The trial court emphasized sanctity of contract, while Chief Judge Wilentz remarked "[W]e suggest that her consent is irrelevant." and "[T]he fact that Mrs. Whitehead 'agreed' to the arrangement is not dispositive...." The two courts' statutory and public policy determinations reflect very different political and moral values.

The doctrine authorizing a court to refuse enforcement of a contract if it violates public policy requires courts to make such determinations. The doctrine is explicitly regulatory, designed to discourage socially harmful activities and protect the integrity of the judiciary.

The practice of surrogate parenting continues to be controversial. While numerous states prohibit paid surrogacy, either by legislation or judicial decision, several others regulate and enforce surrogacy contracts. *See generally* Darra L. Hoffman, *Mama's Baby, Daddy's Maybe: A State-by-State Survey of Surrogacy Laws and Their Disparate Gender Impact*, 35 Wm. Mitchell L. Rev.449 (2008–2009).

C. Lack of Capacity

The ability to enter into contracts and to create relationships that give rise to legally enforceable rights and duties has long been associated individual liberty. In the United

States and elsewhere in the world, this freedom gives an individual agency, the acknowledgement by others that the individual has the ability, as well as the right, to make decisions and exercise control over his or her own actions and possessions.

Subordination of social groups, and of the members of that group, usually involves a limitation on or the deprivation of the right to contract and limits the market activity of particular groups. Restrictions, both in the common law and statutory, were based on race, sex, national origin, and class. During the eighteenth and nineteenth centuries, married women, children, and those with mental illnesses were not permitted legal enforcement of their contracts. In many states and localities, African-Americans, Mexican-Americans, Puerto Ricans, Native Americans, Chinese-Americans, Japanese-Americans, and others were not allowed to own land and were limited in their rights to work and own businesses. The ability of Native Americans to contract is still legally impaired because individuals and tribes must obtain the approval of the federal government for any contracts relating, even indirectly, to Indian lands, *see* 25 U.S.C. § 81, yet Native Americans are otherwise granted the right to contract by federal and state civil rights acts

Nineteenth century capacity doctrine also promoted gender hierarchy. Married women, of whatever racial identification, were deemed incapable of contracting because they were under the legal and moral control of their husbands and thus incapable of independent judgment. The common law, under the rule of coverture, treated married women as legally subsumed by their husbands. Following marriage, only a husband had the capacity to contract. When a married woman worked outside the home, the contract for her employment was between her employer and her husband. *See, e.g., Burton, Burke & Wife v. Marshall*, 4 Gill 487 (Md. Ct. App. 1846) (contract to employ the actress Margaret Burke, parties to the contract were the employer and Burke's husband). *See generally* James Schouler, A Treatise on the Law of Husband and Wife (1882).

In this way and many others, the law has played an important role in the creation and maintenance of economic and social inequality in the United States. Capacity doctrine promoted the belief that men of European descent are intellectually and morally superior to all other people. It reinforced the false ideas that "race" represents significant biological differences and that the genders must be hierarchically ordered. Unfortunately, beliefs so aggressively promoted, so well and deeply cultivated throughout the nation's social and political institutions, cannot be uprooted in our time by mere legislative repeal.

Despite legislative repeal, the legacy of contractual incapacity continues for African-Americans and other people of color in the forms of marginalization, disparate pricing, and racial stereotyping in market transactions. And assumptions about women's incapacity continue to block women from obtaining equality in wages, credit, housing, and other areas of commercial life.

Tales about the obstacles people of color encounter in trying to spend their money in white-owned stores and shops are legendary. People of color are treated as if they were all potential shoplifters, thieves, or deadbeats. There can hardly be a black or brown person in urban America who has not been denied entry to a store, closely watched, snubbed, questioned about her or his ability to pay for an item, or stopped and detained for shoplifting. Salespeople either are slow to wait on blacks and rude when they do; or they are too quick to wait on blacks whom they practically shove out the door. Although anecdotal evidence suggests that men are more likely to encounter such treatment, women are similarly victimized. As an eighteen-year-old female resident of a Harlem housing project put it:

> "Some white people are very rude.... All black females and boys are treated the same—bad—when they go into a white store."

Regina Austin, *"A Nation of Thieves": Securing Black People's Right to Shop and to Sell in White America*, 1994 Utah L. Rev. 147; Patricia J. Williams, The Alchemy of Race and Rights 44–51 (1991) (recounting the experience of being locked out of Benetton's and the salesperson's arrogant rejection of the "gift of my commerce, the lucre of my patronage.").

Human dignity is enhanced by a respect for the agency and autonomy of individuals. In the United States, it is equality, political and only recently social equality, that animates the federal and state legislation addressing systemic bias and discrimination. The first Civil Rights Act in 1866 granted to emancipated slaves in 1866, and " ... all persons within the jurisdiction of the United States ... the same right ... to make and enforce contracts ... as is enjoyed by white citizens." One hundred years later, during the modern Civil Rights Movement, Congress and the Supreme Court revived the moribund statute, now codified at 42 U.S.C. 1981. The Civil Rights Act of 1991 amended § 1981, adding language that made the statute applicable to " ... the making, performance, modification, and termination of contracts, and the enjoyment of all the benefits, privileges, terms and conditions of the contractual relationship."

Consider the efficacy of this legislative remedy in the following case.

Paula Darlene Hampton, Demetria Cooper v. Dillard Department Stores, Inc.

United States Court of Appeals for the Tenth Circuit
247 F.3d 1091 (2001)

Robert Harlan Henry, Circuit Judge.

Paula Darlene Hampton filed suit against Dillard Department Stores, Inc. (Dillard's), claiming that the company had unlawfully interfered with her right to make and enforce a contract in violation of 42 U.S.C.§ 1981.[*] A jury awarded her compensatory and punitive damages based on its findings that (1) Ms. Hampton "was entitled to a free cologne sample as a benefit or privilege of her purchase on April 5, 1996,"; (2) Dillard's "intentionally interfered with her ability to receive a free cologne sample,"; and (3) Ms. Hampton's "race was a motivating factor in Dillard's conduct on April 5, 1996." Dillard's thereafter filed a motion for judgment as a matter of law, which the district court denied. Dillard's now appeals ...

---

[*] 42 U.S.C.A. § 1981 (Equal rights under the law), enacted in the wake of the Emancipation Proclamation and the Civil War, as part of the Civil Rights Acts of 1866, provides as follows:

(a) Statement of equal rights

All persons within the jurisdiction of the United States shall have the same right in every State and Territory to make and enforce contracts, to sue, be parties, give evidence, and to the full and equal benefit of all laws and proceedings for the security of persons and property as is enjoyed by white citizens, and shall be subject to like punishment, pains, penalties, taxes, licenses, and exactions of every kind, and to no other.

(b) "Make and enforce contracts" defined

For purposes of this section, the term "make and enforce contracts" includes the making, performance, modification, and termination of contracts, and the enjoyment of all benefits, privileges, terms, and conditions of the contractual relationship.

(c) Protection against impairment

The rights protected by this section are protected against impairment by nongovernmental discrimination and impairment under color of State law.

The focus of Dillard's appeal is on three questions: (1) whether the fragrance coupon was in fact a benefit of Ms. Hampton's purchase; (2) whether there was indeed intentional interference with Ms. Hampton's redemption of the coupon; and (3) whether the interference was in the end based on racial discrimination. We agree with the district court that these are questions of fact, not law, and the jury made explicit findings as to each. On appellate review, we cannot challenge the jury's findings of fact; instead, we may only ask whether there was a "legally sufficient evidentiary basis for a reasonable jury to find for Ms. Hampton" on each fact. Fed. R. Civ. P. 50(a). Because there was such a basis, we must affirm the district court's order.

I. Background ...

On April 5, 1996, Ms. Hampton and her niece, Demetria Cooper, both African-Americans, were shopping for an Easter outfit for Ms. Cooper's one-year-old son in the Dillard's children's department in Overland Park, Kansas. The plaintiffs had four children with them: Ms. Cooper's son, Ms. Hampton's eight-month-old and seven-year-old daughters, and her elder daughter's friend.

Shortly after they entered the store, Tom Wilson, a Dillard's security officer, noticed them. He observed them for more than fifteen minutes. Mr. Wilson testified that he paid close attention to the party, in part, because they had a stroller with them, because Ms. Cooper had a rolled-up dark cloth item in her hand, and because Ms. Cooper kept looking up at the ceiling and glancing around, as if to check to see if she was being watched. Because his suspicions were aroused, he asked fellow employee Pam Fitzgerel to continue the surveillance in a fitting room in the children's department, where the plaintiffs were trying clothing on Ms. Cooper's one-year-old son. At trial, Ms. Fitzgerel testified that Ms. Cooper was holding a rolled-up cloth item in the fitting room; that she later saw an item under Ms. Cooper's jacket; and that, believing the item to be store merchandise, she contacted Mr. Wilson and told him that she was positive that Ms. Cooper had put something under her coat.

The group left the fitting room and Ms. Hampton proceeded to purchase an outfit for Ms. Cooper's son from the salesclerk in the children's department. When she did so, the sales associate gave Ms. Hampton and Ms. Cooper each a coupon that was redeemable at the fragrance counter for cologne samples. The shopping group then proceeded on to the fragrance counter, which is located where the Dillard's store ends and opens into the Oak Park Mall, to redeem their fragrance coupons.

While the women were in the process of redeeming their coupons and while the women were in a conversation with fragrance consultant Betty Chouteau, Mr. Wilson interrupted them. Referring to Ms. Cooper, he advised Ms. Hampton that "the ... black female had been observed placing something in her coat. He asked to look inside the Dillard's bag carried by Ms. Hampton, took the bag, and emptied the contents on the fragrance counter. Mr. Wilson checked the items against the receipt and determined that they corresponded. Ms. Chouteau testified that she perceived it to be "a rather embarrassing situation" for the women and, upon Mr. Wilson's intervention, she "turned and started talking to other people."

While Mr. Wilson was matching up items to the receipt, Ms. Hampton became visibly upset and told Mr. Wilson that, as a regular customer of Dillard's, she did not appreciate being accused of shoplifting and she did not deserve to be treated this way. Mr. Wilson told her to calm down or he would call the Overland Park police and have her removed from the store. Ms. Hampton asked Mr. Wilson his name and the location of the customer service counter. She then proceeded to the customer service counter and had no more contact with Mr. Wilson. The encounter with Mr. Wilson lasted approximately five minutes. Ms. Hampton and Ms. Cooper subsequently filed suit against Dillard's, alleging false imprisonment under Kansas law and a violation of 42 U.S.C. § 1981....

II. Analysis

A. Ms. Hampton's § 1981 Claim ...

Typically, most litigation involving § 1981 claims has emanated from the right to make and enforce employment contracts ... However, the statute has been applied to discrimination claims arising in the retail sector and restaurant industry, when a contract has been established. *See, e.g., Bobbitt v. Rage, Inc.,* 19 F. Supp. 2d 512, 518–20 (W.D.N.C. 1998) (allowing action to proceed where plaintiffs, who were forced to prepay for food in pizza restaurant, demonstrated that the restaurant altered a fundamental characteristic of the food service based on race); *Washington v. Duty Free Shoppers, Ltd.,* 710 F. Supp. 1288, 1289–90 (N.D. Cal. 1988) (denying summary judgment to defendant where African-American were customers told they needed to show a passport and airline tickets before shopping for duty-paid goods, while other customers were not required to do so).

Applying the prima facie elements to the factual setting of this case, the district court instructed the jury that the plaintiff must establish:

First, that plaintiff was entitled to a free cologne sample as a benefit or privilege of her purchase on April 5, 1996;

Second, that defendant intentionally interfered with plaintiff's right to enjoy the benefits and privileges of that purchase; and

Third that plaintiff's race was a motivating factor in defendant's conduct.

We will discuss each of these elements, beginning with whether there was interference with a contract.

The Coupon as Part of the Purchase Contract

Dillard's challenges whether the fragrance coupon was a benefit of Ms. Hampton's contractual relationship for the purchase of children's wear. According to Dillard's, the coupons were promotional invitations, handed out indiscriminately and not exclusively in connection with a purchase. Dillard's maintains that the coupon was a gift and that it was never intended to confer a right upon its recipient. In addition, Dillard's points to Ms. Cooper's receipt of a coupon as evidence that a purchase was not required to receive the gift.

In rebuttal, Ms. Hampton argues that we must be mindful of the jury's appraisal of the credibility of the witnesses as well as the jury's resolution of factual issues. She and Ms. Cooper testified that, during the time they shopped at the Dillard's store (over an hour), they never saw anyone receive a coupon and saw no one distributing the coupons. The first they saw of the coupons was after Ms. Hampton had purchased merchandise. Furthermore, the sales representative from the fragrance company, Ms. Chouteau, testified that the purpose of the promotional coupon, handed out after a customer of Dillard's had made a purchase, was "to entice the shoppers to come to the fragrance counter so that we could talk to them about our product." All such promotions were supported and agreed to by Dillard's. Finally, Ms. Cooper testified that, upon receipt of the coupons, the children's wear salesperson directed her shopping party toward the appropriate fragrance counter.

Ms. Hampton contends that she performed the steps necessary to act in compliance with the terms and conditions of the offer from Dillard's: she completed a purchase and presented the coupon to the fragrance counter. The performance of these acts, she argues, either constitutes an acceptance or entitles her to "the enjoyment of all benefits, privileges, terms, and conditions of the contractual relationship," as the statute says.

Clearly, the purpose of the statute is to "make it clear that the right to 'make and enforce contracts' free from race discrimination is protected by section 1981." S. Rep. No. 101-315 (1990). Furthermore, the list set forth in subsection (b) of the statute, which gives examples of what might constitute the "making" or "enforcing" of a contract" under the Act, "is intended to be illustrative rather than exhaustive." *Id.* We have clarified "that a § 1981 claim for interference with the right to make and enforce a contract must involve the actual loss of a contract interest, not merely the possible loss of future contract opportunities." *See Wesley*, 42 F. Supp. 2d at 1200 (citing *Phelps*, 886 F.2d at 1267).... Here, Dillard's offered a variance of an option or unilateral contract to Ms. Hampton, and she completed the invited performance in accordance with the terms of the offer. *See Restatement (Second) of Contracts* § 45 ...

Intentional Interference with Redemption of the Coupon

Dillard's also sought judgment as a matter of law because Ms. Hampton suffered no actual loss of a contract right or interest. See Phelps, 886 F.2d at 1267 (emphasizing that actual loss is protected by § 1981, not possible loss). Dillard's contends that Ms. Hampton was not denied a service or product, as required by Morris. At trial, Mr. Wilson testified on behalf of Dillard's that he stopped the women while they were approaching the store's exit and that he did not believe them to be exchanging their coupons for fragrance samples.

A recollection of Mr. Wilson's testimony may explain why the jury and district court reached the decisions that they did:

Q: What did you think Paula Hampton and Demetria Cooper were doing when you approached them?

A: They were getting ready to exit the Dillard's store to go out into the mall.

Q: Okay. Did you notice that they were speaking with a cosmetic associate or a fragrance consultant when you approached the two ladies?

A: No, I did not.

Q: Did you knowingly prevent Paula Hampton from receiving a free cologne sample?

A: No, I did not.

Thus, we have a trained security guard claiming that he did not notice that the women were redeeming a coupon. Indeed, he did not notice that they were shopping or even talking with a salesperson.

This testimony was directly contested by Ms. Hampton and Ms. Cooper. The jury could have resolved this conflict based on their evidence, but the silver bullet may have been the testimony of Ms. Chouteau, the perfume consultant:

Q: Do you recall Paula Hampton and Demetria Cooper and their children coming up to the cosmetics counter?

A: I do.

Q: Do you recall that their discussion with you was interrupted by a Dillard's security officer?

A: Yes, I do....

Q: When Officer Wilson came up and spoke, what did you do then?

A: Well, because it was a rather embarrassing situation and because I was very busy with a lot of other things going on, I turned and started talking to other people at the time with my back to them.

Q: With your back to whom?

A: To the officer and Paula. I mean, I just felt like it was an embarrassing situation for them and I felt uncomfortable, you know, watching, so I turned and went ahead and did what I was supposed to be doing.

Once again, the evidence in the record is sufficient for the jury to determine that Mr. Wilson deliberately interfered with Ms. Hampton's redemption of the coupon and that she suffered an actual loss of a privilege of her contract because of this interruption. Ms. Hampton testified that after he approached her and identified himself while she was at the fragrance counter, Mr. Wilson "took her shopping bag, dumped the contents out on the counter, and compared them to the receipt that was in the bag, and then he shoved everything back at her." After this, Ms. Hampton told Mr. Wilson she was shocked to be accused of shoplifting, and Mr. Wilson subsequently threatened to have her removed from the store.

. . .

Racial Discrimination

Dillard's next contends that it deserved judgment as a matter of law because there is no evidence of racial discrimination. . . .

"A plaintiff who lacks direct evidence of racial discrimination may rely on indirect evidence of discrimination. . . ." *Perry v. Woodward*, 199 F.3d 1126, 1135 (10th Cir. 1999). As noted above, because the issue of intent is one that is often not susceptible to direct proof, the jury considers all the conflicting inferences that the circumstantial evidence may present. *See Washington*, 710 F. Supp. at 1289 (citing *Rogers*, 458 U.S. at 618). . . .

. . . [A]fter a full trial on the merits, "the single overarching issue" on which we focus is whether the adverse action was motivated by race. *Tyler*, 232 F.3d at 812 (setting out approach) . . .

Dillard's contends that Officer Wilson, based on the facts and circumstances, had probable cause to stop Ms. Hampton. However, Dillard's neglects to acknowledge that the jury may have found Mr. Wilson's theory pretextual.

The factfinder's disbelief of the reasons put forward by the defendant (particularly if disbelief is accompanied by a suspicion of mendacity) may, together with the elements of the prima facie case, suffice to show intentional discrimination. Thus, rejection of the defendant's proffered reasons will *permit* the trier of fact to infer the ultimate fact of intentional discrimination. *Reeves v. Sanderson Plumbing Prods., Inc.*, 530 U.S. 133 (2000) (quoting *St. Mary's Honor Ctr. v. Hicks*, 509 U.S. 502, 511 (1993)). As noted above, the jury's conclusions indicate it did not find Mr. Wilson's testimony credible. Thus, "our holding is further fortified by our conclusions that the jury could reasonably infer all defendant's previous justifications were pretextual. If the jury found, as a whole Mr. Wilson was not credible, its decision to reject his proffered reason . . . is, likewise, reasonable." *Tyler*, 232 F.3d at 816.

Ms. Hampton relies primarily on indirect evidence of discrimination. In its memorandum in support of its motion for judgment as a matter of law before the district court, Dillard's defends its security policies as "racially neutral," and contends that there was no evidence that the store's employees had a history of denying services or products to African-American customers. Dillard's fails to acknowledge that the evidence of discriminatory surveillance, although on its own not actionable under § 1981, see Lewis, 948 F. Supp. at 370 (rejected plaintiff's theory of "an unstated, unwritten contract between commercial establishments and the public, that all who enter premises of the former will be treated equally regardless of race" because it would virtually nullify the contract requirement of § 1981), can certainly be viewed as indirect evidence of discrimination. See Hall v. Pennsylvania State Police, 570 F.2d 86, 92 (3d Cir. 1978) (stating that policy to photograph African-American customers of bank "was not the isolated act of an individual employee, but rather the implementation of a policy deliberately adopted by the bank management to offer its services under different terms dependent on race"); Washington, 710 F. Supp. at 1289 (denying defendant's motion for summary judgment where policy of denying services to "suspicious" shoppers targeted African-Americans and stating that "the issue of intent ... is one that is often not susceptible to direct proof, and a court should consider all conflicting inferences that may be presented by the circumstantial evidence in the case").

Ms. Hampton presented multiple forms of indirect evidence of discrimination. She presented testimony from former Dillard's security officers that corroborated the racial surveillance theory. She also presented testimony that African-Americans were frequently "tracked" upon entering the store; that Dillard's implemented race "codes" that highlighted African-American shoppers as suspicious; that African-Americans were singled out as "suspicious" for returning merchandise without a receipt or for moving between departments while carrying merchandise. In addition, store incident reports differentiated shoppers predominantly by race. As to Ms. Hampton specifically, she was noticed and placed under surveillance shortly after entering Dillard's. The district court also noted that Mr. Wilson's "Security Report," despite being less than two pages long, reiterated Ms. Hampton's race twelve times, reflecting implementation of the store's policy and reflecting Mr. Wilson's motivation. Given this abundant evidence, we agree with the district court and hold that the jury's inference of racial discrimination was a reasonable one.

Finally, Dillard's and the dissent strenuously argue that there is no direct evidence or indication that Mr. Wilson acted with an intent to discriminate. As discussed above, the fact that Mr. Wilson has not admitted discrimination ... does not mean there is no evidence of discrimination. As previously noted, there was ample evidence (most tellingly, Mr. Wilson's security report, which reiterated the race of the shoppers a dozen times, and testimony presented to the jury regarding the store's discriminatory coding practices) for the jury to determine that "race was a motivating factor" in Mr. Wilson's interaction with Ms. Hampton. We therefore hold Ms. Hampton presented sufficient evidence that the reasons given by Mr. Wilson for interference with Ms. Hampton's redemption of the contract were pretextual, and the jury reasonably inferred that Dillard's intentionally discriminated against her on the basis of race. See Tyler, 232 F.3d at 816 (reiterating that judgment as a matter of law is appropriate only if "the evidence points but one way, and is susceptible to no reasonable inferences supporting plaintiff's claim").

...

III. Conclusion

For the reasons stated above we AFFIRM the district court's denial of Dillard's motion for judgment as a matter of law and motion for a new trial; we AFFIRM the district court's award of compensatory and punitive damages; we AFFIRM the district court's grant of summary judgment dismissing Ms. Cooper's claims; and we AFFIRM the district court's award of attorney's fees to Ms. Hampton.

Today, most of the direct legal impediments based on race or gender have been repealed. The Federal Civil Rights Act of 1868, 42 U.S.C. § 1981, provides that all people, regardless of race or ethnicity, should have the legal right to contract. This right is given further recognition in the Civil Rights Acts of 1964, the Fair Housing Act, and other civil rights legislation. By the 1970s, the federal civil rights acts and state legislation had abolished most limitations on the contractual capacity of married women, with restrictions remaining only on contracts with their husbands, suretyship contracts, some real property contracts, and contracts relating to the management of community property. *See Restatement (Second) of Contracts* § 12, *comment* d.

---

1. Age Incapacity

Contemporary contract law holds that all children are legally incapable of contracting and adults with mental incapacity are legally incapable of contracting, including, in some cases, adults rendered mentally incapable by alcohol or drug intoxication. The justification for this doctrine has shifted from protection of the status and property interests of dominant groups to protection of children and people with mental incapacity. This justification assumes that children and people with mental incapacity are emotionally and intellectually unable to protect themselves and thus are vulnerable to overreaching by unscrupulous traders and employers. The bargain model of contract assumes that rational actors engage in market transactions to maximize their profits; contemporary capacity doctrine treats children and those with mental impairment, as at least sometimes incapable of rational action and therefore unable to participate well in the market.

Generally, capacity doctrine provides that the contracts of minors are voidable: the party lacking capacity may avoid the contract by *disaffirming* it. *See Restatement (Second) of Contracts* §§ 14, 15. However, the minor, upon reaching the age of majority, or the person with mental incapacity upon recovering capacity, may choose to *ratify* or *affirm* the contract and if performance under the contract is ongoing, continuation of performance may be treated as *implied affirmation*. Moreover, even if the contract is voided, a child or person with mental incapacity may be liable in restitution if the other party provided "necessaries" or "necessities" to the child or person with mental incapacity. *See Restatement (Second) of Contracts* § 12, *comment f*. In apparent conflict with the doctrine of mental incapacity, the Americans with Disabilities Act requires that merchants and others provide *reasonable accommodation* so that persons with mental disabilities can enter contracts and engage in all aspects of commercial life.

The age of majority for purposes of contracting capacity is 18 years in most states; in Alabama, however, the age is 19 years and in Mississippi, it is 21 years. Many states have adopted some criteria for "emancipation" of a child, allowing the child to be deemed capable of contracting before the statutory age of majority. Notice that the term "emancipation" echoes the original justification for the doctrine of incapacity, to protect a father's control, and not the current justification, to protect the child's interest. The criteria for emancipation generally include marriage, military service, and living apart from and independent of parents. Many states also provide a judicial procedure whereby a child can be officially "emancipated" by the court. *See, e.g.,* Cal. Fam. Code§ 7002 (1994). Many states have also enacted provisions allowing children to enter binding contracts of specified types, if approved by a parent or a court. *See, e.g.,* N.Y. Arts & Cult. Aff. Art. 35, *Child Performers and Models*, § 35.03(1) (1994).

What is the magical line that minors cross at 18, 19, or 21 years? Children's rights advocates have argued that the law of age capacity is unjust and empirically unsound. They urge that the rule of contractual incapacity operates not as protection for children, but as a serious restriction on the individual freedom of children.

The United States Census Bureau estimated the number of people between the ages of 10 and 19 years at 42.4 million in 2014 (see Annual Population Estimates at http://factfinder.census.gov). Market researchers estimate teen spending power is roughly $200 billion annually. Social media sites such as Instagram, Facebook, Snapchat, and Twitter have an influence on teen spending, two-thirds of which is comprised of apparel and food. Moreover, the Pew Research Center reported:

> 24% of teens go online "almost constantly," facilitated by the widespread availability of smartphones. Aided by the convenience and constant access provided by mobile devices, especially smartphones, 92% of teens report going online daily—including 24% who say they go online "almost constantly," according to a new study from Pew Research Center. More than half (56%) of teens—defined in this report as those ages 13 to 17—go online several times a day, and 12% report once-a-day use. Just 6% of teens report going online weekly, and 2% go online less often.

> Much of this frenzy of access is facilitated by mobile devices. Nearly three-quarters of teens have or have access to a smartphone and 30% have a basic phone, while just 12% of teens 13 to 17 say they have no cell phone of any type. African-American teens are the most likely of any group of teens to have a smartphone, with 85% having access to one, compared with 71% of both white and Hispanic teens. These phones and other mobile devices have become a primary driver of teen internet use: Fully 91% of teens go online from mobile devices at least occasionally. Among these "mobile teens," 94% go online daily or more often. By comparison, teens who don't access the internet via mobile devices tend to go online less frequently. Some 68% go online at least daily.

> African-American and Hispanic youth report more frequent internet use than white teens. Among African-American teens, 34% report going online "almost constantly" as do 32% of Hispanic teens, while 19% of white teens go online that often.

Amanda Lenhart, Pew Center Research, Teens, Social Media and Technology Overview 2015, 2, April 2015 (footnotes omitted). The online activity leads to other spending including "in-app" purchases. Recently, the Federal Trade Commission has cracked down on internet companies including Google, Amazon.com, and Apple over unauthorized in-app charges incurred by users under the age of 18. Edward Wyatt, Edith Ramirez Is Raising the F.T.C.'s Voice, N.Y. Times, December 21, 2014, http://www.nytimes.com/2014/12/22/business/federal-trade-commission-raises-its-voice-under-its-soft-spoken-chairwoman.html?_r=0.

Yet, while some children are among the United States' largest consumers, others are among the country's poorest residents. 16.1 million children lived in poverty in 2012, more than 40 percent of these poor children living in "extreme poverty," with household incomes of less than half of the federal poverty amount. Infant mortality and preschool child death rates in the United States are higher than most industrialized countries. By the end of 2012, an estimated 4.8 million children lack health insurance coverage and 4 percent of children have unmet dental care needs because their parents cannot afford it. See Center for Disease Control, Summary Health Statistics for U.S. Children: National Health Interview Survey, 2012.

Kim Young v. Phillip Weaver

Court of Civil Appeals of Alabama
883 So.2d 234 (Ala. App. Ct. 2003).

GLENN MURDOCK, JUDGE.

Kim Young appeals from a judgment of the Tuscaloosa Circuit Court awarding damages to Phillip Weaver for alleged breaches by Young of an apartment lease between Young, as tenant, and Weaver, as landlord. We reverse.

In the fall of 2001, Young, who at the time was 18 years old and had been living with her parents all of her life, decided that she "wanted to move out and get away from [her] parents and be on [her] own." Young and a friend, Ashley Springer, also a minor at the time, signed a contract for the lease of an apartment with Weaver on September 20, 2001. No adult signed the lease as a guarantor. Young was employed on a full-time basis at a Lowe's hardware store located in Tuscaloosa at the time she entered into the lease agreement. Young paid a security deposit in the amount of $300; the rent for the apartment was $550 per month, and the lease was set to expire on July 31, 2002.

Young and Springer moved into the apartment in late September and, together, paid rent at the agreed-upon rate for the portion of that month in which they lived in the apartment. Young and Springer continued to live in the apartment during October and most of November 2001; Young moved out near the end of November and returned to live with her parents. Young paid the full amount of her portion[1] of the rent for October and November, but she stopped making any rent payments after she moved out of the apartment.

Young had a dog which stayed in the apartment with the roommates; it is undisputed that the dog damaged part of the floor and the bathroom door in the apartment, causing $270 in damage. Young did not pay for this damage before vacating the apartment. Weaver managed to rent the apartment to someone else in June 2002.

On February 19, 2002, Weaver filed a claim against Young in the Small Claims Court of Tuscaloosa County, seeking damages for the unpaid rent and the damage done by Young's dog to the apartment. The court ruled in favor of Weaver and awarded $1,370 in damages. Young appealed the decision to the Tuscaloosa Circuit Court. The case was tried de novo on December 5, 2002, in a hearing in which the trial court took evidence ore tenus. The circuit court also entered a judgment in favor Weaver and awarded him $1,095, the amount of Young's share of the unpaid rent for December 2001 and January and February 2002, as well as the $270 in damage caused by Young's dog. Young appeals.

Because the trial court took evidence ore tenus, its judgment is given a presumption of correctness and may not be reversed unless it is shown to be unsupported by substantial evidence and plainly and palpably wrong. *See, e.g., Callaway v. E.H. Smith Elec. Contractors, Inc.*, 814 So.2d 893 (Ala. Civ. App. 2001).

Among other things, Young argues on appeal that the apartment was not a "necessity" and that, therefore, as a minor, she was not legally bound by the lease and owes Weaver nothing. We find this argument to be dispositive.[2]

---

1. Young and Springer agreed to share the rent equally. Weaver seeks in this action only to recover that portion of the monthly rent for which Young was responsible, i.e., $275.

2. Our reversal of the trial court's judgment insofar as it awards to Weaver $270 for damage to the apartment caused by Young's dog is also supported by the fact that the record contains undisputed evidence, as noted by Young in her brief to this court, that Weaver was in receipt of a $300 deposit that would be applied to those damages. Weaver does not address this issue in his brief to this court.

Under Alabama law, one who is unmarried and has not reached the age of 19 years is deemed to be a minor, i.e., subject to the disabilities of nonage (although such disabilities may, in certain circumstances, be removed by a judgment of a juvenile court). *See* §26–1–1, §26–13–1 et seq., §30–4–15, and §30–4–16, Ala. Code 1975. Among the disabilities of nonage is the incapacity to make a binding contract: 'It is a well-established general rule at common-law, and recognized in this state, that a minor is not liable on any contract he makes and that he may disaffirm the same.' *Children's Hosp. of Birmingham, Inc. v. Kelley,* 537 So.2d 917, 917 (Ala. Civ. App. 1987), aff'd in pertinent part, rev'd on other grounds, *Ex parte Odem,* 537 So.2d 919 (Ala.1988).

Williams v. Baptist Health Sys., Inc., 857 So.2d 149, 151 (Ala. Civ. App. 2003). However,

Alabama law, like the law of most other states, provides that persons providing 'necessaries'[3] of life to minors may recover the reasonable value of such necessaries irrespective of the existence, or nonexistence, of a (voidable) contract respecting those necessaries. As stated by the Alabama Supreme Court in *Ragan v. Williams,* 127 So. 190 (Ala. 1930), '[w]hen *necessaries* are *furnished* to one who by reason of infancy cannot bind himself by his contract, the law implies an obligation on the part of such person to pay for such "necessaries" out of his own property.' 127 So. at 191.

Williams, 857 So.2d at 151 (emphasis added).

Young does not seek reversal of the trial court's judgment on the ground that the use of the apartment after November 2001 was not "furnished" to her.[4] Instead, her principal argument on appeal is that the apartment was not a necessity. We agree that this case must be disposed of in Young's favor on this basis.

A necessity has been defined as something " 'necessary to the position and condition of the [minor].' " *Ex parte Odem,* 537 So.2d 919, 920 (Ala. 1988) (quoting *Wiggins Estate Co. v. Jeffery,* 19 So.2d 769, 774 (Ala. 1944)). In *Ragan v. Williams,* 127 So. 190, 191 (Ala. 1930), our Supreme Court stated that "[w]hat are 'necessities' within this rule [have been] held to be a relative term … and somewhat flexible" and that "every case stands upon its peculiar facts and reasonable necessities, according to the circumstances of each case; and there is no positive or iron-bound rule by means of which it may be determined what are

---

3. The terms "necessities" and "necessaries" are often used interchangeably in cases in this area of law. For consistency, except when quoting from an authority, this opinion uses the term "necessity" for the concept at issue.

4. "An infant's liability for necessaries is based not upon his or her actual contract to pay for them, but upon a contract implied by law, or in other words, a quasi-contract," 42 Am.Jur.2d Infants §64 (2000) (footnote omitted). Accordingly, it is generally recognized that "[w]hen an infant's contract for necessaries remains executory and the things contracted for have not been furnished him, the infant is not bound by the contract and may repudiate it," id. See 43 C.J.S. Infants §180 (1978) ("To render an infant liable for necessaries they must have been actually furnished; hence [a minor] cannot make a binding executory agreement to purchase necessaries or to pay for necessaries to be supplied him, and he may disaffirm such contract or agreement before it has been performed and recover the unearned portion of the money paid in advance.") (footnotes omitted); Restatement of Restitution §139. See also Ex parte Odem, 537 So.2d 919 (Ala.1988) (describing the obligation of a minor to pay for necessary medical services as "aris[ing] from a quasi-contractual relationship created by operation of law which enforces the implied contract to pay," and holds the minor "liable for the just value of the necessaries"); Ex parte McFerren, 63 So. 159, 159 (Ala. 1913) (observing that "[i]n all cases in which [an infant lessee] has been held liable for rent or in which he has been denied to recover rents paid, he has received some actual benefit from the use of the property as a tenant").

or what are not necessaries." Further, our courts have commented that "the term ['necessity'] is to be made applicable to such things as are obviously requisite for the maintenance of existence of the infant." *Harris v. Raughton*, 73 So.2d 921, 923 (Ala. App. 1954).

Determining whether the subject of a contract is a necessity to a minor entails a two-step analysis:

> It is for the court to determine, as a matter of law, in the first place, whether the things supplied may fall within the general classes of necessaries, and if so, whether there is sufficient evidence to warrant the jury in finding that they are necessary. If either of these preliminary inquiries be decided in the negative, it is the duty of the court to nonsuit the plaintiff who seeks to recover from the [minor]. If they be decided in the affirmative, it is then for the jury to determine whether, under all the circumstances, the things furnished were actually necessary to the position and condition of the [minor], as well as their reasonable value, and whether the [minor] was already sufficiently supplied....

Odem, 537 So.2d at 920 (*quoting Wiggins Estate Co. v. Jeffery*, 19 So.2d at 774). Thus, first a court must determine whether the subject of the contract is generally considered a necessity. If the subject is so considered, then it is for the fact-finder to determine, on the particular facts and circumstances of the case, whether the subject of the contract is, in fact, a necessity to that minor. The first inquiry is a question of law; the second inquiry entails a factual determination.

There is little question that, in general, lodging is considered a necessity. As the *Ragan* Court observed, typical necessities include "things for bodily need — food, support and maintenance, clothing, medicine and medical attention, and lodging." *Ragan*, 127 So. at 191. Thus, the question in this case is whether the trial court erred in concluding as a factual matter that the apartment leased by Young was a necessity for her.

The trial court noted that "Alabama courts have held that lodging is a necessity" and that "[Young] was employed full-time at the time she entered into the contract." Immediately after making those observations, the trial court concluded: "The court finds under the facts of this case the contract was for a necessity." *Id.*

Young contends that the apartment was not a necessity to her because, she argues, her parents did not "kick" her out of their house and they kept her room waiting so that she could return to their home at any time. Young's father testified that every time he talked to his daughter on the telephone while she lived in the apartment he asked her to move back in with them; he also testified that he was willing to take Young back at any time. In essence, because Young's parents were able and willing to house Young at the same time she contracted to lease the apartment, Young argues that in this case the particular lodging at issue was not a necessity.

In support of this contention, Young cites *Harris v. Raughton*, 73 So.2d 921 (Ala. App. 1954). In *Harris*:

> Bremman R. Raughton, a minor, bought an automobile from the appellants. He paid $90 cash as the down payment. According to [Raughton's] testimony, the car would not operate satisfactorily, so in about two days after the sale he returned it to the appellants and demanded a refund of the initial payment. This was refused, and the automobile was left at appellants' place of business.

73 So.2d at 922. Raughton sued Harris and the other appellants to recover his down payment. The evidence showed that Raughton was married and had bought the automobile to use as transportation to and from his place of employment. However, the evidence

also showed that Raughton already owned a truck that he had been using for the same purpose and that he had not disposed of at the time he purchased the new automobile. The court determined that, because Raughton had another vehicle available to him, the automobile in question was not a necessity, and, thus, Raughton was at liberty to void the contract for the purchase of the automobile.

By analogy, Young argues that because she had a place to live provided by her parents still available to her at the time she signed the lease agreement and during the time she lived in the apartment, the apartment was not a necessity. In other words, she argues that the apartment was not " 'necessary to [Young's] position and condition as a [minor]' " at the time she signed the lease. *Odem*, 537 So.2d at 920.

… The undisputed evidence in this case indicates that … Young's parents were willing and able to provide lodging for their daughter at the time she rented the apartment from Weaver.

In *Ragan*, 127 So. 190, the Alabama Supreme Court addressed a case in which a lessor sued a minor lessee for rental payments on a house and the minor pleaded incapacity. The trial court had ruled that the minor had to pay rent for the house. The Supreme Court affirmed, reasoning that

> [t]he testimony, when considered as a whole, shows that the house occupied as the home for the minor and his family, under the circumstances showing his complete emancipation and necessities of earning a livelihood for himself and his immediate family (wife and child), was a necessity for him as a farmer, who was farming for himself and living with his family, apart from his or her family and adjacent to the lands he cultivated.

127 So. at 192.

Ragan is factually distinguishable from the instant case because the situation and condition of Ragan differed markedly from Young's situation and condition. Ragan was emancipated, married, and had children; none of those circumstances are true of Young. Ragan's house was next to the farmland from which he made his living; while Young testified that she worked full-time at Lowe's during the period when she lived in the apartment, she also testified that she continued to work there after she moved back into her parents' residence. Thus, unlike in *Ragan*, Young did not need the apartment to maintain her employment. Finally, Ragan and his family did not live with his parents immediately prior to living in the house in question, and there is no indication that Ragan and his family could have moved in with his parents if they did not live in the house. In contrast, Young had lived with her parents before renting the apartment, and both she and her father testified that she could have moved back into her parents' house at any time during the period that she rented the apartment. In fact, when she left the apartment, Young did move back in to her parents' house and resided there during the very period for which Weaver now seeks to collect rent. In sum, consideration of the factors the *Ragan* Court emphasized in determining that the lodging in question was a necessity in that case supports the conclusion that the lodging in question is not a necessity in the present case.

In contrast to *Ragan*, in *Ex parte McFerren*, 63 So. 159, the Alabama Supreme Court concluded that the leasehold in question was not a necessity. It reached that conclusion on the ground that the minor in that case never actually used the leasehold, a fact which itself demonstrated that the leasehold was not a necessity: "The lease representing nothing that was necessary for the infant, and he, in fact, derived *no benefit* whatever from it." 63 So. at 162. Likewise, in the present case, the fact that the apartment in question was not a necessity for Young, particularly during the post-November 2001 period for which

Weaver seeks to recover rent, is demonstrated by the fact that Young did not reside in the apartment after that date, but returned to live with her parents.

Given the authorities cited above and the particular facts of this case, we conclude that the trial court erred in its determination that the apartment in question was a necessity for Young. Therefore, as a minor, Young is not legally bound under the lease agreement. This result may seem unjust in some ways, but as the Supreme Court observed in *Ex parte McFerren*:

> The above rule [that a minor may disaffirm a contract] may, at times, work a hardship. The law must, however, have a definite policy, and its rules must be fixed. The law has fixed its policy with reference to the protection of infants with regard to their contracts, and those who deal with them, except when actually supplying them with necessaries, deal with them at their peril.

63 So. at 162.

Accordingly, the judgment of the trial court is reversed, and the cause is remanded for the trial court to enter a judgment in favor of Young.

Toshio Mori, Through Anger and Love

(1979)

From a parked automobile Haruo stuck his head out a little and peered across the street. Yes, he was standing by the entrance talking to several men. His old man was talking and laughing as if nothing had happened yesterday. Had he forgotten already? No, his old man couldn't forget that easily. Haruo cautiously drew back and sat on the fender. Five minutes to seven by the City Hall clock. Promptly at seven, he knew, the flower market was going to open. What should he buy? What flowers were most popular, and most profitable? Suddenly he heard footsteps approaching the car. Instantly he was on his feet, and without looking back scurried around the corner. Safely past the corner he increased his pace. At a hundred yards he began to puff with exertion and slackened a bit. Just ahead he spied an alley and ran for it. Puffing and coughing he rested his nine-year-old body, his eyes trained on the sidewalk. Two minutes passed and nobody came after him. Slowly he came out and looked down the street and sighed with relief.

The market was open by now. Well, let the others go in first. He would walk around the block and take his time. Unhurriedly he stopped and looked at the store windows. Every now and then he looked up and down the street. Watching his chance he would slip in the market and make his purchase. He must look out for his old man. Then he must act natural when buying from the wholesalers so they would think that he was buying for his old man. Several minutes ago he was unsure of himself. He couldn't believe that he would be able to go through with it. Now he was sure of himself. He knew what flowers to get and where to get them from. His father bought a lot of things from Matsumoto and Toscana. Matsumoto was a grower of carnations and Toscana raised roses. They knew him well. It would be easy. If only his old man would not appear at the wrong time.

Nearing the market once more Haruo slowed down. His eyes darted from the market entrance to the adjoining wholesale stores. Cautiously he stepped behind the row of parked cars watching for his father. He was not in sight. Should he take a chance now or wait awhile? He watched a number of people coming in and out of the market. Flower business must have been good yesterday. Almost all the florists were present. Should he hurry and buy before the flowers were all gone? Several more florists came out with armfuls of flowers. Haruo became desperate. He hurriedly crossed the street to a spot near the entrance. Growing bolder he peered through the window, watching all sides, and then he saw his father.

His father was in the rear of the market purchasing cyclamen and mixed plants. He looked very much absorbed in the plants. Should he slip in now? Haruo could see Matsumoto, whose table was near the entrance. At least he could get the carnations. Wait a minute. He became suspicious, cautious. Was his old man purposely in the rear so he would fall in a trap? Maybe his old man had seen him a few minutes ago and asked Matsumoto to look out for him. That would be terrible. Then he would have to go back home crawling on his knees. Undoubtedly his father would further humiliate him and kick him out of the house. Maybe Matsumoto did not know. He looked keenly at the carnation grower's face, watching for a tell-tale sign that he was looking out for his old man. No, he did not know. Matsumoto's face was calm and relaxed. His eyes did not shift about. Then he looked in the rear of the market watching for his old man. He was not around. He was gone. Eagerly he walked in heading straight for Matsumoto's table.

Haruo's face fell. Matsumoto's table was bare. Where did his flowers go? Did he sell out? He hesitated in his tracks. Matsumoto's eyes brightened.

"Hello, Haruo!" he cried. "How are you? My, you've grown. And how is your mother?"

"Fine," Haruo said hurriedly. He looked over the table. "Did you sell out? Have you any carnations left?"

"Do you want carnations?" Matsumoto asked. "Let's see. How many do you want?"

"Ten bunches," Haruo said eagerly.

The man looked under the table and started unwrapping a big bundle. "All right, Haruo," he said. "I'll give you ten. Mixed colors?"

"Yes, but give me lots of red."

Matsumoto laughed heartily and his belly shook. "You're a smart boy, Haruo. You know what sells."

Haruo looked about. Matsumoto laughed and talked too loud. He must get away. "Will you please wrap it up?"

"Are you going to take it with you now or is your father coming to pick it up?" he asked.

"I want it now," Haruo said quickly.

Matsumoto hummed a tune and took his time wrapping. Finally he handed over the package. "All right, Haruo."

"How much is it?" Haruo asked.

"Dollar and a half. I'm charging you only fifteen cents a bunch."

"Pay you next time," Haruo said.

"Sure. That's all right," Matsumoto cried, waving his hand.

Haruo fairly ran to Toscana's table. He must hurry. His father might return any minute. His eyes brightened at the sight of Toscana's good roses piled high on his table.

"Hello, boy," called the Italian. "Do you want to buy nice roses? I'll give you a bargain today."

Haruo picked up a bunch to see if the outer petals of the roses were bruised, and then satisfied examined the bases of the stems for the telltale mark of old flowers. Toscana chuckled and picked up several bunches for Haruo to examine.

"All fresh flowers, my boy. No kidding," he said. "You want to buy for your papa?"

"How much?" Haruo asked hurriedly.

Toscana counted off six bunches. "Two dollars to you. A real bargain."

"I'll take it." He said quickly.

Haruo looked about while he waited for the man to finish wrapping. He must get away. Any minute now his old man would be coming back. Which entrance should he take, the front or the rear? Eagerly he accepted the package from Toscana.

"All right, boy," the nurseryman said, nodding and smiling.

With both arms loaded with packages Haruo walked off excitedly. He must hurry. He must catch a bus and ride back to his district and start selling his flowers. . . .

Safely on the bus and bound for his district Haruo leaned back with relief. His father would never find him now. With his feet on the front seat Haruo braced himself. His shoes did not reach the floor. Every now and then he looked into the packages to see if the flowers were all right. A dollar and a half to Matsumoto and two dollars to Toscana. He must pay them next time. He must sell pretty nearly all his flowers to make a good profit. He had ten bunches of carnations and six bunches of roses. That would mean twenty dozen carnations and twelve dozen roses. He must sell cheaper than his old man. How much should he charge? Twenty-five cents a dozen for carnations and thirty-five cents a dozen for roses would be a bargain. Anybody would buy at that price. First, he would go to the shops in the district that knew him. Mazzini, the Browns, Nick, Hamilton Hardware, Rosloff Service Station, Riley, Joe, and the rest. They were friends of his old man. They would be glad to see him.

Haruo took out his pencil and pad and figured. The bus moved and vibrated. Several times the flowers started to slip off the seat. Twenty dozens at twenty-five cents a dozen would be five dollars. Twelve dozen roses at thirty-five would amount to four dollars. Nine dollars for the day! That would be swell. He would give his uncle fifty cents a day for room and board.

The bus stopped and lurched. Haruo looked out of the window. Pretty soon he must get off. He put his pencil and pad in his pocket. He had better start selling right away. He must make good today. If he failed and had to go back begging for forgiveness his old man would laugh at him and give him a stick. No, he couldn't fail. When a boy has run away from home for good he should not think of going home. Even if it killed him he shouldn't. He should move on and take the consequences.

———————

Toshio Mori, a second generation Japanese-American, was born in Oakland, California in 1910. In 1941, he was already a writer and his first collection of stories was about to be published when he was transported with 110,000 other Americans of Japanese descent to an internment camp in Topaz, Utah. Through Anger and Love tells the story of Haruo, a nine-year-old flower seller, who uses his skills as a salesperson to gain independence and, eventually, to connect with others. William Saroyan described Mori as having the "fine heart of a true writer." Mori conveys something of the human condition in his stories. What aspect of the human condition do you find in this story? Does it lead you to draw any conclusions about the infancy doctrine and the capacity of minors to enter into contracts?

———————

Note

Youthful consumers have long been a visible part of commercial exchange. Advertisers in the late 1800s frequently used pictures of babies and young children to sell products, including opium based teething syrup, gasoline, and cigars. *See* Alice L. Muncaster, Helen Sawyer, and Ken Kapson, The Baby Made Me Buy It! A Treasury of Babies Who Sold Yesterday's Products (1991). Today, children are both employed *in* advertising and an important audience *for* advertising. Children's television has been repeatedly criticized for its aggressive advertising techniques, yet efforts to restrict the amount of advertising in television programs directed at children have limited success. Some critics contend that many children's television shows and movies are little more than lengthy commercials for toys and accessories featuring the characters in the shows and movies. Overall, children are an important part of the U.S. economy. Middle-class and wealthy children spend billions of dollars each year and influence how many more billions of dollars of their parents' money is spent.

With less public visibility, children are a significant part of the work force in the United States Although federal and state laws have curtailed the use of child labor in many industries, these laws generally do not apply to family businesses, farm labor, and child performers, among others. Moreover, agencies charged with enforcement of child labor laws are notoriously underfunded, and many businesses violate these laws with apparent impunity.

Children may lack contractual capacity, but their parents can enter into contracts on their behalf. When children are forced to work by their parents, child abuse laws prohibit the most extreme forms of exploitation, but those laws do not address other problems that arise when children are used like property, as a source of income for their parents. A great deal of attention has been paid to this in connection with child stars. The laws in this area, even those that require court approval of contracts by child actors, alter the rules with respect to capacity in a way designed to protect the entertainment industry and to insure the enforceability of contracts. Some protection is usually built in for the child so that some of the money he or she earns will be there when he or she reaches majority. Many critics feel the protection is inadequate. *See, e.g.*, N.Y. Arts & Cult. Aff. Art. 35, *Child Performers and Models* § 35.03(1) (1994), California recently amended its statute to provide even greater protection for the minor child who is a performer.

---

2. Mental Incapacity

Current doctrine provides that a contract entered by a person who is unable to understand the nature of the contract and its obligations is voidable by that person. *See Restatement (Second) of Contracts* § 12. The current justification for this rule is protection of the person who lacks mental capacity. Unlike age incapacity, however, there is no bright line distinguishing those with and without mental capacity, so application of the doctrine is more complex. The main issue is whether the person was or was not able to understand the contract and its consequences, yet evidence on this is often ambiguous, so courts frequently look to the substantive fairness of the contract. If the contract involves an unequal exchange, courts are more likely to think that the person was mentally incapable. If, on the other hand, the terms of the contract appear fair, then courts are less likely to find incompetence. The following case is unusual because the court allows the contract to be avoided on the ground of mental incapacity, even though there was no indication that the terms of the contract were unfair. Upon what evidence did the court base its finding that Bobby Joe Clardy lacked the mental capacity to contract?

Shoals Ford, Inc. v. Maxine Clardy, as conservator for Bobby Joe Clardy

Supreme Court of Alabama
588 So. 2d 879 (1991)

J. GORMAN HOUSTON, JUSTICE

Shoals Ford, Inc., appeals from a judgment based on a jury verdict in favor of Maxine Clardy, as conservator for Bobby Joe Clardy. We affirm.

Ms. Clardy sued Shoals Ford, seeking to have a transaction entered into between Shoals Ford and her husband Bobby Joe for the purchase of a 1989 Ford pickup truck set aside and to recover the monies paid by Bobby Joe to Shoals Ford, alleging that Bobby Joe suffered from a manic-depressive disorder[1] and was in a manic state when he transacted with Shoals Ford to purchase the truck and also alleging that Shoals Ford was negligent,[2] wanton, and willful in dealing with Bobby Joe. She sought compensatory damages, punitive damages, and rescission of the contract. Shoals Ford answered, asserting that it had acted without notice of Bobby Joe's incompetency, that the conservatorship proceeding was not instituted until nearly a month after Bobby Joe had purchased the truck, that the family members had been contributorily negligent in assisting Bobby Joe in purchasing the truck, and that there had been an accord and satisfaction. It amended its answer, adding the affirmative defense of estoppel and pleading "that there was no failure of consideration or undue influence taken of" Bobby Joe in his purchase of the truck and that Ms. Clardy failed to mitigate damages. Both Shoals Ford and Ms. Clardy filed motions for summary judgment, which the trial court denied. Both Shoals Ford and Ms. Clardy moved for a directed verdict, which the trial court denied. The jury returned a verdict in favor of Ms. Clardy in the amount of $6,715.02 in compensatory damages and $18,000 in punitive damages. Shoals Ford filed a motion for new trial or, in the alternative, for judgment notwithstanding the verdict, which the trial court denied. Shoals Ford appeals.

Shoals Ford contends that the evidence was insufficient to sustain the jury's verdict, because, it argues, Ms. Clardy failed to establish the elements necessary for recovery in this case, specifically those elements relating to the incapacity of Bobby Joe at the time he consummated the transaction and took possession of the truck. It contends that the contract was completed, that the truck was delivered, and that Bobby Joe took possession of the truck, all on April 3, 1989, when all of the paperwork was finalized, and that, on that date, Bobby Joe was not incompetent.

Ms. Clardy contends that the evidence establishes that Bobby Joe completed the transaction on April 5, 1989, when he took actual possession of the truck, i.e., when he drove the truck off the lot, and that, on that date, he was incompetent to handle his affairs.

The well-settled law in Alabama is that contracts of insane persons are wholly and completely void. *See Williamson v. Matthews*, 379 So. 2d 1245 (Ala. 1980); Ala. Code § 8-

---

1. Bobby Joe Clardy suffers from a mental disease known as bipolar disorder, which is more commonly called a manic-depressive disorder.
2. Ms. Clardy subsequently withdrew the negligence count.

1-170 (1975). In *McAlister v. Deatherage*, 523 So. 2d 387, 388 (Ala. 1988), quoting from *Weaver v. Carothers*, 228 Ala. 157, 160, 153 So. 201, 202 (1934), this Court explained the cognitive (understanding) test that Alabama adopted in order to determine whether a contract can be avoided because of insanity:

> [To] avoid a contract on the ground of insanity, it must be satisfactorily shown that the party was incapable of transacting the particular business in question. It is not enough that he was the subject of delusions not affecting the subject-matter of the transaction, nor that he was, in other respects, mentally weak. A party cannot avoid a contract, free from fraud or undue influence, on the ground of mental incapacity, unless it can be shown that his insanity ... was of such character that he had no reasonable perception or understanding of the nature and terms of the contract.

Viewing the tendencies of the evidence most favorably to the prevailing party and indulging all reasonable inferences that the jury was free to draw, as required under our applicable standard of review, *see Warren v. Ousley*, 440 So. 2d 1034 (Ala. 1983), we find the following:

On April 1, 1989, Bobby Joe talked to Kelly Cole of Shoals Ford concerning the purchase of a truck; on that day he filled out the initial papers. By April 3, 1989, all the necessary paperwork had been completed and Bobby Joe had signed the necessary documents, but when he went to pick up the truck, he was advised that because of his poor credit rating, Shoals Ford would require a $10,500 down payment instead of the $5,000 down payment previously discussed. On April 5, 1989, Bobby Joe returned to Shoals Ford with the down payment and, at that time, picked up the truck.[3]

According to Ms. Clardy, Bobby Joe had suffered from a manic-depressive disorder for 15 years and was taking lithium to control his condition. She said that she observed in mid-March 1989 that Bobby Joe was becoming manic, but she said that because he was not violent and had not endangered himself or anyone else at that time, she could not involuntarily commit him for treatment. On April 5, 1989, Ms. Clardy received a telephone call from Leslie Clardy Daniel, Ms. Clardy and Bobby Joe's daughter ("the daughter"), concerning Bobby Joe's condition. The daughter told Ms. Clardy that Bobby Joe had threatened her and had obtained $500 from her to make the down payment on a truck he was going to buy from Shoals Ford. Subsequently, Ms. Clardy drove to Shoals Ford and noticed that the truck Bobby Joe had previously looked at, in her presence, was still on the lot. At that time she spoke with a salesperson, and she later telephoned a sales representative with Shoals Ford, concerning Bobby Joe's incompetency and asked that they not allow Bobby Joe to take the truck—that is, she told them that Bobby Joe was not working, that he was ill and would be committed, and that the truck could not be insured. Thereafter, on April 5, 1989, Shoals Ford gave Bobby Joe possession of the truck after he gave it $10,000 as the down payment.[4] Ford Motor Credit Company eventually

---

3. Shoals Ford contends that the procedure it followed with Bobby Joe was what it called a "spot delivery," which is a procedure whereby a purchaser takes delivery before completing the down payment. Thus, it contends that delivery occurred on April 3, 1989, when the necessary paperwork was completed, even though Bobby Joe had not made the down payment and even though he did not actually pick up the truck at that time.

4. Shoals Ford had increased the down payment from $5,000 to $10,500, but accepted the $10,000 amount for the down payment when Ms. Clardy and Bobby Joe's daughter stopped payment on the check the daughter says Bobby Joe forced her to write to him.

repossessed and sold the truck and mailed Ms. Clardy a check for $3,284.98, which left a balance of $6,715.02 of the $10,000 down payment unrecovered by Ms. Clardy.

According to the daughter, when Bobby Joe visited her around April 1, 1989, she tried to get him to resume taking his medicine. He became agitated and went out of control, threw his medicine into a burning pile of leaves, and then left. Around 5 A.M. on April 5, 1989, Bobby Joe returned to the daughter's house, banged on the doors and windows until he awakened the household, threatened their lives, and forced the daughter to write him a check for $500. When he left, the daughter telephoned 911 to report the incident and, as soon as the probate office opened, she telephoned the probate judge to inform him of the situation. She then went to her attorney's office, explained the situation to him, and asked that he prepare a petition to have Bobby Joe involuntarily committed for treatment. While in her attorney's office, she notified the bank to stop payment on the $500 check she had written to Bobby Joe and then called to notify Shoals Ford of Bobby Joe's mental condition, telling a representative that Bobby Joe would be coming in to purchase a truck, specifically describing the particular truck; telling the representative that Bobby Joe was not healthy; and telling the representative that she had filed a petition to have Bobby Joe involuntarily committed. She also asked Shoals Ford to call the Lauderdale County sheriff, a family member, her attorney, Riverbend Center for Mental Health, or the probate office for verification in the event Bobby Joe did appear at the dealership. She further explained to the representative that "buying sprees" was a symptom of Bobby Joe's illness, that he would not be able to make the payments, and that he was not insurable. When she notified Shoals Ford of the situation, it merely stated that if Bobby Joe had the money to purchase the truck, it was "none of her concern." Around 10 A.M. on April 5, 1989, she drove by Shoals Ford and, noticing that the truck was still there, she once again telephoned "to plead" with Shoals Ford to notify her when Bobby Joe arrived. At this time, the representative told her that "it was really not of concern to Shoals Ford."

According to Dr. Joseph W. Glaister, a local psychiatrist who had treated Bobby Joe since 1984, Bobby Joe suffered from a manic depressive illness, manic type, recurrent. Dr. Glaister testified that Bobby Joe's illness was episodic, that his competency could come and go, and that there were stages of the illness when, on mere observation, one might think that Bobby Joe was a slightly excessive, overly friendly individual. He further testified that Bobby Joe had been admitted to the hospital after regular working hours on April 5, 1989, and that when he saw Bobby Joe on April 6, 1989, Bobby Joe was incompetent. Furthermore, according to the testimony of Dr. Glaister, he could not visualize Bobby Joe being otherwise on April 5, 1989.

The daughter's attorney testified that he remembered the events of April 5, 1989, when the daughter contacted him, when he obtained a history of the events of the day, and when he prepared the commitment petition and other documents that were filed with the probate court on that morning. He stated that he did not prepare and file the petition to appoint Ms. Clardy as conservator and limited guardian for Bobby Joe until a month after the petition to commit, because Bobby Joe was hospitalized during that period of time and, in the attorney's opinion, had no opportunity to dissipate his estate.

Based on the foregoing, we hold that there was sufficient evidence to support the jury's verdict that during the period in question — from April 1, 1989 (when Bobby Joe began negotiations to purchase the truck), to April 3, 1989 (when Shoals Ford alleges the transaction was completed), to April 5, 1989 (when Ms. Clardy alleges the transaction was completed) — Bobby Joe was incompetent; that during that period of time, he was incapable of understanding and appreciating the nature, terms, and effect of the contract.

Shoals Ford also contends that the trial court erred in failing to give its requested jury charges and, following timely objection, erred in refusing to cure its errors.

In a jury case, a party is entitled to have its case tried to a jury that is given the appropriate standard by which to reach its decision, and a wrongful refusal of a requested jury charge constitutes a ground for a new trial. *See C.I.T. Financial Services, Inc. v. Bowler*, 537 So. 2d 4 (Ala. 1988). An incorrect, misleading, erroneous, or prejudicial charge may form the basis for granting a new trial. *See Nunn v. Whitworth*, 545 So. 2d 766 (Ala. 1989). However, the refusal of a requested, written instruction, although a correct statement of the law, is not cause for reversal on appeal if it appears that the same rule of law was substantially and fairly given to the jury in the trial court's oral charge. See Rule 51, Ala. R. Civ. P. When examining a charge asserted to be erroneous, this Court looks to the entirety of the charge to see if there is reversible error. *See Grayco Resources Inc. v. Poole*, 500 So. 2d 1030 (Ala. 1986).

The trial court charged the jury as follows:

> I ... charge you that manic depression is a mental illness, but that is not to say that all manic-depressives may be classified as legally insane. Some are and some are not. In order to determine if a person is legally insane, you will have to determine whether or not he, [Bobby Joe] in this case, had sufficient capacity to understand in a reasonable manner the nature and effect of the act he was doing. Or put another way, that he had a reasonable perception or understanding of the nature and terms of the contract. And again, the issue is whether or not he had that mental capacity when he took possession of the truck.

Shoals Ford, objecting to that charge, alleged that the statement about when possession occurred, under the facts of this case, was confusing to the jury and was clearly a misleading statement of the law and the facts in this case. It contends that from the charge, the jury was left with the impression that it was to look only at the events on April 5, 1989 (the date Bobby Joe actually drove the truck from the lot), and not at the events occurring at any previous time (i.e., without regard to the negotiations of April 1, 1989, and the completion of the paperwork on April 3, 1989, which is the date Shoals Ford alleges possession occurred because all of the paperwork had then been completed).

In response to Shoals Ford's objection to this charge, the following colloquy occurred:

> [Shoals Ford's attorney]: I had an objection as to your charging the jury that ... the contract was when the possession was taken and ... in my opinion ... whether or not there was a contract is not in question, but when the contract was is the jury's decision and you kept talking about possession.

> The Court: ... [You] argued that ... [Bobby Joe] took possession on April the 3rd ... and therefore [the fact] that he brought any money in on April the 5th would have nothing to do with it because by that time it was a done deal.

> [Shoals Ford's attorney]: Okay. Well, I just thought it was sort of confusing if they thought ... it was a done deal and [Bobby Joe] didn't take possession until the 5th.

> [Ms. Clardy's attorney]: ... [I] think it was clear that the contract is in effect upon delivery and it's up to [the jury] to decide whether it was the 3rd or the 5th.

> The Court: Right.

From a review of the record, it is apparent, as the trial court noted, that all of the evidence presented by Shoals Ford was intended to prove to the jury that on April 3, 1989, upon completing the negotiations and filling out the necessary paperwork with Bobby Joe, even though Bobby Joe had not made the full down payment and even though he did not pick up the truck, it had delivered the truck to him and he had taken possession of the truck; not on April 5, 1989, when he actually made the full down payment and drove the truck from the dealership. An argument now that the above-quoted jury charge was misleading and confusing to the jury is without merit, especially in light of the fact that the trial court did not mention any specific dates—it did not mention either April 3, 1989, or April 5, 1989, as the date the jury was to consider. Furthermore, under the particular facts of this case, when considering the charge as a single entity, we cannot hold the trial court in error for so charging the jury. Rather, the trial court left the fact-finding function to the jury; it simply guided the jury as to the applicable law.

. . .

Affirmed; application overruled.

Note

The *Restatement (Second) of Contracts* § 15(1)(a) sets forth a cognitive test ("unable to understand in a reasonable manner the nature and consequences of the transaction") and § 15(1)(b) adopts a volitional test ("unable to act in a reasonable manner in relation to the transaction and the other party has reason to know of his condition") for determining mental competency. In *Shoals Ford* what test for determining mental capacity does the court articulate and apply? Re-examine the evidence submitted by the parties and reflect on Oliver Sacks' story of Rebecca in light of the following argument.

In *Silencing the Different Voice: Competency Feminist Theory and Law*, 47 U. Miami L. Rev. 763 (1993), Susan Stefan examines the practices of competency testing in the contexts of health care and the right to die, consent to sexual intercourse, divorce and separation agreements, adoption of children, and the decision to have children. She argues that existing legal definitions of competency and methodologies of assessing competence wrongly assume that competence can be assessed as a fixed and measurable attribute. Instead, she argues, human competence is interactional and an individual's "competence" cannot be known or observed apart from a dynamic of relationship. She observes further that relationships of assessors to assessees are necessarily hierarchical, characterized by dominance and subordination. Stefan identifies a number of interactional factors that shape an assessment of competency: the setting for the assessment (e.g., it matters if this occurs in the home, a law office, the courtroom), the identity of the "expert," the interactions between the expert and the person being assessed, and the perceptions and assumptions of the judge presiding over the determination, including perceptions and assumptions shaped by gender and racial stereotyping. The assumption that competence is fixed and measurable, Stefan argues, focuses attention exclusively on the assessee as if he or she were solely responsible for the quality of communication between the assessor and assessee, and ignores these interactional factors. The following excerpt presents an alternative understanding of competency evaluations.

Oliver Sacks, Rebecca

(1970)

Rebecca was no child when she was referred to our clinic. She was nineteen but, as her grandmother said, "Just like a child in some ways." She could not find her way around the block, she could not confidently open a door with a key; (she could never "see" how the key went, and never seemed to learn). She had left/right confusion, she sometimes put on her clothes the wrong way—inside out, back-to-front, without appearing to notice, or, if she noticed, without being able to get them right. She might spend hours jamming a hand or foot into the wrong glove or shoe—she seemed, as her grandmother said, to have "no sense of space." She was clumsy and ill-coordinated in all her movements—a "klutz," one report said, a "motor moron" another (although when she danced, all her clumsiness disappeared).

Rebecca had a partial cleft palate, which caused a whistling in her speech; short, stumpy fingers, with blunt, deformed nails; and a high, degenerative myopia requiring very thick spectacles—all stigmata of the same congenital condition which had caused her cerebral and mental defects. She was painfully shy and withdrawn, feeling that she was, and had always been, a "figure of fun."

But she was capable of warm, deep, even passionate attachments. She had a deep love for her grandmother, who had brought her up since she was three (when she was orphaned by the death of both parents). She was very fond of nature, and, if she was taken to the city parks and botanical gardens, spent many happy hours there. She was very fond too of stories, though she never learned to read (despite assiduous, and even frantic, attempts), and would implore her grandmother or others to read to her. "She has a hunger for stories," her grandmother said; and fortunately her grandmother loved reading stories and had a fine reading voice which kept Rebecca entranced. And not just stories—poetry too. This seemed a deep need or hunger in Rebecca—a necessary form of nourishment, of reality, for her mind. Nature was beautiful, but mute. It was not enough. She needed the world re-presented to her in verbal images, in language, and seemed to have little difficulty following the metaphors and symbols of even quite deep poems, in striking contrast to her incapacity with simple propositions and instructions. The language of feeling, of the concrete, of image and symbol, formed a world she loved and, to a remarkable extent, could enter. Though conceptually (and "propositionally") inept, she was at home with poetic language, and was herself, in a stumbling, touching way, a sort of "primitive," natural poet. Metaphors, figures of speech, rather striking similitudes, would come naturally to her, though unpredictable, as sudden poetic ejaculations or allusions. Her grandmother was devout, in a quiet way, and this also was true of Rebecca: she loved the lighting of the Sabbath candles, the benisons and orisons which thread the Jewish day; she loved going to the synagogue, where she too was loved (and seen as a child of God, a sort of innocent, a holy fool); and she fully understood the liturgy, the chants, the prayers, rites and symbols of which the Orthodox service consists. All this was possible for her, accessible to her, loved by her, despite gross perceptual and spatio-temporal problems, and gross impairments in every schematic capacity—she could not count change, the simplest calculations defeated her, she could never learn to read or write, and she would average 60 or less in IQ tests (though doing notably better on the verbal than the performance parts of the test).

Thus she was a "moron," a "fool," a "booby," or had so appeared, and so been called, throughout her whole life, but one with an unexpected, strangely moving, poetic power. Superficially she *was* a mass of handicaps and incapacities, with the intense frustrations and anxieties attendant on these; at this level she was, and felt herself to be, a mental cripple—beneath the effortless skills, the happy capacities, of others; but at some deeper level there was no sense of handicap or incapacity, but a feeling of calm and completeness, of being fully alive, of being a soul, deep and high, and equal to all others. Intellectually, then, Rebecca felt a cripple; spiritually she felt herself a full and complete being.

When I first saw her—clumsy, uncouth, all-of-a fumble—I saw her merely, or wholly, as a casualty, a broken creature, whose neurological impairments I could pick out and dissect with precision: a multitude of apraxias and agnosias, a mass of sensorimotor impairments and breakdowns, limitations of intellectual schemata and concepts similar (by Piaget's criteria) to those of a child of eight. A poor thing, I said to myself, with perhaps a "splinter skill," a freak gift, of speech; a mere mosaic of higher cortical functions, Piagetian schemata—most impaired.

The next time I saw her, it was all very different. I didn't have her in a test situation, "evaluating" her in a clinic. I wandered outside—it was a lovely spring day—with a few minutes in hand before the clinic started, and there I saw Rebecca sitting on a bench, gazing at the April foliage quietly, with obvious delight. Her posture had none of the clumsiness which had so impressed me before. Sitting there, in a light dress, her face calm and slightly smiling, she suddenly brought to mind one of Chekov's young women— Irene, Anya, Sonya, Nina—seen against the backdrop of a Chekovian cherry orchard. She could have been any young woman enjoying a beautiful spring day. This was my human, as opposed to my neurological, vision.

As I approached, she heard my footsteps and turned, gave me a broad smile, and wordlessly gestured. "Look at the world," she seemed to say. "How beautiful it is." And then there came out, in Jacksonian spurts, odd, sudden, poetic ejaculation: "spring," "birth," "growing," "stirring," "coming to life," "season," "everything in its time."

. . . .

Why was she so decomposed before, how could she be so recomposed now? I had the strongest feeling of two wholly different modes of thought, or of organization, or of being. The first schematic—pattern-seeing, problem-solving—this is what had been tested, and where she had been found so defective, so disastrously wanting. But the tests had given no inkling of anything *but* the deficits, of anything, so to speak, *beyond* her deficits.

They had given me no hint of her positive powers, her ability to perceive the real world—the world of nature, and perhaps of the imagination—as a coherent, intelligible, poetic whole; her ability to see this, think this, and (when she could) live this; they had given me no intimation of her inner world, which clearly *was* composed and coherent, and approached as something other than a set of problems or tasks.

. . .

Our tests, our approaches, I thought, as I watched her on the bench—enjoying not just a simple but a sacred view of nature—our approach, our "evaluations," are ridiculously inadequate. They only show us deficits, they do not show us powers; they only show us puzzles and schemata, when we need to see music, narrative, play, a being conducting itself spontaneously in its own natural way.

Rebecca, I felt, was complete and intact as "narrative" being, in conditions which allowed her to organize herself in a narrative way; and this was something very important to know, for it allowed one to see her, and her potential, in a quite different fashion from that imposed by the schematic mode.

It was perhaps fortunate that I chanced to see Rebecca in her so-different modes—so damaged and incorrigible in the one, so full of promise and potential in the other—and that she was one of the first patients I saw in our clinic. For what I saw in her, what she showed me, I now saw in them all.

. . .

Then, in November, her grandmother died, and the light, the joy, she had expressed in April now turned into the deepest grief and darkness. She was devastated, but conducted herself with great dignity. Dignity, ethical depth, was added at this time, to form a grave and lasting counterpoint to the light, lyrical self I had especially seen before....

The work of grief was slow, but successful, as Rebecca, even when most stricken, anticipated. It was greatly helped by a sympathetic and supportive great aunt, a sister of her Grannie, who now moved into the house. It was greatly helped by the synagogue, and the religious community, above all by the rites of "sitting shiva," and the special status accorded her as the bereaved one, the chief mourner. It was helped too perhaps by her speaking freely to me. And it has helped also, interestingly, by *dreams*, which she related with animation, and which clearly marked *stages* in the grief-work (*see* Peters, 1983).

...

During the intervening months (between my first seeing her, in April, and her grandmother's death that November), Rebecca—like all our "clients" (an odious word then becoming fashionable, supposedly less degrading than "patients"), was pressed into a variety of workshops and classes, as part of our Developmental and Cognitive Drive (these too were "in" terms at the time).

It didn't work with Rebecca, it didn't work with most of them. It was not, I came to think, the right thing to do, because what we did was to drive them full-tilt upon their limitations, as had already been done, futilely, and often to the point of cruelty, throughout their lives.

...

Rather suddenly, after her grandmother's death, she became clear and decisive. "I want no more classes, no more workshops," she said. "They do nothing for me. They do nothing to bring me together." And then, with that power for the apt model or metaphor I so admired, and which was so well developed in her despite her low IQ, she looked down at the office carpet and said:

"I'm like a sort of living carpet. I need a pattern, a design, like you have on that carpet. I come apart, I unravel, unless there's a design." I looked down at the carpet, as Rebecca said this, and found myself thinking of Sherrington's famous image, comparing the brain/mind to an "enchanted loom," weaving patterns ever-dissolving, but always with meaning. I thought: can one have a raw carpet without design? Could one have the design without the carpet (but this seemed like the smile without the Cheshire cat)? A "living" carpet, as Rebecca was, had to have both—and she especially, with her lack of schematic structure (the warp and woof, the *knit*, of the carpet, so to speak), might indeed unravel without a design (the scenic or narrative structure of the carpet).

"I must have meaning," she went on. "The classes, the odd jobs have no meaning ... What I really love," she added wistfully, "is the theater."

We removed Rebecca from the workshop she hated, and managed to enroll her in a special theater group. She loved this—it composed her; she did amazingly well: she became a complete person, poised, fluent, with style, in each role. And now if one sees Rebecca on stage, for theater and the theater group soon became her life, one would never even guess that she was mentally defective.

———————

Note

Oliver Sacks, M.D. is a physician, a best-selling author, a professor of neurology, and a widely admired public intellectual. The New York Times has referred to him as "the poet laureate of medicine." His book Awakenings, about a group of patients who had survived the great encephalitis lethargica epidemic of the early twentieth century, inspired the 1990 Academy Award-nominated feature film starring Robert De Niro and Robin Williams.

In February 2015, Sacks wrote an Op-Ed piece for the New York Times discussing his diagnosis of terminal cancer and reflecting on his remaining time alive:

> Over the last few days, I have been able to see my life as from a great altitude, as a sort of landscape, and with a deepening sense of the connection of all its parts. This does not mean I am finished with life.
>
> On the contrary, I feel intensely alive, and I want and hope in the time that remains to deepen my friendships, to say farewell to those I love, to write more, to travel if I have the strength, to achieve new levels of understanding and insight.
>
> This will involve audacity, clarity and plain speaking; trying to straighten my accounts with the world. But there will be time, too, for some fun (and even some silliness, as well).

Oliver Sacks, My Own Life, February 19, 2015, http://www.nytimes.com/2015/02/19/opinion/oliver-sacks-on-learning-he-has-terminal-cancer.html.

Sacks' many books, including *The Man Who Mistook His Wife for a Hat*, which includes the essay about Rebecca, are read in courses on ethics, philosophy and sociology. The story of Rebecca illustrates the complex ways in which individuals with neurological diseases experience their lives. Clearly, the doctrine of mental incapacity does not address these experiences in any meaningful way. Indeed, the focus of the doctrine—on "cognitive" and "volitional" "tests"—seems both unworkable and irrelevant when we learn about Rebecca's life.

As with age incapacity, some persons with special intellectual and psychological capacities and other concerned people have argued that contractual disability actually hurts those it purports to protect. Indeed, the mental capacity rules of contract law may conflict with the recently enacted Americans with Disabilities Act. 42 U.S.C. §§ 12101 et. seq. The Act defines "disability" to include a "mental impairment that substantially limits one or more of the major life activities of such individual" (42 U.S.C. § 12102), and provides that:

> No individual shall be discriminated against on the basis of disability in the full and equal enjoyment of the goods, services, facilities, privileges, advantages, or accommodations of any place of public accommodation by any person who owns, leases (or leases to), or operates a place of public accommodation.

42 U.S.C. § 12182. Under the act, "public accommodation" includes hotels, restaurants, and retail stores of all sorts, see 42 U.S.C. § 12181, and "discrimination" includes a failure to take affirmative steps to accommodate special needs, see 42 U.S.C. § 12182.

One important lawyering task is to advise clients of changes in the law that may affect their business operations. What advice would you give Shoals Ford regarding the Americans with Disabilities Act? What might Shoals Ford have done to accommodate Bobby Joe Clardy's special needs and what changes might be implemented to assure that Shoals Fords is in compliance with the Americans with Disabilities Act in its routine transactions?

Chapter Seven

Error or Market Misconduct

In this chapter, we continue to study "defenses" to contract liability. The doctrines of mistake, misunderstanding, misrepresentation, duress, undue influence, and unconscionability deny legal enforcement to private agreements formed as a result of misconduct (or error) that undermines the possibility of free choice. In each of the cases in this chapter that you read, pay close attention to the conduct that triggers the defense, to distinctions between proper and improper market behavior, and to the complex assumptions about human relationships and motivations that shape these doctrines.

A. Mistake of Fact

The Restatement (Second) of Contracts § 151 defines mistake as "a belief that is not in accord with the facts." As the cases below illustrate, courts distinguish between situations in which both parties were mistaken about some important fact, called *mutual mistake*, and situations in which only one party was mistaken, called *unilateral mistake*.

In cases of mutual mistake, some courts will allow an aggrieved party to avoid the contract because neither of the parties had accurate information and thus neither of them intended to form the existing contract. Generally, one party prefers to enforce the contract as is because he will get more than he bargained for and the other party will be "adversely affected." The person adversely affected will attempt to use the doctrine of mutual mistake to rescind or avoid the contract. Mistake will not excuse performance, however, in the case of a party who should have known or should have made an inquiry into the facts before entering into the contract: if one party "assumes the risk of an error." Risk can be allocated contractually to one party (e.g., an "as is" sale) or by established practice between the parties or within the industry (e.g., art sales among collectors).

In cases of unilateral mistake, where only one party is mistaken about a fact, courts usually will enforce the contract, reasoning that it is better to protect the reasonable expectations of the party who did not make the mistake than to save the mistaken party from her or his own error. This rule also has its exceptions. Courts will refuse to enforce contracts when there is unilateral mistake if there is some fault attributable to the non-mistaken party or if enforcement of the contract would be so burdensome to the mistaken party as to be "unconscionable."

A third category of mistake is called *mistake in expression*, where the parties understand the facts correctly and have reached agreement on the contract, but some error is made in transcribing or reducing a contract to written form. In cases of *mistake in expression*, courts will enforce the agreement actually made and order *reformation* of the writing or other erroneous expression.

1. Mutual Mistake of Fact

Todd A. Oliver v. Felisha E. Clark

Nebraska Supreme Court
537 N.W.2d 635 (1995)

JOHN M. GERRARD, JUSTICE

Todd A. Oliver, plaintiff-appellant, brought this action seeking recovery of damages for bodily injuries allegedly sustained on October 7, 1991, in an automobile collision with a vehicle driven by defendant-appellee, Felisha E. Clark. In defense of the action, Clark asserted that on October 25 Oliver received settlement funds and executed a document entitled "Release of All Claims," which released her from all damage claims arising from that accident. On Clark's motion for summary judgment, the district court determined that the release and settlement bound Oliver, and the action was dismissed with prejudice. Oliver appealed to the Nebraska Court of Appeals, assigning as error that there is a question of fact whether such release is binding because of the parties' alleged mutual mistake relating to the nature and extent of the injuries Oliver had sustained in the accident. In order to regulate the caseloads of the appellate courts, we, on our own motion, removed the matter to this court. On the record in this case, we conclude that a genuine issue of fact exists as to whether the parties intended the release to cover the injury which Oliver presently asserts he sustained in the automobile accident. Accordingly, we reverse, and remand for further proceedings.

Factual Background

On October 7, 1991, a pickup truck driven by Clark collided with an automobile driven by Oliver in the Time Out Chicken parking lot on North 30th Street in Omaha, Nebraska. As a result of the collision, Oliver sustained property damage to his automobile and apparently minor injuries to his neck, which produced initial symptomatology of minor pain and swelling of the neck. On October 8, Oliver sought medical treatment from his private physician. X rays failed to indicate any fracture to Oliver's vertebrae, and he was treated and discharged.

On October 22, 1991, Oliver contacted Clark's insurer, indicating that he had received injuries to his back, neck, and arms. On that date, an agent for the insurer offered Oliver $200 to settle his bodily injury claim. Oliver rejected the offer and demanded $1,000 to settle the claim. On October 23, Oliver again contacted the insurer by telephone. During this conversation, Oliver reported that he had received x rays on October 22 and that nothing was wrong with him other than a twisted neck. After some brief negotiations, the agent for the insurer agreed to pay Oliver $500 plus all medical bills incurred to that date in settlement of Oliver's bodily injury claim. Oliver indicated that this settlement was satisfactory to him and stated that he wanted the entire matter settled by October 25.

On October 25, 1991, a document entitled "Release of All Claims" was executed by Oliver in the presence of an agent of the insurer, which document purported to release Clark "from any and all claims ... arising from ... an accident that occurred on or about the 7th day of October 1991 ... [.] [T]his settlement shall apply to all unknown and unanticipated injuries and damages resulting from said accident ... as well as to those now disclosed."

In accordance with the release, Oliver was initially paid $500, and he received additional payments of $1,054 on November 20, 1991, and $34 on December 13 in payment of medical bills incurred prior to the signing of the release.

Following the signing of the release, Oliver's condition progressively deteriorated, and he continued to seek medical treatment regarding severe pain in the area of his neck. On December 5, 1991, Oliver visited Immanuel Medical Center where a CT scan was performed, and Oliver was diagnosed with a transverse fracture of the odontoid of the second cervical vertebra. Stabilization surgery was performed at AMI Saint Joseph Hospital (St. Joseph's) on December 19, which was followed by complications and has resulted in alleged permanent injury to Oliver.

District Court Proceedings

On February 12, 1993, Oliver filed a petition in the district court for Douglas County, alleging negligence on the part of Clark in regard to the automobile accident and seeking damages for permanent injuries and additional medical expenses incurred by Oliver after the signing of the release. Clark filed an answer denying the allegations in Oliver's petition and asserted that Oliver's execution of the document entitled "Release of All Claims" released her from all damage claims arising from the accident. Oliver's reply alleged that at the time of the signing of the release he was not mentally competent to enter into the settlement agreement. Clark subsequently filed a motion for summary judgment in the district court.

At the hearing on Clark's motion for summary judgment, Oliver sought to invalidate the release and settlement on grounds of mutual mistake. Oliver offered his own affidavit, which was received without objection, and attached to the affidavit were records from the Douglas County Board of Mental Health and medical records from St. Joseph's and Immanuel. Oliver's affidavit and the attached medical records reveal that he has a long history of mental illness and, in fact, had been committed by the board of mental health to various institutions for mental health treatment on at least four occasions in the 4 years preceding the accident. In addition, the medical records attached to Oliver's affidavit set forth the initial diagnosis of no fractures on October 8, 1991, the diagnosis of the transverse fracture of the odontoid of the second cervical vertebra on December 5, and the resultant stabilization surgery that was performed on December 19. In opposition to Oliver's claim, Clark offered affidavits of Saralyn Serratore and Diana Thompson, claim representatives of Clark's insurer, which set forth the entire contents of the release of claims and the fact that the insurer paid all sums of money the insurer had agreed to pay pursuant to the terms of the settlement agreement. In addition, Serratore's affidavit revealed that Oliver informed her on November 20 that he was suffering from a psychotic condition known as paranoid schizophrenia.

The district court rejected the claim that a mutual mistake between Oliver and Clark's insurer had occurred and granted summary judgment in favor of Clark, dismissing Oliver's petition with prejudice.

...

Analysis

The crucial question on a motion for summary judgment is whether there exists a "genuine issue as to any material fact." The alleged factual dispute in this appeal concerns whether Oliver's late-diagnosed injury and asserted disability is reached by the release. On a motion for summary judgment, the question is not how a factual issue is to be decided, but whether any real issue of material fact exists....

Mutual Mistake

Nebraska has long followed the majority rule that a settlement agreement which purports to release any and all claims for accident-related damages may be set aside on grounds of mutual mistake where there are injuries of a serious character wholly unknown to the parties which were not taken into consideration when the release was executed. *See, Frahm v. Carlson*, 334 N.W.2d 795 (1983); *Swartz v. Topping*, 213 N.W.2d 718 (1974); *Simpson v. Omaha & C.B. Street R. Co.*, 186 N.W. 1001 (Neb. 1922).

In the seminal *Simpson* case, this court set forth:

> Where one who has sustained personal injuries, and with his attention directed to the known injuries, which are trivial in their nature, contracts for the settlement of his damages with reference thereto, in ignorance of other and more serious injuries, both parties at the time believing that the known injuries are all the injuries sustained, then there is a mutual mistake, and the release, although couched in general terms, should be held not to be a bar to an action for the more serious and unknown injuries.

186 N.W. at 1003.

This court further explained the rule, as follows:

> [T]he true rule is that the mistake must relate to either a present or past fact or facts that are material to the contract of settlement, and not to an opinion as to future conditions as the result of present known facts. A mistake as to the future development of a known injury is a matter of opinion, and is not one of fact, and is not such a mistake as will avoid a release; but, where the mistake is as to the extent of the injury due to unknown conditions or relates to injuries that were wholly unknown, then the release may be avoided, unless it further appears that the parties were contracting with respect to possible unknown injuries, and the releasor intended to relinquish all claims, whether known or unknown.

186 N.W. at 1003.

In *Simpson*, the plaintiff fell while boarding a streetcar. The only known personal injury consisted of a superficial injury to the plaintiff's knee. The $50 release was for torn clothing and the superficial knee injury. After a few months, serious physical and emotional injuries developed. The release recited that the defendant was released "'from any and all cause or causes of action, costs, charges, claim or demand, of whatever name or nature, in any manner arising or to grow out of an accident occurring....'" In *Simpson*, we held that the release was executed under a mutual mistake of the parties, and the plaintiff was not barred from recovery of damages for the injuries that were unknown to both parties at the time the release was executed.

Oliver, to avoid the release in this case, must demonstrate that his present condition is not the result of the development of an injury known at the execution of the release, but is an injury that was wholly unknown at the release's signing. A mistake as to the future development of a known injury is not such a mistake as will avoid a release. *Simpson v. Omaha & C.B. Street R. Co.*, 107 Neb. 779, 186 N.W. 1001 (1922). Put another way, an inaccurate or incomplete diagnosis is often the type of mistake that relates "to either a present or past fact or facts that are material to the contract of settlement" and may lead to a mutual mistake of fact by parties during settlement negotiations. *See id.* Whereas, a mistaken or uncertain prognosis of a known injury is most often a matter of opinion, it is not one of fact and is not such a mistake as will avoid a release.

To ultimately succeed in setting aside the release, Oliver must produce evidence to establish that the parties were not aware of any serious injuries caused by the accident and that the parties contracted for a settlement only with respect to the known minor injuries. In the December 18, 1991, St. Joseph's history and physical form dictated by Dr. Charles Taylon, it was revealed that Oliver saw his private physician the day after the accident and that "cervical spine films were obtained and no fractures were noted. The patient was seen in follow-up in Emergency Department at St. Joseph's. Upon reviewing the films it was not felt the patient had a fracture and he was discharged home." Any fracture-type injury to the cervical vertebra, for which Oliver now seeks recovery, was not disclosed by the x rays taken shortly after the accident. In addition, Serratore's affidavit confirmed that Oliver had contacted the insurer on October 23 and reported that he had received x rays on October 22 and that "nothing was wrong with him other than a twisted neck." Oliver and the insurer reached a settlement agreement on this very same date. This evidence, together with the fact that only $500, plus current medical bills, was paid in consideration for the release, creates an inference that the parties may have been contracting solely for a minor "twisted neck" injury, claimed by Oliver as of October 23, rather than the later-diagnosed fracture of the second cervical vertebra.

. . .

Judgment

Accordingly, we reverse the summary judgment entered against Oliver and remand the cause to the district court for further proceedings consistent with this opinion.

Piano Tuner Finds Problem: Stashed Cash

(1993)

Jake Thielke bought an old piano for $70 at an estate sale and got a surprise: $140,000 was stashed inside.

Thielke and his wife, Diane, asked piano technician Dan Shereda to check it to see if it was worth repairing. Then they watched as Shereda began pulling out neatly wrapped, moldy bundles of $5, $10 and $20 bills from the back of the turn-of-the-century instrument.

Thielke consulted a lawyer, who said the cash still belonged to the estate of Harley Stimm, a Medford barber who also stashed money in a mattress and books before his death in October.

The Thielkes had no regrets about giving up the fortune.

"Morally, we believe we did the right thing," Thielke said. "We talked it over and it didn't feel right to keep it."

Shereda says the piano still needs a lot of work.

---

2. Unilateral Mistake of Fact

Jump-Rope Rhyme

I went upstairs to make my bed.
I made a mistake and bumped my head.
I went downstairs to milk my cow.
I made a mistake and milked the sow.

I went to the kitchen to bake a pie.
I made a mistake and baked a fly.

First Baptist Church of Moultrie v. Barber Contracting Company
Court of Appeals of Georgia
377 S.E.2d 717 (1989)

WILLIAM LEROY McMURRAY, PRESIDING JUDGE

The First Baptist Church of Moultrie, Georgia, invited bids for the construction of a music, education and recreation building. The bids were to be opened on May 15, 1986. They were to be accompanied by a bid bond in the amount of 5 percent of the base bid. The bidding instructions provided, in pertinent part: "Negligence on the part of the bidder in preparing the bid confers no right for the withdrawal of the bid after it has been opened."

Barber Contracting Company ("Barber") submitted a bid for the project in the amount of $1,860,000. The bid provided, in pertinent part: "For and in consideration of the sum of $1.00, the receipt of which is hereby acknowledged, the undersigned agrees that this proposal may not be revoked or withdrawn after the time set for the opening of bids but shall remain open for acceptance for a period of thirty-five (35) days following such time." The bid also provided that if it was accepted within 35 days of the opening of bids, Barber would execute a contract for the construction of the project within 10 days of the acceptance of the bid.

A bid bond in the amount of 5 percent of Barber's bid ($93,000) was issued by The American Insurance Company to cover Barber's bid. With regard to the bid bond, the bid submitted by Barber provided:

> If this proposal is accepted within thirty-five (35) days after the date set for the opening of bids and the undersigned [Barber] fails to execute the contract within ten (10) days after written notice of such acceptance ... the obligation of the bid bond will remain in full force and effect and the money payable thereon shall be paid into the funds of the Owner as liquidated damages for such failure

The bids were opened by the church on May 15, 1986, as planned. Barber submitted the lowest bid. The second lowest bid, in the amount of $1,975,000 was submitted by H & H Construction and Supply Company, Inc. ("H & H").

Barber's president, Albert W. Barber, was present when the bids were opened, and of course, he was informed that Barber was the low bidder. Members of the church building committee informally asked President Barber if changes could be made in the contract to reduce the amount of the bid. He replied that he was sure such changes could be made.

On May 16, 1986, Albert W. Barber informed the architect for the project, William Frank McCall, Jr., that the amount of the bid was in error—the bid should have been $143,120 higher. In Mr. Barber's words:

> [T]he mistake in Barber's bid was caused by an error in totaling the material costs on page 3 of Barber's estimate work sheets. The subtotal of the material cost listed on that page is actually $137,990. The total listed on Barber's summary sheet for the material cost subtotal was $19,214. The net error in addition was $118,776. After adding in mark-ups for sales tax (4 percent), overhead and profit (15 percent), and bond procurement costs (.75 percent), the error was compounded to a total of $143,120 ...

The architect immediately telephoned Billy G. Fallin, co-chairman of the church building committee, and relayed the information which he received from President Barber.

On May 20, 1986, Barber delivered letters to the architect and the church. In the letter to the architect, Barber enclosed copies of its estimate sheets and requested that it be permitted to withdraw its bid. In the letter to the church, Barber stated that it was withdrawing its bid on account of "an error in adding certain estimated material costs." In addition, Barber sought the return of the bid bond from the church.

On May 29, 1986, the church forwarded a construction contract, based upon Barber's bid, to Barber. The contract had been prepared by the architect and executed by the church. The next day, Barber returned the contract to the church without executing it. In so doing, Barber pointed out that its bid had been withdrawn previously.

On July 25, 1986, the church entered into a construction contract for the project with H & H, the second lowest bidder. Through deletions and design changes, the church was able to secure a contract with H & H for $1,919,272.

In the meantime, the church demanded that Barber and The American Insurance Company pay it $93,000 pursuant to the bid bond. The demand was refused.

On May 26, 1987, the church brought suit against Barber and The American Insurance Company seeking to recover the amount of the bid bond. Answering the complaint, defendants denied they were liable to plaintiff.

Thereafter, defendants moved for summary judgment and so did the plaintiff. In support of their summary judgment motions, defendants submitted the affidavit of Albert W. Barber. He averred that in preparing its bid, Barber exercised the level of care ordinarily exercised by contractors submitting sealed bids. In support of its summary judgment motion, the church submitted the affidavit of a building contractor who averred that he would never submit a bid of any magnitude without obtaining assistance in verification and computation.

The trial court denied the summary judgment motions, certified its rulings for immediate review and we granted these interlocutory appeals. *Held*:

> The question for decision is whether Barber was entitled to rescind its bid upon discovering that it was based upon a miscalculation or whether Barber should forfeit its bond because it refused to execute the contract following the acceptance of its bid by the church. We hold that Barber was entitled to rescind its bid.

That equity will rescind a contract upon a unilateral mistake is a generally accepted principle. *See* Corbin on Contracts, §609 (1960). As it is said:

> Where a mistake of one party at the time a contract was made as to a basic assumption on which he made the contract has a material effect on the agreed exchange of performances that is adverse to him, the contract is voidable by him if he does not bear the risk of the mistake ... and (a) the effect of the mistake is such that enforcement of the contract would be unconscionable, or (b) the other party had reason to know of the mistake or his fault caused the mistake.

Restatement (2d) of Contracts, §153 (1979).

The following illustration demonstrates the rule:

> In response to B's invitation for bids on the construction of a building according to stated specifications, A submits an offer to do the work for $150,000. A believes that this is the total of a column of figures, but he has made an error by

inadvertently omitting a $50,000 item, and in fact the total is $200,000. B, having no reason to know of A's mistake, accepts A's bid. If A performs for $150,000, he will sustain a loss of $20,000 instead of making an expected profit of $30,000. If the court determines that enforcement of the contract would be unconscionable, it is voidable by A.

Restatement (2d) of Contracts, §153 (1979) (Illustration 1).

Corbin explains:

> Suppose ... a bidding contractor makes an offer to supply specified goods or to do specified work for a definitely named price, and that he was caused to name this price by an antecedent error of computation. If, before acceptance, the offeree knows, or has reason to know, that a material error has been made, he is seldom mean enough to accept; and if he does accept, the courts have no difficulty in throwing him out. He is not permitted "to snap up" such an offer and profit thereby. If, without knowledge of the mistake and before any revocation, he has accepted the offer, it is natural for him to feel a sense of disappointment at not getting a good bargain, when the offeror insists on withdrawal; but a just and reasonable man will not insist upon profiting by the other's mistake. There are now many decisions to the effect that if the error was a substantial one and notice is given before the other party has made such a change of position that he cannot be put substantially in status quo, the bargain is voidable and rescission will be decreed.

Corbin on Contracts, §609 (1960).

Georgia law is no different. It provides for rescission and cancellation "upon the ground of mistake of fact material to the contract of one party only." OCGA §23-2-31. The mistake must be an "unintentional act, omission, or error arising from ignorance, surprise, imposition, or misplaced confidence." OCGA §23-2-21(a). But relief will be granted even in cases of negligence if the opposing party will not be prejudiced. OCGA §23-2-32.

We can see these principles at work in *M. J. McGough Co. v. Jane Lamb Memorial Hosp.*, 302 F. Supp. 482 (S.D. Iowa 1969). In that case, a bid of $1,957,000 was submitted for a hospital improvement by a contractor. A bond in the amount of $100,000 was given to secure the contractor's bid. The contractor submitted the lowest bid. After the bids were opened, but before its bid was accepted, the contractor informed the hospital that it erroneously transcribed numbers in computing the bid and that, therefore, it underbid the project by $199,800. Nevertheless, the hospital tried to hold the contractor to its bid. When the contractor refused to execute a contract, the hospital awarded the contract to the next lowest bidder. The contractor and surety sought rescission of the bid and the return of the bond. The hospital sued the contractor and surety for damages. The district court allowed the contractor to rescind. Its decision is noteworthy and illuminating. We quote it at length:

> By the overwhelming weight of authority a contractor may be relieved from a unilateral mistake in his bid by rescission under the proper circumstances. *See generally* Annot., 52 A.L.R.2d 792 (1957). The prerequisites for obtaining such relief are: (1) the mistake is of such consequence that enforcement would be unconscionable; (2) the mistake must relate to the substance of the consideration; (3) the mistake must have occurred regardless of the exercise of ordinary care; (4) it must be possible to place the other party in status quo. It is also generally required that the bidder give prompt notification of the mistake and his intention to withdraw....

Applying the criteria for rescission for a unilateral mistake to the circumstances in this case, it is clear that [the contractor] and his surety ... are entitled to equitable relief. The notification of mistake was promptly made, and [the contractor] made every possible effort to explain the circumstances of the mistake to the authorities of [the hospital]. Although [the hospital] argues to the contrary, the Court finds that notification of the mistake was received before acceptance of the bid. The mere opening of the bids did not constitute the acceptance of the lowest bid ... Furthermore, it is generally held that acceptance prior to notification does not bar the right to equitable relief from a mistake in the bid.

The mistake in this case was an honest error made in good faith. While a mistake in and of itself indicates some degree of lack of care or negligence, under the circumstances here there was not such a lack of care as to bar relief....

The mistake here was a simple clerical error. To allow [the hospital] to take advantage of this mistake would be unconscionable. This is especially true in light of the fact that they had actual knowledge of the mistake before the acceptance of the bid. Nor can it be seriously contended that a $199,800 error, amounting to approximately 10 percent of the bid, does not relate directly to the substance of the consideration. Furthermore, [the hospital] has suffered no actual damage by the withdrawal of the bid of [the contractor]. The Hospital has lost only what it sought to gain by taking advantage of [the contractor's] mistake. Equitable considerations will not allow the recovery of the loss of bargain in this situation.

M. J. McGough Co. v. Jane Lamb Memorial Hosp., 302 F.Supp. 482, 485, 486, supra.

In the case *sub judice*, Barber, the contractor, promptly notified the plaintiff that a mistake was made in calculating the amount of the bid. The plaintiff had actual knowledge of the mistake before it forwarded a contract to Barber. The mistake was a "simple clerical error." *M. J. McGough Co. v. Jane Lamb Memorial Hosp.*, 302 F. Supp. 482, 485, *supra*. See OCGA § 23-2-21 (a). It did not amount to negligence preventing equitable relief. *See* OCGA § 23-2-32 (a). Furthermore, it was a mistake which was material to the contract (OCGA § 23-2-31) — it went to the substance of the consideration. (The mistake amounted to approximately seven percent of the bid.) To allow the plaintiff to take advantage of the mistake would not be just. *M. J. McGough Co. v. Jane Lamb Memorial Hosp.*, 302 F. Supp. at 486. *See also Shelton & Co. v. Ellis*, 70 Ga. 297 (1883).

The contention is made that Barber's miscalculation constituted negligence sufficient to prevent relief in equity. See OCGA § 23-2-32 (a). Assuming, arguendo, that the error stemmed from such a want of prudence as to violate a legal duty (OCGA § 23-2-32 (a)), we must nevertheless conclude that Barber is entitled to rescission.

Relief in equity "may be granted even in cases of negligence by the complainant if it appears that the other party has not been prejudiced thereby." OCGA § 23-2-32 (b). It cannot be said that plaintiff was prejudiced by Barber's rescission. After all, plaintiff "lost only what it sought to gain by taking advantage of [the contractor's] mistake." *M. J. McGough Co. v. Jane Lamb Memorial Hosp.*, 302 F. Supp. at 486.

The plaintiff takes the position that rescission is improper since, pursuant to the language set forth in the bid, Barber agreed not to withdraw the bid for a period of 35 days after the bids were opened. It also asserts that the language set forth in the bidding instructions prohibited Barber from withdrawing the bid on the ground of "negligence." We disagree. "[P]rovisions such as these have been considered many times in similar cases, and have never been held effective when equitable considerations dictate otherwise." *M. J. McGough Co. v. Jane Lamb Memorial Hosp.*, 302 F. Supp. 482, 487, *supra*.

The trial court properly denied the plaintiff's (the church's) motion for summary judgment. It erred in denying defendants' (Barber's and The American Insurance Company's) motions for summary judgment.

E. Annie Proulx, The Shipping News

(1993)

Quoyle walked along the wharf, craning to get another look at the Polar Grinder, but it was lost in the rain. A man in a pea jacket and plastic sandals gazed at the rubber boots in Cuddy's Marine Supply Window. Wet, red toes. Said something as Quoyle went past. The liquor store, the marine hardware shop. A long liner drifted toward the fish plant, a figure in yellow oilskins leaning on the rail staring into dimpled water the color of motor oil.

At the end of the wharf, packing crates, a smell of garbage. A small boat was hauled up beside the crates, propped against it a small crayoned board: For Sale. Quoyle looked at the boat. Rain sluiced over the upturned bottom, pattered on the stones.

"You can have it for a hundred." A man leaning in a doorframe, hands draining into his pockets. "Me boy built it but he's gone, now. Won five hundred on the lottery. Took off for the mainland. Where they lives 'mong the snakes." He sniggered "Seek his bloody fuckin' fortune."

"Well, I was just looking at it." But a hundred dollars didn't seem like very much for a boat. It looked all right. Looked sturdy enough. Painted white and grey. Practically new. Must be something wrong with it. Quoyle thumped the side with his knuckles.

"Tell yer what," said the man. "Give me fifty, she's yours."

"Does it leak?" said Quoyle.

"Nah! Don't leak. Sound as a sea ox. Just me boy built it but he's gone now. Good riddance to him, see? I wants to get it out of me sight. I was gonna burn it up," he said shrewdly, taking Quoyle's measure. "So's not to be troubled by the sight of it. Reminding me of the boy."

"No don't burn it," said Quoyle. "Can't go wrong for fifty bucks, can I!" He found a fifty and got a scrawled bill of sale on the back of an envelope. The man's jacket, he saw, was made of some nubby material, ripped, with stains down the side.

"You got a trailer?" The man gestured at the boat, making circles in the air to indicate a rolling motion.

"No. How'll I get it home without one?"

"You'n rent one down at Cuddy's if yer don't mind paying his bloody prices. Or we'll lash it into the bed of yer truck."

"I don't have a truck," said Quoyle. "I've got a station wagon." He never had the right things.

"Why that's almost as good, as long as you doesn't drive too speedy. She'll hang down, y'know, in the front and the back some."

"What kind of boat do you call it, anyway?"

"Ah, its just a speedboat. Get a motor on her and won't you have fun dartin' along the shore!" The man's manner was lively and enthusiastic now. "Soon's this scuddy weather goes off."

In the end, Quoyle rented a trailer and he and the man and half a dozen others who splashed up laughing and hitting the man's shoulder in a way Quoyle ignored, shifted the boat onto the trailer. He headed back to the Gammy Bird. Hell, fifty dollars barely bought dinner for four. The rain ran across the road in waving sheets. The boat wagged.

Saw her. The tall woman in the green slicker. Marching along the edge of the road as usual, her head pushed back. A calm, almost handsome face, ruddy hair in braids wound around her head in an old fashioned coronet. Her hair was wet. She was alone. Looked right at him. They waved simultaneously and Quoyle guessed she must have legs like a marathon runner.

Sauntered into the newsroom and sat at his desk. Only Nutbeem and Tert Card there, Nutbeem half asleep with low atmospheric pressure, his ear against the radio, Card on the phone at the same time whacking the computer keys. Quoyle was going to say something to Nutbeem, but didn't. Instead, worked away on the shipping news. Dull enough, he thought.

SHIPS ARRIVED THIS WEEK.
Bella (Canadian) from the fishing grounds
Farewell (Canadian) from Montreal
Foxfire (Canadian) from Bay Misery
Minatu Maru 54 (Japanese) from the Fishing Grounds
Pescamesca (Portuguese) from the Fishing Grounds
Porto Santo (Panamanian) from the High Seas
Zhok (Russian) from the Fishing Grounds
Ziggurat Zap (U.S.) from the High Seas
And so forth.

At four Quoyle gave the shipping news to Tert Card, whose moist ear lay against the phone receiver, shoulder hunched while he typed. Suffering from the stiff neck again.

Car doors slammed outside, Billy Pretty's voice seesawed. Nutbeem snapped up alertly.

"There's Mr. Jack Buggit and Billy Pretty back from the car wreck. Moose collision while you were gone, Quoyle. Two dead. And the moose."

Saved again, thought Quoyle.

"I hope they got pictures from every angle, enough to carry us through the thin spots," said Tert Card, typing Quoyle's shipping news.

Minutes passed and the door stayed closed. Billy's voice had stopped. Quoyle knew they were looking at his boat. Well, he'd taken the plunge. Smiled, rehearsing a story of how he'd decided on the spur of the moment to buy a boat and get it over, how he almost felt transformed, ready to take on the sea, to seize his heritage.

The door opened. Billy Pretty scuttled in, went straight to his desk without a look at Quoyle. Jack Buggit, hair studded with raindrops, strode halfway across the room, stopped in front of Quoyle's desk, hissed through a mouthful of smoke, "What the hell did you buy that thing for?"

"Why everybody was after me to buy a boat! It looked as good as any of them. It had a good price. I can get back and forth a lot faster now. It's a speedboat."

"It's a shitboat!" said Jack Buggit. "Best thing you can do is get rid of it some dark night." He slammed into his glass office and they heard him mumbling, striking matches, opening and shutting desk drawers. Nutbeem and Tert Card went to the door and stared out at Quoyle's boat.

"What's wrong with it?" asked Quoyle, throwing out his hands. "What's wrong with it? Everybody tells me to buy a boat and when I buy one they tell me I shouldn't have done it."

"I told you," said Billy Pretty, "I told you to buy a nice little rodney, nice little sixteen-foot rodney with a seven-horsepower engine, nice little hull that holds the water, a good lare on it, not too much hollowing, a little boat that bears good under the bows. You bought a wallowing cockeyed bastard no good for nothing but coasting ten feet from shore when it's civil. Hull is as lumpy as a slop sea, there's no motor well, the shape is poor, she'll wallow and throw in water, pitch up and down and rear and sink."

Nutbeem said nothing, but he looked at Quoyle as though, in unwrapping a beribboned gift, he had discovered nylon socks. Billy Pretty started up again.

"That boat was built by a dumb stookawn of a kid, Reeder Gouch's kid that run off about a month after he built it. No ability at all. Not only is it no good for nothing, but it makes you cry to look at it. How could anybody build a boat with a stem got a reverse curve in it? I never seen a boat with a stem like that. They don't make them like that here. Reeder was going to burn it, he said. Too bad he didn't. I told you, get a nice little rodney, that's what you want. Or a motor dory. Or a good speedboat. You ought to fill that thing up with stones and launch it to the bottom. Go down to Nunny Bag Cover and talk to those fellers, Uncle Shag Sismal and Alvin Yark and those fellers. Get one of them to build you a nice little craft. They'll give you something that fits the water, something's got a bit of harmony between the two ends of the boat."

Drumroll of rain. Stupid Man Does Wrong Thing Once More.

The Shipping News, by Annie Proulx, won both the Pulitzer Prize and the National Book Award. In this except, Quoyle, the protagonist in the book, buys a boat that is unsuitable for his purposes. In fact, it is unseaworthy. The character Quoyle is often described in unflattering terms. Should the fact that he is an unsympathetic character enhance or diminish his chances of recovering in a suit against the seller of the boat? What legal doctrine would work best for Quoyle if he wanted to sue Reeder Gouch? What would likely be Quoyle's biggest obstacle to recovery?

---

3. Mistake in Expression

In some cases, the parties reach an actual agreement but make some mistake in the writing or other expression of their agreement. In such cases, the parties were not mistaken. They reached an agreement with full understanding. The only mistake was in *expression of the agreement*. The doctrine of mistake in expression applies to enforce the parties' actual agreement. Reformation of the writing or other expression is an appropriate remedy in such cases. In *First Federal Savings and Loan Association of Nevada v. Racquet Club Condominiums*, 801 P.2d 1360 (Nev. 1990), for example, a partnership sold two condominiums to two individuals: Unit 49 was sold to Benner and Unit 50 was sold to Sampaulesis. First Federal loaned money to both purchasers, and as security for the loans, First Federal was named as the beneficiary on both deeds of trust. However, the deeds of trust for the Benner loan mistakenly listed Unit 50 and the deed of trust for the Sampaulesis loan mistakenly listed Unit 49. After reviewing the evidence, the court ordered *reformation* of the deeds: that is, the court ordered that the documents be changed to reflect the actual agreement of the parties.

B. Misunderstanding

Although the objective theory of interpretation is firmly established, still courts are drawn to a different approach in many cases. Some doctrines explicitly require attention to the parties' actual meaning. The doctrine of misunderstanding is one such doctrine. If one person agrees to sell a ton of wild rice for $4,800, believing that a ton means 2,000 pounds (a short ton), and a second person agrees to buy a ton of wild rice for $4,800, believing that a ton means 2,240 pounds (a metric or long ton), is a contract formed? Under the objective theory, there has been an agreement for the sale of one ton of wild rice. Yet many courts have refused to enforce contracts in situations like this, in which the parties use the same words but they mean something different.

The cases that follow discuss Restatement (Second) § 20, which states that in the case of misunderstanding, there is "no manifestation of mutual assent." What difference is there, if any, between a mistake about a fact, which allows one party to rescind or avoid the contract, and misunderstanding, which can prevent the formation of contract? Roughly, a mistake of fact has to do with facts in the world outside of the contract while misunderstanding refers to differing interpretations of one or more terms in the agreement.

A claim for misunderstanding generally requires two elements: (1) the parties attach materially different meanings to their manifestation; and (2) neither party knows or has reason to know the meaning attached by the other; or each party knows or each party has reason to know the meaning attached by the other. In essence, where the parties attach materially different meanings to a term or terms of the contract and the parties are equally aware or equally unaware of the difference in interpretation, the court will find that there is no contract. If only one party is aware that a different meaning is attached by the other party, the court will enforce the contract on the terms assigned by the party who is not aware of the misunderstanding.

Konic International Corporation v. Spokane Computer Services, Inc.

Court of Appeals of Idaho
109 Idaho 527, 708 P.2d 932 (1985)

Jesse Walters, Chief Judge

Konic International Corporation sued Spokane Computer Services, Inc., to collect the price of an electrical device allegedly sold by Konic to Spokane Computer. The suit was tried before a magistrate sitting without a jury. The magistrate entered judgment for Spokane Computer, concluding there was no contract between the parties because of lack of apparent authority of an employee of Spokane Computer to purchase the device from Konic. The district court, on appeal, upheld the magistrate's judgment. On further appeal by Konic, we also affirm the magistrate's judgment but base our result on reasoning different from that of the lower court.

The magistrate found the following facts. David Young, an employee of Spokane Computer, was instructed by his employer to investigate the possibility of purchasing a surge protector, a device which protects computers from damaging surges of electrical current. Young's investigation turned up several units priced from $50 to $200, none of which, however, were appropriate for his employer's needs. Young then contacted Konic. After discussing Spokane Computer's needs with a Konic engineer, Young was referred to one of Konic's salesmen. Later, after deciding on a certain unit, Young inquired as to the price of the selected item. The salesman responded, "fifty-six twenty." The salesman meant $5,620. Young in turn thought $56.20.

The salesman for Konic asked about Young's authority to order the equipment and was told that Young would have to get approval from one of his superiors. Young in turn prepared a purchase order for $56.20 and had it approved by the appropriate authority. Young telephoned the order and purchase order number to Konic who then shipped the equipment to Spokane Computer. However, because of internal processing procedures of both parties the discrepancy in prices was not discovered immediately. Spokane Computer received the surge protector and installed it in its office. The receipt and installation of the equipment occurred while the president of Spokane Computer was on vacation. Although the president's father, who was also chairman of the board of Spokane Computer, knew of the installation, he only inquired as to what the item was and who had ordered it. The president came back from vacation the day after the surge protector had been installed and placed in operation and was told of the purchase. He immediately ordered that power to the equipment be turned off because he realized that the equipment contained parts which alone were worth more than $56 in value. Although the president then told Young to verify the price of the surge protector, Young failed to do so. Two weeks later, when Spokane Computer was processing its purchase order and Konic's invoice, the discrepancy between the amount on the invoice and the amount on the purchase order was discovered. The president of Spokane Computer then contacted Konic, told Konic that Young had no authority to order such equipment, that Spokane Computer did not want the equipment, and that Konic should remove it. Konic responded that Spokane Computer now owned the equipment and if the equipment was not paid for, Konic would sue for the price. Spokane Computer refused to pay and this litigation ensued.

Following trial, the magistrate found that Young had no actual, implied, or apparent authority to enter into the transaction and, therefore, Spokane Computer did not owe Konic for the equipment.[1] In reaching its decision, the magistrate also noted that when Spokane Computer acquired full knowledge of the facts, it took prompt action to disaffirm Young's purchase.

We agree with the magistrate's result. However, rather than base our decision on the agency principle of apparent authority, as did the trial court, we believe that more basic principles of contract are determinative in this case. "When the result reached by the trial court is correct, but entered on a different theory, we will affirm it on the correct theory." *Goodwin v. Nationwide Insurance Co.*, 656 P.2d 135, 144 (Idaho App. 1982).

Basically what is involved here is a failure of communication between the parties. A similar failure to communicate arose over 100 years ago in the celebrated case of *Raffles v. Wichelhaus*, 2 Hurl. 906, 159 Eng. Rep. 375 (1864), which has become better known as the case of the good ship "Peerless." In *Peerless*, the parties agreed on a sale of cotton which was to be delivered from Bombay by the ship "Peerless." In fact, there were two ships named "Peerless" and each party, in agreeing to the sale, was referring to a different ship. Because the sailing time of the two ships was materially different, neither party was willing to agree to shipment by the "other" Peerless. The court ruled that, because each party had a different ship in mind at the time of the contract, there was in fact no binding contract. The *Peerless* rule later was incorporated into section 71 of the *Restatement of*

---

1. Although the trial court's decision was not explicit about possession of the equipment, the district court, on appeal, determined that Konic was entitled to possession of the equipment.

Contracts and has now evolved into section 20 of *Restatement (Second) of Contracts* (1981). Section 20 states in part:

> (1) There is no manifestation of mutual assent to an exchange if the parties attach materially different meanings to their manifestations and
>
> (a) neither knows or has reason to know the meaning attached by the other.

Comment (c) to section 20 further explains that "even though the parties manifest mutual assent to the same words of agreement, there may be no contract because of a material difference of understanding as to the terms of the exchange." Another authority, Williston, discussing situations where a mistake will prevent formation of a contract, agrees that "where a phrase of contract ... is reasonably capable of different interpretations ... there is no contract." 1 S. Williston, Contracts § 95 (3d ed. 1957).

One commentator on the *Peerless* case, maintaining that the doctrine should be cautiously applied, indicates three principles about the case doctrine that are generally in agreement: (1) "the doctrine applies only when the parties have different understandings of their expression of agreement"; (2) the doctrine does not apply when one party's understanding, because of that party's fault, is less reasonable than the other party's understanding; and (3) parol evidence is admissible to establish the facts necessary to apply the rule. Young, *Equivocation in the Making of Agreements*, 64 Colum. L. Rev. 619 (1964).

The second principle indicates that the doctrine may be applicable to this case because, arguably, both parties' understandings were reasonable. Also, as pointed out by the district court, both parties were equally at fault in contributing to the resulting problems. The third principle is not relevant to the present case.

The first principle is not only directly applicable to the present case, but also corresponds to reasoning used in *Snoderly v. Bower*, 30 Idaho 484, 166 P. 265 (1917), citing the *Peerless* case. In *Snoderly* the court dealt with two parties who had contracted to grow hay. The parties had agreed that, after the hay was harvested and stacked, the hay would "be measured according to government rule." Unfortunately, there were several government rules in use in the vicinity for measuring hay. The court determined that "there was no meeting of the minds of the parties on the question as to what constituted the 'government rule' when the contract was entered into, and that provision in the contract would therefore be void." 30 Idaho at 488, 166 P. at 266, citing *Peerless*. *Snoderly* is somewhat different from the present case because in *Snoderly* both parties apparently wished to keep the benefits of their contract. Our Supreme Court therefore remanded for a determination of the reasonable value of services rendered. In the present case, Spokane Computer did not wish to retain the benefits of Konic's equipment as evidenced by the president's instruction that power to the equipment be turned off immediately and his demand on Konic to remove the equipment.

In the present case, both parties attributed different meanings to the same term, "fifty-six twenty." Thus, there was no meeting of the minds of the parties. With a hundred fold difference in the two prices, obviously price was a material term. Because the "fifty-six twenty" designation was a material term expressed in an ambiguous form to which two meanings were obviously applied, we conclude that no contract between the parties was ever formed. Accordingly, we do not reach the issue of whether Young had authority to order the equipment.

Konic asserts that the conduct of the parties reflects the formation of a contract and, this being a "transaction in goods," the provisions of the *Uniform Commercial Code* should apply. Konic also raises issues based on implied-in-law contract, estoppel, and mistake —

all arguments which have as their basis some form of contract. We conclude that the foregoing analysis is equally applicable to these arguments. The mutual misunderstanding of the parties was so basic and so material that any agreement the parties thought they had reached was merely an illusion.

Although Konic asserts that Spokane Computer was unjustly enriched, the magistrate found no evidence establishing unjust enrichment of Spokane Computer which would support any restitution to Konic. We have held that restitution may sometimes be required even though no contract has materialized. *Dursteler v. Dursteler*, 108 Idaho 230, 697 P.2d 1244 (Ct. App. 1985). However, our review of the record in this case discloses no evidence warranting such a remedy. Therefore, Konic's other theories of recovery are equally unpersuasive.

One final point concerns an issue of attorney fees. Konic contends the magistrate erred in awarding attorney fees to Spokane Computer. However, we have reviewed the record as presented to the district court and can find no evidence that this issue was framed or presented to that court in the appeal from the magistrate division. We will not review issues different from those presented to the intermediate appellate court. *Marvin Centers v. Yehezkely*, 109 Idaho 216, 706 P.2d 105, (Ct. App. 1985). We therefore decline to review the propriety of the magistrate's award of fees to Spokane Computer.

Because this was a suit on a contract for the alleged sale of goods, Spokane Computer is entitled to an award of attorney fees on appeal as the prevailing party, even though no liability under a contract was established. I.C. § 12-120(2). *See e.g., Boise Truck & Equipment, Inc. v. Hafer Logging, Inc.*, 107 Idaho 824, 693 P.2d 470 (Ct. App. 1984). The decision of the district court is affirmed. Costs and attorney fees to respondent, Spokane Computer.

Bud Abbott & Lou Costello, Who's on First?

Abbott and Costello performed their famous "baseball" routine on The Kate Smith Hour on the Columbia Broadcasting System in 1937 and in their movie The Naughty Nineties (1945), and on many other occasions. They developed many variations. Here is one, which is reproduced in an appendix to Bob Thomas, Bud & Lou: The Abbott & Costello Story (1977).

Lou: You know the fellows' names?

Bud: Yes.

Lou: Well, then, who's playin' first?

Bud: Yes.

Lou: I mean the fellow's name on first base.

Bud: Who.

Lou: The fellow's name on first base for St. Louis.

Bud: Who.

Lou: The guy on first base.

Bud: Who is on first base.

Lou: Well, what are you askin' me for?

Bud: I'm not asking you, I'm telling you. Who is on first.

Lou: I'm askin' you, who is on first?

Bud: That's the man's name.

Lou: That's whose name?

Bud: Yes.

Lou: Well, go ahead, tell me.

Bud: Who.

Lou: The guy on first.

Bud: Who.

Lou: The first baseman.

Bud: Who is on first.

Lou: (a new approach): Have you got a first baseman on first?

Bud: Certainly.

Lou: Well, all I'm trying' to find out is what's the guy's name on first base.

Bud: Oh, no, no. What is on *second* base.

Lou: I'm not askin' you who's on second.

Bud: Who's on first.

Lou: That's what I'm tryin' to find out.

Bud: Well, don't change the players around.

Lou: (tension mounting): I'm not changin' anybody.

Bud: Now take it easy.

Lou: What's the guy's name on first base?

Bud: What's the guy's name on *second* base.

Lou: I'm not askin' you who's on second.

Bud: Who's on first.

Lou: I don't know.

Bud: He's on third. We're not talking about him.

Lou: (imploringly): How could I get on third base?

Bud: You mentioned his name.

Lou: If I mentioned the third baseman's name, who did I say is playing third?

Bud: (insistently): No, Who's playing first.

Lou: Stay offa first, will ya?

Bud: Please, now what is it you'd like to know?

Lou: What is the fellow's name on third base?

Bud: What is the fellow's name on *second* base.

Lou: I'm not askin' ya who's on second.

Bud: Who's on first.

Lou: I don't know.

Bud and Lou in unison: Third base!

Lou: (trying a new tack): You got an outfield?

Bud: Certainly.

Lou: St. Louis got a good outfield?

Bud: Oh, absolutely.

Lou: The left fielder's name?

Bud: Why.

Lou: I don't know. I just thought I'd ask.

Bud: Well, I just thought I'd tell you.

Lou: Then tell me who's playing left field.

Bud: Who's playing first.

Lou: Stay outa the infield!

Bud: Don't mention any names out here.

Lou: (firmly): I wanta know what's the fellow's name in left field.

Bud: What is on second.

Lou: I'm not askin' you who's on second.

Bud: Who is on first.

Lou: I don't know!

Bud and Lou: Third base!

(Lou begins making noises.)

Bud: Now take it easy, man.

Lou: And the left fielder's name?

Bud: Why.

Lou: Because.

Bud: Oh, he's center field.

Lou: Wait a minute. You got a pitcher on the team?

Bud: Wouldn't this be a fine team without a pitcher?

Lou: I dunno. Tell me the pitcher's name.

Bud: Tomorrow.

Lou: You don't want to tell me today?

Bud: I'm telling you, man.

Lou: Then go ahead.

Bud: Tomorrow.

Lou: What time?

Bud: What time what?

Lou: What time tomorrow are you gonna tell me who's pitching?

Bud: Now listen, who is not pitching. Who is on—

Lou: (excitedly): I'll break your arm if you say who is on first!

Bud: Then why come up here and ask?

Lou: I want to know what's the pitcher's name!

Bud: What's on second.

Lou: (resigned): I don't know.

Bud and Lou: Third base!

Lou: You gotta catcher?

Bud: Yes.

Lou: The catcher's name.

Bud: Today.

Lou: Today. And Tomorrow's pitching.

Bud: Now you've got it.

Lou: That's all. St. Louis got a couple of days on their team. That's all.

Bud: Well I can't help that. What do you want me to do?

Lou: Gotta catcher.

Bud: Yes.

Lou: I'm a good catcher, too, you know.

Bud: I know that.

Lou: I would like to play for St. Louis.

Bud: Well, I might arrange that.

Lou: I would like to catch. Now Tomorrow's pitching on the team and I'm catching.

Bud: Yes.

Lou: Tomorrow throws the ball and the guy up bunts the ball.

Bud: Yes.

Lou: So when he bunts the ball, me, bein' a good catcher, I want to throw the guy out at first base. So I pick up the ball and throw it to who?

Bud: Now that's the first thing you've said right!

Lou: I don't even know what I'm talking about!

Bud: Well, that's all you have to do.

Lou: I throw it to first base.

Bud: Yes.

Lou: Now who's got it?

Bud: Naturally.

Lou: Who has it?

Bud: Naturally.

Lou: Naturally.

Bud: Naturally.

Lou: I throw the ball to naturally.

Bud: You throw it to who.

Lou: Naturally.

Bud: Naturally, well, say it that way.

Lou: That's what I'm saying!

Bud: Now don't get excited, don't get excited.

Lou: I throw the ball to first base.

Bud: Then who gets it.

Lou: He'd better get it!

Bud: That's it. All right now, don't get excited. Take it easy.

Lou: (frenzied): Now I throw the ball to first base, whoever it is grabs the ball, so the guy runs to second.

Bud: Uh-huh.

Lou: Who picks up the ball and throws it to What. What throws it to I Don't Know. I Don't Know throws it back to Tomorrow. A triple play!

Bud: Yeah, it could be.

Lou: Another guy gets up and it's a long fly ball to center. Why? I don't know. And I don't care.

Bud: What was that?

Lou: I said, I don't care.

Bud: Oh, that's our shortstop.

––––––––––

Herlinda Marie Acedo v. State of Arizona, Department of Public Welfare

Court of Appeals of Arizona
20 Ariz. App. 467, 513 P.2d 1350 (1973)

LEVI RAY HAIRE, JUDGE

The only issue presented by this appeal is whether a natural mother, who voluntarily executes a consent authorizing the placement of her child for adoption, may regain her child after the child has been placed in an adoptive home, solely upon the ground that at the time she signed the requisite consent form she had an unexpressed misconception as to the form's legal significance, which misconception was not the result of any improper actions on the part of the adoption agency. We hold that on the facts here presented, she may not.

The natural mother, hereinafter referred to as petitioner, filed a habeas corpus petition in the trial court, seeking the return of her baby. The evidence shows that the child was born on February 3, 1972 to petitioner, an unmarried woman, who at that time was 18 years of age and a high school graduate. Prior to the child's birth, petitioner had gone to the County Department of Public Welfare, hereinafter referred to as the adoption agency, at which time she decided that it would be best for the unborn baby to give it up for adoption. After the birth of the baby she changed her mind and decided to keep the child.

Petitioner and the baby resided at the home of petitioner's parents until about August 13, 1972, when, although unemployed and in possession of only $20, she moved out of her parents' home, taking the baby with her. On August 14, 1972, only one day after moving, she made another visit to the adoption agency, where the possibility of adoption was again discussed. On August 15, 1972, a welfare worker went to petitioner's temporary residence to discuss the adoption. Petitioner at that time stated that she wanted to place the baby for adoption, and thereafter petitioner accompanied the welfare worker back to her office.

At the office, petitioner was given a "Consent to Place Child for Adoption" form to read, and after reading it was asked if she understood it. She responded that she did, and thereupon signed the form.

The adoption procedure had been explained to petitioner before the consent form was signed. Included in this explanation was the fact that in an adoption proceeding the *adoption* itself is not final until six months after the adoption petition is filed. At no time was there any conversation between petitioner and the representatives of the adoption agency as to petitioner having six months, or any other time period, within which she could, upon request, get her baby back.

In accordance with the written consent, petitioner voluntarily gave her baby to the adoption agency on August 15, 1972. Subsequently, on September 1, 1972, the baby was placed in an adoptive home. During the latter part of August or early September of 1972, petitioner, her $20 expended, returned to her parents' home. On September 4, 1972, petitioner sought to have the baby returned to her and was told that the child had been placed in an adoptive home and that nothing further could be done. On September 8, 1972, petitioner sent to the adoption agency a form prepared by her attorney which purported to revoke her previously given consent. This revocation was received on September 11, 1972. Thereafter petitioner commenced habeas corpus proceedings to have the child returned to her, alleging that the consent for adoption was procured by threats, coercion and fraud.

At the hearing petitioner testified that when she signed the consent form she did not realize its finality, but rather thought she could get her baby back at any time within six months. While no formal findings of fact or conclusions of law were made, the trial judge informally stated at the end of the hearing that "because of the nature of this case," he "would resolve in (petitioner's) favor the fact she was confused about the six months." The court did specifically find that the adoption agency had not engaged in threats, coercion or fraud in obtaining the petitioner's consent, and therefore denied the petition based on *In re Holman's Adoption*, 295 P.2d 372 (1956) and *In re Adoption of Hammer*, 487 P.2d 417 (Ariz. App. 1971). From this denial, petitioner has appealed on the ground that her mistaken belief that she could have her baby back anytime within six months rendered her consent invalid.

. . .

There is no contention that petitioner could not have legally consented to the adoption or that the statutory formalities were not complied with. Nor does petitioner *now* contend that her consent was brought about by fraud, duress, coercion, misrepresentation or other wrongful conduct. Her sole contention on this appeal is that the consent form itself coupled with her conversations with the welfare worker relative to the *adoption* procedure, justified her belief that she could change her mind and get her baby back within six months.

The consent form is entitled "Consent to Place Child for Adoption" and states in relevant part:

> That I have given the matter due consideration, and I believe the best interests of the child will hereby be promoted.

> Now, Therefore, I do hereby *voluntarily and unconditionally consent* to the placement of my said child for adoption with the Coconino County Department

of Public Welfare, P.O. Box 1966, Flagstaff, Arizona 86001 a duly authorized agency for the placing of children for adoption;

> *I hereby surrender custody and relinquish all rights which I may have in the child to said agency*, and I do hereby authorize said agency to take all necessary steps towards the adoption of the child.

> I hereby confer absolute and unrestricted power upon the said agency to consent to the adoption of the child without further notice to me, and with the same force and effect as though I personally gave consent at the time of adoption, and I expressly agree and pledge that I will not interfere in any way with the care, management, or adoption of the child.

> I realize that as a result of this consent to place child for adoption, and by the eventual giving of consent by the said agency, the parent-child relationship between me and the child shall, upon entry of a decree for adoption, be completely terminated and that all the legal rights, privileges, duties, obligations, and other legal consequences of said relationship, shall cease to exist, under A.R.S. Sec. 8-117. (emphasis added).

It should be noted that the form gives *unconditional* consent to the placement of the child, and specifically states that the signer relinquishes all rights in the child. While the last paragraph of the form does speak in *future* terms, we are of the opinion that the form, taken as a whole, clearly indicates that the consent given is immediately effective. There is no language in the form which states or implies that the consenter may change her mind, revoke her consent and thereby regain custody of the child. Moreover, in none of the conversations between petitioner and representatives of the adoption agency was the possibility of petitioner regaining custody discussed.

Based on these conversations and the signing by petitioner of the consent form without any expressed reservations on her part, it was both reasonable and proper for the adoption agency to immediately take steps to secure placement of the child in an adoptive home. Since such placement was secured prior to petitioner's attempted revocation of consent the rule set forth in *In re Holman's Adoption, supra,* is applicable. There the court stated:

> ... we hold that a consent once given by the parent or other persons having the authority to give such consent, may not be revoked *after the child has been placed in the possession of the adoptive parents except for legal cause shown,* as where such consent was procured through fraud, undue influence, coercion or other improper methods.

295 P.2d 372 at 376. (Emphasis in original). *See also, In re Hammer's Adoption, supra.*

Recognizing the rule expressed in *Holman, supra,* the petitioner contends that her unexpressed misinterpretation as to the legal significance of the consent form is sufficient "legal cause" so as to allow her to invalidate what appears to be a voluntary and knowingly executed consent form. We disagree. In *Hamer v. Hope Cottage Children's Bureau, Inc.,* 389 S.W.2d 123 (Tex. App. 1965), the natural mother sought to revoke her consent on the ground she had not read the consent form and thus was ignorant of its contents. The court summarily dealt with this argument stating:

> She admits that on the occasion of several visits and negotiations with Hope Cottage representatives she discussed the adoption of her children, but she does not claim that false representations were made to her. She says simply that she did not read the three documents of consent before signing them. She herself says that nothing was done to prevent her reading them. Having had full

opportunity to read the documents before signing them she will not be permitted to avoid the agreements on the ground that she was mistaken as to or ignorant of their contents.

389 S.W.2d 123 at 126.

Similarly, in *Myers v. Myers*, 188 N.Y.S. 527 (1921), the argument that since the consenter did not realize the effect of the documents he signed, his consent was invalid, was held to be without merit. There, the natural father acknowledged signing certain documents pertaining to adoption, but he maintained that the purport of the documents was not made clear to him, and that he was told and believed that his child would be returned to him any time he desired it. The court held that the father was not to be relieved of the consequences of his acts which were in compliance with the applicable adoption statutes. *See also, Hurley v. St. Martin*, 186 N.E. 596 (Mass. 1933).

We think the policy considerations stated by the Nevada Supreme Court in *Welfare Division of the Department of Health and Welfare v. Maynard*, 445 P.2d 153 (Nev. 1968), in an analogous fact situation, are particularly pertinent. There the court stated:

It is apparent that if in particular cases the unstable whims and fancies of natural mothers were permitted, first, to put in motion all the flow of parental love and expenditure of time, energy and money which is involved in adoption, and then, as casually, put the whole process in reverse, the major purpose of the statute would be largely defeated. Public policy demands that the adoption act should not be nullified by a decision that causes the public to fear the consequences of adopting a child with the full knowledge that their efforts are at the whim and caprice of a natural parent.

445 P.2d 153 at 155.

In *Batton v. Massar*, 369 P.2d 434 (Colo. 1962), the Colorado Supreme Court stated with regard to the trial court's finding that the natural mother did not realize the seriousness and finality of the papers she had signed:

Even though the evidence were such as to warrant the finding made, the facts recited therein are not sufficient ground for setting aside the decrees of adoption.

It is not the law that one may avoid the consequences of his voluntary acts, acts not induced by fraud, duress, coercion, etc., by proof that he or she:

"did not realize the seriousness and finality of the papers she (or he) was signing."

Such a rule of law would render every contract voidable at the whim of the maker.

369 P.2d 434 at 437. (Emphasis added). *See In re List's Adoption*, 211 A.2d 870 (Pa. 1965); *In re Adoption of Pitcher*, 230 P.2d 449 (Cal. App. 1951).

In the fact situation under consideration, we do not deem it necessary to find that petitioner in fact had actual knowledge of the legal significance of the consent form which she executed. In this connection we have considered the trial judge's comment that he would resolve in petitioner's favor "the fact she was confused about the six months" as being equivalent to a finding that petitioner did in fact believe that she could change her mind and revoke her consent at any time within six months.[1] Assuming this to be the

---

1. We are not certain that such an assumption is required by the record. The trial judge also stated, regarding the consent form: "The Court: Part of it may be confusing, I can see, like the six months and the adoption. Part of the form is not confusing such as the first paragraph which says, 'I hereby

case, we find the policy considerations enunciated in the above-cited cases persuasive. Here, by signing the consent form, petitioner, a high school graduate presumably of at least normal intelligence, manifested her intent to relinquish her parental rights in clear and unambiguous terms. When asked if she understood it, she replied in the affirmative. The adoption agency had no way of knowing that she interpreted the agreement to mean other than it stated. Her signature was not obtained by fraud, duress, misrepresentations, coercion or any other wrongful behavior. The adoption agency was obligated to secure an adoptive home for the child at the earliest opportunity. The adoptive parents, whom we note were not made parties or represented here, were likewise justified in accepting the child into their home. To allow the efforts and expectations produced by, and flowing from, petitioner's conduct to be destroyed by her unexpressed misconception, which was neither the result of actions by the adoption agency nor the adoptive parents, would be contrary to the public policy manifested by our adoption statutes. The continued integrity of the adoption procedure demands that a consenter be held to the natural consequences of his or her actions, absent the presence of highly important countervailing policy considerations as discussed in *Holman, supra.*

The fact that the child was in the home of the adoptive parents for only three days before petitioner expressed her desire to have him back, does not alter our conclusion. There must be some readily ascertainable event, upon which adoptive parents can be secure in the knowledge that the child in their home cannot be taken from them solely at the whim of the natural parents. As stated in *Holman, supra,* that event is when the child is first placed in the adoptive home.

The judgment of the superior court is affirmed.

––––––––––––

Note — On Revocation of Consent to Adoption

Should consent to adoption be subject to the normal rules of contract law? Should consent to give up one's parental rights be more or less enforceable than consent to transfer a piece of property and should defenses to enforcement be more or less readily available? Under the laws of Arizona, which remain substantially the same as they were in 1973 when *Acedo* was decided and which are similar to those in many other states, consent to adoption is not valid during a pregnancy or within 72 hours after the birth of the child. Because of that restriction, consent to adoption is more restricted than are other contracts. After the 72-hour period, however, consent to adoption is revocable only for fraud. This means that a biological parent cannot change her mind, cannot decide to breach her contract. Because of this rule, consent to adoption is more strictly enforced than other contracts. In most contracts, a person can breach and will not be forced to perform the contract (will not be forced to "specifically perform") but only to pay damages for the breach (the preference for monetary damages over specific performance will be examined in Chapter Ten). The court in *Acedo* held also that Acedo's consent could not be rescinded on the basis of her misunderstanding of the terms of the consent. The court asserts that this inflexible approach is necessary to maintain "the continued integrity of the adoption process."

The law regarding consent to adoption has received attention in recent years as more adults have sought children to adopt, and the issue of consent is one of several controversial

––––––––––––

surrender custody of the child and relinquish all rights which I may have in the child to said agency.' There's not too much that's ambiguous about that terminology."

issues. Others include "surrogacy" agreements, cross-racial adoptions, adoption by single parents, the parental rights of biological fathers, and adoption by lesbian or gay couples. The Uniform Adoption Act, promulgated by the National Conference of Commissioners on Uniform State Laws and adopted by six states, allows revocation of consent to adoption until eight days following the child's birth. After the eighth day, however, consent to adoption is irrevocable under this Act. Many people criticize this short period of revocation, arguing that it is inadequate to allow the mother, or the father, time to consider alternatives, negotiate with family members, arrange support, and the like. Indeed, physical recovery from a birth alone takes more than eight days for most mothers.

Some states allow new mothers and fathers a longer period of time to revoke a consent to adoption; California, for example, allows 90 days following the child's birth (recently shortened from 180 days). In Wisconsin, a court proceeding is required to validate consents to adoption. Other states allow a period of revocation shorter than the Uniform Adoption Act. As a result of recent national publicity involving Baby Jessica and Baby Richard, several state legislatures have eliminated or shortened the amount of time that biological parents are given to change their minds; in Louisiana, for example, the legislature recently amended its adoption statute to allow no revocation period.

Many argue that the law should allow longer revocation periods for biological parents and that current law has been unduly influenced by a few highly publicized litigated cases. Litigated cases take a long time and for that reason alone an eventual return to the biological parent would often be harmful. But in the overwhelming number of cases in which a biological parent seeks return of the child, the request is made within a few weeks of the consent to adoption. Statutes written to prevent harm to children in litigated cases may be unjustly harsh to biological parents in the vast number of cases.

In addition, some maintain that current law reflects an unjustly harsh judgment of women and men who have agreed, even for a time, to a termination of their parental rights. Scorn for "the bad mother" is a powerful theme in our culture. Do you think that this cultural narrative influences the decisions of legislators and judges in this area?

Ahmad Izadi v. Machado (Gus) Ford, Inc.

Florida Court of Appeals
550 So. 2d 1135 (1989)

ALAN R. SCHWARTZ, CHIEF JUDGE

This is an appeal from the dismissal with prejudice of a three count complaint for damages arising out of the following advertisement placed by the appellee in the February 21, 1988 edition of the Miami Herald:

> The complaint, the allegations of which must at this stage be regarded as true, alleged that the plaintiff Izadi attempted to purchase a 1988 Ford Ranger Pick-Up — the vehicle referred to at the foot of the ad — by tendering Gus Machado Ford $3,595 in cash and an unspecified trade-in. The proposal was made on the basis of his belief that the ad offered $3,000 as a "minimum trade-in allowance" for any vehicle, regardless of its actual value. As is elaborated below, the putative grounds for this understanding were that the $3,000 trade-in figure was prominently referred to at the top of the ad apparently as a portion of the consideration needed to "buy a new Ford" and that it was also designated as the projected deduction from the $7,095 gross cost for the Ranger Pick-Up. Machado,

however, in fact refused to recognize this interpretation of its advertisement and turned Izadi down. In doing so, it apparently relied instead on the infinitesimally small print under the $3,000 figure which indicated it applied only toward the purchase of "any New '88 Eddie Bauer Aerostar or Turbo T-Bird in stock"— neither of which was mentioned in the remainder of the ad—and the statements in the individual vehicle portions that the offer was based on a trade-in that was "*worth* $3,000." Izadi then brought the present action based on claims of breach of contract, fraud and statutory violations involving misleading advertising. We hold that the trial judge erroneously held the contract and misleading advertising counts insufficient, but correctly dismissed the claim for fraud.

1. Breach of Contract.

We first hold, on two somewhat distinct but closely related grounds, that the complaint states a cause of action for breach of an alleged contract which arose when Izadi accepted an offer contained in the advertisement, which was essentially to allow $3,000 toward the purchase of the Ranger for any vehicle the reader-offeree would produce, or, to put the same proposed deal in different words, to sell the Ranger for $3,595, plus any vehicle.

a) It is of course well settled that a completed contract or, as here, an allegedly binding offer must be viewed as a whole, with due emphasis placed upon each of what may be inconsistent or conflicting provisions. *NLRB v. Federbush Co.*, 121 F.2d 954, 957 (2d Cir. 1941) ("Words are not pebbles in alien juxtaposition; they have only a communal existence; and not only does the meaning of each interpenetrate the other, but all in their aggregate take their purport from the setting in which they are used...."); *Durham Tropical Land Corp. v. Sun Garden Sales Co.*, 138 So. 21 (Fla. 1931), *aff'd*, 151 So. 327 (Fla. 1932); *Ross v. Savage*, 63 So. 148 (Fla. 1913); *Transport Rental Systems, Inc. v. Hertz Corp.*, 129 So. 2d 454, 456 (Fla. App. 961) ("The real intention, as disclosed by a fair consideration of all parts of a contract, should control the meaning given to mere words or particular provisions when they have reference to the main purpose."); 11 Fla. Jur. 2d *Contracts* § 121 (1979). In this case, that process might well involve disregarding both the superfine print and apparent qualification as to the value of the trade-in, as contradictory to the far more prominent thrust of the advertisement to the effect that $3,000 will be allowed for any trade-in on any Ford. *Transport Rental Systems, Inc. v. Hertz Corp.*, 129 So. 2d at 456 ("If a contract contains clauses which are apparently repugnant to each other, they must be given such an interpretation as will reconcile them."). We therefore believe that the complaint appropriately alleges[5] that, objectively considered, the advertisement indeed contained just the unqualified $3,000 offer which was accepted by the plaintiff.[6] On the face of the pleadings, the case thus is like many previous ones in which it has been held, contrary to what is perhaps the usual rule, see 1 Williston on Contracts § 27 (W. Jaeger 3d ed. 1957); 1 Corbin, *Contracts* § 25 (1963), that an enforceable contract arises from an offer contained in an advertisement. *R.E. Crummer & Co. v. Nuveen*, 147 F.2d 3 (7th Cir. 1945).

Of course, if an offer were indeed conveyed by an objective reading of the ad, it does not matter that the car dealer may subjectively have not intended for its chosen language to constitute a binding offer. As Williston states:

---

5. We do not now decide what the ultimate construction of the offer may be, or whether the court or the jury should make this determination.

6. It goes almost without saying that the plaintiff's ability eventually to recover on the theories suggested in this opinion depends on the showing that he was, in fact, misled into a genuine—even if unjustified—belief that an offer had been made. If he were merely attempting to take a knowing advantage of imprecise language in the advertisement and did not, in fact, rely upon it, he may not recover.

> [T]he test of the true interpretation of an offer or acceptance is not what the party making it thought it meant or intended it to mean, but what a reasonable person in the position of the parties would have thought it meant.

That rule seems directly to apply to this situation.

b) As a somewhat different, and perhaps more significant basis for upholding the breach of contract claim, we point to the surely permissible conclusion from the carefully chosen language and arrangement of the advertisement itself that Machado—although it did not intend to adhere to the $3,000 trade-in representation—affirmatively, but wrongly sought to make the public believe that it would be honored; that, in other words, the offer was to be used as the "bait" to be followed by a "switch" to another deal when the acceptance of that offer was refused. Indeed, it is difficult to offer any other explanation for the blanket representation of a $3,000 trade-in for *any* vehicle—which is then hedged in sub-microscopic print to apply only to two models which were not otherwise referred to in the ad—or the obvious non-coincidence that the only example of the trade-in for the three vehicles which was set out in the ad was the very same $3,000. This situation invokes the applicability of a line of persuasive authority that a binding offer may be implied from the very fact that deliberately misleading advertising intentionally leads the reader to the conclusion that one exists. *See* Corbin on Contracts § 64, at 139 (Supp. 1989) (where "bait and switch" advertising suspected, public policy "ought to justify a court in holding deceptive advertising to be an offer despite the seller's ... intent not to make any such offer"). In short, the dealer can hardly deny that it did not mean what it purposely misled its customer into believing. This doctrine is expressed in the *Restatement (Second) of Contracts* which states:

§ 20. Effect of Misunderstanding ...

2) The manifestations of the parties are operative in accordance with the meaning attached to them by one of the parties if

(a) that party does not know of any different meaning attached by the first party[.]

Restatement (Second) of Contracts § 20(2)(a) (1981); Restatement (Second) of Contracts § 20(2)(a) comment d ("[I]f one party knows the other's meaning and manifests assent intending to insist on a different meaning, he may be guilty of misrepresentation. Whether or not there is such misrepresentation as would give the other party the power of avoidance, there is a contract under Subsection (2)(a), and the mere negligence of the other party is immaterial."). In *Johnson v. Capital City Ford Co.*, 85 So. 2d 75 (La. App. 1955), the court dealt with a case very like this one, in which the issue was whether a newspaper advertisement stating that any purchaser who bought a 1954 automobile before a certain date could exchange it for a newer model without an extra charge constituted a binding offer. The dealership argued that, despite the plain wording of the advertisement, it had no intention of making an offer, but merely sought to lure customers to the sales lot; it claimed also that, because of the small print at the bottom of the contract, any promises by the purchaser to exchange the vehicle for a later model were not binding. The court rejected these contentions on the holding that a contract had been formed even though the dealership "had an erroneous belief as to what the advertisement, as written, meant, or what it would legally convey." *Johnson*, 85 So. 2d at 80. As the court said:

> There is entirely too much disregard of law and truth in the business, social, and political world of today. It is time to hold men to their primary engagements to tell the truth and observe the law of common honesty and fair dealing. *Johnson*, 85 So. 2d at 82.

We entirely agree.…

3. Statutory Violation.

It follows from what we have said concerning the allegedly misleading nature of the advertisement in making an offer which the advertiser did not intend to keep, that the complaint properly alleged claims for violations of the Florida Deceptive and Unfair Trade Practices Act and the statutory prohibition against misleading advertising.…

Affirmed in part, reversed in part and remanded.

Note

In *Konic*, the court found that the parties had a misunderstanding regarding important terms of their agreements and neither party had reason to know of the other party's understanding, therefore no enforceable contracts existed. In *Acedo*, in contrast, the court found that the written form clearly indicated that Acedo could not revoke her consent to the termination of her parental rights and that Acedo should have known what that meant. In deciding that there was an objectively correct meaning to the disputed term of the contract, the *Acedo* court appeared to use the "outside observer" variation of the objective theory's reasonable person test: looking at the written consent form through the eyes of a "universal" reasonable person positioned outside of the actual circumstances, the court interpreted the meaning of the written words. How might a court have interpreted the agency's words and conduct if they were interpreted according to the understanding of a reasonable person in Acedo's position? What evidence might be admissible to aid in this interpretation? Would the interpretation be different if the court used a socially situated reasonable person test? What evidence might be admissible to aid in that interpretation?

In *Izadi v. Machado Ford*, the court recognized that Izadi misunderstood the advertisement, and that this error could have been corrected if Izadi had read the "infinitesimally small print" more carefully, but nevertheless held that Machado Ford would be liable. Unlike the court in *Acedo*, the *Izadi* court found that, in effect, Izadi's misunderstanding was caused by Machado's "carefully chosen language and arrangement" and that Machado had taken unfair advantage of the misunderstanding. Are the decisions in *Acedo* and *Izadi* reconcilable? Can the different results be justified on the basis of a difference in the facts of the two cases?

What interests are served by the rule preventing the formation of a contract when there is mutual misunderstanding?

C. Misrepresentation

The doctrine of misrepresentation makes a contract voidable (or in some situations entirely void) if it was formed as a consequence of misrepresentation. In addition to being a ground for rescission under the contract doctrine of misrepresentation, a false or misleading statement also may be the basis for a breach of contract action (for breach of warranty), an action to reform the contract, a tort claim for fraud, criminal prosecution, a claim under federal and state unfair and deceptive trade practices acts, a claim under banking regulations, or a variety of other statutory claims. The cases in this section demonstrate the broad range of remedies sought for misrepresentation made in connection with contract formation.

Under the misrepresentation doctrine, a contract is unenforceable if (1) one party makes a statement relevant to the exchange that is not true; (2) the statement is material or fraudulent; (3) the aggrieved party relied on the false information in entering into the contract; and (4) the aggrieved party's reliance was reasonable or justifiable. As to the second element, the doctrine of misrepresentation in contract law, in contrast to tort or criminal law, does not require proof that the speaker knew of or disregarded the falsity of his or her statement, so long as the misinformation is material; that is, important enough to affect the decision of the person who receives it to enter into the contract. Let us assume that the owner of Days-Gone-By Antiques tells Edgar that an antique gas stove was restored by Marisol Hasah, an expert metalworker. Edgar buys the stove and then learns that it was not restored by Marisol Hasah. If Edgar can prove that this was a "material" fact—meaning that a reasonable person would be likely to purchase the stove because of this fact—then Edgar does not have to prove anything about the seller's knowledge or intent when the seller stated that the stove was made by Marisol Hasah. This is known as the "innocent misrepresentation" rule. This rule, like the rule for mistake, focuses on the distortions caused by misinformation. The rule recognizes that false information undermines one of the basic assumptions about a market economy, that the rational economic actor is fully informed. It also reflects beliefs that assent is absent if the real facts of the deal were unknown and that it is unfair to hold someone to a bargain to which he or she has not really assented, regardless of the innocence or blameworthiness of the misrepresentation.

The third element in the defense of misrepresentation is that reliance on the misinformation led the victim to enter the contract. This much is clear in the doctrine. Beyond that, there is little clarity about the causation element. Most courts have held that it is not necessary to prove that the false information was the *only* reason an aggrieved party entered into the contract, but that it was a substantial factor in the decision. Theoretically, at least, this means that the aggrieved party would not have entered the contract if the false statement had not been made. This is essentially a "but-for" test, requiring the aggrieved party to prove a broad negative proposition—that among all imaginable circumstances, there is none in which the contract would have been made without the misrepresentation. In practice the burden of proof is not quite so enormous, because, of course, contract cases are generally subject to a "preponderance of the evidence" test for factual determinations. So as a practical matter, the causation test for misrepresentation asks: does the evidence tend to show that the aggrieved party would not have entered the contract unless the false statement had been made? Some courts, legislators, and consumer advocates, however, have argued that the but-for causation requirement unwisely withholds a remedy from many legitimate claimants. In response, some state consumer protection laws have replaced the but-for causation requirement with more flexible causation tests.

The fourth element, like the test for materiality, also references a reasonableness standard: did the aggrieved party *reasonably* or *justifiably* rely on the false information. Would a reasonable person in the position of the aggrieved party accept the statement as true? The answer depends in part on the relationship between the parties (e.g., was it one that "normally" involves honest communication, as between doctor and patient or parent and child?); on any expertise or special access of the speaker (e.g., the mechanic in charge of the packing machine is especially credible about its condition); and on the availability of independent information (e.g., was the truth written in the contract document? was it readily available in the public records? was it a normal practice to have a rare coin or stamp checked by an expert?). In addition, this element raises basic questions about trust. Should the aggrieved person have trusted the other party even though he was a politician? Should anyone ever trust an oral statement? In real life, people often do trust face-to-face conversations even more than written documents. Should the court just enforce the writing and tell the litigant that he or she should be more suspicious of people? And what about the possibility of gathering information for yourself—do you have a "duty to investigate" everything you are told? If the "victim" could have discovered the truth by carefully reading the contract documents, courts sometimes say that the victim had a "duty to read" the documents, just as the court said in *Acedo v. Arizona*. The next two cases, *Kang v. Harrington* and *Flight Concepts Limited v. The Boeing Company*, both involve the duty to read.

Lawrence S. C. Kang v. W. Dewey Harrington

Supreme Court of Hawaii
587 P.2d 285 (Haw. 1978)

WILLIAM S. RICHARDSON, CHIEF JUSTICE

Appellant, W. Dewey Harrington, appeals from the judgment of the circuit court of the first circuit finding him culpable of fraud with respect to a certain rental agreement. The judgment resulted in the reformation of that agreement and an award of $20,000 punitive damages and $1,800 compensatory damages to appellee, Lawrence S. C. Kang.

Appellee is the owner of a house and lot located at 2927 Hibiscus Place, Honolulu, Hawaii. Appellee's daughter, Dolly Won, lives at 3052 Hibiscus Drive, Honolulu, Hawaii, situated adjacent to the 2927 Hibiscus Place property.

On October 28, 1973, Dolly Won, acting as the agent of appellee, advertised the 2927 Hibiscus Place property as available for rental. On October 29, 1973, Dolly Won met appellant who indicated that he was interested in renting the property. Dolly Won advised appellant that the rent was $450 per month and that no dogs were permitted. Appellant then mentioned that he would be willing to make certain improvements to the property if his dogs would be allowed.

At their next meeting, appellant showed Dolly Won a sketch of the proposed improvements. Appellant stated that he would construct a wall along the ewa [west] side of the property, another wall along the common boundary between the 3052 Hibiscus Drive property and the 2927 Hibiscus Place property and do some terracing and landscaping of the grounds. Consequently, Dolly Won agreed to rent the 2927 Hibiscus Place property to appellant for one year, to permit appellant's dogs and to reduce the rent to $400 per month because of the proposed improvements. Appellant also received an option for an additional one-year term and first consideration in the event that the property was available after the expiration of the second year.

Dolly Won then requested a security deposit of $400 in cash. On November 2, 1973, appellant gave Dolly Won the deposit and a letter of intent which was subsequently signed by both appellant and Dolly Won. The letter, however, stated that the $400 was for the first month's rent of the "house and property located at 3052 Hibiscus from November 6, 1973 for a period of one year with an additional option for a second year at four hundred dollars per month ($400.00) inclusive." Prior to signing the letter the parties revised it to state that the $400 was a security deposit rather than the first month's rent. But no mention was made of the fact that the 3052 Hibiscus Drive property was referred to in the letter instead of the 2927 Hibiscus Place property. Dolly Won then produced the appropriate rental forms but acceded to appellant's request that he be allowed to take them with him to type up at his office.

Appellant returned on November 3, 1973, and gave Dolly Won two copies of the typed-up rental forms to sign. Appellant told Dolly Won that he was in a hurry. Consequently, she initialed and signed all the documents in "a couple minutes" without reading them carefully. The rental agreement prepared by appellant contained an additional provision giving him a perpetual option to rent the 2927 Hibiscus Place property instead of the agreed upon one-year option. The pertinent part of the agreement read as follows:

> 4. Landlord agrees and tenant accepts this lease as a one year lease commencing on November 6, 1973 and ending on November 5, 1974, however at tenants option this lease may be extended for additional similar periods (one year) for the same monthly rate of $400.00 per month. Options are effected by tenants notifying landlord 30 days prior to the expiration date of each year's lease.

Upon taking occupancy of the premises appellant began to make various improvements in addition to the previously agreed upon walls and landscaping. This included, *inter alia*, the enclosure of a patio with screens and sliding glass doors, construction of a concrete patio, electrical and plumbing work, interior repainting and the installation of a picture window, chandelier, sink and appliances.

On or about February 11, 1974, appellant sent a letter to Dolly Won mentioning his long-term intentions with regard to the 2927 Hibiscus Place property and the fact that he had spent and would continue to spend substantial amounts of money to improve the property. On October 3, 1974, Dolly Won received another letter from appellant stating that he had elected to renew his "option for the following year and for many, many years."

On November 25, 1974 appellee filed suit against appellant seeking to reform the rental agreement to limit the option provision to one year and for compensatory damages of $20,000 and punitive damages of $20,000. Appellant answered by alleging that the parties did, in fact, agree to a long-term lease and that appellee had committed an assault and battery against appellant. Appellant sought to reform the rental agreement to provide for a valid fifty-five year lease or declare that the lease was terminated and award appellant his out-of-pocket costs for the improvements. Appellant also sought $30,000 punitive damages for appellee's alleged fraud in construing the rental agreement to relate only to a one-year option and $30,000 punitive damages for appellee's alleged assault and battery against appellant.

The case was heard in the circuit court of the first circuit without a jury. The trial court held that appellant had committed a fraud against appellee in attempting to obtain a perpetual or long-term lease of the 2927 Hibiscus Place property. The rental agreement was reformed to provide for a one-year term with an option for an additional one-year term. Appellee was also given $1,800 compensatory damages and $20,000 punitive damages. The court also held that appellee did not commit an assault and battery against appellant.

On appeal, appellant seeks to set aside the judgment of the circuit court and obtain a new trial....

I. Whether the Trial Court Erred in Finding That Appellant Had Committed a Fraud Against Appellee...

In the instant case, there was a sharp conflict in the testimony of the parties and the other witnesses. Appellant testified that he put the perpetual option provision in because he anticipated a long-term lease. Dolly Won, however, testified that the parties had only agreed to a one-year term with a one-year option for renewal. In light of the conflicting evidence, the trial court specifically found that appellant and his witnesses were not credible. Consequently, the trial court rejected their testimony except when corroborated by other credible evidence. The finding of the trial court with respect to the credibility of the witnesses will necessarily be deferred to. H.R. Civ. P. Rule 52(a) (1972).

The credible evidence accepted by the trial court indicates that appellee, through his agent, Dolly Won, and appellant actually agreed to a one-year rental term with a one-year option for renewal.

The credible evidence also indicates that although appellant was aware of this agreement he, nevertheless, entered into certain acts found by the trial court to be in furtherance of his scheme to obtain a perpetual option or long-term lease of the 2927 Hibiscus Place property. The findings of fact by the trial court with respect to appellant's fraudulent acts are supported by the accepted evidence and are not "clearly erroneous." H.R. Civ. P. Rule 52(a) (1972).

First, appellant was to submit a letter of intent and $400.00 as a security deposit to appellee pursuant to their oral agreement to lease the 2927 Hibiscus Place property for a period of one year with an option for an additional year. Instead, appellant's letter of intent referred to the 3052 Hibiscus Drive property and stated that the $400.00 was for the first month's rent rather than as a security deposit. Although Dolly Won corrected the letter to state that the $400.00 was a security deposit, she failed to notice and correct the fact that the letter referred to the 3052 Hibiscus Drive property instead of the 2927 Hibiscus Place property. The trial court made the finding of fact that appellant intentionally referred to the 3052 Hibiscus Drive property believing that Dolly Won would not notice the inaccurate address. Appellant included the wrong address since, if the letter had correctly referred to the 2927 Hibiscus Place property, it would have negatived appellant's claim to a perpetual option.

Second, in preparing the rental agreement appellant added an extra provision giving him a perpetual option to lease. Then, under the pretext of pressure of time, appellant obtained the hurried approval of Dolly Won without allowing her an opportunity to review and scrutinize the contract.

Third, to support his claim of a perpetual option appellant made numerous improvements to the 2927 Hibiscus Place property other than the ones initially agreed upon.

Finally, in addition to appellant's fraudulent rental agreement and letter of intent, the trial court looked to other acts of appellant that supposedly also constituted his fraud on appellee and made the following findings of fact:

(d) In further pursuance of such fraudulent scheme, Defendant prepared Exhibit 3, which is a xerox copy of a wall plan showing not only the improvements referred to in Findings of Fact No. 4, above, but also many other improvements which had not been previously discussed with agent. This exhibit was intended to support Defendant's claim of a long-term lease and to justify his corollary claim of having expended large sums of money on improvements approved by Plaintiff. In fact, this wall plan was never received by agent and the signature on this exhibit although ostensibly that of agent was placed thereon by Defendant;

(e) Defendant also prepared a letter dated November 9, 1973 (Exhibit 4) addressed to agent, which referred to a wall plan approved by agent on November 8, 1973. Neither this letter nor the wall plan referred to in the letter were received by agent but part of Defendant's fraudulent scheme to obtain a long-term lease ...

Although Dolly Won may have been negligent in failing to correct the letter of intent and the rental agreement and in failing to notice the various improvements, this will not negative appellant's alleged fraud.

Where it appears that one party has been guilty of an intentional and deliberate fraud, by which, to his knowledge, the other party has been misled, or influenced in his action, he cannot escape the legal consequences of his fraudulent conduct by saying that the fraud might have been discovered had the party whom he deceived exercised reasonable diligence and care. *Cummins v. Cummins*, 24 Haw. 116, 122 (1917), quoting from *Linington v. Strong*, 107 Ill. 295, 302 (1883). *See also Anderson v. Knox*, 297 F.2d 702, 711 (9th Cir. 1961).

Thus, the evidence accepted by the lower court indicates that appellant and appellee did agree to a one-year lease with a one-year option of the 2927 Hibiscus Place property. Notwithstanding this agreement the evidence shows that appellant entered into a fraudulent scheme to acquire a perpetual option to lease the subject property. In light of appellant's actions, the lower court did not err in concluding that appellant had committed a fraud on appellee.

...

[In the remainder of the opinion, the court ordered a remittitur of the award of $20,000 in punitive damages, reducing it to $2,500, upheld the $1,800 award for compensatory damages, and upheld the trial court's refusal to allow Harrington any recovery for the improvements he made to the property.]

Note

Courts often evaluate the reason for a person's failure to read and the injustice that would result either from enforcing or from not enforcing the contract. In *Kang*, the Hawai'i Supreme Court decided not to enforce a duty to read against Lawrence Kang and his agent Dolly Won, observing that

Where it appears that one party has been guilty of an intentional and deliberate fraud, by which, to his knowledge, the other party has been misled, or influenced in his action, he cannot escape the legal consequences of his fraudulent conduct by saying that the fraud might have been discovered had the party whom he deceived exercised reasonable diligence and care.

Surely Kang's lawyer would have emphasized that Harrington pressured Dolly Won to sign quickly, saying that he was in a hurry. Do you think that Dolly Won might have perceived W. Dewey Harrington as socially or economically powerful? If so, might this have contributed to her feeling compelled to accommodate his rushed schedule? Do you think the court considered such dynamics of class or gender in evaluating the case? Was race or ethnicity also a factor? Readers familiar with Hawai'i might recognize both ethnic and class identifications in the case: Lawrence S. C. Kang is a Chinese name and W. Dewey Harrington a middle- or upper-class European-American name; Hibiscus Drive is located at the base of Diamond Head Crater, in a traditionally working-class Chinese area that has become one of the most expensive neighborhoods in Honolulu, which means it is one of the most expensive neighborhoods in the United States. Such readers also would recognize the author of the opinion as Chief Justice William S. Richardson, the first Native Hawai'ian appointed to the Hawai'i Supreme Court since statehood, and a strong advocate for fairness, respect for human dignity, and protection of human interdependence in the law.

———————

In *Flight Concepts*, the next case, the Tenth Circuit Court of Appeals decided that Russell P. O'Quinn and Gilman Hill had a duty to read the contract document and that their reason for not reading it, that they trusted BMAC officers when they were told that the document reflected their agreement, was not sufficient to overcome this duty. The plaintiffs alleged misrepresentation in the making of a contract but instead of seeking rescission of the contract, they sought damages measured by the value of the contract they believed they had with Boeing. The district court granted summary judgment in favor of the defendants on the ground that the plaintiffs could not or should not have relied on the defendant's alleged misrepresentations.

Flight Concepts Limited Partnership, Russell P. O'Quinn, Gilman A. Hill, and the Skyfox Corporation v. The Boeing Company

United States Court of Appeals for the Tenth Circuit
38 F.3d 1152 (1994)

EDWIN LEARD MECHEM, SENIOR UNITED STATES DISTRICT JUDGE

This diversity case presents questions of contract interpretation under Kansas law. Plaintiffs appeal the district court's grant of summary judgment to defendants on all counts.

Background

… [T]he plaintiffs (hereinafter "the Skyfox group") modified the Lockheed T-33 aircraft to produce a plane, the Skyfox, envisioned as a low-cost, multiple-role aircraft which would meet the military needs of developing countries as well as the United States. Plaintiffs explored potential marketing options, and eventually gave Boeing Military Airplane Company (hereinafter "BMAC") the exclusive right to produce and sell the airplane worldwide. Under the agreement, plaintiffs would receive a royalty of $150,000 for every Skyfox sold. BMAC never produced or sold any aircraft, and terminated the agreement after two years. Plaintiffs brought suit alleging fraud in the inducement, misrepresentation and concealment; breach of the covenant of good faith and fair dealing; and breach of fiduciary duty. Although plaintiffs challenge the validity of the contract, they request damages calculated as their projected royalty earnings from the sale of 450 Skyfox. Plaintiffs also ask the return of various materials and equipment retained by BMAC after the contract terminated. The district court, after a careful analysis of the evidence and the law, granted summary judgment to defendants on all counts, from which plaintiffs appeal. Plaintiffs repeat their claims of fraud, breach of implied duty and breach of fiduciary duty, and assert the district court erred in finding no disputed material facts on those issues. We affirm.

After meeting several times the parties entered into a series of agreements. In a Memorandum of Understanding, signed April 2, 1985, the parties agreed to enter into an exclusive teaming arrangement to develop a marketing strategy for the Skyfox. The memorandum specifically denied the project, to be pursued in phases, was a partnership. The Memorandum terminated by its own terms on July 1, 1985, and on that date the parties entered into another agreement to continue the feasibility study. The parties negotiated a Proprietary Data Exchange Agreement, effective November 1, 1985, to protect the confidentiality of their technical data. That agreement denied the existence of "a joint venture, partnership or other formal business organization" between the parties. The parties negotiated a Patent and Know-How License Agreement (hereinafter "License Agreement"), entered into on November 27, 1985. The License Agreement gave Boeing "an exclusive, worldwide right and license to utilize Licensor's Know-How and the inventions of Licensed Patents in the manufacture, use and sale of licensed product(s) and any and all other substantial rights." In addition to the royalty for every Skyfox sold, BMAC contracted to pay all taxes and fees associated with any patent application.

The terms of the Licensing Agreement are central to this dispute. Under Article X, BMAC reserved "the right to terminate this Agreement by giving Licensor sixty (60) days notice in writing of such termination, and upon expiration of said sixty (60) days this Agreement shall automatically be terminated." The agreement could also be terminated by mutual written consent of the parties. Article XIII relieves BMAC from any obligation to produce or sell the Skyfox.

Article XIII. No Obligation to Produce

It is the intent of the parties hereto, in consideration of the terms and conditions herein, that BMAC shall be under no obligation whatsoever to produce and/or sell Licensed Product(s) and/or any product utilizing Licensor's Know-How during any part of the term of this License Agreement, and the License Agreement shall not be terminated by Licensor for BMAC's failure to produce and/or sell Licensed Products and/or any product utilizing Licensor's Know-How.

The final subparagraph of the Agreement, under Article XIV, General Provisions, states:

This Agreement embodies the entire understanding between the parties as to a Patent and Know-How License and there are no prior representations, warranties or agreement between the parties relating hereto except for other agreements in writing entered into or which may be entered into between BMAC and Licensor and this Agreement is executed and delivered upon the basis of this understanding. No alteration, waiver or change in any of the terms hereof subsequent to the execution hereof claimed to have been made by any representative of either party shall have any force or effect unless in writing signed by the parties hereto or their duly authorized agents or representatives.

The Skyfox group charges first that BMAC fraudulently induced them to form the contract by promising to invest $25 to $60 million in the Skyfox program when BMAC never intended to spend its own money converting the aircraft. Plaintiffs also allege that BMAC misrepresented its commitment to the project by failing to inform the Skyfox Group that it had plans to develop Project Vision, a plane projected to have similar uses, and that it had access to classified information on government procurement plans. The claims for breach of implied covenant of good faith and fair dealing and breach of fiduciary duty arise from the same facts.

. . .

Discussion

. . .

Fraud in the Inducement, Fraudulent Misrepresentation

Plaintiffs urge this court to look beyond the contract at the verbal assurances defendants gave during negotiations, that BMAC was committed to Skyfox and would support the project financially, to determine that defendants fraudulently induced plaintiffs to sign the Licensing Agreement. Plaintiffs allege defendants' verbal assurances misrepresented the truth in that defendants never intended to invest money in or develop the project.

Under Kansas law, parties to a contract may define the terms of their agreement and, absent fraud, mistake or duress, the contract is enforceable. *Augusta Medical Complex, Inc. v. Blue Cross of Kansas, Inc.*, 227 Kan. 469, 608 P.2d 890, 895 (1980). Where the parties have negotiated and entered into a written contract which addresses the issues negotiated between them, the written contract determines their rights. *Edwards v. Phillips Petroleum Co.*, 187 Kan. 656, 659, 360 P.2d 23, 26 (1961). Parol evidence is inadmissible to introduce statements or representations made during the negotiations that conflict with the written agreement, absent fraudulent misrepresentation. *Edwards*, 187 Kan. at 659. To be actionable, a misrepresentation must relate to a pre-existing or present fact; statements or promises about future occurrences are not actionable. *Id.* An exception exists where evidence establishes that, at the time the promise as to future events was made, the promisor did not intend to perform the promised action. *Id.* at 660. Where the written contract directly contradicts the oral promises made during contract negotiations, the oral promise cannot be construed as fraudulent. *Id.*; *Jack Richards Aircraft Sales, Inc. v. Vaughn*, 203 Kan. 967, 973, 457 P.2d 691, 696 (1969). The Licensing Agreement released BMAC from any obligation to produce aircraft. The fact that the written contract conflicts directly with any oral promises BMAC employees made concurrently erases any effect of those oral promises from the Agreement. Those concurrent oral promises cannot, as a matter of law, establish fraudulent inducement or misrepresentation.

Plaintiff Russell P. O'Quinn, the originator of the Skyfox concept, alleges he had no opportunity to read the Licensing Agreement before he signed it and he would not have signed had he known the Agreement included Article XIII. He argues defendants misrepresented the Agreement to him when they assured him it contained nothing that would hurt him. The plaintiffs were represented throughout the negotiations by able counsel and are themselves experienced and astute businessmen. It was Mr. O'Quinn's duty to read and understand the provisions of the Licensing Agreement. A party cannot void a contract by claiming to be ignorant of its contents. *Albers*, 248 Kan. at 578. Viewing any disputed facts in the light most favorable to plaintiffs, we can find no legal basis for plaintiffs' claims of fraudulent inducement and misrepresentation....

Breach of Fiduciary Duty/Joint Venture

Plaintiffs assert that BMAC had a duty to disclose Boeing's concurrent development of Project Vision and Boeing's illegal receipt of classified information on military procurement, and that the failure to disclose this information during contract negotiations was fraudulent. To establish fraud by concealment under Kansas law, plaintiffs must show the following elements by clear and convincing evidence: (1) that the defendants had factual information plaintiffs did not have and could not have discovered through reasonable diligence; (2) that defendants had a duty to communicate that information to plaintiffs; (3) that the defendants deliberately failed to communicate the information to plaintiffs; (4) that the plaintiffs justifiably relied on defendants to communicate the material information; and (5) that plaintiffs were injured by defendants' failure to communicate the material information. *Lesser v. Neosho County Community College*, 741 F. Supp. 854, 863 (D. Kan. 1990). A material fact is one a reasonable person would consider important in choosing a course of action. *Id.* Suppression of material information is not fraudulent unless the silent party is under some legal obligation to disclose. *DuShane v. Union Nat. Bank*, 223 Kan. 755, 759, 576 P.2d 674, 678 (1978).

In general, the duty to communicate arises from the relationship between the parties. *Id.* at 760, 576 P.2d 674. The duty to disclose arises under Kansas law when there is a fiduciary relationship which may be created by contract or may arise from the relationship of the parties. *Rajala v. Allied Corp.*, 919 F.2d 610, 614 (10th Cir. 1990), *cert. denied*, 500 U.S. 905,

111 S. Ct. 1685, 114 L. Ed. 2d 80 (1991). "A fiduciary relationship imparts a position of peculiar confidence placed by one individual in another. A fiduciary is a person with a duty to act primarily for the benefit of another." *Denison State Bank v. Madeira*, 230 Kan. 684, 691, 640 P.2d 1235, 1241 (1982). A fiduciary relationship may arise from the facts and circumstances of a relationship, but because the fiduciary assumes additional responsibilities within the relationship, the role cannot be established inadvertently. *Rajala* at 614. Under Kansas law, one must consciously assume the responsibilities of a fiduciary. *Id.* at 615.

The record contains no evidence that Boeing or BMAC deliberately assumed the responsibilities of fiduciary in their dealings with the Skyfox group. Nor do the facts as alleged by plaintiffs show that BMAC agreed to act for plaintiffs' benefit. We conclude that defendants were not fiduciaries and had no duty to disclose information to plaintiffs by virtue of that relationship.

Plaintiffs argue a joint venture was formed by the parties that obligated BMAC to communicate material information. A joint venture is an association between two or more people to carry out a business activity for profit. *Modern Air Conditioning, Inc. v. Cinderella Homes, Inc.*, 226 Kan. 70, 76, 596 P.2d 816, 823 (1979). Among the acts or conduct which are indicative of a joint venture, but no single one of which is controlling in the determination, are: (1) the joint ownership and control of property; (2) the sharing of expenses; (3) a community of control over and active participation in the management and direction of the business enterprise; (4) the intention of the parties, express or implied; and (5) the fixing of salaries by joint agreement. *Id.* at 76, 596 P.2d 816. After reviewing the Licensing Agreement it is clear that the parties did not jointly own property or share expenses. BMAC exercised control over its activities and the level of its participation in the Skyfox project. There was no mutual responsibility for the fixing of project salaries. Accepting disputed facts in the light most favorable to plaintiffs, there is no evidence of a joint venture which would obligate BMAC to disclose material information. We find BMAC was, as a matter of law, under no obligation to disclose Project Vision or its access to secured information to the Skyfox group during their negotiations.

Finally, plaintiffs accuse BMAC of having retained data, spare parts and unspecified materials which should be returned to the Skyfox group. The spare parts consist of test wings, a mock cockpit, and a fuselage. Plaintiffs concede that BMAC initially paid for some of the materials but assert, without citing any evidence or authority, that these matters should be resolved at trial. Having found no fiduciary relationship or joint venture between the parties, we must rely on contract language to determine this question.

The Licensing Agreement grants to BMAC any "inventions made by BMAC or jointly by BMAC and Licensor or by Licensor when funded by BMAC or patents and know-how resulting from BMAC's and Licensor's or BMAC funded research and/or development work relating to the Licensed Product(s)...." Under the Proprietary Data Exchange Agreement, proprietary data belongs to the originator. We find no support for plaintiffs' position in any of the agreements before us and agree with the district court's conclusion that the materials were rightly retained by BMAC.

Conclusion

Accepting plaintiffs' version of disputed facts, defendants' behavior through the course of this business relationship does not rise to the level of fraud. Nor can defendants be said to have breached a duty to deal fairly for negotiating a contract with terms favorable to themselves. We affirm the district court's grant of summary judgment to defendants on all claims.

Note

Boeing is reported to be the world's largest commercial aircraft maker and the third largest defense contractor in the United States. The plaintiffs in this case referred to Boeing's recently discovered library of classified defense department documents. In 1989 Boeing pled guilty to a charge of "receiving classified documents" from the Defense Department and paid a fine of $5.2 million dollars. The company was also ordered by the judge who accepted the plea to write a "letter of contrition." A Boeing employee, Richard Lee Fowler, was convicted of illegally obtaining classified documents and sentenced to two years in jail. The court in *Flight Concepts v. Boeing* does not discuss this cache of documents and apparently thought it irrelevant to the plaintiffs' argument that Boeing had no intention of ever keeping its promise to build the Skyfox. Can such intent be inferred from a pattern of conduct by corporate actors that demonstrates the existence of a "win at any cost" culture?

Dominic Gates and Alicia Mundy, Boeing Lawyer Warns of Company's Legal Peril

(2006)

At Boeing's annual leadership retreat earlier this month, the company's top lawyer delivered a devastating worst-case assessment of the potential damage that still looms from the company's recent ethics scandals.

General Counsel Doug Bain's unflinchingly direct speech offers an extraordinary look at the inner workings of a powerful company as it struggles to recover from scandal, retrieve its reputation and ensure ethical behavior in future.

"Was there a culture of 'win at any cost?' Bain asked his audience, some 260 top Boeing executives gathered in Orlando, Fla. "We now know what that cost is."

Bain tallied the severe sanctions he said are possible from two major scandals on Boeing's defense side and for alleged breaches of export laws. Boeing faces possible indictment by U.S. attorneys on both coasts, and the Department of Justice's assessment of damages exceeds $5 billion, he said. In addition, Boeing could be barred from government defense contracts or denied export licenses for both military and commercial sales, he said.

Bain also said 15 company vice presidents have been pushed out for various ethical lapses in recent years. "I found that to be an astronomically high number," he said.

The chilling litany seemed designed to get the attention of any Boeing executive remotely inclined to zone out during all the talk about ethics.

"There are some within the prosecutors' offices that believe that Boeing is rotten to the core," Bain said, according to a copy of the speech provided to The Seattle Times by a company insider. "They talk to us about pervasive misconduct and they describe it in geographic terms of spanning Cape Canaveral to Huntington Beach to Orlando to St. Louis to Chicago. They talk about it in terms of levels within the company that go from non-management engineers to the chief financial officer."

Bain's remarks appear to contradict the widely held expectation that the government sometime this year will agree to a global settlement of the major scandals—with Boeing paying a fine in the hundreds of millions of dollars, and escaping further indictments.

But people familiar with Boeing's position cautioned that a settlement on such terms is still expected.

Boeing spokesman John Dern said Bain was trying to shock his listeners into paying careful attention to ethics—not predicting legal outcomes.

In 2002, Boeing Chief Financial Officer Mike Sears offered a job to Darleen Druyun, chief acquisitions officer at the Air Force, while she was overseeing work on Boeing contracts.

At her sentencing hearing in 2004, Druyun said she favored Boeing on multiple contracts because of favors granted by the company, including hiring her daughter and son-in-law.

The scandal sent Sears and Druyun to jail, forced the resignation of then-CEO Phil Condit and jeopardized major defense contracts, including the Air Force tanker program that would have secured up to 8,000 jobs in Everett.

In 1997, McDonnell Douglas hired an engineer away from Lockheed Martin to work on the Delta IV rocket program. He brought with him proprietary documents, including financial details on Lockheed's planned bid for an Air Force space-rocket competition. Boeing merged with McDonnell Douglas later that year.

After the documents were discovered, three Boeing employees were indicted. The Pentagon stripped Boeing of seven rocket launches and suspended Boeing's rocket division from new government business for 20 months.

In May 2005, Boeing and Lockheed Martin announced a plan—still pending government approval—to merge their space-rocket businesses, including an agreement to drop litigation over the stolen rocket-contract information.

Between 2000 and 2003, Boeing exported commercial jets with a QRS-11 gyrochip in the instrument flight boxes, even though the chip was classified by the State Department as an export-restricted defense item because it can be used to stabilize and steer guided missiles.

The State Department last year prepared civil charges alleging 94 violations of the Arms Control Act. Boeing faces a potential fine of as much as $47 million.

"Bain's talk was intended to be provocative," said Dern. "There was a feeling it was vitally important for people to understand the worst-case potential for what could happen to the company."

Bain, who became general counsel in 1999 and is also a Boeing senior vice president, told the audience that his talk reflected "the perspective of the prosecutors and what they have told us," rather than Boeing's position on the legal issues.

He appeared to take the "scared straight" approach, personalizing the scandals for his executive audience. "These are not ZIP codes," Bain said, as he rattled off the federal prisoner numbers of Darleen Druyun, formerly a top Air Force procurement officer and then a Boeing executive, and Mike Sears, former Boeing chief financial officer.

Repeatedly he asked whether ultimate responsibility resided at the top—with his audience.

"Our jobs as the leaders of this enterprise is to establish a culture that ensures there is no next time," Bain said. "The bottom line is, we just cannot stand another major scandal."

Among Bain's audience was Boeing Chief Executive Jim McNerney, who was aware in advance that the speech would be a downer.

"Good morning," Bain began. "As I walked up here, I think I heard Jim McNerney mutter, 'Here comes Dr. Death.'"

Bain said McNerney had asked for "a candid assessment of our major scandals and how we got there." Bain proceeded to deliver.

He launched into summaries of Boeing's two major scandals and their repercussions.

"The U.S. attorney in Los Angeles is looking at indicting Boeing for violations of the Economic Espionage Act, the Procurement Integrity Act, the False Claims Act and the Major Frauds Act," he said.

"The U.S. attorney in Alexandria, Va., is looking at indicting us for violation of the Conflict of Interest Laws. And both are looking to throw in a few conspiracy and aiding-and-abetting charges, for good measure.

"When we first met with the Department of Justice to see if we could resolve this, it's their view that Boeing's actions have tainted the [Air Force space rocket] EELV contract, the NASA 19-pack contract [a 2002 contract for up to 19 Delta rocket launches], and 27 Darleen Druyun-related contracts. Their estimate of damage is $5 billion to $10 billion."

The Los Angeles attorney's office is investigating the Lockheed Martin documents scandal. In 1997, McDonnell Douglas, which merged with Boeing later that year, hired away an engineer from Lockheed for its Delta space-rocket program. The engineer brought with him thousands of pages of documents containing proprietary pricing information that allegedly helped Boeing underbid its rival and win the biggest share of an Air Force rocket contract.

The Virginia attorney's office is dealing with the Pentagon procurement scandal. In 2002, then-CFO Sears offered a job to Druyun while she was acquisitions officer at the Air Force. She later admitted favoring Boeing on contracts as payback for personal favors, including the hiring of her daughter and son-in-law.

"How come in the year 2000 nobody said, 'Should we really be hiring the relatives of our chief procurement officer of the largest customer we have on the defense side?'" Bain asked.

The first scandal led to Boeing being stripped of the launches it had won, worth about $1 billion, and suspension from further rocket contracts for 20 months. Three employees have been indicted on felonies.

The second sent both Sears and Druyun to jail, forced the resignation of then-CEO Phil Condit and jeopardized major defense contracts, including the Air Force tanker program that would have secured up to 8,000 jobs in Everett.

"If this never happened, we'd be selling tankers to the U.S. government and Italy would not be our only customer," Bain said.

Bain also displayed a list of five areas of State Department concern over Boeing's export of various sensitive technologies. These have cost the company $50 million in fines, he said, not counting an ongoing investigation of charges that Boeing Commercial Airplanes illegally exported a restricted gyroscope embedded inside 737 jets.

"The State Department's view of Boeing is, we just don't get it," Bain said.

Boeing spokesman Dern said global-settlement talks on the two defense scandals are continuing. He added that the $5 billion to $10 billion figures mentioned by Bain "have never been proposed by the government as part of any discussions" of a settlement.

A lawyer experienced in defending companies in criminal cases agreed that a much lower settlement is likely.

"That's funny money," said Victoria Toensing, a partner in Washington, D.C.-based diGenova & Toensing. "The government tries to make it the worst of what it could have been. They use it as leverage."

Boeing already has lost well in excess of $1 billion in revenue through canceled and suspended contracts stemming from the two defense scandals. A person close to the negotiations, who requested anonymity, said the anticipated size of a settlement is on the order of $500 million.

The largest prior settlement of a procurement scandal by a defense contractor was in 1991 when Unisys agreed to pay $190 million.

Spokesmen for both U.S. attorneys offices declined comment.

Toensing also said the Department of Justice (DOJ) has become more cautious about indicting companies since the 2002 indictment of accounting firm Arthur Andersen put the company out of business.

Still, Bain, speaking to his inside audience, vividly focused on the legal threats and possible penalties pending.

Those also include "a presumed denial of export licenses … both on the commercial and the government side," as well as loss of security clearances, a possible resuspension on bidding for space contracts or even total debarment from all government contracts on the defense side, he said.

"We have been trying to resolve these things," Bain said, referring to the ongoing settlement talks. "We have not been successful yet. It is my hope we will be."

Bain repeatedly urged his audience to look inward.

He said 900 of the formal ethics cases brought to the company's Office of Ethics and Business Conduct in 2005 were found to have substance.

He cited an employee survey in which 26 percent of those surveyed said they had observed abusive or intimidating behavior by management.

And of the 15 Boeing vice presidents terminated for ethics violations over the past few years, Bain said two had been ousted for committing crimes and the rest for offenses ranging from expense-account fraud to sexual harassment.

Boeing spokesman Dern said the large number of internal ethics complaints reflects well on Boeing's compliance system.

"We are working hard to promote a culture where people feel like they can raise issues formally and they trust the system," he said. The result is "an ethics system that is working every day and uncovering issues."

As for the employee survey suggesting a high level of management intimidation, "Those are troubling numbers," Dern said. "And numbers that we are working to lower."

At the end of his speech, Bain had one upbeat line.

"I really feel that we've turned the corner and that there's a renewed emphasis and energy on doing the right thing," he said.

Still, as Bain apparently intended, the questions he'd raised and left unanswered hung in the air.

"Do we have a culture of silence? …"

"Where was management throughout this?

"Is the problem the rank and file? Or is the problem us?"

Note

In contract law, the defense of misrepresentation requires proof that the person entered the contract because of a misrepresentation by the other side regarding a material fact. Courts generally distinguish between statements of fact, which may be a ground for a finding of misrepresentation that would allow rescission, and statements of opinion, which generally would not. This distinction is explained by saying that a person should not rely on mere statements of opinion. The rule is subject to exceptions, however, where the person stating an opinion has a fiduciary obligation to the other person, has superior knowledge, or has used deceit. This rule and its exceptions are discussed in *Vokes v. Arthur Murray* below.

Audrey E. Vokes v. Arthur Murray, Inc.

District Court of Appeal of Florida, Second District
212 So. 2d 906 (Fla. App. 1968)

WILLIAM C. PIERCE, JUDGE

This is an appeal by Audrey E. Vokes, plaintiff below, from a final order dismissing with prejudice, for failure to state a cause of action, her fourth amended complaint, hereinafter referred to as plaintiff's complaint.

Defendant Arthur Murray, Inc., a corporation, authorizes the operation throughout the nation of dancing schools under the name of "Arthur Murray School of Dancing" through local franchised operators, one of whom was defendant J. P. Davenport whose dancing establishment was in Clearwater.

Plaintiff Mrs. Audrey E. Vokes, a widow of 51 years and without family, had a yen to be "an accomplished dancer" with the hopes of finding "new interest in life." So, on February 10, 1961, a dubious fate, with the assist of a motivated acquaintance, procured her to attend a "dance party" at Davenport's "School of Dancing" where she whiled away the pleasant hours, sometimes in a private room, absorbing his accomplished sales technique, during which her grace and poise were elaborated upon and her rosy future as "an excellent dancer" was painted for her in vivid and glowing colors. As an incident to this interlude, he sold her eight-hour dance lessons to be utilized within one calendar month therefrom, for the sum of $14.50 cash in hand paid, obviously a baited "come-on."

Thus she embarked upon an almost endless pursuit of the terpsichorean art during which, over a period of less than sixteen months, she was sold fourteen "dance courses" totaling in the aggregate 2302 hours of dancing lessons for a total cash outlay of $31,090.45, all at Davenport's dance emporium. All of these fourteen courses were evidenced by execution of a written "Enrollment Agreement—Arthur Murray's School of Dancing" with the addendum in heavy black print, "No one will be informed that you are taking dancing lessons. Your relations with us are held in strict confidence," setting forth the number of "dancing lessons" and the "lessons in rhythm sessions" currently sold to her from time to time, and always of course accompanied by payment of cash of the realm.

These dance lesson contracts and the monetary consideration therefor of over $31,000 were procured from her by means and methods of Davenport and his associates which went beyond the unsavory, yet legally permissible, perimeter of "sales puffing" and intruded well into the forbidden area of undue influence, the suggestion of falsehood, the suppression of truth, and the free exercise of rational judgment, if what plaintiff alleged in her complaint was true. From the time of her first contact with the dancing school in February, 1961, she was influenced unwittingly by a constant and continuous barrage of flattery, false praise, excessive compliments, and panegyric encomiums, to such extent that it would be not only inequitable, but unconscionable, for a Court exercising inherent chancery power to allow such contracts to stand.

She was incessantly subjected to overreaching blandishment and cajolery. She was assured she had "grace and poise"; that she was "rapidly improving and developing in her dancing skill"; that the additional lessons would "make her a beautiful dancer, capable of dancing with the most accomplished dancers"; that she was "rapidly progressing in the development of her dancing skill and gracefulness," etc., etc. She was given "dance aptitude tests" for the ostensible purpose of "determining" the number of remaining hours [of] instruction needed by her from time to time.

At one point she was sold 545 additional hours of dancing lessons to be entitled to award of the "Bronze Medal" signifying that she had reached "the Bronze Standard," a supposed designation of dance achievement by students of Arthur Murray, Inc.

Later she was sold an additional 926 hours in order to gain the "Silver Medal," indicating she had reached "the Silver Standard," at a cost of $12,501.35.

At one point, while she still had to her credit about 900 unused hours of instructions, she was induced to purchase an additional 24 hours of lessons to participate in a trip to Miami at her own expense, where she would be "given the opportunity to dance with members of the Miami Studio."

She was induced at another point to purchase an additional 123 hours of lessons in order to be not only eligible for the Miami trip but also to become "a life member of the Arthur Murray Studio," carrying with it certain dubious emoluments, at a further cost of $1,752.30.

At another point, while she still had over 1,000 unused hours of instruction she was induced to buy 151 additional hours at a cost of $2,049.00 to be eligible for a "Student Trip to Trinidad," at her own expense as she later learned.

Also, when she still had 1,100 unused hours to her credit, she was prevailed upon to purchase an additional 347 hours at a cost of $4,235.74, to qualify her to receive a "Gold Medal" for achievement, indicating she had advanced to "the Gold Standard."

On another occasion, while she still had over 1,200 unused hours, she was induced to buy an additional 175 hours of instruction at a cost of $2,472.75 to be eligible "to take a trip to Mexico."

Finally, sandwiched in between other lesser sales promotions, she was influenced to buy an additional 481 hours of instruction at a cost of $6,523.81 in order to "be classified as a Gold Bar Member, the ultimate achievement of the dancing studio."

All the foregoing sales promotions, illustrative of the entire fourteen separate contracts, were procured by defendant Davenport and Arthur Murray, Inc., by false representations to her that she was improving in her dancing ability, that she had excellent potential, that she was responding to instructions in dancing grace, and that they were developing her into a beautiful dancer, whereas in truth and in fact she did not develop in her dancing ability, she had no "dance aptitude," and in fact had difficulty in "hearing that musical beat." The complaint alleged that such representations to her "were in fact false and known by the defendant to be false and contrary to the plaintiff's true ability, the truth of plaintiff's ability being fully known to the defendants, but withheld from the plaintiff for the sole and specific intent to deceive and defraud the plaintiff and to induce her in the purchasing of additional hours of dance lessons." It was averred that the lessons were sold to her "in total disregard to the true physical, rhythm, and mental ability of the plaintiff." In other words, while she first exulted that she was entering the "spring of her life," she finally was awakened to the fact there was "spring" neither in her life nor in her feet.

The complaint prayed that the Court decree the dance contracts to be null and void and to be canceled, that an accounting be had, and judgment entered against, the defendants "for that portion of the $31,090.45 not charged against specific hours of instruction given to the plaintiff." The Court held the complaint not to state a cause of action and dismissed it with prejudice. We disagree and reverse.

The material allegations of the complaint must, of course, be accepted as true for the purpose of testing its legal sufficiency. Defendants contend that contracts can only be rescinded for fraud or misrepresentation when the alleged misrepresentation is as to a material fact, rather than an opinion, prediction or expectation, and that the statements and representations set forth at length in the complaint were in the category of "trade puffing," within its legal orbit.

It is true that "generally a misrepresentation, to be actionable, must be one of fact rather than of opinion." *Tonkovich v. South Florida Citrus Industries, Inc.*, 185 So. 2d 710 (Fla. App. 1966); *Kutner v. Kalish*, 173 So. 2d 763 (Fla. App. 1965). But this rule has significant qualifications, applicable here. It does not apply where there is a fiduciary relationship between the parties, or where there has been some artifice or trick employed by the representor, or where the parties do not in general deal at "arm's length" as we understand the phrase, or where the representee does not have equal opportunity to become apprised of the truth or falsity of the fact represented. 14 Fla. Jur. *Fraud and Deceit* § 28; *Kitchen v. Long*, 64 So. 429 (Fla. 1914). As stated by Judge Allen of this Court in *Ramel v. Chasebrook Construction Company*, 135 So. 2d 876 (Fla. App. 1961). "A statement of a party having ... superior knowledge may be regarded as a statement of fact although it would be considered as opinion if the parties were dealing on equal terms."

It could be reasonably supposed here that defendants had "superior knowledge" as to whether plaintiff had "dance potential" and as to whether she was noticeably improving in the art of terpsichore. And it would be a reasonable inference from the undenied averments of the complaint that the flowery eulogiums heaped upon her by defendants as a prelude to her contracting for 1,944 additional hours of instruction in order to attain the rank of the Bronze Standard, thence to the bracket of the Silver Standard, thence to the class of the Gold Bar Standard, and finally to the crowning plateau of a Life Member of the Studio, proceeded as much or more from the urge to "ring the cash register" as from any honest or realistic appraisal of her dancing prowess or a factual representation of her progress.

Even in contractual situations where a party to a transaction owes no duty to disclose facts within his knowledge or to answer inquiries respecting such facts, the law is if he undertakes to do so he must disclose the *whole truth*. *Ramel v. Chasebrook Construction Company, supra*; *Beagle v. Bagwell*, 169 So. 2d 43 (Fla. App. 1964). From the face of the complaint, it should have been reasonably apparent to defendants that her vast outlay of cash for the many hundreds of additional hours of instruction was not justified by her slow and awkward progress, which she would have been made well aware of if they had spoken the "whole truth."

In *Hirschman v. Hodges, etc.*, 51 So. 550 (Fla. 1910), it was said that—" ... what is plainly injurious to good faith ought to be considered as a fraud sufficient to impeach a contract," and that an improvident agreement may be avoided—" ... because of surprise, or mistake, *want of freedom, undue influence, the suggestion of falsehood, or the suppression of truth*." (Emphasis supplied.)

We repeat that where parties are dealing on a contractual basis at arm's length with no inequities or inherently unfair practices employed, the Courts will in general "leave the parties where they find themselves." But in the case sub judice, from the allegations of the unanswered complaint, we cannot say that enough of the accompanying ingredients, as mentioned in the foregoing authorities, were not present which otherwise would have barred the equitable arm of the Court to her. In our view, from the showing made in her complaint, plaintiff is entitled to her day in Court.

It accordingly follows that the order dismissing plaintiff's last amended complaint with prejudice should be and is reversed.

Reversed.

Note — On the Aftermath of Vokes v. Arthur Murray

Do you think part of the world-making in *Vokes v. Arthur Murray* is the representation of women as vulnerable? It is interesting to compare this decision with *Parker v. Arthur Murray*, 295 N.E.2d 487 (Ill App. 1973), involving a 37-year-old, college-educated, unmarried man who paid $24,812 for 2,734 hours of lessons. Like Audrey Vokes, Ryland Parker signed printed forms specifying that the contracts were "non-cancelable" and that "no refunds will be made" and he was "was praised and encouraged regularly by the instructors, despite his lack of progress." Like Vokes, Parker alleged the Arthur Murray's dance instructors had misrepresented his dancing ability and progress and sought rescission of the contracts and return of money allocated to unused lessons. The court granted Parker rescission and return of unused fees, but rested its decision on the ground that Parker had been injured in an automobile accident and therefore was unable to benefit from the dance lessons. The court cited the doctrine of impossibility in support of its finding, but its rationale is closer to the doctrine of frustration. Both impossibility and frustration will be examined in Chapter Eight.

The Federal Trade Commission filed a complaint alleging deceptive trade practices against Arthur Murray, Inc. in 1960. A consent order was entered in which Arthur Murray, Inc. agreed to cease its false advertising, including "bait" or "decoy" promotional schemes; to cease using a variety of coercive practices; and to cease requesting consumers to sign blank contracts. *See In the Matter of Arthur Murray, Inc.*, 57 F.T.C. 306 (1960). The Federal Trade Commission then tried, with mixed success, to enforce this and other decrees against local licensees of Arthur Murray. *See, e.g., Arthur Murray Studio of Washington v. Federal Trade Commission*, 458 F.2d 622 (5th Cir. 1972) (upholding a decree setting a $1,500 limit on contracts for dance lessons). In 1980, pursuant to findings of continuing unfair practices by Arthur Murray International and its licensees, the Federal Trade Commission modified the 1960 decree to require that an absolute unilateral right of cancellation be accorded to all students, with full refund less a modest service fee. *See In the Matter of Arthur Murray, Inc.*, 95 F.T.C. 347 (1980). No reported action was taken by the Federal Trade Commission to enforce the modified decree and in 1985, Arthur Murray International requested that the decree be withdrawn on the ground that the Commission's failure to prosecute similar practices by other dance studios has put Arthur Murray at a competitive disadvantage in the market for franchisees. Request to Reopen and Vacate Consent Order (1985), *In the Matter of Arthur Murray*, 95 F.T.C. 347. Many states have adopted legislation regulating dance studio contracting practices. One of these, the California Dance Studio Act, California Civil Code §§ 1812.50 – 1812.68 (1985), was drafted by law students at Stanford Law School.

Michael I. Meyerson, The Reunification of Contract Law: The Objective Theory of Consumer Form Contracts

47 U. Miami L. Rev. 1263 (1993)

To determine if A has made a legally enforceable promise to B, one must determine whether B "had reason to believe that the first party had that intention." The intent of a speaker or writer is inferred from the perspective of what the listener or reader knew or should have known.

Thus, if owners of property write and sign a piece of paper stating, "We hereby agree to sell to W.O. Lucy the Ferguson Farm complete for $50,000, title satisfactory to buyer," a court can confidently find an intent to sell. Similarly, if Lucy reads and accepts the document, the court may infer an intent to purchase the Ferguson Farm. This is a straightforward application of the rule that "[t]he law imputes to a person an intention corresponding to the reasonable meaning of his words and acts."

Thus, traditionally there has been a so-called duty to read, which binds those who sign or accept a contract to the written terms even if they did not read or understand its content. In cases involving negotiated contracts or experienced businesspeople, this duty to read is consistent with the objective theory because assent can reasonably be inferred from the act of signing a document in such circumstances. One expects the average businessperson to be able to learn the meaning of the contract terms with relative ease and to voice any disagreement with such terms.

There are, however, circumstances where the significance of the same act is quite different. The law has long recognized that unsuspecting recipients of parcel room checks or ticket stubs do not accept, and thus are not bound by, the printed limitations on liability. This principle, too, is consistent with the objective theory because the party printing the ticket, knowing the fine print will not be read, does not have a reasonable belief that the other party assented to the limitations. As the Massachusetts Supreme Judicial Court stated in rejecting a waiver of liability printed on the ticket to an amusement park attraction:

> [A] person of average intelligence and alertness would be unlikely to observe it, and would enter the [ride] in the belief that he had all the rights of the ordinary business visitor with respect to so much of the premises as he was invited to use.

[*Kushner v. McGinnis*, 194 N.E. 106, 108 (Mass. 1935).] The court added that if such a limitation was to be enforceable at all, the ride's proprietor should have "employed adequate means to bring to [the patron's] attention the fact that his invitation was a qualified and conditional one." [*Id.*]

If the objective theory of contracts were correctly applied to consumer form contracts, a similar rule would result. In our current society, the average consumer is unlikely to observe most of the terms in form contracts. They may well know central terms, such as price and quantity, but generally they neither know nor understand subordinate terms, such as those describing recourse in case of breach. Consumers, thus, contract with a reasonable belief that they do not relinquish the rights implied by law for the benefit of the ordinary contracting party.

It is no secret that consumers neither read nor understand standard form contracts.[28] The president of a car rental company hardly believes that renters at the airport rental counter read the front and back of the rental contract before receiving the keys. It is equally unrealistic to state that a reasonable rental car executive would assume that a renter's signature reflects true assent to every term in the contract. The only basis for such a belief would be if the current law mandates such a result *despite* the objective understanding of the rental car executive. Any expectation that the contract terms written by the company's lawyers are enforceable against the consumer is "reasonable" not because the consumer's true intent was objectively ascertained but solely because of the legal rule.

One reason for a contract system founded on objective criteria of assent to ignore the reasonable interpretation of the consumer's intent might be to affect the consumer's behavior. However, consumers do not read form contracts both because it is unreasonable to do so and because businesses do not want consumers to read them prior to signing.

Most consumers fail to read the form contracts that pass before them every day. Consumers simply do not have the time to read them, as exemplified by the car-renter at the airport. They also generally lack the legal background to understand the subordinate clauses. Additionally, because consumers know that the agent behind the counter is not authorized to rewrite the contract,[35] they conclude that there is little to be gained from reading a non-negotiable contract.

Moreover, businesses hardly want the consumer to read form contracts. If the purpose of using a form is to achieve uniformity in transaction, individualized negotiations will defeat that purpose. Additionally, businesses, like consumers, are short of time and prefer not to have their turnover slowed by hordes of consumers pausing to peruse pages of legalese.

Despite wishful commentary to the contrary, there is no evidence that a small cadre of type-A consumers ferrets out the most beneficial subordinate contract terms, permitting the market to protect the vast majority of consumers. Obvious terms, such as pricing and warranties, may be subject to such comparison shopping. It is hard, however, to imagine a sufficient number of prospective consumers refusing to rent a car because the contract contains an unfair forum selection clause.

If consumers do not read and comprehend the subordinate terms of standard form contracts, there can be no subjective agreement to the particular terms. Furthermore, merchants and sellers who know that consumers do not read these terms have no objective basis for claiming that the consumers agreed to those terms. If it is both unreasonable and undesirable to have consumers read these terms, courts should not fashion legal rules in a futile attempt to force consumers to read these terms or to punish those who do not.

The common law of contracts, it seems, has strayed from the path of logical progression. The wrong turn occurred when the perfectly logical assumption that a merchant's signature implied assent to negotiated terms was mistakenly applied to consumer form contracts. The courts abandoned the objective theory in search of a seductive consistency.

---

28. See, e.g., Davis v. M.L.G. Corp., 712 P.2d 985, 992 (Colo. 1986) (automobile rental agent testifying that she had never seen any customer read the reverse side of the rental agreement); Unico v. Owen, 232 A.2d 405, 410 (N.J. 1967) ("The ordinary consumer goods purchaser more often than not does not read the fine print...."); Holiday of Plainview, Ltd. v. Bernstein, 350 N.Y.S.2d 510, 512 (N.Y. Dist. Ct. 1973) (stating that "it is true that defendant (as have many before him and probably many will after him) failed to read the entire contract").

35. "Employees regularly using a form often have only a limited understanding of its terms and limited authority to vary them." Restatement (Second) of Contracts § 211 cmt. b (1979). See, e.g., A & M Produce Co. v. FMC Corp., 186 Cal. Rptr. 114, 125 n.13 (Cal. Ct. App. 1982) (in response to the question whether there is negotiation over form terms, a salesperson stated: "I'm not empowered to do that, sir.").

...

The classical legal view of standard form contracts defies logic and invites great injustice. Essentially, under the twin banners of "freedom of contract" and "duty to read," the law has given drafters of form contracts the power to impose their will on unsuspecting and vulnerable individuals.

The 1918 case of *Morstad v. Atchinson T. & S.F. Railway Co.* [170 P. 886 (N.M. 1918)] demonstrates the resulting hardship and injustice. A railroad worker, Andrew Morstad, was injured while unloading timber. He was taken to a bunk car and was lying on a bed "in an awful pain." The railroad company foreman presented him with a form and said, "[H]ere is something you will have to sign before you go to the hospital." Morstad, who was not wearing his reading glasses, signed the form without reading it. The form was a settlement contract whereby Morstad "agreed" to release the railroad from all liability in exchange for one dollar and transportation to the hospital.

The New Mexico Supreme Court upheld the validity of the release, stating that "[Morstad] was guilty of such gross negligence in not informing himself of the contents of the contract that he is estopped to avoid the same. His lack of knowledge of the contents of the contract was due absolutely to his own negligence." The court opined that "it is the duty of every person to read a contract before he signs the same, if he can read, and it is as much his duty to have the same read and explained to him before he executes it, if he cannot read or understand it."

The court gave several policy rationales for this strict rule. Someone who signs a contract "owes it to the other party to read or have read, the contract ... because the other party has a right to and does conform his own conduct to the requirements of the contract...." The court also noted that permitting Morstad to go beyond the written word would threaten to "destroy all of the efficacy of written contracts." The rule, the court noted in conclusion, "renders written contracts safe and secure, and just what they must be if the business of the world is to be carried on in an orderly fashion."

Classical courts upheld written language, even where the drafter discouraged a semi-literate individual from reading the paper by saying, "it was all a matter of form—it was immaterial." [*Fivey v. Pennsylvania R.R. Co.*, 52 A. 472, 474 (N.J. 1902).] Judges confidently cited, "the well-settled principle that affixing a signature to a contract creates a *conclusive presumption*, except as against fraud, that the signer read, understood, and assented to its terms." Courts moralistically preached that if a person failed to read the contract, "he cannot set up his own carelessness and indolence as a defense." [*McNinch v. Northwest Thresher Co.*, 100 P. 524, 526 (Okla. 1909).]

This classical theory has no basis in either reality or justice. Courts had to create a "conclusive" presumption that the signing party understood the terms because such a presumption was so counter-factual. The drafters of the contracts knew the signing party had not read the terms. There could be no problem of unfair surprise, since the objective understanding of the contract drafter mirrored the subjective reality of the non-drafter.

The other problem with the classical theory was that it permitted drafters of form contracts to abuse their power. There were no safeguards against grotesquely one-sided agreements, drafted to be signed unread.

In response to this problem, judges began resorting to subterfuge to reach the result that should have been obtained directly under basic principles of "objective appearances." Ambiguity, waiver, estoppel, and conditions to contract were used to sidestep unpleasant results, while the courts purportedly followed the path of the earlier decisions.

Many of the finest legal scholars of the twentieth century have tried with limited success to correct these errors, each pointing out the inconsistency in legal reasoning and illustrating a part of the problem. More recently, serious attempts have been made to present a formal solution to the entire area by creating a separate rule for form contracts. The collective wisdom has brought us to the point where contract law can now be reunified, where the objective theory of contracts again applied to all contracts.

Note

Professor Meyerson argues that a correct application of the objective theory of interpretation would lead to the conclusion that a consumer's signature on a document does not necessarily signify the consumer's assent to all of the terms written in the document. Would this argument also apply to some transactions between commercial actors? (Recall "the battle of the forms" and *Uniform Commercial Code* § 2-207 in Chapter Three.) Isn't it striking that this *Uniform Commercial Code* section is based on the explicit recognition that business people do not read documents while courts still routinely impose a duty to read in common law cases? It is not surprising that this issue has become hotly contested in current contract law. In cases involving written documents and allegations of misrepresentation or misunderstanding, lawyers must be aware of the array of available arguments, any one of which may be persuasive to a particular judge.

D. Failure to Disclose

Most civil law systems recognize an obligation of good faith in negotiations. Anglo-American common law traditionally has not recognized such an obligation, maintaining instead that the market functions best when there are "arm's length" transactions, those exchanges between parties who each engage in independent self-interested decision making in a market where there is competition. Anglo-American contract law does regulate negotiating behavior with the doctrines of illegality, public policy, capacity, duress, undue influence, misrepresentation, and unconscionability. There are contracts scholars who feel that in some cases courts are justified in enforcing an obligation to negotiate in good faith. Such doctrines are not designed to disturb the relative informational advantage a party may have. Accordingly, a negotiator generally is not obligated to share information; instead, information is treated as valuable property that people should not be required to transfer. However, legislatures have enacted many exceptions to this rule, requiring disclosure of specific details in particular types of contracts. One well-known example of this legislation is the *Federal Truth in Lending Act*, 15 U.S.C. §§ 1601–1667e. In addition, courts traditionally have held that one party may have a duty to disclose information if that person is in a fiduciary relationship with the other party, as Russel P. Quinn and Gilman A. Hill alleged Boeing had with the Skyfox Group in *Flight Concepts v. Boeing*, above. And more recently, courts have held that a duty to disclose may be enforced if the party has already given partial information and the resulting "half-truth" would be misleading; if the person has important information that is unavailable to the other party; if the person knows that the other party is operating under a mistake; if the party is in a position of trust; or, more controversially, if the information is "material" to the contract.

This recent legislation and case law has had a significant effect on commercial practices, particularly the practices of banks, other large lenders, and real estate agents.

The excerpt below is from *De Officiis*, written in approximately 45–43 BCE by Marcus Cicero, an accomplished Roman rhetor, lawyer, philosopher, and politician; this passage shows the persistence of issues of good faith and morality in contracting practice. *Hill v. Jones*, the first case following the excerpt, imposes a duty to disclose as a corollary of the misrepresentation and mistake doctrines. The next case, *Stambovsky v. Ackley*, imposes a similar duty as a matter of equitable estoppel.

Marcus Cicero, De Officiis, Book III

(c. 45–43 BCE)

... But, as I said above, cases often arise in which expediency may seem to clash with moral rectitude; and so we should examine carefully and see whether their conflict is inevitable or whether they may be reconciled. The following are problems of this sort: suppose, for example, a time of dearth and famine at Rhodes, with provisions at fabulous prices; and suppose that an honest man has imported a large cargo of grain from Alexandria and that to his certain knowledge also several other importers have set sail from Alexandria, and that on the voyage he has sighted their vessels laden with grain and bound for Rhodes; is he to report the fact to the Rhodians or is he to keep his own counsel and sell his own stock at the highest market price? I am assuming the case of a virtuous, upright man, and I am raising the question how a man would think and reason who would not conceal the facts from the Rhodians if he thought that it was immoral to do so, but who might be in doubt whether such silence would really be immoral.

In deciding cases of this kind Diogenes of Babylonia, a great and highly esteemed Stoic, consistently holds one view; his pupil Antipater, a most profound scholar, holds another. According to Antipater all the facts should be disclosed, that the buyer may not be uninformed of any detail that the seller knows; according to Diogenes the seller should declare any defects in his wares, in so far as such a course is prescribed by the common law of the land; but for the rest, since he has goods to sell, he may try to sell them to the best possible advantage, provided he is guilty of no misrepresentation.

"I have imported my stock," Diogenes's merchant will say; "I have offered it for sale; I sell at a price no higher than my competitors—perhaps even lower, when the market is overstocked. Who is wronged?"

"What say you?" comes Antipater's argument on the other side; "it is your duty to consider the interests of your fellow-men and to serve society; you were brought into the world under these conditions and have these inborn principles which you are in duty bound to obey and follow, that your interest shall be the interest of the community and conversely that the interest of the community shall be your interest as well; will you, in view of all these facts, conceal from your fellow-men what relief in plenteous supplies is close at hand for them?"

"It is one thing to conceal," Diogenes will perhaps reply; "not to reveal is quite a different thing. At this present moment I am not concealing from you, even if I am not revealing to you, the nature of the gods or the highest good; and to know these secrets would be of more advantage to you than to know that the price of wheat was down. But I am under no obligation to tell you everything that it may be to your interest to be told."

"Yea," Antipater will say, "but you are, as you must admit, if you will only bethink you of the bonds of fellowship forged by Nature and existing between man and man."

"I do not forget them," the other will reply; "but do you mean to say that those bonds of fellowship are such that there is no such thing as private property? If that is the case, we should not sell anything at all, but freely give everything away."

XIII. In this whole discussion, you see, no one says, "However wrong morally this or that may be, still, since it is expedient, I will do it"; but the one side asserts that a given act is expedient, without being morally wrong, while the other insists that the act should not be done, because it is morally wrong.

Suppose again that an honest man is offering a house for sale on account of certain undesirable features of which he himself is aware but which nobody else knows; suppose it is unsanitary, but has the reputation of being healthful; suppose it is not generally known that vermin are to be found in all the bedrooms; suppose, finally, that it is built of unsound timber and likely to collapse, but that no one knows about it except the owner; if the vendor does not tell the purchaser these facts but sells him the house for far more than he could reasonably have expected to get for it, I ask whether his transaction is unjust or dishonorable.

"Yes," says Antipater, "it is; for to allow a purchaser to be hasty in closing a deal and through mistaken judgment to incur a very serious loss, if this is not refusing 'to set a man right when he has lost his way' (a crime which at Athens is prohibited on pain of public execration), what is? It is even worse than refusing to set a man on his way: it is deliberately leading a man astray."

"Can you say," answers Diogenes, "that he compelled you to purchase, when he did not even advise it? He advertised for sale what he did not like; you bought what you did like. If people are not considered guilty of swindling when they place upon their placards For Sale: A Fine Villa, Well Built, even when it is neither good nor properly built, still less guilty are they who say nothing in praise of their house. For where the purchaser may exercise his own judgment, what fraud can there be on the part of the vendor? But if, again, not all that is expressly stated has to be made good, do you think a man is bound to make good what has not been said? What, pray, would be more stupid than for a vendor to recount all the faults in the article he is offering for sale? And what would be so absurd as for an auctioneer to cry, at the owner's bidding, 'Here is an unsanitary house for sale?' "

In this way, then, in certain doubtful cases moral rectitude is defended on the one side, while on the other side the case of expediency is so presented as to make it appear not only morally right to do what seems expedient, but even morally wrong not to do it.

Note

In this passage, Cicero argued that claims of expediency, or self-interest, are themselves moral claims: they are based on the belief that self-interest is morally good. This position is echoed in neo-classical economics assertion that self-interest is the foundation for rational choice and that the allocation of resources produced by self-interested behavior is best for society. The claim that self-interest is a moral good can be challenged or contested by competing moral claims, such as a claim that generosity is a moral good and is incompatible with self-interest.

Warren G. Hill and Gloria R. Hill v. Ora G. Jones and Barbara R. Jones
Court of Appeals of Arizona
151 Ariz. 81, 725 P.2d 1115 (1986)

BRUCE E. MEYERSON, JUDGE

Must the seller of a residence disclose to the buyer facts pertaining to past termite infestation? This is the primary question presented in this appeal. Plaintiffs Warren G. Hill and Gloria R. Hill (buyers) filed suit to rescind an agreement to purchase a residence. Buyers alleged that Ora G. Jones and Barbara R. Jones (sellers) had made misrepresentations concerning termite damage in the residence and had failed to disclose to them the existence of the damage and history of termite infestation in the residence. The trial court dismissed the claim for misrepresentation based upon a so-called integration clause in the parties' agreement.

Sellers then sought summary judgment on the "concealment" claim arguing that they had no duty to disclose information pertaining to termite infestation and that even if they did, the record failed to show all of the elements necessary for fraudulent concealment. The trial court granted summary judgment, finding that there was "no genuinely disputed issue of material fact and that the law favors the ... defendants." The trial court awarded sellers $1,000.00 in attorney's fees. Buyers have appealed from the judgment and sellers have cross-appealed from the trial court's ruling on attorney's fees.

Facts

In 1982, buyers entered into an agreement to purchase sellers' residence for $72,000. The agreement was entered after buyers made several visits to the home. The purchase agreement provided that sellers were to pay for and place in escrow a termite inspection report stating that the property was free from evidence of termite infestation. Escrow was scheduled to close two months later.

One of the central features of the house is a parquet teak floor covering the sunken living room, the dining room, the entryway and portions of the halls. On a subsequent visit to the house, and when sellers were present, buyers noticed a small "ripple" in the wood floor on the step leading up to the dining room from the sunken living room. Mr. Hill asked if the ripple could be termite damage. Mrs. Jones answered that it was water damage. A few years previously, a broken water heater in the house had in fact caused water damage in the area of the dining room and steps which necessitated that some repairs be made to the floor. No further discussion on the subject, however, took place between the parties at that time or afterwards.

Mr. Hill, through his job as maintenance supervisor at a school district, had seen similar "ripples" in wood which had turned out to be termite damage. Mr. Hill was not totally satisfied with Mrs. Jones's explanation, but he felt that the termite inspection report would reveal whether the ripple was due to termites or some other cause.

The termite inspection report stated that there was no visible evidence of infestation. The report failed to note the existence of physical damage or evidence of previous treatment. The realtor notified the parties that the property had passed the termite inspection. Apparently, neither party actually saw the report prior to close of escrow.

After moving into the house, buyers found a pamphlet left in one of the drawers entitled "Termites, the Silent Saboteurs." They learned from a neighbor that the house had some termite infestation in the past. Shortly after the close of escrow, Mrs. Hill noticed that the wood on the steps leading down to the sunken living room was crumbling. She called an exterminator who confirmed the existence of termite damage to the floor and steps and to wood columns in the house. The estimated cost of repairing the wood floor alone was approximately $5,000.

Through discovery after their lawsuit was filed, buyers learned the following. When sellers purchased the residence in 1974, they received two termite guarantees that had been given to the previous owner by Truly Nolen, as well as a diagram showing termite treatment at the residence that had taken place in 1963. The guarantees provided for semi-annual inspections and annual termite booster treatments. The accompanying diagram stated that the existing damage had not been repaired. The second guarantee, dated 1965, reinstated the earlier contract for inspection and treatment. Mr. Jones admitted that he read the guarantees when he received them. Sellers renewed the guarantees when they purchased the residence in 1974. They also paid the annual fee each year until they sold the home.

On two occasions during sellers' ownership of the house but while they were at their other residence in Minnesota, a neighbor noticed "streamers" evidencing live termites in the wood tile floor near the entryway. On both occasions, Truly Nolen gave a booster treatment for termites. On the second incident, Truly Nolen drilled through one of the wood tiles to treat for termites. The neighbor showed Mr. Jones the area where the damage and treatment had occurred. Sellers had also seen termites on the back fence and had replaced and treated portions of the fence.

Sellers did not mention any of this information to buyers prior to close of escrow. They did not mention the past termite infestation and treatment to the realtor or to the termite inspector. There was evidence of holes on the patio that had been drilled years previously to treat for termites. The inspector returned to the residence to determine why he had not found evidence of prior treatment and termite damage. He indicated that he had not seen the holes in the patio because of boxes stacked there. It is unclear whether the boxes had been placed there by buyers or sellers. He had not found the damage inside the house because a large plant, which buyers had purchased from sellers, covered the area. After investigating the second time, the inspector found the damage and evidence of past treatment. He acknowledged that this information should have appeared in the report. He complained, however, that he should have been told of any history of termite infestation and treatment before he performed his inspection and that it was customary for the inspector to be given such information.

Other evidence presented to the trial court was that during their numerous visits to the residence before close of escrow, buyers had unrestricted access to view and inspect the entire house. Both Mr. and Mrs. Hill had seen termite damage and were therefore familiar with what it might look like. Mr. Hill had seen termite damage on the fence at this property. Mrs. Hill had noticed the holes on the patio but claimed not to realize at the time what they were for. Buyers asked no questions about termites except when they asked if the "ripple" on the stairs was termite damage. Mrs. Hill admitted she was not "trying" to find problems with the house because she really wanted it.

. . .

Duty to Disclose

The principal legal question presented in this appeal is whether a seller has a duty to disclose to the buyer the existence of termite damage in a residential dwelling known to the seller, but not to the buyer, which materially affects the value of the property. For the reasons stated herein, we hold that such a duty exists.

This is not the place to trace the history of the doctrine of *caveat emptor*. Suffice it to say that its vitality has waned during the latter half of the 20th century. *E.g., Richards v. Powercraft Homes, Inc.*, 678 P.2d 427 (Ariz. 1984) (implied warranty of workmanship and habitability extends to subsequent buyers of homes); *see generally Quashnock v. Frost*, 445 A.2d 121 (Pa. 1982); *Ollerman v. O'Rourke Co.*, 288 N.W.2d 95 (Wis. 1980). The modern view is that a vendor has an affirmative duty to disclose material facts where:

1. Disclosure is necessary to prevent a previous assertion from being a misrepresentation or from being fraudulent or material;

2. Disclosure would correct a mistake of the other party as to a basic assumption on which that party is making the contract and if nondisclosure amounts to a failure to act in good faith and in accordance with reasonable standards of fair dealing;

3. Disclosure would correct a mistake of the other party as to the contents or effect of a writing, evidencing or embodying an agreement in whole or in part;

4. The other person is entitled to know the fact because of a relationship of trust and confidence between them.

Restatement (Second) of Contracts § 161 (1981) (hereafter "Restatement"); *see* Restatement (Second) of Torts § 551 (1977).

Arizona courts have long recognized that under certain circumstances there may be a "duty to speak." *Van Buren v. Pima Community College Dist. Bd.*, 546 P.2d 821, 823 (Ariz. 1976); *Batty v. Arizona State Dental Bd.*, 112 P.2d 870, 877 (Ariz. 1941). As the supreme court noted in the context of a confidential relationship, "[s]uppression of a material fact which a party is bound in good faith to disclose is equivalent to a false representation." *Leigh v. Loyd*, 244 P.2d 356, 358 (Ariz. 1952); *National Housing Indus. Inc. v. E.L. Jones Dev. Co.*, 576 P.2d 1374, 1379 (Ariz. 1978).

Thus, the important question we must answer is whether under the facts of this case, buyers should have been permitted to present to the jury their claim that sellers were under a duty to disclose their (sellers') knowledge of termite infestation in the residence. This broader question involves two inquiries. First, must a seller of residential property advise the buyer of material facts within his knowledge pertaining to the value of the property? Second, may termite damage and the existence of past infestation constitute such material facts?

The doctrine imposing a duty to disclose is akin to the well-established contractual rules pertaining to relief from contracts based upon mistake. Although the law of contracts supports the finality of transactions, over the years courts have recognized that under certain limited circumstances it is unjust to strictly enforce the policy favoring finality. Thus, for example, even a unilateral mistake of one party to a transaction may justify rescission. Restatement § 153.

There is also a judicial policy promoting honesty and fair dealing in business relationships. This policy is expressed in the law of fraudulent and negligent misrepresentations. Where a misrepresentation is fraudulent or where a negligent misrepresentation is one of material fact, the policy of finality rightly gives way to the policy of promoting honest dealings between the parties. *See* Restatement § 164(1).

Under certain circumstances nondisclosure of a fact known to one party may be equivalent to the assertion that the fact does not exist. For example "[w]hen one conveys a false impression by the disclosure of some facts and the concealment of others, such concealment is in effect a false representation that what is disclosed is the whole truth." *State v. Coddington*, 662 P.2d 155, 156 (Ariz. App. 1983). Thus, nondisclosure may be equated with and given the same legal effect as fraud and misrepresentation. One category of cases where this has been done involves the area of nondisclosure of material facts affecting the value of property, known to the seller but not reasonably capable of being known to the buyer.

Courts have formulated this "duty to disclose" in slightly different ways. For example, the Florida Supreme Court recently declared "where the seller of a home knows of facts materially affecting the value of the property which are not readily observable and are not known to the buyer, the seller is under a duty to disclose them to the buyer." *Johnson v. Davis*, 480 So. 2d 625, 629 (Fla. 1985) (defective roof in three-year-old home). In California, the rule has been stated this way:

> [W]here the seller knows of facts materially affecting the value or desirability of the property which are known or accessible only to him and also knows that such facts are not known to, or within the reach of the diligent attention and observation of the buyer, the seller is under a duty to disclose them to the buyer.

Lingsch v. Savage, 213 Cal. App. 2d 729, 735, 29 Cal. Rptr. 201, 204 (1963); *contra Ray v. Montgomery*, 399 So. 2d 230 (Ala. 1980); *see generally* W. Prosser & W. Keeton, The Law of Torts§ 106 (5th ed.1984)[2] We find that the Florida formulation of the disclosure rule properly balances the legitimate interests of the parties in a transaction for the sale of a private residence and accordingly adopt it for such cases.

As can be seen, the rule requiring disclosure is invoked in the case of material facts.[3] Thus, we are led to the second inquiry—whether the existence of termite damage in a residential dwelling is the type of material fact which gives rise to the duty to disclose. The existence of termite damage and past termite infestation has been considered by other courts to be sufficiently material to warrant disclosure. *See generally Annot.*, 22 A.L.R.3d 972 (1968).

In *Lynn v. Taylor*, 642 P.2d 131 (Kan. App. 1982), the purchaser of a termite-damaged residence brought suit against the seller and realtor for fraud and against the termite inspector for negligence. An initial termite report found evidence of prior termite infestation and recommended treatment. A second report indicated that the house was termite free. The first report was not given to the buyer. The seller contended that because treatment would not have repaired the existing damage, the first report was not material. The buyer testified that he would not have purchased the house had he known of the first report. Under these circumstances, the court concluded that the facts contained in the first report were material. *See Hunt v. Walker*, 483 S.W.2d 732 (Tenn. App. 1971) (severe damage to the residence by past termite infestation); *Mercer v. Woodard*, 303 S.E.2d 475, 481–82 (Ga. App. 1983) (duty of disclosure extends to fact of past termite damage).

Although sellers have attempted to draw a distinction between live termites[4] and past infestation, the concept of materiality is an elastic one which is not limited by the termites' health. "A matter is material if it is one to which a reasonable person would attach importance in determining his choice of action in the transaction in question." *Lynn v. Taylor*, 642 P.2d at 134–35. For example, termite damage substantially affecting the structural soundness of the residence may be material even if there is no evidence of

---

2. There are variations on this same theme. For example, Pennsylvania has limited the obligation of disclosure to cases of dangerous defects. Glanski v. Ervine, 409 A.2d 425, 430 (Pa. 1979).

3. Arizona has recognized that a duty to disclose may arise where the buyer makes an inquiry of the seller, regardless of whether or not the fact is material. Universal Inv. Co. v. Sahara Motor Inn, Inc., 619 P.2d 485, 487 (Ariz. 1980). The inquiry by buyers whether the ripple was termite damage imposed a duty upon sellers to disclose what information they knew concerning the existence of termite infestation in the residence.

4. Sellers acknowledge that a duty of disclosure would exist if live termites were present. Obde v. Schlemeyer, 353 P.2d 672 (Wash. 1960).

present infestation. Unless reasonable minds could not differ, materiality is a factual matter which must be determined by the trier of fact. The termite damage in this case may or may not be material. Accordingly, we conclude that buyers should be allowed to present their case to a jury.

Sellers argue that even assuming the existence of a duty to disclose, summary judgment was proper because the record shows that their "silence ... did not induce or influence" the buyers. This is so, sellers contend, because Mr. Hill stated in his deposition that he intended to rely on the termite inspection report. But this argument begs the question. If sellers were fully aware of the extent of termite damage and if such information had been disclosed to buyers, a jury could accept Mr. Hill's testimony that had he known of the termite damage he would not have purchased the house.

Sellers further contend that buyers were put on notice of the possible existence of termite infestation and were therefore "chargeable with the knowledge which [an] inquiry, if made, would have revealed." *Godfrey v. Navratil*, 411 P.2d 470, 273 (Ariz. App. 1966) (quoting *Luke v. Smith*, 108 P. 494, 496 (Ariz. 1910)). It is also true that "a party may ... reasonably expect the other to take normal steps to inform himself and to draw his own conclusions." Restatement § 161 comment d. Under the facts of this case, the question of buyers' knowledge of the termite problem (or their diligence in attempting to inform themselves about the termite problem) should be left to the jury.[5]

By virtue of our holding, sellers' cross-appeal is moot. Reversed and remanded.

Jeffrey M. Stambovsky v. Helen V. Ackley and Ellis Realty

Supreme Court, Appellate Division
572 N.Y.S.2d 672 (A.D. 1991)

ISRAEL RUBIN, JUSTICE

Plaintiff, to his horror, discovered that the house he had recently contracted to purchase was widely reputed to be possessed by poltergeists, reportedly seen by defendant seller and members of her family on numerous occasions over the last nine years. Plaintiff promptly commenced this action seeking rescission of the contract of sale. Supreme Court reluctantly dismissed the complaint, holding that plaintiff has no remedy at law in this jurisdiction.

The unusual facts of this case, as disclosed by the record, clearly warrant a grant of equitable relief to the buyer who, as a resident of New York City, cannot be expected to have any familiarity with the folklore of the Village of Nyack. Not being a "local," plaintiff could not readily learn that the home he had contracted to purchase is haunted. Whether the source of the spectral apparitions seen by defendant seller are parapsychic or psychogenic, having reported their presence in both a national publication ("Readers' Digest") and the local press (in 1977 and 1982, respectively), defendant is estopped to deny their existence and, as a matter of law, the house is haunted. More to the point, however, no divination is required to conclude that it is defendant's promotional efforts in publicizing her close encounters with these spirits which fostered the home's reputation in the community. In 1989, the house was included in a five-home walking tour of Nyack and described in a November 27th newspaper article as "a riverfront Victorian (with

---

5. Sellers also contend that they had no knowledge of any existing termite damage in the house. An extended discussion of the facts on this point is unnecessary. Simply stated, the facts are in conflict on this issue.

ghost)." The impact of the reputation thus created goes to the very essence of the bargain between the parties, greatly impairing both the value of the property and its potential for resale. The extent of this impairment may be presumed for the purpose of reviewing the disposition of this motion to dismiss the cause of action for rescission (*Harris v. City of New York*, 542 N.Y.S.2d 550, 552 (A.D.)) and represents merely an issue of fact for resolution at trial.

While I agree with Supreme Court that the real estate broker, as agent for the seller, is under no duty to disclose to a potential buyer the phantasmal reputation of the premises and that, in his pursuit of a legal remedy for fraudulent misrepresentation against the seller, plaintiff hasn't a ghost of a chance, I am nevertheless moved by the spirit of equity to allow the buyer to seek rescission of the contract of sale and recovery of his down payment. New York law fails to recognize any remedy for damages incurred as a result of the seller's mere silence, applying instead the strict rule of caveat emptor. Therefore, the theoretical basis for granting relief, even under the extraordinary facts of this case, is elusive if not ephemeral.

"Pity me not but lend thy serious hearing to what I shall unfold" (William Shakespeare, Hamlet, Act I, Scene V [Ghost]).

From the perspective of a person in the position of plaintiff herein, a very practical problem arises with respect to the discovery of a paranormal phenomenon: "Who you gonna' call?" as the title song to the movie "Ghostbusters" asks. Applying the strict rule of caveat emptor to a contract involving a house possessed by poltergeists conjures up visions of a psychic or medium routinely accompanying the structural engineer and Terminix man on an inspection of every home subject to a contract of sale. It portends that the prudent attorney will establish an escrow account lest the subject of the transaction come back to haunt him and his client—or pray that his malpractice insurance coverage extends to supernatural disasters. In the interest of avoiding such untenable consequences, the notion that a haunting is a condition which can and should be ascertained upon reasonable inspection of the premises is a hobgoblin which should be exorcized from the body of legal precedent and laid quietly to rest.

It has been suggested by a leading authority that the ancient rule which holds that mere non-disclosure does not constitute actionable misrepresentation "finds proper application in cases where the fact undisclosed is patent, or the plaintiff has equal opportunities for obtaining information which he may be expected to utilize, or the defendant has no reason to think that he is acting under any misapprehension" (Prosser, Law of Torts § 106, at 696 [4th ed., 1971]). However, with respect to transactions in real estate, New York adheres to the doctrine of caveat emptor and imposes no duty upon the vendor to disclose any information concerning the premises (*London v. Courduff*, 529 N.Y.S.2d 874 (A.D.) unless there is a confidential or fiduciary relationship between the parties (*Moser v. Spizzirro*, 295 N.Y.S.2d 188 (A.D.), *aff'd*, 252 N.E.2d 632 (N.Y.); *IBM Credit Fin. Corp. v. Mazda Motor Mfg. (USA) Corp.*, 542 N.Y.S.2d 649 (A.D.)) or some conduct on the part of the seller which constitutes "active concealment" (*see*, *17 East 80th Realty Corp. v. 68th Associates*, 569 N.Y.S.2d 647 (A.D.) [dummy ventilation system constructed by seller]; *Haberman v. Greenspan*, 368 N.Y.S.2d 717 [foundation cracks covered by seller]). Normally, some affirmative misrepresentation (*e.g.*, *Tahini Invs., Ltd. v. Bobrowsky*, 470 N.Y.S.2d 431 (A.D.) [industrial waste on land allegedly used only as farm]; *Jansen v. Kelly*, 200 N.Y.S.2d 561 (A.D.) [land containing valuable minerals allegedly acquired for use as campsite]) or partial disclosure (*Junius Constr. Corp. v. Cohen*, 178 N.E. 672 (N.Y.) [existence of third unopened street concealed]; is required to impose upon the seller a duty to communicate undisclosed conditions affecting the premises (*contra*, *Young v. Keith*, 492 N.Y.S.2d 489 (A.D.) [defective water and sewer systems concealed]).

Caveat emptor is not so all-encompassing a doctrine of common law as to render every act of non-disclosure immune from redress, whether legal or equitable.

> In regard to the necessity of giving information which has not been asked, the rule differs somewhat at law and in equity, and while the law courts would permit no recovery of *damages* against a vendor, because of mere concealment of facts *under certain circumstances*, yet if the vendee refused to complete the contract because of the concealment of a material fact on the part of the other, equity would refuse to compel him so to do, because equity only compels the specific performance of a contract which is fair and open, and in regard to which all material matters known to each have been communicated to the other

(*Rothmiller v. Stein*, 38 N.E. 718, 728 [emphasis added]). Even as a principle of law, long before exceptions were embodied in statute law (*see*, *e.g.*, UCC 2-312, 2-313, 2-314, 2-315; 3-417[2][e]), the doctrine was held inapplicable to contagion among animals, adulteration of food, and insolvency of a maker of a promissory note and of a tenant substituted for another under a lease (*see*, *Rothmiller v. Stein*, 38 N.E. at 728 and cases cited therein). Common law is not moribund. Ex facto jus oritur (law arises out of facts). Where fairness and common sense dictate that an exception should be created, the evolution of the law should not be stifled by rigid application of a legal maxim.

The doctrine of caveat emptor requires that a buyer act prudently to assess the fitness and value of his purchase and operates to bar the purchaser who fails to exercise due care from seeking the equitable remedy of rescission (*see*, *e.g.*, *Rodas v. Manitaras*, 552 N.Y.S.2d 618 (A.D.)). For the purposes of the instant motion to dismiss the action pursuant to CPLR 3211(a)(7), plaintiff is entitled to every favorable inference which may reasonably be drawn from the pleadings (*Arrington v. New York Times Co.*, 434 N.E.2d 1319 (N.Y.); *Rovello v. Orofino Realty Co.*, 357 N.E.2d 970 (N.Y.)), specifically, in this instance, that he met his obligation to conduct an inspection of the premises and a search of available public records with respect to title. It should be apparent, however, that the most meticulous inspection and the search would not reveal the presence of poltergeists at the premises or unearth the property's ghoulish reputation in the community. Therefore, there is no sound policy reason to deny plaintiff relief for failing to discover a state of affairs which the most prudent purchaser would not be expected to even contemplate (*see Da Silva v. Musso*, 428 N.E.2d 382 (N.Y.)).

The case law in this jurisdiction dealing with the duty of a vendor of real property to disclose information to the buyer is distinguishable from the matter under review. The most salient distinction is that existing cases invariably deal with the physical condition of the premises (*e.g., London v. Courduff*, 529 N.Y.S.2d 874 [use as a landfill]) and other factors affecting its operation. No case has been brought to this court's attention in which the property value was impaired as the result of the reputation created by information disseminated to the public by the seller (or, for that matter, as a result of possession by poltergeists).

Where a condition which has been created by the seller materially impairs the value of the contract and is peculiarly within the knowledge of the seller or unlikely to be discovered by a prudent purchaser exercising due care with respect to the subject transaction, nondisclosure constitutes a basis for rescission as a matter of equity. Any other outcome places upon the buyer not merely the obligation to exercise care in his purchase but rather to be omniscient with respect to any fact that may affect the bargain. No practical purpose is served by imposing such a burden upon a purchaser. To the contrary, it encourages predatory business practice and offends the principle that equity will suffer no wrong to be without a remedy.

Defendant's contention that the contract of sale, particularly the merger or "as is" clause, bars recovery of the buyer's deposit is unavailing. Even an express disclaimer will not be given effect where the facts are peculiarly within the knowledge of the party invoking it (*Danann Realty Corp. v. Harris*, 5 N.Y.2d 317, 322, 184 N.Y.S.2d 599, 157 N.E.2d 597; *Tahini Invs., Ltd. v. Bobrowsky, supra*). Moreover, a fair reading of the merger clause reveals that it expressly disclaims only representations made with respect to the physical condition of the premises and merely makes general reference to representations concerning "any other matter or things affecting or relating to the aforesaid premises." As broad as this language may be, a reasonable interpretation is that its effect is limited to tangible or physical matters and does not extend to paranormal phenomena. Finally, if the language of the contract is to be construed as broadly as defendant urges to encompass the presence of poltergeists in the house, it cannot be said that she has delivered the premises "vacant" in accordance with her obligation under the provisions of the contract rider.

To the extent New York law may be said to require something more than "mere concealment" to apply even the equitable remedy of rescission, the case of *Junius Construction Corporation v. Cohen*, 178 N.E. 672, *supra*, while not precisely on point, provides some guidance. In that case, the seller disclosed that an official map indicated two as yet unopened streets which were planned for construction at the edges of the parcel. What was not disclosed was that the same map indicated a third street which, if opened, would divide the plot in half. The court held that, while the seller was under no duty to mention the planned streets at all, having undertaken to disclose two of them, he was obliged to reveal the third (*see also, Rosenschein v. McNally*, 233 N.Y.S.2d 254 (N.Y.)).

In the case at bar, defendant seller deliberately fostered the public belief that her home was possessed. Having undertaken to inform the public at large, to whom she has no legal relationship, about the supernatural occurrences on her property, she may be said to owe no less a duty to her contract vendee. It has been remarked that the occasional modern cases which permit a seller to take unfair advantage of a buyer's ignorance so long as he is not actively misled are "singularly unappetizing" (Prosser, Law of Torts § 106, at 696 [4th ed. 1971]). Where, as here, the seller not only takes unfair advantage of the buyer's ignorance but has created and perpetuated a condition about which he is unlikely to even inquire, enforcement of the contract (in whole or in part) is offensive to the court's sense of equity. Application of the remedy of rescission, within the bounds of the narrow exception to the doctrine of caveat emptor set forth herein, is entirely appropriate to relieve the unwitting purchaser from the consequences of a most unnatural bargain.

Accordingly, the judgment of the Supreme Court, New York County (Edward H. Lehner, J.), entered April 9, 1990, which dismissed the complaint pursuant to CPLR 3211(a)(7), should be modified, on the law and the facts and in the exercise of discretion, and the first cause of action seeking rescission of the contract reinstated, without costs.

GEORGE BUNDY SMITH, JUSTICE, DISSENTING

I would affirm the dismissal of the complaint by the motion court.

Plaintiff seeks to rescind his contract to purchase defendant Ackley's residential property and recover his down payment. Plaintiff alleges that Ackley and her real estate broker, defendant Ellis Realty, made material misrepresentations of the property in that they failed to disclose that Ackley believed that the house was haunted by poltergeists. Moreover, Ackley shared this belief with her community and the general public through articles published in *Reader's Digest* (1977) and the local newspaper (1982). In November 1989, approximately two months after the parties entered into the contract of sale but subsequent to the scheduled October 2, 1989 closing, the house was included in a five-house walking tour and again described in the local newspaper as being haunted.

Prior to closing, plaintiff learned of this reputation and unsuccessfully sought to rescind the $650,000 contract of sale and obtain return of his $32,500 down payment without resort to litigation. The plaintiff then commenced this action for that relief and alleged that he would not have entered into the contract had he been so advised and that as a result of the alleged poltergeist activity, the market value and resaleability of the property was greatly diminished. Defendant Ackley has counterclaimed for specific performance.

> It is settled law in New York that the seller of real property is under no duty to speak when the parties deal at arm's length. The mere silence of the seller, without some act or conduct which deceived the purchaser, does not amount to a concealment that is actionable as a fraud (*see Perin v. Mardine Realty Co., Inc.*, 168 N.Y.S.2d 647 (A.D.), *aff'd*, 161 N.E.2d 210 (N.Y.)). The buyer has the duty to satisfy himself as to the quality of his bargain pursuant to the doctrine of caveat emptor, which in New York State still applies to real estate transactions.

London v. Courduff, 529 N.Y.S.2d 874, 875 (A.D.), *app. dism'd*, 534 N.E.2d 332 (N.Y. 1988).

The parties herein were represented by counsel and dealt at arm's length. This is evidenced by the contract of sale that, inter alia, contained various riders and a specific provision that all prior understandings and agreements between the parties were merged into the contract, that the contract completely expressed their full agreement and that neither had relied upon any statement by anyone else not set forth in the contract. There is no allegation that defendants, by some specific act, other than the failure to speak, deceived the plaintiff. Nevertheless, a cause of action may be sufficiently stated where there is a confidential or fiduciary relationship creating a duty to disclose and there was a failure to disclose a material fact, calculated to induce a false belief. *County of Westchester v. Welton Becket Assoc.*, 478 N.Y.S.2d 305, 321 *aff'd*, 485 N.E.2d 1029 (N.Y. 1985). However, plaintiff herein has not alleged and there is no basis for concluding that a confidential or fiduciary relationship existed between these parties to an arm's length transaction such as to give rise to a duty to disclose. In addition, there is no allegation that defendants thwarted plaintiff's efforts to fulfill his responsibilities fixed by the doctrine of caveat emptor. *See London v. Courduff, supra*, 529 N.Y.S.2d at 875.

Finally, if the doctrine of caveat emptor is to be discarded, it should be for a reason more substantive than a poltergeist. The existence of a poltergeist is no more binding upon the defendants than it is upon this court.

Based upon the foregoing, the motion court properly dismissed the complaint.

Maria Elena Llano, In the Family

(1990)

Translated by Beatriz Teleki

When my mother found out that the large mirror in the living room was inhabited, we all gradually went from disbelief to astonishment, and from this to a state of contemplation, ending up by accepting it as an everyday thing.

The fact that the old, spotted mirror reflected the dear departed in the family was not enough to upset our life style. Following the old saying of "let the house burn as long as no one sees the smoke," we kept the secret to ourselves since, after all, it was nobody else's business.

At any rate, some time went by before each one of us would feel absolutely comfortable about sitting down in our favorite chair and learning that, in the mirror, that same chair was occupied by somebody else. For example, it could be Aurelia, my grandmother's sister (1939), and even if cousin Natalie would be on my side of the room, across from her would be the almost forgotten Uncle Nicholas (1927). As could have been expected, our departed reflected in the mirror presented the image of a family gathering almost identical to our own, since nothing, absolutely nothing in the living-room—the furniture and its arrangement, the light, etc.—was changed in the mirror. The only difference was that on the other side it was them instead of us.

I don't know about the others, but I sometimes felt that, more than a vision in the mirror, I was watching an old worn-out movie, already clouded. The deceaseds' efforts to copy our gestures were slower, restrained, as if the mirror were not truly showing a direct image but the reflection of some other reflection.

From the very beginning I knew that everything would get more complicated as soon as my cousin Clara got back from vacation. Because of her boldness and determination, Clara had long given me the impression that she had blundered into our family by mistake. This suspicion had been somewhat bolstered by her being one of the first women dentists in the country. However, the idea that she might have been with us by mistake went away as soon as my cousin hung up her diploma and started to embroider sheets beside my grandmother, aunts and other cousins, waiting for a suitor who actually did show up but was found lacking in one respect or another—nobody ever really found out why.

Once she graduated, Clara became the family oracle, even though she never practiced her profession. She would prescribe painkillers and was the arbiter of fashion; she would choose the theater shows and rule on whether the punch had the right amount of liquor at each social gathering. In view of all this, it was fitting that she take one month off every year to go to the beach.

That summer when Clara returned from her vacation and learned about my mother's discovery, she remained pensive for a while, as if weighing the symptoms before issuing a diagnosis. Afterwards, without batting an eye, she leaned over the mirror, saw for herself that it was true, and then tossed her head, seemingly accepting the situation. She immediately sat by the bookcase and craned her neck to see who was sitting in the chair on the other side. "Gosh, look at Gus," was all she said. There in the very same chair the mirror showed us Gus, some sort of godson of Dad, who after a flood in his hometown came to live with us and had remained there in the somewhat ambiguous character of adoptive poor relation. Clara greeted him amiably with a wave of the hand, but he seemed busy, for the moment, with something like a radio tube and did not pay attention to her. Undoubtedly, the mirror people weren't going out of their way to be sociable. This must have wounded Clara's self-esteem, although she did not let it on.

Naturally, the idea of moving the mirror to the dining-room was hers. And so was its sequel: to bring the mirror near the big table, so we could all sit together for meals.

In spite of my mother's fears that the mirror people would run away or get annoyed because of the fuss, everything went fine. I must admit it was comforting to sit every day at the table and see so many familiar faces, although some of those from the other side were distant relatives, and others, due to their lengthy — although unintentional — absence, were almost strangers. There were about twenty of us sitting at the table every day, and even if their gestures and movements seemed more remote than ours and their meals a little washed-out, we generally gave the impression of being a large family that got along well.

At the boundary between the real table and the other one, on this side, sat Clara and her brother Julius. On the other side was Eulalia (1949), the second wife of Uncle Daniel, aloof and indolent in life, and now the most distant of anyone on the other side. Across from her sat my godfather Sylvester (1952), who even though he was not a blood relative was always a soul relation. I was sad to see that Sylvester had lost his ruddiness, for he now looked like a faded mannequin, although his full face seemed to suggest perfect health. This pallor did not suit the robust Asturian, who undoubtedly felt a bit ridiculous in these circumstances.

For a while we ate all together, without further incidents or problems. We mustn't forget Clara, however, who we had allowed to sit at the frontier between the two tables, the equator separating what was from what was not. Although we paid no attention to the situation, we should have. Compounding our regrettable oversight was the fact that lethargic Eulalia sat across from her so that one night, with the same cordiality with which she had addressed Gus, Clara asked Eulalia to pass the salad. Eulalia affected the haughty disdain of offended royalty as she passed the spectral salad bowl, filled with dull lettuce and grayish semitransparent tomatoes which Clara gobbled up, smiling mischievously at the novelty of it all. She watched us with the same defiance in her eyes that she had on the day she enrolled in a man's subject. There was no time to act. We just watched her grow pale, then her smile faded away until finally Clara collapsed against the mirror.

Once the funeral business was over and we sat back down at the table again, we saw that Clara had taken a place on the other side. She was between cousin Baltazar (1940) and a great-uncle whom we simply called "Ito."

This *fata par* dampened our conviviality somewhat. In a way, we felt betrayed; we felt that they had grievously abused our hospitality. However, we ended up divided over the question of who was really whose guest. It was also plain that our carelessness and

Clara's irrepressible inquisitiveness had contributed to the mishap. In fact, a short time later we realized that there wasn't a great deal of difference between what Clara did before and what she was doing now, and so we decided to overlook the incident and get on with things. Nevertheless, each day we became less and less sure about which side was life and which its reflection, and as one bad step leads to another, I ended up taking Clara's empty place.

I am now much closer to them. I can almost hear the distant rustle of the folding and unfolding of napkins, the slight clinking of glasses and cutlery, the movement of chairs. The fact is that I can't tell if these sounds come from them or from us. I'm obviously not worried about clearing that up. What really troubles me, though, is that Clara doesn't seem to behave properly, with either the solemnity or with the opacity owed to her new position; I don't know how to put it. Even worse, the problem is that I — more than anybody else in the family — may become the target of Clara's machinations, since we were always joined by a very special affection, perhaps because we were the same age and had shared the same children's games and the first anxieties of adolescence

As it happens, she is doing her best to get my attention, and ever since last Monday she has been waiting for me to slip up so she can pass me a pineapple this big, admittedly a little bleached-out, but just right for making juice and also a bit sour, just as she knows I like it.

———————

María Elena Llano (Cuba, 1936–) is a Cuban fiction writer and journalist. Her works include dramatic scripts for theater, television, and radio; short stories; poetry; criticism; and humor. Her short stories have been translated into several languages and are included in a number of anthologies.

The ghosts in this story were part of an extended family. In some cultures or societies the living revere, and sometimes fear, the spirits of their ancestors. The Judge in Stambovsky says the existence of the ghost in that case was a matter of 'local' knowledge; that the buyer, who was a resident of New York City could not be expected to know the folklore of the Village of Nyack. Should this characterization absolve an outsider of responsibility for knowing something about the beliefs of those with whom he deals? What about custom and usage of the trade? Or does this rule only apply when the beliefs are 'irrational' by Western standards and therefore unknowable?

———————

E. Duress

The doctrine of duress makes a contract void or voidable if it was entered as a consequence of physical force or improper threats (e.g., of physical, economic, or other harm) that "overcame" the "will" of the other party. In evaluating these issues, courts attempt to distinguish improper threats (e.g., "If you don't agree to this price, I will break your leg.") from "hard" bargaining (e.g., "I know this is a rare first edition of Corbin on Contracts and you need it to complete your collection of treatises on contract law. I will only sell it to you if you pay twice the price the rare books catalogue says it is worth.") If the threat is improper and the consequences to the victim are grave, then courts consider whether alternatives to the contract were available to the victim.

A victim of duress may not be able to use this doctrine to avoid the contract if the threat came from someone other than the party who is attempting to enforce the contract. The question of responsibility, or the lack of it, for coercive behavior that resulted in a contract is relevant to the claims of one who has already performed or given value under the terms of the contract. While responsibility probably should have been the issue discussed in *United States for the Use of the Trane Company v. Lorna Bond*, the doctrine constrained the court's discussion of the nature of the coercion. The constricted idea of responsibility embodied in this approach allows a party to a contract to benefit from coercion, so long as that party did not actively participate in or have actual knowledge of it.

This rationale is particularly troubling in the relatively common factual setting of *Trane Company*, where the creditor apparently insisted that the primary debtor, Albert Bond, obtain an additional commitment from his wife for the sole benefit of the creditor, without giving the wife anything in return. Isn't it reasonable for some women to refuse such a demand, and isn't it realistic to expect that some men will use the threat of physical injury to overcome their wives' refusals?

The *Restatement (Second)* allows a defense of duress by a third party only where there was actual physical compulsion (e.g., moving another person's hand to sign his or her name — is this a genuine possibility?) or where the party seeking to enforce the contract had reason to know of threats being made by a third party, did not act in good faith, or did not give value or rely on the contract. This rule allows creditors to be indifferent to the predictable consequences of their demands. Moreover, this rule, which distinguishes between physical force that "voids" a contract and threats that merely make a contract "voidable," is exemplary of "conceptualist" or "formalist" reasoning. The problem with a formal approach is that it produces a result that is unjust in light of the actual circumstances in a case. In this case, Lorna Bond's liability meant that her assets and future income would be subject to the debts of Albert Bond and his company.

Despite critiques of the *Restatement (Second)* approach, most courts continue to follow it. *See, e.g., Standard Finance v. Ellis*, 3 Haw. App. 614 (1983). The decision in *Trane Company v. Lorna Bond*, holding that threats of physical injury by a third party may sometimes make a contract void as a result of duress despite lack of specific knowledge by the other party, is unusual because it places the doctrine of duress in historical context and because of its willingness to recognize the role that violence may play in intimate relationships and the responsibility others may have when they unwittingly benefit from that violence.

What are the stories and assumptions about human motivation and interaction that underlie the third party duress issue and arguments? What assumptions about human motivation and interaction underlie the court's analysis in the following case?

———————

United States for the Use of the Trane Company v. Lorna D. Bond

Court of Appeals of Maryland
322 Md. 170, 586 A.2d 734 (1991)

ROBERT C. MURPHY, CHIEF JUDGE

This case has been certified to us by the United States District Court for the District of Columbia, pursuant to the Maryland Uniform Certification of Questions of Law Act,

Maryland Code (1974, 1989 Repl. Vol.), §§ 12-601–12-609 of the Courts and Judicial Proceedings Article.[1] The question of state law presented is "[w]hether a party whose consent to entering a contract is coerced may assert the defense of duress against a party who neither knew of nor participated in the infliction of the coercive acts."

I.

The statement of facts outlined by the federal district court in its certification order discloses that Mech-Con Corporation contracted with the United States in Maryland to perform certain work upon the heating and air-conditioning systems at the Walter Reed Army Medical Center in Washington, D.C. Mech-Con, as principal, and Albert Bond and his wife, Lorna Bond, as sureties, executed a payment bond to cover labor and materials expended by persons working on the project. Mech-Con and Albert Bond subsequently filed petitions in bankruptcy. When Mech-Con failed to comply with certain provisions of the contract, the United States, as plaintiff (for the use of The Trane Company), sued Lorna Bond as the sole defendant to recover on the payment bond which she had signed as surety. Lorna asserted the defense of duress, contending that she was not liable because Albert "physically threatened her and abused her to coerce her to sign a number of documents, including the payment bond, and would not answer her regarding their content." Lorna made no claim that Albert "actually picked up her hand and forced her to sign the contract"; nor did she claim that the plaintiff "knew of any coercive actions taken by defendant's husband." Lorna nevertheless maintains, in reliance upon our 1862 decision in *Central Bank v. Copeland*, 18 Md. 305, that the plaintiff could not enforce the surety agreement against her because, under Maryland law, a person whose consent to a contract is obtained by duress may assert that defense against the other contracting party, even though that party "neither took part in the infliction of duress nor had any knowledge of it."

The plaintiff's motion for summary judgment was opposed by Lorna, and remains pending. The federal district court, believing that "resolution of this motion raises an unsettled issue of Maryland law," has certified the question for our consideration.

II.

The United States contends that the defense of duress cannot be asserted by Lorna to avoid liability on the contract between them because the government was not involved in the infliction of the alleged duress and had no knowledge of it. It argues that the defense of duress is only applicable against the party exerting the duress. It acknowledges, however, that duress may in some instances render a contract absolutely void, and that in such circumstances even an innocent party may not recover on the contract. The government claims that the alleged duress in this case, as described in the certification order, was insufficient as a matter of law to render the contract void because Lorna was not physically forced to sign the contract. Absent such actual physical compulsion, the government maintains that the contract is not void, but is voidable by the victim only if the other contracting party did not rely to its detriment upon the party's assent to the contract. In

---

1. This section provides:

The Court of Appeals may answer questions of law certified to it by the Supreme Court of the United States, a Court of Appeals of the United States, a United States District Court, or the highest appellate court or intermediate appellate court of any other state when requested by the certifying court if there is involved in any proceeding before the certifying court a question of law of this State which may be determinative of the cause then pending in the certifying court and as to which it appears to the certifying court there is no controlling precedent in the Court of Appeals of this State.

other words, the plaintiff argues that where value is given by a contracting party in reliance on the making of the contract, and that party had no knowledge of, or took no part in the exertion of the claimed duress, then the contract is neither void, nor voidable by the alleged victim of the claimed duress. According to the government, nothing in *Central Bank v. Copeland, supra*, requires a different result.

Relying upon *Copeland*, Lorna contends that under Maryland law, duress renders a purported contract void from the beginning, and not merely voidable. She urges that cases in other jurisdictions which hold that the defense of duress cannot be asserted against an innocent contracting party are contrary to *Copeland* and thus are inapposite. Lorna argues that the determination of whether a contract is void turns on whether the duress completely prevented the mutual assent necessary for the formation of a contract, as where the duress forces a person to do an act that the person had no intention of doing, in which event there is no assent and therefore no contract. In making the determination whether she assented to the contract, Lorna suggests that the test is whether the duress exerted upon her amounts to the type of coercion which would make the agreement void, or whether, notwithstanding the coercion, there was an actual expression of assent to the contract. As to this, Lorna asserts that under *Copeland* "the person coerced into executing a contract can raise the defense of duress against a third party who neither participated in nor had knowledge of the coercion."

III.

In *Copeland*, a wife, together with her husband, executed a mortgage on property owned by the wife to secure a debt owed to the mortgagees by the husband. The mortgagees assigned the mortgage to the Central Bank which subsequently sought to sell the property to satisfy the husband's unpaid debt. The wife challenged the validity of the mortgage, claiming that as to her it was void because she lacked capacity to assent to it. In reviewing the evidence, the Court said that the wife

> had been, and was, at the time of executing the mortgage, much enfeebled in health, and suffering nervous and mental depression, caused in part by the harsh conduct of her husband in reference to the proposed transfer of her property, and that her mind was so distracted, confused and reckless, as to induce the belief on the part of her attending physician, that she was incapable of making a valid deed or contract.

Id. at 318.

The evidence further disclosed, the Court said, that the wife's execution of the mortgage was "preceded by personal menaces and threats of her husband to destroy the property by fire, if she did not execute it, and the fact that it was executed and acknowledged involuntarily, as a consequence, cannot be doubted." *Id.* at 318–19. The Court determined that the husband's resort "to measures thus violent and harsh, leads irresistibly to the conclusion, that her consent could not have been obtained otherwise." *Id.* at 319.

Further in its opinion, the Court said that, as to the wife, the validity of the mortgage depended upon the fact of its execution and acknowledgment by her "as her own free and voluntary act," but that her acknowledgment that it was her free and voluntary act was not conclusive. *Id.* at 318. Referring to the legislative enactment which prescribed the form of the acknowledgment, the Court said that it was intended "to guard the wife's title to property against the improper efforts of a husband to wrest it from her, and not to bar from judicial remedy, outrages, by which such an acknowledgment might be extorted." In light of this legislative purpose, the Court explained that a husband "who, by extreme harshness, compels a wife to execute a deed of her property against her will, and then, in the form prescribed by law for her protection, to sanction the wrong inflicted by acknowledging its involuntary execution to be voluntary and without fear, cannot, by reason of the mere formal acknowledgment, entitle himself, nor any one in whose interest such a wrong may be attempted, to set up, and claim upon the deed, as a valid conveyance." *Id.* at 319. In declining to enforce the mortgage against the wife, the court found that the duress exerted upon her by the husband was "so excessive as to subjugate and control the freedom of her will." *Id.*

In the course of its opinion, the Court engaged in the following general discourse of then existing Maryland law:

> The element of obligation upon which a contract may be enforced, springs primarily from the unrestrained mutual assent of the contracting parties, and where the assent of one to a contract is constrained and involuntary, he will not be held obligated or bound by it. A contract, the execution of which is induced by fraud, is void, and a stronger character cannot reasonably be assigned to one, the execution of which is obtained by duress. Artifice and force differ only as modes of obtaining the assent of a contracting party, and a contract to which one assents through imposition or overpowering intimidation, will be declared void, on an appeal to either a court of law or equity to enforce it. The question, whether one executes a contract or deed with a mind and will sufficiently free to make the act binding, is often difficult to determine, but for that purpose a court of equity, unrestrained by the more technical rules which govern courts of law in that respect, will consider all the circumstances from which rational inferences may be drawn, and will refuse its aid against one who, although apparently acting voluntarily, yet, in fact, appears to have executed a contract, with a mind so subdued by harshness, cruelty, extreme distress, or apprehensions short of legal duress, as to overpower and control the will.

Id. at 317–18.

In *Whitridge v. Barry*, 42 Md. 140 (1875), a wife alleged that she assigned her interest in an insurance policy under duress by her husband to satisfy certain of his debts. She claimed that she was "laboring under controlling duress, and had not that necessary freedom, in the exercise of her mental faculties, to make the act binding upon her." *Id.* at 152. The wife testified that she was "fearful of the consequences as to [the husband's] future course, if she failed to sign the paper, as he requested." *Id.* at 153. The Court found that because the wife was advised of the poor state of her husband's financial affairs, "was made familiar with his plans and schemes, and fully impressed, by his persistent importunities, with serious apprehension as to his condition," that there existed "such a pressure upon her ... [as] deprived [her] of that moral agency requisite to a binding act, in the conveyance of her policy, and that she ought not to be held responsible therefor." *Id.* at 152–53. The Court concluded that the wife executed the assignment "under duress and compulsion." *Id.* at 153. It held that while "not every degree of importunity ... is sufficient to invalidate an instrument transferring property; yet if it be such as to deprive the party executing it of her free agency; or such as she is too weak to resist, she ought not to be held responsible therefor." *Id.* at 153–54.

In *First National Bank v. Eccleston*, 48 Md. 145 (1878), a husband and wife executed a deed of trust of certain real estate owned by the wife to secure a debt due by the husband to the bank. Subsequently, the court ordered that the land be sold. The wife, following the husband's death, claimed that the deed was void "because she was forced to sign and acknowledge it by the threats, menaces and ill-treatment of her husband, which in her then weak and enfeebled condition of health, she was unable to resist." 48 Md. at 154.

Accepting the wife's testimony as worthy of credit, the Court held that the deed was void. It recounted the evidence as follows:

> [A]fter this deed had been prepared, the husband took it to his wife and demanded she should sign it without knowing its contents, telling her it was but a matter of form; that she was then near her confinement, in that condition of health and anxiety which required kindness and sympathy; that upon her expressing an unwillingness to sign without some knowledge of what the paper was, he enforced his demand from time to time with curses and oaths, and threats of personal violence, and even of her life, until by these means and the general violence and harshness of his conduct and temper towards her and in her presence, he overpowered her will and resistance; and that he then took her to the City of Washington, where she signed and acknowledged the deed before a notary public without knowing what it contained.

Id. at 160. Two judges dissented, stating that the majority carried the "supposed precedent [of Copeland] to a most dangerous extent." *Id.* at 163. The dissenting judges declared that the evidence was insufficient to vacate the deed "as having been obtained by threats and coercion." *Id.* at 167.

In *Brown v. Pierce*, 7 Wall. 205, an 1869 decision of the Supreme Court of the United States, a conveyance was held void as against an innocent third party who in good faith gave value where the person conveying title to the property was forced to do so under threats of death or violence. The Court said:

> Actual violence is not necessary to constitute duress ... because consent is the very essence of a contract, and, if there be compulsion, there is no actual consent, and moral compulsion, such as that produced by threats to take life or to inflict great bodily harm ... is everywhere regarded as sufficient, in law, to destroy free agency, without which there can be no contract.

7 Wall. at 214. *Accord Baker v. Morton*, 12 Wall. 150, 157–58 (1871).

In *Pierce*, the Supreme Court acknowledged that according to some cases and text writers, "it is only where the threats uttered excite fear of death, or of great bodily harm, or unlawful imprisonment, that a contract, so procured, can be avoided, because, as such courts and authors say, the person threatened with slight injury to the person, or with loss of property, ought to have sufficient resolution to resist such a threat, and to rely upon the law for his remedy." 7 Wall. at 215–16. The Court contrasted this rule with holdings in other cases, specifically mentioning *Copeland*, "that contracts procured by threats of battery to the person, or the destruction of property, may be avoided on the ground of duress, because in such a case there is nothing but the form of a contract, without the substance." *Id.*

Other commentators have noted that at common law, in some circumstances, a contract made under duress could be declared void by the coerced party, even though the duress was not exerted by the other contracting party and that party was unaware of it. 13 Williston on Contracts, § 1622A (3rd ed. 1957); J. Calamari and J. Perillo, Contracts, § 9-2 (3rd ed. 1987). This indeed was Blackstone's view where the contract was coerced by actual imprisonment or fear of loss of life or limb. *See* 1 Blackstone's Commentaries 131 (1897). More specifically, Blackstone stated that "fear of battery ... is no duress; neither is the fear of having one's house burned, or one's goods taken away or destroyed; because in these cases, should the threat be performed, a man may have satisfaction by recovering equivalent damages: but no suitable atonement can be made for the loss of life, or limb." *Id.* Thus, as Williston states at § 1622A, "where duress merely coerces assent it is treated ... like other equitable defenses and cannot be made the basis of attack or defense against one who has acquired legal title to money or tangible property or to a chose in action, for value and in good faith, whether he is the original grantee or promisee or is a purchaser from him."

In *Fairbanks v. Snow*, 13 N.E. 596, 598 (Mass. 1887), Justice Holmes, for the court, said that "if the defendant's hand had been forcibly taken and compelled to hold the pen and write her name, the signature would not have been her act, and if the signature had not been her act, for whatever reason, no contract would have been made, whether the plaintiff knew the facts or not." On the other hand, the court said that when "the so-called 'duress' consists only of threats, and does not go to the height of such bodily compulsion as turns the ostensible party into a mere machine, the contract is only voidable." *Id.* For other cases applying these principles, *see, e.g., Regenold v. Baby Fold, Inc.*, 369 N.E.2d 858, 867 (Ill. 1977); *McCoy v. James T. McMahon Const. Co.*, 216 S.W. 770, 771 (Mo. 1919); *Sheppard v. Frank & Seder*, 161 A. 304 (Pa.1932); *Standard Finance Co., Ltd. v. Ellis*, 657 P.2d 1056, 1061 (Haw. App. 1983). These cases, as well as the Restatement (Second) of Contracts §§ 174, 175 (1981), distinguish between duress by physical compulsion, which may render a contract void, and duress by threat, which renders a contract voidable by the victim except where the other party to the contract in good faith, and without reason to know of the duress, either gives value or relies materially on the contract.

As to when duress by physical compulsion prevents formation of a contract, § 174 of the *Restatement* provides: "If conduct that appears to be a manifestation of assent by a party who does not intend to engage in that conduct is physically compelled by duress, the conduct is not effective as a manifestation of assent."

Comment a to this section states that it applies "to those relatively rare situations in which actual physical force has been used to compel a party to appear to assent to a contract." The result, according to the comment, "is that there is no contract at all or a 'void contract' as distinguished from a voidable one." By way of illustration, the comment states that a void contract is one where the duress involves physical force in compelling the victim to sign the contract.

As to the distinction between void and voidable contracts, *comment* b to § 174 states that a victim of duress may be held to have ratified the contract if it is voidable, but not if it is void. The *comment* further states that a good faith purchaser, on the other hand, "may acquire good title to property if he takes it from one who obtained voidable title by duress but not if he takes it from one who obtained 'void title' by duress." The *comment* further states that it is immaterial under § 174 whether the duress is exercised by a party to the transaction or by a third person.

Section 175 of the *Restatement* addresses when duress by threats makes a contract voidable; it states:

(1) If a party's manifestation of assent is induced by an improper threat by the other party that leaves the victim no reasonable alternative, the contract is voidable by the victim.

(2) If a party's manifestation of assent is induced by one who is not a party to the transaction, the contract is voidable by the victim unless the other party to the transaction in good faith and without reason to know of the duress either gives value or relies materially on the transaction.

Comment a to this section states that the essence of this type of duress is inducement by an improper threat, expressed in words or inferred from words or other conduct. *Comment* b states that a threat, even if improper, does not amount to duress "if the victim has a reasonable alternative to succumbing and fails to take advantage of it." The *Comment* further states that where a threat is one of minor vexation only, toleration of the inconvenience involved may be a reasonable alternative (this being a mixed question of law and fact). *Comment* c states that in order to constitute duress, the improper threat must induce the making of the contract; the test is subjective and calls into question whether the threat actually induces assent on the part of the person claiming to be the victim of duress. As to this, the *comment* explains that all attendant circumstances must be considered, including such matters as the age, background, and relationship of the parties.

Comment e to § 175 states that if a party's assent has been induced by the duress of a third person, rather than that of the other party to the contract, the contract is nevertheless voidable by the victim, except where "the other party has, in good faith and without reason to know of the duress, given value or changes his position materially in reliance on the transaction." In this connection, *comment* e states that § 175 does not protect a party "to whom the duress is attributable under the law of agency."

IV.

In answering the certified question in this case, we consider the principles enunciated in *Copeland* and its progeny, all of which were decided between 1862 and 1878, as well as the later formulation outlined in the Restatement (Second) of Contracts, *supra*. In this regard, in *Food Fair Stores v. Joy*, 389 A.2d 874 (Md. 1978), we considered the contention that a release of civil liability of a store owner, signed by a defendant criminally accused of shoplifting in consideration of the entry of a *nolle prosequi*, was executed under duress. We there noted that the "early test," applied in *Copeland*, was whether execution of the document had been "induced by harshness and threats, and the exercise of an unwarrantable authority, so excessive as to subjugate and control the freedom of [the signatory's] will." We next referred to the definition of "duress," as outlined in § 492 of the first *Restatement of Contracts* (1932), under which courts placed primary emphasis, "on the effect of the wrongful act or threat upon the person claiming to have been ... coerced." 389 A.2d at 887. The controlling factor under the first *Restatement* formulation, we recognized, was the condition, at the time, of the mind of the person subjected to the alleged coercive measures — an essentially subjective test. *Id.* Thus, under § 492 of the first *Restatement*, the decisive question was "whether the person claiming duress entered the particular transaction in such fear as to preclude his exercise of free will and judgment." *Id.* We then observed that under the formulation of the second *Restatement*, there had been a "marked shift in emphasis from the subjective effect of a threat to the nature of the threat itself"; we noted that the earlier requirement of the first *Restatement* "that the threat aroused such fear as to preclude an exercise of 'free will and judgment'" was omitted in the *Restatement (Second) of Contracts* "'because of its vagueness and impracticability.'" *Id.* We concluded in *Food Fair Stores* that, without regard to which test was applied, the release was not the product of duress as a matter of law.

Nothing in *Copeland* or *Eccleston* adopted the principle that mere threats, if succumbed to by the victim, rendered a contract void without regard to innocent third parties who neither knew of nor participated in the infliction of the coercive acts. Rather, these early cases, without distinguishing between physical compulsion and threats of violence, turned on the Court's view of the intensity of the duress exerted upon the victim as it impacted on the victim's will to resist. There is no indication in these cases that the Court rejected the common law rule enunciated by Blackstone, which encompassed threats sufficient to place the victim in fear of actual imprisonment or loss of life or limb for failure to sign the contract.

Necessarily, the determination of duress is dependent upon the circumstances of each individual case. To the extent that the second *Restatement* suggests in § 174 that only physically applied force to directly compel the victim to execute the document will suffice to vitiate a contract as to innocent third parties, we reject such an inflexible rule. Rather, we think it is presently the law of Maryland that a contract may be held void where, in addition to actual physical compulsion, a threat of imminent physical violence is exerted upon the victim of such magnitude as to cause a reasonable person, in the circumstances, to fear loss of life, or serious physical injury, or actual imprisonment for refusal to sign the document. In other words, duress sufficient to render a contract void consists of the actual application of physical force that is sufficient to, and does, cause the person unwillingly to execute the document; as well as the threat of application of immediate physical force sufficient to place a person in the position of the signer in actual, reasonable, and imminent fear of death, serious personal injury, or actual imprisonment.

As earlier indicated, the certified facts before us indicate, without specificity, that Lorna was "physically threatened ... and abused" to coerce her signature as a surety on the payment bond. It is for the District Court, within the framework of the law of this State as set forth in this opinion, to apply that law to the facts of the case in determining whether, as to Lorna, the contract was void for duress. If the contract is not void, but at most only voidable, Lorna may not vitiate it as against an innocent third party.

Note

Many contemporary cases continue to apply a test for duress that asks whether the threat made is one that would be sufficient to "overcome the will" of the person alleging duress. If we think of this as a measure of the magnitude of the threat, then one could argue that the seriousness of the threat that will excuse performance has diminished over time. In some early cases, the test was one that measured the degree of coercion by the strength of will of a "constant and courageous man." Compare that to the test that the Maryland court applied in the case of Lorna Bond.

The following excerpt from *All God's Dangers: The Autobiography of Nate Shaw* is an oral history of the life of Ned Cobb, a member of the Alabama Sharecroppers Union. For more information about Ned Cobb, you can visit the website for the PBS video, The Rise and Fall of Jim Crow, http://www.pbs.org/wnet/jimcrow/stories_people_cobb.html.

The excerpt gives you some idea of the way farming was financed in the South at the turn of the century and the practices that were used by landowners to secure payment of the "furnishing" provided for sharecroppers. How does Nate Shaw describe the relationship between creditors and debtors? Is his view of creditors one that has no currency in contemporary society? Why do you suppose he would not agree to have his wife sign on his loans? What does it mean that Nate Shaw resisted pressure from creditors to add his wife as a signatory? Was there a more compelling reason that would explain why Albert Bond complied with demands that his wife sign on his surety bonds?

Theodore Rosengarten, All God's Dangers: The Life of Nate Shaw
(1974)

... Mr. Albee done come to the house and taken everything my daddy had in the way of stock and farm tools; taken my daddy's cows, his mule, harnesses, while my daddy was waitin in Beaufort jail for Mr. Jasper Clay to get him out. Moved away from Mr. Clay back down to Mr. Todd's place and scuffled around. Mr. Todd took my daddy up, furnished him land to work and helped him out, gave him the cost of a plow and money to buy a horse; my daddy worked that horse two years. And my daddy went — old man Clem Todd agreed for my daddy to get somebody else to furnish him but stay on his place. So my daddy went down there and got in with the Akers in Apafalya. And about the first or second year, Akers cleaned him up.

Ruel Akers' daddy was Dudley Akers. And Dudley Akers and his daddy, which was Ruel Akers' granddaddy, old Hy Akers — used to be a doctor accordin to the name they give him, Dr. Hy Akers — I know they didn't give my daddy a chance to redeem himself. They claimed they had a note against him and they took all he had. In those days, it was out of the knowledge of the colored man to understand that if you gave a man a note on everything you had, exactly how you was subject to the laws. Because the colored man wasn't educated to the laws for his use; they was a great, dark secret to him.

Akers took everything he had except goin in the house and gettin the house furnitures — they'd a got that if my stepmother had signed my daddy's note. Some of em ordered when they gived notes for furnishin, some of em wanted to go in the house and get that woman and have her sign it, too. Well, what was that for? I quickly learnt this: if you furnishes me any amount of money and I give you a note on what you want a note on as a security for the money you furnishin me, that aint enough to satisfy you, you want my wife to sign this note, too. And she come out and sign it — been that way ever since I was a little boy; have a Negro to sign a note, they goin to try to get that woman to stick her mark on that paper. That gets household, kitchen plunder and all. If I wanted supplies in the days I come along after I married my first wife, if I wanted to do any business with a white man for any part of furnishin, I didn't let her go on no notes; she stayed out of it because that would give em a chance to go in the house and get her stuff. O Lord, I have been through tribulations and trials in this world but nobody never has went in my house and got no house furnitures out of there.

Note — On Wife-Beating, Financing Practices, and Third Party Duress

In recommending passage of the Violence Against Women Act of 1994, the Senate Committee on the Judiciary found:

> Violence is the leading cause of injuries to women ages 15 to 44, more common than automobile accidents, muggings, and cancer deaths combined. As many as 4 million women a year are the victims of domestic violence.

S. Rep. No. 138, 103rd Cong., 1st Sess. (1993).

Following hearings in 1990, the Senate Committee concluded:

> Last year, 3 to 4 million women were abused by their husbands — a number greater than the women who were married. And 1.7 million Americans have at some time faced a spouse wielding a knife or a gun.

...

... These crimes have, for too long, been hidden "behind closed doors." The Nation must recognize, as a whole, that these crimes should be taken just as seriously as any other assault. In nineteenth century America, courts drew a curtain around the home, refusing to intervene in cases of spouse abuse. Some courts even sanctioned the "salutary restraint of domestic discipline" but applied the "rule of thumb" limiting "chastisement" to a stick no bigger than a man's thumb. Up until as late as 15 years ago, many jurisdictions refused to arrest and prosecute spouse abusers, even though a comparable assault on the street by a stranger would have led to a lengthy jail term.

A crime, not just a quarrel. The term "domestic violence" may sound tame, but the behavior it describes is far from gentle. Statistics present a chilling picture of just how serious—indeed even lethal—spouse abuse may be. Between 2,000 and 4,000 women die every year from abuse. Every day, four women are killed by their male partners and, in many of those cases, the homicides are the culmination of repeated, but lesser, abuse. One-third of all domestic violence cases, if reported, would be classified by police as felony rape, robbery, or aggravated assault; the remaining two-thirds involve bodily injury at least as serious as the injury inflicted in 90 percent of all robberies and aggravated assaults. Unlike other crimes, spouse abuse is "chronic" violence. It is persistent intimidation and repeated physical injury. Absent intervention "one can almost guarantee that the same woman will be assaulted again and again by the same man." One study showed that, over a 6-month period following a domestic violence incident, one-third of the victims will be subject to another rape, robbery, aggravated or simple assault. And this chronic abuse often escalates. One study showed that in over half of all murders of wives by their husbands, police had been called to the residence five times in the previous year to investigate a domestic violence complaint. Spouse abuse is serious, it is chronic, and it is a problem national in scope. The 3 to 4 million women abused each year are not located in any one area, among any one socio-economic group, or from any particular race, ethnic or religious group. The common perception that battering affects only poor, uneducated, and minority populations, is simply incorrect. No American community and no American family is immune.

... The good news is that, by 1990, significant legal reforms are in place in many States. To counteract the historical presumption against arrest in domestic violence cases, many States have enacted legislation that encourages arrest and some States even require or mandate arrest of spouse abusers. Battered women also have new legal tools: 48 States have what are known as "civil protection" orders—orders that require an abusing spouse to "stay away" and cease violent behavior. These orders are typically easier to obtain than a criminal conviction and their violation may amount to a misdemeanor or require arrest. The bad news, unfortunately, is that both despite and because of these welcome legal reforms, there remains much to be done. First, law reform has not always produced results. Arrests are now authorized, but arrest rates may be as low as 1 for every 100 domestic assaults. Communities may change their policies, but implementation does not follow. The Nation's capital is a case in point: while police protocols tell officers to arrest in domestic violence situations, one study showed that arrests were made in only 5 percent of all cases, and less than 15 percent of cases where the victim was bleeding from wounds. Isolated success stories—like a program in Duluth, Minnesota that drastically reduced domestic violence rates—have not been replicated with any consistency in other communities. And, finally, novel legal remedies, such as the civil protection order, may suffer because of "widespread lack of enforcement." Progress has also created a whole host of new problems. For example, increased authority to arrest and prosecute spouse abusers now strains already overextended police, prosecutors, and courts. In 1987, New York State police dealt with 73,000 family offenses, almost double the number only 3 years before. Arrests tripled in Connecticut after a mandatory arrest law was passed. Not surprisingly, courts and prosecutors are overwhelmed. In Baltimore, two prosecutors and two paralegals provided services to 7,000 victims in 2 years. In Chicago, a doubling of criminal cases swamped the two existing domestic violence courts and required the opening of a third court. The need for shelter further strains States' already limited resources. For a number of women, their only hope of escape is a shelter. But the need for such shelter is chronic and widespread: in one Philadelphia program, three out of every four women are turned away; in Seattle, there are 500 arrests for battering per month, but only 39 beds for battered women; in New York, one program turns away approximately 100 battered women per week. It is shameful, but this society has invested more in our pets than our wives: there are three times as many animal shelters as shelters harboring battered women.

S. Rep. No. 545, 101st Cong., 2nd Sess. (1990).

Financing institutions and other creditors routinely require men to "get their wives to sign" business loans and other business credit arrangements. Advocates for battered women have urged the financial industry to re-examine this practice, arguing that the institutions should do what they can to avoid the risk that some women will be coerced into assuming personal liability on loans or credit granted to their husbands' businesses. At least, advocates urge, financial institutions should have loan officers routinely meet separately with women and give them information about the loan, particularly information about whether the loan will be granted without their assuming liability. Even better, financial institutions should stop asking for spouse's participation. There is no commercial justification for the practice, other than the creditor wants the additional security obtained from requiring spouse to co-sign. Assuming the business and principal owner are approved for a loan or credit on the basis of their own credit-worthiness and willingness to pay, there is no reason for a creditor to require wives or husbands to co-sign except to get free access to additional assets as security. Some defenders of the practice have argued that it is necessary to protect creditors in case the debtor transfers assets to his wife or husband. Yet when a business loan or credit is given to an individual or closely held corporation, the risk to the creditor that the debtor will conceal assets by fraudulently conveying them to his or her spouse is no greater than that the debtor will fraudulently convey them to a friend or other family member (indeed, it is often easier to trace transfers to a spouse than to other recipients). Moreover, the spouse's assumption of personal liability for the loan is far more than mere protection against wrongful transfers of the debtor's assets — it gives the creditor access to additional, separate assets of the spouse. Given the extent of domestic violence, advocates for battered women argue, it is only reasonable, only responsible, for financial institutions to avoid unintentionally encouraging more violence.

The Equal Credit Opportunity Act ("ECOA"), which was enacted in 1974, provides in part, "[a] creditor shall not require the signature of an applicant's spouse or other person, other than a joint applicant, on a credit instrument if the applicant qualifies under the creditor's standards of credit worthiness for the amount and terms of the credit requested." The Official Comments clarify that "when an applicant requests individual credit, a creditor generally may not require the signature of another person unless the creditor has first determined that the applicant alone does not qualify for the credit requested." When an individual applicant fails to meet the creditor's standards "the creditor may require a cosigner, guarantor, endorser, or similar party-but cannot require that it be the spouse."

While the ECOA has been used successfully in some cases to penalize lenders who continued to require a woman to guarantee her spouse's personal debt against her will (*see, e.g., Anderson v. United Finance Co.*, 666 F.2d 1274, 1276–77 (9th Cir. 1982)), its overall effectiveness has been limited in various ways. Courts have interpreted the statute's cause of action to accrue when the note was signed rather than when a potential plaintiff became aware of the violation; this has led to many situations where a spouse could not enforce her affirmative claims under the statute because the applicable statute of limitation had run. *See, e.g., Farrell v. Bank of New Hampshire-Portsmouth*, 929 F.2d 871, 873–74 (1st Cir. 1991) (highlighting the distinction between the accrual date of ECOA from other anti-discrimination statutes). In addition, Regulation B provides a safe harbor provision protecting creditors from liability unless they participated in or had reasonable notice of the violation, which is usually limited to a creditor who took assignment of the debt after the violation.

In *Trane*, Lorna Bond made a duress argument, rather than using the ECOA statute, presumably because the statute does not clearly cover performance or payment bond sureties. The Supreme Court has recently granted certiorari in *Hawkins, et al. v. Community Bank of Raymore*, 2015 U.S. LEXIS 1635 (Mar. 2, 2015), to decide whether wives who are required to join in executing guaranties to a company in which their husbands have an interest are "applicants" within the ECOA and thus protected by its marital-status anti-discrimination provisions. Should this important principle have broader application?

The rule disallowing a defense of third-party duress encourages lending and commercial practices that require the assumption of liability by non-debtor spouses or spouses with no ownership interest in a business because the rule protects banks and other financial institutions from the harmful consequences of this practice. This practice was made illegal by the Equal Credit Opportunity Act, 15 U.S.C. §§ 1691 et. seq. but not in cases where the debtor spouse is not credit worthy. Wouldn't that be precisely the situation where abuse might occur? Because of this rule, creditors have little reason to reevaluate their practices. Because of this rule, moreover, lawyers are taught, and in turn teach others, that women must bear the consequences of male violence on their own.

During the 1760s, when Blackstone's Commentaries on the Laws of England were published, the defense of duress was limited to coercion by physical force or a threat of physical force. Since the mid 20th Century, courts have expanded the defense to include *economic duress*: coercion because of a threat of economic injury. This is now the most common form of duress alleged in litigated cases. The next case is an example.

Toni E. Sosnoff v. Jason D. Carter and Julia Vance Carter

New York Supreme Court, Appellate Division
165 A.D.2d 486, 568 N.Y.S.2d 43 (1991)

Sidney H. Asch, Justice

During the booming 1980s, sophisticated and successful real estate developer Jason Carter entered into a partnership agreement with a wealthy investor and money manager Martin Sosnoff to build a large residential project in Manhattan. Before their venture came to final fruition, the market crash of 1987 took place. Carter alleges that Sosnoff as a result repudiated his partnership obligations. Carter asserts that faced with financial ruin, he was forced to agree to a transformation of Sosnoff's equity investment into a debt and to give Sosnoff a note for this "debt." He contends this constituted economic duress by Sosnoff which presents a viable defense to this action on the note. Countering this legal argument, Sosnoff claims that Carter ratified the creditor-debtor relationship which replaced the partnership by continuing to make payment of interest and principal on the note, for almost two years after the parties entered the new agreement.

Wolfgang Friedmann has pointed out that "For the strong or lucky, freedom of trade just means freedom to expand; it means the survival of the fittest and the eventual destruction of the weak." (Law in a Changing Society 293 [2d ed., Col. U. Press]). To ameliorate the most harsh consequences of economic Darwinism, legal devices such as the Anti-Trust laws, doctrines of unconscionability and impossibility of performance were invented. Among such doctrines is that of economic duress. We are presented in this case with the question of whether or not "economic duress" should be invoked to excuse non-performance.

Plaintiff Toni Sosnoff seeks to recover the principal sum of $7,945,649.55 with interest and costs on a promissory note executed by defendant Jason D. Carter in the face amount of $9,145,648.55 and a written guarantee of payment executed by his wife, defendant Julia Vance Carter, both dated as of July 1, 1988. They were executed in favor of the plaintiff's husband, Martin T. Sosnoff, and thereafter assigned to her.

The defendants do not deny that the July, 1988 note is in default, but assert rather that they were forced to sign the initial November, 1987 note, and guarantee the then modified note and guarantee of July 1988 under economic duress.

In November, 1985, defendant Jason Carter, a real estate developer, who had participated in the rehabilitation of the Ritz Theater on West 48th Street, New York, and Martin Sosnoff, a wealthy investor and money manager who Carter had met through a common accounting firm signed two letter agreements. These provided for the $105,000,000 development of a residential high rise on West 48th Street in Manhattan, to be known as the Ritz Plaza. Their agreement provided that Sosnoff would contribute 80% of the necessary equity and collateral in exchange for 80% of the tax benefits and 50% of the profits.

Subsequently, from November of 1985 to October of 1987, Sosnoff complied with their partnership agreement, contributing his share of the capital and the necessary loan collateral. Defendant Carter, on behalf of the venture, contracted to acquire the real property from the owners of Momma Leone's Restaurant, as well as certain development rights from the owners of the contiguous O'Neill Theater.

Both Sosnoff and Carter obtained a letter of credit from Citibank, made a $1,875,000 payment toward the Momma Leone's acquisition in the agreed 80/20 ratio, took steps to satisfy zoning requirements and pursued various real estate tax benefit programs, including an application to the United States Department of Housing and Urban Development ("HUD") for a permanent mortgage of $90,000,000, signing the requisite application forms as equal principals.

Although the closing of the real estate and development rights was scheduled for November 19, 1987, and Marine Midland Bank officially approved a bridge loan, Martin Sosnoff announced, before then, that he would make no further capital contributions, and that he would not participate in the $20,000,000 bridge loan which he and defendant Carter had obtained from Marine Midland Bank to finance the closing.

Specifically, on November 3, 1987, the very date that Marine Midland approved the bridge loan, Sosnoff's attorney wrote to defendant Carter's attorney, notifying him that

"Martin Sosnoff does not intend to participate in a $20,000,000 proposed commitment from Marine Midland," and expressing "Martin Sosnoff's desire to terminate any relationship" with defendant Carter, requesting that defendant Carter repay "the amounts advanced or otherwise made available by [Sosnoff] or on his behalf...."

Despite a subsequent letter from defendant Carter's attorney urging Sosnoff to remedy his default, participate in the Marine Midland loan and otherwise fulfill his obligations defendants assert Sosnoff refused to honor his commitments.

Further, according to defendant Carter, Sosnoff's refusal to abide by the joint venture agreement threatened a complete collapse of the Ritz project. He claims that this turn of events brought him to the brink of financial ruin because without Sosnoff's participation, the Marine Midland bridge loan was lost and no other bank was willing to lend the $20,000,000 required to purchase the Momma Leone's property and to commence construction on the project. The failure to close would also have constituted a default under the Momma Leone's contract, resulting in the forfeiture of the $1,875,000 cash deposit, causing the owners of Momma Leone's to draw down the letter of credit from Citibank, by then amounting to approximately $4,675,000, on which defendant Carter was personally liable.

Moreover, according to defendants, the day after Sosnoff announced his abandonment of the project, Carter's attorney advised Sosnoff's attorney that Carter was "exploring other financial possibilities ... in an effort to ameliorate the mounting damage exposure."

Nevertheless, according to the defendants, despite Carter's attempt to find someone to replace Sosnoff in the venture shortly before the scheduled November 19, 1987 closing, and under the dire circumstances created by Sosnoff's breach, the best that Carter could do was to obtain a $8.5 million short-term loan from BRT Realty Trust at a high interest rate of 5% above prime, which, by its terms, only provided $4,000,000 toward the scheduled closing, leaving Carter several million dollars short.

Sosnoff then offered to lend the partnership an additional $1.7 million and to convert into cash the $4,675,000 letter of credit from Citibank. This would enable the Momma Leone acquisition to go forward. In exchange for this offer, Sosnoff demanded that the nearly $7.5 million in equity he had previously contributed to the partnership be converted to short-term debt; that defendant Carter release Sosnoff from his obligation to contribute 80% of the partnership's equity; that defendant Carter personally guarantee the combined $9.1 million obligation; and that his wife, defendant Julia Carter, guarantee $1.7 million of that.

The defendants allege that faced with the threat of default on the Momma Leone and O'Neill contracts, they unsuccessfully protested that Sosnoff's proposal amounted to nothing more than the unilateral repudiation of a partnership agreement, and hence were forced to capitulate.

Accordingly, on November 19, 1987, the date of the closing, defendant Carter signed a note on behalf of Sosnoff-Carter Associates, promising to pay Sosnoff $9,145,648.55, plus 9% interest in periodic installments over a 3-year period. Defendants Jason and Julia Carter signed personal guarantees in a release discharging Sosnoff from partnership-related claims, and Sosnoff signed a letter announcing his resignation from the partnership, thereby transforming himself from a major equity investor dependent upon uncertain profits into a lender with a smaller, secured and guaranteed loan.

Although Sosnoff and defendant Carter had signed the application for the mortgage as co-principals, Sosnoff nevertheless refused to consent to make certain minor modifications required by HUD before approving the mortgage, unless defendant Julia Carter agreed to increase her guaranty to cover the full amount of Sosnoff's "loan." Thus, according to defendants, faced with certain financial disaster if Sosnoff carried out his threat to block the HUD loan and thereby destroy the Ritz Plaza project, defendant Julia Carter signed the July, 1988 guaranty as demanded by Sosnoff.

Finally, defendants alleged that defendant Carter was forced to mortgage everything he owned, including his family's residence, in order to keep the Ritz Plaza project alive. Carter also made a number of principal and interest payments to Sosnoff so as to avoid triggering cross-default provisions in the loan agreements entered into by him until May of 1989 when he stopped making any payments on the Sosnoff note. Shortly thereafter, this action was commenced for summary judgment in lieu of complaint pursuant to CPLR 3213.

The Supreme Court denied plaintiff's motion for summary judgment, finding triable issues of fact with respect to the defendants' affirmative defense of economic duress, possible ratification, abatement of duress and as to whether the defendants had acted reasonably, under the circumstances, in disaffirming the note and guarantee, and also upon the court's *sua sponte* determination, that the note and guarantee which the plaintiff had sued upon were not "instruments for the payment of money only" within the meaning of CPLR 3213.

"The applicable law is clear.... [a] contract is voidable on the ground of duress when it is established that the party making the claim was forced to agree to it by means of a wrongful threat precluding the exercise of his free will [citations omitted]" (*Austin Instrument v. Loral Corp.*, 272 N.E.2d 533 (N.Y.)). A demonstration of economic duress can be made by proof that one party to a contract has threatened to breach the agreement by withholding performance unless the other party agrees to some further demand (*805 Third Ave. v. M.W. Realty*, 448 N.E.2d 445 (N.Y.); *Austin Instrument v. Loral Corp., supra.*). This showing of a threatened violation of the contractual obligations by itself ordinarily will not suffice. However, economic duress is established when the facts show that such breach will result in an irreparable injury or harm. (13 Williston on Contracts, [Third Edition], § 1617, pp. 704–705; *Austin Instrument v. Loral Corp.*, 272 N.E.2d at 539).

The defendants in opposition to the summary judgment motion herein, submitted sworn affidavits and exhibits, including agreements between the parties. These documents raise a substantial issue as to whether Sosnoff's repudiation of his partnership obligation just days before the scheduled acquisition of the Ritz Plaza site forced defendants to agree to the promissory note and guaranty, upon which, with the July 1988 modifications, plaintiff brings this action.

Plaintiff asserts that defendants failed to show that there were no other financial alternatives. The mere threat to breach an agreement will not constitute economic duress if the threatened party can obtain performance from some other "source of supply" and the ordinary remedy of an action for breach of contract would be adequate (*Austin Instrument v. Loral Corp.*, 272 N.E.2d at 539). While defendants did not demonstrate beyond doubt that they lacked other funding alternatives, they did show that they explored other financing possibilities, without success. Hence, in their opposition to the summary judgment motion, they met the burden of at least raising a viable issue.

Plaintiff also asserts defendants waived any defense of economic duress by their delay in repudiating the new agreements promptly and by ratifying the debt in making interest and principal payments. One who would disaffirm a contract made under duress must act promptly to repudiate it or be deemed to have elected to affirm (*Bethlehem Steel*

Corp. v. Solow, 405 N.Y.S.2d 80). However, where during the period of acquiescence or at the time of the alleged ratification the disaffirming party is still under the same continuing duress, he has no obligation to repudiate until the duress has ceased (13 Williston on Contracts, [Third Edition], Secs. 1624, 1627; Restatement of Contracts [Second] sec. 381; *Austin Instrument v. Loral Corp.*, 272 N.E.2d at 542). In fact, such continuing economic duress would even have the effect of tolling any period of limitations if the disaffirming party has commenced the action. (*see, Baratta v. Kozlowski*, 464 N.Y.S.2d 803, 807).

Defendant Carter detailed how the dire financial circumstances which compelled him to sign the note continued and alleged that he ceased payments on the note promptly at a point when he believed his other financial backers would not treat that action as a default on their obligations. Further, defendants made a showing, also in opposition, of their repeated protests as to the conduct of Sosnoff. These protests were inconsistent with any act of ratification and were some evidence of defendants' preservation of a claim of economic duress.

Upon a motion for summary judgment, the function of the reviewing court is not to determine the issues but only if there *are* issues. In fulfilling that function, the court must make all reasonable inferences in favor of the party opposing summary judgment. Applying these principles to the facts before us clearly compels the conclusion that the defendants demonstrated the existence of genuine triable issues of fact. Consequently the Supreme Court properly denied summary judgment. In view of this finding, the procedural issue of whether the July 1988 note and guaranty were "instruments for the payment of money only" within the meaning of CPLR 3213 is academic and we do not address it.

Accordingly, the order of the Supreme Court, New York County (Carol Huff, J.), entered on March 27, 1990, which denied plaintiff's motion pursuant to CPLR 3213 for summary judgment in lieu of complaint, should be affirmed, without costs or disbursements.

. . .

————————

F. Undue Influence

The doctrine of undue influence says that a contract entered as a consequence of "undue" persuasion of one party by the other is voidable by the victim. Most often, courts have applied the doctrine only where the person exerting influence was in one of several recognized categories of authority or control, including spouse or lover, lawyer, doctor, and religious or spiritual advisor. In addition, some states recognize situations of presumptive undue influence, the most common being where a person promises to bestow an inheritance on his or her lover. Compare the protection against seduction embodied in this rule with the protection against physical or psychological coercion reflected in the rule of third party duress. In many ways, protection against exploitation by clergy or lovers, as in the case that follows, is more rigorous than protection against physical and psychological abuse. The rule of presumptive undue influence by one who wields power because of a victim's faith or infatuation assumes that the victim will lose perspective, the capacity for critical thought or rational consideration of alternative choices. What other assumptions about human life and motivation underlie this rule? Who is benefited and who is burdened by these assumptions?

Nancy Ferguson v. John F. Jeanes

Court of Appeals of Washington
27 Wash. App. 558, 619 P.2d 369 (1980)

SOLIE M. RINGOLD, JUDGE

John F. Jeanes appeals a judgment rescinding his partnership agreement with Nancy Ferguson and quieting title to certain real property in Ferguson's name. We hold that rescission of a partnership agreement is a proper remedy where the partnership is created through undue influence, and we, therefore, affirm the trial court.

Nancy Ferguson filed a complaint against John F. Jeanes seeking to quiet title to certain real property commonly known as the Kirkview Apartments. Jeanes cross-complained for an accounting, claiming a partnership and one-half interest in the property. At a bench trial, the court concluded that a partnership in the purchase of the subject property was created between the parties through Jeanes' exercise of undue influence over Ferguson. The court rescinded the partnership agreement and quieted title to the property in Ferguson's name. The court awarded Jeanes a judgment for the amount of his capital contribution to the rescinded partnership plus interest.

The trial court's findings of fact reflect its acceptance of Ferguson's testimony and rejection of Jeanes' testimony. Jeanes assigns error to a finding that he lacked credibility on material issues, but he does not assign error to most of the findings. We, therefore, summarize the unchallenged findings and Ferguson's testimony to the extent they reveal the facts necessary to the resolution of this appeal.

Jeanes is a Christian Science Practitioner. He assists in the healing process and maintains a confidential and spiritual relationship with his patients. He met Ferguson in the autumn of 1972 at a time when Ferguson was seriously considering making a full commitment to Christian Science. They soon fell in love and began to seriously consider marriage. Several times a week during their relationship Ferguson obtained treatment from Jeanes. Ferguson testified that she exalted Practitioners in her mind and that she trusted Jeanes because of her affection for him and because of his role as a Practitioner.

In the spring of 1973, Ferguson asked Jeanes to assist her in locating an apartment house to be purchased by her alone. They located the property that is the subject matter of this lawsuit and he advised her concerning the terms of her offer. During the negotiations Jeanes began to encourage Ferguson to allow him to join her as a partner in the purchase and operation of the property in an effort to secure an agreement. Ferguson declined because of her desire for the security that sole ownership would provide. Jeanes became angry and told her that she was ungrateful for all that he had done for her. He stated that her refusal violated the tenets of Christian Science. He told her that she was incapable financially, intellectually and emotionally to purchase and operate the apartment house alone. She testified that his financial argument was the determining factor in her decision to accept him as an equal partner and designate him as a purchaser in the earnest money agreement.

Their offer was accepted but the deed was taken in Ferguson's name alone, at Jeanes' request, for what he said were tax reasons. He did not sign the mortgage, the promissory note and the second deed of trust. While Ferguson advanced nearly $13,000, Jeanes only provided $2,987.50. He stated he had other immediate obligations and would pay later. Other than one $500 payment, Jeanes never paid any more money for the down payment, loan or maintenance and operation expenses.

Whenever Ferguson urged Jeanes to equalize his contribution, he assured her that he would pay at a later date, frequently becoming angry with her for making such requests. On April 1, 1973, continuing to believe that he would pay his share, Ferguson gave Jeanes a written acknowledgment of his partnership interest in the apartment house. Because of their close relationship, Ferguson tolerated the delays and was confident that Jeanes would ultimately provide the money.

This close relationship continued for another 2 years but terminated in July 1975. The parties had brief contact in May 1976 when Ferguson refused to consider Jeanes' suggestion that he might help on an upcoming balloon payment. The next contact between the parties was in August 1977 when Jeanes attempted to secure a quitclaim deed from Ferguson. Ferguson then retained an attorney, who prepared an accounting between the parties and asked Jeanes to review it. Jeanes did not respond to that request. Subsequently, Ferguson proffered a sum of money to reimburse him for the monies he had advanced, but Jeanes did not respond to the accompanying letter nor cash the check. Ferguson continued to successfully operate the apartment building without assistance from Jeanes. She filed this action on March 26, 1978.

Substantial Evidence of Undue Influence

Jeanes assigns error to the trial court's finding of undue influence in the partnership agreement. He contends Ferguson freely and voluntarily decided that she did not have sufficient funds to make the purchase by herself.

The trial court entered several unchallenged findings of fact that are relevant to this issue. (1) Jeanes' performance as a Practitioner had immense influence upon Ferguson and caused her to repose in him an extraordinary amount of trust and confidence. (2) Jeanes' emotional and spiritual influence upon Ferguson made her particularly susceptible to his undue influence in all material dealings between them. (3) Jeanes exercised undue influence over Ferguson in persuading her to return a promissory note he had given her for a $3,900 loan. He brought to bear upon her all of the spiritual and highly charged emotional factors that dominated their relationship by asserting she had no right to the note because of all he had done for her. He told her it was contrary to the tenets of Christian Science to resist returning the note to him. (4) Jeanes used undue influence in persuading Ferguson to take out a loan to purchase hot water heaters for the apartment building and to obligate herself alone on that loan.

In *Pleuss v. Seattle*, 8 Wash. App. 133, 137, 504 P.2d 1191 (1972), we adopted the definition of undue influence found in the *Restatement of Contracts* § 497 (1932):

Where one party is under the domination of another, or by virtue of the relation between them is justified in assuming that the other party will not act in a manner inconsistent with his welfare, a transaction induced by unfair persuasion of the latter, is induced by undue influence and is voidable.

It is not enough that a person is susceptible to undue influence as a result of a confidential relationship. It is also not enough that influence is exerted upon that person. *Severson v. First Baptist Church of Everett*, 34 Wash. 2d 297, 208 P.2d 616 (1949). Persuasion is unfair (or influence is undue) only when it overcomes the will of another such that her own free agency is destroyed. *Binder v. Binder*, 50 Wash. 2d 142, 309 P.2d 1050 (1957). Undue influence must be proved by evidence that is clear, cogent, and convincing. *Tecklenburg v. Washington Gas & Electric Co.*, 40 Wash. 2d 141, 241 P.2d 1172 (1952).

The trial court's unchallenged findings of undue influence by Jeanes in two other transactions between the parties and the unchallenged findings that Ferguson was susceptible to undue influence and placed extraordinary trust in Jeanes must be taken as verities on appeal. *Pannell v. Thompson*, 91 Wash. 2d 591, 589 P.2d 1235 (1979). These facts and the evidence of similar intense spiritual and emotional pressure concerning the partnership agreement provide substantial evidence of undue influence in that transaction. Ferguson's testimony, believed by the trial court, was sufficient to prove by clear, cogent and convincing evidence that her free agency was destroyed when she decided she needed Jeanes' financial assistance and participation in the acquisition of the apartments.

Undue Influence as Basis for Rescission

Jeanes contends that any breach of his agreement to advance funds only permits the court to terminate the partnership and give the parties an accounting. He also argues that even if a finding of undue influence is made, it only permits the court to terminate the partnership and give the parties an accounting under the Uniform Partnership Act, RCW 25.04 (the Act). The Act is silent on the remedies for undue influence in the formation of the agreement. RCW 25.04.390, however, accepts the right to rescission for fraud and misrepresentation. RCW 25.04.050 provides that cases not governed by the Act are controlled by the rules of law and equity.

We hold that partnership agreements, like other contracts, are subject to rescission for undue influence. A partnership cannot be created without the voluntary consent of all alleged partners. *Beebe v. Allison*, 112 Wash. 145, 192 P. 17 (1920). Undue influence makes assent to the partnership involuntary, and unless the unduly influenced party elects to affirm the contract, the appropriate remedy is a rescission that places the parties in the position they were in prior to the invalid agreement. Severson v. First *Baptist Church of Everett, supra*, and *DeCoria v. Red's Trailer Mart, Inc.*, 5 Wash. App. 892, 491 P.2d 241 (1971). Professor Rowley, in his treatise, R. Rowley, Rowley on Partnership §39 at 753–54 (2d ed. 1960), discusses the right to rescission predicated on undue influence: "The usual ground of annulment of the [partnership] contract is fraud or misrepresentation, and mistake has also been held as a ground for rescission. Inadequacy of consideration and undue influence may warrant rescission...."

The Act does not bar rescission. RCW 25.04.390. Furthermore, only valid partnership agreements are subject to the rule that there is no cause of action between partners prior to an accounting. *Dulien Steel, Inc. v. Lampson R.R. Contractors, Inc.*, 12 Wash. App. 232, 529 P.2d 848 (1974). The trial court, therefore, properly invoked the equitable rules of rescission to place the parties in the position they were in prior to the invalid agreement. *DeCoria v. Red's Trailer Mart, Inc., supra*. RCW 25.04.050.

. . .

The judgment of the trial court is affirmed.

G. Unconscionability

The doctrine of unconscionability is a relatively new doctrine. Although courts had characterized some contracts or contract terms as "unconscionable" before the 1940s (most often as justification for refusing specific performance), the doctrine of unconscionability was first articulated as a general rule in drafts of the *Uniform Commercial Code*, written by Karl Llewellyn and circulated during the late 1940s and 1950s. Section 2-302(1) provides:

If the court as a matter of law finds the contract or any clause of the contract to have been unconscionable at the time it was made the court may refuse to enforce the contract, or it may enforce the remainder of the contract without the unconscionable clause, or it may so limit the application of any unconscionable clause as to avoid any unconscionable result.

Paragraph (2) of this section provides:

> When it is claimed or appears to the court that the contract or any clause thereof may be unconscionable the parties shall be afforded a reasonable opportunity to present evidence as to its commercial setting, purpose and effect to aid the court in making the determination.

This was an innovative doctrine, yet it has been widely embraced. The *Restatement (Second) of Contracts* § 208 echoes *U.C.C.* section 2-302, and numerous other statutes incorporate the concept of unconscionability, including some state unfair and deceptive trade practices acts. Karl Llewellyn explained that the doctrine of unconscionability needed to be explicit to allow courts to rule directly on matters that they have addressed surreptitiously in the past:

Frequently courts have adopted other lines of approach to th[e] problem of unfair surprise clauses. They have called upon the rule against trick ... have eviscerated the unfair clause by adverse construction, have manipulated the rules of offer and acceptance to keep the clauses out, or have knocked it out as contrary to public policy or the dominant essence of the contract.... But the cases have been uncertain in application ... and the diversity of reasoning has kept them from providing consistent and accessible lines of guidance for the draftsman or the court—a fact which has led to much unnecessary litigation.

Karl Llewellyn, *Selected Comments on Revised Sales Act* 24–25 (1948) (unpublished) (Karl Llewellyn Papers, Folder J.X.2.h, University of Chicago Law Library). The goal of legal realism is clearly evident in this explanation: judicial decision-making would be improved, Llewellyn and other legal realists argued, if courts articulated the true basis of their decisions and acknowledged important political and moral dimensions of judicial judgment.

Ora Lee Williams v. Walker-Thomas Furniture Company, William Thorne et al. v. Walker-Thomas Furniture Company

United States Court Of Appeals for The District of Columbia Circuit
350 F.2d 445 (1965)

J. Skelly Wright, Circuit Judge:

Appellee, Walker-Thomas Furniture Company, operates a retail furniture store in the District of Columbia. During the period from 1957 to 1962 each appellant in these cases purchased a number of household items from Walker-Thomas, for which payment was to be made in installments. The terms of each purchase were contained in a printed form contract which set forth the value of the purchased item and purported to lease the item to appellant for a stipulated monthly rent payment. The contract then provided, in substance, that title would remain in Walker-Thomas until the total of all the monthly payments made equaled the stated value of the item, at which time appellants could take title. In the event of a default in the payment of any monthly installment, Walker-Thomas could repossess the item.

The contract further provided that "the amount of each periodical installment payment to be made by [purchaser] to the Company under this present lease shall be inclusive of and not in addition to the amount of each installment payment to be made by [purchaser] under such prior leases, bills or accounts; and all payments now and hereafter made by [purchaser] shall be credited pro rata on all outstanding leases, bills and accounts due the Company by [purchaser] at the time each such payment is made." Emphasis added.) The effect of this rather obscure provision was to keep a balance due on every item purchased until the balance due on all items, whenever purchased, was liquidated. As a result, the debt incurred at the time of purchase of each item was secured by the right to repossess all the items previously purchased by the same purchaser, and each new item purchased automatically became subject to a security interest arising out of the previous dealings.

On May 12, 1962, appellant Thorne purchased an item described as a Daveno, three tables, and two lamps, having total stated value of $391.10. Shortly thereafter, he defaulted on his monthly payments and appellee sought to replevy all the items purchased since the first transaction in 1958. Similarly, on April 17, 1962, appellant Williams bought a stereo set of stated value of $514.95.[1] She too defaulted shortly thereafter, and appellee sought to replevy all the items purchased since December, 1957. The Court of General Sessions granted judgment for appellee. The District of Columbia Court of Appeals affirmed, and we granted appellants' motion for leave to appeal to this court.

Appellants' principal contention, rejected by both the trial and the appellate courts below, is that these contracts, or at least some of them, are unconscionable and, hence, not enforceable. In its opinion in *Williams v. Walker-Thomas Furniture Company*, 198 A.2d 914, 916 (D.C. Ct. App. 1964), the District of Columbia Court of Appeals explained its rejection of this contention as follows:

"Appellant's second argument presents a more serious question. The record reveals that prior to the last purchase appellant had reduced the balance in her account to $164. The last purchase, a stereo set, raised the balance due to $678. Significantly, at the time of this and the preceding purchases, appellee was aware of appellant's financial position. The reverse side of the stereo contract listed the name of appellant's social worker and her $218 monthly stipend from the government. Nevertheless, with full knowledge that appellant had to feed, clothe and support both herself and seven children on this amount, appellee sold her a $514 stereo set.

"We cannot condemn too strongly appellee's conduct. It raises serious questions of sharp practice and irresponsible business dealings. A review of the legislation in the District of Columbia affecting retail sales and the pertinent decisions of the highest court in this jurisdiction disclose, however, no ground upon which this court can declare the contracts in question contrary to public policy. We note that were the Maryland Retail Installment Sales Act, Art. 83 §§ 128–153, or its equivalent, in force in the District of Columbia, we could grant appellant appropriate relief. We think Congress should consider corrective legislation to protect the public from such exploitive contracts as were utilized in the case at bar."

We do not agree that the court lacked the power to refuse enforcement to contracts found to be unconscionable. In other jurisdictions, it has been held as a matter of common law that unconscionable contracts are not enforceable.[2] While no decision of this court

---

1. At the time of this purchase her account showed a balance of $164 still owing from her prior purchases. The total of all the purchases made over the years in question came to $1,800. The total payments amounted to $1,400.

2. Campbell Soup Co. v. Wentz, 8 Cir., 172 F.2d 80 (1948); Indianapolis Morris Plan Corporation v. Sparks, 132 Ind.App. 145, 172 N.E.2d 899 (1961); Henningen v. Bloomfield Motors, Inc., 32 N.J. 358, 161 A.2d 69, 84–96 (1960). *Cf.* 1 Corbin, Contracts § 128 (1963).

so holding has been found, the notion that an unconscionable bargain should not be given full enforcement is by no means novel. In *Scott v. United States*, 79 U.S. (12 Wall.) 443, 445, 20 L. Ed. 438 (1870), the Supreme Court stated: " ... If a contract be unreasonable and unconscionable, but not void for fraud, a court of law will give to the party who sues for its breach damages, not according to its letter, but only such as he is equitably entitled to. ..."[3]

Since we have never adopted or rejected such a rule,[4] the question here presented is actually one of first impression.

Congress has recently enacted the Uniform Commercial Code, which specifically provides that the court may refuse to enforce a contract which it finds to be unconscionable at the time it was made. 28 D.C.CODE § 2-302 (Supp. IV 1965). The enactment of this section, which occurred subsequent to the contracts here in suit, does not mean that the common law of the District of Columbia was otherwise at the time of enactment, nor does it preclude the court from adopting a similar rule in the exercise of its powers to develop the common law for the District of Columbia. In fact, in view of the absence of prior authority on the point, we consider the congressional adoption of § 2-302 persuasive authority for following the rationale of the cases from which the section is explicitly derived.[5] Accordingly, we hold that where the element of unconscionability is present at the time a contract is made, the contract should not be enforced.

Unconscionability has generally been recognized to include an absence of meaningful choice on the part of one of the parties together with contract terms which are unreasonably favorable to the other party.[6] Whether a meaningful choice is present in a particular case can only be determined by consideration of all the circumstances surrounding the transaction. In many cases the meaningfulness of the choice is negated by a gross inequality of bargaining power.[7] The manner in which the contract was entered is also relevant to

---

3. *See* Luing v. Peterson, 143 Minn. 6, 172 N.W. 692 (1919); Greer v. Tweed, N.Y.C.P., 13 Abb.Pr., N.S., 427 (1872); Schnell v. Nell, 18 Ind. 29 (1861); and *see generally* the discussion of the English authorities in Hume v. United States, 132 U.S. 406, 10 S.Ct. 134, 33 L.Ed. 393 (1889).

4. While some of the statements in the court's opinion in District of Columbia v. Harlan & Hollingsworth Co., 30 App.D.C. 270 (1908), may appear to reject the rule, in reaching its decision upholding the liquidated damages clause in that case the court considered the circumstances existing at the time the contract was made, See 30 App.D.C. at 279, and applied the usual rule on liquidated damages. *See* 5 Corbin, Contracts §§ 1054–1075 (1964); Note, 72 Yale L.J. 723, 746–755 (1963). *Compare* Jaeger v. O'Donoghue, 57 App.D.C. 191, 18 F.2d 1013 (1927).

5. *See* Comment, § 2-302, Uniform Commercial Code (1962). Compare Note, 45 Va. La. Rev. 583, 590 (1959), where it is predicted that the rule of § 2-302 will be followed by analogy in cases which involve contracts not specifically covered by the section. *Cf.* 1 State of New York Law Revision Commission, Report and Record Of Hearings on the Uniform Commercial Code 108–110 (1954) (remarks of Professor Llewellyn).

6. *See* Henningsen v. Bloomfield Motors, Inc., supra Note 2; Campbell Soup Co. v. Wentz, supra Note 2.

7. *See* Henningsen v. Bloomfield Motors, Inc., supra Note 2, 161 A.2d at 86, and authorities there cited. Inquiry into the relative bargaining power of the two parties is not an inquiry wholly divorced from the general question of unconscionability, since a one-sided bargain is itself evidence of the inequality of the bargaining parties. This fact was vaguely recognized in the common law doctrine of intrinsic fraud, that is, fraud which can be presumed from the grossly unfair nature of the terms of the contract. See the oft-quoted statement of Lord Hardwicke in Earl of Chesterfield v. Janssen, 28 Eng. Rep. 82, 100 (1751):

> " ... [Fraud] may be apparent from the intrinsic nature and subject of the bargain itself; such as no man in his senses and not under delusion would make. ..." And cf. Hume v. United States, supra Note 3, 132 U.S. at 413, 10 S. Ct. at 137, where the Court characterized the English cases as "cases in which one party took advantage of the other's ignorance of

this consideration. Did each party to the contract, considering his obvious education or lack of it, have a reasonable opportunity to understand the terms of the contract, or were the important terms hidden in a maze of fine print and minimized by deceptive sales practices? Ordinarily, one who signs an agreement without full knowledge of its terms might be held to assume the risk that he has entered a one-sided bargain.[8] But when a party of little bargaining power, and hence little real choice, signs a commercially unreasonable contract with little or no knowledge of its terms, it is hardly likely that his consent, or even an objective manifestation of his consent, was ever given to all the terms. In such a case the usual rule that the terms of the agreement are not to be questioned[9] should be abandoned and the court should consider whether the terms of the contract are so unfair that enforcement should be withheld.[10]

In determining reasonableness or fairness, the primary concern must be with the terms of the contract considered in light of the circumstances existing when the contract was made. The test is not simple, nor can it be mechanically applied. The terms are to be considered "in the light of the general commercial background and the commercial needs of the particular trade or case."[11] Corbin suggests the test as being whether the terms are "so extreme as to appear unconscionable according to the mores and business practices of the time and place." 1 Corbin, *op. cit.* Note 2.[12] We think this formulation correctly states the test to be applied in those cases where no meaningful choice was exercised upon entering the contract.

Because the trial court and the appellate court did not feel that enforcement could be refused, no findings were made on the possible unconscionability of the contracts in these cases. Since the record is not sufficient for our deciding the issue as a matter of law, the cases must be remanded to the trial court for further proceedings.

So ordered.

JOHN A. DANAHER, CIRCUIT JUDGE (DISSENTING):

The District of Columbia Court of Appeals obviously was as unhappy about the situation here presented as any of us can possibly be. Its opinion in the Williams case, quoted in the majority text, concludes: "We think Congress should consider corrective legislation to protect the public from such exploitive contracts as were utilized in the case at bar."

---

arithmetic to impose upon him, and the fraud was apparent from the face of the contracts." See also *Greer v. Tweed*, supra *Note 3*.

8. *See* Restatement, Contracts § 70 (1932); *Note*, 63 Harv. La. Rev. 494 (1950). See also Daley v. People's Building, Loan & Savings Ass'n, 59 N.E. 452, 453 (Mass. 1901), in which Mr. Justice Holmes, while sitting on the Supreme Judicial Court of Massachusetts, made this observation:

> " ... Courts are less and less disposed to interfere with parties making such contracts as they choose, so long as they interfere with no one's welfare but their own.... It will be understood that we are speaking of parties standing in an equal position where neither has any oppressive advantage or power ..."

9. This rule has never been without exception. In cases involving merely the transfer of unequal amounts of the same commodity, the courts have held the bargain unenforceable for the reason that "in such a case, it is clear, that the law cannot indulge in the presumption of equivalence between the consideration and the promise." 1 Williston, Contracts § 115 (3d ed. 1957).

10. See the general discussion of "Boiler-Plate Agreements" in Llewellyn, The Common Law Tradition 362–371 (1960).

11. Comment, Uniform Commercial Code § 2-307.

12. *See* Henningsen v. Bloomfield Motors, Inc., supra Note 2; Mandel v. Liebman, 100 N.E.2d 149 (N.Y. 1951). The traditional test as stated in Greer v. Tweed, supra Note 3, 13 Abb.Pr. N.S., at 429, is "such as no man in his senses and not under delusion would make on the one hand, and as no honest or fair man would accept, on the other."

My view is thus summed up by an able court which made no finding that there had actually been sharp practice. Rather the appellant seems to have known precisely where she stood.

There are many aspects of public policy here involved. What is a luxury to some may seem an outright necessity to others. Is public oversight to be required of the expenditures of relief funds? A washing machine, e.g., in the hands of a relief client might become a fruitful source of income. Many relief clients may well need credit, and certain business establishments will take long chances on the sale of items, expecting their pricing policies will afford a degree of protection commensurate with the risk. Perhaps a remedy when necessary will be found within the provisions of the "Loan Shark" law, D.C.Code §§ 26-601 et seq. (1961).

I mention such matters only to emphasize the desirability of a cautious approach to any such problem, particularly since the law for so long has allowed parties such great latitude in making their own contracts. I dare say there must annually be thousands upon thousands of installment credit transactions in this jurisdiction, and one can only speculate as to the effect the decision in these cases will have.[1]

I join the District of Columbia Court of Appeals in its disposition of the issues.

The Square Deal Furniture Company

Deborah Waire Post

Every time I teach *Williams v. Walker-Thomas*, I am transported back in time to my own childhood. My observation of commercial relationships at that time, my experiences as a poor black person living among other working class white and black families on an integrated street in a small city, bear no relation at all to the language of the lower court decision or the dissent on appeal. Nor do they have a strong resemblance to the relationships described by Judge Skelly Wright in his decision. I did not experience retail sales as impersonal or arm's length transactions. And I certainly did not view my parents as un-sophisticated purchasers. My parents were poor, not stupid—and like Ora Williams they dealt regularly with a person from a company like Walker-Thomas. I am pretty sure the extension of credit to my parents had nothing to do with income, assets, debts, or prior credit history. It had a lot to do with the personal relationship between them and the salesman from the Square Deal Furniture Company.

Mrs. Williams was a good credit risk because she had a personal relationship with Walker-Thomas and its agents. There is a lot less risk of default in a personal relationship. Imagine going through a cafeteria line and finding you are a little short of cash. The cashier smiles and lets you take the cup of coffee anyway. You probably will take extra care to stop by and pay for that coffee the next day. You probably would do it even if you knew that the cashier couldn't remember which of the several dozen people he had seen the day before had been given credit. Would you hesitate to take a soda from a soda machine if the machine were out of order and dispensed soda without accepting coins? Would you mail the telephone company the change you find in the coin return?

The representative of the Square Deal Furniture Store was a weekly visitor to our house. In retrospect, I am sure this had something to do with the timing of my parents' weekly

---

1. However, the provision ultimately may be applied or in what circumstances, D.C. Code § 28-2-301 (Supp. IV, 1965) did not become effective until January 1, 1965.

paychecks. When he came, the salesman sat at the kitchen table and drank coffee with my Dad. He talked about lots of things besides the purchases and the payments my parents made. From where we sat as children, he seemed like a family friend. He listened to my parents when they explained they couldn't make a payment that week but would double up the next week. He sympathized when someone got sick. And over the years, he sold us a lot of merchandise. I have vivid memories of the white oxford shirts and plaid skirts we got to start school one year and the "french provincial" sofa, coffee table, and end tables that spruced up our living room for a couple of weeks before they showed signs of premature aging.

The furniture was shoddy, the clothes were fine, but that isn't the point. The point is the relationship that you develop with someone who is given the privileged status of "friend." You pay unless there is a catastrophe—an illness or loss of employment or something like that. And if you can't pay, you return what you did not pay for. But you certainly wouldn't expect someone to show up at your house with a truck and remove everything you had ever purchased.

In contract law, lawyers and judges talk as if the expectations individuals have of one another are created by the pieces of paper they sign. The Walker-Thomas Furniture Company did violence to Mrs. Williams and to the people with whom it dealt on a regular basis. It did violence by charging too much; it did violence by pressuring people to buy more than they could afford; it did violence by threatening harm; it did violence by disregarding friendships. There was bargaining. It was "business." But there was also trust. A salesperson who knows who you are and what you have to do to survive is not going to take more than you can afford to give. And in return, for years at a time, you faithfully make payments that amount to two, three, or even thirty times the market value of the goods you buy. You pay because you can get it on credit and because he will wait to be paid.

These sales are not entirely "arms-length" nor are they completely self-interested. They are based on personal friendship and they depend on personal loyalty. The trial court in Williams called the cross collateralization clause a "sharp practice." Skelly Wright talked about an absence of meaningful choice. But the key to the decision in Williams is surprise. I might even go so far as to call it betrayal.

James Alan McPherson, A Loaf of Bread

(1977)

It was one of those obscene situations, pedestrian to most people, but invested with meaning for a few poor folk whose lives are usually spent outside the imaginations of their fellow citizens. A grocer named Harold Green was caught red-handed selling to one group of people the very same goods he sold at lower prices at similar outlets in better neighborhoods. He had been doing this for many years, and at first he could not understand the outrage heaped upon him. He acted only from habit, he insisted, and had nothing personal against the people whom he served. They were his neighbors. Many of them he had carried on the cuff during hard times. Yet, through some mysterious access to a television station, the poor folk were now empowered to make grand denunciations of the grocer. Green's children now saw their father's business being picketed on the Monday evening news.

No one could question the fact that the grocer had been overcharging the people. On the news even the reporter grimaced distastefully while reading the statistics. His expression said, "It is my job to report the news, but sometimes even I must disassociate myself from it to protect my honor." This, at least, was the impression the grocer's children seemed to bring away from the television. Their father's name had not been mentioned, but there was a close-up of his store with angry black people and a few outraged whites marching in groups of three in front of it. There was also a close-up of his name. After seeing this, they were in no mood to watch cartoons. At the dinner table, disturbed by his children's silence, Harold Green felt compelled to say, "I am not a dishonest man." Then he felt ashamed. The children, a boy and his older sister, immediately left the table, leaving Green alone with his wife. "Ruth, I am not dishonest," he repeated to her.

. . .

"One day this week," she told her husband, "you will give free, for eight hours, anything your customers come in to buy. There will be no publicity, except what they spread by word of mouth. No matter what they say to you, no matter what they take, you will remain silent." She stared deeply into him for what she knew was there. "If you refuse, you have seen the last of your children and myself."

Her husband grunted. Then he leaned toward her. "I will not knuckle under," he said. "I will *not* give!"

"We shall see," his wife told him.

. . .

As for the grocer, from the evening of the television interview he had begun to make plans. Unknown to his wife, he cloistered himself several times with his brother-in-law, an insurance salesman, and plotted a course. He had no intention of tossing steaks to the crowd. "And why should I, Tommy?" he asked his wife's brother, a lean, bald-headed man named Thomas. "I don't cheat anyone. I have never cheated anyone. The businesses I run are always on the up-and-up. So why should I pay?"

"Quite so," the brother-in-law said, chewing an unlit cigarillo. "The world has gone crazy. Next they will say that people in my business are responsible for prolonging life. I have found that people who refuse to believe in death refuse also to believe in the harshness of life. I sell well by saying that death is a long happiness. I show people the realities of life and compare this to a funeral with dignity, *and* the promise of a bundle for every loved one salted away. When they look around hard at life, they usually buy."

"So?" asked Green. Thomas was a college graduate with a penchant for philosophy.

"So," Thomas answered. "You must fight to show these people the reality of both your situation and theirs. How would it be if you visited one of their meetings and chalked out, on a blackboard, the dollars and cents of your operation? Explain your overhead, your security fees, all the additional expenses. If you treat them with respect, they might understand."

Green frowned. "That I would never do," he said. "It would be admission of a certain guilt."

The brother-in-law smiled, but only with one corner of his mouth. "Then you have something to feel guilty about?" he asked.

The grocer frowned at him. "*Nothing!*" he said with great emphasis.

"So?" Thomas said.

The first meeting between the grocer and his brother-in-law took place on Thursday, in a crowded barroom.

At a second meeting, in a luncheonette, it was agreed that the grocer should speak privately with the leader of the group, Nelson Reed. The meeting at which this was agreed took place on Friday afternoon. After accepting this advice from Thomas, the grocer resigned himself to explain to Reed, in as finite detail as possible, the economic structure of his operation. He vowed to suppress no information. He would explain everything: inventories, markups, sale items, inflation, balance sheets, specialty items, overhead, and that mysterious item called profit. This last item, promising to be the most difficult to explain, Green and his brother-in-law debated over for several hours. They agreed first of all that a man should not work for free, then they agreed that it was unethical to ruthlessly exploit. From these parameters, they staked out an area between fifteen and forty percent, and agreed that someplace between these two borders lay an amount of return that could be called fair. This was easy, but then Thomas introduced the factor of circumstance. He questioned whether the fact that one serviced a risky area justified the earning of profits closer to the forty-percent edge of the scale. Green was unsure. Thomas smiled. "Here is a case that will point out an analogy," he said, licking a cigarillo. "I read in the papers that a family wants to sell an electric stove. I call the home and the man says fifty dollars. I ask to come out and inspect the merchandise. When I arrive I see they are poor, have already bought a new stove that is connected, and are selling the old one for fifty dollars because they want it out of the place. The electric stove is in good condition, worth much more than fifty. But because I see what I see I offer forty-five."

Green, for some reason, wrote down this figure on the back of the sales slip for the coffee they were drinking.

The brother-in-law smiled. He chewed his cigarillo. "The man agrees to take forty-five dollars, saying he has had no other calls. I look at the stove again and see a spot of rust. I say I will give him forty dollars. He agrees to this, on condition that I myself haul it away. I say I will haul it away if he comes down to thirty. You, of course, see where I am going."

The grocer nodded. "The circumstances of his situation, his need to get rid of the stove quickly, placed him a position where he has little room to bargain?"

"Yes," Thomas answered. "So? Is it ethical, Harry?"

Harold Green frowned. He had never liked his brother-in-law, and now he thought the insurance agent was being crafty. "But," he answered, "this man does not *have* to sell! It is his choice whether to wait for other calls. It is not the fault of the buyer that the seller is in a hurry. It is the right of the buyer to get what he wants at the lowest price possible. That is the rule. That has *always* been the rule. And the reverse of it applies to the seller as well."

"Yes," Thomas said, sipping coffee from the Styrofoam cup. "But suppose that in addition to his hurry to sell, the owner was also of a weak soul. There are, after all, many such people." He smiled. "Suppose he placed no value on the money?"

"Then," Green answered, "your example is academic. Here we are not talking about real life. One man lives by the code, one man does not. Who is there free enough to make a judgment?" He laughed. "Now you see," he told his brother-in-law. "Much more than a few dollars are at stake. If this one buyer is to be condemned, then so are most people in the history of the world. An examination of history provides the only answer to your question. This code will be here tomorrow, long after the ones who do not honor it are not."

They argued fiercely late into the afternoon, the brother-in-law leaning heavily on his readings. When they parted, a little before five o'clock, nothing had been resolved.

Neither was much resolved during the meeting between Green and Nelson Reed. Reached at home by the grocer in the early evening, the leader of the group spoke coldly at first, but consented finally to meet his adversary at a nearby drugstore for coffee and a talk. They met at the lunch counter, shook hands awkwardly, and sat for a few minutes discussing the weather. Then the grocer pulled two gray ledgers from his briefcase. "You have for years come into my place," he told the man. "In my memory I have always treated you well. Now our relationship has come to this." He slid the books along the counter until they touched Nelson Reed's arm.

Reed opened the top book and flipped the thick green pages with his thumb. He did not examine the figures. "All I know," he said, "is over at your place a can of soup cost me fifty-five cents, and two miles away at your other store for white folks you chargin' thirty-nine cents." He said this with the calm authority of an outraged soul. A quality of condescension tinged with pity crept into his gaze.

The grocer drummed his fingers on the counter top. He twisted his head and looked away, toward shelves containing cosmetics, laxatives, toothpaste. His eyes lingered on a poster of a woman's apple-red lips and milk-white teeth. The rest of the face was missing.

"Ain't no use to hide," Nelson Reed said, as to a child. "*I* know you wrong, *you* know you wrong, and before I finish, *everybody in this city* g'on know you wrong...."

"Before *God*!" Green exclaimed, looking squarely into the face of Nelson Reed. "Before God!" he said again. "*I am not an evil man*!" These last words sounded more like a moan as he tightened the muscles in his throat to lower the sound of his voice. He tossed his left shoulder as if adjusting the sleeve of his coat, or as if throwing of some unwanted weight. Then he peered along the counter top. No one was watching. At the end of the counter the waitress was scrubbing the coffee urn. "Look at these figures, please," he said to Reed.

The man did not drop his gaze. His eyes remained fixed on the grocer's face.

"All right," Green said. "Don't look. I'll tell you what is in these books, believe me if you want. I work twelve hours a day, one day off per week, running my business in three stores. I am not a wealthy person. In one place, in the area you call white, I get by barely by smiling lustily at old ladies, stocking gourmet stuff on the chance I will build a reputation as a quality store. The two clerks there cheat me; there is nothing I can do. In this business you must be friendly with everybody. The second place is on the other side of town, in a neighborhood as poor as this one. I get out there seldom. The profits are not worth the gas. I use the loss there as a write-off against some other properties," he paused.

... "In this area I will admit I make a profit, but it is not so much as you think. But I do not make a profit here because the people are black. I make a profit because a profit is here to be made. I invest more here in window bars, theft losses, insurance, spoilage; I deserve to make more here than at other places." He looked, almost imploringly, at the man seated next to him. "You don't accept this as the right of a man in business?"

Reed grunted. "Did the bear shit in the woods?" he said.

Again Green laughed. He gulped his coffee awkwardly, as if eager to go. Yet his motions slowed once he had set his coffee cup down on the blue plastic saucer. "Place yourself in *my* situation," he said, his voice high and tentative. "If *you* were running my store in this neighborhood, what would be *your* position? Say on a profit scale of fifteen to forty percent, at what point in between would you draw the line?"

Nelson Reed thought. He sipped his coffee and seemed to chew the liquid. "Fifteen to forty?" he repeated.

"Yes."

"I'm a church goin' man," he said. "Closer to fifteen than to forty."

"How close?"

Nelson Reed thought. "In church you tithe ten percent."

"In restaurants you tip fifteen," the grocer said quickly.

"All right," Reed said. "Over fifteen."

"How much over?"

Nelson Reed thought.

"Twenty, thirty, thirty-five?" Green chanted, leaning closer to Reed.

Still the man thought.

"Forty? Maybe even forty-five or fifty?" the grocer breathed in Reed's ear. "In the supermarkets, you know, they have more subtle ways of accomplishing such feats."

Reed slapped his coffee cup with the back of his right hand. The brown liquid swirled across the counter top, wetting the books. "*Damn this!*" he shouted.

Startled, Green rose from his stool.

Nelson Reed was trembling. "I ain't *you*," he said in a deep baritone. "I ain't the *supermarket* neither. All I is is a poor man that works *too* hard to see his pay slip through his fingers like rainwater. All I know is you done *cheat* me, you done *cheat* everybody in the neighborhood, and we organized now to get some of it *back*!" Then he stood and faced the grocer. "My daddy sharecropped down in Mississippi and bought in the company store. He owed them twenty-three years when he died. I paid off five of them years and then run away to up here. Now, I'm a deacon in the Baptist church. I raised my kids the way my daddy raise me and don't bother nobody. Now come to find out, after all my runnin', they done lift that *same company store* up out of Mississippi and slip it down on us here! Well, my daddy was a *fighter*, and if he hadn't owed all them years he would of raise him some hell. Me, I'm steady my daddy's child, plus I got seniority in my union. I'm a free man. Buddy, don't you know *I'm gonna raise me some hell*!"

Harold Green reached for a paper napkin to sop the coffee soaking into his books.

Nelson Reed threw a dollar on top of the books and walked away.

"I *will not* do it!" Harold Green said to his wife that same evening. They were in the bathroom of their home. Bending over the face bowl, she was washing her hair with a towel draped around her neck. The grocer stood by the door, looking in at her. "I will not bankrupt myself tomorrow," he said.

"I've been thinking about it, too," Ruth Green said, shaking her wet hair. "You'll do it, Harry."

"Why should I?" he asked. "You won't leave. You know it was a bluff. I've waited this long for you to calm down. Tomorrow is Saturday. This week has been a hard one. Tonight let's be realistic."

"Of course you'll do it," Ruth Green said. She said it the way she would say "Have some toast." She said, "You'll do it because you want to see your children grow up."

"And for what other reason?" he asked.

She pulled the towel tighter around her neck. "Because you are at heart a moral man."

He grinned painfully.

. . .

All night the grocer thought about this.

Nelson Reed also slept little that Friday night. When he returned home from the drugstore, he reported to his wife as much of the conversation as he could remember. At first he had joked about the exchange between himself and the grocer, but as more details returned to his conscious mind he grew solemn and then bitter. "He ask me to put myself in *his* place," Reed told his wife. "Can you imagine that kind of gumption? I never cheated nobody in my life. All my life I have lived on Bible principles. I am a deacon in the church. I have work all my life for other folks and I don't even own the house I live in." He paced up and down the kitchen, his big arms flapping loosely at his sides. Betty Reed sat at the table, watching. "This here's a low-down, ass-kicking world," he said. "I swear to God it is. All my life I have lived on principle and I ain't got a dime in the bank. Betty," he turned suddenly toward her, "don't you think I'm a fool?"

....

The grocer opened later than usual this Saturday morning, but still it was early enough to make him one of the first walkers in the neighborhood. He parked his car one block from the store and strolled to work. There were no birds singing. The sky in this area was not blue. It was smog-smutted and gray, seeming on the verge of a light rain. The street, as always, was littered with cans, papers, bits of broken glass. As always the garbage cans overflowed. The morning breeze plastered a sheet of newspaper playfully around the sides of a rusted garbage can. For some reason, using his right foot, he loosened the paper and stood watching it slide into the street and down the block. The movement made him feel good. He whistled while unlocking the bars shielding the windows and door of his store. When he had unlocked the main door he stepped in quickly and threw a switch to the right of the jamb, before the shrill sound of the alarm could shatter his mood. Then he switched on the lights. Everything was as it had been the night before. He had already telephoned his two employees and given them the day off. He busied himself doing the usual things—hauling milk and vegetables from the cooler, putting cash in the till—not thinking about the silence of his wife, or the look in her eyes, only an hour before when he left home. He had determined, at some point while driving through the city, that today it would be business as usual. But he expected very few customers.

The first customer of the day was Mrs. Nelson Reed. She came in around nine-thirty a.m. and wandered about the store. He watched her from the checkout counter. She seemed uncertain of what she wanted to buy. She kept glancing at him down the center aisle. His suspicions aroused, he said finally, "Yes, may I help you, Mrs. Reed?" His words caused her to jerk, as if some devious thought had been perceived going through her mind. She reached over quickly and lifted a loaf of whole wheat bread from the rack and walked with it to the counter. She looked at him and smiled. The smile was a broad, shy one, that rare kind of smile one sees on virgin girls when they first confess love to themselves. Betty Reed was a woman of about forty-five. For some reason he could not comprehend, this gesture touched him. When she pulled a dollar from her purse and laid it on the counter, an impulse, from no place he could locate with his mind, seized control of his tongue. "Free," he told Betty Reed. She paused, then pushed the dollar toward him with a firm and determined thrust of her arm. "Free," he heard himself saying strongly, his right palm spread and meeting her thrust with absolute force. She clutched the loaf of bread and walked out of his store.

The next customer, a little girl, arriving well after ten-thirty a.m., selected a candy bar from the rack beside the counter. "Free," Green said cheerfully. The little girl left the candy on the counter and ran out of the store.

...

He felt good about the entire world....

At eleven twenty-five a.m. the pickets arrived.

Two dozen people, men and women, young and old, crowded the pavement in front of his store. Their signs, placards, and voices denounced him as a parasite. The grocer laughed inside himself. He felt lighthearted and wild, like a man drugged. He rushed to the meat counter and pulled a long roll of brown wrapping paper from the rack, tearing it neatly with a quick shift of his body resembling a dance step practiced fervently in his youth. He laid the paper on the chopping block and with the black-inked, felt-tipped marker scrawled, in giant letters, the word FREE. This he took to the window and pasted in place with many strands of Scotch tape. He was laughing wildly. "Free!" he shouted from behind the brown paper. "Free! Free! Free! Free! Free!" He rushed to the door, pushed his head out, and screamed to the confused crowd, "*Free!*" Then he ran back to the counter and stood behind it, like a soldier at attention.

They came in slowly.

Nelson Reed entered first, working his right foot across the dirty tile as if tracking a squiggling worm. The others followed: Lloyd Dukes dragging a placard, Mr. and Mrs. Tyrone Brown, Stanley Harper walking with his fists clenched, Lester Jones with three of his children, Nat Lucas looking sheepish and detached, a clutch of winos, several bashful nuns, ironic-smiling teenagers and a few students. Bringing up the rear was a bearded social scientist holding a tape recorder to his chest. "Free!" the grocer screamed. He threw up his arms in a gesture that embraced, or dismissed, the entire store. "*All free!*" he shouted. He was grinning with the grace of a madman.

. . .

By twelve-ten p.m. the grocer was leaning against the counter, trying to make his mind slow down. Not a man given to drink during work hours, he nonetheless took a swallow from a bottle of wine, a dusty bottle from beneath the wine shelf, somehow overlooked. . . . Somewhat recovered, he was preparing to remember what he should do next when he glanced toward a figure at the door. Nelson Reed was standing there, watching him.

"All gone," Harold Green said. "My friend, Mr. Reed, there is no more." Still the man stood in the doorway, peering into the store.

The grocer waved his arms about the empty room. Not a display case had a single item standing. "All gone," he said again, as if addressing a stupid child. "There is nothing left to get. You, my friend, have come back too late for a second load. I am cleaned out."

Nelson Reed stepped into the store and strode toward the counter. He moved through wine-stained flour, lettuce leaves, red, green, and blue labels, bits and pieces of broken glass. He walked toward the counter.

"All day," the grocer laughed, not quite hysterically now, "all day long I have not made a single cent of profit. The entire day was a loss. This store, like the others, is bleeding me." He waved his arms about the room in a magnificent gesture of uncaring loss. "Now do you understand?" he said. "Now will you put yourself in my shoes? I have nothing here. Come, now, Mr. Reed, would it not be so bad a thing to walk in my shoes?"

"Mr. Green," Nelson Reed said coldly. "My wife bought a loaf of bread in here this mornin'. She forgot to pay you. I, myself, have come here to pay you your money."

"Oh," the grocer said.

. . .

. . . He rang the register with the most casual movement of his finger. The register read fifty-five cents.

Nelson Reed held out a dollar.

"And two cents tax," the grocer said.

The man held out the dollar.

"After all," Harold Green said. "We are all, after all, Mr. Reed, in debt to the government."

He rang the register again. It read fifty-seven cents.

Nelson Reed held out a dollar.

———————

James Alan McPherson, an African-American, won the Pulitzer Prize in 1978 for *Elbow Room*, a collection of short stories, which includes *A Loaf of Bread*. McPherson graduated from Harvard Law School in 1968, three years after the famous case of Williams v. Walker Thomas Furniture Co. was decided in which a "cross collateralization" clause was invalidated because it was unconscionable. The store, Walker Thomas, sold goods to poor and working class people on an installment plan. As long as they maintained an account and continued to buy goods, a balance was maintained on items they purchased in the past. Even when the total amount paid equaled or exceeded the price of most of the goods purchased, any failure to make a payment meant the store could repossess everything it ever sold to the customer.

Some of the practices used by merchants who operate establishments in poor or minority communities, or whose customers are mostly poor or minority, generate resentment. The merchants justify these practices in terms of the greater risk of default by the poor but studies show that the price differential in poor communities, for instance, is much higher than insurance and security costs would warrant. Moreover, these practices generate resentment that is sometimes expressed in ways that harm the business, especially during times of social unrest. What was the practice that upset customers in *A Loaf of Bread*? Did the customers have a reason for being upset? Why wouldn't normal market mechanisms cure this problem? Does the law have a role to play in mediating the dispute between those who sell and those who buy in these situations?

———————

Tony Brower v. Gateway 2000

Supreme Court of New York, Appellate Division
676 N.Y.S.2d 569 (App. Div. 1998)

E. Leo Milonas, J. P.

Appellants are among the many consumers who purchased computers and software products from defendant Gateway 2000 through a direct-sales system, by mail or telephone order. As of July 3, 1995, it was Gateway's practice to include with the materials shipped to the purchaser along with the merchandise a copy of its "Standard Terms and Conditions Agreement" and any relevant warranties for the products in the shipment. The Agreement begins with a "Note to the Customer," which provides, in slightly larger print than the remainder of the document, in a box that spans the width of the page: "This document contains Gateway 2000's Standard Terms and Conditions. By keeping your Gateway 2000 computer system beyond thirty (30) days after the date of delivery, you accept these Terms and Conditions." The document consists of 16 paragraphs, and, as is relevant to this appeal, paragraph 10 of the agreement, entitled "dispute resolution," reads as follows:

"Any dispute or controversy arising out of or relating to this Agreement or its interpretation shall be settled exclusively and finally by arbitration. The arbitration shall be conducted in accordance with the Rules of Conciliation and Arbitration of the International Chamber of Commerce. The arbitration shall be conducted in Chicago, Illinois, U.S.A. before a sole arbitrator. Any award rendered in any such arbitration proceeding shall be final and binding on each of the parties, and judgment may be entered thereon in a court of competent jurisdiction."

Plaintiffs commenced this action on behalf of themselves and others similarly situated for compensatory and punitive damages, alleging deceptive sales practices in seven causes of action, including breach of warranty, breach of contract, fraud and unfair trade practices. In particular, the allegations focused on Gateway's representations and advertising that promised "service when you need it," including around-the-clock free technical support, free software technical support and certain on-site services. According to plaintiffs, not only were they unable to avail themselves of this offer because it was virtually impossible to get through to a technician, but also Gateway continued to advertise this claim notwithstanding numerous complaints and reports about the problem.

Insofar as is relevant to appellants, who purchased their computers after July 3, 1995, Gateway moved to dismiss the complaint based on the arbitration clause in the Agreement. Appellants argued that the arbitration clause is invalid under UCC 2-207, unconscionable under UCC. 2-302 and an unenforceable contract of adhesion. Specifically, they claimed that the provision was obscure; that a customer could not reasonably be expected to appreciate or investigate its meaning and effect; that the International Chamber of Commerce (ICC) was not a forum commonly used for consumer matters; and that because ICC headquarters were in France, it was particularly difficult to locate the organization and its rules. To illustrate just how inaccessible the forum was, appellants advised the court that the ICC was not registered with the Secretary of State, that efforts to locate and contact the ICC had been unsuccessful and that apparently the only way to attempt to contact the ICC was through the United States Council for International Business, with which the ICC maintained some sort of relationship.

In support of their arguments, appellants submitted a copy of the ICC's Rules of Conciliation and Arbitration and contended that the cost of ICC arbitration was prohibitive, particularly given the amount of the typical consumer claim involved. For example, a claim of less than $50,000 required advance fees of $4,000 (more than the cost of most Gateway products), of which the $2000 registration fee was nonrefundable even if the consumer prevailed at the arbitration. Consumers would also incur travel expenses disproportionate to the damages sought, which appellants' counsel estimated would not exceed $1,000 per customer in this action, as well as bear the cost of Gateway's legal fees if the consumer did not prevail at the arbitration; in this respect, the ICC Rules follow the "loser pays" rule used in England. Also, although Chicago was designated as the site of the actual arbitration, all correspondence must be sent to ICC headquarters in France.

...

Finally, we turn to appellants' argument that the [lower] Court should have declared the contract unenforceable, pursuant to UCC 2-302, on the ground that the arbitration clause is unconscionable due to the unduly burdensome procedure and cost for the individual consumer. The [lower] Court found that while a class action lawsuit, such as the one herein, may be a less costly alternative to the arbitration (which is generally less costly than litigation), that does not alter the binding effect of the valid arbitration clause contained in the agreement, (*see, Harris v Shearson Hayden Stone*, 82 A.D.2d 87, 92–93, *affd.* 56 N.Y.2d 627 *for reasons stated below; see also, Matter of Ball [SFX Broadcasting],* 236 A.D.2d 158, *appeal dismissed* 91 N.Y.2d 921).

As a general matter, under New York law, unconscionability requires a showing that a contract is "both procedurally and substantively unconscionable when made" (*Gillman v Chase Manhattan Bank,* 73 N.Y.2d 1, 10). That is, there must be "some showing of 'an absence of meaningful choice on the part of one of the parties together with contract terms which are unreasonably favorable to the other party' (*Matter of State of New York v Avco Fin. Servs.,* 406 N.E.2d. 1075, 1081 (N.Y.)." The *Avco* Court took pains to note, however, that the purpose of this doctrine is not to redress the inequality between the parties but simply to ensure that the more powerful party cannot " 'surprise' " the other party with some overly oppressive term (406 N.E.2d. at 1071).

As to the procedural element, a court will look to the contract formation process to determine if in fact one party lacked any meaningful choice in entering into the contract, taking into consideration such factors as the setting of the transaction, the experience and education of the party claiming unconscionability, whether the contract contained "fine print," whether the seller used "high-pressured tactics" and any disparity in the parties' bargaining power (*Gillman v Chase Manhattan Bank,* 73 N.Y.2d at 11). None of these factors supports appellants' claim here. Any purchaser has 30 days within which to thoroughly examine the contents of their shipment, including the terms of the Agreement, and seek clarification of any term therein (*e.g., Matter of Ball [SFX Broadcasting],* 236 A.D.2d at 161). The Agreement itself, which is entitled in large print "Standard Terms and Conditions Agreement," consists of only three pages and 16 paragraphs, all of which appear in the same size print. Moreover, despite appellants' claims to the contrary, the arbitration clause is in no way "hidden" or "tucked away" within a complex document of inordinate length, nor is the option of returning the merchandise, to avoid the contract, somehow a "precarious" one. We also reject appellants' insinuation that, by using the word "standard," Gateway deliberately meant to convey to the consumer that the terms were standard within the industry, when the document clearly purports to be no more than *Gateway*'s "standard terms and conditions."

With respect to the substantive element, which entails an examination of the substance of the agreement in order to determine whether the terms unreasonably favor one party (*Gillman v Chase Manhattan Bank,* 73 N.Y.2d, at 12), we do not find that the possible inconvenience of the chosen site (Chicago) alone rises to the level of unconscionability. We do find, however, that the excessive cost factor that is necessarily entailed in arbitrating before the ICC is unreasonable and surely serves to deter the individual consumer from invoking the process (*see, Matter of Teleserve Sys. [MCI Telecommunications Corp.],* 230 A.D.2d 585, 594). Barred from resorting to the courts by the arbitration clause in the first instance, the designation of a financially prohibitive forum effectively bars consumers from this forum as well; consumers are thus left with no forum at all in which to resolve a dispute. In this regard, we note that this particular claim is not mentioned in the *Hill* decision, which upheld the clause as part of an enforceable contract.

While it is true that, under New York law, unconscionability is generally predicated on the presence of both the procedural and substantive elements, the substantive element alone may be sufficient to render the terms of the provision at issue unenforceable (*see, Gillman v Chase Manhattan Bank,* 73 N.Y.2d at 12; *Matter of State of New York v Avco Fin. Servs.,* 406 N.E.2d. at 1081; *State of New York v Wolowitz,* 96 A.D.2d 47, 68). Excessive fees, such as those incurred under the ICC procedure, have been grounds for finding an arbitration provision unenforceable or commercially unreasonable (*see, e.g., Matter of Teleserve Sys. [MCI Telecommunications Corp.],* 230 A.D.2d at 593–594).

In [*Filias v. Gateway 2000, Inc.,* 1998 U.S. Dist. LEXIS 20358 (N.D. Ill. 1998)], the Federal District Court stated that it was "inclined to agree" with the argument that selection of the ICC rendered the clause unconscionable, but concluded that the issue was moot because Gateway had agreed to arbitrate before the American Arbitration Association (AAA) and sought court appointment of the AAA pursuant to Federal Arbitration Act (9 USC § 5). The court accordingly granted Gateway's motion to compel arbitration and appointed the AAA in lieu of the ICC. Plaintiffs in that action (who are represented by counsel for appellants before us) contend that costs associated with the AAA process are also excessive, given the amount of the individual consumer's damages, and their motion for reconsideration of the court's decision has not yet been decided. While the AAA rules and costs are not part of the record before us, the parties agree that there is a minimum, nonrefundable filing fee of $500, and appellants claim each consumer could spend in excess of $1,000 to arbitrate in this forum.

Gateway's agreement to the substitution of the AAA is not limited to the Filias plaintiffs. Gateway's brief includes the text of a new arbitration agreement that it claims has been extended to all customers, past, present and future (apparently through publication in a quarterly magazine sent to anyone who has ever purchased a Gateway product). The new arbitration agreement provides for the consumer's choice of the AAA or the ICC as the arbitral body and the designation of any location for the arbitration by agreement of the parties, which "shall not be unreasonably withheld." It also provides telephone numbers at which the AAA and the ICC may be reached for information regarding the "organizations and their procedures."

As noted, however, appellants complain that the AAA fees are also excessive and thus in no way have they accepted defendant's offer, see, UCC 2-209; because they make the same claim as to the AAA as they did with respect to the ICC, the issue of unconscionability is not rendered moot, as defendant suggests. We cannot determine on this record whether the AAA process and costs would be so "egregiously oppressive" that they, too, would be unconscionable, *Avildsen v Prystay*, 171 AD2d 13, 14, *appeal dismissed* 79 NY2d 841. Thus, we modify the order on appeal to the extent of finding that portion of the arbitration provision requiring arbitration before the ICC to be unconscionable and remand to Supreme Court so that the parties have the opportunity to seek appropriate substitution of an arbitrator pursuant to the Federal Arbitration Act, 9 USC § 1 et seq., which provides for such court designation of an arbitrator upon application of either party, where, for whatever reason, one is not otherwise designated, 9 USC § 5.

Appellants make the final argument that the arbitration clause does not apply to the cause of action for false advertising (with respect to the promised round-the-clock service) under various sections of the General Business Law on the ground that there is no mention of arbitration in the technical service contract itself. Although they raise this claim for the first time on this appeal, we find the promise of technical support to be within the scope of arbitration as it is clearly a "dispute or controversy arising out or relating to [the] Agreement or its interpretation." Put another way, the service contract does not apply to some separate product that could be retained while the computer products—and the accompanying agreement—could be returned.

Accordingly, the order of Supreme Court, New York County (Beatrice Shainswit, J.), entered October 21, 1997, which, to the extent appealed from, granted defendants' motion to dismiss the complaint as to appellants on the ground that there was a valid agreement to arbitrate between the parties, should be modified, on the law and the facts, to the extent of vacating that portion of the arbitration agreement as requires arbitration before the International Chamber of Commerce, with leave to the parties to seek appointment of an arbitrator pursuant to 9 USC § 5 and remanding the matter for that purpose, and otherwise affirmed, without costs.

———————

The ALI is currently working on a Restatement of Consumer Law. One of the big issues being debated is the meaning of assent in standardized contracts and, in particular, whether any protection should be provided to consumers where contract boilerplate includes unreasonable or oppressive terms. Under discussion is a revision that would allow parties to use the unconscionability defense as a way of policing the bargain in such cases.

———————

Note

As these cases indicate, there are several different statements of the doctrine of unconscionability. Three are most influential:

1. From Williams v. Walker Thomas

The first is Judge Skelly Wright's statement of the doctrine in *Williams v. Walker Thomas Furniture Co.*, which identifies two elements in unconscionability: "Unconscionability has generally been recognized to include an *absence of meaningful choice on the part of one of the parties together with contract terms which are unreasonably favorable to the other party.*" (Emphasis added).

Judge Wright suggests factors relevant to each of these two elements:

Whether a meaningful choice is present in a particular case can only be determined by consideration of all the circumstances surrounding the transaction. In many cases the meaningfulness of the choice is negated by a gross inequality of bargaining power. The manner in which the contract was entered is also relevant to this consideration. Did each party to the contract, considering his obvious education or lack of it, have a reasonable opportunity to understand the terms of the contract, or were the important terms hidden in a maze of fine print and minimized by deceptive sales practices? ...

In determining reasonableness or fairness, the primary concern must be with the terms of the contract considered in light of the circumstances existing when the contract was made. The test is not simple, nor can it be mechanically applied. The terms are to be considered "in the light of the general commercial background and the commercial needs of the particular trade or case."

2. From the Comment to Uniform Commercial Code Section 2-302

A second influential formulation is in the *Official Comment* to section 2-302 of the *Uniform Commercial Code*:

The basic test is whether, in light of the general commercial background and the commercial needs of the particular trade or case, *the clauses involved are so one-sided* as to be unconscionable under the circumstances at the time of the making of the contract.... *The principal is one of the prevention of oppression and unfair surprise ... and not of disturbance of allocation of risks because of unequal bargaining power.* (Emphasis added.)

3. From Commentary Distinguishing between Procedural and Substantive Unconscionability

A third formulation distinguishes between *procedural unconscionability* ("bargaining naughtiness") and *substantive unconscionability* ("evils in the resulting contract.") Arthur A. Leff, *Unconscionability and the Code—The Emperor's New Clause*, 115 U. Pa. L. Rev. 485, 487 (1967). Traditionally, strong evidence of both procedural and substantive unfairness was necessary to a finding of unconscionability. In the last decade, however, courts have generally shifted to a sliding scale approach, in which a greater quantity of one type of unconscionability will justify a smaller quantity of the other type. Some courts have expanded the sliding scale approach further to hold that "a finding of unconscionability may rest on evidence of either procedural or substantive unconscionability without requiring evidence of both." Melissa T. Lonegrass, *Finding Room for Fairness in Formalism — The Sliding Scale Approach to Unconscionability*, 44 Loy. U. Chi. L.J. 1, 6 (2012).

At this point in its history, the doctrine includes all of the many ideas contained within these formulations. There are, however, some points of consensus: most lawyers would agree with the following:

a) Procedural issues raised by the doctrine include:

- knowledge of the terms: whether each party was able to read and understand the language in which any contract document was written, whether legalese and fine print was used, whether significant or surprising terms were conspicuous, whether attention was drawn to important terms, whether both parties were knowledgeable in the trade or activity of the contract and

- availability of other terms: whether other traders offered different terms, whether the agents negotiating the contract had the authority to change terms, whether one party had monopolistic or oligopolistic power.

b) Substantive issues include:

- one-sidedness of the contract term or terms and

- the strength of any commercial justification.

c) In general, as with other doctrines in U.S. law, courts are more comfortable with the procedural issues raised by this doctrine, because those issues are relatively harmonious with traditional contract law and with the ideology of choice, than with the substantive issues of unfairness or oppression, which raise fundamental questions about the market system of resource allocation.

d) This doctrine leads lawyers and judges into uncharted territory and therefore decisions are often struggling, vague, and inconsistent.

e) The doctrine of unconscionability challenges and subverts other contract law doctrines, including:

- the traditional notion of a duty to read,

- the traditional notion that courts should not inquire into the adequacy of the exchange,

- the assumption in offer and acceptance doctrine that parties negotiate and mutually define contract terms,

- the idea that customs, social practices, and trade practices merely "supplement" a negotiated agreement. Instead, the unconscionability doctrine encourages courts to view these as significant indicators of what people expect of each other, and it leads courts to view shared or communal notions of right and wrong, fair and unfair, just and unjust, as significant to contract interpretation.

Although the need for a doctrine of unconscionability is deeply felt and courts have readily endorsed the doctrine, many courts and legal commentators nevertheless view unconscionability as a renegade doctrine having legitimate origins but challenging the central role of individualism and market ideology in contract law. The doctrine, drawing on the formulations above, involves potentially far-reaching ideas about oppression, unfairness, inequality, and injustice. The following materials explore procedural and substantive issues in unconscionability doctrine.

———————

Brooklyn Union Gas Company v. Rafael Jimeniz

Civil Court of the City of New York
371 N.Y.S.2d 289 (1975)

Norman H. Shilling, Judge

Findings of Fact

Plaintiff, Brooklyn Union Gas Company, is suing defendant Rafael Jimeniz for breach of contract. A verified summons and complaint was served upon the defendant on September 10, 1974 by substituted service. The plaintiff alleges entering into a contract with defendant on or about June 15, 1971 for the delivery and installation of 1 400 Economite Gas Conversion Burner, 1 L400G–A Aquastat, 1 P404A Pressuretrol, 1 Backdraft Diverter. Plaintiff further claims that pursuant to the contract entered into herein the payments to be made by the defendant were deferred for twelve months and that the above items upon delivery and installation had a one year unconditional satisfaction guarantee.

The purported written agreement was presented to the defendant in English only. Defendant, a non-English speaking and writing individual who only spoke and wrote Spanish fluently, admits to signing the papers introduced into evidence by plaintiff, the contract, but also testified that no one ever explained the contract to him. Defendant also testified that when he asked for an interpretation of the contract and an explanation of what the plaintiff's agent, one David H. Mann, said regarding the alleged contract, a woman named Carmen told him to sign it. Plaintiff never sold or negotiated with defendant but induced defendant's tenants to pressure defendant into signing the contract. Plaintiff's agent, Mann, had defendant sign this purported contract at 673 Snediker Avenue, Brooklyn, N.Y. and not at plaintiff's main office at Montague Street, Brooklyn, N.Y. where a Spanish interpreter would have been available.

Defendant could neither write nor speak English and testified to the fact that when one month later he attempted to make a payment at the Montague Street branch, he was told by an employee of the plaintiff that he need not pay for another year. After one year passed defendant started to make payment. On or about May 22, 1973, during the second year, defendant complained to plaintiff that the unit involved herein was not functioning. Plaintiff's field repairmen found that a transformer burned out. An order for the part was placed with plaintiff's office. However, after discovering that defendant had made no payments past 1972, no further action was taken by plaintiff to supply the necessary part. Defendant, not receiving satisfaction, made no attempt to make further payments and plaintiff made no attempt to repair. Defendant further testified that plaintiff's employee, not identified by the defendant, told him if anything ever happened to the unit it would be repaired.

Conclusions of Law

The purported agreement presented to the Court, on its face, seems to be a contract. Absent the testimony adduced at the trial, the normal conclusion would be that a contract had, in fact, been entered into by the parties. However, the purported contract introduced by plaintiff showed three signatures, whereas the defendant's copy only shows his own signature. Under U.C.C. § 2-302 "If the court as a matter of law finds the contract or any clause of the contract to have been unconscionable at the time it was made the court may refuse to enforce the contract."

That is the situation here—this court finds, as a matter of law, that the contract introduced by plaintiff is unconscionable and, thereby, under the U.C.C., unenforceable in this forum. The Court of Appeals has made it plain in *Wilson Trading Corp. v. David Ferguson, Ltd.*, 244 N.E.2d 685, (N.Y. 1968) that whether a contract or any clause of the contract is unconscionable is a matter for the court to decide against the background of the contract's commercial setting, purpose and effect. This court has the power and the discretion to determine whether a contract is unconscionable. It is up to the court as a matter of law to determine if the contract is or is not unconscionable and the court can strike the clause, clauses or the entire contract as a result if it finds the contract to be unconscionable. *Sinkoff Beverage Co. v. Schlitz Brewing Co.*, 273 N.Y.S.2d 364 (1966); *In re Estate of Chance M. Vought, Jr.*, 334 N.Y.S.2d 720 (1972).

> An unconscionable sales contract contains procedural elements involving the contract formation process, which are the use of high pressure sales tactics, failure to disclose the terms of the contract, misrepresentation and fraud on the part of the seller, a refusal to bargain on certain critical terms, clauses hidden in fine print, and unequal bargaining power aggravated by the fact that the consumer in many cases cannot speak English ... The term caveat emptor has been eroded by the code. No longer can a seller hide behind it when acting in an unconscionable manner.

NuDimensions Figure Salons v. Becerra, 340 N.Y.S.2d 268 (1973). The contract must have mutuality of agreement and obligation; if lacking the contract is unenforceable. In making an agreement, the contracting parties create obligations as between themselves—the law of contracts generally contemplate that the parties will meet each other on a footing of social and approximate economic equality. The basic test of unconscionability of a contract is whether under the circumstances existing at the time of the creation of the contract the parties were in equality to each other on all levels. The court can look into the contract to make its determination and ascertain how the contract was printed, whether both parties to the contract spoke English, how the contract was made and if the contract was one-sided. *Triple D & E Inc. v. Van Buren*, 339 N.Y.S.2d 821, *aff'd* 346 N.Y.S.2d 737 (1973).

...

> The doctrine of unconscionability is used by the courts to protect those who are unable to protect themselves and to prevent injustice, both in consumer and non-consumer areas.... [U]nequal bargaining powers and the absence of a meaningful choice on the part of one of the parties, together with contract terms which unreasonably favor the other party, may spell out unconscionability."

Seabrook v. Commuter Housing Co., Inc., 338 N.Y.S.2d 67 (1972). In this case, the defendant had a limited knowledge of the English language and no knowledge of the technical or legal tools of English. The plaintiff never provided an interpreter to explain the contract. The bargaining positions, therefore, were unequal. The defendant was and is, under these facts, unable to protect himself. Since he cannot protect himself, the court must protect him and thus this court declares the contract unconscionable and a nullity.

———————

Note—On the Many Languages Spoken by U.S. Citizens

According to the United States Bureau of the Census, 21 % of persons five years and older in the United States use a language other than English at home. In California, approximately 44%, almost one-half of all people over five years old, use a language other than English at home; in Arizona, Hawai'i, New York, and Texas, more than one-fourth of the residents speak a language other than English. Camille Ryan, Language Use in the United States: 2011 American Community Survey Results (August 2013).

It's important to remember that the United States has never been mono-lingual and that English was not the first language spoken in what is now the United States. Despite this fact, the "English-only" movement has capitalized on fears of the loss of a "common culture" to recruit support for an English-only agenda. Beginning in 1982, with a failed constitutional proposal by the late Senator S.I. Hayakawa (R. Calif.) to make English the official language of the United States, the movement initiatives have included calls for citizenship ceremonies to be performed in English, for ballots to be printed in English only, and for the elimination of bilingual education. Most recently, a recording of the Star Spangled Banner in Spanish, Nuestro Himno, proved to be very controversial, probably because it arose in the context of a national debate about immigration policy. Yet over 150 languages are now spoken in the United States. Besides English and Spanish, the ten languages most frequently spoken at home include Chinese, French, Tagalog, Vietnamese, Italian, Korean, Russian, Polish and Arabic. The demographics projected for 2050 clearly indicate that the United States will continue to become increasingly more culturally diverse. *See generally* Jean Stefancic and Richard Delgado, No Mercy: How Conservative Think Tanks and Foundations Changed America's Social Agenda (1996).

Amy Tan, Mother Tongue

(1990)

I am not a scholar of English or literature. I cannot give you much more than personal opinions on the English language and its variations in this country or others.

I am a writer. And by that definition, I am someone who has always loved language. I am fascinated by language in daily life. I spend a great deal of my time thinking about the power of language—the way it can evoke an emotion, a visual image, a complex idea, or a simple truth. Language is the tool of my trade. And I use them all—all the Englishes I grew up with.

Recently, I was made keenly aware of the different Englishes I do use. I was giving a talk to a large group of people, the same talk I had already given to half a dozen other groups. The nature of the talk was about my writing, my life, and my book, *The Joy Luck Club*. The talk was going along well enough, until I remembered one major difference that made the whole talk sound wrong. My mother was in the room. And it was perhaps the first time she had heard me give a lengthy speech, using the kind of English I have never used with her. I was saying things like "The intersection of memory upon imagination" and "There is an aspect of my fiction that relates to thus-and-thus"—a speech filled with carefully wrought grammatical phrases, burdened, it suddenly seemed to me, with nominalized forms, past perfect tenses, conditional phrases, all the forms of standard English that I had learned in school and through books, the forms of English I did not use at home with my mother.

Just last week, I was walking down the street with my mother, and I again found myself conscious of the English I was using, the English I do use with her. We were talking about the price of new and used furniture and I heard myself saying this: "Not waste money that way." My husband was with us as well, and he didn't notice any switch in my English. And then I realized why. It's because over the twenty years we've been together I've often used that same kind of English with him, and sometimes he even uses it with me. It has become our language of intimacy, a different sort of English that relates to family talk, the language I grew up with.

So you'll have some idea of what this family talk I heard sounds like, I'll quote what my mother said during a recent conversation which I videotaped and then transcribed. During this conversation, my mother was talking about a political gangster in Shanghai who had the same last name as her family's, Du, and how the gangster in his early years wanted to be adopted by her family, which was rich by comparison. Later, the gangster became more powerful, far richer than my mother's family, and one day showed up at my mother's wedding to pay his respects. Here's what she said in part:

"Du Yusong having business like fruit stand. Like off the street kind. He is Du like Du Zong—but not Tsung-ming Island people. The local people call putong, the river east side, he belong to that side local people. That man want to ask Du Zong father take him in like become own family. Du Zong father wasn't look down on him, but didn't take seriously, until that man big like become a mafia. Now important person, very hard to inviting him. Chinese way, came only to show respect, don't stay for dinner. Respect for making big celebration, he shows up. Mean gives lots of respect. Chinese custom. Chinese social life that way. If too important won't have to stay too long. He come to my wedding. I didn't see, I heard it. I gone to boy's side, they have YMCA dinner. Chinese age I was nineteen."

You should know that my mother's expressive command of English belies how much she actually understands. She reads the *Forbes* report, listens to *Wall Street Week*, converses daily with her stockbroker, reads all of Shirley MacLaine's books with ease—all kinds of things I can't begin to understand. Yet some of my friends tell me they understand 50 percent of what my mother says. Some say they understand 80 to 90 percent. Some say they understand none of it, as if she were speaking pure Chinese. But to me, my mother's English is perfectly clear, perfectly natural. It's my mother tongue. Her language, as I hear it, is vivid, direct, full of observation and imagery. That was the language that helped shape the way I saw things, expressed things, made sense of the world.

Lately, I've been giving more thought to the kind of English my mother speaks. Like others, I have described it to people as "broken" or "fractured" English. But I wince when I say that. It has always bothered me that I can think of no other way to describe it other than "broken," as if it were damaged and needed to be fixed, as if it lacked a certain wholeness and soundness. I've heard other terms used, "limited English," for example. But they seem just as bad, as if everything is limited, including people's perceptions of the limited English speaker.

I know this for a fact, because when I was growing up, my mother's "limited" English limited *my* perception of her. I was ashamed of her English. I believed that her English reflected the quality of what she had to say. That is, because she expressed them imperfectly her thoughts were imperfect. And I had plenty of empirical evidence to support me: the fact that people in department stores, at banks, and at restaurants did not take her seriously, did not give her good service, pretended not to understand her, or even acted as if they did not hear her.

My mother has long realized the limitations of her English as well. When I was fifteen, she used to have me call people on the phone to pretend I was she. In this guise, I was forced to ask for information or even to complain and yell at people who had been rude to her. One time it was a call to her stockbroker in New York. She had cashed out her small portfolio and it just so happened we were going to go to New York the next week, our very first trip outside California. I had to get on the phone and say in an adolescent voice that was not very convincing, "This is Mrs. Tan."

And my mother was standing in the back whispering loudly, "Why he don't send me check, already two weeks late. So mad he lie to me, losing me money."

And then I said in perfect English, "Yes, I'm getting rather concerned. You had agreed to send the check two weeks ago, but it hasn't arrived."

Then she began to talk more loudly. "What he want, I come to New York tell him front of his boss, you cheating me?" And I was trying to calm her down, make her be quiet, while telling the stockbroker, "I can't tolerate any more excuses. If I don't receive the check immediately, I am going to have to speak to your manager when I'm in New York next week." And sure enough, the following week there we were in front of this astonished stockbroker, and I was sitting there red-faced and quiet, and my mother, the real Mrs. Tan, was shouting at his boss in her impeccable broken English.

We used a similar routine just five days ago, for a situation that was far less humorous. My mother had gone to the hospital for an appointment, to find out about a benign brain tumor a CAT scan had revealed a month ago. She said she had spoken very good English, her best English, no mistakes. Still, she said, the hospital did not apologize when they said they had lost the CAT scan and she had come for nothing. She said they did not seem to have any sympathy when she told them she was anxious to know the exact diagnosis, since her husband and son had both died of brain tumors. She said they would not give her any more information until the next time and she would have to make another appointment for that. So she said she would not leave until the doctor called her daughter. She wouldn't budge. And when the doctor finally called her daughter, me, who spoke in perfect English—lo and behold—we had assurances the CAT scan would be found, promises that a conference call on Monday would be held, and apologies for any suffering my mother had gone through for a most regrettable mistake.

I think my mother's English almost had an effect on limiting my possibilities in life as well. Sociologists and linguists probably will tell you that a person's developing language skills are more influenced by peers. But I do think that the language spoken in the family, especially in immigrant families which are more insular, plays a large role in shaping the language of the child. And I believe that it affected my results on achievement tests, IQ tests, and the SAT. While my English skills were never judged as poor, compared to math, English could not be considered my strong suit. In grade school I did moderately well, getting perhaps B's, sometimes B-pluses, in English and scoring perhaps in the sixtieth or seventieth percentile on achievement tests. But those scores were not good enough to override the opinion that my true abilities lay in math and science, because in those areas I achieved A's and scored in the ninetieth percentile or higher.

This was understandable. Math is precise; there is only one correct answer. Whereas, for me at least, the answers on English tests were always a judgment call, a matter of opinion and personal experience. Those tests were constructed around items like fill-in-the-blank sentence completion, such as "Even though Tom was _____, Mary thought he was _____." And the correct answer always seemed to be the most bland combinations of thoughts, for example, "Even though Tom was shy, Mary thought he was charming," with the grammatical structure "even though" limiting the correct answer to some sort of semantic opposites, so you wouldn't get answers like, "Even though Tom was foolish, Mary thought he was ridiculous." Well, according to my mother, there were very few limitations as to what Tom could have been and what Mary might have thought of him. So I never did well on tests like that.

The same was true with word analogies, pairs of words in which you were supposed to find some sort of logical, semantic relationship — for example, "*Sunset* is to *nightfall* as _____ is to _____." And here you would be presented with a list of four possible pairs, one of which showed the same kind of relationship: *red* is to *stoplight*, *bus* is to *arrival*, *chills* is to *fever*, *yawn* is to *boring*. Well, I could never think that way. I knew what the tests were asking, but I could not block out of my mind the images already created by the first pair, "*sunset* is to *nightfall*" — and I would see a burst of colors against a darkening sky, the moon rising, the lowering of a curtain of stars. And all the other pairs of words — red, bus, stoplight, boring — just threw up a mass of confusing images, making it impossible for me to sort out something as logical as saying: "A sunset precedes nightfall" is the same as "a chill precedes a fever." The only way I would have gotten that answer right would have been to imagine an associative situation, for example, my being disobedient and staying out past sunset, catching a chill at night, which turns into feverish pneumonia as punishment, which indeed did happen to me.

I have been thinking about all this lately, about my mother's English, about achievement tests. Because lately I've been asked, as a writer, why there are not more Asian Americans represented in American literature. Why are there few Asian Americans enrolled in creative writing programs? Why do so many Chinese students go into engineering? Well, these are broad sociological questions I can't begin to answer. But I have noticed in surveys — in fact, just last week — that Asian students, as a whole, always do significantly better on math achievement tests than in English. And this makes me think that there are other Asian-American students whose English spoken in the home might also be described as "broken" or "limited." And perhaps they also have teachers who are steering them away from writing and into math and science, which is what happened to me.

Fortunately, I happen to be rebellious in nature and enjoy the challenge of disproving assumptions made about me. I became an English major my first year in college, after being enrolled as pre-med. I started writing nonfiction as a freelancer the week after I was told by my former boss that writing was my worst skill and I should hone my talents toward account management.

But it wasn't until 1985 that I finally began to write fiction. And at first I wrote using what I thought to be wittily crafted sentences, sentences that would finally prove I had mastery over the English language. Here's an example from the first draft of a story that later made its way into *The Joy Luck Club*, but without this line: "That was my mental quandary in its nascent state." A terrible line, which I can barely pronounce.

Fortunately, for reasons I won't get into today, I later decided I should envision a reader for the stories I would write. And the reader I decided upon was my mother; because these were stories about mothers. So with this reader in mind — and in fact she did read my early drafts — I began to write stories using all the Englishes I grew up with: the English I spoke to my mother, which for lack of a better term might be described as "simple": the English she used with me, which for lack of a better term might be described as "broken"; my translation of her Chinese, which could certainly be described as "watered down"; and what I imagined to be her translation of her Chinese if she could speak in perfect English, her internal language, and for that I sought to preserve the essence, but neither an English nor a Chinese structure. I wanted to capture what language ability tests can never reveal: her intent, her passion, her imagery, the rhythms of her speech, and the nature of her thoughts.

Apart from what any critic had to say about my writing, I knew I had succeeded where it counted when my mother finished reading my book and gave me her verdict: "So easy to read."

————————

Amy Tan's novels, *The Joy Luck Club*, *The Kitchen God's Wife*, *A Hundred Secret Sense* and *The Bonesetter's Daughter*, have all been bestsellers. Her success is extraordinary — but not unpredictable, given her love of language. And yet, she has said in an interview, "I'm the worst at coming up with the single word, which is the reason why I write novels. I've never been good at multiple choice questions or true/false things because I always want to tell a story. I always want to give exceptions to the rule."

Chapter Eight

Changes after Formation: Impracticability, Frustration, and Agreed Modifications

The doctrines discussed in this (pleasantly short!) chapter concern changes that happen after the contract is made. Sometimes the circumstances that existed at the time the contract was made have changed and one of the parties wants to be excused from the contract, or at least relieved of some part of it. Impossibility/Impracticability of Performance is the argument used when the change has severely increased the difficulty of performance. Frustration of Purpose is the doctrine used by a party who wishes to be excused from performing the contract because the change in circumstances has thwarted the fundamental purpose of the contract. In other cases, the parties agreed to modify an existing contract and one party claims that he or she should not have to abide by the modification. All of these claims raise questions of fate, responsibility, limited power, limited knowledge, and limited choice.

A. Changed Circumstances

Many of our relationships, of varying duration and varying degrees of intimacy, can be called "contractual." We are tenants or landlords, bank customers or bankers; we are debtors or creditors, bailors or bailees, buyers or sellers, partners, agents or principals, employees or employers. Together, these many relationships comprise a social system, a web of interconnections.

For an individual, contracting with others is a way to gain some control over the future and to obtain some security against future risks: renting an apartment gives some assurance of housing; depositing money in a bank is one way to preserve resources for future use; having a job gives some assurance of future income. In this way, contracting is future-oriented, done to give some certainty to an unknowable future. If certainty is the objective, the fact that changes occur should be a good reason to *enforce* contracts, not to *excuse* them: since people make contracts as security for the future, then courts should not excuse people from their contractual obligations merely because unanticipated events occurred. On the other hand, parties who have a contractual arrangement, especially one that endures over time and is not a one off transaction, may expect some flexibility or accommodation when the change that occurs was extreme and unexpected. The doctrines applied in the cases in this chapter attempt to balance these competing interests.

If you and I agree to a lease under which I am to rent your house for a year and pay you $800 a month, what happens if the house burns down before I move in, due to an accident neither of us caused? Can I sue you for breach of contract? Can you sue me if I do not pay you rent? The excuses of impossibility/impracticability and frustration of purpose are asserted by parties seeking to avoid enforcement of a contract because of some change in the circumstances that has made the contract either more burdensome than it was originally (impossibility or impracticability of performance) or less valuable or meaningful than it was originally (frustration of purpose). As you read the cases below, pay attention to the facts courts treat as significant. How does the court balance the competing interests or injuries? What are the political, economic, and moral concerns that inform evaluation of these competing interests and application of these doctrines?

Classical contract theory did not endorse excuses of frustration of purpose or impossibility/impracticability of performance. Legal realists, in contrast, argued that partial or full excuse should be granted, particularly in situations in which people in the same industry, trade, or community normally would make allowance for the difficulty. They argued that the law should reflect community norms, including the norms of compassion and compromise. Karl Llewellyn incorporated this approach into section 2-615 of the *Uniform Commercial Code*, allowing excuse or partial excuse in a variety of situations. The *Restatement (Second) of Contracts* echoes *Uniform Commercial Code* section 2-615 in its section 261.

---

1. Impossibility (or Impracticability) of Performance

Specialty Tires of America, Inc. v. The CIT Group/Equipment Financing, Inc. v. Condere Corporation, Titan Tire Corporation, and Titan International, Inc.

United States District Court, W.D. Pennsylvania
82 F. Supp. 2d 434 (2000)

D. Brooks Smith, District Judge

In this case, Specialty Tires, Inc. ("Specialty") has sued The CIT Group/Equipment Financing, Inc. ("CIT") for breach of contract arising out CIT's failure to deliver eleven tire presses that it had previously contracted to sell to Specialty. CIT, in turn, has filed a third-party complaint against Condere Corporation, Titan Tire Corporation and Titan International, Inc. (collectively "Condere") arising out of the latter's alleged wrongful refusal to permit those presses to be removed from its factory. Specialty has moved for partial summary judgment, arguing that CIT's defenses are without merit, while CIT has moved for full summary judgment on the ground that its performance was excused under the doctrine of impossibility or commercial impracticability,[1] ... For the following reasons, I will grant CIT's motion ...

I.

The material facts of this case are simple and undisputed. In December 1993, CIT, a major equipment leasing company, entered into a sale/leaseback with Condere for eleven tire presses located at Condere's tire plant in Natchez, Mississippi, under which CIT purchased the presses from Condere and leased them back to it for a term of years. CIT retained title to the presses, as well as the right to possession in the event of a default by Condere. In May 1997, Condere ceased making the required lease payments and filed for

---

1. These two terms, while suggesting different levels of difficulty of performance, tend to be used more or less interchangeably, and I will do so as well.

Chapter 11 bankruptcy in the Southern District of Mississippi. In September 1997, Condere rejected the executory portion of the lease agreement, and the bankruptcy court lifted the automatic stay as to CIT's claim involving the presses.

CIT thus found itself, unexpectedly, with eleven tire presses it needed to sell. Maurice "Maury" Taylor, a former minor candidate for President of the United States[3] and the CEO of Condere and Titan International, stated his desire that the presses be removed quickly and advised CIT on how they might be sold. Later, CIT brought two potential buyers to Condere's Natchez plant, where representatives of Condere conducted them on a tour of the facility. Subsequently, Taylor and CIT negotiated concerning Condere's purchase of the presses, but negotiations fell through, after which Taylor again offered his assistance in locating another buyer.

When no buyer was found, CIT decided to advertise the presses. Specialty, a manufacturer of tires that sought to expand its plant in Tennessee, responded, and in early December 1997, representatives of Specialty, CIT and Condere met to conduct an on-site inspection of the equipment. Condere's representative discussed with CIT's personnel and in the presence of Specialty's agents the logistics concerning the removal of the presses. At that meeting, Condere's representative told CIT and Specialty that CIT had an immediate right to possession of the tire presses, and the right to sell them. At no time did any representative of Condere, whether by words or conduct, express any intent to oppose the removal of this equipment. The negotiations proved fruitful, and, in late December 1997, CIT and Specialty entered into a contract for the sale of the presses for $250,000. CIT warranted its title to and right to sell the presses.

Events then took a turn, which led to this lawsuit. When CIT attempted to gain access to the presses to have them rigged and shipped to Specialty, Condere refused to allow this equipment to be removed from the plant. This refusal was apparently because Condere had just tendered a check to CIT for $224,000, without the approval of the bankruptcy court, in an attempt to cure its default under the lease. This unexpected change in position was rejected by CIT, which promptly filed a complaint in replevin in the Southern District of Mississippi to obtain possession. Condere then posted a bond and the replevin court removed the action from the expedited list, scheduling a case management conference for April 1998. It became clear at that juncture that Specialty was not going to obtain its tire presses expeditiously.

CIT then advised Specialty that the presses were subject to the jurisdiction of the bankruptcy court and suggested that Specialty either withdraw its claim to the equipment and negotiate with CIT for a sum of liquidated damages or make a bid for the presses at any auction that might be held by that court. Specialty, as was its right, rejected both suggestions and affirmed the existing contract, demanding performance. To date, Condere has refused to surrender to CIT, and CIT has failed to deliver to Specialty, the tire presses.

Subsequent to the briefing of these motions, the replevin court has issued findings of fact and conclusions of law to the effect that Condere wrongfully retained possession of the presses and that CIT is entitled to remove them immediately. Although Condere may appeal this ruling, CIT has informed Specialty that it is still willing to deliver the presses as soon as it gains possession, and Specialty has indicated its interest in accepting them, in "partial" settlement of its claims.

---

3. *See, e.g.,* Stanley Ziemba, Titan Wheel's Taylor Back at Work, Chicago Tribune, Apr. 10, 1996, at B1, 1996 WL 2660678; Andrew E. Serwer, Taylor: Made for President?, Fortune, Apr. 3, 1995, at 18, 1995 WL 8105190.

...

III.

In the overwhelming majority of circumstances, contractual promises are to be performed, not avoided: *pacta sunt servanda*, or, as the Seventh Circuit loosely translated it, "a deal's a deal." *Waukesha Foundry, Inc. v. Industrial Engineering, Inc.*, 91 F.3d 1002, 1010 (7th Cir. 1996) (citation omitted); *see generally* John D. Calamari & Joseph M. Perillo, *The Law of Contracts* § 13.1, at 495 (4th ed. 1998). This is an eminently sound doctrine, because typically

> a court cannot improve matters by intervention after the fact. It can only destabilize the institution of contract, increase risk, and make parties worse off.... Parties to contracts are entitled to seek, and retain, personal advantage; striving for that advantage is the source of much economic progress. Contract law does not require parties to be fair, or kind, or reasonable, or to share gains or losses equally.

Industrial Representatives, Inc. v. CP Clare Corp., 74 F.3d 128, 131–32 (7th Cir. 1996) (Easterbrook, J.). Promisors are free to assume risks, even huge ones, and promisees are entitled to rely on those voluntary assumptions. Calamari & Perillo, *supra* § 13.16, at 522. Futures contracts, as just one example, are so aleatory that risk-bearing is their sole purpose, yet they are fully enforceable. *See id.* § 13.2, at 496; 4 Ronald A. Anderson, Uniform Commercial Code § 2-615:69 (3d ed. 1997) (performance not excused even if seller is unable to obtain goods).

Even so, courts have recognized, in an evolving line of cases from the common law down to the present, that there are limited instances in which unexpectedly and radically changed conditions render the judicial enforcement of certain promises of little or no utility. This has come to be known, for our purposes, as the doctrines of impossibility and impracticability.[7] Because of the unexpected nature of such occurrences, litigated cases usually involve, not interpretation of a contractual term, but the judicial filling of a lacuna in the parties agreement. Such "gap-filling," however, must be understood for what it is: a court-ordered, as opposed to bargained-for, allocation of risk between the parties. *Albert M. Greenfield & Co. v. Kolea*, 380 A.2d 758, 760 (Pa. 1977). As such, it must be applied sparingly. *Dorn v. Stanhope Steel, Inc.*, 534 A.2d 798, 812 (Pa. Super. Ct. 1987).

Traditionally, there were three kinds of supervening events that would provide a legally cognizable excuse for failing to perform: death of the promisor (if the performance was personal), illegality of the performance, and destruction of the subject matter; beyond that the doctrine has grown to recognize that relief is most justified if unexpected events inflict a loss on one party and provide a windfall gain for the other or where the excuse would save one party from an unexpected loss while leaving the other party in a position no worse than it would have without the contract.[8]

Thus, the *Second Restatement of Contracts* expresses the doctrine of impracticability this way:

---

7. The reported cases on this topic, unfortunately, are not characterized by either consistency or clarity of expression. As one respected treatise puts it, "Students who have concluded a first year contracts course in confusion about the doctrine of impossibility and have since ... found that the cases somehow slip through their fingers when they try to apply them to new situations[ ] may take some comfort in knowing that they are in good company." 1 White & Summers, *supra* § 3-10, at 164.

8. The second of these two grounds is what economists deem a "Pareto optimal" move; that is, an adjustment that makes some parties better off and none worse off than they were initially. For an economic analysis of the law of impossibility, *see* Hon. Richard A. Posner, Economic Analysis of Law § 4.5 (5th ed. 1998).

Where, after a contract is made, a party's performance is made impracticable without his fault by the occurrence of an event the non-occurrence of which was a basic assumption on which the contract was made, his duty to render that performance is discharged, unless the language or the circumstances indicate the contrary.

Restatement (Second) of Contracts § 261 (1981). Article 2 of the U.C.C., which applies to the sale of goods presented by the case sub judice, puts it similarly:

Delay in delivery or non-delivery in whole or in part by a seller ... is not a breach of his duty under a contract for sale if performance as agreed has been made impracticable by the occurrence of a contingency the non-occurrence of which was a basic assumption on which the contract was made....

U.C.C. § 2-615(1).

The principal inquiry in an impracticability analysis, then, is whether there was a contingency the non-occurrence of which was a basic assumption underlying the contract. It is often said that this question turns on whether the contingency was "foreseeable," on the rationale that if it was, the promisor could have sought to negotiate explicit contractual protection. *See Waldinger Corp. v. CRS Group Eng'rs, Inc.*, 775 F.2d 781, 786 (7th Cir. 1985); *Yoffe v. Keller Indus., Inc.*, 443 A.2d 358, 362 (Pa. Super. 1982); *Luria Engineering Co. v. Aetna Cas. & Sur. Co.*, 213 A.2d 151, 153–54 (Pa. Super. 1965). This, however, is an incomplete and sometimes misleading test. Anyone can foresee, in some general sense, a whole variety of potential calamities, but that does not mean that he or she will deem them worth bargaining over. *See* Murray, *supra*, § 112, at 641 ("If 'foreseeable' is equated with 'conceivable', nothing is unforeseeable"). The risk may be too remote, the party may not have sufficient bargaining power, or neither party may have any superior ability to avoid the harm. As my late colleague Judge Teitelbaum recited two decades ago in a famous case of impracticability:

Foreseeability or even recognition of a risk does not necessarily prove its allocation. Parties to a contract are not always able to provide for all the possibilities of which they are aware, sometimes because they cannot agree, often because they are too busy. Moreover, that some abnormal risk was contemplated is probative but does not necessarily establish an allocation of the risk of the contingency which actually occurs.

Aluminum Co. of Am. v. Essex Group, Inc., 499 F.Supp. 53, 76 (W.D.Pa. 1980) (applying Indiana law) (*quoting Transatlantic Financing Corp. v. United States*, 363 F.2d 312 (D.C.Cir.1966) (Skelly Wright, J.)) (internal ellipses omitted); *accord Opera Co. v. Wolf Trap Found.*, 817 F.2d 1094, 1101 (4th Cir.1987) (*also quoting Transatlantic*). So, while the risk of an unforeseeable event can safely be deemed not to have been assumed by the promisor, the converse is not necessarily true. *See Restatement (Second) of Contracts* § 261 cmt. c. Properly seen, then, foreseeability, while perhaps the most important factor,

is at best one fact to be considered in resolving first how likely the occurrence of the event in question was and, second, whether its occurrence, based on past experience, was of such reasonable likelihood that the obligor should not merely foresee the risk but, because of the degree of its likelihood, the obligor should have guarded against it or provided for non-liability against the risk.

Wolf Trap, 817 F.2d at 1102–03.[10]

---

10. Another respected text defines the unforeseeable as "an event so unlikely to occur that reasonable parties see no need explicitly to allocate the risk of its occurrence, although the impact it might have

It is also commonly said that the standard of impossibility is objective rather than subjective–that the question is whether the thing can be done, not whether the promisor can do it. 2 Farnsworth, *Contracts* § 9.6, at 619. This too is more truism than test, although Pennsylvania courts have couched their decisions in this rhetoric. *See Luber v. Luber*, 614 A.2d 771, 774 (Pa. Super. 1992); *Craig Coal Mining Co. v. Romani*, 513 A.2d 437, 439 (Pa. Super. 1986).[11] Indeed, the First Restatement took such an approach, *see* Calamari & Perillo, *supra* § 13.15, at 521, but the Second simply applies "the rationale … that a party generally assumes the risk of his own inability to perform his duty." *Craig Coal*, 513 A.2d at 439 (quoting *Restatement (Second) of Contracts* § 261 cmt. e). This holds particularly when the duty is merely to pay money. *See Luber*, 614 A.2d at 774. It is therefore "preferable to say that such ['subjective'] risks as these are generally considered to be sufficiently within the control of one party that they are assumed by that party." 2 Farnsworth, *supra* § 9.6, at 619–20. It is, of course, essential that the impossibility asserted by the promisor as a defense not have been caused by the promisor. *Id.* § 9.6, at 613–14; *Dorn*, 534 A.2d at 812; *Craig*, 513 A.2d at 440.

Generally speaking, while loss, destruction or a major price increase of fungible goods will not excuse the seller's duty to perform, the rule is different when the goods are unique, have been identified to the contract or are to be produced from a specific, agreed-upon source. In such a case, the nonexistence or unavailability of a specific thing will establish a defense of impracticability. Thus, § 263 of the Second Restatement recites:

> If the existence of a specific thing is necessary for the performance of a duty, its failure to come into existence, destruction, or such deterioration as makes performance impracticable is an event the non-occurrence of which was a basic assumption on which the contract was made.

Moreover, the Supreme Court of Pennsylvania has interpreted this section's predecessor in the First Restatement to apply to, in addition to physical destruction and deterioration, interference by third parties with a specific chattel necessary to the carrying out of the agreement. *Greenfield*, 380 A.2d at 759 (quoting *West v. Peoples First Nat'l Bank & Trust Co.*, 106 A.2d 427 (Pa. 1954)); *accord Yoffe*, 443 A.2d at 362 (acts of third parties sufficient if not foreseeable); *Luria*, 213 A.2d at 153 (same).

Thus, in *Olbum*, the plaintiffs leased the mineral rights of specific portions of their land to a coal mining concern, in exchange for minimum royalty payments extending over four years. After successfully mining the land for a little over a year, defendant ceased its mining operations because the remaining coal had become unmineable and unmerchantable. 459 A.2d at 759. Plaintiffs then sued to recover the remaining royalty payments, but the court held that because the contract depended upon the "continued existence of a particular thing," *id.* at 761, specifically mineable coal, the contract was discharged for supervening impracticability. *Id., passim.*

In *Yoffe*, the promisor owed a contractual duty to file a securities registration statement with the SEC and effect registration within a set time. The SEC, however, unforeseeably undertook an investigation of its accounting practices, delaying the approval and causing

---

would be of such magnitude that the parties would have negotiated over it, had the event been more likely." Calamari & Perillo, *supra*, § 13.18, at 526.

11. I do not mean to suggest that these courts in any way reached the wrong result or engaged in faulty analysis. Rather, in those cases the traditional formulation of the test yielded the unmistakably correct conclusion that the promisor had assumed the risk of his own inability to perform.

damage to the promisee. The court held that, because the third party (SEC)'s actions were unforeseeable, the promisor was discharged. 443 A.2d at 363.

Likewise, in *Selland*, the promisor contracted to sell school bus bodies produced by a particular company, Superior. After the contract was entered into, and without the knowledge of any party, Superior became insolvent and the bodies were never delivered. The promisee then sued the promisor for breach of contract, but the court, applying § 2-615 of the U.C.C., held that the contract was discharged as impracticable. 384 N.W.2d at 492–93.

In *Litman v. Peoples Natural Gas Co.*, 449 A.2d 720 (Pa. Super. 1982), the promisee contracted with defendant gas company to install gas service to an apartment building. Defendant-promisor was unable to perform, however, because the state utility commission subsequently forbade defendant from making any new connections. Plaintiff sued for breach, but the court held that performance was discharged as impossible, owing to the interference of the third-party regulatory body. *Id.* 449 A.2d at 724–25.

Finally, in *Waldinger*, the court applied impracticability to a situation in which a thirdparty engineer unforeseeably required, contrary to industry custom, strict compliance with a standard, making the promisor-defendant's delivery of a compliant machine, as required by contract, impossible. 775 F.2d at 787–89.

The situation presented here is in accord with these cases. To recapitulate, CIT contracted to supply specific tire presses to Specialty. This was not a case of fungible goods; Specialty inspected, and bid for, certain identified, used presses located at the Natchez plant operated by Condere. All parties believed that CIT was the owner of the presses and was entitled to their immediate possession; Condere's representatives stated as much during the inspection visit. Neither Specialty nor CIT had any reason to believe that Condere would subsequently turn an about-face and assert a possessory interest in the presses. The most that can be said is that CIT had a course of dealings with Condere, but nowhere is it argued that there was any history of tortious or opportunistic conduct that would have alerted CIT that Condere would attempt to convert the presses to its own use.

Thus, whether analyzed traditionally in terms of foreseeability, as courts apply that term, or by the risk-exposure methodology outlined *supra*, it is clear that this is not the sort of risk that CIT should have expected to either bear or contract against. In economic terms, which I apply as a "check" rather than as substantive law, it cannot be said with any reliability that either Specialty or CIT was able to avoid the risk of what Condere did at a lower cost. It was "a bolt out of the blue" for both parties. On the other hand, Specialty was in a better position to know what consequences and damages would likely flow from nondelivery or delayed delivery of the presses. This suggests that Specialty is the appropriate party on which to impose the risk, *See* Posner, *supra* § 4.5, at 118; Calamari & Perillo, *supra* § 13.2, at 498. Moreover, judicial discharge of CIT's promise under these circumstances leaves Specialty in no worse a position than it would have occupied without the contract; either way, it would not have these presses, and it has only been able to locate and purchase three similar used presses on the open market since CIT's failure to deliver. On the other hand, CIT is relieved of the obligation to pay damages. Accordingly, excuse for impracticability would appear to be a Pareto-optimal move, note 8, *supra*, increasing CIT's welfare while not harming Specialty. This too is a valid policy reason for imposing the risk of loss on Specialty. *See* Calamari & Perillo, *supra* § 13.1, at 496. Thus, economic analysis confirms as sound policy the result suggested by the caselaw discussed *supra*.

Plaintiff makes much of the argument that there was no "basic assumption" created by Condere upon which Specialty and CIT based their contract, stating that it relied upon

CIT's representations alone. This is specious. As a matter of both law and logic, a basic assumption of any contract for the sale of specific, identified goods is that they are, in fact, available for sale. Accordingly, I reject this contention and conclude that the actions of Condere in detaining the presses presents sufficient grounds on which to base an impracticability defense.

Plaintiff also argues that this is a case only of subjective impossibility, presumably because Condere — which has been holding the presses essentially hostage — could deliver them up to Specialty. Thus, plaintiff contends that only CIT is incapable of performing and therefore should not be excused. This proves too much; in theory, at least, any hold-out party can be brought to the table if the price is high enough, including the parties in the cases discussed *supra*. Certainly, if CIT offered Condere $3 million to surrender the presses, there is little doubt that they would comply, but the law of impracticability does not require such outlandish measures.

In *Lichtenfels*, the promisor was unable to obtain a mining permit because one of ten owners held out for more money, yet the contract to mine was still discharged as impracticable. 531 A.2d at 24–26. Under Pennsylvania law, "impossibility" also encompasses "impracticability because of extreme and unreasonable difficulty, expense or loss involved." *Greenfield*, 380 A.2d at 759. This is simply not a case in which CIT became insolvent and could not perform, or in which the market price of tire presses spiked upward due to a shortage, making the contract unprofitable to CIT. While CIT did assume the risk of its own inability to perform, it did not assume the risk of Condere making it unable to perform by detaining the presses, any more than CIT assumed the risk that thieves would steal the presses from Condere before the latter could deliver them.[12] In sum, this risk was not "sufficiently within the control of [CIT] that [it should be inferred that it was] assumed by that party." 2 Farnsworth, *supra* § 9.6, at 619–20. It was completely within the control of Condere.[13]

Accordingly, I conclude on this record that CIT has made out its defense of impracticability. The ruling of the replevin court, however, indicates that CIT's performance is impracticable only in the temporary sense. Temporary impracticability only relieves the promisor of the obligation to perform as long as the impracticability lasts and for a reasonable time thereafter. *Moudy v. West Va. Pulp & Paper Co.*, 121 A.2d 881, 883 (Pa. 1956); *accord In re 222 Liberty Assocs.*, 101 B.R. 856, 862 (Bankr.E.D.Pa.1989); Calamari & Perillo, *supra* § 13.13, at 519. Once it receives possession of the presses, CIT asserts that it stands ready and willing to perform its contract with Specialty. That issue is not ripe for adjudication and must await a separate lawsuit if CIT should fail to perform after obtaining possession. Suffice it to say that, to the extent Specialty seeks damages for non-delivery of the presses to date, CIT is excused by the doctrine of impracticability and is entitled to full summary judgment.

---

12. In that hypothetical, the thieves could no doubt be induced to hand over the presses for a ransom, and thus someone is "capable" of performing. This shows in stark relief the absurdity of plaintiff's argument.

13. This fact pattern points up the conceptual weakness of the "I cannot do it versus it cannot be done" rendition of the objective/subjective test. Technically, someone could perform, but that someone is in all likelihood a tortfeasor that CIT has had to resort to judicial intervention to bring to heel. Thus, while this case may be seen as one of "I cannot do it," it is still not appropriate to treat as one in which a promisor merely underestimates the financial or technical resources it will need in order to perform.

Note

The doctrine of impossibility was articulated first in cases involving destruction of an essential thing or the death of an essential person. These are established categories of impossibility. Two additional categories are supervening illegality (when legislation or other government regulation makes some part of the contract illegal) and "natural disaster" or "act of God" (when storm, flood, volcano, or some other event of nature makes performance of some part of the contract impossible or impracticable). Courts continue to recognize these categories as presenting the strongest claims of excuse. *See, e.g., Uniform Commercial Code* § 2-613 (Casualty to Identified Goods); *Restatement (Second) of Contracts* §§ 262 (Death or Incapacity of Person Necessary for Performance), 263 (Destruction, Deterioration or Failure to Come into Existence of Thing Necessary for Performance).

Under the influence of legal realists, however, the doctrine has been generalized beyond these categories and has been applied in a wide range of circumstances, as Judge Brooks Smith's opinion in *Specialty Tires* suggests. The general doctrine is now as stated in *Uniform Commercial Code* § 2-615 (Excuse by Failure of Presupposed Conditions) (performance may be excused or delayed if "performance as agreed has been made impracticable by the occurrence of a contingency the non-occurrence of which was a basic assumption on which the contract was made") and *Restatement (Second) of Contracts* § 261 (Discharge By Supervening Impracticability) (same wording). The *United Nations Convention on Contracts for the International Sale of Goods* provides a similar excuse in Article 79 ("A party is not liable for a failure to perform any of his obligations if he proves that the failure was due to an impediment beyond his control and that he could not reasonably be expected to have taken the impediment into account at the time of the conclusion of the contract or to have avoided or overcome it or its consequences.").

Excuse will not be granted, however, if one of the parties explicitly or implicitly (as through trade practice or custom) assumed responsibility for the risk of the contingency or if one party was at fault in creating the problem or in failing to insure against it.

Even under the general doctrine of impracticability, some courts are hesitant to allow excuse where the only changed circumstance is an increase in costs. This issue was the focus of dispute in the next case.

Portland Section of the Council of Jewish Women v. Sisters of Charity of Providence in Oregon

Supreme Court of Oregon
513 P.2d 1183 (Or. 1973)

RALPH M. HOLMAN, JUSTICE

Plaintiff is a charitable corporation organized by Jewish women. Defendant is a charitable corporation which operates the St. Vincent Hospital and Medical Center and is the successor in interest to the Sisters of Charity of Providence of St. Vincent's Hospital. Plaintiff brought this suit to require defendant to perform a contract allegedly made in 1927 between plaintiff and defendant's predecessor which required the hospital, in return for the payment of $5,000, to furnish ward accommodations and services in perpetuity to one person at a time, such person to be designated by plaintiff. Defendant appeals from the trial court's decree specifically enforcing the agreement.

The first question raised by the appeal is whether there was such a contract with defendant's predecessor. The evidence convinces us there was. No signed contract was found by either party. However, unsigned copies of two contracts were found, one dated February 1927 and the other dated March 16, 1927. The two documents were identical except for some minor matters with which we are not directly concerned. Defendant's records disclose an Annual Account of the Financial Archives, under date of December 31, 1958, which has the following entry:

> "Received: $5,000 March 16, 1927, and additional $500.00 April 13, 1945. Obligation in perpetuity with Council of Jewish Women for maintenance of free ward bed for Jewish patients."

Opposite the entry is the following notation:

> "This obligation is faithfully carried out, according to the terms of the agreement."

In addition, defendant's records disclose a journal which lists the names of patients whose charges were written off by St. Vincent's Hospital to the "Jewish Endowed Bed." The first page of the journal is headed,

> "Jewish Endowed Bed 3/16/27."

In addition, other correspondence and documentation were adduced tending to show that there was an agreement to give care to Jewish patients designated by plaintiff.

Defendant makes the argument that, even if some sort of an agreement did exist, there is no evidence of the specific terms of the agreement. We conclude, as the trial judge did, that the unsigned agreement of March 16, 1927, contained the terms of the agreement. It is obvious there was some agreement, and we believe it is not a mere coincidence that the date of the last contract, the date of the payment of the money, and the date at which defendant commenced its journal covering the patients whose charges were written off to the "Jewish Endowed Bed" are the same.

Defendant contends the statute of frauds prevents the agreement from being enforced because there was no writing signed by its predecessor. The payment of the full consideration by plaintiff and the money's acceptance and retention constitute such performance of the contract sufficient to take the agreement out of the statute of frauds. *Stevens v. Good Samaritan Hospital and Medical Ctr.*, 504 P.2d 749 (Or. 1972); *Luckey v. Deatsman*, 343 P.2d 727 (Or. 1959); *Howland v. Iron Fireman Mfg. Co.*, 215 P.2d 380 (Or. 1950). Defendant argues that the performance is not exclusively referable to the contract of March 16, 1927. As previously indicated, the records of the defendant show that it is so referable.

Defendant was incorporated in 1934. The agreement was entered into by its predecessor, the Sisters of Charity of Providence of St. Vincent's Hospital. Since there was no written assumption of the contract by defendant upon defendant's incorporation in 1934, defendant contends that it cannot be required to render specific performance. The evidence indicates that the reason for the reincorporation was a technical limitation on the amount of assets which could be held by the old corporation. After the reincorporation, defendant took over the operation of the hospital and all assets connected therewith including whatever remained of plaintiff's $5,000 or whatever assets were purchased with it. Since the reincorporation was only a technical matter and was for the purpose of uninterruptedly carrying on the business of the old corporation, and since defendant took over all of its predecessor's assets and continued to honor the agreement, defendant is liable on the contract to the same extent as was its predecessor.

In 15 *Fletcher Cyclopedia of Corporations* § 7329, at 633–34 (rev. vol.1961) it is stated:
" ... (W)here a company is merely reincorporated, the new company is liable for the

debts of the old, as where it is formed for the purpose and with the intent of carrying on the business originally planned and intended to be carried on by the old corporation...." (Footnotes omitted.)

...

Defendant's principal defense against specific enforcement of this agreement is that it would work an undue hardship on defendant and on those members of the community using the hospital's services, such hardship being due to the present vastly inflated costs of medical care as compared with the costs of such care when the agreement was made. There is evidence that many new and expensive medical and hospital techniques have been developed which, together with inflation, have increased the cost of defendant's per patient care from a few dollars a day to approximately $140 per day, if all services are utilized.

The problem, though unstated by the parties, is due to the perpetual nature of the agreement[1] and to the inherent risks assumed by the promisor under such an agreement. Although perpetual agreements are disfavored, where clearly provided for they will be enforced according to their terms. *See Zimco Restaurants v. Local 340, Bartenders and Culinary Workers Union*, 331 P.2d 789, 792 (Cal. App. 1958). *Cf. Borough of West Caldwell v. Borough of Caldwell*, 138 A.2d 402, 412–413 (N.J. 1958); *Freeport Sulphur Co. v. Aetna Life Insurance Co.*, 206 F.2d 5, 8, (5th Cir. 1953). All the circumstances of each case must be considered in reaching a conclusion and, if consideration for the promise is fully executed, courts are reluctant to hold the promise terminable. 1 Williston, Contracts 112 § 38 (3d ed. 1957).

Since the contract in this case is clearly perpetual by its terms, the question then becomes whether the defendant assumed the risk of such vastly inflated prices.

The law on the subject of impossibility or hardship is unclear since much of the area is a matter of discretion in enforcing a given contract. However, the modern trend appears to be to allow the defense in more cases than formerly, *see* 6 Corbin, Contracts § 1320, at 321 (1962), though the most restrictive area is still hardship due to increased expense. That is this case. The *Restatement* generally does not allow discharge. It states:

> Except to the extent required by the rules stated in §§ 455–466, facts existing when a bargain is made or occurring thereafter making performance of a promise more difficult or expensive than the parties anticipate, do not prevent a duty from arising or discharge a duty that has arisen. 2 Restatement, Contracts § 467, at 882 (1932).

Corbin's analysis of hardship as a reason for denying specific performance is found in 5A Corbin, Contracts 205 § 1162 (1964):

> ... The remedy (of specific performance) should not be refused ... merely because of the rise or fall of market values that is within the usual contemplation of contractors and the risk of which is usually intended to be assumed when the contract is made. Specific performance will not be refused merely because the contract turned out to be a losing one.
>
> Specific performance should seldom be refused on the ground of changed conditions if nothing has occurred since the making of the bargain that was not within the actual contemplation of the parties when they were bargaining.... (Footnotes omitted.)

---

1. "... first party hereby agrees to furnish ward accommodation in perpetuity to one man, woman or child at a time, such patients to be sent to the hospital of the first party by any reputable physician and with the authorization of the designated official of the second party. The ward accommodation so to be furnished as herein agreed shall include bed, board, care of general nurse, medicine including any anesthetic, when necessary, dressings, laboratory, use of surgery and x-ray."

5A Corbin, Contracts § 1162, at 207–11. *See also* 6 Corbin, Contracts § 1333, at 365 (1962). What is foreseeable in a perpetual contract is difficult to ascertain especially since such contracts are rare.

The law in Oregon on discharge for practical impossibility because of unexpected difficulty or expense is set out in *Savage v. Peter Kiewit Sons' Co.*, 432 P.2d 519 (1968). The court there stated:

> In applying the doctrine of impossibility, courts recognize that unexpected difficulty or expense may approach such an extreme that a practical impossibility exists. *See, e.g., Natus Corporation v. United States*, 371 F.2d 450 (1967). To operate as a discharge, however, the hardship must be so extreme as to be outside any reasonable contemplation of the parties. *Natus Corporation v. United States, supra. And see* Restatement of Contracts § 454 (1932); *Transatlantic Financing Corporation v. United States*, 363 F.2d 312, 315 (D.C. Cir. 1966).
>
> Unexpected difficulties and expense, therefore, whether caused by injunction or by other causes, do not necessarily excuse performance of a contract. The question is whether the unforeseen hazard was one that reasonably should have been guarded against....

432 P.2d at 522. *Accord, Sachs v. Precision Products*, 476 P.2d 199 (Or. 1970); *Schafer v. Sunset Packing*, 474 P.2d 529 (Or. 1970). The cases and texts do not give any exact basis for decision. Subject to equitable principles, it remains in the discretion of this court whether to grant specific performance or not. See *Patecky v. Friend et al.*, 350 P.2d 170 (Or. 1960), where we stated:

> ... Specific performance of a contract is not a matter of right in equity, but is more a matter of grace resting in the sound discretion of the court, controlled by equitable principles. *Wagner v. Savage, as Adm'r.*, 244 P.2d 161 ...

350 P.2d at 175.

We hold that the trial court was correct in decreeing specific performance of the agreement. Even in 1927 it must have been contemplated by the parties that there was a distinct possibility that costs would not remain stable. It was necessarily evident that hospital care was, as it is now, an evolving science in which new treatments and techniques were being developed. Neither are we convinced that the contract presently is impossible of performance or so difficult to perform that equity should give relief therefrom. Defendant's gross receipts at the time of trial were at the rate of approximately $12,000,000 a year. We hold that the hazards of increasing expenses attributable to inflation and new techniques were ones that should and could have been guarded against and that the hardship has not become so extreme as to have been beyond any reasonable contemplation of the parties.

Since both parties to the suit are nonprofit, charitable organizations, the purpose of any contract for hospitalization between the two must logically be presumed to have been for the benefit of the needy. In carrying out their actions and by their performance of the contract the parties have so construed it.[2] It may well be that defendant, in recognition and execution of its philanthropic purposes, was willing to allow the Jewish section of the community to designate those Jews who would be the beneficiaries of defendant's

---

2. The following is an extract from plaintiff's Memorial and Happy Day Fund Report, dated May 4, 1927: " ... the bed is now an established fact and available to our sick poor at St. Vincent Hospital when applied for through the committee." (Emphasis added.)

charity if it would pay at least part of the cost of that charity, and that the $5,000 was never contemplated as being the equivalent of the value of the services such patients would ultimately be given.

Where the contract simply allocates risk and responsibility between two charitable organizations, contrary to the urging of defendant, there is probably no substantial net loss to the community from enforcement. The expenses of care and benefits derived therefrom are merely being distributed through the community in a different way.

The decree of the trial court should be modified slightly to conform with what we believe was the intent of the parties. The Jewish patients to whom defendant is required to give care under the agreement are limited to needy persons who are the legitimate objects of charity.

The decree of the trial court is affirmed as modified. Costs on appeal will be allowed to neither party.

Note

The general doctrine of impossibility or impracticability recognizes a *partial excuse,* where an impediment to performance is partial or temporary. Thus a party asserting the excuse may be relieved from only a part of his or her obligation or for only a limited period of time. In addition, even where a contract is entirely excused, there may be restitutionary claims based on benefits obtained by the parties. The next case involves such a claim.

Roy Cazares and Thomas Tosdal v. Phil Saenz

California Court of Appeal
256 Cal. Rptr. 209 (Cal. App. 1989)

HOWARD B. WIENER, ACTING PRESIDING JUSTICE

On one level, the issue in this case is simply one of attorney's fees. Are plaintiffs Roy Cazares and Thomas Tosdal, former partners in the law firm of Cazares & Tosdal, entitled to one-half of a contingent fee promised them by defendant Phil Saenz when he associated the firm on a particular personal injury case, notwithstanding that Cazares became a municipal court judge before the case was settled? More fundamentally, however, the issue before us requires that we review not only the nature of contingent attorney fee arrangements but also basic contract law regarding ... incapacitation of parties to a contract, and the proper measure of *quantum meruit* recovery in such circumstances. We decide that where one member of a two-person law firm becomes incapable of performing on a contract of association with another lawyer, the obligations of the parties to the contract are discharged if it was contemplated that the incapacitated attorney would perform substantial services under the agreement. We therefore hold that Cazares and Tosdal are not entitled to 50 percent of the contingent fee as provided in the association agreement. They may, however, recover the reasonable value of the legal services rendered before Cazares's incapacitation, prorated on the basis of the original contract price.

Factual and Procedural Background

Defendant Phil Saenz was an attorney of limited experience in November 1978 when he was contacted by the Mexican consulate in San Diego regarding a serious accident involving a Mexican national, Raul Gutierrez.[1] Gutierrez had been burned after touching a power line owned by San Diego Gas & Electric Company (SDG & E). He retained Saenz to represent him in a lawsuit against SDG & E and other defendants. The written retainer agreement authorized Saenz to "retain co-counsel if he deems it necessary" and provided that "[a]ttorney fees shall be 33 1/3% of the net recovery; i.e., after all costs and medical expenses."

Saenz shared office space with the law firm of Cazares & Tosdal, which was composed of partners Roy Cazares and Thomas Tosdal, the plaintiffs in this action.[2] In September 1979, Saenz agreed with Cazares to associate Cazares & Tosdal on the Gutierrez case. According to Saenz, he wanted to work with Cazares because Cazares spoke Spanish and could communicate directly with Gutierrez and because he (Saenz) respected Cazares's work in the Mexican-American community.[3] In contrast, Saenz did not feel comfortable with Tosdal: "Basically, he was an Anglo, a surfer. In my opinion, he was just too liberal for me...." Saenz testified he had no reason to doubt Tosdal's competence as a lawyer.[3] In fact, Saenz did not object to Tosdal's working on the case as long as he (Saenz) had nothing to do with him.

Cazares, on behalf of his firm, and Saenz agreed Saenz would continue to maintain client contact with Gutierrez and would handle a pending immigration matter to prevent Gutierrez from being deported. Saenz also wanted to actively assist in the preparation and trial of the case as a learning experience. Cazares & Tosdal was to handle most of the legal work on the case. Saenz and Cazares orally agreed they would evenly divide the contingent fee on the Gutierrez case.[5] Both Cazares and Saenz testified they expected and assumed Cazares would prosecute the case to its conclusion.

Gutierrez's complaint filed in November 1979 listed both Saenz and Cazares & Tosdal as counsel of record. During the next two and one-half years, Cazares performed most of the legal work in the case. Saenz maintained client contact, performed miscellaneous tasks and attended depositions including some defense depositions, which Cazares did not attend. For all intents and purposes, Tosdal performed no work on the case. Neither Cazares nor Saenz kept time records.

In June 1981, the Cazares & Tosdal partnership dissolved. The two partners decided to retain some cases, including the Gutierrez matter, as partnership assets. No formal

---

1. Saenz had been previously employed in a non-lawyer capacity by the San Diego District Attorney's Office. In that context he had worked with the Mexican consulate on a variety of matters.

2. The law firm of Cazares & Tosdal originally assigned its rights under the association agreement with Saenz to the law firm of Sullivan & Jones which in turn assigned its rights to the law firm of Page, Tucker & Brooks. Page, Tucker & Brooks filed the first amended complaint and, as a result, the caption of the case in the superior court read Page, Tucker & Brooks v. Saenz. While the case was pending in the superior court, Page, Tucker & Brooks assigned its rights back to Roy Cazares and Thomas Tosdal as individuals and judgment was entered in their favor. Accordingly, we have corrected the caption to read as printed above.

3. Saenz testified: "I trusted Roy. He spoke Spanish. He had experience like I had in the community. I know he was sympathetic and what else could I want, Harvard graduate, bright man, so forth. I knew he had a future, and I figure, 'Hey, this is a great guy, we have a lot in common. This is a guy I want to team up with at least through this case. We're compatible....'"

4. Like Cazares, Tosdal attended Harvard Law School, graduating cum laude in 1975.

5. Rule of Professional Conduct Rule 2-108, in effect at the time of the association agreement, provided that any agreement between lawyers to divide a fee must be consented to in writing by the client after full disclosure. Because this rule exists for the benefit of the client, who is not a party to this proceeding, we offer no further comment on the parties' failure to comply with this requirement.

substitution of counsel was filed in the case. Cazares and Saenz moved to a new office and continued to work on the case together for the next year.

In May 1982 Cazares was appointed a municipal court judge. Cazares urged Saenz to seek Tosdal's help in prosecuting the Gutierrez case. Saenz refused. In January 1983, Tosdal wrote Saenz stating that he remained "ready, willing and available to assist you in any aspect of the preparation of the case in which you may desire my aid."

Saenz never responded to Tosdal's offer. Instead, he associated an experienced personal injury attorney, Isam Khoury, to assist him on the Gutierrez case. Saenz also hired a young attorney, Dan Mazella, to do some research work.

In April 1983, Saenz settled the Gutierrez case for $1.1 million, entitling him to a fee slightly in excess of $366,000. Out of that fee, Saenz paid Khoury $40,000 and Mazella $7,000 for their work on the case. About two weeks later, Saenz visited Cazares and offered to pay him $40,000 for his work on the case. Cazares declined, claiming Saenz owed the now defunct Cazares & Tosdal partnership more than $183,000. This litigation ensued.

The case was tried to a referee by stipulation. *See* Code Civ. Proc. § 638. The referee concluded in pertinent part as follows:

> The partnership of Tosdal and Cazares entered into an agreement with Saenz, which was in effect a joint venture agreement. The partnership performed fully up until the time Cazares took the bench. At that time, Saenz rejected any help from the remaining partner, therefore preventing the performance by the partnership in further prosecution of the case. The case of *Jewel v. Boxer*, 156 Cal. App. 3d 171 would appear to govern. The joint venture entered into by [the] partnership [with] Saenz entitled the partnership to receive 50% of the fees received by Defendant Saenz.

The referee went on to conclude that Saenz was entitled to deduct the $47,000 paid to Khoury and Mazella before calculating the 50 percent due Cazares and Tosdal. Accordingly, judgment was entered in favor of Cazares and Tosdal in the amount of $159,833.00 plus interest.

Discussion

I.

The initial question is whether Saenz breached the association agreement with Cazares & Tosdal when, after Cazares's appointment to the municipal court, he refused to work with Tosdal on the Gutierrez case. Here, the referee in effect held that Saenz was *obligated* to accept Tosdal as a substitute for Cazares even though the record firmly establishes both parties to the association agreement contemplated that most if not all of the work on the Gutierrez case would be performed by Cazares. We conclude that Saenz acted within his rights in refusing to work with Tosdal after Cazares became a judge.[6]

---

6. In support of his conclusions, the referee cited Jewel v. Boxer (1984) 203 Cal. Rptr. 13. *Jewel* involved the dissolution of a law partnership and the rights of the partners to contingent fees in cases prosecuted to successful completion by some of the dissolving partners. The Jewel court held that in the absence of an agreement to the contrary, the partnership continued for the purposes of completing and collecting fees on all cases existing at the time of dissolution. There was no issue in the case as to the circumstances which would justify one attorney in refusing to continue working on a case with another attorney or firm with whom he had associated. Nor was there any discussion by the court as to how to measure the reasonable value of legal services rendered under a contingent fee contract where complete performance is made impossible or impracticable by an unforeseen event.

Where a contract contemplates the personal services of a party, performance is excused when that party dies or becomes otherwise incapable of performing. Restatement (Second) of Contracts §§ 261, 262; 1 Witkin, Contracts § 782, in Summary of Cal. Law 705 (9th ed. 1987). Here, the parties contemplated Cazares would personally perform the firm's obligations under the contract with Saenz, which he in fact did for two and one-half years after the execution of the contract. Cazares became legally incapable of performing the contract after his appointment to the bench. *See State Bar of California v. Superior Court*, 278 P. 432 (Cal. 1929). Of course, the contract was not between Saenz and Cazares but between Saenz and the firm of Cazares & Tosdal; thus, performance by the firm was not technically impossible. Nonetheless, the *Restatement (Second) of Contracts* § 262 addresses this issue because its language is not limited to the death or incapacity of a *party* to the contract: "If the existence of a *particular person* is necessary for the performance of a duty, his death or such incapacity as makes performance impracticable is an event the non-occurrence of which was a basic assumption on which the contract was made."[7] (Emphasis added.) Here, both Saenz and Cazares testified that Cazares's prosecution of the case to completion was a "basic assumption on which the contract was made."

. . .

II.

Our decision requires that we remand the case to the trial court for a determination of the reasonable value of the services rendered by Cazares & Tosdal on the *Gutierrez* case. *See* Restatement (Second) of Contracts § 377; *Fracasse v. Brent, supra*, 494 P.2d 9 (Cal.). Because the hourly fee is the prevailing price structure in the legal profession, it is sometimes assumed that the *quantum merui* standard applied to legal services includes nothing more than a reasonable hourly rate multiplied by the amount of time spent on the case. *See, e.g., Paolillo v. American Export Isbrandtsen Lines, Inc.*, 305 F. Supp. 250, 253–254 (S.D.N.Y. 1969). As even Saenz's counsel candidly recognizes, however, this is an overly narrow view of the *quantum meruit* standard applied in the context of a contingent fee agreement which, through no fault of either party, could not be performed.

[I]n seeking *quantum meruit* recovery on a partially performed contingent fee contract, the attorney-plaintiff is not limited to recovering his hourly rate on whatever time has been spent on the case but rather is entitled to an increased amount reflecting the value of the contingency factors as well as the delay in receiving payment for his services. We have further suggested that this "enhanced" fee may be calculated by prorating the original contract price and awarding the appropriate proportion to the partially performing attorney or firm.

The judgment is reversed. The case is remanded to the superior court for further proceedings consistent with this opinion.

Note

In *Saenz*, the court interpreted the contract to require the services of Cazares himself, not merely the services of any lawyer in the firm. When Cazares was appointed judge, he

---

7. Restatement of Contracts § 262 describes a specific type of impracticability of performance supplementing the general statement of the rule in section 261: "Where, after a contract is made, a party's performance is made impracticable without his fault by the occurrence of an event the non-occurrence of which was a basic assumption on which the contract was made, his duty to render that performance is discharged, unless the language or the circumstances indicate to the contrary."

became unavailable to perform the work for Saenz and therefore, the court reasoned, the law firm Cazares & Tosdal was excused from performance of the contract and Saenz also was excused. Saenz was excused because his obligation (to pay the firm 50% of his fee) was contingent (or "dependent") upon the law firm's performance: it is only fair, the court reasoned, that Saenz should not have to pay the full contract price to Cazares & Tosdal if the firm does not have to fully perform. This interdependence of the parties' obligations is developed in the doctrine of constructive conditions, which is examined in Chapter Ten.

---

2. Frustration of Purpose

Raymond Carver, A Small Good Thing

(1993)

Saturday afternoon she drove to the bakery in the shopping center. After looking through a loose-leaf binder with photographs of cakes taped onto the pages, she ordered chocolate, the child's favorite. The cake she chose was decorated with a spaceship and launching pad under a sprinkling of white stars, and a planet made of red frosting at the other end. His name, Scotty, would be in great letters beneath the planet. The baker, who was an older man with a thick neck, listened without saying anything when she told him the child would be eight years old next Monday. The baker wore a white apron that looked like a smock. Straps cut under his arms, went around in back and then to the front again, where they were secured under his heavy waist. He wiped his hands on his apron as he listened to her. He kept his eyes down on the photographs and let her talk. He let her take her time. He'd just come to work and he'd be there all night, baking, and he was in no real hurry.

She gave the baker her name, Ann Weiss, and her telephone number. The cake would be ready on Monday morning, just out of the oven, in plenty of time for the child's party that afternoon. The baker was not jolly. There were no pleasantries between them, just the minimum exchange of words, the necessary information.

...

On Monday morning, the birthday boy was walking to school with another boy. They were passing a bag of potato chips back and forth and the birthday boy was trying to find out what his friend intended to give him for his birthday that afternoon. Without looking, the birthday boy stepped off the curb at an intersection and was immediately knocked down by a car. He fell on his side with his head in the gutter and his legs out in the road. His eyes were closed, but his legs moved back and forth as if he were trying to climb over something. His friend dropped the potato chips and started to cry. The car had gone a hundred feet or so and stopped in the middle of the road. The man in the driver's seat looked back over his shoulder. He waited until the boy got unsteadily to his feet. The boy wobbled a little. He looked dazed, but okay. The driver put the car into gear and drove away.

The birthday boy didn't cry, but he didn't have anything to say about anything either. He wouldn't answer when his friend asked him what it felt like to be hit by a car. He walked home, and his friend went on to school. But after the birthday boy was inside his house and was telling his mother about it — she sitting beside him on the sofa, holding his hands in her lap, saying, "Scotty, honey, are you sure you feel all right, baby?" thinking she would call the doctor anyway — he suddenly lay back on the sofa, closed his eyes, and went limp. When she couldn't wake him up, she hurried to the telephone and called her husband at work. Howard told her to remain calm, remain calm, and then he called an ambulance for the child and left for the hospital himself.

Of course, the birthday party was canceled. The child was in the hospital with a mild concussion and suffering from shock. There'd been vomiting, and his lungs had taken in fluid which needed pumping out that afternoon. Now he simply seemed to be in a very deep sleep—but no coma, Dr. Francis had emphasized, no coma, when he saw the alarm in the parents' eyes. At eleven o'clock that night, when the boy seemed to be resting comfortably enough after the many X-rays and the lab work, and it was just a matter of his waking up and coming around, Howard left the hospital. He and Ann had been at the hospital with the child since that afternoon, and he was going home for a short while to bathe and change clothes.

...

The telephone rang and rang while he unlocked the door and fumbled for the light switch. He shouldn't have left the hospital, he shouldn't have. "Goddamn it!" he said. He picked up the receiver and said, "I just walked in the door!"

"There's a cake here that wasn't picked up," the voice on the other end of the line said.

"What are you saying?" Howard asked.

"A cake," the voice said. "A sixteen-dollar cake."

Howard held the receiver against his ear, trying to understand. "I don't know anything about a cake," he said. "Jesus, what are you talking about?"

"Don't hand me that," the voice said.

Howard hung up the telephone. He went into the kitchen and poured himself some whiskey. He called the hospital. But the child's condition remained the same; he was still sleeping and nothing had changed there. While water poured into the tub, Howard lathered his face and shaved. He'd just stretched out in the tub and closed his eyes when the telephone rang again. He hauled himself out, grabbed a towel, and hurried through the house, saying, "Stupid, stupid," for having left the hospital. But when he picked up the receiver and shouted, "Hello!" there was no sound at the other end of the line. Then the caller hung up.

...

They waited all day, but still the boy did not wake up. Occasionally, one of them would leave the room to go downstairs to the cafeteria to drink coffee and then, as if suddenly remembering and feeling guilty, get up from the table and hurry back to the room. Dr. Francis came again that afternoon and examined the boy once more and then left after telling them he was coming along and could wake up at any minute now. Nurses, different nurses from the night before, came in from time to time.

...

"I'll be right here," he said. "You go on home, honey. I'll keep an eye on things here." His eyes were bloodshot and small, as if he'd been drinking for a long time. His clothes were rumpled. His beard had come out again. She touched his face, and then she took her hand back. She understood he wanted to be by himself for a while, not have to talk or share his worry for a time. She picked her purse up from the nightstand, and he helped her into her coat.

"I won't be gone long," she said.

"Just sit and rest for a little while when you get home," he said. "Eat something. Take a bath. After you get out of the bath, just sit for a while and rest. It'll do you a world of good, you'll see. Then come back," he said. "Let's try not to worry. You heard what Dr. Francis said."

...

She pulled into the driveway and cut the engine. She closed her eyes and leaned her head against the wheel for a minute. She listened to the ticking sounds the engine made as it began to cool. Then she got out of the car. She could hear the dog barking inside the house. She went to the front door, which was unlocked. She went inside and turned on lights and put on a kettle of water for tea. She opened some dog food and fed Slug on the back porch. The dog ate in hungry little smacks. It kept running into the kitchen to see that she was going to stay. As she sat down on the sofa with her tea, the telephone rang.

"Yes!" she said as she answered. "Hello!"

"Mrs. Weiss," a man's voice said. It was five o'clock in the morning, and she thought she could hear machinery or equipment of some kind in the background.

"Yes, yes! What is it?" she said. "This is Mrs. Weiss. This is she. What is it please?" She listened to whatever it was in the background. "Is it Scotty, for Christ's sake?"

"Scotty," the man's voice said. "It's about Scotty, yes. It has to do with Scotty, that problem. Have you forgotten about Scotty?" the man said. Then he hung up.

She dialed the hospital's number and asked for the third floor. She demanded information about her son from the nurse who answered the telephone. Then she asked to speak to her husband. It was, she said, an emergency.

She waited, turning the telephone cord in her fingers. She closed her eyes and felt sick at her stomach. She would have to make herself eat. Slug came in from the back porch and lay down near her feet. He wagged his tail. She pulled at his ear while he licked her fingers. Howard was on the line.

"Somebody just called here," she said. She twisted the telephone cord. "He said it was about Scotty," she cried.

"Scotty's fine," Howard told her. "I mean, he's still sleeping. There's been no change. The nurse has been in twice since you've been gone. A nurse or else a doctor. He's all right."

"This man called. He said it was about Scotty," she told him.

"Honey, you rest for a little while, you need the rest. It must be that same caller I had. Just forget it. Come back down here after you've rested...."

...

"I was drinking a cup of tea," she said, "when the telephone rang. They said it was about Scotty. There was a noise in the background. Was there a noise in the background on that call you had, Howard?"

"I don't remember," he said. "Maybe the driver of the car, maybe he's a psychopath and found out about Scotty somehow. But I'm here with him. Just rest like you were going to do."

...

The doctors called it a hidden occlusion and said it was a one-in-a-million circumstance. Maybe if it could have been detected somehow and surgery undertaken immediately, they could have saved him. But more than likely not. In any case, what would they have been looking for? Nothing had shown up in the tests or in the X-rays.

...

Dr. Francis put his arm around Howard's shoulders. "I'm sorry. God, how I'm sorry." He let go of Howard's shoulders and held out his hand. Howard looked at the hand, and then he took it. Dr. Francis put his arms around Ann once more. He seemed full of some goodness she didn't understand. She let her head rest on his shoulder, but her eyes stayed open. She kept looking at the hospital. As they drove out of the parking lot, she looked back at the hospital.

At home, she sat on the sofa with her hands in her coat pockets. Howard closed the door to the child's room. He got the coffee-maker going and then he found an empty box. He had thought to pick up some of the child's things that were scattered around the living room. But instead he sat down beside her on the sofa, pushed the box to one side, and leaned forward, arms between his knees. He began to weep. She pulled his head over into her lap and patted his shoulder. "He's gone," she said. She kept patting his shoulder. Over his sobs, she could hear the coffee-maker hissing in the kitchen. "There, there," she said tenderly. "Howard, he's gone. He's gone and now we'll have to get used to that. To being alone."

...

Ann hung up the telephone after talking to her sister. She was looking up another number when the telephone rang. She picked it up on the first ring.

"Hello," she said, and she heard something in the background, a humming noise. "Hello!" she said. "For God's sake," she said. "Who is this? What is it you want?"

"Your Scotty, I got him ready for you," the man's voice said. "Did you forget him?"

"You evil bastard!" she shouted into the receiver. "How can you do this, you evil son of a bitch?"

"Scotty," the man said. "Have you forgotten about Scotty?" Then the man hung up on her.

Howard heard the shouting and came in to find her with her head on her arms over the table, weeping. He picked up the receiver and listened to the dial tone.

Much later, just before midnight, after they had dealt with many things, the telephone rang again.

"You answer it," she said. "Howard, it's him, I know." They were sitting at the kitchen table with coffee in front of them. Howard had a small glass of whiskey beside his cup. He answered on the third ring.

"Hello," he said. "Who is this? Hello! Hello!!" The line went dead. "He hung up," Howard said. "Whoever it was."

"It was him," she said. "That bastard. I'd like to kill him," she said. "I'd like to shoot him and watch him kick," she said.

"Ann, my God," he said.

"Could you hear anything?" she said. "In the background? A noise, machinery, something humming?"

"Nothing, really. Nothing like that," he said. "There wasn't much time. I think there was some radio music. Yes, there was a radio going, that's all I could tell. I don't know what in God's name is going on," he said.

She shook her head. "If I could, could get my hands on him." It came to her then. She knew who it was. Scotty, the cake, the telephone number. She pushed the chair away from the table and got up. "Drive me down to the shopping center," she said. "Howard."

"What are you saying?"

"The shopping center. I know who it is who's calling. I know who it is. It's the baker, the son-of-a-bitching baker, Howard. I had him bake a cake for Scotty's birthday. That's who's calling. That's who has the number and keeps calling us. To harass us about the cake. The baker, that bastard."

They drove down to the shopping center. The sky was clear and stars were out. It was cold, and they ran the heater in the car. They parked in front of the bakery. All of the shops and stores were closed, but there were cars at the far end of the lot in front of the movie theater. The bakery windows were dark, but when they looked through the glass they could see a light in the back room and, now and then, a big man in an apron moving in and out of the white, even light. Through the glass, she could see the display cases and some little tables with chairs. She tried the door. She rapped on the glass. But if the baker heard them, he gave no sign. He didn't look in their direction.

They drove around behind the bakery and parked. They got out of the car. There was a lighted window too high up for them to see inside. A sign near the back door said The Pantry Bakery, Special Orders. She could hear faintly a radio playing inside and something creak—an oven door as it was pulled down? She knocked on the door and waited. Then she knocked again, louder. The radio was turned down and there was a scraping sound now, the distinct sound of something, a drawer, being pulled open and then closed.

Someone unlocked the door and opened it. The baker stood in the light and peered out at them. "I'm closed for business," he said. "What do you want at this hour? It's midnight. Are you drunk or something?"

She stepped into the light that fell through the open door. He blinked his heavy eyelids as he recognized her. "It's you," he said.

"It's me," she said. "Scotty's mother. This is Scotty's father. We'd like to come in."

The baker said, "I'm busy now. I have work to do."

She had stepped inside the doorway anyway. Howard came in behind her. The baker moved back. "It smells like a bakery in here. Doesn't it smell like a bakery in here, Howard?"

"What do you want?" the baker said. "Maybe you want your cake? That's it, you decided you want your cake. You ordered a cake, didn't you?"

"You're pretty smart for a baker," she said. "Howard, this is the man who's been calling us." She clenched her fists. She stared at him fiercely. There was a deep burning inside her, an anger that made her feel larger than herself, larger than either of these men.

"Just a minute here," the baker said. "You want to pick up your three-day-old cake? That it? I don't want to argue with you, lady. There it sits over there, getting stale.... It's no good to me, no good to anyone now. It cost me time and money to make that cake. If you want it, okay, if you don't that's okay, too. I have to get back to work." He looked at them and rolled his tongue behind his teeth.

"More cakes," she said. She knew she was in control of it, of what was increasing in her. She was calm.

"Lady, I work sixteen hours a day in this place to earn a living," the baker said. He wiped his hands on his apron. "I work night and day in here, trying to make ends meet." A look crossed Ann's face that made the baker move back and say, "No trouble, now." He reached to the counter and picked up a rolling pin with his right hand and began to tap it against the palm of his other hand. "You want the cake or not? I have to get back to work. Bakers work at night," he said again. His eyes were small, mean-looking, she thought, nearly lost in the bristly flesh around his cheeks. His neck was thick with fat.

"I know bakers work at night," Ann said. "They make phone calls at night, too. You bastard," she said.

The baker continued to tap the rolling pin against his hand. He glanced at Howard. "Careful, careful," he said to Howard.

"My son's dead," she said with a cold, even finality. "He was hit by a car Monday morning. We've been waiting with him until he died. But, of course, you couldn't be expected to know that, could you? Bakers can't know everything—can they, Mr. Baker? But he's dead. He's dead, you bastard!" Just as suddenly as it had welled in her, the anger dwindled, gave way to something else, a dizzy feeling of nausea. She leaned against the wooden table that was sprinkled with flour, put her hands over her face, and began to cry, her shoulders rocking back and forth. "It isn't fair," she said. "It isn't, isn't fair."

Howard put his hand at the small of her back and looked at the baker. "Shame on you," Howard said to him. "Shame."

The baker put the rolling pin back on the counter. He undid his apron and threw it on the counter. He looked at them, and then he shook his head slowly. He pulled a chair out from under the card table that held papers and receipts, an adding machine, and a telephone directory. "Please sit down," he said. "Let me get you a chair," he said to Howard. "Sit down now, please." The baker went into the front of the shop and returned with two little wrought-iron chairs. "Please sit down, you people."

Ann wiped her eyes and looked at the baker. "I wanted to kill you," she said. "I wanted you dead."

The baker had cleared a space for them at the table. He shoved the adding machine to one side, along with the stacks of notepaper and receipts. He pushed the telephone directory onto the floor, where it landed with a thud. Howard and Ann sat down and pulled their chairs up to the table. The baker sat down, too.

"Let me say how sorry I am," the baker said, putting his elbows on the table. "God alone knows how sorry. Listen to me, I'm just a baker. I don't claim to be anything else. Maybe once, maybe years ago, I was a different kind of human being. I've forgotten, I don't know for sure. But I'm not any longer, if I ever was. Now I'm just a baker. That don't excuse my doing what I did, I know. But I'm deeply sorry. I'm sorry for your son, and sorry for my part in this," the baker said. He spread his hands out on the table and turned them over to reveal his palms. "I don't have any children myself, so I can only imagine what you must be feeling. All I can say to you now is that I'm sorry. Forgive me, if you can," the baker said. "I'm not an evil man, I don't think. Not evil, like you said on the phone. You got to understand what it comes down to is I don't know how to act anymore, it would seem. Please," the man said, "let me ask you if you can find it in your hearts to forgive me?"

It was warm inside the bakery. Howard stood up from the table and took off his coat. He helped Ann from her coat. The baker looked at them for a minute and then nodded and got up from the table. He went to the oven and turned off some switches. He found cups and poured coffee from an electric coffee-maker. He put a carton of cream on the table, and a bowl of sugar.

"You probably need to eat something," the baker said. "I hope you'll eat some of my hot rolls. You have to eat and keep going. Eating is a small, good thing in a time like this," he said.

He served them warm cinnamon rolls just out of the oven, the icing still runny. He put butter on the table and knives to spread the butter. Then the baker sat down at the table with them. He waited. He waited until they each took a roll from the platter and began to eat. "It's good to eat something," he said, watching them. "There's more. Eat up. Eat all you want. There's all the rolls in the world in here."

They ate rolls and drank coffee. Ann was suddenly hungry, and the rolls were warm and sweet. She ate three of them, which pleased the baker. Then he began to talk. They listened carefully. Although they were tired and in anguish, they listened to what the baker had to say. They nodded when the baker began to speak of loneliness, and of the sense of doubt and limitation that had come to him in his middle years. He told them what it was like to be childless all these years. To repeat the days with the ovens endlessly full and endlessly empty. The party food, the celebrations he'd worked over. Icing knuckle-deep. The tiny wedding couples stuck into cakes. Hundreds of them, no, thousands by now. Birthdays. Just imagine all those candles burning. He had a necessary trade. He was a baker. He was glad he wasn't a florist. It was better to be feeding people. This was a better smell anytime than flowers.

"Smell this," the baker said, breaking open a dark loaf. "It's a heavy bread, but rich." They smelled it, then he had them taste it. It had the taste of molasses and coarse grains. They listened to him. They ate what they could. They swallowed the dark bread. It was like daylight under the fluorescent trays of light. They talked on into the early morning, the high, pale cast of light in the windows, and they did not think of leaving.

———————

Raymond Carver maintained that great literature is life-connected, life-affirming, and life-changing. "In the best fiction," he wrote "the central character, the hero or heroine, is also the 'moved' character, the one to whom something happens in the story that makes a difference. Something happens that changes the way that character looks at himself and hence the world." A small good thing describes a relationship that begins with the kind of impersonal dealings that we associate with isolated transactions. Is the doctrine of frustration of purpose an expression of the sentiments that you find expressed in this story? How so?

———————

Brenner v. Little Red School House, Ltd.

Supreme Court of North Carolina
274 S.E.2d 206 (N.C. 1981)

. . .

By his complaint filed 17 July 1979, plaintiff sought a refund of the $100.00 confirmation fee and $972.00 advanced tuition which he had paid to defendant pursuant to a contract by which defendant agreed to enroll plaintiff's son in the fourth grade class of defendant school and to teach him for the 1978–1979 school session. The contract provided in pertinent part as follows:

> We understand that the tuition is $1,080.00 per year, payable in advance on the first day of school, no portion refundable. We also understand that upon your approval we may elect to pay tuition in $100.00 per month installments with interest according to published schedule, but that such election does not in any wise modify the stipulation that tuition is payable in advance.

> Enclosed is our $100.00 confirmation fee which will reserve our student a place for the coming year. This confirmation fee is to be applied to the yearly tuition only after all other installments, interest and other charges are paid.

Plaintiff was divorced on 21 January 1973 by an order which also awarded custody of the couple's minor son to his former wife. Plaintiff continued to make payments for the support of the child, including the tuition required to enable the child to attend defendant school for several years. Prior to the beginning of the 1978–79 school term, plaintiff paid defendant $1,072.00 pursuant to the contract. Subsequently, plaintiff's former wife refused to allow the child to attend the school at any time during the 1978–79 term.

Plaintiff's complaint stated that the contract at issue was void and unenforceable for lack of consideration or failure of consideration, and therefore all payments made thereunder should be refunded to avoid unjustly enriching defendant.

. . .

The Court of Appeals reversed the trial court's decision granting plaintiff's motion for summary judgment and remanded for entry of judgment in favor of defendant. Plaintiff appeals to this Court as a matter of right pursuant to G.S. 7A-30(2).

J. William Copeland, Justice

Plaintiff sets forth several arguments in support of his allegation that the Court of Appeals erred in reversing the trial court's order entering summary judgment in his favor. We have carefully reviewed each of plaintiff's contentions and find that summary judgment could not properly be granted in favor of either party. For the reasons stated below, we reverse that portion of the Court of Appeals' decision that remanded the case for entry of summary judgment in favor of defendant.

Plaintiff-appellant first contends that the doctrine of impossibility of performance and frustration of purpose should apply in this case to bring about a rescission of the contract. Impossibility of performance is recognized in this jurisdiction as excusing a party from performing under an executory contract if the subject matter of the contract is destroyed without fault of the party seeking to be excused from performance. *Sechrest v. Forest Furniture Co.*, 141 S.E.2d 292 (N.C. 1965). Plaintiff's former wife's refusal to send the child to defendant school did not destroy the subject matter of the contract; it was still possible for the child to attend the school. The doctrine of impossibility of performance clearly has no bearing on this case.

In support of the applicability of the doctrine of frustration of purpose, plaintiff argues that his former wife's refusal to allow the child to attend defendant school was a fundamental change in conditions that destroyed the object of the contract and resulted in a failure of consideration. Judge Harry C. Martin agreed with plaintiff and dissented on this basis, discussing the doctrine of frustration of purpose at length. While we agree with Judge Martin's general discussion of the law concerning frustration of purpose, we hold that the doctrine does not apply to bring about a rescission under the facts of this case.

The doctrine of frustration of purpose is discussed in 17 Am. Jur. 2d, *Contracts* § 401 (1964) as follows:

> Changed conditions supervening during the term of a contract sometimes operate as a defense excusing further performance on the ground that there was an implied condition in the contract that such a subsequent development should excuse performance or be a defense, and this kind of defense had prevailed in some instances even though the subsequent condition that developed was not one rendering performance impossible. . . . In such instances, . . . the defense

doctrine applied has been variously designated as that of "frustration" of the purpose or object of the contract or "commercial frustration."

Although the doctrines of frustration and impossibility are akin, frustration is not a form of impossibility of performance. It more properly relates to the consideration for performance. Under it performance remains possible, but is excused whenever a fortuitous event supervenes to cause a failure of the consideration or a practically total destruction of the expected value of the performance. The doctrine of commercial frustration is based upon the fundamental premise of giving relief in a situation where the parties could not reasonably have protected themselves by the terms of the contract against contingencies that later arose.

If the frustrating event was reasonably foreseeable, the doctrine of frustration is not a defense. In addition, if the parties have contracted in reference to the allocation of the risk involved in the frustrating event, they may not invoke the doctrine of frustration to escape their obligations. 17A C.J.S. *Contracts* § 463(2) (1963). *See also Perry v. Champlain Oil Co.*, 134 A.2d 65 (N.H. 1957).

In the present case, plaintiff contracted to pay the tuition for the entire school year in advance of the first day of school. In consideration therefor, defendant promised to hold a place in the school for plaintiff's child, to make all preparations necessary to educate the child for the school year, and to actually teach the child during that period. Both parties received valuable consideration under the terms of the contract. After receiving plaintiff's tuition payment, defendant reserved a space for plaintiff's child, made preparations to teach the child, and at all times during the school year kept a place open for the child. This performance by defendant was sufficient consideration for plaintiff's tuition payment. A school such as defendant must make arrangements for the education of its pupils on a yearly basis, prior to the commencement of the school year. Many of these arrangements are based upon the number of pupils enrolled, for example, the teaching materials to be ordered, the number of teachers to be hired, and the desks and other equipment that will be used by the children. In addition, private schools are often limited in the number of pupils that can be accommodated, so that the reservation of a space for one child may prevent another's enrollment in the school. Had it been advised before the first day of school that plaintiff's child would not be in attendance, defendant might have been able to fill the vacant position. After the start of the school year, the probability of filling the position decreased substantially, thus to allow plaintiff to recover the tuition paid might deprive defendant of income it would have received had the contract not been entered into. Therefore, although plaintiff did not receive the full consideration contemplated by the contract, he received consideration sufficient to avoid the application of the doctrine of frustration of purpose. There was no substantial destruction of the value of the contract.

Furthermore, we find the doctrine of frustration of purpose inapplicable on an additional basis. Although the parties could not have been expected to foresee the exact actions of plaintiff's former wife in refusing to send the child to defendant school, the possibility that the child might not attend was foreseeable and appears expressly provided for in the contract. The contract states that tuition is "payable in advance of the first day of school, no portion refundable." This provision allocates to plaintiff the risk that the child will not attend, and prevents the application of the doctrine of frustration of purpose.

Since the doctrine of frustration of purpose does not apply and the terms of the contract are clear and unambiguous, the courts are bound to enforce it as written. *Crockett v. First Federal Savings and Loan Association of Charlotte*, 224 S.E.2d 580 (N.C. 1976); *Weyerhaeuser*

Co. v. Carolina Power & Light Co., 127 S.E.2d 539 (N.C. 1962). This holding is consistent with prior cases in this jurisdiction that state that a contract providing for the nonrefundable payment of tuition is enforceable as written, regardless of the nonattendance of the pupil, where the failure to attend is not caused by some fault on the part of the school. *Horner School v. Wescott*, 32 S.E.2d 885 (N.C. 1899). Our decision is also in accord with the majority of jurisdictions in this country. *J.J. & L. Investment Co. v. Minaga*, 487 P.2d 561 (Colo. App. 1971).

Defendant argues that even if the contract is not rescinded, this Court should find it unconscionable and refuse to enforce it. We disagree. A court will generally refuse to enforce a contract on the ground of unconscionability only when the inequality of the bargain is so manifest as to shock the judgment of a person of common sense, and where the terms are so oppressive that no reasonable person would make them on the one hand, and no honest and fair person would accept them on the other. *Hume v. United States*, 132 U.S. 406 (1889); *Christian v. Christian*, 365 N.E.2d 849 (N.Y. 1977). In determining whether a contract is unconscionable, a court must consider all the facts and circumstances of a particular case. If the provisions are then viewed as so one-sided that the contracting party is denied any opportunity for a meaningful choice, the contract should be found unconscionable. *In re Friedman*, 407 N.Y.S.2d 999 (1978); *Collins v. Uniroyal Inc.*, 315 A.2d 30 (N.J. 1973), *aff'd* 315 A.2d 16 (N.J. 1974). *See, e.g.*, G.S. 25A-43(c).

After considering all the facts before the trial court, we hold that the contract at issue cannot be declared unenforceable on the grounds of unconscionability. There was no inequality of bargaining power between the parties. Plaintiff was not forced to accept defendant's terms, for there were other private and public schools available to educate the child. The clause providing the tuition payments would be non-refundable is reasonable when considered in light of the expense to defendant in preparing to educate the child and in reserving a space for him. The bargain was one that a reasonable person of sound judgment might accept. "Ordinarily, when parties are on equal footing, competent to contract, enter into an agreement on a lawful subject, and do so fairly and honorably, the law does not permit inquiry as to whether the contract was good or bad, whether it was wise or foolish." *Robertson v. Williams*, 83 S.E.2d 811, 814 (N.C. 1954). The contract is enforceable as written.

...

However, we find that by his allegation that Ms. Ballinger agreed to refund the tuition paid, plaintiff raised an issue of fact sufficient to avoid the entry of summary judgment against him. If Ms. Ballinger did agree to refund plaintiff's payment, her agreement would constitute an enforceable modification of the provision of the contract prohibiting a refund. Where, as in this case, a contract has been partially performed, an agreement to alter its terms is treated as any other contract and must be supported by consideration. *Wheeler v. Wheeler*, 263 S.E.2d 763 (N.C. 1980); *Lenoir Memorial Hospital, Inc. v. Stancil*, 139 S.E.2d 901 (N.C. 1965). In return for defendant's promise to refund the tuition paid, plaintiff would relinquish his right to have his child educated in defendant school. Defendant received a benefit in being relieved of the responsibility to teach the child for the school year. It is well established that any benefit, right, or interest bestowed upon the promisor, or any forbearance, detriment, or loss undertaken by the promisee, is sufficient consideration to support a contract. *Carolina Helicopter Corp. v. Cutler Realty Co.*, 139 S.E.2d 362 (N.C. 1964); 17 C.J.S. *Contracts* §74 (1963). We believe that there was consideration sufficient to support an agreement by Ms. Ballinger to refund plaintiff's payment, if such an agreement was made. Whether such an agreement was reached is a material fact to be determined by the jury. Summary judgment is properly granted only if all the evidence before the court indicates that there is no genuine issue as to any material fact and that one party is entitled to judgment as a matter of law. The burden of establishing the absence of any triable issue of fact is on the party moving for summary judgment. *Econo-Travel Motor Hotel Corp. v. Taylor*, 271 S.E.2d 54 (N.C. 1980); *Middleton v. Myers*, 261 S.E.2d (N.C. 1980); 108 G.S. 1A-1, Rule 56(c). Plaintiff failed to meet his burden to prove, as a matter of law, that an enforceable agreement to refund his payments existed. Hence, the trial court erred in granting plaintiff's motion for summary judgment. Likewise, defendant did not prove, as a matter of law, that no agreement to refund plaintiff's payment was made, and that portion of the Court of Appeal's opinion which remanded to the trial court for entry of summary judgment in favor of defendant was also in error.

For the reasons stated, we reverse the decision of the Court of Appeals and remand to that court with instructions to remand to the District Court, Guilford County, for a new trial.

B. Agreed Modifications and the Pre-Existing Duty Rule

Classical contract theory provides that a promise to do something one is already obligated to do cannot be sufficient consideration for a return promise. The court in *White v. Village of Homewood* (Chapter Four), cited this rule as one ground for its decision not to enforce White's agreement releasing the Village from any liability for injuries caused by the test for firefighters. The court in *White* reasoned that since the fire department was statutorily required to allow applicants to take the firefighters' test, its agreement to let White take the test was not sufficient consideration for her promise to release the department from liability for its negligence. This is the *pre-existing duty rule*.

Where the pre-existing obligation was created in a contract between the parties (rather than by statute or contract with some other entity), the *pre-existing duty rule* means that *contract modifications* are not enforceable unless both parties agree to do something in addition to what the contract originally required. Classical contract theory embraced this rule as a salutary check on abuse of power within contracting relationships. So, for example, if Trinh Thi May and Herbert Weinberg have agreed that Trinh will paint Weinberg's house for $3,000 (the original contract), and they later agree to increase the price to $4,000 for the same amount of painting (the modification), courts would say that Weinberg's promise to pay Trinh the additional $1,000 is not enforceable, as she did not promise to do anything other than what she was obligated to do under the original contract (the pre-existing duty rule).

As the next case indicates, one rationale for this rule was to prevent coercive threats to breach a contract. The rule enabled courts to refuse enforcement of a coerced modification, even though economic duress was not recognized, at that time, as a defense to contract enforcement.

Yet under current duress doctrine, economic duress is a defense and thus the pre-existing duty rule seems less persuasive. Indeed, the rule has been harshly criticized as unrealistic and ideologically rigid. There are many reasons why people may want to modify existing contracts, even when the modification results in an increased burden for only one party. Businesspeople routinely assume long-term contracts will require adjustments and expect flexibility of both parties. This is particularly true for businesspeople from countries and cultures that have not been influenced by U.S. contract theory. *See* Hiroshi Wagatsuma & Arthur Rosett, *Cultural Attitudes Towards Contract Law: Japan and the United States Compared*, below.

In recent years, U.S. courts have frequently refused to apply the pre-existing duty rule to contract modifications undertaken in good faith, particularly where there have been unanticipated changes in circumstances. *See* Restatement (Second) of Contracts § 89. *Section* 2-209(1) of the *Uniform Commercial Code* explicitly rejects the rule for contracts involving the sale of goods: "An agreement modifying a contract within this Article needs no consideration to be binding."

In keeping with the practice in most of the world, the *United Nations Convention on Contracts for the International Sale of Goods* provides for enforcement of agreed modifications. Article 29(1) provides: "A contract may be modified or terminated by the mere agreement of the parties."

The following cases involve the traditional pre-existing duty rule and its modern reformations.

Alaska Packers' Ass'n v. Domenico et al.

United States Circuit Court of Appeals, Ninth Circuit
117 F. 99 (9th Cir. 1902)

Erskine M. Ross, Circuit Judge

The libel in this case was based upon a contract alleged to have been entered into between the libelants and the appellant corporation on the 22d day of May, 1900, at Pyramid Harbor, Alaska, by which it is claimed the appellant promised to pay each of the libelants, among other things, the sum of $100 for services rendered and to be rendered. In its answer the respondent denied the execution, on its part, of the contract sued upon, averred that it was without consideration, and for a third defense alleged that the work performed by the libelants for it was performed under other and different contracts than that sued on, and that, prior to the filing of the libel, each of the libelants was paid by the respondent the full amount due him thereunder, in consideration of which each of them executed a full release of all his claims and demands against the respondent.

The evidence shows without conflict that on March 26, 1900, at the city and county of San Francisco, the libelants entered into a written contract with the appellants, whereby they agreed to go from San Francisco to Pyramid Harbor, Alaska, and return, on board such vessel as might be designated by the appellant, and to work for the appellant during the fishing season of 1900, at Pyramid Harbor, as sailors and fishermen, agreeing to do "regular ship's duty, both up and down, discharging and loading; and to do any other work whatsoever when requested to do so by the captain or agent of the Alaska Packers' Association." By the terms of this agreement, the appellant was to pay each of the libelants $50 for the season, and two cents for each red salmon in the catching of which he took part.

On the 15th day of April, 1900, 21 of the libelants signed shipping articles by which they shipped as seamen on the Two Brothers, a vessel chartered by the appellant for the voyage between San Francisco and Pyramid Harbor, and also bound themselves to perform the same work for the appellant provided for by the previous contract of March 26th; the appellant agreeing to pay them therefor the sum of $60 for the season, and two cents each for each red salmon in the catching of which they should respectively take part.

Unloading the Catch, Louis Breslow.

Under these contracts, the libelants sailed on board the Two Brothers for Pyramid Harbor, where the appellants had about $150,000 invested in a salmon cannery. The libelants arrived there early in April of the year mentioned, and began to unload the vessel and fit up the cannery. A few days thereafter, to wit, May 19th, they stopped work in a body, and demanded of the company's superintendent there in charge $100 for services in operating the vessel to and from Pyramid Harbor, instead of the sums stipulated for in and by the contracts; stating that unless they were paid this additional wage they would stop work entirely, and return to San Francisco.

The evidence showed, and the court below found, that it was impossible for the appellant to get other men to take the places of the libelants, the place being remote, the season short and just opening; so that, after endeavoring for several days without success to induce the libelants to proceed with their work in accordance with their contracts, the company's superintendent, on the 22d day of May, so far yielded to their demands as to instruct his clerk to copy the contracts executed in San Francisco, including the words "Alaska Packers' Association" at the end, substituting, for the $50 and $60 payments, respectively, of those contracts, the sum of $100, which document, so prepared, was signed by the libelants before a shipping commissioner whom they had requested to be brought from Northeast Point; the superintendent, however, testifying that he at the time told the libelants that he was without authority to enter into any such contract, or to in any way alter the contracts made between them and the company in San Francisco.

Upon the return of the libelants to San Francisco at the close of the fishing season, they demanded pay in accordance with the terms of the alleged contract of May 22d, when the company denied its validity, and refused to pay other than as provided for by the contracts of March 26th and April 15th, respectively. Some of the libelants, at least, consulted counsel, and, after receiving his advice, those of them who had signed the shipping articles before the shipping commissioner at San Francisco went before that officer, and received the amount due them thereunder, executing in consideration thereof a release in full, and the others paid at the office of the company, also receipting in full for their demands.

On the trial in the court below, the libelants undertook to show that the fishing nets provided by the respondent were defective, and that it was on that account that they demanded increased wages. On that point, the evidence was substantially conflicting, and the finding of the court was against the libelants, the court saying:

> The contention of libelants that the nets provided them were rotten and unserviceable is not sustained by the evidence. The defendants' interest required that libelants should be provided with every facility necessary to their success as fishermen, for on such success depended the profits defendant would be able to realize that season from its packing plant, and the large capital invested therein. In view of this self-evident fact, it is highly improbable that the defendant gave libelants rotten and unserviceable nets with which to fish. It follows from this finding that libelants were not justified in refusing performance of their original contract.

The evidence being sharply conflicting in respect to these facts, the conclusions of the court, who heard and saw the witnesses, will not be disturbed. *The Alijandro*, 56 F. 621 (9th Cir. 1893).

The real questions in the case as brought here are questions of law, and, in the view that we take of the case, it will be necessary to consider but one of those. Assuming that the appellant's superintendent at Pyramid Harbor was authorized to make the alleged contract of May 22d, and that he executed it on behalf of the appellant, was it supported by a sufficient consideration? From the foregoing statement of the case, it will have been seen that the libelants agreed in writing, for certain stated compensation, to render their services to the appellant in remote waters where the season for conducting fishing operations is extremely short, and in which enterprise the appellant had a large amount of money invested; and, after having entered upon the discharge of their contract, and at a time when it was impossible for the appellant to secure other men in their places, the libelants, without any valid cause, absolutely refused to continue the services they were under contract to perform unless the appellant would consent to pay them more money.

Consent to such a demand, under such circumstances, if given, was, in our opinion, without consideration, for the reason that it was based solely upon the libelants' agreement to render the exact services, and none other, that they were already under contract to render. The case shows that they willfully and arbitrarily broke that obligation. As a matter of course, they were liable to the appellant in damages, and it is quite probable, as suggested by the court below in its opinion, that they may have been unable to respond in damages. But we are unable to agree with the conclusions there drawn, from these facts, in these words:

> Under such circumstances, it would be strange, indeed, if the law would not permit the defendant to waive the damages caused by the libelants' breach, and enter into the contract sued upon, — a contract mutually beneficial to all the parties thereto, in that it gave to the libelants reasonable compensation for their labor, and enabled the defendant to employ to advantage the large capital it had invested in its canning and fishing plant.

Certainly, it cannot be justly held, upon the record in this case, that there was any voluntary waiver on the part of the appellant of the breach of the original contract. The company itself knew nothing of such breach until the expedition returned to San Francisco, and the testimony is uncontradicted that its superintendent at Pyramid Harbor, who, it is claimed, made on its behalf the contract sued on, distinctly informed the libelants that he had no power to alter the original or to make a new contract, and it would, of course, follow that, if he had no power to change the original, he would have no authority to waive any rights thereunder.

The circumstances of the present case bring it, we think, directly within the sound and just observations of the supreme court of Minnesota in the case of *King v. Railway Co.*, 63 N.W. 1105 (Minn.):

> No astute reasoning can change the plain fact that the party who refuses to perform, and thereby coerces a promise from the other party to the contract to pay him an increased compensation for doing that which he is legally bound to do, takes an unjustifiable advantage of the necessities of the other party. Surely it would be a travesty on justice to hold that the party so making the promise for extra pay was estopped from asserting that the promise was without consideration. A party cannot lay the foundation of an estoppel by his own wrong, where the promise is simply a repetition of a subsisting legal promise. There can be no consideration for the promise of the other party, and there is no warrant for inferring that the parties have voluntarily rescinded or modified their contract. The promise cannot be legally enforced, although the other party has completed his contract in reliance upon it.

In *Lingenfelder v. Brewing Co.*, 15 S.W. 844, the court, in holding void a contract by which the owner of a building agreed to pay its architect an additional sum because of his refusal to otherwise proceed with the contract, said:

> It is urged upon us by respondents that this was a new contract. New in what? Jungenfeld was bound by his contract to design and supervise this building. Under the new promise, he was not to do anything more or anything different. What benefit was to accrue to Wainwright? He was to receive the same service from Jungenfeld under the new, that Jungenfeld was bound to tender under the original, contract. What loss, trouble, or inconvenience could result to Jungenfeld

that he had not already assumed? No amount of metaphysical reasoning can change the plain fact that Jungenfeld took advantage of Wainwright's necessities, and extorted the promise of five per cent. on the refrigerator plant as the condition of his complying with his contract already entered into. Nor had he even the flimsy pretext that Wainwright had violated any of the conditions of the contract on his part. Jungenfeld himself put it upon the simple proposition that "if he, as an architect, put up the brewery, and another company put up the refrigerating machinery, it would be a detriment to the Empire Refrigerating Company," of which Jungenfeld was president. To permit plaintiff to recover under such circumstances would be to offer a premium upon bad faith, and invite men to violate their most sacred contracts that they may profit by their own wrong. That a promise to pay a man for doing that which he is already under contract to do is without consideration is conceded by respondents. The rule has been so long imbedded in the common law and decisions of the highest courts of the various states that nothing but the most cogent reasons ought to shake it. (Citing a long list of authorities.)

. . .

What we hold is that, when a party merely does what he has already obligated himself to do, he cannot demand an additional compensation therefor; and although, by taking advantage of the necessities of his adversary, he obtains a promise for more, the law will regard it as nudum pactum, and will not lend its process to aid in the wrong.

. . .

It results from the views above expressed that the judgment must be reversed, and the cause remanded, with directions to the court below to enter judgment for the respondent, with costs. It is so ordered.

———————

Star of Alaska

When the *Balclutha* went aground in 1904, the Alaska Packers Association purchased her where she lay for the non-princely sum of $500. After extensive repairs, they renamed her *Star of Alaska* (all Alaska Packer iron and steel sailing vessels had a "Star" prefix to their names).

During this career, the ship sailed up the West Coast from Alameda, California, carrying supplies and cannery workers. *Star of Alaska* anchored out in Chignik Bay, Alaska, during April. After the supplies were unloaded and the cannery workers had settled into the company's camp ashore, only a ship keeper or two remained on board. In early September, her hold packed with cases of canned salmon, *Star of Alaska* started the 2,400-mile voyage back to San Francisco Bay. She was considered a fast sailer, averaging better than twenty-two days for the trip north and fifteen days when homeward bound.

During the winter, the ship was laid up with the rest of the Alaska Packer's fleet of thirty-odd vessels in Alameda, where shipwrights performed maintenance and renovation. In 1911, the poop deck was extended to house Italian and Scandinavian fishermen. Later, additional bunks were added in the 'tween deck for Chinese cannery workers. As *Balclutha*, the ship carried a crew of twenty-six men; on *Star of Alaska*, over 200 men made the trip north.

Star of Alaska was the only sailing ship the Alaska Packers sent north in 1930, and when she returned that September she, too, was retired.

Hiroshi Wagatsuma & Arthur Rosett, Cultural Attitudes towards Contract Law: Japan and the United States Compared

2 Pacific Basin L.J. 76 (1983)

In many Japanese contracts there are clauses such as, "if in the future a dispute arises between the parties with regard to the rights and duties provided in this contract, the parties will confer in good faith," (*sie-i o motte Kyo–gi suru*), or in a similar situation, " ... will settle the dispute harmoniously by consultation" (*kyo–gi ni yori enman ni kaiketsu suru*). These "confer-in-good-faith" and "harmonious-settlement" clauses reveal the basic nature of the Japanese contract. Kawashima's interpretation of the meaning of such clauses is accurate. He says,

> in Japanese contract the parties not only do not stipulate in a detailed manner the rights and duties under the contract, but also think that even the rights and duties provided for the written agreement are tentative rather than definite. Accordingly, when a dispute arises, they think it desirable at that time to fix such rights and duties by means of *ad hoc* consultation. Therefore, even something such as the due date of a debt is not thought of as something strictly defined but as fixed "give or take a few days." The creditor who demands payment of the penalty for delay when payment is only a day or two overdue is thought of as a shylock or an inflexible person. Therefore, it is possible to state that a confer-in-good-faith clause, even if it is not written in a contract document, is, so to speak, tacitly implied in all contracts.[9]

...

Anglo-American commercial law is primarily the result of common law judicial rulings, not statutory code analysis. These rules arose through a lawyer-dominated process of case decision in relationships that had gone wrong and therefore demanded court intervention. They are not modeled on how things are supposed to work among cooperative businesspersons with healthy ongoing relationships. They emphasize the competitive and antagonistic dimensions of such reality rather than the cooperative and supportive aspects. Looked at the way described above, commercial law can be seen as a kind of medicine for pathological situations, for failed agreements, in which smooth commercial relations have broken down and cooperative transactions have turned sour and ended in conflict. The rules that have emerged over the last century and a half are framed from the perspective of the "doctor" called in to minister to the sick transaction and to resolve the dispute.

Returning to the Japanese situation, it should be clear by now that the so-called traditional Japanese attitude toward contract is not essentially different from that prevalent among American businesspersons. The difference is that in the West contract is used to define rights and duties of the parties by detailed provisions when good-will and trust between the parties have broken down, while the Japanese tend to insist upon the continuing effectiveness of good-will and trust in every situation.

---

9. T. Kawashima, Nihonjin no Ho– Ishiki (The Legal Consciousness of the Japanese) (1967); Kawashima, The Legal Consciousness of Contract in Japan, 7 Law in Japan: An Annual 1 (1974).

To repeat the medical metaphor, Westerners use contract as a medical device to save a sick relationship in case a relationship loses its original healthy trust, while Japanese social norms demand that the relationship always be healthy. People are forced to behave as if their relationship were continuously healthy even when the bond based upon mutual trust has been damaged. It is as though people are afraid of taking medicine lest they should become really ill because taking a medicine is admitting that one is actually sick. While in the American mind, the function of contract is to anticipate possible future strife and trouble as well as to pre-define disputes and enunciate rights, contract in the Japanese mind is a symbolic expression or reflection of mutual trust that is expected to work favorably for both parties in case of future trouble and never to break down.

Lester L. Quigley, Jr. and Veronna Kay Lovell, as Guardians and Conservators of Lester L. Quigley, Sr. v. Donald M. Wilson and Janis D. Wilson

Court of Appeals of Iowa
474 N.W.2d 277 (Iowa 1991)

Leo Oxberger, Chief Judge

In 1980 Lester Quigley, Sr. sold his farm on contract to Donald and Janis Wilson. The Wilsons made the installment payments until 1985. In 1985, the Wilsons assigned the contract to Forrest Hatfield. Sometime prior to February 1986, Hatfield informed the Wilsons he could no longer make the payments and returned the farm to them. Donald Wilson then met with Quigley, Sr. to inform him they were also unable to make the upcoming March 1, 1986 payment. After negotiations, Quigley, Sr. and the Wilsons agreed to reduce the contract price along with some other changes from the original contract terms. Both parties signed an agreement dated March 7, 1986, created by Quigley, Sr.'s attorney, which reduced their negotiations to writing. Quigley, Sr.'s attorney later recorded the agreement. The Wilsons made all payments due under the 1986 agreement.

Quigley, Sr. is quite elderly and has resided in a nursing home since 1985. In 1988 Quigley, Sr. established a voluntary conservatorship appointing his two children, Lester L. Quigley, Jr. and Veronna Kay Lovell, co-conservators for himself.

The co-conservators filed this lawsuit September 12, 1988, against the Wilsons, seeking a declaratory judgment that the Wilsons were in default of the 1980 contract. The Wilsons filed an answer generally denying the claims and asserting the 1986 agreement modified the 1980 contract.

The day before trial the plaintiffs filed a trial brief and motion for partial judgment on the pleadings. They alleged the 1986 agreement was unenforceable due to lack of consideration. The district court overruled the motion finding lack of consideration was not a triable issue because the plaintiffs failed to specially plead it as an affirmative defense.

The case proceeded to trial. The jury found Lester Quigley, Sr. was mentally competent when he entered into the 1986 agreement. The court then held a bench trial on the equitable issues of fraud and undue influence. The court entered a verdict in favor of the Wilsons, finding the 1986 agreement enforceable.

The co-conservators appeal. They contend the issue of lack of consideration should have been submitted to the jury because a reply pleading was unnecessary. They argue the exclusion of the issue prejudiced their case and further assert that based on their defense of lack of consideration, the court should have granted their motion for partial judgment and directed the verdict in their favor. They also claim they were entitled to a jury trial on the equitable as well as legal issues.

Initially, we consider the proper scope of review. The essential character of a cause of action and the relief it seeks, as shown by the complaint, determine whether an action is at law or equity. *Mosebach v. Blythe*, 282 N.W.2d 755, 758 (Iowa App. 1979). Where the primary right of the plaintiff arises from nonperformance of a contract, where the remedy is money, and where the damages are full and certain, remedies are usually provided at law. *Id.* The issues of Quigley, Sr.'s competency to enter into a contract and whether a lack of consideration invalidated the 1986 agreement are triable at law, therefore, our scope of review of these issues is on assigned error only.

. . .

Although we find the trial court erred in its rationale for refusing to allow the plaintiffs to develop their lack of consideration defense to the jury, we do not find reversible error. If a basis exists for affirming the trial court, we will do so regardless of whether that basis was relied upon by the trial court. *See Anderson v. Yearous*, 249 N.W.2d 855, 863 (Iowa 1977).

In the trial court's findings of fact and conclusions of law the court stated the 1986 agreement appeared to constitute a waiver within the meaning of *In re Guardianship of Collins*, 327 N.W.2d 230 (Iowa 1982). In *Collins*, Ms. Collins decided to eliminate the interest requirement on a land contract in which she was the seller and change the contract to be paid over 12 years instead of the original 24 years. Ms. Collins persisted in her desire, even though counseled it was not a particularly advantageous change. The contract was changed to conform to Ms. Collins' desires and the buyers made payments under the new agreement. Subsequently, a voluntary conservatorship was established for Ms. Collins and the conservator brought suit claiming Ms. Collins was incompetent when she entered the new agreement and the agreement was invalid because it lacked consideration.

The trial court rejected the conservator's contention Ms. Collins was incompetent when she entered the new agreement, but did find the new agreement invalid because it was a modification lacking consideration. *Id.* at 232–33. The supreme court found the agreement constituted a valid waiver stating:

> This court has long held that contract rights can be waived. Waiver is the voluntary or intentional relinquishment of a known right. It can be express or implied. The essential elements are the existence of a right, actual or constructive knowledge of it, and an intention to give it up. No consideration is required. Nor is prejudice necessary.

Id. at 233–34.

The distinguishing factor between the case at bar and the *Collins* case is that in *Collins* the vendor simply made a unilateral decision to waive her right to interest so each payment made by the buyer went entirely toward principal, whereas, Quigley, Sr. and the Wilsons renegotiated a new price and payment schedule.

In the case at bar it could be said that Quigley, Sr. waived the $89,500 difference between the original price of $210,000 and the amended price of $120,500. However, it is difficult to describe the changing of a payment schedule providing for annual payments of $7,000 plus interest to one providing for annual payments of $1,562.50 plus interest along with the changing of the due date for a balloon payment from March 1, 1988, to March 1,

1996 as simply a waiver of payments. Additionally, the amendment provides for changes in the insurance requirements and allows for sale of the mobile home on the property.

These changes constitute more than the seller abandoning a contractual right arising from a contract. They create new and different obligations to be performed by the buyer. We therefore limit waiver to situations where a party to a contract abandons a right that party has under a contract. We categorize situations where contracting parties incur different duties and obligations from those in their original contract as modifications.

Therefore, we do not find the case at bar establishes a waiver, but rather a modification that normally does require consideration. *See Recker v. Gustafson*, 279 N.W.2d 744, 759 (Iowa 1979). In *Recker* which dealt with an oral "modification" to an oral land contract, the court discussed the Iowa law on sufficiency of consideration to support a modification or replacement of a contract. In *Recker* the court quoted the *Restatement (Second) of the Law of Contracts*§ 89D that provides: "A promise modifying a duty under a contract not fully performed on either side is binding (a) if the modification is fair and equitable in view of circumstances not anticipated by the parties when the contract was made." ... *Id*. at 758.

The *Recker* court also quoted from comment b, Illustration 4 of the *Restatement* § 89D:

> [t]he reason modification must rest in circumstances not "anticipated" as part of the context in which the contract was made, but a frustrating event may be unanticipated for this purpose if it was not adequately covered, even though it was foreseen as a remote possibility. When such a reason is present, the relative financial strength of the parties, the formality with which the modification is made, the extent to which it is performed or relied on and other circumstances may be relevant to show or negate imposition or unfair surprise.

Id.

The *Recker* court declined to adopt the *Restatement* position because no unanticipated circumstances existed in the case other than a desire for more money. However, the court did not discount its application in appropriate circumstances in the future.

We find the case at bar an appropriate circumstance for the adoption of the *Restatement's* position. The unanticipated circumstances were the drastic decrease in the value of the land coupled with the seller's concern about tax repercussions from reacquiring the land and the fact the Wilsons had not received any income from the farm for the previous year. Additionally, the new agreement followed negotiations lasting over a period of time, the document was written by the seller's attorney, the trial court found the reduced price was roughly the fair market value of the property at the time the re-negotiations occurred, and the buyers had already paid $58,000 toward principal on the original contract and the balance of the new contract price was $62,500. Additionally, we find it significant the jury found Quigley, Sr. was competent when he entered the 1986 agreement and the trial court found no undue influence or fraudulent misrepresentation involved in the agreement. These factors lead us to find this is a situation where it is appropriate to find the modification fair and equitable and does not require proof of additional consideration.

Although we do not rely on the trial court's reasoning that no consideration was necessary because the 1986 agreement was a waiver, we reach the same result by adopting the Restatement's position and therefore we affirm the trial court's refusal to allow the issue of consideration to be litigated. *See Anderson v. Yearous*, 249 N.W.2d at 863. Based on this decision, the trial court also correctly denied the plaintiff's motion for partial judgment and directed verdict.

...

Affirmed.

David Shribman, Iowa's Story Is America's

(2000)

In the last 100 years, rebellion has flared twice.

It came first when Henry Wallace's readers — isolated, their children in bad schools, their homes without electric lights or indoor plumbing — were excluded from the prosperity of the 1920s.... In the 1920s, Iowa led the nation in bank suspensions. By 1932, farm products were selling for half, or less, of their average price in the 1920s. In the first nine months of 1932 alone, 257 Iowa farms were sold at foreclosure. The situation was so bad, Iowa farmers came to believe that state testing of cattle for bovine tuberculosis was a conspiracy to lower meat prices. The result was the Iowa Cow War, a mass protest by farmers determined to prevent veterinarians from performing the test.

Soon the Cow War led to war in the streets and in the chambers of the state Legislature. With grain prices frighteningly low, pitchfork-wielding farmers invaded the Capitol. Farmers blocked all 10 highways leading into Sioux City, sometimes with spiked telephone poles, hoping to prevent any milk from entering the city and calling for a "farmers' holiday." Mobs halted farm foreclosures in Pocahontas, Dakota City, and Roland. The effort to stop foreclosures led angry farmers in LeMars, in the western part of the state, to drag a judge from his bench, strip him down to his long johns, put him on a truck, threaten him with castration, and nearly hang him.

"People think of Iowa as a pretty quiet place," says George Mills, 93, who covered the farm rebellion for the Marshalltown *Times Republican*. "But it was pretty wild in this state."

It was pretty wild, too, a half-century later, when the rural credit crisis of the 1980s brought Iowa's family-farm culture under new strains and pressures. With land prices dropping and farm debt growing, farmers were caught in a classic squeeze. By the end of 1986, two dozen banks in Iowa had failed, along with farm-implement manufacturers and dealerships.

"The '80s was a decade when many Iowans affected by the economic crisis lost whatever innocence they had left, when the social fabric of long-standing personal and community relationships, built on mutual trust and common purpose, unraveled in the heat of economic chaos and unleashed market forces," wrote David Ostendorf, who was a cofounder of Prairie Fire Rural Action, perhaps the principal group of farm activists in the 1980s.

The continuing struggle to preserve the family farm is a symbol of larger struggles in Iowa and across the country. In the years from 1973 to 1987, a period that marked the ascendancy of the corporation from coast to coast and across international boundaries, Iowa lost 22,000 farms. In the past half-century, more than 100,000 family farms have disappeared from Iowa.

Farm Equipment Store, Inc. v. White Farm Equipment Company

Court of Appeals of Indiana

596 N.E.2d 274 (Ind. App. 1992)

GEORGE B. HOFFMAN, JUDGE

Appellant-plaintiff Farm Equipment Store, Inc. appeals the grant of partial summary judgment to White Farm Equipment Company.

One issue is dispositive of this appeal: whether Allied modified the dealership contract.

The facts relevant to this appeal disclose that Allied Products Corporation (Allied) manufactures farm machinery through its division White-New Idea Farm Equipment Company. It distributes these products through dealers. Farm Equipment Store, Inc. (Farm Equipment) executed a dealer agreement with Allied in February of 1986 and was an Allied dealer until June of 1988.

Before serving as a dealer for Allied, Farm Equipment was a dealer for White Farm Equipment Company (White Farm), a Delaware corporation that declared bankruptcy in 1985. In late 1985, Allied acquired certain assets from White Farm in the bankruptcy proceeding, including the White line of tractors and field implements and the right to market those lines through a division of Allied. Allied acquired these White Farm assets from the bankruptcy estate free of any obligations White Farm had to its dealers.

After acquiring the White Farm assets, Allied entered into new dealership agreements with certain of White Farm's former dealers. Allied and Farm Equipment signed a dealer agreement in 1986. On June 14, 1988, Allied sent a letter to Farm Equipment terminating the dealer agreement without notice. After termination, Farm Equipment returned approximately $40,000.00 in repair parts it had purchased from Allied. Farm Equipment also sought to return additional parts that it had not purchased from Allied. Farm Equipment valued these parts at approximately $210,000.00. Allied refused to accept the return of these parts.

On August 24, 1988, Farm Equipment filed suit against Allied alleging four claims. None of these claims are a part of this appeal. On March 13, 1991, Farm Equipment filed an amended complaint alleging that the dealership agreement had been modified "through a course of dealing" to require that Allied "accept return of repair parts purchased by [Farm Equipment] from [Allied's] predecessors in title and interest."

Allied requested summary judgment. After a hearing, the trial court granted partial summary judgment to Allied. Farm Equipment appeals the trial court's finding that there was no modification of the written dealership agreement as to the return of parts upon termination.

Review of a summary judgment requires an appellate court to employ the same standard as the trial court by determining whether a genuine issue of material fact exists, and any doubt in this regard must be resolved in favor of the non-moving party. *Lee v. Schroeder*, 529 N.E.2d 349, 352 (Ind. App. 1988). Summary judgment is proper when conflicting facts and inferences exist as to some elements of a claim if there is no dispute as to facts that are dispositive of the matter. *Id.*

Since the contract was one for the sale of goods, it is governed by the *Uniform Commercial Code* (U.C.C.), as it has been adopted in Indiana, Ind. Code § 26-1-2-101, *et seq.* (1988 ed.).

The parties entered into the dealership contract in 1986. Attached to the contract was a schedule of terms and discounts. This schedule was deemed incorporated into the contract under the contract provisions.

In the schedule of terms and discounts, a provision for annual returns was provided:

Annual Returns—During the time the Dealer's Sales Contract is in effect, the Dealer [Farm Equipment] may return repair parts for credit subject to the following provisions:

1. The return privilege shall be limited to an amount not to exceed 10% of the Dealer's stock order purchase of repair parts at billing net prices during the previous twelve month period ending October 31st.

2. Repair parts eligible for return will be those parts purchased from the Company [Allied] and that are included in the Company's current Returnable Parts List[.]

. . .

At the request of the Company, Dealer will provide proof to the satisfaction of the Company, that the parts sought to be returned were purchased by the Dealer pursuant to and during the term of a Dealer Sales and Service Contract in effect between the Dealer and White-New Idea Farm Equipment Company, A Division of Allied Products Corporation, and not from any predecessor company or other entity.

Farm Equipment alleges that, under the annual parts return clause, Allied not only accepted repair parts purchased from it but also repair parts purchased from Allied's predecessors.

Farm Equipment acknowledges the no oral modification and non-waiver clauses in the contract: "This Agreement may not be altered, modified, amended or changed, in whole or in part, except in writing and executed by [Allied] and [Farm Equipment] in the same manner as is provided for the execution of this Agreement" and

Failure of either party to enforce any of the provisions of this Agreement or any rights with respect thereto or failure to exercise any election provided for herein shall in no way be considered to be a waiver of such provisions, rights or elections or in any way affect the validity of this Agreement.

The contract also had a "Repurchase on Termination" provision. This clause obligated Allied, upon termination of the contract, to repurchase from Farm Equipment unsold repair parts in Farm Equipment's inventory that Farm Equipment had purchased from Allied:

c. Repair Parts. Upon termination of this contract, [Allied] agrees to repurchase and [Farm Equipment] agrees to sell and to deliver ... those parts purchased from [Allied] hereunder then on hand unsold, which are in [Allied's] opinion new and salable, and that are included in [Allied's] current Parts Return List.

. . .

d. Limitation of Repurchase Obligation. The Obligation of [Allied] to repurchase ... repair parts is limited to those ... repair parts purchased by [Farm Equipment] from [Allied] under this Agreement.

Upon termination of the contract, Allied repurchased those repair parts that had been purchased from it. However, Allied refused to repurchase the repair parts purchased from Allied's predecessors.

Farm Equipment argues that by accepting repair parts purchased from Allied's predecessors under the Annual Parts Return Program, Allied modified the contract through a "course of performance" to permit return of the repair parts purchased from Allied's predecessors. Therefore, Farm Equipment contends that the modification of the return provision of the Annual Parts Return Program also modifies the repurchase provisions of the contract requiring Allied to repurchase repair parts purchased from Allied's predecessors. Although Farm Equipment acknowledges that there were no oral modification and non-waiver provisions in the contract, Farm Equipment believes that Allied has waived these provisions pursuant to the *Uniform Commercial Code* (U.C.C.).

Two sections of the U.C.C., § 2-208 and § 2-209, are cited in support of Farm Equipment's argument. § 2-208(1) and (3) explain "course of performance"

> (1) Where the contract for sale involves repeated occasions for performance by either party with knowledge of the nature of the performance and opportunity for objection to it by the other, any course of performance accepted or acquiesced in without objection shall be relevant to determine the meaning of the agreement.
>
> ...
>
> (3) Subject to the provisions of 2-209 on modification and waiver, such course of performance shall be relevant to show a waiver or modification of any term inconsistent with such course of performance.

Farm Equipment asserts that when Allied accepted the repair parts, which had been purchased from Allied's predecessors, under the Annual Parts Return Program, Allied established a "course of performance" permitting return of repair parts purchased from Allied's predecessors. Therefore, Farm Equipment argues, Allied is obligated to accept return of these repair parts under the contract as modified.

The U.C.C. states the following regarding modification and waiver:

> (2) A signed agreement that excludes modification or rescission, except by a signed writing, cannot be otherwise modified or rescinded....
>
> ...
>
> (4) Although an attempt at modification or rescission does not satisfy the requirements of subsection (2) or (3) [Statute of Frauds], it can operate as a waiver.

[U.C.C.] § 2-209(2) and (4)

Allied contends Farm Equipment is prevented from modifying the agreement under [U.C.C.] § 2-209(2) since there was a no oral modification clause. Furthermore, since a non-waiver provision was included in the contract, Allied claims that waiver under [U.C.C.] § 2-209(4) is not possible. Farm Equipment, on the other hand, argues that under [U.C.C.] § 2-209(4) Allied waived its no oral modification and non-waiver provisions through a "course of performance."

Both parties cite to *Marlowe v. Argentine Naval Comm'n* 808 F.2d 120 (D.C.Cir. 1986), in support of their arguments. It is true, as Allied notes, that the *Marlowe* court rejected plaintiff's oral modification of the contract due to the fact that the contract permitted only written modifications. The *U.C.C.* statute cited in the decision corresponds to [U.C.C.] § 2-209(2). Likewise, the court refused to permit plaintiff's waiver theory under the U.C.C., which section corresponds with [U.C.C.] § 2-209(4), since the contract had a non-waiver clause. But as *Farm Equipment* points out, the court, in dicta, declared that had there been a "course of performance" established between the parties, it would seem harsh to read the contract provisions so strictly as to preclude waiver. *Id.* at 124.

There appears to be a split of authority on whether a party's "course of performance" can override no oral modification or non-waiver provisions in a contract. Some courts strictly construe such provisions precluding a party's "course of performance" from operating as a modification or waiver. Other courts believe that these no oral modification or non-waiver provisions are subject to modification or waiver like any other term in the contract. *Westinghouse Credit Corp. v. Shelton* 645 F.2d 869, 873 (10th Cir. 1981). However, whether such a waiver or modification occurred is a question of fact for the fact-finder, which would make summary judgment inappropriate.

A question of fact as to whether Allied waived or modified the terms in the contract is not present in this case. The provision that Farm Equipment claims Allied modified was the Annual Parts Return provision. Although Farm Equipment claims that this provision and the provision for Repurchase on Termination are "identical" making a modification of one provision an automatic modification of the other, this is not true. The two provisions are similar in certain respects but not identical.

Obviously, the Annual Parts Return provision applies when the contract is still in effect, while the Repurchase on Termination provision is effective after the contract has been terminated. But more importantly, Farm Equipment only received a credit under the Annual Parts Return Program. This credit was limited to no more than 10% of the dealer's purchases from Allied during the previous year. For 1987, this amounted to approximately $4,000.00–$5,000.00.

Under the Repurchase on Termination provisions, Allied had to repurchase the repair parts. The repurchase of its own parts cost approximately $40,000.00. Repurchase of the parts from its predecessors would have cost approximately $210,000.00.

The evidence presented demonstrated that the Annual Parts Return Program was for the mutual benefit of both parties. However, Allied is not receiving any such increased sales volume and economic benefit under the Repurchase on Termination clause. Similarly, the Annual Parts Return Program evinces goodwill between the parties. This is not necessary upon termination.

Therefore, while the two provisions may appear similar at first glance, they have fundamental differences. Allied may not be forced to accept predecessors' repair parts under the termination clause just because it did so under the annual return clause of the contract. A modification or waiver of one part of the contract dealing with returns does not automatically result in a wholesale waiver or modification of other return provisions in the contract.

Any modification or waiver on Allied's part is restricted to those specific terms in the Annual Parts Return Program. The Repurchase on Termination clause is a separate and different clause and should be treated as such. The trial court properly granted summary judgment on this issue to Allied.

Affirmed.

Jane Smiley, A Thousand Acres

(1993)

We might as well have had a catechism:
What is a farmer?
A farmer is a man who feeds the world.

What is a farmer's first duty?
To grow more food.
What is a farmer's second duty?
To buy more land.
What are the signs of a good farm?
Clean fields, neatly painted buildings, breakfast at six,
no debts, no standing water.
How do you know a good farmer when you meet him?
He will not ask you for any favors.

———————

Chapter Nine

Understanding Contractual Obligations: Interpretation and Implied Terms

If an enforceable contract is formed, what are its terms and what do they mean? In Chapter Three, we looked at the objective theory of interpretation and at the rule that interpretation should usually be based on the understanding of a "reasonable person" in the position of the recipient of a communication. The doctrines examined in this chapter operate against the background of the objective theory: assuming that the express terms of a contract should be interpreted from the perspective of a reasonable person, but also that it is fair to imply terms when (1) the parties have signaled assent to these terms in their behavior over time; or (2) the parties are members of a community where the particular practice or interpretation is customary. Some implied terms are normative—implied where a literal reading of the terms of a contract without a term that limits discretion of one party, would defeat the reasonable expectations of the other party.

Section A begins with examples of implied terms: terms inferred from the conduct of the parties, the arrangement and function of the transaction, and the customs of an industry or trade. These are the unspoken understandings and expectations that each party brings to the transaction. Implied terms are crucial to every successful contract, yet they can be hotly contested, particularly when the contracting partners have different experiences and interests.

Many implied terms are based entirely on local history and circumstances: the man who delivers magazines to my uncle's newsstand, for example, knows to put them on the box in the back of the stand, because then they will stay dry if it rains. Other implied terms are based on more general conditions: it is generally understood by those who deal with hardware stores that deliveries will be made between 8 a.m. and 5 p.m. but not on Sunday unless the store owner agrees. Among the many implied terms in this more general category are those that implicate contested values like decency, good faith, and commercial reasonableness.

Section B focuses on express terms articulated by the parties, either orally or in writing. This section begins with the parol evidence rule. This rule can limit the evidence that is admissible as evidence in a trial to prove the meaning of the terms of an agreement or to establish the existence of terms in an agreement. In both cases, the parol evidence rule asks whether the parties intended a written document to have special significance as evidence of their agreement. We will then look at several doctrines applicable to interpretation of express terms, including the maxims of formal interpretation, the "plain meaning rule," contextual interpretation, trade usage, and reasonable expectations.

In a dispute over the meaning of the terms in a contract, contract theory often creates an opposition between individual autonomy and social justice; between economic freedom or liberty and politics or morality. When determining individual goals and desires, contemporary courts look beyond the parties' spoken or written words to the circumstances and history of their relationship. Courts interpret contracts according to commonplace ideas about human relationships. Inasmuch as these commonplaces are informed by familiar political, moral, and economic beliefs, they bring matters of social justice into the interpretation of individual agreements. In the process of interpretation, the distinction between individual and collective concerns tends to blur.

A. Implied Terms — Unspoken Understandings and Expectations

Classical contract theory assumes that parties generally express every important term of their agreements and that this expression is the contract between them. If, in the occasional case, parties have failed to articulate every part of their agreement, courts can "fill in the gaps" with terms supplied by prior dealings between the parties, by trade usage, and by general norms of reasonableness or good faith.

Contemporary contract law, strongly influenced by the legal realist movement of the 1930s, 1940s, and 1950s, employs a broader, more encompassing definition of agreement. The *Uniform Commercial Code*, for example, defines "agreement" as "the bargain of the parties in fact, as found in their language or by implication from other circumstances including course of dealing or usages of trade or course of performance ..." Uniform Commercial Code § 1-201(3). This broad definition of agreement recognizes that it is rarely possible or even worthwhile for parties to articulate every important term of their agreement. Inevitably, some important understandings and expectations will be left unspoken, if only because they seem so obvious or so unlikely to occur.

From this perspective, negotiated terms (or "dickered terms") are seen as only part of the agreed terms, many of which are implied but unspoken. If the parties have dealt with each other in the past, then they bring expectations based on those past dealings. Similarly, if they participate in or with a trade, they then bring expectations and understandings based on the established practices of that trade; inasmuch as they are members of a larger community and culture, they then bring unspoken expectations of that community and culture; and since they have some understanding of the purposes and structures of the present transaction, they bring unspoken expectations and understandings tied to those purposes and structures. In the legal realist model, these unspoken expectations and understandings are as central to the contract as are any of the express terms.

The materials in this part focus on three prominent sources or kinds of evidence used to establish the existence of an implied term: (1) trade practices, community norms, and other regular routines; (2) best efforts, good faith, and similar communal norms; and (3) the interpretive presumptions and implied terms that courts sanction. The purpose of this part is not to catalogue every source or kind of implied term, but instead to provide an introduction into how courts evaluate implied terms.

---

1. Trade Practices, Community Norms, and Other Regular Routines

Trade practices, community norms, regular routines of all sorts, are the background understandings and expectations against which particular transactions occur.

Nanakuli Paving and Rock Company v. Shell Oil Company, Inc.

United States Court of Appeals for the Ninth Circuit
664 F.2d 772 (1981)

WALTER E. HOFFMAN, DISTRICT JUDGE

Appellant Nanakuli Paving and Rock Company (Nanakuli) initially filed this breach of contract action against appellee Shell Oil Company (Shell) in Hawaiian State Court in February 1976. Nanakuli, the second largest asphaltic paving contractor in Hawaii, had bought all its asphalt requirements from 1963 to 1974 from Shell under two long-term supply contracts; its suit charged Shell with breach of the later 1969 contract. The jury returned a verdict of $220,800 for Nanakuli on its first claim, which is that Shell breached the 1969 contract in January 1974, by failing to price protect Nanakuli on 7200 tons of asphalt at the time Shell raised the price for asphalt from $44 to $76. Nanakuli's theory is that price-protection, as a usage of the asphaltic paving trade in Hawaii, was incorporated into the 1969 agreement between the parties, as demonstrated by the routine use of price protection by suppliers to that trade, and reinforced by the way in which Shell actually performed the 1969 contract up until 1974. Price protection, appellant claims, required that Shell hold the price on the tonnage Nanakuli had already committed because Nanakuli had incorporated that price into bids put out to or contracts awarded by general contractors and government agencies. The District Judge set aside the verdict and granted Shell's motion for judgment n.o.v., which decision we vacate. We reinstate the jury verdict because we find that, viewing the evidence as a whole, there was substantial evidence to support a finding by reasonable jurors that Shell breached its contract by failing to provide protection for Nanakuli in 1974. We do not believe the evidence in this case was such that, giving Nanakuli the benefit of all inferences fairly supported by the evidence and without weighing the credibility of the witnesses, only one reasonable conclusion could have been reached by the jury. *Cockrum v. Whitney*, 479 F.2d 84, 85–86 (9th Cir. 1973).

Nanakuli offers two theories for why Shell's failure to offer price protection in 1974 was a breach of the 1969 contract. First, it argues, all material suppliers to the asphaltic paving trade in Hawaii followed the trade usage of price protection and thus it should be assumed, under the U.C.C., that the parties intended to incorporate price protection into their 1969 agreement. This is so, Nanakuli continues, even though the written contract provided for price to be "Shell's Posted Price at time of delivery," F.O.B. Honolulu. Its proof of a usage that was incorporated into the contract is reinforced by evidence of the commercial context, which under the U.C.C. should form the background for viewing a particular contract. The full agreement must be examined in light of the close, almost symbiotic relations between Shell and Nanakuli on the island of Oahu, whereby the expansion of Shell on the island was intimately connected to the business growth of Nanakuli. The U.C.C. looks to the actual performance of a contract as the best indication of what the parties intended those terms to mean. Nanakuli points out that Shell had price protected it on the two occasions of price increases under the 1969 contract other than the 1974 increase. In 1970 and 1971, Shell extended the old price for four and three months, respectively, after an announced increase. This was done, in the words of Shell's agent in Hawaii, in order to permit Nanakuli's to "chew up" tonnage already committed at Shell's old price.[4]

. . .

Shell presents three arguments for upholding the judgment n. o. v. or, on cross appeal, urging that the District Judge erred in admitting certain evidence. First, it says, the District Court should not have denied Shell's motion in limine to define trade, for purposes of trade usage evidence, as the sale and purchase of asphalt in Hawaii, rather than expanding the definition of trade to include other suppliers of materials to the asphaltic paving trade. Asphalt, its argument runs, was the subject matter of the disputed contract and the only product Shell supplied to the asphaltic paving trade.[5] Shell protests that the judge, by expanding the definition of trade to include the other major suppliers to the asphaltic paving trade, allowed the admission of highly prejudicial evidence of routine price protection by all suppliers of aggregate.[6] Asphaltic concrete paving is formed by mixing paving asphalt with crushed rock, or aggregate, in a "hot-mix" plant and then pouring the mixture onto the surface to be paved. . . . Shell's final argument is that, even assuming . . . that the broad trade definition was correct and evidence of trade usages by aggregate suppliers was admissible, price protection could not be construed as reasonably consistent with the express price term in the contract, in which case the *Code* provides that the express term controls.

We hold that the judge did not abuse his discretion in defining the applicable trade, for purposes of trade usages, as the asphaltic paving trade in Hawaii, rather than the purchase and sale of asphalt alone, given the unusual, not to say unique, circumstances: the smallness of the marketplace on Oahu; the existence of only two suppliers on the island; the long and intimate connection between the two companies on Oahu, including the background of how the development of Shell's asphalt sales on Oahu was inextricably linked to Nanakuli's own expansion on the island; the knowledge of the aggregate business on the part of Shell's Hawaiian representative, Bohner; his awareness of the economics of Nanakuli's bid estimates, which included only two major materials, asphalt and aggregate; his familiarity with realities of the Hawaiian marketplace in which all government agencies refused to include escalation clauses in contract awards and thus pavers would face tremendous losses on price increases if all their material suppliers did not routinely offer them price protection; and Shell's determination to build Nanakuli up to compete for those lucrative government contracts with the largest paver on the island, Hawaiian Bitumuls, which was supplied by the only other asphalt company on the islands, Chevron,

---

4. Price protection was practiced in the asphaltic paving trade by either extending the old price for a period of time after a new one went into effect or charging the old price for a specified tonnage, which represented work committed at the old price. In addition, several months' advance notice was given of price increases.

5. Shell's argument would, in effect, eliminate all trade usage evidence. First, it argues that its own acts were irrelevant as mere waivers, not acts in the course of the performance of the contract. Second, it contends that all acts of price protection by the only other asphalt supplier in Hawaii, Chevron, the marketing division of Standard Oil Company, were irrelevant to prove trade usage because Chevron at one time owned all or part of the paving company it supplied and routinely price protected Hawaiian Bitumuls. The court correctly refused to bar that evidence since the one-time relationship between the two went to the weight, not the admissibility, of the evidence. Nanakuli was given permission to offer evidence in rebuttal that Chevron price protected other customers in California with whom it had no such relationship in the event Shell tried to impeach that evidence.

6. The judge excluded evidence of price protection usage by suppliers of cement because cement was too infrequently used in the production of asphaltic paving and, when used, formed too small a percentage of the finished product.

and which was routinely price protected on materials. We base our holding on the reading of the Code Comments as defining trade more broadly than transaction and as binding parties not only to usages of their particular trade but also to usages of trade in general in a given locality. This latter seems an equitable application of usage evidence where the usage is almost universally practiced in a small market such as was Oahu in the 1960s before Shell signed its 1969 contract with Nanakuli.[7] ...

Lastly we hold that, although the express price terms of Shell's posted price of delivery may seem, at first glance, inconsistent with a trade usage of price protection at time of increases in price, a closer reading shows that the jury could have reasonably construed price protection as consistent with the express term. We reach this holding for several reasons. First, we are persuaded by a careful reading of the U.C.C., one of whose underlying purposes is to promote flexibility in the expansion of commercial practices and which rather drastically overhauls this particular area of the law. The Code would have us look beyond the printed pages of the contract to usages and the entire commercial context of the agreement in order to reach the "true understanding" of the parties. Second, decisions of other courts in similar situations have managed to reconcile such trade usages with seemingly contradictory express terms where the prior course of dealings between the parties, trade usages, and the actual performance of the contract by the parties showed a clear intent by the parties to incorporate those usages into the agreement or to give to the express term the particular meaning provided by those usages, even at times varying the apparent meaning of the express terms. Third, the delineation by thoughtful commentators of the degree of consistency demanded between express terms and usage is that a usage should be allowed to modify the apparent agreement, as seen in the written terms, as long as it does not totally negate it. We believe the usage here falls within the limits set forth by commentators and generally followed in the better reasoned decisions. The manner in which price protection was actually practiced in Hawaii was that it only came into play at times of price increases and only for work committed prior to those increases on non-escalating contracts. Thus, it formed an exception to, rather than a total negation of, the express price term of "Shell's Posted Price at time of delivery." Our decision is reinforced by the overwhelming nature of the evidence that price protection was routinely practiced by all suppliers in the small Oahu market of the asphaltic paving trade and therefore was known to Shell; that it was a realistic necessity to operate in that market and thus vital to Nanakuli's ability to get large government contracts and to Shell's continued business growth on Oahu; and that it therefore constituted an intended part of the agreement, as that term is broadly defined by the Code, between Shell and Nanakuli.

I. History of Nanakuli-Shell Relations before 1973

Nanakuli, a division of Grace Brothers, Ltd., a Hawaiian corporation, is the smaller of the two major paving contractors on the island of Oahu, the larger of the two being Hawaiian Bitumuls (H.B.). Nanakuli first entered the paving business on Oahu in 1948, but it only began to move into the largest Oahu market, Honolulu, in the mid-1950s. Until 1964 or so, Nanakuli only got small paving jobs, such as service stations, driveways, and

---

7. We uphold the court's ruling to admit evidence of trade usage after 1969 to show that Nanakuli's expectation that Shell would go along with that usage was justified, given the continued practice of price protection by all suppliers after 1969. We decline to decide whether the Code allows such admission under normal circumstances, a practice which may well lead to confusion of the issue, but we uphold the ruling as harmless error given the admissibility of evidence of post-1969 price protection by Shell and Chevron as evidence of good faith by Shell in 1974 and the harmless nature of the minimal evidence of price protection by aggregate suppliers after 1969.

small subdivision streets; it was not in a position to compete with H.B. for government contracts for major roads, airports, and other large jobs. In the early sixties Nanakuli owner Walter Grace began to negotiate a mutually advantageous arrangement with Shell whereby Shell, which had a small market percentage and no asphalt terminals in Hawaii, would sign a long-term supply contract with Nanakuli that would commit Nanakuli to buy its asphalt requirements from Shell. On the other hand, Nanakuli would be helped to expand its paving business on Oahu through a guaranteed supply and a discount on its asphalt prices. Nanakuli's growth would expand the market for Shell's asphalt on the island, which would justify Shell's capital investment of a half a million dollars on Oahu, to which asphalt would be brought in heated tankers from Shell's refinery in Martinez, California.

Shell signed two five-year contracts in 1963: a supply contract with Nanakuli itself and a distributorship with Grace, which provided for a $2 commission on all Nanakuli's sales. In fact, almost all Nanakuli's sales were to itself and thus the commission operated, according to Shell's Hawaiian representative, Bohner, primarily as a discount mechanism. Lennox, who succeeded Grace as president in 1965 at Grace's death, testified that its purpose was "to make us competitive in our paving operation with our competitor (H.B.) who is much larger than ourselves because they were a distributor for the Standard Oil Company's asphalt operation." Lennox and Smith, who joined Nanakuli as vice-president in 1965 and eventually succeeded Lennox, both saw Nanakuli's and Shell's relationship as that of partners. That characterization was not denied by Bohner, Shell's Hawaiian representative from 1964 to 1978, who, in fact, essentially corroborated their description of the close relations between the two companies. As a symbol of that relationship, Nanakuli painted its trucks "Shell white," placed Shell's logo on those trucks, chose the same orange as used by Shell for its own logo, and put the Shell logo on its stationary.

...

In 1968, two top Shell asphalt officials came from the mainland to discuss Nanakuli's expansion: Blee from San Francisco and Lewis from New York. Together with Bohner and Nanakuli's Lennox and Smith, they met with officials of Nanakuli's bank to discuss the loan and repayment schedule. The three contracts were finally signed after long negotiations on April 1, 1969 ... a supply contract, a distributorship contract, and volume discount letter, all three to last until December 31, 1975, at which point each would have the option to cancel on six-months' notice, with a minimum duration of over seven years, April 1, 1969, to July 1, 1976. Such long-term contracts were certainly unusual for Shell and this one was probably unique among Shell's customers, at least by 1974.

II. Trade Usage Before and After 1969

The key to price protection being so prevalent in 1969 that both parties would intend to incorporate it into their contract is found in one reality of the Oahu asphaltic paving market: the largest paving contracts were let by government agencies and none of the three levels of government—local, state, or federal—allowed escalation clauses for paving materials. If a paver bid at one price and another went into effect before the award was made, the paving company would lose a great deal of money, since it could not pass on increases to any government agency or to most general contractors. Extensive evidence was presented that, as a consequence, aggregate suppliers routinely price protected paving contractors in the 1960s and 1970s, as did the largest asphaltic supplier in Oahu, Chevron.

...

IV. Shell-Nanakuli Relations, 1973–74

Two important factors form the backdrop for the 1974 failure by Shell to price protect Nanakuli: the Arab oil embargo and a complete change of command and policy in Shell's asphalt management. The jury was read a page or so from the World Book about the events and effect of the partial oil embargo, which shortened supplies and increased the price of petroleum, of which asphalt is a byproduct. The federal government imposed direct price controls on petroleum, but not on asphalt. Despite the international importance of those events, the jury may have viewed the second factor as of more direct significance to this case. The structural changes at Shell offered a possible explanation for why Shell in 1974 acted out of step with, not only the trade usage and commercially reasonable practices of all suppliers to the asphaltic paving trade on Oahu, but also with its previous agreement with, or at least treatment of, Nanakuli.

Bohner testified to a big organizational change at Shell in 1973 when asphalt sales were moved from the construction sales to the commercial sales department. In addition, by 1973 the top echelon of Shell's asphalt sales had retired. Lewis and Blee, who had negotiated the 1969 contract with Nanakuli, were both gone. Their duties were taken over by three men: Fuller in San Mateo, California, District Manager for Shell Sales, Lawson, and Chippendale, who was Shell's regional asphalt manager in Houston. When the philosophy toward asphalt pricing changed, apparently no one was left who was knowledgeable about the peculiarities of the Hawaiian market or about Shell's long-time relations with Nanakuli or its 1969 agreement, beyond the printed contract.

...

We conclude that the decision to deny Nanakuli price protection was made by new Houston management without a full understanding of Shell's 1969 agreement with Nanakuli or any knowledge of its past pricing practices toward Nanakuli. If Shell did commit itself in 1969 to price protect Nanakuli, the Shell officials who made the decisions affecting Nanakuli in 1974 knew nothing about that commitment. Nor did they make any effective effort to find out. They acted instead solely in reliance on the 1969 contract's express price term, devoid of the commercial context that the Code says is necessary to an understanding of the meaning of the written word. Whatever the legal enforceability of Nanakuli's right, Nanakuli officials seem to have acted in good faith reliance on its right, as they understood it, to price protection and rightfully felt betrayed by Shell's failure to act with any understanding of its past practices toward Nanakuli.

V. Scope of Trade Usage

The validity of the jury verdict in this case depends on four legal questions. First, how broad was the trade to whose usages Shell was bound under its 1969 agreement with Nanakuli: did it extend to the Hawaiian asphaltic paving trade or was it limited merely to the purchase and sale of asphalt, which would only include evidence of practices by Shell and Chevron? Second, were the two instances of price protection of Nanakuli by Shell in 1970 and 1971 waivers of the 1969 contract as a matter of law or was the jury entitled to find that they constituted a course of performance of the contract? Third, could the jury have construed an express contract term of Shell's posted price at delivery as reasonably consistent with a trade usage and Shell's course of performance of the 1969 contract of price protection, which consisted of charging the old price at times of price increases, either for a period of time or for specific tonnage committed at a fixed price in non-escalating contracts? Fourth, could the jury have found that good faith obliged Shell to at least give advance notice of a $32 increase in 1974, that is, could they have found that the commercially reasonable standards of fair dealing in the trade in Hawaii in 1974 were to give some form of price protection?

We approach the first issue in this case mindful that an underlying purpose of the U.C.C. as enacted in Hawaii is to allow for liberal interpretation of commercial usages. The *Code* provides, "This chapter shall be liberally construed and applied to promote its underlying purposes and policies." Haw. Rev. Stat. §490:1-102(1). Only three purposes are listed, one of which is "(t)o permit the continued expansion of commercial practices through custom, usage and agreement of the parties; ..." *Id.* §490:1-102(2)(b). The drafters of the *Code* explain:

This Act is drawn to provide *flexibility* so that, since it is intended to be a semipermanent piece of legislation, it will provide its own machinery for *expansion of commercial practices.* It is intended to make it possible for the law embodied in this Act to be *developed* by the courts in the light of *unforeseen and new circumstances and practices* ...

The text of each section should be *read in the light of the purpose and policy* of the rule or principle in question, as also of the Act as a whole, and the application of the language should be *construed narrowly or broadly*, as the case may be, in *conformity with the purposes and policies* involved.

... (T)he Code seeks to avoid ... interference with evolutionary growth ...

This principle of *freedom of contract is subject* to specific *exceptions* found elsewhere in the Act.... [An example being the bar on contractual exclusion of the requirement of good faith, although the parties can set out standards for same.] ... *In this connection,* section 1-205 incorporating into the agreement *prior course of dealing and usages of trade is of particular importance.*

Id., Comments 1 & 2 (emphasis supplied). We read that to mean that courts should not stand in the way of new commercial practices and usages by insisting on maintaining the narrow and inflexible old rules of interpretation. We seek the definition of trade usage not only in the express language of the *Code* but also in its underlying purposes, defining it liberally to fit the facts of the particular commercial context here.

The *Code* defines usage of trade as "any practice or method of dealing having such regularity of observance in a *place, vocation or trade* as to justify an expectation that it will be observed with respect to the transaction in question." *Id.* §490:1-205(2) (emphasis supplied). We understand the use of the word "or" to mean that parties can be bound by a usage common to the place they are in business, even if it is not the usage of their particular vocation or trade. That reading is borne out by the repetition of the disjunctive "or" in subsection 3, which provides that usages "in the vocation or trade in which they are engaged or of which they are or should be aware give particular meaning to and supplement or qualify terms of an agreement." *Id.* §490:1-205(3). The drafters' Comments say that trade usage is to be used to reach the "commercial meaning of the agreement" by interpreting the language "as meaning what it may fairly be expected to mean to parties involved in the particular transaction in a *given locality* or in a given *vocation or trade.*" *Id.,* Comment 4 (emphasis supplied). The inference of the two subsections and the Comment, read together, is that a usage need not necessarily be one practiced by members of the party's own trade or vocation to be binding if it is so commonly practiced in a locality that a party should be aware of it. Subsection 5 also shows the importance of the place where the usage is practiced: "An applicable usage of trade in the place where any part of performance is to occur shall be used in interpreting the agreement as to that part of the performance." The validity of this interpretation is additionally demonstrated by the Comment of the drafters: "Subsection (3), giving the prescribed effect to usages of which the parties 'are or should be aware', reinforces the provision of subsection (2) requiring not universality but only the described 'regularity of observance' of the practice or method. This subsection also reinforces the point of subsection (2) that such usages may be either *general to trade or particular to a special branch of trade.*" *Id.*, Comment 7 (emphasis supplied). This language indicates that Shell would be bound not only by usages of sellers of asphalt but by more general usages on Oahu, as long as those usages were so regular in their observance that Shell should have been aware of them. This reading of the *Code*, in our opinion, achieves an equitable result. A party is always held to conduct generally observed by members of his chosen trade because the other party is justified in so assuming unless he indicates otherwise. He is held to more general business practices to the extent of his actual knowledge of those practices or to the degree his ignorance of those practices is not excusable: they were so generally practiced he should have been aware of them.

...

Shell argued not only that the definition of trade was too broad, but also that the practice itself was not sufficiently regular to reach the level of a usage and that Nanakuli failed to show with enough precision how the usage was carried out in order for a jury to calculate damages. The extent of a usage is ultimately a jury question. The *Code* provides, "The existence and scope of such a usage are to be proved as facts." Haw. Rev. Stat. § 490:1-205(2). The practice must have "such regularity of observance ... as to justify an expectation that it will be observed...." *Id.* The Comment explains:

> The ancient English tests for "custom" are abandoned in this connection. Therefore, it is not required that a usage of trade be "ancient or immemorial," "universal" or the like ... [F]ull recognition is thus available for new usages and for usages currently observed by the great majority of decent dealers, even though dissidents ready to cut corners do not agree.

Id., Comment 5. The Comment's demand that "not universality but only the described 'regularity of observance'" is required reinforces the provision only giving "effect to usages of which the parties 'are or should be aware'" *Id.*, Comment 7. A "regularly observed" practice of protection, of which Shell "should have been aware," was enough to constitute a usage that Nanakuli had reason to believe was incorporated into the agreement.

Nanakuli went beyond proof of a regular observance. It proved and offered to prove that price protection was probably a universal practice by suppliers to the asphaltic paving trade in 1969. It had been practiced by H.C. & D. since at least 1962, by P.C. & A. since well before 1960, and by Chevron routinely for years, with the last specific instance before the contract being March, 1969, as shown by documentary evidence. The only usage evidence missing was the behavior by Shell, the only other asphalt supplier in Hawaii, prior to 1969. That was because its only major customer was Nanakuli and the judge ruled prior course of dealings between Shell and Nanakuli inadmissible. Shell did not point in rebuttal to one instance of failure to price protect by any supplier to an asphalt paver in Hawaii before its own 1974 refusal to price protect Nanakuli. Thus, there clearly was enough proof for a jury to find that the practice of price protection in the asphaltic paving trade existed in Hawaii in 1969 and was regular enough in its observance to rise to the level of a usage that would be binding on Nanakuli and Shell.

...

VII. Express Terms as Reasonably Consistent with Usage ...

Perhaps one of the most fundamental departures of the *Code* from prior contract law is found in the parol evidence rule and the definition of an agreement between two parties. Under the *U.C.C.*, an agreement goes beyond the written words on a piece of paper.

" 'Agreement' means the bargain of the parties in fact as found in their language or by implication from other circumstances including course of dealing or usage of trade or course of performance as provided in this chapter (sections 490:1-205 and 490:2-208)." *Id.* §490:1-201(3). Express terms, then, do not constitute the entire agreement, which must be sought also in evidence of usages, dealings, and performance of the contract itself. The purpose of evidence of usages, which are defined in the previous section, is to help to understand the entire agreement.

> (Usages are) a factor in reaching the commercial meaning of the agreement which the parties have made. The language used is to be interpreted as meaning what it may fairly be expected to mean to parties involved in the particular commercial transaction in a given locality or in a given vocation or trade. . . . Part of the agreement of the parties . . . is to be sought for in the usages of trade which furnish the background and give particular meaning to the language used, and are the framework of common understanding controlling any general rules of law which hold only when there is no such understanding.

Id. §490:1-205, Comment 4. Course of dealings is more important than usages of the trade, being specific usages between the two parties to the contract. "(C)ourse of dealing controls usage of trade." *Id.* §490:1-205(4). It "is a sequence of previous conduct between the parties to a particular transaction which is fairly to be regarded as establishing a common basis of understanding for interpreting their expressions and other conduct." *Id.* §490:1-205(1). Much of the evidence of prior dealings between Shell and Nanakuli in negotiating the 1963 contract and in carrying out similar earlier contracts was excluded by the court.

A commercial agreement, then, is broader than the written paper and its meaning is to be determined not just by the language used by them in the written contract but "by their action, read and interpreted in the light of commercial practices and other surrounding circumstances. The measure and background for interpretation are set by the commercial context, which may explain and supplement even the language of a formal or final writing." *Id.*, Comment 1. Performance, usages, and prior dealings are important enough to be admitted always, even for a final and complete agreement; only if they cannot be reasonably reconciled with the express terms of the contract are they not binding on the parties. "The express terms of an agreement and an applicable course of dealing or usage of trade shall be construed wherever reasonable as consistent with each other; but when such construction is unreasonable express terms control both course of dealing and usage of trade and course of dealing controls usage of trade." *Id.* §490:1-205(4).

. . .

Our study of the *Code* provisions and Comments, then, form the first basis of our holding that a trade usage to price protect pavers at times of price increases for work committed on nonescalating contracts could reasonably be construed as consistent with an express term of seller's posted price at delivery. Since the agreement of the parties is broader than the express terms and includes usages, which may even add terms to the agreement,[34] and since the commercial background provided by those usages is vital to an understanding of the agreement, we follow the Code's mandate to proceed on the as-

---

34. "The agreement of the parties includes that part of their bargain found in course of dealing, usage of trade, or course of performance. These sources are relevant not only to the interpretation of express contract terms, but may themselves constitute contract terms." White & Summers, Uniform Commercial Code §3-3 at 84 (1972).

sumption that the parties have included those usages unless they cannot reasonably be construed as consistent with the express terms....

[In an omitted section, the court discusses numerous federal and state cases in which evidence of trade usage, course of dealing, and course of performance were analyzed as evidence of a contract.]

Some guidelines can be offered as to how usage evidence can be allowed to modify a contract. First, the court must allow a check on usage evidence by demanding that it be sufficiently definite and widespread to prevent unilateral post-hoc revision of contract terms by one party....

[Professor Kirst] offers a second guideline:

> Because the stock printed forms cannot always reflect the changing methods of business, members of the trade may do business with a standard clause in the forms that they ignore in practice. If the trade consistently ignores obsolete clauses at variance with actual trade practices, a litigant can maintain that it is reasonable that the courts also ignore the clauses. Similarly, members of a trade may handle a particular subset of commercial transactions in a manner consistent with written terms because the writing cannot provide for all variations or contingencies. Thus, if the trade regards an express term and a trade usage as consistent because the usage is not a complete contradiction but only an occasional but definite exception to a written term, the courts should interpret the contract according to the usage.

Kirst, [Usage of Trade and Course of Dealing: Subversion of the UCC Theory, 177 U. Ill. Law Forum 811,] 824. Levie, [Trade Usage and Custom Under the Common Law and the Uniform Commercial Code, 40 N.Y.U. L. Rev. 1101 (1965)], at 1112, writes, "Astonishing as it will seem to most practicing attorneys, under the Code it will be possible in some cases to use custom to contradict the written agreement.... Therefore usage may be used to 'qualify' the agreement, which presumably means to 'cut down' express terms although not to negate them entirely." Here, the express price term was "Shell's Posted Price at time of delivery." A total negation of that term would be that the buyer was to set the price. It is a less than complete negation of the term that an unstated exception exists at times of price increases, at which times the old price is to be charged, for a certain period or for a specified tonnage, on work already committed at the lower price on nonescalating contracts. Such a usage forms a broad and important exception to the express term, but does not swallow it entirely. Therefore, we hold that, under these particular facts, a reasonable jury could have found that price protection was incorporated into the 1969 agreement between Nanakuli and Shell and that price protection was reasonably consistent with the express term of seller's posted price at delivery.

...

Note

The significance of trade usages was the focus of heated debate during the drafting of the *United Nations Convention on Contracts for the International Sale of Goods.* Representatives of Third World nations argued that traders from the Western industrialized nations had developed customs and usages that operated to exclude and disadvantage Third World traders. These representatives argued that contract interpretation should subject communal meanings and usages to standards of fairness and justice. *See* Elizabeth

Hayes Patterson, *United Nations Convention on Contracts for the International Sale of Goods: Unification and the Tension Between Compromise and Domination*, 2 Stan. J. Int'l L. 263–303 (1986); Amy Kastely, *Unification and Community: A Rhetorical Analysis of the United Nations Sales Convention*, 8 Nw. J. Int'l L. & Bus. 574 (1988).

Fisher v. Congregation Bnai Yitzhok

Superior Court of Pennsylvania
110 A.2d 881 (1955)

WILLIAM E. HIRT, JUDGE

Plaintiff is an ordained rabbi of the orthodox Hebrew faith. He however does not officiate except on occasion as a professional rabbi-cantor in the liturgical service of a synagogue. The defendant is an incorporated Hebrew congregation with a synagogue in Philadelphia. Plaintiff, in response to defendant's advertisement in a Yiddish newspaper, appeared in Philadelphia for an audition before a committee representing the congregation. As a result, a written contract was entered into on June 26, 1950, under the terms of which plaintiff agreed to officiate as cantor at the synagogue of the defendant congregation "for the High Holiday Season of 1950," at six specified services during the month of September 1950. As full compensation for the above services the defendant agreed to pay plaintiff the sum of $1,200.

The purpose upon which the defendant congregation was incorporated is thus stated in its charter: "The worship of Almighty God according to the faith, discipline, forms and rites of the orthodox Jewish religion." And up to the time of the execution of the contract the defendant congregation conducted its religious services in accordance with the practices of the orthodox Hebrew faith. On behalf of the plaintiff there is evidence that under the law of the Torah and other binding authority of the Jewish law, men and women may not sit together at services in the synagogue. In the orthodox synagogue, where the practice is observed, the women sit apart from the men in a gallery, or they are separated from the men by means of a partition between the two groups. The contract in this case is entirely silent as to the character of the defendant as an orthodox Hebrew congregation and the practices observed by it as to the seating at the services in the synagogue. At a general meeting of the congregation on July 12, 1950, on the eve of moving into a new synagogue, the practice of separate seating by the defendant formerly observed was modified and for the future the first four rows of seats during religious services were set aside exclusively for the men, and the next four rows for the women, and the remainder for mixed seating of both men and women. When plaintiff was informed of the action of the defendant congregation in deviating from the traditional practice as to separate seating, he through his attorney notified the defendant that he, a rabbi of the orthodox faith, would be unable to officiate as cantor because "this would be a violation of his beliefs." Plaintiff persisted in the stand taken that he would not under any circumstances serve as cantor for defendant as long as men and women were not seated separately. And when defendant failed to rescind its action permitting men and women to sit together during services, plaintiff refused to officiate. It then was too late for him to secure other employment as cantor during the 1950 Holiday season except for one service that paid him $100, and he brought suit for the balance of the contract price.

The action was tried before the late Judge Fenerty, without a jury, who died before deciding the issue. By agreement the case was disposed of by the late President Judge

Frank Smith "on the notes of testimony taken before Judge Fenerty." At the conclusion of the trial, counsel had stipulated that the judge need not make specific findings of fact in his decision. This waiver applied to the disposition of the case by Judge Smith. Nevertheless Judge Smith did specifically find that defendant, at the time the contract was entered into, "Was conducting its services according to the Orthodox Hebrew Faith." Judge Smith accepted the testimony of three rabbis learned in Hebrew law, who appeared for plaintiff, to the effect: "That Orthodox Judaism required a definite and physical separation of the sexes in the synagogue." And he also considered it established by the testimony that an orthodox rabbi-cantor "could not conscientiously officiate in a 'trefah' synagogue, that is, one that violates Jewish law"; and it was specifically found that the old building which the congregation left, "had separation in accordance with Jewish orthodoxy." The ultimate finding was for the plaintiff in the sum of $1,100 plus interest. And the court entered judgment for the plaintiff on the finding. In this appeal it is contended that the defendant is entitled to judgment as a matter of law.

. . .

In determining the right of recovery in this case the question is to be determined under the rules of our civil law, and the ancient provision of the Hebrew law relating to separate seating is read into the contract only because implicit in the writing as to the basis— according to the evidence—upon which the parties dealt. *Cf. Canovaro v. Brothers of Order of H. of St. Aug.*, 191 A. 140, 150 (Pa.). In our law the provision became a part of the written contract under a principle analogous to the rule applicable to the construction of contracts in the light of custom or immemorial and invariable usage. It has been said that: "When a custom or usage is once established, in absence of express provision to the contrary it is considered a part of a contract and binding on the parties though not mentioned therein, the presumption being that they knew of and contracted with reference to it." 1 Henry, Pa. Evid., 4th Ed., § 203. *Cf.* Restatement, Contracts § 248(2) and § 249. In this case there was more than a presumption. From the findings of the trial judge supported by the evidence it is clear that the parties contracted on the common understanding that the defendant was an orthodox synagogue which observed the mandate of the Jewish law as to separate seating. That intention was implicit in this contract though not referred to in the writing, and therefore must be read into it. It was on this ground that the court entered judgment for plaintiff in this case.

Judgment affirmed.

---

2. Best Efforts, Good Faith, and Similar Communal Norms

Decisions giving weight to trade practices, custom, and community norms in determining the content of contracts challenge the classical idea that contracts are freely created by individuals and not imposed on individuals by society. While most lawyers are willing to concede that the customs of a particular industry are part of actual agreements, there is much disagreement regarding norms of good faith, reasonable care, best efforts, professional skill, merchantable quality, and the like. While many courts have interpreted contracts to include duties of good faith and both the *Uniform Commercial Code* section 1-304 and the *Restatement (Second) of Contracts* section 205 provide that every contract includes an obligation of good faith, many lawyers and judges continue to view this duty as an external, socially-imposed standard of behavior. Similarly, although various statutes and judicial decisions interpret contracts to include obligations of reasonableness or professional skill, merchantable quality, and best efforts, some judges and lawyers continue to see these as externally-imposed requirements. Implicit in this "internal-external" debate is the idea that externally-imposed obligations are less legitimate than self-imposed ones. What is the justification for that idea? Is it persuasive? What are the political, ethical, and economic consequences of this idea? Who does it benefit and who does it burden?

In *Wood v. Lucy, Lady Duff Gordon*, 118 N.E. 214 (N.Y. 1917) (which we read in chapter 4 on Consideration and Illusory Promises), Justice Benjamin Cardozo, a highly respected and very influential jurist, offers a third source for an implied obligation:

> *The implication of a promise here finds support in many circumstances. The defendant gave an exclusive privilege.* She was to have no right for at least a year to place her own indorsement or market her own designs except through the agency of the plaintiff. The acceptance of the exclusive agency was an assumption of its duties. *We are not to suppose that one party was to be placed at the mercy of the other.*
>
> ...
>
> ... Without an implied promise, the transaction cannot have such business efficacy, as both parties must have intended that at all events it should have.... It is true, of course, as the Appellate Division has said, that if he was under no duty to try to market designs or to place certificates of indorsement, his promise to account for profits or take out copyrights would be valueless. But in determining the intention of the parties the promise has a value. It helps to enforce the conclusion that the plaintiff had some duties. His promise to pay the defendant one-half of the profits and revenues resulting from the exclusive agency and to render accounts monthly was a promise to use reasonable efforts to bring profits and revenues into existence. [Emphasis added.]

In this passage, Justice Cardozo suggests that recognizing an implied obligation of best efforts is necessary to make the parties' arrangement effective and is consistent with shared values of reciprocity. In this way, Justice Cardozo collapses the supposed distinction between internally and externally imposed obligations. He suggests that people normally intend to comply with social norms and that there is no necessary conflict between individual choice and social control.

The cases in this section allow you to see the various ideas and issues associated with the doctrine of good faith. In the first case, *Reid v. Key Bank*, Judge Bownes grapples with whether a duty of good faith exists and, if so, what is the relationship between that duty and the statutory prohibition on racial discrimination. Both examine the Bank's exercise of its discretion in deciding whether to extend a loan. Should these obligations have the same standard of proof? Are they redundant?

The case after *Reid* also involves one party's exercise of discretion. In *Simcala, Inc. v. American Coal Trade, Inc.*, American Coal Trade agreed to supply Simcala's needs for coal and of course Simcala had discretion in determining its needs for coal; this was a typical "requirements contract." In contracts, in which one party was given discretion to evaluate matters of importance to the other party, courts readily hold that the discretion must be exercised in good faith, yet they struggle to define the content of that obligation.

So what does good faith mean? Although all U.S. jurisdictions have recognized a duty of good faith in all or some contracts, the scope and definition of this duty is complicated and controversial, particularly in contracts that do not fit the "traditional" categories.

There is little doubt that the duty of good faith is violated when one party prevents the other from performing the contract. Even before the general doctrine of good faith was articulated, numerous courts held that a party breached a contract if she interfered with (prevented, hindered) the other party from performing the contract. Today, cases involving prevention or hindrance are easily decided under the doctrine of good faith. Similarly, there is little doubt that the duty of good faith is violated if a party exercises discretion under the contract to hurt the other party or to seize a large profit (or "windfall") at the expense of the other party. As we have seen, courts routinely recognize an obligation of "reasonableness" in the exercise of contractual discretion.

Beyond these traditionally recognized areas, however, the existence and meaning of the duty of good faith is less clear. As Judge Bownes discusses below in *Reid v. Key Bank*, courts have distinguished between an "objective" test (reasonable person, commercial reasonableness, fair dealing) and a "subjective" test (honesty in fact). Revisions to the *U.C.C.* change the definition of good faith from simply "honesty in fact" to "honesty in fact and the observance of reasonable commercial standards of fair dealing," incorporating both tests. Still other definitions have been offered by commentators, including the definition of "bad faith" as the attempt to recapture opportunities foregone by entering the contract (e.g., trying to convert the use of leased property), Steve Burton, *Breach of Contract and the Common Law Duty to Perform in Good Faith*, 94 Harv. L. Rev. 369 (1980), and the definition of good faith as *excluding* behavior inconsistent with common standards of decency, fairness, and reasonableness. Robert Summers, *The General Duty of Good Faith — Its Recognition and Conceptualization*, 67 Cornell L. Rev. 810 (1982).

The comments to *Restatement (Second) of Contracts* section 205 endorse a flexible definition of good faith, similar to that proposed by Professor Summers:

> The phrase "good faith" is used in a variety of contexts, and its meaning varies somewhat with the context. Good faith performance or enforcement of a contract emphasizes faithfulness to an agreed common purpose and consistency with the justified expectations of the other party; it excludes a variety of types of conduct characterized as involving "bad faith" because they violate community standards of decency, fairness or reasonableness.

Restatement (Second) of Contracts § 205, Comment a.

> Subterfuges and evasions violate the obligation of good faith in performance even though the actor believes his conduct to be justified. But the obligation goes further; bad faith may be overt or may consist of inaction, and fair dealing may require more than honesty. A complete catalogue of types of bad faith is impossible, but the following types are among those which have been recognized in judicial decisions: evasion of the spirit of the bargain, lack of diligence and slacking off, willful rendering of imperfect performance, abuse of power to specify terms, and interference with or failure to cooperate in the other party's performance.

Restatement (Second) of Contracts § 205, Comment d.

A flexible definition of good faith need not be unpredictable. As one court observed:

> This [flexible standard] does not mean that decisions as to what constitutes bad faith must be ad hoc and standardless. Without attempting to give positive content to the phrase "good faith," it is possible to set forth operational standards by which good faith can be distinguished from bad faith within a particular context.

Best v. United States National Bank of Oregon, 739 P.2d 554, 558 (Ore. 1987).

———

Paul Reid and Mary J. Reid v. Key Bank of Southern Maine, Inc.

United States Court of Appeals for the First Circuit
821 F.2d 9 (1987)

HUGH H. BOWNES, CIRCUIT JUDGE

Plaintiffs Paul and Mary J. Reid brought a seventeen-count action in United States District Court for the District of Maine against Key Bank of Southern Maine, Inc., defendant. Plaintiffs alleged various federal and state claims resulting from the actions of Depositors Trust Co. of Southern Maine (Depositors), Key Bank's predecessor in interest. The suit grew out of the circumstances surrounding the termination by Depositors of plaintiffs' credit arrangement with it. A jury trial resulted in a verdict for plaintiffs on one of the counts and an award of damages. Both parties have appealed.

I. Summary of the Facts

In mid-1975, Paul Reid approached Depositors to obtain financing for the establishment of a painting business. From 1976 through 1979, Depositors granted Reid a series of loans which Reid used for the operation of his business, Pro Paint and Decorating. During this period, Peter H. Traill was the loan officer responsible for Reid's accounts, Marco F. DeSalle was the president of the bank, and Henry Lawson was, for a time, an assistant vice-president.

On March 2, 1979, Reid and Depositors entered into a $25,000 commercial credit agreement. The agreement was variously explained at trial as a "line of credit" and an "incomplete loan." However defined, it was the largest amount of credit Depositors had yet extended to Reid. Reid sought the credit primarily to finance work he was performing at the Bucksport Housing Project for Nickerson & O'Day, Inc., a general contractor.

In mid-May, 1979, Traill telephoned Reid and informed him that Depositors would not grant him any further advances under the March agreement. Reid had thought at the time that this halt of further advances might only be temporary. Defendant claimed that Traill sent Reid a follow-up letter on May 18, 1979, stating that Depositors would no longer honor overdrafts on Reid's accounts and suggesting that Reid restructure his debts with another lender. Reid denied receiving the letter and alleged that it was never, in fact, sent to him. On May 29, 1979, Nickerson & O'Day sent a check to Depositors as payment for Reid's work at the Bucksport Housing Project. The check was for $6,507.90. It was made out to Depositors and to Pro Paint pursuant to an agreement between Depositors and Reid whereby Reid assigned his accounts receivable to Depositors as security for the March loan. Depositors credited $2,500 to the account of Pro Paint and applied the remaining $4,007.90 to offset part of the outstanding balance on Reid's March loan. Reid claimed that Depositors undertook this action without his authorization.

Reid claimed that another check was also inappropriately handled by Depositors. He testified that on June 8, 1979, he gave Traill a check for an amount somewhere between eleven and fifteen thousand dollars. Reid contended that this check represented the proceeds for work he performed at Brunswick Naval Air Station. He alleged that Depositors converted the check and used it to offset part of the balance on the March loan. Defendant strongly contested this claim and implied at trial that the check in question existed only in Reid's imagination.

On September 20, 1979, Reid received a past-due notice on the March loan. The notice requested payment of $694.84 in interest and stated that the payment had been due on

September 5, 1979. Reid testified that this was the first notice he had received concerning the March loan.

On November 5, 1979, Depositors repossessed Reid's personal automobile and one of his vans. Reid discovered one of the vehicles in a lot and attempted to drive it away. He testified that he did not know it had been repossessed and thought it had been stolen. On a complaint by Lawson, Reid was arrested in connection with this incident and was placed for a time in jail.

Reid's business collapsed and he lost his four vehicles and his home. On November 7, 1979, Reid filed a Chapter 13 bankruptcy proceeding which was converted to a Chapter 11 proceeding in January, 1980. Mrs. Reid suffered emotional problems and drug dependency. The couple separated for a period of a year and a half.

The Reids, who are black, claimed that Depositors acted in bad faith to limit and then terminate their credit. They also claimed that Depositors' actions were motivated by racial prejudice. Defendant claimed that Depositors acted in good faith to secure its financial interests when it learned of Reid's personal difficulties and mismanagement of his business; it denied that its actions were racially motivated.

At trial, the district court directed a verdict for defendant on plaintiffs' claims for violations of the Fair Credit Reporting Act and for breach of fiduciary duties. Plaintiffs withdrew their claims for interference with contractual relations and wrongful dishonoring of checks. The jury found for defendant on plaintiffs' claims for violation of the express terms of the credit agreement, racial discrimination, two counts for infliction of emotional distress, and failure to comply with Article 9 of the *Uniform Commercial Code*. The jury found for plaintiffs on their pendent state claim for breach of the March loan agreement based on violation of an implied covenant of good faith and fair dealing. It awarded plaintiffs $100,000 in compensatory and $500,000 in exemplary damages; the exemplary damages award was struck by the court. Both parties have appealed. In Part II, we address defendant's arguments on appeal; in Parts III–VI we address those of plaintiffs.

II. Implied Covenant of Good Faith and Fair Dealing

A. The Existence of the Cause of Action in Maine

Plaintiffs' recovery in contract was based on the theory that when Depositors, in May 1979, and thereafter, shut off Reid's credit and took steps to realize upon its collateral, it violated an implied covenant of good faith contained in the March loan agreement between plaintiffs and Depositors. The district court took as self-evident the proposition that Maine contract law required good faith performance. *See generally* Burton, *Breach of Contract and the Common Law Duty to Perform in Good Faith*, 94 Harv. L. Rev. 369 (1980). The *Uniform Commercial Code*, as adopted by Maine, states: "Every contract or duty within this Title imposes an obligation of good faith in its performance or enforcement." 4 Me. Rev. Stat. Ann. tit. 11, § 1-203 (1964). That this obligation carries with it a cause of action seems clear from another provision of the *Code*: "Any right or obligation declared by this Title is enforceable by action unless the provision declaring it specifies a different and limited effect." *Id.* at § 1-106(2). *See also* Restatement (Second) of Contracts § 205 (1979).

We interpret the Maine cases making reference to the general duty of good faith in light of this general acceptance of the principle. The Maine Supreme Judicial Court has explicitly recognized the U.C.C.'s "broad requirements of good faith, commercial reasonableness and fair dealing." *Schiavi Mobile Homes, Inc. v. Gironda*, 463 A.2d 722, 724–25 (Me. 1983) (citing *U.C.C.* §§ 1-203, 2-103 & 1-106, Comment 1). In addition, some aspects of the present case concern the handling of Reid's bank accounts with Depositors and would thus be governed by the standard of "good faith" and "ordinary care" under section 4-103 of the *U.C.C. See C-K Enterprises v. Depositors Trust Co.*, 438 A.2d 262, 265 (Me. 1981).

In *Linscott v. State Farm Mutual Auto Ins. Co.*, 368 A.2d 1161 (Me. 1977), the court discussed whether a duty of good faith existed between an insurer and a third-party tort claimant. The court stated that, while such a duty is "implicit" in the contract between an insurer and its insured, the essentially "adversary" relationship between an insurer and a third-party claimant precludes the finding of such an implicit duty in their dealings. Defendant would have us view the court's finding of a good faith duty between the insurer and the insured as exceptional; under defendant's interpretation, an "adversary" relationship, whether contractual or not, would have no good faith requirement.

We cannot agree with this reading of *Linscott*. The general principles of modern contract law, as embodied in Maine's *Uniform Commercial Code* and recognized in *Schiavi*, mandate that we interpret *Linscott* as finding no duty of good faith toward a third-party claimant primarily because of the absence of a contractual relationship. We view the Maine court as implicitly recognizing that contractual relationships of the present nature are governed by a requirement of good faith performance. We do not think that this duty to perform in good faith is altered merely by calling the contractual relationship "adversary."

Defendant next argues that a cause of action based on the duty is not generally accepted, even if the principle of good faith performance has been widely acknowledged. Defendant cites several cases finding no such cause of action in their jurisdictions. *See, e.g., Management Assistance, Inc. v. Computer Dimensions, Inc.*, 546 F. Supp. 666 (N.D. Ga. 1982), *aff'd*, 747 F.2d 708 (11th Cir. 1984). These cases generally cite as their authority *Chandler v. Hunter*, 340 So. 2d 818, 821 (Ala. App. 1976), for the proposition that no jurisdiction has been found that allows such a cause of action.

We reject the applicability of *Chandler* and the cases based on it for two reasons. First, a determination that no such cause of action exists would conflict with the clear meaning of section 1-203 of the U.C.C., particularly when read in conjunction with section 1-106(2). We assume that the Maine courts would adhere to the plain language of these provisions, as well as to generally accepted modern contract principles. Secondly, the fact that numerous jurisdictions have allowed recovery on theories of breach of good faith refutes the empirical assumption upon which *Chandler* appears to have been based. *See, e.g., K.M.C. Co. v. Irving Trust Co.*, 757 F.2d 752 (6th Cir. 1985) (suit under New York law by borrower against lender for arbitrary termination of credit); *Power Motive Corp. v. Mannesmann Demag Corp.*, 617 F. Supp. 1048 (D. Colo. 1985) (Ohio law); *Fortune v. National Cash Register Co.*, 364 N.E.2d 1251 (Mass. 1977) (Massachusetts law). *See also Atlas Truck Leasing, Inc. v. First NH Banks, Inc.*, 808 F.2d 902 (1st Cir. 1987) (interpreting New Hampshire law).

B. The "Demand" Provision

Defendant argues that the "demand" provision of the note establishing the credit agreement precludes a good faith requirement in this case, even if such a requirement is recognized in general. Defendant contends that this exception to the general good faith requirement is mandated by section 1-208 of the *U.C.C.*, as interpreted by the *U.C.C.* Comment to the section. Section 1-208 states:

§ 1-208. Option to accelerate at will.

A term providing that one party or his successor in interest may accelerate payment or performance or require collateral or additional collateral "at will" or "when he deems himself insecure" or in words of similar import shall be construed to mean that he shall have power to do so only if he in good faith believes that the prospect of payment or performance is impaired....

The *U.C.C.* Comment observes: "Obviously this section has no application to demand instruments or obligations whose very nature permits call at any time with or without reason."

We turn, therefore, to the documents establishing the loan to see whether they clearly gave Depositors the right to demand payment or terminate the relationship on demand and without cause. The "Secured Interest Note," dated March 2, 1979, states in its opening paragraph: "On Demand, after date, for value received, [Paul Reid d/b/a Pro Paint & Decorating] ... promise[s] to pay to the order of [Depositors] ... Twenty-five Thousand and no/100 Dollars with interest at 13.75 per cent per annum payable quarterly."

This provision appears, at first glance, to be an unambiguous demand clause. It cannot, however, possibly be read literally in the context of the kind of agreement entered into here. Although the note seems to grant Depositors the right to immediate repayment of $25,000 "on demand," Reid had not yet received that sum of money from the bank. Indeed, he was never to receive the full amount. The "demand" provision thus cannot represent the beginning and end of the inquiry into the time term of the contract.

DeSalle, president of Depositors, testified to similar effect at trial, based on his knowledge of banking practices. He said that the "demand" provision in such an agreement is to be interpreted in light of the other conditions in the note and that a bank could not simply terminate the agreement capriciously. He also thought that the absence of a time term in such a note indicated the likelihood that the schedule for repayment of the principal was governed by a verbal agreement between the loan officer and the debtor. In view both of our reading of the document and of DeSalle's testimony about banking practices, we find that the "demand" provision in the note should not be understood as a completely integrated agreement on the time term of the contract. *See Astor v. Boulos Co.*, 451 A.2d 903, 905 (Me. 1982); Restatement (Second) of Contracts § 209 (1979).

Furthermore, the documents establishing the loan place conditions on the acceleration of payment or termination of the agreement. The "Secured Interest Note" provides for various conditions which would "render" the obligation "payable on demand." The "Security Agreement," also signed March 2, 1979, lists a series of events whose occurrence would signify that Reid would be in "default." The presence of such conditions in both documents indicates that the agreement could not simply be terminated at the whim of the parties; rather, the right of termination or acceleration was subjected to various limitations. The detailed enumeration of events that would "*render*" the note "payable on demand," or which would put Reid in "default," shows the qualified and relative nature of any "demand" provision. It would be illogical to construe an agreement, providing for repayment or default in the event of certain contingencies, as permitting the creditor, in the absence of the occurrence of those contingencies, to terminate the agreement without any cause whatsoever. Under such a construction, the enumerated conditions would be rendered meaningless. We find, therefore, that the documents establishing the loan defeat neither the legal obligation nor the justifiable expectation of the parties that the contract be performed in good faith.

C. The Standard

Defendant challenges the district court's formulation of the test of "good faith" in its instruction to the jury. Defendant claims that the judge instructed the jury that the test for good faith comprises both an objective and a subjective component. Defendant argues that under Maine law an objective standard, such as a "reasonable man" test, may only be applied in cases involving the sales of goods that fall under Article 2 of the *U.C.C.* Otherwise, defendant claims, any consideration of "good faith" should be limited to its subjective definition in section 1-201(19) as "honesty in fact."

We have examined the judge's original instructions as well as his subsequent clarification of those instructions to determine the precise nature of the test submitted to the jury. In regard to the contract claim, the judge initially formulated two standards. First, he stated that the contract, as a whole, was subject to a "covenant of good faith and fair dealing." Second, with specific reference to the claim that Depositors inappropriately disposed of Reid's collateral, he stated that the bank had a duty to act in a "commercially reasonable manner." In setting the latter standard, he cited Article 9 of the *U.C.C. See* 5 Me. Rev. Stat. Ann. tit. 11, §§ 9-501–504. He then twice defined "good faith" in terms indicating a purely subjective standard. He concluded the instruction, however, by reformulating the "good faith" test as including an objective standard of reasonableness.

The jury later requested that the judge clarify these instructions. In his new instructions, the judge clearly formulated a subjective standard for good faith:

> Now good faith is defined as honesty in fact. One acts with good faith, in general, when one acts honestly.

> Good faith means that one acts without any improper motivation. One acts with the truth and not for some ulterior motive that is unconnected with the substance of the agreement in question when one is acting with good faith.

The judge again referred to the "commercially reasonable" standard only in connection with Article 9 violations.

We find, therefore, that the judge ultimately instructed the jury to decide the issue of good faith under the subjective standard. "Honesty in fact" is required under all interpretations of the duty of good faith under section 1-203. Thus, even if we agreed with defendant that the Maine courts would limit an objective standard for good faith to Article 2 cases, we would not find a fatal error in the judge's instructions here.

D. Sufficiency of Evidence

Finally, defendant contends that there was insufficient evidence to support a finding of an absence of good faith, particularly in view of the jury's failure to find that racial discrimination had been an "effective factor" in the termination of Reid's credit at Depositors. We disagree. We affirm the district court's holding that evidence concerning the manner in which Depositors conducted their dealings with Reid was sufficient to support a jury verdict of bad faith and was not based on mere speculation. The standard for defendant's motion for a judgment notwithstanding the verdict was whether the evidence, viewed in the light most favorable to plaintiffs, would lead to the conclusion that no reasonable jury could have found for plaintiffs on the good faith issue. This heavy burden was not met by defendant.

We think the jury could have reasonably inferred that Depositors' actions were not taken in good faith. The March, 1979, credit agreement represented the largest amount of credit extended to Reid by the bank, and could be seen as the culmination of an ongoing and mutually beneficial relationship. The jury could have found that by mid-May, when Reid's line of credit was abruptly shut off, he was not in default and his overall position had not changed that significantly, especially as the bank did not first register complaints to him or ask him to alter his conduct in some manner. The bank's president testified that it was customary before cutting off a customer's line of credit to send notices in advance and call the customer to the bank for discussion. This was not done as to Reid, nor was any convincing reason advanced by the bank for not doing so. (The bank, indeed, did not even call as a witness the officer who had dealt directly with Reid and could have best explained why the bank acted as it did.) The jury could have found that in restricting Reid's credit when and as it did the bank was motivated by ulterior considerations, not a good faith concern for its financial security. The jury could have found that the bank decided in bad faith and without notice to terminate the credit relationship as a whole. The jury might have viewed the bank's actions to restrict and terminate Reid's credit to be in bad faith in part because they were taken only a short time after the bank had shown confidence in Reid and had given him grounds to rely on the continuation of the relationship. The jury might have inferred bad faith from these actions of the bank, even if it did not believe that racial prejudice was the effective factor that motivated the bank's bad faith. In sum, the jury could have reasonably found that the bank acted in bad faith in precipitously and without warning halting further advances on which it knew Reid's business depended, in failing to make a sufficient effort to negotiate alternative solutions to any problems it perceived in its relationship with Reid, and in failing to give notice that it intended to terminate the relationship entirely. The evidence concerning these and other aspects of Depositors' actions provided a sufficient basis for a jury finding that the bank's actions were not taken in good faith.

III. Exemplary Damages

The jury awarded plaintiffs $500,000 in exemplary damages. This award clearly related to the finding of a breach of the implied covenant of good faith because the jury found for defendant on all other counts. The district judge struck the exemplary damages award, stating that he had specifically charged the jury that exemplary damages could not be awarded on a contract claim in Maine.

Plaintiffs contest the district court's finding that it had not submitted to the jury the issue of exemplary damages on the contract claim. Our examination of the record supports the district court's finding. There is no merit in plaintiffs' procedural argument. Plaintiffs also argue that exemplary damages are available in Maine in exceptional circumstances.

Under Maine law, "[a]s a general rule, exemplary damages are not recoverable for a breach of contract." *Forbes v. Wells Beach Casino, Inc.*, 409 A.2d 646, 655 (Me. 1979). Plaintiffs argue that this "general rule" admits of an exception when the breach amounts to an independent, recoverable tort. This view of the general state of the doctrine of exemplary damages is not without merit. *See, e.g., In re Blier Cedar Co.*, 7 B.R. 195, 196 (D. Me. 1980) (interpreting Maine law as containing the "tort" exception).

We need not, however, reach this legal question here because there are no recoverable torts to which the exemplary damages could attach. The jury found for defendant on the conversion count, plaintiffs withdrew their claim for intentional interference with contractual relations and wrongful dishonoring of checks, and the court directed a verdict for defendant on the count for breach of fiduciary duties. Even if we were to accept plaintiffs' legal argument, therefore, we would not find exemplary damages appropriate in this case.

. . .

Affirmed. No costs to either party.

Note

In the 1960s, the civil rights movement transformed the sensibility of many people in the United States with respect to race and to systemic discrimination. The violence against those who sought to integrate public accommodations like lunch counters and public transportation, or to register black voters and enroll black children in white public schools, for example, was visible to the entire nation, or at least to anyone who had access to a television set. Eventually racism, or overt racism at least, was stigmatized. Moral condemnation of racism led to anti-discrimination statutes like the Equal Credit Opportunity Act, 15 U.S.C. 1691, which took effect in 1968.

But the moral censure of racism that promoted racial equality was not sustained. In the decades that the followed the Civil Rights movement, the United States Supreme Court declared that discrimination required proof of discriminatory intent or discriminatory purpose in Equal Protection and Title VII cases that alleged discriminatory treatment. *See, e.g.*, Washington v. Davis, 426 U.S. 229 (1976); Wards Cove Packing Co. v. Atonio, 490 U.S. 642 (1989). Attempts to use racial categories to increase integration were rejected when the standard of "strict scrutiny" was applied to the use of racial categories with no distinction between attempts to remedy the legacy of past discrimination (benign discrimination) and invidious discrimination. The most recent example is Parents Involved in Community Schools v. Seattle School District No. 1, 551 U.S. 701 (2007).

Racial bias is often covert. While it is sometimes expressed in a form that we recognize as racial animus, more often it takes the form of implicit, or unconscious, bias. Charles R. Lawrence III, *The Id, the Ego, and Equal Protection: Reckoning with Unconscious Racism*, 39 Stan. L. Rev. 317 (1987); David O. Sears, *A Perspective on Implicit Prejudice from Survey Research, Psychological Inquiry*, Vol. 15, No. 4 (2004). Do you think that implicit bias might explain the way the officers at Key Bank treated Paul Reid? Is the reluctance to call someone "racist" because of the stigma that attaches to that term a reason why a jury might prefer to find for the plaintiff on the basis of a violation of the implied obligation of good faith rather than the civil rights statute? *See generally* Kerry Kawakami, Elizabeth Dunn, Francine Karmali and John F. Dovidio, *Mispredicting Affective and Behavioral Responses to Racism*, 323 Science 276–278 (2009).

Simcala, Inc. v. American Coal Trade, Inc.

Supreme Court of Alabama
821 So. 2d 197 (2001)

CHAMP LYONS, JR. JUSTICE

American Coal Trade, Inc. ("ACT") commenced an action against Simcala, Inc., alleging a breach of contract arising from Simcala's failure to perform its agreement to purchase its estimated coal requirements from ACT. Following a bench trial, the trial court entered a final judgment in favor of ACT and against Simcala in the amount of $101,850 in lost profits and $10,690 in interest, plus costs.

We affirm.

I. Facts and Background

Simcala, the buyer, issued a purchase order dated January 12, 1998, pursuant to which it estimated it would purchase, during 1998, from ACT 17,500 tons of "Black Creek" coal at $78.50 per ton. The purchase order stated that the order was a blanket order for 1998 and that "the above [i.e., 17,500 tons] is an approximate quantity and to be shipped as required." Simcala also included in the purchase order chemical and size specifications for the coal.

During 1998, Simcala actually purchased only 7,200 tons of coal from ACT, representing 41% of the estimated amount. Simcala ordered approximately 6,000 tons of coal from ACT between January and mid-May. Simcala suspended its orders in mid-May because of problems with its furnace and it purchased no coal from ACT from mid-May to the end of June. Simcala claims that the furnace problems were caused by the poor quality of the ACT coal, but it does not argue that the coal failed to meet the specifications in the purchase order. Simcala resumed orders for coal at the end of June and purchased approximately 1,200 tons during July and August.

The mine from which ACT obtained its coal to fulfill the Simcala purchase order closed in August 1998. However, throughout September, ACT's supplier had a surplus of coal from that mine and ACT had asked Simcala to purchase some of this surplus coal. Simcala, however, ordered no coal in September.

In early October, Simcala ordered 600 tons of coal from ACT. However, ACT did not deliver the coal because by October its supplier had sold the surplus coal from the closed mine to another buyer. ACT offered uncontroverted evidence that by mid-October it would have had another source had Simcala ordered any additional coal, but Simcala did not order any additional coal from ACT.

The trial court found no evidence that Simcala's reduction in the amount of coal it ordered and the eventual cessation of its orders were in bad faith. However, the court found that Simcala's purchase of only 41% of its estimated needs for the year was "unreasonably disproportionate" under § 7-2-306(1), Ala. Code 1975, and it held, therefore, that Simcala had breached the contract. The trial court also found that ACT's profit would have been $10.50 for each ton of coal had Simcala purchased the full amount estimated. Thus, the court, as previously noted, awarded ACT lost profits of $101,850, and interest in the amount of $10,690, and taxed costs to Simcala.[1]

Section 7-2-306(1), part of Alabama's version of the Uniform Commercial Code, states:

> "A term which measures the quantity by the output of the seller or the requirements of the buyer means such actual output or requirements as may occur in good faith, *except that no quantity unreasonably disproportionate to any stated estimate* or in the absence of any stated estimate to any normal or otherwise comparable prior output or requirements *may be tendered or demanded*." (Emphasis added).

Simcala argues that the "unreasonably disproportionate" language contained in § 7-2-306(1) applies only to amounts exceeding the estimates in requirements contracts, not to lesser amounts than the estimates. Thus, Simcala claims it was entitled to reduce its requirements—even to zero—so long as it did not do so in bad faith; it further claims that the trial court correctly found it was not acting in bad faith when it reduced its purchases below the estimate in the purchase order. In the alternative, Simcala argues that even if the "unreasonably disproportionate" language applies to decreases from estimates, its performance was excused because, it says, ACT breached the contract when it was unable to meet Simcala's order for 600 tons of coal in early October.

The question presented is one of first impression in Alabama: Whether § 7-2-306(1), Ala. Code 1975, permits a buyer purchasing pursuant to a requirements contract to reduce its requirements to a level unreasonably disproportionate to an agreed-upon estimate so

---

1. The trial court based its calculation of damages on the difference between the 7,800 tons of coal Simcala purchased or ordered—including 600 tons ACT did not deliver—and Simcala's estimated requirements—17,500 tons.

long as it is acting in good faith. The trial court interpreted § 7-2-306(1) to mean that a requirements-contract buyer who has provided the seller an estimate of its requirements may not reduce its requirements to a level unreasonably disproportionate to that estimate, even when it does so in good faith. The trial court concluded that the reduction in this case was unreasonable. The trial court's interpretation of § 7-2-306(1) involves a question of law; it is reviewed de novo by an appellate court, without any presumption of correctness. *Aetna Cas. & Sur. Co. v. Mitchell Bros., Inc.,* 814 So.2d 191, 195 (Ala.2001).

II. Application of § 7-2-306(1)

"Words used in a statute must be given their natural, plain, ordinary, and commonly understood meaning, and where plain language is used a court is bound to interpret that language to mean exactly what it says." *IMED Corp. v. Systems Eng'g Assocs. Corp.,* 602 So.2d 344, 346 (Ala.1992), quoted in *Ex parte Fann,* 810 So.2d 631, 633 (Ala.2001). Our primary obligation is to "ascertain and give effect to the intent of the Legislature as that intent is expressed through the language of the statute." *Ex parte Krothapalli,* 762 So.2d 836, 838 (Ala. 2000). Moreover, we must presume " 'that every word, sentence, or provision was intended for some useful purpose, has some force and effect, and that some effect is to be given to each, and also that no superfluous words or provisions were used.' " *Ex parte Children's Hosp. of Alabama,* 721 So.2d 184 (Ala. 1998), quoting *Sheffield v. State,* 708 So.2d 899, 909 (Ala. Crim. App. 1997). *See also Elder v. State,* 50 So. 370, 371 (Ala. 1909) (stating that it is unreasonable to presume that the Legislature intended the words it used to be meaningless).

Because this case presents a question of first impression concerning language used in the Uniform Commercial Code, "we look for guidance to the Uniform Commercial Code itself, the official Comments to the Code, the writings of commentators, and the case law of other jurisdictions." *Massey Ferguson Credit Corp. v. Wells Motor Co.,* 374 So.2d 319, 321 (Ala. 1979). Comment 3 of the official comments to § 7-2-306 states:

"If an estimate of output or requirements is included in the agreement, no quantity unreasonably disproportionate to it may be tendered or demanded. Any minimum or maximum set by the agreement shows a clear limit on the intended elasticity. In similar fashion, *the agreed estimate is to be regarded as a center around which the parties intend the variation to occur.*" (Emphasis added.)

The use of the word "center" clearly indicates that the drafters intended to prohibit both unreasonably disproportionate increases *and* decreases from the estimates in a requirements contract. To interpret § 7-2-306(1) to prohibit only unreasonably disproportionate increases, but not decreases, would make the description in official comment 3 of an estimate as a "center around which the parties intend the variation to occur" mere surplus verbiage.

Simcala emphasizes official comment 2 in support of its argument that § 7-2-306(1) prohibits only unreasonably disproportionate increases. Comment 2 states:

"Reasonable elasticity in the requirements is expressly envisaged by this section and *good faith variations from prior requirements are permitted even when the variation may be such as to result in discontinuance.* A shut-down by a requirements buyer for lack of orders might be permissible when a shut-down merely to curtail losses would not. *The essential test is whether the party is acting in good faith.*" (Emphasis in Simcala's brief.)

While comment 3 begins with the words, "If an estimate ... is included...," comment 2 does not mention estimates. Comment 2 addresses the general limitation of "good faith," which applies when there is no agreed-upon estimate. *See Orange & Rockland Utils., Inc.*

v. Amerada Hess Corp., 397 N.Y.S.2d 814, 818–19 (1977). The specificity of comment 3, however, dealing with estimates, displaces the generality of comment 2. Comment 3 therefore applies in the special case, like this one, where the parties have agreed on an estimate. Thus, the drafters' comments to § 7-2-306 support the conclusion that the statute applies both to unreasonably disproportionate increases and decreases from agreed-upon estimates.

Some federal courts and other state courts have previously addressed this question. *Brewster of Lynchburg, Inc. v. Dial Corp.,* 33 F.3d 355, 365 (4th Cir. 1994) (predicting direction of Arizona law); *Atlantic Track & Turnout Co. v. Perini Corp.,* 989 F.2d 541, 544–45 (1st Cir. 1993) (predicting direction of Massachusetts law on an output contract); *Empire Gas Corp. v. American Bakeries Co.,* 840 F.2d 1333, 1335 (7th Cir. 1988) (predicting direction of Illinois law); *R.A. Weaver & Associates, Inc. v. Asphalt Constr., Inc.,* 587 F.2d 1315, 1321–22 (D.C.Cir. 1978) (predicting direction of District of Columbia law); *Canusa Corp. v. A & R Lobosco, Inc.,* 986 F.Supp. 723, 729 (E.D.N.Y. 1997) (predicting direction of New York law as to an output contract). Most of these courts have resolved this issue in favor of the party in Simcala's position, holding that unreasonably disproportionate decreases are permissible so long as the buyer has acted in good faith, but that unreasonably disproportionate increases are impermissible. However, in *Romine v. Savannah Steel Co.,* 160 S.E.2d at 661, the Georgia Court of Appeals interpreted the statute to apply to deviations both above and below the stated estimate. Of course, while these decisions from other jurisdictions may be persuasive, this Court is not bound by federal or other state court decisions construing the laws of other states, even though the law being construed may be identical to Alabama law. *Weems v. Jefferson-Pilot Life Ins., Co.,* 663 So.2d 905, 913 (Ala. 1995).

Several courts that have reached the opposite conclusion have candidly acknowledged that by its plain meaning, the statute prohibits unreasonably disproportionate decreases from estimates. *Brewster,* 33 F.3d at 364 ("Although this statute may appear to prescribe *both* unreasonably disproportionate increases and reductions in a buyer's requirements, judicial interpretations of this statute provide otherwise."), *Empire Gas,* 840 F.2d at 1337 ("The proviso does not distinguish between the buyer who demands more than the stated estimate and the buyer who demands less, and therefore if read literally it would forbid a buyer to take (much) less than the stated estimate."), *R.A. Weaver & Assocs.,* 587 F.2d at 1322 ("The limiting language of Section 2-306(1) accordingly would seem to preclude appellant's reducing its requirements to zero, for zero would appear the quintessential 'disproportionate amount.'").

Courts interpreting analogous provisions of § 7-2-306(1) to allow unreasonably disproportionate decreases from stated estimates if those decreases are in good faith emphasize concerns over market impact that would flow from following the plain meaning of the statute. See, e.g., *Atlantic Track & Turnout Co.,* 989 F.2d at 545 ("an obligation to buy approximately a stated estimate of goods would pose a significant burden on buyers as it would force them to make inefficient business judgments"); *Empire Gas,* 840 F.2d at 1338 ("If the obligation were not just to refrain from buying a competitor's goods but to buy approximately the stated estimate ... the contract would be altogether more burdensome to the buyer.").

While other courts may be willing to look beyond the language chosen by their legislatures, we have repeatedly reaffirmed the fundamental principle of statutory construction that, where possible, words must be given their plain meaning. See, e.g., *Ex parte Smallwood,* 511 So.2d 537, 539 (Ala.2001); *Ex parte Krothapalli,* 762 So.2d at 838; *IMED Corp.,* 602 So.2d at 346. The plain language of § 7-2-306(1) admits of only one interpretation—that both unreasonably disproportionate increases and reductions in estimates are forbidden. See *Brewster*, 33 F.3d at 364; *Empire Gas*, 840 F.2d at 1337.

As we have repeatedly stated, the function of this Court is "'to say what the law is, not what it should be.'" *Ex parte Achenbach*, 783 So.2d 4, 7 (Ala.2000), quoting *DeKalb County LP Gas Co. v. Suburban Gas, Inc.*, 729 So.2d 270, 276 (Ala. 1998). To hold as Simcala requests we do—that the statute forbids only unreasonably disproportionate increases but not decreases—would require us to presume that the Legislature did not intend the ordinary meaning of the words that it chose to use in its enactment. We conclude that the interpretation supported by the plain meaning of the language of the statute and by the official comments is that §7-2-306(1) prohibits unreasonably disproportionate decreases made in good faith. If adverse effects on market conditions warrant a different result, it is for the Legislature, not this Court, to amend the statute.

The trial court found no evidence that Simcala had acted in bad faith in reducing its requirements, but it found that Simcala had breached the contract because its actual purchases of coal—7,200 tons—were unreasonably disproportionate to its stated esti-mate—17,500 tons. Simcala does not challenge the finding that its actual purchases from ACT were unreasonably disproportionate to the estimate. Under our construction of §7-2-306(1), even assuming Simcala's good faith, Simcala breached its requirements contract with ACT by demanding an unreasonably disproportionate reduction from its stated estimate. Thus, further discussion of the trial court's finding that Simcala had acted in good faith is unnecessary....

IV. Conclusion

Simcala was obligated under §7-2-306(1) to purchase an amount not unreasonably disproportionate to its stated estimate of 17,500 tons. ACT did not breach the contract. Thus, Simcala remained obligated under the contract.

The judgment of the trial court is affirmed.

Thomas Woodall, Justice, dissenting

The majority has employed the plain-meaning rule of statutory construction so as to defeat the obvious purpose of §7-2-306(1), Ala. Code 1975. In doing so, it has ignored another fundamental rule of statutory construction:

"A literal interpretation of a statute will not be blindly adopted when it would defeat the purpose of the statute, if any other reasonable construction can be given to the language in dispute. *Burton Manufacturing Co. v. State*, 469 So.2d 620 (Ala. Civ. App. 1985)." *McClain v. Birmingham Coca-Cola Bottling Co.*, 578 So.2d 1299, 1301 (Ala. 1991).

One obvious purpose of §7-2-306(1) is to treat a requirements contract differently than a contract to purchase a specific quantity of goods. However, under the majority's interpretation of that section, Simcala is required to pay to ACT the latter's anticipated profits on the entire quantity of coal, which the purchase order clearly indicated was only "an approximate quantity and to be shipped as required." Not only is that holding inconsistent with the purpose of the statute, it is also inconsistent with the majority's own conclusion that Simcala's purchase of some lesser amount "not unreasonably dis-proportionate to its stated estimate" would not be actionable.

It is presumptuous for the majority to conclude that "[t]he plain language of §7-2-306(1) admits of only one interpretation—that both unreasonably disproportionate increases and reductions in estimates are forbidden." In fact, there is another reasonable construction that can be given to the language in dispute, one that would be more consistent with the obvious purpose of the statute. Indeed, as the majority points out, most of the federal and state courts that have addressed the relevant question "have resolved this issue in favor of the party in Simcala's position, holding that unreasonably disproportionate decreases are permissible so long as the buyer has acted in good faith, but that unreasonably disproportionate increases are impermissible." I would adopt this more reasonable construction, and would hold that the trial court's finding that Simcala acted in good faith in ordering the coal it required precludes any recovery by ACT. Therefore, I respectfully dissent.

United Airlines, Inc. v. Good Taste, Inc., d/b/a Saucy Sisters Catering

Alaska Supreme Court
982 P.2d 1259 (Alaska 1999)

ALEXANDER O. BRYNER, JUSTICE

United Airlines terminated a catering contract with Saucy Sisters Catering in Anchorage. Saucy Sisters sued, claiming fraud, breach of contract, and breach of the implied covenant of good faith and fair dealing. The trial court dismissed the breach of contract claim but allowed the other claims to be tried. A jury, finding no fraud but a breach of the implied covenant, awarded Saucy Sisters damages. We hold that under Illinois law, which the parties agree governs, the contract could be terminated at will, and the implied covenant did not require United to have a legitimate business reason for termination. We therefore remand for entry of judgment for United.

I. Facts and Proceedings

The background facts are undisputed; the trial court summarized them concisely as follows:

> In 1987, United contacted Saucy Sisters' President and invited her to bid on United's in-flight catering contract. Shortly after United's invitation, Saucy Sisters entered into discussions/negotiations with United regarding the particulars of the catering contract and the obligations of the parties.
>
> On March 14, 1988, United awarded Saucy Sisters the catering contract. As a result of being awarded the contract, and in order to meet United's operation requirements for contracting caterers, Saucy Sisters expanded its operation extensively, spending roughly one million dollars in the process. [Footnote omitted.] A "Catering Agreement" ("Agreement") was signed by the parties and was performed for approximately one year. On May 18, 1989, United gave Saucy Sisters a ninety (90) day notice of termination by which it notified Saucy Sisters that its performance under the Agreement would terminate as of August 15, 1989. The Agreement was terminated August 15, 1989.
>
> United's ninety day termination notice was in accordance with a no-cause termination provision found in the Catering Agreement. The provision states:
>
> Term: The term of this Agreement shall commence on May 1, 1988, and shall continue for a period of 3 years(s) [sic]; provided, however, either party may terminate this Agreement upon ninety (90) days' prior written notice.
>
> The facts surrounding this termination provision are at the center of this dispute. In its version of the facts, Saucy Sisters alleges that Roger Groth, United's contracting representative, assured Saucy Sisters that United had never used the

ninety-day termination provision in the past and that the provision existed only to provide United with an "out" in the event United chose not to fly to Anchorage in the future. Saucy Sisters claims it would not have undertaken such a massive and expensive expansion effort at the risk of a no-cause, ninety-day termination notice but for Roger Groth's allegedly fraudulent representations regarding the restrictions on the termination provision. United fails to dispute these facts anywhere in the record, but stated during oral argument that Roger Groth would testify that he never made such statements regarding the termination provision.

Saucy Sisters sued United, alleging wrongful termination of the Catering Agreement, fraud, and breach of the covenant of good faith and fair dealing. The parties filed opposing motions for summary judgment: United sought judgment on all three claims; Saucy Sisters moved for judgment on its claim of fraud. Superior Court Judge Brian C. Shortell ruled on these motions. Relying on Section 22 of the Agreement, Judge Shortell initially found that Illinois law would apply to all claims. The judge went on to find: (1) that the facts surrounding the fraud claim were disputed and should go to the jury; (2) that the ninety-day termination clause was an unambiguous no-cause termination provision and that United did not breach the express terms of that clause; and (3) that a genuine factual dispute existed as to Saucy Sisters' covenant of good faith and fair dealing claim, which was permissible under Illinois law, despite existence of a no-cause termination clause.

As to the implied covenant claim, the judge specifically stated:

> Applied to the facts of the instant case, the covenant of good faith and fair dealing may impose limits on the manner in which either of the parties could exercise the broad discretion given them by the no-cause termination clause found in Section III.... [A]lthough the implied covenant of good faith and fair dealing does not create an enforceable legal duty to be nice or to behave decently in a general way, it may require both United and Saucy Sisters to exercise the discretion afforded to them by the termination clause in a manner consistent with the reasonable expectation of both parties. This means that even though United did not breach the express terms of Section III of the Catering Agreement, it might still be found to have breached the contract by breaching the implied covenant of good faith and fair dealing. Whether United acted in such a way as to breach that covenant is a question of fact to be decided at trial. (Citation omitted.)

United unsuccessfully moved for reconsideration of this ruling. Later, at the close of evidence at trial, it unsuccessfully moved for a directed verdict on the covenant claim. The jury returned a verdict finding that United had not engaged in fraud but had breached the covenant of good faith and fair dealing. The jury awarded Saucy Sisters $1,541,000 in damages. After adding prejudgment interest, costs, and attorney's fees to the verdict, Judge Shortell entered judgment in Saucy Sisters' favor for $3,604,843.57. United moved for a judgment notwithstanding the verdict and, in the alternative, for a new trial. Judge Shortell denied these motions.

II. Discussion

United appeals, claiming that the superior court misconstrued Illinois law in denying United's motion for summary judgment on Saucy Sisters' claim for breach of the implied covenant of good faith and fair dealing.

...

Under Illinois Law, the Trial Court Erred in Denying United's Motion for Summary Judgment on Saucy Sisters' Covenant of Good Faith and Fair Dealing Claim.

United asserts that Illinois law does not permit an implied covenant of good faith and fair dealing to supplant the clear language of a contract allowing termination without cause. According to United, because the disputed Agreement clearly and unambiguously allowed either party to terminate upon ninety days' notice and did not require good cause for termination, the trial court erred in finding the implied covenant applicable and in denying United summary judgment on this claim.

Saucy Sisters responds that the ninety-day termination clause gave both parties broad discretion to terminate their agreement. In such situations, Saucy Sisters argues, Illinois law applies the implied covenant of good faith and fair dealing as a limit on the permissible bounds of contractual discretion. Thus, in Saucy Sisters' view, the implied covenant applied in this case, and the trial court properly allowed this claim to go to the jury.

We review orders denying summary judgment de novo and affirm if we find that a genuine issue of material fact exists or that the moving party is not entitled to judgment as a matter of law. In deciding if a genuine issue of material fact exists, we draw all reasonable inferences in favor of the non-moving party. Here, the primary dispute concerning the trial court's summary judgment ruling centers on the correct interpretation of Illinois law. This is a purely legal question that we decide independently, based on our review and evaluation of applicable Illinois precedent.

The covenant of good faith and fair dealing is well accepted in Illinois, and its broad contours are firmly established: the covenant is implied in every contract.[11] The implied covenant guides the construction of contracts without creating independent duties for the contracting parties.[12] Its implied terms cannot modify the express terms of the contract.[13]

The covenant operates to define the intent of contracting parties when a contract is ambiguous or when it vests the parties with broad discretion as to its performance.[14] In cases involving unambiguous contracts that vest broad discretion in one of the parties, the covenant operates by constraining that party to exercise its discretion reasonably and fairly: "not arbitrarily, capriciously, or in a manner inconsistent with the reasonable expectation of the parties."[15]

Of course, a contractual no-cause termination clause may accurately be characterized as vesting the parties with broad discretion as to the termination of their contract; for this reason, it might be plausible to argue in the case of a no-cause termination clause that the implied covenant requires the parties to terminate reasonably — that is, for some legitimate reason. This is essentially the view that Saucy Sisters advocated at trial. And in denying United's pretrial motion for summary judgment on the implied covenant claim, the court adopted Saucy Sisters' theory:

> [A]lthough the implied covenant of good faith and fair dealing does not create an enforceable legal duty to be nice or to behave decently in a general way, it may require both United and Saucy Sisters to exercise the discretion afforded to them by the termination clause in a manner consistent with the reasonable expectation of both parties.

Saucy Sisters thereafter relied on this theory at trial. It expressly argued to the jury that even if United made no misrepresentations concerning the ninety-day no-cause termination

---

11. *See* Martindell v. Lake Shore Nat'l Bank, 154 N.E.2d 683, 690 (Ill. 1958).

12. See Echo, Inc. v. Whitson Co., 121 F.3d 1099, 1105–06 (7th Cir. 1997); Anderson v. Burton Assocs., Ltd., 578 N.E.2d 199, 203 (Ill. App. 1991).

13. See Northern Trust Co. v. VIII South Mich. Assocs., 657 N.E.2d 1095, 1104 (Ill. App. 1995).

14. See id.

15. Id.

clause, the implied covenant prevented it from violating Saucy Sisters' reasonable expectation that the agreement would be terminated only for a legitimate business reason:

> [Y]ou can't terminate for an arbitrary or capricious reason or to prevent the other party from obtaining reasonably anticipated benefits. You can't violate those reasonable expectations just because you find a better deal. Just because it's now in your financial interest to walk away from the agreement that you made.

Saucy Sisters invoked the same theme in opposing United's motions for judgment notwithstanding the verdict and a new trial on the implied covenant claim:

> [T]he United catering contract gave both parties discretion. There was, however, no express provision saying either party could exercise that discretion unreasonably. Accordingly, the implied covenant of good faith and fair dealing was applicable, and neither party was permitted to terminate the contract for arbitrary and capricious reasons.

Applying this view of the law to the facts here, Saucy Sisters insisted that the jury's verdict on the implied covenant claim should be upheld because "reasonable jurors could have found that [Saucy Sisters] performed the contract properly, that any problems in performance were caused by United, and that United terminated the contract without any legitimate business reason whatsoever."

But as far as we can determine, Illinois courts have never held the implied covenant to require good cause or a legitimate business reason for terminating a contract with an express no-cause termination provision. To the contrary, Illinois courts seem to have recognized consistently that "terminable-at-will contracts are generally held to permit termination for any reason, good cause or not, *or for no cause at all.*"[16] The courts have likewise recognized that applying the implied covenant to limit the terms of a no-cause termination provision would be "incongruous" with this general rule[17] and might "eviscerate the at will doctrine altogether."[18]

Several courts have reconciled this tension between no-cause termination clauses and the implied good faith covenant by explaining that parties to contracts with such clauses must reasonably expect the possibility of termination for any reason or no reason at all.[19] But in any event, the prevailing rule in Illinois, however rationalized, unmistakably favors the provisions of an express no-cause contract over potentially conflicting demands of the implied covenant: "[T]he duty of good faith and fair dealing does not override the

---

16. Jespersen v. Minnesota Mining & Mfg. Co., 681 N.E.2d 67, 71 (Ill. App. 1997) (citing Alderman Drugs, Inc. v. Metropolitan Life Ins. Co., 515 N.E.2d 689 (Ill. App. 1987)) (emphasis added), aff'd, 700 N.E.2d 1014 (Ill. App. 1998). see also Digital Equip. Corp. v. Uniq Digital Tech., Inc., 73 F.3d 756, 759–60 (7th Cir. 1996) (holding that a termination clause allowing for termination of a distributorship contract at the end of any year could not be modified by the duty of good faith even though the manufacturer relied on the contract and invested $1 million in facilitating the needs of the contract); Gordon v. Matthew Bender & Co., 562 F.Supp. 1286, 1290 (N.D.Ill. 1983) (holding that if the implied obligation to deal in good faith were allowed to create a cause of action in an employment-at-will situation, it would "eviscerate the at will doctrine altogether"); Harrison v. Sears, Roebuck & Co., 546 N.E.2d 248, 256 (Ill. App. 1989) (holding that putting implied restrictions on an employment-at-will contract would be inconsistent with the express terms of the contract which allowed for termination at any time).

17. Harrison, 546 N.E.2d at 256.

18. Gordon, 562 F.Supp. at 1290.

19. *See* Beraha v. Baxter Health Care Corp., 956 F.2d 1436, 1444–45 (7th Cir. 1992); Nichols Motorcycle Supply Inc. v. Dunlop Tire Corp., 913 F.Supp. 1088, 1143 (N.D.Ill. 1995) (vacated in part pursuant to settlement, September 18, 1995).

clear right to terminate at will, since no obligation can be implied which would be inconsistent with and destructive of the unfettered right to terminate at will."[20]

To be sure, some Illinois precedent hints that the implied covenant might apply in particular at-will termination situations. In *Hentze v. Unverfehrt,* the Illinois Court of Appeals, finding bad faith conduct that amounted to "opportunistic advantage-taking," held the implied covenant applicable when a company terminated an at-will dealership contract and engaged in a variety of other bad-faith tactics specifically aimed at driving one of two competing dealers out of business.[21]

Saucy Sisters relies heavily on *Hentze.* It asserts that, as interpreted in *Hentze,* "[T]he covenant of good faith and fair dealing requires, at a minimum, a proper motive to exercise the power [of termination without cause]." Because, in Saucy Sisters' view, the evidence at trial supported the conclusion that United ended its catering contract to seek a more lucrative arrangement with a competing caterer (Marriott), Saucy Sisters asserts that United's action, under *Hentze*'s approach, amounted to impermissible advantage-taking: "[A] party engages in opportunistic advantage-taking in Illinois when exercising the reserved power to terminate unreasonably and with an improper motive[.]"

But Saucy Sisters reads *Hentze* too broadly. The *Hentze* court took pains to acknowledge that, under the settled Illinois rule, the defendant company, DECO, "had the right to terminate the [dealership] contract for no reason at all."[22] So too, the *Hentze* court emphasized that, "[h]ad DECO merely ... sent Hentze a termination letter ..., we would be hard-pressed to find any absence of good faith."[23] The court thus made clear that its invocation of the implied covenant rested not on DECO's termination of the contract without, as Saucy Sisters puts it, "a proper motive to exercise the power," but rather on DECO's deliberate efforts to drive Hentze out of business by using other "tactics ... [that] went far beyond the intendments of any at-will clause."[24]

In short, the opportunistic advantage-taking described in *Hentze* was considerably more than an absence of the "legitimate business reason" that Saucy Sisters insists is a necessary ingredient for a valid at-will termination under Illinois law; it was instead a subjectively improper purpose — the malicious goal of driving Hentze out of business — combined with a variety of objectively unfair tactics designed to achieve that goal.[25]

Stripped of its implied covenant trappings, Saucy Sisters' broad reading of *Hentze* — its contention that United could not act arbitrarily or capriciously, but instead was required to have a legitimate business reason for termination — amounts to a claim that United could terminate the catering contract only for cause. But, as we have seen, this claim cannot be countenanced under Illinois law. The settled rule in Illinois remains that a contract expressly terminable at will may be ended for any reason or no reason at all.[26] *Hentze* does indicate that Illinois law might provide a measure of protection against a ter-

---

20. Jespersen, 681 N.E.2d at 71.
21. 604 N.E.2d 536, 539–40 (Ill. App. 1992).
22. *Id.* 604 N.E.2d at 540.
23. *Id.*
24. *Id.*
25. So described in *Hentze,* the practices prohibited by the implied covenant of good faith and fair dealing resemble the kind of opportunistic advantage-taking this court has recognized as impermissible under Alaska's law governing the implied covenant. *See, e.g.,* Mitford v. de Lasala, 666 P.2d 1000, 1007 (Alaska 1983). And, like Illinois courts, we have recognized that this prohibition against subjectively improper opportunism does not convert an at-will contract into a contract requiring good cause for termination. *see* Ramsey v. City of Sand Point, 936 P.2d 126, 133 (Alaska 1997).
26. *See* Jespersen, 681 N.E.2d at 71.

mination specifically motivated by bad faith and accompanied by unfair tactics.[27] But Saucy Sisters neither alleged nor proved "opportunistic advantage-taking"[28] of this kind. To the contrary, Saucy Sisters' complaint alleged no ulterior motive or subjective bad faith on United's part for terminating the contract, and its evidence at trial suggested only that United might have ended the contract in order to strike a better bargain with Marriott, not — as United claimed — because of Saucy Sisters' poor performance.

United's alleged desire for a more advantageous arrangement with Marriott certainly might not amount to "good cause" for terminating Saucy Sisters' contract, and from Saucy Sisters' perspective termination for this reason might even amount to arbitrary or capricious conduct, carried out for no legitimate business reason. But under Illinois law, the goal of achieving higher profits from a lower-bidding supplier is not itself inherently impermissible and does not amount to opportunistic advantage-taking; neither does reliance on an express at-will termination clause to attain this goal evince subjective bad faith or amount to an objectively unfair tactic.

Citing *Dayan v. McDonald's Corporation,*[29] the dissent concludes that Illinois would invoke the implied covenant to preclude United from terminating its contract "in a manner inconsistent with the reasonable expectations of the parties." But *Dayan* does not support this conclusion.[31] Instead, it narrowly limits its broad view of the implied covenant to franchise contracts, noting that this view reflects "judicial concern over longstanding abuses in franchise relationships, particularly contract provisions giving the franchisor broad unilateral powers of termination at will."[32] And even in franchise cases, *Dayan* seemingly would apply its broad interpretation of the good faith requirement only when "the exercise of discretion [is] vested *in one of* the parties to a contract."[33]

In fact, *Dayan* expressly recognizes that Illinois law applies a narrower interpretation of the implied covenant outside the area of franchise contracts. *Dayan* describes Illinois law as holding that the covenant protects at-will employees only when a termination is "inspired by an improper motive, such as a desire to deprive the employee of health or pension benefits[.]"[34]

This is essentially the rule of law that we conclude Illinois would apply to the present case. As a matter of Illinois law, the appropriateness of this narrow view of the implied covenant — rather than *Dayan*'s broader franchise rule — seems apparent given that the contract at issue here does not involve a franchise. Moreover, the contract's termination clause applied not just to United but to Saucy Sisters as well, giving both parties contractual discretion to terminate at will upon ninety days' notice.

That Illinois law would narrowly construe the implied covenant's effect on this contract seems unmistakable in light of *Jespersen v. Minnesota Mining and Manufacturing Co.*[35] The Illinois Court of Appeals there emphatically rejected a claim that the implied covenant barred termination of an at-will distributorship contract without good cause:

---

27. *See* Hentze, 604 N.E.2d at 540.

28. *Id.* 604 N.E.2d at 539.

29. 466 N.E.2d 958 (Ill. App. 1984).

31. Seegmiller v. Western Men, Inc., 437 P.2d 892 (Utah 1968), also mentioned by the dissent, fails to support the dissent's conclusion because, like Dayan, it involves a franchise contract. Moreover, because the franchise at issue in Seegmiller was terminated for good cause, Seegmiller's interpretation of the good faith covenant is dictum.

32. Dayan, 466 N.E.2d at 973.

33. *Id.* 466 N.E.2d at 972 (emphasis added).

34. *Id.*

35. 681 N.E.2d 67 (Ill. App. 1997), aff'd, 700 N.E.2d 1014 (Ill. 1998).

[T]erminable-at-will contracts are generally held to permit termination for any reason, good cause or not, or for no cause at all. Mindful that every contract carries the duty of good faith and fair dealing, as a matter of law, absent express disavowal by the parties, the duty of good faith and fair dealing does not override the clear right to terminate at will, since no obligation can be implied which would be inconsistent with and destructive of the unfettered right to terminate at will.[36]

The Illinois Supreme Court recently affirmed the decision of the court of appeals, observing, "Both parties here enjoyed the right to terminate the agreement at will, which means they could terminate the agreement for any reason or no reason without committing a breach of contract."[37]

In sum, we conclude that the trial court was mistaken in ruling that the implied covenant of good faith and fair dealing might "require both United and Saucy Sisters to exercise the discretion afforded to them by the termination clause in a manner consistent with the reasonable expectation of both parties." Under Illinois law, Saucy Sisters could not reasonably expect something other than what it expressly bargained for: a contract expressly terminable for any cause or no cause upon ninety days' notice. Because we conclude that the court erred in submitting Saucy Sisters' implied covenant claim to the jury, we reverse the judgment against United.[38] Our disposition makes it unnecessary to consider any other arguments raised on appeal or cross-appeal.

III. Conclusion

We affirm the trial court's order granting United summary judgment on Saucy Sisters' breach of contract claim, but reverse its order denying United summary judgment on the implied covenant claim. Accordingly, we vacate the judgment and remand for entry of judgment in favor of United.

Warren Matthews, Chief Justice, dissenting.

While I agree with the majority that Illinois law "favors the provisions of an express no-cause contract over potentially conflicting demands of the implied covenant [of good faith and fair dealing]," that type of contract is not at issue in this case. If this contract creates a right to terminate for no cause, the right exists because of a legal inference, not because that right is explicitly stated. I believe that a different legal inference should be drawn: that either party could terminate the contract for no cause if the reason for termination was consistent with the parties' reasonable expectations.[2]

This reading is consistent with the implied covenant of good faith and fair dealing as expressed in section 205 of the Restatement (Second) of Contracts: "Every contract imposes

---

36. *Id.* 681 N.E.2d at 71 (citations omitted).

37. 700 N.E.2d at 1017.

38. Saucy Sisters asserts that United waived its right to appeal the implied covenant issue by failing to object to, or propose alternative versions of, the jury instruction concerning the covenant. But this instruction merely paraphrased Saucy Sisters' interpretation of Illinois law governing the implied covenant. The trial court expressly adopted this interpretation of Illinois law in denying United's pretrial motion for summary judgment on the implied covenant claim and tacitly adhered to it in summarily denying United's mid-trial motion for directed verdict on the claim; later, the court again tacitly adhered to this interpretation in denying United's post-trial motions for JNOV and a new trial. Given these circumstances, United did not waive its right to appeal by failing to object separately to the implied covenant instruction. *see* Landers v. Municipality of Anchorage, 915 P.2d 614, 617 (Alaska 1996); *cf.* Brown v. Estate of Jonz, 591 P.2d 532, 534 (Alaska 1979).

2. See 3A Arthur Corbin, Corbin on Contracts § 654A, at 114 (1999 Supp.).

upon each party a duty of good faith and fair dealing in its performance and enforcement." The Supreme Court of Illinois has adopted a similar rule: "Every contract implies good faith and fair dealing between the parties...."[3] A review of *Martindell* and the Illinois Appellate Court cases cited in the majority opinion gives me no reason to think that Illinois law respecting the covenant of good faith and fair dealing is inconsistent with the Restatement's discussion of the covenant.

According to the Restatement, good faith enforcement "emphasizes faithfulness to an agreed common purpose and consistency with the justified expectations of the other party."[4] One type of violation recognized by the Restatement is the "abuse of a power ... to terminate the contract."[5] As authority for this comment the Restatement draws on various types of cases, including those involving franchise terminations. [6]

The covenant of good faith and fair dealing was discussed in *Dayan v. McDonald's Corp.*[7] a franchise termination case involving Illinois law. The court reviewed its understanding of Illinois law regarding the covenant in terms materially indistinguishable from the Restatement:

> As the above authorities demonstrate, the doctrine of good faith performance imposes a limitation on the exercise of discretion vested in one of the parties to a contract. In describing the nature of that limitation the courts of this state have held that a party vested with contractual discretion must exercise that discretion reasonably and with proper motive, and may not do so arbitrarily, capriciously, or in a manner inconsistent with the reasonable expectations of the parties.[8]

Dayan confirms my view that the termination clause in the present case—since it does not state that the contract may be canceled without cause—should be construed to incorporate the covenant. Quoting with approval from a Utah case which held that the implied covenant of good faith limited the power of the franchisor to terminate a franchise agreement without good cause where, by its terms, the franchise was terminable upon sixty days written notice to the franchisee, the court in *Dayan* stated:

> when parties enter into a contract of this character, and there is no express provision that it may be cancelled without cause, it seems fair and reasonable to assume that both parties entered into the arrangement in good faith, intending that if the service is performed in a satisfactory manner it will not be cancelled arbitrarily.[9]

The majority opinion dismisses the significance of *Dayan* by reading into it an artificial limitation. But *Dayan* gives no indication that its holding is limited to cases involving franchises, and there is no logic to such a rule. Franchise cases are not a special subcategory of contract law, but merely a type of contract case that reflects an imbalance of power between contracting parties. The *Restatement of Contracts* uses franchise cases as appropriate examples to illustrate general rules of contract law.[11] Similarly, the "unilateral power[ ]" of the franchisor is not a significant distinguishing element. The problem is that the fran-

---

3. Martindell v. Lake Shore Nat'l Bank, 15 Ill.2d 272, 154 N.E.2d 683, 690 (1958).

4. Restatement (Second) of Contracts § 205 cmt. a (1981).

5. *Id.* at cmt. e.

6. *See id.*, Reporter's Note to § 205, cmt. e.

7. 466 N.E.2d at 972.

8. 466 N.E.2d at 972 (citations omitted).

9. Id. (quoting Seegmiller v. Western Men, Inc., 437 P.2d 892 (Utah 1968)).

11. *See* Restatement (Second) of Contracts § 205, Reporter's Note to cmt. e (1981) (citing various franchise and non-franchise cases to illustrate concept of good faith in enforcement).

chisee—the economically weaker party—must spend large amounts to begin business and then is at risk of losing the investment based on the decision of the franchisor—the economically stronger party. The problem is not solved by giving the weaker party a similar power of termination. In other words, to use the *Dayan* parties as an example, Dayan's vulnerability to termination of his franchise by McDonald's is hardly changed by giving him the power to terminate the franchise. This is the situation in the present case.[12]

While it would be sufficient to end the analysis here, the following observations concerning the covenant's application to the facts of this case seem worth making.

Determining the reasonable expectations of contracting parties is not necessarily an easy task. Contract language must be considered along with the parties' discussions and the purposes of the contract.[13] And it may be useful to ask what the parties would have done had they considered the precise issue when the contract was formed. The Supreme Court of Delaware addressed this recently in *DuPont v. Pressman*:[14]

> The Covenant is best understood as a way of "implying terms in the agreement." It is a way of "honoring the reasonable expectations created by the autonomous expressions of the contracting parties."
>
> One method of analyzing the Covenant is to ask what the parties likely would have done if they had considered the issue involved. "[I]s it clear from what was expressly agreed upon that the parties who negotiated the express terms of the contract would have agreed to proscribe the act later complained of ... had they thought to negotiate with respect to that matter?" [T]he Covenant "is a stab at approximating the terms the parties would have negotiated had they foreseen the circumstances that have given rise to their dispute."

Both parties knew that Saucy Sisters must undergo expensive renovations in order to serve United. Saucy Sisters claims a cost of $600,000. We might ask what the parties would have done had Saucy Sisters asked United whether United could terminate the contract either soon after start up or at any time during the three-year term solely because a competitor offered better terms. I think the answer would have been that United would forego that power. Had United asserted the right to terminate to get better terms, there likely would have been no contract. Saucy Sisters would probably not have spent what for it was a small fortune had United overtly reserved the right to make a better deal during the three-year period.

> Most cases invoking the obligation to perform in good faith can be synthesized using the following principle: a party performs in bad faith by using discretion in performance for reasons outside the justified expectations of the parties arising from their agreement. Distinguishing allowed from disallowed reasons—opportunities forgone from opportunities preserved on entering a contract—will often be easy. But the distinction will be difficult in some cases. Specific disallowed reasons may be inferred from the express contract terms in light of the ordinary course of business and customary practice, in accordance with the usual principles of contract interpretation. It is not hard to infer from a fixed contract price, for

---

12. The court also dismisses the rule as described by Seegmiller as dictum. While it is true that the holding in Seegmiller rested on other grounds, the language does reflect the general rule accepted by Illinois courts.

13. See Steven J. Burton & Eric G. Andersen, Contractual Good Faith: Formation, Performance, Breach, Enforcement § 2.3 (1995).

14. 679 A.2d 436, 443 (Del. 1996) (citations omitted) (alteration in original).

example, that the parties have forgone opportunities to take advantage of market price fluctuations.[15]

Thus, in my view, early termination by United motivated by a desire to contract with a competitor on better terms would have contradicted the justified expectations of Saucy Sisters.

In light of the foregoing, I believe that summary judgment in favor of United was therefore correctly denied. Whether particular conduct qualifies as good faith is a question of law for the court.[16] But whether United in fact acted with an impermissible motive was properly a question for the jury.[17] No question has been raised as to whether the jury was correctly instructed. I would therefore affirm the judgment on the question of liability.[18]

Note — On Legal Realism and the Duty of Good Faith

In *Wood v. Lucy, Lady Duff Gordon,* 118 N.E. 214 (1917), Judge Cardozo cast doubt on the purported distinction between individual and social standards of behavior. Judge Cardozo suggests that courts should assume that parties expect to treat each other fairly, just as they expect to follow established trade practices or their regular course of dealing.

Are implied obligations of good faith, implied warranties of merchantability, implied standards of reasonableness and the like matters of individual choice or social control? Do these correspond to the actual expectations of the parties or are they imposed on the parties as edicts of public policy? In Cardozo's analysis, these questions are irrelevant. If a social standard of behavior is fair and just, then people generally will expect to follow it in their contractual relationships. This collapsing of individual and social values, and the accompanying recognition of a normative component in factual determinations, is characteristic of legal realist analysis. *See* Kenneth M. Casebeer, *Escape from Liberalism: Fact and Value in Karl Llewellyn,* 1977 Duke L.J. 671.

---

3. Interpretive Presumptions and Implied Terms

Scattered throughout contract decisions are various "presumptions" favoring or disfavoring an assortment of implied terms. In many states, for example, there are presumptions that employment for an indefinite period of time (even "permanent employment") is implicitly terminable for any reason or for no reason at all. This is the "at will" employment doctrine that we saw in *Worley v. Wyoming Bottling* (Chapter Four). In many states, there is a presumption in favor of terms requiring arbitration of all disputes arising under a contract. These presumptions and others influence courts as they engage in the process of articulating implied terms. As you read the next case excerpt, pay close attention to the court's use, evaluation, and justification for presumptions regarding medical benefits.

---

15. Burton & Anderson, supra, § 2.3.3 at 57.

16. 3A Corbin on Contracts § 655B, at 116–17 (1999 Supp.).

17. *See id.*

18. United also raises a question as to whether the damage award is consistent with Illinois law. Given my dissenting position, I have not addressed this question.

Jeffrey Poole et al v. City of Waterbury et al.

Connecticut Supreme Court

831 A.2d 211 (Conn. 2003)

JOETTE KATZ, JUDGE

The dispositive issue in this appeal is whether the trial court properly concluded that the plaintiffs, a group of 114 retired firefighters and widows of retired firefighters for the named defendant, the city of Waterbury (city), have a vested right to the specific medical benefits prescribed under the collective bargaining agreement in effect at the time that the firefighters retired. The defendants claim that the trial court improperly: (1) construed the collective bargaining agreements as providing the plaintiffs with a vested lifetime right to the specific medical benefits they had at the time of the retirees' retirement; (2) concluded that No. 01-1 of the 2001 Special Acts (S.A.01-1) did not authorize the defendant oversight board to modify the plan; and (3) granted permanent injunctive relief in the form of reinstatement of the specific medical benefits in light of the city's financial crisis. We conclude that, although the plaintiffs have a vested right to medical benefits generally, they do not have a vested right to the specific benefits prescribed in the collective bargaining agreement in effect at the time of the retirees' retirement. Accordingly, we reverse the judgment of the trial court.

...

The record reveals the following facts and procedural history. For some time prior to 1986, the city provided medical benefits to retired city firefighters, but those benefits were not included expressly in the city's collective bargaining agreements. Beginning in 1986, the city and the Waterbury Fire Fighters Association, Local 1339, a labor union in which each of the retirees was a member until his retirement, negotiated a series of collective bargaining agreements, each of which included a provision for retirees' medical benefits, effective: July 1, 1986, through June 30, 1989 ("1986 agreement"); July 1, 1989, through June 30, 1992 ("1989 agreement"); July 1, 1992, through June 30, 1995 ("1992 agreement"); and July 1, 1995, through June 30, 1999 ("1995 agreement"). The 1986 agreement provided, in article XXXIII, § 16, that the city "shall continue in full force and effect the benefits for each retiree and each employee who retires or dies after July 1, 1986, his spouse, and each eligible dependent of such retiree or employee...." The provision thereafter set forth the scope of the benefits, a basic plan supplemented by various home and office, major medical and prescription drug riders (indemnity plan), which was to be provided "at no cost to those eligible" pursuant to article XXXIII, § 16a, of the agreement. The 1989, 1992 and 1995 agreements provided similar indemnity plans, but referred only to providing such benefits to employees who retired after the execution of the agreement, and not to those employees who already had retired. The 1995 agreement imposed two additional terms: (1) § 16 of article XXXIII provided that the prescribed "medical benefits for retirees ... may be substituted for similar—but in no event, less—medical benefits if the City and the Coalition of City Unions agree on a modified insurance plan for City employees"; and (2) § 17 of that article mandated participation in medicare [sic] for retirees who had attained the age of sixty-five, had received medical benefits under the agreement and were eligible for medicare [sic], with the city providing supplemental insurance. At the expiration of the 1995 agreement in June of 1999, the city and the union had not yet agreed on terms for a successor agreement. After negotiations failed to result in a consensus, the matter was submitted for binding arbitration.

During the course of the negotiations between the city and the union, the state legislature determined that it had to take certain action because, as a result of many years of gross fiscal mismanagement, the city was in a state of financial crisis. See S.A. 01-1, § 1. Specifically, the city had underfunded its pensions for years and was paying its pension liabilities out of the city's general fund. In addition, the city had been paying health care benefits, the cost of which were rapidly rising, out of the city's general fund. As a result of these and other liabilities, the city's bond rating had been downgraded. The crisis threatened not only the city, but also the fiscal reputation of the state, which acts essentially as guarantor of certain of the city's obligations.

To address the crisis, the legislature enacted S.A. 01-1, effective upon its passage on March 9, 2001. See footnote 4 of this opinion. [sic] In accordance with the special act, the city was required to undertake certain fiscal and management controls. As a further measure, the legislature created the oversight board to ensure that order was restored to the city's finances. S.A. 01-1, §§ 10 and 11. The special act confers broad authority on the oversight board to take the necessary measures to accomplish this goal. S.A. 01-1, § 11. The oversight board's authority encompasses, inter alia, the power to set aside city contracts, under certain circumstances, and to serve as the arbitration panel with respect to labor contracts subject to binding arbitration. S.A. 01-1, § 11(a)(5) and (b)(7).

Pursuant to its authority, the oversight board acted as the arbitrator in the collective bargaining dispute between the city and the union. On December 14, 2001, the oversight board issued an arbitration award prescribing the city's obligations, effective retroactively from July 1, 1999, through June 30, 2004 (1999 agreement). Article XXXIII, § 16, of the 1999 agreement set forth the following terms regarding medical benefits: "Those employees who are participating in the City's medical insurance plan at the time of retirement ... shall be eligible to participate in such medical insurance plan which the City provides to its active bargaining unit employees, as such plans may change pursuant to any successor collective bargaining agreement, subject to the same conditions as may exist at any time for such active employees." Under the 1999 agreement, active employees, and therefore retirees, received medical benefits pursuant to a managed care plan with a preferred provider organization, rather than the traditional indemnity plan provided under previous agreements. Additional changes under the 1999 agreement included, inter alia, a requirement of a small copayment for office and home visits.

On March 14, 2002, the plaintiffs filed in the Superior Court an application for prejudgment remedy, seeking temporarily to enjoin the defendants from altering the plaintiffs' existing medical benefits. The plaintiffs also filed the complaint in this action, seeking temporary and permanent injunctive relief, as well as damages, and alleging that the defendants' conduct constituted: (1) a breach of contract; (2) an ultra vires act; (3) a taking under the state and federal constitutions; and (4) an impairment of contract rights in violation of the federal constitution. Thereafter, the parties stipulated that the temporary injunction hearing also would serve as the hearing on the plaintiffs' claim for permanent injunctive relief. At hearings on the matter, the court heard testimony from various city officials and several of the plaintiffs as to the city's prior practices with respect to the provision of specific medical benefits to retirees. The court also heard testimony from city officials regarding the city's financial crisis and the various measures the city had taken as a result, which affected the plaintiffs, other city employees and city residents generally.

On August 14, 2002, the trial court issued its memorandum of decision, concluding that the defendants had breached the plaintiffs' vested contractual right to the specific indemnity plan provided under the pre-1999 collective bargaining agreements. In its memorandum of decision, the trial court first examined the factual context in which the issues arose. It recognized the magnitude of the financial crisis facing the city and noted the oversight board's estimate of $2 million in savings resulting from the conversion of all of the city's retired employees to managed health care plans. The court concluded that "[t]he failure of the city to bring prudent cost controls to retiree health benefits will create serious difficulties for the city in enacting the types of conservative budgets mandated by [S.A.] 01-1." The court then noted certain differences in cost and availability of services and service providers between the managed care plan provided under the 1999 agreement and the indemnity plan provided under the pre-1999 agreements. The court concluded that, "[although] a managed health care plan is inherently less flexible than a traditional indemnity plan, it is by no means certain from the evidence that a given beneficiary will always fare worse under the new health care plan...." Nonetheless, the court concluded that "[t]he plaintiffs here have succeeded in showing that there are significant differences between the traditional indemnity plans currently provided to them and the proposed managed care plan. The court cannot conclude that the differences are trivial, even though the plaintiffs have not shown that over their life expectancy they will suffer a specific quantifiable loss."

The court next turned to the legal issues. It first determined that the question of whether the plaintiffs have a vested right to the specific medical benefits was governed by ordinary contract principles. Applying those principles, the court pointed to certain language in the pre-1999 agreements providing that the city "'shall continue in full force and effect the benefits for each employee who retires or dies on or after the execution of this agreement.'" The court noted competing interpretations by the parties as to the meaning of that phrase, and then turned to examine certain extrinsic evidence, specifically, testimony related to the city's prior practice of continuing benefits for retirees beyond the expiration of the agreements. The court concluded that, "[t]he way the city and the current and former union membership jointly interpreted the provisions of these contracts for almost two decades clearly indicates the intent of the parties to create a vested right to the health benefits that each firefighter elected on retirement." The court rejected the defendants' contention that S.A. 01-1 empowered the oversight board to modify vested rights obtained under collective bargaining agreements.

With respect to the plaintiffs' remedies, the court concluded that the plaintiffs had demonstrated that injunctive relief was appropriate ... order[ed] that the defendants "take all necessary steps to reinstate each plaintiff to the health care plan in which each plaintiff was enrolled prior to the involuntary conversion to the managed health care plan on or about April 1, 2002, unless the plaintiff requests not to be so reinstated."

The defendants also submitted an application for a stay of the permanent injunction, which the trial court denied. Thereafter, the defendants filed with this court a motion for an emergency temporary stay and a motion for review of the trial court's denial of its application for a stay of the permanent injunction. This court granted both motions and the relief requested therein. This certified appeal followed....

The defendants raise three claims on appeal. First, they contend that the trial court improperly determined that the plaintiffs had a vested right to the specific medical benefits in effect under the collective bargaining agreement at the time the retirees retired.... We agree with the defendants' first claim and therefore do not reach the [other] two claims.

The issue of whether the trial court properly determined that the plaintiffs had a vested right to the specific medical benefits under the collective bargaining agreement in effect at the time of the retirees' retirement requires us to resolve two questions. The first question is whether the plaintiffs' right to benefits survived the termination of the collective bargaining agreements and thereby vested.

. . .

A.

A preliminary question raised by the parties in the present case is whether, in order to interpret the agreements to determine whether the right to benefits survived the agreements' termination, a particular legal presumption should be imposed, either against vesting or in favor of vesting. This question has been the subject of extensive debate, both in the courts and in academia. *See generally* C. Fisk, "Lochner Redux: The Renaissance of Laissez-Faire Contract in the Federal Common Law of Employee Benefits," 56 Ohio St. L.J. 153 (1995); D. Weckstein, "The Problematic Provision and Protection of Health and Welfare Benefits for Retirees," 24 San Diego L. Rev. 101 (1987); D. Sondgeroth, note, "High Hopes: Why Courts Should Fulfill Expectations of Lifetime Retiree Health Benefits in Ambiguous Collective Bargaining Agreements," 42 B.C. L. Rev. 1215 (2001).

The defendants contend that, pursuant to our decisions in *Pineman v. Oechslin*, 488 A.2d 803 (Conn. 1985), and *Fennell v. Hartford*, 681 A.2d 934 (Conn. 1996), as well as case law from other jurisdictions, we should impose a presumption against vesting in the absence of unambiguous express vesting language. Conversely, the plaintiffs urge us to reject such a presumption and to rely on case law imposing a presumption in favor of vesting. This issue raises a question of law over which we exercise plenary review. *DeLeo v. Nusbaum*, 821 A.2d 744 (Conn. 2003).

The Connecticut cases cited by the defendants are inapposite. In *Pineman v. Oechslin*, 488 A.2d 803, the issue was whether state employees had a vested, contractual right to benefits under the State Employees Retirement Act, General Statutes § 5-152 et seq. Our decision therein resolving that question in the negative was predicated on the absence of express language in that act evincing an intent to create a contract. *Id.* at 416; accord *Cece v. Felix Industries, Inc.*, 728 A.2d 505 (Conn. 1999). In the present case, there is no question that the collective bargaining agreements at issue are contracts. Moreover, although our decision in Pineman recognized that such contractual obligations should not be construed lightly because of their binding effect on future legislatures, we also recognized two other issues relevant to the present case: (1) that retirement benefits are not mere gratuities; and (2) that employees have enforceable rights once they satisfy the eligibility criteria under the State Employees Retirement Act. *Pineman v. Oechslin*, supra. In *Fennell v. Hartford*, we concluded that a pension manual created and distributed by the defendant city pension commission was not an implied contract because the pension commission did not have the authority to confer benefits not provided for by the city's charter. By contrast, there is no doubt in the present case that the city had the authority to enter into an express contract and confer the benefits at issue.

As to the case law from other jurisdictions cited by both parties, we note that most of it arises in the context of claims in which the Employee Retirement Income Security Act of 1974 (ERISA), 29 U.S.C. § 1001 et seq., is at issue. ERISA does not apply to government sponsored benefit plans. See 29 U.S.C. § 1003(b). The courts applying ERISA uniformly hold that, although the law does not require the vesting of health insurance plans, as it does for pension plans, employers may create vested rights in such benefits when the intent is expressed unambiguously. *American Federation of Grain Millers v. International Multifoods Corp.*, 116 F.3d 976, 980 (2d Cir. 1997). From that starting point, however, several different approaches have emerged. Some courts impose a presumption that there is no vesting in the absence of a written, unambiguous expression of intent to do so, whereas others impose a presumption in favor of vesting if there is some ambiguity in the language conferring the benefit. *See Rossetto v. Pabst Brewing Co.*, 217 F.3d 539, 543 (7th Cir. 2000) *see generally* D. Sondgeroth, 42 B.C. L. Rev. at 1229–42 (discussing different presumptions applied and rationales offered in support thereof).

In our view, the rationales articulated for either presumption are not particularly persuasive. The courts imposing a presumption against vesting base that approach largely on their construction of ERISA—drawing an adverse inference from Congress' decision to require vesting for pension rights, but not to include a comparable requirement for welfare benefits. *See, e.g., International Union, United Automobile, Aerospace & Agricultural Implement Workers of America, U.A.W. v. Skinner Engine Co.*, 188 F.3d 130, 137–38 (3d Cir. 1999); id., at 139 (citing several courts that apply this rationale); *see also* C. Fisk, 56 Ohio St. L.J. at 172–73. In the absence of a comparable statutory scheme in the present case, no such adverse inference is warranted. Moreover, we agree with the Court of Appeals for the Seventh Circuit that, although requiring express terms, such as "vested," "accrued" or "guaranteed," facilitates the court's function in interpreting contracts, that rationale is an inadequate basis for imposing such a requirement when the parties' intent otherwise can be ascertained. *Bidlack v. Wheelabrator Corp.*, 993 F.2d at 607; accord *Anchorage v. Gentile*, 922 P.2d 248, 256–57 (Alaska, 1996). Conversely, those courts that impose a presumption in favor of vesting rely on the status-based nature of retirement benefits and shift the burden to the employer to disprove vesting based on a contractual ambiguity. *See Maurer v. Joy Technologies, Inc.*, 212 F.3d 907, 914–17 (6th Cir.2000) (reiterating holding of *International Union, United Automobile, Aerospace & Agricultural Implement Workers of America v. Yard-Man, Inc.*, 716 F.2d 1476 (6th Cir. 1983), seminal case articulating this view); *Roth v. Glendale*, 614 N.W.2d 467 (Wis. 2000), and cases cited therein. In our view, this burden shifting is inconsistent with the principle that contractual obligations generally cease at the termination of a collective bargaining agreement. *See Litton Financial Printing Division v. National Labor Relations Board*, 501 U.S. at 207; *United Food & Commercial Workers International Union v. Gold Star Sausage Co.*, 897 F.2d at 1026.

We also conclude that neither presumption adequately takes into account the competing and significant policy concerns at issue. From the employer's perspective, courts should not impose lightly an indefinite financial obligation when, unlike with pension plans, the employer lacks the ability to predict or control costs. Indeed, this concern is of heightened importance in the public employment sphere. A municipality must ensure its fiscal integrity to provide not only benefits for past and future employees, but also necessary services to its residents. Furthermore, courts should hesitate to presume a vesting intent when the result could well be to discourage employers from providing such benefits in the first instance. *See* C. Fisk, 56 Ohio St. L.J. at 159 ("[s]tringent regulation to protect employees will increase the cost of benefits to employers and thus, at some point, will create an incentive for employers to exercise their prerogative not to provide benefits at all").

From the employee's perspective, the promise of health insurance benefits at retirement may be a significant inducement in determining employment. *Roth v. Glendale* 614 N.W.2d 467; A. Sulentic, "Promises, Promises: Using the Parol Evidence Rule to Manage Extrinsic Evidence in ERISA Litigation," 3 U. Pa. J. Lab. & Emp. L. 1, 2 n.6 and accompanying text (2000–2001); cf. *Bender v. Bender*, 785 A.2d 197 (Conn. 2001) (noting in context of pensions benefits, "employers frequently use lucrative retirement packages in lieu of additional salary to attract and retain desirable employees"). Employees reasonably relying on ambiguous terms as making such a promise may be put in an untenable position when their employer unilaterally withdraws or substantially diminishes benefit insurance— incurring a substantial financial burden for which they had not planned at a time when it is least affordable, if they can obtain coverage at all. *See Law Enforcement Labor Services, Inc. v. Mower*, 483 N.W.2d 696, 701 (Minn. 1992); *see generally* P. Frostin & D. Salisbury, "Retiree Health Benefits: Savings Needed to Fund Health Care in Retirement" (Employee Benefit Research Institute, February 2003) p. 13, fig. 9 (comparing cost of health coverage for retiree covered by employer health plan with retiree not covered by plan).

Therefore, we reject both presumptions and conclude that the best course is to apply our well established principles of contract interpretation.

. . .

[The court affirmed the trial court's determination that the contracts had given the retirees' vested rights to health insurance but reversed the finding that the contracts did not allow any changes to the health benefits. The court found instead that the defendants were entitled to make reasonable changes and that the changes in dispute were reasonable.]

B. Interpreting Express Terms

While the process of construing implied terms focuses on the enormity of unspoken understandings and expectations among people, the interpretation of express terms focuses on the fluidity of language and the contingency of expressed human desire. In this Part we will first discuss the parol evidence rule, which exists to give effect to parties' efforts to bestow special authority on written expression. Then we will look at the interpretation of integrated written documents and at the persistent, if futile, appeal to "plain meaning." The third part of this section will examine the "reasonable expectations" doctrine and the challenge of complex adhesion contracts.

1. Parol Evidence Rule and the Exclusion of Evidence

The parol evidence rule assumes that parties will sometimes want to give special authority or significance to a written statement of some or all of their agreement and purports to carry out this desire by excluding evidence that would conflict with such a writing. This assumption about parties' desires is controversial. Most legal systems do not make such an assumption — they do not have a parol evidence rule — and many lawyers in the United States have criticized the assumption. The international representatives who drafted the *United Nations Convention on Contracts for the International Sale of Goods* decided not to adopt a parol evidence rule for international transactions because it was unrealistic and unduly cumbersome. Indeed, business people from other nations find it incredible that people in the United States would think it possible to write down every aspect of a contract or that a final statement of an agreement should be made immune from dispute.

In addition to being controversial, the parol evidence rule in Anglo-American law is complex and confusing. In 1898, well-known Harvard Professor James Bradley Thayer remarked of the parol evidence rule: "Few things are darker than this, or fuller of subtle difficulties." James Bradley Thayer, A Preliminary Treatise on Evidence at the Common Law 390 (1898). A generation later, in 1923, Professor John Henry Wigmore quoted Thayer and added: "[A]nd this condition of the law all members of the profession will concede. . . . [I]t is not strange that the so-called Parol Evidence rule is attended with a confusion and an obscurity which make it the most discouraging subject in the whole field of Evidence." 5 John Henry Wigmore, *Wigmore on Evidence* § 2400, at 235–36 (2d ed. 1923).

The assumption that parties will sometimes want to give special authority or significance to a written statement of their agreement is the first element of the parol evidence rule. In its second element, the doctrine assumes that if people do want to give special significance to a writing, they want that significance to be one of two sorts. Either:

1) the parties meant the writing to be a *final* statement of the terms stated in the writing, but not to be a *complete* statement of all of the terms of the agreement, in which case evidence of prior or contemporaneous agreements that *conflict* with the written terms should **not** be admitted, but evidence of *supplementary* terms should be admitted (this is "partial integration"); or

2) the writing was meant to be both a *final* and *complete* statement of all of the terms of the agreement, in which case evidence of prior or contemporaneous agreements *regarding the transaction* should **not** be admitted (this is "full integration").

And note: the parol evidence rule operates to exclude only evidence of *prior or contemporaneous* agreements: the parol evidence rule *does not apply* to evidence regarding agreements made *after* the writing.

Thus, if one party objects to the admission of evidence on the basis of the parol evidence rule, the first question is whether the parties wanted the writing to have special significance: whether it was *integrated. See Betaco, Inc. v. Cessna Aircraft Co.*, below. If the answer to this question is yes, then the court must decide if the parties intended the writing to be partially or fully integrated (that is, whether the parties intended the document to be a *final* statement of the terms contained therein (partial integration) or a *final and complete* statement of the entire agreement (full integration)). Most courts will look at all of the available evidence to decide the parties' intentions regarding integration, although some courts focus only on the document itself, particularly when the document contains an explicit statement that the writing is final or complete (such clauses are called *integration clauses* or *merger clauses*).

If the court decides that the writing was intended to be partially integrated, then the next issue is whether the offered evidence of a prior or contemporaneous agreement would *contradict* the final terms in the writing (in which case it should be excluded) or whether it would prove *supplementary terms* (in which case it should be admitted).

If the court decides that the writing was intended to be fully integrated, the court must exclude all evidence involving matters that are part of the agreement, unless the evidence falls into one of the exceptions listed below. Agreements which the court concludes are *separate* from the agreement contained in the writing can be proved and enforced.

The general exceptions or limitations to the parol evidence rule are:

1) evidence is admissible to *explain a term* even if the writing is integrated—many courts say that evidence is admissible to explain a term only if the term is *ambiguous* or that evidence is admissible only to prove a meaning to which the writing is "reasonably susceptible";

2) evidence of *trade usages* or of *prior dealings* between the parties is always admissible because that evidence is a strong indication of the unspoken (implied) understandings and expectations between the parties (this is provided explicitly in the *Uniform Commercial Code* § 2-202(a) and is followed by some courts in cases not governed by the *Uniform Commercial Code*);

3) evidence regarding *defenses* to the formation and enforcement of the contract, including incapacity, misunderstanding, mistake, misrepresentation, duress, undue influence, unconscionability, illegality, public policy, lack of consideration, and the like should be admissible even though the writing is integrated. In some cases, however, courts will reject claimed defenses of misrepresentation on the ground that the alleged victim should not have relied on the misrepresentation if it was inconsistent with the integrated writing. Recall, in Chapter Seven, *Flight Concepts Limited v. The Boeing Company*, where the court entered summary judgment for the defendants on allegations of misrepresentation because the misrepresentations were contradicted in the contract document, and *Kang v. Harrington*, where the court allowed the action for reformation and damages despite the writing.

In addition, courts may apply the parol evidence rule broadly or narrowly in order to avoid injustice in particular situations. Where the writings are part of an *adhesion contract* (that is where the contract is offered on a take-it-or-leave-it basis to someone who needs the contract), for example, courts may be reluctant to apply the parol evidence rule to exclude evidence of additional or even contradictory oral representations. In other cases, courts may be particularly rigid in applying the rule in other situations where the admission of evidence would cause injustice, as in collective bargaining contexts. *See Merk et al. v. Jewel Food Stores*, below.

Betaco, Inc. v. Cessna Aircraft Co.

United States Court of Appeals for the Seventh Circuit
32 F.3d 1126 (1994)

Ilana Rovner, Circuit Judge

Betaco, Inc. ("Betaco") agreed in 1990 to purchase a six-passenger CitationJet from the Cessna Aircraft Company ("Cessna"). Betaco's decision was based in part on Cessna's representation in a cover letter accompanying the purchase agreement that the new jet was "much faster, more efficient and has more range than the popular Citation I," a model with which Betaco was familiar. After advancing $150,000 toward the purchase of the new plane, Betaco became convinced that the CitationJet would not have a greater range than the Citation I with a full passenger load and decided to cancel the purchase. When Cessna refused to return Betaco's deposit, Betaco filed suit in diversity claiming, inter alia, that Cessna had breached an express warranty that the CitationJet had a greater range than the Citation I. The district court rejected Cessna's contention that the purchase agreement signed by the parties was a fully integrated document that precluded Betaco's attempt to rely on this warranty. A jury concluded that the cover letter's representation as to the range of the plane did amount to an express warranty and that Cessna had breached this warranty, and Betaco was awarded damages of $150,000 with interest. We reverse the district court's entry of partial summary judgment in favor of Betaco on the threshold integration issue, concluding that a question of fact exists as to the parties' intent that can be resolved only after a factual hearing before the district court.

I. Background ...

Betaco is a Delaware corporation headquartered in Indiana; it is a holding company that acquires aircraft for sale or lease to other companies and also for the personal use of J. George Mikelsons, the company owner. Betaco leases aircraft to Execujet and also to American Transair, an airline that Mikelsons founded in 1973 and of which he is the chairman and chief executive. Both companies interlock with Betaco. Mikelsons is himself an experienced pilot.

In late 1989, Betaco became interested in a new aircraft known as the CitationJet to be manufactured by Cessna, a Kansas corporation. Mikelsons contacted Cessna and asked for information about the forthcoming plane. On January 25, 1990, Cessna forwarded to Mikelsons a packet of materials accompanied by a cover letter which read as follows:

Dear Mr. Mikelsons:

We are extremely pleased to provide the material you requested about the phenomenal new CitationJet.

Although a completely new design, the CitationJet has inherited all the quality, reliability, safety and economy of the more than 1600 Citations before it. At 437 miles per hour, the CitationJet is much faster, more efficient, and has more range than the popular Citation I. And its luxurious first-class cabin reflects a level of comfort and quality found only in much larger jets.

And you get all this for less than an ordinary turboprop!

If you have questions or need additional information about the CitationJet, please give me a call. I look forward to discussing this exciting new airplane with you.

Sincerely,

Robert T. Hubbard
Regional Manager

Enclosed with Hubbard's letter was a twenty-three page brochure providing general information about the CitationJet, including estimates of the jet's anticipated range and performance at various fuel and payload weights. A purchase agreement was also enclosed. The preliminary specifications attached and incorporated into that agreement as "Exhibit A" indicated that the CitationJet would have a full fuel range of 1,500 nautical miles, plus or minus four percent, under specified conditions.

Mikelsons signed the purchase agreement on January 29, 1990 and returned it to Cessna, whose administrative director, Ursula Jarvis, added her signature on February 8, 1990. The agreement occupied both sides of a single sheet of paper. As completed by the parties, the front side reflected a purchase price of $2.495 million and a preliminary delivery date of March, 1994, with Betaco reserving the right to opt for an earlier delivery in the event one were possible. The payment terms required Betaco to make an initial deposit of $50,000 upon execution of the contract, a second deposit of $100,000 when Cessna gave notice that the first prototype had been flown, and a third deposit of $125,000 at least six months in advance of delivery. The balance was to be paid when the plane was delivered. The agreement expressly incorporated the attached preliminary specifications, although Cessna reserved the right to revise them "whenever occasioned by product improvements or other good cause as long as such revisions do not result in a reduction in performance standards." Item number 9 on the front page stated: "The signatories to this Agreement verify that they have read the complete Agreement, understand its contents and have full authority to bind and hereby do bind their respective parties."

Following this provision, in a final paragraph located just above the signature lines (written in capital lettering that distinguished this provision from the preceding provisions), the agreement stated:

PURCHASER AND SELLER ACKNOWLEDGE AND AGREE BY EXECUTION OF THIS AGREEMENT THAT THE TERMS AND CONDITIONS ON REVERSE

SIDE HEREOF ARE EXPRESSLY MADE PART OF THIS AGREEMENT. EXCEPT FOR THE EXPRESS TERMS OF SELLER'S WRITTEN LIMITED WARRANTIES PERTAINING TO THE AIRCRAFT, WHICH ARE SET FORTH IN THE SPEC-IFICATION (EXHIBIT A), SELLER MAKES NO REPRESENTATIONS OR WAR-RANTIES EXPRESS OR IMPLIED, OF MERCHANTABILITY, FITNESS FOR ANY PARTICULAR PURPOSE, OR OTHERWISE WHICH EXTEND BEYOND THE FACE HEREOF OR THEREOF. THE WRITTEN LIMITED WARRANTIES OF SELLER ACCOMPANYING ITS PRODUCT ARE IN LIEU OF ANY OTHER OBLIGATION OR LIABILITY WHATSOEVER BY REASON OF THE MANU-FACTURE, SALE, LEASE OR USE OF THE WARRANTED PRODUCTS AND NO PERSON OR ENTITY IS AUTHORIZED TO MAKE ANY REPRESENTA-TIONS OR WARRANTIES OR TO ASSUME ANY OBLIGATIONS ON BEHALF OF SELLER. THE REMEDIES OF REPAIR OR REPLACEMENT SET FORTH IN SELLER'S WRITTEN LIMITED WARRANTIES ARE THE ONLY REMEDIES UNDER SUCH WARRANTIES OR THIS AGREEMENT. IN NO EVENT SHALL SELLER BE LIABLE FOR ANY INCIDENTAL OR CONSEQUENTIAL DAMAGES, INCLUDING, WITHOUT LIMITATION, LOSS OF PROFITS OR GOODWILL, LOSS OF USE, LOSS OF TIME, INCONVENIENCE, OR COM-MERCIAL LOSS. THE ENGINES AND ENGINE ACCESSORIES ARE SEPA-RATELY WARRANTED BY THEIR MANUFACTURER AND ARE EXPRESSLY EXCLUDED FROM THE LIMITED WARRANTIES OF SELLER. THE LAWS OF SOME STATES DO NOT PERMIT CERTAIN LIMITATIONS ON WAR-RANTIES OR REMEDIES. IN THE EVENT THAT SUCH A LAW APPLIES, THE FOREGOING EXCLUSIONS AND LIMITATIONS ARE AMENDED IN-SOFAR AND ONLY INSOFAR, AS REQUIRED BY SAID LAW.

On the reverse side, the agreement included the following integration clause among its "General Terms":

This agreement is the only agreement controlling this purchase and sale, express or implied, either verbal or in writing, and is binding on Purchaser and Seller, their heirs, executors, administrators, successors or assigns. This Agreement, including the rights of Purchaser hereunder, may not be assigned by Purchaser except to a wholly-owned subsidiary or successor in interest by name change or otherwise and then only upon the prior written consent of Seller. Purchaser ac-knowledges receipt of a written copy of this Agreement which may not be modified in any way except by written agreement executed by both parties.

In early 1992, Paul Ruley and another Betaco employee visited Cessna's facilities in order to select the radio and navigational equipment to be installed in the plane. In the course of his work as an administrator for Execujet and American Transair, Ruley assesses the suitability of aircraft for particular charter flights based on the distance, passenger load, fuel, aircraft weight, and runway requirements. After his visit to Cessna, Ruley completed some calculations concerning the CitationJet and showed them to Mikelsons. By Ruley's estimate, the new jet would have a greater range than its predecessor, the Citation I, when carrying three to five passengers; but with a full passenger load of six (plus two crew members), the CitationJet would have a range no greater than or slightly less than that of the Citation I. Ruley also believed that the new plane would not meet the full fuel range of 1,500 nautical miles set forth in the preliminary specifications.

After seeing Ruley's numbers, Mikelsons contacted Cessna in March or April 1992. The testimony at trial was in conflict as to exactly what Cessna personnel told Mikelsons about the range of the new plane. In any case, Mikelsons was not satisfied that the

CitationJet would live up to his expectations and decided to cancel the purchase. On April 16, 1992, Mick Hoveskeland of Cessna wrote to Mikelsons accepting the cancellation and offering to apply Betaco's deposit toward the purchase of another aircraft. Cessna subsequently refused Betaco's demand for a return of the deposit, however, invoking the contract's proviso that "all cash deposits shall be retained by [Cessna] not as a forfeiture but as liquidated damages for default if this Agreement is canceled or terminated by [Betaco] for any cause whatsoever...." Betaco proceeded to file this suit.

...

II. Analysis

The sole issue before us is whether the district court erred in concluding that the contract signed by Betaco and Cessna was not a fully integrated contract containing a complete and exclusive statement of the parties' agreement. Cessna does not challenge the jury's determination that Hubbard's representation as to the relative range of the CitationJet constituted an express warranty. Rather, Cessna's contention is that because the purchase agreement was, contrary to the district court's determination, fully integrated, Betaco was precluded from attempting to establish any additional warranty via extrinsic evidence (in this case, Hubbard's cover letter). Both parties agree that we should look to Kansas law in resolving this issue; their contract contains a provision that both the agreement and the parties' legal relationship shall be determined in accordance with Kansas commercial law, including the *Uniform Commercial Code ("U.C.C.")* as adopted by the Kansas legislature.

The provision of the U.C.C. that is central to this case is U.C.C. section 2-202, found at section 84-2-202 of the Kansas Statutes:

> Final written expression: Parol or extrinsic evidence. Terms with respect to which the confirmatory memoranda of the parties agree or which are otherwise set forth in a writing intended by the parties as a final expression of their agreement with respect to such terms as are included therein may not be contradicted by evidence of any prior agreement or of a contemporaneous oral agreement but may be explained or supplemented
>
> (a) by course of dealing or usage of trade (section 84-1-205) or by course of performance (section 84-2-208); and
>
> (b) by evidence of consistent additional terms unless the court finds the writing to have been intended also as a complete and exclusive statement of the terms of the agreement.

Kan. Stat. Ann. § 84-2-202. The parties agree that they intended the signed purchase contract as a final expression of the terms set forth within its four corners. Betaco, however, has relied on Hubbard's cover letter as evidence of a "consistent additional term" of the agreement. Section 2-202(b) bars that evidence (and thus Betaco's claim for breach of the warranty in Hubbard's letter) if the parties intended the signed contract to be the "complete and exclusive" statement of their agreement.

An initial question arises as to the appropriate standard of review. Cessna urges us to review the district court's decision de novo, whereas Betaco contends that the court's ruling was a factual determination that we may review for clear error only.

Although the rule set forth in section 2-202 is superficially a rule of evidence, Kansas does not treat it as such: ..."The parol evidence rule is not a rule of evidence, but of substantive law. Its applicability is for the court to determine, and, when the result is reached it is a conclusion of substantive law.'" *In re Estate of Goff*, 379 P.2d 225, 234 (1963) (*quoting Phipps v. Union Stock Yards Nat'l Bank*, 140 Kan. 193, 34 P.2d 561, 563 (1934).

We have likewise treated the rule as a substantive one, and have accordingly considered the determination of whether or not an agreement was completely integrated to be a legal determination subject to de novo review.

Betaco correctly points out, however, that insofar as this determination turns on the intent of the contracting parties, it poses a factual question. *See Willner* [*v. University of Kansas*, 848 F.2d 1020 (10th Cir. 1988) (per curiam), *cert. denied*, 488 U.S. 1011, 109 S. Ct. 797, 102 L. Ed. 2d 788 (1989)] at 1022 n.3; *Transamerica Oil Corp. v. Lynes, Inc.*, 723 F.2d 758, 763 (10th Cir. 1983). Thus, in cases where the integration assessment amounts to "a predominantly factual inquiry, revolving around the unwritten intentions of the parties instead of interpretation of a formal integration clause," courts have treated the district court's determination as a finding of fact subject to review only for clear error. *Northwest Cent. Pipeline Corp. v. JER Partnership*, 943 F.2d 1219, 1225 (10th Cir. 1991); *Transamerica Oil*, 723 F.2d at 763; *see also In re Pearson Bros. Co.*, 787 F.2d 1157, 1161 (7th Cir. 1986) ("When a court interpreting a contract goes beyond the four corners of the contract and considers extrinsic evidence, the court's determination of the parties' intent is a finding of fact.").

Yet, in this case, the district court decided the question on summary judgment. Essentially, the court determined that the evidence before it could only be construed in one way, and that Betaco was entitled to judgment as a matter of law on the integration issue. Thus, the precise question before us is not who should prevail *ultimately* on the integration issue, but whether it was appropriate to enter partial summary judgment in favor of Betaco and against Cessna on the matter. Our review of that particular determination is of course, de novo, as it would be in any other appeal from the grant of summary judgment. We examine the record in the light most favorable to Cessna, granting it the benefit of all reasonable inferences that may be drawn from the evidence. "If we find a genuine issue as to any fact which might affect the outcome of the case, summary judgment will have been inappropriate and we will reverse." *Frey v. Fraser Yachts*, 29 F.3d 1153, 1156 (7th Cir. 1994).

The familiar rule of contractual interpretation is that absent an ambiguity, the intent of the parties is to be determined from the face of the contract, without resort to extrinsic evidence. *Metropolitan Life Ins. Co. v. Strand*, 1994 WL 242599, at 4 (Kan. June 3, 1994); Yet, the drafters of section 2-202 rejected any presumption that a written contract sets forth the parties' entire agreement. *See* Kan. Stat. Ann.§ 84-202, Official U.C.C. Comment (1). Instead, in ascertaining whether the parties intended their contract to be completely integrated, a court looks beyond the four corners of the document to the circumstances surrounding the transaction, "including the words and actions of the parties." *Burge v. Frey*, 545 F. Supp. 1160, 1170 (D. Kan. 1982). *Mid Continent Cabinetry* identifies the relevant considerations: The focus is on the intent of the parties. *Sierra Diesel Injection Service v. Burroughs Corp.*, 890 F.2d 108, 112 (9th Cir. 1989). Section 2-202 does not offer any tests for determining if the parties intended their written agreement to be integrated. Comment three to § 2-202 offers one measure of when a statement is complete and exclusive: "If the additional terms are such that, if agreed upon, they would certainly have been included in the document in the view of the court, then evidence of their alleged making must be kept from the trier of fact." The courts have looked to several factors, not just the writing, in deciding if the writing is integrated. These factors include merger or integration clauses, B. Clark & C. Smith, The Law of Product Warranties ¶ 4.04 [1] and [2] at 4-37-4-40 (1984) (1990 Supp.); disclaimer clauses, *see, e.g., St. Croix Printing Equipment, Inc. v. Rockwell Intern. Corp.*, [428 N.W.2d 877, 880 (Minn. App. 1988)]; the nature and scope of prior negotiations and any alleged extrinsic terms, J. White and R. Summers, Uniform Commercial Code§ 2-10 at 108 (3d ed. 1988); and the sophistication of the parties, *Sierra*

Diesel Injection Service, 890 F.2d at 112. *See also Transamerica Oil*, 723 F.2d at 763; *Ray Martin Painting, Inc. v. Ameron, Inc.*, 638 F. Supp. 768, 773 (D. Kan. 1986).

We look first to the warranty limitation and integration clauses of the purchase agreement, as these speak directly to the completeness and exclusivity of the contract. The warranty limitation clause states that "except for the express terms of seller's written limited warranties pertaining to the aircraft, which are set forth in the specification, [Cessna] makes no representations or warranties express or implied, of merchantability, fitness for any particular purpose, or otherwise *which extend beyond the face hereof or thereof*" (Emphasis supplied.) The clause goes on to admonish the buyer that no individual is authorized to make representations or warranties on behalf of Cessna. On its face, this clause might be construed to disavow the types of representations found in Hubbard's letter to Mikelsons. However, as a general rule, express warranties, once made, cannot be so easily disclaimed. Section 2-316(1) of the Kansas U.C.C. provides that "subject to the provisions of this article on parol or extrinsic evidence (K.S.A. §84-2-202), negation or limitation [of an express warranty] is inoperative to the extent such construction is unreasonable." Kan. Stat. Ann. §84-2-316(1); *see L.S. Heath & Son, Inc. v. AT&T Info. Sys., Inc.*, 9 F.3d 561, 570 (7th Cir. 1993). The commentary explains that the purpose of this provision is to "protect a buyer from unexpected and unbargained language of disclaimer." Kans. Stat. Ann. 84-2-16(1), Official *U.C.C.*ain Comment (1). On the other hand, the disclaimer rule is, by its express terms, subject to the provisions of section 2-202 (*see* Kan. Stat. Ann. 84-2-316(1) & Kansas Comment 1983); thus, if the signed contract is deemed fully integrated, the plaintiff is precluded from attempting to establish any express warranty outside the signed contract. *Jordan v. Doonan Truck & Equip., Inc.*, 552 P.2d 881, 884 (Kan. 1976).

We thus turn to the integration clause of the contract. Although not dispositive, "the presence of a merger clause is strong evidence that the parties intended the writing to be the complete and exclusive agreement between them...." *L.S. Heath & Co.*, 9 F.3d at 569 (citing *Sierra Diesel*, 890 F.2d at 112; R. Anderson, Uniform Commercial Code, §2-202:25 (1983). Here the clause states that "this agreement is the *only* agreement controlling this purchase and sale, express or implied, either verbal or in writing, and is binding on Purchaser and Seller" and that the agreement "may not be modified in any way except by written agreement executed by both parties" (Emphasis supplied.) The language is simple and straightforward; and Betaco does not suggest that a reasonable buyer would find it difficult to comprehend. On the other hand, Betaco does note, as the district court did, that this was, like most other provisions in the contract, a preprinted clause that was not the subject of negotiation by the parties. Yet, that fact alone does not render the provision unenforceable. *See Northwestern Nat'l Ins. Co. v. Donovan*, 916 F.2d 372, 377 (7th Cir. 1990). The clause was not buried in fine print, nor was it written so as to be opaque. *See id.* It was relegated to the back of the contract rather than the front, but the front page admonished the signatories in bold, capitalized lettering that the terms on the back were part of the agreement, and although the reverse side contained a number of provisions, they were neither so many nor so complicated that the reader would have given up before he or she reached the integration clause. Mikelsons signed the contract, and there is no dispute that he had the opportunity to review it in as much detail as he wished before signing it. Under these circumstances, the integration provision should have come as no surprise to Betaco. *Compare Transamerica Oil*, 723 F.2d at 763 (where plaintiff's order was taken over telephone, document that plaintiff received and signed upon delivery did not constitute fully integrated agreement); *Hemmert*, 663 F. Supp. at 1553 (same). In our view, therefore, the clause is strong evidence that the parties intended and agreed for the signed contract to be the complete embodiment of their agreement.

The district court focused on another circumstance that courts frequently consider in assessing the degree to which a contract is integrated: is the term contained in a purported warranty outside the contract one that the parties would have included in the contract itself had they intended it to be part of the agreement? U.C.C. § 2-202, Official Comment (3). The court thought that Hubbard's representation as to the relative range of the CitationJet was not such a term, although neither the court nor Betaco has cited any evidence in the record to support that proposition. The court did note that "the representation made by Mr. Hubbard was not so formally presented nor central to the purchase that Mr. Mikelsons of Betaco would most likely have insisted it be included, especially where the Purchase Agreement was a standard form. The representation did not include the word 'warranty,' a red flag that might have clued a non-attorney into the necessity of including it in the Purchase Agreement." Our analysis is somewhat different on this score, however.

We are not persuaded that the range of the aircraft was not something that certainly would be included in the agreement. On the contrary, the specifications made part of the contract do contain an express representation as to the range of the CitationJet, and, in fact, it was that warranty that formed the basis for Count I of Betaco's complaint. In that sense, an extraneous reference to the range of the aircraft arguably is less like a supplemental term on a subject as to which the contract is otherwise silent, and more like a potentially conflicting term that section 2-202 would explicitly exclude from admission into evidence. *See generally Souder v. Tri-County Refrigeration Co.*, 373 P.2d 155, 159–60 (Kan. 1962) (noting the distinction between using extrinsic evidence to explain or supplement the contract and using it to vary the terms of the agreement).

The context of the representation does not alter our analysis in this regard. It may well be, as the district court emphasized, that because the statement as to the relative range of the CitationJet was contained in the cover letter accompanying the purchase agreement, Mr. Mikelsons may have given it more weight than he would a more isolated statement. At the same time, as the court pointed out, the reference was informal, without language that might alert the reader that the contract should include a comparable provision. *Id.* But in our view, one might just as readily infer from this that the contents of the letter were not meant to supplement the purchase agreement. Recall the wording of the passage on which Betaco relies: "At 437 miles per hour, the CitationJet is much faster, more efficient, and has more range than the popular Citation l." Like the balance of the letter, this statement is long on adjectives and short on details—how much faster? how much more efficient? how much more range? . . . .

. . .

[In an omitted section, the court quotes from the specifications incorporated into the agreement.]

[This] summary of the aircraft's performance capabilities is, in stark contrast to the letter, quite precise and quite explicit about the assumptions underlying each of the estimates. Given the marked difference in style and detail between these specifications and the indeterminate braggadocio in the cover letter, we find it somewhat implausible that the parties might have considered the "more range" reference to be part of their agreement yet failed to include it in the purchase contract with the level of specificity characteristic of that document.

Finally, we do not find it particularly significant that Mikelsons did not consult a lawyer before signing the purchase agreement. Again, the contract was neither lengthy nor obtuse. Nor was this a contract of adhesion. These were two seemingly sophisticated parties entering into a commercial agreement, and Mikelsons' significant experience as a pilot, as an airline executive, and as a purchaser of an earlier model of the Citation aircraft surely went a long way toward balancing whatever advantage Cessna may have enjoyed as the drafter of the agreement. *See Bowers Mfg. Co. v. Chicago Mach. Tool Co.*, 453 N.E.2d 61, 66 (Ill. App. 1983) ("the courts are less reluctant to hold educated businessmen to the terms of contracts to which they have entered than consumers dealing with skilled corporate sellers") (quoted with approval in *Ray Martin Painting*, 638 F. Supp. at 773); *see also Binks Mfg. Co. v. National Presto Indus., Inc.*, 709 F.2d 1109, 1116 (7th Cir. 1983)). Furthermore, there is no evidence that the contract was tainted by fraud, mutual mistake, or any other circumstance that would call into question the binding nature of the agreement. *See generally Prophet* [*v. Builders, Inc.* 462 P.2d 122, 126 (Kan. 1969)]. That Betaco chose not to have the contract reviewed by an attorney before Mikelsons signed it does not, standing alone, permit Betaco to escape the operation of the terms it signed on to, including the integration clause. As the Kansas Supreme Court has stated:

> This court follows the general rule that a contracting party is under a duty to learn the contents of a written contract before signing it. *Sutherland v. Sutherland*, 358 P.2d 776 (Kan. 1961). We have interpreted this duty to include the duty to obtain a reading and explanation of the contract, and we have held that the negligent failure to do so will estop the contracting party from avoiding the contract on the ground of ignorance of its contents. *Maltby v. Sumner*, 219 P.2d 395 (Kan. 1950). As a result of this duty, a person who signs a written contract is bound by its terms regardless of his or her failure to read and understand its terms.

Rosenbaum v. Texas Energies, Inc., 736 P.2d 888, 891–92 (Kan, 1987). That we would make this assumption should come as no surprise to Betaco, for in signing the contract, Mikelsons also assented to its provision that the signatories to this agreement verify that they have read the complete Agreement, understand its contents and have full authority to bind and hereby do bind their respective parties.

The circumstances identified by the district court do not, in sum, establish as a matter of law that the purchase agreement was not fully integrated and that extrinsic evidence of additional, consistent terms was therefore admissible. Nor has Betaco identified anything more in the record that would support partial summary judgment in its favor on this question. The district court's decision to grant partial summary judgment in favor of Betaco and against Cessna therefore must be reversed, and the jury's verdict (which was based upon the extrinsic evidence admitted pursuant to the district court's summary judgment ruling) must be vacated.

Two options remain for us at this juncture: we may reverse the denial of Cessna's cross motion for partial summary judgment and deem the signed purchase agreement fully integrated as a matter of law (thus entitling Cessna to judgment on Count 11) or, in the event we detect factual disputes that preclude this determination on summary judgment, remand the case for a bench hearing (as the applicability of section 2-202 is, as we have noted above, a question for the court rather than the jury). We are somewhat surprised to note that although the parties ask us to draw diametrically opposed conclusions from the evidence bearing on the integration issue, neither has ever (either on appeal or in the district court) suggested that a factual hearing might be necessary in order to resolve their dispute. Instead, both parties appear confident that the issue can simply be decided one way or the other based on the summary judgment record presented to the district court.

If the only evidence offered on the question of whether the parties meant the signed purchase agreement to be fully integrated had been the two documents on which the district court relied—the agreement itself (and in particular, the warranty limitation and integration clauses of that agreement) along with the cover letter from Hubbard—we might be inclined to agree that no hearing was necessary to assess the parties' intent. The purchase agreement contains, as we have discussed above, a straightforward integration clause which, coupled with the express disclaimer of other warranties, suggests that the parties' understanding did not extend beyond the four corners of the signed contract. Against that, the very casual nature of the cover letter's remark attributing "more range" to the new CitationJet than its predecessor is, at best, only weak evidence to the contrary, particularly when the contract itself addresses the range of the new aircraft in quite specific terms. Thus, we would be most reluctant to hold that Hubbard's letter, standing alone, would provide enough support for the notion that the contract was not a complete reflection of the parties' understanding to avoid summary judgment.

But there is a bit more to the evidence that Betaco tendered. In a brief affidavit, Mikelsons offered the following background averments regarding Hubbard's "more range" remark:

3. In late 1989 and prior to my receipt of Robert Hubbard's letter of January 25, 1990, and my execution of the Purchase Agreement dated January 29, 1990, I had several telephone conversations with Mr. Hubbard and other Cessna representatives who were aware of my interest in possibly purchasing a CitationJet.

4. During those conversations, I expressed the requirement that the CitationJet have or possess greater range (that is, available flying distance) than the Cessna Citation I which Betaco owned and that I occasionally flew. The Cessna representatives assured me that the range of the CitationJet was greater than the range of the Citation I.

5. I specifically relied on the verbal representations and statements of Cessna representatives and Robert Hubbard's letter confirming his prior verbal representation that the range of the CitationJet was greater than that of the Citation I when I executed the Purchase Agreement.

Again to our surprise, neither party has so much as mentioned these averments in the briefing, but we find them to be significant. In part they bear on a question that the jury has already decided—did Cessna expressly warrant that the CitationJet had a range greater than the Citation I? But they also bear in part on whether the purchase agreement, although it did address the range of the CitationJet, set forth the parties' entire understanding as to the range capabilities of the plane, particularly as compared to the earlier model. If, in fact, there were substantial discussions preceding Betaco's commitment to the purchase of the CitationJet focusing specifically on the range of the new jet vis à vis the Citation I, one might infer that the signed agreement did not, ultimately, embody the complete agreement between the parties. In that respect, the case could be viewed as being more like *Transamerica Oil*, for example, where the court concluded that the parties' agreement extended beyond the signed "Sales and Service Invoice" to include the representations that the plaintiff had seen in trade journals and the assurances that the seller had given it over the telephone prior to the purchase. 723 F.2d at 761, 763. We do not mean to suggest that the evidence ought to be viewed in that way, of course. Although Mikelsons' affidavit appears to characterize Hubbard's letter as the culmination of prior discussions about the range of the new plane, the wording of the letter is far more consistent with that of a standard promotional letter than a confirmation of prior discussions concerning what Betaco contends was an essential contract term. Moreover, as we have noted, Mikelsons was an apparently sophisticated businessman who had the opportunity to review the contract at length before deciding to purchase, very much in contrast to the situation in *Transamerica Oil*. Still, as we consider the merits of Cessna's cross-motion for summary judgment, we must take care to give Betaco the benefit of every reasonable inference that may be drawn from the record. Construed favorably to Betaco, we believe that Mikelsons' affidavit raises a question of fact as to whether the parties considered the purchase contract to be the complete and exclusive statement of their agreement.

Both parties seem to have forgotten that where competing inferences may be drawn from facts that are otherwise undisputed, summary judgment is improper. *See Texas Refrigeration Supply, Inc. v. FDIC*, 953 F.2d 975, 982 (5th Cir. 1992) (*citing Phillips Oil Co. v. OKC Corp.*, 812 F.2d 265, 274 n. 15 (5th Cir.), *cert. denied*, 484 U.S. 851, 108 S. Ct. 152, 98 L. Ed. 2d 107 (1987)). Just as we believe that plausible inferences from the record rendered partial summary judgment in Betaco's favor on the integration issue improper, so we believe that contrary inferences preclude summary judgment in favor of Cessna. We therefore remand the case for a hearing in which the district judge will sit as a finder of fact and decide, based on whatever evidence the parties choose to submit, whether the parties intended the purchase agreement to be the complete embodiment of their understanding or not. In the event the court answers this question in the affirmative, of course, the rule set forth in section 2-202 would bar Betaco's warranty claim and compel the entry of final judgment in Cessna's favor on Count II of the complaint. We express no opinion as to the appropriate outcome of this hearing; that is a matter for the district court to decide based on the totality of the circumstances and the resolution of the competing inferences that the evidence permits.

III. Conclusion

Because we find that the record before the court on summary judgment was reasonably subject to contrary assessments of whether the parties intended their signed contract to be the complete embodiment of their agreement, we reverse the entry of partial summary judgment against Cessna on this question and vacate the final judgment subsequently entered in favor of Betaco on Count II of the complaint. The case is remanded for a factual hearing before the bench on the integration issue and for appropriate disposition based on the outcome of that hearing. Circuit Rule 36 shall not apply on remand.

Note

On remand from this decision, the district court held a hearing on whether the parties intended the document they signed to be a final and complete embodiment of their agreement. After conducting that hearing, the district court decided that the parties did not intend the writing to be a complete statement of their agreement and thus admitted evidence of the express warranty. On appeal, the Seventh Circuit Court of Appeals reversed this determination, holding that the document was fully integrated, that the express warranty should have been excluded, and that final judgment should be entered in favor of Cessna. *Betaco Inc. v. The Cessna Aircraft Company*, 103 F.3d 1281 (7th Cir. 1996) ("Betaco II").

The Seventh Circuit determination that the writing was fully integrated is controversial, however, because it disregards the district court's finding on the credibility of Betaco's witness, Mikelsons, and it apparently disregards the UCC's directive in section 2-316(1) that express warranties are to be given effect despite conflicting written terms.

Mikelsons claimed to have had discussions with representatives at Cessna. Cessna denied that any such conversations took place. In circumstances like this, the commentary to UCC § 2-316 suggests that the parol evidence rule may protect sellers against "false allegations of oral warranties." UCC § 2-316, comment 2. The district court believed Mikelsons. The court found his statements credible because the conduct of Mikelsons and Cessna subsequent to the formation of the contract was consistent with Mikelsons' version of events. Judge Rovner, writing for the court of appeals, says that she accepts the district court's finding that Mikelsons was telling the truth but nevertheless finds that the writing was fully integrated and that the evidence regarding the conversation must be excluded.

In the course of her opinion, Judge Rovner also suggests that the presence of a disclaimer of warranty alone "calls into question the viability of a breach of warranty claim based on an extrinsic writing" like the cover letter. Yet UCC § 2-316(1) provides that "when there is a conflict between an express warranty and disclaimers of express warranties, the disclaimer is inoperative." Although UCC § 2-316(1) does provide that the parol evidence rule may apply to exclude evidence regarding express terms, this provision should not be read to say that the mere existence of a conflict supports exclusion of the express warranty, as Judge Rovner suggests.

Kelly Merk, Joseph Staszewski, and Vickie Menagh et al., on Behalf of Themselves and all Others Similarly Situated v. Jewel Food Stores, American Stores Company, Incorporated, and United Food and Commercial Workers Union Local No. 881, AFL-CIO and CLC

United States Court of Appeals for the Seventh Circuit
945 F.2d 889 (1991)

RICHARD DICKSON CUDAHY, CIRCUIT JUDGE

This case involves application of the parol evidence rule to the unique context of collective bargaining agreements. Specifically, we must determine the legal significance of secret oral negotiations between union officials and company management that modify central terms of a collective bargaining agreement which was submitted to the union membership for ratification without any notice that it would be conditioned by additional terms.

I.

The relevant facts are as follows. Jewel Food Stores (Jewel) operates approximately 180 supermarkets in and around Chicago, employing over 15,000 workers who are represented by Local 881 of the United Food and Commercial Workers Union (the Union). In September 1982, Jewel and the Union began negotiating a new collective bargaining agreement (the CBA) to run from September 15, 1982 to June 15, 1985. Negotiations culminated in a contract which was reduced to writing and ratified by the Union membership on January 27, 1983. The CBA established wage rates, vacation leave and other terms of employment for the duration of the contract. Section 4.1 of the CBA, in particular, specified that "During the term of this Agreement, the Employer agrees to pay not less than the minimum wage rates set out in Appendix A."

Had the CBA embodied the entire agreement between the parties, this case would have been easily resolved. But the outcome of negotiations was not so straightforward. Anxious about the potential entry into the Chicago market of warehouse competitors such as Cub Foods, Jewel insisted that the CBA contain a "most favored nations" clause, a provision that would allow it to match the wages of unionized competitors opening in the Chicago market after the start of the contract term. The Union refused this demand throughout the negotiations, and the final compact did not include a most favored nations clause. Just before the CBA was approved, however, Union president Fred Burki and two Jewel representatives—Neil Petronella, chief negotiator, and Marsh Collins, corporate vice president—forged a secret deal at an informal hallway meeting late in the evening of January 23, 1983. The precise terms of that deal are in dispute: Union officials claim that all they promised was to "sit and discuss" Jewel's competitive position once Cub Foods entered the Chicago market whereas Jewel executives contend that they agreed to "an economic reopener with full reservation of rights." An economic reopener provision permits the company to reopen all economic terms of the CBA upon occurrence of the condition precedent. Negotiations may then proceed as if the parties were bargaining over a totally new contract, and both sides retain their respective economic weapons, including the Union's right to strike and the company's right to lock out or unilaterally implement a final offer after bargaining to impasse. Whatever the terms of the secret oral agreement between Union officials and Jewel management, both sides affirm that it was never disclosed to or ratified by the Union rank and file even though ratification is required under the Union constitution and bylaws.

Cub Foods' entry into the Chicago market in 1983 precipitated this dispute. Shortly thereafter, Jewel announced the reopening of contract negotiations. On February 26, 1984, when negotiations reached impasse, Jewel unilaterally implemented its final offer, cutting the wages of its employees below levels mandated by the CBA. Jewel slashed wages by as much as $1.25 an hour and reduced vacation and personal day benefits as well. The Union immediately filed an unfair labor practice complaint and sued to compel arbitration. The district court ordered Jewel to arbitrate. After an arduous course of negotiations, the Union and Jewel finally resolved their longstanding dispute on the eve of expiration of the CBA: Jewel agreed to award backpay to its current employees while the Union pledged to relinquish its unfair labor practice complaint and the district court suit. At Jewel's insistence, however, the settlement abandoned the plaintiffs in this case—a class comprising approximately 2,000 Jewel employees who retired, quit or were fired during the protracted 15-month battle.

Claiming the back wages to which they believed they were rightfully entitled under the CBA, plaintiffs filed suit against the Union for breach of its duty of fair representation and against Jewel for breach of contract. The district court granted summary judgment for the Union, ruling that the Union owed no duty of fair representation to former employees. 641 F. Supp. 1024 (N.D. Ill. 1986). In an interlocutory appeal, this Circuit upheld the district court's ruling, 848 F.2d 761 (7th Cir. 1988), and the Supreme Court denied certiorari, 488 U.S. 956 (1988).

Plaintiffs' breach of contract action against Jewel, however, proceeded to a one-week jury trial. After the jury returned a verdict in favor of Jewel, plaintiffs moved for judgment notwithstanding the verdict and, in the alternative, for a new trial. The district court denied both motions, examining and rejecting each of plaintiffs' arguments in turn. Invoking the parol evidence rule, plaintiffs first contested the district court's admission of extrinsic evidence regarding the oral reopener to modify the provisions of the written CBA. But the district court submitted the parol evidence issue to the jury because it was not clear from the face of the CBA whether it was intended to embody the parties' entire agreement. The jury determined that the CBA was not integrated and the district court apparently agreed with this conclusion, upholding the jury's verdict as supported by the evidence. The district court also dismissed plaintiff's second argument, ruling that oral modifications to a written CBA do not violate national labor policy. Finally, it held that lack of ratification did not

render the oral reopener agreement invalid. The jury found waiver of the ratification requirement based upon evidence of a past practice of adherence to unratified side agreements.
The district court agreed with the jury's conclusion but broadly declared that, in any event,
Jewel had a right to rely on the unratified oral reopener absent clear notice that the Union
was acting in bad faith against the interests of its members.

On appeal, plaintiffs challenge the verdict against them on the following grounds. First,
they claim that the district court improperly admitted evidence of the oral reopener
agreement in violation of the parol evidence rule. Second, they argue that the oral reopener
agreement should not have been enforced because it violated the Union's constitutional
requirement that significant terms of the labor contract be ratified by union members.
Third, they contend that section 8(d) of the Labor Management Relations Act (LMRA)
and national labor policy militate against enforcement of a clandestine oral reopener
agreement that contradicts the terms of the written and ratified CBA. Fourth, they maintain
that the district court committed numerous evidentiary errors, entitling them to a new
trial. Finally, they contest the district court's dismissal of their claim for punitive damages.

II.

We review the district court's denial of judgment notwithstanding the verdict de novo,
applying federal common law (rather than the law of any state) to this suit for breach of
a collective bargaining agreement. *See Mohr v. Metro East Mfg. Co.*, 711 F.2d 69 (7th Cir.
1983). For Congress has accorded labor contracts a special status, authorizing the courts
to fashion a body of federal common law governing their enforcement. *See Textile Workers
Union v. Lincoln Mills*, 353 U.S. 448, 456 (1957) ("[T]he substantive law to apply in [breach
of contract] suits under §301(a) is federal law, which the Courts must fashion from the
policy of our national labor laws."). This special solicitude reflects the fact that the collective
bargaining agreement is more than a mere contract—it is "the charter instrument of a
system of industrial self-government." *United Steelworkers of America v. American Mfg.
Co.*, 363 U.S. 564, 570 (1960) (Brennan, J., concurring). Ordinary common law contract
principles, therefore, cannot simply be imported whole into the labor context and mech-
anistically applied to collective bargaining agreements. To foster industrial peace and
stability, we must instead read collective bargaining agreements with sensitivity to considerations of national labor policy....

We must first determine whether the parol evidence rule bars the admission of testimony
regarding the secret oral agreement. The parol evidence rule provides that evidence of
prior or contemporaneous agreements or negotiations may not be introduced to contradict
the terms of a partially or completely integrated writing. *See* Restatement (Second) of
Contracts §215. A writing is deemed fully integrated if the parties intend it to be the
expression of their entire agreement. If they intend the writing to be the final expression
of the terms it contains but not a complete expression of all the terms agreed upon—
some terms remaining unwritten—the agreement is termed partially integrated. *See* E.
Farnsworth, Contracts 452 (1982). If a writing is only partially integrated, evidence of
prior or contemporaneous agreements is admissible to supplement its terms though not
to contradict it. If an agreement is completely integrated, however, not even evidence of
a "consistent additional term" may be introduced to elucidate the writing. *See id.*;
Restatement (Second) of Contracts §215.

Whether a writing is fully integrated is generally a question of law to be resolved by a
court. *See Calder v. Camp Grove State Bank*, 892 F.2d 629, 631–32 (7th Cir. 1990); E.
Farnsworth, Contracts 460. A judge and not a jury should ordinarily answer this threshold
question because it often requires going beyond the four corners of the written document

and scrutinizing the very extrinsic evidence whose admissibility is at issue. *See* E. Farnsworth, Contracts 456 n.25 ("[I]f there seems to be some circularity in examining the very evidence whose admissibility is at stake in order to determine its admissibility, it may help to keep in mind that this examination is made as a matter of law in order to determine whether the evidence shall go to the trier of fact."). But the district court entrusted the issue of integration to the jury because the CBA did not on its face clearly indicate whether it was intended to incorporate all the terms of the contract. The jury accordingly heard testimony regarding the oral agreement and concluded that the CBA was not intended to be a complete integration of all the parties' understandings. Because the district court concurred in the jury's verdict that the CBA was not integrated, the parol evidence rule did not apply. Hence the secret side agreement could be introduced to vary or contradict the terms of the written CBA.

We agree that the parties did not intend the written terms of the CBA to embody their entire agreement, for neither the Union nor Jewel denies the existence of an additional oral term to the contract—they only dispute its content. Union officials claim that all they promised was to "sit and discuss" Jewel's competitive position once Cub Foods entered the Chicago market. Jewel executives maintain, on the other hand, that they agreed to "an economic reopener with full reservation of rights conditioned on the entry of Cub Foods into the Chicago market." Because both sides concede that there was an additional oral term to their contract, it necessarily follows that the written terms of the CBA did not represent a full integration. And once the CBA was found not integrated as a matter of law, it was proper for the jury to resolve the additional factual question of the precise terms of the oral promise. The jury ultimately believed Jewel's version of the story, concluding that the parties had orally agreed to reopen the economic terms of the contract in the event Cub Foods penetrated the Chicago market. The oral reopener, therefore, became an enforceable part of the CBA.[1]

Mechanical application of the parol evidence rule would thus permit Jewel to introduce testimony regarding the oral side agreement. Yet our analysis of the parol evidence issue cannot proceed in a vacuum, abstracted from the particular setting in which it arose. Because this secret oral reopener undercuts obligations specified in a collective bargaining agreement, it inevitably implicates national labor policy. The critical question before us, then, is whether national labor policy allows enforcement of a clandestine oral side agreement that alters fundamental terms of the written and ratified collective bargaining agreement.

As the Supreme Court has recognized, a collective bargaining agreement is more than just a contract—it erects a system of industrial self-government. *See United Steelworkers*, 363 U.S. at 570. Indeed, certain terms of the collective bargaining agreement are deemed so important that their negotiation is mandated by law. *See Ford Motor Co. v. National Labor Relations Bd.*, 441 U.S. 488 (1979). Yet the laws regulating labor relations would have little substance if the central provisions of the collective compact could be nullified by means of secret side agreements. Union officials and management would then be free quietly to barter away basic guarantees contained in the collective bargaining agreement and relied upon by all union members. In a slightly different context, Judge Easterbrook

---

1. The jury could in theory have reached another conclusion: it could have determined that the CBA represented a partial integration, at least as to basic economic terms such as wage rates and the duration of the contract. The jury could have found that the written CBA embodied the entire agreement of the parties as to these fundamental terms. Had the jury so concluded, parol testimony could not have been admitted to contradict the CBA although it might still have been introduced to supplement the CBA with respect to collateral matters.

forcefully emphasized the hazards of oral side agreements that alter the terms of a written contract: "[D]efenses based on ... oral side agreements ... are as a class the defenses most likely to breed litigation even when asserted in good faith, and they create manifold opportunities for manipulation by crafty operators." *Central States Southeast and Southwest Areas Pension Fund v. Gerber Truck Service, Inc.*, 870 F.2d 1148, 1154 (7th Cir. 1989) (en banc). To avert industrial strife, collective bargaining agreements must be more secure than garden variety contracts. Accordingly, we hold that national labor policy forbids introduction of prior or contemporaneous secret agreements to contradict fundamental terms of a ratified collective bargaining contract. This secret oral reopener is, therefore, inadmissible and unenforceable as a matter of federal law.

...

The district court's decision is therefore reversed and remanded for further proceedings consistent with this opinion.

FRANK H. EASTERBROOK, CIRCUIT JUDGE, DISSENTING

An employer, fearing a rival with a reputation for low wages (more to the point, low prices) demands a most-favored-nations clause, under which it would receive the benefit of any concessions the union makes to the rival. Unions prefer not to make such bargains. A strike looms: the employer will not sign a contract without a most-favored-nations clause, and the union will not sign a contract with one.

At the last minute they agree to replace the contested clause with a reopener. Although the contract is to run for three years, if the dreaded competitor enters the market sooner either side may renew negotiations with the usual privileges: after good faith bargaining to impasse, the employer may implement its final offer, the union may strike, or both. *Electrical Workers Local 47 v. NLRB*, 927 F.2d 635 (D.C. Cir. 1991). A reopener can work in either side's favor depending on economic conditions. It does not modify or contradict any other term of the contract; it is part of the terms, giving each side an option.

The rival entered; the employer exercised the right to reopen; union and employer bargained to impasse, and the employer implemented its final offer. When the dust settled the union retained the fundamental terms of the contract (including wages) and won back pay for its members. But it did not seek back pay for employees who left the firm before that settlement. These employees tried to tax the union with breach of its duty of fair representation but lost. *Merk v. Jewel Companies, Inc.*, 848 F.2d 761 (7th Cir. 1988). So also the ex-employees lost their contract suit against the employer. A jury determined that the deal was as I have described it, that the plaintiffs received their contractual due.

The reason this case went to a jury at all is that the reopener was oral, while the bulk of the pact was written. But as the union conceded that there had been an oral side agreement, disputing only the employer's description of its content, the parol evidence rule did not prevent the jury from determining whose version is correct. My colleagues agree with the trial judge that the doctrines applied to commercial cases enforce that oral agreement. Had this been a long-term contract for coal with an oral agreement to renegotiate the price if a low-cost strip mine should open, or a contract to build a skyscraper with an oral agreement to renegotiate the number of stories if the real estate market should collapse, the agreement could be enforced.

But not when the commodity is labor, the majority says. If my colleagues thought there was some problem with the feeble enforcement of the parol evidence rule in modern litigation, I would share their concern. The parol evidence rule and the statute of frauds reduce the costs of fabrication, litigation, and error—at the expense of making the bargaining process less flexible and withholding enforcement of some bargains. Most courts today think the costs of strict insistence on written instruments excessive. Whether they are right in believing this is an interesting question. What the majority does, however, is not signal a revival of the writing requirement; it maintains, instead, that labor law is different. What, then, is the source of the difference?

My colleagues point to "national labor policy," which they say mandates that "collective bargaining agreements must be more secure than garden variety contracts." Labor policy may be found in labor statutes. It turns out that the National Labor Relations Act does not forbid oral agreements. Quite the contrary, the Act requires only one sort of agreement to be in writing. Pension plans must be written down, and the writings will be strictly enforced on command of both labor, 29 U.S.C. § 186(c)(5)(B), and pension, 29 U.S.C. § 1145, laws. *See Central States Pension Fund v. Gerber Truck Service, Inc.*, 870 F.2d 1148 (7th Cir. 1989) (in banc). When Congress singles out one kind of agreement for a strict writing requirement (as it did to protect the interests of the pension plans, which are not present at the bargaining table), it makes sense to infer that labor and management may decide for themselves how formal the rest of their dealings shall be. If labor policy really emphasized stability (and protection of workers from their own leaders' "backroom deals,") the NLRA would require the commitment of all agreements to writing, would require leaders to submit them to vote by members, and would require the written pact to be circulated far enough in advance of the vote that it could be digested and intelligently debated. Labor law requires none of these things, as my colleagues concede, *id.* at 895. By any reckoning, ordinary commercial contracts — to which §§ 2-201, 2-202, and 2-209 of the *Uniform Commercial Code* apply — are more secure against disputes about oral colloquies than are labor agreements governed by § 8(d) of the NLRA, 29 U.S.C. § 158(d). Labor law emphasizes flexibility, not certainty.

Flexibility is a commodity negotiators value, and not only because it is impossible to write down all of the understandings and practices (even all of the "important" understandings and practices) that make up the terms and conditions of employment. Collective bargaining agreements are relational contracts. They do not settle all important terms; rather they establish a framework within which the parties compose their differences.

It is perverse to say that the contracting process in labor must be more formal than the contracting process in shipping or construction or natural resources. You can define how much coal to sell and where to deliver it; you can set the duration of a charter party. Labor agreements govern the ongoing relations among thousands of persons and affect matters not so easy to specify. Rigidity backfires. Competitive conditions and technology change. Labor relations must change too, even over so short a period as three years. Failure to adjust to new developments means failure in product markets (look at the automobile and railroad industries), and when the employer slips in product markets labor takes the fall. If a low-price rival enters and siphons business, a firm bound to pay high wages will lay off many workers. Layoffs hurt the employees with the shortest tenure — that is, the persons who are plaintiffs in this case. Greater flexibility promotes responses in the marketplace that may benefit both sides.

Ongoing accommodation is a hallmark of labor relations. Representatives of labor and management meet continually to discuss both individual grievances and more general questions. Changes may ensue, with or without written agreements. "[T]he parties to a CBA [collective bargaining agreement] may tacitly acquiesce to an amendment of the agreement through their course of dealing." *Matuszak v. Torrington Co.*, 927 F.2d 320, 324 (7th Cir. 1991). Because labor and management recognize that even this process cannot be comprehensive, they deputize arbitrators to resolve still more issues. Arbitrators sometimes are limited to grievances, but more commonly their powers extend to all interpretive debates. Courts regularly say that arbitrators are not bound by the parol evidence rule, that because collective bargaining agreements are incomplete, and so much of labor relations consists in oral understandings, arbitrators may use these oral exchanges to supplement or even contradict the written terms. *E.g., SEPTA v. Railroad Signalmen*, 882 F.2d 778, 784 (3d Cir. 1989); *Loveless v. Eastern Air Lines*, 681 F.2d 1272, 1279–80 (11th Cir. 1982). If my colleagues are right, these decisions must be wrong.

The Supreme Court has said repeatedly that labor relations require more flexibility than the common law allows — not, as my colleagues hold, more formality. *E.g., Transportation — Communication Employees v. Union Pacific R.R.*, 385 U.S. 157, 160–61 (1966) ("A collective bargaining agreement is not ... governed by the same old common-law concepts which control such private contracts.... In order to interpret such an agreement it is necessary to consider the scope of other related collective bargaining agreements, as well as the practice, usage and custom pertaining to all such agreements."); *United Steelworkers v. Warrior & Gulf Navigation Co.*, 363 U.S. 574, 578–81 (1960); *McKinney v. Missouri-Kansas-Texas R.R.*, 357 U.S. 265, 273–74 (1958). *See also Consolidated Rail Corp. v. Railway Labor Executives' Association*, 491 U.S. 299, 308–09 (1989) (describing "flexibility" as a hallmark of labor relations under both the NLRA and the Railway Labor Act and adjuring courts not to disfavor informal arrangements).

Flexibility entails giving labor and management the option of having a fully integrated agreement, of banning oral side agreements, as well as the option of coming to partially-written, partially-oral understandings. My colleagues concede that this agreement, which lacked an integration clause, did not ban oral understandings. Our question is whether labor law forbids such side agreements even when the parties decide against an integrated writing. A handful of cases say that it does; the majority relies on *Gatliff Coal Co. v. Cox*, 152 F.2d 52 (6th Cir. 1945), and a smattering of unreviewed decisions by district courts, all more than a generation old. *Gatliff* rests in part on the premise that the NLRA "contemplates that a collective bargaining agreement be in writing," 152 F.2d at 56, which it obtained by misreading *H.J. Heinz Co. v. NLRB*, 311 U.S. 514, 523–26 (1941). *Heinz* holds that it is an unfair labor practice for the employer, having reached an agreement with the union, to refuse to sign a document embodying its agreement. That labor is entitled to a written memorial of a bargain hardly shows that labor is *forbidden* to reach oral understandings with management. *Gatliff* dealt with a common problem: a member of a multi-employer bargaining unit refused to sign the pact the association reached with the union, pleading that local officials said that it would not have to. Today a belated effort to withdraw from a multi-employer unit would be dealt with as an unfair labor practice, *see Charles D. Bonanno Linen Service, Inc. v. NLRB*, 454 U.S. 404 (1982), and not as a problem of parol evidence. After the Labor Board resolved the multi-employer unit problem in 1958, *Retail Associates, Inc.*, 120 N.L.R.B. 388 (1958), *Gatliff* vanished without a trace.[1] More

---

1. My colleagues think it significant that I have not found a case disapproving *Gatliff* by name. Guilty as charged. Plea in mitigation: As other courts take no notice of *Gatliff*, there are no citations to collect. The Supreme Court has never cited *Gatliff*. No court of appeals has cited it since 1964, when Lewis v. Owens, 338 F.2d 740, 742 (6th Cir. 1964), pointedly declined to rely on it. *Gatliff* has been cited by courts of appeals a total of three times: Clothing Workers v. NLRB, 324 F.2d 228, 231 (2d Cir. 1963); Lewis v. Lowry, 322 F.2d 453, 456 (4th Cir. 1963) (in banc), and *Owens*. *Lowry*, like *Owens*, cites *Gatliff* without endorsing its conclusion that labor policy bars oral agreements that would be permitted by the parol evidence rule. *Clothing Workers* includes *Gatliff* in a string citation for the proposition established in *Heinz*: that the employer must sign a formal document if the union demands one. *Gatliff*'s conclusion that an employer may not withdraw from a unit after agreement has been reached is unimpeachable, given *Bonanno* and *Retail Associates*. The reason *Gatliff* gave has been abandoned, and the one that replaced it in *Bonanno* and *Retail Associates* does not assist the plaintiffs. A natural person missing for seven years is presumed dead. Justice Holmes remarked that "the reports

recent cases in the Supreme Court (*e.g., Conrail* and *Union Pacific*), in the sixth circuit (*e.g., Sargent*), in our own circuit (*e.g., Matuszak*), and in other circuits take a different approach to contractual formalities. For example, the fifth circuit believes that the parol evidence rule does not apply at all in labor law. *Manville Forest Products, Inc. v. Paperworkers Union*, 831 F.2d 72, 75–76 (5th Cir. 1987). Going to the extreme opposite from my colleagues, *Manville* said that "national labor policy" forbids labor and management to have a fully integrated contract no matter how strongly they prefer the benefits of certainty.[2] *See also Westinghouse Elevators of Puerto Rico, Inc. v. S.I.U. de Puerto Rico*, 583 F.2d 1184 (1st Cir. 1978); *cf. Bokunewicz v. Purolator Products, Inc.*, 907 F.2d 1396, 1401–02 (3d Cir. 1990). I am no more enamored of an approach that dishonors attempts to put everything in writing than I am of an approach that dishonors oral agreements when the parties did not want their writings to be complete. There is a happy middle ground: parties may choose for themselves.

...

Neither the parol evidence rule nor the union's ratification requirement vitiates an oral reopener agreement. My colleagues fuse two unsatisfactory theories: "Taken individually ... none of plaintiffs' arguments may be dispositive. Read together, however, they clearly illuminate the grave dangers posed by a backroom deal that is secretly negotiated between union officials and company management without the knowledge or consent of the union rank and file." Here the majority announces that the 1983 reopener was *bad* for the employees—despite its disclaimer of authority to inquire into this question. This is special pleading. Reopeners are OK when they help the employees but not when they help the employer. Such a disposition bears no resemblance to a rule of law. It is a thumb on the scales of justice.

---

2. The Interpretation of Terms in an Integrated Writing

The rationale for the objective theory of interpretation is that actual subjective intent is difficult to determine and it is unjust to give significance to "secret" intentions. The objective theory, through the "reasonable person" standard, directs courts' attention to outward evidence of intent and purports to protect those who would rely on such outward

---

of a given jurisdiction in the course of a generation take up pretty much the whole body of the law, and restate it from the present point of view." The Path of the Law, 10 Harv. L. Rev. 457, 458 (1897), reprinted in Collected Legal Papers 167, 169 (1920). *Gatliff* has been missing for seven years plus a generation, which speaks more eloquently than express disapproval.

2. The majority insists, 945 F.2d at 899 n.4, that cases such as *Manville* "hold only that parol evidence may be considered to resolve ambiguities or fill in gaps in a written collective bargaining agreement." This is the argument from triviality. More to come in the text below. Two observations here: First, none of the other courts of appeals believes that this matters. Second, I am baffled by the refrain that a reopener is specially grave because it "conflicts" with "fundamental" provisions of the agreement. With what provision does it conflict? If the reopener had been written down we would not say that the contract had an internal contradiction. A reopener is an option to bargain in midterm, and options do not "conflict" with the provisions that control in the event they are not exercised. At all events, what I find significant about these cases is not that their subjects are grave or trivial, but that these courts hold that oral agreements trump written ones. The writing in *Manville* contained a zipper clause—language specifying that the pact was fully integrated and waiving all right to bargain during the term of the agreement. The court of appeals held that such a clause may be ignored. That is why these cases represent the polar opposite to the majority's position. They say that the parties cannot achieve an integrated collective bargaining agreement.

manifestations. As the materials in Chapter Three indicate, this approach now dominates contract law. Within the objective approach, however, there is currently a deep tension between formal and contextual methods of interpretation. Formal interpretation assumes that words have determinate meanings independent of particular contexts. This approach, often associated with the "plain meaning rule," has periodically gained favor among lawyers in England and the United States, and it continues to be attractive to many judges and lawyers in the U.S. But formal interpretation was vigorously criticized by the legal realists in the 1930s and 1940s, and current law strongly favors contextual interpretation, which presumes that words have meaning only within a context of social interaction and thus that words must be interpreted within the context in which they were used. To understand contract interpretation issues and arguments, one must be familiar with both the formal and the contextual approach and be aware of the strengths and weaknesses of each.

An additional concern influencing courts as they interpret some documents is the phenomenon known as "adhesion contracts." These are typically printed forms presented to an individual by a representative of the other party in circumstances in which actual negotiation is not possible or expected. This is the "take it or leave it" document so familiar in mass marketing. Typically, the representative presenting the document does not have authority to change any of its terms, so the individual has no reason to try to negotiate. In many cases no one, not even the store manager, has such authority. Faced with this reality, individuals typically do not even read the document before signing it, because there is no reason to do so other than the remote possibility that it is so shockingly unfair that the individual will forego the contract. Most individuals assume that there is some government or industry regulation that will prohibit the most egregious terms (and this is largely correct) and that business people generally are concerned enough about their reputation to refrain from including such terms.

So how should these documents be interpreted, assuming, as we must, that they are not usually read before they are signed and they function to define the relationship between the author and a large, unspecified, "public"?

These are the issues examined in this subpart.

---

a. Formal Maxims of Interpretation

Some courts have placed great weight on maxims of interpretation, using them as if they were decoding devices, capable of revealing determinate meanings in express terms. Contemporary courts rarely ascribe such significance to the maxims of interpretation, but they do use them for guidance or support.

Edwin Patterson, The Interpretation and Construction of Contracts

64 Colum. L. Rev. 833 (1964)

In this brief treatment we can only quote a list of standard maxims, which may not be complete. The ones most often phrased in Latin are given first:

1. *Noscitur a sociis.* The meaning of a word in a series is affected by others in the same series; or, a word may be affected by its immediate context. The example for the next maxim may be taken to illustrate this one.

2. *Ejusdem generis.* A general term joined with a specific one will be deemed to include only things that are like (of the same genus as) the specific one. This one if applied usually leads to a restrictive interpretation. *E.g., S* contracts to sell *B* his farm together with the

"cattle, hogs, and other animals." This would probably not include S's favorite house-dog, but might include a few sheep that S was raising for the market.

3. *Expressio unius exclusio alterius.* If one or more specific items are listed, without any more general or inclusive terms, other items although similar in kind are excluded. *E.g.,* S contracts to sell B his farm together with "the cattle and hogs on the farm." This language would be interpreted to exclude the sheep and S's favorite house-dog.

4. *Ut magis valeat quam pereat.* By this maxim an interpretation that makes the contract valid is preferred to one that makes it invalid.

5. *Omnia praesumuntur contra proferentem.* This maxim states that if a written contract contains a word or phrase which is capable of two reasonable meanings, one of which favors one party and the other of which favors the other, that interpretation will be preferred which is less favorable to the one by whom the contract was drafted. This maxim favors the party of lesser bargaining power, who has little or no opportunity to choose the terms of the contract, and perforce accepts one drawn by the stronger party. Such [are] "contracts of adhesion".... However, the maxim is commonly invoked in cases that do not reveal any disparity of bargaining power between the parties.

6. *Interpret contract as a whole.* A writing or writings that form part of the same transaction should be interpreted together as a whole, that is, every term should be interpreted as a part of the whole and not as if isolated from it. This maxim expresses the contextual theory of meaning, which is, perhaps, a truism.

7. "*Purpose of the parties.*" "The principal apparent purpose of the parties is given great weight in determining the meaning to be given to manifestations of intention or to any part thereof." This maxim must be used with caution. In fact, the two parties to a (bargain) contract necessarily have different purposes, and if these are apparent, then the court can construe a principal or common purpose from the two as a guide to the interpretation of language or the filling of gaps. Thus a contract to sell, buy, and export scrap copper was construed to make the buyer's obtaining of an export license a condition of the seller's promise to deliver. However, if the purposes of the parties are obscure the court may well fall back upon "plain meaning."

8. *Specific provision is exception to a general one.* If two provisions of a contract are inconsistent with each other and if one is "general" enough to include the specific situation to which the other is confined, the specific provision will be deemed to qualify the more general one, that is, to state an exception to it. A lease of a truck-trailer provided that the lessee should be absolutely liable for loss or damage to the vehicle, yet another clause stated that no party's liability should be increased by this contract. It was held that the former was more specific and therefore controlled the general provision, hence the lessee was liable. A careful draftsman would have stated the former as an exception to the latter, and the court in effect does it for him.

9. *Handwritten or typed provisions control printed provisions.* Where a written contract contains both printed provisions and handwritten or typed provisions, and the two are inconsistent, the handwritten or typed provisions are preferred. This maxim is based on the inference that the language inserted by handwriting or by typewriter for this particular contract is a more recent and more reliable expression of their intentions than is the language of a printed form. While this maxim is used in interpreting insurance contracts and other contracts of adhesion, it is also applicable to all contracts drawn up on a printed form.

10. *Public interest preferred.* If a public interest is affected by a contract, that interpretation or construction is preferred which favors the public interest. The proper scope of application of this rule seems doubtful. It may have some appropriate uses in construing contracts

between private parties. However, as applied to government contracts it would, if applied, be used to save the taxpayers' money as against those contracting with the government. But this is not, it is believed, a standard of interpretation or construction uniformly applied to government contracts.

This battery of maxims is never fired all together. The judge or other interpreter-construer of a contract may, by making prudent choices, possibly obtain some useful guides for his reasoning and justifications for his conclusion.

---

b. Contextual Meaning

The following excerpt describes the interpretive approach of the *Restatement (Second) of Contracts*. Judge Robert Braucher was the first Reporter and a principal drafter of the *Restatement (Second)*.

Robert Braucher, Interpretation and Legal Effect in the Second Restatement of Contracts

81 Colum. L. Rev. 13 (1981)

Perhaps the most significant change from the original *Restatement* is an increased emphasis on the context in which a contract is made and on the meanings attached by the parties to their words and conduct. In the original *Restatement* it was recognized that "evidence of surroundings is always admissible,"[7] but that statement was buried in comment; the black letter and other comments suggested that meanings were supplied by "the law" in accordance with some six conceivable "standards of interpretation," that "a contract may have a meaning different from that which either party supposed it to have," that general or limited usage was controlling except where it produced "an uncertain or ambiguous result," and that "the ordinary sense of words both singly and in collocation is adhered to" in the absence of absurdity or inconsistency. One is reminded of the "plain meaning rule," now largely discarded in the realm of statutory interpretation.

The revision abandons the apparatus of "standards of interpretation," which had not proved useful in judicial decisions or in law teaching. The reporter's note calls attention to a dictum of Mr. Justice Holmes with respect to the meaning of constitutional and statutory language, emphasizing the importance of context. Following Professor Corbin's recommendation, the stated rules do not depend on a preliminary determination of "ambiguity." Rules on usage of trade, course of dealing, and course of performance are rephrased in the terminology of the *Uniform Commercial Code*. The net effect is to de-emphasize meaning supplied by rules of construction existing in the law and to direct attention to the context in which the parties make their agreement.

John Cheever, Artemis, the Honest Well Digger

(1974)

His father had chosen his name, thinking it referred to artesian wells. It wasn't until Artemis was a grown man that he discovered he had been named for the chaste goddess of the hunt. He didn't seem to mind and, anyhow, everybody called him Art.

---

7. Restatement of Contracts § 235 Comment f (1932).

. . .

It was sixteen days after his return from Moscow that he got his first letter from Natasha. His address on the envelope was in English, but there was a lot of Cyrillic writing and the stamps were brilliantly colored. The letter disconcerted his mother and had, she told him, alarmed the postman. To go to Russia was one thing, but to receive letters from that strange and distant country was something else. "My darling," Natasha had written. "I dreamed last night that you and I were a wave on the Black Sea at Yalta. I know you haven't seen that part of my country, but if one were a wave, moving toward shore, one would be able to see the Crimean Mountains covered with snow. In Yalta sometimes when there are roses in bloom, you can see snow falling on the mountains. When I woke from the dream, I felt elevated and relaxed and I definitely had the taste of salt in my mouth. I must sign this letter Fifi, since nothing so irrational could have been written by your loving Natasha."

He answered her letter that night. "Dearest Natasha, I love you. If you will come to this country, I will marry you. I think of you all the time and I would like to show you how we live — the roads and trees and the lights of the cities. It is very different from the way you live. I am serious about all this, and if you need money for the plane trip, I will send it. If you decided that you didn't want to marry me, you could go home again. Tonight is Halloween. I don't suppose you have that in Russia. It is the night when the dead are supposed to rise, although they don't, of course, but children wander around the streets disguised as ghosts and skeletons and devils and you give them candy and pennies. Please come to my country and marry me."

. . .

He got her reply in ten days. "I like to think that our letters cross and I like to think of them flapping their wings at each other somewhere over the Atlantic. I would love to come to your country and marry you or have you marry me here, but we cannot do this until there is peace in the world. I wish we didn't have to depend upon peace for love. I went to the country on Saturday and the birds and the birches and the pines were soothing. I wish you had been with me. A Unitarian doctor of divinity came to the office yesterday looking for an interpreter. He seemed intelligent and I took him around Moscow myself. He told me I didn't have to believe in God to be a Unitarian. God, he told me, is the progress from chaos to order to human responsibility. I always thought God sat on the clouds, surrounded by troops of angels, but perhaps he lives in a submarine, surrounded by divisions of mermaids. Please send me a snapshot and write again. Your letters make me very happy."

"I am enclosing a snapshot," he wrote. "It's three years old. It was taken at the Wakusha Reservoir. This is the center of the Northeast watershed. I think of you all the time. I woke at three this morning thinking of you. It was a nice feeling. I like the dark. The dark seems to me like a house with many rooms. Sixty or seventy. At night now after work I go skating. I suppose everybody in Russia must know how to skate. I know that Russians play hockey, because they usually beat the Americans in the Olympics. Three to two, seven to two, eight to one. It is beginning to snow. Love, Artemis . . ."

. . .

As he returned from work one night, his mother told him that someone had called from the county seat and said that the call was urgent. Artemis guessed that it must be the Internal Revenue Service. He had had difficulty trying to describe to them the profit and loss in looking for water. He was a conscientious citizen and he called the number. A stranger identified himself as Mr. Cooper and he didn't sound like the Internal Revenue

Service. Cooper wanted to see Artemis at once. "Well, you see," Artemis said, "it's my bowling night. Our team is tied for first place and I'd hate to miss the games if we could meet some other time." Cooper was agreeable and Artemis told him where he was working and how to get there. Cooper said he would be there at ten in the morning and Artemis went bowling.

In the morning it began to snow. It looked like a heavy storm. Cooper showed up at ten. He did not get out of his car, but he was so very pleasant that Artemis guessed he was a salesman. Insurance.

"I understand that you've been in Russia."

"Well, I was only there for forty-eight hours. They canceled my visa. I don't know why."

"But you've been corresponding with Russia."

"Yes, there's this girl. I went out with her once. We write to each other."

"The State Department is very much interested in your experience. Undersecretary Hurlow would like to talk to you."

"But I didn't really have any experience. I saw some churches and had three chicken dinners and then they sent me home."

"Well, the Undersecretary is interested. He called yesterday and again this morning. Would you mind going to Washington?"

. . .

Except for a very small desk, there was nothing businesslike about the office. There were colored rugs, sofas, pictures, and flowers. Mr. Hurlow was a very tall man who seemed tired or perhaps unwell. "It was good of you to come, Mr. Bucklin. I'll go straight to the point. I have to go to the Hill at eleven. You know Natasha Funaroff."

"I took her out once. We had dinner and sat in a park."

"You correspond with her."

"Yes."

"Of course, we've monitored your letters. Their government does the same. Our intelligence feels that your letters contain some sort of information. She, as the daughter of a marshal, is close to the government. The rest of her family were shot. She wrote that God might sit in a submarine, surrounded by divisions of mermaids. That same day was the date of our last submarine crisis. I understand that she is an intelligent woman and I can't believe that she would write anything so foolish without it having a second meaning. Earlier she wrote that you and she were a wave on the Black Sea. The date corresponds precisely to the Black Sea maneuvers. You sent her a photograph of yourself beside the Wakusha Reservoir, pointing out that this was the center of the Northeast watershed. This, of course, is not classified information, but it all helps. Later you write that the dark seems to you like a house divided into seventy rooms. This was written ten days before we activated the Seventieth Division. Would you care to explain any of this?"

"There's nothing to explain. I love her."

"That's absurd. You said yourself that you only saw her once. How can you fall in love with a woman you've only seen once? I can't at the moment threaten you, Mr. Bucklin. I can bring you before a committee, but unless you're willing to be more cooperative, this would be a waste of our time. We feel quite sure that you and your friend have worked out a cipher. I can't forbid you to write, of course, but we can stop your letters. What I would like is your patriotic cooperation. Mr. Cooper, whom I believe you met, will call on you once a week or so and give you the information or rather the misinformation that we would like you to send to Russia, couched, of course, in your cipher, your descriptions of the dark as a house."

"I couldn't do that, Mr. Hurlow. It would be dishonest to you and to Natasha."

. . .

He never heard again from the State Department. Had they made a mistake? Were they fools or idle? He would never know. He wrote Natasha four very circumspect letters, omitting his hockey and bowling scores. There was no reply.

. . .

———————

This short story first appeared in Playboy Magazine in 1973 and was published in a collection of short stories by John Cheever that won the Pulitzer Prize in 1979. What does this short story tell you about the relationship between context and meaning? Artemis and his girlfriend came from different counties, different cultures and spoke different languages. Artemis and the state department officials with whom he dealt come from the same country and speak the same language. With whom did Artemis have the most trouble communicating?

———————

Note

For examples of the contextual emphasis described by Judge Braucher, please read sections 202, 203, 206, and 207 of the *Restatement (Second) of Contracts*. The *United Nations Convention on Contracts for the International Sale of Goods* also adopts a contextual approach to contract interpretation. *See, e.g.,* Article 8. What concerns may lead a court to adopt either a formal or a contextual approach to interpretation? Proponents of formalism argue that clear rules of interpretation allow people to predict the extent of their legal liability and thus enhance their ability to act freely. Proponents of contextualism also claim to enhance freedom, arguing that courts ought not to impose their own meanings on parties' language (meanings which may be quite strange to the parties themselves) and ought instead to give effect to the particular meanings and understandings of the parties' community or trade.

———————

c. The Ambiguity Rule and the "Ambiguity" of Language

As we have seen, the traditional parol evidence rule begins with the question whether the parties intended to express their final and/or compete agreement in a writing. This question must be answered by the court prior to deciding what may or may not be admitted into the evidentiary record. In other words, in a jury case, the court will hold a hearing without the jury being present.*

At that hearing, the court must review the document, hear testimony, examine any other evidence of the parties intent, and make a decision. If the court determines that the parties did intend to express their final and complete agreement in the writing, then

———————

* Although the division of responsibility between court and jury (between the judge and the trier of fact) suggested in this paragraph is consistent with most interpretations of the parol evidence rule in contemporary U.S. Contract law, there are variations among different jurisdictions. These variations, however, have little bearing on the central dispute between Justice Traynor and Judge Kozinski in the following cases.

the court should characterize the writing as "fully integrated," and should exclude all prior or contemporary evidence ("extrinsic evidence") regarding the agreement.

There is, however, an exception to this general exclusion, which is that some extrinsic evidence can be admitted if it is relevant to the meaning of an "ambiguous" term in the integrated writing. If one of the parties offers evidence under this exception, then the court must make another preliminary ruling, which is whether the writing term identified by the proponent of the extrinsic evidence is "ambiguous." Here is where serious disagreements arise. Some courts maintain that the rationale of the parol evidence rule requires the court to look only at the written term, aided by no more than a dictionary, to determine if the word or phrase in the writing has two meanings, neither of which is clear in the writing. Others assert that this "four corners" approach is not required by the logic of the parol evidence rule and that, to the contrary, the purpose of the parol evidence rule is to carry out the parties intention, not to thwart it through imposition of an un-realistically formal understanding of human language. The only way to accurately discern the parties intention, this view would argue, is to understand the wider context in which its words selected. In response, advocates of the "four corners" view assert that their opponents' approach would open the door to groundless fantasy, allowing anyone to invent whatever meaning to a word that served his or her interests

This is the dispute that you will see in the next two cases, in which two very smart and highly respected judges take conflicting positions on the question of how a court should decide whether extrinsic evidence should be admitted to help explain the meaning of an ambiguous term in an integrated writing. As you read each case, pay close attention to how each judge explains and justifies the approach he takes and to how each judge responds to criticism of his approach.

Pacific Gas and Electric Company v. G. W. Thomas Drayage & Rigging Company

Supreme Court of California
442 P.2d 641 (Cal. 1968)

Roger J. Traynor, Chief Justice

Defendant appeals from a judgment for plaintiff in an action for damages for injury to property under an indemnity clause of a contract.

In 1960 defendant entered into a contract with plaintiff to furnish the labor and equipment necessary to remove and replace the upper metal cover of plaintiff's steam turbine. Defendant agreed to perform the work "at (its) own risk and expense" and to "indemnify" plaintiff "against all loss, damage, expense and liability resulting from ... injury to property, arising out of or in any way connected with the performance of this contract." Defendant also agreed to procure not less than $50,000 insurance to cover liability for injury to property. Plaintiff was to be an additional named insured, but the policy was to contain a cross-liability clause extending the coverage to plaintiff's property.

During the work the cover fell and injured the exposed rotor of the turbine. Plaintiff brought this action to recover $25,144.51, the amount it subsequently spent on repairs. During the trial it dismissed a count based on negligence and thereafter secured judgment on the theory that the indemnity provision covered injury to all property regardless of ownership.

Defendant offered to prove by admissions of plaintiff's agents, by defendant's conduct under similar contracts entered into with plaintiff, and by other proof that in the indemnity clause the parties meant to cover injury to property of third parties only and not to plaintiff's property. Although the trial court observed that the language used was "the classic language for a third party indemnity provision" and that "one could very easily conclude that ... its whole intendment is to indemnify third parties," it nevertheless held that the "plain language" of the agreement also required defendant to indemnify plaintiff for injuries to plaintiff's property. Having determined that the contract had a plain meaning, the court refused to admit any extrinsic evidence that would contradict its interpretation.

When a court interprets a contract on this basis, it determines the meaning of the instrument in accordance with the " ... extrinsic evidence of the judge's own linguistic education and experience." (3 Corbin on Contracts (1960 ed.) (1964 Supp. § 579, p. 225, fn. 56.) The exclusion of testimony that might contradict the linguistic background of the judge reflects a judicial belief in the possibility of perfect verbal expression. (9 Wigmore on Evidence (3d ed. 1940) § 2461, p. 187.) This belief is a remnant of a primitive faith in the inherent potency[2] and inherent meaning of words.

The test of admissibility of extrinsic evidence to explain the meaning of a written instrument is not whether it appears to the court to be plain and unambiguous on its face, but whether the offered evidence is relevant to prove a meaning to which the language of the instrument is reasonably susceptible. (*Continental Baking Co. v. Katz*, 439 P.2d 889 (Cal. 1968))

A rule that would limit the determination of the meaning of a written instrument to its four-corners merely because it seems to the court to be clear and unambiguous, would either deny the relevance of the intention of the parties or presuppose a degree of verbal precision and stability our language has not attained.

Some courts have expressed the opinion that contractual obligations are created by the mere use of certain words, whether or not there was any intention to incur such obligations. Under this view, contractual obligations flow, not from the intention of the parties but from the fact that they used certain magic words. Evidence of the parties' intention therefore becomes irrelevant.

In this state, however, the intention of the parties as expressed in the contract is the source of contractual rights and duties. A court must ascertain and give effect to this intention by determining what the parties meant by the words they used. Accordingly, the exclusion of relevant, extrinsic evidence to explain the meaning of a written instrument could be justified only if it were feasible to determine the meaning the parties gave to the words from the instrument alone.

If words had absolute and constant referents, it might be possible to discover contractual intention in the words themselves and in the manner in which they were arranged. Words, however, do not have absolute and constant referents. "A word is a symbol of thought but has no arbitrary and fixed meaning like a symbol of algebra or chemistry, ..." (*Pearson v. State Social Welfare Board* 353 P.2d 33, 39 (Cal. 1960)) The meaning of particular words or groups of words varies with the " ... verbal context and surrounding circumstances

---

2. E.g., "The elaborate system of taboo and verbal prohibitions in primitive groups; the ancient Egyptian myth of Khern, the apotheosis of the word, and of Thoth, the Scribe of Truth, the Giver of Words and Script, the Master of Incantations; the avoidance of the name of God in Brahmanism, Judaism and Islam; totemistic and protective names in medieval Turkish and Finno-Ugrian languages; the misplaced verbal scruples of the "Pré cieuses"; the Swedish peasant custom of curing sick cattle smitten by witchcraft, by making them swallow a page torn out of the psalter and put in dough...." Ullman, The Principles of Semantics 43 (1963 ed.). (See also Ogden and Richards, The Meaning of Meaning (rev. ed. 1956) pp. 24–47.)

and purposes in view of the linguistic education and experience of their users and their hearers or readers (not excluding judges).... A word has no meaning apart from these factors; much less does it have an objective meaning, one true meaning." (Corbin, *The Interpretation of Words and the Parol Evidence Rule* (1965) 50 Cornell L. Rev. 161, 187.) Accordingly, the meaning of a writing

> ... can only be found by interpretation in the light of all the circumstances that reveal the sense in which the writer used the words. The exclusion of parol evidence regarding such circumstances merely because the words do not appear ambiguous to the reader can easily lead to the attribution to a written instrument of a meaning that was never intended. (Citations omitted.)

(*Universal Sales Corp. v. Cal. Press Mfg. Co.*, *supra*, 128 P.2d 665, 679 (Cal.) (concurring opinion).

Although extrinsic evidence is not admissible to add to, detract from, or vary the terms of a written contract, these terms must first be determined before it can be decided whether or not extrinsic evidence is being offered for a prohibited purpose. The fact that the terms of an instrument appear clear to a judge does not preclude the possibility that the parties chose the language of the instrument to express different terms. That possibility is not limited to contracts whose terms have acquired a particular meaning by trade usage, but exists whenever the parties' understanding of the words used may have differed from the judge's understanding.

Accordingly, rational interpretation requires at least a preliminary consideration of all credible evidence offered to prove the intention of the parties. (Civ. Code § 1647; Code Civ. Proc. § 1860; *see also* 9 Wigmore on Evidence, § 2470, fn. 11, p. 227.) Such evidence includes testimony as to the "circumstances surrounding the making of the agreement ... including the object, nature and subject matter of the writing ..." so that the court can "place itself in the same situation in which the parties found themselves at the time of contracting." (*Universal Sales Corp. v. Cal. Press Mfg. Co.*, 128 P.2d 665, 671 (Cal.). If the court decides, after considering this evidence, that the language of a contract, in the light of all the circumstances, is "fairly susceptible of either one of the two interpretations contended for...." (*Balfour v. Fresno C. & I. Co.* 44 P. 876, 877 (Cal. 1895)), extrinsic evidence relevant to prove either of such meanings is admissible.

In the present case the court erroneously refused to consider extrinsic evidence offered to show that the indemnity clause in the contract was not intended to cover injuries to plaintiff's property. Although that evidence was not necessary to show that the indemnity clause was reasonably susceptible of the meaning contended for by defendant, it was nevertheless relevant and admissible on that issue. Moreover, since that clause was reasonably susceptible of that meaning, the offered evidence was also admissible to prove that the clause had that meaning and did not cover injuries to plaintiff's property. Accordingly, the judgment must be reversed.

...

———————

Note

G.W. Thomas's attorney argued that the indemnity term is standard or "boilerplate" and therefore has a particular meaning for lawyers familiar with contracts made in the drayage and rigging trades. The trial court rejected this argument. If the meaning of legal language is at issue, isn't it appropriate to consider the "linguistic background" of those who have been trained in the law, the background shared by lawyers who draft contracts and judges who interpret them? Do lawyers prefer formal interpretive rules? If the decision in *Pacific Gas and Electric Company* produces a result which is consistent with the common understanding of what an indemnification provision means, why does Judge Kozinski take exception in the next case to Judge Traynor's opinion?

Trident Center v. Connecticut General Life Insurance Company

United States Court of Appeals for the Ninth Circuit
847 F.2d 564 (1988)

ALEX KOZINSKI, CIRCUIT JUDGE

The parties to this transaction are, by any standard, highly sophisticated business people: Plaintiff is a partnership consisting of an insurance company and two of Los Angeles' largest and most prestigious law firms; defendant is another insurance company. Dealing at arm's length and from positions of roughly equal bargaining strength, they negotiated a commercial loan amounting to more than $56 million. The contract documents are lengthy and detailed; they squarely address the precise issue that is the subject of this dispute; to all who read English, they appear to resolve the issue fully and conclusively.

Plaintiff nevertheless argues here, as it did below, that it is entitled to introduce extrinsic evidence that the contract means something other than what it says. This case therefore presents the question whether parties in California can ever draft a contract that is proof to evidence. Somewhat surprisingly, the answer is no.

Facts

The facts are rather simple. Sometime in 1983 Security First Life Insurance Company and the law firms of Mitchell, Silberberg & Knupp and Manatt, Phelps, Rothenberg & Tunney formed a limited partnership for the purpose of constructing an office building complex on Olympic Boulevard in West Los Angeles. The partnership, Trident Center, the plaintiff herein, sought and obtained financing for the project from defendant, Connecticut General Life Insurance Company. The loan documents provide for a loan of $56,500,000 at 12 percent interest for a term of 15 years, secured by a deed of trust on the project. The promissory note provides that "[m]aker shall not have the right to prepay the principal amount hereof in whole or in part" for the first 12 years. In years 13–15, the loan may be prepaid, subject to a sliding prepayment fee. The note also provides that in case of a default during years 1–12, Connecticut General has the option of accelerating the note and adding a 10 percent prepayment fee.

Everything was copacetic for a few years until interest rates began to drop. The 12 percent rate that had seemed reasonable in 1983 compared unfavorably with 1987 market rates and Trident started looking for ways of refinancing the loan to take advantage of the lower rates. Connecticut General was unwilling to oblige, insisting that the loan could not be prepaid for the first 12 years of its life, that is, until January 1996.

Trident then brought suit in state court seeking a declaration that it was entitled to prepay the loan now, subject only to a 10 percent prepayment fee. Connecticut General promptly removed to federal court and brought a motion to dismiss, claiming that the loan documents clearly and unambiguously precluded prepayment during the first 12 years. The district court agreed and dismissed Trident's complaint. The court also "sua sponte, sanction[ed] the plaintiff for the filing of a frivolous lawsuit." Trident appeals both aspects of the district court's ruling.

Discussion

I.

Trident makes two arguments as to why the district court's ruling is wrong. First, it contends that the language of the contract is ambiguous and proffers a construction that it believes supports its position. Second, Trident argues that, under California law, even seemingly unambiguous contracts are subject to modification by parol or extrinsic evidence. Trident faults the district court for denying it the opportunity to present evidence that the contract language did not accurately reflect the parties' intentions.

A. The Contract

As noted earlier, the promissory note provides that Trident "shall not have the right to prepay the principal amount hereof in whole or in part before January 1996." It is difficult to imagine language that more clearly or unambiguously expresses the idea that Trident may not unilaterally prepay the loan during its first 12 years. Trident, however, argues that there is an ambiguity because another clause of the note provides that "[i]n the event of a prepayment resulting from a default hereunder or the Deed of Trust prior to January 10, 1996 the prepayment fee will be ten percent (10%)." Trident interprets this clause as giving it the option of prepaying the loan if only it is willing to incur the prepayment fee.

We reject Trident's argument out of hand. In the first place, its proffered interpretation would result in a contradiction between two clauses of the contract; the default clause would swallow up the clause prohibiting Trident from prepaying during the first 12 years of the contract. The normal rule of construction, of course, is that courts must interpret contracts, if possible, so as to avoid internal conflict. *See Brobeck, Phleger & Harrison v. Telex Corp.*, 602 F.2d 866, 872 (9th Cir.), *cert. denied*, 444 U.S. 981, 100 S. Ct. 483, 62 L. Ed. 2d 407 (1979) (California law).

In any event, the clause on which Trident relies is not on its face reasonably susceptible to Trident's proffered interpretation. Whether to accelerate repayment of the loan in the event of default is entirely Connecticut General's decision. The contract makes this clear at several points. *See* Note at 4 ("in each such event [of default], the entire principal indebtedness, or so much thereof as may remain unpaid at the time, shall, *at the option of Holder*, become due and payable immediately" (emphasis added)); *id.* at 7 ("[i]n the event Holder exercises its *option to accelerate* the maturity hereof ..." (emphasis added)); Deed of Trust ¶ 2.01, at 25 ("in each such event [of default], Beneficiary *may* declare all sums secured hereby immediately due and payable ..." (emphasis added)). Even if Connecticut General decides to declare a default and accelerate, it "may rescind any notice of breach or default." *Id.* ¶ 2.02, at 26. Finally, Connecticut General has the option of doing nothing at all: "Beneficiary reserves the right at its sole option to waive noncompliance by Trustor with any of the conditions or covenants to be performed by Trustor hereunder." *Id.* ¶ 3.02, at 29.

Once again, it is difficult to imagine language that could more clearly assign to Connecticut General the exclusive right to decide whether to declare a default, whether and when to accelerate, and whether, having chosen to take advantage of any of its remedies, to rescind the process before its completion.

Trident nevertheless argues that it is entitled to precipitate a default and insist on acceleration by tendering the balance due on the note plus the 10 percent prepayment fee. The contract language, cited above, leaves no room for this construction. It is true, of course, that Trident is free to stop making payments, which may then cause Connecticut

General to declare a default and accelerate. But that is not to say that Connecticut General would be required to so respond. The contract quite clearly gives Connecticut General other options: It may choose to waive the default, or to take advantage of some other remedy such as the right to collect "all the income, rents, royalties, revenue, issues, profits, and proceeds of the Property." Deed of Trust ¶ 1.18, at 22. By interpreting the contract as Trident suggests, we would ignore those provisions giving Connecticut General, not Trident, the exclusive right to decide how, when and whether the contract will be terminated upon default during the first 12 years.

In effect, Trident is attempting to obtain judicial sterilization of its intended default. But defaults are messy things; they are supposed to be. Once the maker of a note secured by a deed of trust defaults, its credit rating may deteriorate; attempts at favorable refinancing may be thwarted by the need to meet the trustee's sale schedule; its cash flow may be impaired if the beneficiary takes advantage of the assignment of rents remedy; default provisions in its loan agreements with other lenders may be triggered. Fear of these repercussions is strong medicine that keeps debtors from shirking their obligations when interest rates go down and they become disenchanted with their loans. That Trident is willing to suffer the cost and delay of a lawsuit, rather than simply defaulting, shows far better than anything we might say that these provisions are having their intended effect. We decline Trident's invitation to truncate the lender's remedies and deprive Connecticut General of its bargained-for protection.

B. Extrinsic Evidence

Trident argues in the alternative that, even if the language of the contract appears to be unambiguous, the deal the parties actually struck is in fact quite different. It wishes to offer extrinsic evidence that the parties had agreed Trident could prepay at any time within the first 12 years by tendering the full amount plus a 10 percent prepayment fee. As discussed above, this is an interpretation to which the contract, as written, is not reasonably susceptible. Under traditional contract principles, extrinsic evidence is inadmissible to interpret, vary or add to the terms of an unambiguous integrated written instrument. *See* 4 S. Williston [A Treatise on the Law of Contracts], § 631, at 948–49 [(3d ed. 1961)]; 2 B. Witkin, California Evidence § 981, at 926 (3d ed. 1986).

Trident points out, however, that California does not follow the traditional rule. Two decades ago the California Supreme Court in *Pacific Gas & Electric Co. v. G.W. Thomas Drayage & Rigging Co.*, 442 P.2d 641 (Cal. 1968), turned its back on the notion that a contract can ever have a plain meaning discernible by a court without resort to extrinsic evidence. The court reasoned that contractual obligations flow not from the words of the contract, but from the intention of the parties. "Accordingly," the court stated, "the exclusion of relevant, extrinsic, evidence to explain the meaning of a written instrument could be justified only if it were feasible to determine the meaning the parties gave to the words from the instrument alone." 442 P.2d 641 (Cal.). This, the California Supreme Court concluded, is impossible: "If words had absolute and constant referents, it might be possible to discover contractual intention in the words themselves and in the manner in which they were arranged. Words, however, do not have absolute and constant referents." *Id.* In the same vein, the court noted that "[t]he exclusion of testimony that might contradict the linguistic background of the judge reflects a judicial belief in the possibility of perfect verbal expression. This belief is a remnant of a primitive faith in the inherent potency and inherent meaning of words." 442 P.2d 641, 645 (citation and footnotes omitted).

Under *Pacific Gas,* it matters not how clearly a contract is written, nor how completely it is integrated, nor how carefully it is negotiated, nor how squarely it addresses the issue before the court: the contract cannot be rendered impervious to attack by evidence. If one side is willing to claim that the parties intended one thing but the agreement provides for another, the court must consider extrinsic evidence of possible ambiguity. If that evidence raises the specter of ambiguity where there was none before, the contract language is displaced and the intention of the parties must be divined from self-serving testimony offered by partisan witnesses whose recollection is hazy from passage of time and colored by their conflicting interests. *See Delta Dynamics, Inc. v. Arioto*, 446 P.2d 785, 789 (Cal. 1968)) (Mosk, J., dissenting). We question whether this approach is more likely to divulge the original intention of the parties than reliance on the seemingly clear words they agreed upon at the time. *See generally Morta v. Korea Ins. Co.*, 840 F.2d 1452, 1460 (9th Cir. 1988).

Pacific Gas casts a long shadow of uncertainty over all transactions negotiated and executed under the law of California. As this case illustrates, even when the transaction is very sizeable, even if it involves only sophisticated parties, even if it was negotiated with the aid of counsel, even if it results in contract language that is devoid of ambiguity, costly and protracted litigation cannot be avoided if one party has a strong enough motive for challenging the contract. While this rule creates much business for lawyers and an occasional windfall to some clients, it leads only to frustration and delay for most litigants and clogs already overburdened courts.

It also chips away at the foundation of our legal system. By giving credence to the idea that words are inadequate to express concepts, *Pacific Gas* undermines the basic principle that language provides a meaningful constraint on public and private conduct. If we are unwilling to say that parties, dealing face to face, can come up with language that binds them, how can we send anyone to jail for violating statutes consisting of mere words lacking "absolute and constant referents"? How can courts ever enforce decrees, not written in language understandable to all, but encoded in a dialect reflecting only the "linguistic background of the judge"? Can lower courts ever be faulted for failing to carry out the mandate of higher courts when "perfect verbal expression" is impossible? Are all attempts to develop the law in a reasoned and principled fashion doomed to failure as "remnant[s] of a primitive faith in the inherent potency and inherent meaning of words"?

Be that as it may. While we have our doubts about the wisdom of *Pacific Gas*, we have no difficulty understanding its meaning, even without extrinsic evidence to guide us. As we read the rule in California, we must reverse and remand to the district court in order to give plaintiff an opportunity to present extrinsic evidence as to the intention of the parties in drafting the contract. It may not be a wise rule we are applying, but it is a rule that binds us. *Erie R.R. Co. v. Tompkins*, 304 U.S. 64, 78 (1938).

II.

In imposing sanctions on plaintiff, the district court stated:

> Pursuant to Fed. R. Civ. P. 11, the Court, *sua sponte*, sanctions the plaintiff for the filing of a frivolous lawsuit. The Court concludes that the language in the note and deed of trust is plain and clear. No reasonable person, much less firms of able attorneys, could possibly misunderstand this crystal-clear language. Therefore, this action was brought in bad faith.

Having reversed the district court on its substantive ruling, we must, of course, also reverse it as to the award of sanctions. While we share the district judge's impatience with this litigation, we would suggest that his irritation may have been misdirected. It is difficult to blame plaintiff and its lawyers for bringing this lawsuit. With this much money at stake, they would have been foolish not to pursue all remedies available to them under the applicable law. At fault, it seems to us, are not the parties and their lawyers but the legal system that encourages this kind of lawsuit. By holding that language has no objective meaning, and that contracts mean only what courts ultimately say they do, *Pacific Gas* invites precisely this type of lawsuit. With the benefit of 20 years of hindsight, the California Supreme Court may wish to revisit the issue. If it does so, we commend to it the facts of this case as a paradigmatic example of why the traditional rule, based on centuries of experience, reflects the far wiser approach.

Conclusion

The judgment of the district court is reversed. The case is remanded for reinstatement of the complaint and further proceedings in accordance with this opinion. The parties shall bear their own costs on appeal.

Note

Are Justice Traynor's and Judge Kozinski's views of contract interpretation, as articulated in these two opinions, reconcilable? Might it be possible to have a "plain meaning rule" that would discourage contests of meaning where the parties are part of a single trade, business, or community but would allow such claims where the parties do not share contracting practices? This might be a "situated" plain meaning rule.

Frigaliment Importing Co. v. B.N.S. International Sales Corp.

United States District Court Southern District of New York
190 F. Supp. 116 (S.D.N.Y. 1960)

HENRY FRIENDLY, CIRCUIT JUDGE

The issue is, what is chicken? Plaintiff says "chicken" means a young chicken, suitable for broiling and frying. Defendant says "chicken" means any bird of that genus that meets contract specifications on weight and quality, including what it calls "stewing chicken" and plaintiff pejoratively terms "fowl." Dictionaries give both meanings, as well as some others not relevant here. To support its, plaintiff sends a number of volleys over the net; defendant essays to return them and adds a few serves of its own. Assuming that both parties were acting in good faith, the case nicely illustrates Holmes' remark "that the making of a contract depends not on the agreement of two minds in one intention, but on the agreement of two sets of external signs—not on the parties' having meant the same thing but on their having said the same thing." *The Path of the Law, in* Collected Legal Papers, p. 178. I have concluded that plaintiff has not sustained its burden of persuasion that the contract used "chicken" in the narrower sense.

The action is for breach of the warranty that goods sold shall correspond to the description, New York Personal Property Law, McKinley's Consol. Laws, c. 41, §95. Two contracts are in suit. In the first, dated May 2, 1957, defendant, a New York sales corporation, confirmed the sale to plaintiff, a Swiss corporation, of

US Fresh Frozen Chicken, Grade A, Government Inspected, Eviscerated

21/2–3 lbs. and 11/2–2 lbs. each

all chicken individually wrapped in cryovac, packed in secured fiber cartons or wooden boxes, suitable for export

75,000 lbs.... 21/2–3 lbs @ ... $33.00;

25,000 lbs.... 11/2–2 lbs @ ... $36.50

per 100 lbs. FAS New York

scheduled May 10, 1957 pursuant to instructions from Penson & Co., New York.

The second contract, also dated May 2, 1957, was identical save that only 50,000 lbs. of the heavier "chicken" were called for, the price of the smaller birds was $37 per 100 lbs., and shipment was scheduled for May 30. The initial shipment under the first contract was short but the balance was shipped on May 17. When the initial shipment arrived in Switzerland, plaintiff found, on May 28, that the 21/2–3 lbs. birds were not young chicken suitable for broiling and frying but stewing chicken or "fowl"; indeed, many of the cartons and bags plainly so indicated. Protests ensued. Nevertheless, shipment under the second contract was made on May 29, the 2½–3 lbs. birds again being stewing chicken. Defendant stopped the transportation of these at Rotterdam.

This action followed. Plaintiff says that, notwithstanding that its acceptance was in Switzerland, New York law controls under the principle of *Rubin v. Irving Trust Co.*, 113 N.E.2d 424, 431 (N.Y. 1953); defendant does not dispute this, and relies on New York decisions. I shall follow the apparent agreement of the parties as to the applicable law.

Since the word "chicken" standing alone is ambiguous, I turn first to see whether the contract itself offers any aid to its interpretation. Plaintiff says the 1½–2 lbs. birds necessarily had to be young chicken since the older birds do not come in that size, hence the 2½–3 lbs. birds must likewise be young. This is unpersuasive—a contract for "apples" of two different sizes could be filled with different kinds of apples even though only one species came in both sizes. Defendant notes that the contract called not simply for chicken but for "US Fresh Frozen Chicken, Grade A, Government Inspected." It says the contract thereby incorporated by reference the Department of Agriculture's regulations, which favor its interpretation; I shall return to this after reviewing plaintiff's other contentions.

The first hinges on an exchange of cablegrams which preceded execution of the formal contracts. The negotiations leading up to the contracts were conducted in New York between defendant's secretary, Ernest R. Bauer, and a Mr. Stovicek, who was in New York for the Czechoslovak government at the World Trade Fair. A few days after meeting Bauer at the fair, Stovicek telephoned and inquired whether defendant would be interested in exporting poultry to Switzerland. Bauer then met with Stovicek, who showed him a cable from plaintiff dated April 26, 1957, announcing that they "are buyer" of 25,000 lbs. of chicken 2½–3 lbs. weight, Cryovac packed, grade A Government inspected, at a price up to 33 cents per pound, for shipment on May 10, to be confirmed by the following morning, and were interested in further offerings. After testing the market for price, Bauer accepted, and Stovicek sent a confirmation that evening. Plaintiff stresses that, although these and subsequent cables between plaintiff and defendant, which laid the basis for the additional quantities under the first and for all of the second contract, were predominantly in German, they used the English word "chicken"; it claims this was done because it understood "chicken" meant young chicken whereas the German word, "Huhn," included both "Brathuhn" (broilers) and "Suppenhuhn" (stewing chicken), and that defendant, whose officers were thoroughly conversant with German, should have realized this.[2] Whatever force this argument might otherwise have is largely drained away by Bauer's testimony that he asked Stovicek what kind of chickens were wanted, received the answer "any kind

---

2. These cables were in German; "chicken," "broilers" and, on some occasions, "fowl," were in English.

of chickens," and then, in German, asked whether the cable meant "Huhn" and received an affirmative response. Plaintiff attacks this as contrary to what Bauer testified on his deposition in March, 1959, and also on the ground that Stovicek had no authority to interpret the meaning of the cable. The first contention would be persuasive if sustained by the record, since Bauer was free at the trial from the threat of contradiction by Stovicek as he was not at the time of the deposition; however, review of the deposition does not convince me of the claimed inconsistency. As to the second contention, it may well be that Stovicek lacked authority to commit plaintiff for prices or delivery dates other than those specified in the cable; but plaintiff cannot at the same time rely on its cable to Stovicek as its dictionary to the meaning of the contract and repudiate the interpretation given the dictionary by the man in whose hands it was put. *See* Restatement of the Law of Agency, 2d § 145; 2 Mecham, Agency§ 1781 (2d ed. 1914); *Park v. Moorman Mfg. Co.*, 1952, 121 Utah 339, 241 P.2d 914, 919, 40 A.L.R. 2d 273; *Henderson v. Jimmerson*, Tex. Civ. App. 1950, 234 S.W.2d 710, 717–718. Plaintiff's reliance on the fact that the contract forms contain the words "through the intermediary of _____" with the blank not filled, as negating agency, is wholly unpersuasive; the purpose of this clause was to permit filling in the name of an intermediary to whom a commission would be payable, not to blot out what had been the fact.

Plaintiff's next contention is that there was a definite trade usage that "chicken" meant "young chicken." Defendant showed that it was only beginning in the poultry trade in 1957, thereby bringing itself within the principle that "when one of the parties is not a member of the trade or other circle, his acceptance of the standard must be made to appear" by proving either that he had actual knowledge of the usage or that the usage is "so generally known in the community that his actual individual knowledge of it may be inferred." 9 Wigmore, Evidence (3d ed. 1940) 2464. Here there was no proof of actual knowledge of the alleged usage; indeed, it is quite plain that defendant's belief was to the contrary. In order to meet the alternative requirement, the law of New York demands a showing that "the usage is of so long continuance, so well established, so notorious, so universal and so reasonable in itself, as that the presumption is violent that the parties contracted with reference to it, and made it a part of their agreement." *Walls v. Bailey*, 49 N.Y. 464, 472–73 (1872).

Plaintiff endeavored to establish such a usage by the testimony of three witnesses and certain other evidence. Strasser, resident buyer in New York for a large chain of Swiss co-operatives, testified that "on chicken I would definitely understand a broiler." However, the force of this testimony was considerably weakened by the fact that in his own transactions the witness, a careful businessman, protected himself by using "broiler" when that was what he wanted and "fowl" when he wished older birds. Indeed, there are some indications, dating back to a remark of Lord Mansfield, *Edie v. East India Co.*, 2 Burr. 1216, 1222 (1761), that no credit should be given "witnesses to usage, who could not adduce instances in verification." 7 Wigmore, Evidence(3d ed. 1940) § 1954; *see McDonald v. Acker, Merrall & Condit Co.*, 182 N.Y.S. 607 (N.Y. App. 1920). While Wigmore thinks this goes too far, a witness' consistent failure to rely on the alleged usage deprives his opinion testimony of much of its effect. Niesielowski, an officer of one of the companies that had furnished the stewing chicken to defendant, testified that "chicken" meant "the male species of the poultry industry. That could be a broiler, a fryer or a roaster," but not a stewing chicken; however, he also testified that upon receiving defendant's inquiry for "chickens," he asked whether the desire was for "fowl or frying chickens" and, in fact, supplied fowl, although taking the precaution of asking defendant, a day or two after plaintiff's acceptance of the contracts in suit, to change its confirmation of its order from "chickens," as defendant had originally prepared it, to "stewing chickens." Dates, an employee of Urner-Barry Company, which publishes a daily market report on the poultry trade, gave it as his view that the trade meaning of "chicken" was "broilers and fryers." In addition to this opinion testimony, plaintiff relied on the fact that the Urner-Barry service, the Journal of Commerce, and Weinberg Bros. & Co. of Chicago, a large supplier of poultry, published quotations in a manner which, in one way or another, distinguish between "chicken," comprising broilers, fryers and certain other categories, and "fowl," which, Bauer acknowledged, included stewing chickens. This material would be impressive if there were nothing to the contrary. However, there was, as will now be seen.

Defendant's witness Weininger, who operates a chicken eviscerating plant in New Jersey, testified "Chicken is everything except a goose, a duck, and a turkey. Everything is a chicken, but then you have to say, you have to specify which category you want or that you are talking about." Its witness Fox said that in the trade "chicken" would encompass all the various classifications. Sadina, who conducts a food inspection service, testified that he would consider any bird coming within the classes of "chicken" in the Department of Agriculture's regulations to be a chicken. The specifications approved by the General Services Administration include fowl as well as broilers and fryers under the classification "chickens." Statistics of the Institute of American Poultry Industries use the phrases "Young chickens" and "Mature chickens," under the general heading "Total chickens." and the Department of Agriculture's daily and weekly price reports avoid use of the word "chicken" without specification.

Defendant advances several other points which it claims affirmatively support its construction. Primary among these is the regulation of the Department of Agriculture, 7 C.F.R. § 70.300–70.370, entitled, "Grading and Inspection of Poultry and Edible Products Thereof." and in particular 70.301 which recited:

Chickens. The following are the various classes of chickens:

> (a) Broiler or fryer ...
> (b) Roaster ...
> (c) Capon ...
> (d) Stag ...
> (e) Hen or stewing chicken or fowl ...
> (f) Cock or old rooster ...

Defendant argues, as previously noted, that the contract incorporated these regulations by reference. Plaintiff answers that the contract provision related simply to grade and Government inspection and did not incorporate the Government definition of "chicken," and also that the definition in the Regulations is ignored in the trade. However, the latter contention was contradicted by Weininger and Sadina; and there is force in defendant's argument that the contract made the regulations a dictionary, particularly since the reference to Government grading was already in plaintiff's initial cable to Stovicek.

Defendant makes a further argument based on the impossibility of its obtaining broilers and fryers at the 33 cents price offered by plaintiff for the 2½–3 lbs. birds. There is no substantial dispute that, in late April, 1957, the price for 2½–3 lbs. broilers was between 35 and 37 cents per pound, and that when defendant entered into the contracts, it was well aware of this and intended to fill them by supplying fowl in these weights. It claims that plaintiff must likewise have known the market since plaintiff had reserved shipping space on April 23, three days before plaintiff's cable to Stovicek, or, at least, that Stovicek was chargeable with such knowledge. It is scarcely an answer to say, as plaintiff does in its brief, that the 33 cents price offered by the 2½–3 lbs. "chickens" was closer to the prevailing 35 cents price for broilers than to the 30 cents at which defendant procured fowl. Plaintiff must have expected defendant to make some profit—certainly it could not have expected defendant deliberately to incur a loss.

Finally, defendant relies on conduct by the plaintiff after the first shipment had been received. On May 28 plaintiff sent two cables complaining that the larger birds in the first shipment constituted "fowl." Defendant answered with a cable refusing to recognize plaintiff's objection and announcing "We have today ready for shipment 50,000 lbs. chicken 2½–3 lbs. 25,000 lbs. broilers 1½–2 lbs.," these being the goods procured for shipment under the second contract, and asked immediate answer "whether we are to ship this merchandise to you and whether you will accept the merchandise." After several other cable exchanges, plaintiff replied on May 29:

Confirm again that merchandise is to be shipped since resold by us if not enough pursuant to contract chickens are shipped the missing quantity is to be shipped within ten days stop we resold to our customers pursuant to your contract chickens grade A you have to deliver us said merchandise we again state that we shall make you fully responsible for all resulting costs.

Defendant argues that if plaintiff was sincere in thinking it was entitled to young chickens, plaintiff would not have allowed the shipment under the second contract to go forward, since the distinction between broilers and chickens drawn in defendant's cablegram must have made it clear that the larger birds would not be broilers. However, plaintiff answers that the cables show plaintiff was insisting on delivery of young chickens and that defendant shipped old ones at its peril. Defendant's point would be highly relevant on another disputed issue—whether if liability were established, the measure of damages should be the difference in market value of broilers and stewing chicken in New York or the larger difference in Europe, but I cannot give it weight on the issue of interpretation. Defendant points out also that plaintiff proceeded to deliver some of the larger birds in Europe, describing them as "poulets"; defendant argues that it was only when plaintiff's customers complained about this that plaintiff developed the idea that "chicken" meant "young chicken." There is little force in this in view of plaintiff's immediate and consistent protests.

When all the evidence is reviewed, it is clear that defendant believed it could comply with the contracts by delivering stewing chicken in the 2½–3 lbs. size. Defendant's subjective intent would not be significant if this did not coincide with an objective meaning of "chicken." Here it did coincide with one of the dictionary meanings, with the definition in the Department of Agriculture Regulations to which the contract made at least oblique reference, with at least some usage in the trade, with the realities of the market, and with what plaintiff's spokesman had said. Plaintiff asserts it to be equally plain that plaintiff's own subjective intent was to obtain broilers and fryers; the only evidence against this is the material as to market prices and this may not have been sufficiently brought home. In any event it is un-necessary to determine that issue. For plaintiff has the burden of showing that "chicken" was used in the narrower rather than in the broader sense, and this it has not sustained.

This opinion constitutes the Court's findings of fact and conclusions of law. Judgment shall be entered dismissing the complaint with costs.

———————

Note

– On Frigaliment as a Misunderstanding Case

Judge Friendly later expressed doubt about his analysis in *Frigaliment Importing*. In a dissenting opinion in *Dadorian Export Co. v. United States*, 291 F.2d 178, 187 n.4 (2d Cir.

1961), Judge Friendly suggested that *Raffles v. Wichelhaus* might have provided a better line of analysis — that *Frigaliment Importing* involved a mutual misunderstanding and therefore the court should have found that no contract existed. However, Friendly suggested, Frigaliment still should have borne the losses caused by the misunderstanding "because of defendant's not unjustifiable change of position." *Id.* Why should Frigaliment have borne responsibility for B.N.S.'s "change of position" if there was a mutual misunderstanding? In *Raffles* itself, the buyer refused to take delivery and the court held that it was not in breach of contract. In *Frigaliment*, the buyer did receive the goods, but protested that they were not in conformity to the contract. If, as under *Raffles*, no contract was formed, then Frigaliment would be liable in restitution, wouldn't it, for the value of the benefit it received? The value of the benefit presumably was the market price of the stewers.

– On the United Nations Sales Convention

Frigaliment Importing Company is a Swiss corporation and B.N.S. International Sales Corporation is a U.S. firm. As both Switzerland and the United States have ratified the *United Nations Convention on Contracts for the International Sale of Goods*, today this dispute would be governed by the *Convention* unless the parties had agreed to another jurisdiction when the contract was made. *See* Articles 1, 6. How might this dispute be resolved under the *Convention*?

The applicable provisions are Articles 7 and 8, and perhaps Article 9. Under Article 8(1), "statements made by and other conduct of a party are to be interpreted according to his intent where the other party knew or could not have been unaware what that intent was." The first communication between Frigaliment and B.N.S. was the cable of April 27, 1957 from Frigaliment Importing. Frigaliment maintained that its intent in that cable was to order broilers and that is why it used the English word "chicken" (which it understood to mean a "young" version of the animal, as opposed to a "hen" or a "rooster.") Under Article 8(1), this meaning would prevail if "the other party knew or could not have been unaware of what that intent was." If the case were heard today, the attorneys would focus testimony on this issue.

Piecing together the evidence recited by Judge Friendly, B.N.S. knew that there was a significant market distinction between young animals, called broilers and fryers, and older hens, called stewers. B.N.S. also knew that Frigaliment offered 33 cents a pound. It is difficult to evaluate the evidence on market prices that Judge Friendly gives, because they are not identified as growers' or packers' prices or as wholesale or retail prices. B.N.S. also knew that Frigaliment chose to use the word "chicken" as the only English word in its German-language cable. Frigaliment argued that the use of the English word should have given B.N.S., whose officers spoke German, an indication of its intended meaning, but the court apparently rejected this assertion. (Upon what basis was this assertion rejected? Should Frigaliment's attorney have presented German experts?) At the very least, B.N.S. knew, as Frigaliment apparently did not know, that the English term "chicken" is ambiguous and that the ambiguity would have significant economic consequence in this transaction. Given its knowledge of the ambiguity, how could B.N.S. have *not* concluded that Frigaliment would want the more valuable birds rather than the less valuable ones? Looking at the correspondence in this way, B.N.S.'s behavior appears oriented toward determining whether it could "get away with" shipping stewers, rather than toward ascertaining exactly what Frigaliment wanted. Article 7(1) provides: "In the interpretation of this *Convention*, regard is to be had ... to the need to promote ... the observance of good faith in international trade." As Professor John Honnold, Chief of the United Nations International Trade Law Branch and Secretary to the United Nations Commission on International Trade Law (UNCITRAL) during the period of drafting of the *Convention*, observed, "[a] theme that underlies numerous articles of the *Convention* is the duty to communicate information needed by the other party — a recognition that the consummation of a sales transaction involves interrelated steps that depend on cooperation." John Honnold, Uniform Law for International Sales 131 (1982); *see also id.* at 138–41 (discussing Article 8's application to a *Raffles v. Wichelhaus* situation).

If, on the other hand, a reasonable person in B.N.S.'s position and life experience would not have known that the word "chicken" was significantly ambiguous and could have been unaware that Frigaliment wanted the more valuable bird, then Article 8(2) would apply. Under Article 8(2), a communication is to be interpreted "according to the understanding that a reasonable person of the same kind as the other party would have had in the same circumstances." And under 8(3), "[i]n determining ... the understanding a reasonable person would have had, due consideration is to be given to all relevant circumstances of the case including the negotiations, any practices which the parties have established between themselves, usages and any subsequent conduct of the parties." Under this provision, the question becomes how would a reasonable person "of the same kind" as B.N.S. have interpreted the cable? What is B.N.S.'s "kind"? What characteristics matter? Is it significant that Bauer and other officers live in the United States, in New York, that they speak German and English, and that they are new to the poultry trade? What other characteristics are relevant?

Should Frigaliment have inquired into B.N.S.'s experience in the trade? Judge Friendly acknowledges that people in the poultry trade do generally understand the word "chicken" to mean young, male fryers or broilers or at least that they feel it necessary to specify "stewers" or "fowl" or "hens" for birds of the type that B.N.S. delivered. Trade usages are discussed further in Article 9. Under 9(1), "The parties are bound by any usage to which they have agreed and by any practices which they have established between themselves," and under 9(2), "The parties are considered, unless otherwise agreed, to have impliedly made applicable to their contract or its formation a usage of which the parties knew or ought to have known and which in international trade is widely known to, and regularly observed by, parties to contracts of the type involved in the particular trade concerned." If this case were litigated under the *Convention*, the attorneys would direct their discovery and evidence to the criteria of Article 9(2), that is, to whether this is "a usage ... which in international trade is widely known to, and regularly observed by, parties to contracts of the type involved in the particular trade concerned."

What if a reasonable person of the kind of B.N.S.'s officers would think that the word "chicken" was inherently ambiguous, that it could mean either broilers or stewers, and that there is a big economic difference between the two? Would a reasonable person in B.N.S.'s position, of B.N.S.'s type, believe in good faith that Frigaliment would want the less valuable alternative or that it would be indifferent to the choice between them? Under both the *United Nations Sales Convention* and domestic contract law, this dispute involves what obligation, if any, a person in B.N.S.'s situation has to make further inquiries. If Frigaliment misunderstood the English word "chicken," thinking that it has a clear meaning when it does not, what obligation does B.N.S. have to clarify the meaning between it and Frigaliment? Did B.N.S. take advantage of Frigaliment's misunderstanding? Bauer did ask Stovicek what kind of chickens Frigaliment wanted, and Stovicek answered "any kind of chickens." Speaking in German, Bauer then asked if the cable meant "Huhn" and Stovicek answered affirmatively. Would a reasonable person in Bauer's position think that Stovicek was acting as a representative of Frigaliment? Judge Friendly concluded that Stovicek was acting as Frigaliment's agent, at least for negotiating purposes. Would Stovicek's answers lead a reasonable person of Bauer's kind to think that the confusion had been resolved in favor of a definition that included stewers? Here again, more evidence is needed on German usage, particularly as this was shared among Bauer, Stovicek, and the Frigaliment officers.

---

3. The Reasonable Expectation Doctrine and "Blanket Assent" — Interpretation of Standard Form Contracts

Courts have struggled with contracts involving standard form writings, particularly in transactions involving mass marketing, individual consumers, or both. Classical contract law emphasized the importance of written terms, yet in modern practice, printed form documents often are not read, important terms are buried in fine print or legalese, or the people forming the contract do not have authority to negotiate any changes to the printed terms. In such cases, courts are reluctant to say that the printed terms reflect the actual or even the objective agreement between the parties. In these cases, the "duty to read" doctrine seems inept and a signature on a printed form document might not fairly indicate agreement to all of the terms contained therein. The materials in this subsection focus on the doctrine of reasonable expectations, which courts have developed to interpret insurance policies and other complex consumer transactions, and on Karl Llewellyn's important contribution to the interpretation of standard form contracts, the idea of "blanket assent."

Regional Bank of Colorado, N.A. v. St. Paul Fire and Marine Insurance Company

United States Court of Appeals for the Tenth Circuit
35 F.3d 494 (1994)

Earl E. O'Connor, Senior District Judge

Appellant St. Paul Fire and Marine Insurance Company ("St. Paul") appeals from a grant of summary judgment in favor of appellee Regional Bank of Rifle ("Regional Bank"). We exercise jurisdiction pursuant to 28 U.S.C. § 1291 and affirm.

Regional Bank, the insured, filed an action for a declaratory judgment with respect to coverage and duty to defend on a claim for carbon monoxide poisoning under the comprehensive general liability ("CGL") insurance policy issued by St. Paul's. The policy contained a "pollution exclusion" clause. The case was submitted on cross motions for summary judgment with the following stipulated facts:

1. At all times relevant hereto plaintiff [Regional Bank] had in effect a policy of insurance issued by defendant [St. Paul's]....

2. On January 27, 1988, Debra Seibert rented an apartment for occupancy by herself and her minor son from plaintiff. At that time, Debra Seibert was pregnant with her daughter, Brandy Loague. At the time, plaintiff owned this apartment.

3. After sleeping in the above-referenced apartment on the night of January 29, 1988, Ms. Seibert and her son were taken to the Hospital suffering from inhalation of carbon monoxide allegedly emitted from a faulty wall heater in the apartment.

4   As a result of their carbon monoxide inhalation, Ms. Seibert and her son filed Civil Action No. 89-CV-291 against the plaintiff herein in the Garfield County District Court (the "Garfield Action"). This case remains pending.

5.   The parties hereto agree that the sole issue to be decided in this case is whether [the subject policy] provides, up to its applicable limits, coverage to the plaintiff for the damages and injuries allegedly suffered by Ms. Seibert, her son and daughter in the Garfield Action. More specifically, the issue before the Court is whether [the subject policy's] Pollution Exclusion excludes coverage for the injuries and damages allegedly caused by Ms. Seibert, her unborn daughter and her son's carbon monoxide inhalation. This Exclusion reads, in pertinent part, as follows:

Exclusions—What This Agreement Won't Cover

Pollution. We won't cover bodily injury, property damage or medical expenses that result from pollution at or from:

—your premises;

—a waste site; or

—your work site

. . .

Pollution means the actual, alleged or threatened discharge, dispersal, release or escape of pollutants.

Pollutants mean any solid, liquid, gaseous, or thermal irritant or contaminant, including:

—smoke, vapors, soot, fumes;

—acids, alkalis, chemicals; and

—waste

Your premises means any premises you own, rent, lease or occupy. It also includes premises you no longer own, rent, lease or occupy.

. . .

Under Colorado law, absent an ambiguity, "an insurance policy must be given effect according to the plain and ordinary meaning of its terms." *Terranova v. State Farm Mut. Auto. Ins. Co.*, 800 P.2d 58, 60 (Colo. 1990). "A court may not rewrite an unambiguous policy nor limit its effect by a strained construction. A policy term is ambiguous if it is reasonably susceptible to more than one meaning." *Terranova*, 800 P.2d at 60. Insurance contracts are not to be technically construed, but are to be "construed as they would be understood by a person of ordinary intelligence." *State Farm Mut. Auto. Ins. Co. v. Nissen*, 851 P.2d 165, 167 (Colo. 1993).

In *Davis v. M.L.G. Corp.*, 712 P.2d 985, 989 (Colo. 1986), the court referred to the "general rules of construction" of "true" insurance contracts as follows:

If there remains any doubt, the terms should be read in the sense which the insurer had reason to believe they would be interpreted by the ordinary reader and purchaser. The test to be applied is not what the insurer intended by his words, but what the ordinary reader and purchaser would have understood them to mean.

The scope of an agreement is not to be determined in a vacuum. *Id.* at 990. Rather, the court looks to the reasonable expectations of an ordinary policyholder to give effect to the ordinary and popular meaning of words. *Id.* "The interpretation which makes a contract fair and reasonable is selected over that which yields a harsh or unreasonable result." *Id.*

Moreover, "to benefit from an exclusionary provision in a particular contract of insurance the insurer must establish that the exemption claimed applies in the particular case, and that the exclusions are not subject to any other reasonable interpretation." *Broderick Investment Co.* [*v. Hartford Accident & Indem. Co.*, 954 F.2d 601 (10th Cir. 1992) at 606 (applying Colorado law); *Hecla Mining Co. v. New Hampshire Ins. Co.*, 811 P.2d 1083, 1090 (Colo. 1991) (interpreting an exclusion for sudden and unexpected pollution).

In construing the policy to provide coverage, the district court did not expressly find the policy ambiguous, but held that the policy did not exclude coverage for injuries sustained by tenants of the Bank who were exposed to carbon monoxide emitted from a faulty heater. The court looked to what coverage a reasonable person in the position of the policyholder would have expected and held that "a reasonable policyholder would expect a CGL policy to give him complete comprehensive coverage, including coverage for home accidents such as this." The court reasoned that the broad interpretation of the exclusion urged by St. Paul's was unreasonable because it would exclude coverage for inhalation of smoke (an irritant) caused by a fire on the premises, but not for burns resulting from that same fire.

. . .

We believe that the Colorado Supreme Court would apply the rule of reasonable expectations in construing the terms of the policy here, regardless of whether or not the policy was found to be ambiguous. *See Nissen*, 851 P.2d at 168; *but see, Ohio Casualty Ins. v. Imperial Contractors, Inc.*, 765 P.2d 1060, 1062 (Colo. App. 1988) (inferring, without citation to any authority, that the reasonable expectation doctrine does not apply absent an ambiguity).

In *Nissen*, the Colorado Supreme Court quoted Robert E. Keeton, *Basic Text on Insurance Law* § 6.3(a), at 351 (1971): "The objectively reasonable expectations of applicants and intended beneficiaries regarding the terms of insurance contracts will be honored even though painstaking study of the policy provisions would have negated those expectations." 851 P.2d at 168. In *Chacon* [*v. American Family Mutual Insurance Co.*, 788 P.2d 748 (Colo. 1990)], the court interpreted an unambiguous policy in light of what "a reasonable person would have understood the contract to mean." Similarly, the Colorado Court of Appeals cited *Collister v. Nationwide Life Ins. Co.*, 388 A.2d 1346, 1353 (Pa. 1978), with approval in *Sanchez* [*v. Connecticut Gen. Life Ins. Co.*, 681 P.2d 974 (Colo. Ct. App. 1984)]. The court in *Collister*, 388 A.2d at 1353, stated, "[R]egardless of the ambiguity, or lack thereof, inherent in a given set of insurance documents (whether they be applications, conditional receipts, riders, policies, or whatever), the public has a right to expect that they will receive something of comparable value in return for the premium paid."

St. Paul's argues that the plain and ordinary meaning of the terms used in the pollution exclusion clause excludes coverage for the event in question here, i.e., personal injuries caused by exposure to carbon monoxide emissions. There is little doubt that if the heater malfunction had caused a fire and injured the tenants, there would have been coverage. However, St. Paul's urges that because the malfunction caused carbon monoxide emissions, coverage is excluded by the "absolute" pollution exclusion clause of the policy. St. Paul's argues that carbon monoxide is a gaseous irritant and thus, bodily injury caused by exposure to it on the insured's "premises" was excluded from coverage.

The interpretation purported by St. Paul's stretches the plain meaning of the policy exclusion. When viewed in isolation, the terms "irritant" and "contaminant" are "virtually boundless, for 'there is no substance or chemical in existence that would not irritate or damage some person or property.'" *Pipefitters Welfare Educ. Fund v. Westchester Fire Ins. Co.*, 976 F.2d 1037, 1043 (7th Cir. 1992) (a reasonable policyholder would expect discharge of PCB-laden oil to be excluded by the pollution exclusion clause) (quoting *Westchester Fire Ins. Co. v. City of Pittsburgh*, 768 F. Supp. 1463 (D. Kan. 1991)). The *Pipefitters* court stated:

> Without some limiting principle, the pollution exclusion clause would extend far beyond its intended scope, and lead to some absurd results. To take but two simple examples, reading the clause broadly would bar coverage for bodily injuries suffered by one who slips and falls on the spilled contents of a bottle of Draino, and for bodily injury caused by an allergic reaction to chlorine in a public pool. Although Draino and chlorine are both irritants or contaminants that cause, under certain conditions, bodily injury or property damage, one would not ordinarily characterize these events as pollution.

976 F.2d at 1037. In a similar vein, the court in *Westchester Fire Ins. Co. v. City of Pittsburgh*, 768 F. Supp. 1463, 1470 (D. Kan. 1991), observed, "[t]he terms 'irritant' and 'contaminant'... cannot be read in isolation, but must be construed as substances generally recognized as polluting the environment." They must occur in a setting such that they would be recognized as a toxic or particularly harmful substance in industry or by governmental regulators. *Id.*

The pollution exclusion at issue here excludes coverage for bodily injury and medical expenses caused by pollution on the insured's premises. "Pollutant" is defined as "any solid, liquid, gaseous, or thermal irritant or contaminant, including: smoke, vapors, ... fumes; ..." The terms "irritant" and "contaminant" are not defined in the policy. *Webster's New International Dictionary* 1197 (3d ed. 1986) defines "irritant" as "tending to produce irritation or inflammation; something that irritates or excites; an agent by which irritation is produced." This somewhat circular definition begs the question. A reasonable policy holder would not understand the policy to exclude coverage for anything that irritates. "Irritant" is not to be read literally and in isolation, but must be construed in the context of how it is used in the policy, i.e., defining "pollutant."

While a reasonable person of ordinary intelligence might well understand carbon monoxide is a pollutant when it is emitted in an industrial or environmental setting, an ordinary policyholder would not reasonably characterize carbon monoxide emitted from a residential heater which malfunctioned as "pollution." It seems far more reasonable that a policyholder would understand the exclusion as being limited to irritants and contaminants commonly thought of as pollution and not as applying to every possible irritant or contaminant imaginable.

Affirmed

Note

In interpreting the insurance policy, the court asked what would be the "reasonable expectations of an ordinary policyholder." Why did the court choose this standard? The court reasoned that the reasonable expectations of an ordinary policyholder define the "plain and ordinary meaning" of the contract terms and that an interpretation based on such reasonable expectations is fair. " '[R]egardless of the ambiguity, or lack thereof, inherent in a given set of insurance documents..., the public has a right to expect that they will receive something of comparable value in return for the premium paid.' " This contextual analysis is explicitly concerned with the risk that the drafter of lengthy and complicated documents will include terms that diminish the value of the exchange to the other party, and it acknowledges this inequality of power between insurance companies and purchasers of insurance.

Recall the formal maxims set out at the beginning of this section. Many of them draw upon rules of grammar or formal logic and some upon notions of public policy, such as the maxims favoring an interpretation that makes the contract valid and an interpretation that favors the public interest. The maxim *omnia praesumunter contra proferentem*, resolving doubtful interpretations against the drafter, reflects concern for inequality of opportunity and information. *See* Edwin Patterson, *The Interpretation and Construction of Contracts*, 64 Colum. L. Rev. 833 (1964). This concern is manifest in the reasonable expectations doctrine as well.

Contextual interpretation is now firmly rooted in contemporary contract law, even though formal arguments continue to carry weight with some courts. Throughout both contextual and formal interpretation, courts interpret individuals' words and behavior through lenses colored by moral, political, and economic concerns. In these and many other doctrines, one can see the public character of "private" contracts.

Laurie Kindel Fett, The Reasonable Expectations Doctrine: An Alternative to Bending and Stretching Traditional Tools of Contract Interpretation

18 Wm. Mitchell L. Rev. 1113 (1992)

The majority of Americans own insurance policies. They pay premiums for insurance coverage that is difficult if not impossible to understand. In fact, most Americans find their policies so confusing that they do not even read them. As a result, insurance companies can present a policyholder with standard policies without ever giving the policyholder the opportunity to negotiate the terms. Negotiating policies individually would likely put insurance companies out of business because of the enormous cost or render insurance coverage so costly that only the rich could afford it. Presently, policyholders have to accept the standard forms because the only alternative is to forego insurance, which could be disastrous.

Courts interpret insurance policies with this inequality in mind,[2] recognizing that policyholders rarely have an opportunity to negotiate their policies and often are forced to accept provisions or exclusions which they do not want. Since insurance policies are standardized forms, usually the only differences from policy to policy are marketing, service, and premiums. By using traditional contract interpretation tools, the courts attempt to effectuate the intent of the parties while giving the policyholder an extra measure of protection. Often these tools create rights for the policyholder that extend beyond those discernable from the actual language of the policy.

Although courts frequently use traditional tools to interpret insurance contracts, these tools sometimes are inadequate to determine the parties' intent or resolve the inequality created by the policyholder's lack of bargaining power. Insurance policies may require additional safeguards in situations where the traditional tools do not apply. By recognizing that the policyholder may have expectations of coverage different from the explicit language

---

2. Robert H. Jerry, II, Understanding Insurance Law § 25C, at 104 (1987). Jerry correctly observes that no real contract negotiation occurs in the sale and marketing of insurance policies. Instead, policyholders are confronted with a take-it-or-leave-it choice. In most transactions, the policyholder does not even receive the policy until after the policyholder pays the first premium. *id.* § 25C, at 104–05.

of the policy, courts further protect policyholders from their lack of bargaining power. This additional safeguard is the reasonable expectations doctrine. The doctrine of reasonable expectations allows the court to impose liability on the insurer for misleading the policyholder or to mandate coverage when it seems fair to do so.

Note

In addition to insurance companies, numerous other businesses use standard forms for consumer transactions. Judges, lawyers and scholars have struggled to develop lines of analysis of standard form contracting that will yield satisfactory results. The fundamental problem is that contract law assumes the possibility of individual bargaining and negotiation, while the practice of standard form contracting is based on the economic efficiency of standardized transactions and the absence of individualized negotiation. If both parties have not agreed to the "terms" in a standard form, then how should courts treat them? Are they binding on the non-drafting party? If so, upon what basis and with what limits? If exchanges do occur, then surely the parties had some sort of agreement, but of what significance are "boilerplate terms"? Although numerous arguments have been made and various models of analysis suggested, Karl Llewellyn's "blanket assent" idea, explained in the excerpt below, has been the single most influential.

Karl Llewellyn's concerns about standard form contracts are even more salient today, where consumers routinely click "I agree" to contract terms without reading them. This has been a theme throughout the book, seen most vividly in the chapters on assent (offer and acceptance) and defenses (misrepresentation and the duty to read). What effect should these issues have on courts charged with interpreting the parties' intentions, when it is clear the parties did not actually read the terms they are "agreeing" to?

Karl Llewellyn's blanket assent analysis is incorporated into section 211 of the *Restatement (Second) of Contracts*:

§ 211. Standardized Agreements

(1) Except as stated in Subsection (3), where a party to an agreement signs or otherwise manifests assent to a writing and has reason to believe that like writings are regularly used to embody terms of agreements of the same type, he adopts the writing as an integrated agreement with respect to the terms included in the writing.

(2) Such a writing is interpreted wherever reasonable as treating alike all those similarly situated, without regard to their knowledge or understanding of the standard terms of the writing.

(3) Where the other party has reason to believe that the party manifesting such assent would not do so if he knew that the writing contained a particular term, the term is not part of the agreement.

Chapter Ten

Understanding Contractual Obligations: Liability

This chapter focuses on several doctrines related to contractual liability: constructive conditions, substantial performance, express conditions, the perfect tender rule, and anticipatory repudiation. We have seen these doctrines at work in several cases already; here we focus on them directly.

Any failure to fully perform one's obligations according to the terms of a contract is a breach of contract, giving rise to legal liability. The doctrines in this Chapter address two sets of complications to this simple statement. The first of these involve the effect of one party's breach of contract on the obligations of the other. Must the aggrieved party continue to perform her obligations, or can she treat the contract as terminated and arrange for a substitute? The doctrines examined in Part A guide analysis of these issues. The second set of complications involve various responses that a defendant may make to the allegation that she has breached the contract. The doctrines examined in Parts B–D address some of these issues.

A. Constructive Conditions, Breach of Contract and Substantial Performance

Under the doctrine of constructive conditions, a court analyzes the relationship between the parties' promises. A constructive condition is a relationship between two promises that the court describes or defines (constructs) by drawing an analogy to express conditions. In brief, an "express condition" is defined as "an event, not certain to occur, which must occur, unless its non-occurrence is excused, before performance under a contract becomes due." Restatement (Second) of Contracts § 224. We will examine the doctrine of express conditions in greater detail in Part B of this Chapter, but what is most important at this point is that an express condition is a term of the parties agreement that they have agreed upon. An express term may be articulated by the parties or it may be implied in their words and conduct, but on some level, it is agreed upon. A "constructive condition," in contrast, is a characterization imposed by the court in order to analyze the effect of one party's breach on the other's obligations.

In most cases, a significant breach by one party should release the other party from the contract. Say Deanne Williams promises to pay $5,000 for a used car and New Deal Autos promises to deliver it to her on Thursday. If the seller fails to deliver the car, surely Deanne should not have to pay New Deal Autos the $5,000. In such a case, a court would conclude that New Deal Autos' delivery of the car is a constructive condition of Deanne's obligation to pay. Since the constructive condition was not satisfied, Deanne is not obligated to pay. In the same way, New Deal Autos would not have to deliver the car if Deanne was not prepared to pay the $5,000 for the car. New Deal Auto's promise to deliver the car and Deanne's promise to pay are not "true" or express conditions like those examined later. Rather, by implying constructive conditions a court can determine whether to impose liability where the constructive condition has not been fulfilled.

Courts consider two questions about the relationship between two promises:

(1) what is the effect of breach of one promise on the other party's promise? and/or

(2) in what order must the promises be performed?

Fulfillment of one promise is said to be a constructive condition of a return promise made by the other party if the promises are dependent. One consequence of this characterization is that a serious breach of the promise will usually have the effect of completely releasing or excusing the other person from his or her promise. This result seems sensible.

This outcome appears so clearly correct that courts presume that cross-promises are dependent: in order to characterize two promises as independent (not constructive conditions of each other), there must be affirmative evidence indicating that the parties wanted the obligations to be independent. Sometimes, though, there is good reason to treat obligations as independent. Here is an example:

> In a development partnership, one party promises to obtain financing, supply materials, and build the foundation while the other party promises to obtain necessary permits, oversee architectural plans, and hire subcontractors for construction of the building.

In a case like this, where each party has undertaken several different tasks, the parties may agree that some or all of their obligations are independent of the others or a court may decide that the purpose of the contract would be better served by treating one obligation, to obtain permits, for example, as independent of some or all of the other party's obligations, e.g., to supply materials. If these obligations are deemed to be independent, then the first party's breach of her promise to supply materials will not release the second party from his obligation to obtain permits. The second party may be entitled to damages caused by the first party's breach, but the second party still must perform her obligations under the contract.

The second important issue addressed by the doctrine of constructive conditions is the order in which performances are to occur. In January, Trinh hires Chris, a renowned carpenter, to build oak cabinets for $50,000, to be completed by May 5. Trinh agrees to make a down payment of $5,000, but nothing else is said about when payment is due. Generally, courts presume that dependent promises are concurrent, because that gives each party some protection. This is the "cash on the barrelhead" model of exchange. If I am going to deliver the car to you, complete with keys and title, I want your money first; but if you are going to give me money, you want the car keys first. So we'll do a simultaneous switch. This is a concurrent exchange. It is presumed in the doctrine because it is the preference of most people who enter contracts.

A different legal presumption applies, however, where the performances take significantly different periods of time to complete. Where the performance of one party takes a long period of time (as in employment, service contracts, or specially manufactured goods), courts will characterize the time-consuming performance as a condition precedent to the other party's performance. This presumption originated in judges' protection of the interests of employers. The comments to section 234 of the Restatement (Second) of Contracts explain this history:

> Centuries ago, the principle became settled that where work is to be done by one party and payment is to be made by the other, the performance of the work must precede payment, in the absence of a showing of contrary intention. It is sometimes supposed, that this principle grew out of employment contracts, and reflects a conviction that employers as a class are more likely to be responsible than are workmen paid in advance.

See also Patterson, Constructive Conditions of Exchange, 42 Colum. L. Rev. 903, 919 (1942).

Courts in the nineteenth and early twentieth centuries applied this presumption because of an underlying assumption that a worker will not work if he or she is paid in advance. It is better to protect employers against this risk, they reasoned, than to protect workers against the risk that an employer will not pay them for work already done. A third alternative, to presume that contracts in which one performance takes time require periodic performance, such as partial payment for work, apparently was rejected as too burdensome to employers.

As the comment to section 234 suggests, however, this presumption puts the party who must perform first at risk. In an effort to reduce this risk, courts and legislatures have developed some countervailing protections. Legislation protects employees by requiring that they be paid periodically. The construction industry developed a custom and use of "progress payments" which are made periodically during the process of construction and common law courts developed the notions of "divisibility"—enforcing the parts of a contract where the performance and the payment corresponded to one another. A major reform, a rejection of the notion of independent covenants, is found in the doctrine of substantial performance articulated by Justice Cardozo in *Jacob & Youngs v. Kent*, below.

Jacob & Youngs, Inc. v. George Edward Kent

Court of Appeals of New York
230 N.Y. 239, 129 N.E. 889 (1921)

Benjamin Cardozo, Justice

The plaintiff built a country residence for the defendant at a cost of upwards of $77,000, and now sues to recover a balance of $3,483.46, remaining unpaid. The work of construction ceased in June, 1914, and the defendant then began to occupy the dwelling. There was no complaint of defective performance until March, 1915. One of the specifications for the plumbing work provides that—

> "All wrought-iron pipe must be well galvanized, lap welded pipe of the grade known as 'standard pipe' of Reading manufacture."

The defendant learned in March, 1915, that some of the pipe, instead of being made in Reading, was the product of other factories. The plaintiff was accordingly directed by the architect to do the work anew. The plumbing was then encased within the walls except in a few places where it had to be exposed. Obedience to the order meant more than the substitution of other pipe. It meant the demolition at great expense of substantial parts of the completed structure. The plaintiff left the work untouched, and asked for a certificate that the final payment was due. Refusal of the certificate was followed by this suit.

The evidence sustains a finding that the omission of the prescribed brand of pipe was neither fraudulent nor willful. It was the result of the oversight and inattention of the plaintiff's subcontractor. Reading pipe is distinguished from Cohoes pipe and other brands only by the name of the manufacturer stamped upon it at intervals of between six and seven feet. Even the defendant's architect, though he inspected the pipe upon arrival, failed to notice the discrepancy. The plaintiff tried to show that the brands installed, though made by other manufacturers, were the same in quality, in appearance, in market value, and in cost as the brand stated in the contract—that they were, indeed, the same thing, though manufactured in another place. The evidence was excluded, and a verdict directed for the defendant. The Appellate Division reversed, and granted a new trial.

We think the evidence, if admitted, would have supplied some basis for the inference that the defect was insignificant in its relation to the project. The courts never say that one who makes a contract fills the measure of his duty by less than full performance. They do say, however, that an omission, both trivial and innocent, will sometimes be atoned for by allowance of the resulting damage, and will not always be the breach of a condition to be followed by a forfeiture. *Spence v. Ham*, 163 N.Y. 220, 57 N.E. 412, 51 L. R. A. 238; *Woodward v. Fuller*, 80 N.Y. 312; *Glacius v. Black*, 67 N.Y. 563, 566; *Bowen v. Kimbell*, 203 Mass. 364, 370, 89 N.E. 542, 133 Am. St. Rep. 302. The distinction is akin to that between dependent and independent promises, or between promises and conditions. Anson on Contracts (Corbin's Ed.) § 367; 2 Williston on Contracts § 842. Some promises are so plainly independent that they can never by fair construction be conditions of one another. *Rosenthal Paper Co. v. Nat. Folding Box & Paper Co.*, 226 N.Y. 313, 123 N.E. 766; *Bogardus v. N. Y. Life Ins. Co.*, 101 N.Y. 328, 4 N.E. 522. Others are so plainly dependent that they must always be conditions. Others, though dependent and thus conditions when there is departure in point of substance, will be viewed as independent and collateral when the departure is insignificant. 2 Williston on Contracts §§ 841, 842; *Eastern Forge Co. v. Corbin*, 182 Mass. 590, 592, 66 N.E. 419; *Robinson v. Mollett, L. R.*, 7 Eng. & Ir. App. 802, 814; *Miller v. Benjamin*, 142 N.Y. 613, 37 N.E. 631. Considerations partly of justice and partly of presumable intention are to tell us whether this or that promise shall be placed in one class or in another. The simple and the uniform will call for different remedies from the multifarious and the intricate. The margin of departure within the range of normal expectation upon a sale of common chattels will vary from the margin to be expected upon a contract for the construction of a mansion or a "skyscraper." There will be harshness sometimes and oppression in the implication of a condition when the thing upon which labor has been expended is incapable of surrender because united to the land, and equity and reason in the implication of a like condition when the subject-matter, if defective, is in shape to be returned. From the conclusion that promises may not be treated as dependent to the extent of their uttermost minutiae without a sacrifice of justice, the progress is a short one to the conclusion that they may not be so treated without a perversion of intention. Intention not otherwise revealed may be presumed to hold in contemplation the reasonable and probable. If something else is in view, it must not be left to implication. There will be no assumption of a purpose to visit venial faults with oppressive retribution.

Those who think more of symmetry and logic in the development of legal rules than of practical adaptation to the attainment of a just result will be troubled by a classification where the lines of division are so wavering and blurred. Something, doubtless, may be said on the score of consistency and certainty in favor of a stricter standard. The courts have balanced such considerations against those of equity and fairness, and found the latter to be the weightier. The decisions in this state commit us to the liberal view, which is making its way, nowadays, in jurisdictions slow to welcome it. *Dakin & Co. v. Lee*, 1916, 1 K. B. 566, 579. Where the line is to be drawn between the important and the trivial cannot be settled by a formula. "In the nature of the case precise boundaries are impossible." 2 Williston on Contracts § 841. The same omission may take on one aspect or another according to its setting. Substitution of equivalents may not have the same significance in fields of art on the one side and in those of mere utility on the other. Nowhere will change be tolerated, however, if it is so dominant or pervasive as in any real or substantial measure to frustrate the purpose of the contract. *Crouch v. Gutmann*, 134 N.Y. 45, 51, 31 N.E. 271, 30 Am. St. Rep. 608. There is no general license to install whatever, in the builder's judgment, may be regarded as "just as good." *Easthampton L. & C. Co., Ltd., v. Worthington*, 186 N.Y. 407, 412, 79 N.E. 323. The question is one of degree, to be answered, if there is doubt, by the triers of the facts (*Crouch v. Gutmann; Woodward v. Fuller, supra*), and, if the inferences are certain, by the judges of the law (*Easthampton L. & C. Co., Ltd. v. Worthington, supra*). We must weigh the purpose to be served, the desire to be gratified, the excuse for deviation from the letter, the cruelty of enforced adherence. Then only can we tell whether literal fulfillment is to be implied by law as a condition. This is not to say that the parties are not free by apt and certain words to effectuate a purpose that performance of every term shall be a condition of recovery. That question is not here. This is merely to say that the law will be slow to impute the purpose, in the silence of the parties, where the significance of the default is grievously out of proportion to the oppression of the forfeiture. The willful transgressor must accept the penalty of his transgression. *Schultze v. Goodstein*, 180 N.Y. 248, 251, 73 N.E. 21; *Desmond-Dunne Co. v. Friedman-Doscher Co.*, 162 N.Y. 486, 490, 56 N.E. 995. For him there is no occasion to mitigate the rigor of implied conditions. The transgressor whose default is unintentional and trivial may hope for mercy if he will offer atonement for his wrong. *Spence v. Ham, supra.*

In the circumstances of this case, we think the measure of the allowance is not the cost of replacement, which would be great, but the difference in value, which would be either nominal or nothing. Some of the exposed sections might perhaps have been replaced at moderate expense. The defendant did not limit his demand to them, but treated the plumbing as a unit to be corrected from cellar to roof. In point of fact, the plaintiff never reached the stage at which evidence of the extent of the allowance became necessary. The trial court had excluded evidence that the defect was unsubstantial, and in view of that ruling there was no occasion for the plaintiff to go farther with an offer of proof. We think, however, that the offer, if it had been made, would not of necessity have been defective because directed to difference in value. It is true that in most cases the cost of replacement is the measure. *Spence v. Ham, supra*. The owner is entitled to the money which will permit him to complete, unless the cost of completion is grossly and unfairly out of proportion to the good to be attained. When that is true, the measure is the difference in value. Specifications call, let us say, for a foundation built of granite quarried in Vermont. On the completion of the building, the owner learns that through the blunder of a subcontractor part of the foundation has been built of granite of the same quality quarried in New Hampshire. The measure of allowance is not the cost of reconstruction. "There may be omissions of that which could not afterwards be supplied exactly as called for by the contract without taking down the building to its foundations, and at the same time the omission may not affect the value of the building for use or otherwise, except so slightly as to be hardly appreciable." *Handy v. Bliss*, 204 Mass. 513, 519, 90 N.E. 864, 134 Am. St. Rep. 673. *Cf. Foeller v. Heintz*, 137 Wis. 169, 178, 118 N.W. 543, 24 L. R. A. (N.S.) 321; *Oberlies v. Bullinger*, 132 N.Y. 598, 601, 30 N.E. 999; 2 Williston on Contracts

§ 805, p. 1541. The rule that gives a remedy in cases of substantial performance with compensation for defects of trivial or inappreciable importance has been developed by the courts as an instrument of justice. The measure of the allowance must be shaped to the same end.

The order should be affirmed, and judgment absolute directed in favor of the plaintiff upon the stipulation, with costs in all courts.

Chester B. McLaughlin, Justice

I dissent. The plaintiff did not perform its contract. Its failure to do so was either intentional or due to gross neglect which, under the uncontradicted facts, amounted to the same thing, nor did it make any proof of the cost of compliance, where compliance was possible.

Under its contract it obligated itself to use in the plumbing only pipe (between 2,000 and 2,500 feet) made by the Reading Manufacturing Company. The first pipe delivered was about 1,000 feet and the plaintiff's superintendent then called the attention of the foreman of the subcontractor, who was doing the plumbing, to the fact that the specifications annexed to the contract required all pipe used in the plumbing to be of the Reading Manufacturing Company. They then examined it for the purpose of ascertaining whether this delivery was of that manufacture and found it was. Thereafter, as pipe was required in the progress of the work, the foreman of the subcontractor would leave word at its shop that he wanted a specified number of feet of pipe, without in any way indicating of what manufacture. Pipe would thereafter be delivered and installed in the building, without any examination whatever. Indeed, no examination, so far as appears, was made by the plaintiff, the subcontractor, defendant's architect, or any one else, of any of the pipe except the first delivery, until after the building had been completed. Plaintiff's architect then refused to give the certificate of completion, upon which the final payment depended, because all of the pipe used in the plumbing was not of the kind called for by the contract. After such refusal, the subcontractor removed the covering or insulation from about 900 feet of pipe which was exposed in the basement, cellar, and attic, and all but 70 feet was found to have been manufactured, not by the Reading Company, but by other manufacturers, some by the Cohoes Rolling Mill Company, some by the National Steel Works, some by the South Chester Tubing Company, and some which bore no manufacturer's mark at all. The balance of the pipe had been so installed in the building that an inspection of it could not be had without demolishing, in part at least, the building itself.

I am of the opinion the trial court was right in directing a verdict for the defendant. The plaintiff agreed that all the pipe used should be of the Reading Manufacturing Company. Only about two-fifths of it, so far as appears, was of that kind. If more were used, then the burden of proving that fact was upon the plaintiff, which it could easily have done, since it knew where the pipe was obtained. The question of substantial performance of a contract of the character of the one under consideration depends in no small degree upon the good faith of the contractor. If the plaintiff had intended to, and had, complied with the terms of the contract except as to minor omissions, due to inadvertence, then he might be allowed to recover the contract price, less the amount necessary to fully compensate the defendant for damages caused by such omissions. *Woodward v. Fuller*, 80 N.Y. 312; *Nolan v. Whitney*, 88 N.Y. 648. But that is not this case. It installed between 2,000 and 2,500 feet of pipe, of which only 1,000 feet at most complied with the contract. No explanation was given why pipe called for by the contract was not used, nor that any effort made to show what it would cost to remove the pipe of other manufacturers and install that of the Reading Manufacturing Company. The

Subject to HIS Approval

Time, That Tough Old Tester of everything in this world, writes the final "Okay" on the materials that go into the house you build. For Time alone can tell whether those materials are worthy—whether they will serve you faithfully through the years, or whether they will cause you expense and trouble long before your house has completed its allotted span.

In the important matter of piping, so vital to the permanence of any building, Time has spoken clearly. His verdict—today as eighty years ago—is Genuine *Puddled* Wrought Iron for lasting pipe economy and satisfaction. No other pipe material has proved so successful in withstanding *all* the attacks of Time and his henchmen.

Reading 5-Point Pipe is made of Genuine *Puddled* Wrought Iron—that rust-resisting, strain-defying metal. That is why you can forget pipe repairs and replacements for the rest of your life, on the day you install it.

Use only Reading 5-Point Nipples with Reading 5-Point Pipe . . . you'll know them by the indented spiral band.

READING IRON COMPANY, Reading, Pennsylvania

For Your Protection. This Indented Spiral forever Marks

All

5 POINT PIPE
READING
GENUINE PUDDLED WROUGHT IRON

GENUINE PUDDLED WROUGHT IRON
READING PIPE
DIAMETERS RANGING FROM ⅛ TO 20 INCHES

Science and Invention Have Never Found a Satisfactory Substitute for Genuine Puddled Wrought Iron

defendant had a right to contract for what he wanted. He had a right before making payment to get what the contract called for. It is no answer to this suggestion to say that the pipe put in was just as good as that made by the Reading Manufacturing Company, or that the difference in value between such pipe and the pipe made by the Reading Manufacturing Company would be either "nominal or nothing." Defendant contracted for pipe made by the Reading Manufacturing Company. What his reason was for requiring this kind of pipe is of no importance. He wanted that and was entitled to it. It may have been a mere whim on his part, but even so, he had a right to this kind of pipe, regardless of whether some other kind, according to the opinion of the contractor or experts, would have been "just as good, better, or done just as well." He agreed to pay only upon condition that the pipe installed were made by that company and he ought not to be compelled to pay unless that condition be performed. *Schultze v. Goodstein*, 180 N.Y. 248, 73 N.E. 21; *Spence v. Ham, supra*; *Steel S. & E. C. Co. v. Stock*, 225 N.Y. 173, 121 N.E. 786; *Van Clief v. Van Vechten*, 130 N.Y. 571, 29 N.E. 1017; *Glacius v. Black*, 50 N.Y. 145, 10 Am. Rep. 449; *Smith v. Brady*, 17 N.Y. 173, and authorities cited on page 185, 72 Am. Dec. 442. The rule, therefore, of substantial performance, with damages for unsubstantial omissions, has no application. *Crouch v. Gutmann*, 134 N.Y. 45, 31 N.E. 271, 30 Am. St. Rep. 608; *Spence v. Ham*, 163 N.Y. 220, 57 N.E. 412, 51 L. R. A. 238.

What was said by this court in *Smith v. Brady*, supra, is quite applicable here:

> I suppose it will be conceded that every one has a right to build his house, his cottage or his store after such a model and in such style as shall best accord with his notions of utility or be most agreeable to his fancy. The specifications of the contract become the law between the parties until voluntarily changed. If the owner prefers a plain and simple Doric column, and has so provided in the agreement, the contractor has no right to put in its place the more costly and elegant Corinthian. If the owner, having regard to strength and durability, has contracted for walls of specified materials to be laid in a particular manner, or for a given number of joists and beams, the builder has no right to substitute his own judgment or that of others. Having departed from the agreement, if performance has not been waived by the other party, the law will not allow him to allege that he has made as good a building as the one he engaged to erect. He can demand payment only upon and according to the terms of his contract, and if the conditions on which payment is due have not been performed, then the right to demand it does not exist. To hold a different doctrine would be simply to make another contract, and would be giving to parties an encouragement to violate their engagements, which the just policy of the law does not permit.

17 N.Y. 186, 72 Am. Dec. 442.

I am of the opinion the trial court did not err in ruling on the admission of evidence or in directing a verdict for the defendant.

For the foregoing reasons I think the judgment of the Appellate Division should be reversed and the judgment of the Trial Term affirmed.

————

Richard Danzig, The Capability Problem in Contract Law

(2004)

A basic question worth asking yourself both in pondering an individual case and in assessing the performance of a judicial system, is: why do people engage in litigation? Interviews with surviving contemporaries, a study of the records in the case, and research in collateral contemporary materials (newspapers, Who's Who, phone books, land records, etc.) permit the following description of the events leading up to the litigation in *Jacob and Youngs v. Kent*.

George Edward Kent, the defendant in this case, was a successful New York lawyer who maintained two offices and two apartments in Manhattan as well as the mansion in Jericho (Long Island) whose construction provoked this litigation. In addition, George Kent acquired substantial wealth and political connections by his marriage (at age 38) to a daughter of W.R. Grace, then the owner of a large shipping line, and later Mayor of New York.

In 1913 when the Kents decided to build on land Mrs. Kent had acquired in Jericho during an earlier period, they hired an architect, William Wells Bosworth of New York City, who drew plans and specifications for a mansion on the property. In response to these plans Jacob and Youngs, a substantial, though not eminent, New York construction firm, tendered a "proposal" (an estimate of cost) for construction which was accepted. The contract and specifications for construction reprinted above were drawn and dated May 5 and May 7, 1913.

Why was pipe manufactured by the Philadelphia and Reading Iron and Coal Company specified? If Mr. Kent had a professional or financial connection with the Reading Company it remains buried. His surviving daughters, one born in 1898, another in 1911, are unaware of any such connection, as is his personal secretary of 20 years. While the latter entered Kent's employ in 1927, he saw most of Kent's papers and was consequently aware of his stockholdings and major clients for some years before that. In addition veteran employees at the remnants of what were the Reading Companies have never heard of a Kent or Grace connection and no member of either family shows up in the companies' annual reports as a director or officer from 1915–1945.

The contract specified a standard of pipe which cost 30% more than steel pipe—then the most widely used (and now the almost universally used) pipe. The makers of wrought iron pipe, however, claimed that the savings due to durability and low maintenance more than made up for the added expense.[1] The years from 1905–1920 saw a peak in the popularity of wrought iron pipe. For example Byers Co. reported a rise in the use of wrought iron pipe from 40–50% of the total market in New York City in the "few years" previous to 1916.[2] This rise occurred, according to Byers, not in "cheap buildings sold to the public at large," but rather "in skyscraper construction as well as in other large buildings planned and constructed with expertness and care."[3] As an example of such a building a Byers publication printed a picture of a house built in Southampton, Long Island, another area like Jericho into which wealthy New Yorkers were moving after 1910. The house is very like that constructed for the Kents.

The Reading Company was by its account the largest manufacturer of wrought iron pipe in the country, having provided it for such famous New York buildings as the Metropolitan Life Insurance Building and the Chrysler Building.[4] Indeed, its 1911 brochure asserted that "the majority of the modern and most prominent buildings in New York City are equipped with Reading wrought iron pipe" and that "many leading architects and engineers have drawn their specifications in favor of wrought iron pipe, in instances prohibiting steel pipe entirely."[5]

Interestingly, as this last comment suggests, these trade publications made their comparative claims not so much with reference to their competitors who made wrought

---

1. A.M. Byers Co., The Selection of Pipe for Modern Buildings 7 (1916).

2. *Id.* at 12.

3. *Id.*

4. Reading Iron Co., Court of Actual Experience: Wrought Iron Pipe v. Steel Pipe 37 (9th ed., 1911).

5. *Id.*, p. 2.

iron pipe, as to those who made steel pipe. According to a pipe wholesaler interviewed in New York City in 1975, genuine wrought iron pipe was manufactured in the pre-war period by four largely noncompeting companies: Reading, Cohoes, Byers and Southchester. According to this informant, all of these brands "were of the same quality and price. The manufacturer's name would make absolutely no difference in pipe or in price."

The testimony prepared for the Kent trial was to the same effect. If one reads between and around objections and exclusions of evidence it is apparent that Jacob and Youngs were prepared to show equality of price, weight, size, appearance, composition, and durability for all four major brands of wrought iron pipe. Indeed, in addition to other witnesses, an employee of the Reading Company was prepared to testify to this effect. Probably because of this evidence, Kent's briefs on appeal conceded that "experts could have testified that the substitute pipe was the same in quality in all respects...."[6] It appears that this concession crystallized into a "stipulation" before argument in the Court of Appeals, and that Cardozo's reference was to this when he directed a judgment for Jacob and Youngs.

Why then was Reading Pipe specified? Apparently because it was the normal trade practice to assure wrought iron pipe quality by naming a manufacturer. In contemporary trade bulletins put out by Byers and Reading, prospective buyers were cautioned that some steel pipe manufacturers used iron pipe and often sold under misleading names like "wrought pipe." To avoid such inferior products, Byers warned: "When wrought iron pipe is desired, the specifications often read 'genuine wrought iron pipe' but as this does not always exclude wrought iron containing steel scrap, it is safer to mention the name of a manufacturer known not to use scrap." Reading's brochure said: "If you want the best pipe, specify 'Genuine wrought iron pipe made from Puddled Pig Iron' and have the Pipe-Fitter furnish you with the name of the manufacturer."[7]

The contract makes it especially clear that the use of Reading was primarily as a standard. Specification twenty-two says: "Where any particular brand of manufactured article is specified, it is to be considered as a standard. Contractors desiring to use another shall first make application in writing to the Architect stating the difference in cost and obtain their written approval of change." (Jacob and Youngs stressed the implications of the first sentence in their court of appeals brief.[8])

Why, given a realistic indifference to the maker of the pipe, did Kent refuse to pay for anything but Reading Pipe through three levels of litigation? Mr. Kent, according to some

---

6. Appellant's Brief, New York Court of Appeals, p. 13.

7. This area of plumbing metallurgy had apparently been productive of conflict between builders and owners. The Reading pamphlet cited above, at p. 2 notes: "In some cases, where wrought iron was specified and steel pipe was substituted, it resulted after discovery in heavy fines to the contractor, and in some instances the steel pipe was ordered torn out and replaced with wrought iron pipe at a large expense." The Appellants' Brief in *Jacob and Youngs*, p. 13–14, quoted from *Shultze v. Goodstein*, 180 N.Y. 248, 73 N.E. 21, a case in which some type of pipe, probably steel, was substituted for the specified iron pipe. In that case, complete performance as to iron pipe was deemed a condition to the buyer's duty to pay. (The case is cited by McLaughlin in dissent, but Cardozo passed it off as a case relevant only to willful breaches.)

8. The imprecision of the specifications is underscored by the fact that apparently it was not possible to make *lap welded* wrought iron in all sizes (1/4"–2" in diameter) necessary for such a house. (Trial testimony of Parke H. Holton, a pipe marketing expert from Nason Mfg. Co. *And see* BYERS PIPE, a magazine put out by Byers Co. in July 1921, bulletin no. 34 which shows that lap welding is only done on pipes of 11/4, 11/2, and 2". A different kind of welding is used on smaller pipe.) Thus it is apparent that the specifications could NOT have been met. *See also* testimony by Henry S. Carland, a sales Representative for Reading, showing that the specifications called for a non-existent pipe.) This evidence was ruled inadmissible on the ground both sides had accepted the specifications in the contract.

who knew him, carried cost consciousness "to the extreme point." As one put it: "The old man would go all over town to save a buck." Perhaps having paid the extra cost of wrought iron pipe, he felt cheated when not indisputably assured of the highest quality and purity with which Reading's name was associated. However, a Reading representative's willingness to testify for the plaintiff, and the apparent ability of Jacob and Youngs to show the equality of Byers, Cohoes, Southchester and Reading pipes (an equality probably realized by Kent's architect) suggest that Kent may have seized upon the pipe substitution as an expression of other dissatisfactions in his relationship with Jacob and Youngs. A summary of the construction process was revealed during the suit suggests anything but a harmonious relationship between builder and owner.

The first shipment of pipe arrived in June 1913, soon after the contract was signed. It was examined by Youngs, his foreman, Wallace Heidtman, and the subcontractor's worker, Louis Simpson. At this point, Heidtman reminded Simpson that the "specification calls for Reading." (Testimony of Simpson, Heidtman, Youngs). This batch, probably 1000 feet (or two fifths of the total used in the house) was found to be Reading. Note that it was built into the foundation and was the least discoverable later. Thus while only 70 of the 700–800 feet of pipe exposed in cellar and attic were of Reading Pipe (testimony of William H. Healy, architect's assistant) it is not surprising that more Reading wasn't found. After that point, none of the three, nor Healy, whose duties included "in a general way" making sure the specifications were met, examined any later shipments of pipe. (Testimony of Healy, Simpson, Youngs.) Simpson was to blame for not ordering Reading Pipe. (This, by his own testimony.) His error was probably negligent. Healy, the architect's watchdog, may share some of the blame as Jacob and Youngs argued in their brief and as Cardozo hinted in his opinion. Kent later hired Healy on a full time basis to prepare for trial.

As the work progressed, additional work became necessary in the amount of $7,244.44. (Complaint, paragraph 4.) While work was originally to be completed on the fifteenth of December, 1913, a modification was written and signed on the twenty-third of that month, extending the contract for an unspecified time and adding $580.00 to Kent's bill. (Complaint, paragraphs 6, 12, 13.) The reason given for the delay is that "the defendant failed to perform what he was to do under the said contract in time so the plaintiff's work could be completed by the said time," and because of "the defaults and delays of defendant." This language parallels one excuse for delay allowed in Art. III of the contract. The only duty which Kent seems to have owed Jacob and Youngs was to make payment, although the missing specifications may have detailed some preparatory work which Kent or his agents were to have done. Thus the delay and need for modification may have hinged on other troubles causing Kent to withhold payment at certain points. Paragraph 8 of the complaint notes "certain alterations and omissions entitled the defendant to a deduction of $4,031.41." Here again, there is evidence of unhappiness on Kent's part with work done by Jacob and Youngs. The whole price paid under the subcontract for the plumbing was only $6,000, so the earlier disputes were over equally large aspects of the contract.

The Kents moved into the house in June 1914, after twice as much time had passed for completion as the contract specified. Yet, even Jacob and Youngs averred no more in their complaint than that "substantial completion" occurred by November 13, 1914. At that time a new modification entitled Jacob and Youngs to $240, and specified several "minor details of work" yet to be completed. The $3,483.46 outstanding on the contract would not be paid until these defaults were cured. (Complaint, paragraphs 14, 15.)

Moreover, though Kent occupied the house in June 1914 and work stopped except for "minor details" by November, Jacob and Youngs had not received the final payment or certificate by March 1915, 2 years after the contract was signed, and 1 ½ years after it was to have been completed. (World War I began in Europe in the summer of 1914, probably complicating supply conditions). Yet until then, Reading pipe was never mentioned as a subject of dispute. In fact, on October 10, 1914 Healy had written the subcontracting plumber on behalf of his principal, as follows:

New York
October 10, 1914

Re: Kent Residence
McKenna Bros.,
Westbury, L.I.

Gentlemen:

In response to the request in your letter to us under date of October 6th, we write to inform you that your work at the above residence is satisfactory. It is understood that this statement in no way releases you from obligations as per your contract and guarantee.

Yours very truly,
W.W. Bosworth
per H

WH/K

On March 19, 1915, Jacob and Youngs received a letter from Bosworth noting that some non-Reading pipe had been discovered. Healy, Bosworth's assistant, probably discovered the error. According to his testimony he was employed by Kent full time at some point. Kent's lawyer went out of his way to be sure that Healy not explain the nature of that employment, but it is plausible to suppose that Healy's satisfaction with the plumbing, expressed in the letter of the previous October, changed to dissatisfaction at Kent's prompting. Perhaps Healy then set to looking for specification errors by Jacob and Youngs. Jacob and Youngs hinted in their brief that were Youngs allowed to testify what he was told by the architect as to why the certificate was withheld, it would show that it was solely at Kent's insistence.[9]

Later in March, Youngs, Healy, McKenna (the plumbing subcontractor) and representatives from Reading and Cohoes examined about 150' of pipe and found some to be Cohoes, some Reading, and most unmarked. (Testimony of John A. McKenna.) A March 19 letter demanded that Jacob and Youngs replace the offending pipe. It was from the architect and followed the procedure in article IV of the contract, for dealing with unsatisfactory work or materials. By Nov. 23, 1915, the pipe had not been replaced and a letter from Bosworth to Jacob and Youngs referred to still other details of work yet undone, as well as reiterating the replacement demand.

On January 16, 1916, Bosworth sent a letter to Jacob and Youngs giving the latter three days notice of termination unless the builders replaced the pipe, as specified in article V of the contract. After this nothing seems to have happened until November 10, 1916 when Jacob and Youngs formally demanded and was refused the architect's certificate. These delays are intriguing, but unexplained. One wonders if Kent believed himself absolved of the duty to pay as of January 1916, only to receive a new demand for the architect's certificate in November and a legal complaint in December. Perhaps, also, it was Jacob and Youngs' initial intention to forget the $3,400 still owing, but some new pressure led the firm to change its mind.

---

9. Appellee's Brief, New York Court of Appeals, pp. 6–7.

The complaint was filed on December 11, 1916. Paragraph three alleged "That … the plaintiff proceeded to perform the conditions of said contract on its part to be performed, and furnished and delivered substantially all the materials and performed substantially all the work required by the said contract on the part of the plaintiff to be furnished and performed." On December 29, 1916, Kent responded by denying the claim of substantial performance.

B. Express or True Conditions

As we have seen, the *Restatement (Second) of Contracts* defines a "condition" as "an event, not certain to occur, which must occur, unless its non-occurrence is excused, before performance under a contract becomes due." *Restatement (Second) of Contracts* § 224. A condition (or a "true condition" as some lawyers call it) is a contract term that the parties explicitly or implicitly created in order to allocate risks, impose incentives, or otherwise structure their relationship. The purpose of the doctrine of *express or true conditions* is to give effect to the parties' agreement that the occurrence (or non-occurrence) of some specific event is necessary before one or the other of the parties has an obligation to perform the contract.

In each of the following examples, there is a condition — the elimination of basketball team from the playoffs, ability to purchase antique wood, payment by a certain date — that qualifies each of the promised performances. In each case, understanding the condition will be an important step in determining whether a breach and resulting liability has occurred.

> Ruthann promises to build a deck on Brad's house by May 1, if the Eagles Basketball Team (of which Ruthann is a member) is eliminated from the league playoffs, and Brad promises to pay Ruthann $1,800 upon completion of the deck.

In this example, the elimination of the Eagles is a condition to Ruthann's obligation to build the deck by May 1. If the team is not eliminated, then Ruthann is not obligated to build and Brad cannot enforce the contract against her unless satisfaction of the condition is waived or excused.

> Eugene promises to repair Harriet's antique sandalwood table, if he is able to purchase sandalwood costing less than $500 for replacement pieces, and Harriet promises to pay Eugene $1,250 for the completed work.

In this example, Eugene's purchasing sandalwood costing less than $500 for replacement pieces is a condition to his obligation to repair the table. If Eugene is not able to purchase the wood in the specified price range, then he is not obligated to repair the table, unless the condition is waived or excused.

> Annette promises to produce a training film for Beto's Fabric Company, if Beto gives notice that he wants to exercise his option by paying her $4,000 on or before July 1.

Beto's paying $4,000 on or before July 1 is a condition of Annette's obligation to produce the film. If Beto fails to pay $4,000 on or before July 1, Annette is not obligated to produce the film, unless the condition is waived or excused.

These examples illustrate one important legal consequence of a condition: performance is not due if the event does not occur unless the condition is waived or excused. The examples also illustrate several reasons why parties may want to specify conditions in their contract: in the first example, the condition allocates to Brad the risk that Ruthann will be too busy playing basketball to work on the deck before May 1; in the second, the condition places a maximum price on the materials that Eugene will have to purchase, and thus limits the risk of an increase in the cost of his materials. In the third example, the condition gives Beto an option; if he decides that he does not want the film, then Beto simply won't pay, and the contract will end, without liability on either party. Annette, on the other hand, has ensured that she will know by July 1 whether Beto wants the film, and if he does, she will be paid on or before that day.

The doctrine of conditions establishes a set of concepts and rules designed to give effect to the parties' desire to qualify their obligations in a way that takes certain risks into account. Traditionally, the doctrine distinguished between a "condition precedent" (an event that must occur before the obligation becomes due) and a "condition subsequent" (an event that terminates an obligation that is presently due). All of the examples above involve conditions precedent. The classic example of a condition subsequent is a notice requirement in an insurance policy. Think of a simple fire insurance policy: the company will pay if a fire causes damage to the property, so long as the insured notifies the company within thirty days of the fire. Under traditional doctrine, the fire would be a condition precedent to the company's obligation to pay, and the insured giving notice would be a condition subsequent. The *Restatement (Second)* rejects this distinction, observing that almost all conditions function as conditions precedent (e.g., one can easily say that notice is a condition precedent to the insurance company's obligation to pay) and that the distinction causes unnecessary confusion. *See Restatement (Second) of Contracts* § 224, Comment e.

Like promises, conditions can be express or implied. All of the examples above involve express conditions, but consider the following:

> In a lease, the landlord promises to maintain the premises in good condition. One of the kitchen pipes begins to leak. After several days, the leaking water damages the tenant's furniture. The tenant calls a plumber who repairs the leak and then sues the landlord for the cost of the repairs and the damage to his furniture.

In such a case, the court is likely to hold that the landlord's obligation to repair the plumbing is subject to the implied condition that the tenant notify the landlord of leaks and other problems. If the tenant does not tell the landlord about the leak, then the landlord's obligation to repair does not arise. *See Wal-Noon Corp. v. Hill*, 119 Cal. Rep. 646, 45 Cal. App. 3d 605 (1975) (notice is an implied condition of a landlord's obligation to repair).

---

1. Covenant or Condition: Why It Matters

In the next case in this section, the court examines the consequences of a court's decision that a term is an express condition that must be satisfied before one of the parties is obligated to perform the contract instead of a promise that the court would treat as a constructive condition. The discussion highlights the requirement of strict compliance with respect to an express condition. When a condition is not satisfied, the party for whose benefit the condition operates is not obligated to perform the contract. This is true whether the condition is one beyond the control of the party who wishes to enforce the contract or is a promissory condition such as delivery of notice. If there is no obligation to perform, the other party may suffer a significant loss. It may be the loss of the expected profit or benefit from the contract or it may be that there have been expenses incurred and money expended in preparation for performance. This is the "forfeiture" referenced in *Jacob and Youngs v. Kent*.

The quote from Professor Williston's treatise in the *Oppenheimer & Co. Inc. v. Oppenheim, Appel, Dixon & Co.* opinion notes that the courts will apply a standard of substantial compliance "to do justice and avoid hardship." Likewise, in *Jacob & Youngs v. Kent*, Judge Cardozo describes the doctrine of substantial performance as an equitable doctrine designed to offer protection from forfeiture to one who innocently breaches a contract in some relatively minor way.

There were only two instances when the doctrine of substantial performance would not apply. Cardozo, quoting *Spence v. Ham*, suggested that the doctrine should not be available for someone who intentionally breaches:

> The willful transgressor must accept the penalty of his transgression. *Schultze v. Goodstein*, 180 N.Y. 248, 251, 73 N.E. 21; *Desmond-Dunne Co. v. Friedman-Doscher Co.*, 162 N.Y. 486, 490, 56 N.E. 995. For him there is no occasion to mitigate the rigor of implied conditions. The transgressor whose default is unintentional and trivial may hope for mercy if he will offer atonement for his wrong.

This limitation is echoed in the *Restatement (Second) of Contracts* § 241: one of the factors to be considered in deciding whether there has been a significant breach is the "extent to which the behavior of the party failing to perform or to offer to perform comports with standards of good faith and fair dealing."

Nor could the doctrine of substantial performance be applied, according to Cardozo, when the parties " … by apt and certain words to effectuate a purpose that performance of every term shall be a condition of recovery." In the cases that follow you will see the tension that exists between competing ideals in contract law: deference to the will of the parties expressed in carefully worded contractual language and an aversion, particularly in cases of unequal bargaining power, to harsh terms that result in a forfeiture. Note the strategies the courts use to deal with the latter situation.

Oppenheimer & Co., Inc., v. Oppenheim, Appel, Dixon & Co.

Court of Appeals of New York
660 N.E.2d 415 (1995)

CARMEN BEAUCHAMP CIPARICK, J.

The parties entered into a letter agreement setting forth certain conditions precedent to the formation and existence of a sublease between them. The agreement provided that there would be no sublease between the parties "unless and until" plaintiff delivered to defendant the prime landlord's written consent to certain "tenant work" on or before a specified deadline. If this condition did not occur, the sublease was to be deemed "null and void." Plaintiff provided only oral notice on the specified date. The issue presented is whether the doctrine of substantial performance applies to the facts of this case. We conclude it does not for the reasons that follow.

I.

In 1986, plaintiff Oppenheimer & Co. moved to the World Financial Center in Manhattan, a building constructed by Olympia & York Company (O & Y). At the time of its move, plaintiff had three years remaining on its existing lease for the 33rd floor of the building known as One New York Plaza. As an incentive to induce plaintiff's move, O & Y agreed to make the rental payments due under plaintiff's rental agreement in the event plaintiff was unable to sublease its prior space in One New York Plaza.

In December 1986, the parties to this action entered into a conditional letter agreement to sublease the 33rd floor. Defendant already leased space on the 29th floor of One New York Plaza and was seeking to expand its operations. The proposed sublease between the parties was attached to the letter agreement. The letter agreement provided that the proposed sublease would be executed only upon the satisfaction of certain conditions. Pursuant to paragraph 1 (a) of the agreement, plaintiff was required to obtain "the Prime Landlord's written notice of confirmation, substantially to the effect that [defendant] is a subtenant of the Premises reasonably acceptable to Prime Landlord." If such written notice of confirmation were not obtained "on or before December 30, 1986, then this letter agreement and the Sublease ... shall be deemed null and void and of no further force and effect and neither party shall have any rights against nor obligations to the other."

Assuming satisfaction of the condition set forth in paragraph 1 (a), defendant was required to submit to plaintiff, on or before January 2, 1987, its plans for "tenant work" involving construction of a telephone communication linkage system between the 29th and 33rd floors. Paragraph 4 (c) of the letter agreement then obligated plaintiff to obtain the prime landlord's "written consent" to the proposed "tenant work" and deliver such consent to defendant on or before January 30, 1987. Furthermore, if defendant had not received the prime landlord's written consent by the agreed date, both the agreement and the sublease were to be deemed "null and void and of no further force and effect," and neither party was to have "any rights against nor obligations to the other." Paragraph 4 (d) additionally provided that, notwithstanding satisfaction of the condition set forth in paragraph 1 (a), the parties "agree not to execute and exchange the Sublease unless and until ... the conditions set forth in paragraph (c) above are timely satisfied."

The parties extended the letter agreement's deadlines in writing and plaintiff timely satisfied the first condition set forth in paragraph 1 (a) pursuant to the modified deadline. However, plaintiff never delivered the prime landlord's written consent to the proposed tenant work on or before the modified final deadline of February 25, 1987. Rather, plaintiff's attorney telephoned defendant's attorney on February 25 and informed defendant that the prime landlord's consent had been secured. On February 26, defendant, through its attorney, informed plaintiff's attorney that the letter agreement and sublease were invalid for failure to timely deliver the prime landlord's written consent and that it would not agree to an extension of the deadline. The document embodying the prime landlord's written consent was eventually received by plaintiff on March 20, 1987, 23 days after expiration of paragraph 4 (c)'s modified final deadline.

Plaintiff commenced this action for breach of contract, asserting that defendant waived and/or was estopped by virtue of its conduct[9] from insisting on physical delivery of the prime landlord's written consent by the February 25 deadline. Plaintiff further alleged in its complaint that it had substantially performed the conditions set forth in the letter agreement.

At the outset of trial, the court issued an order in limine barring any reference to substantial performance of the terms of the letter agreement. Nonetheless, during the

---

9. Plaintiff argued that it could have met the deadline, but failed to do so only because defendant, acting in bad faith, induced plaintiff into delaying delivery of the landlord's consent. Plaintiff asserted that the parties had previously extended the agreement's deadlines as a matter of course.

course of trial, the court permitted the jury to consider the theory of substantial performance, and additionally charged the jury concerning substantial performance. Special interrogatories were submitted. The jury found that defendant had properly complied with the terms of the letter agreement, and answered in the negative the questions whether defendant failed to perform its obligations under the letter agreement concerning submission of plans for tenant work, whether defendant by its conduct waived the February 25 deadline for delivery by plaintiff of the landlord's written consent to tenant work, and whether defendant by its conduct was equitably estopped from requiring plaintiff's strict adherence to the February 25 deadline. Nonetheless, the jury answered in the affirmative the question, "Did plaintiff substantially perform the conditions set forth in the Letter Agreement?," and awarded plaintiff damages of $ 1.2 million.

Defendant moved for judgment notwithstanding the verdict. Supreme Court granted the motion, ruling as a matter of law that "the doctrine of substantial performance has no application to this dispute, where the Letter Agreement is free of all ambiguity in setting the deadline that plaintiff concededly did not honor." The Appellate Division reversed the judgment on the law and facts, and reinstated the jury verdict. The Court concluded that the question of substantial compliance was properly submitted to the jury and that the verdict should be reinstated because plaintiff's failure to deliver the prime landlord's written consent was inconsequential.

This Court granted defendant's motion for leave to appeal and we now reverse.

II.

Defendant argues that no sublease or contractual relationship ever arose here because plaintiff failed to satisfy the condition set forth in paragraph 4 (c) of the letter agreement. Defendant contends that the doctrine of substantial performance is not applicable to excuse plaintiff's failure to deliver the prime landlord's written consent to defendant on or before the date specified in the letter agreement and that the Appellate Division erred in holding to the contrary. Before addressing defendant's arguments and the decision of the court below, an understanding of certain relevant principles is helpful.

A condition precedent is "an act or event, other than a lapse of time, which, unless the condition is excused, must occur before a duty to perform a promise in the agreement arises" (Calamari and Perillo, Contracts § 11-2, at 438 [3d ed]; see, Restatement [Second] of Contracts § 224; see also, *Merritt Hill Vineyards v Windy Hgts. Vineyard*, 61 NY2d 106, 112–113). Most conditions precedent describe acts or events which must occur before a party is obliged to perform a promise made pursuant to an existing contract, a situation to be distinguished conceptually from a condition precedent to the formation or existence of the contract itself (*see, M.K. Metals v Container Recovery Corp.*, 645 F2d 583). In the latter situation, no contract arises "unless and until the condition occurs" (Calamari and Perillo, Contracts § 11-5, at 440 [3d ed]).

Conditions can be express or implied. Express conditions are those agreed to and imposed by the parties themselves. Implied or constructive conditions are those "imposed by law to do justice" (Calamari and Perillo, Contracts § 11-8, at 444 [3d ed]). Express conditions must be literally performed, whereas constructive conditions, which ordinarily arise from language of promise, are subject to the precept that substantial compliance is sufficient. The importance of the distinction has been explained by Professor Williston:

> "Since an express condition ... depends for its validity on the manifested intention of the parties, it has the same sanctity as the promise itself. Though the court may regret the harshness of such a condition, as it may regret the harshness of a promise, it must, nevertheless, generally enforce the will of the

parties unless to do so will violate public policy. Where, however, the law itself has imposed the condition, in absence of or irrespective of the manifested intention of the parties, it can deal with its creation as it pleases, shaping the boundaries of the constructive condition in such a way as to do justice and avoid hardship." (5 Williston, Contracts § 669, at 154 [3d ed].)

In determining whether a particular agreement makes an event a condition courts will interpret doubtful language as embodying a promise or constructive condition rather than an express condition. This interpretive preference is especially strong when a finding of express condition would increase the risk of forfeiture by the obligee (*see*, Restatement (Second) of Contracts § 227 (1)).

Interpretation as a means of reducing the risk of forfeiture cannot be employed if "the occurrence of the event as a condition is expressed in unmistakable language" (Restatement (Second) of Contracts § 229, comment a, at 185; *see*, § 227, comment b [where language is clear, "(t)he policy favoring freedom of contract requires that, within broad limits, the agreement of the parties should be honored even though forfeiture results"]). Nonetheless, the nonoccurrence of the condition may yet be excused by waiver, breach or forfeiture. The Restatement posits that "[t]o the extent that the non-occurrence of a condition would cause disproportionate forfeiture, a court may excuse the non-occurrence of that condition unless its occurrence was a material part of the agreed exchange" (Restatement (Second) of Contracts § 229).

Turning to the case at bar, it is undisputed that the critical language of paragraph 4 (c) of the letter agreement unambiguously establishes an express condition precedent rather than a promise, as the parties employed the unmistakable language of condition ("if," "unless and until"). There is no doubt of the parties' intent and no occasion for interpreting the terms of the letter agreement other than as written.

Furthermore, plaintiff has never argued, and does not now contend, that the nonoccurrence of the condition set forth in paragraph 4 (c) should be excused on the ground of forfeiture.[10] Rather, plaintiff's primary argument from the inception of this litigation has been that defendant waived or was equitably estopped from invoking paragraph 4 (c). Plaintiff argued secondarily that it substantially complied with the express condition of delivery of written notice on or before February 25th in that it gave defendant oral notice of consent on the 25th.

Contrary to the decision of the Court below, we perceive no justifiable basis for applying the doctrine of substantial performance to the facts of this case. The flexible concept of substantial compliance "stands in sharp contrast to the requirement of strict compliance that protects a party that has taken the precaution of making its duty expressly conditional" (2 Farnsworth, Contracts § 8.12, at 415 [2d ed. 1990]). If the parties "have made an event a condition of their agreement, there is no mitigating standard of materiality or substantiality applicable to the non-occurrence of that event" (Restatement [Second] of Contracts § 237, comment d, at 220). Substantial performance in this context is not sufficient, "and if relief is to be had under the contract, it must be through excuse of the non-occurrence of the condition to avoid forfeiture" (*id.; see, Brown-Marx Assocs. v Emigrant Sav. Bank*, 703 F2d 1361, 1367–1368 [11th Cir]; *see also*, Childres, Conditions in the Law of Contracts, 45 NYU L Rev 33, 35).

---

10. The Restatement defines the term "forfeiture" as "the denial of compensation that results when the obligee loses [its] right to the agreed exchange after [it] has relied substantially, as by preparation or performance on the expectation of that exchange" (§ 229, comment *b*).

Here, it is undisputed that plaintiff has not suffered a forfeiture or conferred a benefit upon defendant. Plaintiff alludes to a $ 1 million licensing fee it allegedly paid to the prime landlord for the purpose of securing the latter's consent to the subleasing of the premises. At no point, however, does plaintiff claim that this sum was forfeited or that it was expended for the purpose of accomplishing the sublease with defendant. It is further undisputed that O & Y, as an inducement to effect plaintiff's move to the World Financial Center, promised to indemnify plaintiff for damages resulting from failure to sublease the 33rd floor of One New York Plaza. Consequently, because the critical concern of forfeiture or unjust enrichment is simply not present in this case, we are not presented with an occasion to consider whether the doctrine of substantial performance is applicable, that is, whether the courts should intervene to excuse the nonoccurrence of a condition precedent to the formation of a contract.

The essence of the Appellate Division's holding is that the substantial performance doctrine is universally applicable to all categories of breach of contract, including the nonoccurrence of an express condition precedent. However, as discussed, substantial performance is ordinarily not applicable to excuse the nonoccurrence of an express condition precedent.

. . .

Plaintiff's reliance on the well-known case of *Jacob & Youngs v Kent* (230 NY 239) is misplaced. There, a contractor built a summer residence and the buyer refused to pay the remaining balance of the contract price on the ground that the contractor used a different type of pipe than was specified in the contract. The buyer sought to enforce the contract as written. This would have involved the demolition of large parts of the structure at great expense and loss to the seller. This Court, in an opinion by then-Judge Cardozo, ruled for the contractor on the ground that "an omission, both trivial and innocent, will sometimes be atoned for by allowance of the resulting damage, and will not always be the breach of a condition to be followed by a forfeiture" (230 NY, at 241). But Judge Cardozo was careful to note that the situation would be different in the case of an express condition:

> "This is not to say that the parties are not free by apt and certain words to effectuate a purpose that performance of every term shall be a condition of recovery. That question is not here. This is merely to say that the law will be slow to impute the purpose, in the silence of the parties, where the significance of the default is grievously out of proportion to the oppression of the forfeiture" (*id.*, at 243–244).

The quoted language contradicts the Appellate Division's proposition that the substantial performance doctrine applies universally, including when the language of the agreement leaves no doubt that an express condition precedent was intended (*see*, 205 AD2d, at 414). More importantly, *Jacob & Youngs* lacks determinative significance here on the additional ground that plaintiff conferred no benefit upon defendant. The avoidance-of-forfeiture rationale which engendered the rule of *Jacob & Youngs* is simply not present here, and the case therefore "should not be extended by analogy where the reason for the rule fails" (*Van Iderstine Co. v Barnet Leather Co.*, 242 NY 425, 434).

The lease renewal and insurance cases relied upon by plaintiff are clearly distinguishable and explicable on the basis of the risk of forfeiture existing therein. For example, in *Sy Jack Realty Co. v Pergament Syosset Corp.* (27 NY2d 449, 452), this Court gave effect to a late notice of lease renewal. Importantly, while we reaffirmed the general rule "that notice, when required to be 'given' by a certain date, is insufficient and ineffectual if not received within the time specified," we held that the prior courts properly invoked the rule that equity "relieves against ... forfeitures of valuable lease terms when default in notice has not prejudiced the landlord" (id., quoting *Jones v Gianferante*, 305 NY 135, 138; *see also, J. N. A. Realty Corp. v Cross Bay Chelsea*, 42 NY2d 392, 397 ["when a tenant in possession under an existing lease has neglected to ... renew, he might suffer a forfeiture if he has made valuable improvements on the property"]). We stated: "Since a long-standing location for a retail business is an important part of the good will of that enterprise, the tenant stands to lose a substantial and valuable asset" (*id.*, 22 NY2d, at 453).

III.

In sum, the letter agreement provides in the clearest language that the parties did not intend to form a contract "unless and until" defendant received written notice of the prime landlord's consent on or before February 25, 1987. Defendant would lease the 33rd floor from plaintiff only on the condition that the landlord consent in writing to a telephone communication linkage system between the 29th and 33rd floors and to defendant's plans for construction effectuating that linkage. This matter was sufficiently important to defendant that it would not enter into the sublease "unless and until" the condition was satisfied. Inasmuch as we are not dealing here with a situation where plaintiff stands to suffer some forfeiture or undue hardship, we perceive no justification for engaging in a "materiality-of-the-nonoccurrence" analysis. To do so would simply frustrate the clearly expressed intention of the parties. Freedom of contract prevails in an arm's length transaction between sophisticated parties such as these, and in the absence of countervailing public policy concerns there is no reason to relieve them of the consequences of their bargain. If they are dissatisfied with the consequences of their agreement, "the time to say so [was] at the bargaining table" (*Maxton, supra*, at 382).

Finally, the issue of substantial performance was not for the jury to resolve in this case. A determination whether there has been substantial performance is to be answered, "if the inferences are certain, by the judges of the law" (*Jacob & Youngs v Kent*, 230 NY 239, 243, supra).

Accordingly, the order of the Appellate Division should be reversed, with costs, and the complaint dismissed.

---

2. Excuse of Conditions

As the court in the preceding case acknowledged, a condition can be excused by a court if the condition violates public policy or if it will cause a "disproportionate forfeiture" of the benefit of the bargain expected by one of the parties. *See* Restatement (Second) of Contracts §§ 185, 229.

For example, Mitchell promises to sell a condominium to his daughter Leeza for $120,000 on the condition that she divorce her husband. In all jurisdictions, a contract term encouraging divorce is against public policy. In this case, a court could excuse the condition or it could declare the entire contract unenforceable under the doctrine of public policy that we examined in Chapter Six. Notice the different result: If the court excuses the condition, then Mitchell is obligated to sell the condominium to Leeza for $120,000; if the court declares the entire contract unenforceable, Mitchell does not have to sell Leeza the condominium.

A second basis for excusing a condition and imposing liability is based in good faith and fair dealing. When the party has unjustly prevented the condition from happening or otherwise contributed to the failure of a condition that would trigger that party's liability the court will excuse the condition. For example, a seller tried to assert that it was not obligated to sell real property to prospective buyers because the buyers had not met the deadline to qualify for a mortgage loan. This assertion against its obligation to sell was disallowed because the seller may have substantially hindered the loan approval process. *Khadka v. American Home Mortg. Servicing, Inc.*, 37 Misc.3d 1214 (2012).

In addition, a court will excuse the condition and impose liability when one party to the contract stands to lose a great deal and the condition is relatively minor. This is most likely to occur when one side has performed on the contract and the other side received those services and benefited from them. So, for example, in *Visual Software Solutions, et al. v. Managed Healthcare Associates, et al.*, 2001 WL 1159741 (E.D. Pa. 2001), one company acquired another and entered into employment contracts with the founders of the acquired company. Payments under the acquisition contract were conditioned on the former owners/employees periodically submitting "Certificates of Compliance," evidence that they had complied with the terms of their employment contracts. The employees failed to submit a Certificate of Compliance and the employer refused to make the periodic payment, even though the employees had, in fact, complied with their employment contracts. The court excused the condition to avoid disproportionate forfeiture and required the buyer/employer to make the payment. *But c.f., Dove v. Rose Acre Farms*, 434 N.E. 2d. 931 (1982) (employee who was eligible for bonus could not recover because he did not satisfy condition that he be present at work every day.)

Although courts can excuse a condition, before resorting to an overt act of judicial activism, courts prefer to use interpretive strategies to avoid a disproportionate forfeiture. A court will treat the clause not as a condition, but rather as a promise. The court in the following case, *MidAmerica Construction Management, Inc. v. Mastec North America, Inc.*, cites the Texas Court of Appeals' consideration of this presumptive strategy.

MidAmerica Construction concerns a dispute over payments to a subcontractor. The dispute involves the conditional payment clauses included in many construction contracts. The clauses are designed to protect a general contractor who has obligations to pay subcontractors, but who wants to wait until receiving its payment on the general contract before paying the subcontractors. The court describes two types of express conditions: "pay-if-paid" and "pay-when-paid." Despite the similarity in these terms, they are treated very differently. The court also discusses the fact that some states have enacted limitations on these terms and two state courts refuse to enforce the terms as against public policy.

MidAmerica Construction Management, Inc. v. Mastec North America, Inc., a Florida Corporation and Renegade of Idaho, Inc.

U.S. Court of Appeals
436 F.3d 1257 (10th Cir. 2006)

DAVID M. EBEL, CIRCUIT JUDGE

In this case, we must determine whether a contract between two defendant general contractors and a plaintiff subcontractor requires the general contractors to pay the subcontractor for the work the subcontractor performed only if the general contractors are first paid on their own contract with the project owner. In making this determination, we address the type of language that constitutes a "pay-if-paid" clause under both Texas and New Mexico law in a contract for a private-sector construction project.

We Affirm the district court's grant of summary judgment to Defendants MasTec North America, Inc. ("MasTec") and Renegade of Idaho, Inc. ("Renegade") on the claim of

Plaintiff MidAmerica Construction Management, Inc. ("MidAmerica") that Defendants breached their contract with Plaintiff by refusing to pay Plaintiff for the work Plaintiff performed under the contract. We do so because we determine that (1) the contract contains a "pay-if-paid" clause; (2) this clause is enforceable under both Texas and New Mexico law; and (3) as a result, Defendants need not at the present time pay Plaintiff for the work that Plaintiff performed under the contract, because Defendants have not been paid by project owner PathNet, Inc. ("PathNet") for that work.

Background

PathNet hired Defendant Renegade to help construct the New Mexico and Texas portions of a fiber optic network. Defendant MasTec subsequently purchased Renegade. On January 31, 2001, Defendants hired Plaintiff as a subcontractor to help install a buried conduit for fiber optic line. The parties' agreement was embodied in a written contract (the "Subcontract Agreement").

Plaintiff began performing under the Subcontract Agreement. Defendants made an initial payment of approximately $127,000 to Plaintiff in March 2001 for work performed in January and February of that year. However, after PathNet filed for bankruptcy in April 2001, Defendants refused to make any further payments to Plaintiff because Defendants asserted that they had not received payment from PathNet for the work Plaintiff performed.

In November 2003, Plaintiff brought suit against Defendants in the United States District Court for the Western District of Oklahoma, contending that Defendants owed it approximately $1.9 million for work performed under the Subcontract Agreement. The district court denied Plaintiff's motion for partial summary judgment and granted Defendants' counter-motion for summary judgment on all Plaintiff's claims. Specifically, the district court held that a provision in the Subcontract Agreement that provides that "all payments to Subcontractor by Contractor are expressly contingent upon and subject to receipt of payment for the work by Contractor from Owner," was unambiguous and makes Defendants (Contractor) receipt of payment for the work from PathNet (Owner) a condition precedent to payment of Plaintiff (Subcontractor). Thus, unless and until Defendants receive payment for the work in question from PathNet, Defendants have no duty to pay Plaintiff and Plaintiff acquires no right to enforce the promise of payment.

The court stated that:

> applying either New Mexico or Texas law or the law of both states, the court enforces the contract as written and holds that Defendants have no obligation to pay Plaintiff unless or until PathNet pays Defendants.

...

Plaintiff appealed from the district court's order and judgment.

Discussion

I. Jurisdiction, Standard of Review, and Choice of Law

...

As is explained more fully below, we conclude that the Subcontract Agreement contains a "pay-if-paid" clause that is enforceable under both Texas and New Mexico law, making PathNet's payment of Defendants a condition precedent to Defendants' obligation to pay Plaintiff. Enforcing this clause does not yield a result that violates the law or public policy of Oklahoma. There are no Oklahoma cases interpreting "pay-if-paid" clauses, *See* John B. Hayes, Survey of Payment Provision and Trust Fund Statute: Oklahoma, 24 Construction Law. 20 (2004)—and thus there are no Oklahoma cases stating that Oklahoma does not enforce such clauses. One frequently-cited Tenth Circuit case applying Oklahoma law, *Byler v. Great Am. Ins. Co.*, 395 F.2d 273 (10th Cir. 1968), suggests that Oklahoma courts would enforce a contractual provision that conditions payment upon the happening of a future event—such as payment of a general contractor by a project owner—if required to do so by plain and unambiguous contractual language. *See id.* at 276–77; *See also United States v. Mann*, 197 F.2d 39, 40–42 (10th Cir. 1952); *Moore v. Continental Cas. Co.*, 366 F. Supp. 954, 955–56 (W.D. Okla. 1973). There is no constitutional or statutory prohibition against "pay-if-paid" clauses in Oklahoma.[3] Therefore, we apply Texas and New Mexico law in interpreting the Subcontract Agreement.

II. The "Pay-if-Paid" Clause in the Subcontract Agreement

A. Legal and Contractual Framework

Construction contracts often contain provisions referred to as "pay-when-paid" and "pay-if-paid" clauses. *See* Robert F. Carney & Adam Cizek, Payment Provisions in Construction Contracts and Construction Trust Fund Statutes: A Fifty-State Survey, 24 Construction Law. 5 (2004). Courts have not uniformly applied these terms. *See id.* ("Some courts refer to both provisions as 'pay-when-paid' clauses …"). Still, the terms "pay-when-paid" and "pay-if-paid" refer to distinct types of contractual clauses:

> A typical "pay-when-paid" clause might read: "Contractor shall pay subcontractor within seven days of contractor's receipt of payment from the owner." Under such a provision in a construction subcontract, a contractor's obligation to pay the subcontractor is triggered upon receipt of payment from the owner. Most courts hold that this type of clause at least means that the contractor's obligation to make payment is suspended for a reasonable amount of time for the contractor to receive payment from the owner. The theory is that a "pay-when-paid" clause creates a timing mechanism only. Such a clause does not create a condition precedent to the obligation to ever make payment, and it does not expressly shift the risk of the owner's nonpayment to the subcontractor. …
>
> A typical "pay-if-paid" clause might read: "Contractor's receipt of payment from the owner is a condition precedent to contractor's obligation to make

---

3. As is explained more fully below, statutory prohibitions against "pay-if-paid" clauses typically take one of two forms: an anti-waiver provision in a state's mechanic's lien statute, or an outright ban on conditional payment provisions. Some legislatures also restrict the application of "pay-if-paid" clauses in order to permit subcontractors to pursue bond claims or lien actions. However, the Oklahoma legislature has not adopted any such measures that relate to "pay-if-paid" clauses in contracts for private-sector construction projects.

In November 2004—after the parties entered into the Subcontract Agreement, Plaintiff brought suit against Defendants, and the district court granted summary judgment to Defendants—the Oklahoma legislature's Fair Pay for Construction Act took effect. *See* Okla. Stat. tit. 15, §§ 621–627 (2004), *renumbered as* tit. 61, §§ 221–227 (2005). The act provides that:

> the following are against the public policy of this state and are void and unenforceable:
> 1. A provision, covenant, clause or understanding in, collateral to or affecting a construction contract that makes the contract subject to the laws of another state or that requires any litigation, arbitration or other dispute resolution proceeding arising from the contract to be conducted in another state;…

Okla. Stat. tit. 15, § 627(B). We need not decide whether the act applies retroactively to the Subcontract Agreement because the act provides that " 'construction contract' means a written contract or subcontract awarded … for the purpose of making any public improvements or constructing any public building or making repairs to or performing maintenance on the same." Id. tit. 15, § 622(1); tit. 61, § 222 (emphasis added). Thus, the act could not apply to the Subcontract Agreement, which is for the purpose of constructing a private fiber optic network.

payment to the subcontractor; the subcontractor expressly assumes the risk of the owner's nonpayment and the subcontract price includes this risk." Under a "pay-if-paid" provision in a construction contract, receipt of payment by the contractor from the owner is an express condition precedent to the contractor's obligation to pay the subcontractor. A "pay-if-paid" provision in a construction subcontract is meant to shift the risk of the owner's nonpayment under the subcontract from the contractor to the subcontractor. In many jurisdictions, courts will enforce a "pay-if-paid" provision only if that language is clear and unequivocal. Judges generally will find that a "pay-if-paid" provision does not create a condition precedent, but rather a reasonable timing provision, where the "pay-if-paid" provision is ambiguous.

Id. at 5–6 (footnotes omitted).

In this case, the Subcontract Agreement provides:

Upon final acceptance of the Work by Contractor and Owner, Contractor will pay Subcontractor for the Work at the prices and schedule and in the manner described on the Work Order(s); provided that, all payments to Subcontractor by Contractor are expressly contingent upon and subject to receipt of payment for the Work by Contractor from Owner, even if (a) Contractor has posted a payment bond with Owner or (b) the Primary Contract is on a "cost plus" or other reimbursement basis requiring the Contractor to pay subcontractors prior to being reimbursed by Owner.

B. Interpretation Under Texas Law

The Texas Supreme Court has not definitively determined where the line between "pay-if-paid" and "pay-when-paid" clauses should be drawn....

In *Gulf Construction Co. v. Self*, 676 S.W.2d 624 (Tex. Ct. App. 1984), the Texas Court of Appeals stated:

A condition precedent may be either a condition to the formation of a contract or to an obligation to perform an existing agreement. Conditions may, therefore, relate either to the formation of contracts or liability under them. Conditions precedent to an obligation to perform are those acts or events, which occur subsequently to the making of the contract, that must occur before there is a right to immediate performance and before there is a breach of contractual duty. While no particular words are necessary for the existence of a condition, such terms as "if," "provide that," "on condition that," or some other phrase that conditions performance, usually connote an intent for a condition rather than a promise. In the absence of such a limiting clause, whether a certain contractual provision is a condition, rather than a promise, must be gathered from the contract as a whole and from the intent of the parties.... Where the intent of the parties is doubtful or where a condition would impose an absurd or impossible result, then the agreement should be interpreted as creating a covenant rather than a condition. Also, it is a rule of construction that a forfeiture, by finding a condition precedent, is to be avoided when possible under another reasonable reading of the contract.... The rule ... is that:

Since forfeitures are not favored, courts are inclined to construe the provisions in a contract as covenants rather than as conditions. If the terms of the contract are fairly susceptible of an interpretation which will prevent a forfeiture, they will be so construed.

> Generally, a writing is construed most strictly against its author and in such a manner as to reach a reasonable result consistent with the apparent intention of the parties.

Id. at 627–28 (citations omitted); *see also Criswell v. European Crossroads Shopping Ctr., Ltd.*, 792 S.W.2d 945, 948 (Tex. 1990) (laying out the interpretive approach to be used in resolving a dispute between an owner and an engineer using nearly identical language).

In this case, as noted above, the Subcontract Agreement provides that "all payments to Subcontractor by Contractor are expressly contingent upon and subject to receipt of payment for the Work by Contractor from Owner, even if ... the Primary Contract is on a 'cost plus' or other reimbursement basis requiring the Contractor to pay subcontractors prior to being reimbursed by Owner." The Subcontract Agreement contains the necessary conditional language to make PathNet's payment of Defendants a condition precedent to Defendants' obligation to pay Plaintiff. Instead of using timing-related terms like "until," which are indicative of a "pay-when-paid" clause, *cf. Self,* 676 S.W.2d at 627, the Subcontract Agreement uses phrases associated with conditionality. Indeed, the phrases "expressly contingent upon" and "subject to" in the Subcontract Agreement are similar to the words "if," "provide that," and "on condition that" cited in Self as being indicative of the creation of a condition precedent. *See* Black's Law Dictionary (8th ed. 2004) (defining "contingent" as "dependent on something else; conditional"); *see also A.J. Wolfe Co. v. Baltimore Contractors,* 244 N.E.2d 717, 720–21 (Mass. 1969) ("In the absence of a clear provision that payment to the subcontractor is to be directly contingent upon the receipt by the general contractor of payment from the owner, such a provision should be viewed only as postponing payment by the general contractor for a reasonable time after requisition....") (emphasis added). While the Subcontract Agreement might have been more explicit, *cf. Carney & Cizek, supra* (noting that a typical "pay-if-paid" clause might state that "the subcontractor expressly assumes the risk of the owner's nonpayment and the subcontract price includes this risk"), the Subcontract Agreement's failure to say all that it might have said is not enough to throw the intent of the contracting parties into doubt. *Cf. Self,* 676 S.W.2d at 628.

. . .

Case law from other jurisdictions does not provide "convincing evidence," *Thermatool Corp.,* 278 F.3d at 1132, that the Texas Supreme Court would not employ the *Self* approach. In *Thomas J. Dyer Co. v. Bishop International Engineering Co.,* 303 F.2d 655, 661 (6th Cir. 1962)—the seminal case on the enforceability of "pay-if-paid" or "pay-when-paid" clauses—the Sixth Circuit stated:

> Normally and legally, the insolvency of the owner will not defeat the claim of the subcontractor against the general contractor. Accordingly, in order to transfer this normal credit risk incurred by the general contractor from the general contractor to the subcontractor, the contract between the general contractor and subcontractor should contain an express condition clearly showing that to be the intention of the parties.

Id. at 660–61; ... The fact that the approach used in Dyer and its progeny is similar to the *Self* approach lends credence to the conclusion that the Texas Supreme Court would employ the *Self* approach.

. . .

Thus, the clear conditional language in the Subcontract Agreement marks it as a "pay-if-paid" clause enforceable under Texas law. As such, we hold that under Texas law

Defendants are not obligated to pay Plaintiff for the work that Plaintiff performed under the Subcontract Agreement unless and until PathNet pays Defendants for that work.

C. Interpretation Under New Mexico Law

No New Mexico court has yet determined the enforceability of a "pay-if-paid" or "pay-when-paid" provision. Both parties contend that a recent New Mexico statute—the Retainage Act, N.M. Stat. Ann. §§ 57-28-1-57-28-11—sheds light on the way that the New Mexico Supreme Court would interpret the Subcontract Agreement. The Retainage Act states, in pertinent part, that:

> all construction contracts shall provide that payment for amounts due, except for retainage, shall be paid within twenty-one days after the owner receives an undisputed request for payment.... All construction contracts shall provide that contractors and subcontractors make prompt payment to their subcontractors and suppliers for amounts owed for work performed on the construction project within seven days after receipt of payment from the owner, contractor or sub-contractor.... These payment provisions apply to all tiers of contractors, sub-contractors, and suppliers.

N.M. Stat. Ann. § 57-28-5(A), (C).

Plaintiff argues that because the Retainage Act mandates prompt payment to subcontractors, New Mexico would be likely to find that a "pay-if-paid" clause in a contract for a private-sector construction project—a clause that might interfere with payments to subcontractors—is against public policy. Defendants argue that the text of the act, by including the phrase "after receipt of payment from the owner," endorses contingent payments.

However, the fact that the New Mexico legislature has enacted this provision sheds little light on whether a New Mexico court would enforce a bargained-for "pay-if-paid" clause in a contract for a private-sector construction project. *See Statesville Roofing & Heating Co. v. Duncan*, 702 F. Supp. 118, 122 (W.D.N.C. 1988) (noting that a prior version of North Carolina's equivalent of the Retainage Act "addresses only the issue of what is to be done when the general [contractor] has already been paid. It says nothing about what happens when the owner does not pay.").[4]

Thus, we must look outside New Mexico for guidance on how the New Mexico Supreme Court would interpret the Subcontract Agreement. As noted above, the general weight and trend of authority holds that enforceable "pay-if-paid" clauses may be created in contracts for private-sector construction projects by using language clearly indicating the intent to create a condition precedent. *See also* Richard A. Lord, 8 Williston on Contracts § 19:58 (2004) ("It has long been the rule that, if the parties clearly do intend that the risk of nonpayment be borne by the subcontractor, and clearly express that intent by making the right of the subcontractor to be paid expressly conditional on the receipt of such payment by the contractor from the owner, they may by contract allocate that risk, and the courts will enforce that freely bargained-for allocation of risk."). Only a handful of states have determined that clearly drafted "pay-if-paid" clauses in contracts for pri-vate-sector construction projects are not enforceable on public policy grounds. Since it appears that the New Mexico Supreme Court would not find a clearly drafted "pay-if-

---

4. Neither party contends that the Texas equivalent of the Retainage Act, Tex. Prop. Code Ann. §§ 28.001–28.010, sheds light on the way that the Texas Supreme Court would interpret the Subcontract Agreement. If the parties were to make such an argument, the argument would fail for the reasons discussed in connection with this analysis of the New Mexico Retainage Act.

paid" clause in a contract for a private-sector construction project unenforceable for the reasons expressed by these other states, it follows that the New Mexico Supreme Court likely would find the "pay-if-paid" clause in the Subcontract Agreement to be enforceable under New Mexico law. *See* Hendrick, Spangler & Wedge, *supra*, at 23 ("Except for those states where conditional payment provisions are unenforceable as a matter of public policy, a conditional payment provision will be enforced if the clause utilizes the term 'condition' or 'condition precedent,' and if it is clear and unambiguous that the subcontractor assumed the risk of owner nonpayment."); *see also id.* at 27 ("Except for the jurisdictions which have, by statute, barred conditional payment provisions, all courts enforce 'pay-if-paid' clauses, particularly where they are unambiguous, and clearly provide that payment from the owner is a condition precedent to payment to the subcontractor.").

The highest courts in two states have voided "pay-if-paid" provisions in contracts for private-sector construction projects as against public policy because such clauses violate the antiwaiver protections in the states' mechanic's lien statutes. *See William R. Clarke Corp. v. Safeco Ins. Co.*, 938 P.2d 372, 374 (Cal. 1997) ("Pay if paid provisions ... are contrary to the public policy of this state and therefore unenforceable because they effect an impermissible indirect waiver or forfeiture of the subcontractors' constitutionally protected mechanic's lien rights in the event of nonpayment by the owner."); *West-Fair Elec. Contractors v. Aetna Cas. & Sur. Co.*, 661 N.E.2d 967, 971 (N.Y. 1995) ("[A] pay-when-paid provision which forces the subcontractor to assume the risk that the owner will fail to pay the general contractor is void and unenforceable as contrary to public policy set forth in the Lien Law § 34 [which states that 'any contract, agreement or understanding whereby the right to file or enforce any [mechanic's] lien ... is waived, shall be void as against public policy and wholly unenforceable'].”). However, because New Mexico does not have an express antiwaiver provision in its mechanic's lien laws, cf. N.M. Stat. Ann. § 48-2A-12(B) (referring to a "signed waiver of lien"), the reasoning in *Clarke* and *West-Fair* does not apply....

Some state legislatures have prohibited conditional payment provisions in contracts for private-sector construction projects. *See* N.C. Gen. Stat. § 22C-2 ("Payment by the owner to a contractor is not a condition precedent for payment to a subcontractor and payment by a contractor to a subcontractor is not a condition precedent for payment to any other subcontractor, and an agreement to the contrary is unenforceable."); Wis. Stat. § 779.135(3) (rendering void "provisions making a payment to a general contractor from any person who does not have a contractual agreement with the subcontractor or supplier a condition precedent to a general contractor's payment to a subcontractor or a supplier"). However, the New Mexico legislature has enacted no statutory measure analogous to those adopted by these other states. In the absence of guidance from the New Mexico legislature, we decline to craft a state policy prohibiting the use of clearly worded "pay-if-paid" clauses.

Thus, it appears that the New Mexico Supreme Court would interpret the Subcontract Agreement as containing an enforceable "pay-if-paid" clause and would enforce the clear condition in this contract as drafted by the parties. As such, we hold that under New Mexico law Defendants are not obligated to pay Plaintiff for the work that Plaintiff performed under the Subcontract Agreement unless and until PathNet pays Defendants for that work.

III. Defendants' Partial Payment to Plaintiff

Plaintiff argues that a partial payment that Defendants made to Plaintiff establishes that the parties intended that Plaintiff should be paid regardless of whether Defendants were paid by PathNet. Plaintiff's argument fails under both Texas and New Mexico law.

Under Texas law,

if a written contract is worded so that it can be given a definite or certain legal meaning, then it is unambiguous. An ambiguity does not arise simply because the parties offer conflicting interpretations. Rather, a contract is ambiguous only if two or more meanings are genuinely possible after application of the pertinent rules of interpretation to the face of the instrument. Parol evidence is not admissible for the purpose of creating an ambiguity. Only when a contract is first determined to be ambiguous may the court admit extraneous evidence to determine the true meaning of the instrument.

Coastal Mart, Inc. v. Southwestern Bell Telephone Co., 154 S.W.3d 839, 843 (Tex. App. 2005). In this case, the Subcontract Agreement's consideration of whether payment from PathNet is a condition precedent to Defendants' obligation to pay Plaintiff "can be given a definite or certain legal meaning." Thus, under Texas law external evidence like the partial payment may not be considered in interpreting the alleged "pay-if-paid" clause in the agreement.

Under New Mexico law:

an ambiguity exists in an agreement when the parties' expressions of mutual assent lack clarity. The question whether an agreement contains an ambiguity is a matter of law to be decided by the trial court. The court may consider collateral evidence of the circumstances surrounding the execution of the agreement in determining whether the language of the agreement is unclear. If the evidence presented is so plain that no reasonable person could hold any way but one, then the court may interpret the meaning as a matter of law.

Mark V, Inc. v. Mellekas, 114 N.M. 778, 845 P.2d 1232, 1235 (N.M. 1993) (citations omitted). Because the partial payment made here was not part of the circumstances surrounding the execution of the contract, this post-formation conduct would not be considered by New Mexico for the purposes of creating an ambiguity under the contract. In any event, that payment does not shed light on Defendants' intent in contracting. The fact that Defendants made a single partial payment to Plaintiff before receiving payment from PathNet may be attributable to a host of factors, including a desire to maintain a cooperative working relationship with Plaintiff, provide an incentive for Plaintiff's continued performance, or allow Plaintiff operating capital to purchase supplies. Defendants' single partial payment does not signal a desire on the part of Defendants to be liable for all payments to Plaintiff even if PathNet did not pay Defendants. The payment neither creates an ambiguity in the agreement nor provides evidence of the parties' intent sufficient to overcome the indication of Defendants' intent expressed in the plain text of the Subcontract Agreement.

Therefore, the partial payment that Defendants made to Plaintiff does not establish that the parties intended that Plaintiff should be paid regardless of whether Defendants were paid by PathNet. As such, the payment does not disturb our conclusion that under both Texas and New Mexico law Defendants are not obligated to pay Plaintiff for the work that Plaintiff performed under the Subcontract Agreement unless and until PathNet pays Defendants for that work.[5]

---

5. Plaintiff does not raise the argument that the partial payment modified or waived the alleged "pay-if-paid" clause, stating in its brief that:

[Defendants] ... and the district court ... discuss this [partial payment] issue in terms of waiver and rely on the provision in the Subcontract Agreement providing that the contract "may not be amended except by a writing...." ... However, [Plaintiff]'s argument in this regard is not based on waiver. Rather, [Plaintiff] asserts only that the payment is evidence of the parties' intent and their interpretation of their obligations pursuant to the Subcontract

IV. The "Termination Clause" in the Subcontract Agreement

Our conclusion that the parties intended PathNet's payment of Defendants to be a condition precedent to Defendants' obligation to pay Plaintiff is buttressed by an additional clause in the Subcontract Agreement that provides:

> If the Primary Contract to which a Work Order refers is terminated, suspended or delayed for any reason.... Subcontractor will only be entitled to recover from Owner such amounts as are payable to Contractor for the portion of the Work completed by Subcontractor, less Contractor's anticipated gross profit from the work. Subcontractor is not entitled to mobilization, start-up, demobilization or other amounts, or consequential, special, incidental, liquidated or punitive damages, or for commercial loss or lost profits, unless such amounts or damages are awarded to Contractor, in which case Subcontractor may recover such amounts or damages for the portion of the Work completed by Subcontractor less the same percentage constituting Contractor's gross profit retained by Contractor from all other amounts payable by Owner. Subcontractor will not be entitled to any other remedy for a termination, suspension or delay under this Section ... including any amounts directly from Contractor. (Emphasis added.)

We need not and do not consider whether this provision — which the court below characterized as a "termination clause" — is sufficient on its own to constitute an enforceable "pay-if-paid" clause. Rather, the termination clause sheds light on the parties' intent in agreeing to the "expressly contingent" language in the "pay-if-paid" provision discussed above. The termination clause makes clear that following the termination, suspension, or delay of the contract between PathNet and Defendants, Plaintiff's remedy under nearly all circumstances is to seek reimbursement from PathNet — not Defendants.[6] There is no definition in the Subcontract Agreement for the phrase "terminated, suspended or delayed," nor are the words used in the phrase defined individually. However, the fact that the phrase is part of the larger expression "terminated, suspended or delayed for any reason" makes clear that the phrase is to be given a broad reading. Thus, the termination clause

---

Agreement and the provision for payment contained in the work order.

Accordingly, we need not consider this issue. Even if we were to consider whether the payment modified the Subcontract Agreement, we would find, like the district court, that because the Subcontract Agreement provides that it "may not be amended except by a writing signed by each of the parties," and may not be modified or waived except in a writing signed by both parties, Defendants' single payment to Plaintiff could not effect a modification or waiver of the payment term making payment of Plaintiff "expressly contingent upon and subject to receipt of payment" by Defendants from PathNet.

To the extent that Plaintiff argues that a work order issued by Defendants to Plaintiff modifies or waives the "pay-if-paid" clause in the Subcontract Agreement, that argument is without merit. The fact that the work order does not reiterate the "pay-if-paid" clause, and instead states only that Plaintiff must present a release of lien before final payment will be made, does not undercut the condition precedent created by the "pay-if-paid" clause. In general such an order does not alter the main terms of the contract, but rather serves as an execution document under the contract. For a work order to alter a condition precedent to payment under a contract, the order must contain a more direct expression of an intent to modify those terms than does the work order in this case. Any tension between the work order's requirement that Plaintiff present a release of lien before receiving final payment, and the original contract's statement that Plaintiff waived all lien rights on signing the contract, is irrelevant for purposes of interpreting the "pay-if-paid" clause.

6. Based on the termination clause, it is at least arguable that Plaintiff should be able to seek a recovery directly from Defendants if Defendants are awarded mobilization, start-up, demobilization or other amounts, or consequential, special, incidental, liquidated or punitive damages, or commercial loss or lost profits. However, we need not conclusively determine whether this is the case because there is no indication in the record that Defendants were awarded such sums.

was triggered by PathNet's breach of its contract with Renegade based on PathNet's bankruptcy, even though PathNet did not formally negotiate an end to the contract. Therefore, the termination clause supports our conclusion that since PathNet terminated its contract with Defendants without paying Defendants for Plaintiff's work, Plaintiff cannot now seek to recover from Defendants the amount that Plaintiff asserts it is owed.

Conclusion

For the foregoing reasons, we AFFIRM the judgment of the district court.

---

3. Waiver of Conditions

The following case involves Timothy Munro's claim against Kenneth Woodring for a sewer line connection. Munro's claim depends on a finding that the condition that would trigger Woodring's liability occurred or was waived. In the context of a conditional obligation (here, the obligation to connect the sewer if required by the county) courts define "waiver" as "the intentional relinquishment of a known right." Thus, a waiver requires 1) the existence of a right, advantage or benefit; 2) actual or constructive knowledge of the existence of the right; and 3) an intention to relinquish the right. As we saw in our examination of agreed modifications in Chapter Eight, a waiver may be expressed in words or implied from the conduct of the party such that the other party would believe that a right has been given up intentionally. The court found that Woodring expressly waived the condition by agreeing to cover any costs related to the sewer connection instead of pursuing or preserving an option to pursue the exemption from Sussex County. Notice that the court in this case refers to a "condition precedent," even though as noted above, the *Restatement (Second)* rejects this distinction.

Timothy J. Munro v. Beazer Home Corporation Kenwood Development LLC & Kenneth S. Woodring

Court Of Common Pleas of Delaware, Sussex
2011 Del. C.P. LEXIS 16, 2011 WL 2651910 (Not Reported in A.3d)

ROSEMARY BETTS BEAUREGARD, JUDGE

Plaintiff Timothy Munro brings this action for damages alleging that defendants promised to connect his property to the Fenwick Island Sewer District and failed to do so. In addition to breach of contract against all parties, Munro brings an action in fraud against Defendant Kenneth Woodring and an action in quantum meruit against Defendant Beazer Homes Corporation. Both defendants deny liability or, in the alternative, assert the other is liable. Finally, the parties stipulate that Woodring's sole proprietorship, Kenwood Development Co., is a nominal party only and that Woodring assumed personal liability for all Kenwood contracts material to the litigation.

There are essentially two issues: (1) Was Woodring or Beazer contractually obligated to connect Munro's home to the Fenwick Island Sewer District; and (2) if so, did Munro suffer any damages?

At the conclusion of the trial on this matter, the Court reserved decision and requested that the parties submit their closing arguments in writing. After carefully reviewing the parties' submissions, the Court finds in favor of Munro and Beazer and against Woodring for the reasons stated herein.

Factual Background

Woodring is a Maryland-based real estate developer who, during the late 1990s, operated in Sussex County, Delaware. Woodring, with the help of two third-party investors, purchased a parcel of land now known as Ashley Manor for approximately $300,000.

The Ashley Manor parcel is located northwest of Fenwick Island, a popular beach community. Woodring and his investors purchased the parcel with the intention of developing it into a large residential community, complete with a community pool and club house. As for the prospective residents, Woodring envisaged their "average age ... [to be] between 65 and 75. Not the type of people to be running thru [sic] the woods ..."; that is to say, Woodring intended to create a relaxing retirement community by the beach.

Before Woodring could begin construction of the Ashley Manor development, however, he needed to rezone the parcel. At the time of its purchase, Ashley Manor sat in an agricultural residential district. This would not suit the large retirement community planned by Woodring. Thus, Woodring and his landscape architects submitted an application to the Sussex County Council to rezone the Ashley Manor parcel into a high density residential district.

Woodring's application was a partial success. The Sussex County Council agreed to rezone the Ashley Manor parcel into a high density residential district on the condition that Woodring connect it and adjacent properties to the Fenwick Island Sanitary Sewer District. Satisfaction of this condition required the approval of adjacent landowners whose properties were served by privately owned septic systems.

Woodring's architects first proposed to accomplish the necessary connection through a series of subterranean easements. Pursuant to this proposal, Woodring planned to run eight-inch diameter pipes from the Ashley Manor parcel in a southeasterly direction across adjacent properties and, ultimately, connect the pipes to a pump station within the Sewer District. One of these planned easements would run through the property of Timothy Munro.

Munro did not share Woodring's desire to bring sewer services to the area. It was Munro's view that his new septic system capably served his needs and he did not want to pay any additional expenses associated with a sewer connection. Moreover, Munro feared that the future residents of Ashley Manor would trespass across his land by way of the proposed easement toward a convenience store located across the street. Accordingly, Munro objected to Woodring's initial plan.

In response, Woodring submitted a new proposal that avoided the need for an easement across Munro's property. The new proposal, however, did not avoid the annexation of Munro's property into the Sewer District. Thus, Woodring still required Munro's acquiescence to the plan.

The rezoning was vital to Woodring's success with the Ashley Manor project. Woodring, therefore, approached Munro to gain his approval. After some negotiation, Munro agreed to remove this objection of Woodring's second proposal as consideration for the first of two agreements ("first contract"):

> In consideration for your cooperation in the expansion of the sewer district, we hereby agree to be responsible for any monetary impact this may have on your property. This would include Front Foot Benefit Charges, increase in property taxes and if required, connection fees and cost of sewer service.

Sussex County allows for exemptions for sewer connections under certain circumstances. Kenwood Development Co. [i.e., Woodring's sole proprietorship] accepts the responsibility for filing any documents if an exemption is required.

This agreement will be for a period of 10 years from date of sewer services availability.

Pursuant to this agreement, Munro sent a letter to Sussex County Council and removed his objection to Woodring's second proposal. Woodring, however, never sought an exemption on behalf of Munro.

Despite his contractual obligation to withhold his opposition to the Sewer District expansion, Munro renewed his objection less than one year later at a public hearing. Evidently, Munro still had concerns, perhaps new concerns, regarding the expansion of the Sewer District. The Council, therefore, reserved its decision on Woodring's second proposal and provided Woodring and Munro an opportunity to discuss possible solutions. The parties' negotiations produced a second agreement ("second contract"):

> As we discussed ... the expansion of the sewer district will eliminate the possibility in the future for you to construct a replacement LPP septic system to serve your personal residence. This letter is offered to confirm an agreement we discussed as follows:
>
>> At such time that Ashley Manor residential planned community is constructed, and the gravity sewer piping is installed ... to serve Ashley Manor, a small diameter force main will be installed from [the gravity sewer] to your residence. The force main as currently envisioned will be approximately one (1) inch in diameter ... The cost of installation of the force main will be borne entirely by the Ashley Manor developer.[14]

In a subsequent letter, Woodring assured Munro that the foregoing agreement incorporated the original contract.

Munro, thereafter, removed his second objection to Woodring's proposal. As a result, the Sussex County Board adopted a resolution to expand the Sewer District to include Ashley Manor and, incidentally, the Munro property.

Despite his success in securing all the necessary approvals for the Ashley Manor development, Woodring could not maintain ownership of the project long enough to see construction begin. A business dispute between Woodring and his investors required the intervention of the Court of Chancery which resolved the conflict by ordering a partition of the property. As a result, Woodring and his fellow investors entered into negotiations with Beazer, a home builder and dealer.

Beazer ultimately agreed to purchase Ashley Manor from Woodring and his investors for $4,275,000. The Agreement of Sale contained a Due Diligence Clause whereby Beazer reserved the right to walk away freely if dissatisfied with the information provided by Woodring. The parties twice executed amendments to the agreement which, together, extended the due diligence period to over 100 days.

During this time, Woodring provided Beazer access to a series of private business documents. These documents included a federal wetlands delineation and boundary survey, a series of preliminary site plans, letters associated with an environmental impact study, letters concerning zoning approval, agreements with a local water company, and a copy of minutes from the Sussex County Council hearing wherein the Council approved the expansion of the Sewer District. To the Court's knowledge, the copy of these minutes is the only document that gives mention of Munro. The minutes do not document any obligation to connect Munro to the Sewer District.

---

14. Emphasis in original.

In addition, Beazer had access to any publicly accessible information concerning the Ashley Manor development held by State agencies. A memorandum drafted by Woodring's architects and provided to Beazer during the due diligence period recommended that "[a]dditional research should be undertaken at the Sussex County Planning and Zoning Department, Sussex County Engineering Department, Delaware Department of Transportation, Sussex Conservation District, Natural Resources Conservation Services, DNREC, and the Office of The State Fire Marshall."

The Court heard testimony that information held by these agencies contained references to the Munro-Woodring contracts. Despite the architects' recommendations, Beazer did not inspect these public resources.

After the due diligence period expired, but before settlement, Beazer assigned the Agreement of Sale to Beazer's general contractor, Ashley Manor, LLC, which ultimately settled on the property. Prior to closing, Woodring and his investors assigned "all their rights, title, and interest in all Plans and other Development Data prepared by and/or acquired by and utilized by Seller's engineer ... to secure the approval of the Preliminary Site Plan ..."

Ashley Manor, LLC began construction of the retirement community sometime after settlement and, in the process, connected it to the Sewer District. At this time, however, the subcontractor responsible for Ashley Manor's sewer connection refused to connect Munro.

Munro contacted his counsel in this case soon after it became apparent that Ashley Manor's subcontractor did not intend to connect Munro's property to the Sewer District. Munro's counsel, thereafter, dispatched a letter to both Beazer and Woodring demanding assurance that the parties intend to honor the Munro-Woodring contracts by performing a sewer connection and by paying any economic impact incurred to Munro associated with the Sewer District expansion.

In response, then-counsel for Beazer denied any knowledge of the Munro-Woodring contracts and indicated that it had no intention of performing any obligation undertaken by Woodring. Woodring, likewise, denied any liability for the Munro-Woodring contracts. Instead, Woodring stated that Beazer assumed his prior obligations at the time of its purchase of the Ashley Manor development.

At the present time, Munro's property remains unconnected to the Sewer District. Although the Court heard some testimony that it is possible for Munro to obtain an exemption from Sussex County's requirement that residents living within the Sewer District connect to the sewer, neither Munro nor any of the defendants have applied for one. Woodring, however, testified that he is ready to do so now. Even so, such exemptions are discretionary with Sussex County Council and not guaranteed. Moreover, it is clear that, even with an exemption, Munro would be required by the County to purchase a sewer connection should his septic system fail in the future.

In light of the foregoing, Munro alleges that Woodring undertook a contractual obligation to connect his home to the Sewer District and failed to do so. Alternatively, Munro argues that Beazer assumed Woodring's obligation in connection with its purchase of the Ashley Manor development. Both defendants deny liability or, in the alternative, assert that the other is liable. In addition, Munro argues that, even if Beazer did not assume a contractual obligation to connect Munro to the Sewer District, it is liable for the unjust benefit it incurred through Woodring's alleged breach. Finally, Munro brought an action against Woodring for common law fraud. The Court, however, did not hear any evidence concerning this claim. Munro's fraud claim is, therefore, dismissed at this time.

Analysis

Breach of Contract

The first issue is whether the two contracts, when read together or independently, impose an enforceable contractual obligation on Woodring to connect Munro to the Sewer District. The defendants argue that the first contract is not presently enforceable because, although it does impose such an obligation, that obligation was conditional on Munro's need to connect to the Sewer District in the first instance. The Court finds instead that Woodring waived the alleged condition through both his conduct and by express promise.

Delaware courts adhere to the objective theory of contracts. Unless a contract is ambiguous or there exists a suggestion of mistake, fraud, or duress, our courts give effect to the contract as it is written and understood by a reasonable third-party.[24] In doing so here, the Court looks only to the plain meaning of the terms found within the four corners of the agreement.[25]

In the first contract, Woodring expressly assumed liability "for any monetary impact" the sewer expansion had on Munro's property, including "connection fees and costs of sewer service ... for 10 years from date of sewer service availability." The Court finds that it was reasonable for Munro to expect, based on this language, that Woodring assumed a contractual obligation to connect Munro's property to the sewer. The additional term "if required," however, raises a supplemental issue as to whether the parties intended to make this obligation conditional.

Express language in a contract that qualifies a promise to perform upon the happening of a stated event creates what is known as a condition precedent.[27] A condition precedent is an event that, although not certain to occur, must occur before performance under a contract becomes due.[28] Courts interpret language such as "if," "as soon as," or "provided that" as the express creation of a condition. Even if such language is used and a condition precedent is created, it may be waived when a party conducts itself in such a way that evidences such an intention.[29] Consideration is not necessary to support a waiver if the condition precedent is inserted into the contract for the waiving party's benefit.[30]

The Court finds that the parties' inclusion of the phrase "if required" is sufficient for the creation of a condition precedent. Further, a reasonable interpretation of the condition is that Woodring's performance obligation arises only if Sussex County deems Munro's sewer connection necessary. This interpretation of the condition is supported by the language of the contract itself: "Sussex County allows for exemptions for sewer connections under certain circumstances. Kenwood Development Co. [i.e., Woodring's sole proprietorship] accepts the responsibility for filing any documents if an exemption is required."

Woodring argues, however, that the condition precedent has not been satisfied because Sussex County has yet to require Munro to connect to the sewer. Notwithstanding this contention, the Court finds that Woodring waived the condition precedent in two ways:

First, Woodring's conduct following execution of the contract evidences his intent to waive the condition. Woodring "accept[ed] the responsibility for filing any documents if

---

24. Osborn ex rel. v. Kemp, 991 A.2d 1153, 1159 (Del. 2010).

25. *Id.*

27. 17A Am. Jur. 2d Contracts § 455.

28. Restatement (Second) of Contracts § 224 (1981).

29. Pouls v. Windmill Estates, LLC, 2010 Del. Super. LEXIS 244, 2010 WL 2348648 (Del. Super. June 10, 2010).

30. *Id.* at n. 9; *see also,* 17A Am. Jur. 2d Contracts § 637.

an exemption is required." Woodring and his architects learned that an exemption was required only a few months after the execution of the contract upon receipt of a letter from the Sussex County Engineering Department which stated precisely that. Despite this understanding, Woodring testified that he did not bother to file the necessary exemption application with Sussex County until faced with the present litigation. If Woodring intended to secure the benefit of the condition precedent, he would have followed through with the exemption application process and made certain that a sewer connection was unnecessary.

Second, Woodring expressly waived the condition precedent through the language of the second agreement. That agreement provides that "[a]t such time that the Ashley Manor residential planned community is constructed, and that the gravity sewer piping is installed along Route 20 to serve Ashley Manor, a small diameter force main will be installed from the Route 20 gravity sewer to your residence." The language "[a]t such time" and "will be" effectively eliminate the function of the condition.

Beazer contends that the second agreement should be disregarded because it is a modification of the initial contract and lacks valid consideration. Specifically, Beazer posits that the purported consideration for the modification was Munro's promise to withhold his objection to the Sewer District expansion. Beazer argues that Munro had a preexisting duty that arose from the first contract to withhold his objection and such past consideration cannot supply new consideration for a subsequent modification.

While it is true that the modification is unenforceable because it is supported only by past consideration, lack of consideration does not bar enforcement of a waiver. Woodring inserted the condition into the initial contract for his benefit — it served as a means by which Woodring could avoid performance. His unconditional promise to undertake the sewer connection, regardless of whether or not a sewer connection was required, effectuates an express waiver of this benefit.

Accordingly, the Court finds that Woodring owed Munro an enforceable obligation to connect Munro's home to the sewer.

...

[Editors: In the omitted discussion, the Court finds Beazer is not liable either under a theory of third party assignment or quantum meruit]

Damages

As discussed above, Woodring owed Munro an obligation to connect Munro's property to the sewer. Woodring breached this obligation by repudiating the contract.[41] Accordingly, Woodring must pay Munro damages.

...

Based on the first contract, which the Court found to be enforceable, Munro reasonably expected Woodring to pay for any economic impact the expansion of the Sewer District had on his property. The parties stipulate that this includes System Connection Charges, Permit Fees, Service Charges, and Sewer Assessment Charges. These charges and fees amount to $7,413.

In addition, the Court finds that the first contract also contemplates the actual construction of the sewer connection. At trial, Munro's expert plumber testified that such a connection will cost Munro $14,300....

---

41. Restatement (Second) of Contracts §§ 251 and 253 (1981).

The Court is convinced after hearing the evidence and submissions of the parties, that Munro has proven his reasonable damages in the amount of $21,713.00.

Conclusion

For the foregoing reasons, the Court finds that Plaintiff has proven its claim of breach of contract against Defendant Woodring by a preponderance of the evidence. Therefore, judgment is entered against Woodring in the amount of $21,713.00, together with pre- and post-judgment interest at the legal rate of 5.75 percent plus costs. The Court finds in favor of Defendants Kenwood Development Co. and Beazer Homes Corporation on this claim.

The Court finds that Plaintiff has failed to prove its remaining claims by a preponderance of the evidence. Accordingly, judgment is entered in favor of Defendant Woodring on Plaintiff's claim for fraud. Additionally, on Plaintiff's claim for quantum meruit, judgment is entered in favor of Defendant Beazer Homes Corporation.

Finally, the Court finds that Defendant Woodring failed to prove its cross-claim against Defendant Beazer Homes Corporation. Therefore, judgment is entered in favor of Defendant Beazer Homes Corporation on that claim.

---

4. The Preference for Characterizing a Term as a Promise rather than an Express Condition

If you think back to our discussion of the doctrines of constructive conditions and substantial performance, you will understand an additional aspect of the doctrine of express conditions: There is a preference in favor of interpreting a term as a promise rather than an express condition. Let's look at the logic behind that preference.

Contract doctrine allows courts to characterize contract terms in one of two ways. A contract term may be:

1) a "promise" (a commitment to do or not to do something), or

2) a "condition" (an event that must occur, unless excused, before performance of an obligation becomes due)

The characterization of a term as a condition or a promise can be controversial, because very different legal consequences flow from the different characterizations; the most significant differences are in the effect of non-occurrence or nonperformance; the extent of deviation permitted; and the ways that the term can be modified or excused. These differences can be summarized as follows:

1) Promises:

Effect of Non-Occurrence:

If a promise is not performed, then the promisor is liable for breach of contract and may be required to pay damages or be subject to an order of specific performance.

Extent of Non-Conformity:

Most promises (although not all) are subject to the doctrine of substantial performance.

Modification or Excuse:

> In general, a promise can be modified only by mutual agreement, and the modification must satisfy the consideration requirement or some exception to it. These exceptions (discussed in Chapter Eight) include *Uniform Commercial Code* section 2-209, which allows enforcement of a good faith modification without consideration in a contract for the sale of goods, and *Restatement (Second) of Contracts* section 89, which allows enforcement of a modification without consideration made in response to an unanticipated change in the circumstances of the contract.

2) Conditions:

Effect of Non-Occurrence:

> If a condition is not fulfilled, then the obligation it qualifies does not become due. There will be no liability for either party.

Extent of Non-Conformity:

> The doctrine of conditions requires that conditions must be *strictly fulfilled*. If a condition does not occur in precisely the way indicated by the contract term, then the conditioned performance does not become due.

Modification or Excuse:

> Conditions can be unilaterally waived by the party whose performance is conditioned. Waiver does not require mutual agreement nor consideration. In addition, a condition can be excused by the court in order to avoid disproportionate forfeiture by a party.

Because these different characterizations have different legal consequences, parties often disagree on the appropriate characterization of a term. In one case involving the sale of a house, for example, the contract specified that the seller would provide proof of a title insurance commitment on or before July 10. The seller did not provide this proof until July 15. If the proof of title insurance was a condition, then it clearly was not strictly fulfilled and the buyer's obligation to buy would never arise. If, on the other hand, the title insurance was a promise, then the court could find that the seller had substantially performed the obligation by submitting the proof on July 15. The court applied the preference in favor of construing terms as promises in order to achieve a more flexible structure to the contract:

> We recognize that where a contract unequivocally conditions the purchaser's performance on the seller's undertaking to provide a title insurance commitment, the failure of the seller to strictly comply with the condition will excuse the purchaser's duty of performance under the contract. *See Merritt Hill Vineyards, Inc. v. Windy Heights Vineyard, Inc.*, 460 N.E.2d 1077 (N.Y. 1984) (seller's obligation to furnish title insurance policy and mortgage confirmation was construed as a condition rather than a promise, where the requirements were contained in a section of the contract entitled "Conditions Precedent to Purchaser's Obligation to Close"). Where, however, there is doubt as to whether a contractual provision is intended as a promise or a condition, it is preferable to construe the provision as a promise, thereby avoiding the potentially harsh effects of a forfeiture that can result in some cases by a contrary construction.

In deciding how to characterize a term, a court must evaluate the parties' intentions and the legal consequences that will result from alternative characterizations. The analysis looks both backward — to the parties' intentions — and forward — to the legal consequences of different characterizations. A court will consider the parties' words and behavior, the overall purpose or function of the contract, and any relevant practices in the trade or community. The words "provided that," "subject to," and "in the event that" suggest a condition, while "promise," "commit," "agree to," and "obligate" suggest a promise. Looking at the overall purpose and function of the contract, a court will consider which characterization would result in legal consequences that would most closely approximate the parties' goals. In addition, evidence of relevant practices in the trade or community can be significant to the characterization of a term just as it was in *Nanakuli Paving* (in Chapter 9): the norms and expectations of the trade or community may reveal other possible purposes of the agreement, or may shed light on the meaning of particular words and phrases. Finally, courts have articulated a preference for characterizing a term as a promise, rather than a condition or a promissory condition, because the doctrine of substantial performance allows flexibility, which courts assume that parties intend in most situations, while the rule of strict fulfillment imposes a rigidity that seems at odds with common expectations.

5. Other Protections for Parties Who Must Perform First

Despite its limitations, the doctrine of substantial performance does provide some protection for workers who, under the doctrine of constructive conditions, are required to complete their performance before the other party's obligation (most often it is an obligation to pay) arises. In *Jacob & Youngs*, the court presumed that the builder would have to perform, at least substantially perform, before Kent would be obligated to make the last payment due under the contract. The rule of substantial performance protects workers by assuring that they will be paid even if the performance involved a minor breach. Additional protection is offered by the doctrine of divisible contracts, the use of restitution in favor of a party in breach, and legislation requiring periodic payment of wages.

The doctrine of *divisible contracts* allows courts to treat a single contract as if it were two or more separate contracts. If a party has substantially performed one part of the contract and seriously breached the rest, then under the divisible contract doctrine, he or she would be entitled to payment for the completed work. Assume, for example, that Muriel Yazee, a landscaper, contracts to build a fishpond on a one acre plot of land and to make an irrigated apple orchard on another part of the same land, and the owner, Desmond O'Grady, promises to pay her a total of $20,000. In negotiating the contract and in the contract document, the parties have specified that $11,000 will be for the fishpond and $9,000 for the apple orchard and that the fishpond will be built before the apple orchard. Assume further that Muriel built the fishpond to the specifications she agreed upon with Desmond except the pond is five feet narrower than planned. Muriel has only begun to level the land for the apple orchard, however, and financial difficulties have led her to abandon the project. Desmond has refused to pay Muriel any part of the $20,000, arguing that her promises were constructive conditions to his obligation to pay and that her breach was serious, amounting to almost half of her performance under the contract, and therefore his obligation to pay never arose. The court may hold that the contract is divisible into one contract for the fishpond and one for the apple orchard and that Muriel substantially performed the fishpond contract and therefore is entitled to payment of $11,000, minus whatever damages would compensate Desmond for Muriel's failure to build the pond as wide as required. As to the apple orchard, Desmond's obligation to pay would be excused because of Muriel's serious breach, and Muriel would have to pay Desmond damages for the breach (which would most likely be measured by however much more than $9,000 Desmond will have to pay someone else to do the job).

The divisible contract doctrine does provide some protection for workers. The doctrine is quite limited, however, because courts generally will not apply it where the parties have not clearly spelled out distinct terms for distinct parts of a contract. Say another of Muriel's contracts specified that she would plant 100 trees at a cost of $100 per tree, for a total of $10,000. Most courts would not be willing to treat that contract as divisible into 100 separate contracts, or even into two contracts for 50 trees each. Courts are not willing to apply the doctrine in such cases because it appears to conflict with freedom of contract and free market values associated with the bargain principle.

Another protection for one who has to perform first is restitution. Traditionally, restitution was not available for one who has "unclean hands"—who has in some way misbehaved in the situation. This rule meant that a person who had breached a contract could not recover in restitution for benefits retained by the other party. For example, assume the contract between Muriel and Desmond was for the fishpond only: Muriel would build a fishpond according to Desmond's specifications, which included a bricked walkway and three wooden benches, and Desmond would pay her $11,000. Assume further that Muriel dug out the pond and built a dam, but stopped work before building the brick walk and benches. Desmond probably is not obligated to pay her anything under the contract, because her performance is a constructive condition precedent to his obligation to pay, and she has not substantially performed the contract, so his obligation to pay never arose. Yet Desmond got the pond, including a dam. He could hire someone else to build the walk and benches, pay them maybe $3,000, and get the whole project completed at $8,000 less than what he expected it to cost. Is this just? Many courts have held that despite her wrongdoing, Muriel ought to recover in restitution for the fair market value of the work she has done for Desmond. She did breach the contract, so courts might be inclined to give her a low estimation of market value, but still most would grant her some recovery.

The most significant protections for workers, however, are not judicial doctrines. Most state and some federal legislation provide that most workers must be paid no less frequently than every month. These statutes require periodic payment employment contracts, in effect overruling the presumption in the doctrine of constructive conditions as it applies to employment contracts. In addition, many independent contractors, construction companies, suppliers, and the like have sufficient bargaining power to insist on periodic payments in their contracts. These more powerful contractors thus require their "employers" to forego the doctrinal presumption against periodic payments.

C. On the Rule of Perfect Tender in the Uniform Commercial Code

Rejecting the doctrine of substantial performance, section 2-601 of the *Uniform Commercial Code* establishes a rule of perfect tender for the seller under a contract for the sale of goods:

§ 2-601 Buyer's Rights on Improper Delivery

Subject to the provisions of this Article on breach in installment contracts (Section 2-612) and unless otherwise agreed under the sections on contractual limitations of remedy (Sections 2-718 and 2-719), *if the goods or the tender of delivery fail in any respect to conform to the contract,* the buyer may

(a) reject the whole; or

(b) accept the whole; or

(c) accept any commercial unit or units and reject the rest.

(Emphasis added).

Section 2-703 gives a more detailed description of situations in which a seller can cancel the contract because of a breach by the buyer, but courts have held that there is no requirement that the buyer's breach be substantial or material in order to warrant the remedy of cancellation:

§ 2-703 Seller's Remedies in General.

Where the buyer wrongfully rejects or revokes acceptance of goods or fails to make a payment due on or before delivery or repudiates with respect to a part or the whole, then with respect to any goods directly affected and, if the breach is of the whole contract (Section 2-612), then also with respect to the whole un-delivered balance, the aggrieved seller may

(a) withhold delivery of such goods;

(b) stop delivery by any bailee as hereafter provided (Section 2-705);

(c) proceed under the next section respecting goods still unidentified to the con-tract;

(d) resell and recover damages as hereafter provided (Section 2-706);

(e) recover damages for non-acceptance (Section 2-708) or in a proper case the price (Section 2-709);

(f) cancel.

Yet Karl Llewellyn, principal drafter of Article Two of the *Uniform Commercial Code,* believed that the traditional rule of perfect tender for sales contracts was unwise, unjust, and unrealistic. He advised against section 2-601 and, after losing that argument, argued strongly in favor of other provisions that would temper its effect. While section 2-601 was retained, Llewellyn was successful in securing several moderating provisions. The most important of these are section 2-612, which adopts a rule of substantial impairment for installment contracts, section 2-608, which requires proof of substantial impairment for revocation of acceptance, and section 2-508, which establishes a seller's right to cure in some situations. The following case involves the *U.C.C.* rule of perfect tender and some related provisions.

Ernest Ramirez and Adele Ramirez v. Autosport

Supreme Court of New Jersey
88 N.J. 277, 440 A.2d 1345 (1982)

Stewart G. Pollock, Justice

This case raises several issues under the *Uniform Commercial Code* ("the *Code*" and "*UCC*") concerning whether a buyer may reject a tender of goods with minor defects and whether a seller may cure the defects. We consider also the remedies available to the buyer, including cancellation of the contract. The main issue is whether plaintiffs, Mr. and Mrs.

Ramirez, could reject the tender by defendant, Autosport, of a camper van with minor defects and cancel the contract for the purchase of the van.

The trial court ruled that Mr. and Mrs. Ramirez rightfully rejected the van and awarded them the fair market value of their trade-in van. The Appellate Division affirmed in a brief per curiam decision which, like the trial court opinion, was unreported. We affirm the judgment of the Appellate Division.

I.

Following a mobile home show at the Meadowlands Sports Complex, Mr. and Mrs. Ramirez visited Autosport's showroom in Somerville. On July 20, 1978 the Ramirezes and Donald Graff, a salesman for Autosport, agreed on the sale of a new camper and the trade-in of the van owned by Mr. and Mrs. Ramirez. Autosport and the Ramirezes signed a simple contract reflecting a $14,100 purchase price for the new van with a $4,700 trade-in allowance for the Ramirez van, which Mr. and Mrs. Ramirez left with Autosport. After further allowance for taxes, title and documentary fees, the net price was $9,902. Because Autosport needed two weeks to prepare the new van, the contract provided for delivery on or about August 3, 1978.

On that date, Mr. and Mrs. Ramirez returned with their checks to Autosport to pick up the new van. Graff was not there so Mr. White, another salesman, met them. Inspection disclosed several defects in the van. The paint was scratched, both the electric and sewer hookups were missing, and the hubcaps were not installed. White advised the Ramirezes not to accept the camper because it was not ready.

Mr. and Mrs. Ramirez wanted the van for a summer vacation and called Graff several times. Each time Graff told them it was not ready for delivery. Finally, Graff called to notify them that the camper was ready. On August 14 Mr. and Mrs. Ramirez went to Autosport to accept delivery, but workers were still touching up the outside paint. Also, the camper windows were open, and the dining area cushions were soaking wet. Mr. and Mrs. Ramirez could not use the camper in that condition, but Mr. Leis, Autosport's manager, suggested that they take the van and that Autosport would replace the cushions later. Mrs. Ramirez counteroffered to accept the van if they could withhold $2,000, but Leis agreed to no more than $250, which she refused. Leis then agreed to replace the cushions and to call them when the van was ready.

On August 15, 1978 Autosport transferred title to the van to Mr. and Mrs. Ramirez, a fact unknown to them until the summer of 1979. Between August 15 and September 1, 1978 Mrs. Ramirez called Graff several times urging him to complete the preparation of the van, but Graff constantly advised her that the van was not ready. He finally informed her that they could pick it up on September 1.

When Mr. and Mrs. Ramirez went to the showroom on September 1, Graff asked them to wait. And wait they did—for one and a half hours. No one from Autosport came forward to talk with them, and the Ramirezes left in disgust.

On October 5, 1978 Mr. and Mrs. Ramirez went to Autosport with an attorney friend. Although the parties disagreed on what occurred, the general topic was whether they should proceed with the deal or Autosport should return to the Ramirezes their trade-in van. Mrs. Ramirez claimed they rejected the new van and requested the return of their trade-in. Mr. Lustig, the owner of Autosport, thought, however, that the deal could be salvaged if the parties could agree on the dollar amount of a credit for the Ramirezes. Mr. and Mrs. Ramirez never took possession of the new van and repeated their request for the return of their trade-in. Later in October, however, Autosport sold the trade-in to an innocent third party for $4,995. Autosport claimed that the Ramirez' van had a book value of $3,200 and claimed further that it spent $1,159.62 to repair their van. By subtracting the total of those two figures, $4,159.62, from the $4,995.00 sale price, Autosport claimed a $600–700 profit on the sale.

On November 20, 1978 the Ramirezes sued Autosport seeking, among other things, rescission of the contract. Autosport counterclaimed for breach of contract.

II.

Our initial inquiry is whether a consumer may reject defective goods that do not conform to the contract of sale. The basic issue is whether under the *UCC*, adopted in New Jersey as N.J.S.A. 12A:1-101 *et seq.*, a seller has the duty to deliver goods that conform precisely to the contract. We conclude that the seller is under such a duty to make a "perfect tender" and that a buyer has the right to reject goods that do not conform to the contract. That conclusion, however, does not resolve the entire dispute between buyer and seller. A more complete answer requires a brief statement of the history of the mutual obligations of buyers and sellers of commercial goods.

In the nineteenth century, sellers were required to deliver goods that complied exactly with the sales agreement. *See Filley v. Pope*, 115 U.S. 213, 220, 6 S. Ct. 19, 21, 29 L. Ed. 372, 373 (1885) (buyer not obliged to accept otherwise conforming scrap iron shipped to New Orleans from Leith, rather than Glasgow, Scotland, as required by contract); *Columbian Iron Works & Dry-Dock Co. v. Douglas*, 84 Md. 44, 47, 34 A. 1118, 1120–1121 (1896) (buyer who agreed to purchase steel scrap from United States cruisers not obliged to take any other kind of scrap). That rule, known as the "perfect tender" rule, remained part of the law of sales well into the twentieth century. By the 1920's the doctrine was so entrenched in the law that Judge Learned Hand declared "(t)here is no room in commercial contracts for the doctrine of substantial performance." *Mitsubishi Goshi Kaisha v. J. Aron & Co., Inc.*, 16 F.2d 185, 186 (2d Cir. 1926).

The harshness of the rule led courts to seek to ameliorate its effect and to bring the law of sales in closer harmony with the law of contracts, which allows rescission only for material breaches. *LeRoy Dyal Co. v. Allen*, 161 F.2d 152, 155 (4th Cir. 1947). *See* 5 Corbin, Contracts § 1104 at 464 (1951); 12 Williston, Contracts § 1455 at 14 (3d ed. 1970). Nevertheless, a variation of the perfect tender rule appeared in the *Uniform Sales Act. N.J.S.A.* 46:30-75 (purchasers permitted to reject goods or rescind contracts for any breach of warranty); N.J.S.A. 46:30-18 to -21 (warranties extended to include all the seller's obligations to the goods). *See* Honnold, Buyer's Right of Rejection, A Study in the Impact of Codification Upon a Commercial Problem, 97 U. Pa. L. Rev. 457, 460 (1949). The chief objection to the continuation of the perfect tender rule was that buyers in a declining market would reject goods for minor nonconformities and force the loss on surprised sellers. *See* Hawkland, Sales and Bulk Sales Under the Uniform Commercial Code, 120–122 (1958), cited in N.J.S.A. 12A:2-508, New Jersey Study Comment 3.

To the extent that a buyer can reject goods for any nonconformity, the *UCC* retains the perfect tender rule. Section 2-106 states that goods conform to a contract "when they are in accordance with the obligations under the contract". N.J.S.A. 12A:2-106. Section 2-601 authorizes a buyer to reject goods if they "or the tender of delivery fail in any respect to conform to the contract." N.J.S.A. 12A:2-601. The *Code*, however, mitigates the harshness of the perfect tender rule and balances the interests of buyer and seller. *See Restatement (Second) Contracts* § 241 comment (b) (1981). The *Code* achieves that result through its provisions for revocation of acceptance and cure. N.J.S.A. 12A:2-608, 2-508.

Initially, the rights of the parties vary depending on whether the rejection occurs before or after acceptance of the goods. Before acceptance, the buyer may reject goods for any nonconformity. N.J.S.A. 12A:2-601. Because of the seller's right to cure, however, the buyer's rejection does not necessarily discharge the contract. N.J.S.A. 12A:2-508. Within the time set for performance in the contract, the seller's right to cure is unconditional. *Id.*, subsec. (1); *see id.*, Official Comment 1. Some authorities recommend granting a breaching party a right to cure in all contracts, not merely those for the sale of goods. *Restatement (Second) Contracts*, ch. 10, especially §§ 237 and 241. Underlying the right to cure in both kinds of contracts is the recognition that parties should be encouraged to communicate with each other and to resolve their own problems. *Id.*, Introduction p. 193.

The rights of the parties also vary if rejection occurs after the time set for performance. After expiration of that time, the seller has a further reasonable time to cure if he believed reasonably that the goods would be acceptable with or without a money allowance. N.J.S.A. 12A:2-508(2). The determination of what constitutes a further reasonable time depends on the surrounding circumstances, which include the change of position by and the amount of inconvenience to the buyer. N.J.S.A. 12A:2-508, Official Comment 3. Those circumstances also include the length of time needed by the seller to correct the nonconformity and his ability to salvage the goods by resale to others. *See Restatement (Second) Contracts* § 241 comment (d). Thus, the *Code* balances the buyer's right to reject nonconforming goods with a "second chance" for the seller to conform the goods to the contract under certain limited circumstances. N.J.S.A. 12A:2-508, New Jersey Study Comment 1.

After acceptance, the *Code* strikes a different balance: the buyer may revoke acceptance only if the nonconformity substantially impairs the value of the goods to him. N.J.S.A. 12A:2-608. *See Herbstman v. Eastman Kodak Co.*, 68 N.J. 1, 9, 342 A.2d 181 (1975). *See generally*, Priest, *Breach and Remedy for the Tender of Non-Conforming Goods under the Uniform Commercial Code: An Economic Approach*, 91 Harv. L. Rev. 960, 971–973 (1978). This provision protects the seller from revocation for trivial defects. *Herbstman, supra*, 68 N.J. at 9, 342 A.2d 181. It also prevents the buyer from taking undue advantage of the seller by allowing goods to depreciate and then returning them because of asserted minor defects. *See* White & Summers, Uniform Commercial Code § 8-3 at 391 (2 ed. 1980). Because this case involves rejection of goods, we need not decide whether a seller has a right to cure substantial defects that justify revocation of acceptance. *See Pavesi v. Ford Motor Co.*, 155 N.J. Super. 373, 378, 382 A.2d 954 (App. Div. 1978) (right to cure after acceptance limited to trivial defects) and White & Summers, *supra*, § 8-4 at 319 n.76 (open question as to the relationship between §§ 2-608 and 2-508).

Other courts agree that the buyer has a right of rejection for any nonconformity, but that the seller has a countervailing right to cure within a reasonable time. *Marine Mart Inc. v. Pearce*, 252 Ark. 601, 480 S.W.2d 133, 137 (1972). *See Intermeat, Inc. v. American Poultry, Inc.*, 575 F.2d 1017, 1024 (2d Cir. 1978); *Moulton Cavity & Mold., Inc. v. Lyn-Flex Industries*, 396 A.2d 1024, 1027 n.6 (Me. 1979); *Uchitel v. F. R. Tripler & Co.*, 107 Misc. 2d 310, 316, 434 N.Y.S.2d 77, 81 (App. Term 1980); *Rutland Music Services, Inc. v. Ford Motor Co.*, 422 A.2d 248, 249 (Vt. 1980). *But see McKenzie v. Alla-Ohio Coals*, Inc., 29 U.C.C. Rep. 852, 856–857 (D.D.C. 1979).

One New Jersey case, *Gindy Mfg. Corp. v. Cardinale Trucking Corp.*, suggests that, because some defects can be cured, they do not justify rejection. 111 N.J. Super. 383, 387 n.1, 268 A.2d 345 (Law Div. 1970). *Accord, Adams v. Tremontin*, 42 N.J. Super. 313, 325, 126 A.2d 358 (App. Div. 1956) (Uniform Sales Act). *But see Sudol v. Rudy Papa Motors*, 175 N.J. Super. 238, 240–41, 417 A.2d 1133 (D. Ct. 1980) (§ 2-601 contains perfect tender rule). Nonetheless, we conclude that the perfect tender rule is preserved to the extent of permitting a buyer to reject goods for any defects. Because of the seller's right to cure, rejection does not terminate the contract. Accordingly, we disapprove the suggestion in *Gindy* that curable defects do not justify rejection.

A further problem, however, is identifying the remedy available to a buyer who rejects goods with insubstantial defects that the seller fails to cure within a reasonable time. The *Code* provides expressly that when "the buyer rightfully rejects, then with respect to the goods involved, the buyer may cancel." N.J.S.A. 12A:2-711. "Cancellation" occurs when either party puts an end to the contract for breach by the other. N.J.S.A. 12A:2-106(4). Nonetheless, some confusion exists whether the equitable remedy of rescission survives under the *Code. Compare Ventura v. Ford Motor Corp.*, 173 N.J. Super. 501, 503, 414 A.2d 611 (Ch. Div. 1980), *aff'd* 180 N.J. Super. 45, 433 A.2d 801 (App. Div. 1981) (rescission under *UCC*) and *Pavesi v. Ford Motor Corp.*, *supra*, 155 N.J. Super. at 377, 382 A.2d 954 (equitable remedies still available since not specifically superseded, § 1-103) with *Edelstein v. Toyota Motors Dist.*, 176 N.J. Super. 57, 63–64, 422 A.2d 101 (App. Div. 1980) (under *UCC* rescission is revocation of acceptance) and *Sudol v. Rudy Papa Motors*, *supra*, 175 N.J. Super. at 241–242, 417 A.2d 1133 (under *UCC*, rescission no longer exists as such).

The *Code* eschews the word "rescission" and substitutes the terms "cancellation," "revocation of acceptance," and "rightful rejection." N.J.S.A. 12A:2-106(4); 2-608; and 2-711 & Official Comment 1. Although neither "rejection" nor "revocation of acceptance" is defined in the *Code*, rejection includes both the buyer's refusal to accept or keep delivered goods and his notification to the seller that he will not keep them. White & Summers, *supra*, § 8-1 at 293. Revocation of acceptance is like rejection, but occurs after the buyer has accepted the goods. Nonetheless, revocation of acceptance is intended to provide the same relief as rescission of a contract of sale of goods. N.J.S.A. 12A:2-608 Official Comment 1; N.J. Study Comment 2. In brief, revocation is tantamount to rescission. *See Herbstman v. Eastman Kodak Co.*, *supra*, 68 N.J. at 9, 342 A.2d 181; *accord, Peckham v. Larsen Chevrolet-Buick-Oldsmobile, Inc.*, 99 Idaho 675, 677, 587 P.2d 816, 818 (1978) (rescission and revocation of acceptance amount to the same thing). Similarly, subject to the seller's right to cure, a buyer who rightfully rejects goods, like one who revokes his acceptance, may cancel the contract. N.J.S.A. 12A:2-711 & Official Comment 1. We need not resolve the extent to which rescission for reasons other than rejection or revocation of acceptance, e.g., fraud and mistake, survives as a remedy outside the *Code. Compare* N.J.S.A. 12A:1-103 and White & Summers, *supra*, § 8-1, p. 295, with N.J.S.A. 12A:2-721. Accordingly, we approve *Edelstein* and *Sudol*, which recognize that explicit *Code* remedies replace rescission, and disapprove *Ventura* and *Pavesi* to the extent they suggest the *UCC* expressly recognizes rescission as a remedy.

Although the complaint requested rescission of the contract, plaintiffs actually sought not only the end of their contractual obligations, but also restoration to their pre-contractual position. That request incorporated the equitable doctrine of restitution, the purpose of which is to restore plaintiff to as good a position as he occupied before the contract. Corbin, *supra*, § 1102 at 455. In *UCC* parlance, plaintiffs' request was for the cancellation of the contract and recovery of the price paid. N.J.S.A. 12A:2-106(4), 2-711.

General contract law permits rescission only for material breaches, and the *Code* restates "materiality" in terms of "substantial impairment." *See Herbstman v. Eastman Kodak Co.*, *supra*, 68 N.J. at 9, 342 A.2d 181; *id.* at 15, 342 A.2d 181 (Conford, J., concurring). The *Code* permits a buyer who rightfully rejects goods to cancel a contract of sale. N.J.S.A. 12A:2-711. Because a buyer may reject goods with insubstantial defects, he also may cancel the contract if those defects remain uncured. Otherwise, a seller's failure to cure minor defects would compel a buyer to accept imperfect goods and collect for any loss caused by the nonconformity. N.J.S.A. 12A:2-714.

Although the *Code* permits cancellation by rejection for minor defects, it permits revocation of acceptance only for substantial impairments. That distinction is consistent with other *Code* provisions that depend on whether the buyer has accepted the goods. Acceptance creates liability in the buyer for the price, N.J.S.A. 12A:2-709(1), and precludes rejection. N.J.S.A. 12A:2-607(2); N.J.S.A. 12A:2-606, New Jersey Study Comment 1. Also, once a buyer accepts goods, he has the burden to prove any defect. N.J.S.A. 12A:2-607(4); White & Summers, *supra*, § 8-2 at 297. By contrast, where goods are rejected for not conforming to the contract, the burden is on the seller to prove that the nonconformity was corrected. *Miron v. Yonkers Raceway*, Inc., 400 F.2d 112, 119 (2d Cir. 1968).

Underlying the *Code* provisions is the recognition of the revolutionary change in business practices in this century. The purchase of goods is no longer a simple transaction in which a buyer purchases individually-made goods from a seller in a face-to-face transaction. Our economy depends on a complex system for the manufacture, distribution, and sale of goods, a system in which manufacturers and consumers rarely meet. Faceless manufacturers mass-produce goods for unknown consumers who purchase those goods from merchants exercising little or no control over the quality of their production. In an age of assembly lines, we are accustomed to cars with scratches, television sets without knobs and other products with all kinds of defects. Buyers no longer expect a "perfect tender." If a merchant sells defective goods, the reasonable expectation of the parties is that the buyer will return those goods and that the seller will repair or replace them.

Recognizing this commercial reality, the *Code* permits a seller to cure imperfect tenders. Should the seller fail to cure the defects, whether substantial or not, the balance shifts again in favor of the buyer, who has the right to cancel or seek damages. N.J.S.A. 12A:2-711. In general, economic considerations would induce sellers to cure minor defects. *See generally* Priest, *supra*, 91 Harv. L. Rev. 973–974. Assuming the seller does not cure, however, the buyer should be permitted to exercise his remedies under N.J.S.A. 12A:2-711. The *Code* remedies for consumers are to be liberally construed, and the buyer should have the option of canceling if the seller does not provide conforming goods. *See* N.J.S.A. 12A:1-106.

To summarize, the *UCC* preserves the perfect tender rule to the extent of permitting a buyer to reject goods for any nonconformity. Nonetheless, that rejection does not automatically terminate the contract. A seller may still effect a cure and preclude unfair rejection and cancellation by the buyer. N.J.S.A. 12A:2-508, Official Comment 2; N.J.S.A. 12A:2-711, Official Comment 1.

III.

The trial court found that Mr. and Mrs. Ramirez had rejected the van within a reasonable time under N.J.S.A. 12A:2-602. The court found that on August 3, 1978 Autosport's salesman advised the Ramirezes not to accept the van and that on August 14, they rejected delivery and Autosport agreed to replace the cushions. Those findings are supported by substantial credible evidence, and we sustain them. *See Rova Farms Resort v. Investors Ins. Co.*, 65 N.J. 474, 483–484, 323 A.2d 495 (1974). Although the trial court did not find whether Autosport cured the defects within a reasonable time, we find that Autosport did not effect a cure. Clearly the van was not ready for delivery during August, 1978 when Mr. and Mrs. Ramirez rejected it, and Autosport had the burden of proving that it had corrected the defects. Although the Ramirezes gave Autosport ample time to correct the defects, Autosport did not demonstrate that the van conformed to the contract on September 1. In fact, on that date, when Mr. and Mrs. Ramirez returned at Autosport's invitation, all they received was discourtesy.

On the assumption that substantial impairment is necessary only when a purchaser seeks to revoke acceptance under N.J.S.A. 12A:2-608, the trial court correctly refrained from deciding whether the defects substantially impaired the van. The court properly concluded that plaintiffs were entitled to "rescind"—i.e., to "cancel"—the contract.

Because Autosport had sold the trade-in to an innocent third party, the trial court determined that the Ramirezes were entitled not to the return of the trade-in, but to its fair market value, which the court set at the contract price of $4,700. A buyer who rightfully rejects goods and cancels the contract may, among other possible remedies, recover so much of the purchase price as has been paid. N.J.S.A. 12A:2-711. The *Code*, however, does not define "pay" and does not require payment to be made in cash.

A common method of partial payment for vans, cars, boats and other items of personal property is by a "trade-in." When concerned with used vans and the like, the trade-in market is an acceptable, and perhaps the most appropriate, market in which to measure damages. It is the market in which the parties dealt; by their voluntary act they have established the value of the traded-in article. *See Frantz Equipment Co. v. Anderson*, 37 N.J. 420, 431–32, 181 A.2d 499 (1962) (in computing purchaser's damages for alleged breach of uniform conditional sales law, trade-in value of tractor was appropriate measure); *accord, California Airmotive Corp. v. Jones*, 415 F.2d 554, 556 (6th Cir. 1969). In other circumstances, a measure of damages other than the trade-in value might be appropriate. *See Chemical Bank v. Miller Yacht Sales*, 173 N.J. Super. 90, 103, 413 A.2d 619 (App. Div. 1980) (in determining value of security interest in boat, court rejected both book value and contract trade-in value and adopted resale value as appropriate measure of damages).

The ultimate issue is determining the fair market value of the trade-in. This Court has defined fair market value as "the price at which the property would change hands between a willing buyer and a willing seller when the former is not under any compulsion to buy and the latter is not under any compulsion to sell, both parties having reasonable knowledge of relevant facts." *In re Estate of Romnes*, 79 N.J. 139, 144, 398 A.2d 543 (1978). Although the value of the trade-in van as set forth in the sales contract was not the only possible standard, it is an appropriate measure of fair market value.

For the preceding reasons, we affirm the judgment of the Appellate Division.

Note—Breach Provisions in the United Nations Convention on Contracts for the International Sale of Goods

The *United Nations Convention on Contracts for the International Sale of Goods* has a rule of *fundamental breach* that significantly restricts a party's power to cancel a contract in the event of a breach. Article 49 provides: "The buyer may declare the contract avoided: (a) if the failure by the seller to perform any of his obligations under the contract or this *Convention* amounts to a fundamental breach of contract ..." and Article 64 provides: "The Seller may declare the contract avoided: (a) if the failure of the buyer to perform any of his obligations under the contract or this *Convention* amounts to a fundamental breach of contract...." Fundamental breach is defined in Article 25:

> A breach of contract committed by one of the parties is fundamental if it results in such detriment to the other party as substantially to deprive him of what he is entitled to expect under the contract, unless the party in breach did

not foresee and a reasonable person of the same kind in the same circumstances would not have foreseen such a result.

Underlying the requirement of a fundamental breach is a recognition that cancellation often deprives one party of compensation for time, energy, and resources already committed to the contract and thus risks unjust forfeiture and windfall benefits. Under the doctrine of fundamental breach, parties are required to work together to correct whatever problems have developed. This approach is reflected as well in Articles 47 and 48, which allow the buyer to extend the time for performance in the event of the seller's delay and recognize a seller's right to cure defective performance in many cases. Article 47 provides:

> (1) The buyer may fix an additional period of time of reasonable length for performance by the seller of his obligations.
>
> (2) Unless the buyer has received notice from the seller that he will not perform within the period so fixed, the buyer may not, during that period, resort to any remedy for breach of contract. However, the buyer is not deprived thereby of any right he may have to claim damages for delay in performance.

Article 48 provides:

> Subject to Article 49, the seller may, even after the date for delivery, remedy at his own expense any failure to perform his obligations, if he can do so without unreasonable delay and without causing the buyer unreasonable inconvenience or uncertainty of reimbursement by the seller of expenses advanced by the buyer. However, the buyer retains any right to claim damages as provided for in this Convention.

While explicit cooperation requirements are rare in U.S. contract law, they are common in the world's other legal systems and are reflected in the *United Nations Convention on Contracts for the International Sale of Goods*.

D. Anticipatory Breach and Related Doctrines

What if the time for performance of a contract has not yet arrived, but one party *says* that he or she will not perform the contract or *acts* as if he or she will not perform; must the other person wait for the time for performance, hoping that the first party will come through, or can he or she treat the these words or actions as the equivalent of a breach of contract? Assume that Chun Hwan agreed to buy a van from Daphne Weinberger: Daphne promised to deliver the van on June 1 and Hwan promised to pay $2,500 on May 1 and the remaining $2,500 at the time of delivery. On April 26, Hwan received a letter from Daphne saying "I have decided I want to give the car to my nephew. Sorry." Must Hwan still pay Daphne $2,500 on May 1? He is worried that if he does pay the money, he still may never get the car, but if he doesn't pay the money, he may be in breach of the contract.

What can Hwan do to protect himself? Can he suspend or cancel the contract because Daphne seems unlikely to perform? Must he wait until the time for delivery specified in the contract arrives? And if Hwan does wait for the time for performance, can the seller later claim that he should have acted more quickly to minimize the damages he may suffer from the seller's breach? Many people would think that Daphne's letter is a breach of the contract, Hwan should not have to pay the first $2,500, he should be free to buy a van elsewhere if he can, and he should be able to sue Daphne for breach of contract without waiting until June 1. This common sense approach is embodied in the doctrine of *anticipatory breach*. Under this doctrine, an express or implied repudiation of a contract may be treated as an immediate breach of contract. *See* Restatement (Second) of Contracts section 251 and CISG Article 71.

The doctrine of *anticipatory breach* or *anticipatory repudiation* would allow Hwan to treat Daphne's repudiation as a present breach of contract. Yet this doctrine is not always sufficient to protect people in Hwan's position, because words and behavior are often ambiguous. What if Daphne had written: "I have told my nephew that he can have my van"? Is this a *repudiation* of the contract? What if Daphne had written no letter, but Hwan had overheard Daphne's nephew say that she had given him the van? What if Hwan had merely seen Daphne's nephew driving the van?

It is often difficult to assess whether a party has repudiated a contract, and the price for being wrong is high. In this situation, Hwan risks breaching the contract himself if he fails to pay on May 1 and a court later decides that Daphne had not repudiated the contract. By the same token, if Hwan decides to pay on May 1st and Daphne later breaches, she may argue that he failed to fulfill his duty to mitigate damages that he should not have paid the $2,500 and should have immediately looked for a substitute van. The following case involves these issues.

H. B. Taylor v. Elizabeth and Ellwood Johnston

Supreme Court of California
15 Cal. 3d 130, 539 P.2d 425, 123 Cal. Rptr. 641 (1975)

Raymond L. Sullivan, Justice

In this action for damages for breach of contract defendants Elizabeth and Ellwood Johnston, individually and as copartners doing business as Old English Rancho, appeal from a judgment entered after a nonjury trial in favor of plaintiff H. B. Taylor and against them in the amount of $132,778.05 and costs.

Plaintiff was engaged in the business of owning, breeding, raising and racing thoroughbred horses in Los Angeles County. Defendants were engaged in a similar business, and operated a horse farm in Ontario, California, where they furnished stallion stud services. In January 1965 plaintiff sought to breed his two thoroughbred mares, Sunday Slippers and Sandy Fork to defendants' stallion Fleet Nasrullah. To that end, on January 19 plaintiff and defendants entered into two separate written contracts—one pertaining to Sunday Slippers and the other to Sandy Fork. Except for the mare involved the contracts were identical. We set forth in the margin the contract covering Sunday Slippers.[1]

---

1. Original

Important
Please Sign Original and Return as Quickly as Possible
Retaining Duplicate for Your Own File.

January 8, 1965

Old English Rancho
Route 1, Box 224-A
Ontario, California 91761
Gentlemen:
    I hereby confirm my reservation for one services to the stallion Fleet Nasrullah for

The contract provided that Fleet Nasrullah was to perform breeding services upon the respective mares in the year 1966 for a fee of $3,500, payable on or before September 1, 1966. If the stud fee was paid in full and the mares failed to produce a live foal (one that stands and nurses without assistance) from the breeding a return breeding would be provided the following year without additional fee.

On October 4, 1965, defendants sold Fleet Nasrullah to Dr. A. G. Pessin and Leslie Combs II for $1,000,000 cash and shipped the stallion to Kentucky. Subsequently Combs and Pessin syndicated the sire by selling various individuals 36 or 38 shares, each share entitling the holder to breed one mare each season to Fleet Nasrullah. Combs and Pessin each reserved three shares.

On the same day defendants wrote to plaintiff advising the latter of the sale and that he was 'released' from his 'reservations' for Fleet Nasrullah.[2] Unable to reach defendants by telephone, plaintiff had his attorney write to them on October 8, 1965, insisting on performance of the contracts. Receiving no answer, plaintiff's attorney on October 19 wrote a second letter threatening suit. On October 27, defendants advised plaintiff by letter that arrangements had been made to breed the two mares to Fleet Nasrullah in Kentucky.[3] However, plaintiff later learned that the mares could not be boarded at Spendthrift Farm where Fleet Nasrullah was standing stud and accordingly arranged with Clinton Frazier of Elmhurst Farm to board the mares and take care of the breeding.

In January 1966 plaintiff shipped Sunday Slippers and Sandy Fork to Elmhurst Farm. At that time, however, both mares were in foal and could not be bred, since this can occur only during the five-day period in which they are in heat. The first heat period normally occurs nine days, and the second heat period thirty days, after foaling. Succeeding heat periods occur every 21 days.

On April 17, 1966, Sunday Slippers foaled and Frazier immediately notified Dr. Pessin. The latter assured Frazier that he would make the necessary arrangements to breed the

---

the year 1966.

Terms: $3,500.00 — guarantee Live Foal.

FEE is due and payable on or before Sept. 1, 1966.

IF stud fee is paid in full, and mare fails to produce a live foal (one that stands and nurses without assistance) from this breeding, a return breeding the following year to said mare will be granted at no additional stallion fee.

FEE is due and payable prior to sale of mare or prior to her departure from the state. If mare is sold or leaves the state, no return breeding will be granted. 'Stud Certificate to be given in exchange for fees paid.

Veterinarian Certificate due in lieu of payment if mare is barren.

I hereby agree That OLD ENGLISH RANCHO shall in no way be held responsible for accidents of any kind or disease.

Mare: Sunday Slippers   Mr. H. B. Taylor
Roan filly 1959   112 North Evergreen street
Moolah Bux-maoli-ormesby   Burbank, California 91505
(Veterinary certificate must accompany all barren mares.)
Stakes winner of $64,000.00
last raced in 1962
    /s/ H. B. Taylor

2. Defendants' letter stated in part: "We wish to inform you that FLEET NASRULLAH has been sold and will stand the 1966 season in Kentucky. You are, therefore, released from your reservations made to the stallion."

3. Defendants' letter stated in part: "Mr. Johnston has made arrangements for you to breed SANDY FORK ... and SUNDAY SLIPPERS ... to FLEET NASRULLAH for the 1966 season. Therefore, you should communicate with Dr. A. G. Pessin of Spendthrift Farm, Lexington, Kentucky to finalize breeding arrangements...."

mare to Fleet Nasrullah. On April 26, the ninth day after the foaling, Frazier, upon further inquiry, was told by Dr. Pessin to contact Mrs. Judy who had charge of booking the breedings and had handled these matters with Frazier in the past. Mrs. Judy, however, informed Frazier that the stallion was booked for that day but would be available on any day not booked by a shareholder. She indicated that she was acting under instructions but suggested that he keep in touch with her while the mare was in heat.

Sunday Slippers came into heat again on May 13, 1966. Frazier telephoned Mrs. Judy and attempted to book the breeding for May 16.[4] She informed him that Fleet Nasrullah had been reserved by one of the shareholders for that day, but that Frazier should keep in touch with her in the event the reservation was canceled. On May 14 and May 15 Frazier tried again but without success; on the latter date, Sunday Slippers went out of heat.

On June 4, the mare went into heat again. Frazier again tried to book a reservation with Fleet Nasrullah but was told that all dates during the heat period had been already booked. He made no further efforts but on June 7, on plaintiff's instructions, bred Sunday Slippers to a Kentucky Derby winner named Chateaugay for a stud fee of $10,000.

Sandy Fork, plaintiff's other mare awaiting the stud services of Fleet Nasrullah, foaled on June 5, 1966. Frazier telephoned Mrs. Judy the next day and received a booking to breed the mare on June 14, the ninth day after foaling. On June 13, 1966, however, she canceled the reservation because of the prior claim of a shareholder. Frazier made no further attempts and on June 14 bred Sandy Fork to Chateaugay.

Shortly after their breeding, it was discovered that both mares were pregnant with twins. In thoroughbred racing twins are considered undesirable since they endanger the mare and are themselves seldom valuable for racing. Both mares were therefore aborted. However, plaintiff was not required to pay the $20,000 stud fees for Chateaugay's services because neither mare delivered a live foal.

The instant action for breach of contract proceeded to trial on plaintiff's fourth amended complaint, which alleged two causes of action, the first for breach of the two written contracts, the second for breach of an oral agreement. Defendants' cross-complained for the stud fees. The court found the facts to be substantially as stated above and further found and concluded that by selling Fleet Nasrullah defendants had "put it out of their power to perform properly their contracts," that the conduct of defendants and their agents Dr. Pessin and Mrs. Judy up to and including June 13, 1966, constituted a breach[5] and plaintiff "was then justified in treating it as a breach and repudiation of their contractual

---

4. Frazier did not seek to breed Sunday Slippers on May 13, 1966, because the mare's follicle had not yet ruptured, conception can occur up to 12 hours after rupture of the follicle. Accordingly, Frazier normally tried to book a breeding for three days after the onset of heat.

5. We set forth the significant paragraph of the findings at length:

When defendants sold Fleet Nasrullah in 1965 to a purchaser who shipped him to Kentucky, defendants put it out of their power to perform properly their contracts with plaintiff. Those contracts did not require that plaintiff's rights to the breeding services of Fleet Nasrullah should be relegated to a secondary or subordinate position to that of any other person, whether he be a holder of shares in the stallion or not. No such conditions were stated in the contracts and none can be inferred therefrom. From the conduct of the defendants, their agent Dr. Pessin, and their subagent Mrs. Judy, plaintiff was justified in concluding that the defendants were just giving him the runaround and had no intention of performing their contract in the manner required by its terms and as required by the covenant of good faith and fair dealing. Their conduct and that of their agent Dr. Pessin, and their subagent Mrs. Judy up to and including June 13, 1966 constituted a breach of defendants' breeding contracts with plaintiff (plaintiff's Exhibits 8, 9 and 10) and plaintiff was then justified in treating it as a breach and repudiation of their contractual obligation to him.

obligations to him," and that defendants unjustifiably breached the contracts but plaintiff did not.[6] The court awarded plaintiff damages for defendants' breach in the sum of $103,122.50 ($99,800 net damage directly sustained plus $3,322.50 for reasonable costs and expenses for mitigation of damages). "Because of defendants' wholly unwarranted, high-handed, and oppressive breach of their contractual obligation to plaintiff, the plaintiff is entitled to recover from the defendants pre-judgment interest at the rate of 7% per annum on the sum of $99,800.00 from August 1, 1968...." It was concluded that defendants should take nothing on their cross-complaint. Judgment was entered accordingly. This appeal followed.

Defendants' main attack on the judgment is two-pronged. They contend: First, that they did not at any time repudiate the contracts; and second, that they did not otherwise breach the contracts because performance was made impossible by plaintiff's own actions. To put it another way, defendants argue in effect that the finding that they breached the contracts is without any support in the evidence. Essentially they take the position that on the uncontradicted evidence in the record, as a matter of law there was neither anticipatory nor actual breach. As will appear, we conclude that the trial court's decision was based solely on findings of anticipatory breach and that we must determine whether such decision is supported by the evidence.

Nevertheless both aspects of defendants' argument require us at the outset to examine the specifications for performance contained in the contracts. (*See* fn. 1, *ante.*) We note that the reservation for "one services" for Fleet Nasrullah was "for the year 1966." As the evidence showed, a breeding is biologically possible throughout the calendar year, since mares regularly come into heat every 21 days, unless they are pregnant. The contracts therefore appear to contemplate breeding with Fleet Nasrullah at any time during the calendar year 1966. The trial court made no finding as to the time of performance called for by the contracts.[7] There was testimony to the effect that by custom in the thoroughbred racing business the breeding is consummated in a "breeding season" which normally extends from January until early July, although some breeding continues through August. It is possible that the parties intended that the mares be bred to Fleet Nasrullah during the 1966 breeding season rather than the calendar year 1966.[8]

However, in our view, it is immaterial whether the contract phrase "for the year 1966" is taken to mean the above breeding season or the full calendar year since in either event the contract period had not expired by June 7 and June 14, 1966, the dates on which Sunday Slippers and Sandy Fork respectively were bred to Chateaugay[9] and by which time, according to the findings (*see* fn. 5, *ante*) defendants had repudiated the contracts. There can be no *actual* breach of a contract until the time specified therein for performance has arrived. *Gold Min. & Water Co. v. Swinerton* (1943) 142 P.2d 22, 32; 1 Witkin, Summary of Cal. Law (8th ed.) § 629, p. 536; *see* Rest. 2d Contracts (Tent. Draft No. 8, 1973) § 260.

---

6. The court concluded that "The defendants unjustifiably breached these contracts; the plaintiff did not breach these contracts."

7. The trial court was not compelled to specify the exact time for performance because it concluded that defendants had breached the contracts by anticipatory repudiation, i.e., a breach which occurs prior to the time for performance.

8. Perhaps the fact that the stud fees were due to be paid September 1, 1966, at the close of the breeding season supports such a conclusion. Moreover, defendants concede without argument that the trial court impliedly found the time of performance to be the breeding season.

9. Both Sunday Slippers and Sandy Fork would have had at least one more heat during the 1966 breeding season—that of Sunday Slippers commencing on June 26, 1966, and that of Sandy Fork commencing on July 7, 1966.

Although there may be a *breach by anticipatory repudiation*; "(b)y its very name an essential element of a true anticipatory breach of a contract is that the repudiation by the promisor occur before his performance is due under the contract." *Gold Min. & Water Co. v. Swinerton, supra,* 142 P.2d at p. 27 (Ca.). In the instant case, because under either of the above interpretations the time for performance had not yet arrived, defendants' breach as found by the trial court was of necessity an anticipatory breach and must be analyzed in accordance with the principles governing such type of breach. To these principles we now direct our attention.

Anticipatory breach occurs when one of the parties to a bilateral contract repudiates the contract. The repudiation may be express or implied. An express repudiation is a clear, positive, unequivocal refusal to perform *Guerrieri v. Severini* 330 P.2d 635, 641 (Ca. 1958); *Gold Min. & Water Co. v. Swinerton, supra,* 142 P.2d 22, 32 (Ca.); *Whitney Inv. Co. v. Westview Dev. Co.* (1969) 78 Cal. Rptr. 302, 310 (Cal. App.); *Atkinson v. District Bond Co.* 43 P.2d 867, 872 (Ca. App. 1935); an implied repudiation results from conduct where the promisor puts it out of his power to perform so as to make substantial performance of his promise impossible *Zogarts v. Smith* (1948) 194 P.2d 143 (Ca. App.); 1 Witkin, Summary of Cal. Law (8th ed.) § 632, pp. 538–39; 4 Corbin, Contracts (1951) § 984, pp. 949–51).

When a promisor repudiates a contract, the injured party faces an election of remedies: he can treat the repudiation as an anticipatory breach and immediately seek damages for breach of contract, thereby terminating the contractual relation between the parties, or he can treat the repudiation as an empty threat, wait until the time for performance arrives and exercise his remedies for actual breach if a breach does in fact occur at such time. *Guerrieri v. Severini, supra,* 51 Cal. 2d 12, 18–19, 330 P.2d 635. However, if the injured party disregards the repudiation and treats the contract as still in force, and the repudiation is retracted prior to the time of performance, then the repudiation is nullified and the injured party is left with his remedies, if any, invocable at the time of performance. *Id.,* at pp. 19–20, 330 P.2d 635; *Salot v. Wershow* (1958) 157 Cal. App. 2d 352, 357–58, 320 P.2d 926; *see Cook v. Nordstrand* (1948) 83 Cal. App. 2d 188, 194–95, 188 P.2d 282; *Atkinson v. District Bond Co., supra,* 5 Cal. App. 2d 738, 743–44, 43 P.2d 867.

As we have pointed out, the trial court found that the whole course of conduct of defendants and their agents Dr. Pessin and Mrs. Judy from the time of the sale of Fleet Nasrullah up to and including June 13, 1966, amounted to a repudiation which plaintiff was justified in treating as an anticipatory breach. (*See* fn. 5, *ante.*) However, when the principles of law governing repudiation just described are applied to the facts constituting this course of conduct as found by the trial court, it is manifest that such conduct cannot be treated as an undifferentiated continuum amounting to a single repudiation but must be divided into two separate repudiations.

First, defendants clearly repudiated the contracts when, after selling Fleet Nasrullah and shipping him to Kentucky, they informed plaintiff "[y]ou are, therefore, released from your reservations made to the stallion." However, the trial court additionally found that "[p]laintiff did not wish to be 'released' from his 'reservations'... insist[ed] on performance of the stud service agreements ... [and] threaten[ed] litigation if the contracts were not honored by defendants...." Accordingly defendants arranged for performance of the contracts by making Fleet Nasrullah available for stud service to plaintiff in Kentucky through their agents Dr. Pessin and Mrs. Judy. Plaintiff elected to treat the contracts as in force and shipped the mares to Kentucky to effect the desired performance. The foregoing facts lead us to conclude that the subsequent arrangements by defendants to make Fleet Nasrullah available to service plaintiff's mares in Kentucky constituted a retraction of the repudiation. Since at this time plaintiff had not elected to treat the repudiation as an anticipatory breach[10] and in fact had shipped the mares to Kentucky in reliance on defendants' arrangements, this retraction nullified the repudiation. Thus, plaintiff was then left with his remedies that might arise at the time of performance.

The trial court found that after the mares had arrived in Kentucky, had delivered the foals they were then carrying and were ready for servicing by Fleet Nasrullah, plaintiff was justified in concluding from the conduct of defendants, their agent Dr. Pessin, and their subagent Mrs. Judy, that "defendants were just giving him the runaround and had no intention of performing their contract in the manner required by its terms" and in treating such conduct "as a breach and repudiation of their contractual obligation to him." See fn. 5, ante. Since, as we have explained, defendants retracted their original repudiation, this subsequent conduct amounts to a finding of a second repudiation.

There is no evidence in the record that defendants or their agents Dr. Pessin and Mrs. Judy ever stated that Sunday Slippers and Sandy Fork would not be serviced by Fleet Nasrullah during the 1966 breeding season or that they ever refused to perform. Frazier, plaintiff's agent who made arrangements for the breeding of the mares admitted that they had never made such a statement to him.[11] Accordingly, there was no *express* repudiation or unequivocal refusal to perform. *Guerrieri v. Severini, supra,* 51 Cal. 2d 12, 18, 330 P.2d 635; *Atkinson v. District Bond Co., supra,* 5 Cal. App. 2d 738, 743–44, 43 P.2d 867.

The trial court's finding of repudiation, expressly based on the "conduct of the defendants" and their agents suggests that the court found an implied repudiation. However, there is no implied repudiation, i.e., by conduct equivalent to an unequivocal refusal to perform, unless "the promisor *puts it out of his power to perform.*" *Zogarts v. Smith, supra,* 86 Cal. App. 2d 165, 172–73, 194 P.2d 143; 1 Witkin, Summary of Cal. Law (8th ed.) § 632, p. 538; 4 Corbin, Contracts, *supra,* § 984, pp. 949–51; *Rest.2d Contracts* (Tent. Draft No. 8, 1973) §§ 268, 274. Once the mares arrived in Kentucky, defendants had the power to perform the contracts; Fleet Nasrullah could breed with the mares. No subsequent conduct occurred to render this performance impossible. Although plaintiff was subordinated to the shareholders with respect to the priority of reserving a breeding time with Fleet Nasrullah, there is no evidence in the record that this subordination of reservation rights rendered performance impossible. Rather it acted to postpone the time of performance, which still remained within the limits prescribed by the contracts. It rendered performance more difficult to achieve; it may even have cast doubt upon the eventual accomplishment of performance; it did not render performance impossible.[12]

---

10. Plaintiff concedes that the repudiation was not "accepted by plaintiff."

11. "Q.... At any time, did Mrs. Judy or anyone else ever tell you that she could not or would not breed either mare to Fleet Nasrullah before the end of 1966? ..."THE WITNESS: No."

12. Plaintiff suggests that this conduct, namely delaying plaintiff's breeding until a day not reserved by a shareholder, amounted to an anticipatory breach because Mrs. Judy inserted a condition to defendants' performance, which as the trial court found was not contemplated by the contracts. Assuming arguendo that this conduct might have amounted to a breach of contract by improperly delaying performance, at most it would have constituted only a partial breach — insufficiently material to terminate the contracts (*see Rest. 2d Contracts* (Tent. Draft No. 8, 1973) §§ 262, 266, 268, 274). It did not constitute a repudiation of the contracts which was the sole basis of the trial court's decision since "(t)o justify the adverse party in treating the renunciation as a breach, the refusal to perform must be of the whole contract or of a covenant going to the whole consideration...." (*Atkinson v. District Bond Co., supra,* 5 Cal. App. 2d 738, 743, 43 P.2d 867, 869.).

Because there was no repudiation, express or implied, there was no anticipatory breach. Plaintiff contends that defendants' conduct, as found by the trial court, indicated that "defendants were just giving him the runaround and had no intention of performing their contract" and therefore that this conduct was the equivalent of an express and un-equivocal refusal to perform. Plaintiff has not presented to the court any authority in California in support of his proposition that conduct which has not met the test for an implied repudiation, i.e., conduct which removed the power to perform, may nonetheless be held to amount to the equivalent of an express repudiation and thus constitute an anticipatory breach. Without addressing ourselves to the question whether some conduct could ever be found equal to an express repudiation, we hold that defendants' conduct in this case as a matter of law did not constitute an anticipatory breach.

To constitute an express repudiation, the promisor's statement, or in this case conduct, must amount to an unequivocal refusal to perform:

> A mere declaration, however, of a party of an intention not to be bound will not of itself amount to a breach, so as to create an effectual renunciation of the contract; for one party cannot by any act or declaration destroy the binding force and efficacy of the contract. To justify the adverse party in treating the renunciation as a breach, the refusal to perform must be of the whole contract ... and must be distinct, unequivocal, and absolute.

Atkinson v. District Bond Co., *supra*, 5 Cal. App. 2d 738, 743, 43 P.2d 867, 869.

To recapitulate, Sandy Fork was in foal in January 1966, the commencement of the 1966 breeding season, and remained so until June 5, 1966. Throughout this period Fleet Nasrullah could not perform his services as contracted due solely to the conduct of plaintiff in breeding Sandy Fork in 1965. Biologically the first opportunity to breed Sandy Fork was on June 14, 1966, nine days after foaling. Frazier telephoned Mrs. Judy on June 6, 1966, and received a booking with Fleet Nasrullah for June 14, 1966. On June 13 Mrs. Judy telephoned Frazier and informed him she would have to cancel Sandy Fork's reservation for the following day because one of the shareholders insisted on using that day. Mrs. Judy gave no indication whatsoever that she could not or would not breed Sandy Fork on any of the following days in that heat period or subsequent heat periods. Frazier made no further attempts to breed Sandy Fork with Fleet Nasrullah. Thus, plaintiff, who delayed the possibility of performance for five months, asserts that the delay of performance oc-casioned by defendants' cancellation of a reservation on the first day during the six-month period that plaintiff made performance possible amounts to an unequivocal refusal to perform, even though there was adequate opportunity for Fleet Nasrullah to perform within the period for performance specified in the contract and even though defendants never stated any intention not to perform. We conclude that as a matter of law this conduct did not amount to an unequivocal refusal to perform and therefore did not constitute an anticipatory breach of the contract covering Sandy Fork.

Sunday Slippers foaled on April 17, 1966, first came into heat on April 26 and then successively on May 13 and June 4, 1966. Mrs. Judy informed Frazier that she would breed Sunday Slippers on any day that one of the shareholders did not want to use the stallion. Frazier unsuccessfully sought to breed the mare on April 26, May 14, May 15, and June 4, 1966, Fleet Nasrullah being reserved on those dates. Mrs. Judy continued to assure Frazier that the breeding would occur. Sunday Slippers was due to come into heat again twice during the breeding season: June 25 and July 16, 1966. At most this conduct amounts to delay of performance and a warning that performance might altogether be precluded if a shareholder were to desire Fleet Nasrullah's services on all the remaining days within the period specified for performance in which Sunday Slippers was in heat. We conclude that as a matter of law this conduct did not amount to an unequivocal refusal to perform and therefore did not constitute an anticipatory breach of the contract covering Sunday Slippers.

In sum, we hold that there is no evidence in the record supportive of the trial court's finding and conclusion that defendants repudiated and therefore committed an anticipatory breach of the contracts.

In view of the foregoing conclusion we need not consider defendants' remaining contentions.

The judgment is reversed.

Song of the Horse

A Nineteenth-Century Papago Song, translated by James Denison

Black hair rope is what you used in roping me.
You treated me badly.
You even threw me down and tied me.
Not satisfied with that, you tied a knot in my tail.
That made me disgusted.

Note

Sections 2-609 and 2-610 of the *Uniform Commercial Code* establish a process for communication and clarification of a party's intention and ability to perform that might have helped H.B. Taylor. These sections are echoed in *Restatement (Second) of Contracts* section 251.

AMF, Incorporated v. McDonald's Corporation

United States Court of Appeals for the Seventh Circuit
536 F.2d 1167 (1976)

WALTER J. CUMMINGS, CIRCUIT JUDGE

AMF, Incorporated, filed this case in the Southern District of New York in April 1972. It was transferred to the Northern District of Illinois in May 1973. AMF seeks damages for the alleged wrongful cancellation and repudiation of McDonald's Corporation's ("McDonald's") orders for sixteen computerized cash registers for installation in restaurants owned by wholly-owned subsidiaries of McDonald's and for seven such registers ordered by licensees of McDonald's for their restaurants. In July 1972, McDonald's of Elk Grove, Inc. sued AMF to recover the $20,385.28 purchase price paid for a prototype computerized cash register and losses sustained as a result of failure of the equipment to function satisfactorily. Both cases were tried together during a fortnight in December 1974. A few months after the completion of the bench trial, the district court rendered a memorandum opinion and order in both cases in favor of each defendant. The only appeal is from the eight judgment orders dismissing AMF's complaints against McDonald's and the seven licensees.[1] We affirm.

The district court's memorandum opinion and order are unreported. Our statement of the pertinent facts is culled from the 124 findings of fact contained therein or from the record itself.

In 1966, AMF began to market individual components of a completely automated restaurant system, including its model 72C computerized cash register involved here. The 72C cash register then consisted of a central computer, one to four input stations, each with a keyboard and cathode ray tube display, plus the necessary cables and controls.

In 1967 McDonald's representatives visited AMF's plant in Springdale, Connecticut, to view a working "breadboard" model 72C to decide whether to use it in McDonald's restaurant system. Later that year, it was agreed that a 72C should be placed in a McDonald's restaurant for evaluation purposes.

In April 1968, a 72C unit accommodating six input stations was installed in McDonald's restaurant in Elk Grove, Illinois. This restaurant was a wholly-owned subsidiary of McDonald's and was its busiest restaurant. Besides functioning as a cash register, the 72C was intended to enable counter personnel to work faster and to assist in providing data for accounting reports and bookkeeping. McDonald's of Elk Grove, Inc. paid some $20,000 for this prototype register on January 3, 1969. AMF never gave McDonald's warranties governing reliability or performance standards for the prototype.

At a meeting in Chicago on August 29, 1968, McDonald's concluded to order sixteen 72C's for its company-owned restaurants and to cooperate with AMF to obtain additional orders from its licensees. In December 1968, AMF accepted McDonald's purchase orders for those sixteen 72C's. In late January 1969, AMF accepted seven additional orders for 72C's from McDonald's licensees for their restaurants.[2] Under the contract for the sale of all the units, there was a warranty for parts and service. AMF proposed to deliver the first unit in February 1969, with installation of the remaining twenty-two units in the first half of 1969. However, AMF established a new delivery schedule in February 1969, providing for deliveries to commence at the end of July 1969 and to be completed in January 1970, assuming that the first test unit being built at AMF's Vandalia, Ohio, plant was built and satisfactorily tested by the end of July 1969. This was never accomplished.

During the operation of the prototype 72C at McDonald's Elk Grove restaurant, many problems resulted, requiring frequent service calls by AMF and others. Because of its poor performance, McDonald's had AMF remove the prototype unit from its Elk Grove restaurant in late April 1969.

At a March 18, 1969, meeting, McDonald's and AMF personnel met to discuss the performance of the Elk Grove prototype. AMF agreed to formulate a set of performance and reliability standards for the future 72C's, including "the number of failures permitted at various degrees of seriousness, total permitted downtime, maximum service hours and cost." Pending mutual agreement on such standards, McDonald's personnel asked that production of the twenty-three units be held up and AMF agreed.

On May 1, 1969, AMF met with McDonald's personnel to provide them with performance and reliability standards. However, the parties never agreed upon such

1. AMF's lawsuits against said licensees were governed by the parent case and were dismissed in the light of the district court's memorandum opinion and order entered in AMF's case against McDonald's.

2. An eighth order was canceled and is not involved in this lawsuit.

standards. At that time, AMF did not have a working machine and could not produce one within a reasonable time because its Vandalia, Ohio, personnel were too inexperienced. After the May 1st meeting, AMF concluded that McDonald's had canceled all 72C orders. The reasons for the cancellation were the poor performance of the prototype, the lack of assurances that a workable machine was available and the unsatisfactory conditions at AMF's Vandalia, Ohio, plant where the twenty-three 72C's were to be built.

On July 29, 1969, McDonald's and AMF representatives met in New York. At this meeting it was mutually understood that the 72C orders were canceled and that none would be delivered.

In its conclusions of law, the district court held that McDonald's and its licensees had entered into contracts for twenty-three 72C cash registers but that AMF was not able to perform its obligations under the contracts (*see* note, 1, *supra*). Citing section 2-610 of the *Uniform Commercial Code* (Ill. Rev. Stats. (1975) ch. 26, §2-610)[3] and Comment 1 thereunder,[4] the court concluded that on July 29, McDonald's justifiably repudiated the contracts to purchase all twenty-three 72C's.

Relying on Section 2-609 and 2-610 of the *Uniform Commercial Code* (Ill. Rev. Stats. (1975) ch. 26, §§2-609 and 2-610),[5] the court decided that McDonald's was warranted in repudiating the contracts and therefore had a right to cancel the orders by virtue of section 2-711 of the *Uniform Commercial Code* (Ill. Rev. Stats. (1975) ch. 26, §2-711).[6] Accordingly, judgment was entered for McDonald's.

---

3. Section 2-610 provides:
Anticipatory Repudiation. When either party repudiates the contract with respect to a performance not yet due the loss of which will substantially impair the value of the contract to the other, the aggrieved party may
   (a) for a commercially reasonable time await performance by the repudiating party; or
   (b) resort to any remedy for breach (Section 2-703 or Section 2-711), even though he has notified the repudiating party that he would await the latter's performance and has urged retraction; and
   (c) in either case suspend his own performance or proceed in accordance with the provisions of this Article on the seller's right to identify goods to the contract notwithstanding breach or to salvage unfinished goods (Section 2-704).
4. Official Comment 1 is reproduced in *Uniform Commercial Code Annotated* 401 (1968) and need not be considered in the disposition of this case.
5. Section 2-609 provides:
Right to Adequate Assurance of Performance.
   (1) A contract for sale imposes an obligation on each party that the other's expectation of receiving due performance will not be impaired. When reasonable grounds for insecurity arise with respect to the performance of either party the other may in writing demand adequate assurance of due performance and until he receives such assurance may if commercially reasonable suspend any performance for which he has not already received the agreed return.
   (2) Between merchants the reasonableness of grounds for insecurity and the adequacy of any assurance offered shall be determined according to commercial standards.
   (3) Acceptance of any improper delivery or payment does not prejudice the aggrieved party's right to demand adequate assurance of future performance.
   (4) After receipt of a justified demand failure to provide within a reasonable time not exceeding 30 days such assurance of due performance as is adequate under the circumstances of the particular case is a repudiation of the contract.
6. Section 2-711 provides:
Buyer's Remedies in General; Buyer's Security Interest in Rejected Goods.
   (1) Where the seller fails to make delivery or repudiates or the buyer rightfully rejects or justifiably revokes acceptance then with respect to any goods involved, and with respect to the whole if the breach goes to the whole contract (Section 2-612), the buyer may

The findings of fact adopted by the district court were a mixture of the court's own findings and findings proposed by the parties, some of them modified by the court. AMF has assailed ten of the 124 findings of fact, but our examination of the record satisfies us that all have adequate support in the record and support the conclusions of law.

Whether in a specific case a buyer has reasonable grounds for insecurity is a question of fact. Comment 3 to *UCC* § 2-609; Anderson, Uniform Commercial Code, § 2-609 (2d ed. 1971). On this record, McDonald's clearly had "reasonable grounds for insecurity" with respect to AMF's performance. At the time of the March 18, 1969, meeting, the prototype unit had performed unsatisfactorily ever since its April 1968 installation. Although AMF had projected delivery of all twenty-three units by the first half of 1969, AMF later scheduled delivery from the end of July 1969 until January 1970. When McDonald's personnel visited AMF's Vandalia, Ohio, plant on March 4, 1969, they saw that none of the 72C systems was being assembled and learned that a pilot unit would not be ready until the end of July of that year. They were informed that the engineer assigned to the project was not to commence work until March 17th. AMF's own personnel were also troubled about the design of the 72C, causing them to attempt to reduce McDonald's order to five units. Therefore, under section 2-609 McDonald's was entitled to demand adequate assurance of performance by AMF.[7]

However, AMF urges that section 2-609 of the *UCC* (note 5 *supra*) is inapplicable because McDonald's did not make a written demand of adequate assurance of due performance. In *Pittsburgh-Des Moines Steel Co. v. Brookhaven Manor Water Co.*, 532 F.2d 572, 581 (7th Cir. 1976), we noted that the *Code* should be liberally construed[8] and therefore rejected such "a formalistic approach" to section 2-609.[9] McDonald's failure to

---

cancel and whether or not he has done so may in addition to recovering so much of the price as has been paid

    (a) 'cover' and have damages under the next section as to all the goods affected whether or not they have been identified to the contract; or

    (b) recover damages for non-delivery as provided in this Article (Section 2-713).

(2) Where the seller fails to deliver or repudiates the buyer may also

    (a) if the goods have been identified recover them as provided in this Article (Section 2-502); or

    (b) in a proper case obtain specific performance or replevy the goods as provided in this Article (Section 2-716).

(3) On rightful rejection or justifiable revocation of acceptance a buyer has a security interest in goods in his possession or control for any payments made on their price and any expenses reasonably incurred in their inspection, receipt, transportation, care and custody and may hold such goods and resell them in like manner as an aggrieved seller (Section 2-706).

7. McDonald's was justified in seeking assurances about performance standards at the March 18th meeting. The parts and service warranty in the contracts for the twenty-three 72C's was essentially a limitation of remedy provision. Under UCC § 2-719(2) (Ill. Rev. Stats. (1975) ch. 26, § 2-719(2)) if the 72C cash registers failed to work or could not be repaired within a reasonable time, the limitation of remedy provision would be invalid, and McDonald's would be entitled to pursue all other remedies provided in Article 2. *See* Riley v. Ford Motor Co., 442 F.2d 670, 673 (5th Cir. 1971); Earl M. Jorgensen Co. v. Mark Construction Co., 540 P.2d 978, 985–987 (Hawaii 1975). Because McDonald's would have a right to reject the machines if they proved faulty after delivery and then to cancel the contract, it was consistent with the purposes of section 2-609 for McDonald's to require assurances that such eventuality would not occur. *See* Comment 1 to UCC § 2-719.

8. UCC section 1-102(1) provides that the Code "shall be liberally construed and applied to promote its underlying purposes and policies" (Ill. Rev. Stats. (1975) ch. 26, § 1-102(1)).

9. *See also* Copylease Corp. of America v. Memorex Corp., 403 F. Supp. 625, 631 (S.D.N.Y. 1975); Kunian v. Development Corp. of America, 334 A.2d 427, 433 (Conn. S. Ct. 1973). A passing reference was made to *UCC* section 609's written requirement for a demand in National Ropes, Inc. v. National

make a written demand was excusable because AMF's Mr. Dubosque's testimony and his April 2 and 18, 1969, memoranda about the March 18th meeting showed AMF's clear understanding that McDonald's had suspended performance until it should receive adequate assurance of due performance from AMF.

After the March 18th demand, AMF never repaired the Elk Grove unit satisfactorily nor replaced it. Similarly, it was unable to satisfy McDonald's that the twenty-three machines on order would work. At the May 1st meeting, AMF offered unsatisfactory assurances for only five units instead of twenty-three. The performance standards AMF tendered to McDonald's were unacceptable because they would have permitted the 72C's not to function properly for 90 hours per year, permitting as much as one failure in every fifteen days in a busy McDonald's restaurant. Also, as the district court found, AMF's Vandalia, Ohio, personnel were too inexperienced to produce a proper machine. Since AMF did not provide adequate assurance of performance after McDonald's March 18th demand, *UCC* section 2-609(1) permitted McDonald's to suspend performance. When AMF did not furnish adequate assurance of due performance at the May 1st meeting, it thereby repudiated the contract under section 2-609(4). At that point, section 2-610(b) (note 3 *supra*) permitted McDonald's to cancel the orders pursuant to section 2-711 (note 6, *supra*), as it finally did on July 29, 1969.

In seeking reversal, AMF relies on *Pittsburgh-Des Moines Steel Co. v. Brookhaven Manor Water Co., supra,* 532 F.2d at 581. There we held a party to a contract could not resort to *UCC* section 2-609 since there was no demonstration that reasonable grounds for insecurity were present. That case is inapt where, as here, McDonald's submitted sufficient proof in that respect. But that case does teach that McDonald's could cancel the orders under sections 2-610 and 2-711 because of AMF's failure to give adequate assurance of due performance under section 2-609.

AMF also relies heavily on *Stewart-Decatur Security Systems v. Von Weise Gear Co.,* 517 F.2d 1136 (8th Cir. 1975), but it did not involve the provisions of the *Commercial Code* that are before us. There the buyer had agreed to purchase production line models of a previously approved prototype. Here McDonald's contracted to purchase workable 72C's, not copies of the worthless Elk Grove prototype.

Judgment Affirmed.

Diving Service, Inc., 513 F.2d 53, 61 (5th Cir. 1975). However, the court held that section 2-609 was not applicable because there was no finding that the seller had reasonable grounds for insecurity and because the record would not support such a finding.

Chapter Eleven

Remedies

One party breaches a contract. The doctrines examined in Chapter Ten may allow the aggrieved party to suspend or cancel his or her performance under the contract in response to a breach. Some lawyers call this a "defensive remedy," because it enables the aggrieved party to protect against even greater loss. In addition, the aggrieved party can sue for breach of contract and if liability is established, the court can require the breaching party to perform the contract ("specific performance"), pay money to the aggrieved party ("damages"), comply with any remedy specified in the agreement (e.g., "liquidated damages," or other agreed remedies), or any combination of these three.

Think of a contract involving something that is important to you—maybe a job, an apartment, or an airline ticket home. Three weeks ago you found an apartment you can afford, within walking distance of the law school, with bright sunny windows and a view of the park. You completed an application; the rental officer, Alan, shook your hand and said you could move in at the beginning of the month. You signed a printed lease and paid a $1,000 deposit. Anticipating the apartment, you bought a new couch, table, and chairs for $825, and you spent all week-end searching for second-hand kitchen supplies. Less than an hour ago you went to the rental office to pick up the apartment key. A man named Jake introduced himself as the rental officer. You asked for Alan, and Jake said Alan didn't work there anymore. You asked about the apartment and Jake said a new tenant moved in yesterday. Then Jake got a telephone call, quickly said good-bye, and rushed out the door.

So how do you feel? How would you explain the situation to a friend? You really wanted that apartment and the rental company promised you could rent it—the rental agent signed a lease with you! Plus you are out at least $1,825; you can't get your money back from the furniture store; and you wasted a whole weekend! They have your $1,000! This is just wrong!

The principles of bargain, reliance, and restitution resurface here as different ways of measuring the harm done when someone fails to perform a contract. If you find a comparable apartment, it might cost you more money. If you cannot cancel the contract for the furniture you purchased, the furniture is unsuitable for the substitute apartment you find, or you end up living at home with your parents for another year, your out of pocket expenditures may be wasted. Most disturbing of all, the other party is walking away with your money! Each of these scenarios describes an infringement of your interests. The lease agreement gives you a legitimate expectation that you will have a place to live that will cost a certain amount and be in a certain location. You trusted the company to fulfill its promise and you spent money relying on the lease. And of course it is unjust for the rental company to keep your $1,000.

So what's a fair remedy? If you sue the rental company, should the judge order them to rent the apartment to you, reimburse you for the $1,825, and return your $1,000 deposit? No, the company breached its contract, but you aren't entitled to recover all losses you may have sustained. The different measurements of injury can also be classified in terms of the three overarching principles that we have been discussing: the bargain principle gives rise to damages measured by the benefit that you expected to gain from the bargain. The reliance interest measures injury in terms of expenses incurred in the belief that you had a new apartment, and the restitution interest would result in the disgorgement of the money received by the landlord.

As we have seen throughout this course, the values associated with bargain, reliance, and restitution are important throughout contemporary contract law. Contract remedies, however, are focused primarily on protecting the expectation interest. As the Uniform Commercial Code puts it, remedies should be shaped "to the end that the aggrieved party may be put in as good a position as if the other party had fully performed." (UCC § 1-305) When a court decides that a contract is enforceable, then the remedy for breach should give the aggrieved party the equivalent of what he or she would have gotten if the contract were performed, no more and no less. Theoretically, then, the remedy should give the plaintiff the "benefit of the bargain." This chapter begins with the remedy that is most likely to give the injured party the benefit of the bargain—specific performance.

A. Benefit of the Bargain: Specific Performance

What is the best way to put the disappointed tenant in as good a position as he would have been in if the rental company had fully performed its contract? Shouldn't the judge simply order the rental company to rent the apartment to the plaintiff on the exact terms of the lease agreement?

If a court did issue an order like this, the contract remedy would be termed "specific performance of the contract." The traditional rule is that specific performance will be ordered only if "there is no adequate remedy at law"—meaning that monetary damages (the only remedy that early English "law courts" could order) will not adequately compensate the plaintiff. In addition, specific performance will be ordered only if the acts required of the defendant were clear, if performance will not be unfairly difficult for the defendant, and only if performance of the contract will not violate some public policy or have a negative impact on the public.

Recently courts have granted specific performance more readily and commentators have endorsed this change. The *UCC* and the *Restatement (Second) of Contracts* both support use of the remedy in a broad range of situations. Specific performance is still an "exceptional" remedy, but it is certainly available in appropriate cases.

Adam D. Sokoloff et al. v. Harriman Estates Development Corp.

New York Court of Appeals
754 N.E.2d 184 (2001)

HOWARD A. LEVINE, JUDGE

On this appeal, we review the dismissal on the pleadings ... of plaintiffs' cause of action seeking specific performance of an alleged contract. The facts as alleged in the complaint and other averments submitted in opposition to the motion to dismiss are as follows. In March 1998, plaintiffs purchased land in the Village of Sands Point, Nassau County, in contemplation of building a new home on the property. For a total of $65,000, defendant

Harriman Estates Development Corp., a residential contractor, offered to provide plaintiffs with certain pre-construction services, including furnishing an "architectural and site plan/landscape design" and assisting them in obtaining a building permit. The offer was set forth by Harriman in a March 12, 1998 letter, which established a payment schedule and requested payment of a $10,000 retainer fee. Plaintiffs accepted the offer by paying Harriman the retainer fee. Thereafter, following several meetings between plaintiffs, Harriman and defendant Frederick Ercolino, an architect, the architectural plans were finalized, filed with the Village and approved.

Although plaintiffs paid Harriman a total of $55,000 for the architectural plans and other services, and tendered the remaining balance due under the terms of their agreement with Harriman, Harriman and Ercolino refused to allow plaintiffs to use these plans to build their home. After plaintiffs rejected Harriman's offer to build the home for an estimated cost of $1,895,000 (a sum significantly greater than Harriman's earlier estimates), Harriman for the first time informed plaintiffs that the architectural plans could not be used to construct the house unless it was hired as the builder. Harriman predicated its claim to the exclusive use of the plans on the terms of a contract it had entered into with Ercolino in May 1998 for the "Sokoloff Residence."

Plaintiffs then brought this action against Harriman and Ercolino for specific performance of the "contract dated March 12, 1998" (the first cause of action) and for replevin of the architectural plans (the second cause of action). With respect to the first cause of action, seeking specific performance, plaintiffs alleged that Harriman was acting as their agent in procuring architectural drawings and plans from Ercolino, that the plans were unique and based upon a design conceived by them and that they had no adequate remedy at law. Plaintiffs requested an order directing Harriman and Ercolino to permit them to use the architectural plans....

. . .

Harriman moved to dismiss the complaint for failure to state a cause of action. Supreme Court granted the motion in part by dismissing the cause of action for replevin, leaving intact plaintiffs' cause of action for specific performance. On Harriman's appeal, ... the Appellate Division reversed, [and] dismissed the specific performance claim.... We granted leave to appeal and now reverse.

We reject Harriman's assertion that specific performance is an inappropriate remedy because the architectural plans are not unique and a dollar value can be placed on the purchase of replacement plans. In general, specific performance will not be ordered where money damages "would be adequate to protect the expectation interest of the injured party" Restatement [Second] of Contracts § 359. Specific performance is a proper remedy, however, where "the subject matter of the particular contract is unique and has no established market value."

The decision whether or not to award specific performance is one that rests in the sound discretion of the trial court. In determining whether money damages would be an adequate remedy, a trial court must consider, among other factors, the difficulty of proving damages with reasonable certainty and of procuring a suitable substitute performance with a damages award (see, Restatement [Second] of Contracts § 360). Specific performance is an appropriate remedy for a breach of contract concerning goods that "are unique in kind, quality or personal association" where suitable substitutes are unobtainable or unreasonably difficult or inconvenient to procure (see, id., comment c).

In this case, plaintiffs have alleged that "[t]he architectural plans and drawings are unique in that they are based upon a design conceived by the plaintiffs," and that without specific performance they "would have to change their requirements" as to the design of their new home. These allegations are sufficient to withstand a motion to dismiss for failure to state a cause of action. Whether money damages would adequately compensate plaintiffs for loss of these allegedly unique architectural plans is a matter to be resolved at a later stage, not on a motion to dismiss the complaint....

Accordingly, the order of the Appellate Division should be reversed, with costs, and the motion of defendant Harriman Estates Development Corp. to dismiss the first cause of action of the complaint against it denied.

Note

As Judge Levine observes, Anglo-American contract law has treated specific performance as an "exceptional" remedy for breach of contract, available only when monetary compensatory damages are inadequate. The general rule was sometimes stated as allowing specific performance only where the item contracted for was "unique" (and land was generally considered unique).

Several reasons are given for the preference for compensatory damages over specific performance. One is historical. By the seventeenth century, a dual system of courts developed in England: the common law courts, which were restricted to specified writs or orders, and the Chancery or Equity Courts. By delegated authority, the common law courts issued writs in the name of the King. If a person felt he or she had been injured by another, the aggrieved person would seek action by the courts, acting in the King's stead. The common law courts could issue writs or orders only in specified circumstances. In order to obtain relief, a complaint had to satisfy one of the specified circumstances (e.g., trespass, debt, special trespass).

By the thirteenth century, the writ system became formal and rigid and no new writs or causes of action could be created. Unable to recover in the common law courts, some people petitioned the King for special relief and the King assigned these petitions to the Chancellor, who eventually set up courts to hear the petitions. These courts developed a separate system of jurisprudence called equity and remedies that are equitable. While the common law courts were confined to awards of monetary damages, Equity courts had the power to issue injunctions and other affirmative relief. By the seventeenth century, the Chancery or Equity Courts were well established and were viewed with competitive suspicion by common law judges. Under this dual system of courts, then, the rule allowing injunctive relief (or "specific performance") for breach of contract only when there is no adequate remedy at law originated as a jurisdictional requirement. The rule required, in essence, that a person seek relief first from the common law and then, only if the legal remedy was inadequate, from equity. This rationale lost much of its political significance with the merger of courts of law and equity in England in 1854 and in most of the United States before the end of the nineteenth century. Yet some jurisdictional distinctions still do exist, as in the distinction in the state of Pennsylvania between the Pennsylvania Board of Arbitration of Claims, which has jurisdiction over monetary claims against government agencies but not over claims for injunctive relief, and the Commonwealth Courts, which do have authority to hear claims for specific performance.

A second rationale for the rule favoring damages over specific performance in the United States has focused on the imbalance of power created when one party can be ordered to perform work or other contractual obligations. Forced labor under an order of specific performance is too much like involuntary servitude prohibited by the Thirteenth Amendment to the United States Constitution, or peonage, outlawed by 42 U.S.C.S. 1994, a Reconstruction Era statute. Concern with the use of specific performance to force people to work remains, as *Beverly Glen Music, Inc. v. Warner Communications, Inc.*, below, demonstrates.

The third argument that has been used in opposition to specific performance is the idea that breach of contract is morally neutral. So long as expectation damages are paid, this argument asserts, there is no social interest in contract compliance and "a man should be free to breach his contract." More recently, law and economics scholars have argued that some breaches of contract are desirable because they result in a more efficient allocation of resources. *See, e.g.,*Richard Posner, Economic Analysis of Law 88–90 (2d ed. 1977). Others disagree with this reasoning, concluding that efficiency is served best by respecting a plaintiff's choice of compensatory or specific relief. *See, e.g.*, Anthony Kronman, *Specific Performance*, 45 U. Chi. L. Rev. 351 (1978); Alan Schwartz, *The Case for Specific Performance*, 89 Yale L.J. 271 (1979).

The use of specific performance remains controversial in current law. Based on an evaluation of more than fourteen hundred cases, Professor Douglas Laycock concluded that the rule allowing specific performance only upon a showing of no adequate remedy at law is effectively dead. Although courts continue to recite the rule, Laycock found that in most cases, courts award specific performance if plaintiffs request it, and that in those cases where specific relief is denied, courts are motivated by concern for judicial expense or other administrative concerns. Douglas Laycock, *The Death of the Irreparable Injury Rule*, 103 Harv. L. Rev. 687 (1990).

For domestic transactions involving the sale or lease of goods, sections 2-716 (Buyer's Right to Specific Performance or Replevin), 2-709 (Action for the Price), 2A-521 (Lessee's Right to Specific Performance or Replevin), and 2A-529 (Lessor's Action for the Rent) of the *Uniform Commercial Code* allow specific performance in a wide range of cases. For international transactions in goods, the *United Nations Convention on Contracts for the International Sale of Goods* provides specific performance in Articles 46(1) ("The buyer may require performance by the seller of his obligations unless the buyer has resorted to a remedy which is inconsistent with this requirement.") and 62 ("The seller may require the buyer to pay the price, take delivery or perform his other obligations, unless the seller has resorted to a remedy which is inconsistent with this requirement.).

Beverly Glen Music, Inc. v. Warner Communications, Inc. and Anita Baker

California Court of Appeal
178 Cal. App. 3d 1142 (1986)

ROBERT KINGSLEY, ACTING PRESIDING JUSTICE

The plaintiff appeals from an order denying a preliminary injunction against the defendant, Warner Communications, Inc. We affirm.

Facts

In 1982, plaintiff Beverly Glen Music, Inc. signed to a contract a then-unknown singer, Anita Baker. Ms. Baker recorded an album for Beverly Glen which was moderately successful, grossing over one million dollars. In 1984, however, Ms. Baker was offered a considerably better deal by defendant Warner Communications. As she was having some difficulties with Beverly Glen, she accepted Warner's offer and notified plaintiff that she was no longer willing to perform under the contract. Beverly Glen then sued Ms. Baker and sought to have her enjoined from performing for any other recording studio. The injunction was denied, however, as, under *Civil Code* section 3423, subdivision Fifth, California courts will not enjoin the breach of a personal service contract unless the service is unique in nature and the performer is guaranteed annual compensation of at least $6,000, which Ms. Baker was not.

Following this ruling, the plaintiff voluntarily dismissed the action against Ms. Baker. Plaintiff, however, then sued Warner Communications for inducing Ms. Baker to breach her contract and moved the court for an injunction against Warner to prevent it from employing her. This injunction, too, was denied, the trial court reasoning that what one was forbidden by statute to do directly, one could not accomplish through the back door. It is from this ruling that the plaintiff appeals.

Discussion

From what we can tell, this is a case of first impression in California. While there are numerous cases on the general inability of an employer to enjoin his former employee from performing services somewhere else, apparently no one has previously thought of enjoining the new employer from accepting the services of the breaching employee. While we commend the plaintiff for its resourcefulness in this regard, we concur in the trial court's interpretation of the maneuver.

"It is a familiar rule that a contract to render personal services cannot be specifically enforced." *Foxx v. Williams* 52 Cal. Rptr. 896, 907 (Cal. Ct. App. 1966) An unwilling employee cannot be compelled to continue to provide services to his employer either by ordering specific performance of his contract, or by injunction. To do so runs afoul of the Thirteenth Amendment's prohibition against involuntary servitude. *Poultry Producers Etc. v. Barlow* (1922) 208 P. 93, 102 (Cal.). However, beginning with the English case of *Lumley v. Wagner* (1852) 42 Eng. Rep. 687, courts have recognized that, while they cannot directly enforce an affirmative promise (in the *Lumley* case, Miss Wagner's promise to perform at the plaintiff's opera house), they can enforce the negative promise implied therein (that the defendant would not perform for someone else that evening). Thus, while it is not possible to compel a defendant to perform his duties under a personal service contract, it is possible to prevent him from employing his talents anywhere else. The net effect is to pressure the defendant to return voluntarily to his employer by denying him the means of earning a living. Indeed, this is its only purpose, for, unless the defendant relents and honors the contract, the plaintiff gains nothing from having brought the injunction.

The California Legislature, however, did not adopt this principle when in 1872 it enacted *Civil Code* section 3423, subdivision Fifth, and *Code of Civil Procedure* section 526, subdivision 5. These sections both provided that an injunction could not be granted: "To prevent the breach of a contract the performance of which would not be specifically enforced." In 1919, however, these sections were amended, creating an exception for: "a contract in writing for the rendition or furnishing of personal services from one to another where the minimum compensation for such service is at the rate of not less than six thousand dollars per annum and where the promised service is of a special, unique, unusual, extraordinary or intellectual character...."

The plaintiff has already unsuccessfully argued before the trial court that Ms. Baker falls within this exception. It has chosen not to appeal that judgment, and is therefore barred from questioning that determination now. The sole issue before us then is whether plaintiff—although prohibited from enjoining Ms. Baker from performing herself—can seek to enjoin all those who might employ her and prevent them from doing so, thus achieving the same effect.

We rule that plaintiff cannot. Whether plaintiff proceeds against Ms. Baker directly or against those who might employ her, the intent is the same: to deprive Ms. Baker of her livelihood and thereby pressure her to return to plaintiff's employ. Plaintiff contends that this is not an action against Ms. Baker but merely an equitable claim against Warner to deprive it of the wrongful benefits it gained when it "stole" Ms. Baker away. Thus, plaintiff contends, the equities lie not between the plaintiff and Ms. Baker, but between plaintiff and the predatory Warner Communications company. Yet if Warner's behavior has actually been predatory, plaintiff has an adequate remedy by way of damages. An injunction adds nothing to plaintiff's recovery from Warner except to coerce Ms. Baker to honor her contract. Denying someone his livelihood is a harsh remedy. The Legislature has forbidden it but for one exception. To expand this remedy so that it could be used in virtually all breaches of a personal service contract is to ignore over one hundred years of common law on this issue. We therefore decline to reverse the order.

The order is affirmed.

Lea S. VanderVelde, The Gendered Origins of the Lumley Doctrine: Binding Men's Consciences and Women's Fidelity
101 Yale L.J. 775 (1992)

In the familiar case of *Lumley v. Wagner*, the English Court of Equity held that although opera singer Johanna Wagner could not be ordered to perform her contract, she would be enjoined from singing at any competing music hall for the term of the contract. *Lumley* is usually lauded in first year contracts courses as a just and fair decision, one that illustrates the proper distinction between equitable orders that force performance (unworkable and unjust) and equitable orders that prevent performance (sometimes workable, usually practical, and not necessarily unjust).

Contracts classes, however, rarely consider the central labor issue: whether an injunction preventing an employee from quitting and working elsewhere violates the American tradition of free labor and the right to quit employment. In American employment law, the *Lumley* rule was a regressive development. The beneficial side of the rule, that the opera singer would not be ordered to perform, was already secured by the Thirteenth Amendment.[5] Before *Lumley* took hold in American courts, employers had considerably less leverage to compel the continued service of employees under contract. With the *Lumley* rule in effect, employers could shut employees out of work unless they returned to work for them for the remainder of the employment contract, a term which sometimes lasted several years. An employer holding the power of an injunction over an employee could dictate the terms on which that employee would be free to work elsewhere.

The *Lumley* rule's regressive effect was expressly denounced by a leading American jurist at its first introduction in the labor emancipatory era following the Civil War; yet it quiescently attained the status of the dominant common law rule in American courts by the 1890s. How did the rule of *Lumley v. Wagner* come to be incorporated into the canon of rules pertaining to equitable intervention in cases of departing employees? Why,

---

5. While *Lumley v. Wagner* was decided in 1852 in England, it was not noticed by American courts until considerably later. *See* Ford v. Jermon, 6 Phila. 6 (Dist. Ct. 1865).

of all the nineteenth-century opinions on the subject, was *Lumley*, rather than other rulings decided by equally eminent American judges constructed into the canon of law?

The answer appears to be related to the gendered context in which the rule was examined at the time that American courts constructed the canon. Suits involving the services of women constituted the core of cases and provided the central contextual focus in which the rule was examined. Many more actresses than actors were sued under this cause of action. Indeed, in the nineteenth century, all of the prominent cases in this line involved the services of women, and only women performers were subjected to permanent injunctions against performing elsewhere for the duration of the contract. In the corpus of reported cases, no male performer was ever permanently enjoined from quitting and performing elsewhere during the entire nineteenth century.

The fact that suits over women dominate this line of cases appears to be more than a coincidence. On no other topic of employment litigation, save the tort of seduction, do women figure so prominently in the leading cases. This concentration of women litigants is anomalous in the nineteenth century, an era when women were unlikely to be parties to any employment litigation. Both legal and cultural constraints discouraged women from working for wages. If they were married, the doctrine of coverture submerged women's legal identity under their husbands'. Thus, it is indeed unusual to find that on a gender-neutral legal issue like an employee's right to quit, women's cases would so considerably outnumber men's cases in a profession where women worked alongside men. Moreover, it is unusual that these women's cases would be raised to establish the standard.

... I offer a tentative explanation of this phenomenon: that the *Lumley* rule's reception in the United States was facilitated by the fact that the majority of cases that employers won were cases involving women. I have chosen the term "gendered" to describe this phenomenon because the term covers a broad range of gender-specific elements that recur in this line of cases. These include sexist behavior, sex role typing, unequal treatment, charged language of a gender-specific nature, and sexual harassment. However, the pattern is complex. The phenomenon was not a simple one of misogyny or sexism, and it did not appear uniformly in every case involving a woman employee. Deeper cultural constructions of the role of women in the public workplace, particularly the very public workplace of the stage, explain the phenomenon better than would attributions of sexism to the few key individuals involved. A woman appearing in public on the stage posed a particular challenge to the dominant norm of the Victorian Era that women were supposed to remain in the privacy of the home.

... [U]nlike male actors, nineteenth-century women performers were less likely to be viewed as free and independent employees. Nineteenth-century women were generally perceived as relationally bound to men. In this line of cases, that perception of women manifested itself in the need to bind actresses to their male theater managers. Moreover, in the view of the dominant culture, women performers were more likely to be perceived as subordinate than were their male counterparts. The decisions in this line of cases reflect larger "belief systems out of which knowledge is constructed, [belief systems that] place constraints on thought [and] that have real consequences for the behavior of individuals who live within them."[17] This conceptualization of women in the nineteenth century paved the way for the adoption of the *Lumley* rule in America.

The story that emerges is one of reversal of a legal rule due in large part to the increasing presence of women in the acting profession. When *Lumley* first appeared in the United States, the cultural repulsion to anything that even hinted of slavery led to its unequivocal

---

17. Alice Kessler-Harris, A Woman's Wage: Historical Meanings and Social Consequences 1 (1990).

rejection. But later in the century, the cultural aversion to mastery had lessened and no longer seemed to apply to men's domination of women in particular. In the later cases, courts were harsher upon women defendants who attempted to leave their employment than they were in the few parallel cases involving men. And, in the later cases, courts were harsher upon women than they had been earlier in the century. By the end of the century, the courts' subjugation of actresses to the control of theater managers surpassed even the language of their contracts and became an incident of a status classification constructed largely by the courts, rather than the consequence of any voluntary agreement between the parties.[19]

Although no court articulated gender as a factor influencing its decision,[20] the tone of the opinions as well as the pattern of results demonstrates that the courts of New York, where the core cases were litigated, were unable to ignore differential cultural constructions of women's proper behavior as reflected in the larger society and in other legal rules. Women's attempts to control their worklives and to assert their agency and independence by terminating employment that they no longer found desirable was no more to be tolerated than the emerging trend of women's attempts to divorce their husbands.[23] Although courts deciding employment cases spoke of "binding men's consciences," they rarely did so when presented with male defendants.[24] The courts appeared more willing and even eager to sanction what they perceived as women's infidelity to their male employers.

Acting was one of the few professions open to women in the nineteenth century. Actresses vastly outnumbered professional women in most other fields. Thus, these cases represent the best evidence of nineteenth-century legal treatment of relatively independent, professional working women. In certain respects, the status of actresses was the highest working women could hope to attain. No other profession in the nineteenth century offered women greater autonomy and income. The freer atmosphere of the theater community allowed women to enjoy lifestyle privileges and liberties forbidden to other middle class American women.

In other respects, actresses were a population at risk. Outside of the theater community, members of the acting profession, particularly actresses, were viewed with suspicion. In the words of historian Claudia Johnson:

> Because of the religious objections to the theater in the nineteenth century, an actress was pulled in antipodal directions, for at the same time that she was

---

19. *See* [*e.g.*,] … Duff v. Russell, 14 N.Y.S. 134 (Super. Ct. 1891), *aff'd*, 31 N.E. 622 (N.Y. Ct. App. 1892); Hoyt v. Fuller, 19 N.Y.S. 962 (Super. Ct. 1892); and Edwards v. Fitzgerald (N.Y. Sup. Ct. 1895), *cited in* Hammerstein v. Sylva, 124 N.Y.S. 535, 539–40 n.1 (Sup. Ct. 1910).

20. These 19th-century cases differ from contemporary laws and customs that explicitly excluded women from various businesses and professions. *See, e.g.*, Bradwell v. Illinois, 83 U.S. (16 Wall.) 130 (1872) (barring woman from practicing law on gender grounds). In exclusion cases, gender discrimination was explicitly articulated, discussed, and elaborated. In the actress cases presented here, however, no one argued for the exclusion of women from the stage, perhaps because it was not in the interests of the theater owners, actors, or actresses. The disparate treatment was channeled instead into subordinating the women by tying them to theater owners' control. Hence, gender considerations are much more submerged in the judicial texts.

23. Mary S. Jones, An Historical Geography of Changing Divorce Law in the United States 32 (1978).

24. For the list of men's cases that did not result in permanent injunctions, *see infra* notes 242, 251, 259. The only published opinions binding male employees to their employers involved preliminary injunctions: Hayes v. Willio, 11 Abb. Pr. (n.s.) 167 (N.Y.C.P. 1871), *rev'd on other grounds*, 4 Daly's Rep. 259 (N.Y.C.P. 1872); American Ass'n Base-Ball Club v. Pickett, 8 Pa. C. 232 (C.P. 1890). Neither of these cases resulted in a permanent injunction for the term of the contract.

excoriated, she was afforded in the theater one of the very few opportunities not only to earn independence and a living wage but also, ironically, to gain a measure of self-respect. Above all, this disparaged profession gave her, if she were ambitious and talented, the possibility of economic and professional equality with men which she could find nowhere else.[30]

To discover that actresses were more constrained by the courts than were actors is to demonstrate the bounds of their employment liberty. To discover that actresses were more constrained than actors is to illustrate that access to a profession on terms basically parallel to those offered men does not guarantee full equality of privileges and liberties. The developments in this Article tell a cautionary tale of women seeking and gaining greater independence in a profession.

Second, these developments are particularly important because the *Lumley* rule gained such prominence and eventually came to apply to all professional performers. The historical pattern suggests that gender played an important role in building *Lumley* into a legal canon. As a result, one can examine how a legal rule originally accepted in the heavily gendered context of actresses' cases eventually came to subordinate male performers to their employers as well. The point is not only that, in keeping with prevailing cultural biases, some courts and employers accorded actresses disparate treatment based on gender. Rather, gender was a catalyst that transformed this aspect of the legal status of an entire class of professional working people. What *Lumley* wrought came to apply to all manner of employed people: actors, actresses, dancers, singers, musicians, radio commentators, booking agents, baseball players, boxers, jockeys, public school music teachers, artists, inventors, retail sales people, and managers.[32] Courts of equity no longer viewed employees under contract as partners or free laborers; instead, they were seen as legally subordinate to their employers.

Third, this social history of a prominent remedies rule contributes to the ongoing debate over the proper use of equitable powers.[33] It demonstrates that an employer's ability to enjoin valuable employees from moving to other jobs has been a contested issue of labor policy for well over a century....

. . .

B. Monetary Damages for Breach of Contract

1. Expectation, Reliance, and Restitution Interests

The expectation measure is the amount of money that would put the aggrieved party in the position she or he would have been in if the contract had been performed. It is a

---

30. Claudia D. Johnson, American Actress — Perspective on the Nineteenth Century (1984) at 37.

32. *See* David Tannenbaum, *Enforcement of Personal Service Contracts in the Entertainment Industry*, 42 Cal. L. Rev. 18, 19–23 (1954) (citing cases applying *Lumley*); *see also* George A. Kessler & Co. v. Chappelle, 77 N.Y.S. 285 (App. Div. 1902) (champagne salesman); E. Jaccard Jewelry Co. v. O'Brien, 70 Mo. App. 432 (1897) (jewelry salesman); Burney v. Ryle, 17 S.E. 986 (Ga. 1893) (insurance company manager); Strobridge Lithographing Co. v. Crane, 12 N.Y.S. 898 (Sup. Ct. 1890) (lithographic sketch artist); Wollensak v. Briggs, 20 Ill. App. 50 (1886) (inventor).

33. *See* Anthony T. Kronman, *Specific Performance*, 45 U.Chi. L. Rev. 351 (1978); Alan Schwartz, *The Myth that Promisees Prefer Supracompensatory Remedies: An Analysis of Contracting for Damage Measures*, 100 Yale L.J. 369 (1990).

"go forward" measure that tries to reproduce what would have happened if the defendant had performed as required by the contract.

If a court finds that expectation is not the best measure in a particular case, the court may use the alternative measures of reliance or restitution to determine monetary damages. In contrast to expectation damages, the reliance measure is a "go-back" remedy, designed to compensate the plaintiff for expenditures made and opportunities foregone by the plaintiff in reliance on the contract; that is, reliance damages are designed to put the plaintiff in the position he or she was in before the contract was made. The restitution measure, in contrast, is designed to take away from the breaching party any benefit she or he obtained from the contract; the restitution measure is a "defendant-give-back" remedy.

Alice Sullivan v. James H. O'Connor

Supreme Judicial Court of Massachusetts
296 N.E.2d 183 (1973)

BENJAMIN KAPLAN, JUSTICE

The plaintiff patient secured a jury verdict of $13,500 against the defendant surgeon for breach of contract in respect to an operation upon the plaintiff's nose. The substituted consolidated bill of exceptions presents questions about the correctness of the judge's instructions on the issue of damages.

The declaration was in two counts. In the first count, the plaintiff alleged that she, as patient, entered into a contract with the defendant, a surgeon, wherein the defendant promised to perform plastic surgery on her nose and thereby to enhance her beauty and improve her appearance; that he performed the surgery but failed to achieve the promised result; rather the result of the surgery was to disfigure and deform her nose, to cause her pain in body and mind, and to subject her to other damage and expense. The second count, based on the same transaction, was in the conventional form for malpractice, charging that the defendant had been guilty of negligence in performing the surgery. Answering, the defendant entered a general denial.

On the plaintiff's demand, the case was tried by jury. At the close of the evidence, the judge put to the jury, as special questions, the issues of liability under the two counts, and instructed them accordingly. The jury returned a verdict for the plaintiff on the contract count, and for the defendant on the negligence count. The judge then instructed the jury on the issue of damages.

As background to the instructions and the parties' exceptions, we mention certain facts as the jury could find them. The plaintiff was a professional entertainer, and this was known to the defendant. The agreement was as alleged in the declaration. More particularly, judging from exhibits, the plaintiff's nose had been straight, but long and prominent; the defendant undertook by two operations to reduce its prominence and somewhat to shorten it, thus making it more pleasing in relation to the plaintiff's other features. Actually the plaintiff was obliged to undergo three operations, and her appearance was worsened. Her nose now had a concave line to about the midpoint, at which it became bulbous; viewed frontally, the nose from bridge to midpoint was flattened and broadened, and the two sides of the tip had lost symmetry. This configuration evidently could not be improved by further surgery. The plaintiff did not demonstrate, however, that her change of appearance had resulted in loss of employment. Payments by the plaintiff covering the defendant's fee and hospital expenses were stipulated at $622.65.

The judge instructed the jury, first, that the plaintiff was entitled to recover her out-of-pocket expenses incident to the operations. Second, she could recover the damages flowing directly, naturally, proximately, and foreseeably from the defendant's breach of promise. These would comprehend damages for any disfigurement of the plaintiff's nose — that is, any change of appearance for the worse — including the effects of the consciousness of such disfigurement on the plaintiff's mind, and in this connection the jury should consider the nature of the plaintiff's profession. Also consequent upon the defendant's breach, and compensable, were the pain and suffering involved in the third operation, but not in the first two. As there was no proof that any loss of earnings by the plaintiff resulted from the breach, that element should not enter into the calculation of damages.

By his exceptions the defendant contends that the judge erred in allowing the jury to take into account anything but the plaintiff's out-of-pocket expenses (presumably at the stipulated amount). The defendant excepted to the judge's refusal of his request for a general charge to that effect, and, more specifically, to the judge's refusal of a charge that the plaintiff could not recover for pain and suffering connected with the third operation or for impairment of the plaintiff's appearance and associated mental distress.[1]

The plaintiff on her part excepted to the judge's refusal of a request to charge that the plaintiff could recover the difference in value between the nose as promised and the nose as it appeared after the operations. However, the plaintiff in her brief expressly waives this exception and others made by her in case this court overrules the defendant's exceptions; thus she would be content to hold the jury's verdict in her favor.

We conclude that the defendant's exceptions should be overruled.

It has been suggested on occasion that agreements between patients and physicians by which the physician undertakes to effect a cure or to bring about a given result should be declared unenforceable on grounds of public policy. *See Guilmet v. Campbell*, 188 N.W.2d 601, 620 (Mich.) (dissenting opinion). But there are many decisions recognizing and enforcing such contracts, *see* Annotation, 43 A.L.R. 3d 1221, 1225, 1229–33, and the law of Massachusetts has treated them as valid, although we have had no decision meeting head on the contention that they should be denied legal sanction. *Small v. Howard*, 128 Mass. 131; *Gabrunas v. Miniter*, 193 N.E. 551 (Mass.); *Forman v. Wolfson*, 98 N.E.2d 615 (Mass.). These causes of action are, however, considered a little suspect, and thus we find courts straining sometimes to read the pleadings as sounding only in tort for negligence, and not in contract for breach of promise, despite sedulous efforts by the pleaders to pursue the latter theory. *See Gault v. Sideman*, 191 N.E.2d 436 (Ill. App.); Annot., *supra*, at 1225, 1238–44.

It is not hard to see why the courts should be unenthusiastic or skeptical about the contract theory. Considering the uncertainties of medical science and the variations in the physical and psychological conditions of individual patients, doctors can seldom in good faith promise specific results. Therefore it is unlikely that physicians of even average integrity will in fact make such promises. Statements of opinion by the physician with some optimistic coloring are a different thing, and may indeed have therapeutic value. But patients may transform such statements into firm promises in their own minds, especially when they have been disappointed in the event, and testify in that sense to sympathetic juries. If actions for breach of promise can be readily maintained, doctors, so it is said, will be frightened into practicing "defensive medicine." On the other hand, if these

---

1. The defendant also excepted to the judge's refusal to direct a verdict in his favor, but this exception is not pressed and could not be sustained.

actions were outlawed, leaving only the possibility of suits for malpractice, there is fear that the public might be exposed to the enticements of charlatans, and confidence in the profession might ultimately be shaken. *See* Miller, *The Contractual Liability of Physicians and Surgeons*, 1953 Wash. U. L.Q. 413, 416–23. The law has taken the middle of the road position of allowing actions based on alleged contract, but insisting on clear proof. Instructions to the jury may well stress this requirement and point to tests of truth, such as the complexity or difficulty of an operation as bearing on the probability that a given result was promised. *See Annotation*, 43 A.L.R. 3d 1225, 1225–1227.

If an action on the basis of contract is allowed, we have next the question of the measure of damages to be applied where liability is found. Some cases have taken the simple view that the promise by the physician is to be treated like an ordinary commercial promise, and accordingly that the successful plaintiff is entitled to a standard measure of recovery for breach of contract—"compensatory" ("expectancy") damages, an amount intended to put the plaintiff in the position he would be in if the contract had been performed, or, presumably, at the plaintiff's election, "restitution" damages, an amount corresponding to any benefit conferred by the plaintiff upon the defendant in the performance of the contract disrupted by the defendant's breach. *See* Restatement: Contracts § 329 and comment a, §§ 347, 384(1). Thus in *Hawkins v. McGee*, 146 A. 641 (N.H.), the defendant doctor was taken to have promised the plaintiff to convert his damaged hand by means of an operation into a good or perfect hand, but the doctor so operated as to damage the hand still further. The court, following the usual expectancy formula, would have asked the jury to estimate and award to the plaintiff the difference between the value of a good or perfect hand, as promised, and the value of the hand after the operation. (The same formula would apply, although the dollar result would be less, if the operation had neither worsened nor improved the condition of the hand.) If the plaintiff had not yet paid the doctor his fee, that amount would be deducted from the recovery. There could be no recovery for the pain and suffering of the operation, since that detriment would have been incurred even if the operation had been successful; one can say that this detriment was not "caused" by the breach. But where the plaintiff by reason of the operation was put to more pain that he would have had to endure, had the doctor performed as promised, he should be compensated for that difference as a proper part of his expectancy recovery. It may be noted that on an alternative count for malpractice the plaintiff in the *Hawkins* case had been nonsuited; but on ordinary principles this could not affect the contract claim, for it is hardly a defense to a breach of contract that the promisor acted innocently and without negligence. The New Hampshire court further refined the *Hawkins* analysis in *McQuaid v. Michou*, 157 A. 881 (N.H.), all in the direction of treating the patient-physician cases on the ordinary footing of expectancy. *See McGee v. United States Fid. & Guar. Co.*, 53 F.2d 953 (1st Cir.) (later development in the *Hawkins* case); *Cloutier v. Kasheta*, 197 A.2d 627 (N.H.); *Lakeman v. LaFrance*, 156 A.2d 123 (N.H.).

Other cases, including a number in New York, without distinctly repudiating the *Hawkins* type of analysis, have indicated that a different and generally more lenient measure of damages is to be applied in patient-physician actions based on breach of alleged special agreements to effect a cure, attain a stated result, or employ a given medical method. This measure is expressed in somewhat variant ways, but the substance is that the plaintiff is to recover any expenditures made by him and for other detriment (usually not specifically described in the opinions) following proximately and foreseeably upon the defendant's failure to carry out his promise. *Robins v. Finestone*, 127 N.E.2d 330 (N.Y.). *Cf. Carpenter v. Moore*, 322 P.2d 125 (Wash.). This, be it noted, is not a "restitution" measure, for it is not limited to restoration of the benefit conferred on the defendant (the fee paid) but includes other expenditures, for example, amounts paid for medicine and nurses; so also it would seem according to its logic to take in damages for any worsening of the plaintiff's condition due to the breach. Nor is it an "expectancy" measure, for it does not appear to contemplate recovery of the whole difference in value between the condition as promised and the condition actually resulting from the treatment. Rather the tendency of the formulation is to put the plaintiff back in the position he occupied just before the parties entered upon the agreement, to compensate him for the detriments he suffered in reliance upon the agreement. This kind of intermediate pattern of recovery for breach of contract is discussed in the suggestive article by Fuller and Perdue, *The Reliance Interest in Contract Damages*, 46 Yale L.J. 52, 373, where the authors show that, although not attaining the currency of the standard measures, a "reliance" measure has for special reasons been applied by the courts in a variety of settings, including noncommercial settings. *See* 46 Yale L.J. at 396–401.[2]

For breach of the patient-physician agreements under consideration, a recovery limited to restitution seems plainly too meager, if the agreements are to be enforced at all. On the other hand, an expectancy recovery may well be excessive. The factors, already mentioned, which have made the cause of action somewhat suspect, also suggest moderation as to the breadth of the recovery that should be permitted. Where, as in the case at bar and in a number of the reported cases, the doctor has been absolved of negligence by the trier, an expectancy measure may be thought harsh. We should recall here that the fee paid by the patient to the doctor for the alleged promise would usually be quite disproportionate to the putative expectancy recovery. To attempt, moreover, to put a value on the condition that would or might have resulted, had the treatment succeeded as promised, may sometimes put an exceptional strain on the imagination of the fact finder. As a general consideration, Fuller and Perdue argue that the reasons for granting damages for broken promises to the extent of the expectancy are at their strongest when the promises are made in a business context, when they have to do with the production or distribution of goods or the allocation of functions in the market place; they become weaker as the context shifts from a commercial to a noncommercial field. 46 Yale L.J. at 60–63.

There is much to be said, then, for applying a reliance measure to the present facts, and we have only to add that our cases are not unreceptive to the use of that formula in special situations. We have, however, had no previous occasion to apply it to patient-physician cases.[3]

---

2. Some of the exceptional situations mentioned where reliance may be preferred to expectancy are those in which the latter measure would be hard to apply or would impose too great a burden; performance was interfered with by external circumstances; the contract was indefinite. *See* 46 Yale L.J. at 373–386; 394–396.

3. In Mt. Pleasant Stable Co. v. Steinberg, 131 N.E. 295 (Mass.), the plaintiff company agreed to supply teams of horses at agreed rates as required from day to day by the defendant for his business. To prepare itself to fulfill the contract and in reliance on it, the plaintiff bought two "Cliest" horses at a certain price. When the defendant repudiated the contract, the plaintiff sold the horses at a loss and in its action for breach claimed the loss as an element of damages. The court properly held that the plaintiff was not entitled to this item as it was also claiming (and recovering) its lost profits (expectancy) on the contract as a whole. *Cf.* Noble v. Ames Mfg. Co., 112 Mass. 492. (The loss on sale of the horses is analogous to the pain and suffering for which the patient would be disallowed a recovery in Hawkins v. McGee, 146 A. 641 (N.H.), because he was claiming and recovering expectancy damages.) The court in the *Mt. Pleasant* case referred, however, to Pond v. Harris, 113 Mass. 114, as a contrasting situation where the expectancy could not be fairly determined. There the defendant had wrongfully revoked an agreement to arbitrate a dispute with the plaintiff (this was before such agreements were made specifically enforceable). In an action for the breach, the plaintiff was held entitled to recover for his preparations for the arbitration which had been rendered useless and a waste, including the

The question of recovery on a reliance basis for pain and suffering or mental distress requires further attention. We find expressions in the decisions that pain and suffering (or the like) are simply not compensable in actions for breach of contract. The defendant seemingly espouses this proposition in the present case. True, if the buyer under a contract for the purchase of a lot of merchandise, in suing for the seller's breach, should claim damages for mental anguish caused by his disappointment in the transaction, he would not succeed; he would be told, perhaps, that the asserted psychological injury was not fairly foreseeable by the defendant as a probable consequence of the breach of such a business contract. *See* Restatement: Contracts § 341 and comment a. But there is no general rule barring such items of damage in actions for breach of contract. It is all a question of the subject matter and background of the contract, and when the contract calls for an operation on the person of the plaintiff, psychological as well as physical injury may be expected to figure somewhere in the recovery, depending on the particular circumstances. The point is explained in *Stewart v. Rudner*, 84 N.W.2d 816 (Mich.). *Cf. Frewen v. Page*, 131 N.E. 475 (Mass.); *McClean v. University Club*, 97 N.E.2d 174 (Mass.). Again, it is said in a few of the New York cases, concerned with the classification of actions for statute of limitations purposes, that the absence of allegations demanding recovery for pain and suffering is characteristic of a contract claim by a patient against a physician, that such allegations rather belong in a claim for malpractice. *See Robins v. Finestone*, 127 N.E.2d 330 (N.Y.); *Budoff v. Kessler*, 153 N.Y.S.2d 654. These remarks seem unduly sweeping. Suffering or distress resulting from the breach going beyond that which was envisaged by the treatment as agreed, should be compensable on the same ground as the worsening of the patient's condition because of the breach. Indeed it can be argued that the very suffering or distress "contracted for" — that which would have been incurred if the treatment achieved the promised result — should also be compensable on the theory underlying the New York cases. For that suffering is "wasted" if the treatment fails. Otherwise stated, compensation for this waste is arguably required in order to complete the restoration of the status quo ante.[4]

In the light of the foregoing discussion, all the defendant's exceptions fail: the plaintiff was not confined to the recovery of her out-of-pocket expenditures; she was entitled to

---

plaintiff's time and trouble and his expenditures for counsel and witnesses. The context apparently was commercial but reliance elements were held compensable when there was no fair way of estimating an expectancy. *See, generally,* Annot., 17 A.L.R.2d 1300. A noncommercial example is Smith v. Sherman, 4 Cush. 408, 413–14, suggesting that a conventional recovery for breach of promise of marriage included a recompense for various efforts and expenditures by the plaintiff preparatory to the promised wedding.

4. Recovery on a reliance basis for breach of the physician's promise tends to equate with the usual recovery for malpractice, since the latter also looks in general to restoration of the condition before the injury. But this is not paradoxical, especially when it is noted that the origins of contract lie in tort. *See* Farnsworth, *The Past of Promise: An Historical Introduction to Contract*, 69 Col. L. Rev. 576, 594–96; Breitel, J. in Stella Flour & Feed Corp. v. National City Bank, 136 N.Y.S.2d 139 (dissenting opinion). A few cases have considered possible recovery for breach by a physician of a promise to sterilize a patient, resulting in birth of a child to the patient and spouse. If such an action is held maintainable, the reliance and expectancy measures would, we think, tend to equate, because the promised condition was preservation of the family status quo. *See* Custodio v. Bauer, 251 Cal. App. 2d 303, Jackson v. Anderson, 230 So. 2d 503 (Fla. App.). *Cf.* Troppi v. Scarf, 187 N.W.2d 511 (Mich. App.). *But cf.* Ball v. Mudge, 391 P.2d 201 (Wash.); Doerr v. Villate, 220 N.E.2d 767 (Ill. App.); Shaheen v. Knight, 11 Pa. D. & C.2d 41. *See also* ANNOTATION, 27 A.L.R.3d 906. It would, however, be a mistake to think in terms of strict "formulas." For example, a jurisdiction which would apply a reliance measure to the present facts might impose a more severe damage sanction for the willful use by the physician of a method of operation that he undertook not to employ.

recover also for the worsening of her condition,[5] and for the pain and suffering and mental distress involved in the third operation. These items were compensable on either an expectancy or a reliance view. We might have been required to elect between the two views if the pain and suffering connected with the first two operations contemplated by the agreement, or the whole difference in value between the present and the promised conditions, were being claimed as elements of damage. But the plaintiff waives her possible claim to the former element, and to so much of the latter as represents the difference in value between the promised condition and the condition before the operations.

Plaintiff's exceptions waived.

Defendant's exceptions overruled.

Eric P. Nash, What's a Life Worth?

(1994)

According to lawyers … Forget about all men being created equal. Or that death is the great equalizer. Last year, wrongful death compensatory damages went from a low of $62,987, for a 37-year-old iron worker and father of two who was killed in a construction accident in Florida, to $10 million, for a 19-year-old man shot to death in the parking lot of an apartment complex that was found to have provided insufficient security. Women tend to receive smaller verdicts than men, but even a small income earned by a woman is looked upon favorably by a jury in making its decision. Last year, the low verdict was $28,000, for a woman in her 60's who was killed when a driver ran an obstructed stop sign; the county was found negligent in maintaining the visibility of the stop sign. The high was $11.3 million, for a 29-year-old woman with two small children. Her car burst into flames after it was hit in a head-on collision, and the manufacturer of the fuel pump was found liable because of a defective fuel pump. . . .

According to Jim Hogshire, author of "Sell Yourself to Science," on the world black market a heart can go for about $20,000. Blood is worth $120 a pint (an average size adult has about ten pints of blood). A liver is worth up to $150,000 a slice, because a partial liver will regenerate itself. Bone marrow sells for $10,000 a quart, which, mixed with blood, represents about 5 to 10 percent of the bone marrow in an adult male body. Lungs sell for $25,000 for a whole one or just a lobe. Kidneys sell for $10,000 to $50,000 each. Skin is worth $50 a patch. A woman's eggs are worth $2,000 per harvest, usually several hundred eggs at a time (females are born with millions of eggs). A shot of sperm goes for about $50.

---

2. Persistent Issues in the Measurement of Expectation Damages

The calculation of expectation damages is an exercise in imagination, in thinking "what would have happened if … ?" In arguing for expectation damages, lawyers must be able to imagine and then argue for a particular version of what might have been, but never was.

---

5. That condition involves a mental element and appraisal of it properly called for consideration of the fact that the plaintiff was an entertainer. *Cf.* McQuaid v. Michou, 157 A. 881 (N.H.) (discussion of continuing condition resulting from physician's breach).

The expectation measure for damages is supposed to compensate the injured party for "all losses caused by the breach"—that is, to give the plaintiff the monetary value of all that he would have had if the contract had been fully performed plus any additional expenses caused by the breach (minus, of course, the value of everything he saved as a consequence of the breach, including costs not incurred because he stopped performance, value received because he was able to salvage materials, and so on). The *Restatement (Second)* section 347 provides a check-list of sorts with items to consider as you envision and assess expectation damages:

> [As a general rule, subject to the other limitations,] the injured party has a right to damages based on his expectation interest as measured by
>
> (a) the loss in the value to him of the other party's performance caused by its failure or deficiency, plus
>
> (b) any other loss, including incidental or consequential loss, caused by the breach, less
>
> (c) any cost or other loss that he has avoided by not having to perform (Emphasis added)

This check-list helps one to focus on the different items of loss, cost, and savings that will result in most breach of contract cases. It is not a "formula" into which one can plug predetermined values, but is instead a guide to collecting details that one might not otherwise see.

In *Sullivan v. O'Conner*, for example, the check-list can help sort through the details:

> (a) The loss in value to her of the other party's performance ... that loss would be the difference in value between the wonderful "straight and short" nose that O'Conner promised and the "bulbous" nose that the doctor delivered. Assuming we can translate these into monetary figures, that is one important element in Ms. Sullivan's expectation damages. But are there other elements?
>
> (b) *any other loss,* including incidental or consequential loss, *caused by the breach* ... that would include any expenses, any pain and suffering, and any lost income caused by the third surgery that was necessary because the doctor did not perform the contract as promised. Did Ms. Sullivan actually gain anything or avoid any costs because of the breach?
>
> (c) *any cost or other loss that he has avoided* by not having to perform. If Ms. Sullivan did not pay the doctor, then that is a savings that should be subtracted from her losses....

It is one thing to talk about damages in a theoretical way and quite another to figure out what the damages are in a particular case. The calculation of damages is seldom straight forward and this check-list is merely a beginning. Plaintiff and defendant may argue for different measures of damages—expectancy, reliance or restitution—but even when they agree on the type of damages that are appropriate, they may introduce conflicting evidence on the amount of prospective profits, expenses, losses, and savings. Courts affirm the general principle that damages do not have to be proved with mathematical precision or certainty, but they also require that damages be proved with reasonable certainty, as you will see further on in this chapter.

a. Valuation

As the *Sullivan* case demonstrates, valuation is not an easy task, especially when dealing with something without a ready market. Is the "market" a superior assessor of value? Even if the value of a service or thing has a well-defined market (for example, real property) there is likely to be a large discrepancy between the values determined by each of the parties. The following case involves determining the amount of compensation due the Nez Perce Indians as a consequence of an unconscionable price term for land that the tribe ceded to the United States. What valuation problems did the Court of Claims face and how did it come up with the final figure?

"No man owns any part of the earth. No man can sell what he does not own."

Tuekakas, leader of the Nez Percé and father of Chief Joseph (c. 1850)

Nez Percé Tribe of Indians v. The United States

United States Court of Claims
176 Ct. Cl. 815 (1966)
On Appeal from the Indian Claims Commission*

Don N. Laramore, Judge, delivered the opinion of the court

In this case the Nez Percé Tribe of Indians appeals from a decision of the Indian Claims Commission that it is not entitled to a recovery under section 2, clauses (3) and (5) of the Indian Claims Commission Act.[6]

Appellant claims additional compensation for the reservation lands which it ceded to the United States by the Agreement of May 1, 1893, ratified August 15, 1894. Prior to the Agreement, appellant owned a treaty reservation in northern Idaho which contained some 762,000 acres. Under the Agreement, part of the reservation was allotted to individual Indians and to the Tribe for trust lands. The remaining land, comprising 549,559 acres, was ceded to the appellee for a purchase price of $2.97 per acre. The appellant contended before the Commission that the ceded lands had a fair market value of $12.63 per acre on August 15, 1894, the agreed valuation date. The appellee argued that the evidence supported a value of $1.29 per acre. The Commission indicated that the evidence would support a value of $4 per acre as a maximum, but decided that the $2.97 per acre which the appellant received was not sufficiently less than the maximum $4 value to be considered "unconscionable." In addition, the Commission concluded that appellant had not succeeded in establishing that there was any fraud or duress or unfair and dishonorable dealing in connection with the negotiations and execution of the Agreement. In a concurring opinion, Commissioner Scott wrote that he personally found the discrepancy unconscionable, particularly viewed in gross — i.e., the $1.03 difference multiplied by the 549,559 acres involved amounts to $566,045.77. However, he felt bound by precedents indicating that the discrepancy must be "very gross." We are of the view that there is substantial evidence in the record indicating a value of $4 per acre, but unlike the Commission, we think this is

----

*. [Editors: The Indian Claims Commission was created in 1946 for the purpose of resolving "ancient" claims by Indian tribes against the government. Congress dissolved the Indian Claims Commission in 1978, transferring its 102 remaining cases to the Court of Claims. When the United States Claims Court was created in 1982, the entire jurisdiction of the Court of Claims was transferred to the new court.]

6. 60 Stat. 1049, 1050 (1946). Clauses (3) and (5) of section 2 provide: "The Commission shall hear and determine the following claims against the United States on behalf of any Indian tribe ... : (3) claims which would result if the treaties, contracts, and agreements between the claimant and the United States were revised on the ground of fraud, duress, [or] unconscionable consideration ... ; (5) claims based upon fair and honorable dealings that are not recognized by any existing rule of law or equity."

a minimum figure. We agree with the Commission that the appellant has not shown fraud or duress or that the dealings were other than "fair and honorable." We disagree, however, with the Commission's view of the law of unconscionable consideration and, accordingly reverse and remand the case for further proceedings.

By way of background, the Nez Percé Tribe in 1855 ceded to the United States a tremendous area in the Territory of Washington which then included what is now part of the present State of Washington and northern Idaho. This agreement or treaty was ratified in 1859. In its Article II, the agreement provided for a large reservation, a portion of which was later ceded in 1894 and is involved here. The relevant portion of the 1859 reservation was located in northern Idaho just east of Lewiston. The area consisted mainly of a high and gently undulating plateau cut into blocks by canyons. The rainfall, climate, and soils, were generally favorable for the raising of cereal crops, especially wheat. The area was an extension of the Palouse country and had similar soils. Slightly over one-half of the ceded area had a highest and best use for agriculture. Somewhat less than one-quarter of the ceded area had a highest and best use as timberland. These areas contained a good commercial grade of timber for which there was an expanding local market. The remaining land was classified as range land and was well-suited for livestock grazing.

By 1894, the Lewiston area was fairly well-settled and growing. The city itself was founded in 1861 at the confluence of the Snake and Clearwater Rivers, the latter running through the northern part of the reservation. It was the first capital of the Idaho territory and by 1867 was the population center of the Walla Walla Valley.

In 1890, the neighboring counties to the reservation had substantial amounts of acreage under cultivation. Thus, Nez Percé, Shoshone, and Idaho counties reported 48,339 cultivated acres; the figure for Whitman, Garfield, Columbia, and Asotin counties was 237,558 acres. This indicates that both the market (presumably in Lewiston) and transportation facilities adequately served the area. The Clearwater River was navigable for river transportation for a short distance into the subject area. Rail transportation was available a short distance outside, to the north. There were also wagon trails across the reservation.

The 1893 Agreement gave the Indians first choice through the allotment provision. These allotments, totaling 180,657 acres, were generally scattered throughout the reservation excepting some concentration around the existing Indian settlements in the northwest section of the ceded area. The soil and topographical maps suggest that the Indians chose wisely. About two-thirds of the lands selected by them were in the most favorable land classification. Their selection of the lands in the northwest section might be explained by their proximity to Lewiston and better river transportation. Their selection of the most northwestern plateau lands above the Clearwater River is probably best explained by the fact that the Palouse soil area (apparently the best wheat-growing area) continues south to this plateau and the railroad is closest to this area.

The unallotted or ceded lands were opened to the public on November 18, 1895, and the best lands were taken very quickly. There were 507 homestead filings in the first 13 days following the reservation's opening. The Agreement of 1893 and the proclamation opening the lands to settlement provided that settlers pay $3.75 per acre for agricultural lands and $5 per acre for stone, timber and mineral lands. During the first five years 68 percent of the land was taken, and by 1905, 10 years after the lands had been opened, 87 percent was taken. A total of 449,160 acres was acquired free under the homestead laws; 14,800 agricultural acres were bought for the statutory $3.75 per acre; 9,320 timber acres were bought for the statutory $5 per acre; 27,200 acres were reserved for state schools;

7,880 acres were retained by the United States for public use or leased for grazing; 4,240 acres were placed in public water reserve; and the remaining 36,400 acres were reserved for miscellaneous uses such as for churches and power sites.

The picture we get, in summary, is that of a large tract of virgin land (about 850 square miles) adaptable to varied uses, the 1894 market value of which was necessarily lowered by its sheer size, the necessity of substantial development expenditures, and its lesser degree of accessibility to markets than other nearby areas. In addition to these negatives, there was the supply and demand factor as such; that is to say, the northern Idaho area, although no doubt relatively populous for a new territory, simply did not have the kind of population growth that exerts a real inflationary bias on land values. Whatever pressure there was to settle new land, and there obviously was some pressure as the very fact of the Nez Percé cession suggests, it was probably deferrable. It is significant to note in this connection that the 1894 valuation date falls at the low point of the so-called "Cleveland Depression." Farm product prices were markedly affected during this period, so it is reasonable to assume that land values were diminished as well. Such generalities, of course, do not give the answer to the question of fact we must resolve; they are at best common sense guidelines, useful in viewing the evidence to determine whether the value of the cession in 1894 was closer to $4 per acre than it was to $12 per acre.

The principal evidence on valuation is contained in the two appraisal reports and the testimony of the parties' expert witnesses. Appellant relies on the testimony of William C. Brown, appellee on the testimony of Homer Hoyt. Both appraisers arrived at their ultimate value figures ($11.89 per acre for Brown; $1.29 per acre for Hoyt) primarily by looking to so-called "comparable sales." In addition, they looked to the topography, soil conditions, transportation availability—to name a few other factors—and have supplied us with a substantial record of maps, photographs, and charts to buttress their conclusions. In evaluating this volume of material, the Commission concentrated on the "comparable sales" in areas proximate to the reservation, and struck a balance between what it considered to be the extreme positions of the experts. Thus, the Commission observed that appellant's expert Brown looked to many land transactions with prices exceeding $20 per acre which occurred in well-settled areas where the land was frequently of better quality, transportation was superior, and rainfall was more plentiful. In addition, it noted that many of the sales were of farms which were improved—i.e., with fences, buildings, watering facilities— and which had been settled for some years before the valuation date. So it concluded, as did Brown, that these sales would have to be discounted to make them "comparable" to the reservation land. Brown used a 20 percent discount; the Commission obviously used something greater. On the other hand, the Commission observed that appellee's expert, Hoyt, considered many less sales in his analysis and in many instances looked to distant lands not in any way comparable to the ceded lands. The Commission, in effect, concluded that Hoyt over-discounted the value of the lands which both he and Brown considered, and improperly considered lands beyond the zone of even bare comparability.

We agree with the Commission that Brown was overly optimistic and Hoyt overly pessimistic. We are also in accord with the Commission's apparent inclination toward Brown's basic method. However, in concluding that the evidence shows that the land was worth a minimum and not a maximum of $4 per acre, we have viewed the evidence, and particularly the appraisal method used by Brown, somewhat differently from the Commission. Brown's report shows the average sales price of agricultural lands in the counties in which parts of the ceded tract were located ("tract counties") to be $15.70 per acre. This was the result of the investigation of 174 sales covering 38,335 acres. Timberland sales averaged $13.38 per acre in these counties and range land $4.54 per acre. For so-called "comparable counties" — i.e., counties neighboring the counties in which parts of the reservation were located — Brown found sales price averages to be somewhat lower than in the tract counties. Averaging the tract county and comparable county figures, he determined that agricultural land in the tract area in 1894 was worth $15.42 per acre, timberland $13.01 per acre, and range land $4.11 per acre. He multiplied these averages by the tract acreage in each of these categories to arrive at a value for the entire half-million acres of $11.89 per acre.

In computing the average sales price figures in the first step above, Brown applied a 20 percent discount to the actual sales price. Stated differently, he discounted the $19.80 per acre average sales price of tract and comparable county agricultural land to $15.42. This discount he felt was necessary to reflect the fact that the $19.80 per acre average included improvements to the land and improvements on the land, e.g., the value of buildings and fixtures, plowing, watering facilities and fencing. In addition, he applied a scale of discounts to arrive at the $19.80, these discounts to take into account the purchasing power of the dollar in the area (i.e., the price index from 1890–1900). We have no quarrel with the latter discounts. We do think, however, that the 20 percent discount may be unrealistically low. Brown went to great effort to document his 20 percent figure, and perhaps so far as it goes it is accurate. We think it should be expanded to cover not just the value of the improvements to the "comparable" land, but also to cover the "real" cost of improving the ceded land. This broadens the concept of discount to make the comparison to the tract county and comparable county lands more meaningful. The topography alone suggests there were substantial barriers to bringing in the labor and material necessary to improve the land to the degree that land was improved on the Palouse plateau which was nearer the railroads and population "centers." While we cannot supply a precise figure for the proper discount, we think something in the range of 25 percent may better take into account the premium which "improved" land in the other areas could have commanded over the ceded lands.

In addition to the improvement discount, we think the land values in other areas, if they are to be used as the guide here, should be further discounted to take account of the remoteness of the ceded land. Brown made no such discount. Granting that a railroad came within two miles of the northern boundary and that the Clearwater River was regularly navigable at least for a few miles in the northwest part, the topography was such that transportation of wheat, hay, or timber would have been readily accessible in a relatively limited part of the ceded area, and the allotment map suggests that the Indians chose the prime land in the most accessible areas. Accordingly, we feel that a purchaser of the ceded area would have expected to pay some percent less than the price he would have expected to pay for land on the Palouse plateau or near the Snake River, for example — both being areas considered as comparable by Brown. This might have been 20 to 25 percent.

Finally, we note regarding Brown's method, that he made no discount for size. We think this is an extremely important feature entering into market value. A purchaser of over one-half million acres simply would not pay what 1,000 purchasers of 500 acres each would be willing to pay. Of course, the Indians were in a sense compelled to cede the land, while they might have preferred to sell it piecemeal over a number of years to the hypothetical 1,000 purchasers of 500 acres each. So we are loath to allow the government to get a bargain because it compelled the Indians to cede the land. It is simply the fact, however, that in buying such a large, undeveloped tract, the government undertook the project of dividing and selling the land. Cf. Miami Tribe of Oklahoma v. United States, 9 Ind. Cl. Comm. 1, 17 (1960), aff'd by order, 159 Ct. Cl. 593 (1962). These are expenses the Indians were saved by selling the land as a unit. In addition, by buying the land and holding it pending disposition, the government lost the interest on the amount of the purchase price for the period prior to resale. Any purchaser of a large tract necessarily must take account of the "interest cost" of holding land pending resale. How much of a discount is warranted by the size it is difficult to say. We think, however, that something in the range of 20–25 percent might be reasonable.

By adding together a 25 percent discount for improvements, a 20–25 percent discount for remoteness and inaccessibility, a 20–25 percent discount for size, and applying this to Brown's "comparable" sales, it is possible to come up with a figure fairly close to $4— i.e., $20 per acre less 65 to 75 percent equals $5 to $7. This is, of course, the roughest form of estimating. We do not suggest that these discounts either were used by the Commission or should have been. We do not know how it arrived at the conclusion that "a figure as high as $4.00 per acre might be indicated ... [,] [b]ut in no event ... could [it] have exceeded $4.00 per acre." In our review of the opinion, findings of fact, and record to determine whether there is substantial evidence to support a $4 figure, we have had to consider what the Commission might have had in mind. We think the discounts, which of course can be conveniently altered to produce a wide spectrum of possible values, are a reasonable approximation of what the Commission did. It should be clear, however, that the discounts we have said might be within a range of reasonableness are in no sense absolutes; they are but steps in analyzing the reasonableness of the Commission's conclusion in the light of the evidence. Property appraisal is an inexact science at best; this is particularly so when the valuation date is 70 years distant from the appraisal date. So any discounts other than those which can be documented (e.g., Brown's 20 percent discount for improvements) will necessarily be left to conjecture—the reasonableness of which is largely a matter of common sense.

To reiterate, we think that the $4 per acre figure is supported by substantial evidence. It is, however, at the threshold, and not at the ceiling as the Commission determined. We think the overwhelming weight of the evidence shows that the Commission should have found the $4 figure to be the minimum. In so concluding, we have considered the Brown and Hoyt comparable sales analyses, giving more weight to Brown's. Since none of the sales were strictly comparable, we have looked to the discounting methods which were used by the appraisers implicitly or explicitly to make the other sales comparable. To Brown's method of discounting improvements we have added additional discounts for remoteness and size. Also in our thinking has been the effect of the 1894 depression on property values and the effect of the allotments. Finally, we have thought it significant that the 1894 Treaty provided for a sales price of $3.75 per acre for agricultural land and $5 per acre for timberland, and a substantial amount of acreage was bought by settlers after 1894 at these prices. No doubt the government would be entitled to some premium over its purchase price ($2.97 per acre here), but the very size of the premium here suggests that the bargain was too good.

The question then arises as to whether the difference between the $2.97 per acre paid to the Indians and the $4 per acre minimum value is sufficiently large as to be unconscionable under section 2 of the Indian Claims Commission Act. 60 Stat. 1049, 1050. In *Osage Nation v. United States*, 1 Ind. Cl. Comm. 43 (1948), the Commission was called upon to define "unconscionable consideration" as used in the Act. It concluded that the dividing line between what is grossly inadequate consideration and what is merely inadequate was a peculiarly factual question. In affirming the Commission's approach, this court wrote:

> Appellants urge that no showing of actual fraud is required for relief on the grounds of unconscionable consideration. There are cases which seem to support

both views, but it appears that only where the inequality of the bargain is very gross, does disparity of price alone justify a conclusion that the consideration was unconscionable. As to what is "very gross," the courts have provided no exact formula and each case must be carefully considered on its own particular facts and circumstances. [Emphasis added.]

[119 Ct. Cl. 592, 666, 97 F. Supp. 381, 421, cert. denied, 342 U.S. 896 (1951).] The "facts and circumstances" inquiry has always been crucial in each case, and there is no ready-made test. Thus, although this court's cases holding that a particular consideration was unconscionable have involved discrepancies of over 100 percent (the percentage difference between the actual value and the amount paid), there has been no indication that lesser percentage discrepancies are exempt from the challenge of unconscionability. *See Sac and Fox Tribe of Indians of Oklahoma v. United States,* 167 Ct. Cl. 710, 340 F. 2d 368 (1964), *Otoe and Missouria Tribe v. United States,* 131 Ct. Cl. 593, 131 F. Supp. 265, cert. denied, 350 U.S. 848 (1955); *Osage Nation of Indians v. United States, supra.* The Commission has, however, taken the strict view that discrepancies considerably less than 100 percent are not unconscionable. In *Miami Tribe v. United States,* 6 Ind. Cl. Comm. 513 (1958), it held that payment of 63 percent (a 59 percent discrepancy) of the true value was not unconscionable. In the present case it has held that a payment of 75 percent (a 33 1/3 percent discrepancy) is not unconscionable. *See also Pottawatomie Tribe v. United States,* 3 Ind. Cl. Comm. 10, 61 (1954). We think that the Commission has relied too much on the bare percentage discrepancy.

In the present case, inquiry into all the "facts and circumstances" puts the situation in a somewhat different light. Specifically, it is significant to us that the ceded area was comprised of 549,559 acres. The $1.03 difference between the amount paid and the market value multiplied by this acreage totals $566,045.77. Granting that this represents the same 33 1/3 percent discrepancy, it has a different taste. Half a million dollars in 1894 was a very substantial sum. When we consider that the Agreement provided that $1,000,000 of the total $1,626,222 consideration was to be put in trust to earn five percent interest and that it is likely that the $566,045.77 discrepancy would have similarly been put in trust at interest, the discrepancy becomes still more significant. The trust provided that a $50,000 distribution would be made one year after ratification with semi-annual $150,000 distributions thereafter—five percent interest to accrue on the unpaid balance. Agreement of May 1, 1893, Article III. Assuming that the $566,045.77 discrepancy had been put into the trust in 1894, no part of it would have been distributed for about five years, and then it would have taken two years to distribute the corpus alone. As a very rough estimate, the interest would have been close to $200,000 for the duration that the discrepancy hypothetically would have been held in trust. When added to the $566,045.77 discrepancy, this interest component raises the percentage discrepancy from 33 1/3 percent to about 50 percent.

...

There remains the question of whether the appellant is entitled to interest on its recovery. Appellant now seeks interest on the theory that if the United States had paid an amount equal to the fair market value of the land at the time of the cession, this additional sum would have drawn interest in the same manner and at the same rate as provided for the $1,000,000 held in trust under the Agreement's Article III. It is, of course, well established that interest does not run on claims against the United States unless there is an express statutory or contract provision to the contrary or unless there is a showing of delay in payment for lands "taken" in contravention of the Fifth Amendment. 28 U.S.C. § 2516(a) (1964 ed.). *United States v. Alcea Band of Tillamooks,* 341 U.S. 48, 49 (1951). Thus appellant's burden here is to show that the Agreement as ratified would have given it five percent interest on the differential amount had it been paid to the trust in 1894. The Agreement is quite specific. Article III, supra, provides that the Nez Percé Indians shall be paid $1,626,222 exactly; the $626,222 portion to be paid "to said Indians per capita as soon as practicable after the ratification of this Agreement," the "remainder of said sum" (equaling $1,000,000) to be held in trust. Earlier in this opinion, we speculated that had the government paid the fair market value in 1894, it probably would have agreed to hold the extra money in trust in the same manner as the $1,000,000. However, that speculation was appropriate only as it related to the question of whether the consideration was unconscionable. In determining whether the Agreement should be read so as to give appellant interest on the difference between the price paid and the fair market value, it is not enough for us to be able to say that probably a larger payment would have been put into the trust. Article III did not make the trust open-ended. It was to receive "the remainder" of a specific sum. What would have happened had the sum been larger it is impossible for us to say. This is not a case like the *Pawnee Tribe v. United States*, 56 Ct. Cl. 1, 15 (1920), in which this court awarded interest on an amount which the agreement specified but which the United States had for some unknown reason never paid. The Agreement here specified a sum to bear interest, and that sum apparently was paid and did bear interest; the sum claimed here is over and above the amount specified in the Agreement. In short, the Agreement has reference only to the amount that was actually agreed upon and gives no warrant for reading in a requirement that any sum determined in the future to be the fair market value should bear interest.

Accordingly, the decision of the Indian Claims Commission is reversed, and the case is remanded for further proceedings in conformity with this opinion.

Note

The Ni Mii Pu lived in an area that is now divided among the states of Washington, Oregon, Idaho, and Montana. The Tribe was named "Nez Percé" by members of the Lewis and Clark Expedition in 1805. Members of the Tribe reportedly were helpful to the expedition, and a Nez Percé guide accompanied Lewis and Clark down the rivers that are now the Snake and Columbia. The Tribe now uses both its traditional name and the name Nez Percé, *see* Noon Ni Mii Pu (We the People): Nez Percé Tribe's Tradition Lives On [publication of the Nez Percé Tribe].

In 1855, at the Walla Walla Council, the Nez Percé reluctantly agreed to cede some of their land in exchange for money and various government services, including schools and a hospital. At the time of this Council, one observer estimated the population of the Tribe to be approximately 3,300. The Agreement was ratified in 1859, as the court described. Gold was discovered on the reservation in 1860, and European-Americans invaded the area. Observers estimated that ten thousand outsiders mined gold from the Nez Percé reservation during 1860 and 1861. It is estimated that approximately fifty million dollars' worth of gold was stolen from the Nez Percé reservation during the 1860s.

Following the discovery of gold, the United States government pressured the Tribe to give up its reservation. And in 1863, some Nez Percé leaders agreed to cede a portion of the tribal land, but other Nez Percé chiefs, including Tuekakas and his son Joseph, did not agree. In early 1877, war broke out. Several divisions of the United States Army, led by General O.O. Howard, were deployed against the Tribe. Although the military encounters were fairly even in outcome, the Nez Percé were outnumbered by the U.S. military, and the tribe was driven from its lands. In October 5, 1877, Chief Joseph and most of the surviving Nez Percé tribe surrendered to General Howard. The Nez Percé were then taken as captives to Fort Leavenworth.

In 1885, after years of great suffering, a surviving population of approximately 270 Nez Percé were allowed to return to the northwest, where, over the impassioned objection of the Tribe, they were divided into two reservations. One hundred and eighteen were taken under military force to the Lapwai Reservation in Northern Idaho. The remaining one hundred and fifty, including Chief Joseph, were taken to the Colville Reservation in Washington. The Agreement of May 1, 1893, the subject of this litigation, was negotiated with the small number of Nez Percé survivors on the Lapwai Reservation. *See generally*, Merrill D. Beal, "I Will Fight No More Forever": Chief Joseph and the Nez Percé War (1963); Harvey Chalmers, The Last Stand of the Nez Percé: Destruction of a People (1962).

---

b. The Risk of Windfall: The Choice between Cost of Completion and Diminution in Value

Recall *Jacob & Youngs v. Kent*. Judge Cardozo found that Jacob & Youngs did breach their contract with Kent, but that the builders had "substantially performed" their contract obligations. Therefore, Cardozo decided, Kent was still obligated to pay for the house, but he was also entitled to damages (a set off) for Jacob & Youngs' breach. So a problem of valuation was presented: was the owner entitled to the cost of ripping out the walls and installing Reading Pipe or the difference in value to Kent of a house-with-Reading-pipe that Jacob & Youngs promised and the house-with-Cohoes-pipe that they delivered?

That's a tough question. Let's imagine the hearing: Kent's attorney says "My client made the free choice to buy Reading pipe, that's what he wants, and at this point it will cost $100,000 to get that (by tearing down walls etc.) so that is the amount of my client's loss." Jacob & Youngs' attorney says "no, the value of the house is what your client could sell it for, and the market research clearly shows that the difference in price between the house with Cohoes pipe instead of Reading pipe will be $50. That is it value of his loss from my client's breach of contract."

What if, by the time of this hearing, another company—hired by Kent—had already replaced the Cohoes with Reading pipe and Kent had already paid them $100,000? Is there any doubt that Kent's recovery from Jacob & Young should be based on the $100,000? For some reason, we would think, Kent really likes Reading pipe. Maybe it is sentimental, maybe aesthetic, but he really does value Reading pipe a lot more than most people do. We would be puzzled, but that is not a good reason to deny the higher measure.

The problem Judge Cardozo faced in the actual *Jacob & Youngs v. Kent* was not that Kent may have been foolish enough to replace the pipes. The problem was the high risk that Kent would be "over-compensated" by an award based on the cost of repair—that Kent would keep the Cohoes pipe and the money. When a court takes a utilitarian approach to this kind of problem, asking not whether the owner really wants Reading Pipe but whether there is any real value in having Reading Pipe, cost of completion damages are likely to be seen as a form of economic waste. Another approach that may be taken by a court would be to focus on the risk of a windfall and should ask "how likely is it that the plaintiff will actually do the repairs?"

American Standard, Inc. and Westinghouse Air Brake Company v. Harold Schectman and United States Fire Insurance Company

Supreme Court, Appellate Division
80 A.D.2d 318 (1981)

STEWART F. HANCOCK, JUSTICE

Plaintiffs have recovered a judgment on a jury verdict of $90,000 against defendant for his failure to complete grading and to take down certain foundations and other subsurface structures to one foot below the grade line as promised. Whether the court should have charged the jury, as defendant Schectman requested, that the difference in value of plaintiffs' property with and without the promised performance was the measure of the damage is the main point in his appeal.[1] We hold that the request was properly denied and that the cost of completion—not the difference in value—was the proper measure. Finding no other basis for reversal, we affirm.

Until 1972, plaintiffs operated a pig iron manufacturing plant on land abutting the Niagara River in Tonawanda. On the 26-acre parcel were, in addition to various industrial and office buildings, a 60-ton blast furnace, large lifts, hoists and other equipment for transporting and storing ore, railroad tracks, cranes, diesel locomotives and sundry implements and devices used in the business. Since the 1870's plaintiffs' property, under several different owners, had been the site of various industrial operations. Having decided to close the plant, plaintiffs on August 3, 1973 made a contract in which they agreed to convey the buildings and other structures and most of the equipment to defendant, a demolition and excavating contractor, in return for defendant's payment of $275,000 and his promise to remove the equipment, demolish the structures and grade the property as specified.

We agree with Trial Term's interpretation of the contract as requiring defendant to remove all foundations, piers, headwalls, and other structures, including those under the surface and not visible and whether or not shown on the map attached to the contract, to a depth of approximately one foot below the specified grade lines.[2] The proof from plaintiffs' witnesses and the exhibits, showing a substantial deviation from the required grade lines and the existence above grade of walls, foundations and other structures, support the finding, implicit in the jury's verdict, that defendant failed to perform as

---

1. The judgment in the amount of $122,434.60 including interest and costs is jointly and severally against both defendants, viz., Harold Schectman, the contracting party, and the company which issued the performance bond, United States Fire Insurance Company. Inasmuch as the interests of both defendants here are identical, for the purpose of this appeal and for the sake of simplicity we treat the defendants as one: i.e., the contracting party, Harold Schectman. A third-party action commenced by the bonding company on an indemnity agreement between it and defendant Schectman and others is not part of this appeal. The appeal is also taken from an order denying defendant's motion to set aside the verdict and for a new trial.

2. Paragraph 7 of the Agreement states in pertinent part:

7. After the Closing Date, Purchaser shall demolish all of the Improvements on the North Tonawanda Property included in the sale to Purchaser, cap the water intake at the pumphouse end, and grade and level the property, all in accordance with the provisions of Exhibit C and C sub 1 attached hereto.

Exhibit C (Notes on demolition and grading) contains specifications for the grade levels for four separate areas shown on Map C sub 1 and the following instruction: "Except as otherwise excepted all structures and equipment including foundations, piers, headwalls, etc. shall be removed to a depth approximately one foot below grade lines as set forth above. Area common to more than one area will be faired to provide reasonable transitions, it being intended to provide a reasonably attractive vacant plot for resale."

agreed. Indeed, the testimony of defendant's witnesses and the position he has taken during his performance of the contract and throughout this litigation (which the trial court properly rejected), viz., that the contract did not require him to remove all subsurface foundations, allow no other conclusion.

We turn to defendant's argument that the court erred in rejecting his proof that plaintiffs suffered no loss by reason of the breach because it makes no difference in the value of the property whether the old foundations are at grade or one foot below grade and in denying his offer to show that plaintiffs succeeded in selling the property for $183,000 — only $3,000 less than its full fair market value. By refusing this testimony and charging the jury that the cost of completion (estimated at $110,500 by plaintiffs' expert), not diminution in value of the property, was the measure of damage the court, defendant contends, has unjustly permitted plaintiffs to reap a windfall at his expense. Citing the definitive opinion of Chief Judge Cardozo in *Jacob & Youngs, Inc. v. Kent*, 230 N.Y. 239, 129 N.E. 889, he maintains that the facts present a case "of substantial performance" of the contract with omissions of "trivial or inappreciable importance" p. 245, 129 N.E. 889, and that because the cost of completion was "grossly and unfairly out of proportion to the good to be attained," p. 244, 129 N.E. 889, the proper measure of damage is diminution in value.

The general rule of damages for breach of a construction contract is that the injured party may recover those damages which are the direct, natural and immediate consequence of the breach and which can reasonably be said to have been in the contemplation of the parties when the contract was made, *see* 13 N.Y. Jur., Damages, §§ 46, 56; *Chamberlain v. Parker*, 45 N.Y. 569; *Hadley v. Baxendale*, 9 Exch. 341, 156 Eng. Reprint 145; Restatement: Contracts § 346. In the usual case where the contractor's performance has been defective or incomplete, the reasonable cost of replacement or completion is the measure, *see, Bellizzi v. Huntley Estates*, 3 N.Y.2d 112, 164 N.Y.S.2d 395, 143 N.E.2d 802; *Spence v. Ham*, 163 N.Y. 220, 57 N.E. 412; *Condello v. Stock*, 285 App. Div. 861, 136 N.Y.S.2d 507, *mod. on other grounds*, 1 N.Y.2d 831, 1 N.Y.S.2d 216; *Along-The-Hudson Co. v. Ayres*, 170 App. Div. 218, 156 N.Y.S. 58; 13 N.Y. Jur. *Damages* § 56, p. 502; Restatement, Contracts, § 346. When, however, there has been a substantial performance of the contract made in good faith but defects exist, the correction of which would result in economic waste, courts have measured the damages as the difference between the value of the property as constructed and the value if performance had been properly completed, *see Jacob & Youngs, Inc. v. Kent*, *supra*; *H. P. Droher and Sons v. Toushin*, 250 Minn. 490, 85 N.W.2d 273; Restatement, Contracts § 346, subd. [1], par. [a], cl. [ii], p. 573; comment b, p. 574; 13 N.Y. Jur.*Damages*, § 58; Ann. 76 A.L.R.2d 805, § 4, pp. 812–815. *Jacob & Youngs* is illustrative. There, plaintiff, a contractor, had constructed a house for the defendant which was satisfactory in all respects save one: The wrought iron pipe installed for the plumbing was not of Reading manufacture, as specified in the contract, but of other brands of the same quality. Noting that the breach was unintentional and the consequences of the omission trivial, and that the cost of replacing the pipe would be "grievously out of proportion," *Jacob & Youngs, Inc. v. Kent, supra*, 230 N.Y. p. 244, 129 N.E. 889 to the significance of the default, the court held the breach to be immaterial and the proper measure of damage to the owner to be not the cost of replacing the pipe but the nominal difference in value of the house with and without the Reading pipe.

Not in all cases of claimed "economic waste" where the cost of completing performance of the contract would be large and out of proportion to the resultant benefit to the property have the courts adopted diminution in value as the measure of damage. Under the *Restatement* rule, the completion of the contract must involve "unreasonable economic waste" and the illustrative example given is that of a house built with pipe different in name from but equal in quality to the brand stipulated in the contract as in *Jacob & Youngs, Inc. v. Kent, supra,* Restatement, Contracts § 346, subd. [1], par. [a], cl. [ii], p. 573; Illustration 2, p. 576. In *Groves v. John Wunder Co.,* 205 Minn. 163, 286 N.W. 235, plaintiff had leased property and conveyed a gravel plant to defendant in exchange for a sum of money and for defendant's commitment to return the property to plaintiff at the end of the term at a specified grade — a promise defendant failed to perform. Although the cost of the fill to complete the grading was $60,000 and the total value of the property, graded as specified in the contract, only $12,160 the court rejected the "diminution in value" rule, stating:

> The owner's right to improve his property is not trammeled by its small value. It is his right to erect thereon structures which will reduce its value. If that be the result, it can be of no aid to any contractor who declines performance. As said long ago in *Chamberlain v. Parker,* 45 N.Y. 569, 572: "A man may do what he will with his own, ... and if he chooses to erect a monument to his caprice or folly on his premises, and employs and pays another to do it, it does not lie with a defendant who has been so employed and paid for building it, to say that his own performance would not be beneficial to the plaintiff."

Groves v. John Wunder Co., supra, 205 Minn., p. 168, 286 N.W. 235.

The "economic waste" of the type which calls for application of the "diminution in value" rule generally entails defects in construction which are irremediable or which may not be repaired without a substantial tearing down of the structure as in *Jacob & Youngs, see Bellizzi v. Huntley Estates,* 3 N.Y.2d 112, 115, 164 N.Y.S.2d 395, 143 N.E.2d 802, *supra; Groves v. John Wunder Co., supra; W. G. Slugg Seed & Fertilizer, Inc. v. Paulson Lbr.,* 62 Wis. 2d 220, 214 N.W.2d 413; Restatement, Contracts § 346, Illustrations 2, 4, pp. 576–577; Ann. 76 A.L.R.2d 805 § 4, pp. 812–815.

Where, however, the breach is of a covenant which is only incidental to the main purpose of the contract and completion would be disproportionately costly, courts have applied the diminution in value measure even where no destruction of the work is entailed, *see, e. g., Peevyhouse v. Garland Coal & Min. Co.,* 382 P.2d 109 [Okla.], *cert. denied* 375 U.S. 906, 84 S. Ct. 196, 11 L. Ed. 2d 145, holding [contrary to *Groves v. John Wunder Co., supra*] that diminution in value is the proper measure where defendant, the lessee of plaintiff's lands under a coal mining lease, failed to perform costly remedial and restorative work on the land at the termination of the lease. The court distinguished the "building and construction" cases and noted that the breach was of a covenant incidental to the main purpose of the contract which was the recovery of coal from the premises to the benefit of both parties; and *see Avery v. Fredericksen & Westbrook,* 67 Cal. App. 2d 334, 154 P.2d 41.

It is also a general rule in building and construction cases, at least under *Jacob & Youngs* in New York, *see Groves v. John Wunder Co., supra;* Ann. 76 A.L.R.2d 805, § 6, pp. 823–826, that a contractor who would ask the court to apply the diminution of value measure "as an instrument of justice" must not have breached the contract intentionally and must show substantial performance made in good faith, *Jacob & Youngs, Inc. v. Kent, supra,* 230 N.Y. pp. 244, 245, 129 N.E. 889.

In the case before us, plaintiffs chose to accept as part of the consideration for the promised conveyance of their valuable plant and machines to defendant his agreement to grade the property as specified and to remove the foundations, piers and other structures to a depth of one foot below grade to prepare the property for sale. It cannot be said that the grading and the removal of the structures were incidental to plaintiffs' purpose of "achieving a reasonably attractive vacant plot for resale," *compare Peevyhouse v. Garland*

Coal & Min. Co., *supra*. Nor can defendant maintain that the damages which would naturally flow from his failure to do the grading and removal work and which could reasonably be said to have been in the contemplation of the parties when the contract was made would not be the reasonable cost of completion, *see* 13 N.Y. Jur., Damages §§ 46, 56; *Hadley v. Baxendale*, *supra*. That the fulfillment of defendant's promise would (contrary to plaintiffs' apparent expectations) add little or nothing to the sale value of the property does not excuse the default. As in the hypothetical case posed in *Chamberlain v. Parker*, 45 N.Y. 569, *supra*, cited in *Groves v. John Wunder Co.*, *supra*, of the man who "chooses to erect a monument to his caprice or folly on his premises, and employs and pays another to do it," it does not lie with defendant here who has received consideration for his promise to do the work "to say that his own performance would not be beneficial to the plaintiff[s]," *Chamberlain v. Parker*, *supra*, p. 572.

Defendant's completed performance would not have involved undoing what in good faith was done improperly but only doing what was promised and left undone, *compare Jacob & Youngs, Inc. v. Kent*, *supra*; Restatement, Contracts § 346, Illustration 2, p. 576. That the burdens of performance were heavier than anticipated and the cost of completion disproportionate to the end to be obtained does not, without more, alter the rule that the measure of plaintiffs' damage is the cost of completion. Disparity in relative economic benefits is not the equivalent of "economic waste" which will invoke the rule in *Jacob & Youngs, Inc. v. Kent*, *supra*, see *Groves v. John Wunder Co.*, *supra*. Moreover, faced with the jury's finding that the reasonable cost of removing the large concrete and stone walls and other structures extending above grade was $90,000, defendant can hardly assert that he has rendered substantial performance of the contract or that what he left unfinished was "of trivial or inappreciable importance," *Jacob & Youngs, Inc. v. Kent*, *supra*, 230 N.Y. p. 245, 129 N.E. 889. Finally, defendant, instead of attempting in good faith to complete the removal of the underground structures, contended that he was not obliged by the contract to do so and, thus, cannot claim to be a "transgressor whose default is unintentional and trivial [and who] may hope for mercy if he will offer atonement for his wrong," *Jacob & Youngs, Inc. v. Kent*, *supra*, p. 244, 129 N.E. 889. We conclude, then, that the proof pertaining to the value of plaintiffs' property was properly rejected and the jury correctly charged on damages.

The judgment and order should be affirmed.

Note

Is it appropriate to consider the motivation or blameworthiness of the defendant when considering what method of valuation to use? Should the court give weight to aesthetic, social, and political values that inform the choice of the plaintiff or merely to pecuniary values? In either case, the approach seems to conflict with classical contract theory's assumption that contract performance and breach are morally neutral. No blame attaches if the defendant decides that it is better to breach than to perform, to pay the plaintiff for the loss in value rather than lose money completing performance. That choice is no different from the situation where the defendant breaches believing that he can make more money by breaching the contract, paying damages, and selling to someone else at a higher price. Generally speaking, contract law leaves a party free to do so and no additional penalty ought to be exacted because of the conscious decision to breach.

As *American Standard* indicates, Judge Cardozo's decision established an important line of cases that conflict with the claimed moral neutrality of the classical approach. For further discussion, *see* Carol Chomsky, *Of Spoil Pits and Swimming Pools: Reconsidering the Measure of Damages for Construction Contracts*, 75 Minn. L. Rev. 1445 (1991) (criticizing the current rule as permitting "too much discretion, allowing courts to reject the remedy of completion cost based on their own unarticulated subjective evaluation of the harm. This, in turn, results in inconsistent holdings and, frequently, under-compensation of the owner"); Judith L. Maute, *Peevyhouse v. Garland Coal & Mining Co. Revisited: The Ballad of Willie and Lucille*, 89 Nw. U. L. Rev. 1341 (1995) (providing rich contextual details of the *Peevyhouse* litigation, criticizing the decision, and giving reasons to believe that the Oklahoma Supreme Court was tainted by improper judicial bias in favor of Garland Coal's lawyer).

c. Pecuniary versus Non-Pecuniary Loss

While damages for breach of contract are supposed to compensate the aggrieved party for his or her losses, the rule against damages for non-pecuniary loss results in under-compensation in many cases. The "normal" assumption is that breach of contract causes only economic injury. If you remember the hypothetical with which we began this chapter, you may feel anger or disappointment when the rental agent tells you that you cannot have the apartment you expected to have, you may be distressed at the prospect of looking for another place, but, for the most part, those injuries are not compensable.

The origin of the rule against compensation for non-pecuniary loss is obscure. It was reinvigorated by classical contract theorists who argued that aesthetic and emotional values are inappropriate in rough and tumble market transactions and that legal recognition of these values would be incompatible with the moral neutrality of contract. The continued viability of the rule appears to depend upon the seldom-questioned commonplace that aesthetic or emotional losses are trivial and inappropriate in this context.

In *Sullivan v. O'Connor*, the court rejected the idea that non-pecuniary losses could never be compensated and offered a qualification to the general rule:

> We find expressions in the decisions that pain and suffering (or the like) are simply not compensable in actions for breach of contract. The defendant seemingly espouses this proposition in the present case. True, if the buyer under a contract for the purchase of a lot of merchandise, in suing for the seller's breach, should claim damages for mental anguish caused by his disappointment in the transaction, he would not succeed; he would be told, perhaps, that the asserted psychological injury was not fairly foreseeable by the defendant as a probable consequence of the breach of such a business contract. *See* Restatement: Contracts § 341 cmt. a. But there is no general rule barring such items of damage in actions for breach of contract. It is all a question of the subject matter and background of the contract, and when the contract calls for an operation on the person of the plaintiff, psychological as well as physical injury may be expected to figure somewhere in the recovery, depending on the particular circumstances.

Many courts have held that damages for non-pecuniary losses should be awarded if the contract involved non-pecuniary values. The contract in *Sullivan v. O'Connor*, as in other cases concerning surgical or other medical treatment, clearly involved physical well-being—that was one of the purposes for which the contract was made. It was foreseeable, as the court found, that a breach of contract would result in additional pain and suffering for Sullivan, and thus it was appropriate to award damages to compensate for this non-pecuniary loss. Upon what basis do the courts allow recovery for non-pecuniary loss in *Deitsch v. The Music Company* and *Liberty Homes v. Epperson*? Do you agree with those decisions? What is the rationale for the general rule disapproving non-pecuniary losses? Is it consistent with market ideology? Is it consistent with dominant moral and political beliefs? Who is burdened by this rule, and who is benefited?

Carla Deitsch et al. v. The Music Company

Hamilton County Municipal Court
6 Ohio Misc. 2d 6, 453 N.E.2d 1302 (1983)

Mark Painter, Judge

This is an action for breach of contract. Plaintiffs and defendant entered into a contract on March 27, 1980, whereby defendant was to provide a four-piece band at plaintiffs' wedding reception on November 8, 1980. The reception was to be from 8:00 p.m. to midnight. The contract stated "wage agreed upon—$295.00," with a deposit of $65, which plaintiffs paid upon the signing of the contract.

Plaintiffs proceeded with their wedding, and arrived at the reception hall on the night of November 8, 1980, having employed a caterer, a photographer and a soloist to sing with the band. However, the four-piece band failed to arrive at the wedding reception. Plaintiffs made several attempts to contact defendant but were not successful. After much wailing and gnashing of teeth, plaintiffs were able to send a friend to obtain some stereo equipment to provide music, which equipment was set up at about 9:00 p.m.

This matter came on to be tried on September 28, 1982. Testimony at trial indicated there were several contacts between the parties from time to time between March and November 1980. The testimony of plaintiff Carla Deitsch indicated that she had taken music to the defendant several weeks prior to the reception and had received a telephone call from defendant on the night before the wedding confirming the engagement. Defendant's president testified that he believed the contract had been canceled, since the word "canceled" was written on his copy of the contract. There was no testimony as to when that might have been done, and no one from defendant-company was able to explain the error. There was also testimony that defendant's president apologized profusely to the mother of one of the plaintiffs, stating that his "marital problems" were having an effect on his business, and it was all a grievous error.

The court finds that defendant did in fact breach the contract and therefore that plaintiffs are entitled to damages. The difficult issue in this case is determining the correct measure and amount of damages.

Counsel for both parties have submitted memoranda on the issue of damages. However, no cases on point are cited. Plaintiffs contend that the *entire* cost of the reception, in the amount of $2,643.59, is the correct measure of damages. This would require a factual finding that the reception was a total loss, and conferred no benefit at all on the plaintiffs. Defendant, on the other hand, contends that the only measure of damages which is proper is the amount which plaintiffs actually lost, that is, the $65 deposit. It is the court's opinion that neither measure of damages is proper; awarding to plaintiffs the entire sum of the reception would grossly over-compensate them for their actual loss, while the simple return of the deposit would not adequately compensate plaintiffs for defendant's breach of contract.

Therefore, we have to look to other situations to determine whether there is a middle ground, or another measure of damages which would allow the court to award more than the deposit, but certainly less than the total cost of the reception.

It is hornbook law that in any contract action, the damages awarded must be the natural and probable consequence of the breach of contract or those damages which were within the contemplation of the parties at the time of making the contract. *Hadley v. Baxendale* (1854), 9 Exch. 341, 156 Eng. Rep. 145.

Certainly, it must be in the contemplation of the parties that the damages caused by a breach by defendant would be greater than the return of the deposit—that would be no damages at all.

The case that we believe is on point is *Pullman Company v. Willett* (Richland App. 1905), 7 Ohio C.C. (N.S.) 173, *affirmed* (1905), 72 Ohio St. 690, 76 N.E. 1131. In that case, a husband and wife contracted with the Pullman Company for sleeping accommodations on the train. When they arrived, fresh from their wedding, there were no accommodations, as a result of which they were compelled to sit up most of the night and change cars several times. The court held that since the general measure of damages is the loss sustained, damages for the deprivation of the comforts, conveniences, and privacy for which one contracts in reserving a sleeping car space are not to be measured by the amount paid therefor. The court allowed compensatory damages for the physical inconvenience, discomfort and mental anguish resulting from the breach of contract, and upheld a jury award of $125. The court went on to state as follows:

> It is further contended that the damages awarded were excessive. We think not. The peculiar circumstances of this case were properly [a] matter for the consideration of the jury. The damages for deprivation of the comforts, conveniences and privacy for which he had contracted and agreed to pay *are not to be measured by the amount to be paid therefor.* He could have had cheaper accommodations had he so desired, but that he wanted these accommodations under the circumstances of this case was but natural and commendable, and we do not think that the record fails to show any damages, but, on the contrary it fully sustains the verdict and would, in our opinion, sustain even a larger verdict had the jury thought proper to fix a larger amount. (Emphasis added.)

Pullman Company v. Willett, supra, at 177–78; *see, also,* 49 Ohio Jur. 2d 191, Sleeping Car Companies, Section 6.

Another similar situation would be the reservation of a room in a hotel or motel. Surely, the damages for the breach of that contract could exceed the mere value of the room. In such a case, the Hawaii Supreme Court has held the plaintiff was "not limited to the narrow traditional contractual remedy of out-of-pocket losses alone." *Dold v. Outrigger Hotel* (1972), 54 Haw. 18, 22, 501 P.2d 368, at 371–372.

The court holds that in a case of this type, the out-of-pocket loss, which would be the security deposit, or even perhaps the value of the band's services, where another band could not readily be obtained at the last minute, would not be sufficient to compensate plaintiffs. Plaintiffs are entitled to compensation for their distress, inconvenience, and the diminution in value of their reception. For said damages, the court finds that the compensation should be $750. Since plaintiffs are clearly entitled to the refund of their security deposit, judgment will be rendered for plaintiffs in the amount of $815 and the costs of this action.

Judgment accordingly.

Denise Chávez, The Wedding

(1995)

If my marriage is going to be like my wedding, then I'm in for a lot of trouble. For one thing, that Saturday there was a tornado watch all day. We never have tornadoes in Agua Oscura. I don't know anyone that's ever seen one either....

So here I am walking up the aisle, by myself, no one to walk me up. When I get to the front, I trip over Mr. Dosamantes' lap robe. He's in a wheelchair sitting up there on the groom's side, but his blanket is over on the bride's side of the pews. This is Our Lady of Grace Church. The grandmother's idea. I wanted to say our vows in Juárez and spend the night over there at Sylvia's listening to mariachis, but no way.

I nearly trip and I drag the blanket with me as Hector pulls it back. Then El Gonie picks it up. Soveida is out of her pew, and Lupita's maid starts giggling. I get mad, but then Hector looks at me, and I say *Jesus, just settle down*, with my eyes, and I walk up to the altar. The priest is up there. I don't like the way he looks. All skinny and like he's about to tell you how holy he is.... And the guy doesn't have a sense of humor. And what's even worse, the priest keeps forgetting my name.

"Do you ... ah ... ah ... take Hector for your lawful, wedded, husband ... Hector, do you take ... ah ... ah ... ah ... as your ... ah ... lawful wedded wife?"

"Ada," I say. "A-d-a." The priest can't remember my name, and we have to pay him for the honor of marrying us! Then. Out comes this ring that looks like it came out of a Cracker Jack box. I don't like it, but I put the damn thing on anyway, only it doesn't fit. It's too tight. Which reminds me of the saying: The way you get married shows how your life together as man and wife is going to be. A tight fit, I think.

I can barely get the ring on, but I finally do, and then it's time for the I do's.

I can hardly hear Hector, he sounds like he's about thirteen years old. We "I do" at the same time, and then we laugh and then we "I do" again at the same time. Everyone in the church starts laughing, and I get embarrassed. Then Hector forgets to lift up the veil when he goes to kiss me. More laughter. La Virgie steps in to lift it up, and Hector misses my mouth, so I grab him and cheers break out. Now he's embarrassed and we walk down the aisle: man, wife, and baby. Mr. Dosamantes' wheelchair is finally out of the way. Everyone stands up and we go outside where they throw birdseed.

"Birdseed? What happened to the rice, Soveida? I always wanted rice!"

"Rice isn't good for the birds, Ada. They say it's better to have birdseed. The birds choke on the rice."

"Shit! This is my wedding and I wanted rice."

"Forget it babes, we're having rice at the reception," says Hector.

"That's Spanish rice, Hector, not the kind of rice I'm talking about. I wanted Uncle Ben's converted rice."

"Sorry, Ada," says Soveida.

And I say, "Whose damn wedding is this, anyway?"

———————

Liberty Homes, Inc. v. Darniece B. Epperson and Fred R. Epperson

Supreme Court of Alabama
581 So. 2d 449 (1991)

JANIE SHORES, JUSTICE

During the summer of 1985, the Eppersons visited Harlan Trailer Sales, Inc., a Liberty mobile home dealer. John Harlan, owner of Harlan Trailer Sales, Inc., told the Eppersons that he sold only Liberty homes, and he recommended that they view certain mobile homes that were manufactured by Liberty that were on display in Leeds, Alabama.

The Eppersons returned to Harlan's office, which contained a Liberty plaque and brochures illustrating the types of homes Liberty manufactured. The Eppersons gave Harlan certain specifications for a custom-built Liberty double-wide mobile home, which was to have certain changes from a standard production model, including changing room sizes, adding a fireplace, changing the kitchen and bathroom arrangement, and adding a closet. Harlan assured the Eppersons that he would handle all arrangements for their special order.

On July 11, 1985, a Liberty salesman filled out an on-line production order for the Eppersons' home. Liberty knew the home was to be specially manufactured for the Eppersons, because the on-line production order identified the Eppersons as the customers. This production order was attached to a clip-board and traveled with the home as it went down the production line.

Once the home was manufactured, it was delivered in two separate sections to the Harlan Trailer Sales lot, where the Eppersons saw it for the first time. On July 25, 1987, the Eppersons signed an agreement to purchase the mobile home. The contract specified that the purchase price was $25,982.50, and it incorporated a security agreement. Long-term financing was provided by Green Tree Acceptance, Inc., and the monthly payments were $319.82.

Upon Harlan's recommendation, the Eppersons contacted Bruce Carswell who hooked up the electrical system to the mobile home. The Eppersons moved in on August 2, 1987.

While moving into the home, Mr. Epperson received an electrical shock when he leaned against the metal frame of a living room window, located on the front of the mobile home. Marie Griggs, a friend of the Eppersons who helped them move, was also shocked when she leaned on the front door frame. Bruce Carswell went to the Eppersons' home to investigate the problem and was shocked when he touched the front door handle.

Once Harlan was notified of the problem, he sent William Stockman, an employee of Alabama Electric Company, to correct it. Stockman hooked to the door and window frame a meter that measures voltage. The meter indicated that a 150-volt electric current was running through the frames. Believing that a "hot" wire was in contact with the frames and causing them to carry electrical current, Stockman replaced the wire with a "jumper wire" that rerouted the current away from the frames. Harlan paid Stockman for making the repairs and sent the bill to Liberty. In September 1985, the GFI receptacle (an electrical outlet) in the master bathroom broke. Harlan's workers replaced the receptacle.

Throughout the first year in their new home, the Eppersons noticed dimming of the lights. Mrs. Epperson stated that the power supply to the vacuum cleaner, toaster, and television would also fluctuate. Although the Eppersons notified Harlan about the power fluctuation, the problem was never remedied.

In February 1986, the home started to buckle in the center where the two sections of the home were joined. Harlan releveled the home in order to stop the buckling. Harlan was also called to repair a leak in the roof over the children's bedroom; however, the leak was never repaired to the Eppersons' satisfaction.

Because the power supply continued to be inconsistent, the Eppersons again contacted Harlan, who told them he would no longer help them because he believed their warranty had expired. When asked for a copy of the wiring diagram to their home, Harlan suggested that they call Mr. Steve Carroll of Liberty. According to the Eppersons, Mr. Carroll denied that any wiring diagram existed. Mr. Carroll denies ever having this telephone conversation with the Eppersons.

On the morning of January 13, 1988, Mrs. Epperson heard a "staticky radio sound" coming from the living room window area, and saw blue sparks shooting out from around the window. Mr. Epperson turned the power supply off and used his foot and a hammer to knock the plasterboard away. Behind the insulation he found melted, smoldering wires and scorched insulation and 2 by 4's. Mr. Stockman came to the home and cut the burned wires and installed a temporary system so that the plugs and lights would work.

Mr. Epperson alleges that Harlan denied responsibility based upon his belief that the warranty had expired. Epperson also alleges that Mr. Steve Carroll of Liberty promised he would send someone to the Eppersons' home to make repairs. No Liberty representative came. Harlan and Carroll deny having any conversation with the Eppersons.

Carroll finally sent Mr. Gary Chancey to the Eppersons in response to a letter by Mrs. Epperson concerning the sparks and the scorched wall materials. Chancey claimed he was not qualified to make the wiring repairs and suggested that Epperson get the same person who had made the temporary repairs to make permanent wiring changes, and he said it would be done at Liberty's expense. Epperson took Chancey's advice and got Stockman to make the repairs, with Liberty's knowledge.

During the summer of 1988, the power supply in the kitchen began fluctuating, and in September the entire rear half of the home lost power. A-1 City Electric Company fixed the problem temporarily. The Eppersons again contacted Liberty in order to get a wiring diagram for their home, but they never received a response.

In October 1988, the Eppersons' attorney wrote Liberty, and Liberty sent Mr. Tommy Law, a repairman, to investigate the situation. According to the Eppersons, Mr. Law stated that their mobile home would have to be completely rewired and that they should find alternative housing while the repairs were being made. Shortly after Law's visit, the Eppersons rented and moved into a friend's single-wide mobile home. The Eppersons incurred the cost of hooking up utilities to their rental home, storing extra furniture, and paying rent. Living in the smaller home was an inconvenience, because the conditions were very cramped and there was a lack of privacy.

In addition to the cramped living conditions, Mrs. Epperson worried about the possibility that the home could catch fire and worried that if it did she might not be able to get her children out of the home. The Eppersons installed battery-powered smoke detectors and conducted family fire drills.

Having made 37 payments on their home to Green Tree Acceptance, Inc., the Eppersons ceased making payments. Their double-wide home was repossessed, and Green Tree sued the Eppersons for the balance of their loan. The Eppersons reached a settlement with Green Tree.

On November 18, 1988, the Eppersons sued Liberty, alleging breach of contract, breach of express and implied warranties, and fraud....

...

III. Contract

Liberty argues that it should have no liability to the Eppersons because, it says, there was no contract between them. A manufacturer, such as Liberty, may be held liable in contract if the dealer with which the plaintiff contracted was an agent for the manufacturer. *Massey-Ferguson, Inc. v. Laird*, 432 So. 2d 1259 (Ala. 1983). Both Fred and Darniece Epperson testified that Harlan's office was located in a Liberty mobile home and that it contained brochures and pamphlets. Mr. Epperson testified that he saw a Liberty plaque and he said that Harlan indicated to him "that he sold nothing other than for a new manufacturer, Liberty, and other than that he sold nothing but used mobile homes." Harlan also recommended that the Eppersons purchase a Liberty home. Using these facts, the jury could have concluded that Harlan was Liberty's agent and, thus, that Liberty was liable to the Eppersons based upon their contract with Harlan.

Liberty argues that the trial court erred when it denied Liberty's motion for directed verdict, j.n.o.v., or new trial. Liberty claims that the Eppersons could not receive damages for mental anguish in a breach of contract claim. In general, damages recoverable for a breach of contract do not include damages for mental anguish. *Sanford v. Western Life Insurance Co.*, 368 So. 2d 260 (Ala. 1979). Damages for mental anguish can be recovered, however, "where the contractual duty or obligation is so coupled with matters of mental concern or solicitude, or with the feelings of the party to whom the duty is owed, that a breach of that duty will necessarily or reasonably result in mental anguish or suffering." *B & M Homes, Inc. v. Hogan*, 376 So. 2d 667, 671 (Ala. 1979) (quoting earlier cases).

In *Alabama Power Co. v. Harmon*, 483 So. 2d 386 (Ala. 1986), Alabama Power Company failed to provide Harmon with electrical service as it had promised to do. Harmon's mobile home was rendered uninhabitable because of the company's failure to supply electricity. There was evidence that Harmon had to rely upon his friends and upon other family members to provide housing and that this fact caused him to suffer emotional distress. Based upon these facts, this Court upheld the award of damages for mental distress.

In the present case, the Eppersons contracted with Harlan to purchase a home specially manufactured by Liberty. Understood in this contract was the belief that the home would be constructed to carry electrical current safely. The plaintiffs' evidence indicated that it was not so constructed; therefore, the jury could find a breach of contract. There was evidence that the Eppersons suffered mental anguish as a result of the electrical problems with their home, and the evidence, therefore, supported the jury's verdict. Therefore, the trial court did not err in denying a directed verdict, in refusing to set the verdict aside, or in denying a new trial.

. . .

Affirmed.

---

bell hooks, Homeplace: A Site of Resistance

(1990)

Oh! that feeling of safety, of arrival, of homecoming when we finally reached the edges of her yard, when we could see the soot black face of our grandfather, Daddy Gus, sitting in his chair on the porch, smell his cigar, and rest on his lap....

I speak of this journey as leading to my grandmother's house, even though our grandfather lived there too. In our young minds houses belonged to women, were their special domain, not as property, but as places where all that truly mattered in life took place—the warmth and comfort of shelter, the feeding of our bodies, the nurturing of our souls. There we learned dignity, integrity of being, there we learned to have faith. The folks who made this life possible, who were our primary guides and teachers, were black women.

Their lives were not easy. Their lives were hard. They were black women who for the most part worked outside the home serving white folks, cleaning their houses, washing their clothes, tending their children—black women who worked in the fields or in the streets, whatever they could do to make ends meet, whatever was necessary. Then they returned to their homes to make life happen there. This tension between service outside one's home, family, and kin network, service provided to white folks which took time and energy, and the effort of black women to conserve enough of themselves to provide service (care and nurturance) within their own families and communities is one of the many factors that has historically distinguished the lot of black women in patriarchal white supremacist society from that of black men. Contemporary black struggle must honor this history of service just as it must critique the sexist definition of service as women's "natural role."

... Historically, African-American people believed that the construction of a homeplace, however fragile and tenuous (the slave hut, the wooden shack), had a radical political dimension. Despite the brutal reality of racial apartheid, of domination, one's homeplace was the one site where one could freely confront the issue of humanization, where one could resist. Black women resisted by making homes where all black people could strive to be subjects, not objects, where we could be affirmed in our minds and hearts despite poverty, hardship, and deprivation, where we could restore to ourselves the dignity denied us on the outside in the public world.

---

3. Limitations on Damages: Causation, Certainty, Foreseeability, and Mitigation

Contract doctrine imposes four important limitations on damages for breach of contract: first, the claimed damages must be shown to have been caused by the breach of contract; second, damages must be proved with *reasonable certainty*; third, expectation damages are not recoverable unless they were *reasonably foreseeable* when the contract was made; and fourth, damages are not recoverable if the aggrieved party could have taken reasonable steps to limit the extent of his or her loss. This last rule is referred to as the "*duty to mitigate*" damages.

---

a. Causation

In this section we look at the important issue of causation. In order to recover damages for breach of contract, a plaintiff must show that the claimed losses were *caused by* the breach of contract. Generally, proving causation will require evidence sufficient to allow the trier of fact to conclude that the loss would not have occurred if the contract had been fully performed (this is a "but-for" test: "but for the breach of contract, this loss would not have occurred").

Gavin L. McDonald v. John P. Scripps Newspaper et al.

257 Cal.Rptr. 473 (Cal. Ct. App., 2d. Dist. 1989)

Justice Arthur Gilbert

Question—When should an attorney say "no" to a client? Answer—When asked to file a lawsuit like this one.

Master Gavin L. McDonald did not win the Ventura County Spelling Bee. Therefore, through his guardian ad litem,[1] he sued. Gavin alleges that contest officials improperly allowed the winner of the spelling bee to compete. Gavin claimed that had the officials not violated contest rules, the winner "would not have had the opportunity" to defeat him. The trial court wisely sustained a demurrer to the complaint without leave to amend.

We affirm because two things are missing here—causation and common sense. Gavin lost the spelling bee because he spelled a word wrong. Gavin contends that the winner of the spelling bee should not have been allowed to compete in the contest. Gavin, however, cannot show that but for the contest official's allowing the winner to compete, he would have won the spelling bee.

In our puzzlement as to how this case even found its way into court, we are reminded of the words of a romantic poet.

> "The [law] is too much with us; late and soon,
> Getting and spending, we lay waste our powers:
> Little we see in Nature that is ours;
> We have given our hearts away, a sordid boon!"

(Wordsworth, The World Is Too Much With Us (1807) with apologies to William Wordsworth, who we feel, if he were here, would approve.)

Facts

Gavin was a contestant in the 1987 Scripps Howard National Spelling Bee, sponsored in Ventura County by the newspaper, the Ventura County Star-Free Press. The contest is open to all students through the eighth grade who are under the age of 16. Gavin won competitions at the classroom and school-wide levels. This earned him the chance to compete against other skilled spellers in the county-wide spelling bee. The best speller in the county wins a trip to Washington D.C. and a place in the national finals. The winner of the national finals is declared the national champion speller.

Gavin came in second in the county spelling bee. Being adjudged the second best orthographer in Ventura County is an impressive accomplishment, but pique overcame self-esteem. The spelling contest became a legal contest.

We search in vain through the complaint to find a legal theory to support this metamorphosis. Gavin alleges that two other boys, Stephen Chen and Victor Wang, both of whom attended a different school, also competed in the spelling contest. Stephen had originally lost his school-wide competition to Victor. Stephen was asked to spell the word "horsy." He spelled it "h-o-r-s-e-y." The spelling was ruled incorrect. Victor spelled the same word "h-o-r-s-y." He then spelled another word correctly, and was declared the winner.

---

1. We do not hold Gavin responsible.

Contest officials, who we trust were not copy editors for the newspaper sponsoring the contest, later discovered that there are two proper spellings of the word "horsy," and that Stephen's spelling was correct after all.[2]

Contest officials asked Stephen and Victor to again compete between themselves in order to declare one winner. Victor, having everything to lose by agreeing to this plan, refused. Contest officials decided to allow both Victor and Stephen to advance to the county-wide spelling bee, where Gavin lost to Stephen.

Taking Vince Lombardi's aphorism to heart, "Winning isn't everything, it's the only thing," Gavin filed suit against the Ventura County Star-Free Press and the Scripps Howard National Spelling Bee alleging breach of contract, breach of implied covenant of good faith and fair dealing, and intentional and negligent infliction of emotional distress.

In his complaint, Gavin asserts that contest officials violated spelling bee rules by allowing Stephen Chen to compete at the county level. He suggests that had Stephen not progressed to the county-wide competition, he, Gavin, would have won. For this leap of faith he seeks compensatory and punitive damages.

The trial court sustained Scripps's demurrer without leave to amend because the complaint fails to state a cause of action. The action was dismissed, and Gavin appeals.

Discussion

Gavin asserts that he has set forth the necessary elements of a cause of action for breach of contract, and that these elements are: "(1) The contract; (2) Plaintiff's performance; (3) Defendant's breach; (4) Damage to plaintiff. 4 Witkin, California Procedure, Pleading, § 464 (3rd Ed. 1985)."

Gavin's recitation of the law is correct, but his complaint wins no prize. He omitted a single word in the fourth element of an action for breach of contract, which should read "damage to plaintiff therefrom." (4 Witkin, Cal. Procedure (3d ed. 1985) Pleading, § 464, p. 504, italics added.) Not surprisingly, the outcome of this case depends on that word. (2) A fundamental rule of law is that "whether the action be in tort or contract compensatory damages cannot be recovered unless there is a causal connection between the act or omission complained of and the injury sustained." (*Capell Associates, Inc. v. Central Valley Security Co.* (1968) 260 Cal.App.2d 773, 779; *State Farm Mut. Auto. Ins. Co. v. Allstate Ins. Co.* (1970) 9 Cal.App.3d 508, 528 [88 Cal.Rptr. 246]; Civ. Code, §§ 3300, 3333.)

The erudite trial judge stated Gavin's shortcoming incisively. "I see a gigantic causation problem...." Relying on the most important resource a judge has, he said, "common sense tells me that this lawsuit is nonsense."

Even if Gavin and Scripps had formed a contract which Scripps breached by allowing Stephen Chen to compete at the county level in violation of contest rules, nothing would change. Gavin cannot show that he was injured by the breach. Gavin lost the spelling bee because he misspelled a word, and it is irrelevant that he was defeated by a contestant who "had no right to advance in the contest."

Gavin argues that had the officials "not violated the rules of the contest, Chen would not have advanced, and would not have had the opportunity to defeat" Gavin. Of course,

---

2. "[H]orsey also horsy 1: relating to, resembling, or suggestive of a horse 2: addicted to or having to do with horses or horse racing or characteristic of the manners, dress, or tastes of horsemen." (Webster's Third New Internat. Dict. (1961) p. 1093.)

it is impossible for Gavin to show that he would have spelled the word correctly if Stephen were not his competitor. Gavin concedes as much when he argues that he would not have been damaged if defeated by someone who had properly advanced in the contest. That is precisely the point.

Gavin cannot show that anything would have been different had Stephen not competed against him. Nor can he show that another competitor would have also misspelled that or another word, thus allowing Gavin another opportunity to win. (4) "It is fundamental that damages which are speculative, remote, imaginary, contingent, or merely possible cannot serve as a legal basis for recovery." (*Earp v. Nobmann* (1981) 175 Cal.Rptr. 767.)

Gavin offers to amend the complaint by incorporating certain rules of the spelling bee which purportedly show that the decision to allow Stephen to advance in the competition was procedurally irregular. This offer to amend reflects a misunderstanding of the trial court's ruling. The fatal defect in the complaint is that Gavin cannot show that but for Stephen Chen's presence in the spelling bee, Gavin would have won.

"The general rule is that it is an abuse of discretion to sustain a demurrer without leave to amend unless the complaint shows that it is incapable of amendment. [Citation.] But it is also true that where the nature of plaintiff's claim is clear, but under substantive law no liability exists, leave to amend should be denied, for no amendment could change the result." (*Berkeley Police Assn. v. City of Berkeley*, (1977) 143 Cal.Rptr. 255)

The third cause of action, states that plaintiff has suffered humiliation, indignity, mortification, worry, grief, anxiety, fright, mental anguish, and emotional distress, not to mention loss of respect and standing in the community. These terms more appropriately express how attorneys who draft complaints like this should feel.

A judge whose prescience is exceeded only by his eloquence said that " … Courts of Justice do not pretend to furnish cures for all the miseries of human life. They redress or punish gross violations of duty, but they go no farther; they cannot make men virtuous: and, as the happiness of the world depends upon its virtue, there may be much unhappiness in it which human laws cannot undertake to remove." (*Evans v. Evans* (1790) Consistory Court of London.) Unfortunately, as evidenced by this lawsuit, this cogent insight, although as relevant today as it was nearly 200 years ago, does not always make an impression on today's practitioner.

In *Shapiro v. Queens County Jockey Club* (1945) [53 N.Y.S.2d 135], plaintiff's horse was the only horse to run the full six furlongs in the sixth race at Aqueduct Race Track after racing officials declared a false start. A half hour later the sixth race was run again, and plaintiff's horse came in fifth out of a total of six.

The *Shapiro* court held that plaintiff had no cause of action against the race track. Plaintiff could not support the theory that his horse would have won the second time around if all the other horses had also run the six furlongs after the false start. Plaintiff was not content to merely chalk up his loss to a bad break caused by the vicissitudes of life. The lesson to be learned is that all of us, like high-strung horses at the starting gate, are subject to life's false starts. The courts cannot erase the world's imperfections.

The Georgia Supreme Court in *Georgia High School Ass'n v. Waddell* (1981) 285 S.E.2d 7, decided it was without authority to review the decision of a football referee regarding the outcome of the game. The court stated that the referee's decision did not present a justiciable controversy. (3c) Nor does the decision of the spelling bee officials present a justiciable controversy here.

Our decision at least keeps plaintiff's bucket of water from being added to the tidal wave of litigation that has engulfed our courts.[3]

Sanctions—A close call

Causation has been counsel's nemesis. Its absence makes Gavin's quest for "justice" an illusory one. The lack of causation in the complaint is the cause for dismissal of the complaint. Counsel could not show us or the trial court how an amendment could cure the complaint. The lesson should have been learned at the trial court. As the law disregards trifles (Civ. Code, § 3533), so, too, one should not trifle with the Court of Appeal. (6) The filing of an appeal here, for a case so trivial, and so lacking in merit, makes it a likely candidate for sanctions.

To counsel's credit, we are convinced that he did not prosecute this appeal for an improper motive or to delay the effect of an adverse judgment. He, therefore, at least avoids two criteria set forth in *In re Marriage of Flaherty* (1982) 646 P.2d 179. This case, however, lacks merit, and we cannot conceive of a reasonable attorney who would disagree with this appraisal.

Falling within a criterion of Flaherty, however, does not in and of itself compel sanctions. The *Flaherty* court warned that "any definition must be read so as to avoid a serious chilling effect on the assertion of litigants' rights on appeal.... An appeal that is simply without merit is not by definition frivolous and should not incur sanctions. Counsel should not be deterred from filing such appeals out of a fear of reprisals." (*In re Marriage of Flaherty*, supra, 31 Cal.3d at p. 650.)

It is creative and energetic counsel who from time to time challenge existing law and question past policies. This insures that the law be a living and dynamic force. Although noble aims were not advanced here, we are mindful of the caution in *Flaherty* that the borderline between appeals that are frivolous and those that simply have no merit is vague, and that punishment should be used sparingly "to deter only the most egregious conduct." (*In re Marriage of Flaherty, supra*, 31 Cal.3d at pp. 650651.) We therefore decline to impose sanctions, but we hope this opinion will serve as a warning notice for counsel to be discerning when drawing the line between making new law or wasting everyone's time.

Advice to Gavin and an aphorism or two

Gavin has much to be proud of. He participated in a spelling bee that challenged the powers of memory and concentration. He met the challenge well but lost out to another contestant. Gavin took first in his school and can be justifiably proud of his performance.

It is this lawsuit that is trivial, not his achievement. Our courts try to give redress for real harms; they cannot offer palliatives for imagined injuries.

Vince Lombardi may have had a point, but so did Grantland Rice—It is "not that you won or lost—but how you played the game".

As for the judgment of the trial court, we'll spell it out. A-F-I-R-M-E-D. Appellant is to pay respondent's costs on appeal.

---

3. Judge Irving Kaufman of the Second Circuit Court of Appeals, in a speech, has spoken of the alarming tidal wave of litigation in this country that shows no signs of abatement. (Cherna v. Cherna (Fla. Dist. Ct. App. 1983) 427 So.2d 395, 396, fn. 2.)

b. "Reasonable Certainty"

A further requirement is that the aggrieved party must prove that any anticipated benefits, the loss of which are part of the damage claim, were "reasonably certain" to have occurred. In other words, the plaintiff cannot be compensated as if all of his dreams and speculations would have occurred. In the following case, *Halliburton v. Eastern Cement,* the court has to decide whether the plaintiff should be able to recover all that he hoped to gain from the transaction. In its analysis, the court mentions two distinctions that are helpful: the difference between general and consequential damages and the difference between established businesses and new ones.

General and Consequential Damages

General damages represent the simple difference between what was promised (a pneumatic cement pumping system that worked) and what was delivered (a pneumatic cement pumping system that didn't work). This item of loss is not speculative. If the machine was defective, it probably was not worth the purchase price. The harm to a buyer can be computed without raising the issue of whether the damages are reasonable certainty. Consequential damages, in contrast, represent the losses that happened as a consequence of the aggrieved party not being able to use what was promised (a pneumatic cement pumping system that worked) to make more money. One challenge to consequential damages will often be the allegation that such damages are uncertain or speculative.

In some situations, it is easy to prove that the expected gains would have occurred. Let's assume Julia owns an embroidery company. Every year she registers with the School District as one of several companies that will sell school uniforms with the school name embroidered on the shirt. Every year she sells about 1000 school shirts. She buys the plain white shirts from a wholesale supplier, Sam, for $5.00 each. Julia then embroiders each one and sells them at Uniform Sale Day for $15.00 each. In June, Julia ordered 1000 of the plain white shirts from Sam to be delivered at the beginning of July. Without explanation, Sam delayed delivery for 4 weeks and, despite her hard work, Julia could not complete more than 200 shirts by August 1. On sale day she sold all 200 of the shirts, but she could have sold the full 1000, as she had every year in the past. It is certain that she would have earned an additional $8,000 in damages if Sam had not breached the contract. But what if Julia had never sold shirts to the school district before? What if this were a new enterprise on which she was embarking?

Reasonable Certainty and "New Enterprises"

As the court notes, the traditional rule was that new enterprises could not prove lost profits with reasonable certainty. As you read the next case, look closely at the reasonable certainty issue and the court's analysis. Do you agree with the court?

Halliburton Company v. Eastern Cement Corporation

Florida Court of Appeals
672 So. 2d 844 (1996)

GARY M. FARMER, JUDGE

This is the second appearance of this case before us. In its previous manifestation, we reversed a directed verdict which had ruled as a matter of law that the "no warranty disclaimer" in seller's offer trumped the express warranty provision in buyer's acceptance. *Eastern Cement Corp. v. Halliburton Co.*, 600 So.2d 469 (Fla. 4th DCA), *rev. denied*, 613 So.2d 4 (Fla.1992). We determined that the two varying provisions canceled each other, and that the remaining contract implied statutory warranties of fitness for a particular purpose and merchantability. Having so decided, we added: "under section [2.715], Florida Statutes (1989), the buyer can recover both incidental and consequential damages when these implied warranties are read into the contract." 600 So.2d at 472.

. . .

Turning to the subject of remedies for breach of contract, we reject buyer's "for-want-of-a-nail" argument under which the trial court allowed the jury to award damages in this action involving the sale of goods. Essentially the buyer argued that if the goods sold, a single pneumatic cement pumping system, had been as warranted, it would then have purchased four additional systems and, thence, after chartering a vessel for a long term, would have exploited the systems by entering the containerized cargo business. The jury accepted this evidence because it awarded damages representing the profits lost from the proposed containerized cargo business with the four additional systems operating as planned. Seller argues that buyer's damages were too remote and speculative to go to the jury.

Ordinarily, where the buyer has accepted non-conforming goods and sued for breach, as in this case, the buyer is entitled to general, incidental and consequential damages, which in a proper case may be an amalgam of some or all three. [Florida's UCC § 2.714] ... provides that the measure of general damages is the difference between the value of the goods accepted and their value as warranted. Section [2.714(3)] provides that incidental and consequential damages may be recovered "in a proper case."

Consequential damages are defined in the Code to be:

> "[a]ny loss resulting from general or particular requirements and needs of which the seller at the time of contracting had reason to know and which could not reasonably be prevented by cover or otherwise; and
>
> (b) injury to person or property proximately resulting from any breach of warranty."

[2.715(2)].

As the leading text on the UCC points out, "[t]he most commonly litigated and thus the most often sought after item of consequential damages is lost profits." White & Summers, 1 Uniform Commercial Code 3rd, § 10-4, at 518. As this text also points out, to recover lost profits the buyer must generally satisfy the judicial requirements of foreseeability and certainty. *Id.*

The courts previously drew a distinction about lost profits between established businesses and those not yet begun. *See, e.g., New Amsterdam Cas. Co. v. Utility Battery Mfg. Co.*, 122 Fla. 718, 166 So. 856 (1935) (claimant allowed to show lost profits as to established business by competent proof); *Innkeepers Int'l, Inc. v. McCoy Motels Ltd.*, 324 So.2d 676 (Fla. 4th DCA 1975), *cert. denied*, 336 So.2d 106 (Fla.1976) (recovery for lost profits not generally allowed for new business with no history) … ; *but see Twyman v. Roell,* 123 Fla. 2, 166 So. 215 (1936) (proof of lost profits for unestablished business allowable provided there is "yardstick" by which such profits may be measured). More recently, however, in *W.W. Gay Mech. Contractor, Inc. v. Wharfside Two Ltd.,* 545 So.2d 1348 (Fla.1989), the court explained and modified its previous holdings:

> "In New Amsterdam this Court held that prospective business profits are generally too speculative and dependent on changing circumstances to be recovered. New Amsterdam provided an exception allowing the plaintiff to show the amount of his loss by competent proof. However, this exception only applied to the interruption of an established business. Twyman, on the other hand, did not limit recovery to established businesses. There, the Court stated that, if there is a 'yardstick' by which prospective profits can be measured, they will be allowed if proven. 123 Fla. at 6, 166 So. at 217. The Court provided further that the 'uncertainty which defeats recovery in such cases' is the cause of the damage rather than the amount. 'If from proximate estimates of witnesses a satisfactory conclusion can be reached, it is sufficient if there is such certainty as satisfies the mind of a prudent and impartial person.' Id. at 7–8, 166 So. at 218.
>
> "We follow the holding in *Twyman.* A business can recover lost prospective profits regardless of whether it is established or has any 'track record.' The party must prove that 1) the defendant's action caused the damage and 2) there is some standard by which the amount of damages may be adequately determined."

545 So.2d at 1350–51. Hence, although we regard buyer's evidence as to the indispensable yardstick in this case to be unusually weak, we find it necessary to concentrate our attention on the evidence relating to the cause of the damage rather than the amount.

The issue of causation begins with a legal inquiry that, if satisfied, ends with a factual inquiry. This is so because the cause for any contemporary event can, if one is inclined to do so, be connected in a seemingly logical chain of circumstances and occurrences all the way back to creation. But the law imposes boundaries on the inquiry. Justice Cardozo once spoke of:

> "that common-sense accommodation of judgment to kaleidoscopic situations which characterizes the law in its treatment of problems of causation. One could carry the search for causes backward, almost without end. [c.o.] Instead, there has been a selective process which picks the substantial causes out of the web and lays the other ones aside.… To set bounds to the pursuit, the courts have formulated the distinction between controversies that are basic and those that are collateral, between disputes that are necessary and those that are merely possible. We shall be lost in a maze if we put that compass by."

Gully v. First National Bank in Meridian, 299 U.S. 109, 117–118, 57 S.Ct. 96, 100, 81 L.Ed. 70 (1936). In short, the facts relating to causation must first satisfy legal restraints, i.e. the legal limits to how deeply into history the law will allow the cause for an event to be traced.

Here, the link of unrealized future events necessary to establish the loss is founded on the buyer's testimony that it lost $24+ million because the defect in the one system actually sold prevented the buyer from going into a new business in which 4 other systems would have been necessarily purchased and, with them, the profits would surely have flowed.[9] An expert opinion from an outside economist with a Ph.D. projecting future revenues,

---

9. We recognize that the actual testimony as to the lost profits came from an expert witness, and not the buyer directly, but that is a meaningless distinction under the facts of this case.

profits and economic probabilities for the anticipated success of a prospective new business venture may provide a reasonable measure in a proper case for the loss of prospective profits in a business not yet begun, but it hardly addresses the causal relationship inquiry as to the proximate results of the breach itself.

Buyer's own evidence shows that the connection between the one system and the future business is, as a matter of law, too remote, too speculative, and too theoretical. The lost profits would purportedly have resulted from the operation of 4 additional systems, which the buyer says it *would* have purchased sometime in the future if the one system sold under the contract in suit had performed as warranted. There was not even a proposed contract for the future purchase of these 4 additional systems, and no discussion between buyer and seller as to possible terms. This future business would have been collateral and secondary to the business for which the single contractual system was purchased. Buyer had no personnel with experience in shipping containerized cargo. No express type of cargo was specified. The suggested scheme was not evidenced by formal plans, by proposed budgets, by specific site plans, by the formation of a new legal entity, or by anything that would have moved from an aspiration to a concrete (pun intended) plan.

All that was offered was a hope of commercial fortune hanging from a thin thread of "what-ifs" — buoyed by the buyer's after-the-fact testimonial conviction that success and profits would surely have been there for the taking. The evidence forming the necessary chain of causation between the defects in the single system sold under the contract in suit and any possible future profits lost in the containerized cargo business comes down to little more than pure speculation. Buyer's evidence as to causation is as reliable as the "investment" at the $2 window.

It is in short, as seller argues, the nail that lost the kingdom. To borrow from *Ohoud Establishment for Trade & Contracts v. Tri-State Contracting & Trading Corporation*, 523 F.Supp. 249 (D.N.J.1981), cited by seller:

> "The court would have little difficulty in submitting the loss of the shoe, the horse, and probably the rider to a jury if caused by the sale of a defective nail or the failure to deliver the nail as agreed. The loss of the battle creates a doubtful question, but the loss of the kingdom is so remote as to bar its submission to a jury."

523 F.Supp. at 255. The court added: "[i]f the manufacturer of the nail becomes responsible for the loss of the kingdom, then we may not have any more nails." 523 F.Supp. at 257.

. . .

Therefore, we affirm the jury verdict on liability but reverse the damages and remand to the trial judge to strike any award for lost profits for the future containerized cargo business.[7]

George Herbert, The Temple

(1633)

For want of a nail, the shoe was lost;
For want of a shoe, the horse was lost;

---

7. As seller has conceded that there is evidence to support the award of $928,000 in direct consequential damages in the operation of the single system purchased, we remand for the entry of judgment in that amount only.

For want of a horse, the rider was lost;
For want of a rider the battle is lost;
For want of a battle the kingdom is lost.
All for the loss of a horseshoe nail.

---

c. Foreseeability

The requirement of foreseeability sets another limitation on expectation damages. The doctrine provides that an aggrieved party may not recover for consequential damages of a type that was not reasonably foreseeable at the time the contract was made. The leading case on foreseeability of contract damages is *Hadley v. Baxendale*, below. The reported decision in *Hadley v. Baxendale* is odd, as you will see, because the facts stated at the beginning of the case, apparently written by a court reporter, seem to conflict in an important way with the facts assumed by the court. So when you read the case, remember that most subsequent courts and commentators have assumed that the court reporter's summary was simply incorrect. What do you think?

Hadley v. Baxendale
Court of Exchequer
156 Eng. Rep. 145 (1854)

At the trial before Crompton, J., at the last Gloucester Assizes, it appeared that the plaintiffs carried on an extensive business as millers at Gloucester; and that, on the 11th of May, their mill was stopped by a breakage of the crank shaft by which the mill was worked. The steam-engine was manufactured by Messrs. Joyce & Co., the engineers, at Greenwich, and it became necessary to send the shaft as a pattern for a new one to Greenwich. The fracture was discovered on the 12th, and on the 13th the plaintiffs sent one of their servants to the office of the defendants, who are the well known carriers trading under the name of Pickford & Co., for the purpose of having the shaft carried to Greenwich. The plaintiff's servant told the clerk that the mill was stopped, and that the shaft must be sent immediately; and in answer to the inquiry when the shaft would be taken, the answer was, that if it was sent up by twelve o'clock any day, it would be delivered at Greenwich on the following day. On the following day the shaft was taken by the defendants, before noon, for the purpose of being conveyed to Greenwich, and the sum of £2,4s was paid for its carriage for the whole distance; at the same time the defendant's clerk was told that a special entry, if required, should be made to hasten its delivery. The delivery of the shaft at Greenwich was delayed by some neglect; and the consequence was, that the plaintiffs did not receive the new shaft for several days after they would otherwise have done, and the working of their mill was thereby delayed, and they thereby lost the profits they would otherwise have received.

On the part of the defendants, it was objected that these damages were too remote, and that the defendants were not liable with respect to them. The learned Judge left the case generally to the jury, who found a verdict with £25 damages beyond the amount paid into Court.

Whateley, in last Michaelmas Term, obtained a rule nisi for a new trial, on the ground of misdirection.

BARON SIR EDWARD HALL ALDERSON

We think that there ought to be a new trial in this case; but, in so doing, we deem it to be expedient and necessary to state explicitly the rule which the Judge, at the next trial, ought, in our opinion, to direct the jury to be governed by when they estimate the damages.

It is, indeed, of the last importance that we should do this; for, if the jury are left without any definite rule to guide them, it will, in such cases as these, manifestly lead to the greatest injustice. The Courts have done this on several occasions; and, in *Blake v. Midland Railway Company* (18 Q.B. 93), the Court granted a new trial on this very ground, that the rule had not been definitely laid down to the jury by the learned Judge at Nisi Prius.

"There are certain established rules," this Court says, in *Alder v. Keighley* (15 M. & W. 117), "according to which the jury ought to find." And the Court, in that case adds: "and here there is a clear rule, that the amount which would have been received if the contract had been kept, is the measure of damages if the contract is broken."

Now we think the proper rule in such a case as the present is this: — Where two parties have made a contract which one of them has broken, the damages which the other party ought to receive in respect of such breach of contract should be such as may fairly and reasonably be considered either arising naturally, i.e., according to the usual course of things, from such breach of contract itself, or such as may reasonably be supposed to have been in the contemplation of both parties, at the time they made the contract, as the probable result of the breach of it. Now, if the special circumstances under which the contract was actually made were communicated by the plaintiffs to the defendants, and thus known to both parties, the damages resulting from the breach of such a contract, which they would reasonably contemplate, would be the amount of injury which would ordinarily follow from a breach of contract under these special circumstances so known and communicated. But, on the other hand, if these special circumstances were wholly unknown to the party breaking the contract, he, at the most, could only be supposed to have had in his contemplation the amount of injury which would arise generally, and in the great multitude of cases not affected by any special circumstances, from such a breach of contract. For, had the special circumstances been known, the parties might have specially provided for the breach of contract by special terms as to the damages in that case; and of this advantage it would be very unjust to deprive them. Now the above principles are those by which we think the jury ought to be guided in estimating the damages arising out of any breach of contract. It is said, that other cases such as breaches of contract in the non-payment of money, or in the not making a good title to land, are to be treated as exceptions from this, and as governed by a conventional rule. But as, in such cases, both parties must be supposed to be cognizant of that well-known rule, these cases may, we think, be more properly classed under the rule above enunciated as to cases under known special circumstances, because there both parties may reasonably be presumed to contemplate the estimation of the amount of damages according to the conventional rule. Now, in the present case, if we are to apply the principles above laid down, we find that the only circumstances here communicated by the plaintiffs to the defendants at the time the contract was made, were, that the article to be carried was the broken shaft of a mill, and that the plaintiffs were the millers of that mill. But how do these circumstances show reasonably that the profits of the mill must be stopped by an unreasonable delay in the delivery of the broken shaft by the carrier to the third person? Suppose the plaintiffs had another shaft in their possession put up or putting up at the time, and that they only wished to send back the broken shaft to the engineer who made it; it is clear that this would be quite consistent with the above circumstances, and yet the unreasonable delay in the delivery would have no effect upon the intermediate profits of the mill. Or, again, suppose that, at the time of the delivery to the carrier, the machinery of the mill had been in other respects defective, then, also, the same results would follow. Here it is true that the shaft was actually sent back to serve as a model for a new one, and that the want of a new one was the only cause of the stoppage of the mill, and that the loss of profits really arose from not sending down the new shaft in proper time, and that this arose from the delay in delivering the broken one to serve as a model. But it is obvious that, in the great multitude of cases of millers sending off broken shafts to third persons by a carrier under ordinary circumstances, such consequences would not, in all probability, have occurred; and these special circumstances were here never communicated by the plaintiffs to the defendants. It follows, therefore, that the loss of profits here cannot reasonably be considered such a consequence of the breach of contract as could have been fairly and reasonably contemplated by both the parties when they made this contract. For such loss would neither have flowed naturally from the breach of this contract in the great multitude of such cases occurring under ordinary circumstances, nor were the special circumstances, which, perhaps, would have made it a reasonable and natural consequence of such breach of contract, communicated to or known by the defendants. The Judge ought, therefore, to have told the jury, that, upon the facts then before them, they ought not to take the loss of profits into consideration at all in estimating the damages. There must therefore be a new trial in this case.

Rule absolute.

---

d. Mitigation

The duty to mitigate damages imposes on the person who has been injured by a breach an obligation to take reasonable steps to reduce his or her losses. Also known as the doctrine of avoidable consequences, an injured party who is found to have failed to mitigate consequential damages will not be able to collect the damages that it could have avoided. The doctrine applies after the breach and while some harm can be avoided. The nonbreaching party need only make reasonable efforts and expenditures to minimize damages. Why does an injured party owe this duty? Is it an economic concern with the avoidance of waste? Or perhaps an ethical claim that one ought not to wallow in one's injuries? Debate over the duty to mitigate puts the breaching party in the position of blaming the innocent party for some failure to act, and courts sometimes impose a heavy burden of persuasion on the breaching party on such issues. What, fairly, should an aggrieved party be required to do or to accept in order to reduce his or her losses?

The first case in this section looks at circumstances in which the injured party has a "duty" to mitigate damages. Note that the consequence of failing to mitigate damages does not result in a breach of duty claim by the other party. Rather, the injured party's recovery for the harm caused by the breach of contract is reduced by the amount of damages that could have been avoided. The second case in this section looks at the issue of reasonable efforts in the employment context. How far do the breached parties in these circumstances have to go in order to recover the benefit of the bargain denied by the breach of contract?

G. Emery Davis, Alice Davis, Michael Davis, and Rayce Davis v. First Interstate Bank, and Sam Davis, Neva Davis, Jim Davis, and Carol Davis v. First Interstate Bank of Idaho, N.A.

Supreme Court of Idaho
765 P.2d 680 (1988)

STEPHEN BISTLINE, JUSTICE.

This case involves starving sheep and a promise to lend money. The plaintiffs, Emery and Sam Davis, own sheep which run together. The defendant bank concedes it had a valid contract with plaintiffs to lend money for the sheep ranching operation—and that the bank breached this contract when it failed to lend the plaintiffs money in December of 1983. The trial court granted defendant's motion for summary judgment on the ground that plaintiffs failed to mitigate their damages by seeking alternative financing. We reverse.

Plaintiffs Emery Davis (and his family) and Sam Davis (and his family) own separate sheep ranches, but the sheep run together. In 1982 plaintiffs began financing their operations through defendant First Interstate Bank of Idaho (bank). The bank made the plaintiffs an operating loan commencing in 1982. Plaintiffs were unable to pay the full amount at the end of the 1982 budget year. In 1983 the bank continued to finance plaintiffs. The parties negotiated for financing in 1984, but were unable to reach an agreement. This dispute centers on the bank's refusal to finance plaintiffs for the 1984 budget year. For the purposes of summary judgment, the bank concedes that it had a contractual duty to lend plaintiffs money for the sheep ranching operation for the year commencing in December of 1983, and that it breached this duty when it failed to do so.

Plaintiffs subsequently brought suit, seeking recovery under four separate causes of action: (1) breach of contract, resulting in starved, malnourished sheep; (2) gross negligence, with a prayer for punitive damages, for failure to notify plaintiffs that their operation would not be financed; (3) damages for loss of credit standing; (4) damages for extreme humiliation, anguish, mental and physical distress and suffering resulting from intentional harassment. Plaintiffs made a timely demand for jury trial.

The trial judge granted the bank's motion for summary judgment on the basis that plaintiffs failed to mitigate their damages. Specifically, the trial court found that plaintiffs did not take any action to obtain an alternate source of financing.

The scope of review when a grant of summary judgment is challenged on appeal is limited to determining only whether there exist genuine issues of material fact and whether the prevailing party is entitled to judgment as a matter of law. *Gro–Mor, Inc. v. Butts,* 712 P.2d 721 (Idaho Ct. App. 1985). *See also* I.R.C.P. 56(c). Facts in the existing record, including all reasonable inferences arising therefrom must be liberally construed in favor of the nonmoving party; the court must look to the totality of the motions, affidavits, depositions, pleadings, and attached exhibits, not merely to portions of the record in isolation. *Anderson v. City of Pocatello,* 731 P.2d 171 (Idaho 1986).

The duty to mitigate, also known as the doctrine of avoidable consequences, provides that a plaintiff who is injured by actionable conduct of the defendant, is ordinarily denied recovery for damages which could have been avoided by reasonable acts, including reasonable expenditures, after the actionable conduct has taken place. D. Dobbs, *Remedies* § 3.7, at 186 (1973). *See also Casey v. Nampa & Meridian Irrigation Dist.,* 379 P.2d 409, 412 (Idaho 1963). The burden of proof is on the party causing the alleged damage, *Eliopulos v. Kondo Farms, Inc.,* 643 P.2d 1085, 1090 (Idaho Ct. App.1982), the bank in this instance. The reasonableness of the method selected to minimize damages is an issue to be resolved by the jury. *Casey, supra,* 379 P.2d at 412, cited in *Eliopulos, supra,* 643 P.2d at 1090.

For the purposes of summary judgment, the bank concedes that it had a contractual duty to lend plaintiffs money for their sheep ranching operation for the year commencing in December of 1983. The bank further concedes for summary judgment purposes that it breached this contractual agreement when it failed to lend plaintiffs money in December of 1983. The district court granted summary judgment in favor of the bank on the ground that once the bank breached its contract, plaintiffs failed to seek alternative means of financing. The basis for the district court's ruling, however, is not supported by the record.

The affidavit of Sam Davis unequivocally avers that once the bank failed to honor its commitment to lend the needed money, he then sought alternative financing at both the Idaho First National Bank and the Farmers Home Administration. Financial statements were filled out at both institutions (exhibits A and B), but Sam Davis was told that he lacked sufficient collateral.[1] These facts must be construed most favorably to plaintiffs. Sam Davis tried to obtain alternative financing. The law, however, does not demand that he so obtain it: "The doctrine [of avoidable consequences] requires reasonable effort to mitigate damages. Thus, if reasonable, the efforts need not be successful." J. Colamari [sic] & J. Perillo, Contracts § 14–5, Avoidable Consequences at 539 (2d ed. 1977). We conclude that there exists a question of material fact, appropriate for resolution by a jury, as to whether plaintiffs exercised reasonable care to mitigate their damages. Thus, summary judgment was erroneously granted.

Furthermore, it is questionable whether plaintiffs were under a duty to mitigate at all. The affidavit of Sam Davis states that bank officials assured plaintiffs that the bank would not let the sheep starve.[2]

Professor McCormick in his *Handbook on the Law of Damages* § 38, at 141 (1935), notes that under the doctrine of avoidable consequences, there is no duty to act where the wrongdoer gives assurances:

---

1. The affidavit of Sam Davis provides:
   When First Interstate did not honor its commitment to provide the money for the supplemental feed for the ewes I then made contact to Idaho First National Bank and Farmers Home Administration to see if we could get some sort of financing to take care of the necessary feed. First Interstate also cut me out of the money it agreed to pay for the feed to finish fattening out the lambs. When I went to Idaho First National Bank in Rexburg and filled out a financial statement, they flat out told me that without any collateral they could loan me no money. I got the same response at Farmers Home Administration in Rexburg.
2. The affidavit of Sam Davis provides:
   During the first week of December 1983 it was extremely cold and we had a terrible blizzard which dumped a lot of snow. The ewes were without adequate feed and we knew from our past experience that they had to be fed supplemental feed pellets in order to prevent malnutrition. My uncle Emery made contact with First Interstate Bank to explain the need for the supplemental feed right after the blizzard. Tom Lloyd assured him that they would take care of the sheep.
I went into First Interstate Bank during the first of December when the next to the last load of lambs were sold and asked Tom Lloyd what we were going to do about getting grain to those pregnant ewes who were in dire need of supplementary feed. He spoke with Phil Davies in Boise and told me that 'The bank would furnish us money to take care of the sheep on a day to day basis.'

[T]he plaintiff's failure to act to guard against injury will not affect his recovery where such failure was due to assurances given him by the defendant himself.

Thus, the assurances of bank officials informing plaintiffs that the sheep would be cared for on a day to day basis preclude summary judgment on the basis that plaintiff failed to mitigate damages. If the ultimate trier of fact should determine the bank assured plaintiffs that the sheep would be cared for, no duty to mitigate would arise.

Finally, even assuming, *arguendo,* that plaintiffs were required to mitigate damages and failed to do so by seeking alternative financing, summary judgment would not be appropriate as to all causes of action. Not only did the plaintiffs allege an action for breach of contract, but also for gross negligence and infliction of mental and physical distress. These causes of action sound in tort, and, based on our review of the complaint, are unrelated to the facts underlying the breach of contract claim. Thus, even if plaintiffs are held duty-bound to mitigate damages under the contract claim, it may be that no corresponding duty would arise as to the claims sounding in tort.

We reverse the summary judgment. The cause is remanded to the district court for further proceedings.

Costs to appellants; no attorney fees on appeal.

Shirley MacLaine Parker v. Twentieth Century-Fox Film Corp.

Supreme Court of California
3 Cal. 3d 176, 474 P.2d 689, 89 Cal. Rptr. 737 (1970)

Louis H. Burke, Justice

Defendant Twentieth Century-Fox Film Corporation appeals from a summary judgment granting to plaintiff the recovery of agreed compensation under a written contract for her services as an actress in a motion picture. As will appear, we have concluded that the trial court correctly ruled in plaintiff's favor and that the judgment should be affirmed.

Plaintiff is well known as an actress, and in the contract between plaintiff and defendant is sometimes referred to as the "Artist." Under the contract, dated August 6, 1965, plaintiff was to play the female lead in defendant's contemplated production of a motion picture entitled "Bloomer Girl." The contract provided that defendant would pay plaintiff a minimum "guaranteed compensation" of $53,571.42 per week for 14 weeks commencing May 23, 1966, for a total of $750,000. Prior to May 1966 defendant decided not to produce the picture and by a letter dated April 4, 1966, it notified plaintiff of that decision and that it would not "comply with our obligations to you under" the written contract.

By the same letter and with the professed purpose "to avoid any damage to you," defendant instead offered to employ plaintiff as the leading actress in another film tentatively entitled "Big Country, Big Man" (hereinafter, "Big Country"). The compensation offered was identical, as were 31 of the 34 numbered provisions or articles of the original contract. Unlike "Bloomer Girl," however, which was to have been a musical production, "Big Country" was a dramatic "western type" movie. "Bloomer Girl" was to have been filmed in California; "Big Country" was to be produced in Australia. Also, certain terms in the proffered contract varied from those of the original. Plaintiff was given one week within which to accept; she did not and the offer lapsed. Plaintiff then commenced this action seeking recovery of the agreed guaranteed compensation.

Shirley MacLaine on broadway, 1984. Martha Swope © TIME Inc.

The complaint sets forth two causes of action. The first is for money due under the contract; the second, based upon the same allegations as the first, is for damages resulting from defendant's breach of contract. Defendant in its answer admits the existence and validity of the contract, that plaintiff complied with all the conditions, covenants and promises and stood ready to complete the performance, and that defendant breached and "anticipatorily repudiated" the contract. It denies, however, that any money is due to plaintiff either under the contract or as a result of its breach, and pleads as an affirmative defense to both causes of action plaintiff's allegedly deliberate failure to mitigate damages, asserting that she unreasonably refused to accept its offer of the leading role in "Big Country."

Plaintiff moved for summary judgment under *Code Civ. P.* §437c, the motion was granted, and summary judgment for $750,000 plus interest was entered in plaintiff's favor. This appeal by defendant followed.

The familiar rules are that the matter to be determined by the trial court on a motion for summary judgment is whether facts have been presented which give rise to a triable factual issue. The court may not pass upon the issue itself. Summary judgment is proper only if the affidavits or declarations[8] in support of the moving party would be sufficient to sustain a judgment in his favor and his opponent does not by affidavit show facts sufficient to present a triable issue of fact. The affidavits of the moving party are strictly construed, and doubts as to the propriety of summary judgment should be resolved

---

8. In this opinion "affidavits" includes "declarations under penalty of perjury." (*See* Code Civ. Proc. §2015.5.)

against granting the motion. Such summary procedure is drastic and should be used with caution so that it does not become a substitute for the open trial method of determining facts. The moving party cannot depend upon allegations in his own pleadings to cure deficient affidavits, nor can his adversary rely upon his own pleadings in lieu or in support of affidavits in opposition to a motion; however, a party can rely on his adversary's pleadings to establish facts not contained in his own affidavits. *Slobojan v. Western Travelers Life Ins. Co.*, 70 Cal. 2d 432, 436–37, 74 Cal. Rptr. 895, 450 P.2d 271 (1969), and cases cited. Also, the court may consider facts stipulated to by the parties and facts which are properly the subject of judicial notice.

As stated, defendant's sole defense to this action which resulted from its deliberate breach of contract is that in rejecting defendant's substitute offer of employment plaintiff unreasonably refused to mitigate damages.

The general rule is that the measure of recovery by a wrongfully discharged employee is the amount of salary agreed upon for the period of service, less the amount which the employer affirmatively proves the employee has earned or with reasonable effort might have earned from other employment. *W. F. Boardman Co. v. Petch*, 186 Cal. 476, 484, 199 P. 1047 (1921); *DeAngeles v. Roos Bros., Inc.*, 244 Cal. App. 2d 434, 441–42, 52 Cal. Rptr. 783 (1966). However, before projected earnings from other employment opportunities not sought or accepted by the discharged employee can be applied in mitigation, the employer must show that the other employment was comparable, or substantially similar, to that of which the employee has been deprived; the employee's rejection of or failure to seek other available employment of a different or inferior kind may not be resorted to in order to mitigate damages. *Gonzales v. Internat. Assn. of Machinists*, 213 Cal. App. 2d 817, 822–24, 29 Cal. Rptr. 190 (1963).

In the present case defendant has raised no issue of *reasonableness of efforts* by plaintiff to obtain other employment; the sole issue is whether plaintiff's refusal of defendant's substitute offer of "Big Country" may be used in mitigation. Nor, if the "Big Country" offer was of employment different or inferior when compared with the original "Bloomer Girl" employment, is there an issue as to whether or not plaintiff acted reasonably in refusing the substitute offer. Despite defendant's arguments to the contrary, no case cited or which our research has discovered holds or suggests that reasonableness is an element of a wrongfully discharged employee's option to reject, or fail to seek, different or inferior employment lest the possible earnings therefrom be charged against him in mitigation of damages.[9]

Applying the foregoing rules to the record in the present case, with all intendments in favor of the party opposing the summary judgment motion—here, defendant—it is clear that the trial court correctly ruled that plaintiff's failure to accept defendant's tendered substitute employment could not be applied in mitigation of damages because the offer of the "Big Country" lead was of employment both different and inferior, and that no factual dispute was presented on that issue. The mere circumstance that "Bloomer Girl" was to be

---

9. Instead, in each case the reasonableness referred to was that of the *efforts* of the employee to obtain other employment that was not different or inferior; his right to reject the latter was declared as an unqualified rule of law. Thus, Gonzales v. Internat. Assn. of Machinists, *supra*, 213 Cal. App. 2d 817, 823–24, 29 Cal. Rptr. 190, 194, holds that the trial court correctly instructed the jury that plaintiff union member, a machinist, was required to make "such *efforts* as the average [member of his union] desiring employment would make at that particular time and place" (italics added); but, further, that the court *properly rejected* defendant's *offer of proof of* the *availability of other kinds of employment* at the same or higher pay than plaintiff usually received and all outside the jurisdiction of his union, as plaintiff could not be required to accept different employment or a nonunion job....

a musical review calling upon plaintiff's talents as a dancer as well as an actress, and was to be produced in the City of Los Angeles, whereas "Big Country" was a straight dramatic role in a "Western Type" story taking place in an opal mine in Australia, demonstrates the difference in kind between the two employments; the female lead as a dramatic actress in a western style motion picture can by no stretch of imagination be considered the equivalent of or substantially similar to the lead in a song-and-dance production.

Additionally, the substitute "Big Country" offer proposed to eliminate or impair the director and screenplay approvals accorded to plaintiff under the original "Bloomer Girl" contract, and thus constituted an offer of inferior employment. No expertise or judicial notice is required in order to hold that the deprivation or infringement of an employee's rights held under an original employment contract converts the available "other employment" relied upon by the employer to mitigate damages, into inferior employment which the employee need not seek or accept.

Statements found in affidavits submitted by defendant in opposition to plaintiff's summary judgment motion, to the effect that the "Big Country" offer was not of employment different from or inferior to that under the "Bloomer Girl" contract, merely repeat the allegations of defendant's answer to the complaint in this action, constitute only conclusionary assertions with respect to undisputed facts, and do not give rise to a triable factual issue so as to defeat the motion for summary judgment.

In view of the determination that defendant failed to present any facts showing the existence of a factual issue with respect to its sole defense — plaintiff's rejection of its substitute employment offer in mitigation of damages — we need not consider plaintiff's further contention that for various reasons, including the provisions of the original contract, plaintiff was excused from attempting to mitigate damages.

The judgment is affirmed.

RAYMOND L. SULLIVAN, ACTING CHIEF JUSTICE, DISSENTING

The basic question in this case is whether or not plaintiff acted reasonably in rejecting defendant's offer of alternate employment. The answer depends upon whether that offer (starring in "Big Country, Big Man") was an offer of work that was substantially similar to her former employment (starring in "Bloomer Girl") or of work that was of a different or inferior kind. To my mind this is a factual issue which the trial court should not have determined on a motion for summary judgment. The majority have not only repeated this error but have compounded it by applying the rules governing mitigation of damages in the employer-employee context in a misleading fashion. Accordingly, I respectfully dissent.

The familiar rule requiring a plaintiff in a tort or contract action to mitigate damages embodies notions of fairness and socially responsible behavior which are fundamental to our jurisprudence. Most broadly stated, it precludes the recovery of damages which, through the exercise of due diligence, could have been avoided. Thus, in essence, it is a rule requiring reasonable conduct in commercial affairs. This general principle governs the obligations of an employee after his employer has wrongfully repudiated or terminated the employment contract. Rather than permitting the employee simply to remain idle during the balance of the contract period, the law requires him to make a reasonable effort to secure other employment. He is not obliged, however, to seek or accept any and all types of work which may be available. Only work which is in the same field and which is of the same quality need be accepted.[10]

---

10. This qualification of the rule seems to reflect the simple and humane attitude that it is too severe to demand of a person that he attempt to find and perform work for which he has no training

Over the years the courts have employed various phrases to define the type of employment which the employee, upon his wrongful discharge, is under an obligation to accept. Thus in California alone it has been held that he must accept employment which is "substantially similar" *Lewis v. Protective Security Life Ins. Co.*, 208 Cal. App. 2d 582, 584, (1962); *De La Falaise v. Gaumont-British P. Corp.*, 103 P.2d 447 (Cal. App. 1940); "comparable employment" *Erler v. Five Points Motors, Inc.*, 249 Cal. App. 2d 560, 562 (1967); *Harris v. Nat. Union, etc., Cooks and Stewards*, 254 P.2d 673 (Cal. App. 1953); employment "in the same general line of the first employment" *Rotter v. Stationers Corporation*, 186 Cal. App. 2d 170, 172 (1960); "equivalent to his prior position" *DeAngeles v. Roos Bros., Inc.*, 244 Cal. App. 2d 434, 443 (1966); "employment in a similar capacity" *Silva v. McCoy*, 259 Cal. App. 2d 256, 260 (1968); employment which is "not ... of a different or inferior kind." ... *Gonzales v. Internat. Assn. of Machinists*, 213 Cal. App. 2d 817, 822 (1963).[11]

For reasons which are unexplained, the majority cite several of these cases yet select from among the various judicial formulations which contain one particular phrase, "Not of a different or inferior kind," with which to analyze this case. I have discovered no historical or theoretical reason to adopt this phrase, which is simply a negative restatement of the affirmative standards set out in the above cases, as the exclusive standard. Indeed, its emergence is an example of the dubious phenomenon of the law responding not to rational judicial choice or changing social conditions, but to unrecognized changes in the language of opinions or legal treatises. However, the phrase is a serviceable one and my concern is not with its use as the standard but rather with what I consider its distortion.

The relevant language excuses acceptance only of employment which is of a *different kind*. *Gonzales v. Internat. Assn. of Machinists, supra*, 213 Cal. App. 2d 817. It has never been the law that the mere existence of *differences between two jobs in the same field* is sufficient, as a matter of law, to excuse an employee wrongfully discharged from one from accepting the other in order to mitigate damages. Such an approach would effectively eliminate any obligation of an employee to attempt to minimize damage arising from a wrongful discharge. The only alternative job offer an employee would be required to accept would be an offer of his former job by his former employer.

Although the majority appear to hold that there was a difference "in kind" between the employment offered plaintiff in "Bloomer Girl" and that offered in "Big Country," an examination of the opinion makes crystal clear that the majority merely point out differences between the two *films* (an obvious circumstance) and then apodictically assert that these constitute a difference in the *kind of employment*. The entire rationale of the majority boils down to this: that the *"mere circumstances"* that "Bloomer Girl" was to be a musical review while "Big Country" was a straight drama "demonstrates the difference in kind" since a female lead in a western is not "the equivalent of or substantially similar to" a lead in a musical. This is merely attempting to prove the proposition by repeating it. It shows that the vehicles for the display of the star's talents are different but it does not prove that her employment as a star in such vehicles is of necessity different *in kind* and either inferior or superior.

I believe that the approach taken by the majority (a superficial listing of differences with no attempt to assess their significance) may subvert a valuable legal doctrine. The inquiry in cases such as this should not be whether differences between the two jobs exist

or experience. Many of the older cases hold that one need not accept work in an inferior rank or position nor work which is more menial or arduous. This suggests that the rule may have had its origin in the bourgeois fear of resubmergence in lower economic classes.

11. *See also* 28 A.L.R. 736, 740–42; 15 Am. Jur. 431.

(there will always be differences) but whether the differences which are present are substantial enough to constitute differences in the *kind* of employment or, alternatively, whether they render the substitute work employment of an *inferior kind*.

It seems to me that *this* inquiry involves, in the instant case at least, factual determinations which are improper on a motion for summary judgment. Resolving whether or not one job is substantially similar to another or whether, on the other hand, it is of a different or inferior kind, will often (as here) require a critical appraisal of the similarities and differences between them in light of the importance of these differences to the employee. This necessitates a weighing of the evidence, and it is precisely this undertaking which is forbidden on summary judgment. *Garlock v. Cole*, 199 Cal. App. 2d 11, 14 (1962).

This is not to say that summary judgment would never be available in an action by an employee in which the employer raises the defense of failure to mitigate damages. No case has come to my attention, however, in which summary judgment has been granted on the issue of whether an employee was obliged to accept available alternate employment. Nevertheless, there may well be cases in which the substitute employment is so manifestly of a dissimilar or inferior sort, the declarations of the plaintiff so complete and those of the defendant so conclusionary and inadequate that no factual issues exist for which a trial is required. This, however, is not such a case.

It is not intuitively obvious, to me at least, that the leading female role in a dramatic motion picture is a radically different endeavor from the leading female role in a musical comedy film. Nor is it plain to me that the rather qualified rights of director and screenplay approval contained in the first contract are highly significant matters either in the entertainment industry in general or to this plaintiff in particular. Certainly, none of the declarations introduced by plaintiff in support of her motion shed any light on these issues.[12]

Nor do they attempt to explain why she declined the offer of starring in "Big Country, Big Man." Nevertheless, the trial court granted the motion, declaring that these approval rights were "critical" and that their elimination altered "the essential nature of the employment."

---

12. Plaintiff's declaration states simply that she has not received any payment from defendant under the "Bloomer Girl" contract and that the only persons authorized to collect money for her are her attorney and her agent.

The declaration of Herman Citron, plaintiff's theatrical agent, alleges that prior to the formation of the "Bloomer Girl" contract he discussed with Richard Zanuck, defendant's vice president, the conditions under which plaintiff might be interested in doing "Big Country"; that it was Zanuck who informed him of Fox's decision to cancel production of "Bloomer Girl" and queried him as to plaintiff's continued interest in "Big Country"; that he informed Zanuck that plaintiff was shocked by the decision, had turned down other offers because of her commitment to defendant for "Bloomer Girl" and was not interested in "Big Country." It further alleges that "Bloomer Girl" was to have been a musical review which would have given plaintiff an opportunity to exhibit her talent as a dancer as well as an actress and that "Big Country" was a straight dramatic role; the former to have been produced in California, the latter in Australia. Citron's declaration concludes by stating that he has not received any payment from defendant for plaintiff under the "Bloomer Girl" contract.

Benjamin Neuman's declaration states that he is plaintiff's attorney; that after receiving notice of defendant's breach he requested Citron to make every effort to obtain other suitable employment for plaintiff; that he (Neuman) rejected defendant's offer to settle for $400,000 and that he has not received any payment from defendant for plaintiff under the "Bloomer Girl" contract. It also sets forth correspondence between Neuman and Fox which culminated in Fox's final rejection of plaintiff's demand for full payment.

The plaintiff's declarations were of no assistance to the trial court in its effort to justify reaching this conclusion on summary judgment. Instead, it was forced to rely on judicial notice of the definitions of "motion picture," "screenplay" and "director" and then on judicial notice of practices in the film industry which were purportedly of "common knowledge." This use of judicial notice was error. Evidence Code section 451, subdivision (e) was never intended to authorize resort to the dictionary to solve essentially factual questions which do not turn upon conventional linguistic usage. More important, however, the trial court's notice of "facts commonly known" violated Evidence Code section 455, subdivision (a). Before this section was enacted there were no procedural safeguards affording litigants an opportunity to be heard as to the propriety of taking judicial notice of a matter or as to the tenor of the matter to be noticed. Section 455 makes such an opportunity (which may be an element of due process, *see* Evid. Code § 455, Law Revision Com. Comment (a)) mandatory and its provisions should be scrupulously adhered to. "Judicial notice can be a valuable tool in the adversary system for the lawyer as well as the court," Kongsgaard, *Judicial Notice*, 18 Hastings L.J. 117, 140 (1966), and its use is appropriate on motions for summary judgment. Its use in this case, however, to determine on summary judgment issues fundamental to the litigation without complying with statutory requirements of notice and hearing is a highly improper effort to "cut the Gordian knot of involved litigation." *Silver Land & Dev. Co. v. California Land Title Co.*, 248 Cal. App. 2d 241, 242 (1967).

The majority do not confront the trial court's misuse of judicial notice. They avoid this issue through the expedient of declaring that neither judicial notice nor expert opinion (such as that contained in the declarations in opposition to the motion)[13] is necessary to reach the trial court's conclusion. *Something*, however, clearly *is* needed to support this conclusion. Nevertheless, the majority make no effort to justify the judgment through an examination of the plaintiff's declarations. Ignoring the obvious insufficiency of these declarations, the majority announce that "the deprivation or infringement of an employee's rights held under an original employment contract" changes the alternate employment offered or available into employment of an inferior kind.

I cannot accept the proposition that an offer which eliminates *any* contract right, regardless of its significance, is, as a matter of law, an offer of employment of an inferior

---

13. Fox filed two declarations in opposition to the motion; the first is that of Frank Ferguson, Fox's chief resident counsel. It alleges, in substance, that he has handled the negotiations surrounding the "Bloomer Girl" contract and its breach; that the offer to employ plaintiff in "Big Country" was made in good faith and that Fox would have produced the film if plaintiff had accepted; that by accepting the second offer plaintiff was not required to surrender any rights under the first (breached) contract nor would such acceptance have resulted in a modification of the first contract; that the compensation under the second contract was identical; that the terms and conditions of the employment were substantially the same and not inferior to the first; that the employment was in the same general line of work and comparable to that under the first contract; that plaintiff often makes pictures on location in various parts of the world; that article 2 of the original contract which provides that Fox is not required to use the artist's services is a standard provision in artists' contracts designed to negate any implied covenant that the film producer promises to play the artist in or produce the film; that it is not intended to be an advance waiver by the producer of the doctrine of mitigation of damages. The second declaration is that of Richard Zanuck. It avers that he is Fox's vice president in charge of production; that he has final responsibility for casting decisions; that he is familiar with plaintiff's ability and previous artistic history; that the offer of employment for "Big Country" was in the same general line and comparable to that of "Bloomer Girl"; that plaintiff would not have suffered any detriment to her image or reputation by appearing in it; that elimination of director and script approval rights would not injure plaintiff; that plaintiff has appeared in dramatic and western roles previously and has not limited herself to musicals; and that Fox would have complied with the terms of its offer if plaintiff had accepted it.

kind. Such an absolute rule seems no more sensible than the majority's earlier suggestion that the mere existence of differences between two jobs is sufficient to render them employment of different kinds. Application of such per se rules will severely undermine the principle of mitigation of damages in the employer-employee context.

I remain convinced that the relevant question in such cases is whether or not a particular contract provision is so significant that its omission *creates* employment of an inferior kind. This question is, of course, intimately bound up in what I consider the ultimate issue: whether or not the employee acted reasonably. This will generally involve a factual inquiry to ascertain the importance of the particular contract term and a process of weighing the absence of that term against the countervailing advantages of the alternate employment. In the typical case, this will mean that summary judgment must be withheld.

In the instant case, there was nothing properly before the trial court by which the importance of the approval rights could be ascertained, much less evaluated. Thus, in order to grant the motion for summary judgment, the trial court misused judicial notice. In upholding the summary judgment, the majority here rely upon per se rules which distort the process of determining whether or not an employee is obliged to accept particular employment in mitigation of damages.

I believe that the judgment should be reversed so that the issue of whether or not the offer of the lead role in "Big Country, Big Man" was of employment comparable to that of the lead role in "Bloomer Girl" may be determined at trial.

Note

In *Parker*, the breaching party, Twentieth Century-Fox, made an offer to Shirley MacLaine Parker, the aggrieved party, which might have reduced the damages resulting from its breach. Must an aggrieved party deal with the breaching party? What risks might that entail for the aggrieved party? Recall *Sosnoff v. Carter* (Chapter Seven) and *Alaska Packers' Ass'n v. Domenico* (Chapter Eight), in which parties alleged they had been coerced into entering a new contract with someone who had breached a contract. Professor Robert A. Hillman has suggested five factors that should be considered in deciding whether an aggrieved party ought to be required to deal with the breaching party in order to mitigate damages: whether the injured party can reduce her injury by accepting the new offer; whether the injured party still can perform her obligations; whether the new offer is the best offer available; whether the aggrieved party will be able to pursue rights under the original contract; and whether the breaching party can provide adequate assurance of performance on the new terms. *See* Robert A. Hillman *Keeping the Deal Together after Material Breach — Common Law Mitigation Rules, the UCC, and the Restatement (Second) of Contracts*, 47 U. Col. L. Rev. 553 (1976). Under these standards, would Shirley MacLaine Parker be required to accept the new offer by Twentieth Century-Fox? Compare Professor Murray's approach:

> [T]he tendency is to say that when the relationship which the particular contract involves is a highly personal one, as in employment cases, so that the dealing further with the defaulter might prove to be particularly distasteful to the innocent promisee, the offer need not be accepted. On the other hand, in cases involving more impersonal relationships, the view has been taken that the defaulter's offer must be accepted (i.e., will be deemed a "mitigating" opportunity) provided it is not made by way of compromise or in substitution of the performance under the original contract.

J. Murray, Contracts §§ 164, 227, at 465 (1974).

Professor Murray distinguishes between personal and impersonal contract relationships. Is this distinction clear? In *Parker*, might it be "distasteful" to Shirley MacLaine Parker to deal further with Twentieth Century? How does the court analyze this issue?

Bloomer Girl was based upon the life of Amelia Bloomer, a mid-nineteenth century feminist, suffragist, and abolitionist, and *Big Country* is a Western. As Professor Mary Jo Frug argues, *Big Country* "would offer a leading actress the inferior kind of leading role westerns have typically offered to women. Like Miss Kitty in "Gunsmoke," a woman in a western is usually very much subordinated to the main focus of such films — the cowboy hero." Mary Jo Frug, Postmodern Legal Feminism 89 (1992). Professor Frug observes:

> It will seem unjust, to some readers, that Shirley MacLaine is apparently going to get $750,000, after this decision, for doing nothing. The mitigation rule seems to lose all of its muscle as a result of this "different or inferior" qualification. Would MacLaine have been entitled to damages if she had refused the lead in *Annie Hall*, because that extremely successful film is not a musical? Would she have been denied damages if she turned down *Springtime for Hitler*? How can you tell?

Id.

C. The UCC Remedies Provisions: Market, Cover, Resale, and Other Measures of Damages

The UCC sets forth a panoply of separate remedies for buyers and sellers of goods: "all things (including specially manufactured goods) which are moveable at the time of identification to the contract." (2-104). These remedies reflect the underlying principles of putting the aggrieved party in as good a position as if the other party had performed and requiring commercially reasonable conduct. Together these principles protect the expectation interests of the parties and protect the parties from predatory or commercially unreasonable or retaliatory behavior by the other party. Although the Code allows the aggrieved party to choose the remedy, the aggrieved party must also comply with the specific requirements for each remedy.

1. General Remedies for Buyers when Sellers Have Breached

If the seller tenders the goods but they are non-conforming, the buyer may:

1) *reject the goods* within a reasonable time and notify the seller of rejection within a reasonable time (2-601, 2-602);

2) *revoke acceptance* if there is a substantial impairment of the value of the goods to the buyer, and the buyer has accepted the goods with the seller's assurances that the non-conformity will be cured, or the defect was not discoverable upon a reasonable inspection (2-608); or

3) *accept the non-conforming goods* and give notice to the seller within a reasonable time after breach is discovered or should have been discovered of the intent to claim a breach with respect to the accepted goods. (2-607(3)(a)).

If the buyer rightfully rejects or justifiably revokes acceptance, or if the seller fails to tender the goods at all, the buyer may then either cover (2-712) (make substitute purchases); recover damages under a market measure of damages, "hypothetical cover," (2-713); or, if the goods are unique or cover is otherwise not possible, sue for specific performance (2-716).

If the buyer chooses to cover (more technically, to make good faith purchases of substitute goods without unreasonable delay), the measure of recovery under 2-712 is the difference between the cost of cover and the contract price. Cover may reduce the litigation difficulty, time, and expense of proving market price.

If the buyer chooses to recover damages under 2-713, the measure of recovery is the difference between the contract price and the market price at the time buyer learned of the breach. The buyer may pursue this remedy when there is no longer a need for the goods, or no reasonable substitute exists, or the buyer has failed to make a commercially reasonable cover. Although the buyer has the choice of remedy, there are potential difficulties for the buyer. For example, a failure to cover could bar recovery of consequential damages that would have been avoided by covering (2-715(2)). Also, if the disappointed buyer could have procured substitute goods, the buyer will be barred from the remedies of replevin and specific performance (2-716).

In addition to the damages for breach under 2-712 and 2-713, the buyer may also recover consequential and incidental damages (2-715). Pre-Code cases held that consequential damages could be recovered if they were foreseeable—that is, the seller knew at the time of contracting the buyer's purpose in making the purchase and no substitute would be available in the event of breach. Adopting the rule of *Hadley v. Baxendale*, the Code allows recovery of consequential damages, "any loss resulting from general or particular requirements and needs of which the seller at the time of contracting had reason to know and which could not be reasonably be prevented by cover or otherwise." (2-715(2)). The seller may be found to "have reason to know" where there are market shortages of the goods, or where the seller controls brand name goods, or has exclusive control over patented goods, or where the seller knows the goods will be used as part of a manufacturing process.

The Code adds the category of incidental damages which includes expenses reasonably incurred in the inspection, receipt, transportation and care and custody of goods rightfully rejected, any commercially reasonable charges, expenses or commissions in connection with effectuating cover, and any other reasonable expenses incident to the delay or other breach. (2-715(1)).

If the buyer chooses to keep the goods despite their defects, the measure of recovery is the difference between the value of the goods accepted and the value of the goods as warranted. (2-714(2)). Value is determined at the time and place of acceptance and an objective market standard is used. Breach of warranty recovery can also include consequential damages.

2. General Remedies for Sellers when Buyers Have Breached

If the buyer wrongfully rejects, revokes acceptance, fails to make payment when due, or repudiates all or a part of the goods, under the general remedies set forth in 2-703, the aggrieved seller may:

1. withhold delivery
2. stop delivery by any bailee (2-705)

3. proceed with manufacture under 2-704 respecting goods still unidentified to the contract (or identify unfinished goods and treat as subject of resale)

4. resell and recover damages (2-706)

5. recover damages for non-acceptance or repudiation (2-708)

6. in a proper case (e.g., where goods can't be resold) recover the price (2-709)

7. cancel the contract.

Under the resale option (2-706), the seller must properly notify the breaching buyer of the intent to resell and must resell in good faith and in a commercially reasonable manner. The seller may recover the difference between the contract price and the resale price plus incidental damages less any expenses saved as a result of the breach by the buyer. As damages for non-acceptance or repudiation (2-708(1)), the seller may recover the difference between the contract price and the market price at the time and place of tender price plus incidental damages less any expenses saved as a result of the breach by the buyer. However, when 2-708(1) is inadequate to put the seller in as good a position as performance, then 2-708(2) allows the seller to recover its profit (including reasonable overhead) plus incidental damages (2-710), with due allowance for costs reasonably incurred and due credit for payments or proceeds of sale.

The most common situation in which 2-708(2) applies is where the seller is a "lost volume" seller. A "lost volume" seller is one who has more items to sell than he or she can find buyers to buy. For such a seller, every lost sale means a lost profit. Think, for example, about a seller who does not have a large volume of things to sell: Graciela wants to sell her 1965 Volvo Sedan. Craig agrees to buy the Volvo for $35,000. If Craig breaches the contract, Graciela must try to sell the Volvo to someone else. If she finds another buyer who will pay her $30,000, then she is entitled to damages of $5,000 from Craig (under 2-706) or if she decides not to resell the car, Graciela is entitled to the difference between the contract price ($35,000) and the market price (the Blue Book price could be used).

Now think of a volume seller: Rosemary has a car lot full of Kia Spectras, and she can get more from the manufacturer. Rosemary's problem is to find as many buyers as she can. Gene agrees to buy a Kia Spectra from Rosemary and then breaches his contract. Even if another buyer immediately walks onto the lot and buys a Kia, that is not a replacement sale. A car would have been available to sell to the new buyer even without Gene's breach. Rosemary has lost her profit on the sale to Gene. If you were to calculate Rosemary's damages under 2-706 or 2-708(1), you will probably end up with $0. Under 2-708(2), Rosemary, a "lost volume" seller, could recover the profit she has lost when a buyer breaches.

The next case considers the seller's choice of remedies under 2-706 and 2-708(1).

Peace River Seed Co-Operative, Ltd. v. Proseeds Mktg.

Supreme Court of Oregon
322 P.3d 531 (2014)

THOMAS A. BALMER, C. J.

In this breach of contract case, we examine the availability of different remedies under the Uniform Commercial Code (UCC) for an aggrieved seller of goods after a buyer breaches a contract to purchase those goods. Specifically, we consider the relationship between ORS 72.7080(1), which measures a seller's damages as the difference between the unpaid contract price and the market price at the time and place for tender, and ORS 72.7060, which measures a seller's damages as the difference between the contract price and the resale price. We examine those provisions to determine whether an aggrieved seller who has resold goods can recover a greater amount of damages using the market price measure of damages than the seller would recover using the resale price measure of damages. Plaintiff, a seller seeking damages from a buyer that breached contracts to purchase goods, argued at trial that it was entitled to recover its market price damages. The trial court determined that plaintiff was entitled to the lesser of its market price damages or its resale price damages, and the court ultimately awarded plaintiff its resale price damages. The Court of Appeals reversed and remanded, because the court determined that plaintiff could recover its market price damages, even though it had resold some of the goods at issue. *Peace River Seed Co-Op v. Proseeds Marketing*, 293 P.3d 1058 (Ore. App. 2012). The Court of Appeals also reversed the trial court's decision not to award plaintiff its attorney fees under the parties' contracts, and remanded for the trial court to determine whether the parties intended the ambiguous contract term "charges for collection" to include attorney fees. *Id.* at 724–25. For the reasons that follow, we agree that plaintiff was entitled to recover its market price damages, even if those damages exceeded plaintiff's resale price damages. We conclude, however, that plaintiff is not entitled to recover its attorney fees under the parties' contracts.

Facts and Proceedings Below

The facts material to our discussion are mostly undisputed. Peace River Seed Co-Operative ("plaintiff") is a Canadian company that buys grass seed from and sells grass seed for grass seed producers. Proseeds Marketing ("defendant") is an Oregon corporation that purchases grass seed from various sources to resell to end users. A broker prepared and the parties agreed to multiple contracts for defendant to purchase from plaintiff the total production of grass seed from a certain number of acres for a fixed price over a period of two years. The contracts incorporated the NORAMSEED Rules for the Trade of Seeds for Planting, which have been adopted by the American and Canadian Seed Trade Associations to govern the trade of seed. The NORAMSEED Rules provide that the UCC applies to transactions within the United States, and both parties have litigated this case under the UCC.

Under the contracts, defendant was to provide shipping and delivery instructions to plaintiff. During the contract period, however, the price of grass seed fell dramatically. Although defendant initially provided shipping instructions and plaintiff shipped conforming seed, defendant eventually refused to provide shipping instructions for delivery of additional seed under the contracts. After multiple requests for shipping instructions, and defendant's continued refusal to provide them, plaintiff cancelled the contracts. Over the next three years, plaintiff was able to sell at least some of the seed that defendant had agreed to purchase to other buyers.

The parties submitted their contract dispute to arbitration. Following an arbitrator's award in plaintiff's favor, plaintiff sought to enforce the award in court, and the trial court entered judgment over defendant's objection. Defendant appealed, and the Court of Appeals remanded for trial after concluding that the arbitration was not binding. *Peace River Seed Co-Op v. Proseeds Marketing*, 132 P.3d 31 (Ore. App.), *rev. den.*, 140 P.3d 1133 (Ore. 2006). In the subsequent bench trial, the court concluded that defendant had breached the contracts and that plaintiff had been entitled to cancel the contracts and seek damages. When the trial court awarded plaintiff its damages, the court noted that the parties had entered into fixed price contracts, "regardless of the market price at the time of harvest and shipment," and the court explained that "[e]ach party takes certain risks and hopes for certain benefits in this type of a contract." Nonetheless, the court concluded that plaintiff had an "obligation to mitigate damages" and was "not entitled to recover damages in an amount greater than actually incurred." Accordingly, the trial court awarded plaintiff the lesser of two measures of damages: the difference between the unpaid contract price and the market price (the measure under ORS 72.7080(1)) or the difference between the contract price and the resale price (the measure under ORS 72.7060). The trial court directed plaintiff to submit calculations of each measure of damages.

Both parties sought reconsideration. At a hearing on those motions, the trial court stated that it would not be "absolutely one-hundred percent convinced" about the appropriate measure of damages until it could see how each party calculated market price damages and resale price damages. The trial court acknowledged that plaintiff previously had submitted its calculation of market price damages and had proven those damages, but the court also directed the parties to calculate damages to account for any seed that had been resold. Subsequently, defendant submitted its analysis of damages based on the prices that plaintiff had received when it resold. Plaintiff criticized defendant's analysis and stuck by its calculation of market price damages, without submitting an analysis of damages based on resale prices.

Each party's calculation of damages for one of the breached contracts, contract 1874, illustrates the implications of using the market price or the resale price to calculate damages. The evidence at trial showed that the contract price for contract 1874 was $0.72 per pound. Plaintiff sought damages of $3,736.00 for that contract, apparently based on a market price of $0.64 per pound, resulting in a contract price minus market price differential of $0.08 per pound for 46,700 pounds of seed not accepted by defendant.[1] Defendant argued, however, that plaintiff had resold at least some of that seed for $0.75 per pound, $0.03 per pound above the contract price and $0.11 per pound above plaintiff's market price calculation. Thus, according to defendant, plaintiff did not have any damages for that resold seed because plaintiff had resold for more than the contract price. If plaintiff recovered $0.08 per pound in market price damages, in addition to the $0.75 per pound that plaintiff allegedly had received on the resale, plaintiff ultimately would recover $0.83 per pound, which was $0.11 more than the contract price.[2]

For that same contract, however, where the contract price was $0.72 per pound, defendant noted that some of the seed had been resold for $0.60 per pound. That meant that the resale price damages would be $0.12 per pound. That is, for at least some of the resold seed from contract 1874, plaintiff's resale price damages of $0.12 per pound would exceed plaintiff's claimed market price damages of $0.08 per pound. In sum, the parties' calculations of damages for contract 1874 showed that, with regard to some seed, the market price damage calculation would lead to a larger award, but that, with regard to other seed, the resale price damage calculation would lead to a larger award. On the whole, however, defendant calculated that plaintiff would receive a smaller amount of damages using the resale price measure of damages than plaintiff calculated that it would receive using the market price measure of damages.

---

1. Market price is calculated "at the time and place for tender." ORS 72.7080(1). At trial, the evidence established a somewhat different market price, but that difference does not affect the legal analysis.

2. Even if plaintiff could not recover its market price damages, plaintiff would have received $0.03 per pound more than the contract price because plaintiff allegedly resold for more than the contract price. That is a result, however, that the UCC explicitly allows. *See* ORS 72.7060(6) ("The seller is not accountable to the buyer for any profit made on any resale.").

The trial court awarded plaintiff damages using the resale price measure of damages as calculated by defendant.[3] The trial court reasoned that plaintiff had not calculated damages as ordered by the court. The court stated that "even if Plaintiff [was] correct that Defendant's calculations [were] somehow flawed or incorrect, no alternative calculation ha[d] been offered." Thus, the trial court concluded that it was "left with no option but to accept Defendant's calculation." The trial court also denied plaintiff's request for attorney fees. The court concluded that plaintiff had not adequately alleged its request for attorney fees, and, on the merits, rejected plaintiff's argument that it was entitled to recover attorney fees under a provision of the NORAMSEED Rules, which the parties had incorporated into their contracts. Those rules allowed a seller to recover "charges for collection of payment" if the buyer did not pay in full and immediately when due. Rather than construing the phrase "charges for collection of payment," however, the trial court stated that the term "fees" in the NORAMSEED Rules was ambiguous, and the court purported to construe the term against plaintiff as the drafter of the contracts that had incorporated those rules.[4]

Plaintiff appealed. As relevant on review, plaintiff argued that the trial court erred in not awarding plaintiff its market price damages under ORS 72.7080(1) or its attorney fees under the NORAMSEED Rules. *Peace River*, 253 Ore. App. at 711, 722–23.

The Court of Appeals reversed and remanded. On the first issue, the court noted that, at least on its face, the UCC allows a seller to recover damages as calculated under either ORS 72.7060 (contract price less resale price) or ORS 72.7080(1) (contract price less market price). *Id.* at 713. After reviewing the relevant statutory provisions, the court went on to conclude that, "[i]n the absence of a restriction within the UCC that precludes an aggrieved seller from seeking its remedy pursuant to ORS 72.7080 if the seller has resold, we would decline to impose such a restriction." *Id.* at 715. In support of that conclusion, the court explained that, once the buyer breaches, the buyer loses any right to control the goods or to "insist upon a different measure of damages." *Id.* at 716–17. Moreover, the court noted, market price damages require the buyer to fulfill only the bargain to which it agreed. Id. at 717. Although the court acknowledged that the UCC policy is that remedies should put an aggrieved party "in as good a position as if the other party had fully performed," ORS 71.3050(1), the court concluded that the intent of the UCC is to allow an aggrieved seller to recover market price damages, even if the seller has resold the goods. *Id.* at 715–16 n 7. The court remanded the case for a proper calculation of plaintiff's market price damages. *Id.* at 717.

On the issue of attorney fees, the Court of Appeals determined that the trial court had erred in its contract interpretation analysis by both interpreting the wrong contract term and failing to follow the contract interpretation framework in *Yogman v. Parrott*, 937 P.2d 1019 (Ore. 1997). *Peace River*, 253 Ore. App. at 723–25. Applying the *Yogman* analysis, the Court of Appeals first determined that the relevant contract term, "charges for collection," was ambiguous. The court went on to note that the trial court had failed to determine the intent of the parties as necessary under the second step of *Yogman*. *Id.* at 724. Because the court concluded that there was some evidence in the record of the parties'

---

3. Although we refer to defendant's calculation of damages as plaintiff's resale price damages, where defendant could not identify a resale, it appears that defendant used a market price calculation. Because the parties' dispute centers on the trial court's decision to use the resale price measure of damages where possible, we use the shorthand "resale price damages" to refer to defendant's calculation of damages, which the trial court awarded plaintiff.

4. Neither party contends that the reasoning that the trial court applied in its contract interpretation analysis is correct. The term "fees" does not appear in the NORAMSEED Rules, and plaintiff did not draft the parties' contracts.

intent regarding that contract term, the court remanded to the trial court to consider the parties' intent in the first instance. *Id.* at 725.

Defendant sought review and now urges this court to reverse the Court of Appeals and affirm the trial court on both issues.

An Aggrieved Seller's Remedies Under The UCC

The UCC provides a variety of remedies to an aggrieved seller. *See* ORS 72.7030 (providing an index of a seller's remedies). As noted, the issue in this case is whether an aggrieved seller who has resold goods can recover the difference between the unpaid contract price and the market price under ORS 72.7080(1), even when market price damages would exceed resale price damages under ORS 72.7060.

Commentators and courts have taken two different approaches to this issue. Relying on the text and context of the sellers' remedies provisions, some commentators have argued that the drafters of the UCC intended for sellers to be able to recover either market price damages or resale price damages, even if the seller resold the goods for more than the market price. *See, e.g.*, Henry Gabriel, The Seller's Election of Remedies Under the Uniform Commercial Code: An Expectation Theory, 23 Wake Forest L Rev 429, 429 (1988) (arguing that an aggrieved seller "should be allowed to elect between the two remedies regardless of the seller's good faith post-breach activities concerning the non-accepted goods"); Ellen A. Peters, Remedies for Breach of Contracts Relating to the Sale of Goods Under the Uniform Commercial Code: A Roadmap for Article Two, 73 Yale LJ 199, 260 (1963) (arguing for a "non-restrictive reading of the various remedies sections to preserve full options to use or to ignore substitute transactions as a measure of damages"). On the other hand, Professors White and Summers, whose view has been adopted by a number of courts, have argued that the UCC's general policy is that damages should put a seller only in "as good a position as if the other party had fully performed," ORS 71.3050(1), meaning a seller who has resold should not be allowed to recover more in market price damages than it could recover in resale price damages. James J. White, Robert S. Summers and Robert A. Hillman, 1 Uniform Commercial Code §8:13, 689 (6th ed. 2012) (so stating). We agree with those commentators who have observed that the drafters did not clearly resolve this issue. *See, e.g., id.* at 691 (noting that the UCC and the comments are "equivocal" about whether a seller can recover more under section 2-708(1) than it could recover under section 2-706); Gabriel, 23 Wake Forest L Rev at 430 (noting "the failure of the drafters to clearly resolve the problem of election between sections 2-706 and 2-708(1)"). Nonetheless, we conclude that the text, context, and legislative history of the sellers' remedies provisions support a seller's right to recover either market price damages or resale price damages, even if market price damages lead to a larger recovery.

We analyze the relevant statutory provisions using the framework described in *State v. Gaines*, 206 P.3d 1042, 1045 (Ore. 2009). We begin by examining the statute's text and context to determine the legislature's intent regarding a seller's remedies under the UCC. Because the relevant statutes are part of the UCC, we also consider the official UCC comments as an indication of the legislature's intent. *Security Bank v. Chiapuzio*, 747 P.2d 335, 339 n.6 (Ore. 1987) (noting that the Oregon legislature took note of the official comments of the UCC, which are "statements of the purpose of each section"). In addition, "the legislative intent to make the UCC a uniform code makes relevant the decisions of other courts that have examined these questions and the discussions of the questions by scholars in the field, especially those scholars who participated in drafting the UCC." *Id.* We also examine legislative history. The Oregon legislature enacted the UCC in 1961 "with little debate or discussion of the legislative intent," but the UCC was proposed so that

Oregon could "obtain the same advantages that other states had gained from the adoption of a uniform and comprehensive set of commercial statutes." *Id.* Given "the legislative intent to make the UCC a uniform code," *id.*, we consider prior drafts of the UCC, as drafted by the National Conference of Commissioners on Uniform State Laws (NCCUSL), as part of the legislative history. *Cf. Datt v. Hill*, 227 P.3d 714, 719 (Ore. 2010) (examining history of uniform act in interpreting Oregon statute taken from that act).

Before examining the statutory scheme, however, we briefly review the law as it existed prior to the enactment of the UCC in Oregon. At common law, an aggrieved seller

> "ha[d] the election of three remedies: (1) To hold the property for the purchaser, and to recover of him the entire purchase money; (2) to sell it, after notice to the purchaser, as his agent for that purpose, and recover the difference between the contract price and that realized on the sale; (3) to retain it as his own, and recover the difference between the contract and market prices at the time and place of delivery[.]"

Krebs Hop Co. v. Livesley, 118 P 165, 166 (Ore. 1911). *Krebs Hop Co.* suggests that, before Oregon adopted the UCC, an aggrieved seller had to elect between remedies, and if the seller resold the goods, it had elected its remedy and could recover only resale price damages, but not market price damages. *See* Gabriel, 23 Wake Forest L Rev at 446 (explaining that, under pre-UCC law, an aggrieved seller who resold the goods was assumed to have elected the resale remedy and was barred from using an inconsistent remedy, such as market price damages). Although the UCC retained some aspect of each of the remedies available at common law, as explained below, it specifically rejected the doctrine of election of remedies. *See* Legislative Comment 1 to ORS 72.7030, reprinted in Legislative Counsel Committee, Oregon's Uniform Commercial Code with Comments and Index and Tables 101 (1962) (noting that the UCC chapter on sales "reject[s] any doctrine of election of remedy as a fundamental policy"); Peters, 73 Yale LJ at 204 n 16 (noting that many sections of the UCC were "designed to mitigate the effect of prior law insofar as it forced a choice of remedy on the party aggrieved without regard to the adequacy of compensation").

When a buyer breaches a contract for the sale of goods, ORS 72.7030 provides a seller with an index of remedies:

> "Where the buyer wrongfully rejects or revokes acceptance of goods or fails to make a payment due on or before delivery or repudiates with respect to a part or the whole, then with respect to any goods directly affected and, if the breach is of the whole contract as provided in ORS
>
> 72.6120, then also with respect to the whole undelivered balance, the aggrieved seller may:
>
> "...
>
> "(4) Resell and recover damages as provided in ORS 72.7060.[5]

---

5. ORS 72.7060(1) provides,
"Under the conditions stated in ORS 72.7030 on seller's remedies, the seller may resell the goods concerned or the undelivered balance thereof. Where the resale is made in good faith and in a commercially reasonable manner the seller may recover the difference between the resale price and the contract price together with any incidental damages allowed under the provisions of ORS 72.7100, but less expenses saved in consequence of the buyer's breach."

"(5) Recover damages for nonacceptance as provided in ORS 72.7080 or in a proper case the price as provided in ORS 72.7090.[6]

"(6) Cancel."

That section lists the seller's remedies, which, as relevant here, include resale price damages, ORS 72.7060, and market price damages, ORS 72.7080. Moreover, it lists those remedies without any limiting conjunction, such as "or," that might suggest that the remedies are mutually exclusive. In contrast, a similar index of a buyer's remedies after a seller's breach provides that the buyer may "(a) 'Cover' and have damages ... or (b) Recover damages for nondelivery." ORS 72.7110(1) (emphasis added.) Thus, although the buyer's index of remedies suggests that a buyer who covers may be precluded from seeking market price damages, the seller's index of remedies does not contain a similar limitation if the seller chooses to resell. It follows that the text of ORS 72.7030 supports plaintiff's argument that a seller who has resold is not necessarily limited to its resale price damages under ORS 72.7060, but has the option of seeking to recover market price damages under ORS 72.7080.

The UCC comments to the statute describing a seller's remedies confirm that interpretation. Although the comments acknowledge that, in a particular case, the pursuit of one remedy may prevent a seller from obtaining certain damages, the comments also state that the UCC chapter on sales "reject[s] any doctrine of election of remedy as a fundamental policy and thus the remedies are essentially cumulative in nature and include all of the available remedies for breach." Legislative Comment 1 to ORS 72.7030 at 101; *id.* ("Whether the pursuit of one remedy bars another depends entirely on the facts of the individual case."). In contrast, the comments to the statute describing a buyer's market price remedy explain that that remedy "is completely alternative to 'cover' under ORS 72.7120 and applies *only when and to the extent that the buyer has not covered.*" Legislative Comment 5 to ORS 72.7130 at 110 (emphasis added). Thus, while the comments to the statute describing a seller's remedies expressly reject the doctrine of election of remedies, the comments to the statute describing a buyer's market price remedy appear to adopt that doctrine. Those comments further indicate that a seller who resells goods after a buyer's breach would not be considered to have "elected" the resale remedy and thus would not be precluded from seeking a larger damage recovery using the market price measure of damages.

The text of ORS 72.7060, which sets forth the seller's resale remedy, similarly suggests that a seller who resells goods is not necessarily precluded from using the market price measure of damages, even if it leads to a larger recovery. ORS 72.7060(1) states that "the seller may resell the goods concerned or the undelivered balance thereof," which suggests that an aggrieved seller is not required to resell. (Emphasis added.) *See* White, Summers and Hillman, 1 Uniform Commercial Code § 8:6 at 671 ("Resale is not mandatory."). Similarly, the text of ORS 72.7060 indicates that a seller who resells is not required to seek damages using the resale remedy. *See* ORS 72.7060(1) ("Where the resale is made in good faith and in a commercially reasonable manner the seller may recover the difference

---

6. ORS 72.7080(1) provides,

"Subject to subsection (2) of this section [with respect to lost profits] and to the provisions of ORS 72.7230 with respect to proof of market price, the measure of damages for nonacceptance or repudiation by the buyer is the difference between the market price at the time and place for tender and the unpaid contract price together with any incidental damages provided in ORS 72.7100, but less expenses saved in consequence of the buyer's breach."

between the resale price and the contract price …." (Emphasis added.)). In fact, the unqualified text of ORS 72.7080(1) seems to suggest that market price is in fact the default measure of damages. *See* ORS 72.7080(1) ("Subject to … the provisions of ORS 72.7230 with respect to proof of market price, the measure of damages for nonacceptance or repudiation by the buyer is the difference between the market price at the time and place for tender and the unpaid contract price …." (Emphasis added.)). Thus, the text of the remedy provisions does not limit a seller who resells to its resale price damages.

As defendant notes, however, one of the comments to ORS 72.7060 does indicate that the drafters intended ORS 72.7060 to be a seller's primary remedy, and did not intend to allow a seller to recover more under the market price remedy. Comment 2 to ORS 72.7060 explains that "[f]ailure to act properly under ORS 72.7060 deprives the seller of the measure of damages there provided and relegates him to that provided in ORS 72.7080 [market price damages]." Legislative Comment 2 to ORS 72.7060 at 104 (emphasis added). That language suggests that the comment drafters viewed market price damages as less favorable, but it does not indicate why they viewed them that way. The pejorative language used in the comments does not necessarily lead to the conclusion that a seller who resells cannot use the market price remedy or must use the resale price remedy if it would yield the same or a smaller amount of damages than the market price remedy. That language instead could indicate that market price damages are considered less favorable because market price is often hard to prove, as many commentators have noted. *See, e.g.*, Henry J. Bailey III, 1 The Oregon Uniform Commercial Code § 2.140, 279 (2d ed 1990) (noting that the remedy under ORS 72.7080(1) "is often a less advantageous remedy for the seller because of difficulty of proof of market price"). As a result, that comment language is not dispositive, particularly in light of the text of the remedy provisions.

Turning to legislative history, prior drafts of the UCC provide additional insight into the drafters' intent to allow a seller to recover its market price damages, even if the seller has resold. In particular, in an earlier draft of the section describing the resale price remedy, section 2-706, one of the comments stated that that section provided

> "'the *exclusive* measure of the seller's damages where the resale has been made in accordance with the requirements of this section. Evidence of market or current prices at any particular time or place is relevant only on the question of whether the seller acted with commercially reasonable care and judgment in making the resale.'"

See Gabriel, 23 Wake Forest L Rev at 436 (quoting UCC § 2-706 cmt 3 (May 1949 Draft) (emphasis added)). Under that version of the UCC, a seller who had met the resale requirements would be required to use the resale price measure of damages. That comment later was revised, however, and when Oregon adopted the UCC, the comment included language that also had been in the 1949 draft comment, but the mandatory language had been removed, leaving only the permissive wording: "If the seller complies with the prescribed standard of duty in making the resale, he may recover from the buyer the damages provided for in subsection (1)." Legislative Comment 3 to ORS 72.7060 at 104 (emphasis added). That shift, from resale as the exclusive remedy to resale as a permissible remedy, indicates that the drafters intended for a seller to be able to choose to recover market price damages, even after reselling under ORS 72.7060.

Defendant argues, however, that even if a seller who resells can recover market price damages under ORS 72.7080(1), those damages cannot exceed the seller's resale price damages. Defendant primarily relies on the general policy statement set forth in ORS 71.3050 to support its argument. ORS 71.3050(1) provides,

"The remedies provided by the Uniform Commercial Code must be liberally administered to the end that the aggrieved party may be put *in as good a position as if the other party had fully performed* but consequential damages, special damages or penal damages may not be had except as specifically provided in the Uniform Commercial Code or by other rule of law."

(Emphasis added.) Defendant reasons that the reference in ORS 71.3050(1) to putting an aggrieved party "in as good a position as if the other party had fully performed" acts as a limit on the damages that a party can receive. Commentators and courts likewise have relied on that provision in concluding that a seller's market price damages should be limited to the actual loss suffered, by taking into account any goods that have been resold. *See, e.g.,* White, Summers and Hillman, 1 Uniform Commercial Code § 8:13 at 689 ("We conclude that a seller should not be permitted to recover more under 2-708(1) [market price damages] than under 2-706 [resale price damages] .... Section 1-305 indicates that a seller who has resold may not invoke 2-708(1)."); Coast Trading Co. v. Cudahy Co., 592 F.2d 1074, 1081–83 (9th Cir 1979) (adopting approach of White and Summers and reducing section 2-708(1) market price damages of seller who conducted commercially unreasonable resale to what seller could have recovered under section 2-706 if resale had been commercially reasonable); *Tesoro Petroleum Corp. v. Holborn Oil Co.,* 145 Misc. 2d 715, 547 NYS 2d 1012, 1016–17 (NY Sup Ct 1989) (adopting approach of White and Summers and limiting seller to resale price damages because higher market price damages would create a "windfall" inconsistent with the general policy of the UCC).

The text of ORS 71.3050(1) indicates that the drafters of the UCC intended a seller's remedies to be compensatory. *See* Legislative Comment 1 to *former* ORS 71.1060 at 6 (1963), *amended and renumbered* as ORS 71.3050 (2009) (noting that statute is intended to "make it clear that compensatory damages are limited to compensation"). The text of that section, however, also provides that the remedies in the UCC are to be "liberally administered." ORS 71.3050(1); *see also* Legislative Comment 4 to ORS 72.7030 at 101 ("It should also be noted that the Uniform Commercial Code requires its remedies to be liberally administered ...."). Nonetheless, we agree with defendant that the general policy of compensation provided in ORS 71.3050(1) must be taken into account.

We do not agree, however, that that policy necessarily limits an aggrieved seller who has resold to its resale price damages. Defendant argues that if it had fully performed, plaintiff could expect to recover only the contract price, and that limiting plaintiff to the difference between the contract price and the resale price therefore gives it the benefit of its bargain. As Professor Gabriel notes, however, limiting a seller to its resale price damages does not account fully for either party's expectations upon entering into the contract. He explains that a seller expects to be able to recover the difference between the contract price and the market price because it is the "logical and expected measure of damages," and because the ability to recover market price damages "is the natural assumption the seller makes in return for the risk inherent in the contract that the sale may not turn out to be economically beneficial to the seller. That the seller then resells the goods in no way diminishes this expectancy regarding the first contract." Gabriel, 23 Wake Forest L Rev at 449, 453. From the buyer's perspective, he argues that "the [buyer] has specific obligations and will suffer the consequences of the failure to perform these obligations because this is the [buyer's] expectation." *Id.* at 450. In other words, contrary to defendant's argument, an aggrieved seller expects to be able to recover market price damages under the contract, and a breaching buyer expects to have to fulfill its obligation to the seller—even if a seller resells and recovers market price damages, "the buyer's obligation is no more than the right the buyer originally conferred upon the seller." *Id.* at 449.

Moreover, limiting an aggrieved seller to its resale price damages ignores the risk for which the parties bargained. When parties bargain for fixed price contracts, each party assumes the risk of market price fluctuations. The parties are willing to take that risk because of the benefits that they might receive: if the market price decreases, the seller benefits, and if the market price increases, the buyer benefits. In a fixed price contract, therefore, market price damages represent the risk for which both parties bargained.[7] *Cf. id.* ("The logical and expected measure of damages is the contract price-market price differential. This measure of damages is the risk the buyer assumed by entering into the contract; it is the right conferred upon the seller by the buyer." (Emphasis added.)).[8] For those reasons, we conclude that a seller can recover market price damages, even if the seller resells some of the goods at above the market price at the time and place for tender.

Defendant argues, however, that that conclusion does not account for an aggrieved party's duty to mitigate, which is consistent with the UCC's policy of minimizing damages. See Legislative Comment 1 to former ORS 71.1060 at 6 (1963) ("[T]he Code elsewhere makes it clear that damages must be minimized.");[9] Roy Ryden Anderson, 1 Damages Under the Uniform Commercial Code § 1:6, 11–12 (2012)(noting that the duty to mitigate is "implicit in every damage remedy" and typically is justified under section 1-305). We do not understand the duty to mitigate to be a limit on a seller's market price damages because, as noted, the text demonstrates and commentators agree that a seller is not required to resell goods after a buyer's breach. If the duty to mitigate does not require the aggrieved seller to resell its goods, we do not think that the duty to mitigate can require the seller to use the resale price measure of damages. *See* Gabriel, 23 Wake Forest L Rev at 445 ("The seller has no obligation to resell, and the failure to resell the goods does not affect the right to proceed under section 2-708(1). If non-action by the seller does not impact on the statutory right under section 2-708(1), common sense dictates that an affirmative act by the seller to resell should not have any impact on that right." (Footnote omitted.)). The comments to the resale remedy provision also acknowledge that the seller who resells does so for its own benefit, and not for the benefit of the breaching party as mitigation. *See* Legislative Comment 2 to ORS 72.7060 at 104 (noting that the seller resells "in his own behalf, for his own benefit and for the purpose of fixing his damages"); cf. ORS 72.7060(6) ("The seller is not accountable to the buyer for any profit made on any resale."). Therefore, the principle of mitigation does not appear to limit an aggrieved

---

7. We do not, however, foreclose the right of a seller of goods under a fixed price contract to recover resale price damages under ORS 72.7060.

8. Professor Gabriel's explanation also responds to the argument that to permit a seller to recover market price damages when it has resold some or all of the goods confers an improper "windfall" on the seller. If a seller is limited to its resale price damages, it is just as accurate to say that the breaching buyer has received a "windfall," because the seller's success in reselling reduces the damages that the buyer must pay—and not because of anything the buyer did, but only because of the seller's successful efforts. As discussed in the text, the UCC imposes no obligation on the seller to resell, and the buyer's expectation, at the time the buyer entered into the contract, was that it might have to pay market price damages if it breached the contract. The point is not that one party or the other gets an undeserved "windfall," but rather that the provisions of the UCC, as we have interpreted them here, determine the rights and obligations of each party and therefore what is expected of each party and what each may expect of the other, as well as the consequences of either party's breach. The result we reach here is consistent with those expectations. *See generally* Gabriel, 23 Wake Forest L Rev at 453.

9. After that comment, the drafters cite to ORS 72.7060(1), which is the seller's resale remedy, and ORS 72.7120(2), which is the buyer's cover remedy. As already noted, however, the text demonstrates—and commentators agree—that neither resale nor cover is mandatory, so we do not understand that citation to imply that a seller must resell to mitigate its damages.

seller's recovery to resale price damages under ORS 72.7060; the seller may instead seek market price damages under ORS 72.7080(1).

In sum, when viewed in light of the bargained-for market risks and the UCC's rejection of the doctrine of election of remedies, the text, context, and legislative history of the sellers' remedy provisions demonstrate that an aggrieved seller can seek damages under either ORS 72.7080(1) or ORS 72.7060. That means that an aggrieved seller can seek damages under ORS 72.7080(1) even if the seller has resold the goods and market price damages exceed resale price damages.

Returning to the facts of this case, the trial court limited plaintiff's damages to resale price damages under ORS 72.7060. We have determined that plaintiff is entitled to market price damages under ORS 72.7080(1). Plaintiff asks us not to remand for calculation of those damages, as the Court of Appeals did. *See Peace River*, 253 Ore. App. at 717 (concluding that "the case must be remanded for a proper calculation of [plaintiff's] damages"). Instead, plaintiff argues that this court should remand with instructions to award plaintiff its market price damages as previously calculated. Plaintiff argues that the trial court made a specific finding accepting its calculation of those damages, and then improperly deducted certain resales from that amount. Because of that initial finding, plaintiff asserts that any additional calculation of its damages under ORS 72.7080(1) is unnecessary. Defendant responds that the trial court never made a finding accepting plaintiff's calculation of its damages under ORS 72.7080(1). Moreover, defendant notes, the record does not identify the amount that the trial court attributed to plaintiff's resales, which means that this court cannot simply work backwards from the trial court's award. Thus, defendant argues, this court must remand for calculation of plaintiff's market price damages.

As noted, after the trial court issued its initial letter opinion concluding that defendant had breached the contracts and directing plaintiff to calculate both its resale price damages and its market price damages, defendant filed a motion for reconsideration. Among other things, that motion challenged plaintiff's calculation of its market price damages. At the hearing on defendant's motion, defense counsel emphasized that plaintiff had the burden of proving its damages, and the trial court responded, "[T]hey have proven they have been damaged and they have proven in my opinion the numbers that they presented at trial. I'm just not sure whether they are entitled to all of that or something lesser based upon our discussion here."[10] Although the trial court appeared to accept plaintiff's calculation of market price damages, the court stated that it had not decided the amount of damages or how to determine those damages because, the court explained, "I am not absolutely one-hundred percent convinced what the measure is until I see completely how you each calculate your damages to some degree[.]"

Following that hearing, defendant submitted a calculation of plaintiff's resale price damages, and although plaintiff argued that that calculation was incorrect, plaintiff did not submit its own calculation of resale price damages. In the trial court's subsequent

---

10. Earlier in the hearing, the trial court also stated that "the simplest and easiest thing for me to say would be to calculate [damages] [plaintiff's] way," but the court was not sure whether the market price remedy was the proper measure of damages. The court went on to state, "[W]hat I'm saying to [defense counsel] is that I need him to tell me why that's not what I should do because, you know, the other side of it is that the argument could be—and—and this is a little bit where I am—that you [plaintiff] have proven your damages and you have given me evidence of that proof and you have given me a basis for that calculation. And so, based upon that, you have presented to me a prima facie case for your damages. Okay."

ruling awarding damages, the court acknowledged that it had "informed the parties at the close of evidence that a prima facie case for damages had been presented at trial," but the court noted that it had directed the parties to calculate the damages using the measure of damages directed by the court. Moreover, the court stated, "it could well be argued that Plaintiff has not in fact proved their damages," and the court went on to note that it "would have been within [its] discretion to have found Plaintiff did not adequately prove damages." Nonetheless, the court explained that it had given plaintiff time to provide a calculation of the measure of damages that accounted for resales. Because plaintiff did not do so, the court reasoned that it was "left with no option but to accept Defendant's calculation" using the resale price measure of damages.

The trial court did not award plaintiff its market price damages under ORS 72.7080(1), presumably because the court concluded that plaintiff was not entitled to that measure of damages — defendant's calculation of resale price damages was the "lesser of the two calculations offered. Nonetheless, the trial court did state that plaintiff had proven its damages at trial. Even after defendant challenged plaintiff's market price damage calculation, the trial court concluded that plaintiff had presented a prima facie case for its market price damages. Moreover, although defendant suggests that the "record in this case does not permit this court to identify the amount the trial court attributed to [plaintiff's] resales," the amount that the trial court attributed to plaintiff's resales is irrelevant in determining plaintiff's market price damages because market price damages and resale price damages are separate remedies. The trial court ordered that plaintiff be awarded "[t]he lesser of its resale price damages or its market price damages. Thus, because we have concluded that plaintiff is entitled to recover its market price damages, on remand, the trial court should award plaintiff its market price damages as calculated in Exhibit 409.[11] The trial court also awarded plaintiff prejudgment interest on its damages. Defendant did not raise that issue in the Court of Appeals. Because we have concluded that the measure of damages awarded by the trial court was erroneous, on remand the trial court should calculate prejudgment interest on the damages set out in Exhibit 409 and include the appropriate sum in its judgment.[12]

Attorney Fees

[Editors: In an omitted section, the court interprets the meaning of the contract by looking at the usage of trade and the parties' intent. If the contract provided for recovery of attorney fees, then those fees would be added to the damages.]

In sum, plaintiff did not present evidence that the parties' contracts, through incorporation of the NORAMSEED Rule allowing a seller to recover "charges for collection of payment," provide for plaintiff to recover its attorney fees. That is, plaintiff did not demonstrate through text and context, including trade usage, or through evidence of the parties' intent, that the term "charges for collection" includes attorney fees.[17]

---

11. Defendant states in its brief that it has paid the judgment entered against it by the trial court. The parties can address on remand the appropriate amount of the award, taking into account amounts defendant already has paid.

12. Because we conclude that plaintiff is entitled to recover damages under ORS 72.7080(1), we do not address the parties' discussion of lost volume sellers. *See* White, Summers and Hillman, 1 Uniform Commercial Code § 8:13 at 692, § 8:15 at 700 (explaining that a lost volume seller would have made a sale to the breaching buyer and to the party who purchased the goods after breach and noting that resale price damages are not a proper measure of damages for a lost volume seller).

17. Plaintiff argues that we should resolve any remaining ambiguity by applying ORS 42.260, which provides,

"When the terms of an agreement have been intended in a different sense by the parties,

Conclusion

For the reasons explained above, we conclude that plaintiff can recover its market price damages under ORS 72.7080(1). Because the trial court determined that plaintiff had proven its market price damages at trial, but later declined to award those damages for reasons that we have concluded were legally erroneous, plaintiff is entitled to recover market price damages in the amount calculated in plaintiff's Exhibit 409, together with prejudgment interest on that amount. However, we agree with the trial court, although for different reasons, that plaintiff is not entitled to recover its attorney fees under the NORAMSEED Rule that allows a seller to recover "charges for collection."

The decision of the Court of Appeals is affirmed in part and reversed in part. The judgment of the circuit court is affirmed in part and reversed in part, and the case is remanded to the circuit court.

D. Contract Terms Regarding Remedies

1. Liquidated Damages Clause

Under the principle of "freedom of contract," terms in a contract that specify an appropriate measure of damages or other remedy should be respected and enforced by courts. Yet in contemporary law, such terms are sometimes viewed with some suspicion, and may not be readily or absolutely enforceable. In the case that follows we see how one court treated this contractual term.

Michael E. Kvassay, d/b/a Kvassay Exotic Foods v. Albert Murray, et al.

Court of Appeals of Kansas
15 Kan. App. 2d 426, 808 P.2d 896 (1991)

RICHARD B. WALKER, DISTRICT JUDGE

Plaintiff Michael Kvassay, d/b/a Kvassay Exotic Foods, appeals the trial court's finding that a liquidated damages clause was unenforceable and from the court's finding that damages for lost profits were not recoverable. Kvassay contends these damages occurred when Great American Foods, Inc., (Great American) breached a contract for the purchase of baklava. Great American and Albert and Deana Murray, principals of Great American, cross-appeal the trial court's ruling that Kvassay could pierce Great American's corporate veil to collect damages awarded at trial.

On February 22, 1984, Kvassay, who had been an independent insurance adjuster, contracted to sell 24,000 cases of baklava to Great American at $19.00 per case. Under the contract, the sales were to occur over a one-year period and Great American was to be Kvassay's only customer. The contract included a clause which provided: "If Buyer

---

that sense is to prevail, against either party, in which the party supposed the other understood it. When different constructions of a provision are otherwise equally proper, that construction is to be taken which is most favorable to the party in whose favor the provision was made." Plaintiff has not shown, however, either that defendant "supposed" that plaintiff understood the term "charges for collection" to include attorney fees or that plaintiff's construction of that term is "equally proper" in comparison to defendant's construction.

refuses to accept or repudiates delivery of the goods sold to him, under this Agreement, Seller shall be entitled to damages, at the rate of $5.00 per case, for each case remaining to be delivered under this Contract."

Problems arose early in this contractual relationship with checks issued by Great American being dishonored for insufficient funds. Frequently one of the Murrays issued a personal check for the amount due. After producing approximately 3,000 cases, Kvassay stopped producing the baklava because the Murrays refused to purchase any more of the product.

The Murrays formed Sunshine Ceramics, Inc., in 1974. The company was inactive during the late 1970's and early 1980's and failed to make a number of required corporate filings. In August 1984, the name of the corporation was changed to Great American Foods, Inc. The Murrays also operated fast food restaurants in Wichita under the name of Great American Subs, Inc., and controlled an entity named Murray Investments. The Murrays conducted business for all of their entities and personal business from one street location in Wichita. In August 1984, the Murrays opened a bank account in the name of Great American Distributors, Inc., although no incorporation papers were ever filed. The Murrays frequently paid the bills of their various entities with personal checks and often wrote checks to themselves on corporate accounts. In addition, there were times when one entity would pay the Murrays' personal expenses or the expense of other Murray entities.

In April 1985, Kvassay filed suit for damages arising from the collapse of his baklava baking business. Great American counterclaimed and, in May 1988, the trial court sustained a defense motion to bifurcate the case. The court conducted bench hearings on the validity of the liquidated damages clause and the question of piercing the corporate veil. The trial court ruled that liquidated damages could not be recovered and that Great American's corporate veil could be pierced by Kvassay....

A jury trial on the issues of breach of contract and damages was held in February 1990.... On the second day of trial, before any evidence on the question of loss of profits had been presented, the trial court ruled that lost profits were not recoverable and barred Kvassay from presenting any evidence on that question. The jury returned verdicts in Kvassay's favor and awarded him a total of $35,673.99.

Kvassay first attacks the trial court's ruling that the amount of liquidated damages sought by him was unreasonable and therefore the liquidated damages clause was unenforceable.

Kvassay claimed $105,000 in losses under the liquidated damages clause of the contract, representing $5 per case for the approximately 21,000 cases of baklava which he was not able to deliver. The trial court determined that Kvassay's use of expected profits to formulate liquidated damages was improper because the business enterprise lacked duration, permanency, and recognition. The court then compared Kvassay's previous yearly income (about $20,000) with the claim for liquidated damages ($105,000) and found "the disparity becomes so great as to make the clause unenforceable."

Since the contract involved the sale of goods between merchants, the *Uniform Commercial Code* governs. *See* K.S.A. 84-2-102. "The *Code* does not change the pre-*Code* rule that the question of the propriety of liquidated damages is a question of law for the court." 4 Anderson, Uniform Commercial Code§ 2-718:6, p. 572 (3d ed. 1983). Thus, this court's scope of review of the trial court's ruling is unlimited. *Hutchinson Nat'l Bank & Tr. Co. v. Brown*, 753 P.2d 1299 (Kan. App.), *rev. denied* 243 Kan. 778 (1988).

Liquidated damages clauses in sales contracts are governed by K.S.A. 84-2-718, which reads in part:

(1) Damages for breach by either party may be liquidated in the agreement but only at an amount which is reasonable in the light of the anticipated or actual harm caused by the breach, the difficulties of proof of loss, and the inconvenience or nonfeasibility of otherwise obtaining an adequate remedy. A term fixing unreasonably large liquidated damages is void as a penalty.

To date, the appellate courts have not interpreted this section of the *UCC* in light of facts similar to those presented in this case. In ruling on this issue, the trial court relied on rules governing liquidated damages as expressed in *U.S.D. No. 315 v. DeWerff*, 626 P.2d 1206 (Kan. App. 1981). *DeWerff*, however, involved a teacher's breach of an employment contract and was not governed by the *UCC*. Thus, the rules expressed in that case should be given no effect if they differ from the rules expressed in 84-2-718.

In *DeWerff*, this court held a "stipulation for damages upon a future breach of contract is valid as a liquidated damages clause if the set amount is determined to be reasonable and the amount of damages is difficult to ascertain." 6 Kan. App. 2d at 78, 626 P.2d 1206. This is clearly a two-step test: Damages must be reasonable and they must be difficult to ascertain. Under the *UCC*, however, reasonableness is the only test. K.S.A. 84-2-718. K.S.A. 84-2-718 provides three criteria by which to measure reasonableness of liquidated damages clauses: (1) anticipated or actual harm caused by breach; (2) difficulty of proving loss; and (3) difficulty of obtaining an adequate remedy.

In its ruling, the trial court found the liquidated damages clause was unreasonable in light of Kvassay's income before he entered into the manufacturing contract with Great American. There is no basis in 84-2-718 for contrasting income under a previous unrelated employment arrangement with liquidated damages sought under a manufacturing contract. Indeed, the traditional goal of the law in cases where a buyer breaches a manufacturing contract is to place the seller "'in the same position he would have occupied if the vendee had performed his contract.'" *Outcault Adv. Co. v. Citizens Nat'l Bank*, 234 P. 988 (Kan. 1925). Thus, liquidated damages under the contract in this case must be measured against the anticipated or actual loss under the baklava contract as required by 84-2-718. The trial court erred in using Kvassay's previous income as a yardstick.

Was the trial court correct when it invalidated the liquidated damages clause, notwithstanding the use of an incorrect test? If so, we must uphold the decision even though the trial court relied on a wrong ground or assigned an erroneous reason for its decision. *Sutter Bros. Constr. Co. v. City of Leavenworth*, 708 P.2d 190 (Kan. 1985). To answer this question, we must look closer at the first criteria for reasonableness under 84-2-718, anticipated or actual harm done by the breach.

Kvassay produced evidence of anticipated damages at the bench trial showing that, before the contract was signed between Kvassay and Great American, Kvassay's accountant had calculated the baklava production costs. The resulting figure showed that, if each case sold for $19, Kvassay would earn a net profit of $3.55 per case after paying himself for time and labor. If he did not pay himself, the projected profit was $4.29 per case. Nevertheless, the parties set the liquidated damages figure at $5 per case. In comparing the anticipated damages of $3.55 per case in lost net profit with the liquidated damages of $5 per case, it is evident that Kvassay would collect $1.45 per case or about 41 percent over projected profits if Great American breached the contract. If the $4.29 profit figure is used, a $5 liquidated damages award would allow Kvassay to collect 71 cents per case or about 16 1/2 percent over projected profits if Great American breached the contract.

An examination of these pre-contract comparisons alone might well lead to the conclusion that the $5 liquidated damages clause is unreasonable because enforcing it would result in a windfall for Kvassay and serve as a penalty for Great American. A term fixing unreasonably large liquidated damages is void as a penalty under 84-2-718.

A better measure of the validity of the liquidated damages clause in this case would be obtained if the actual lost profits caused by the breach were compared to the $5 per case amount set by the clause. However, no attempt was made by Kvassay during the bench trial to prove actual profits or actual costs of production. Thus, the trial court could not compare the $5 liquidated damages clause in the contract with the actual profits lost by the breach. It was not until the jury trial that Kvassay attempted to prove his actual profits lost as part of his damages. Given the trial court's ruling that lost profits were not recoverable and could not be presented to the jury, it is questionable whether the court would have permitted evidence concerning lost profits at the bench trial.

The trial court utilized an impermissible factor to issue its ruling on the liquidated damages clause and the correct statutory factors were not directly addressed. We reverse the trial court on this issue and remand for further consideration of the reasonableness of the liquidated damages clause in light of the three criteria set out in 84-2-718 and our ruling on recoverability of lost profits which follows.

. . .

[Editors: In an omitted discussion, the court discussed the requirement of reasonable certainty of proof of lost profits.]

Given the quantity of evidence offered to prove the profitability of Kvassay's business, it is clear the trial court was premature in ruling, as a matter of law, that lost profits could not be proved. Kvassay should have been permitted to offer his evidence and meet his burden of proof on damages.

. . .

The trial court's decisions with respect to liquidated damages and lost profits are reversed and the case is remanded for a new trial on those issues....

Note — Liquidated Damages Clauses

The $5 per case clause in the contract between Kvassay and Great American was a "liquidated damages" clause. If the amount of liquidated damages is a good faith estimate of actual damages likely to result from a breach of contract, such a clause can avoid protracted litigation and facilitate post-breach settlement. The danger, however, is that one party will specify liquidated damages greater than an estimate of actual damages, in an attempt to impose a penalty on breach by the other party that would function as a disincentive to breach. Contractual penalties have long been viewed with suspicion, and classical contract theorists argued against enforcement of penalty clauses even if they were freely negotiated. Although free market values would suggest deference to such agreed clauses, an important tenet of classical contract theory holds that parties ought to be free to breach their contracts, subject only to payment of expectation damages. This tenet led classical theorists to oppose awards of punitive damages for breach of contract and to prohibit enforcement of penalty clauses. *Uniform Commercial Code* section 2-718, applied by the court in *Kvassay*, states the current law regarding liquidated damages clauses for contracts involving goods; a similar rule applies to other sorts of contracts:

> Damages for breach by either party may be liquidated in the agreement but only
> at an amount which is reasonable in the light of the anticipated or actual harm

caused by the breach, the difficulties of proof of loss, and the inconvenience or nonfeasibility of otherwise obtaining an adequate remedy. A term fixing unreasonably large liquidated damages is void as a penalty.

Restatement (Second) of Contracts § 356(1)

---

2. Limitation of Liability Clauses

Jimmie Elsken, Administrator of the Estate of Patricia Ann Elsken v. Network Multi-Family Security Corporation

Supreme Court of Oklahoma
838 P.2d 1007 (1992)

RUDOLPH HARGRAVE, JUSTICE

We are presented with three questions certified to this Court from the United States District Court for the Northern District of Oklahoma, pursuant to 20 O.S. §§ 1601 *et seq.*, to wit:

1. Whether, under Oklahoma law, a contractual limitation of liability for personal injury is valid and enforceable? and

2. Whether, under Oklahoma law, the limitation of liability clause contained in the Residential Alarm Security Agreement is valid and enforceable? and

3. Whether, under Oklahoma law, the indemnification and hold harmless clause is valid and enforceable.

We answer question number one as follows: A contractual limitation of liability for personal injury in a burglar alarm service contract may be valid and enforceable, as discussed herein.

We answer question number two as follows: If the Residential Alarm Services Agreement submitted was properly executed by both parties, and if the parties dealt at arm's length, then such limitation of liability clause would be valid and enforceable to limit liability for ordinary negligence.

We answer question number three in the affirmative.

The questions were submitted to this Court on a limited stipulation of facts for purpose of the certified questions only. The facts submitted are as follows: On April 11, 1988, Patricia Ann Elsken was found dead in her apartment, the victim of an apparent homicide. At the time of her death, Patricia Ann Elsken was leasing Apartment No. 1416 of the Windsail Apartments under a lease agreement. Patricia Ann Elsken signed the Residential Alarm Security Agreement, but did not initial the back side of the agreement in the spaces provided. The alarm was working on the day in question. There was no sign of forced entry into Patricia Ann Elsken's apartment. The trial court has made determinations as found in its Order of October 4, 1990, which include that there was no defect in the mechanism of the security system, or regarding proper maintenance. Further, the Court held that the Defendant bears no liability for the independent criminal act of Ms. Elsken's killer which resulted in her death. The only issue remaining is whether Defendant's failure to respond to the signaled intrusion was a contributory cause to Ms. Elsken's death. An alarm signal went off from Patricia Elsken's apartment at 10:33 a.m. on the morning of April 11, 1988. Patricia Elsken was found dead later that day. Brentwood Properties, Ltd., was the management corporation managing the apartment complex. They are no longer a party to the lawsuit. Johnstown Properties, Inc., has been granted summary judgment on the grounds it was not in charge of properties at the time of Patricia Elsken's death. An alarm signal was received at Network at 10:33 a.m., April 11, 1988. When no answer was received to the telephone call to Patricia Elsken's apartment, the apartment complex manager was called and told Network to disregard the alarm at 10:38 a.m.

We have upheld a limitation of liability clause in a burglar alarm service contract against allegations that such a clause was violative of public policy. *Fretwell v. Protection Alarm Co.*, 764 P.2d 149 (Okla. 1988). We note at the outset that courts have made a distinction between clauses that seek to exempt a contracting party from his own negligence and those that seek to limit the liability of the contracting party. *See, Branch v. Mobil Oil Corp.*, 772 F. Supp. 570 (W.D. Okla. 1991), *Fischer v. Atlantic Richfield*, 774 F. Supp. 616 (W.D. Okla. 1989), *Mohawk Drilling Co. v. McCullough Tool Co.*, 271 F.2d 627 (10th Cir. 1959).

Indeed, Oklahoma statutes specifically provide that a contract having as its object, directly or indirectly, to *exempt* anyone from responsibility for his own fraud or willful injury to the person or property of another or violation of law are against the policy of the law. 15 O.S. 1991 § 212. Title 15 O.S. 1991 § 212.1 (eff. date January 1, 1986) provides that any notice given by a business entity that provides services or facilities for profit to the general public which seeks to exempt the business entity from liability for personal injury caused by or resulting from negligence on its part or that of its employees shall be deemed void as against public policy and wholly unenforceable.[14] The clause in the case at bar is a limitation of liability.

In *Hargrave v. Canadian Valley Electric*, 792 P.2d 50 (Okla. 1990), while we recognized the court's power to void contracts for violation of public policy, we noted:

> We must remain mindful that contracts should not be declared void on the ground of public policy except in those cases that are free from doubt. Prejudice to the public interest must hence be clearly apparent before a court is justified in pronouncing a solemn agreement to be of no effect.... Contracts must stand unless it clearly appears that public right or public weal is contravened.

Courts repeatedly have upheld limitation of liability provisions in burglar alarm contracts as not violative of public policy, *see, Morgan Co. v. Minnesota Mining & Mfg. Co.*, 246 N.W.2d 443 (Minn. 1976), and cases cited therein at p. 447, even when applied to a claim for personal injury. *Schrier v. Beltway Alarm Co.*, 533 A.2d 1316 (Md. App. 1987). Courts have refused to uphold limitation of liability clauses where the defendant's conduct constituted gross negligence. *Sommer v. Federal Signal Corp.*, 571 N.Y.S.2d 228 (A.D. 1 Dept. 1991), *Arell's Fine Jewelers, Inc. v. Honeywell*, 537 N.Y.S.2d 365 (A.D. 4 Dept. 1989).

In *Schrier, supra*, Mr. Schrier, on behalf of Veteran's Liquor, entered into an "Alarm Protection Agreement" with Beltway Alarm Co. for the installation of a "central station connected hold-up" system. The parties also entered into a second contract calling for continued maintenance of the system. Both the contracts contained language limiting Beltway's liability for loss or damage due to a breach of the contract or negligence in performance by Beltway. Schrier was shot and severely wounded during a hold-up of the

---

14. Oklahoma's Uniform Commercial Code, Sales, at 12A O.S. § 2-719, prohibits limitation of consequential damages for injury to the person in the case of consumer goods, as prima facie unconscionable.

liquor store. He alleged that he activated two alarm buttons during the robbery, prior to the shooting and that Beltway delayed fourteen minutes in notifying the police department. He alleged that, but for the delay, he would not have been shot. Schrier argued that the contract contained an invalid liquidated damages clause and that the limitation of liability clause was void as against public policy, particularly because personal injury was involved. The court rejected all of Schrier's arguments and upheld the $250.00 limitation of liability provision. In rejecting the argument that the limitation clause was invalid as against public interest the court noted, at page 1323, that the burglar alarm industry is not performing a police function or public service.

The courts' holdings have been based on several factors: that the security company is not an insurer, the extreme difficulty of predicting the nature and extent of any loss, the difficulty or impossibility of ascertaining what portion of any loss sustained is attributable to the alarm company's failure to perform, and the uncertain nature of occurrences that might cause injury or loss.

In *Fretwell, supra,* plaintiff homeowners brought a negligence action against defendant corporation which had installed and monitored a burglar-alarm system in plaintiff's home. Plaintiffs claimed that defendant failed to notify the police department of a cut in their telephone line that carried the alarm system, that defendant failed to enter the house to check the residence, although having been given a key for that purpose, and that defendant failed to contact persons listed to be notified in the event of an alarm. The contract limited liability of defendant to $50.00, and contained an indemnification clause. The contract stated that defendant was not an insurer and contained a liquidated damages provision. The contract further stated that if plaintiffs wanted defendants to assume a greater liability or responsibility than that set out in the agreement, an additional price must be quoted. The issue was the effect of the contract upon the damages allowed in the negligence action. We said, at pp. 151–52:

> It reasonably follows that since the contract established the duty, any lawful limitations in the contract may also limit the liability of the tortfeasor. The clause in the case at bar makes no attempt to reasonably forecast just compensation for harm caused, it is clearly an attempt to limit damages. The contract wording is "The liability of Protection shall be limited to the sum of $50.00 or the actual loss of the subscriber, whichever ... is the lesser."
>
> The contract before this Court explicitly states that the alarm company is not an insurer and offers to increase the monthly payment if insurance is desired. We conclude that the contractual provision before this Court is neither unconscionable nor against public policy. Therefore the damages to the Fretwells is limited to Fifty dollars.

The contract (Residential Alarm Services Agreement) in the case at bar contains a Limitation of Liability section. This section states in bold capital letters that neither client nor Network is an insurer, and that insurance for any type of loss shall be obtained by Resident. The Limitation of Liability section sets out at paragraph 3.3 that Resident acknowledges that it is impractical and extremely difficult to fix the actual damages, if any, that may proximately result from a failure of client or Network to perform any of their respective obligations, or the failure of the system to operate properly, because of, among other things, the uncertainty of determining value of the Resident's property, uncertainty of the response time of dispatched parties, inability to ascertain what portion of any loss would be proximately caused by the system's failure, and the uncertain nature of occurrences that might cause injury or death to Resident or any other person which the system was designed to detect or avert. Paragraph 3.4 of the Residential Alarm Security Agreement's Limitation of Liability section provides:

> Resident understands and agrees that if either Client or Network should be found liable for loss or damage due to failure of the System in any respect whatsoever, including but not limited to monitoring, Client's and Network's collective liability shall not exceed a sum equal to Two hundred fifty dollars ($250.00) and this liability shall be exclusive. CLIENT AND NETWORK ARE NOT INSURERS AND RESIDENT ASSUMES ALL RESPONSIBILITY FOR OBTAINING INSURANCE TO COVER LOSSES OF ALL TYPES. The provisions of this section shall apply if death, loss or damage, irrespective of cause or origin, results directly or indirectly, to persons or property, from performance or nonperformance of the obligations imposed by this Agreement, or from negligence, active or otherwise, of Client, Network, their agents, employees, legal representatives or assigns.

Paragraph 3.5 provides that Resident understands and agrees that for Network to assume a greater liability, Resident may obtain from Network increased liability by paying an additional charge directly to Network.

The stipulation of facts for purposes of this certified question state that Resident signed the Residential Alarm Security Agreement. She is presumed to have read the provisions thereof and there is no allegation that she did not. We do not know whether the parties were in an unequal bargaining position. Assuming that the parties were not in an unequal bargaining position, the above limitation of liability would be binding and enforceable as to defendant's actions constituting ordinary negligence.

We have held a limitation of liability clause valid in a burglar alarm/security systems contract. Plaintiffs assert that the limitation of liability clause should not operate to limit liability for personal injury. We view the issue as being whether one contracting party in a burglar alarm contract can contractually limit its liability for ordinary negligence in performance of the contract, and we find that it can, provided that the parties have equal bargaining power.

The third question presented is whether under Oklahoma law the indemnification and hold harmless clause is valid and enforceable. Indemnity is governed by 15 O.S. 1981 §§ 421–430. The indemnification clause in the Residential Alarm Security Agreement is:

> 4.1 In the event any person not a party to this Agreement shall make any claim or file any lawsuit against Client or Network for any reason relating to the duties and obligations of Client or Network pursuant to this Agreement, including, but not limited to, the design, installation, maintenance, operation or non-operation of the System, or the providing of monitoring, patrol or extended maintenance services, Resident agrees to indemnify, defend and hold Client and Network harmless from any and all such claims and lawsuits, including the payment of all damages, expenses, costs and attorney's fees, whether such claims be based upon alleged intentional conduct, active or passive negligence or strict or product liability on the part of Client, Network, their agents, employees, legal representatives or assigns.

We held a virtually identical indemnification clause valid in *Fretwell, supra*. We rejected there the argument that the indemnity clause was unenforceable because it sought to indemnify the appellant from its own negligence. We said that where the intention to indemnify is unequivocally clear from an examination of the contract, such agreement is enforceable. An examination of the indemnification clause in the Residential Alarm Security Agreement clearly expresses an intention to indemnify Network from its own negligence and we find the agreement to be enforceable. Accordingly, we answer the third question in the affirmative.

Note

After the Supreme Court of Oklahoma clarified Oklahoma law in the preceding case, the Federal District Court in the Northern District of Oklahoma dismissed the case against Network Multi-family Security Corporation. This was affirmed by the 10th Circuit Court of Appeals in *Jimmie Elsken v. Network Multi-family Security Corporation,* 49 F.3d 1470 (1995). According to the 10th Circuit, a "plain reading" of the contract, which included a term stating that the signatory read the contract, meant that Ms. Elsken was bound by the contract even if she did not read it; even if there was evidence — in the form of an affidavit of the apartment manager — that she never read the contract. The fact that the contract included a place for initials next to the limitation of liability provision did not mean that more or additional assent was needed to make this term effective, especially since the language on the front of the contract said that the tenant had read and agreed to terms on the back.

The reference in the Oklahoma Supreme Court decision to the possible unequal bargaining power of the two parties was handled by the 10th Circuit in the following way:

> ... Ms. Elsken fails to highlight law and sufficient facts showing the existence of unequal bargaining power between Network and Patricia Elsken. She simply notes for the court that the contract was presented to Patricia Elsken "on a take-it-or-leave-it basis" and residents were not permitted to make changes to the Services Agreement. From these assertions alone a fact finder would be unable to determine that Patricia Elsken was in a bargaining position that would render the Services Agreement unenforceable.

Network Multi-family is a wholly owned subsidiary of Protection One, a company whose stock is publically traded. Protection One had revenues in 2003 of $263 million. The company markets its services to apartment complexes, not tenants. What follows is some of the representations made on Protection One's website.

> Industry surveys indicate that residents choose their apartment homes because of safety and security measures provided by the property.... Safety and security are primary concerns of apartment residents today, and they know the value of an intrusion alarm. Hence, providing in-unit monitored alarms to your residents can help generate higher rates ... In many cases, it isn't actual crime, but the fear of crime that motivates apartment residents when choosing their new apartment home. They know monitored alarms are a proven deterrent to crime, and they request alarms in their apartment homes. Residents appreciate the peace of mind they enjoy with an in-unit monitored alarm system, even in the most crime-free neighborhoods.

Should Jimmie Elsken have had to include in her pleadings facts that showed the defendant was a wholly owned subsidiary of a publicly traded company with revenues of several million dollars? Should she have challenged not only the limitation of liability but also the liquidated damages provision? Does $250 seem unreasonably low to you? The promotional material for Protection One states that tenants are looking for the "peace of mind" that an alarm or security system gives them and that "peace of mind" has a value that can be quantified. It translates into the fee that is paid for the service and higher rents that can be charged in buildings with alarm systems. Does $250 represent a fair estimate of the loss sustained when the security system doesn't operate as promised?

Jonathan Franzen, The Corrections
(2001)

Caroline's fevered imaginings notwithstanding, the house appeared to be intact. Gary eased the car up the driveway past the bed of hostas and euonymus from which, just as she'd said, another SECURITY BY NEVEREST sign had been stolen. Since the beginning of the year, Gary had planted and lost five SECURITY BY NEVEREST signs. It galled him to be flooding the market with worthless signage, thereby diluting the value of the SECURITY BY NEVEREST as a burglary deterrent. Here in the heart of Chestnut Hill, needless to say, the sheet-metal currency of the Neverest and Western Civil Defense and ProPhilaTex signs in every front yard was backed by full faith and credit of floodlights and retinal scanners, emergency batteries, buried hotlines, and remotely securable doors; but elsewhere in northwest Philly, down through Mount Airy into Germantown and Nicetown where the sociopaths had their dealings and their dwellings, there existed a class of bleeding-heart homeowners who hated what it might say about their "values" to buy their own home-security systems but whose liberal "values" did not preclude stealing Gary's SECURITY BY NEVEREST signs on an almost weekly basis and planting them in their own yards ... "I guess I'll go put out another sign." Gary said.

"You should nail it to a tree," Caroline said. "Take it off its stick and nail it to a tree."

Nearly unmanned by disappointed expectation, Gary filled his chest with air and coughed, "The idea, Caroline, is that there be a certain classiness and subtlety to the message we're projecting? A certain word-to-the-wise quality? When you have to *chain* your sign to a tree to keep it from getting stolen—"

"I said nail."

"It's like announcing to the sociopaths. We're whipped! Come and get us! Come and get us!"

"I didn't say chain. I said nail."

Caleb reached for the remote and raised the TV volume.

Gary went to the basement and from a flat cardboard carton took the last of the six signs that a Neverest representative had sold to him in bulk. Considering the cost of a Neverest home-security system, the signs were unbelievably shoddy. The placards were unevenly painted and attached by fragile aluminum rivets to posts of rolled sheet metal too thin to be hammered into the ground (you had to dig a hole).

Caroline didn't look up when he retuned to the kitchen. [...] Leaving the door wide open, he went to the front yard and planted the new Neverest sign in the old sterile hole. When he came back a minute later, the door was locked again. He took his keys out and turned the deadbolt and pushed the door open to the extent the chain permitted, triggering the excuse-me-please alarm inside. He shoved on the door, stressing its hinges. He considered putting his shoulder to it and ripping out the chain. With a grimace and a shout Caroline jumped up and clutched her back and stumbled over to enter code within the thirty-second limit.

"Gary," she said, "just knock."

"I was in the front yard," he said. "I was fifty feet away. Why are you setting the alarm?"

———————

Figgie International, Inc. v. Destileria Serralles, Inc.

United States Court Of Appeals
190 F.3d 252 (4th Cir. 1999)

WILLIAM B. TRAXLER, CIRCUIT JUDGE

This action arises out of a sales agreement between Destileria Serralles, Inc. ("Serralles"), a bottler of rum, and Figgie International, Inc. ("Figgie"), a manufacturer of bottle-labeling equipment. Following Figgie's unsuccessful attempts to provide satisfactory bottle labeling equipment to Serralles under the agreement, Serralles returned the equipment and received a refund of the purchase price.

When a dispute arose as to whether Serralles was entitled to damages for breach of the agreement, Figgie instituted this declaratory judgment action, seeking a determination that Serralles is limited under the agreement to the exclusive remedy of repair, replacement, or return of the equipment. *See* S.C. Code Ann. § 36-2-719 (Law. Coop. 1976). Serralles, on the other hand, contends that it is entitled to the full array of remedies provided by the South Carolina Uniform Commercial Code (the "UCC" or "Code"). *See* S.C. Code Ann. §§ 36-2-712, -714, and -715 (Law. Co-op. 1976). The district court granted Figgie's motion for summary judgment and denied Serralles' motion for partial summary judgment. Finding no error in the district court's judgment, we affirm.

I.

Serralles, a distributor of rum and other products, operates a rum bottling plant in Puerto Rico. In June 1993, Serralles and Figgie entered into a written agreement under which Figgie was to provide bottle-labeling equipment capable of placing a clear label on a clear bottle of "Cristal" rum within a raised glass oval. When the bottle labeling equipment was installed in the Serralles plant in April 1994, however, problems arose immediately. Over the course of the next several months, Figgie attempted to repair the equipment to achieve satisfactory performance. However, by November 1994, the equipment still did not work properly, prompting Figgie to refund the purchase price and Serralles to return the equipment.

Additionally, Serralles requested that Figgie pay for alleged losses caused by the failure of the equipment to perform as expected and by the delay in obtaining alternative equipment. Unable to reach a compromise, Figgie instituted this declaratory judgment action, asserting that it owed no further obligations to Serralles under the agreement because Serralles' remedy for breach was limited to repair, replacement, or refund—both under the written terms and conditions of the sales agreement and pursuant to usage of trade in the bottle-labeling industry.

With regard to the alleged limitation of remedy in the sales agreement, Figgie asserts that standard terms and conditions accompanying the sales agreement contained the following language:

Buyer's exclusive remedies for all claims arising out of this agreement and the transaction to which it pertains shall be the right to return the product at buyer's expense, and, at seller's option, receive repayment of the purchase price plus reasonable depreciation for the repair and/or replacement of the product.... Seller shall not be subject to any other obligations or liabilities whatsoever with respect to this transaction, and shall under no circumstances be liable for delays, or for any consequential, contingent or incidental damages.

Figgie, however, has been unable to produce the original sales agreement, asserting that it was lost during a business reorganization. Hence, Figgie is forced to rely upon standard terms and conditions that purportedly accompanied every sales agreement entered into during the time that the Serralles agreement was executed. Serralles, on the other hand, has produced its copy of the agreement, the last page of which stated that "this quotation is made subject to the additional general terms and conditions of sale printed on the reverse hereof," but the reverse side of the page is blank. Figgie asserts that the absence of the general terms and conditions on Serralles' copy is most certainly a copying mistake, whereas Serralles asserts that they were never part of the agreement.

Although conceding at oral argument that a factual dispute exists as to whether the written standards and conditions accompanied the original sales agreement, Figgie asserts that it is nevertheless entitled to summary judgment because, under the UCC, usage of trade in the bottle-labeling industry would supplement the sales agreement with the identical limited remedy of repair, replacement, or refund. *See* S.C. Code Ann. §36-1-205(3) (Law. Co-op. 1976). Serralles, of course, disputes that usage of trade imposes this limitation and, alternatively, asserts that because the limited remedy has "failed of its essential purpose," S.C. Code Ann. §36-2-719(2), it is entitled to the full array of remedies provided by the UCC.

. . .

III.

We first address Serralles' contention that the district court erred in granting Figgie's motion for summary judgment. Specifically, the district court concluded that usage of trade in the bottle-labeling industry supplemented the agreement between Figgie and Serralles with the limited remedy of repair, replacement, or return in the event of a breach. Serralles disputes that usage of trade supplies such a limited remedy and, in any event, contends that the limited remedy failed of its essential purpose.

Because the crux of this appeal centers on whether the agreement between the parties limited Serralles' remedy for breach to repair, replacement, or refund of the purchase price, we begin with the language of S.C. Code Ann. §36-2-719, which governs modifications or limitations to the remedies otherwise provided by the UCC for the breach of a sales agreement. Section 36-2-719 provides that:

(1) Subject to the provisions of subsections (2) and (3) of this section and of the preceding section (§36-2-318) [*sic*] on liquidation of damages,

(a) the agreement may provide for remedies in addition to or in substitution for those provided in this chapter and may limit or alter the measure of damages recoverable under this chapter, as by limiting the buyer's remedies to return of the goods and repayment of the price or to repair and replacement of nonconforming goods or parts; and

(b) resort to a remedy as provided is optional unless the remedy is expressly agreed to be exclusive, in which case it is the sole remedy.

(2) Where circumstances cause an exclusive or limited remedy to fail of its essential purpose, remedy may be had as provided in this act.

(3) Consequential damages may be limited or excluded unless the limitation or exclusion is unconscionable. Limitation of consequential damages for injury to the person in the case of consumer goods is prima facie unconscionable but limitation of damages where the loss is commercial is not.

Under these provisions, parties to a commercial sales agreement may provide for remedies in addition to those provided by the UCC, or limit themselves to specified remedies in lieu of those provided by the UCC. An "agreement" for purposes of the UCC is defined as "the bargain of the parties in fact as found in their language or by implication from other circumstances including course of dealing or usage of trade...." S.C. Code Ann. §36-1-201(3) (Law. Co-op. 1976) (emphasis added). In turn, the Code provides that "[a] course of dealing between parties and any usage of trade in the vocation or trade in which they are engaged or of which they are or should be aware give particular meaning to and supplement or qualify terms of an agreement." S.C. Code Ann. §36-1-205(3); *see also Weisz Graphics v. Peck Indus. Inc.*, 403 S.E.2d 146, 150 (S.C. Ct. App. 1991) (holding that industry standard supplemented the express provisions of a written contract).

"Usage of trade" is defined as "any practice or method of dealing having such regularity of observance in a place, vocation or trade as to justify an expectation that it will be observed with respect to the transaction in question...." S.C. Code Ann. §36-1-205(2) (Law. Coop. 1976). Where possible and reasonable, an applicable course of dealing or usage of trade will be construed as consistent with the agreement's express terms. *See* S.C. Code Ann. §36-1-205(4) (Law. Co-op. 1976).

A.

Serralles contends that the district court erred in concluding that usage of trade in the bottle-labeling industry supplemented the agreement between these parties with the limited remedy of repair, replacement, or refund. We disagree.

In support of its motion for summary judgment, Figgie submitted several affidavits of persons with extensive experience in the bottle labeling and packaging industry, attesting that sellers in the industry always limit the available remedies in the event of a breach to repair, replacement, or return, and specifically exclude consequential damages. While Serralles asserts that it did not "acquiesce" in this practice, it has offered no evidence to contradict the affidavits submitted by Figgie. Accordingly, the district court correctly concluded that usage of trade would limit Serralles to the exclusive remedy of repair, replacement, or return.

Serralles also contends that it cannot be limited to the remedy of repair, replacement, or return because the written agreement does not "explicitly" state that this remedy is exclusive. As noted previously, S.C. Code Ann. §36-2-719(1)(b) states that "resort to a remedy as provided [for under subsection (1)(a)] is optional unless the remedy is expressly agreed to be exclusive, in which case it is the sole remedy." Relying upon the case of *Myrtle Beach Pipeline Corp. v. Emerson Elec. Co.*, 843 F. Supp. 1027 (D.S.Cir. 1993), aff'd, 46 F.3d 1125 (4th Cir. 1995) (unpublished), which held that "the [UCC] requires that the exclusivity of a limited remedy be made explicit ... and failure to do so will result in the limited remedy's being construed as an optional additional remedy and will not preclude the availability of other remedies under the Code," id. at 1041, Serralles contends that a limited remedy imposed or implied by trade usage cannot be an exclusive remedy because it is neither "expressly agreed to" nor "explicit." We disagree.

Section 36-2-719 provides that the "agreement" between the parties may limit remedies. Section 36-1-201(3) defines "agreement" as including terms "implied from other circumstances including course of dealing or usage of trade," and §36-1-205 reiterates that usage of trade will supplement and qualify the terms of an agreement provided it can be reasonably construed as being consistent with the written terms. It seems clear to us that, pursuant to these provisions, usage of trade will supplement agreements and may indeed impose an exclusive remedy in the event of a breach. In so holding, we agree with those circuits which have rejected the contention that a limited remedy cannot be exclusive if imposed by usage of trade. *See Western Indus. Inc. v. Newcor Canada Ltd.*, 739 F.2d

1198, 1204–05 (7th Cir. 1984) (rejecting contention that trade custom cannot limit liability because § 2-719(1)(b) of the UCC provides that resort to a remedy is optional unless expressly agreed to be exclusive); *Transamerica Oil Corp. v. Lynes, Inc.*, 723 F.2d 758, 766 (10th Cir. 1983) (holding that, under the UCC, "usage of trade may add an exclusive remedy to an agreement"); *Posttape Assoc. v. Eastman Kodak Co.*, 537 F.2d 751, 756–57 (3d Cir. 1976) (holding that "the totality of the agreement … must include a provision, present in the trade usage, or otherwise expressed, that the limited remedy is an exclusive one"). And we note that *Myrtle Beach Pipeline* is not to the contrary. In that case, the district court held that it would not construe a remedy—provided for by the written terms of the agreement—as being exclusive unless such exclusivity was explicitly set forth in the same agreement. *Myrtle Beach Pipeline* neither addressed nor involved the imposition of an exclusive or limited remedy by usage of trade.

B.

Having determined that usage of trade supplemented the agreement between the parties with the exclusive remedy of repair, replacement, or return, we turn to Serralles' contention that the limited remedy "failed of its essential purpose," entitling it to nevertheless pursue the full array of UCC remedies. *See* S.C. Code Ann. § 36-2-719(2). We conclude that it did not.

Section 36-2-719(1)(a) specifically contemplates that parties to an agreement may, as they did in this case, limit available remedies in the event of a breach to "return of the goods and repayment of the price or to repair and replacement of nonconforming goods or parts." Section 36-2-719(2), however, provides that the general remedies of the UCC will apply, notwithstanding an agreed-upon exclusive remedy, if the "circumstances cause [the remedy] … to fail of its essential purpose." Under this provision, "where an apparently fair and reasonable clause because of circumstances fails in its purpose or operates to deprive either party of the substantial value of the bargain, it must give way to the general remedy provisions of[the Code].'" *Bishop Logging Co. v. John Deere Indus. Equip. Co.*, 455 S.E. 2d 183 (S.C. Ct. App. 1995) (quoting S.C. Code Ann. § 36-2-719, Official Comment 1). In the instant case, however, there is no evidence that the limited remedy of repair, replacement, or return has failed of its essential purpose or that the contracting parties have been deprived of the substantial value of the bargain.

Serralles argues that Figgie, by first attempting to repair the equipment, elected to pursue repair as the exclusive remedy and, thereby, forgo enforcement of the remedy of return and reimbursement. From this premise, Serralles contends that Figgie's failure to repair the machines resulted in the remedy failing of its essential purpose. We find no support in the language of the UCC or in the cases interpreting it for this novel argument, and no evidence that this contemplated remedy of return and refund, once invoked, failed of its essential purpose.

While Serralles is correct that a limited remedy of repair or replacement can fail of its essential purpose where the seller's repair or replacement is unsuccessful, *see Bishop Logging*, 455 S.E.2d at 192–93, Serralles' remedies were limited to repair, replacement, or return, *see Marr Enter., Inc. v. Lewis Refrigeration Co.*, 556 F.2d 951 (9th Cir. 1976) (holding that a limited remedy of repair or refund did not fail of its essential purpose). Figgie installed the bottle-labeling equipment in April and, over the course of the next several months, attempted to find solutions to resolve the problems encountered. In November, when attempts to fix the equipment had so far failed, the equipment was returned and the purchase price refunded. Hence, the remedies invoked were exactly those envisioned by § 36-2-719(1)(a) and contemplated by the agreement.

Serralles' contention that a seller eliminates the remedy of "refund" simply by electing to attempt repair or replacement is unpersuasive. On the contrary, one would expect a manufacturer or seller to first attempt to repair or replace equipment in order to meet its contractual obligations to the purchaser, and only resort to a return and refund if unsuccessful in doing so—particularly in the context of an agreement between two commercial entities for the purchase of sophisticated equipment.[1] Accordingly, the district court correctly concluded that the limited remedy of repair, replacement, or return did not fail of its essential purpose.

C.

Serralles' final contention is that Figgie made various representations and guarantees during the months following initial installation of the equipment that should be construed as new agreements not subject to a limited remedy, or as modifications to or waivers of the limited remedy provision in the original agreement. For example, Serralles relies upon Figgie's assurances that it was "committed 100% to the success of the . . . project," that it would continue efforts to meet the obligations under the agreement, that it expected to work out the labeling problems, that it "guaranteed and [took] full responsibility" for resolving the problems, and that it remained committed to "ensure completely satisfactory performance of the . . . equipment . . . as soon as possible."

Having reviewed the communications, we find no evidence of an intent on the part of either party to modify the existing contractual relationship or to create a new one. Rather, it is clear that all of the communications relied upon by Serralles took place while Figgie was attempting to repair the equipment in accordance with the limited remedy available under the original sales agreement. Serralles has directed us to no statement or promise by Figgie which could reasonably be interpreted as specifying additional remedies which would be available in the event Figgie was unsuccessful in its attempts to first repair the equipment. Nor is there any evidence of an agreement by Figgie to waive the existing limitation of remedy in exchange for the opportunity to repair the equipment.[2]

. . .

V.

For the foregoing reasons, we conclude that the district court did not err in denying Serralles' motion for partial summary judgment or in granting Figgie's motion for summary judgment. Accordingly, the judgment below is affirmed.

---

1. We do not suggest, of course, that a limited remedy of repair, replacement, or refund can never fail of its essential purpose. For example, the court in Marr indicated that such a remedy may indeed fail of its essential purpose if defects or problems are "not . . . detectable until such a late time that under the totality of the circumstances . . . a refund of the purchase price would have been totally inadequate." *Id.* at 955. Serralles, however, was aware of the problems from the outset and actively participated in the attempts to repair.

2. The district court held that, even assuming "there was a meeting of the minds in the written communications between the parties and that each new promise or guarantee created a contract to provide a working labeling machine," Figgie was entitled to summary judgment because any such new contracts would also be subject to the limited remedy supplied by trade usage. Because it is clear to us that no new contracts were created as a matter of law, we need not decide whether usage of trade would supply a limited remedy to subsequent contracts to repair.

Chapter Twelve

Third Party Interests

A. Third Party Beneficiaries

Third party beneficiary doctrine can be simply stated: an *intended beneficiary* of a contract can sue for enforcement, subject to the same defenses applicable to the promisee, and he or she may have a right to object to modifications of the contract if he or she has relied upon it or formally consented to it. The category of intended beneficiary is then further divided into that of donee beneficiary and creditor beneficiary. An *incidental beneficiary* does not have any enforceable rights under the contract. Complications arise in the determination whether one is an *intended* or an *incidental* *beneficiary*.

The doctrine of third party beneficiaries rests on a recognition of interconnectedness that is different from and sometimes in conflict with notions of mutual assent and market ideology. Market ideology in the United States—the set of common economic beliefs and practices—tends to view transactions as autonomous: each party is expected to benefit from the transaction and to bear his or her costs for the transaction, with little effect on others, except in unusual cases. Consistent with this view of autonomous transactions, classical contract theory treats most contracts as having little impact on anyone other than the contracting parties. Third party beneficiary doctrine represents a limited, and historically controversial, exception to this approach. While the doctrine was recognized in some states during the end of the nineteenth century, it met with much resistance in other states. In Massachusetts, for example, courts refused to recognize the doctrine until 1978. And in England, courts, with some limited exceptions, consistently rejected it until Parliament enacted the Contracts (Rights of Third Parties) Act of 1999, which provides for enforcement of contract terms by third parties when the contract so provides. The idea of allowing someone who was not a party to a contract, that is, who was not in privity, to sue for its breach conflicts with core assumptions of contract law.

The third party beneficiary doctrine is narrowly circumscribed, so as to minimize or obscure this fundamental conflict. The doctrine permits a third party to sue for breach of contract only if the original parties "intended" to benefit that party. In this way, the doctrine reaffirms the primacy and control of the contracting parties.

Courts differ, however, in their interpretation of this element of "intention." As you read the next case, pay close attention to how the court evaluates this element.

763

L.A.C., a Minor, by and through her Next Friend, D.C. v. Ward Parkway Shopping Center Company, L.P.

Supreme Court of Missouri
75 S.W.3d 247 (2002)

WILLIAM RAY PRICE, JR, JUDGE

I.   Summary

L.A.C., a minor, claims that she was raped at the Ward Parkway Shopping Mall. She brought suit against ... the security company hired by them to provide security services for the mall. The trial court granted summary judgment for the defendants ...

We reverse, because ... the contract between the owners and managers of the mall and the security company clearly and directly provided for the safety of the mall's business invitees and, as a third party creditor beneficiary, plaintiff can bring suit against the security company for breach of that contract ...

II. Factual and Procedural Background

...

In March 15, 1997, L.A.C., a twelve-year old minor, went to Ward Parkway Shopping Center to see a movie with her friend, A.G. After leaving the movie, she and a group of friends gathered in a common area. Also with the group was a fifteen-year old boy, whom plaintiff had met the previous weekend.

While she talked to this young man, he grabbed her purse and ran off with it into a hallway. She followed, demanding its return. The young man replied, "No, not till you give me a kiss." She complied, and the young man returned her purse. But as she turned to walk away, the young man grabbed her, and said, "Let's do it."

The young man picked her up and began to carry her. Plaintiff screamed, hitting him on the back and demanding to be put down. Friends nearby refused to help her because the boy was older and bigger and had a gun showing. The young man briefly put her down, but then said, "[W]e're going to do this," picked her up and carried her into the "catwalk," a walkway connecting the mall to a parking lot. In the catwalk, despite her struggles, the young man raped her.

After the plaintiff was picked up and began screaming, her friend went downstairs and within a minute found an IPC security guard. She told the guard that her friend was in trouble and needed help. The guard dismissed her, saying that the young man was just playing. A.G. then went upstairs and found another IPC officer near the arcade. After explaining what happened, that officer also dismissed her, accusing her of trying to "get some boys for messing with [the girls]."

After her second failed attempt to get help, A.G. saw L.A.C. again. At first, in a state of shock and warned by her assailant to be silent, plaintiff said nothing. However, after a couple of minutes, she broke down and cried, telling her friend that the young man had raped her. Plaintiff reported the rape to the police and received treatment that night at a hospital. Her assailant was arrested the next day and eventually found to have committed rape by the juvenile division of the circuit court.

Ward Parkway Shopping Center Company, L.P. (WPSCC) and W.S.C. Associates, L.P. (WSC) both own and operate the Ward Parkway Shopping Center (the mall), and G.G. Management (GG) provides management services at the mall pursuant to a management agreement (these parties will be referred to collectively as the Ward Parkway Group). IPC

International Corporation (IPC) is a security company with whom GG contracted to provide security for the mall....

The contract between the mall management and IPC contains a number of relevant provisions. Two are especially important. First, IPC security officers are empowered to detain individuals when necessary to protect mall customers from risk of serious injury:

> I.3.H. Under normal circumstances, an employee or agent of the CONTRACTOR, shall avoid making an arrest of any kind; provided, however, the employees or agents of the CONTRACTOR may detain an individual when necessary to protect either that individual or mall customers or employees from risk of serious injury. [emphasis supplied]

Second, IPC and mall management both agreed to cooperate to determine the proper work hours and staffing to "provide adequate security to the mall."

> I.4. HOURS & STAFFING—The daily and weekly schedule of security man-hours and coverage at each location shall be determined by the Manager, subject to input from CONTRACTOR. The hours and number of Security Officers required will change periodically. The Manager has the right to change hours and personnel coverage....

> VI.5. Manager and Contractor shall agree upon the proper level of staffing needed to provide adequate security to Mall [sic]. Upon agreement, the staffing level shall be conclusively deemed for all purposes to be a material representation by Contractor to Manager that the staffing level is one which will provide full and adequate security to the Mall. CONTRACTOR will be able to provide additional security staff for grand opening events on an "as needed" basis. Officers will be in uniform, and ready for duty at the start of their assigned shifts. [emphasis supplied]

The contract also assigns specific duties to IPC security officers, including making frequent, random rounds of the premises to check for safety hazards.[2] Security officers are required to be watchful for criminal activities and report any such observations to mall management:

> I.3.B. Report immediately to representatives designated by the Manager any unusual incidents, hazardous conditions, accidents, defects, suspicious activities, or criminal activities observed during the shift.

> C. Prepare for the Manager at the end of each shift, a security log report noting therein all incidents, accidents, suspicious activities, hazardous conditions or criminal activities observed. Unless other provisions are made by the parties, all reports shall be prepared on standard log forms, provided by the Manager.

> D. Perform such other duties and enforce rules and regulations as are mutually agreed upon by the parties that are reduced to writing, and that are made available

---

2. I.3.A. Make frequent, random rounds of the premises, the common areas of the center, sidewalks, parking lots, ring roads, checking gates, doors, windows, and lights. Make frequent, random motorized patrols of the parking lots and ring roads, and perform other Security tasks as instructed by manager....
I. CONTRACTOR shall instruct Security Officers to patrol assigned areas; observe activities; conduct routine rounds of the interior and exterior of the premises and complete reports. CONTRACTOR shall provide training to its employees to insure such employees know the general orders for Security Officers and the special orders for any post to which he/she is assigned. CONTRACTOR's officers shall safeguard equipment and material against damage, theft, loss or unauthorized use; and stay alert for any security or safety hazards at all times.

to the Security Officers assigned to each location by representatives of the Manager.

IPC agreed to bind its employees to a Policy and Procedures Manual published by IPC:

> I.3.J. Manager has adopted a comprehensive Security Orders Policy and Procedures Manual (herein "the manual".) The manual includes Manager's instructions to CONTRACTOR and a copy of Manager's Safety Regulations. CONTRACTOR and its employees shall be familiar with and will adhere to those instructions and regulations at all times. CONTRACTOR shall disseminate such manual to all Security Officers and shall insure that said Security Officers comply with the content thereof.

IPC agreed to be familiar with and adhere to these instructions and regulations at all times. Two passages from the manual expressly indicate:

> The ultimate goal of any successful shopping center Owner, Developer or Manager is the continued patronage of customers to the mall. In each Center, Mall Management endeavors to create a safe, orderly atmosphere in which customers may relax and shop without undue concern for their own safety. In order to sustain and insure this positive atmosphere, the management of your Center has retained the services of IPC International Corporation to provide Mall Public Safety Services.

> You have been chosen to be a member of the Public Safety Staff by individuals who feel that you have the potential to be a true asset to the organization—one who has the right combination of knowledge, experience, education, judgment and positive appearance to understand and perform the varied responsibilities of an IPC Mall Public Safety Officer. Given the proper "tools" of knowledge which follow in this manual, you will have everything that you need to perform your duties in an effective and professional manner. It is up to you to earn the respect and confidence of those for whom and with whom you work.

Finally, IPC also distributed a training manual to its employees, which stated:

> The personal safety of yourself, fellow Officers, customers and tenants to the mall is the absolute priority at all times ...

> Our clients are most concerned with the well being of visitors, customers and employees of the shopping center. It is for this reason that Public Safety personnel are present.... [T]he responsibility for the safety of life and property within the center is shared by tenant stores, civil authorities, center management (through the Public Safety Service) and each individual person who visits the center.

Plaintiff brought suit against ... IPC for breach of contract as a third party beneficiary of the management and security contracts. After discovery, ... IPC moved for judgment on the pleadings. In support of its response to the motions, plaintiff submitted ... IPC incident reports and Kansas City police department records. The IPC records are detailed reports of incidents involving criminal activity that occurred at the mall. Some of the submitted police records correlate with some of the IPC reports.... The IPC incident reports describe a number of crimes, violent and non-violent, that were reportedly perpetrated on the premises of the Ward Parkway mall within the three years prior to the incident. The reports include one sexual assault, one robbery and abduction, thirteen armed or attempted armed robberies, nine strong-arm or otherwise violent robberies, four aggravated assaults and twenty-eight simple assaults. The IPC reports also include nine incidents labeled "battery," which range from an improper touching, to a fight, to an assault during an attempted theft of an automobile. Three reports indicate unlawful use of a firearm, including one involving a suspect who pointed a weapon at officers after a robbery. (A large number of the proffered IPC reports indicate non-violent crimes, such as one instance of sexual misconduct and numerous instances of disorderly conduct, stalking and public indecency.) In all, at least seventy-five of the crimes were violent ...

Many of these crimes, especially some of the most violent, involved female victims. In 1996, a female store manager was abducted and the victim of an armed robbery. Just a few months prior to the incident in this case, a mother and daughter were both robbed at gunpoint in the parking lot. At least three other armed robberies involved female victims and male offenders, as well as virtually every reported strong-armed robbery. Women were also victims of a number of assaults and violent purse snatchings. A statistical analysis of crimes at the shopping center prepared by IPC indicates that a disproportionate number of victims of crime at the mall were women....

In addition to the incident reports detailing criminal activity that occurred on the premises of the shopping center, plaintiff submitted deposition testimony of various corporate officers ...

An executive vice president of IPC answered affirmatively that rape in isolated areas of a mall is a security concern of the company and that rape is "a crime that we are constantly vigilant for in all areas of the shopping center."

A 1995 security audit conducted for the mall management by IPC that indicated the catwalk area was frequented by "unruly youth" and had been the site of a "high level of incidents." The audit identified a number of security issues that IPC suggested should be implemented to improve safety at the shopping center. These proposals included enhancing the lighting in the catwalk area and conducting an evaluation to determine if an additional security officer should be deployed on Friday and Saturday evenings.[4] The audit noted that the lights along the base of the wall of the theater exits, near the catwalk, were not illuminated.

The trial court granted ... IPC's motion for judgment on the pleadings on all claims. In granting judgment for IPC, the trial court considered depositions, affidavits, documents and other evidence outside of the pleadings. We, therefore, review the grant of the motion for dismissal on the pleadings as a grant of a motion for summary judgment.

Plaintiff appeals ... the judgment against her on her contract claims against IPC....

III.

Plaintiff, of course, is not a signatory party to the IPC contract. The validity of her claim rests up [sic] whether she can make her claim as a third party beneficiary. "A third party beneficiary is one who is not privy to a contract or its consideration but who may nonetheless maintain a cause of action for breach of the contract." *Andes v. Albano*, 853 S.W.2d 936, 942 (Mo. banc 1993). "Only those third parties for whose primary benefit the parties contract may maintain an action." *Id.* "[I]t is not necessary for the parties to the contract to have as their 'primary object' the goal of benefiting the third parties, but only that the third parties be primary beneficiaries." *Id.*

"The intention of the parties is to be gleaned from the four corners of the contract, and if uncertain or ambiguous, from the circumstances surrounding its execution." *Terre Du Lac Ass'n. v. Terre Du Lac, Inc.*, 737 S.W.2d 206, 213 (Mo. App. 1987). "Third party beneficiary rights depend on, and are measured by, the terms of the contract between

---

4. The crime occurred on Saturday, March 15, 1997.

the promisor and the promisee." *Id.* "Although it is not necessary that the third party beneficiary be named in the contract, the terms of the contract must express directly and clearly an intent to benefit an identifiable person or class." *Id.*

There are three types of third party beneficiaries: donee, creditor and incidental. The first two categories may recover, the third may not. *Kansas City N.O. Nelson Co. v. Mid-Western Construction Co. of Missouri, Inc.,* 782 S.W.2d 672, 677 (Mo. App. 1989). "A person is a donee beneficiary if the purpose of the promisee in obtaining the promise of all or part of the performance thereof is to make a gift to the beneficiary or to confer upon him a right against the promisor to some performance neither due nor supposed nor asserted to be due from the promisee to the beneficiary." *Id.* "A person is a creditor beneficiary if the performance of the promise will satisfy an actual or supposed or asserted duty of the promisee to the beneficiary." *Id.* "Finally, if the person is neither a donee beneficiary nor a creditor beneficiary, he is an incidental beneficiary."

As previously indicated, the owners and the operators of the mall had a duty to take reasonable precautions to protect mall customers from violent crime. The Ward Parkway Group contracted with IPC for this very purpose. Brief review of certain provisions of the IPC contract make this clear.

[Editors: Here the Court reviews the same contract sections quoted above, Sections I.3.H, I.4, VI.5, I.3.B–D, I.3.J, and the same paragraphs from the IPC Policy and Procedures Manual.]

There can be no doubt that the Ward Parkway Group contracted with IPC to assist it in its duty to take reasonable measures to protect mall customers from criminal activity. We especially note the language of the IPC contract, paragraph VI.5, indicating that "Upon agreement, the staffing level shall be conclusively deemed for all purposes to be a material representation by Contractor to Manager that the staffing level is one which will provide full and adequate security to Mall [sic]." As such, plaintiff is a creditor beneficiary of the contract and has a right to bring suit and recover if she can also establish breach that caused damages.

. . .

STEPHEN N. LIMBAUGH, JR., CHIEF JUSTICE, DISSENTING.

I respectfully dissent.

. . .

The simple answer on the [breach of contract] claim [against IPC] is that plaintiff cannot be a third-party beneficiary if it is determined in the first instance, as I would hold, that Ward Parkway, the mall owner, had no duty to protect plaintiff. Under the majority's analysis, plaintiff is a "creditor beneficiary" because the performance of IPC's promise to provide security for the mall "will satisfy an actual or supposed or asserted duty that the mall owners owed to plaintiff." Absent that duty, however, there can be no creditor beneficiary.

The claim that the security contract imposes a duty on IPC is directly contrary to the long-established precedent of this Court that a party not privy to a contract may not use the duties created thereunder as a basis for tort. *Roddy v. Mo. Pac. Ry. Co.,* 15 S.W. 1112 (Mo. 1891). The majority relies upon an exception discussed in dicta in *Wolfmeyer v. Otis Elevator Co.,* 262 S.W.2d 18, 22 (Mo. 1953), that "a defendant, by entering into a contract, may place himself in such a relation toward third persons as to impose upon him an obligation to act in such a way that they will not be injured." In *Westerhold v. Carroll,* 419 S.W.2d 73, 77–79 (Mo. 1967), however, this Court clarified its comments in *Wolfmeyer* by holding that the exception to privity that allows a third party to sue in tort for breach of the contract is very limited and narrow and applies only in cases where the relationship between the third party and the contracting party was so close "as to approach that of privity." *Id.* at 78. The Court also emphasized that where the purpose of the privity requirement is to prevent exposing the parties to "unlimited liability to an unlimited number of persons," the general rule should remain in effect. *Id.* In this case, there certainly is no relationship between plaintiff and IPC so close "as to approach that of privity," and to disregard the privity requirement would indeed subject the security company to unlimited liability to an unlimited number of persons — the many thousands of patrons and employees of the mall — which is exactly what *Westerhold* forbids.

Finally, the majority holds that IPC's duty to act arose when plaintiff's friend, A.G., informed two IPC officers of the abduction. The majority's reasoning is that the situation fits into the "first special facts and circumstances" exception where "a person, known to be violent, is present on the premises or an individual is present who has conducted himself so as to indicate danger and sufficient time exists to prevent injury." *Faheen, By and Through Hebron v. City Parking Corp.,* 734 S.W.2d at 273. First, this argument is not raised by the plaintiff at any point. Second, the exception to which the majority refers is inapposite. It applies only where a person is previously known to be dangerous, based upon that person's "character, past conduct and tendencies." *Scheibel v. Hillis,* 531 S.W.2d 285, 288 (Mo. banc 1976).

For these reasons, I would affirm the judgments entered by the circuit court.

Notes

a. On the Distinction between Creditor and Donee Beneficiaries

In analyzing whether the plaintiffs were "intended beneficiaries" in the contract between the Ward Parkway Group and IPC, the court employed a traditional distinction in third party beneficiary doctrine between two types of intended beneficiaries, "donee beneficiaries" and "creditor beneficiaries." The *Restatement (Second) of Contracts* rejected these labels because they have no legal significance: both are intended beneficiaries and both should have a right to enforce the contract. Thus, the Restatement incorporates these concepts into the broader definition in Section 302:

§ 302. Intended and Incidental Beneficiaries

(1) Unless otherwise agreed between promisor and promisee, a beneficiary of a promise is an intended beneficiary if recognition of a right to performance in the beneficiary is appropriate to effectuate the intention of the parties and either

    (a) the performance of the promise will satisfy an obligation of the promisee to pay money to the beneficiary; or

    (b) the circumstances indicate that the promisee intends to give the beneficiary the benefit of the promised performance.

(2) An incidental beneficiary is a beneficiary who is not an intended beneficiary.

The commentary to this section states: "[t]he type of beneficiary covered by Subsection (1)(a) is often referred to as a "creditor beneficiary." The commentary further states:

Where the promised performance is not paid for by the recipient, discharges no right that he has against anyone, and is apparently designed to benefit him, the promise is often referred to as a "gift promise." The beneficiary of such a promise is often referred to as a "donee beneficiary"; he is an intended beneficiary under Subsection (1)(b).

When the court found that L.A.C. was a creditor beneficiary, what obligation did Ward Parkway owe to her that I.P.C.'s performance would satisfy? A typical creditor beneficiary transaction treats the performance of a promise as an asset of the promisee who wishes to extinguish a debt owed to the third party.

> Holly purchases a bicycle from Fox for $500, promising to pay Fox next week. Lawrence owes Holly $500 and they agree that Lawrence will repay Holly by delivering the $500 to Fox next week.

In this example Fox is a creditor beneficiary of the contract between Holly and Lawrence.

A life insurance contract in which the insurer agrees to pay the policy proceeds to a named beneficiary upon the death of the insured party is a typical example of a contract involving a donee beneficiary.

b. On Government Contracts

Government programs designed to carry out some public goal or to benefit some identifiable sector of the public are often implemented through contracts between the government and some private entity. The government may employ a construction company to build a library, for example, or may hire a paving company to build a road. In such cases, a breach by the construction company or by the paving company will have its greatest impact on the surrounding community, not on the government itself. In such cases, there are two separate doctrines that may support a community member's claim for damages caused by the breach—the third party beneficiary doctrine and the doctrine of implied causes of action. The implied cause of action doctrine provides that some government legislation implicitly authorizes the courts to provide a remedy for individuals who are harmed by violation of the statute. You will see the interplay of these two doctrines in the next case, *Henry Horner Mothers Guild v. The Chicago Housing Authority.*

In recent years, however, both of these doctrines have been significantly restricted and legal scholars have noted the hostility of the courts, including the U.S. Supreme Court, to citizen access to the courts to enforce statutory mandates. *See e.g.*, Pamela S. Karlan, *Disarming the Private Attorney General*, 2003 U. Ill. L. Rev. 183.

c. On Contract "Externalities"

Many contracts involve activities that will impact third parties. A homeowner's contract with a landscaping company to plant trees may provide much needed shade to a neighbor's yard. An oil company's contract for the operation of hydraulic fracturing equipment may contaminate an entire community's groundwater. See e.g., Thomas H. Darraha, Avner Vengosha, Robert B. Jackson, Nathaniel R. Warner, and Robert J. Poredae, *Noble gases identify the mechanisms of fugitive gas contamination in drinking-water wells overlying the Marcellus and Barnett Shales*, Proceedings of the National Academy of Sciences, vol. 111, no. 39, (documenting fugitive gas contamination in drinking-water wells overlying the Marcellus and Barnett Shales in Texas).

Economists would call these effects "externalities"—benefits or costs of the contracts that fall to people other than the contracting parties—and free market ideology, which features discrete, autonomous, market transactions, generally assumes that such externalized effects are rare. On the other hand, if sufficiently proved, market ideology generally supports government action responding to such externalized effects: where the public is benefited, market economics generally would support government policies to encourage such contracts, by subsidizing the construction of baseball stadiums, for example, by granting public funds to support scientific research, or by giving tax exemptions to public-service organizations (e.g., charitable and other non-profit organizations). Similarly, if externalized costs are proved, market economics would support zoning regulations, pollution control requirements, and licensing fees that prevent or reduce some of the "externalized" costs. In practice, however, market ideology too often blinds business and governmental leaders, leading them to ignore externalized costs of private industry and governmental action. The controversy about the existence and causes of global climate change, for example, may actually be a debate about the externalized costs of the production and of using fossil fuels.

———————

Henry Horner Mothers Guild, et al. v. The Chicago Housing Authority, et al.

United States District Court for the Northern District of Illinois
780 F. Supp. 511 (1991)

JAMES BLOCK ZAGEL, DISTRICT JUDGE

Plaintiffs filed a five-count complaint against the Chicago Housing Authority ("CHA"), Vincent Lane (as chairman of the CHA), the United States Department of Housing and Urban Development ("HUD"), and Jack Kemp (as the secretary of HUD). Plaintiffs assert Counts I, IV, and V of their complaint against defendants CHA and Lane (collectively "the CHA defendants"). The CHA defendants seek dismissal of those counts under Fed. R. Civ. P. 12(b)(6).

Plaintiffs bring Count I pursuant to 42 U.S.C. § 1983, charging the CHA defendants with a violation of plaintiffs' rights under § 1437p of the United States Housing Act

"Swingset, Henry Horner Homes, Chicago," photo by Patricia Evans.

("Housing Act"). 42 U.S.C. § 1441, *et seq.* Count IV alleges a breach of the Annual Contributions Contract ("ACC") between HUD and the CHA; plaintiffs assert that they are third party beneficiaries of the ACC. Finally, plaintiffs allege in Count V that the CHA defendants have breached their lease agreements with Henry Horner tenants.

For purposes of defendants' 12(b)(6) motion, the court must accept the well pleaded allegations of the complaint as true, and shall draw reasonable inferences in the light most favorable to plaintiff. *Bethlehem Steel Corp. v. Bush*, 918 F.2d 1323, 1326 (7th Cir. 1990); *Yeksigian v. Nappi*, 900 F.2d 101, 102 (7th Cir. 1990). Furthermore, the record is limited to the complaint and defendants may not challenge the allegations of the complaint. *Webster v. New Lenox School Dist. No. 122*, 917 F.2d 1004, 1005 (7th Cir. 1990); *Gomez v. Illinois State Bd. of Educ.*, 811 F.2d 1030, 1039 (7th Cir. 1987).[5]

I. Housing Act Claim (Count I)

The CHA is a public housing authority that administers federally subsidized and assisted low rent housing programs pursuant to the Housing Act. 42 U.S.C. § 1441 *et seq.* Plaintiffs are a class composed of residents at the Henry Horner Homes and applicants for public housing. Plaintiffs allege that the CHA's failure to maintain the Henry Horner Homes resulted in their substantial deterioration, such that half the units have been vacated and the remaining units exist in a state of perpetual disrepair. Plaintiffs further allege that as a result of the CHA's neglect, the buildings have become health and fire hazards and the unoccupied units have been overrun with vandals, trespassers and drug dealers. According to plaintiffs, this combination of deterioration and vacancy has resulted in a constructive or *de facto* demolition of the Henry Horner developments.

The Housing Act establishes conditions under which a public housing authority may demolish or dispose of existing public housing units. Section 1437p(d) provides that a public housing agency "shall not take any action to demolish or dispose of a public housing project without obtaining the approval of the Secretary and satisfying the conditions specified in subsections (a) and (b) of this section." 42 U.S.C. § 1437p(d) (1991). Subsection (a) requires a public housing authority to secure the approval of the Secretary of HUD before demolishing or disposing of the development. 42 U.S.C. § 1437p(a). Subsection (b) requires that the public housing authority consult with tenants and tenant councils who will be affected by the demolition or disposition, and to provide assistance and alternative units to any displaced tenants. 42 U.S.C. § 1437p(b).

Plaintiffs contend that because defendants have not satisfied the requirements enumerated in subsections (a) and (b) for demolition or disposal of the Henry Horner developments, their § 1983 claim alleging a violation of their rights under § 1437p(d) states a claim upon which this Court can grant relief. In response, the CHA defendants concede that they have not met the requirements of subsections (a) and (b). They contend, however, that de facto or constructive demolition is not actionable under § 1437p(d) and seek dismissal on those grounds.

---

5. Defendants attached an affidavit of George Phillips, a former housing manager of the Henry Horner developments, as an exhibit to their reply memorandum. The affidavit states that 102 tenants have moved into the Horner developments since January 1991. Plaintiffs assert that because defendants have presented matters outside of the pleadings the court should treat this 12(b)(6) motion as a motion for summary judgment. The Court will not consider the Phillips affidavit in ruling on defendants' motion because the affidavit does not, as a whole, refute the allegations of the complaint. Therefore, defendants' 12(b)(6) motion will not be treated as a motion for summary judgment.

A. Actual v. De Facto Demolition

The CHA defendants argue that § 1437p(d) does not cover a public housing agency's omission or failure to act that leads to a state of disrepair of a building or housing project. Under defendants' interpretation, until a public housing agency takes active measures to tear down a public housing project or makes an affirmative decision to demolish a project, a public housing tenant does not possess an enforceable right under § 1437p(d). Not surprisingly, plaintiffs disagree. They contend that the requirements of § 1437p(d) apply to any type of conduct by a housing authority that results in the destruction of all or part of a housing project. Under plaintiffs' reading of the Act, conduct that destroys a project—in the sense that the housing units would not longer be habitable—is governed by § 1437p(d) regardless of whether such conduct is characterized as affirmative conduct or passive neglect.

To resolve this dispute, the Court must decide whether the words "any action" contained in § 1437p(d) can reasonably be construed to encompass an omission or failure to act. In answering this question, the decision in *Edwards v. District of Columbia*, 821 F.2d 651 (D.C. Cir.1987), is instructive. The *Edwards* court held that although § 1437p may have created a private cause of action for actual demolition of a public housing development, § 1437p did not create enforceable rights that would be violated by a de facto demolition. *Edwards*, 821 F.2d at 657–658, 660. Senior District Judge Will, sitting by designation on the *Edwards* court, dissented. Judge Will stated that "§ 1437p, in order to be meaningful and effective, also prohibits a [public housing authority], acting without prior HUD authorization, from condemning a project to death as effectively as if it were physically demolished by abandoning and neglecting it." *Id.* at 666.

Congress responded to the circuit court's decision in *Edwards* by amending § 1437p to include subsection (d). Subsection (d) and its legislative history supplied the congressional intent that Judge Wald, in *Edwards*, appropriately found lacking when she concluded that the pre-amendment § 1437p did not create an enforceable right that could be violated by a de facto demolition. This subsection clarified that Congress intended that:

> no [public housing authority] shall take *any steps* toward demolition and disposition without having satisfied the statutory criteria. This provision is intended to correct an erroneous interpretation by the United States Court of Appeals for the D.C. Circuit in *Edwards v. District of Columbia* and shall be fully enforceable by tenants of and applicants of the housing that is threatened. H.R. Conf. Rep. No. 426, 100th Cong., 1st Sess. (1987), *reprinted in* 1987 U.S. Code Cong. & Admin.News 3317, 3458 (emphasis supplied).

The Court agrees that "in light of this amendment and its legislative history, there can be no doubt that Congress intended that § 1437p create enforceable rights." *Concerned Tenants Ass'n of Father Panik Village v. Pierce*, 685 F. Supp. 316, 320 (D. Conn. 1988). *Accord Tinsley v. Kemp*, 750 F. Supp. 1001, 1008 (W.D. Mo. 1990). There is some disagreement among the courts, however, regarding the scope of these rights and whether a de facto demolition implicates the rights protected by § 1437p. Since Congress amended § 1437p, two of the three courts to address the issue have interpreted subsection (d) as prohibiting conduct that results in a constructive or de facto demolition of public housing. *Compare Tinsley*, 750 F. Supp. at 1007–8 and *Concerned Tenants*, 685 F. Supp. at 321 *with Dessin v. Housing Authority of Fort Meyers*, No. 90-232, slip op. (M.D. Fla. Sept. 27, 1990).[6]

---

6. The court in *Dessin* dismissed the plaintiffs' Housing Act claim on ripeness grounds. *Dessin*, No. 90-232, slip op. at 5. Nevertheless, the court went on to express its disagreement with *Tinsley* and *Concerned Tenants*, which interpreted § 1437p(d) to allow a cause of action by current or potential

Defendants urge that subsection (d) be interpreted narrowly, as applying only to plans to tear down or raze a property. *See Dessin*, No. 90-232, slip op. at 7. According to defendants, a reading of the statute to include de facto demolition would constitute an unwarranted expansion of the statute's language. In light of Congress' rejection of *Edwards* and concomitant amendment of § 1437p, as well as the language of subsection (d) and its legislative history, the court declines to embrace defendants' narrow reading of § 1437p(d).

Both the language of the statute and the legislative history reveal that § 1437p(d) should be construed more broadly than defendants' interpretation allows. The statute and legislative history prohibit "any action" and "any step" toward demolition of a public housing project. This language is, by its nature, broad; it is crafted to encompass a wide range of conduct on the part of a public housing authority. Indeed, nothing in the statute or legislative history suggests that Congress intended to limit the right conferred in subsection (d) by exempting certain types of conduct. Thus, neither the statute nor legislative history support a distinction between actual and de facto demolition. *Concerned Tenants*, 685 F. Supp. at 321. "The use of the words 'any action' and 'any step' can only be reasonably construed to encompass conduct, including an omission or a failure to act, by a public housing agency that would result in the destruction of all or part of a housing project ..." *Id.*

Defendants' narrow construction of subsection (d) is at odds with Congress' intent in enacting § 1437p: to prohibit the destruction of public housing projects without HUD approval. *Id.*; *Tinsley*, 750 F. Supp. at 1007.

> Because the result—the unapproved destruction of a housing project—is the same whether done by a wrecking ball and bulldozers or by neglect that renders the units uninhabitable, the requirements of § 1437p should apply to both actual and de facto demolitions. To conclude otherwise would allow public housing agencies to evade the law by simply allowing housing projects to fall into decay and disrepair.

Concerned Tenants, 685 F. Supp. at 321.

Moreover, the language of the statute is not limited to demolition. The Act prohibits "any action to demolish or dispose of a housing project or a portion of a housing project ..." 42 U.S.C. § 1437p(d). The use of this language further supports a less narrow construction of the subsection than that urged by defendants. Congress not only prohibited demolition, but also steps taken to otherwise dispose of public housing units. For example, under subsection (d) a housing authority cannot eliminate public housing units by selling the buildings or converting them to another use without first obtaining HUD approval and satisfying the conditions outlined in § 1437p(d).

In sum, the Court finds that § 1437p(d) creates an enforceable right against conduct that results in the de facto demolition of public housing. In so doing, the Court does not reach the far more difficult problem of what would have to be proved to show de facto demolition. Plaintiffs have stated a claim for which relief may be granted sufficient to overcome a motion to dismiss.

---

tenants when a housing authority has constructively demolished public housing by failure to maintain. The passages of *Dessin* discussing the validity of an action for de facto demolition under subsection (d) are not essential to the court's decision, which rested on the ripeness doctrine. The court's general observations about subsection (d) are therefore dicta, which is "not entitled to the full weight usually given judicial decisions ..." *Matter of Cassidy*, 892 F.2d 637, 640 (7th Cir. 1990) (citing *United States v. Crawley*, 837 F.2d 291 (7th Cir. 1988)). Even if the court's conclusions about subsection (d) were integral to the analytical foundation of its holding, this Court would decline to follow the *Dessin* court's interpretation of § 1437p(d) for the reasons stated in this opinion.

II. Breach of the Annual Contributions Contract (Count IV)

Defendants CHA and Lane also argue that Count IV of the complaint, alleging breach of the Annual Contributions Contract ("ACC"), also fails to state a claim. The ACC is a contract under which the CHA agrees to maintain public housing in a safe and sanitary condition in exchange for HUD funds. 42 U.S.C. §§ 1437c, 1437g. Defendants contend that plaintiffs are not intended beneficiaries under the ACC. Therefore, defendants reason, plaintiffs do not have standing to assert a breach of contract claim under the ACC.

The Seventh Circuit has held that public housing tenants can be considered third party beneficiaries for certain types of contracts between HUD and public housing authorities. *Holbrook v. Pitt*, 643 F.2d 1261 (7th Cir. 1981). Other courts have held that the ACC, in particular, confers third party beneficiary status on public housing tenants. *See Ashton v. Pierce*, 716 F.2d 56, 66 (D.C. Cir. 1983), *modified on other grounds*, 723 F.2d 70 (D.C. Cir. 1983); *Knox Hill Tenant Council v. Washington*, 448 F.2d 1045, 1057–58 (D.C. Cir. 1971); *Tinsley*, 750 F. Supp. at 1012; *Concerned Tenants*, 685 F. Supp. at 324. Moreover, the *Holbrook* court stated that a third party may have enforceable rights under a contract if the contract were made for the third party's direct benefit. *Holbrook*, 643 F.2d at 1270.[7]

Under the standard enunciated in *Holbrook*, plaintiffs qualify as third party beneficiaries of the ACC. The ACC calls for the CHA to develop and administer each housing development "to achieve the well-being and advancement of the tenants thereof." It also requires the CHA "at all times [to] operate each Project ... solely for the purpose of providing decent, safe and sanitary dwellings ... within the financial reach of Families of Low Income." The terms of the contract thus communicate that the purpose of the contract is to benefit public housing tenants, as well as low-income families generally, who are applicants and potential applicants of public housing.

Defendants' motion to dismiss Count IV is denied.

. . .

Note

The Henry Horner Mothers Guild was formed in 1983 by Maurine Woodson. With funding from the MacArthur Foundation and the Woods Charitable Fund, for the purpose of community organizing, the Mothers Guild eventually began working with William P. Wilen, a lawyer first at the Legal Assistance Foundation in Chicago and then at the Sargeant Shriver National Center on Poverty Law. *See* William P. Wilen, *The Horner Model: Successfully Redeveloping Public Housing*, 1 Nw. J. L & Soc. Pol'y 62 (2006). The case you just read was filed as a class action suit against the Chicago Housing Authority (CHA) and the United States Department of Housing and Urban Development (HUD). In 1995, the litigants entered into a consent decree which was amended as the plans for the Henry Horner redevelopment proceeded. The Horner plaintiffs continued to be involved and a Horner Working Group which included legal counsel for the Horner plaintiffs and a representative of the Horner residents committee, chose the developer that was to build Phase II of the housing that was to replace the original Henry Horner public housing.

---

7. Federal common law governs plaintiffs' third party beneficiary claims because "the outcome of this action could directly affect significant obligations of the United States." *Concerned Tenants*, 685 F. Supp. at 322. *Accord* Holbrook, 643 F.2d at 1270 n. 16.

The CHA embarked on a $1.5 Plan for Transformation in 2001. The Plan, an ambitious blueprint for reforming public housing in Chicago, involved the demolition of high-rise tenements and the creation of mixed-income, mixed-race communities throughout Chicago. Unfortunately, the Plan did not follow the Henry Horner model, which included paced demolition to ease displacement, social services to assist with relocation, and tracking relocated families to assure suitable resettlement. The federal General Accounting Office praised this model for national public housing reform.

In cases that were decided after Henry Horner Mothers Guild, courts held that tenants are not intended beneficiaries of annual contributions contracts with H.U.D. *See, e.g., Diane Simmons and John Chase et al. v. Charleston Housing Authority*, 881 F. Supp. 225 (S.D.W.Va. 1995); *Carmelia Velez v. Henry Cisneros*, 850 F. Supp. 1257, 1275 (1994) (asserting that allowing third party beneficiary claims would subject the federal government to the diverse state rules on third party beneficiaries and would result in extensive liability for the federal government).

Should the test for third party beneficiary standing under a contract with the government be the same as under contracts between private citizens or entities? Should it be the same as the test for an implied right of action under a regulatory statute? The United States Housing Act offers subsidies for local housing authorities willing to create low cost housing. In exchange for the subsidies, local housing authorities agree to comply with rent caps and other requirements, including those discussed in *Henry Horner Mothers Guild*. Yet like most regulatory programs, enforcement responsibility rests on government agencies with limited resources and independent priorities. Allowing tenants to sue for enforcement adds an additional enforcement mechanism just as the provision of private causes of action under many statutes enhances enforcement through "private attorney general" litigation.

Over the last three decades, the federal and state courts have severely limited the ability of private citizens to enforce the provisions in government contracts or to enforce the terms in statutes that impose duties on entities or organizations that are regulated by the government. This hostility to the third party beneficiary doctrine and to implied rights of action under state and federal statutes takes the form of a presumption that all groups and private citizens are simply incidental beneficiaries of government contracts. Some statutes do explicitly provide for action by individual citizens, particularly the consumer protection statutes like the Deceptive Trade Practices Act discussed in the following case.

Bruce M. Cooper; John W. Romito; Roy L. Baker; Whitney Taylor Thompson, individually and on behalf of all other persons similarly situated v. Charter Communications Entertainments I, LLC; Charter Communications, Inc.

United States Court of Appeals for the First Circuit
760 F.3d 103 (2014)

WILLIAM J. KAYATTA, CIRCUIT JUDGE.

In the aftermath of a substantial snowstorm, four customers sued cable provider Charter Communications Entertainment I, LLC, and its parent company, Charter Communications, Inc. (collectively, "Charter"), on behalf of themselves and a putative class of others claimed to be similarly situated. The plaintiffs contend that Charter violated contractual, statutory, and common law duties by failing to provide credits to its customers for their loss of cable, internet, and telephone service during the storm. We hold that the district court properly exercised its jurisdiction under the Class Action Fairness Act, 28 U.S.C. § 1332(d), but erred in granting Charter's motion to dismiss. We therefore vacate in part the district court's opinion and remand for further proceedings.

I. Background

Except where otherwise noted, the facts in this opinion are taken from the plaintiffs' complaint, with all reasonable inferences drawn in the plaintiffs' favor. *See Maloy v. Ballori-Lage*, 744 F.3d 250, 251 (1st Cir. 2014). We bear in mind, however, that in assessing jurisdictional issues, we must weigh the evidence without favoring either party. *Valentin v. Hosp. Bella Vista*, 254 F.3d 358, 364 (1st Cir. 2001).

Plaintiffs Bruce Cooper, John Romito, Roy Baker, and Whitney Taylor Thompson are residents of Massachusetts who purchase cable television, internet, or telephone services from Charter. The district court has not yet considered any motion for class certification, so for now they are the only plaintiffs.

Beginning on October 29, 2011, Massachusetts experienced a severe snow storm that damaged trees, made travel impossible on many roads, and took down power and cable lines. During the storm, the plaintiffs did not receive services from Charter, either because they lost electrical power and therefore could not use television or internet devices, or because Charter's own equipment failed to provide service even where power was available, or due to some combination of the two.

Cooper, Romito, and Baker filed the complaint in this case in Massachusetts state court on November 22, 2011. Two weeks later, having not yet served the complaint on Charter, the plaintiffs' attorneys sent the company a demand letter seeking relief on behalf of the three original plaintiffs and others similarly situated. This letter was later incorporated into the plaintiffs' first amended and second amended complaints, the latter of which is the operative complaint here. The demand letter specified when the three customers' services were interrupted. According to the letter, for example, Cooper and Baker lost service at 6:00 pm on October 29, 2011, and did not receive it again until 3:00 pm on November 7, 2011. As to Thompson, who was added as the fourth plaintiff after the demand letter was sent, the record contains no information regarding when her service was interrupted, aside from the allegation in the amended complaint that her interruption lasted more than twenty-four consecutive hours.

A month after receiving the plaintiffs' demand, Charter sent a letter to their attorneys, informing them that Charter had issued credits to the accounts of Cooper, Baker, and Romito, which the company said fully compensated them for the time they were without service.

After the first amended complaint was served on Charter in February 2012, the company removed the case to federal court, invoking the Class Action Fairness Act. Charter then filed a motion to dismiss, asserting that the plaintiffs' claims were moot and that the complaint failed to state a claim. *See* Fed. R. Civ. P. 12(b)(1), (b)(6). The district court ruled that removal was proper and granted Charter's motion to dismiss. The court found that the claims of Cooper, Baker, and Romito were moot because they had received credits covering the time they were without service. The court also found that, as to the fourth plaintiff, Thompson, the complaint failed to state a claim. This appeal followed.

. . .

III. Analysis.

. . .

C. Failure to State a Claim

Each of the plaintiffs' claims arises under Massachusetts statutory or common law, and so we look to that law in assessing the plausibility of their claims. *See Daigle v. Maine Med. Ctr., Inc.*, 14 F.3d 684, 689 (1st Cir. 1994).

With one exception, the plaintiffs' claims revolve around a provision in Massachusetts law requiring that:

> In the event a license is issued [to provide cable service], each licensee shall agree to the following: ... (l) In the event its service to any subscriber is interrupted for twenty-four or more consecutive hours, it will grant such subscriber a pro rata credit or rebate.

Mass. Gen. Laws ch. 166A, § 5.

Charter has indeed included such language in its licensing agreements, almost verbatim, albeit with the presumably reasonable limiting gloss that credits or rebates need be provided only when "the interruption was not caused by the Subscriber and the Licensee knew or should have known of the service interruption."

The parties dispute how to interpret the statute's language, and thus the nearly identical language of the licensing agreements. Charter asserts that the statutorily-mandated language only requires the company to provide credits or rebates to subscribers who ask for them. We reject this claim as inconsistent with the statute's actual language. The language imposes no such limitation, instead flatly imposing a duty to provide a credit or rebate to any subscriber whose service is interrupted for sufficient duration. Charter nevertheless claims that the legislature would have used the plural form, "subscribers," rather than the term "any subscriber," if it intended cable providers to give credits to all subscribers who lost service. Charter does not cite any legal precedent, nor any grammatical rule, to support its argument, and we find it illogical: the statute's language plainly applies without limitation to all subscribers who lose service for twenty-four hours or more, just as a rule prohibiting "any person" less than thirty-five years old from becoming president applies to all such people despite its use of the singular word "person." *See* U.S. Const. art. II, § 1, cl. 4. Similarly, we see no basis for Charter's claim that the legislature would have used the term "automatic" if it intended cable providers to grant refunds to all subscribers who lost service. Although inclusion of that word in the statute would have provided belt-and-suspenders support for our conclusion, it does not follow that the word's absence leads us to disregard the clear meaning of the words the legislature actually used.

Even the implicit limitation made express in Charter's agreement—that Charter knows or should have known of the interruption—is not so limited as to apply only when Charter's knowledge arises from a consumer complaint or request. If Charter knows, for example, that it is not transmitting to an entire area because one of its own facilities is not passing along a signal, we can conceive of no reason why the Massachusetts legislature would have intended—but not written into the statute—a requirement that subscribers in that area must communicate to Charter what it already knows or should know in order to receive a credit.

Of course we do not know—or suggest—that Charter failed to provide a credit or rebate to subscribers whom it knew (or should have known) suffered a service interruption for twenty-four or more hours. Also not raised by this appeal is when exactly service is "interrupted" under the statute.[5] On a review of dismissal of this complaint under Rule

---

5. Charter argues as a matter of fact that the plaintiffs' service interruption was outside its control, and as a matter of law that it was therefore not obligated to provide credits. As this appeal provides

12(b)(6), rather, we assume that plaintiffs suffered a covered service interruption, of which Charter was aware, simply because it is plausibly alleged.

We therefore assume that Charter has conducted itself and is currently asserting a right to continue conducting itself in a manner that we find to be violative of the licensing term that Massachusetts' legislature viewed as sufficiently important as to be a required term of all such licensing agreements. The question is whether plaintiffs can maintain a private cause of action as a result of this assumed breach. We now analyze that question, bearing in mind that the following discussion, to the extent it considers claims for damages, applies only to plaintiff Thompson.

1. Contract Claims

The plaintiffs contend that they can sue as third-party beneficiaries to enforce the licensing agreements incorporating the statutory mandate. Under Massachusetts law, to prevail on a third-party beneficiary claim, a plaintiff must establish that the "language and circumstances of the contract show that the parties to the contract clearly and definitely intended the beneficiary to benefit from the promised performance." *Cumis Ins. Soc'y, Inc. v. BJ's Wholesale Club, Inc.*, 918 N.E.2d 36, 44 (Mass. 2009) (internal quotation marks, alterations omitted). Because government contracts by their very nature tend to benefit the public, Massachusetts courts apply a presumption against finding third-party liability in assessing those contracts, overcome only where the language and circumstances of the contract make it particularly clear that the parties intended members of the public to possess enforcement power. *See MacKenzie v. Flagstar Bank, FSB*, 738 F.3d 486, 491 (1st Cir. 2013) (applying Massachusetts law). In assessing attempts by third parties to enforce government contracts, we pay special heed to "[t]he distinction between an intention to benefit a third party and an intention that the third party should have the right to enforce that intention," with only the latter supporting third-party enforcement. 9 J. Murray, Corbin on Contracts § 45.6, p. 92 (rev. ed. 2007) (quoted in *Laguer v. OneWest Bank, FSB*, 31 Mass.L.Rptr. 14 (Mass. Super. Feb. 27, 2013)).

Here, the plaintiffs submitted with their complaint a copy of one licensing agreement between Charter and a Massachusetts municipality. We will assume for the purposes of this opinion that the agreement is identical in all material respects to any other licensing agreement, with a different municipality, that might apply to the plaintiffs' claims. The contract requires Charter to "grant a pro rata credit or rebate to any Subscriber whose entire Cable Service is interrupted for twenty-four (24) or more consecutive hours, if the interruption was not caused by the Subscriber and the Licensee knew or should have known of the service interruption." The plaintiffs are correct that this provision seems intended to benefit cable customers such as themselves, and the contract requires Charter to make payment directly to those customers, lending support to their claim. *See Pub. Serv. Co. of New Hampshire v. Hudson Light & Power Dep't*, 938 F.2d 338, 342 (1st Cir. 1991). The contract provision thus resembles the illustration offered by the Second Restatement of Contracts of a government contract that does create enforceable rights in third parties: "A, a municipality, enters into a contract with B, by which B promises to build a subway and to pay damages directly to any person who may be injured by the work of construction." Restatement (Second) of Contracts § 313 illus. 3 (1981); *see also MacKenzie*, 738 F.3d at 491 (relying on this section of the restatement in applying Massachusetts law).

---

no occasion to find facts, we also express no view whatsoever on Charter's proffered reading of the law.

We are nevertheless persuaded by the language of the contract as a whole that the parties did not intend individuals to hold power to enforce it. The contract includes a separate section that spells out in detail how the contract can be enforced. According to the contract, the municipality may seek specific performance, monetary damages, or revocation of the license. It must first notify Charter of an alleged breach, then wait thirty days for Charter to either cure the default or explain why it feels no cure is required. If the municipality is not satisfied, it must schedule a public hearing at which Charter may offer evidence. Only after those requirements have been fulfilled may the municipality pursue a remedy. Where the parties have provided such specific and elaborate procedures as prerequisites to enforcement, we cannot treat the plaintiffs' attempt to circumvent those procedures as consistent with the parties' intent.[6]

We note that the dismissal of the plaintiffs' third-party beneficiary claim does not deprive them of any opportunity for relief under the licensing agreement. Rather, in situations in which an elected local government holds enforcement power, citizens can seek recourse by acting through the political process to cause the municipality to seek a remedy in the form of credits for all affected consumers. But because the agreement here cannot plausibly support a third-party beneficiary claim, the political process is the plaintiffs' only recourse to secure enforcement of the agreements qua agreements.... Finally, the plaintiffs' claim for breach of the duty of good faith and fair dealing fails because, for the reasons we have described above, the plaintiff's complaint does not establish any contractual relationship between them and Charter. *See MacKenzie*, 738 F.3d at 493.

2. The Massachusetts Unfair and Deceptive Trade Practices Statute

Although third-party beneficiary principles provide no basis on which the plaintiffs can sue Charter for breach of its promise to municipalities, Massachusetts' legislature has provided an alternative path to a similar destination, without requiring any inquiry into common law notions of intended beneficiaries. Specifically, Chapter 93A of the Massachusetts code authorizes consumers to sue for "[u]nfair methods of competition and unfair or deceptive acts or practices in the conduct of any trade or commerce." Mass. Gen. Laws ch. 93A, § 2(a).

In considering whether a particular act or practice violates the unfairness prong of Chapter 93A, Massachusetts courts assess: "(1) whether the practice is within at least the penumbra of some common-law, statutory, or other established concept of unfairness; (2) whether it is immoral, unethical, oppressive, or unscrupulous; and (3) whether it causes substantial injury to consumers (or competitors or other businessmen)." *Massachusetts Eye & Ear Infirmary v. QLT Phototherapeutics, Inc.*, 412 F.3d 215, 243 (1st Cir. 2005) (quoting *PMP Assocs., Inc. v. Globe Newspaper Co.*, 321 N.E.2d 915, 918 (Mass. 1975)) (internal alterations omitted). For the practice to fall within the penumbra of a statute's concept of unfairness, it need not actually violate the statute. Otherwise, there would have been no need for the Massachusetts Supreme Judicial Court to refer to penumbras. *Cf. Kattar v. Demoulas*, 433 Mass. 1, 12–13, 739 N.E.2d 246 (2000) (holding that Chapter 93A "makes conduct unlawful which was not unlawful under the common law or any prior statute" (internal alteration omitted)). Furthermore, because "there is no limit to

---

6. Although neither party cites Astra USA, Inc. v. Santa Clara County, California, 131 S. Ct. 1342 (2011), it provides further support for our decision. *See id.* at 1347 (rejecting under federal common law an attempt by a third party to enforce a government contract where the contract incorporated statutory obligations, and suits by third parties "would undermine the [government's] efforts" to enforce the obligations "harmoniously and on a uniform ... basis").

human inventiveness in this field," Massachusetts courts evaluate unfair and deceptive trade practice claims based on the circumstances of each case. Id. at 13 (internal quotation marks, alteration omitted). In general, the evaluation of what constitutes an unfair trade practice is for the finder of fact, subject to the court's performance of a legal gate-keeping function. *Milliken & Co. v. Duro Textiles, LLC*, 887 N.E.2d 244, 258 (Mass. 2008).

A recent decision by the Massachusetts Supreme Judicial Court makes clear that a failure by Charter to pay a credit in accord with its statutorily-imposed contractual obligation would likely violate Chapter 93A. *See Casavant v. Norwegian Cruise Line Ltd.*, 952 N.E.2d 908, 911 (2011). In *Casavant*, a state regulation required sellers of travel services to disclose refund policies to consumers. *Id.* The regulations further provided that, should a seller fail to disclose its refund policy to a customer who had purchased services, the customer could cancel his or her contract and receive a full refund. Id. Analyzing a cruise line's failure to provide a refund in accordance with these regulations, Massachusetts' highest court found such a clear violation of Chapter 93A that it reversed a contrary conclusion by the factfinder. *Id.* at 504–05.

To be sure, this case differs from *Casavant* in that no regulation literally required that Charter provide credits to consumers. Rather, a regulation required Charter to promise it would do so in specified circumstances. But actually providing a credit is certainly within at least the penumbra of the statutory mandate that Charter promise to provide credits. Why, after all, would the legislature have required Charter to promise to pay if it did not intend for Charter to do so? And if Charter breached such a promise, it caused precisely the injury to consumers that the legislature sought to avoid. Whether such a breach violated 93A as a matter of law, as in *Casavant*, we need not decide at this stage. We need only decide whether the alleged conduct plausibly makes out a Chapter 93A claim. It most certainly does.

We acknowledge that this conclusion seems at first blush at odds with our conclusion regarding the third party beneficiary claim. Any such appearance is misleading. To the extent a duty is merely created by contract, it makes sense that Massachusetts law would leave it to the contracting parties to decide who can enforce it. To the extent that the duty also emanates from a legislative judgment that it reflects fair treatment of customers, however, the state legislature by enacting Chapter 93A has opted to let consumers seek relief in court. In short, the Massachusetts legislature created two potential causes of action in the event of a breach by Charter: an action for breach of contract, and an action under Chapter 93A, each subject to different procedures and remedies. The fact that Massachusetts, like other states, allows the contracting parties to decide who can maintain an action for breach of the contract does not mean that Massachusetts has allowed the contracting parties to take away the consumers' rights under Chapter 93A.

3. Unjust Enrichment, Money Had and Received

Finally, the plaintiffs' complaint asserts claims for unjust enrichment and money had and received based on their own individual dealings with Charter.[7] Both claims rest on

---

7. We have described these causes of action as "very close in character—one rooted in common law and the other equity jurisprudence." Jelmoli Holding, Inc. v. Raymond James Fin. Servs., Inc., 470 F.3d 14, 21 (1st Cir. 2006). Their elements are as follows: "Money had and received is based on money, or its equivalent, which in equity and good conscience should be returned to the claimant and is often styled as money that should be returned where one is unjustly enriched at another's expense. Unjust enrichment is an equitable claim with the same elements save that it is not limited to enrichment by money, or its equivalent." *Id.* at 17 n.2 (internal citations and quotation marks omitted).

the notion that Charter unfairly benefited by collecting money from the plaintiffs for services not actually rendered.

Charter's only preserved argument against these claims is that "an express contract governs the relationship between the Plaintiffs and Charter," precluding any quasi-contract claim.[8] Charter is correct that damages for breach of contract and unjust enrichment are mutually exclusive. *See Platten v. HG Bermuda Exempted Ltd.*, 437 F.3d 118, 130 (1st Cir. 2006) ("Massachusetts law does not allow litigants to override an express contract by arguing unjust enrichment."). Nevertheless, it is generally permissible to pursue alternative theories at the pleading stage. *See* Fed. R. Civ. P. 8(d). And, in any event, we cannot determine at this stage of the case whether Charter is correct that an express contract between the parties exists. In assessing a motion to dismiss, we focus narrowly on the plaintiffs' complaint along with any incorporated documents. The plaintiffs say that their complaint should not be interpreted as raising any claim based on a contract between them and Charter, and the complaint undisputedly did not incorporate any such contract, including the several formal contracts that Charter later submitted. Although we suspect that there is indeed an express contract between the parties that will, by its existence, foreclose a claim for unjust enrichment, we simply cannot say now that it is implausible to think otherwise.[9]

Consequently, we decline to find that the plaintiffs' complaint forecloses their quasi-contract claims.

IV. Conclusion

For the reasons outlined above, we affirm the district court's exercise of jurisdiction under the Class Action Fairness Act but vacate the district court's grant of Charter's motion to dismiss under Federal Rules of Civil Procedure 12(b)(1) and 12(b)(6). Costs are taxed against the appellees.

So ordered.

Notes

a. On the Rights of an Intended Beneficiary

As a general rule, intended beneficiaries "stand in the shoes" of the promisee, able to assert no greater claims than the promisee could assert and subject to whatever defenses, based on the contract, that the promisor could assert against the promisee. *See* Restatement (Second) of Contracts section 309. An intended beneficiary's claim is also subject to an enforceable modification agreed between the promisor and the promisee, unless the intended beneficiary has relied upon the contract to his or her detriment or has assented to the contract at the request of the promisor or the promisee. *See* Restatement (Second) of Contracts section 311.

b. On Third Party Promissory Estoppel Claims

Section 90 of the *Restatement (Second) of Contracts* mentions the possibility of foreseeable reliance by third persons:

---

8. Because it was not raised below, we will not consider Charter's alternative argument that the claims are "deficient for lack of sufficient pleading."

9. Rules 26(f)(3)(B) and 56 of the Federal Rules of Civil Procedure offer the district court plenty of discretion to have the parties fish or cut bait on this specific issue without any prolonged discovery, expense, or delay.

A promise which the promisor should reasonably expect to induce action or forbearance on the part of the promisee *or a third person* and which does induce
such action or forbearance is binding if injustice can be avoided only by
enforcement of the promise. The remedy granted for breach may be limited as
justice requires. (Emphasis added.)

The Commentary to this section makes clear the drafters' belief that third persons who have
foreseeably relied on a promise should be able to sue for enforcement of the promise:

> c. Reliance by third persons. If a promise is made to one party for the benefit of
> another, it is often foreseeable that the beneficiary will rely on the promise. En-
> forcement of the promise in such cases rests on the same basis and depends on
> the same factors as in cases of reliance by the promisee. Justifiable reliance by
> third persons who are not beneficiaries is less likely, but may sometimes reinforce
> the claim of the promisee or beneficiary.

Illustrations:

5. A holds a mortgage on B's land. To enable B to obtain a loan, A promises B in
   writing to release part of the land from the mortgage upon payment of a stated
   sum. As A contemplated, C lends money to B on a second mortgage, relying on
   A's promise. The promise is binding and may be enforced by C.

6. A executes and delivers a promissory note to B, a bank, to give B a false appearance
   of assets, deceive the banking authorities, and enable the bank to continue to
   operate. After several years B fails and is taken over by C, a representative of B's
   creditors. A's note is enforceable by C.

7. A and B, husband and wife, are tenants by the entirety of a tract of land. They
   make an oral promise to B's niece C to give her the tract. B, C and C's husband
   expend money in building a house on the tract and C and her husband take
   possession and live there for several years until B dies. The expenditures by B and
   by C's husband are treated like those by C in determining whether justice requires
   enforcement of the promise against A.

For a case adopting this provision and allowing a third person to sue for breach of a
promise upon which she had relied, *see Benjamin Ravelo and Marlene Ravelo v. County
of Hawaii*, 658 P.2d 883 (Haw. 1983) (The county promised Benjamin Ravelo that he
would be hired as a police officer; in reliance on that promise, Marlene Ravelo, Benjamin's
wife, quit her job on the island of Oahu and moved herself and her family to the island
of Hawai'i).

c. Third Party Professional Malpractice Claims

Professional malpractice can be the basis for contract and tort claims. Some jurisdictions
interpret service contracts, including contracts for professional services, to include implied
obligations of best efforts or reasonable skill, so that a failure to use best effort or reasonable
skill would give rise to a breach of contract action. In addition, the traditional tort of
misfeasance continues in the tort action for negligence in the performance of an assumed
task. In order to establish the tort of negligence, however, one must establish that the
alleged tortfeasor owed a duty to the injured plaintiff. One way a tort duty can be established
is through contract and through the status of an intended beneficiary of a contract. In
this context, then, a plaintiff's standing to bring a tort claim for negligence would depend
upon whether they were an intended beneficiary of a professional service contract. The
following case is an example of this connection.

Erika Fabian v. Ross M. Lindsay, III and Lindsay and Lindsay, LLC

Supreme Court of South Carolina
765 S.E.2d 132 (2014)

JUSTICE DONALD W. BEATTY

Erika Fabian (Appellant) brought this action for legal malpractice and breach of contract by a third-party beneficiary, alleging attorney Ross M. Lindsay, III and his law firm Lindsay & Lindsay (collectively, Respondents) made a drafting error in preparing a trust instrument for her late uncle and, as a result, she was effectively disinherited. Appellant appeals from a circuit court order dismissing her action under Rule 12(b)(6), SCRCP for failure to state a claim and contends South Carolina should recognize a cause of action, in tort and in contract, by a third-party beneficiary of a will or estate planning document against a lawyer whose drafting error defeats or diminishes the client's intent. We agree, and we reverse and remand for further proceedings.

I. Facts

A. The Trust Agreement

The facts, in the light most favorable to Appellant, are as follows. On May 25, 1990, Appellant's uncle, Dr. Denis Fabian, executed a trust agreement that was drafted by Respondents. Dr. Fabian was then around 80 years old and his wife, Marilyn Fabian, whom he had married in 1973, was about twenty years younger. Dr. Fabian made his wife the life beneficiary of the trust.

Mrs. Fabian had two adult daughters from a prior marriage. Dr. Fabian then had one living brother, Eli Fabian, who was in his 70s and not in good health. Dr. Fabian also had two nieces, Miriam Fabian, who was Eli's daughter, and Appellant, who was the daughter of Dr. Fabian's predeceased brother, Zoltan Fabian. Dr. Fabian was aware of Appellant's loss of both her father and her mother at an early age.

Dr. Fabian died on February 5, 2000, and his brother Eli died a few weeks later. Thus, Eli survived Dr. Fabian, but not Mrs. Fabian, who held the life interest in the trust. At Dr. Fabian's death, the trust was valued at approximately $13 million.

Appellant had been told by Dr. Fabian and his wife that she was being provided for in Dr. Fabian's estate plan. She alleges that at the time of Dr. Fabian's death, everyone involved in the matter was under the impression that, when Mrs. Fabian passed, one-half of Dr. Fabian's estate was going to Appellant and Miriam, with the other half to be distributed to Mrs. Fabian's two children.

After Dr. Fabian's death, however, Respondents mailed a letter and two pages from the trust agreement to Appellant and informed her that she would not be receiving anything from Dr. Fabian's trust upon Mrs. Fabian's future death because the share that would have been distributed to her would, instead, be distributed to Eli's estate. Since Appellant's cousin Miriam was Eli's only heir, Miriam would now stand to be the beneficiary of both her share and Appellant's share. The distribution provision at issue in the trust agreement drafted by Respondents reads as follows:

> *Upon or after the death of the survivor of my said spouse and me*, my Trustee shall divide this Trust as then constituted into two (2) separate shares so as to provide One (1) share for the children of Marilyn K. Fabian and One (1) share for my brother, Eli Fabian. If either of my wife's children predceases (sic) her, the predeceased child's share shall be distributed to his or her issue per stirpes. *If my said brother, Eli Fabian, predeceases me*, then one half of *his share* shall be

distributed to his daughter, Miriam Fabian, or her issue per stirpes, and the other half of *his share* shall be distributed to my niece, Erica (sic) Fabian [Appellant], or her issue per stirpes.

(Emphasis added.) Appellant maintains the first sentence makes it abundantly clear that the division and distribution of the trust corpus is to occur only *after* the death of *both* Dr. Fabian and his wife. In addition, Respondents knew that Dr. Fabian wanted Eli's share of the trust to pass to the two named nieces if Eli was not alive at the time of distribution to receive his share. However, the use of the word "me" in the last sentence has effectively defeated her uncle's intentions by inadvertently disinheriting her. She contends this drafting error has resulted in an "unexpected windfall" to one cousin (Miriam), who has now received an unintended double share, and the "devastating" disinheritance of the other cousin (Appellant).

B. Reformation Action

In response to this situation, Appellant filed an action for reformation of the trust agreement. Two of the three trustees, Mrs. Fabian, who held the life interest, and Walter Pikul, Dr. Fabian's long-time business advisor, agreed with Appellant that the trust document contained a drafting error that thwarted Dr. Fabian's intent, and they concurred in Appellant's request for reformation on the basis the error made the trust ambiguous. In contrast, Appellant's cousin Miriam, who stood to reap the windfall of receiving a double share, strenuously opposed reformation, as did the drafting attorney, respondent Ross M. Lindsay, III, who maintained the trust document was unambiguous and did not need correction.

After years of escalating litigation expenses, Appellant accepted a settlement paid for by the trust. The trust was not reformed, but the parties stipulated that Appellant was not releasing any claim she had against Respondents in their capacity as Dr. Fabian's estate planning attorneys who had drafted the instrument and counseled Dr. Fabian on the creation of the trust.

C. Action for Professional Negligence & Breach of Contract

Appellant filed the current action against Respondents as the drafters of the trust agreement in which she claims to hold an intended beneficial interest. She asserted a tort claim for professional negligence (attorney malpractice) and a claim for breach of contract on behalf of a third-party beneficiary. Respondents promptly moved to dismiss Appellant's claims under Rule 12(b)(6), SCRCP for failure to state a cause of action.

The circuit court granted the motion to dismiss, finding Appellant could not assert a claim for legal malpractice because South Carolina law recognizes no duty in the absence of an attorney-client relationship. In addition, the court stated no South Carolina court had ever recognized a breach of contract action by an intended beneficiary of estate planning documents, stating: "To the contrary, the Supreme Court has characterized such a cause of action as merely one of a variety of theories which fall under the umbrella of 'legal malpractice,' which requires privity."[1] The court concluded Respondents were

---

1. The circuit court relied upon Rydde v. Morris, 675 S.E.2d 431, 432 (S.C. 2009), in which this Court held "an attorney owes no duty to a prospective beneficiary of a *nonexistent* will." (Emphasis added.) We noted some jurisdictions had relaxed privity requirements to allow a cause of action where an attorney failed to draft a will in conformity with the testator's wishes, but not for cases involving a nonexistent document. *Id. at* 647–48, 675 S.E.2d at 433–34. *Rydde* is not controlling as it involves a distinguishable issue that implicates different legal and policy considerations, as suggested in *Rydde* itself.

"immune from liability" to Appellant under any theory for their alleged error in drafting the trust document. Appellant appealed, and this Court certified the appeal from the Court of Appeals pursuant to Rule 204(b), SCACR. We thereafter granted a motion by the Greenville Estate Planning Study Group to file an amicus curiae brief in support of Respondents.

. . .

III. Law/Analysis

A. Privity Under Existing Law

In dismissing Appellant's claims, the circuit court essentially found Appellant was not in privity with Respondents and therefore failed to establish a viable cause of action. "'Privity' denotes [a] mutual or successive relationship to the same rights of property." *Thompson v. Hudgens*, 159 S.E. 807, 812 (S.C. 1931) (citation omitted); *see also* Black's Law Dictionary 1394 (10th ed. 2014) (defining "privity" as "[t]he connection or relationship between two parties, each having a legally recognized interest in the same subject matter (such as a transaction, proceeding, or piece of property); mutuality of interests"). South Carolina courts have equated privity with standing. *See Maners v. Lexington Cnty. Sav. & Loan Ass'n*, 267 S.E.2d 422, 423 (S.C. 1980) (affirming the trial judge's determination that "appellant had no standing to allege [her claim] because she was not in privity with respondent").

An early case by the United States Supreme Court adopted the concept of privity from an English decision, *Winterbottom v. Wright*, 152 Eng. Rep. 402 (Exch.) (1842), and applied it to hold an attorney was not liable to a bank that relied on his erroneous certification that his client had good title to land. *See Nat'l Sav. Bank v. Ward*, 100 U.S. 195 (1879) (discussing *Winterbottom*'s limitation of recovery in another context to those having privity of contract). The Supreme Court noted there were exceptions, however, for instances of fraud, collusion, and like circumstances. *Id.* at 205–06.

Privity for legal malpractice has traditionally been established by the existence of an attorney-client relationship. *See generally Rydde v. Morris*, 675 S.E.2d 431, 435 (S.C. 2009) (stating "existing law [] imposes a privity requirement as a condition to maintaining a legal malpractice claim in South Carolina"). "A plaintiff in a legal malpractice action must establish four elements: (1) the existence of an attorney-client relationship, (2) a breach of duty by the attorney, (3) damage to the client, and (4) proximate causation of the client's damages by the breach." *RFT Mgmt. Co. v. Tinsley & Adams L.L.P.*, 732 S.E.2d 166, 170 (S.C. 2012).

Appellant contends the current appeal presents an opportunity not available in prior cases for South Carolina to join the vast majority of states allowing intended third-party beneficiaries to bring claims against the lawyer who prepared the defective will or estate planning document. *See Chastain v. Hiltabidle*, 673 S.E.2d 826 (S.C. Ct. App. 2009) (stating whether a duty exists in regard to an alleged wrong is a question of law for the court). Appellant argues a lawyer's negligence in preparing an estate or testamentary document impacts three potential classes of plaintiffs: (1) the client, (2) the decedent's estate, and (3) the intended beneficiaries. As she aptly states:

> [O]f the three possible plaintiffs, only the beneficiaries have the motivation and sufficient damages to bring a malpractice claim. The client is deceased and the estate lacks a cause of action or damages or both. Indeed, because the ben-eficiaries were supposed to be the beneficial owners of estate assets, only the ben-eficiaries suffer directly due to the lawyer's negligence. If no cause of action is available to the beneficiaries, the negligent drafting lawyer is effectively immune

from liability. Therefore, only the beneficiaries suffer the loss caused by the lawyer's negligence.

In the 1950s, after observing the problems created by the traditional privity requirement, jurisdictions in the United States began abandoning strict privity as an absolute bar to claims for legal malpractice. A majority of jurisdictions now recognize a cause of action by a third-party beneficiary of a will or estate planning document against the lawyer whose drafting error defeats or diminishes the client's intent, although they have done so using a variety of tests and formulations, whether in tort, contract, or both. Max N. Pickelsimer, Comment, *Attorney Malpractice in Will Drafting: Will South Carolina Expand Privity to Impose a Duty to Intended Beneficiaries of a Will?*, 58 S.C. L. Rev. 581, 581–86 (2007) (discussing the origin and evolution of privity in the United States); *see also* Joan Teshima, Annotation, *Attorney's Liability, to One Other Than Immediate Client, for Negligence in Connection with Legal Duties*, 61 A.L.R.4th 615 (1988 & Supp. 2014) (collecting cases considering the legal theories for imposing civil liability upon an attorney for damages to a nonclient directly caused by the attorney's professional negligence).

> The jurisdictions that have eased the strict privity requirement typically use one of the following three approaches to determine whether the intended beneficiary of a will has standing to bring an action for legal malpractice: (1) the balancing of factors test, which originated in California; (2) 'the Florida-Iowa rule[']; and (3) breach of contract based on a third-party beneficiary contract theory.

Pickelsimer, *supra*, at 586 (footnotes omitted).

B. Theories for Imposing Liability in Tort or Contract

(1) Balancing of Factors Test

In an influential decision emanating from California in 1958, the rule on privity in legal malpractice actions began to evolve throughout the United States. In *Biakanja v. Irving*, 320 P.2d 16 (Cal. 1958), the court held that where the defendant negligently prepared an invalid will, the beneficiary could recover for her loss in tort even though she was not in privity with the defendant. Although the defendant in that case was a notary public and not an attorney, the court also overruled prior cases involving attorneys.

The holding in *Biakanja* was formally extended to attorneys a few years later in *Lucas v. Hamm*, 364 P.2d 685 (Cal. 1961). In *Lucas*, the court allowed recovery both in tort and as a third-party beneficiary to a contract. In discussing whether to impose tort liability, the Lucas court reiterated all but one of the factors it originally delineated in *Biakanja* and stated, "[T]he determination whether in a specific case the defendant will be held liable to a third person not in privity is a matter of policy and involves the balancing of various factors, among which are the extent to which the transaction was intended to affect the plaintiff, the foreseeability of harm to him, the degree of certainty that the plaintiff suffered injury, the closeness of the connection between the defendant's conduct and the injury, and the policy of preventing future harm." *Id.* at 687 (citing *Biakanja*, 320 P.2d at 19).

Applying these factors, the court reasoned that "one of the main purposes which the transaction between defendant and the testator intended to accomplish was to provide for the transfer of property to plaintiffs; the damage to plaintiffs in the event of invalidity of the bequest was clearly foreseeable; it became certain, upon the death of the testator without change of the will, that plaintiffs would have received the intended benefits but for the asserted negligence of defendant; and if persons such as plaintiffs are not permitted to recover for the loss resulting from negligence of the draftsman, no one would be able to do so, and the policy of prevent[ing] future harm would be impaired." *Id.* at 688.

The court then noted since the defendant in this case was an attorney, it "must consider an additional factor not present in *Biakanja*, namely, whether the recognition of liability to beneficiaries of wills negligently drawn by attorneys would impose an undue burden on the profession." *Id.* The court found although in some situations liability could be large and unpredictable, this was also true for any attorney's liability to his client, and the extension of liability to beneficiaries injured by a negligently drawn will does not place an undue burden on the profession, particularly when taking into consideration that the opposite conclusion would cause the innocent beneficiary to bear the entire loss of the attorney's professional negligence. *Id.*

Other jurisdictions have engaged in a similar or modified "balancing of factors" analysis to generally determine whether an attorney should be liable to a third party in the absence of strict privity. *See e.g., Fickett v. Super. Ct.,* 558 P.2d 988, 990 (Ariz. Ct. App. 1976) (citing *Biakanja* and *Lucas* and stating "[w]e are of the opinion that the better view is that the determination of whether, in a specific case, the attorney will be held liable to a third person not in privity is a matter of policy and involves the balancing of various factors. . . ."); *Pizel v. Zuspann,* 795 P.2d 42, 51 (Kan. 1990) ("We find the California cases persuasive. We conclude that an attorney may be liable to parties not in privity based upon the balancing test developed by the California courts."); *Donahue v. Shughart, Thomson & Kilroy, P.C.,* 900 S.W.2d 624, 629 (Mo. 1995) (en banc) ("[T]he question of legal duty of attorneys to non-clients will be determined by weighing the factors in the modified balancing test.").

(2) The Florida-Iowa Rule

In the event this Court joins the majority of jurisdictions allowing a third party beneficiary to seek recovery for the improper drafting of a will or estate planning document, Respondents and the amicus urge this Court to adopt an alternative theory of recovery known as the "Florida-Iowa Rule." It provides:

> An attorney preparing a will has a duty not only to the testator-client, but also to the testator's intended beneficiaries, who may maintain a legal malpractice action against the attorney on theories of either tort (negligence) or contract (third-party beneficiaries). However, liability to the testamentary beneficiary can arise only if, due to the attorney's professional negligence, the testamentary intent, *as expressed in the will*, is frustrated, and the beneficiary's legacy is lost or diminished as a direct result of that negligence.

DeMaris v. Asti, 426 So. 2d 1153, 1154 (Fla. Dist. Ct. App. 1983) (citations omitted); *see also Schreiner v. Scoville,* 410 N.W.2d 679, 683 (Iowa 1987) ("[W]e hold a cause of action ordinarily will arise only when as a direct result of the lawyer's professional negligence the testator's intent as expressed in the testamentary instruments is frustrated in whole or in part and the beneficiary's interest in the estate is either lost, diminished, or unrealized."). A few other jurisdictions have also adopted this theory. *See, e.g., Mieras v. DeBona,* 550 N.W.2d 202 (Mich. 1996) (stating the beneficiary named in a will may bring a tort-based action for negligence in drafting the will, but the court will not look to extrinsic evidence).

Respondents' desire, in the absence of this Court's retention of strict privity, is to promote the Florida-Iowa Rule because its essential feature, the imposition of a ban on all extrinsic evidence, obviously makes it more difficult for a plaintiff to establish a claim. *See* Joan Teshima, Annotation, *What Constitutes Negligence Sufficient to Render Attorney Liable to Person Other Than Immediate Client,* 61 A.L.R.4th 464, 480 (1988) ("Some courts have ruled in this situation that evidence extrinsic to the will cannot be admitted to prove the testator's intent, thus making it impossible, or virtually so, for a thwarted beneficiary to prove his case against an attorney.").

Appellant understandably opposes this theory. As she correctly asserts: "The fundamental flaw in the Florida-Iowa [R]ule is that it focuses on the testamentary documents prepared by the lawyer rather than the source of the beneficiary's claim, which is not the allegedly defective will or trust document, but instead is the client-lawyer agreement that was intended to satisfy the client's testamentary intent. The proper approach in cases like this one where latent ambiguities exist in the will, trust agreement, or estate plan would be to allow the admission of extrinsic evidence to establish the client's intent as is generally allowed in a typical will contest."

The Florida-Iowa Rule is actually based on a California case, *Ventura County Humane Society v. Holloway*, 115 Cal. Rptr. 464, 468 (Ct. App. 1974), which held the plaintiff had standing under the balancing of factors test articulated in *Biakanja* and *Lucas*, but in doing so, the court stated "[a]n attorney may be held liable to the testamentary beneficiaries only ... [i]f due to the attorney's professional negligence the testamentary intent expressed in the will is frustrated and the beneficiaries clearly designated by the testator lose their legacy as a direct result of such negligence." *See Pickelsimer, supra,* at 589 (discussing the genesis of the Florida-Iowa Rule).

Appellant's argument for rejecting the Florida-Iowa Rule and its prohibition on extrinsic evidence finds support from the fact that a California district court has specifically observed that other courts applying the Rule have "read *Ventura* too broadly" because extrinsic evidence "was not at issue in *Ventura*," and the case does not stand for the proposition that inquiries should be limited to the testamentary document to the exclusion of all other evidence. *Creighton Univ. v. Kleinfeld*, 919 F. Supp. 1421, 1425 n.5 (E.D. Cal. 1995). To the contrary, extrinsic evidence is often "vital" to proving an attorney's drafting error. *Id.*

For these reasons, we reject the Florida-Iowa Rule and hold extrinsic evidence is not barred, as it is often essential to the pursuit of a claim. *See Jewish Hosp. of St. Louis, Mo. v. Boatmen's Nat'l Bank of Belleville*, 633 N.E.2d 1267, 1273–76 (holding an attorney who drafted a will owed a duty in contract or tort to the remainder beneficiaries of a testamentary trust; under either theory, the non-client beneficiary must demonstrate that they are in the nature of a third-party intended beneficiary of the relationship between the attorney and the client, and evidence of intention is derived from a consideration of all of the circumstances surrounding the parties at the time of the execution of the will).

(3) Third-Party Beneficiary of Contract Theory

Another theory recognized for recovery is based on a third-party beneficiary approach. South Carolina law already generally recognizes a breach of contract claim for a third-party beneficiary of a contract and we find this principle is appropriate here.

"Generally, one not in privity of contract with another cannot maintain an action against him in breach of contract, and any damage resulting from the breach of a contract between the defendant and a third-party is not, as such, recoverable by the plaintiff." *Windsor Green Owners Ass'n v. Allied Signal, Inc.*, 605 S.E.2d 750, 752 (S.C.Ct. App. 2004) (citation omitted). "However, if a contract is made for the benefit of a third person, that person may enforce the contract if the contracting parties intended to create a direct, rather than an incidental or consequential, benefit to such third person." *Id.* (citation omitted).

Courts in other jurisdictions have expressly extended this principle to frustrated third-party beneficiaries of estate instruments, although some have done so as a breach of contract action while others have used the "third-party beneficiary" principle as a basis to allow recovery in negligence. Some jurisdictions have recognized that a plaintiff may choose to proceed in contract, tort, or both. *See, e.g., Lucas,* 364 P.2d at 689 & n.2; *Stowe v. Smith,* 441 A.2d 81, 84 (Conn. 1981); *Blair v. Ing,* 21 P.3d 452, 464 (Haw. 2001).

In *Lucas,* in addition to allowing tort recovery, the California court found "that intended beneficiaries of a will who lose their testamentary rights because of failure of the attorney who drew the will to properly fulfill his obligations under his contract with the testator may recover as third-party beneficiaries." 364 P.2d at 689. The court stated, "Obviously the main purpose of a contract for the drafting of a will is to accomplish the future transfer of the estate of the testator to the beneficiaries named in the will, and therefore it seems improper to hold ... that the testator intended only 'remotely' to benefit those persons." *Id.* at 688. The court found this main purpose and "intent can be effectuated, in the event of a breach by the attorney, only by giving the beneficiaries a right of action, [so] we should recognize, as a matter of policy, that they are entitled to recover as third-party beneficiaries." *Id.* at 689. Moreover, the court noted the general rule is "where a case sounds in both tort and contract, the plaintiff will ordinarily have freedom of election between the two actions." *Id.* at 689 n.2.

We find this reasoning sound and adopt it here. We also find persuasive *Guy v. Liederbach,* 459 A.2d 744, 746 (Pa. 1983) to the extent that the Pennsylvania court stated it would allow recovery as to *named* beneficiaries:

> [W]hile important policies require privity (an attorney-client or analogous professional relationship, or a specific undertaking) to maintain an action in negligence for professional malpractice, a named legatee of a will may bring suit as an intended third party beneficiary of the contract between the attorney and the testator for the drafting of a will which specifically names the legatee as a recipient of all or part of the estate.

The court found the grant of standing to a narrow class of third-party beneficiaries was appropriate based on the *Restatement (Second) of Contracts* § 302 (1979), "where the intent to benefit the plaintiff is clear and the promisee (testator) is unable to enforce the contract," as named legatees would otherwise have no recourse for failed legacies that resulted from attorney malpractice. *Id.* at 747.

Recognizing a cause of action is not a radical departure from the existing law of legal malpractice that requires a lawyer-client relationship, which is equated with privity and standing. Where a client hires an attorney to carry out his intent for estate planning and to provide for his beneficiaries, there is an attorney-client relationship that forms the basis for the attorney's duty to carry out the client's intent. This intent in estate planning is directly and inescapably for the benefit of the third-party beneficiaries. Thus, imposing an avenue for recourse in the beneficiary, where the client is deceased, is effectively enforcing the client's intent, and the third party is in privity with the attorney. It is the breach of the attorney's duty to the client that is the actionable conduct in these cases. *See* Dennis J. Horan & George W. Spellmire, Jr., Attorney Malpractice: Prevention and Defense 2-1 to 2-5 (1989) (discussing directly intended beneficiaries of the attorney-client relationship); *see also Gaar v. N. Myrtle Beach Realty Co.,* 339 S.E.2d 887, 889 (S.C.Ct. App. 1986) ("In his professional capacity the attorney is not liable, except to his client and those in privity with his client, for injury allegedly arising out of the performance of his professional activities." (emphasis added)); *Thompson v. Hudgens,* 159 S.E. 807, 812 (S.C. 1931) ("Generally speaking, the heir is in privity with his ancestor....").

In these circumstances, retaining strict privity in a legal malpractice action for negligence committed in preparing will or estate documents would serve to improperly immunize this particular subset of attorneys from liability for their professional negligence. Joining the majority of states that have recognized causes of action is the just result. This does not impose an undue burden on estate planning attorneys as it merely puts them in the same position as most other legal professionals by making them responsible for their professional negligence to the same extent as attorneys practicing in other areas.

In sum, today we affirmatively recognize causes of action both in tort and in contract by a third-party beneficiary of an existing will or estate planning document against a lawyer whose drafting error defeats or diminishes the client's intent. The focus of a will or estate document is, inherently, on third-party beneficiaries. That being the case, the action typically does not arise until the client is deceased. *See Stowe*, 441 A.2d at 83 (stating "merely drafting and executing a will creates no vested right in the legatee until the death of the testatrix"); Ronald E. Mallen & Jeffrey M. Smith, Legal Malpractice § 36:12, at 1288 (2014) ("Since litigation concerning errors in the preparation of a will necessarily arrives after the client's death, the plaintiff usually is an allegedly injured or omitted beneficiary....").

Specifically as to tort actions, the balancing test propounded by the California courts provides a valuable framework in evaluating the considerations that support adoption of a cause of action. *See Donahue*, 900 S.W.2d at 627 ("That balancing test has been cited with approval by most jurisdictions which have considered the issue." (citing Ronald E. Mallen & Jeffrey M. Smith, Legal Malpractice § 7.11, at 383 (3d ed. 1983)). As discussed previously, we reject the Florida-Iowa Rule for its narrow application and ban on extrinsic evidence. As to contract actions for third-party beneficiaries, we find the reasoning in Lucas and Guy particularly persuasive, and we adopt Guy's limitation on recovery to persons who are named in the estate planning document or otherwise identified in the instrument by their status (e.g., my children and grandchildren, my wife's children).

One court that still retains strict privity, but struggled greatly in doing so, is particularly notable for a vigorous joint dissent in which the justices pointedly remarked:

> With an obscure reference to "the greater good," [ ] the Court unjustifiably insulates an entire class of negligent lawyers from the consequences of their wrongdoing, and unjustly denies legal recourse to the grandchildren for whose benefit Ms. Barcelo hired a lawyer in the first place....

...

> ... [T]he Court's decision means that, as a practical matter, no one has the right to sue for the lawyer's negligent frustration of the testator's intent. A flaw in a will or other testamentary document is not likely to be discovered until the client's death. And, generally, the estate suffers no harm from a negligently drafted testamentary document.

Barcelo v. Elliott, 923 S.W.2d 575, 579–80 (Tex. 1996) (Cornyn & Abbott, JJ., dissenting) (citations and footnotes omitted). The justices asserted the majority "gives no consideration to the fair adjustment of the loss between the parties, one of the traditional objectives of tort law," and "[t]hese grounds for the imposition of a legal duty in tort law generally, which apply to lawyers in every other context, are no less important in estate planning." *Id.* at 580. We agree with these observations and find there are compelling policy reasons supporting recognition of these claims.

IV. Conclusion

We recognize a cause of action, in both tort and contract, by a third-party beneficiary of an existing will or estate planning document against a lawyer whose drafting error defeats or diminishes the client's intent. Recovery under either cause of action is limited to persons who are named in the estate planning document or otherwise identified in the instrument by their status. Where the claim sounds in both tort and contract, the plaintiff may elect a recovery. We apply this holding in the instant appeal and to cases pending on appeal as of the date of this opinion. As a result, we reverse the order dismissing Appellant's complaint and remand the matter to the circuit court for further proceedings consistent with this opinion.

Reversed and Remanded.

JUSTICE JOHN W. KITTREDGE, CONCURRING

I concur in the majority opinion except as may concern the applicable burden of proof, which is not addressed in the majority opinion. I agree with Justice Pleicones that the burden of proof should be the clear and convincing standard.

JUSTICE COSTA M. PLEICONES, CONCURRING

I agree with the majority that we should recognize a cause of action for legal malpractice brought on behalf of a person in Appellant's position. As I believe this cause of action should properly sound only in tort, I write separately. Further, I would hold that a decision should only apply prospectively, but that Appellant may pursue her claim to finality under the guidelines announced today.

I agree that public policy considerations dictate a relaxation of the strict privity requirement for purposes of asserting a legal malpractice claim against an attorney who drafts an estate planning document. *See Russo v. Sutton*, 422 S.E.2d 750, 753 (S.C. 1992) ("We have not hesitated to act in the past when it has become apparent that the public policy of the State is offended by outdated rules of law."); *see also Auric v. Continental Cas. Co.*, 331 N.W.2d 325, 329 (Wis. 1983) (relaxing the requirement of strict privity in the context of a legal malpractice action based on public policy considerations because the possibility of liability for negligent drafting of an estate planning instrument is one way to make an attorney accountable for his negligence). Likewise, I agree that an attorney owes a duty only to a beneficiary named in an estate planning instrument or identified as such by status in the instrument. *See Lucas v. Hamm*, 364 P.2d 685, 687 (Cal. 1961) (stating the policy reasons, such as the foreseeability of harm to the named-beneficiary, that support the imposition of a duty); *see also* Restatement (Third) of the Law Governing Lawyers § 51(3)(a) (2000) (stating a lawyer owes a duty to a non-client when "the lawyer knows that a client intends as one of the primary objectives of the representation that the lawyer's services benefit the non-client"). Thus, I agree that Appellant may assert a legal malpractice claim against Respondent based on Respondent's status as a named beneficiary in the trust instrument.

I also write separately as I would require a beneficiary asserting such a legal malpractice claim to prove by clear and convincing evidence that the attorney breached the duty owed to the beneficiary, and the beneficiary suffered damages which were proximately caused by the attorney's breach. *See* S.C. Code Ann. § 62-2-601(B) (Supp. 2013) (noting the burden of proof is clear and convincing evidence in a will reformation action); *see, e.g., Pivnick v. Beck*, 762 A.2d 653, 654 (N.J. 2000) (adopting the clear and convincing burden of proof when a non-client brings a legal malpractice claim on the basis that a lawyer was negligent in drafting an estate planning document).

I respectfully differ from the majority's recognition of a breach of contract action based on a beneficiary's supposed status as a third-party beneficiary. While I acknowledge, as the majority sets forth in great detail, that many jurisdictions recognize a breach of contract action on this basis,[1] I would rely on precedent from this Court and find that a legal mal-practice action, which is a form of professional negligence brought by a third-party who lacks privity, sounds only in tort. *See Tommy L. Griffin Plumbing & Heating Co. v. Jordan, Jones & Goulding, Inc.*, 463 S.E.2d 85, 88 (S.C. 1995) (finding a professional negligence action sounds in tort). Moreover, while I agree with the majority that evidence extrinsic to the four corners of the estate planning instrument is admissible to prove whether a lawyer breached his duty in drafting the instrument, I believe characterizing such evidence as "extrinsic" in a legal malpractice context is a misnomer because the evidence sought to be admitted does not "relate to a contract."[2]

Finally, I disagree with allowing "cases pending on appeal as of the date of the opinion" the opportunity to pursue a legal malpractice action in this context. Instead, I would hold that while Appellant may pursue her claim to finality, our decision should only apply prospectively. *See Toth v. Square D Co.*, 377 S.E.2d 584, 586–87 (S.C. 1989) ("Prospective application is required when liability is created where formerly none existed."). I would allow Appellant the benefit of pursuing her claim because our decision today recognizes a duty that has been foreshadowed by this Court. *See Rydde v. Morris*, 675 S.E.2d 431, 433 (S.C. 2009) (noting, albeit in dicta, that generally an attorney owes a duty to a non-client intended beneficiary of an executed will where it is shown that the testator's intent has been defeated or diminished by negligence on the part of the attorney, resulting in loss to the beneficiary); *see also* Joan Teshima, Annotation, *Attorney's Liability, to One Other Than Immediate Client, for Negligence in Connection with Legal Duties*, 61 A.L.R.4th 615 (1988 & Supp. 2014) (compiling cases from a majority of jurisdictions recognizing that an estate planning attorney may be liable to a beneficiary named or one identified as such by her status in an estate planning instrument).

Whether Appellant can prevail on her legal malpractice claim is a question for the fact finder and is one in which we do not answer today. Therefore, I concur with the majority's reversal of the circuit court's Rule 12(b)(6) dismissal because Appellant has stated a viable cause of action in tort based on Respondent's purportedly negligent drafting of the trust instrument.

Charles Dickens, Bleak House

(1853)

London. Michaelmas Term lately over, and the Lord Chancellor sitting in Lincoln's Inn Hall. Implacable November weather. As much mud in the streets, as if the waters had but newly retired from the face of the earth, and it would not be wonderful to meet a Megalosaurus, forty feet long or so, waddling like an elephantine lizard up Holburn Hill. Smoke lowering down from chimney-pots, making a soft black drizzle, with flakes of soot in it as big as full-grown snow-flakes — gone into mourning, one might imagine, for the death of the sun. Dogs, undistinguishable in mire. Horses, scarcely better; splashed to their very blinkers. Foot passengers, jostling one another's umbrellas, in a general infection of ill-temper, and losing their foothold at street-corners, where tens of thousands of other foot passengers have been slipping and sliding since the day broke (if this day

----

1. *See, e.g.,* Lucas, 364 P.2d at 689.
2. *See* Black's Law Dictionary 637 (9th ed. 2009) (defining extrinsic evidence as evidence "relating to a contract but not appearing on the face of the contract because it comes from other sources, such as statements between the parties or the circumstances surrounding the agreement").

ever broke), adding new deposits to the crust upon crust of mud, sticking at those points tenaciously to the pavement, and accumulating at compound interest.

Fog everywhere. Fog up the river, where it flows among green aits and meadows; fog down the river, where it rolls defiled among the tiers of shipping, and the waterside pollutions of a great (and dirty) city. Fog on the Essex marshes, fog on the Kentish heights. Fog creeping into the cabooses of collier-brigs; fog lying out on the yards, and hovering in the rigging of great ships; fog drooping on the gunwales of barges and small boats. Fog in the eyes and throats of ancient Greenwich pensioners, wheezing by the firesides of their wards; fog in the stem and bowl of the afternoon pipe of the wrathful skipper, down in his close cabin; fog cruelly pinching the toes and fingers of his shivering little 'prentice boy on deck. Chance people on the bridges peeping over the parapets into a nether sky of fog, with fog all round them, as if they were up in a balloon, and hanging in the misty clouds.

. . .

On such an afternoon, if ever, the Lord High Chancellor ought to be sitting here—as here he is—with a foggy glory round his head, softly fenced in with crimson cloth and curtains, addressed by a large advocate with great whiskers, a little voice, and an interminable brief, and outwardly directing his contemplation to the lantern in the roof, where he can see nothing but fog. On such an afternoon, some score of members of the High Court of Chancery bar ought to be—as here they are—mistily engaged in one of the ten thousand stages of an endless cause, tripping one another up on slippery precedents, groping knee-deep in technicalities, running their goat-hair and horse-hair warded heads against walls of words, and making a pretense of equity with serious faces, as players might. On such an afternoon, the various solicitors in the cause, some two or three of whom have inherited it from their fathers, who made a fortune by it, ought to be—as are they not?—ranged in a line, in a long matted well (but you might look in vain for Truth at the bottom of it), between the registrar's red table and the silk gowns, with bills, cross-bills, answers, rejoinders, injunctions, affidavits, issues, references to masters, masters' reports, mountains of costly nonsense, piled before them. Well may the court be dim, with wasting candles here and there, well may the fog hang heavy in it, as if it would never get out; well may the stained glass windows lose their colour, and admit no light of day into the place; well may the uninitiated from the streets, who peep in through the glass panes in the door, be deterred from entrance by its owlish aspect, and by the drawl languidly echoing to the roof from the padded dais where the Lord High Chancellor looks into the lantern that has no light in it, and where the attendant wigs are all stuck in a fog-bank! This is the Court of Chancery; which has its decaying houses and its blighted lands in every shire; which has its worn-out lunatic in every madhouse, and its dead in every churchyard; which has its ruined suitor, with his slipshod heels and threadbare dress, borrowing and begging through the round of every man's acquaintance; which gives to monied might the means abundantly of wearying out the right; which so exhausts finances, patience, courage, hope; so overthrows the brain and breaks the heart; that there is not an honourable man among its practitioners who would not give—who does not often give—the warning, "Suffer any wrong that can be done you rather than come here!"

Who happen to be in the Lord Chancellor's court this murky afternoon besides the Lord Chancellor, the counsel in the cause, two or three counsel who are never in any cause, and the well of solicitors before mentioned? There is the registrar below the Judge, in wig and gown; and there are two or three maces, or petty-bags, or privy purses, or whatever they may be, in legal court suits. These are all yawning; for no crumb of amusement ever falls from *Jarndyce and Jarndyce* (the cause in hand), which was squeezed dry years upon years ago. The short-hand writers, the reporters of the court, and the reporters of newspapers, invariably decamp with the rest of the regulars when *Jarndyce and Jarndyce* comes on. Their places are a blank. Standing on a seat at the side of the hall, the better to peer into the curtained sanctuary, is a little mad old woman in a squeezed bonnet, who is always in court, from its sitting to its rising, and always expecting some incomprehensible judgment to be given in her favour. Some say she really is, or was, a party to a suit; but no one knows for certain, because no one cares. She carries some small litter in a reticule which she calls her documents; principally consisting of paper matches and dry lavender. A sallow prisoner has come up, in custody, for the half-dozenth time, to make a personal application "to purge himself of his contempt;" which, being a solitary surviving executor who has fallen into a state of conglomeration about accounts of which it is not pretended that he had ever any knowledge, he is not at all likely ever to do. In the meantime his prospects in life are ended....

Jarndyce and Jarndyce drones on. This scarecrow of a suit has, in course of time, become so complicated, that no man alive knows what it means. The parties understand it least; but it has been observed that no two Chancery lawyers can talk about it for five minutes, without coming to a total disagreement as to all the premises. Innumerable children have been born into the cause; innumerable young people have married into it; innumerable old people have died out of it. Scores of persons have deliriously found themselves made parties in *Jarndyce and Jarndyce*, without knowing how or why; whole families have inherited legendary hatreds with the suit.

B. Assignment of Rights and Delegation of Duties (and "Assignment of a Contract")

1. Assignment of Rights

The doctrine of assignment rests on the idea that contract rights are analogous to items of tangible property. As one leading decision announced: "Henceforth in all Courts a debt must be regarded as a piece of property capable of legal assignment in the same sense as a bale of goods." *Fitzroy v. Cave*, 2 K.B. 364 (1905). If a contract right is property, then it can be bought, sold, or given away. An "assignment" is a contract in which an existing contract right is transferred. Other rights also can be assigned, including rights under some licenses and permits, and rights in legal claims.

Yet the idea that a contract right is a piece of property, subject to transfer, has been hotly debated. During the seventeenth, eighteenth, and nineteenth centuries, many maintained that the assignment of contract rights is an injustice that the law ought not sanction. Lord Coke was an influential proponent of this view; he wrote:

> And first was observed the great wisdom and policy of the sages and founders of our law, who have provided, that no possibility, right, title, nor thing in action, shall be granted or assigned to strangers, for that would be the course of multiplying of contentions and suits, of great oppression of the people, and chiefly of terre-tenents, and the subversion of the due and equal execution of justice.

Lord Coke, *Lampert's Case*, 10 Coke, 46b (1612). The subversion of justice Lord Coke feared flows from the substitution of creditors without the debtor's consent. This view maintains that debt is a personal relationship that involves an imbalance of power and a serious risk of abuse, and a debtor should be able to choose the person to whom he or she becomes indebted. It does matter, some argue, whether one is indebted to one's trusted friend, an unscrupulous bully, or an indifferent institution.

This view prevailed in common law courts throughout the seventeenth and most of the eighteenth centuries. Yet during this period, Chancery judges did enforce assignments of rights and under their authority, assignment came to be an important component in credit transactions. By the end of the nineteenth century, the credit industry had taken root, and all courts were pressured to give effect to assignment as a financing tool. The "transfer of debt" came to be viewed as a foundation for modern economic development. Professor Macleod wrote with the extravagance of the nineteenth century middle-class:

> If we were asked — Who made the discovery which has most deeply affected the fortunes of the human race? We think, after full consideration, we might safely answer — The man who first discovered that a Debt is a Saleable Commodity.

1 Henry Macleod, Principles of Economical Philosophy 481 (2d ed. 1872).

Evening News Association v. Peterson

United States District Court for the District of Columbia
477 F. Supp. 77 (1979)

BARRINGTON D. PARKER, DISTRICT JUDGE

The question presented in this litigation is whether a contract of employment between an employee and the owner and licensee of a television station, providing for the employee's services as a newscaster-anchorman, was assigned when the station was sold and acquired by a new owner and licensee.

Plaintiff Evening News Association (Evening News) a Michigan Corporation, acquired station WDVM-TV (Channel 9) a District of Columbia television station from Post-Newsweek Stations, Inc. (Post-Newsweek) in June of 1978. At that time, the defendant Gordon Peterson was and had been employed for several years as a newscaster-anchorman by Post-Newsweek. This defendant is a citizen of the State of Maryland. The plaintiff claims that Peterson's employment contract was assignable without the latter's consent, was indeed assigned, and thus otherwise enforceable. The defendant contends, however, that his Post-Newsweek contract required him to perform unique and unusual services and because of the personal relationship he had with Post-Newsweek the contract was not assignable.

Mr. Peterson was employed by the plaintiff for more than one year after the acquisition and received the compensation and all benefits provided by the Post-Newsweek contract. In early August, 1979, he tendered his resignation to the plaintiff. At that time the defendant had negotiated an employment contract with a third television station located in the District of Columbia, a competitor of the plaintiff. The Evening News then sued Peterson, seeking a declaration of the rights and legal relations of the parties under the contract and permanent injunctive relief against the defendant.

Following an accelerated briefing schedule and an expedited bench trial on the merits, the Court concludes that the contract was assignable and that Evening News is entitled to appropriate permanent injunctive relief against the defendant Gordon Peterson.

In accordance with Rule 52(a) Fed. R. Civ. P., the Court's findings of fact and conclusions of law in support of that determination are set forth.

Findings of Fact

The defendant was employed by Post-Newsweek Stations, Inc. from 1969 to 1978. During that period he negotiated several employment contracts. Post-Newsweek had a license to operate television station WTOP-TV (Channel 9) in the District of Columbia. In June of 1978, following approval by the Federal Communications Commission, Post-Newsweek sold its operating license to Evening News and Channel 9 was then designated WDVM-TV. A June 26, 1978, Bill of Sale and Assignment and Instrument of Assumption and Indemnity between the two provided in pertinent part:

> PNS has granted, bargained, sold, conveyed and assigned to ENA, ... all the property of PNS ... including, ... all right, title and interest, legal or equitable, of PNS in, to and under all agreements, contracts and commitments listed in Schedule A hereto....

When Evening News acquired the station, Peterson's Post-Newsweek employment contract, dated July 1, 1977, was included in the Bill of Sale and Assignment. The contract was for a three-year term ending June 30, 1980, and could be extended for two additional one-year terms, at the option of Post-Newsweek. The significant and relevant duties and obligations under that contract required Peterson:

> to render services as a news anchorman, and to perform such related services as news gathering, writing and reporting, and the organization and preparation of program material, to the extent required by the Stations, as are consistent with (his) primary responsibility as a news anchorman.... (To participate) personally as a newsman, announcer, on-the-air personality or other performer in any news, public affairs, documentary, news analysis, interview, special events or other program or segment of any program, designated by ... and to the extent required by the Stations ... as may reasonably be required by the Stations....

As compensation the defendant was to receive a designated salary which increased each year from 1977 through the fifth (option) year. Post-Newsweek was also obligated to provide additional benefits including term life insurance valued at his 1977 base salary, disability insurance, an annual clothing allowance and benefits to which he was entitled as provided in an underlying collective bargaining agreement with the American Federation of Television and Radio Artists.

There was no express provision in the 1977 contract concerning its assignability or nonassignability. However, it contained the following integration clause: "This agreement contains the entire understanding of the parties ... and this agreement cannot be altered or modified except in a writing signed by both parties."

A.

Aside from the various undisputed documents and exhibits admitted into evidence, there were sharp conflicts in testimony concerning various events and what was said and done by the parties and their representatives, both before and after the Evening News' acquisition. As trier of fact, having heard and seen the several witnesses testify and after assessing and determining their credibility, the Court makes the following additional findings.

The defendant's duties, obligations and performance under the 1977 contract did not change in any significant way after the Evening News' acquisition. In addition, the Evening News met all of its required contract obligations to the defendant and its performance after acquisition in June, 1978, was not materially different from that of Post-Newsweek.

Mr. Peterson testified that he had "almost a family relationship" with James Snyder, News Director, and John Baker, Executive Producer, for Post-Newsweek, which permitted and promoted a free exchange of ideas, frank expressions of dissent and criticism and open lines of communication. These men left Channel 9 when Post-Newsweek relinquished its license, and they have since been replaced by Evening News personnel. According to Mr. Peterson, the close relationship and rapport which existed between him and them was an important factor as he viewed the contract; these relationships made the contract in his view nonassignable and indeed their absence at the Evening News prevented defendant from contributing his full efforts. Even if Mr. Peterson's contentions are accepted, it should be noted that he contracted with the Post-Newsweek corporation and not with the News Director and Executive Producer of that corporation. Indeed, the 1977 contract makes no reference to either officer, except to provide that vacations should be scheduled and coordinated through the News Director. Had the defendant intended to condition his performance on his continued ability to work with Snyder and Baker, one would have expected the contract to reflect that condition.

The close, intimate and personal relationship which Mr. Peterson points to as characterizing his association with Post-Newsweek and its personnel, was highly subjective and was supported only by his testimony. The Court cannot find that Peterson contracted with Post-Newsweek in 1977 to work with particular individuals or because of a special policy-making role he had been selected to perform in the newsroom. For the fourteen-month period of Peterson's employment at the Evening News, there is no showing that he was in any way circumscribed, limited in his work or otherwise disadvantaged in his performance. Nor is there any credible evidence that the News Director or other top personnel of Evening News were rigid, inflexible, warded off any of Mr. Peterson's criticisms or even that at any time he gave suggestions and criticisms which were ignored or rejected. Finally, the Court does not find that Post-Newsweek contracted with Peterson because of any peculiarly unique qualities or because of a relationship of personal confidence with him.

B.

In his direct testimony, Mr. Peterson expressed a degree of disappointment because of Evening News' failure to keep apace with advances in technology and to seize opportunities for live in-depth coverage of current events. He characterized the plaintiff's news coverage as "less aggressive" than what he had experienced with Post-Newsweek.

On cross-examination, however, he was shown an exhibit comparing the broadcast of special assignments reported and produced by him for two one-year periods, one before and one after the June, 1978 acquisition. While he admitted to its accuracy with some reservation, the exhibit clearly showed that a comparable number of such assignments of similar quality, were broadcast within the two years. He also conceded that for the same period Evening News received two Peabody awards, an award for best editorials, and a number of Emmy awards for public affairs exceeding those received in prior years by Post-Newsweek. Finally, he acknowledged that Channel 9 still maintained the highest ratings for audience viewing among the television stations in the Washington, D.C. market area.

A great amount of testimony was generated as to when Peterson learned of the Evening News' acquisition and what then occurred relative to the assignment of the contract. The testimony on this issue was conflicting, largely cumulative and as now viewed, over-emphasized by the parties. The Court finds that the defendant gained first knowledge of a possible sale and transfer of the station in December, 1977. At that time, the president of Post-Newsweek publicly announced to the station's employees, including Peterson, that an agreement in principle had been reached, subject to approval by the Federal Communications Commission. At no time from December, 1977, until December, 1978, did the defendant or his attorney ever indicate or venture an opinion that the contract was not assignable. Indeed, through at least April, 1979, the defendant's attorney made representations that assignment of the contract presented no problem to his client.

In summary, the Court finds that the performance required of Mr. Peterson under the 1977 contract was (1) not based upon a personal relationship or one of special confidence between him and Post-Newsweek or its employees, and (2) was not changed in any material way by the assignment to the Evening News.

Conclusions of Law

There is diversity of citizenship; the amount in controversy exceeds $10,000; and the Court has jurisdiction over this proceeding by virtue of 28 U.S.C. § 1332.

A.

The distinction between the assignment of a right to receive services and the obligation to provide them is critical in this proceeding. This is so because duties under a personal services contract involving special skill or ability are generally not delegable by the one obligated to perform, absent the consent of the other party. The issue, however, is not whether the personal services Peterson is to perform are delegable but whether Post-Newsweek's right to receive them is assignable.

Contract rights as a general rule are assignable. *Munchak Corp. v. Cunningham*, 457 F.2d 721 (4th Cir. 1972); *Meyer v. Washington Times Co.*, 76 F.2d 988 (D.C. Cir.) *cert. denied* 295 U.S. 734 (1935); 4 A. Corbin, Contracts § 865 (1951); Restatement (First) of Contracts § 151 (1932). This rule, however, is subject to exception where the assignment would vary materially the duty of the obligor, increase materially the burden of risk imposed by the contract, or impair materially the obligor's chance of obtaining return performance. Corbin § 868; Restatement § 152. There has been no showing, however, that the services required of Peterson by the Post-Newsweek contract have changed in any material way since the Evening News entered the picture. Both before and after, he anchored the same news programs. Similarly he has had essentially the same number of special assignments since the transfer as before. Any additional policy-making role that he formerly enjoyed and is now denied was neither a condition of his contract nor factually supported by other than his own subjective testimony.

The general rule of assignability is also subject to exception where the contract calls for the rendition of personal services based on a relationship of confidence between the parties. *Munchak*, 457 F.2d at 725; *Meyer*, 64 App. D.C. at 219, 76 F.2d at 989. As Corbin has explained this limitation on assignment:

> In almost all cases where a "contract" is said to be non-assignable because it is "personal," what is meant is not that the contractor's right is not assignable, but that the performance required by his duty is a personal performance and that an attempt to perform by a substituted person would not discharge the contractor's duty.

Corbin § 865. In *Munchak*, the Court concluded that a basketball player's personal services contract could be assigned by the owner of the club to a new owner, despite a contractual prohibition on assignment to another club, on the basis that the services were to the club. The Court found it "inconceivable" that the player's services "could be affected by the personalities of successive corporate owners." 457 F.2d at 725. The policy against the assignment of personal service contracts, as the Court noted, "is to prohibit an assignment of a contract in which the obligor undertakes to serve only the original obligee." 457 F.2d at 726.

Given the silence of the contract on assignability, its merger clause, and the usual rule that contract rights are assignable, the Court cannot but conclude on the facts of this case that defendant's contract was assignable. Mr. Peterson's contract with Post-Newsweek gives no hint that he was to perform as other than a newscaster-anchorman for their stations. Nor is there any hint that he was to work with particular Post-Newsweek employees or was assured a policy-making role in concert with any given employees. Defendant's employer was a corporation, and it was for Post-Newsweek Stations, Inc. that he contracted to perform. The corporation's duties under the contract did not involve the rendition of personal services to defendant; essentially they were to compensate him. Nor does the contract give any suggestion of a relation of special confidence between the two or that defendant was expected to serve the Post-Newsweek stations only so long as the latter had the license for them.

B.

As noted, the 1977 contract contained a clause providing that the entire understanding between the parties was contained within the four corners of the agreement. The contract contains no provision relating to assignment. The defendant's counsel asserts, however, that an ambiguity exists and he therefore seeks to introduce certain exhibits and other extrinsic evidence for purposes of explaining and discerning the intentions of the parties. Specifically, he seeks to introduce four documents: an earlier 1973 contract; a draft of a proposed 1974 contract; the final 1974 contract; and a letter of 1975 from the president of Post-Newsweek to the defendant. The Court reserved decision on admissibility of the exhibits and now rules that they are inadmissible for the purposes intended by the defendant. The 1977 contract makes no reference to any prior agreements, to any negotiations between the parties, or specifically to the four proffered exhibits. To make use of them to show the intention of the parties in 1977, or to show what happened in past contract negotiations, simply asks too much.

The Court does not share the defendant's belief that silence on the issue of assignability creates ambiguity, and he fails to provide any legal authority to warrant such an inference. An unsupported assertion that ambiguity exists is insufficient to give a different meaning to a contract when there is in fact no contractual provision. For the Court to accept the defendant's exhibits in an effort to explain the parties' intent would modify and enlarge the provisions of the agreement and bestow upon the defendant an advantage which he did not originally have. The law of this Circuit is clearly set forth in *Clayman v. Goodman Properties, Inc.*, 518 F.2d 1026, 1033 (D.C. Cir. 1973), where Circuit Judge Robinson said in part:

> [W]e perceive no basis for resort to evidence depicting the circumstances surrounding the making of the contract before us. We need do little more than reiterate that [t]he parol evidence rule requires that "[w]hen two parties have made a contract and have expressed it in a writing to which they have both assented as the complete and accurate integration of that contract, evidence, whether parol or otherwise, of antecedent understandings and negotiations will not be admitted for the purpose of varying or contradicting the writing."

The consequences which the law attaches to a written contract are as much a part of it as the terms it sets forth, and the legal effect of the contract can no more be changed or modified by parol evidence than it could have had it been made express.

The contract before the Court, as the agreement in *Clayman*, contains a merger clause stating that the contract embodies the final and exclusive understanding of the parties. Such a stipulation is given full effect in this jurisdiction absent the Court's finding of any ambiguity in the contract. *Lee v. Flintkote Co.*, 593 F.2d 1275, 1281 (D.C. Cir. 1979).

C.

Plaintiff's argument that defendant has waived any objection to the assignment by accepting the contract benefits and continuing to perform for the Evening News for over a year has perhaps some merit. If defendant has doubts about assignability, he should have voiced them when he learned of the planned transfer or at least at the time of transfer. His continued performance without reservation followed by the unanticipated tender of his resignation did disadvantage Evening News in terms of finding a possible replacement for him and possibly in lost revenues. The Court, however, concludes that the contract was assignable in the first instance and thus it is not necessary to determine whether defendant's continued performance constitutes a waiver of objection to the assignment.

During the course of this trial Edwin W. Pfeiffer, an executive officer of WDVM-TV, testified that Mr. Peterson allegedly stated "if the Judge decides I should stay, I will stay." Assuming that he did not overstate Mr. Peterson's position and that Mr. Peterson was quoted in appropriate context, the television audience of the Washington, D.C. metropolitan area should anticipate his timely reappearance as news anchorman for station WDVM-TV. Of course, the avenue of appeal is always available.

An order consistent with this Memorandum Opinion will be entered. Counsel for the plaintiff shall submit immediately an appropriate order.

Note

Assignments of accounts receivable (money due from customers to whom credit has been granted) are involved in several common commercial financing arrangements. In one version, the accounts are sold to a financial institution at a discount (an amount somewhat less than the principal amount due under the accounts). Sometimes the merchant continues to collect payments from customers and then turns them over to the financial institution; sometimes the customers are told to make payments directly to the assignee. In some such arrangements, the sales of accounts are "with recourse," meaning that the merchant will pay the financial institution if a customer fails to pay; in others the sale is "without recourse," meaning that the financial institution will assume the risk of nonpayment by a customer. Generally, a sale without recourse will be at a much lower price than a sale with recourse. In another financing arrangement, the financial institution loans money to the merchant, taking an assignment of accounts receivable as *security* against a possible default in repayment by the merchant.

The importance granted assignments of contract rights in current law is most evident in the treatment of contract clauses that purport to *prohibit* assignments. Regarding rights to money for goods sold or leased or for services rendered, Uniform Commercial Code section 9-406(c) provides that any attempt to restrict the right to assign such contract rights is ineffective. By this provision, the Uniform Commercial Code gives greater weight to maintaining the credit industry than to traditional concerns of contractual freedom. For assignments of other contract rights, Uniform Commercial Code section 2-210(3) and Restatement (Second) of Contracts, section 322(1) provide that a contract term that purports to restrict assignment of "the contract" is to be construed as barring only a delegation of duties, not an assignment of rights.

There are few significant limitations on assignment of contract rights. Some states and federal laws limit assignments of wages by employees and assignments of rights to payment under contracts with the United States government. Proponents of these legislative limitations argue they are necessary to protect employers and the U.S. government from the difficulties and hardships that result from assignment of debt, to which other obligors are exposed. And, in contrast to the result in *Evening News Association*, some states bar assignment of a non-compete clause in an employment contract unless the employee consents to the assignment.

If a contract right is validly assigned, then the assignee has the right to insist that the obligor direct performance of the contract to him or her. Until notified of the assignment, the obligor may continue to perform as before, but once notified that performance should be redirected, an obligor is in breach of contract if he or she fails to comply. The assignee's rights under the contract are subject to any defenses available against the assignor that arose prior to the assignment (that is, the assignee *stands in the shoes* of the assignor at the time of the assignment). *See* Restatement (Second) of Contracts, section 336. In some contracts, an obligor waives his or her right to assert defenses against an assignee. The purpose of this waiver is to make the assignment more valuable to potential assignees. Under the Uniform Commercial Code, such a waiver is effective to prevent the obligor from asserting a defense if the assignee purchases the contract right without knowledge of the defense, *see* Uniform Commercial Code § 9-403. In consumer transactions, however, such waivers are prohibited by a regulation promulgated by the Federal Trade Commission and by many state consumer protection statutes. *See, e.g.,* General Statutes of North Carolina § 25A-25 (Preservation of consumers' claims and defenses); *see also* Uniform Consumer Credit Code § 3-307.

Equico Lessors, Inc., etc. v. A. Moneim Ramadan, M.D., etc.

First District Court of Appeal of Florida
493 So. 2d 516 (1986)

Edward T. Barfield, Judge

Equico Lessors appeals a final judgment rendered for Ramadan in Equico's action to enforce an equipment lease assigned to Equico by the original lessor. The trial court determined that there was a sufficiently close connection between Equico, as assignee, and the assignor of the lease so as to set aside the lease's waiver of defenses clause, allowing Ramadan, the lessee, to assert breach of warranty claims against Equico. We disagree and reverse.

On November 14, 1980, Ramadan signed a lease with Hastings Capital Corporation for a computerized energy management system for his Gainesville office building. The unit was manufactured by a subsidiary of Hastings and was installed by a Gainesville heating and cooling company. Hastings claimed the system would reduce the building's electricity consumption.

Prior to execution of the lease, Equico conducted a credit check on Ramadan after Hastings approached Equico about a future assignment of the yet-to-be executed lease. Equico also set the financial terms of the lease. Ten days after Ramadan signed the lease, Hastings Capital assigned the lease to Equico. This was effected by completion of a pre-printed assignment clause that named Equico as the assignee. Ramadan's personal guaranty of the lease was also assigned to Equico by execution of a pre-printed assignment clause, which again named Equico as assignee.

The lease contained a waiver of defenses clause as to any assignee of the lease.[1] The clause provided that an assignee would be free of all defenses or claims Ramadan, as lessee, may have against Hastings Capital, as lessor.

The expected series of horribles followed. The leased equipment failed to perform and repeated attempts to repair it were unsuccessful. According to Ramadan, the system not only failed to save any energy, it resulted in greater energy use. One year after signing the lease, Ramadan had the equipment removed by the installer and stopped making lease payments. Hastings Capital and its subsidiary went out of business. Equico then brought this suit against Ramadan for the balance of the payments due on the lease. Ramadan raised the defenses of misrepresentation and of failure of consideration and counterclaimed on a breach of warranty.

Equico initially obtained summary judgment, claiming the waiver of defenses clause precluded Ramadan's defenses. On appeal, this court reversed the summary judgment, finding that there was a question of fact as to whether Equico was so closely connected to Hastings Capital, the original lessor, or to the transaction as to deny Equico the benefits of the waiver of defenses clause. *Ramadan v. Equico Lessors*, Inc., 448 So. 2d 60 (Fla. Dist. Ct. App. 1984).

The case proceeded to trial. Equico's assistant vice president testified while it supplied the printed forms used to execute the lease, there was no prior agreement that the lease would indeed be assigned to Equico. Equico assumed the lease would be assigned and prepared the lease and related documents on that assumption. Ramadan testified he did not know Equico was a potential party to the lease until he signed the lease. However, he had been contacted by Equico during the credit check.

The trial court rendered judgment for Ramadan. It found that there was a sufficiently close connection between Equico and Hastings Capital to preclude Equico from taking the lease as a holder in due course and asserting the waiver of defenses clause against Ramadan. The court found the consideration of the lease failed and Equico could not recover the balance of the lease payments. Ramadan was allowed to recover on his counterclaim in the amount of the lease payments he had made.

Florida's *Uniform Commercial Code* contains a provision that validates waiver of defenses clauses in contracts or leases.[2] The purpose of this statutory provision is to treat the assignee like a holder in due course of a negotiable instrument. *See* 19C Fla. Stat. Ann. 240, (1966), Uniform Commercial Code Comment. Such clauses are designed to facilitate financing of transactions by insulating an innocent or unknowing purchaser of the contract,

---

1. Paragraph 17 of the lease stated:
   It is understood that Lessor contemplates assigning this Agreement, and that said assignee may assign the same. All rights of Lessor in the equipment and hereunder may be assigned, pledged, mortgaged, transferred, or otherwise disposed of, either in whole or in part, without notice to Lessee. The assignee's rights shall be free from all defenses, set-offs or counterclaims which Lessee may be entitled to assert against Lessor. No such assignee shall be obligated to perform any duty, covenant or condition required to be performed by Lessor under the terms of this Agreement.
2. Section 679.206, Florida Statutes, provides that:
   (1) Subject to any statute or decision which establishes a different rule for buyers or lessees of consumer goods, an agreement by a buyer or lessee that he will not assert against an assignee any claim or defense which he may have against the seller or lessor is enforceable by an assignee who takes his assignment for value, in good faith and without notice of a claim or defense, except as to the defense of a type which may be asserted against a holder in due course of a negotiable instrument under the chapter on commercial paper.

lease or financing note from disputes over the underlying transaction. Such clauses reduce the risk to assignees in taking such assignments and thereby encourage the financing of transactions by assuring a market for those wishing to assign contracts and leases.

However, because of the great protection such a clause gives an assignee, such as Equico, it is only valid when the assignment is taken for value, in good faith and without knowledge of a defense or claim. *Leasing Service Corp. v. River City Construction, Inc.*, 743 F.2d 871 (11th Cir. 1984). The close connection doctrine acts as an evidentiary rule by which the good faith of an assignee is tested. *Are v. Barnett Bank of Miami Beach, NA*, 330 So. 2d 250 (Fla. Dist. Ct. App. 1976). It is not a rule of law that says if a close connection appears, then the assignee will be denied the benefit of a waiver of defenses clause. In a commercial setting, more than just a close connection must be shown before an assignee will be denied the status of a holder in due course under § 679.206(1), Florida Statutes.

Courts have applied this test in cases involving both consumer and commercial transactions. *See, Are v. Barnett Bank of Miami Beach, N.A.*, 330 So. 2d 250 (Fla. Dist. Ct. App. 1976) (close connection not found in assignment of installment sale contract on motor home used in business.); *Rehurek v. Chrysler Credit Corp.*, 262 So. 2d 452 (Fla. 2d D.C.A. 1972) (close connection found between assignee and assignor in assignment of installment sales contract for consumer purchase of automobile); *First New England Financial Corp. v. Woffard*, 421 So. 2d 590 (Fla. Dist. Ct. App. 1982) (close connection found in consumer purchase of yacht). However, the courts have been more protective of consumers when enforcing such clauses than of business parties.

In *Are v. Barnett Bank*, 330 So. 2d at 250, the court refused to find the assignee bank had not taken the assignment in good faith. There the buyer had purchased on an installment sales contract a motor home for use in his business. The contract was assigned to the bank. The buyer refused to continue payments after one year. The court held the facts showed that the bank as financier was not closely connected to the seller when the contract was assigned. Further, the bank was not an integral part of the selling dealer's business operations. Thus there was no question of fact that the bank did not purchase the contract in good faith nor with notice of the purchaser's claims of defects.

Courts in other jurisdictions also require a greater showing of close connection between the assignee and the assignor and the underlying commercial transaction before invalidating a particular waiver of defenses clause. In *Leasing Service Corp. v. River City Construction Inc.*, 743 F.2d at 871, the 11th Circuit said the defendant needed to show the assignee's knowledge of the seller's fraudulent acts or its significant participation in the original transaction. The assignee's supplying the forms for the underlying lease was not sufficient as such a practice was common in commercial transactions.[3]

In *Equico Lessors, Inc. v. Rockville Reminder, Inc.*, 492 A.2d 528 (Conn. App. Ct. 1985), Equico Lessors (the appellant in the instant case) was denied the protection of a waiver of defenses clause upon a showing that Equico had knowledge of the guarantee which the commercial lessee alleged was breached. The facts of that case are strikingly similar to the instant case. The transaction involved the lease of energy saving equipment with a guarantee of minimum savings in electric bills. Equico supplied pre-printed forms for the transaction with assignment clauses showing Equico as assignee. Equico's employees explained how the forms were to be completed and were present when the guarantee of

---

3. Walter E. Heller & Co. v. Convalescent Home of the First Church of Deliverance, 365 N.E.2d 1285 (Ill. App. 1977); ITT Industrial Credit Co. v. Milo Concrete Co., 229 S.E.2d 814 (N.C. App. 1976) and Valmont Credit Corp. v. McIlrany, 344 N.W.2d 691 (S.D. 1984).

energy savings was discussed with the lessor's salesmen. The lease in question was assigned to Equico at about the same time it was executed. On these facts, given Equico's prior knowledge of the seller's guarantee, and therefore of potential claims that might arise, Equico was found to be closely tied to the transaction and denied judgment.

Here, the evidence of a close connection consisted of Equico's supplying pre-printed forms for the lease between Hastings Capital and Ramadan; the lease and personal guaranty contained pre-printed assignment clauses naming Equico as assignee; and Equico conducted a credit check on Ramadan before the lease was executed. Equico had taken assignments of approximately 30 leases from Hastings in the past with a total value of $250,000. However, there was no evidence of a standing agreement that Hastings Capital would assign to Equico all the leases it executed or that Equico agreed to take all assignments from Hastings Capital.

There was no showing in this transaction that Equico had knowledge of the performance guarantee made by Hastings. Equico had no knowledge of the equipment's failure before the assignment or of Ramadan's potential claims. Further, Equico did not solicit Ramadan but only agreed to finance the arrangement after Hastings Capital representatives had arranged the transaction.

The evidence offered by Ramadan was insufficient to justify setting aside the waiver of defenses clause. The trial court therefore erred in entering judgment for Ramadan. The final judgment is reversed and the case is remanded to the trial court to enter judgment for appellant.

---

2. Delegation of Duties, Including "Assignment of a Contract"

A delegation of duties is an arrangement in which someone who owes a contractual obligation arranges to have another person do the work. A delegation is a contract between the delegator (the original obligor) and the delegate: the delegate promises to do whatever it is that the delegator is obligated to do. Say Martina Chowalski has contracted to sand the floors in William Besset's store for $3,000. Martina may hire Sophia Negretti to do the sanding. Martina may pay Sophia $3,000 to do the work, but more likely, she will pay Sophia less, say $2,400, keeping the $600 as her profit for arranging and overseeing the job. Sophia may be an employee of Martina or she may be an independent subcontractor.

Arrangements like this are prevalent in the construction industry and in many manufacturing and distribution industries. Yet the doctrine of delegation of duties is much more restrictive than the doctrine of assignment of rights. While courts and legislators view assignments as clearly beneficial to the financial industry and seldom hear the complaints of individual debtors who would object to the practice, courts and legislators see delegations of duties in a different light. The groups benefited by the practice of delegation are the contract performers, the people, like Martina or Sophia, who are obligated to do some work or supply some goods. These groups are not as influential as the financial industry. Moreover, the groups that object to delegation are those who, like William, have employed others to do work or supply goods. For a variety of reasons, courts have tended to view delegations of duties as socially harmful, or at least not socially beneficial. From Williams' perspective, a delegation of Martina's duty has little value and carries some risk. He may have hired Martina because of some specific characteristic: perhaps her good reputation or her skill. After the delegation, Sophia does the work, and William may feel shortchanged.

The delegation doctrine provides that a delegation is not valid if it will "change the quality or character of the performance." *See* Restatement (Second) of Contracts section 318. In the following case, *Sally Beauty Company, Inc. v. Nexxus Products Company, Inc.*, the majority holds that the delegation of duties under the distribution contract is invalid because the proposed delegate is a competitor of the obligee. Judge Richard Posner dissented from this decision, arguing that the delegation does not present the risk to the obligee's interests that the majority perceives. Implicit in Posner's decision is the idea that delegations, like assignments, are socially beneficial and should be encouraged by the law. Upon what basis might one argue that delegations are socially beneficial?

In our example, Martina transfers only the contract duties. In *Sally Beauty Company*, Best Barber & Beauty Supply Company "assigned its contract" with Nexxus to Sally Beauty. As a general rule, the phrase "assignment of a contract" means that the transferor has both assigned the contract rights and delegated the contract duties. *See* Uniform Commercial Code section 2-210(4):

> (4) An assignment of "the contract" or of "all my rights under the contract" or an assignment in similar general terms is an assignment of rights and unless the language or the circumstances (as in an assignment for security) indicate the contrary, it is a delegation of performance of the duties of the assignor and its acceptance by the assignee constitutes a promise by him to perform those duties. This promise is enforceable by either the assignor or the other party to the original contract.

Sally Beauty Company, Inc. v. Nexxus Products Company, Inc.

United States Court of Appeals for the Seventh Circuit
801 F.2d 1001 (1986)

RICHARD D. CUDAHY, CIRCUIT JUDGE

Nexxus Products Company ("Nexxus") entered into a contract with Best Barber & Beauty Supply Company, Inc. ("Best"), under which Best would be the exclusive distributor of Nexxus hair care products to barbers and hair stylists throughout most of Texas. When Best was acquired by and merged into Sally Beauty Company, Inc. ("Sally Beauty"), Nexxus cancelled the agreement. Sally Beauty is a wholly-owned subsidiary of Alberto-Culver Company ("Alberto-Culver"), a major manufacturer of hair care products and a competitor of Nexxus'. Sally Beauty claims that Nexxus breached the contract by cancelling; Nexxus asserts by way of defense that the contract was not assignable or, in the alternative, not assignable to Sally Beauty. The district court granted Nexxus' motion for summary judgment, ruling that the contract was one for personal services and therefore not assignable. We affirm on a different theory—that this contract could not be assigned to the wholly-owned subsidiary of a direct competitor under section 2-210 of the *Uniform Commercial Code*.

I.

Only the basic facts are undisputed and they are as follows. Prior to its merger with Sally Beauty, Best was a Texas corporation in the business of distributing beauty and hair care products to retail stores, barber shops and beauty salons throughout Texas. Between March and July 1979, Mark Reichek, Best's president, negotiated with Stephen Redding, Nexxus' vice-president, over a possible distribution agreement between Best and Nexxus. Nexxus, founded in 1979, is a California corporation that formulates and markets hair care products. Nexxus does not market its products to retail stores, preferring to sell them to independent distributors for resale to barbers and beauticians. On August 2, 1979, Nexxus executed a distributorship agreement with Best, in the form of a July 24, 1979 letter from Reichek, for Best, to Redding, for Nexxus:

Dear Steve:

It was a pleasure meeting with you and discussing the distribution of Nexus Products. The line is very exciting and we feel we can do a substantial job with it — especially as the exclusive distributor in Texas (except El Paso). If I understand the pricing structure correctly, we would pay $1.50 for an item that retails for $5.00 (less 50%, less 40% off retail), and Nexus will pay the freight charges regardless of order size. This approach to pricing will enable us to price the items in the line in such a way that they will be attractive and profitable to the salons. Your offer of assistance in promoting the line seems to be designed to simplify the introduction of Nexus Products into the Texas market. It indicates a sincere desire on your part to assist your distributors. By your agreeing to underwrite the cost of training and maintaining a qualified technician in our territory, we should be able to introduce the line from a position of strength. I am sure you will let us know at least 90 days in advance should you want to change this arrangement. By offering to provide us with the support necessary to conduct an annual seminar (ie. mailers, guest artisit [sic]) at your expense, we should be able to reenforce our position with Nexus users and introduce the product line to new customers in a professional manner. To satisfy your requirement of assured payment for merchandise received, each of our purchase orders will be accompanied by a Letter of Credit that will become negotiable when we receive the merchandise. I am sure you will agree that this arrangement is fairest for everybody concerned. While we feel confident that we can do an outstanding job with the Nexus line and that the volume we generate will adequately compensate you for your continued support, it is usually best to have an understanding should we no longer be distributing Nexus Products — either by our desire or your request. Based on our discussions, cancellation or termination of Best Barber & Beauty Supply Co., Inc. as a distributor can only take place on the anniversary date of our original appointment as a distributor — and then only with 120 days prior notice. If Nexus terminates us, Nexus will buy back all of our inventory at cost and will pay the freight charges on the returned merchandise. Steve, we feel that the Nexus line is exciting and very promotable. With the program outlined in this letter, we feel it can be mutually profitable and look forward to a long and successful business relationship. If you agree that this letter contains the details of our understanding regarding the distribution of Nexus Products, please sign the acknowledgment below and return one copy of this letter to me.

Very truly yours,

/s/ Mark E. Reichek

President

Acknowledged /s/ Stephen Redding

Date 8/2/79.

In July 1981 Sally Beauty acquired Best in a stock purchase transaction and Best was merged into Sally Beauty, which succeeded to Best's rights and interests in all of Best's contracts. Sally Beauty, a Delaware corporation with its principal place of business in Texas, is a wholly-owned subsidiary of Alberto-Culver. Sally Beauty, like Best, is a distributor of hair care and beauty products to retail stores and hair styling salons. Alberto-Culver is a major manufacturer of hair care products and, thus, is a direct competitor of Nexxus in the hair care market.[1]

Shortly after the merger, Redding met with Michael Renzulli, president of Sally Beauty, to discuss the Nexxus distribution agreement. After the meeting, Redding wrote Renzulli a letter stating that Nexxus would not allow Sally Beauty, a wholly-owned subsidiary of a direct competitor, to distribute Nexxus products:

> As we discussed in New Orleans, we have great reservations about allowing our Nexxus Products to be distributed by a company which is, in essence, a direct competitor. We appreciate your argument of autonomy for your business, but the fact remains that you are totally owned by Alberto-Culver. Since we see no way of justifying this conflict, we cannot allow our products to be distributed by Sally Beauty Company.

In August 1983 Sally Beauty commenced this action by filing a complaint in the Northern District of Illinois, claiming that Nexxus had violated the federal antitrust laws and breached the distribution agreement. In August 1984 Nexxus filed a counterclaim alleging violations of the Lanham Act, the Racketeer Influenced and Corrupt Organizations Act ("RICO") and the unfair competition laws of North Carolina, Tennessee and unidentified "other states." On October 22, 1984 Sally Beauty filed a motion to dismiss the counterclaims arising under RICO and "other states' law." Nexxus filed a motion for summary judgment on the breach of contract claim the next day.

The district court ruled on these motions in a Memorandum Opinion and Order dated January 31, 1985. It granted Sally's motion to dismiss the two counterclaims and also granted Nexxus' motion for summary judgment. In May 1985 it dismissed the remaining claims and counterclaims (pursuant to stipulation by the parties)[2] and directed the entry of an appealable final judgment on the breach of contract claim.

II.

Sally Beauty's breach of contract claim alleges that by acquiring Best, Sally Beauty succeeded to all of Best's rights and obligations under the distribution agreement. It further alleges that Nexxus breached the agreement by failing to give Sally Beauty 120 days notice prior to terminating the agreement and by terminating it on other than an anniversary date of its formation. Nexxus, in its motion for summary judgment, argued that the distribution agreement it entered into with Best was a contract for personal services, based upon a relationship of personal trust and confidence between Reichek and the Redding family. As such, the contract could not be assigned to Sally without Nexxus' consent.

In opposing this motion Sally Beauty argued that the contract was freely assignable because (1) it was between two corporations, not two individuals and (2) the character of the performance would not be altered by the substitution of Sally Beauty for Best. It also argued that "the Distribution Agreement is nothing more than a simple, non-exclusive

---

1. The appellant does not appear to dispute the proposition that Alberto-Culver is Nexxus' direct competitor, see Reply Brief at 8–10; rather it disagrees only with Nexxus' contention that performance by Sally Beauty would necessarily be unacceptable. *See infra.*

2. One of the two antitrust counts had already been dismissed by stipulation of the parties in May 1984.

contract for the distribution of goods, the successful performance of which is in no way dependent upon any particular personality, individual skill or confidential relationship."

In ruling on this motion, the district court framed the issue before it as "whether the contract at issue here between Best and Nexxus was of a personal nature such that it was not assignable without Nexxus' consent." It ruled:

> The court is convinced, based upon the nature of the contract and the circumstances surrounding its formation, that the contract at issue here was of such a nature that it was not assignable without Nexxus's consent. First, the very nature of the contract itself suggests its personal character. A distribution agreement is a contract whereby a manufacturer gives another party the right to distribute its products. It is clearly a contract for the performance of a service. In the court's view, the mere selection by a manufacturer of a party to distribute its goods pre-supposes a reliance and confidence by the manufacturer on the integrity and abilities of the other party.... In addition, in this case the circumstances surrounding the contract's formation support the conclusion that the agreement was not simply an ordinary commercial contract but was one which was based upon a relationship of personal trust and confidence between the parties. Specifically, Stephen Redding, Nexxus's vice-president, travelled to Texas and met with Best's president personally for several days before making the decision to award the Texas distributorship to Best. Best itself had been in the hair care business for 40 years and its president Mark Reichek had extensive experience in the industry. It is reasonable to conclude that Stephen Redding and Nexxus would want its distributor to be experienced and knowledgeable in the hair care field and that the selection of Best was based upon personal factors such as these.

The district court also rejected the contention that the character of performance would not be altered by a substitution of Sally Beauty for Best: "Unlike Best, Sally Beauty is a subsidiary of one of Nexxus' direct competitors. This is a significant distinction and in the court's view, it raises serious questions regarding Sally Beauty's ability to perform the distribution agreement in the same manner as Best."

We cannot affirm this summary judgment on the grounds relied on by the district court. Under Fed. R. Civ. P. 56(c) summary judgment may be granted only where there is no genuine issue as to any material fact and the moving party is entitled to judgment as a matter of law. The burden on the movant is stringent: "all doubts as to the existence of material fact must be resolved against the movant." *Moore v. Marketplace Restaurant, Inc.*, 754 F.2d 1336, 1339 (7th Cir. 1985), quoting *Dreher v. Sielaff*, 636 F.2d 1141, 1143 n. 4 (7th Cir. 1980). Nexxus did not meet its burden on the question of the parties' reasons for entering into this agreement. Although it might be "reasonable to conclude" that Best and Nexxus had based their agreement on "a relationship of personal trust and confidence," and that Reichek's participation was considered essential to Best's performance, this is a finding of fact. *See Phillips v. Oil, Inc.*, 104 S.W.2d 576, 579 (Tex. Civ. App. 1937, *writ ref'd n.r.e.*) (question whether contract was entered into because of parties' "personal confidence and trust" is for the determination of trier of fact). Since the parties submitted conflicting affidavits on this question, the district court erred in relying on Nexxus' view as representing undisputed fact in ruling on this summary judgment motion. *See Cedillo v. Local 1, International Association of Bridge & Structural Iron Workers*, 603 F.2d 7, 11 (7th Cir. 1979) ("questions of motive and intent are particularly inappropriate for summary adjudication").

We may affirm this summary judgment, however, on a different ground if it finds support in the record. *United States v. Winthrop Towers*, 628 F.2d 1028, 1037 (7th Cir.

1980). Sally Beauty contends that the distribution agreement is freely assignable because it is governed by the provisions of the *Uniform Commercial Code* (the "*UCC*" or the "*Code*"), as adopted in Texas. We agree with Sally that the provisions of the *UCC* govern this contract and for that reason hold that the assignment of the contract by Best to Sally Beauty was barred by the *UCC* rules on delegation of performance, UCC § 2-210(1), Tex. Bus & Com. Code Ann. § 2-210(a) (Vernon 1968).

III.

The *UCC* codifies the law of contracts applicable to "transactions in goods." UCC § 2-102, Tex. Bus. & Com. Code Ann. § 2-102 (Vernon 1968). Texas applies the "dominant factor" test to determine whether the *UCC* applies to a given contract or transaction: was the essence of or dominant factor in the formation of the contract the provision of goods or services? *Montgomery Ward & Co., Inc. v. Dalton*, 665 S.W.2d 507, 511 (Tex. Ct. App. 1984) (contract for repair of roof predominantly involves services). No Texas case addresses whether a distribution agreement is a contract for the sale of goods, but the rule in the majority of jurisdictions is that distributorships (both exclusive and non-exclusive) are to be treated as sale of goods contracts under the *UCC*. See [*e.g.,*] *Kirby v. Chrysler Corp.*, 554 F. Supp. 743 (D. Md. 1982) (automobile dealership).

Several ... courts note that "a distributorship agreement is more involved than a typical sales contract," *Quality Performance Lines* [*v. Yoho Automotive*, Inc., 609 P.2d 1340 (Utah 1980)] at 1342, but apply the *UCC* nonetheless because the sales aspect in such a contract is predominant. This is true of the contract at issue here (as embodied in the July 24, 1979 letter from Reichek to Redding). Most of the agreed-to terms deal with Nexxus' sale of its hair care products to Best. We are confident that a Texas court would find the sales aspect of this contract dominant and apply the majority rule that such a distributorship is a contract for "goods" under the *UCC*.

IV.

The fact that this contract is considered a contract for the sale of goods and not for the provision of a service does not, as Sally Beauty suggests, mean that it is freely assignable in all circumstances. The delegation of performance under a sales contract (whether in conjunction with an assignment of rights, as here, or not) is governed by *UCC* section 2-210(1), Tex. Bus. & Com. Code § 2-210(a) (Vernon 1968). The *UCC* recognizes that in many cases an obligor will find it convenient or even necessary to relieve himself of the duty of performance under a contract, *see* Official Comment 1, UCC § 2-210 ("[T]his section recognizes both delegation of performance and assignability as normal and permissible incidents of a contract for the sale of goods."). The *Code* therefore sanctions delegation except where the delegated performance would be unsatisfactory to the obligee: "A party may perform his duty through a delegate unless otherwise agreed to or unless the other party has a substantial interest in having his original promisor perform or control the acts required by the contract." UCC § 2-210(1), Tex. Bus. & Com. Code Ann. § 2-210(a) (Vernon 1968). Consideration is given to balancing the policies of free alienability of commercial contracts and protecting the obligee from having to accept a bargain he did not contract for.

We are concerned here with the delegation of Best's duty of performance under the distribution agreement, as Nexxus terminated the agreement because it did not wish to accept Sally Beauty's substituted performance.[6] Only one Texas case has construed section

---

6. If this contract is assignable, Sally Beauty would also, of course, succeed to Best's rights under the distribution agreement. But the fact situation before us must be distinguished from the assignment

2-210 in the context of a party's delegation of performance under an executory contract. In *McKinnie v. Milford*, 597 S.W.2d 953 (Tex. Ct. App. 1980), the court held that nothing in the *Texas Business and Commercial Code* prevented the seller of a horse from delegating to the buyer a pre-existing contractual duty to make the horse available to a third party for breeding. "[I]t is clear that Milford [the third party] had no particular interest in not allowing Stewart [the seller] to delegate the duties required by the contract. Milford was only interested in getting his two breedings per year, and such performance could only be obtained from McKinnie [the buyer] after he bought the horse from Stewart." *Id.* at 957. In *McKinnie*, the Texas court recognized and applied the *UCC* rule that bars delegation of duties if there is some reason why the non-assigning party would find performance by a delegate a substantially different thing than what he had bargained for.

In the exclusive distribution agreement before us, Nexxus had contracted for Best's "best efforts" in promoting the sale of Nexxus products in Texas. UCC § 2-306(2), Tex. Bus. & Com. Code Ann. § 2-306(b) (Vernon 1968), states that "[a] lawful agreement by either buyer or seller for exclusive dealing in the kind of goods concerned imposes unless otherwise agreed an obligation by the seller to use best efforts to supply the goods and by the buyer to use best efforts to promote their sale." This implied promise on Best's part was the consideration for Nexxus' promise to refrain from supplying any other distributors within Best's exclusive area. *See* Official Comment 5, UCC § 2-306. It was this contractual undertaking which Nexxus refused to see performed by Sally.

In ruling on Nexxus' motion for summary judgment, the district court noted: "Unlike Best, Sally Beauty is a subsidiary of one of Nexxus' direct competitors. This is a significant distinction and in the court's view, it raises serious questions regarding Sally Beauty's ability to perform the distribution agreement in the same manner as Best." In *Berliner Foods Corp. v. Pillsbury Co.*, 633 F. Supp. 557 (D. Md. 1986), the court stated the same reservation more strongly on similar facts. Berliner was an exclusive distributor of Haagen-Dazs ice cream when it was sold to Breyer's, manufacturer of a competing ice cream line. Pillsbury Co., manufacturer of Haagen-Dazs, terminated the distributorship and Berliner sued. The court noted, while weighing the factors for and against a preliminary injunction, that "it defies common sense to require a manufacturer to leave the distribution of its products to a distributor under the control of a competitor or potential competitor." *Id.* at 559–60. We agree with these assessments and hold that Sally Beauty's position as a wholly-owned subsidiary of Alberto-Culver is sufficient to bar the delegation of Best's duties under the agreement.

We do not believe that our holding will work the mischief with our national economy that the appellants predict. We hold merely that the duty of performance under an exclusive distributorship may not be delegated to a competitor in the market place—or the wholly-owned subsidiary of a competitor—without the obligee's consent. We believe that such a rule is consonant with the policies behind section 2-210, which is concerned with preserving the bargain the obligee has struck. Nexxus should not be required to accept the "best efforts" of Sally Beauty when those efforts are subject to the control of Alberto-Culver. It is entirely reasonable that Nexxus should conclude that this performance would be a different thing than what it had bargained for. At oral argument, Sally Beauty argued

---

of contract rights that are no longer executory (e.g., the right to damages for breach or the right to payment of an account), which is considered in *UCC* section 2-210(2), Tex. Bus. & Com. Code Ann. § 2-210(b) (Vernon 1968), and in several of the authorities relied on by appellants. The policies underlying these two situations are different and, generally, the *UCC* favors assignment more strongly in the latter. *See* UCC § 2-210(2) (non-executory rights assignable even if agreement states otherwise).

that the case should go to trial to allow it to demonstrate that it could and would perform the contract as impartially as Best. It stressed that Sally Beauty is a "multi-line" distributor, which means that it distributes many brands and is not just a conduit for Alberto-Culver products. But we do not think that this creates a material question of fact in this case. When performance of personal services is delegated, the trier merely determines that it is a personal services contract. If so, the duty is per se nondelegable. There is no inquiry into whether the delegate is as skilled or worthy of trust and confidence as the original obligor: the delegate was not bargained for and the obligee need not consent to the substitution.[9] And so here: it is undisputed that Sally Beauty is wholly owned by Alberto-Culver, which means that Sally Beauty's "impartial" sales policy is at least acquiesced in by Alberto-Culver—but could change whenever Alberto-Culver's needs changed. Sally Beauty may be totally sincere in its belief that it can operate "impartially" as a distributor, but who can guarantee the outcome when there is a clear choice between the demands of the parent-manufacturer, Alberto-Culver, and the competing needs of Nexxus? The risk of an unfavorable outcome is not one which the law can force Nexxus to take. Nexxus has a substantial interest in not seeing this contract performed by Sally Beauty, which is sufficient to bar the delegation under section 2-210, Tex. Bus. Com. Code Ann. § 2-210 (Vernon 1968). Because Nexxus should not be forced to accept performance of the distributorship agreement by Sally, we hold that the contract was not assignable without Nexxus' consent.

The judgment of the district court is affirmed.

RICHARD POSNER, CIRCUIT JUDGE, DISSENTING

My brethren have decided, with no better foundation than judicial intuition about what businessmen consider reasonable, that the *Uniform Commercial Code* gives a supplier an absolute right to cancel an exclusive-dealing contract if the dealer is acquired, directly or indirectly, by a competitor of the supplier. I interpret the *Code* differently.

Nexxus makes products for the hair and sells them through distributors to hair salons and barbershops. It gave a contract to Best, cancellable on any anniversary of the contract with 120 days' notice, to be its exclusive distributor in Texas. Two years later Best was acquired by and merged into Sally Beauty, a distributor of beauty supplies and wholly owned subsidiary of Alberto-Culver. Alberto-Culver makes "hair care" products, too, though they mostly are cheaper than Nexxus's, and are sold to the public primarily through grocery stores and drugstores. My brethren conclude that because there is at least a loose competitive relationship between Nexxus and Alberto-Culver, Sally Beauty cannot—as a matter of law, cannot, for there has been no trial on the issue—provide its "best efforts" in the distribution of Nexxus products. Since a commitment to provide best efforts is read into every exclusive-dealing contract by section 2-306(2) of the *Uniform Commercial Code*, the contract has been broken and Nexxus can repudiate it. Alternatively, Nexxus had "a substantial interest in having his original promisor perform or control the acts required by the contract," and therefore the delegation of the promisor's (Best's) duties to Sally Beauty was improper under section 2-210(1).

---

9. Of course, the obligee makes such an assessment of the prospective delegate. If it thinks the delegated performance will be as satisfactory, it is of course free to consent to the delegation. Thus, the dissent is mistaken in its suggestion that we find it improper—a "conflict of interest"—for one competitor to distribute another competitor's products. Rather, we believe only that it is commercially reasonable that the supplier in those circumstances have consented to such a state of affairs. To borrow the dissent's example, Isuzu allows General Motors to distribute its cars because it considers this arrangement attractive. Nor is distrust of one's competitors a trait unique to lawyers (as opposed to ordinary businessmen), as the dissent may be understood to suggest.

My brethren's conclusion that these provisions of the *Uniform Commercial Code* entitled Nexxus to cancel the contract does not leap out from the language of the provisions or of the contract; so one would expect, but does not find, a canvass of the relevant case law. My brethren cite only one case in support of their conclusion: a district court case from Maryland, *Berliner Foods Corp. v. Pillsbury Co.*, 633 F. Supp. 557 (D. Md. 1986), which, since it treated the contract at issue there as one for personal services, *id.* at 559 (a characterization my brethren properly reject for the contract between Nexxus and Best), is not helpful. *Berliner* is the latest in a long line of cases that make the propriety of delegating the performance of a distribution contract depend on whether or not the contract calls for the distributor's personal (unique, irreplaceable, distinctive, and therefore nondelegable) services. *See, e.g., Bancroft v. Scribner*, 72 Fed. 988 (9th Cir. 1896); *Detroit Postage Stamp Service Co. v. Schermack*, 146 N.W. 144 (Mich. 1914); *W.H. Barber Agency Co. v. Co-Op. Barrel Co.*, 158 N.W. 38 (Minn. 1916); *Paige v. Faure*, 127 N.E. 898 (N.Y. 1920). By rejecting that characterization here, my brethren have sawn off the only limb on which they might have sat comfortably.

A slightly better case for them (though not cited by them) is *Wetherell Bros. Co. v. United States Steel Co.*, 200 F.2d 761, 763 (1st Cir. 1952), which held that an exclusive sales agent's duties were nondelegable. The agent, a Massachusetts corporation, had agreed to use its "best endeavors" to promote the sale of the defendant's steel in the New England area. The corporation was liquidated and its assets sold to a Pennsylvania corporation that was not shown to be qualified to conduct business in Massachusetts, the largest state in New England. On these facts the defendant was entitled to treat the liquidation and sale as a termination of the contract. The *Wetherell* decision has been understood to depend on its facts. *See Jennings v. Foremost Dairies, Inc.*, 235 N.Y.S.2d 566, 574 (1962); 4 Corbin on Contracts, 1971 Pocket Part § 865, at p. 128. The facts of the present case are critically different. So far as appears, the same people who distributed Nexxus's products for Best (except for Best's president) continued to do so for Sally Beauty. Best was acquired, and continues, as a going concern; the corporation was dissolved, but the business wasn't. Whether there was a delegation of performance in any sense may be doubted. *Cf Rossetti v. City of New Britain*, 303 A.2d 714, 718–19 (Conn. 1972). The general rule is that a change of corporate form—including a merger—does not in and of itself affect contractual rights and obligations. *United States Shoe Corp. v. Hackett*, 793 F.2d 161, 163–64 (7th Cir. 1986).

The fact that Best's president has quit cannot be decisive on the issue whether the merger resulted in a delegation of performance. The contract between Nexxus and Best was not a personal-services contract conditioned on a particular individual's remaining with Best. *Compare Jennings v. Foremost Dairies, Inc., supra*, 235 N.Y.S.2d at 574. If Best had not been acquired, but its president had left anyway, as of course he might have done, Nexxus could not have repudiated the contract.

No case adopts the per se rule that my brethren announce. The cases ask whether, as a matter of fact, a change in business form is likely to impair performance of the contract. *Wetherell* asked this. So did *Arnold Productions, Inc. v. Favorite Films Corp.*, 298 F.2d 540, 543–44 (2d Cir. 1962), and *Des Moines Blue Ribbon Distributors, Inc. v. Drewrys Ltd.*, 129 N.W.2d 731, 738–39 (Iowa 1964). *Green v. Camlin*, 92 S.E.2d 125, 127 (S.C. 1956), has some broad language which my brethren might have cited; but since the contract in that case forbade assignment it is not an apt precedent.

My brethren find this a simple case—as simple (it seems) as if a lawyer had undertaken to represent the party opposing his client. But notions of conflict of interest are not the same in law and in business, and judges can go astray by assuming that the legal-services industry is the pattern for the entire economy. The lawyerization of America has not reached that point. Sally Beauty, though a wholly owned subsidiary of Alberto-Culver, distributes "hair care" supplies made by many different companies, which so far as appears compete with Alberto-Culver as vigorously as Nexxus does. Steel companies both make fabricated steel and sell raw steel to competing fabricators. General Motors sells cars manufactured by a competitor, Isuzu. What in law would be considered a fatal conflict of interest is in business a commonplace and legitimate practice. The lawyer is a fiduciary of his client; Best was not a fiduciary of Nexxus.

Selling your competitor's products, or supplying inputs to your competitor, sometimes creates problems under antitrust or regulatory law—but only when the supplier or distributor has monopoly or market power and uses it to restrict a competitor's access to an essential input or to the market for the competitor's output, as in *Otter Tail Power Co. v. United States*, 410 U.S. 366 (1973), or *FTC v. Brown Shoe Co.*, 384 U.S. 316 (1966), or *United Air Lines, Inc. v. CAB*, 766 F.2d 1107, 1114–15 (7th Cir. 1985). There is no suggestion that Alberto-Culver has a monopoly of "hair care" products or Sally Beauty a monopoly of distributing such products, or that Alberto-Culver would ever have ordered Sally Beauty to stop carrying Nexxus products. Far from complaining about being squeezed out of the market by the acquisition, Nexxus is complaining in effect about Sally Beauty's refusal to boycott it!

How likely is it that the acquisition of Best could hurt Nexxus? Not very. Suppose Alberto-Culver had ordered Sally Beauty to go slow in pushing Nexxus products, in the hope that sales of Alberto-Culver "hair care" products would rise. Even if they did, since the market is competitive Alberto-Culver would not reap monopoly profits. Moreover, what guarantee has Alberto-Culver that consumers would be diverted from Nexxus to it, rather than to products closer in price and quality to Nexxus products? In any event, any trivial gain in profits to Alberto-Culver would be offset by the loss of goodwill to Sally Beauty; and a cost to Sally Beauty is a cost to Alberto-Culver, its parent. Remember that Sally Beauty carries beauty supplies made by other competitors of Alberto-Culver; Best alone carries "hair care" products manufactured by Revlon, Clairol, Bristol-Myers, and L'Oreal, as well as Alberto-Culver. Will these powerful competitors continue to distribute their products through Sally Beauty if Sally Beauty displays favoritism for Alberto-Culver products? Would not such a display be a commercial disaster for Sally Beauty, and hence for its parent, Alberto-Culver? Is it really credible that Alberto-Culver would sacrifice Sally Beauty in a vain effort to monopolize the "hair care" market, in violation of section 2 of the Sherman Act? Is not the ratio of the profits that Alberto-Culver obtains from Sally Beauty to the profits it obtains from the manufacture of "hair care" products at least a relevant consideration?

Another relevant consideration is that the contract between Nexxus and Best was for a short term. Could Alberto-Culver destroy Nexxus by failing to push its products with maximum vigor in Texas for a year? In the unlikely event that it could and did, it would be liable in damages to Nexxus for breach of the implied best-efforts term of the distribution contract. Finally, it is obvious that Sally Beauty does not have a bottleneck position in the distribution of "hair care" products, such that by refusing to promote Nexxus products vigorously it could stifle the distribution of those products in Texas; for Nexxus has found alternative distribution that it prefers—otherwise it wouldn't have repudiated the contract with Best when Best was acquired by Sally Beauty.

Not all businessmen are consistent and successful profit maximizers, so the probability that Alberto-Culver would instruct Sally Beauty to cease to push Nexxus products vigorously in Texas cannot be reckoned at zero. On this record, however, it is slight. And there is no principle of law that if something happens that trivially reduces the probability that a dealer will use his best efforts, the supplier can cancel the contract. Suppose there had been no merger, but the only child of Best's president had gone to work for Alberto-Culver as a chemist. Could Nexxus have canceled the contract, fearing that Best (perhaps unconsciously) would favor Alberto-Culver products over Nexxus products? That would be an absurd ground for cancellation, and so is Nexxus's actual ground. At most, so far as the record shows, Nexxus may have had grounds for "insecurity" regarding the performance by Sally Beauty of its obligation to use its best efforts to promote Nexxus products, but if so its remedy was not to cancel the contract but to demand assurances of due performance. *See* UCC § 2-609; Official Comment 5 to § 2-306. No such demand was made. An anticipatory repudiation by conduct requires conduct that makes the repudiating party unable to perform. Farnsworth, Contracts 636 (1982). The merger did not do this. At least there is no evidence it did. The judgment should be reversed and the case remanded for a trial on whether the merger so altered the conditions of performance that Nexxus is entitled to declare the contract broken.

Hunter Tract Improvement Company v. S. H. Stone et al.

Supreme Court of Washington
58 Wash. 661, 109 P. 112 (1910)

RALPH O. DUNBAR, JUSTICE

Appellant platted, as Mount Baker addition to the city of Seattle, a tract of land adjoining Lake Washington, containing about two hundred and ten acres, and gave to the city of Seattle about twenty-five acres of this land for parks and boulevards, including the lake frontage, and in other ways attempted to make it desirable for first-class residences, and a great many people had bought lots in said addition. One Marguerite Foy had secured a contract for the purchase of lot 14 in block 18 in said addition, and had assigned the same to a woman of the negro race, Susie Stone, wife of the respondent S. H. Stone, who is also a negro. The assignment was approved on the back of the contract, and said S. H. Stone and wife, Susie Stone, were about to commence the erection of a private residence for themselves on said lot.

Thereupon the appellant brought this action against S. H. Stone and wife and Marguerite Foy, respondents herein, to obtain a cancellation of said assignment to Susie Stone, upon the ground that the contract made with Marguerite Foy could not be binding until the assignment should be accepted and approved by the appellant, and that the purported approval and acceptance of the assignment to Susie Stone was induced by mistake as to the race of said Susie Stone and of her husband, and that the said Susie Stone and her husband wilfully and wrongfully concealed from the appellant the fact that they were of the negro race, knowing all the time that the appellant would not consent to or approve of the assignment to a person or persons of the negro race.

There were other provisions of the complaint in relation to the failure to pay interest, but it was conceded upon the trial that the interest had been paid, and this ground for rescission is abandoned upon this appeal. The answer admitted the assignment, admitted the fact that the respondents Susie Stone and S. H. Stone were colored people, but denied all allegations of knowledge of the conditions asserted in the complaint, or of any fraud on their part. The court upon the trial of the cause found in favor of the defendants, and dismissed the action. From judgment of dismissal, this appeal is taken.

It is the appellant's contention that it is injured from the fact that the addition will become less popular and less valuable if negroes are allowed to erect and maintain residences in said addition, and that it had promised and agreed with divers and sundry parties to whom it had sold that negroes would not be allowed to purchase any of the lots of this addition or to maintain residences thereon. The main contention is based upon the first assignment of error, viz., that the court refused to find that it was agreed by the parties to the contract, and so set forth therein (referring to the contract between Marguerite Foy and appellant), that no assignment of the said contract, or of any rights thereunder, should be valid until the same should be accepted and approved by this plaintiff, and this finding requested was in accordance with paragraph 4 of the complaint. We do not think the court erred in not making this finding as requested. A great many other assignments are discussed by the appellant, which it seems to us are not material, in consideration of the conclusion we have reached on the assignment just mentioned. It may be conceded that the general propositions of law stated by the appellant are correctly stated, and that the authorities cited sustain such proposition, viz., that the parties to a contract may in terms prohibit its assignment so that neither personal representatives nor assignees can succeed to any rights in virtue of it or be bound by its obligations; or that a party has a right to select and determine with whom he will contract, and cannot have another person thrust upon him without his consent. But these principles, and authorities cited to sustain them, are not in point as we view this contract.

Appellant quotes somewhat extensively from the case of *La Rue v. Groezinger*, 24 Pac. 42 (Cal.) where a contract by which A. agreed to sell, and B. to buy, all the grapes of a certain standard which A. might raise in a certain vineyard during a certain period, was declared to be assignable by A. But in the course of the opinion, the court used the language set forth in appellant's brief, to the effect that, though a contract may not expressly say that it is not transferable, yet if there are equivalent expressions or language which excludes the idea of performance by another, it is not assignable; citing *Shultz & Co. v. Johnson's Adm'r*, 5 B. Mon. (Ky.) 497. An examination of that case shows that S. contracted with J. to receive, and pay for at a certain price, all the hemp which J. could raise for six successive years on not less than one hundred or more than one hundred and sixty acres of land, of his own raising. J. died, and in a suit by his administrator for refusing to receive and pay for a crop raised after the death of J., held that the contract was personal and that it could not be performed by J's administrator, the court holding that there was a personal equation in that case which could not be disregarded; that S. contracted with reference to the requisite skill and experience which J. was known to possess, and that by the especial terms of the contract he could not be compelled to take the production of any one else. But the court, in *La Rue v. Groezinger, supra*, shows conclusively by its announcement that it would not have held such a contract as the one in question nonassignable, for it proceeds to say:

> ... If the language does not exclude the idea of performance by another, and the nature of the thing contracted for, or the circumstances of the case, do not show that the skill, credit, or other personal quality or circumstance of the party was a distinctive characteristic of the thing stipulated for, or a material inducement to the contract,—then the contract was assignable, under the provisions above quoted ... And while it is to be conceded that men have perfect liberty to contract with whom they choose, and to exclude the idea of performance by another, yet in the absence of anything indicating such an intention, we do not think that the courts should indulge in speculation as to possible prejudice or fancied preference. It should not assume that the parties were influenced by unusual or conjectural motives merely because some men might be so affected under similar circumstances.

The whole opinion is an argument against appellant's contention.

But instead of there being special circumstances in this contract to indicate that the intention of the parties was that it should not be assignable, the contract itself expressly provides for an assignment in the eighth clause, which is as follows: "Where the words vendor or vendee appear, it is understood to include heirs, assigns, successors or legal representatives." It is true that, after the form of assignment on the back of the contract, the following words appear: "This assignment is hereby accepted and approved." But this is no part of the contract. The contract was completed, signed, and acknowledged by the parties, and this provision was not incorporated in that agreement, and the parties to the contract can in no way be bound by it. It was evidently incorporated simply as a provision for a novation, and for the purpose of releasing the original contractor and accepting the obligation of the assignee in lieu thereof. There being, then, no obligation on the part of the assignee to have this assignment approved, it is immaterial whether the approval was made through mistake or otherwise. Certain it is that there would have been no protection to the appellant under this contract, in respect to the condition it is complaining of, if it had executed a deed to Marguerite Foy, and she had seen fit to deed the same to the respondents Stone, or to make any contract that she saw fit to make with relation to the land.

We think there is no merit in the appeal, and the judgment must be affirmed.

———————

Appendix

Some Authoritative Texts in Contract Law

A. Uniform Commercial Code

Article 1

Part 1. General Provisions

§ 1-101. Short Titles

(a)   This [Act] may be cited as the *Uniform Commercial Code*.

(b)   This article may be cited as *Uniform Commercial Code*-General Provisions

§ 1-102. Scope of Article.

This article applies to a transaction to the extent that it is governed by another article of [the *Uniform Commercial Code*].

§ 1-103. Construction of [*Uniform Commercial Code*] to Promote Its Purposes and Policies; Applicability of Supplemental Principles of Law.

(a)   [The *Uniform Commercial Code*] must be liberally construed and applied to promote its underlying purposes and policies, which are:

(1) to simplify, clarify, and modernize the law governing commercial transactions;

(2) to permit the continued expansion of commercial practices through custom, usage, and agreement of the parties; and

(3) to make uniform the law among the various jurisdictions.

(b)   Unless displaced by the particular provisions of [the *Uniform Commercial Code*], the principles of law and equity, including the law merchant and the law relative to capacity to contract, principal and agent, estoppel, fraud, misrepresentation, duress, coercion, mistake, bankruptcy, and other validating or invalidating cause supplement its provisions.

Official Comment

1.   The *Uniform Commercial Code* is drawn to provide flexibility so that, since it is intended to be a semi-permanent and infrequently amended piece of legislation, it will provide its own machinery for expansion of commercial practices. It is intended to make it possible for the law embodied in the *Uniform Commercial Code* to be applied by the courts in the light of unforeseen and new circumstances and practices. The proper construction of the *Uniform Commercial Code* requires, of course, that its interpretation and application be limited to its reason.

...

The *Uniform Commercial Code* should be construed in accordance with its underlying purposes and policies. The text of each section should be read in the light of the purpose and policy of the rule or principle in question, as also of the *Uniform Commercial Code* as a whole, and the application of the language should be construed narrowly or broadly, as the case may be, in conformity with the purposes and policies involved.

2. *Applicability of supplemental principles of law.* Subsection (b) states the basic relationship of the *Uniform Commercial Code* to supplemental bodies of law. The *Uniform Commercial Code* was drafted against the backdrop of existing bodies of law, including the common law and equity, and relies on those bodies of law to supplement it provisions in many important ways. At the same time, the *Uniform Commercial Code* is the primary source of commercial law rules in areas that it governs, and its rules represent choices made by its drafters and the enacting legislatures about the appropriate policies to be furthered in the transactions it covers. Therefore, while principles of common law and equity may supplement provisions of the *Uniform Commercial Code*, they may not be used to supplant its provisions, or the purposes and policies those provisions reflect, unless a specific provision of the *Uniform Commercial Code* provides otherwise. In the absence of such a provision, the *Uniform Commercial Code* preempts principles of common law and equity that are inconsistent with either its provisions or its purposes and policies.

    The language of subsection (b) is intended to reflect both the concept of supplementation and the concept of preemption. Some courts, however, had difficulty in applying the identical language of former Section 1-103 to determine when other law appropriately may be applied to supplement the *Uniform Commercial Code*, and when that law has been displaced by the Code. Some decisions applied other law in situations in which that application, while not inconsistent with the text of any particular provision of the *Uniform Commercial Code*, clearly was inconsistent with the underlying purposes and policies reflected in the relevant provisions of the Code. *See, e.g., Sheerbonnet, Ltd. v. American Express Bank, Ltd.,* 951 F. Supp. 403 (S.D.N.Y. 1995). In part, this difficulty arose from Comment 1 to former Section 1-103, which stated that "this section indicates the continued applicability to commercial contracts of all supplemental bodies of law except insofar as they are explicitly displaced by this Act." The "explicitly displaced" language of that Comment did not accurately reflect the proper scope of *Uniform Commercial Code* preemption, which extends to displacement of other law that is inconsistent with the purposes and policies of the *Uniform Commercial Code*, as well as with its text.

3. *Application of subsection (b) to statutes.* The primary focus of Section 1-103 is on the relationship between the *Uniform Commercial Code* and principles of common law and equity as developed by the courts. State law, however, increasingly is statutory. Not only are there a growing number of state statutes addressing specific issues that come within the scope of the *Uniform Commercial Code*, but in some States many general principles of common law and equity have been codified. When the other law relating to a matter within the scope of the *Uniform Commercial Code* is a statute, the principles of subsection (b) remain relevant to the court's analysis of the relationship between that statute and the *Uniform Commercial Code*, but other principles of statutory interpretation that

specifically address the interrelationship between statutes will be relevant as well. In some situations, the principles of subsection (b) still will be determinative. For example, the mere fact that an equitable principle is stated in statutory form rather than in judicial decisions should not change the court's analysis of whether the principle can be used to supplement the *Uniform Commercial Code* under subsection (b), equitable principles may supplement provisions of the *Uniform Commercial Code* only if they are consistent with the purposes and policies of the *Uniform Commercial Code* as well as its text. In other situations, however, other interpretive principles addressing the interrelationship between statutes may lead the court to conclude that the other statute is controlling, even though it conflicts with the *Uniform Commercial Code*. This, for example, would be the result in a situation where the other statute was specifically intended to provide additional protection to a class of individuals engaging in transactions covered by the *Uniform Commercial Code*.

4. *Listing not exclusive.* The list of sources of supplemental law in subsection (b) is intended to be merely illustrative of the other law that may supplement the *Uniform Commercial Code*, and is not exclusive. No listing could be exhaustive. Further, the fact that a particular section of the *Uniform Commercial Code* makes express reference to other law is not intended to suggest the negation of the general application of the principles of subsection (b). Note also that the word "bankruptcy" in subsection (b), continuing the use of that word from former Section 1-103, should be understood not as a specific reference to federal bankruptcy law but, rather as a reference to general principles of insolvency, whether under federal or state law.

Part 2. General Definitions and Principles of Interpretation

§ 1-201. General Definitions.

(a) Unless the context otherwise requires, words or phrases defined in this section, or in the additional definitions contained in other articles of [the *Uniform Commercial Code*] that apply to particular articles or parts thereof, have the meanings stated.

(b) Subject to definitions contained in other articles of [the *Uniform Commercial Code*] that apply to particular articles or parts thereof:

(2) "Aggrieved party" means a party entitled to pursue a remedy.

(3) "Agreement," as distinguished from "contract," means the bargain of the parties in fact, as found in their language or inferred from other circumstances, including course of performance, course of dealing, or usage of trade as provided in Section 1-303.

(8) "Burden of establishing" a fact means the burden of persuading the trier of fact that the existence of the fact is more probable than its nonexistence.

(10) "Conspicuous", with reference to a term, means so written, displayed, or presented that a reasonable person against which it is to operate ought to have noticed it. Whether a term is "conspicuous" or not is a decision for the court. Conspicuous terms include the following:

(A) a heading in capitals equal to or greater in size than the surrounding text, or in contrasting type, font, or color to the surrounding text of the same or lesser size; and

(B) language in the body of a record or display in larger type than the surrounding text, or in contrasting type, font, or color to the surrounding text of the same size, or set off from surrounding text of the same size by symbols or other marks that call attention to the language.

(11) "Consumer" means an individual who enters into a transaction primarily for personal, family, or household purposes.

(12) "Contract," as distinguished from "agreement," means the total legal obligation that results from the parties' agreement as determined by [the *Uniform Commercial Code*] as supplemented by any other applicable laws.

(14) "Defendant" includes a person in the position of defendant in a counterclaim, cross claim, or third party claim.

(20) "Good faith," except as otherwise provided in Article 5, means honesty in fact and the observance of reasonable commercial standards of fair dealing.

(32) "Remedy" means any remedial right to which an aggrieved party is entitled with or without resort to a tribunal.

(34) "Right" includes remedy.

(36) "Send" in connection with a writing, record, or notice means:

(A) to deposit in the mail or deliver for transmission by any other usual means of communication with postage or cost of transmission provided for and properly addressed and, in the case of an instrument, to an address specified thereon or otherwise agreed, or if there be none to any address reasonable under the circumstances; or

(B) In any other way to cause to be received any record or notice within the time it would have arrived if properly sent.

(37) "Signed" includes using any symbol executed or adopted with present intention to adopt or accept a writing.

(40) "Term" means a portion of an agreement that relates to a particular matter.

(43) "Writing" includes printing, typewriting, or any other intentional reduction to tangible form. "Written" has a corresponding meaning.

Official Comments

3. "Agreement." Derived from former Section 1201. As used in the *Uniform Commercial Code* the word is intended to include full recognition of usage of trade, course of dealing, course of performance and the surrounding circumstances as effective parts thereof, and of any agreement permitted under the provisions of the *Uniform Commercial Code* to displace a stated rule of law. Whether an agreement has legal consequences is determined by applicable provisions of the *Uniform Commercial Code* and, to the extent provided in Section 1-103, by the law of contracts.

§ 1-202. Notice; Knowledge.

(a)   Subject to subsection (f), a person has "notice" of a fact if the person:

(1) has actual knowledge of it;

(2) has received a notice or notification of it; or

(3) from all the facts and circumstances known to the person at the time in question, has reason to know that it exists.

(b)   "Knowledge" means actual knowledge. "Knows" has a corresponding meaning.

(c) "Discover," "learn," or words of similar import refer to knowledge rather than to reason to know.

(d) A person "notifies" or "gives" a notice or notification to another person by taking such steps as may be reasonably required to inform the other person in ordinary course, whether or not the other person actually comes to know of it.

(e) Subject to subsection (f), a person "receives" a notice or notification when:

(1) it comes to that person's attention; or

(2) it is duly delivered in a form reasonable under the circumstances at the place of business through which the contract was made or at another location held out by that person as the place for receipt of such communications.

(f) Notice, knowledge, or a notice or notification received by an organization is effective for a particular transaction from the time it is brought to the attention of the individual conducting that transaction and, in any event, from the time it would have been brought to the individual's attention if the organization had exercised due diligence. An organization exercises due diligence if it maintains reasonable routines for communicating significant information to the person conducting the transaction and there is reasonable compliance with the routines. Due diligence does not require an individual acting for the organization to communicate information unless the communication is part of the individual's regular duties or the individual has reason to know of the transaction and that the transaction would be materially affected by the information.

§ 1-205. Reasonable Time; Seasonableness.

(a) Whether a time for taking an action required by [the *Uniform Commercial Code*] is reasonable depends on the nature, purpose, and circumstances of the action.

(b) An action is taken seasonably if it is taken at or within the time agreed or, if no time is agreed, at or within a reasonable time.

§ 1-206. Presumptions.

Whenever [the *Uniform Commercial Code*] creates a "presumption" with respect to a fact, or provides that a fact is "presumed," the trier of fact must find the existence of the fact unless and until evidence is introduced that supports a finding of its nonexistence.

Part 3. Territorial Applicability and General Rules

§ 1-302. Variation by Agreement.

(a) Except as otherwise provided in subsection (b) or elsewhere in [the *Uniform Commercial Code*], the effect of provisions of [the *Uniform Commercial Code*] may be varied by agreement.

(b) The obligations of good faith, diligence, reasonableness, and care prescribed by [the *Uniform Commercial Code*] may not be disclaimed by agreement. The parties, by agreement, may determine the standards by which the performance of those obligations is to be measured if those standards are not manifestly unreasonable. Whenever [the *Uniform Commercial Code*] requires an action to be taken within a reasonable time, a time that is not manifestly unreasonable may be fixed by agreement.

(c) The presence in certain provisions of [the Uniform Commercial Code] of the phrase "unless otherwise agreed," or words of similar import, does not imply that the effect of other provisions may not be varied by agreement under this section.

Official Comment

1.   Subsection (a) states affirmatively at the outset that freedom of contract is a principle of the *Uniform Commercial Code*: "the effect" of its provisions may be varied by "agreement." The meaning of the statute itself must be found in its text, including its definitions, and in appropriate extrinsic aids; it cannot be varied by agreement. But the *Uniform Commercial Code* seeks to avoid the type of interference with evolutionary growth found in pre-Code cases such as Manhattan Co. v. Morgan, 242 N.Y. 38, 150 N.E. 594 (1926). Thus, private parties cannot make an instrument negotiable within the meaning of Article 3 except as provided in Section 3-104; nor can they change the meaning of such terms as "bona fide purchaser," "holder in due course," or "due negotiation," as used in the *Uniform Commercial Code*. But an agreement can change the legal consequences that would otherwise flow from the provisions of the *Uniform Commercial Code*. "Agreement" here includes the effect given to course of dealing, usage of trade and course of performance by Sections 1-201 and 1-303; the effect of an agreement on the rights of third parties is left to specific provisions of the *Uniform Commercial Code* and to supplementary principles applicable under Section 1-103. The rights of third parties under Section 9 317 when a security interest is unperfected, for example, cannot be destroyed by a clause in the security agreement.

     This principle of freedom of contract is subject to specific exceptions found elsewhere in the *Uniform Commercial Code* and to the general exception stated here. The specific exceptions vary in explicitness: the statute of frauds found in Section 2-201, for example, does not explicitly preclude oral waiver of the requirement of a writing, but a fair reading denies enforcement to such a waiver as part of the "contract" made unenforceable; Section 9 602, on the other hand, is a quite explicit limitation on freedom of contract. Under the exception for "the obligations of good faith, diligence, reasonableness and care prescribed by [the *Uniform Commercial Code*]," provisions of the *Uniform Commercial Code* prescribing such obligations are not to be disclaimed. However, the section also recognizes the prevailing practice of having agreements set forth standards by which due diligence is measured and explicitly provides that, in the absence of a showing that the standards manifestly are unreasonable, the agreement controls. In this connection, Section 1-303 incorporating into the agreement prior course of dealing and usages of trade is of particular importance.

     Subsection (b) also recognizes that nothing is stronger evidence of a reasonable time than the fixing of such time by a fair agreement between the parties. However, provision is made for disregarding a clause which whether by inadvertence or overreaching fixes a time so unreasonable that it amounts to eliminating all remedy under the contract. The parties are not required to fix the most reasonable time but may fix any time which is not obviously unfair as judged by the time of contracting.

2.   An agreement that varies the effect of provisions of the *Uniform Commercial Code* may do so by stating the rules that will govern in lieu of the provisions varied. Alternatively, the parties may vary the effect of such provisions by stating that their relationship will be governed by recognized bodies of rules or principles

applicable to commercial transactions. Such bodies of rules or principles may include, for example, those that are promulgated by intergovernmental authorities such as UNCITRAL or Undercoat (see, e.g., Undercoat Principles of International Commercial Contracts), or non-legal codes such as trade codes.

3. Subsection (c) is intended to make it clear that, as a matter of drafting, phrases such as "unless otherwise agreed" have been used to avoid controversy as to whether the subject matter of a particular section does or does not fall within the exceptions to subsection (b), but absence of such words contains no negative implication since under subsection (b) the general and residual rule is that the effect of all provisions of the *Uniform Commercial Code* may be varied by agreement.

§ 1-303. Course of Performance, Course of Dealing, and Usage of Trade.

(a) A "course of performance" is a sequence of conduct between the parties to a particular transaction that exists if:

  (1) the agreement of the parties with respect to the transaction involves repeated occasions for performance by a party; and

  (2) the other party, with knowledge of the nature of the performance and opportunity for objection to it, accepts the performance or acquiesces in it without objection.

(b) A "course of dealing" is a sequence of conduct concerning previous transactions between the parties to a particular transaction that is fairly to be regarded as establishing a common basis of understanding for interpreting their expressions and other conduct.

(c) A "usage of trade" is any practice or method of dealing having such regularity of observance in a place, vocation, or trade as to justify an expectation that it will be observed with respect to the transaction in question. The existence and scope of such a usage must be proved as facts. If it is established that such a usage is embodied in a trade code or similar record, the interpretation of the record is a question of law.

(d) A course of performance or course of dealing between the parties or usage of trade in the vocation or trade in which they are engaged or of which they are or should be aware is relevant in ascertaining the meaning of the parties' agreement, may give particular meaning to specific terms of the agreement, and may supplement or qualify the terms of the agreement. A usage of trade applicable in the place in which part of the performance under the agreement is to occur may be so utilized as to that part of the performance.

(e) Except as otherwise provided in subsection (f), the express terms of an agreement and any applicable course of performance, course of dealing, or usage of trade must be construed whenever reasonable as consistent with each other. If such a construction is unreasonable:

  (1) express terms prevail over course of performance, course of dealing, and usage of trade;

  (2) course of performance prevails over course of dealing and usage of trade; and

  (3) course of dealing prevails over usage of trade.

(f) Subject to Section 2-209 and Section 2A-208, a course of performance is relevant to show a waiver or modification of any term inconsistent with the course of performance.

(g)   Evidence of a relevant usage of trade offered by one party is not admissible unless that party has given the other party notice that the court finds sufficient to prevent unfair surprise to the other party.

Official Comment

1.   The *Uniform Commercial Code* rejects both the "lay dictionary" and the "conveyancer's" reading of a commercial agreement. Instead the meaning of the agreement of the parties is to be determined by the language used by them and by their action, read and interpreted in the light of commercial practices and other surrounding circumstances. The measure and background for interpretation are set by the commercial context, which may explain and supplement even the language of a formal or final writing.

2.   "Course of dealing," as defined in subsection (b), is restricted, literally, to a sequence of conduct between the parties previous to the agreement. A sequence of conduct after or under the agreement, however, is a "course of performance." "Course of dealing" may enter the agreement either by explicit provisions of the agreement or by tacit recognition.

3.   The *Uniform Commercial Code* deals with "usage of trade" as a factor in reaching the commercial meaning of the agreement that the parties have made. The language used is to be interpreted as meaning what it may fairly be expected to mean to parties involved in the particular commercial transaction in a given locality or in a given vocation or trade. By adopting in this context the term "usage of trade," the *Uniform Commercial Code* expresses its intent to reject those cases which see evidence of "custom" as representing an effort to displace or negate "established rules of law." A distinction is to be drawn between mandatory rules of law such as the Statute of Frauds provisions of Article 2 on Sales whose very office is to control and restrict the actions of the parties, and which cannot be abrogated by agreement, or by a usage of trade, and those rules of law (such as those in Part 3 of Article 2 on Sales) which fill in points which the parties have not considered and in fact agreed upon. The latter rules hold "unless otherwise agreed" but yield to the contrary agreement of the parties. Part of the agreement of the parties to which such rules yield is to be sought for in the usages of trade which furnish the background and give particular meaning to the language used, and are the framework of common understanding controlling any general rules of law which hold only when there is no such understanding.

4.   A usage of trade under subsection (c) must have the "regularity of observance" specified. The ancient English tests for "custom" are abandoned in this connection. Therefore, it is not required that a usage of trade be "ancient or immemorial," "universal," or the like. Under the requirement of subsection (c) full recognition is thus available for new usages and for usages currently observed by the great majority of decent dealers, even though dissidents ready to cut corners do not agree. There is room also for proper recognition of usage agreed upon by merchants in trade codes.

5.   The policies of the *Uniform Commercial Code* controlling explicit unconscionable contracts and clauses (Sections 1-304, 2-302) apply to implicit clauses that rest on usage of trade and carry forward the policy underlying the ancient requirement that a custom or usage must be "reasonable." However, the emphasis is shifted. The very fact of commercial acceptance makes out a prima facie case that the usage is reasonable, and the burden is no longer on the usage to establish itself

as being reasonable. But the anciently established policing of usage by the courts is continued to the extent necessary to cope with the situation arising if an unconscionable or dishonest practice should become standard.

6. Subsection (d), giving the prescribed effect to usages of which the parties "are or should be aware," reinforces the provision of subsection (c) requiring not universality but only the described "regularity of observance" of the practice or method. This subsection also reinforces the point of subsection (c) that such usages may be either general to trade or particular to a special branch of trade.

7. Although the definition of "agreement" in Section 1-201 includes the elements of course of performance, course of dealing, and usage of trade, the fact that express reference is made in some sections to those elements is not to be construed as carrying a contrary intent or implication elsewhere. Compare Section 1-302(c).

8. In cases of a well established line of usage varying from the general rules of the *Uniform Commercial Code* where the precise amount of the variation has not been worked out into a single standard, the party relying on the usage is entitled, in any event, to the minimum variation demonstrated. The whole is not to be disregarded because no particular line of detail has been established. In case a dominant pattern has been fairly evidenced, the party relying on the usage is entitled under this section to go to the trier of fact on the question of whether such dominant pattern has been incorporated into the agreement.

9. Subsection (g) is intended to insure that this Act's liberal recognition of the needs of commerce in regard to usage of trade shall not be made into an instrument of abuse.

§ 1-304. Obligation of Good Faith.

Every contract or duty within [the Uniform Commercial Code] imposes an obligation of good faith in its performance and enforcement.

Official Comment

1. This section sets forth a basic principle running throughout the *Uniform Commercial Code*. The principle is that in commercial transactions good faith is required in the performance and enforcement of all agreements or duties. While this duty is explicitly stated in some provisions of the *Uniform Commercial Code*, the applicability of the duty is broader than merely these situations and applies generally, as stated in this section, to the performance or enforcement of every contract or duty within this Act. It is further implemented by Section 1-303 on course of dealing, course of performance, and usage of trade. This section does not support an independent cause of action for failure to perform or enforce in good faith. Rather, this section means that a failure to perform or enforce, in good faith, a specific duty or obligation under the contract, constitutes a breach of that contract or makes unavailable, under the particular circumstances, a remedial right or power. This distinction makes it clear that the doctrine of good faith merely directs a court towards interpreting contracts within the commercial context in which they are created, performed, and enforced, and does not create a separate duty of fairness and reasonableness which can be independently breached.

2. "Performance and enforcement" of contracts and duties within the *Uniform Commercial Code* include the exercise of rights created by the *Uniform Commercial Code*.

§ 1-305. Remedies to Be Liberally Administered.

(a)   The remedies provided by [the *Uniform Commercial Code*] must be liberally administered to the end that the aggrieved party may be put in as good a position as if the other party had fully performed but neither consequential or special damages nor penal damages may be had except as specifically provided in [the *Uniform Commercial Code*] or by other rule of law.

(b)   Any right or obligation declared by [the *Uniform Commercial Code*] is enforceable by action unless the provision declaring it specifies a different and limited effect.

Official Comment

1.   Subsection (a) is intended to effect three propositions. The first is to negate the possibility of unduly narrow or technical interpretation of remedial provisions by providing that the remedies in the *Uniform Commercial Code* are to be liberally administered to the end stated in this section. The second is to make it clear that compensatory damages are limited to compensation. They do not include consequential or special damages, or penal damages; and the *Uniform Commercial Code* elsewhere makes it clear that damages must be minimized. Cf. Sections 1-304, 2-706(1), and 2-712(2). The third purpose of subsection (a) is to reject any doctrine that damages must be calculable with mathematical accuracy. Compensatory damages are often at best approximate: they have to be proved with whatever definiteness and accuracy the facts permit, but no more. Cf. Section 2-204(3).

2.   Under subsection (b), any right or obligation described in the *Uniform Commercial Code* is enforceable by action, even though no remedy may be expressly provided, unless a particular provision specifies a different and limited effect. Whether specific performance or other equitable relief is available is determined not by this section but by specific provisions and by supplementary principles. Cf. Sections 1-103, 2-716.

3.   "Consequential" or "special" damages and "penal" damages are not defined in the *Uniform Commercial Code*; rather, these terms are used in the sense in which they are used outside the *Uniform Commercial Code*.

Article 2 Sales — Selected Sections

Part 1. Short Title, General Construction, and Subject Matter

§ 2-102 Scope; Certain Security and Other Transactions Excluded from this Article.

Unless the context otherwise requires, this Article applies to transactions in goods; it does not apply to any transaction which although in the form of an unconditional contract to sell or present sale is intended to operate only as a security transaction nor does this Article impair or repeal any statute regulating sales to consumers, farmers or other specified classes of buyers.

§ 2-103 Definitions and Index of Definitions.

(1)   In this Article unless the context otherwise requires ...

(b) "Good faith" in the case of a merchant means honesty in fact and the observance of reasonable commercial standards of fair dealing in the trade.

§ 2-104 Definitions: "Merchant" "Between Merchants" "Financing Agency"

(1)   "Merchant" means a person who deals in goods of the kind or otherwise by his occupation holds himself out as having knowledge or skill peculiar to the practices or goods involved in the transaction or to whom such knowledge or skill may be attributed by his employment of an agent or broker or other intermediary who by his occupation holds himself out as having such knowledge or skill.

(3)   "Between merchants" means in any transaction with respect to which both parties are chargeable with the knowledge or skill of merchants.

§ 2-105 Definitions: Transferability; "Goods"; "Future" Goods; "Lot"; "Commercial Unit."

(1)   "Goods" means all things (including specially manufactured goods) which are movable at the time of identification to the contract for sale other than the money in which the price is to be paid, investment securities (Article 8), and things in action. "Goods" also includes the unborn young of animals and growing crops and other identified things attached to realty as described in the section on goods to be severed from realty (Section 2-107).

§ 2-106 Definitions: "Contract"; "Agreement"; "Contract for Sale"; "Sale"; "Present Sale"; "Conforming" to Contract; "Termination"; "Cancellation".

(1)   In this Article unless the context otherwise requires "contract" and "agreement" are limited to those relating to the present or future sale of goods. "Contract for sale" includes both a present sale of goods and a contract to sell goods at a future time. A "sale" consists in the passing of title from the seller to the buyer for a price (Section 2-401). A "present sale" means a sale which is accomplished by the making of the contract.

Part 2. Form, Formation and Readjustment of Contract

§ 2-201 Formal Requirements; Statute of Frauds.

(1)   Except as otherwise provided in this section a contract for the sale of goods for the price of $500 or more is not enforceable by way of action or defense unless there is some writing sufficient to indicate that a contract for sale has been made between the parties and signed by the party against whom enforcement is sought or by his authorized agent or broker. A writing is not insufficient because it omits or incorrectly states a term agreed upon but the contract is not enforceable under this paragraph beyond the quantity of goods shown in such writing.

(2)   Between merchants if within a reasonable time a writing in confirmation of the contract and sufficient against the sender is received and the party receiving it has reason to know its contents, it satisfies the requirements of subsection (1) against such party unless written notice of objection to its contents is given within ten days after it is received.

(3)   A contract which does not satisfy the requirements of subsection (1) but which is valid in other respects is enforceable

(a) if the goods are to be specially manufactured for the buyer and are not suitable for sale to others in the ordinary course of the seller's business and the seller, before notice of repudiation is received and under circumstances which reasonably indicate that the goods are for the buyer, has made either a substantial beginning of their manufacture or commitments for their procurement; or

(b) if the party against whom enforcement is sought admits in his pleading, testimony or otherwise in court that a contract for sale was made, but the contract is not enforceable under this provision beyond the quantity of goods admitted; or

(c) with respect to goods for which payment has been made and accepted or which have been received and accepted (Section 2-606).

§ 2-202 Final Written Expression: Parol or Extrinsic Evidence.

Terms with respect to which the confirmatory memoranda of the parties agree or which are otherwise set forth in a writing intended by the parties as a final expression of their agreement with respect to such terms as are included therein may not be contradicted by evidence of any prior agreement or of a contemporaneous oral agreement but may be explained or supplemented

(a)   by course of dealing or usage of trade (Section 1-205) or by course of performance (Section 2-208); and

(b)   by evidence of consistent additional terms unless the court finds the writing to have been intended also as a complete and exclusive statement of the terms of the agreement.

Official Comment

Purposes:

1.   This section definitely rejects:

(a) Any assumption that because a writing has been worked out which is final on some matters, it is to be taken as including all the matters agreed upon;

(b) The premise that the language used has the meaning attributable to such language by rules of construction existing in the law rather than the meaning which arises out of the commercial context in which it was used; and

(c) The requirement that a condition precedent to the admissibility of the type of evidence specified in paragraph (a) is an original determination by the court that the language used is ambiguous.

2.   Paragraph (a) makes admissible evidence of course of dealing, usage of trade and course of performance to explain or supplement the terms of any writing stating the agreement of the parties in order that the true understanding of the parties as to the agreement may be reached. Such writings are to be read on the assumption that the course of prior dealings between the parties and the usages of trade were taken for granted when the document was phrased. Unless carefully negated they have become an element of the meaning of the words used. Similarly, the course of actual performance by the parties is considered the best indication of what they intended the writing to mean.

3.   Under paragraph (b) consistent additional terms, not reduced to writing, may be proved unless the court finds that the writing was intended by both parties as a complete and exclusive statement of all the terms. If the additional terms are such that, if agreed upon, they would certainly have been included in the document in the view of the court, then evidence of their alleged making must be kept from the trier of fact.

§ 2-204 Formation in General.

(1)   A contract for sale of goods may be made in any manner sufficient to show agreement, including conduct by both parties which recognizes the existence of such a contract.

(2)   An agreement sufficient to constitute a contract for sale may be found even though the moment of its making is undetermined.

(3)   Even though one or more terms are left open a contract for sale does not fail for indefiniteness if the parties have intended to make a contract and there is a reasonably certain basis for giving an appropriate remedy.

§ 2-205 Firm Offers.

An offer by a merchant to buy or sell goods in a signed writing which by its terms gives assurance that it will be held open is not revocable, for lack of consideration, during the time stated or if no time is stated for a reasonable time, but in no event may such period of irrevocability exceed three months; but any such term of assurance on a form supplied by the offeree must be separately signed by the offeror.

§ 2-206 Offer and Acceptance in Formation of Contract.

(1)   Unless otherwise unambiguously indicated by the language or circumstances

(a) an offer to make a contract shall be construed as inviting acceptance in any manner and by any medium reasonable in the circumstances;

(b) an order or other offer to buy goods for prompt or current shipment shall be construed as inviting acceptance either by a prompt promise to ship or by the prompt or current shipment of conforming or nonconforming goods, but such a shipment of nonconforming goods does not constitute an acceptance if the seller seasonably notifies the buyer that the shipment is offered only as an accommodation to the buyer.

(2)   Where the beginning of a requested performance is a reasonable mode of acceptance an offeror who is not notified of acceptance within a reasonable time may treat the offer as having lapsed before acceptance.

§ 2-207 Additional Terms in Acceptance or Confirmation.

(1)   A definite and seasonable expression of acceptance or a written confirmation which is sent within a reasonable time operates as an acceptance even though it states terms additional to or different from those offered or agreed upon, unless acceptance is expressly made conditional on assent to the additional or different terms.

(2)   The additional terms are to be construed as proposals for addition to the contract. Between merchants such terms become part of the contract unless:

(a) the offer expressly limits acceptance to the terms of the offer;

(b) they materially alter it; or

(c) notification of objection to them has already been given or is given within a reasonable time after notice of them is received.

(3)   Conduct by both parties which recognizes the existence of a contract is sufficient to establish a contract for sale although the writings of the parties do not otherwise establish a contract. In such case the terms of the particular contract consist of those terms on which the writings of the parties agree, together with any supplementary terms incorporated under any other provisions of this Act.

Official Comment

1.   This section is intended to deal with two typical situations. The one is the written confirmation, where an agreement has been reached either orally or by informal correspondence between the parties and is followed by one or both of the parties

sending formal memoranda embodying the terms so far as agreed upon and adding terms not discussed. The other situation is offer and acceptance, in which a wire or letter expressed and intended as an acceptance or the closing of an agreement adds further minor suggestions or proposals such as "ship by Tuesday," "rush," "ship draft against bill of lading inspection allowed," or the like. A frequent example of the second situation is the exchange of printed purchase order and acceptance (sometimes called "acknowledgment") forms. Because the forms are oriented to the thinking of the respective drafting parties, the terms contained in them often do not correspond. Often the seller's form contains terms different from or additional to those set forth in the buyer's form. Nevertheless, the parties proceed with the transaction.

2.   Under this Article a proposed deal which in commercial understanding has in fact been closed is recognized as a contract. Therefore, any additional matter contained in the confirmation or in the acceptance falls within subsection (2) and must be regarded as a proposal for an added term unless the acceptance is made conditional on the acceptance of the additional or different terms.

3.   Whether or not additional or different terms will become part of the agreement depends upon the provisions of subsection (2). If they are such as materially to alter the original bargain, they will not be included unless expressly agreed to by the other party. If, however, they are terms which would not so change the bargain they will be incorporated unless notice of objection to them has already been given or is given within a reasonable time.

4.   Examples of typical clauses which would normally "materially alter" the contract and so result in surprise or hardship if incorporated without express awareness by the other party are: a clause negating such standard warranties as that of merchantability or fitness for a particular purpose in circumstances in which either warranty normally attaches; a clause requiring a guaranty of 90% or 100% deliveries in a case such as a contract by cannery, where the usage of the trade allows greater quantity leeways; a clause reserving to the seller the power to cancel upon the buyer's failure to meet any invoice when due; a clause requiring that complaints be made in a time materially shorter than customary or reasonable.

5.   Examples of clauses which involve no element of unreasonable surprise and which therefore are to be incorporated in the contract unless notice of objection is seasonably given are: a clause setting forth and perhaps enlarging slightly upon the seller's exemption due to supervening causes beyond his control, similar to those covered by the provision of this Article on merchant's excuse by failure of presupposed conditions or a clause fixing in advance any reasonable formula of proration under such circumstances; a clause fixing a reasonable time for complaints within customary limits, or in the case of a purchase for sub-sale, providing for inspection by the sub-purchaser; a clause providing for interest on overdue invoices or fixing the seller's standard credit terms where they are within the range of trade practice and do not limit any credit bargained for; a clause limiting the right of rejection for defects which fall within the customary trade tolerances for acceptance "with adjustment" or otherwise limiting remedy in a reasonable manner (*see* Sections 2-718 and 2-719).

6.   If no answer is received within a reasonable time after additional terms are proposed, it is both fair and commercially sound to assume that their inclusion has been assented to. Where clauses on confirming forms sent by both parties

conflict, each party must be assumed to object to a clause of the other conflicting with one on the confirmation sent by himself. As a result the requirement that there be notice of objection which is found in subsection (2) is satisfied and the conflicting terms do not become a part of the contract. The contract then consists of the terms originally expressly agreed to, terms on which the confirmations agree, and terms supplied by this Act, including subsection (2). The written confirmation is also subject to Section 2-201. Under that section a failure to respond permits enforcement of a prior oral agreement; under this section a failure to respond permits additional terms to become part of the agreement.

7. In many cases, as where goods are shipped, accepted and paid for before any dispute arises, there is no question whether a contract has been made. In such cases, where the writings of the parties do not establish a contract, it is not necessary to determine which act or document constituted the offer and which the acceptance. See Section 2-204. The only question is what terms are included in the contract, and subsection (3) furnishes the governing rule.

§ 2-208 Course of Performance or Practical Construction.

(1) Where the contract for sale involves repeated occasions for performance by either party with knowledge of the nature of the performance and opportunity for objection to it by the other, any course of performance accepted or acquiesced in without objection shall be relevant to determine the meaning of the agreement.

(2) The express terms of the agreement and any such course of performance, as well as any course of dealing and usage of trade, shall be construed whenever reasonable as consistent with each other; but when such construction is unreasonable, express terms shall control course of performance and course of performance shall control both course of dealing and usage of trade (Section 1-205).

(3) Subject to the provisions of the next section on modification and waiver, such course of performance shall be relevant to show a waiver or modification of any term inconsistent with such course of performance.

§ 2-209 Modification, Rescission, and Waiver.

(1) An agreement modifying a contract within this Article needs no consideration to be binding.

(2) A signed agreement which excludes modification or rescission except by a signed writing cannot be otherwise modified or rescinded, but except as between merchants such a requirement on a form supplied by the merchant must be separately signed by the other party.

(3) The requirements of the statute of frauds section of this Article (Section 2-201) must be satisfied if the contract as modified is within its provisions.

(4) Although an attempt at modification or rescission does not satisfy the requirements of subsection (2) or (3) it can operate as a waiver.

(5) A party who has made a waiver affecting an executory portion of the contract may retract the waiver by reasonable notification received by the other party that strict performance will be required of any term waived, unless the retraction would be unjust in view of a material change of position in reliance on the waiver.

§ 2-210 Delegation of Performance; Assignment of Rights.

(1) A party may perform his duty through a delegate unless otherwise agreed or unless the other party has a substantial interest in having his original promisor

perform or control the acts required by the contract. No delegation of performance relieves the party delegating of any duty to perform or any liability for breach.

(2) Unless otherwise agreed all rights of either seller or buyer can be assigned except where the assignment would materially change the duty of the other party, or increase materially the burden or risk imposed on him by his contract, or impair materially his chance of obtaining return performance. A right to damages for breach of the whole contract or a right arising out of the assignor's due performance of his entire obligation can be assigned despite agreement otherwise.

(3) Unless the circumstances indicate the contrary a prohibition of assignment of "the contract" is to be construed as barring only the delegation to the assignee of the assignor's performance.

(4) An assignment of "the contract" or of "all my rights under the contract" or an assignment in similar general terms is an assignment of rights and unless the language or the circumstances (as in an assignment for security) indicate the contrary, it is a delegation of performance of the duties of the assignor and its acceptance by the assignee constitutes a promise by him to perform those duties. This promise is enforceable by either the assignor or the other party to the original contract.

(5) The other party may treat any assignment which delegates performance as creating reasonable grounds for insecurity and may without prejudice to his rights against the assignor demand assurances from the assignee (Section 2-609).

Part 3. General Obligation and Construction of Contract

§ 2-301 General Obligations of Parties.

The obligation of the seller is to transfer and deliver and that of the buyer is to accept and pay in accordance with the contract.

§ 2-302 Unconscionable Contract or Clause.

(1) If the court as a matter of law finds the contract or any clause of the contract to have been unconscionable at the time it was made the court may refuse to enforce the contract, or it may enforce the remainder of the contract without the unconscionable clause, or it may so limit the application of any unconscionable clause as to avoid any unconscionable result.

(2) When it is claimed or appears to the court that the contract or any clause thereof may be unconscionable the parties shall be afforded a reasonable opportunity to present evidence as to its commercial setting, purpose, and effect to aid the court in making the determination.

Official Comment

Purposes:

1. This section is intended to make it possible for the courts to police explicitly against the contracts or clauses which they find to be unconscionable. In the past such policing has been accomplished by adverse construction of language, by manipulation of the rules of offer and acceptance or by determinations that the clause is contrary to public policy or to the dominant purpose of the contract. This section is intended to allow the court to pass directly on the unconscionability of the contract or particular clause therein and to make a conclusion of law as to its unconscionability. The basic test is whether, in the light of the general com-

mercial background and the commercial needs of the particular trade or case, the clauses involved are so one-sided as to be unconscionable under the circumstances existing at the time of the making of the contract. Subsection (2) makes it clear that it is proper for the court to hear evidence upon these questions. The principle is one of the prevention of oppression and unfair surprise (Cf. Campbell Soup Co. v. Wentz, 172 F.2d 80, 3d Cir. 1948) and not of disturbance of allocation of risks because of superior bargaining power....

§ 2-305 Open Price Term.

(1) The parties if they so intend can conclude a contract for sale even though the price is not settled. In such a case the price is a reasonable price at the time for delivery if

(a) nothing is said as to price; or

(b) the price is left to be agreed by the parties and they fail to agree; or

(c) the price is to be fixed in terms of some agreed market or other standard as set or recorded by a third person or agency and it is not so set or recorded.

(2) A price to be fixed by the seller or by the buyer means a price for him to fix in good faith.

(3) When a price left to be fixed otherwise than by agreement of the parties fails to be fixed through fault of one party the other may at his option treat the contract as canceled or himself fix a reasonable price.

(4) Where, however, the parties intend not to be bound unless the price be fixed or agreed and it is not fixed or agreed there is no contract. In such a case the buyer must return any goods already received or if unable so to do must pay their reasonable value at the time of delivery and the seller must return any portion of the price paid on account.

§ 2-306 Output, Requirements and Exclusive Dealings.

(1) A term which measures the quantity by the output of the seller or the requirements of the buyer means such actual output or requirements as may occur in good faith, except that no quantity unreasonably disproportionate to any stated estimate or in the absence of a stated estimate to any normal or otherwise comparable prior output or requirements may be tendered or demanded.

(2) A lawful agreement by either the seller or the buyer for exclusive dealing in the kind of goods concerned imposes unless otherwise agreed an obligation by the seller to use best efforts to supply the goods and by the buyer to use best efforts to promote their sale.

Official Comment

2. Under this Article, a contract for output or requirements is not too indefinite since it is held to mean the actual good faith output or requirements of the particular party. Nor does such a contract lack mutuality of obligation since, under this section, the party who will determine quantity is required to operate his plant or conduct his business in good faith and according to commercial standards of fair dealing in the trade so that his output or requirements will approximate a reasonably foreseeable figure. Reasonable elasticity in the requirements is expressly envisaged by this section and good faith variations from prior requirements are permitted even when the variation may be such as to result in discontinuance. A shutdown by a requirements buyer for lack of orders might

be permissible when a shutdown merely to curtail losses would not. The essential test is whether the party is acting in good faith. Similarly, a sudden expansion of the plant by which requirements are to be measured would not be included within the scope of the contract as made but normal expansion undertaken in good faith would be within the scope of this section. One of the factors in an expansion situation would be whether the market price had risen greatly in a case in which the requirements contract contained a fixed price. Reasonable variation of an extreme sort is exemplified in *Southwest Natural Gas Co. v. Oklahoma Portland Cement Co.*, 102 F.2d 630 (C.C.A.10, 1939). This Article takes no position as to whether a requirements contract is a provable claim in bankruptcy.

3.   If an estimate of output or requirements is included in the agreement, no quantity unreasonably disproportionate to it may be tendered or demanded. Any minimum or maximum set by the agreement shows a clear limit on the intended elasticity. In similar fashion, the agreed estimate is to be regarded as a center around which the parties intend the variation to occur.

§ 2-308 Absence of Specified Place for Delivery.

Unless otherwise agreed

(a) the place for delivery of goods is the seller's place of business or if he has none his residence; but

(b) in a contract for sale of identified goods which to the knowledge of the parties at the time of contracting are in some other place, that place is the place for their delivery; and

(c) documents of title may be delivered through customary banking channels.

§ 2-309 Absence of Specific Time Provisions; Notice of Termination.

(1)   The time for shipment or delivery or any other action under a contract if not provided in this Article or agreed upon shall be a reasonable time.

(2)   Where the contract provides for successive performances but is indefinite in duration it is valid for a reasonable time but unless otherwise agreed may be terminated at any time by either party.

(3)   Termination of a contract by one party except on the happening of an agreed event requires that reasonable notification be received by the other party and an agreement dispensing with notification is invalid if its operation would be unconscionable.

§ 2-310 Open Time for Payment or Running of Credit; Authority to Ship Under Reservation.

(1)   Unless otherwise agreed

(a) payment is due at the time and place at which the buyer is to receive the goods even though the place of shipment is the place of delivery; and

(b) if the seller is authorized to send the goods he may ship them under reservation, and may tender the documents of title, but the buyer may inspect the goods after their arrival before payment is due unless such inspection is inconsistent with the terms of the contract (Section 2-513); and

(c) if delivery is authorized and made by way of documents of title otherwise than by subsection (b) then payment is due at the time and place at which the buyer is to receive the documents regardless of where the goods are to be received; and

(d) where the seller is required or authorized to ship the goods on credit the credit period runs from the time of shipment but postdating the invoice or delaying its dispatch will correspondingly delay the starting of the credit period.

§ 2-311 Options and Cooperation Respecting Performance.

(1) An agreement for sale which is otherwise sufficiently definite (subsection (3) of Section 2-204) to be a contract is not made invalid by the fact that it leaves particulars of performance to be specified by one of the parties. Any such specification must be made in good faith and within limits set by commercial reasonableness.

(2) Unless otherwise agreed specifications relating to assortment of the goods are at the buyer's option and except as otherwise provided in subsections (1)(c) and (3) of Section 2-319 specifications or arrangements relating to shipment are at the seller's option.

(3) Where such specification would materially affect the other party's performance but is not seasonably made or where one party's cooperation is necessary to the agreed performance of the other but is not seasonably forthcoming, the other party in addition to all other remedies

(a) is excused for any resulting delay in his own performance; and

(b) may also either proceed to perform in any reasonable manner or after the time for a material part of his own performance treat the failure to specify or to cooperate as a breach by failure to deliver or accept the goods.

§ 2-312 Warranty of Title and Against Infringement; Buyer's Obligation Against Infringement.

(1) Subject to subsection (2) there is in a contract for sale a warranty by the seller that

(a) the title conveyed shall be good, and its transfer rightful; and

(b) the goods shall be delivered free from any security interest or other lien or encumbrance of which the buyer at the time of contracting has no knowledge.

(2) A warranty under subsection (1) will be excluded or modified only by specific language or by circumstances which give the buyer reason to know that the person selling does not claim title in himself or that he is purporting to sell only such right or title as he or a third person may have.

(3) Unless otherwise agreed a seller who is a merchant regularly dealing in goods of the kind warrants that the goods shall be delivered free of the rightful claim of any third person by way of infringement or the like but a buyer who furnishes specifications to the seller must hold the seller harmless against any such claim which arises out of compliance with the specifications.

§ 2-313 Express Warranties by Affirmation, Promise, Description, Sample.

(1) Express warranties by the seller are created as follows:

(a) Any affirmation of fact or promise made by the seller to the buyer which relates to the goods and becomes part of the basis of the bargain creates an express warranty that the goods shall conform to the affirmation or promise.

(b) Any description of the goods which is made part of the basis of the bargain creates an express warranty that the goods shall conform to the description.

> (c) Any sample or model which is made part of the basis of the bargain creates an express warranty that the whole of the goods shall conform to the sample or model.

(2)   It is not necessary to the creation of an express warranty that the seller use formal words such as "warrant" or "guarantee" or that he have a specific intention to make a warranty, but an affirmation merely of the value of the goods or a statement purporting to be merely the seller's opinion or commendation of the goods does not create a warranty.

Official Comments

Purposes of Changes: To consolidate and systematize basic principles with the result that:

1.   "Express" warranties rest on "dickered" aspects of the individual bargain, and go so clearly to the essence of that bargain that words of disclaimer in a form are repugnant to the basic dickered terms. "Implied" warranties rest so clearly on a common factual situation or set of conditions that no particular language or action is necessary to evidence them and they will arise in such a situation unless unmistakably negated. This section reverts to the older case law insofar as the warranties of description and sample are designated "express" rather than "implied."

2.   Although this section is limited in its scope and direct purpose to warranties made by the seller to the buyer as part of a contract for sale, the warranty sections of this Article are not designed in any way to disturb those lines of case law growth which have recognized that warranties need not be confined either to sales contracts or to the direct parties to such a contract. They may arise in other appropriate circumstances such as in the case of bailments for hire, whether such bailment is itself the main contract or is merely a supplying of containers under a contract for the sale of their contents. The provisions of Section 2-318 on third party beneficiaries expressly recognize this case law development within one particular area. Beyond that, the matter is left to the case law with the intention that the policies of this Act may offer useful guidance in dealing with further cases as they arise

3.   The present section deals with affirmations of fact by the seller, descriptions of the goods or exhibitions of samples, exactly as any other part of a negotiation which ends in a contract is dealt with. No specific intention to make a warranty is necessary if any of these factors is made part of the basis of the bargain. In actual practice affirmations of fact made by the seller about the goods during a bargain are regarded as part of the description of those goods; hence no particular reliance on such statements need be shown in order to weave them into the fabric of the agreement. Rather, any fact which is to take such affirmations, once made, out of the agreement requires clear affirmative proof. The issue normally is one of fact.

4.   In view of the principle that the whole purpose of the law of warranty is to determine what it is that the seller has in essence agreed to sell, the policy is adopted of those cases which refuse except in unusual circumstances to recognize a material deletion of the seller's obligation. Thus, a contract is normally a contract for a sale of something describable and described. A clause generally disclaiming "all warranties, express or implied" cannot reduce the seller's obligation with respect to such description and therefore cannot be given literal effect under Section 2-316.

This is not intended to mean that the parties, if they consciously desire, cannot make their own bargain as they wish. But in determining what they have agreed upon good faith is a factor and consideration should be given to the fact that the probability is small that a real price is intended to be exchanged for a pseudo-obligation.

5.   Paragraph (1)(b) makes specific some of the principles set forth above when a description of the goods is given by the seller. A description need not be by words. Technical specifications, blueprints and the like can afford more exact description than mere language and if made part of the basis of the bargain goods must conform with them. Past deliveries may set the description of quality, either expressly or impliedly by course of dealing. Of course, all descriptions by merchants must be read against the applicable trade usages with the general rules as to merchantability resolving any doubts.

6.   The basic situation as to statements affecting the true essence of the bargain is no different when a sample or model is involved in the transaction. This section includes both a "sample" actually drawn from the bulk of goods which is the subject matter of the sale, and a "model" which is offered for inspection when the subject matter is not at hand and which has not been drawn from the bulk of the goods. Although the underlying principles are unchanged, the facts are often ambiguous when something is shown as illustrative, rather than as a straight sample. In general, the presumption is that any sample or model just as any af-firmation of fact is intended to become a basis of the bargain. But there is no escape from the question of fact. When the seller exhibits a sample purporting to be drawn from an existing bulk, good faith of course requires that the sample be fairly drawn. But in mercantile experience the mere exhibition of a "sample" does not of itself show whether it is merely intended to "suggest" or to "be" the character of the subject-matter of the contract. The question is whether the seller has so acted with reference to the sample as to make him responsible that the whole shall have at least the values shown by it. The circumstances aid in answering this question. If the sample has been drawn from an existing bulk, it must be regarded as describing values of the goods contracted for unless it is accompanied by an unmistakable denial of such responsibility. If, on the other hand, a model of merchandise not on hand is offered, the mercantile presumption that it has become a literal description of the subject matter is not so strong, and particularly so if modification on the buyer's initiative impairs any feature of the model.

7.   The precise time when words of description or affirmation are made or samples are shown is not material. The sole question is whether the language or samples or models are fairly to be regarded as part of the contract. If language is used after the closing of the deal (as when the buyer when taking delivery asks and receives an additional assurance), the warranty becomes a modification, and need not be supported by consideration if it is otherwise reasonable and in order (Section 2-209).

8.   Concerning affirmations of value or a seller's opinion or commendation under subsection (2), the basic question remains the same: What statements of the seller have in the circumstances and in objective judgment become part of the basis of the bargain? As indicated above, all of the statements of the seller do so unless good reason is shown to the contrary. The provisions of subsection (2) are included, however, since common experience discloses that some statements or predictions cannot fairly be viewed as entering into the bargain. Even as to

false statements of value, however, the possibility is left open that a remedy may be provided by the law relating to fraud or misrepresentation.

§ 2-314 Implied Warranty: Merchantability; Usage of Trade.

(1)   Unless excluded or modified (Section 2-316), a warranty that the goods shall be merchantable is implied in a contract for their sale if the seller is a merchant with respect to goods of that kind. Under this section the serving for value of food or drink to be consumed either on the premises or elsewhere is a sale.

(2)   Goods to be merchantable must be at least such as

(a) pass without objection in the trade under the contract description; and

(b) in the case of fungible goods, are of fair average quality within the description; and

(c) are fit for the ordinary purposes for which such goods are used; and

(d) run, within the variations permitted by the agreement, of even kind, quality and quantity within each unit and among all units involved; and

(e) are adequately contained, packaged, and labeled as the agreement may require; and

(f) conform to the promises or affirmations of fact made on the container or label if any.

(3)   Unless excluded or modified (Section 2-316) other implied warranties may arise from course of dealing or usage of trade.

§ 2-315 Implied Warranty: Fitness for Particular Purpose.

Where the seller at the time of contracting has reason to know any particular purpose for which the goods are required and that the buyer is relying on the seller's skill or judgment to select or furnish suitable goods, there is unless excluded or modified under the next section an implied warranty that the goods shall be fit for such purpose.

§ 2-316 Exclusion or Modification of Warranties.

(1)   Words or conduct relevant to the creation of an express warranty and words or conduct tending to negate or limit warranty shall be construed wherever reasonable as consistent with each other; but subject to the provisions of this Article on parol or extrinsic evidence (Section 2-202) negation or limitation is inoperative to the extent that such construction is unreasonable.

(2)   Subject to subsection (3), to exclude or modify the implied warranty of merchantability or any part of it the language must mention merchantability and in case of a writing must be conspicuous, and to exclude or modify any implied warranty of fitness the exclusion must be by a writing and conspicuous. Language to exclude all implied warranties of fitness is sufficient if it states, for example, that "There are no warranties which extend beyond the description on the face hereof."

(3)   Notwithstanding subsection (2)

(a) unless the circumstances indicate otherwise, all implied warranties are excluded by expressions like "as is", "with all faults" or other language which in common understanding calls the buyer's attention to the exclusion of warranties and makes plain that there is no implied warranty; and

(b) when the buyer before entering into the contract has examined the goods or the sample or model as fully as he desired or has refused to examine the goods there is no implied warranty with regard to defects which an examination ought in the circumstances to have revealed to him; and

(c) an implied warranty can also be excluded or modified by course of dealing or course of performance or usage of trade.

(4) Remedies for breach of warranty can be limited in accordance with the provisions of this Article on liquidation or limitation of damages and on contractual modification of remedy (Sections 2-718 and 2-719).

Official Comment

1. This section is designed principally to deal with those frequent clauses in sales contracts which seek to exclude "all warranties, express or implied." It seeks to protect a buyer from unexpected and unbargained language of disclaimer by denying effect to such language when inconsistent with language of express warranty and permitting the exclusion of implied warranties only by conspicuous language or other circumstances which protect the buyer from surprise.

2. The seller is protected under this Article against false allegations of oral warranties by its provisions on parol and extrinsic evidence and against unauthorized representations by the customary "lack of authority" clauses. This Article treats the limitation or avoidance of consequential damages as a matter of limiting remedies for breach, separate from the matter of creation of liability under a warranty. If no warranty exists, there is of course no problem of limiting remedies for breach of warranty. Under subsection (4) the question of limitation of remedy is governed by the sections referred to rather than by this section.

3. Disclaimer of the implied warranty of merchantability is permitted under subsection (2), but with the safeguard that such disclaimers must mention merchantability and in case of a writing must be conspicuous.

4. Unlike the implied warranty of merchantability, implied warranties of fitness for a particular purpose may be excluded by general language, but only if it is in writing and conspicuous.

5. Subsection (2) presupposes that the implied warranty in question exists unless excluded or modified. Whether or not language of disclaimer satisfies the requirements of this section, such language may be relevant under other sections to the question whether the warranty was ever in fact created. Thus, unless the provisions of this Article on parol and extrinsic evidence prevent, oral language of disclaimer may raise issues of fact as to whether reliance by the buyer occurred and whether the seller had "reason to know" under the section on implied warranty of fitness for a particular purpose.

7. Paragraph (a) of subsection (3) deals with general terms such as "as is," "as they stand," "with all faults," and the like. Such terms in ordinary commercial usage are understood to mean that the buyer takes the entire risk as to the quality of the goods involved. The terms covered by paragraph (a) are in fact merely a particularization of paragraph (c) which provides for exclusion or modification of implied warranties by usage of trade.

§2-318 Third Party Beneficiaries of Warranties Express or Implied.

Alternative A

A seller's warranty whether express or implied extends to any natural person who is in the family or household of his buyer or who is a guest in his home if it is reasonable to expect that such person may use, consume or be affected by the goods and who is injured in person by breach of the warranty. A seller may not exclude or limit the operation of this section.

Alternative B

A seller's warranty whether express or implied extends to any natural person who may reasonably be expected to use, consume or be affected by the goods and who is injured in person by breach of the warranty. A seller may not exclude or limit the operation of this section.

Alternative C

A seller's warranty whether express or implied extends to any person who may reasonably be expected to use, consume or be affected by the goods and who is injured by breach of the warranty. A seller may not exclude or limit the operation of this section with respect to injury to the person of an individual to whom the warranty extends.

Part 5. Performance

§ 2-508. Cure by Seller of Improper Tender or Delivery; Replacement.

(1) Where any tender or delivery by the seller is rejected because nonconforming and the time for performance has not yet expired, the seller may seasonably notify the buyer of his intention to cure and may then within the contract time make a conforming delivery.

(2) Where the buyer rejects a nonconforming tender which the seller had reasonable grounds to believe would be acceptable with or without money allowance the seller may if he seasonably notifies the buyer have a further reasonable time to substitute a conforming tender.

Part 6. Breach, Repudiation and Excuse

§ 2-601 Buyer's Rights on Improper Delivery.

Subject to the provisions of this Article on breach in installment contracts (Section 2-612) and unless otherwise agreed under the sections on contractual limitations of remedy (Sections 2-718 and 2-719), if the goods or the tender of delivery fail in any respect to conform to the contract, the buyer may

(a) reject the whole; or

(b) accept the whole; or

(c) accept any commercial unit or units and reject the rest.

§ 2-602. Manner and Effect of Rightful Rejection.

(1) Rejection of goods must be within a reasonable time after their delivery or tender. It is ineffective unless the buyer seasonably notifies the seller.

§ 2-606. What Constitutes Acceptance of Goods.

(1) Acceptance of goods occurs when the buyer

(a) after a reasonable opportunity to inspect the goods signifies to the seller that the goods are conforming or that he will take or retain them in spite of their nonconformity; or

(b) fails to make an effective rejection (subsection (1) of Section 2-602), but such acceptance does not occur until the buyer has had a reasonable opportunity to inspect them; or

(c) does any act inconsistent with the seller's ownership; but if such act is wrongful as against the seller it is an acceptance only if ratified by him.

(2) Acceptance of a part of any commercial unit is acceptance of that entire unit.

§ 2-607. Effect of Acceptance; Notice of Breach; Burden of Establishing Breach After Acceptance; Notice of Claim or Litigation to Person Answerable Over.

(1) The buyer must pay at the contract rate for any goods accepted.

(2) Acceptance of goods by the buyer precludes rejection of the goods accepted and if made with knowledge of a nonconformity cannot be revoked because of it unless the acceptance was on the reasonable assumption that the nonconformity would be seasonably cured but acceptance does not of itself impair any other remedy provided by this Article for nonconformity.

(3) Where a tender has been accepted

(a) the buyer must within a reasonable time after he discovers or should have discovered any breach notify the seller of breach or be barred from any remedy; and

(b) if the claim is one for infringement or the like (subsection (3) of Section 2-312) and the buyer is sued as a result of such a breach he must so notify the seller within a reasonable time after he receives notice of the litigation or be barred from any remedy over for liability established by the litigation.

(4) The burden is on the buyer to establish any breach with respect to the goods accepted.

(5) Where the buyer is sued for breach of a warranty or other obligation for which his seller is answerable over

(a) he may give his seller written notice of the litigation. If the notice states that the seller may come in and defend and that if the seller does not do so he will be bound in any action against him by his buyer by any determination of fact common to the two litigations, then unless the seller after seasonable receipt of the notice does come in and defend he is so bound.

(b) if the claim is one for infringement or the like (subsection (3) of Section 2-312) the original seller may demand in writing that his buyer turn over to him control of the litigation including settlement or else be barred from any remedy over and if he also agrees to bear all expense and to satisfy any adverse judgment, then unless the buyer after seasonable receipt of the demand does turn over control the buyer is so barred.

(6) The provisions of subsections (3), (4) and (5) apply to any obligation of a buyer to hold the seller harmless against infringement or the like (subsection (3) of Section 2-312).

§ 2-608 Revocation of Acceptance in Whole or in Part.

(1) The buyer may revoke his acceptance of a lot or commercial unit whose nonconformity substantially impairs its value to him if he has accepted it

(a) on the reasonable assumption that its nonconformity would be cured and it has not been seasonably cured; or

(b) without discovery of such nonconformity if his acceptance was reasonably induced either by the difficulty of discovery before acceptance or by the seller's assurances.

(2) Revocation of acceptance must occur within a reasonable time after the buyer discovers or should have discovered the ground for it and before any substantial change in condition of the goods which is not caused by their own defects. It is not effective until the buyer notifies the seller of it.

(3) A buyer who so revokes has the same rights and duties with regard to the goods involved as if he had rejected them.

§ 2-609 Right to Adequate Assurance of Performance.

(1) A contract for sale imposes an obligation on each party that the other's expectation of receiving due performance will not be impaired. When reasonable grounds for insecurity arise with respect to the performance of either party the other may in writing demand adequate assurance of due performance and until he receives such assurance may if commercially reasonable suspend any performance for which he has not already received the agreed return.

(2) Between merchants the reasonableness of grounds for insecurity and the adequacy of any assurance offered shall be determined according to commercial standards.

(3) Acceptance of any improper delivery or payment does not prejudice the aggrieved party's right to demand adequate assurance of future performance.

(4) After receipt of a justified demand failure to provide within a reasonable time not exceeding thirty days such assurance of due performance as is adequate under the circumstances of the particular case is a repudiation of the contract.

Official Comment

1. The section rests on the recognition of the fact that the essential purpose of a contract between commercial men is actual performance and they do not bargain merely for a promise, or for a promise plus the right to win a lawsuit and that a continuing sense of reliance and security that the promised performance will be forthcoming when due, is an important feature of the bargain. If either the willingness or the ability of a party to perform declines materially between the time of contracting and the time for performance, the other party is threatened with the loss of a substantial part of what he has bargained for. A seller needs protection not merely against having to deliver on credit to a shaky buyer, but also against having to procure and manufacture the goods, perhaps turning down other customers. Once he has been given reason to believe that the buyer's performance has become uncertain, it is an undue hardship to force him to continue his own performance. Similarly, a buyer who believes that the seller's deliveries have become uncertain cannot safely wait for the due date of performance when he has been buying to assure himself of materials for his current manufacturing or to replenish his stock of merchandise.

3. Subsection (2) of the present section requires that "reasonable" grounds and "adequate" assurance as used in subsection (1) be defined by commercial rather than legal standards. The express reference to commercial standards carries no connotation that the obligation of good faith is not equally applicable here....

Thus a buyer who falls behind in "his account" with the seller, even though the items involved have to do with separate and legally distinct contracts, impairs the seller's expectation of due performance. Again, under the same test, a buyer who requires precision parts which he intends to use immediately upon delivery, may have reasonable grounds for insecurity if he discovers that his seller is making defective deliveries of such parts to other buyers with similar needs. Thus, too, in a situation such as arose in *Jay Dreher Corporation v. Delco Appliance Corporation*, 93 F.2d 275 (C.C.A.2, 1937), where a manufacturer gave a dealer an exclusive franchise for the sale of his product but on two or three occasions breached the exclusive dealing clause, although there was no default in orders, deliveries or payments under the separate sales contract between the parties, the aggrieved dealer would be entitled to suspend his performance of the contract for sale under the present section and to demand assurance that the exclusive dealing contract would be lived up to. There is no need for an explicit clause tying the exclusive franchise into the contract for the sale of goods since the situation itself ties the agreements together.

The nature of the sales contract enters also into the question of reasonableness. For example, a report from an apparently trustworthy source that the seller had shipped defective goods or was planning to ship them would normally give the buyer reasonable grounds for insecurity....

4. What constitutes "adequate" assurance of due performance is subject to the same test of factual conditions. For example, where the buyer can make use of a defective delivery, a mere promise by a seller of good repute that he is giving the matter his attention and that the defect will not be repeated, is normally sufficient. Under the same circumstances, however, a similar statement by a known corner-cutter might well be considered insufficient without the posting of a guaranty or, if so demanded by the buyer, a speedy replacement of the delivery involved. By the same token where a delivery has defects, even though easily curable, which interfere with easy use by the buyer, no verbal assurance can be deemed adequate which is not accompanied by replacement, repair, money allowance, or other commercially reasonable cure.

§ 2-610 Anticipatory Repudiation.

When either party repudiates the contract with respect to a performance not yet due the loss of which will substantially impair the value of the contract to the other, the aggrieved party may

(a) for a commercially reasonable time await performance by the repudiating party; or

(b) resort to any remedy for breach (Section 2-703 or Section 2-711), even though he has notified the repudiating party that he would await the latter's performance and has urged retraction; and

(c) in either case suspend his own performance or proceed in accordance with the provisions of this Article on the seller's right to identify goods to the contract notwithstanding breach or to salvage unfinished goods (Section 2-704).

§ 2-611 Retraction of Anticipatory Repudiation.

(1) Until the repudiating party's next performance is due he can retract his repudiation unless the aggrieved party has since the repudiation canceled or materially changed his position or otherwise indicated that he considers the repudiation final.

(2) Retraction may be by any method which clearly indicates to the aggrieved party that the repudiating party intends to perform, but must include any assurance justifiably demanded under the provisions of this Article (Section 2-609).

(3)   Retraction reinstates the repudiating party's rights under the contract with due excuse and allowance to the aggrieved party for any delay occasioned by the repudiation.

§ 2-612 "Installment Contract"; Breach.

(1)   An "installment contract" is one which requires or authorizes the delivery of goods in separate lots to be separately accepted, even though the contract contains a clause "each delivery is a separate contract" or its equivalent.

(2)   The buyer may reject any installment which is nonconforming if the nonconformity substantially impairs the value of that installment and cannot be cured or if the nonconformity is a defect in the required documents; but if the nonconformity does not fall within subsection (3) and the seller gives adequate assurance of its cure the buyer must accept that installment.

(3)   Whenever nonconformity or default with respect to one or more installments substantially impairs the value of the whole contract there is a breach of the whole. But the aggrieved party reinstates the contract if he accepts a nonconforming installment without seasonably notifying of cancellation or if he brings an action with respect only to past installments or demands performance as to future installments.

§ 2-613 Casualty to Identified Goods.

Where the contract requires for its performance goods identified when the contract is made, and the goods suffer casualty without fault of either party before the risk of loss passes to the buyer, or in a proper case under a "no arrival, no sale" term (Section 2-324) then

(a) if the loss is total the contract is avoided; and

(b) if the loss is partial or the goods have so deteriorated as no longer to conform to the contract the buyer may nevertheless demand inspection and at his option either treat the contract as avoided or accept the goods with due allowance from the contract price for the deterioration or the deficiency in quantity but without further right against the seller.

§ 2-614 Substituted Performance.

(1)   Where without fault of either party the agreed berthing, loading, or unloading facilities fail or an agreed type of carrier becomes unavailable or the agreed manner of delivery otherwise becomes commercially impracticable but a commercially reasonable substitute is available, such substitute performance must be tendered and accepted.

(2)   If the agreed means or manner of payment fails because of domestic or foreign governmental regulation, the seller may withhold or stop delivery unless the buyer provides a means or manner of payment which is commercially a substantial equivalent. If delivery has already been taken, payment by the means or in the manner provided by the regulation discharges the buyer's obligation unless the regulation is discriminatory, oppressive or predatory.

§ 2-615 Excuse by Failure of Presupposed Conditions.

Except so far as a seller may have assumed a greater obligation and subject to the preceding section on substituted performance:

(a) Delay in delivery or non-delivery in whole or in part by a seller who complies with paragraphs (b) and (c) is not a breach of his duty under a contract for sale if performance as agreed has been made impracticable by the occurrence of a contingency the nonoccurrence of which was a basic assumption on which the contract was made or by compliance in good faith with any applicable foreign or domestic governmental regulation or order whether or not it later proves to be invalid.

(b) Where the causes mentioned in paragraph (a) affect only a part of the seller's capacity to perform, he must allocate production and deliveries among his customers but may at his option include regular customers not then under contract as well as his own requirements for further manufacture. He may so allocate in any manner which is fair and reasonable.

(c) The seller must notify the buyer seasonably that there will be delay or non-delivery and, when allocation is required under paragraph (b), of the estimated quota thus made available for the buyer.

Official Comment

4.   Increased cost alone does not excuse performance unless the rise in cost is due to some unforeseen contingency which alters the essential nature of the performance. Neither is a rise or a collapse in the market in itself a justification, for that is exactly the type of business risk which business contracts made at fixed prices are intended to cover. But a severe shortage of raw materials or of supplies due to a contingency such as war, embargo, local crop failure, unforeseen shutdown of major sources of supply or the like, which either causes a marked increase in cost or altogether prevents the seller from securing supplies necessary to his performance, is within the contemplation of this section. (*See Ford & Sons, Ltd., v. Henry Leetham & Sons, Ltd.*, 21 Com. Cas. 55 (1915, K.B.D.).)

5.   Where a particular source of supply is exclusive under the agreement and fails through casualty, the present section applies rather than the provision on destruction or deterioration of specific goods. The same holds true where a particular source of supply is shown by the circumstances to have been contemplated or assumed by the parties at the time of contracting. (*See Davis Co. v. Hoffmann LaRoche Chemical Works*, 166 N.Y.S. 179 (1917) and *International Paper Co. v. Rockefeller*, 146 N.Y.S. 371 (1914).) There is no excuse under this section, however, unless the seller has employed all due measures to assure himself that his source will not fail. (*See Canadian Industrial Alcohol Co., Ltd., v. Dunbar Molasses Co.*, 179 N.E. 383 (N.Y. 1932) and *Washington Mfg. Co. v. Midland Lumber Co.*, 194 P. 777 (Wash 1921).)

In the case of failure of production by an agreed source for causes beyond the seller's control, the seller should, if possible, be excused since production by an agreed source is without more a basic assumption of the contract. Such excuse should not result in relieving the defaulting supplier from liability nor in dropping into the seller's lap an unearned bonus of damages over. The flexible adjustment machinery of this Article provides the solution under the provision on the obligation of good faith. A condition to his making good the claim of excuse is the turning over to the buyer of his rights against the defaulting source of supply to the extent of the buyer's contract in relation to which excuse is being claimed.

6.   In situations in which neither sense nor justice is served by either answer when the issue is posed in flat terms of "excuse" or "no excuse," adjustment under the various provisions of this Article is necessary, especially the sections on good faith, on insecurity and assurance and on the reading of all provisions in the

light of their purposes, and the general policy of this Act to use equitable principles in furtherance of commercial standards and good faith.

§ 2-616 Procedure on Notice Claiming Excuse.

(1) Where the buyer receives notification of a material or indefinite delay or an allocation justified under the preceding section he may by written notification to the seller as to any delivery concerned, and where the prospective deficiency substantially impairs the value of the whole contract under the provisions of this Article relating to breach of installment contracts (Section 2-612), then also as to the whole,

    (a) terminate and thereby discharge any unexecuted portion of the contract; or

    (b) modify the contract by agreeing to take his available quota in substitution.

(2) If after receipt of such notification from the seller the buyer fails so to modify the contract within a reasonable time not exceeding thirty days the contract lapses with respect to any deliveries affected.

(3) The provisions of this section may not be negated by agreement except in so far as the seller has assumed a greater obligation under the preceding section.

Part 7. Remedies

§ 2-703 Seller's Remedies in General.

Where the buyer wrongfully rejects or revokes acceptance of goods or fails to make a payment due on or before delivery or repudiates with respect to a part or the whole, then with respect to any goods directly affected and, if the breach is of the whole contract (Section 2-612), then also with respect to the whole undelivered balance, the aggrieved seller may

    (a) withhold delivery of such goods;

    (b) stop delivery by any bailee as hereafter provided (Section 2-705);

    (c) proceed under the next section respecting goods still unidentified to the contract;

    (d) resell and recover damages as hereafter provided (Section 2-706);

    (e) recover damages for non-acceptance (Section 2-708) or in a proper case the price (Section 2-709);

    (f) cancel.

§ 2-704 Seller's Right to Identify Goods to the Contract Notwithstanding Breach or to Salvage Unfinished Goods.

(1) An aggrieved seller under the preceding section may

    (a) identify to the contract conforming goods not already identified if at the time he learned of the breach they are in his possession or control;

    (b) treat as the subject of resale goods which have demonstrably been intended for the particular contract even though those goods are unfinished.

(2) Where the goods are unfinished an aggrieved seller may in the exercise of reasonable commercial judgment for the purposes of avoiding loss and of effective realization either complete the manufacture and wholly identify the goods to the contract or cease manufacture and resell for scrap or salvage value or proceed in any other reasonable manner.

§ 2-706 Seller's Resale Including Contract for Resale.

(1) Under the conditions stated in Section 2-703 on seller's remedies, the seller may resell the goods concerned or the undelivered balance thereof. Where the resale is made in good faith and in a commercially reasonable manner the seller may recover the difference between the resale price and the contract price together with any incidental damages allowed under the provisions of this Article (Section 2-710), but less expenses saved in consequence of the buyer's breach.

(2) Except as otherwise provided in subsection (3) or unless otherwise agreed resale may be at public or private sale including sale by way of one or more contracts to sell or of identification to an existing contract of the seller. Sale may be as a unit or in parcels and at any time and place and on any terms but every aspect of the sale including the method, manner, time, place and terms must be commercially reasonable. The resale must be reasonably identified as referring to the broken contract, but it is not necessary that the goods be in existence or that any or all of them have been identified to the contract before the breach.

(3) Where the resale is at private sale the seller must give the buyer reasonable notification of his intention to resell.

(4) Where the resale is at public sale

(a) only identified goods can be sold except where there is a recognized market for a public sale of futures in goods of the kind; and

(b) it must be made at a usual place or market for public sale if one is reasonably available and except in the case of goods which are perishable or threaten to decline in value speedily the seller must give the buyer reasonable notice of the time and place of the resale; and

(c) if the goods are not to be within the view of those attending the sale the notification of sale must state the place where the goods are located and provide for their reasonable inspection by prospective bidders; and

(d) the seller may buy.

(5) A purchaser who buys in good faith at a resale takes the goods free of any rights of the original buyer even though the seller fails to comply with one or more of the requirements of this section.

(6) The seller is not accountable to the buyer for any profit made on any resale. A person in the position of a seller (Section 2-707) or a buyer who has rightfully rejected or justifiably revoked acceptance must account for any excess over the amount of his security interest, as hereinafter defined (subsection (3) of Section 2-711).

§ 2-708 Seller's Damages for Non-acceptance or Repudiation.

(1) Subject to subsection (2) and to the provisions of this Article with respect to proof of market price (Section 2-723), the measure of damages for non-acceptance or repudiation by the buyer is the difference between the market price at the time and place for tender and the unpaid contract price together with any incidental damages provided in this Article (Section 2-710), but less expenses saved in consequence of the buyer's breach.

(2) If the measure of damages provided in subsection (1) is inadequate to put the seller in as good a position as performance would have done then the measure of damages is the profit (including reasonable overhead) which the seller would

have made from full performance by the buyer, together with any incidental damages provided in this Article (Section 2-710), due allowance for costs reasonably incurred and due credit for payments or proceeds of resale.

§ 2-709 Action for the Price.

(1) When the buyer fails to pay the price as it becomes due the seller may recover, together with any incidental damages under the next section, the price

(a) of goods accepted or of conforming goods lost or damaged within a commercially reasonable time after risk of their loss has passed to the buyer; and

(b) of goods identified to the contract if the seller is unable after reasonable effort to resell them at a reasonable price or the circumstances reasonably indicate that such effort will be unavailing.

(2) Where the seller sues for the price he must hold for the buyer any goods which have been identified to the contract and are still in his control except that if resale becomes possible he may resell them at any time prior to the collection of the judgment. The net proceeds of any such resale must be credited to the buyer and payment of the judgment entitles him to any goods not resold.

(3) After the buyer has wrongfully rejected or revoked acceptance of the goods or has failed to make a payment due or has repudiated (Section 2-610), a seller who is held not entitled to the price under this section shall nevertheless be awarded damages for non-acceptance under the preceding section.

§ 2-710 Seller's Incidental Damages.

Incidental damages to an aggrieved seller include any commercially reasonable charges, expenses or commissions incurred in stopping delivery, in the transportation, care and custody of goods after the buyer's breach, in connection with return or resale of the goods or otherwise resulting from the breach.

§ 2-711 Buyer's Remedies in General; Buyer's Security Interest in Rejected Goods.

(1) Where the seller fails to make delivery or repudiates or the buyer rightfully rejects or justifiably revokes acceptance then with respect to any goods involved, and with respect to the whole if the breach goes to the whole contract (Section 2-612), the buyer may cancel and whether or not he has done so may in addition to recovering so much of the price as has been paid

(a) "cover" and have damages under the next section as to all the goods affected whether or not they have been identified to the contract; or

(b) recover damages for non-delivery as provided in this Article (Section 2-713).

(2) Where the seller fails to deliver or repudiates the buyer may also

(a) if the goods have been identified recover them as provided in this Article (Section 2-502); or

(b) in a proper case obtain specific performance or replevy the goods as provided in this Article (Section 2-716).

(3) On rightful rejection or justifiable revocation of acceptance a buyer has a security interest in goods in his possession or control for any payments made on their price and any expenses reasonably incurred in their inspection, receipt, transportation, care and custody and may hold such goods and resell them in like manner as an aggrieved seller (Section 2-706).

§ 2-712 "Cover"; Buyer's Procurement of Substitute Goods.

(1)   After a breach within the preceding section the buyer may "cover" by making in good faith and without unreasonable delay any reasonable purchase of or contract to purchase goods in substitution for those due from the seller.

(2)   The buyer may recover from the seller as damages the difference between the cost of cover and the contract price together with any incidental or consequential damages as hereinafter defined (Section 2-715), but less expenses saved in consequence of the seller's breach.

(3)   Failure of the buyer to effect cover within this section does not bar him from any other remedy.

§ 2-713 Buyer's Damages for Non-Delivery or Repudiation.

(1)   Subject to the provisions of this Article with respect to proof of market price (Section 2-723), the measure of damages for non-delivery or repudiation by the seller is the difference between the market price at the time when the buyer learned of the breach and the contract price together with any incidental and consequential damages provided in this Article (Section 2-715), but less expenses saved in consequence of the seller's breach.

(2)   Market price is to be determined as of the place for tender or, in cases of rejection after arrival or revocation of acceptance, as of the place of arrival.

§ 2-714 Buyer's Damages for Breach in Regard to Accepted Goods.

(1)   Where the buyer has accepted goods and given notification (subsection (3) of Section 2-607) he may recover as damages for any nonconformity of tender the loss resulting in the ordinary course of events from the seller's breach as determined in any manner which is reasonable.

(2)   The measure of damages for breach of warranty is the difference at the time and place of acceptance between the value of the goods accepted and the value they would have had if they had been as warranted, unless special circumstances show proximate damages of a different amount.

(3)   In a proper case any incidental and consequential damages under the next section may also be recovered.

§ 2-715 Buyer's Incidental and Consequential Damages.

(1)   Incidental damages resulting from the seller's breach include expenses reasonably incurred in inspection, receipt, transportation and care and custody of goods rightfully rejected, any commercially reasonable charges, expenses or commissions in connection with effecting cover and any other reasonable expense incident to the delay or other breach.

(2)   Consequential damages resulting from the seller's breach include

    (a) any loss resulting from general or particular requirements and needs of which the seller at the time of contracting had reason to know and which could not reasonably be prevented by cover or otherwise; and

    (b) injury to person or property proximately resulting from any breach of warranty.

§ 2-716 Buyer's Right to Specific Performance of Replevin.

(1)   Specific performance may be decreed where the goods are unique or in other proper circumstances.

(2)   The decree for specific performance may include such terms and conditions as to payment of the price, damages, or other relief as the court may deem just.

(3)   The buyer has a right of replevin for goods identified to the contract if after reasonable effort he is unable to effect cover for such goods or the circumstances reasonably indicate that such effort will be unavailing or if the goods have been shipped under reservation and satisfaction of the security interest in them has been made or tendered.

Official Comment

Purposes of Changes: To make it clear that:

1.   The present section continues in general prior policy as to specific performance and injunction against breach. However, without intending to impair in any way the exercise of the court's sound discretion in the matter, this Article seeks to further a more liberal attitude than some courts have shown in connection with the specific performance of contracts of sale.

2.   In view of this Article's emphasis on the commercial feasibility of replacement, a new concept of what are "unique" goods is introduced under this section. Specific performance is no longer limited to goods which are already specific or ascertained at the time of contracting. The test of uniqueness under this section must be made in terms of the total situation which characterizes the contract. Output and requirements contracts involving a particular or peculiarly available source or market present today the typical commercial specific performance situation, as contrasted with contracts for the sale of heirlooms or priceless works of art which were usually involved in the older cases. However, uniqueness is not the sole basis of the remedy under this section for the relief may also be granted "in other proper circumstances" and inability to cover is strong evidence of "other proper circumstances".

§ 2-717 Deduction of Damages from the Price.

The buyer on notifying the seller of his intention to do so may deduct all or any part of the damages resulting from any breach of the contract from any part of the price still due under the same contract.

§ 2-718 Liquidation or Limitation of Damages; Deposits.

(1)   Damages for breach by either party may be liquidated in the agreement but only at an amount which is reasonable in the light of the anticipated or actual harm caused by the breach, the difficulties of proof of loss, and the inconvenience or non-feasibility of otherwise obtaining an adequate remedy. A term fixing unreasonably large liquidated damages is void as a penalty.

(2)   Where the seller justifiably withholds delivery of goods because of the buyer's breach, the buyer is entitled to restitution of any amount by which the sum of his payments exceeds

(a) the amount to which the seller is entitled by virtue of terms liquidating the seller's damages in accordance with subsection (1), or

(b) in the absence of such terms, twenty per cent of the value of the total performance for which the buyer is obligated under the contract or $500, whichever is smaller.

(3)   The buyer's right to restitution under subsection (2) is subject to offset to the extent that the seller establishes

(a) a right to recover damages under the provisions of this Article other than subsection (1), and

(b) the amount or value of any benefits received by the buyer directly or indirectly by reason of the contract.

(4) Where a seller has received payment in goods their reasonable value or the proceeds of their resale shall be treated as payments for the purposes of subsection (2); but if the seller has notice of the buyer's breach before reselling goods received in part performance, his resale is subject to the conditions laid down in this Article on resale by an aggrieved seller (Section 2-706).

§ 2-719 Contractual Modification or Limitation of Remedy.

(1) Subject to the provisions of subsections (2) and (3) of this section and of the preceding section on liquidation and limitation of damages,

(a) the agreement may provide for remedies in addition to or in substitution for those provided in this Article and may limit or alter the measure of damages recoverable under this Article, as by limiting the buyer's remedies to return of the goods and repayment of the price or to repair and replacement of non-conforming goods or parts; and

(b) resort to a remedy as provided is optional unless the remedy is expressly agreed to be exclusive, in which case it is the sole remedy.

(2) Where circumstances cause an exclusive or limited remedy to fail of its essential purpose, remedy may be had as provided in this Act.

(3) Consequential damages may be limited or excluded unless the limitation or exclusion is unconscionable. Limitation of consequential damages for injury to the person in the case of consumer goods is prima facie unconscionable but limitation of damages where the loss is commercial is not.

Article 9 Secured Transactions — Selected Sections on Assignment

§ 9-403. Agreement Not to Assert Defenses Against Assignee

(a) [**"Value."**] In this section, "value" has the meaning provided in Section 3 303(a).

(b) [**Agreement not to assert claim or defense.**] Except as otherwise provided in this section, an agreement between an account debtor and an assignor not to assert against an assignee any claim or defense that the account debtor may have against the assignor is enforceable by an assignee that takes an assignment:

(1) for value;

(2) in good faith;

(3) without notice of a claim of a property or possessory right to the property assigned; and

(4) without notice of a defense or claim in recoupment of the type that may be asserted against a person entitled to enforce a negotiable instrument under Section 3-305(a).

(c) [**When subsection (b) not applicable.**] Subsection (b) does not apply to defenses of a type that may be asserted against a holder in due course of a negotiable instrument under Section 3-305(b).

(d) [**Omission of required statement in consumer transaction.**] In a consumer transaction, if a record evidences the account debtor's obligation, law other than this article requires that the record include a statement to the effect that the rights of an assignee are subject to claims or defenses that the account debtor could assert against the original obligee, and the record does not include such a statement:

(1) the record has the same effect as if the record included such a statement; and

(2) the account debtor may assert against an assignee those claims and defenses that would have been available if the record included such a statement.

§ 9-406. Discharge Of Account Debtor; Notification Of Assignment; Identification And Proof Of Assignment; Restrictions On Assignment Of Accounts, Chattel Paper, Payment Intangibles, And Promissory Notes Ineffective

(a)   [**Discharge of account debtor; effect of notification.**] Subject to subsections (b) through (i), an account debtor on an account, chattel paper, or a payment intangible may discharge its obligation by paying the assignor until, but not after, the account debtor receives a notification, authenticated by the assignor or the assignee, that the amount due or to become due has been assigned and that payment is to be made to the assignee. After receipt of the notification, the account debtor may discharge its obligation by paying the assignee and may not discharge the obligation by paying the assignor.

(b)   [**When notification ineffective.**] Subject to subsection (h), notification is ineffective under subsection (a):

(1) if it does not reasonably identify the rights assigned;

(2) to the extent that an agreement between an account debtor and a seller of a payment intangible limits the account debtor's duty to pay a person other than the seller and the limitation is effective under law other than this article; or

(3) at the option of an account debtor, if the notification notifies the account debtor to make less than the full amount of any installment or other periodic payment to the assignee, even if:

(A) only a portion of the account, chattel paper, or payment intangible has been assigned to that assignee;

(B) a portion has been assigned to another assignee; or

(C) the account debtor knows that the assignment to that assignee is limited.

(c)   [**Proof of assignment.**] Subject to subsection (h), if requested by the account debtor, an assignee shall seasonably furnish reasonable proof that the assignment has been made. Unless the assignee complies, the account debtor may discharge its obligation by paying the assignor, even if the account debtor has received a notification under subsection (a).

(d)   [**Term restricting assignment generally ineffective.**] Except as otherwise provided in subsection (e) and Sections 2A-303 and 9-407, and subject to subsection (h), a term in an agreement between an account debtor and an assignor or in a promissory note is ineffective to the extent that it:

(1) prohibits, restricts, or requires the consent of the account debtor or person obligated on the promissory note to the assignment or transfer of, or the creation, attachment, perfection, or enforcement of a security interest in, the account, chattel paper, payment intangible, or promissory note; or

(2) provides that the assignment or transfer or the creation, attachment, perfection, or enforcement of the security interest may give rise to a default, breach, right

of recoupment, claim, defense, termination, right of termination, or remedy under the account, chattel paper, payment intangible, or promissory note.

(e) **[Inapplicability of subsection (d) to certain sales.]** Subsection (d) does not apply to the sale of a payment intangible or promissory note.

(f) **[Legal restrictions on assignment generally ineffective.]** Except as otherwise provided in Sections 2A-303 and 9-407 and subject to subsections (h) and (i), a rule of law, statute, or regulation that prohibits, restricts, or requires the consent of a government, governmental body or official, or account debtor to the assignment or transfer of, or creation of a security interest in, an account or chattel paper is ineffective to the extent that the rule of law, statute, or regulation:

  (1) prohibits, restricts, or requires the consent of the government, governmental body or official, or account debtor to the assignment or transfer of, or the creation, attachment, perfection, or enforcement of a security interest in the account or chattel paper; or

  (2) provides that the assignment or transfer or the creation, attachment, perfection, or enforcement of the security interest may give rise to a default, breach, right of recoupment, claim, defense, termination, right of termination, or remedy under the account or chattel paper.

(g) **[Subsection (b)(3) not waivable.]** Subject to subsection (h), an account debtor may not waive or vary its option under subsection (b)(3).

(h) **[Rule for individual under other law.]** This section is subject to law other than this article which establishes a different rule for an account debtor who is an individual and who incurred the obligation primarily for personal, family, or household purposes.

(i) **[Inapplicability to healthcare insurance receivable.]** This section does not apply to an assignment of a healthcare insurance receivable.

B. United Nations Convention on Contracts for the International Sale of Goods
1980 WL 574487 (I.E.L.) (Apr. 11, 1980)

Part I: Sphere of Application and General Provisions

Chapter I: Sphere of Application
Article 1

  (1) This Convention applies to contracts of sale of goods between parties whose places of business are in different States:

   (a) when the States are Contracting States; or

   (b) when the rules of private international law lead to the application of the law of a Contracting State.

  (2) The fact that the parties have their places of business in different States is to be disregarded whenever this fact does not appear either from the contract or from

any dealings between, or from information disclosed by, the parties at any time before or at the conclusion of the contract.

(3)   Neither the nationality of the parties nor the civil or commercial character of the parties or of the contract is to be taken into consideration in determining the application of this Convention.

Article 2

This Convention does not apply to sales:

(a) of goods bought for personal, family or household use, unless the seller, at any time before or at the conclusion of the contract, neither knew nor ought to have known that the goods were bought for any such use;

(b) by auction;

(c) on execution or otherwise by authority of law;

(d) of stocks, shares, investment securities, negotiable instruments or money;

(e) of ships, vessels, hovercraft or aircraft;

(f) of electricity.

Article 3

(1) Contracts for the supply of goods to be manufactured or produced are to be considered sales unless the party who orders the goods undertakes to supply a substantial part of the materials necessary for such manufacture or production.

(2) This Convention does not apply to contracts in which the preponderant part of the obligations of the party who furnishes the goods consists in the supply of labour or other services.

Article 4

This Convention governs only the formation of the contract of sale and the rights and obligations of the seller and the buyer arising from such a contract. In particular, except as otherwise expressly provided in this Convention, it is not concerned with:

(a) the validity of the contract or of any of its provisions or of any usage;

(b) the effect which the contract may have on the property in the goods sold.

Article 5

This Convention does not apply to the liability of the seller for death or personal injury caused by the goods to any person.

Article 6

The parties may exclude the application of this Convention or, subject to article 12, derogate from or vary the effect of any of its provisions.

Chapter II: General Provisions

Article 7

(1)   In the interpretation of this Convention, regard is to be had to its international character and to the need to promote uniformity in its application and the observance of good faith in international trade.

(2)   Questions concerning matters governed by this Convention which are not expressly settled in it are to be settled in conformity with the general principles on which it is based or, in the absence of such principles, in conformity with the law applicable by virtue of the rules of private international law.

Article 8

(1)   For the purposes of this Convention statements made by and other conduct of a party are to be interpreted according to his intent where the other party knew or could not have been unaware what that intent was.

(2)   If the preceding paragraph is not applicable, statements made by and other conduct of a party are to be interpreted according to the understanding that a reasonable person of the same kind as the other party would have had in the same circumstances.

(3)   In determining the intent of a party or the understanding a reasonable person would have had, due consideration is to be given to all relevant circumstances of the case including the negotiations, any practices which the parties have established between themselves, usages and any subsequent conduct of the parties.

Article 9

(1)   The parties are bound by any usage to which they have agreed and by any practices which they have established between themselves.

(2)   The parties are considered, unless otherwise agreed, to have impliedly made applicable to their contract or its formation a usage of which the parties knew or ought to have known and which in international trade is widely known to, and regularly observed by, parties to contracts of the type involved in the particular trade concerned.

Article 10

For the purposes of this Convention:

(a) if a party has more than one place of business, the place of business is that which has the closest relationship to the contract and its performance, having regard to the circumstances known to or contemplated by the parties at any time before or at the conclusion of the contract;

(b) if a party does not have a place of business, reference is to be made to his habitual residence.

Article 11

A contract of sale need not be concluded in or evidence by writing and is not subject to any other requirements as to form. It may be proved by any means, including witnesses.

Article 12

Any provision of Article 11, Article 29 or Part II of this Convention that allows a contract of sale or its modification or termination by agreement or any offer, acceptance or other indication of intention to be made in any form other than in writing does not apply where any party has his place of business in a Contracting State which has made a declaration under article 96 of this Convention. The parties may not derogate from or vary the effect of this article.

Article 13

For the purposes of this Convention 'writing' includes telegram and telex.

Part II: Formation of the Contract

Article 14

(1)   A proposal for concluding a contract addressed to one or more specific persons constitutes an offer if it is sufficiently definite and indicates the intention of the

offeror to be bound in case of acceptance. A proposal is sufficiently definite if it indicates the goods and expressly or implicitly fixes or makes provision for determining the quantity and the price.

(2)   A proposal other than one addressed to one or more specific persons is to be considered merely as an invitation to make offers, unless the contrary is clearly indicated by the person making the proposal.

Article 15

(1)   An offer becomes effective when it reaches the offeree.

(2)   An offer, even if it is irrevocable, may be withdrawn if the withdrawal reaches the offeree before or at the same time as the offer.

Article 16

(1)   Until a contract is concluded an offer may be revoked if the revocation reaches the offeree before he has dispatched an acceptance.

(2)   However, an offer cannot be revoked:

(a) if it indicates, whether by stating a fixed time for acceptance or otherwise, that it is irrevocable; or

(b) if it was reasonable for the offeree to rely on the offer as being irrevocable and the offeree has acted in reliance on the offer.

Article 17

An offer, even if it is irrevocable, is terminated when a rejection reaches the offeror.

Article 18

(1)   A statement made by or other conduct of the offeree indicating assent to an offer is an acceptance. Silence or inactivity does not in itself amount to acceptance.

(2)   An acceptance of an offer becomes effective at the moment the indication of assent reaches the offeror. An acceptance is not effective if the indication of assent does not reach the offeror within the time he has fixed or, if no time is fixed, within a reasonable time, due account being taken of the circumstances of the transaction, including the rapidity of the means of communication employed by the offeror. An oral offer must be accepted immediately unless the circumstances indicate otherwise.

(3)   However, if, by virtue of the offer or as a result of practices which the parties have established between themselves or of usage, the offeree may indicate assent by performing an act, such as one relating to the dispatch of the goods or payment of the price, without notice to the offeror, the acceptance is effective at the moment the act is performed, provided that the act is performed within the period of time laid down in the preceding paragraph.

Article 19

(1)   A reply to an offer which purports to be an acceptance but contains additions, limitations or other modifications is a rejection of the offer and constitutes a counter-offer.

(2)   However, a reply to an offer which purports to be an acceptance but contains additional or different terms which do not materially alter the terms of the offer

constitutes an acceptance, unless the offeror, without undue delay, objects orally to the discrepancy or dispatches a notice to that effect. If he does not so object, the terms of the contract are the terms of the offer with the modifications contained in the acceptance.

(3)   Additional or different terms relating, among other things, to the price, payment, quality and quantity of the goods, place and time of delivery, extent of one party's liability to the other or the settlement of disputes are considered to alter the terms of the offer materially.

Article 20

(1)   A period of time for acceptance fixed by the offeror in a telegram or a letter begins to run from the moment the telegram is handed in for dispatch or from the date shown on the letter or, if no such date is shown, from the date shown on the envelope. A period of time for acceptance fixed by the offeror by telephone, telex or other means of instantaneous communication, begins to run from the moment that the offer reaches the offeree.

(2)   Official holidays or non-business days occurring during the period for acceptance are included in calculating the period. However, if a notice of acceptance cannot be delivered at the address of the offeror on the last day of the period because that day falls on an official holiday or a non-business day at the place of business of the offeror, the period is extended until the first business day which follows.

Article 21

(1)   A late acceptance is nevertheless effective as an acceptance if without delay the offeror orally so informs the offeree or dispatches a notice to that effect.

(2)   If a letter or other writing containing a late acceptance shows that it has been sent in such circumstances that if its transmission had been normal it would have reached the offeror in due time, the late acceptance is effective as an acceptance unless, without delay, the offeror orally informs the offeree that he considers his offer as having lapsed or dispatches a notice to that effect.

Article 22

An acceptance may be withdrawn if the withdrawal reaches the offeror before or at the same time as the acceptance would have become effective.

Article 23

A contract is concluded at the moment when an acceptance of an offer becomes effective in accordance with the provisions of this Convention.

Article 24

For the purposes of the Part of the Convention, an offer, declaration of acceptance or any other indication of intention "reaches" the addressee when it is made orally to him or delivered by any other means to him personally, to his place of business or mailing address or, if he does not have a place of business or mailing address, to his habitual residence.

C. Restatement (Second) of Contracts (1981)

Foreword

The *Restatement of the Law of Contracts* was approved and promulgated by the American Law Institute in May 1932, the first of the original Restatements to be finished. With Professor Samuel Williston as Chief Reporter and Professor Arthur L. Corbin as a Special Adviser and the Reporter on Remedies, the work was a legendary success, exercising enormous influence as an authoritative exposition of the subject. It is implicit in the concept of restatement that the work should be kept current by periodic reexamination and revision. The discharge of that continuing responsibility was made possible by a grant to the Institute in 1952 from the A. W. Mellon Educational and Charitable Trust of Pittsburgh, Pennsylvania, the endowment that supports Restatement, Second. The program has thus far produced completed works in Agency (1958), Trusts (1959), Torts (1965, 1977, 1979), Conflict of Laws (1971), and Property (Landlord and Tenant) (1977), in addition to the present volumes and the work on Judgments, which is now in press. Efforts in other fields are under way, including Property (Donative Transfers) and Restitution. *Restatement, Second, of the Law of Contracts* was begun in 1962 and completed by the Institute in 1979. During the intervening years, fourteen tentative drafts, the first of which appeared in 1964, were submitted for consideration. Contracts was thus on the agenda of the Annual Meetings in every year but two from 1964 through 1979. Professor Robert Braucher of the Harvard Law School served as Reporter for approximately the first half of this period, resigning on his appointment to the Supreme Judicial Court of Massachusetts in January 1971. He was succeeded as Reporter by Professor E. Allan Farnsworth of Columbia University School of Law, who carried the project to completion. The Institute is grateful to the Reporters for their leadership, their scholarship, their judgment and their drafting skills, which are pervasively reflected in these volumes.

Chapter 1. Meaning of Terms

§ 1 Contract Defined.

A contract is a promise or a set of promises for the breach of which the law gives a remedy, or the performance of which the law in some way recognizes as a duty.

§ 2 Promise; Promisor; Promisee; Beneficiary.

(1) A promise is a manifestation of intention to act or refrain from acting in a specified way, so made as to justify a promisee in understanding that a commitment has been made.

(2) The person manifesting the intention is the promisor.

(3) The person to whom the manifestation is addressed is the promisee.

(4) Where performance will benefit a person other than the promisee, that person is a beneficiary.

§ 3 Agreement Defined; Bargain Defined.

An agreement is a manifestation of mutual assent on the part of two or more persons. A bargain is an agreement to exchange promises or to exchange a promise for a performance or to exchange performances.

§ 4 How a Promise May Be Made.

A promise may be stated in words either oral or written, or may be inferred wholly or partly from conduct.

Chapter 2. Formation of Contracts — Parties and Capacity

§ 12 Capacity to Contract.

(1) No one can be bound by contract who has not legal capacity to incur at least voidable contractual duties. Capacity to contract may be partial and its existence in respect of a particular transaction may depend upon the nature of the transaction or upon other circumstances.

(2) A natural person who manifests assent to a transaction has full legal capacity to incur contractual duties thereby unless he is

(a) under guardianship, or

(b) an infant, or

(c) mentally ill or defective, or

(d) intoxicated.

§ 14 Infants.

Unless a statute provides otherwise, a natural person has the capacity to incur only voidable contractual duties until the beginning of the day before the person's eighteenth birthday.

§ 15 Mental Illness or Defect.

(1) A person incurs only voidable contractual duties by entering into a transaction if by reason of mental illness or defect

(a) he is unable to understand in a reasonable manner the nature and consequences of the transaction, or

(b) he is unable to act in a reasonable manner in relation to the transaction and the other party has reason to know of his condition.

(2) Where the contract is made on fair terms and the other party is without knowledge of the mental illness or defect, the power of avoidance under Subsection (1) terminates to the extent that the contract has been so performed in whole or in part or the circumstances have so changed that avoidance would be unjust. In such a case a court may grant relief as justice requires.

§ 16 Intoxicated Persons.

A person incurs only voidable contractual duties by entering into a transaction if the other party has reason to know that by reason of intoxication

(a) he is unable to understand in a reasonable manner the nature and consequences of the transaction, or

(b) he is unable to act in a reasonable manner in relation to the transaction.

Chapter 3. Formation of Contracts—Mutual Assent

§ 17 Requirement of a Bargain.

(1)   Except as stated in Subsection (2), the formation of a contract requires a bargain in which there is a manifestation of mutual assent to the exchange and a consideration.

(2)   Whether or not there is a bargain a contract may be formed under special rules applicable to formal contracts or under the rules stated in §§ 82–94.

§ 20 Effect of Misunderstanding.

(1)   There is no manifestation of mutual assent to an exchange if the parties attach materially different meanings to their manifestations and

    (a) neither party knows or has reason to know the meaning attached by the other; or

    (b) each party knows or each party has reason to know the meaning attached by the other.

(2)   The manifestations of the parties are operative in accordance with the meaning attached to them by one of the parties if

    (a) that party does not know of any different meaning attached by the other, and the other knows the meaning attached by the first party; or

    (b) that party has no reason to know of any different meaning attached by the other, and the other has reason to know the meaning attached by the first party.

§ 22 Mode of Assent: Offer and Acceptance.

(1)   The manifestation of mutual assent to an exchange ordinarily takes the form of an offer or proposal by one party followed by an acceptance by the other party or parties.

(2)   A manifestation of mutual assent may be made even though neither offer nor acceptance can be identified and even though the moment of formation cannot be determined.

§ 24 Offer Defined.

An offer is the manifestation of willingness to enter into a bargain, so made as to justify another person in understanding that his assent to that bargain is invited and will conclude it.

§ 25 Option Contracts.

An option contract is a promise which meets the requirements for the formation of a contract and limits the promisor's power to revoke an offer.

§ 26 Preliminary Negotiations.

A manifestation of willingness to enter into a bargain is not an offer if the person to whom it is addressed knows or has reason to know that the person making it does not intend to conclude a bargain until he has made a further manifestation of assent.

§ 29 To Whom an Offer Is Addressed.

(1)   The manifested intention of the offeror determines the person or persons in whom is created a power of acceptance.

(2) An offer may create a power of acceptance in a specified person or in one or more of a specified group or class of persons, acting separately or together, or in anyone or everyone who makes a specified promise or renders a specified performance.

§ 30 Form of Acceptance Invited.

(1) An offer may invite or require acceptance to be made by an affirmative answer in words, or by performing or refraining from performing a specified act, or may empower the offeree to make a selection of terms in his acceptance.

(2) Unless otherwise indicated by the language or the circumstances, an offer invites acceptance in any manner and by any medium reasonable in the circumstances.

§ 32 Invitation of Promise or Performance.

In case of doubt an offer is interpreted as inviting the offeree to accept either by promising to perform what the offer requests or by rendering the performance, as the offeree chooses.

§ 33 Certainty.

(1) Even though a manifestation of intention is intended to be understood as an offer, it cannot be accepted so as to form a contract unless the terms of the contract are reasonably certain.

(2) The terms of a contract are reasonably certain if they provide a basis for determining the existence of a breach and for giving an appropriate remedy.

(3) The fact that one or more terms of a proposed bargain are left open or uncertain may show that a manifestation of intention is not intended to be understood as an offer or as an acceptance.

§ 34 Certainty and Choice of Terms; Effect of Performance or Reliance.

(1) The terms of a contract may be reasonably certain even though it empowers one or both parties to make a selection of terms in the course of performance.

(2) Part performance under an agreement may remove uncertainty and establish that a contract enforceable as a bargain has been formed.

(3) Action in reliance on an agreement may make a contractual remedy appropriate even though uncertainty is not removed.

§ 35 The Offeree's Power of Acceptance.

(1) An offer gives to the offeree a continuing power to complete the manifestation of mutual assent by acceptance of the offer.

(2) A contract cannot be created by acceptance of an offer after the power of acceptance has been terminated in one of the ways listed in § 36.

§ 36 Methods of Termination of the Power of Acceptance.

(1) An offeree's power of acceptance may be terminated by

(a) rejection or counteroffer by the offeree, or

(b) lapse of time, or

(c) revocation by the offeror, or

(d) death or incapacity of the offeror or offeree.

(2) In addition, an offeree's power of acceptance is terminated by the nonoccurrence of any condition of acceptance under the terms of the offer.

§ 39 Counteroffers.

(1) A counteroffer is an offer made by an offeree to his offeror relating to the same matter as the original offer and proposing a substituted bargain differing from that proposed by the original offer.

(2) An offeree's power of acceptance is terminated by his making of a counteroffer, unless the offeror has manifested a contrary intention or unless the counteroffer manifests a contrary intention of the offeree.

§ 40 Time When Rejection or Counteroffer Terminates the Power of Acceptance.

Rejection or counteroffer by mail or telegram does not terminate the power of acceptance until received by the offeror, but limits the power so that a letter or telegram of acceptance started after the sending of an otherwise effective rejection or counteroffer is only a counteroffer unless the acceptance is received by the offeror before he receives the rejection or counteroffer.

§ 41 Lapse of Time.

(1) An offeree's power of acceptance is terminated at the time specified in the offer, or, if no time is specified, at the end of a reasonable time.

(2) What is a reasonable time is a question of fact, depending on all the circumstances existing when the offer and attempted acceptance are made.

(3) Unless otherwise indicated by the language or the circumstances, and subject to the rule stated in § 49, an offer sent by mail is seasonably accepted if an acceptance is mailed at any time before midnight on the day on which the offer is received.

§ 42 Revocation by Communication from Offeror Received by Offeree.

An offeree's power of acceptance is terminated when the offeree receives from the offeror a manifestation of an intention not to enter into the proposed contract.

§ 43 Indirect Communication of Revocation.

An offeree's power of acceptance is terminated when the offeror takes definite action inconsistent with an intention to enter into the proposed contract and the offeree acquires reliable information to that effect.

§ 45 Option Contract Created by Part Performance or Tender.

(1) Where an offer invites an offeree to accept by rendering a performance and does not invite a promissory acceptance, an option contract is created when the offeree tenders or begins the invited performance or tenders a beginning of it.

(2) The offeror's duty of performance under any option contract so created is conditional on completion or tender of the invited performance in accordance with the terms of the offer.

Comment

a. *Offer limited to acceptance by performance only.* This Section is limited to cases where the offer does not invite a promissory acceptance. Such an offer has often been referred to as an "offer for a unilateral contract." Typical illustrations are found in offers of rewards or prizes and in noncommercial arrangements among relatives and friends. See Comment b to § 32. As to analogous cases arising under offers which give the offeree power to accept either by performing or by promising to perform, as he chooses, see §§ 32, 62.

. . .

d.   Beginning to perform. If the invited performance takes time, the invitation to perform necessarily includes an invitation to begin performance. In most such cases the beginning of performance carries with it an express or implied promise to complete performance. See § 62. In the less common case where the offer does not contemplate or invite a promise by the offeree, the beginning of performance nevertheless completes the manifestation of mutual assent and furnishes consideration for an option contract. See § 25. If the beginning of performance requires the cooperation of the offeror, tender of part performance has the same effect. Part performance or tender may also create an option contract in a situation where the offeree is invited to take up the option by making a promise, if the offer invites a preliminary performance before the time for the offeree's final commitment.

Illustrations:

4. A offers a reward for the return of lost property. In response to the offer, B searches for the property and finds it. A then notifies B that the offer is revoked. B makes a tender of the property to A conditional on payment of the reward, and A refuses. There is a breach of contract by A.

5. A, a magazine, offers prizes in a subscription contest. At a time when B has submitted the largest number of subscriptions, A cancels the contest. A has broken its contract with B.

6. A writes to her daughter B, living in another state, an offer to leave A's farm to B if B gives up her home and cares for A during A's life, B remaining free to terminate the arrangement at any time. B gives up her home, moves to A's farm, and begins caring for A. A is bound by an option contract.

7. A offers to sell a piece of land to B, and promises that if B incurs expense in employing experts to appraise the property the offer will be irrevocable for 30 days. B hires experts and pays for their transportation to the land. A is bound by an option contract.

8. In January A, an employer, publishes a notice to his employees, promising a stated Christmas bonus to any employee who is continuously in A's employ from January to Christmas. B, an employee hired by the week, reads the notice and continues at work beyond the expiration of the current week. A is bound by an option contract, and if B is continuously in A's employ until Christmas a notice of revocation of the bonus is ineffective.

e.   Completion of performance. Where part performance or tender by the offeree creates an option contract, the offeree is not bound to complete performance. The offeror alone is bound, but his duty of performance is conditional on completion of the offeree's performance. If the offeree abandons performance, the offeror's duty to perform never arises. See § 224, defining "condition," and Illustration 4 to that Section. But the condition may be excused, for example, if the offeror prevents performance, waives it, or repudiates. *See* Comment b to § 225 and §§ 239, 278.

f.   Preparations for performance. What is begun or tendered must be part of the actual performance invited in order to preclude revocation under this Section. Beginning preparations, though they may be essential to carrying out the contract or to accepting the offer, is not enough. Preparations to perform may, however, constitute justifiable reliance sufficient to make the offeror's promise binding under § 87(2).

In many cases what is invited depends on what is a reasonable mode of acceptance. *See* § 30. The distinction between preparing for performance and beginning performance in such cases may turn on many factors: the extent to which the offeree's conduct is clearly referable to the offer, the definite and substantial character of that conduct, and the extent to which it is of actual or prospective benefit to the offeror rather than the offeree, as well as the terms of the communications between the parties, their prior course of dealing, and any relevant usages of trade.

Illustration:

9.   A makes a written promise to pay $5,000 to B, a hospital, "to aid B in its humanitarian work." Relying upon this and other like promises, B proceeds in its humanitarian work, expending large sums of money and incurring large liabilities. Performance by B has begun, and A's offer is irrevocable.

g.   *Agency contracts.* This Section frequently applies to agency arrangements, particularly offers made to real estate brokers. Sometimes there is a return promise by the agent, particularly if there is an agreement for exclusive dealing, since such an agreement normally imposes an obligation on the agent to use best efforts. See *Uniform Commercial Code* § 2-306(2); compare *Restatement, Second, Agency* § 378. In other cases the agent does not promise to act, but the principal must compensate him if he does act. The rules governing the principal's duty of compensation are stated in detail in Chapter 14 of the *Restatement, Second, Agency*, particularly §§ 443–57.

§ 48 Death or Incapacity of Offeror or Offeree.

An offeree's power of acceptance is terminated when the offeree or offeror dies or is deprived of legal capacity to enter into the proposed contract.

§ 50 Acceptance of Offer Defined; Acceptance by Performance; Acceptance by Promise.

(1)   Acceptance of an offer is a manifestation of assent to the terms thereof made by the offeree in a manner invited or required by the offer.

(2)   Acceptance by performance requires that at least part of what the offer requests be performed or tendered and includes acceptance by a performance which operates as a return promise.

(3)   Acceptance by a promise requires that the offeree complete every act essential to the making of the promise.

§ 53 Acceptance by Performance; Manifestation of Intention Not to Accept.

(1)   An offer can be accepted by the rendering of a performance only if the offer invites such an acceptance.

(2)   Except as stated in § 69, the rendering of a performance does not constitute an acceptance if within a reasonable time the offeree exercises reasonable diligence to notify the offeror of non-acceptance.

(3)   Where an offer of a promise invites acceptance by performance and does not invite a promissory acceptance, the rendering of the invited performance does not constitute an acceptance if before the offeror performs his promise the offeree manifests an intention not to accept.

§ 54 Acceptance by Performance; Necessity of Notification to Offeror.

(1)   Where an offer invites an offeree to accept by rendering a performance, no notification is necessary to make such an acceptance effective unless the offer requests such a notification.

(2)   If an offeree who accepts by rendering a performance has reason to know that the offeror has no adequate means of learning of the performance with reasonable promptness and certainty, the contractual duty of the offeror is discharged unless

(a) the offeree exercises reasonable diligence to notify the offeror of acceptance, or

(b) the offeror learns of the performance within a reasonable time, or

(c) the offer indicates that notification of acceptance is not required.

§ 56 Acceptance by Promise; Necessity of Notification to Offeror.

Except as stated in § 69 or where the offer manifests a contrary intention, it is essential to an acceptance by promise either that the offeree exercise reasonable diligence to notify the offeror of acceptance or that the offeror receive the acceptance seasonably.

§ 58 Necessity of Acceptance Complying with Terms of Offer.

An acceptance must comply with the requirements of the offer as to the promise to be made or the performance to be rendered.

§ 59 Purported Acceptance Which Adds Qualifications.

A reply to an offer which purports to accept it but is conditional on the offeror's assent to terms additional to or different from those offered is not an acceptance but is a counteroffer.

§ 60 Acceptance of Offer Which States Place, Time or Manner of Acceptance.

If an offer prescribes the place, time or manner of acceptance its terms in this respect must be complied with in order to create a contract. If an offer merely suggests a permitted place, time or manner of acceptance, another method of acceptance is not precluded.

§ 61 Acceptance Which Requests Change of Terms.

An acceptance which requests a change or addition to the terms of the offer is not thereby invalidated unless the acceptance is made to depend on an assent to the changed or added terms.

§ 62 Effect of Performance by Offeree Where Offer Invites either Performance or Promise.

(1)   Where an offer invites an offeree to choose between acceptance by promise and acceptance by performance, the tender or beginning of the invited performance or a tender of a beginning of it is an acceptance by performance.

(2)   Such an acceptance operates as a promise to render complete performance.

§ 63 Time When Acceptance Takes Effect.

Unless the offer provides otherwise,

(a) an acceptance made in a manner and by a medium invited by an offer is operative and completes the manifestation of mutual assent as soon as put out of the offeree's possession, without regard to whether it ever reaches the offeror; but

(b) an acceptance under an option contract is not operative until received by the offeror.

§ 69 Acceptance by Silence or Exercise of Dominion.

(1)   Where an offeree fails to reply to an offer, his silence and inaction operate as an acceptance in the following cases only:

(a) Where an offeree takes the benefit of offered services with reasonable opportunity to reject them and reason to know that they were offered with the expectation of compensation.

(b) Where the offeror has stated or given the offeree reason to understand that assent may be manifested by silence or inaction, and the offeree in remaining silent and inactive intends to accept the offer.

(c) Where because of previous dealings or otherwise, it is reasonable that the offeree should notify the offeror if he does not intend to accept.

(2) An offeree who does any act inconsistent with the offeror's ownership of offered property is bound in accordance with the offered terms unless they are manifestly unreasonable. But if the act is wrongful as against the offeror it is an acceptance only if ratified by him.

Chapter 4. Formation of Contracts — Consideration

§ 71 Requirement of Exchange; Types of Exchange.

(1) To constitute consideration, a performance or a return promise must be bargained for.

(2) A performance or return promise is bargained for if it is sought by the promisor in exchange for his promise and is given by the promisee in exchange for that promise.

(3) The performance may consist of

(a) an act other than a promise, or

(b) a forbearance, or

(c) the creation, modification, or destruction of a legal relation.

(4) The performance or return promise may be given to the promisor or to some other person. It may be given by the promisee or by some other person.

Comment:

a. *Other meanings of "consideration."* The word "consideration" has often been used with meanings different from that given here. It is often used merely to express the legal conclusion that a promise is enforceable. Historically, its primary meaning may have been that the conditions were met under which an action of assumpsit would lie. It was also used as the equivalent of the quid pro quo required in an action of debt. A seal, it has been said, "imports a consideration," although the law was clear that no element of bargain was necessary to enforcement of a promise under seal. On the other hand, consideration has sometimes been used to refer to almost any reason asserted for enforcing a promise, even though the reason was insufficient. In this sense we find references to promises "in consideration of love and affection," to "illegal consideration," to "past consideration," and to consideration furnished by reliance on a gratuitous promise.

Consideration has also been used to refer to the element of exchange without regard to legal consequences. Consistent with that usage has been the use of the phrase "sufficient consideration" to express the legal conclusion that one requirement for an enforceable bargain is met. Here § 17 states the element of exchange required for a contract enforceable as a bargain as "a consideration."

Thus "consideration" refers to an element of exchange which is sufficient to satisfy the legal requirement; the word "sufficient" would be redundant and is not used.

b.   *"Bargained for."* In the typical bargain, the consideration and the promise bear a reciprocal relation of motive or inducement: the consideration induces the making of the promise and the promise induces the furnishing of the consideration. Here, as in the matter of mutual assent, the law is concerned with the external manifestation rather than the undisclosed mental state: it is enough that one party manifests an intention to induce the other's response and to be induced by it and that the other responds in accordance with the inducement. See § 81; compare § 19, 20. But it is not enough that the promise induces the conduct of the promisee or that the conduct of the promisee induces the making of the promise; both elements must be present, or there is no bargain. Moreover, a mere pretense of bargain does not suffice, as where there is a false recital of consideration or where the purported consideration is merely nominal. In such cases there is no consideration and the promise is enforced, if at all, as a promise binding without consideration under § 82–94. See Comments b and c to § 87.

Illustrations:

1. A offers to buy a book owned by B and to pay B $10 in exchange therefor. B accepts the offer and delivers the book to A. The transfer and delivery of the book constitute a performance and are consideration for A's promise. See *Uniform Commercial Code* § 2-106, 2-301. This is so even though A at the time he makes the offer secretly intends to pay B $10 whether or not he gets the book, or even though B at the time he accepts secretly intends not to collect the $10.

2. A receives a gift from B of a book worth $10. Subsequently A promises to pay B the value of the book. There is no consideration for A's promise. This is so even though B at the time he makes the gift secretly hopes that A will pay him for it. As to the enforcement of such promises, see § 86.

3. A promises to make a gift of $10 to B. In reliance on the promise B buys a book from C and promises to pay C $10 for it. There is no consideration for A's promise. As to the enforcement of such promises, see § 90.

4. A desires to make a binding promise to give $1000 to his son B. Being advised that a gratuitous promise is not binding, A writes out and signs a false recital that B has sold him a car for $1000 and a promise to pay that amount. There is no consideration for A's promise.

5. A desires to make a binding promise to give $1000 to his son B. Being advised that a gratuitous promise is not binding, A offers to buy from B for $1000 a book worth less than $1. B accepts the offer knowing that the purchase of the book is a mere pretense. There is no consideration for A's promise to pay $1000.

c.   *Mixture of bargain and gift.* In most commercial bargains there is a rough equivalence between the value promised and the value received as consideration. But the social functions of bargains include the provision of opportunity for free individual action and exercise of judgment and the fixing of values by private action, either generally or for purposes of the particular transaction. Those functions would be impaired by judicial review of the values so fixed. Ordinarily, therefore, courts do not inquire into the adequacy of consideration, particularly where one or both of the values exchanged are difficult to measure. See § 79.

Even where both parties know that a transaction is in part a bargain and in part a gift, the element of bargain may nevertheless furnish consideration for the entire transaction.

On the other hand, a gift is not ordinarily treated as a bargain, and a promise to make a gift is not made a bargain by the promise of the prospective donee to accept the gift, or by his acceptance of part of it. This may be true even though the terms of gift impose a burden on the donee as well as the donor. See Illustration 2 to § 24. In such cases the distinction between bargain and gift may be a fine one, depending on the motives manifested by the parties. In some cases there may be no bargain so long as the agreement is entirely executory, but performance may furnish consideration or the agreement may become fully or partly enforceable by virtue of the reliance of one party or the unjust enrichment of the other. Compare § 90.

Illustrations:

6. A offers to buy a book owned by B and to pay B $10 in exchange therefor. B's transfer and delivery of the book are consideration for A's promise even though both parties know that such books regularly sell for $5 and that part of A's motive in making the offer is to make a gift to B. See § 79, 81.

7. A owns land worth $10,000 which is subject to a mortgage to secure a debt of $5,000. A promises to make a gift of the land to his son B and to pay off the mortgage, and later gives B a deed subject to the mortgage. B's acceptance of the deed is not consideration for A's promise to pay the mortgage debt.

8. A and B agree that A will advance $1000 to B as a gratuitous loan. B's promise to accept the loan is not consideration for A's promise to make it. But the loan when made is consideration for B's promise to repay.

d.   *Types of consideration.* Consideration may consist of a performance or of a return promise. Consideration by way of performance may be a specified act of forbearance, or any one of several specified acts or forbearances of which the offeree is given the choice, or such conduct as will produce a specified result. Or either the offeror or the offeree may request as consideration the creation, modification or destruction of a purely intangible legal relation. Not infrequently the consideration bargained for is an act with the added requirement that a certain legal result shall be produced. Consideration by way of return promise requires a promise as defined in § 2. Consideration may consist partly of promise and partly of other acts or forbearances, and the consideration invited may be a performance or a return promise in the alternative. Though a promise is itself an act, it is treated separately from other acts. *See* § 75.

Illustrations:

9. A promises B, his nephew aged 16, that A will pay B $1000 when B becomes 21 if B does not smoke before then. B's forbearance to smoke is a performance and if bargained for is consideration for A's promise.

10. A says to B, the owner of a garage, "I will pay you $100 if you will make my car run properly." The production of this result is consideration for A's promise.

11. A has B's horse in his possession. B writes to A, "If you will promise me $100 for the horse, he is yours." A promptly replies making the requested promise. The property in the horse at once passes to A. The change in ownership is consideration for A's promise.

12. A promises to pay B $1,000 if B will make an offer to C to sell C certain land for $25,000 and will leave the offer open for 24 hours. B makes the requested offer and forbears to revoke it for 24 hours, but C does not accept. The creation of a power of acceptance in C is consideration for A's promise.

13. A mails a written order to B, offering to buy specified machinery on specified terms. The order provides "Ship at once." B's prompt shipment or promise to ship is consideration for A's promise to pay the price. See § 32; *Uniform Commercial Code* § 2-206(1)(b).

e. *Consideration moving from or to a third person.* It matters not from whom the consideration moves or to whom it goes. If it is bargained for and given in exchange for the promise, the promise is not gratuitous.

Illustrations:

14. A promises B to guarantee payment of a bill of goods if B sells the goods to C. Selling the goods to C is consideration for A's promise.

15. A makes a promissory note payable to B in return for a payment by B to C. The payment is consideration for the note.

16. A, at C's request and in exchange for $1 paid by C, promises B to give him a book. The payment is consideration for A's promise.

17. A promises B to pay B $1, in exchange for C's promise to A to give A a book. The promises are consideration for one another.

18. A promises to pay $1,000 to B, a bank, in exchange for the delivery of a car by C to A's son D. The delivery of the car is consideration for A's promise.

§ 72 Exchange of Promise for Performance.

Except as stated in §§ 73 and 74, any performance which is bargained for is consideration.

§ 73 Performance of Legal Duty.

Performance of a legal duty owed to a promisor which is neither doubtful nor the subject of honest dispute is not consideration; but a similar performance is consideration if it differs from what was required by the duty in a way which reflects more than a pretense of bargain.

§ 74 Settlement of Claims.

(1) Forbearance to assert or the surrender of a claim or defense which proves to be invalid is not consideration unless

   (a) the claim or defense is in fact doubtful because of uncertainty as to the facts or the law, or

   (b) the forbearing or surrendering party believes that the claim or defense may be fairly determined to be valid.

(2) The execution of a written instrument surrendering a claim or defense by one who is under no duty to execute it is consideration if the execution of the written instrument is bargained for even though he is not asserting the claim or defense and believes that no valid claim or defense exists.

§ 77 Illusory and Alternative Promises.

A promise or apparent promise is not consideration if by its terms the promisor or purported promisor reserves a choice of alternative performances unless

(a) each of the alternative performances would have been consideration if it alone had been bargained for; or

(b) one of the alternative performances would have been consideration and there is or appears to the parties to be a substantial possibility that before the promisor exercises his choice events may eliminate the alternatives which would not have been consideration.

Comment:

a.   *Illusory promises.* Words of promise which by their terms make performance entirely optional with the "promisor" do not constitute a promise. See Comment e to § 2; compare § 76. In such cases there might theoretically be a bargain to pay for the utterance of the words, but in practice it is performance which is bargained for. Where the apparent assurance of performance is illusory, it is not consideration for a return promise. A different rule applies, however, where performance is optional, not by the terms of the agreement, but by virtue of a rule of law. See § 5 (defining "term"), § 78.

Illustrations:

1. A offers to deliver to B at $2 a bushel as many bushels of wheat, not exceeding 5,000, as B may choose to order within the next 30 days. B accepts, agreeing to buy at that price as much as he shall order from A within that time. B's acceptance involves no promise by him, and is not consideration.

2. A promises B to act as B's agent for three years from a future date on certain terms; B agrees that A may so act, but reserves the power to terminate the agreement at any time. B's agreement is not consideration, since it involves no promise by him.

§ 78 Voidable and Unenforceable Promises.

The fact that a rule of law renders a promise voidable or unenforceable does not prevent it from being consideration.

§ 79 Adequacy of Consideration; Mutuality of Obligation.

If the requirement of consideration is met, there is no additional requirement of

(a) a gain, advantage, or benefit to the promisor or a loss, disadvantage, or detriment to the promisee; or

(b) equivalence in the values exchanged; or

(c) "mutuality of obligation."

Comment

a.   *Rationale.* In such typical bargains as the ordinary sale of goods each party gives up something of economic value, and the values exchanged are often roughly or exactly equivalent by standards independent of the particular bargain. Quite often promise is exchanged for promise, and the promised performances are sometimes divisible into matching parts. See § 31. Hence it has sometimes been said that consideration must consist of a "benefit to the promisor" or a "detriment to the promisee"; it has frequently been claimed that there was no consideration because the economic value given in exchange was much less than that of the promise or the promised performance; "mutuality of obligation" has been said to be essential to a contract. But experience has shown that these are not essential elements of a bargain or of an enforceable contract, and they are negated as requirements by the rules stated in §§ 71–78. This Section makes that negation explicit.

b.   *Benefit and detriment.* Historically, the common law action of debt was said to require a quid pro quo, and that requirement may have led to statements that consideration must be a benefit to the promisor. But contracts were enforced in the common law action of assumpsit without any such requirement; in actions of assumpsit the emphasis was rather on the harm to the promisee, and detrimental reliance on a promise may still be the basis of contractual relief. *See* §90. But reliance is not essential to the formation of a bargain, and remedies for breach have long been given in cases of exchange of promise for promise where neither party has begun to perform. Today when it is said that consideration must involve a detriment to the promisee, the supposed requirement is often qualified by a statement that a "legal detriment" is sufficient even though there is no economic detriment or other actual loss. It is more realistic to say simply that there is no requirement of detriment.

Illustrations:

1. A contracts to sell property to B. As a favor to B, who is C's friend, and in consideration of A's performance of the contract, C guarantees that B will pay the agreed price. A's performance is consideration for C's promise. See §73.

2. A has executed a document in the form of a guaranty which imposes no obligation on A and has no value. B's surrender of the document to A, if bargained for, is consideration for a promise by A to pay $10,000. Compare §74.

c.   *Exchange of unequal values.* To the extent that the apportionment of productive energy and product in the economy are left to private action, the parties to transactions are free to fix their own valuations. The resolution of disputes often requires a determination of value in the more general sense of market value, and such values are commonly fixed as an approximation based on a multitude of private valuations. But in many situations there is no reliable external standard of value, or the general standard is inappropriate to the precise circumstances of the parties. Valuation is left to private action in part because the parties are thought to be better able than others to evaluate the circumstances of particular transactions. In any event, they are not ordinarily bound to follow the valuations of others.

Ordinarily, therefore, courts do not inquire into the adequacy of consideration. This is particularly so when one or both of the values exchanged are uncertain or difficult to measure. But it is also applied even when it is clear that the transaction is a mixture of bargain and gift. See Comment c to §71. Gross inadequacy of consideration may be relevant to issues of capacity, fraud and the like, but the requirement of consideration is not a safeguard against imprudent and improvident contracts except in cases where it appears that there is no bargain in fact.

Illustrations:

3. A borrows $300 from B to enable A to begin litigation to recover a gold mine through litigation, and promises to repay $10,000 when he recovers the mine. The loan is consideration for the promise.

4. A is pregnant with the illegitimate child of B, a wealthy man. A promises to give the child A's surname and B's given name, and B promises to provide for the support and education of the child and to set up a trust of securities to provide the child with a minimum net income of $100 per week until he reaches the age of 21. The naming of the child is consideration for B's promise.

d.   *Pretended exchange.* Disparity in value, with or without other circumstances, sometimes indicates that the purported consideration was not in fact bargained for but was a mere formality or pretense. Such a sham or "nominal" consideration does not satisfy the requirement of § 71. Promises are enforced in such cases, if at all, either as promises binding without consideration under §§ 8294 or as promises binding by virtue of their formal characteristics under § 6. See, for example, §§ 95109 on contracts under seal.

Illustrations:

5. In consideration of one cent received, A promises to pay $600 in three yearly installments of $200 each. The one cent is merely nominal and is not consideration for A's promise.

6. A dies leaving no assets and owing $4000 to the B bank. C, A's widow, promises to pay the debt, and B promises to make no claim against A's estate. Without some further showing, B's promise is a mere formality and is not consideration for C's promise.

e.   *Effects of gross inadequacy.* Although the requirement of consideration may be met despite a great difference in the values exchanged, gross inadequacy of consideration may be relevant in the application of other rules. Inadequacy "such as shocks the conscience" is often said to be a "badge of fraud," justifying a denial of specific performance. See § 364(1)(c). Inadequacy may also help to justify rescission or cancellation on the ground of lack of capacity (see §§ 15, 16), mistake, misrepresentation, duress or undue influence (see Chapters 6 and 7). Unequal bargains are also limited by the statutory law of usury, by regulation of the rates of public utilities and some other enterprises, and by special rules developed for the sale of an expectation of inheritance, for contractual penalties and forfeitures (see §§ 229, 356), and for agreements between secured lender and borrower (*see Restatement of Security* § 55, *Uniform Commercial Code* § 9-501).

f.   *Mutuality.* The word "mutuality," though often used in connection with the law of Contracts, has no definite meaning. "Mutual assent" as one element of a bargain is the subject of Topic 2 of this Chapter. "Mutuality of remedy" is dealt with in Comment c to § 363. Clause (c) of this Section negates any supposed requirement of "mutuality of obligation." Such a requirement has sometimes been asserted in the form, "Both parties must be bound or neither is bound." That statement is obviously erroneous as applied to an exchange of promise for performance; it is equally inapplicable to contracts governed by §§ 82-94 and to contracts enforceable by virtue of their formal characteristics under § 6. Even in the ordinary case of the exchange of promise for promise, § 78 makes it clear that voidable and unenforceable promises may be consideration. The only requirement of "mutuality of obligation" even in cases of mutual promises is that stated in §§ 76- 77.

§ 81 Consideration as Motive or Inducing Cause.

(1)   The fact that what is bargained for does not of itself induce the making of a promise does not prevent it from being consideration for the promise.

(2)   The fact that a promise does not of itself induce a performance or return promise does not prevent the performance or return promise from being consideration for the promise.

§ 86 Promise for Benefit Received.

(1)   A promise made in recognition of a benefit previously received by the promisor from the promisee is binding to the extent necessary to prevent injustice.

(2)   A promise is not binding under Subsection (1)

(a) if the promisee conferred the benefit as a gift or for other reasons the promisor has not been unjustly enriched; or

(b) to the extent that its value is disproportionate to the benefit.

Comment

a.   *"Past consideration"; "moral obligation."* Enforcement of promises to pay for benefit received has sometimes been said to rest on "past consideration" or on the "moral obligation" of the promisor, and there are statutes in such terms in a few states. Those terms are not used here: "past consideration" is inconsistent with the meaning of consideration stated in § 71, and there seems to be no consensus as to what constitutes a "moral obligation." The mere fact of promise has been thought to create a moral obligation, but it is clear that not all promises are enforced. Nor are moral obligations based solely on gratitude or sentiment sufficient of themselves to support a subsequent promise.

Illustrations:

1. A gives emergency care to B's adult son while the son is sick and without funds far from home. B subsequently promises to reimburse A for his expenses. The promise is not binding under this Section.

2. A lends money to B, who later dies. B's widow promises to pay the debt. The promise is not binding under this Section.

3. A has immoral relations with B, a woman not his wife, to her injury. A's subsequent promise to reimburse B for her loss is not binding under this Section.

b.   *Rationale.* Although in general a person who has been unjustly enriched at the expense of another is required to make restitution, restitution is denied in many cases in order to protect persons who have had benefits thrust upon them. *See Restatement of Restitution* §§ 1, 2, 112. In other cases restitution is denied by virtue of rules designed to guard against false claims, stale claims, claims already litigated, and the like. In many such cases a subsequent promise to make restitution removes the reason for the denial of relief, and the policy against unjust enrichment then prevails. *Compare Restatement, Second, Agency* § 462 on ratification of the acts of a person who officiously purports to act as an agent. Enforcement of the subsequent promise sometimes makes it unnecessary to decide a difficult question as to the limits on quasi-contractual relief.

Many of the cases governed by the rules stated in §§ 82–85 are within the broader principle stated in this Section. But the broader principle is not so firmly established as those rules, and it may not be applied if there is doubt whether the objections to restitution are fully met by the subsequent promise. Facts such as the definite and substantial character of the benefit received, formality in the making of the promise, part performance of the promise, reliance on the promise or the probability of such reliance may be relevant to show that no imposition results from enforcement.

c.   *Promise to correct a mistake.* One who makes a mistake in the conferring of a benefit is commonly entitled to restitution regardless of any promise. But restitution is often denied to avoid prejudice to the recipient of the benefit. Thus restitution of the value of services or of improvements to land or chattels may require a payment which the recipient cannot afford. *See Restatement of Restitution* §§ 41, 42. Where a subsequent promise shows that the usual protection is not needed in the particular case, restitution is granted to the extent promised.

Illustrations:

   4. A is employed by B to repair a vacant house. By mistake A repairs the house next door, which belongs to C. A subsequent promise by C to pay A the value of the repairs is binding.

   5. A pays B a debt and gets a signed receipt. Later B obtains a default judgment against A for the amount of the debt, and A pays again. B's subsequent promise to refund the second payment if A has a receipt is binding.

   d.   *Emergency services and necessaries.* The law of restitution in the absence of promise severely limits recovery for necessaries furnished to a person under disability and for emergency services. *See Restatement of Restitution* §§ 113-17, 139. A subsequent promise in such a case may remove doubt as to the reality of the benefit and as to its value, and may negate any danger of imposition or false claim. A positive showing that payment was expected is not then required; an intention to make a gift must be shown to defeat restitution.

Illustrations:

   6. A finds B's escaped bull and feeds and cares for it. B's subsequent promise to pay reasonable compensation to A is binding.

   7. A saves B's life in an emergency and is totally and permanently disabled in so doing. One month later B promises to pay A $15 every two weeks for the rest of A's life, and B makes the payments for 8 years until he dies. The promise is binding.

   e.   *Benefit conferred as a gift.* In the absence of mistake or the like, there is no element of unjust enrichment in the receipt of a gift, and the rule of this Section has no application to a promise to pay for a past gift. Similarly, when a debt is discharged by a binding agreement, the transaction is closed even though full payment is not made. But marginal cases arise in which both parties understand that what is in form a gift is intended to be reimbursed indirectly, or in which a subsequent promise to pay is expressly contemplated. Enforcement of the subsequent promise is proper in some such cases.

Illustrations:

   8. A submits to B at B's request a plan for advertising products manufactured by B, expecting payment only if the plan is adopted. Because of a change in B's selling arrangements, B rejects the plan without giving it fair consideration. B's subsequent promise to reimburse A's expenses in preparing the plan is binding.

   9. A contributes capital to B, an insurance company, on the understanding that B is not liable to reimburse A but that A will be reimbursed through salary and commissions. Later A withdraws from the company and B promises to pay him ten percent of premiums received until he is reimbursed. The promise is binding.

   f.   *Benefit conferred pursuant to contract.* By virtue of the policy of enforcing bargains, the enrichment of one party as a result of an unequal exchange is not regarded as unjust, and this Section has no application to a promise to pay or perform more or to accept less than is called for by a preexisting bargain between the same parties. Compare §§ 79, 89. Similarly, if a third person receives a benefit as a result of the performance of a bargain, this Section does not make binding the subsequent promise of the third person to pay extra compensation to the performing party. But a promise to pay in substitution for the return performance called for by the bargain may be binding under this Section.

Illustration:

> 10. A digs a well on B's land in performance of a bargain with B's tenant C. C is unable to pay as agreed, and B promises to pay A the reasonable value of the well. The promise is binding.

§ 87 Option Contract.

(1)   An offer is binding as an option contract if it

(a) is in writing and signed by the offeror, recites a purported consideration for the making of the offer, and proposes an exchange on fair terms within a reasonable time; or

(b) is made irrevocable by statute.

(2)   An offer which the offeror should reasonably expect to induce action or forbearance of a substantial character on the part of the offeree before acceptance and which does induce such action or forbearance is binding as an option contract to the extent necessary to avoid injustice.

Comment

e.   *Reliance.* Subsection (2) states the application of § 90 to reliance on an unaccepted offer, with qualifications which would not be appropriate in some other types of cases covered by § 90. It is important chiefly in cases of reliance that is not part performance. If the beginning of performance is a reasonable mode of acceptance, it makes the offer fully enforceable under § 45 or § 62; if not, the offeror commonly has no reason to expect part performance before acceptance. But circumstances may be such that the offeree must undergo substantial expense, or undertake substantial commitments, or forego alternatives, in order to put himself in a position to accept by either promise or performance. The offer may be made expressly irrevocable in contemplation of reliance by the offeree. If reliance follows in such cases, justice may require a remedy. *Compare Restatement, Second, Torts* § 325; *Restatement, Second, Agency* § 378. But the reliance must be substantial as well as foreseeable.

Full-scale enforcement of the offered contract is not necessarily appropriate in such cases. Restitution of benefits conferred may be enough, or partial or full reimbursement of losses may be proper. Various factors may influence the remedy: the formality of the offer, its commercial or social context, the extent to which the offeree's reliance was understood to be at his own risk, the relative competence and the bargaining position of the parties, the degree of fault on the part of the offeror, the ease and certainty of proof of particular items of damage and the likelihood that unprovable damages have been suffered.

Illustrations:

> 4. A leases a farm to B and later gives B an "option" to buy the farm for $15,500 within five years. With A's approval, B makes permanent improvements in the

farm buildings, builds roads, drains and dams, and contours plow land, using his own labor and expending several thousand dollars. Toward the end of the five years, A purports to revoke the option, demanding a higher price. B then gives written notice of acceptance in accordance with the terms of the offer. Specific performance by A may be decreed.

5. A offers to B a "blanket arrangement" to buy "poultry grown by you" at stated prices. As contemplated, B buys 7,000 baby chicks and begins raising them for sale to A as "broilers." Thereafter A purports to revoke the offer. B has the rights of an aggrieved seller under a contract for the sale of 7,000 "broilers."

6. A submits a written offer for paving work to be used by B as a partial basis for B's bid as general contractor on a large building. As A knows, B is required to name his subcontractors in his general bid. B uses A's offer and B's bid is accepted. A's offer is irrevocable until B has had a reasonable opportunity to notify A of the award and B's acceptance of A's offer.

§ 89 Modification of Executory Contract.

A promise modifying a duty under a contract not fully performed on either side is binding

(a) if the modification is fair and equitable in view of circumstances not anticipated by the parties when the contract was made; or

(b) to the extent provided by statute; or

(c) to the extent that justice requires enforcement in view of material change of position in reliance on the promise.

Comment

a. *Rationale.* This Section relates primarily to adjustments in ongoing transactions. Like offers and guaranties, such adjustments are ancillary to exchanges and have some of the same presumptive utility. *See* §§ 72, 87, 88. Indeed, paragraph (a) deals with bargains which are without consideration only because of the rule that performance of a legal duty to the promisor is not consideration. See § 73. This Section is also related to § 84 on waiver of conditions: it may apply to cases in which § 84 is inapplicable because a condition is material to the exchange or risk. As in cases governed by § 84, relation to a bargain tends to satisfy the cautionary and channeling functions of legal formalities. See Comment c to § 72. The Statute of Frauds may prevent enforcement in the absence of reliance. *See* §§ 149–50. Otherwise formal requirements are at a minimum.

b. *Performance of legal duty.* The rule of § 73 finds its modern justification in cases of promises made by mistake or induced by unfair pressure. Its application to cases where those elements are absent has been much criticized and is avoided if paragraph (a) of this Section is applicable. The limitation to a modification which is "fair and equitable" goes beyond absence of coercion and requires an objectively demonstrable reason for seeking a modification. Compare *Uniform Commercial Code* § 2-209 Comment. The reason for modification must rest in circumstances not "anticipated" as part of the context in which the contract was made, but a frustrating event may be unanticipated for this purpose if it was not adequately covered, even though it was foreseen as a remote possibility. When such a reason is present, the relative financial strength of the parties, the formality with which the modification is made, the extent to which it is performed or relied on and other circumstances may be relevant to show or negate imposition or unfair surprise.

The same result called for by paragraph (a) is sometimes reached on the ground that the original contract was "rescinded" by mutual agreement and that new promises were then made which furnished consideration for each other. That theory is rejected here because it is fictitious when the "rescission" and new agreement are simultaneous, and because if logically carried out it might uphold unfair and inequitable modifications.

Illustrations:

1. By a written contract A agrees to excavate a cellar for B for a stated price. Solid rock is unexpectedly encountered and A so notifies B. A and B then orally agree that A will remove the rock at a unit price which is reasonable but nine times that used in computing the original price, and A completes the job. B is bound to pay the increased amount.

2. A contracts with B to supply for $300 a laundry chute for a building B has contracted to build for the Government for $150,000. Later A discovers that he made an error as to the type of material to be used and should have bid $1,200. A offers to supply the chute for $1000, eliminating overhead and profit. After ascertaining that other suppliers would charge more, B agrees. The new agreement is binding.

3. A is employed by B as a designer of coats at $90 a week for a year beginning November 1 under a written contract executed September 1. A is offered $115 a week by another employer and so informs B. A and B then agree that A will be paid $100 a week and in October execute a new written contract to that effect, simultaneously tearing up the prior contract. The new contract is binding.

4. A contracts to manufacture and sell to B 2,000 steel roofs for corn cribs at $60. Before A begins manufacture a threat of a nationwide steel strike raises the cost of steel about $10 per roof, and A and B agree orally to increase the price to $70 per roof. A thereafter manufactures and delivers 1700 of the roofs, and B pays for 1,500 of them at the increased price without protest, increasing the selling price of the corn cribs by $10. The new agreement is binding.

5. A contracts to manufacture and sell to B 100,000 castings for lawn mowers at 50 cents each. After partial delivery and after B has contracted to sell a substantial number of lawn mowers at a fixed price, A notifies B that increased metal costs require that the price be increased to 75 cents. Substitute castings are available at 55 cents, but only after several months delay. B protests but is forced to agree to the new price to keep its plant in operation. The modification is not binding.

c. *Statutes. Uniform Commercial Code* § 2-209 dispenses with the requirement of consideration for an agreement modifying a contract for the sale of goods. Under that section the original contract can provide against oral modification, and the requirements of the Statute of Frauds must be met if the contract as modified is within its provisions; but an ineffective modification can operate as a waiver. The Comment indicates that extortion of a modification without legitimate commercial reason is ineffective as a violation of the duty of good faith imposed by the Code. A similar limitation may be applicable under statutes which give effect to a signed writing as a substitute for the seal, or under statutes which give effect to acceptance by the promisee of the modified performance. In some States statutes or constitutional provisions flatly forbid the payment of extra compensation to Government contractors.

d.   *Reliance.* Paragraph (c) states the application of § 90 to modification of an executory contract in language adapted from *Uniform Commercial Code* § 2-209. Even though the promise is not binding when made, it may become binding in whole or in part by reason of action or forbearance by the promisee or third persons in reliance on it. In some cases the result can be viewed as based either on estoppel to contradict a representation of fact or on reliance on a promise. Ordinarily reliance by the promisee is reasonably foreseeable and makes the modification binding with respect to performance by the promisee under it and any return performance owed by the promisor. But as under § 84 the original terms can be reinstated for the future by reasonable notification received by the promisee unless reinstatement would be unjust in view of a change of position on "his part. Compare *Uniform Commercial Code* § 2-209(5).

Illustrations:

6.   A defaults in payment of a premium on a life insurance policy issued by B, an insurance company. Pursuant to the terms of the policy, B notifies A of the lapse of the policy and undertakes to continue the insurance until a specified future date, but by mistake specifies a date two months later than the insured would be entitled to under the policy. On inquiry by A two years later, B repeats the mistake, offering A an option to take a cash payment. A fails to do so, and dies one month before the specified date. B is bound to pay the insurance.

7.   A is the lessee of an apartment house under a 99year lease from B at a rent of $10,000 per year. Because of war conditions many of the apartments become vacant, and in order to enable A to stay in business B agrees to reduce the rent to $5,000. The reduced rent is paid for five years. The war being over, the apartments are then fully rented, and B notifies A that the full rent called for by the lease must be paid. A is bound to pay the full rent only from a reasonable time after the receipt of the notification.

8.   A contracts with B to carry a shipment of fish under refrigeration. During the short first leg of the voyage the refrigeration equipment on the ship breaks down, and A offers either to continue under ventilation or to hold the cargo at the first port for later shipment. B agrees to shipment under ventilation but later changes his mind. A receives notification of the change before he has changed his position. A is bound to ship under refrigeration.

§ 90 Promise Reasonably Inducing Action or Forbearance.

(1)   A promise which the promisor should reasonably expect to induce action or forbearance on the part of the promisee or a third person and which does induce such action or forbearance is binding if injustice can be avoided only by enforcement of the promise. The remedy granted for breach may be limited as justice requires.

(2)   A charitable subscription or a marriage settlement is binding under Subsection (1) without proof that the promise induced action or forbearance.

Comment

a.   *Relation to other rules.* Obligations and remedies based on reliance are not peculiar to the law of contracts. This Section is often referred to in terms of "promissory estoppel," a phrase suggesting an extension of the doctrine of estoppel. Estoppel prevents a person from showing the truth contrary to a representation of fact made by him after another has relied on the representation. *See Restatement, Second, Agency* § 8B; *Restatement, Second, Torts* §§ 872, 894. Reliance is also a significant feature of numerous rules in the law of negligence, deceit and restitution. I §§ 354, 378; *Restatement, Second, Torts* §§ 323, 537; *Restatement of Restitution* § 55. In some cases those rules and this Section overlap; in others they provide analogies useful in determining the extent to which enforcement is necessary to avoid injustice.

It is fairly arguable that the enforcement of informal contracts in the action of assumpsit rested historically on justifiable reliance on a promise. Certainly reliance is one of the main bases for enforcement of the half-completed exchange, and the probability of reliance lends support to the enforcement of the executory exchange. See Comments to §§ 72, 75. This Section thus states a basic principle which often renders inquiry unnecessary as to the precise scope of the policy of enforcing bargains. Sections 8789 state particular applications of the same principle to promises ancillary to bargains, and it also applies in a wide variety of non-commercial situations. *See, e.g.*, § 94.

Illustration:

1. A, knowing that B is going to college, promises B that A will give him $5,000 on completion of his course. B goes to college, and borrows and spends more than $5,000 for college expenses. When he has nearly completed his course, A notifies him of an intention to revoke the promise. A's promise is binding and B is entitled to payment on completion of the course without regard to whether his performance was "bargained for" under § 71.

b.   *Character of reliance protected.* The principle of this Section is flexible. The promisor is affected only by reliance which he does or should foresee, and enforcement must be necessary to avoid injustice. Satisfaction of the latter requirement may depend on the reasonableness of the promisee's reliance, on its definite and substantial character in relation to the remedy sought, on the formality with which the promise is made, on the extent to which the evidentiary, cautionary, deterrent and channeling functions of form are met by the commercial setting or otherwise, and on the extent to which such other policies as the enforcement of bargains and the prevention of unjust enrichment are relevant. *Compare* Comment to § 72. The force of particular factors varies in different types of cases: thus reliance need not be of substantial character in charitable subscription cases, but must in cases of firm offers and guaranties. Compare Subsection (2) with §§ 87, 88.

Illustrations:

2. A promises B not to foreclose, for a specified time, a mortgage which A holds on B's land. B thereafter makes improvements on the land. A's promise is binding and may be enforced by denial of foreclosure before the time has elapsed.

3. A sues B in a municipal court for damages for personal injuries caused by B's negligence. After the one year statute of limitations has run, B requests A to discontinue the action and start again in the superior court where the action can be consolidated with other actions against B arising out of the same accident. A does so. B's implied promise that no harm to A will result bars B from asserting the statute of limitations as a defense.

4. A has been employed by B for 40 years. B promises to pay A a pension of $200 per month when A retires. A retires and forbears to work elsewhere for several years while B pays the pension. B's promise is binding.

c. *Reliance by third persons.* If a promise is made to one party for the benefit of another, it is often foreseeable that the beneficiary will rely on the promise. Enforcement of the promise in such cases rests on the same basis and depends on the same factors as in cases of reliance by the promisee. Justifiable reliance by third persons who are not beneficiaries is less likely, but may sometimes reinforce the claim of the promisee or beneficiary.

Illustrations:

5. A holds a mortgage on B's land. To enable B to obtain a loan, A promises B in writing to release part of the land from the mortgage upon payment of a stated sum. As A contemplated, C lends money to B on a second mortgage, relying on A's promise. The promise is binding and may be enforced by C.

6. A executes and delivers a promissory note to B, a bank, to give B a false appearance of assets, deceive the banking authorities, and enable the bank to continue to operate. After several years B fails and is taken over by C, a representative of B's creditors. A's note is enforceable by C.

7. A and B, husband and wife, are tenants by the entirety of a tract of land. They make an oral promise to B's niece C to give her the tract. B, C and C's husband expend money in building a house on the tract and C and her husband take possession and live there for several years until B dies. The expenditures by B and by C's husband are treated like those by C in determining whether justice requires enforcement of the promise against A.

d. *Partial enforcement.* A promise binding under this section is a contract, and full-scale enforcement by normal remedies is often appropriate. But the same factors which bear on whether any relief should be granted also bear on the character and extent of the remedy. In particular, relief may sometimes be limited to restitution or to damages or specific relief measured by the extent of the promisee's reliance rather than by the terms of the promise. See §§ 84, 89; compare *Restatement, Second, Torts* § 549 on damages for fraud. Unless there is unjust enrichment of the promisor, damages should not put the promisee in a better position than performance of the promise would have put him. See §§ 344, 349. In the case of a promise to make a gift it would rarely be proper to award consequential damages which would place a greater burden on the promisor than performance would have imposed.

Illustrations:

8. A applies to B, a distributor of radios manufactured by C, for a "dealer franchise" to sell C's products. Such franchises are revocable at will. B erroneously informs A that C has accepted the application and will soon award the franchise, that A can proceed to employ salesmen and solicit orders, and that A will receive an initial delivery of at least 30 radios. A expends $1,150 in preparing to do business, but does not receive the franchise or any radios. B is liable to A for the $1,150 but not for the lost profit on 30 radios. **Compare Restatement, Second, Agency** § 329.

9. The facts being otherwise as stated in Illustration 8, B gives A the erroneous information deliberately and with C's approval and requires A to buy the assets

of a deceased former dealer and thus discharge C's "moral obligation" to the widow. C is liable to A not only for A's expenses but also for the lost profit on 30 radios.

10. A, who owns and operates a bakery, desires to go into the grocery business. He approaches B, a franchisor of supermarkets. B states to A that for $18,000 B will establish A in a store. B also advises A to move to another town and buy a small grocery to gain experience. A does so. Later B advises A to sell the grocery, which A does, taking a capital loss and foregoing expected profits from the summer tourist trade. B also advises A to sell his bakery to raise capital for the supermarket franchise, saying "Everything is ready to go. Get your money together and we are set." A sells the bakery taking a capital loss on this sale as well. Still later, B tells A that considerably more than an $18,000 investment will be needed, and the negotiations between the parties collapse. At the point of collapse many details of the proposed agreement between the parties are unresolved. The assurances from B to A are promises on which B reasonably should have expected A to rely, and A is entitled to his actual losses on the sales of the bakery and grocery and for his moving and temporary living expenses. Since the proposed agreement was never made, however, A is not entitled to lost profits from the sale of the grocery or to his expectation interest in the proposed franchise from B.

11. A is about to buy a house on a hill. Before buying he obtains a promise from B, who owns adjoining land, that B will not build on a particular portion of his lot, where a building would obstruct the view from the house. A then buys the house in reliance on the promise. B's promise is binding, but will be specifically enforced only so long as A and his successors do not permanently terminate the use of the view.

12. A promises to make a gift of a tract of land to B, his son-in-law. B takes possession and lives on the land for 17 years, making valuable improvements. A then dispossesses B, and specific performance is denied because the proof of the terms of the promise is not sufficiently clear and definite. B is entitled to a lien on the land for the value of the improvements, not exceeding their cost.

f.   *Charitable subscriptions, marriage settlements, and other gifts.* One of the functions of the doctrine of consideration is to deny enforcement to a promise to make a gift. Such a promise is ordinarily enforced by virtue of the promisee's reliance only if his conduct is foreseeable and reasonable and involves a definite and substantial change of position which would not have occurred if the promise had not been made. In some cases, however, other policies reinforce the promisee's claim. Thus the promisor might be unjustly enriched if he could reclaim the subject of the promised gift after the promisee has improved it.

Subsection (2) identifies two other classes of cases in which the promisee's claim is similarly reinforced. American courts have traditionally favored charitable subscriptions and marriage settlements, and have found consideration in many cases where the element of exchange was doubtful or nonexistent. Where recovery is rested on reliance in such cases, a probability of reliance is enough, and no effort is made to sort out mixed motives or to consider whether partial enforcement would be appropriate.

Illustrations:

15. A promises B $5000, knowing that B desires that sum for the purchase of a parcel of land. Induced thereby, B secures without any payment an option

to buy the parcel. A then tells B that he withdraws his promise. A's promise is not binding.

16. A orally promises to give her son B a tract of land to live on. As A intended, B gives up a homestead elsewhere, takes possession of the land, lives there for a year and makes substantial improvements. A's promise is binding.

17. A orally promises to pay B, a university, $100,000 in five annual installments for the purposes of its fundraising campaign then in progress. The promise is confirmed in writing by A's agent, and two annual installments are paid before A dies. The continuance of the fundraising campaign by B is sufficient reliance to make the promise binding on A and his estate.

18. A and B are engaged to be married. In anticipation of the marriage A and his father C enter into a formal written agreement by which C promises to leave certain property to A by will. A's subsequent marriage to B is sufficient reliance to make the promise binding on C and his estate.

Chapter 5. The Statute of Frauds

§ 139 Enforcement by Virtue of Action in Reliance.

(1)   A promise which the promisor should reasonably expect to induce action or forbearance on the part of the promisee or a third person and which does induce the action or forbearance is enforceable notwithstanding the Statute of Frauds if injustice can be avoided only by enforcement of the promise. The remedy granted for breach is to be limited as justice requires.

(2)   In determining whether injustice can be avoided only by enforcement of the promise, the following circumstances are significant:

(a) the availability and adequacy of other remedies, particularly cancellation and restitution;

(b) the definite and substantial character of the action or forbearance in relation to the remedy sought;

(c) the extent to which the action or forbearance corroborates evidence of the making and terms of the promise, or the making and terms are otherwise established by clear and convincing evidence;

(d) the reasonableness of the action or forbearance;

(e) the extent to which the action or forbearance was foreseeable by the promisor.

Chapter 6. Mistake

§ 151 Mistake Defined.

A mistake is a belief that is not in accord with the facts.

§ 152 When Mistake of Both Parties Makes a Contract Voidable.

(1)   Where a mistake of both parties at the time a contract was made as to a basic assumption on which the contract was made has a material effect on the agreed

exchange of performances, the contract is voidable by the adversely affected party unless he bears the risk of the mistake under the rule stated in § 154.

(2)   In determining whether the mistake has a material effect on the agreed exchange of performances, account is taken of any relief by way of reformation, restitution, or otherwise.

§ 153 When Mistake of One Party Makes a Contract Voidable.

Where a mistake of one party at the time a contract was made as to a basic assumption on which he made the contract has a material effect on the agreed exchange of performances that is adverse to him, the contract is voidable by him if he does not bear the risk of the mistake under the rule stated in § 154, and

(a)   the effect of the mistake is such that enforcement of the contract would be unconscionable, or

(b)   the other party had reason to know of the mistake or his fault caused the mistake.

§ 154 When a Party Bears the Risk of a Mistake.

A party bears the risk of a mistake when

(a)   the risk is allocated to him by agreement of the parties, or

(b)   he is aware, at the time the contract is made, that he has only limited knowledge with respect to the facts to which the mistake relates but treats his limited knowledge as sufficient, or

(c)   the risk is allocated to him by the court on the ground that it is reasonable in the circumstances to do so.

§ 155 When Mistake of Both Parties as to Written Expression Justifies Reformation.

Where a writing that evidences or embodies an agreement in whole or in part fails to express the agreement because of a mistake of both parties as to the contents or effect of the writing, the court may at the request of a party reform the writing to express the agreement, except to the extent that rights of third parties such as good faith purchasers for value will be unfairly affected.

Chapter 7. Misrepresentation, Duress and Undue Influence

§ 159 Misrepresentation Defined.

A misrepresentation is an assertion that is not in accord with the facts.

§ 160 When Action Is Equivalent to an Assertion (Concealment).

Action intended or known to be likely to prevent another from learning a fact is equivalent to an assertion that the fact does not exist.

§ 161 When Nondisclosure Is Equivalent to an Assertion.

A person's nondisclosure of a fact known to him is equivalent to an assertion that the fact does not exist in the following cases only:

(a)   where he knows that disclosure of the fact is necessary to prevent some previous assertion from being a misrepresentation or from being fraudulent or material.

(b)   where he knows that disclosure of the fact would correct a mistake of the other party as to a basic assumption on which that party is making the contract and if nondisclosure of the fact amounts to a failure to act in good faith and in accordance with reasonable standards of fair dealing.

(c) where he knows that disclosure of the fact would correct a mistake of the other party as to the contents or effect of a writing, evidencing or embodying an agreement in whole or in part.

(d) where the other person is entitled to know the fact because of a relation of trust and confidence between them.

§ 162 When a Misrepresentation Is Fraudulent or Material.

(1) A misrepresentation is fraudulent if the maker intends his assertion to induce a party to manifest his assent and the maker

(a) knows or believes that the assertion is not in accord with the facts, or

(b) does not have the confidence that he states or implies in the truth of the assertion, or

(c) knows that he does not have the basis that he states or implies for the assertion.

(2) A misrepresentation is material if it would be likely to induce a reasonable person to manifest his assent, or if the maker knows that it would be likely to induce the recipient to do so.

§ 163 When a Misrepresentation Prevents Formation of a Contract.

If a misrepresentation as to the character or essential terms of a proposed contract induces conduct that appears to be a manifestation of assent by one who neither knows nor has reasonable opportunity to know of the character or essential terms of the proposed contract, his conduct is not effective as a manifestation of assent.

§ 164 When a Misrepresentation Makes a Contract Voidable.

(1) If a party's manifestation of assent is induced by either a fraudulent or a material misrepresentation by the other party upon which the recipient is justified in relying, the contract is voidable by the recipient.

(2) If a party's manifestation of assent is induced by either a fraudulent or a material misrepresentation by one who is not a party to the transaction upon which the recipient is justified in relying, the contract is voidable by the recipient, unless the other party to the transaction in good faith and without reason to know of the misrepresentation either gives value or relies materially on the transaction.

§ 167 When a Misrepresentation Is an Inducing Cause.

A misrepresentation induces a party's manifestation of assent if it substantially contributes to his decision to manifest his assent.

§ 168 Reliance on Assertions of Opinion.

(1) An assertion is one of opinion if it expresses only a belief, without certainty, as to the existence of a fact or expresses only a judgment as to quality, value, authenticity, or similar matters.

(2) If it is reasonable to do so, the recipient of an assertion of a person's opinion as to facts not disclosed and not otherwise known to the recipient may properly interpret it as an assertion

(a) that the facts known to that person are not incompatible with his opinion, or

(b) that he knows facts sufficient to justify him in forming it.

§ 169 When Reliance on an Assertion of Opinion Is Not Justified.

To the extent that an assertion is one of opinion only, the recipient is not justified in relying on it unless the recipient

(a) stands in such a relation of trust and confidence to the person whose opinion is asserted that the recipient is reasonable in relying on it, or

(b) reasonably believes that, as compared with himself, the person whose opinion is asserted has special skill, judgment or objectivity with respect to the subject matter, or

(c) is for some other special reason particularly susceptible to a misrepresentation of the type involved.

§ 171 When Reliance on an Assertion of Intention Is Not Justified.

(1) To the extent that an assertion is one of intention only, the recipient is not justified in relying on it if in the circumstances a misrepresentation of intention is consistent with reasonable standards of dealing.

(2) If it is reasonable to do so, the promisee may properly interpret a promise as an assertion that the promisor intends to perform the promise.

§ 172 When Fault Makes Reliance Unjustified.

A recipient's fault in not knowing or discovering the facts before making the contract does not make his reliance unjustified unless it amounts to a failure to act in good faith and in accordance with reasonable standards of fair dealing.

§ 173 When Abuse of a Fiduciary Relation Makes a Contract Voidable.

If a fiduciary makes a contract with his beneficiary relating to matters within the scope of the fiduciary relation, the contract is voidable by the beneficiary, unless

(a) it is on fair terms, and

(b) all parties beneficially interested manifest assent with full understanding of their legal rights and of all relevant facts that the fiduciary knows or should know.

§ 174 When Duress by Physical Compulsion Prevents Formation of a Contract.

If conduct that appears to be a manifestation of assent by a party who does not intend to engage in that conduct is physically compelled by duress, the conduct is not effective as a manifestation of assent.

§ 175 When Duress by Threat Makes a Contract Voidable.

(1) If a party's manifestation of assent is induced by an improper threat by the other party that leaves the victim no reasonable alternative, the contract is voidable by the victim.

(2) If a party's manifestation of assent is induced by one who is not a party to the transaction, the contract is voidable by the victim unless the other party to the transaction in good faith and without reason to know of the duress either gives value or relies materially on the transaction.

§ 176 When a Threat Is Improper.

(1) A threat is improper if

(a) what is threatened is a crime or a tort, or the threat itself would be a crime or a tort if it resulted in obtaining property,

(b) what is threatened is a criminal prosecution,

(c) what is threatened is the use of civil process and the threat is made in bad faith, or

(d) the threat is a breach of the duty of good faith and fair dealing under a contract with the recipient.

(2)   A threat is improper if the resulting exchange is not on fair terms, and

(a) the threatened act would harm the recipient and would not significantly benefit the party making the threat,

(b) the effectiveness of the threat in inducing the manifestation of assent is significantly increased by prior unfair dealing by the party making the threat, or

(c) what is threatened is otherwise a use of power for illegitimate ends.

§ 177 When Undue Influence Makes a Contract Voidable.

(1)   Undue influence is unfair persuasion of a party who is under the domination of the person exercising the persuasion or who by virtue of the relation between them is justified in assuming that that person will not act in a manner inconsistent with his welfare.

(2)   If a party's manifestation of assent is induced by undue influence by the other party, the contract is voidable by the victim.

(3)   If a party's manifestation of assent is induced by one who is not a party to the transaction, the contract is voidable by the victim unless the other party to the transaction in good faith and without reason to know of the undue influence either gives value or relies materially on the transaction.

Chapter 8. Unenforceability on Grounds of Public Policy

§ 178 When a Term Is Unenforceable on Grounds of Public Policy.

(1)   A promise or other term of an agreement is unenforceable on grounds of public policy if legislation provides that it is unenforceable or the interest in its enforcement is clearly outweighed in the circumstances by a public policy against the enforcement of such terms.

(2)   In weighing the interest in the enforcement of a term, account is taken of

(a) the parties' justified expectations,

(b) any forfeiture that would result if enforcement were denied, and

(c) any special public interest in the enforcement of the particular term.

(3)   In weighing a public policy against enforcement of a term, account is taken of

(a) the strength of that policy as manifested by legislation or judicial decisions,

(b) the likelihood that a refusal to enforce the term will further that policy,

(c) the seriousness of any misconduct involved and the extent to which it was deliberate, and

(d) the directness of the connection between that misconduct and the term.

§ 179 Bases of Public Policies Against Enforcement.

A public policy against the enforcement of promises or other terms may be derived by the court from

(a) legislation relevant to such a policy, or

(b) the need to protect some aspect of the public welfare, as is the case for the judicial policies against, for example,

    (i) restraint of trade (§§ 186-188),

    (ii) impairment of family relations (§§ 189-191), and

    (iii) interference with other protected interests (§§ 192-196, 356).

§ 185 Excuse of a Condition on Grounds of Public Policy

To the extent that a term requiring the occurrence of a condition is unenforceable under the rule stated in § 178, a court may excuse the non-occurrence of the condition unless its occurrence was an essential part of the agreed exchange.

§ 186 Promise in Restraint of Trade.

(1) A promise is unenforceable on grounds of public policy if it is unreasonably in restraint of trade.

(2) A promise is in restraint of trade if its performance would limit competition in any business or restrict the promisor in the exercise of a gainful occupation.

§ 187 Non-Ancillary Restraints on Competition.

A promise to refrain from competition that imposes a restraint that is not ancillary to an otherwise valid transaction or relationship is unreasonably in restraint of trade.

§ 188 Ancillary Restraints on Competition.

(1) A promise to refrain from competition that imposes a restraint that is ancillary to an otherwise valid transaction or relationship is unreasonably in restraint of trade if

    (a) the restraint is greater than is needed to protect the promisee's legitimate interest, or

    (b) the promisee's need is outweighed by the hardship to the promisor and the likely injury to the public.

(2) Promises imposing restraints that are ancillary to a valid transaction or relationship include the following:

    (a) a promise by the seller of a business not to compete with the buyer in such a way as to injure the value of the business sold;

    (b) a promise by an employee or other agent not to compete with his employer or other principal;

    (c) a promise by a partner not to compete with the partnership.

§ 189 Promise in Restraint of Marriage.

A promise is unenforceable on grounds of public policy if it is unreasonably in restraint of marriage.

§ 190 Promise Detrimental to Marital Relationship.

(1) A promise by a person contemplating marriage or by a married person, other than as part of an enforceable separation agreement, is unenforceable on grounds of public policy if it would change some essential incident of the marital relationship in a way detrimental to the public interest in the marriage relationship. A separation agreement is unenforceable on grounds of public policy unless it

is made after separation or in contemplation of an immediate separation and is fair in the circumstances.

(2)   A promise that tends unreasonably to encourage divorce or separation is unenforceable on grounds of public policy.

§ 191 Promise Affecting Custody.

A promise affecting the right of custody of a minor child is unenforceable on grounds of public policy unless the disposition as to custody is consistent with the best interest of the child.

§ 192 Promise Involving Commission of a Tort.

A promise to commit a tort or to induce the commission of a tort is unenforceable on grounds of public policy.

§ 193 Promise Inducing Violation of Fiduciary Duty.

A promise by a fiduciary to violate his fiduciary duty or a promise that tends to induce such a violation is unenforceable on grounds of public policy.

§ 194 Promise Interfering with Contract with Another.

A promise that tortuously interferes with performance of a contract with a third person or a tortuously induced promise to commit a breach of contract is unenforceable on grounds of public policy.

§ 195 Term Exempting from Liability for Harm Caused Intentionally, Recklessly or Negligently.

(1)   A term exempting a party from tort liability for harm caused intentionally or recklessly is unenforceable on grounds of public policy.

(2)   A term exempting a party from tort liability for harm caused negligently is unenforceable on grounds of public policy if

(a) the term exempts an employer from liability to an employee for injury in the course of his employment;

(b) the term exempts one charged with a duty of public service from liability to one to whom that duty is owed for compensation for breach of that duty, or

(c) the other party is similarly a member of a class protected against the class to which the first party belongs.

(3)   A term exempting a seller of a product from his special tort liability for physical harm to a user or consumer is unenforceable on grounds of public policy unless the term is fairly bargained for and is consistent with the policy underlying that liability.

§ 196 Term Exempting from Consequences of Misrepresentation.

A term unreasonably exempting a party from the legal consequences of a misrepresentation is unenforceable on grounds of public policy.

§ 197 Restitution Generally Unavailable.

Except as stated in§§ 198 and 199, a party has no claim in restitution for performance that he has rendered under or in return for a promise that is unenforceable on grounds of public policy unless denial of restitution would cause disproportionate forfeiture.

§ 198 Restitution in Favor of Party Who Is Excusably Ignorant or Is Not Equally in the Wrong.

A party has a claim in restitution for performance that he has rendered under or in return for a promise that is unenforceable on grounds of public policy if

(a) he was excusably ignorant of the facts or of legislation of a minor character, in the absence of which the promise would be enforceable, or

(b) he was not equally in the wrong with the promisor.

Chapter 9. The Scope of Contractual Obligations

§ 201 Whose Meaning Prevails.

(1) Where the parties have attached the same meaning to a promise or agreement or a term thereof, it is interpreted in accordance with that meaning.

(2) Where the parties have attached different meanings to a promise or agreement or a term thereof, it is interpreted in accordance with the meaning attached by one of them if at the time the agreement was made

(a) that party did not know of any different meaning attached by the other, and the other knew the meaning attached by the first party; or

(b) that party had no reason to know of any different meaning attached by the other, and the other had reason to know the meaning attached by the first party.

(3) Except as stated in this Section, neither party is bound by the meaning attached by the other, even though the result may be a failure of mutual assent.

§ 202 Rules in Aid of Interpretation.

(1) Words and other conduct are interpreted in the light of all the circumstances, and if the principal purpose of the parties is ascertainable it is given great weight.

(2) A writing is interpreted as a whole, and all writings that are part of the same transaction are interpreted together.

(3) Unless a different intention is manifested,

(a) where language has a generally prevailing meaning, it is interpreted in accordance with that meaning;

(b) technical terms and words of art are given their technical meaning when used in a transaction within their technical field.

(4) Where an agreement involves repeated occasions for performance by either party with knowledge of the nature of the performance and opportunity for objection to it by the other, any course of performance accepted or acquiesced in without objection is given great weight in the interpretation of the agreement.

(5) Wherever reasonable, the manifestations of intention of the parties to a promise or agreement are interpreted as consistent with each other and with any relevant course of performance, course of dealing, or usage of trade.

§ 203 Standards of Preference in Interpretation.

In the interpretation of a promise or agreement or a term thereof, the following standards of preference are generally applicable:

(a) an interpretation which gives a reasonable, lawful, and effective meaning to all the terms is preferred to an interpretation which leaves a part unreasonable, unlawful, or of no effect;

    (b) express terms are given greater weight than course of performance, course of dealing, and usage of trade, course of performance is given greater weight than course of dealing or usage of trade, and course of dealing is given greater weight than usage of trade;

    (c) specific terms and exact terms are given greater weight than general language;

    (d) separately negotiated or added terms are given greater weight than standardized terms or other terms not separately negotiated.

§ 205 Duty of Good Faith and Fair Dealing.

Every contract imposes upon each party a duty of good faith and fair dealing in its performance and its enforcement.

§ 206 Interpretation Against the Draftsman.

In choosing among the reasonable meanings of a promise or agreement or a term thereof, that meaning is generally preferred which operates against the party who supplies the words or from whom a writing otherwise proceeds.

§ 207 Interpretation Favoring the Public.

In choosing among the reasonable meanings of a promise or agreement or term thereof, a meaning that serves the public interest is generally preferred.

§ 208 Unconscionable Contract or Term.

If a contract or term thereof is unconscionable at the time the contract is made a court may refuse to enforce the contract, or may enforce the remainder of the contract without the unconscionable term, or may so limit the application of any unconscionable term as to avoid any unconscionable result.

§ 209 Integrated Agreements

    (1)   An integrated agreement is a writing or writings constituting a final expression of one or more terms of an agreement.

    (2)   Whether there is an integrated agreement is to be determined by the court as a question preliminary to determination of a question of interpretation or to application of the parol evidence rule.

    (3)   Where the parties reduce an agreement to a writing which in view of its completeness and specificity reasonably appears to be a complete agreement, it is taken to be an integrated agreement unless it is established by other evidence that the writing did not constitute a final expression.

§ 210 Completely and Partially Integrated Agreements.

    (1)   A completely integrated agreement is an integrated agreement adopted by the parties as a complete and exclusive statement of the terms of the agreement.

    (2)   A partially integrated agreement is an integrated agreement other than a completely integrated agreement.

    (3)   Whether an agreement is completely or partially integrated is to be determined by the court as a question preliminary to determination of a question of interpretation or to application of the parol evidence rule.

§ 211 Standardized Agreements.

    (1)   Except as stated in Subsection (3), where a party to an agreement signs or otherwise manifests assent to a writing and has reason to believe that like writings are regularly used to embody terms of agreements of the same type, he adopts the

writing as an integrated agreement with respect to the terms included in the writing.

(2)   Such a writing is interpreted wherever reasonable as treating alike all those similarly situated, without regard to their knowledge or understanding of the standard terms of the writing.

(3)   Where the other party has reason to believe that the party manifesting such assent would not do so if he knew that the writing contained a particular term, the term is not part of the agreement.

§ 212 Interpretation of Integrated Agreement.

(1)   The interpretation of an integrated agreement is directed to the meaning of the terms of the writing or writings in the light of the circumstances, in accordance with the rules stated in this Chapter.

(2)   A question of interpretation of an integrated agreement is to be determined by the trier of fact if it depends on the credibility of extrinsic evidence or on a choice among reasonable inferences to be drawn from extrinsic evidence. Otherwise a question of interpretation of an integrated agreement is to be determined as a question of law.

§ 213 Effect of Integrated Agreement on Prior Agreements (Parol Evidence Rule).

(1)   A binding integrated agreement discharges prior agreements to the extent that it is inconsistent with them.

(2)   A binding completely integrated agreement discharges prior agreements to the extent that they are within its scope.

(3)   An integrated agreement that is not binding or that is voidable and avoided does not discharge a prior agreement. But an integrated agreement, even though not binding, may be effective to render inoperative a term which would have been part of the agreement if it had not been integrated.

§ 214 Evidence of Prior or Contemporaneous Agreements and Negotiations.

Agreements and negotiations prior to or contemporaneous with the adoption of a writing are admissible in evidence to establish

(a)   that the writing is or is not an integrated agreement;

(b)   that the integrated agreement, if any, is completely or partially integrated;

(c)   the meaning of the writing, whether or not integrated;

(d)   illegality, fraud, duress, mistake, lack of consideration, or other invalidating cause;

(e)   ground for granting or denying rescission, reformation, specific performance, or other remedy.

§ 215 Contradiction of Integrated Terms.

Except as stated in the preceding Section, where there is a binding agreement, either completely or partially integrated, evidence of prior or contemporaneous agreements or negotiations is not admissible in evidence to contradict a term of the writing.

§ 216 Consistent Additional Terms.

(1)   Evidence of a consistent additional term is admissible to supplement an integrated agreement unless the court finds that the agreement was completely integrated.

(2)   An agreement is not completely integrated if the writing omits a consistent additional agreed term which is

(a) agreed to for separate consideration, or

(b) such a term as in the circumstances might naturally be omitted from the writing.

§ 217 Integrated Agreement Subject to Oral Requirement of a Condition.

Where the parties to a written agreement agree orally that performance of the agreement is subject to the occurrence of a stated condition, the agreement is not integrated with respect to the oral condition.

§ 218 Untrue Recitals; Evidence of Consideration.

(1)   A recital of a fact in an integrated agreement may be shown to be untrue.

(2)   Evidence is admissible to prove whether or not there is consideration for a promise, even though the parties have reduced their agreement to a writing which appears to be a completely integrated agreement.

§ 219 Usage.

Usage is habitual or customary practice.

§ 220 Usage Relevant to Interpretation.

(1)   An agreement is interpreted in accordance with a relevant usage if each party knew or had reason to know of the usage and neither party knew or had reason to know that the meaning attached by the other was inconsistent with the usage.

(2)   When the meaning attached by one party accorded with a relevant usage and the other knew or had reason to know of the usage, the other is treated as having known or had reason to know the meaning attached by the first party.

§ 221 Usage Supplementing an Agreement.

An agreement is supplemented or qualified by a reasonable usage with respect to agreements of the same type if each party knows or has reason to know of the usage and neither party knows or has reason to know that the other party has an intention inconsistent with the usage.

§ 222 Usage of Trade.

(1)   A usage of trade is a usage having such regularity of observance in a place, vocation, or trade as to justify an expectation that it will be observed with respect to a particular agreement. It may include a system of rules regularly observed even though particular rules are changed from time to time.

(2)   The existence and scope of a usage of trade are to be determined as questions of fact. If a usage is embodied in a written trade code or similar writing the interpretation of the writing is to be determined by the court as a question of law.

(3)   Unless otherwise agreed, a usage of trade in the vocation or trade in which the parties are engaged or a usage of trade of which they know or have reason to know gives meaning to or supplements or qualifies their agreement.

§ 223 Course of Dealing.

(1)   A course of dealing is a sequence of previous conduct between the parties to an agreement which is fairly to be regarded as establishing a common basis of understanding for interpreting their expressions and other conduct.

(2)   Unless otherwise agreed, a course of dealing between the parties gives meaning to or supplements or qualifies their agreement.

§ 224 Condition Defined.

A condition is an event, not certain to occur, which must occur, unless its nonoccurrence is excused, before performance under a contract becomes due.

§ 225 Effects of the Nonoccurrence of a Condition.

(1) Performance of a duty subject to a condition cannot become due unless the condition occurs or its nonoccurrence is excused.

(2) Unless it has been excused, the nonoccurrence of a condition discharges the duty when the condition can no longer occur.

(3) Nonoccurrence of a condition is not a breach by a party unless he is under a duty that the condition occur.

§ 226 How an Event May Be Made a Condition.

An event may be made a condition either by the agreement of the parties or by a term supplied by the court.

§ 227 Standards of Preference with Regard to Conditions.

(1) In resolving doubts as to whether an event is made a condition of an obligor's duty, and as to the nature of such an event, an interpretation is preferred that will reduce the obligee's risk of forfeiture, unless the event is within the obligee's control or the circumstances indicate that he has assumed the risk.

(2) Unless the contract is of a type under which only one party generally undertakes duties, when it is doubtful whether

(a) a duty is imposed on an obligee that an event occur, or

(b) the event is made a condition of the obligor's duty, or

(c) the event is made a condition of the obligor's duty and a duty is imposed on the obligee that the event occur, the first interpretation is preferred if the event is within the obligee's control.

(3) In case of doubt, an interpretation under which an event is a condition of an obligor's duty is preferred over an interpretation under which the nonoccurrence of the event is a ground for discharge of that duty after it has become a duty to perform.

§ 228 Satisfaction of the Obligor as a Condition.

When it is a condition of an obligor's duty that he be satisfied with respect to the obligee's performance or with respect to something else, and it is practicable to determine whether a reasonable person in the position of the obligor would be satisfied, an interpretation is preferred under which the condition occurs if such a reasonable person in the position of the obligor would be satisfied.

§ 229 Excuse of a Condition to Avoid Forfeiture.

To the extent that the nonoccurrence of a condition would cause disproportionate forfeiture, a court may excuse the nonoccurrence of that condition unless its occurrence was a material part of the agreed exchange.

Chapter 10. Performance and Non-Performance

§ 231 Criterion for Determining When Performances Are to Be Exchanged under an Exchange of Promises.

Performances are to be exchanged under an exchange of promises if each promise is at least part of the consideration for the other and the performance of each promise is to be exchanged at least in part for the performance of the other.

§ 232 When It Is Presumed That Performances Are to Be Exchanged under an Exchange of Promises.

Where the consideration given by each party to a contract consists in whole or in part of promises, all the performances to be rendered by each party taken collectively are treated as performances to be exchanged under an exchange of promises, unless a contrary intention is clearly manifested.

§ 233 Performance at One Time or in Installments.

(1)   Where performances are to be exchanged under an exchange of promises, and the whole of one party's performance can be rendered at one time, it is due at one time, unless the language or the circumstances indicate the contrary.

(2)   Where only a part of one party's performance is due at one time under Subsection (1), if the other party's performance can be so apportioned that there is a comparable part that can also be rendered at that time, it is due at that time, unless the language or the circumstances indicate the contrary.

§ 234 Order of Performances.

(1)   Where all or part of the performances to be exchanged under an exchange of promises can be rendered simultaneously, they are to that extent due simultaneously, unless the language or the circumstances indicate the contrary.

(2)   Except to the extent stated in Subsection (1), where the performance of only one party under such an exchange requires a period of time, his performance is due at an earlier time than that of the other party, unless the language or the circumstances indicate the contrary.

§ 250 When a Statement or an Act Is a Repudiation

A repudiation is

(a)   a statement by the obligor to the obligee indicating that the obligor will commit a breach that would of itself give the obligee a claim for damages for total breach under § 243, or

(b)   a voluntary affirmative act which renders the obligor unable or apparently unable to perform without such a breach.

§ 251 When a Failure to Give Assurance May Be Treated as a Repudiation

(1)   Where reasonable grounds arise to believe that the obligor will commit a breach by nonperformance that would of itself give the obligee a claim for damages for total breach under § 243, the obligee may demand adequate assurance of due performance and may, if reasonable, suspend any performance for which he has not already received the agreed exchange until he receives such assurance.

(2)   The obligee may treat as a repudiation the obligor's failure to provide within a reasonable time such assurance of due performance as is adequate in the circumstances of the particular case.

Chapter 11. Impracticability of Performance and Frustration of Purpose

§ 261 Discharge By Supervening Impracticability.

Where, after a contract is made, a party's performance is made impracticable without his fault by the occurrence of an event the nonoccurrence of which was a basic assumption on which the contract was made, his duty to render that performance is discharged, unless the language or the circumstances indicate the contrary.

§ 262 Death or Incapacity of Person Necessary for Performance.

If the existence of a particular person is necessary for the performance of a duty, his death or such incapacity as makes performance impracticable is an event the nonoccurrence of which was a basic assumption on which the contract was made.

§ 263 Destruction, Deterioration or Failure to come into Existence of Thing Necessary for Performance.

If the existence of a specific thing is necessary for the performance of a duty, its failure to come into existence, destruction, or such deterioration as makes performance impracticable is an event the nonoccurrence of which was a basic assumption on which the contract was made.

§ 264 Prevention By Governmental Regulation or Order.

If the performance of a duty is made impracticable by having to comply with a domestic or foreign governmental regulation or order, that regulation or order is an event the nonoccurrence of which was a basic assumption on which the contract was made.

§ 269 Temporary Impracticability or Frustration.

Impracticability of performance or frustration of purpose that is only temporary suspends the obligor's duty to perform while the impracticability or frustration exists but does not discharge his duty or prevent it from arising unless his performance after the cessation of the impracticability or frustration would be materially more burdensome than had there been no impracticability or frustration.

Chapter 12. Discharge by Assent or Alteration

§ 280 Novation.

A novation is a substituted contract that includes as a party one who was neither the obligor nor the obligee of the original duty.

Chapter 13. Joint and Several Promisors and Promisees

§ 288 Promises of the Same Performance.

(1) Where two or more parties to a contract make a promise or promises to the same promisee, the manifested intention of the parties determines whether they promise that the same performance or separate performances shall be given.

(2) Unless a contrary intention is manifested, a promise by two or more promisors is a promise that the same performance shall be given.

Chapter 14 Contract Beneficiaries

§ 302 Intended and Incidental Beneficiaries.

(1) Unless otherwise agreed between promisor and promisee, a beneficiary of a promise is an intended beneficiary if recognition of a right to performance in the beneficiary is appropriate to effectuate the intention of the parties and either

> (a) the performance of the promise will satisfy an obligation of the promisee to pay money to the beneficiary; or
>
> (b) the circumstances indicate that the promisee intends to give the beneficiary the benefit of the promised performance.

(2) An incidental beneficiary is a beneficiary who is not an intended beneficiary.

§ 308 Identification of Beneficiaries.

It is not essential to the creation of a right in an intended beneficiary that he be identified when a contract containing the promise is made.

§ 309 Defenses Against the Beneficiary.

(1) A promise creates no duty to a beneficiary unless a contract is formed between the promisor and the promisee; and if a contract is voidable or unenforceable at the time of its formation the right of any beneficiary is subject to the infirmity.

(2) If a contract ceases to be binding in whole or in part because of impracticability, public policy, nonoccurrence of a condition, or present or prospective failure of performance, the right of any beneficiary is to that extent discharged or modified.

(3) Except as stated in Subsections (1) and (2) and in § 311 or as provided by the contract, the right of any beneficiary against the promisor is not subject to the promisor's claims or defenses against the promisee or to the promisee's claims or defenses against the beneficiary.

(4) A beneficiary's right against the promisor is subject to any claim or defense arising from his own conduct or agreement.

Chapter 15. Assignment and Delegation

§ 317 Assignment of a Right.

(1) An assignment of a right is a manifestation of the assignor's intention to transfer it by virtue of which the assignor's right to performance by the obligor is extinguished in whole or in part and the assignee acquires a right to such performance.

(2) A contractual right can be assigned unless

> (a) the substitution of a right of the assignee for the right of the assignor would materially change the duty of the obligor, or materially increase the burden or risk imposed on him by his contract, or materially impair his chance of obtaining return performance, or materially reduce its value to him, or
>
> (b) the assignment is forbidden by statute or is otherwise inoperative on grounds of public policy, or
>
> (c) assignment is validly precluded by contract.

§ 318 Delegation of Performance of Duty.

(1) An obligor can properly delegate the performance of his duty to another unless the delegation is contrary to public policy or the terms of his promise.

(2) Unless otherwise agreed, a promise requires performance by a particular person only to the extent that the obligee has a substantial interest in having that person perform or control the acts promised.

(3) Unless the obligee agrees otherwise, neither delegation of performance nor a contract to assume the duty made with the obligor by the person delegated discharges any duty or liability of the delegating obligor.

§ 322 Contractual Prohibition of Assignment.

(1)   Unless the circumstances indicate the contrary, a contract term prohibiting assignment of "the contract" bars only the delegation to an assignee of the performance by the assignor of a duty or condition.

(2)   A contract term prohibiting assignment of rights under the contract, unless a different intention is manifested,

(a) does not forbid assignment of a right to damages for breach of the whole contract or a right arising out of the assignor's due performance of his entire obligation;

(b) gives the obligor a right to damages for breach of the terms forbidding assignment but does not render the assignment ineffective;

(c) is for the benefit of the obligor, and does not prevent the assignee from acquiring rights against the assignor or the obligor from discharging his duty as if there were no such prohibition.

§ 328 Interpretation of Words of Assignment; Effect of Acceptance of Assignment.

(1)   Unless the language or the circumstances indicate the contrary, as in an assignment for security, an assignment of "the contract" or of "all my rights under the contract" or an assignment in similar general terms is an assignment of the assignor's rights and a delegation of his unperformed duties under the contract.

(2)   Unless the language or the circumstances indicate the contrary, the acceptance by an assignee of such an assignment operates as a promise to the assignor to perform the assignor's unperformed duties, and the obligor of the assigned rights is an intended beneficiary of the promise.

Caveat: The Institute expresses no opinion as to whether the rule stated in Subsection (2) applies to an assignment by a purchaser of his rights under a contract for the sale of land.

§ 336 Defenses Against an Assignee.

(1)   By an assignment the assignee acquires a right against the obligor only to the extent that the obligor is under a duty to the assignor; and if the right of the assignor would be voidable by the obligor or unenforceable against him if no assignment had been made, the right of the assignee is subject to the infirmity.

(2)   The right of an assignee is subject to any defense or claim of the obligor which accrues before the obligor receives notification of the assignment, but not to defenses or claims which accrue thereafter except as stated in this Section or as provided by statute.

(3)   Where the right of an assignor is subject to discharge or modification in whole or in party by impracticability, public policy, nonoccurrence of a condition, or present or prospective failure of performance by an obligee, the right of the assignee is to that extent subject to discharge or modification even after the obligor receives notification of the assignment.

(4)   An assignee's right against the obligor is subject to any defense or claim arising from his conduct or to which he was subject as a party or a prior assignee because he had notice.

Chapter 16. Remedies

§ 344 Purposes of Remedies.

Judicial remedies under the rules stated in this *Restatement* serve to protect one or more of the following interests of a promisee:

(a) his "expectation interest," which is his interest in having the benefit of his bargain by being put in as good a position as he would have been in had the contract been performed,

(b) his "reliance interest," which is his interest in being reimbursed for loss caused by reliance on the contract by being put in as good a position as he would have been in had the contract not been made, or

(c) his "restitution interest," which is his interest in having restored to him any benefit that he has conferred on the other party.

§ 345 Judicial Remedies Available.

The judicial remedies available for the protection of the interests stated in § 344 include a judgment or order

(a) awarding a sum of money due under the contract or as damages,

(b) requiring specific performance of a contract or enjoining its nonperformance,

(c) requiring restoration of a specific thing to prevent unjust enrichment,

(d) awarding a sum of money to prevent unjust enrichment,

(e) declaring the rights of the parties, and

(f) enforcing an arbitration award.

§ 347 Measure of Damages in General.

Subject to the limitations stated in §§ 35053, the injured party has a right to damages based on his expectation interest as measured by

(a) the loss in the value to him of the other party's performance caused by its failure or deficiency, plus

(b) any other loss, including incidental or consequential loss, caused by the breach, less

(c) any cost or other loss that he has avoided by not having to perform.

§ 348 Alternatives to Loss in Value of Performance.

(1) If a breach delays the use of property and the loss in value to the injured party is not proved with reasonable certainty, he may recover damages based on the rental value of the property or on interest on the value of the property.

(2) If a breach results in defective or unfinished construction and the loss in value to the injured party is not proved with sufficient certainty, he may recover damages based on

(a) the diminution in the market price of the property caused by the breach, or

(b) the reasonable cost of completing performance or of remedying the defects if that cost is not clearly disproportionate to the probable loss in value to him.

(3) If a breach is of a promise conditioned on a fortuitous event and it is uncertain whether the event would have occurred had there been no breach, the injured

party may recover damages based on the value of the conditional right at the time of breach.

§ 349 Damages Based on Reliance Interest.

As an alternative to the measure of damages stated in § 347, the injured party has a right to damages based on his reliance interest, including expenditures made in preparation for performance or in performance, less any loss that the party in breach can prove with reasonable certainty the injured party would have suffered had the contract been performed.

§ 350 Avoidability as a Limitation on Damages.

(1)   Except as stated in Subsection (2), damages are not recoverable for loss that the injured party could have avoided without undue risk, burden or humiliation.

(2)   The injured party is not precluded from recovery by the rule stated in Subsection (1) to the extent that he has made reasonable but unsuccessful efforts to avoid loss.

§ 351 Unforeseeability and Related Limitations on Damages.

(1)   Damages are not recoverable for loss that the party in breach did not have reason to foresee as a probable result of the breach when the contract was made.

(2)   Loss may be foreseeable as a probable result of a breach because it follows from the breach

(a) in the ordinary course of events, or

(b) as a result of special circumstances, beyond the ordinary course of events, that the party in breach had reason to know.

(3)   A court may limit damages for foreseeable loss by excluding recovery for loss of profits, by allowing recovery only for loss incurred in reliance, or otherwise if it concludes that in the circumstances justice so requires in order to avoid dispro-portionate compensation.

§ 352 Uncertainty as a Limitation on Damages.

Damages are not recoverable for loss beyond an amount that the evidence permits to be established with reasonable certainty.

§ 356 Liquidated Damages and Penalties

(1)   Damages for breach by either party may be liquidated in the agreement but only at an amount that is reason-able in the light of the anticipated or actual loss caused by the breach and the difficulties of proof of loss. A term fixing unreasonably large liquidated damages is unenforceable on grounds of public policy as a penalty.

(2)   A term in a bond providing for an amount of money as a penalty for non-occurrence of the condition of the bond is unenforceable on grounds of public policy to the extent that the amount exceeds the loss caused by such non-occurrence.

§ 357 Availability of Specific Performance and Injunction.

(1)   Subject to the rules stated in §§ 35969, specific performance of a contract duty will be granted in the discretion of the court against a party who has committed or is threatening to commit a breach of the duty.

(2)   Subject to the rules stated in §§ 35969, an injunction against breach of a contract duty will be granted in the discretion of the court against a party who has committed or is threatening to commit a breach of the duty if

(a) the duty is one of forbearance, or

(b) the duty is one to act and specific performance would be denied only for reasons that are inapplicable to an injunction.

§ 358 Form of Order and Other Relief.

(1) An order of specific performance or an injunction will be so drawn as best to effectuate the purposes for which the contract was made and on such terms as justice requires. It need not be absolute in form and the performance that it requires need not be identical with that due under the contract.

(2) If specific performance or an injunction is denied as to part of the performance that is due, it may nevertheless be granted as to the remainder.

(3) In addition to specific performance or an injunction, damages and other relief may be awarded in the same proceeding and an indemnity against future harm may be required.

§ 359 Effect of Adequacy of Damages.

(1) Specific performance or an injunction will not be ordered if damages would be adequate to protect the expectation interest of the injured party.

(2) The adequacy of the damage remedy for failure to render one part of the performance due does not preclude specific performance or injunction as to the contract as a whole.

(3) Specific performance or an injunction will not be refused merely because there is a remedy for breach other than damages, but such a remedy may be considered in exercising discretion under the rule stated in § 357.

§ 360 Factors Affecting Adequacy of Damages.

In determining whether the remedy in damages would be adequate, the following circumstances are significant:

(a) the difficulty of proving damages with reasonable certainty,

(b) the difficulty of procuring a suitable substitute performance by means of money awarded as damages, and

(c) the likelihood that an award of damages could not be collected.

§ 362 Effect of Uncertainty of Terms.

Specific performance or an injunction will not be granted unless the terms of the contract are sufficiently certain to provide a basis for an appropriate order.

D. Restatement (Third) of Restitution and Unjust Enrichment (2011)

§ 1 Restitution and Unjust Enrichment

A person who is unjustly enriched at the expense of another is subject to liability in restitution.

Comment

a. Liability in restitution. Liability in restitution derives from the receipt of a benefit whose retention without payment would result in the unjust enrichment of the defendant at the expense of the claimant. While the paradigm case of unjust enrichment is one in which the benefit on one side of the transaction corresponds to an observable loss on the other, the consecrated formula "at the expense of another" can also mean "in violation of the other's legally protected rights," without the need to show that the claimant has suffered a loss. *See* § 3.

The usual consequence of a liability in restitution is that the defendant must restore the benefit in question or its traceable product, or else pay money in the amount necessary to eliminate unjust enrichment.

The identification of unjust enrichment as an independent basis of liability in common-law legal systems—comparable in this respect to a liability in contract or tort—was the central achievement of the 1937 Restatement of Restitution. That conception of the subject is carried forward here. The use of the word "restitution" to describe the cause of action as well as the remedy is likewise inherited from the original Restatement, despite the problems this usage creates. There are cases in which the essence of a plaintiff's right and remedy is the reversal of a transfer, and thus a literal "restitution," without regard to whether the defendant has been enriched by the transfer in question. Conversely, there are cases in which the remedy for unjust enrichment gives the plaintiff something—typically, the defendant's wrongful gain—that the plaintiff did not previously possess. See Comments *c* and *e*.

Such is the inherent flexibility of the concept of unjust enrichment that almost every instance of a recognized liability in restitution might be referred to the broad rule of the present section. The same flexibility means that the concept of unjust enrichment will not, by itself, yield a reliable indication of the nature and scope of the liability imposed by this part of our legal system. It is by no means obvious, as a theoretical matter, how "unjust enrichment" should best be defined; whether it constitutes a rule of decision, a unifying theme, or something in between; or what role the principle would ideally play in our legal system. Such questions preoccupy much academic writing on the subject. This Restatement has been written on the assumption that the law of restitution and unjust enrichment can be usefully described without insisting on answers to any of them....

§ 2 Limiting Principles

(1) The fact that a recipient has obtained a benefit without paying for it does not of itself establish that the recipient has been unjustly enriched.

(2) A valid contract defines the obligations of the parties as to matters within its scope, displacing to that extent any inquiry into unjust enrichment.

(3) There is no liability in restitution for an unrequested benefit voluntarily conferred, unless the circumstances of the transaction justify the claimant's intervention in the absence of contract.

(4) Liability in restitution may not subject an innocent recipient to a forced exchange: in other words, an obligation to pay for a benefit that the recipient should have been free to refuse.

§ 3 Wrongful Gain

A person is not permitted to profit by his own wrong.

§ 22 Performance of Another's Duty

(1) A person who performs another's duty to a third person or to the public is entitled to restitution from the other as necessary to prevent unjust enrichment, if the circumstances justify the decision to intervene without request.

(2) Unrequested intervention may be justified in the following circumstances:

    (a) the claimant may be justified in paying another's money debt if there is no prejudice to the obligor in substituting a liability in restitution for the original obligation;

    (b) the claimant may be justified in performing another's duty to furnish necessaries to a third person, to avoid imminent harm to the interests of the third person; and

    (c) the claimant may be justified in performing another's duty to the public, if performance is urgently required for the protection of public health, safety, or general welfare.

(3) There is no unjust enrichment and no claim in restitution by the rule of this section except insofar as the claimant's intervention has relieved the defendant of an otherwise enforceable obligation.

Index